Les canadianismes sont clairement indiqués
Canadianisms clearly labelled

aubaine *nf Can (achat avantageux)* bargain

auditeur, -trice *nm,f* (**a**) *(chargé de l'audit)* auditor ▫ **auditeur des détaillants** retail auditor; **auditeur externe** external auditor; **auditeur interne** internal auditor; **auditeur marketing** marketing auditor (**b**) *Admin* **auditeur la Cour des comptes** = junior official at the French Audit Office

Le signe = introduit une explication quand il n'y a pas de traduction possible
Explanations introduced by = when no translation possible

Chaque nouvelle catégorie sémantique est précédée d'une lettre en gras entre parenthèses
New sense category introduced by bold letter in brackets

avancer *vt* (**a**) *(dans le temps)* to advance, to bring forward; **la réunion a été avancée du 14 au 7** the meeting has been brought forward from the 14th to the 7th (**b**) *(financirement)* **avancer de l'argent qn** to advance money to sb; *(prter)* to lend sb money; **avancer un mois d'appointements qn** to advance sb a month's salary, to pay sb a month's salary in advance

avilir 1 *vt (monnaie)* to depreciate, to devalue; *(prix)* to bring down
2 s'avilir *vpr (biens)* to depreciate, to decrease in value

Les verbes pronominaux ressortent clairement
French reflexive verbs given special status

Les équivalents culturels sont précédés du signe ≃
Cultural equivalents introduced by ≃

avoué *nm Jur Br* ≃ solicitor, *Am* ≃ attorney

bailleur, -eresse *nm,f* (**a**) **bailleur de fonds** *(investisseur)* (financial) backer; *(associé passif)* *Br* sleeping partner, *Am* silent partner (**b**) *Jur* lessor

La différence entre les termes britanniques et américains donnés en traduction est clairement indiquée
Differences in British and American translations clearly labelled

Chaque nouvelle catégorie grammaticale est traitée à la ligne et précédée d'un numéro en gras
New grammatical category introduced by bold numeral, placed on a new line

baisser 1 *vt (prix, loyer)* to lower, to reduce, to bring down; **faire baisser le cot de la vie** to lower or reduce or bring down the cost of living; **la concurrence fait baisser les prix** competition brings prices down
2 *vi (prix, actions)* to fall; *(stocks)* to be running low; **le dollar a baisseé** the dollar has weakened

Les variantes orthographiques renvoient à la forme la plus courante
Alternative spellings are cross-referred to the most common form

banquable = **bancable**

Des informations supplémentaires apparaissent en italiques entre parenthèses
Additional information shown in italic in brackets

banqueroute *nf Jur* bankruptcy; **faire banqueroute** to go b... **fraud...** *frauduleuse* fraud... **queroute simple** b... *ties amounting to a br...*

...teurs de ...enseignent sur ...de langue
...language ...ark informal usages

bénef *nm Fam (abré...*

HARRAP'S
BUSINESS
DICTIONARY • DICTIONNAIRE
English-French • Français-Anglais

HARRAP'S
BUSINESS
DICTIONARY · DICTIONNAIRE
English-French · Français-Anglais

HARRAP

This edition first published in Great Britain in 2003
by Chambers Harrap Publishers Ltd
7 Hopetoun Crescent
Edinburgh EH7 4AY

Previous edition published 1999

ISBN 0245 50506 7 (France)
ISBN 0245 60714 5 (UK)

Dépôt légal : décembre 2002

Designed and typeset by Chambers Harrap Publishers Ltd, Edinburgh
Printed in France by MAME

Project manager and English lexicographer/
Directrice de projet et lexicographe anglophone
Anna Stevenson

French lexicographer/Lexicographe francophone
Georges Pilard

with/avec
Nadia Cornuau
Gearóid Cronin
Nicolas Dupuy
José A. Gálvez
Rachel Skeet

Publishing manager/Direction éditoriale
Patrick White

Prepress/Prépresse
Clair Cameron
Vienna Leigh

Specialist consultants/Consultants spécialistes
Barbara Campbell
Teacher of Business English,
Institute of Applied Linguistics, Edinburgh

Iain Davidson BA Hons, MA, TESOL
Business Communication Consultant

Marc Fermin DEA
Lecturer in Modern Languages,
Glasgow Caledonian University, University of Paisley

Nicole Génard
Université d'Angers

Maddy Glas, Docteur de la Sorbonne
Professeur de Français des Affaires, INSEAD

Jean-François Trinquecoste
Maître de Conférences,
Université Montesquieu-Bordeaux IV

Peter Walton
ESSEC, Paris

Trademarks
Words considered to be trademarks have been designated in this dictionary by the symbol ®. However, no judgement is implied concerning the legal status of any trademark by virtue of the presence or absence of such a symbol.

Marques déposées
Les termes considérés comme des marques déposées sont signalés dans ce dictionnaire par le symbole ®. Cependant, la présence ou l'absence de ce symbole ne constitue nullement une indication quant à la valeur juridique de ces termes.

Contents

Table des matières

Preface

In the four years since the last edition of the **Harrap's Business Dictionary** was published, there have been many advances in the business world, with the Internet and mobile phone technology playing an increasingly important role and the single currency now firmly established in many European countries. The vocabulary of business has evolved too, and new terms such as **B2B**, **viral marketing**, **écotaxe** and **Medef** all feature in this edition. As before, all areas of business are well represented, with terms from fields as diverse as marketing, finance, the Stock Exchange and the European Union all covered. Colloquial business terms, together with the language of everyday office life, also have their place in this book (**bean counter**, **paper clip**, **zinzin** and **surligneur**).

As in the previous edition, we have sought to help the reader by providing extra information in the form of **context** and **practical help**.

Context is provided by giving many translated examples within entries, together with several hundred quotations from the French, British and American business press. These quotations are presented in boxes after the relevant entry and show the use of the word or expression in the real business world.

Practical help is provided in the form of a revised and expanded two-colour supplement which comprises:

- an extensive guide to French business communication, including fully annotated sample letters, e-mails, faxes, memos and CVs, together with useful phrases, letter-writing conventions, information on job applications and telephone conversations.
- A lively description of the differences between business meetings in French- and English-speaking countries, including the phrases you will hear and want to use.
- Advice on working with an interpreter that will help make both your and the interpreter's job easier.
- Tables giving information on nations of the world and their respective currencies and official languages.
- Tables of information on French, Belgian and Swiss administrative divisions.
- Model French financial statements with a short explanation of the different accounting traditions in France, Britain and the US.

It is our hope that this new edition will prove an invaluable resource for all students of business French and businesspeople who liaise with their counterparts in the French-speaking world.

Préface

Depuis la dernière édition du **Harrap's Business** il y a quatre ans, le monde des affaires a connu un grand nombre de changements. La technologie Internet et la téléphonie mobile jouent un rôle de plus en plus important, et la monnaie unique est maintenant bien établie dans de nombreux pays européens. Le vocabulaire des affaires a lui aussi évolué, et de nouveaux termes tels que **B2B**, **viral marketing**, **écotaxe** et **Medef** sont désormais traités dans la présente édition. Comme auparavant, l'ouvrage couvre tous les domaines des affaires et comporte des termes issus aussi bien du marketing, de la finance, que de la Bourse ou de l'Union européenne. Y figurent également des termes familiers utilisés dans certains domaines, ainsi que des termes employés quotidiennement au travail (**bean counter**, **paper clip**, **zinzin** et **surligneur**).

Comme dans l'édition précédente, nous avons cherché à aider l'utilisateur en lui apportant des informations supplémentaires sous forme de **contextes** et **d'aide pratique**.

La **mise en contexte** est assurée par de nombreux exemples figurant avec leur traduction dans le corps des entrées, ainsi que par la présence de centaines de citations extraites de la presse française, britannique et américaine. Ces citations sont présentées dans des encadrés à la fin des entrées correspondantes et montrent comment les termes en question sont réellement utilisés dans le monde des affaires.

L'**aide pratique** à l'utilisateur est constituée d'un supplément en couleur revu et augmenté qui comprend :

- Un guide approfondi de communication commerciale en anglais, comprenant des modèles de lettres, d'e-mails, de fax, de notes de service et de C.V. avec annotations, ainsi que des expressions utiles, les conventions à respecter lors de l'élaboration d'une lettre, des informations sur les candidatures et les conversations téléphoniques.
- Un article sur les différences entre les réunions d'affaires dans les pays francophones et anglophones, dans lequel l'utilisateur trouvera également les expressions les plus utiles et les plus fréquemment utilisées.
- Un article contenant de nombreux conseils pour faciliter à la fois la tâche de l'homme d'affaires travaillant avec un interprète et le travail de l'interprète lui-même.
- Un tableau des États du monde comprenant la monnaie et la/les langue(s) officielle(s) de chaque nation.
- La liste des divisions administratives de certains pays anglophones, ainsi qu'un tableau contenant les cinquante états américains.
- Des modèles de bilans financiers anglais avec une brève explication des différentes techniques de comptabilité en France, en Grande-Bretagne et aux États-Unis.

Nous espérons que cette nouvelle édition apportera une aide précieuse aux étudiants d'anglais commercial, ainsi qu'aux hommes et femmes d'affaires en contact avec leurs homologues anglophones.

Labels
Indications d'usage

English	Abbreviation	Français
gloss [introduces an explanation]	=	glose [introduit une explication]
cultural equivalent [introduces a translation which has a roughly equivalent status in the target language]	≃	équivalent culturel [introduit une traduction dont les connotations dans la langue cible sont comparables]
abbreviation	*abbr, abrév*	abréviation
accounting	*Acct*	comptabilité
adjective	*adj*	adjectif
administration	*Admin*	administration
adverb	*adv*	adverbe
North American English	*Am*	anglais américain
no longer in existence or renamed	*Anciennement*	terme n'ayant plus cours
insurance	*Assur*	assurances
auxiliary	*aux*	auxiliaire
banking	*Banking, Banque*	banque
Belgian French	*Belg*	belgicisme
Stock Exchange	*Bourse*	Bourse
British English	*Br*	anglais britannique
Canadian French	*Can*	canadianisme
accounting	*Compta*	comptabilité
computing	*Comptr*	informatique
customs	*Customs*	douanes
conjunction	*conj*	conjonction
customs	*Douanes*	douanes
economics	*Econ, Écon*	économie
European Union	*EU*	Union européenne
feminine	*f*	féminin
familiar	*Fam*	familier
finance	*Fin*	finance
no longer in existence or renamed	*Formerly*	terme n'ayant plus cours
insurance	*Ins*	assurances
law	*Jur, Law*	droit
masculine	*m*	masculin
masculine and feminine noun [same form for both genders, eg comptable *mf*]	*mf*	nom masculin et féminin [formes identiques]
masculine and feminine noun [different form in the feminine, eg conseiller(ère) *m,f*]	*m,f*	nom masculin et féminin [formes différentes]
marketing	*Mktg*	marketing
noun	*n*	nom
feminine noun	*nf*	nom féminin
feminine plural noun	*nfpl*	nom féminin pluriel

masculine noun	*nm*	nom masculin
masculine and feminine noun [same form for both genders, eg **comptable** *nmf*]	*nmf*	nom masculin ou féminin [formes identiques]
masculine and feminine noun [different form in the feminine, eg **conseiller, -ère** *nm,f*]	*nm,f*	nom masculin et féminin [formes différentes au féminin]
masculine plural noun	*nmpl*	nom masculin pluriel
computing	*Ordinat*	informatique
plural	*pl*	pluriel
prefix	*pref, préf*	préfixe
preposition	*prep, prép*	préposition
pronoun	*pron*	pronom
Stock Exchange	*St Exch*	Bourse
suffix	*suff*	suffixe
Swiss French	*Suisse*	helvétisme
telephone and telecommunications	*Tel, Tél*	téléphone et télécommunications
European Union	*UE*	Union européenne
verb	*v*	verbe
intransitive verb	*vi*	verbe intransitif
impersonal verb	*v impersonnel*	verbe impersonnel
reflexive verb	*vpr*	verbe pronominal
transitive verb	*vt*	verbe transitif
transitive verb used with a preposition [eg **postuler à** (to apply for); il a **postulé à** ce poste (he has applied for this job)]	*vt ind*	verbe transitif indirect [par exemple : **postuler à**; il a **postulé à** ce poste]
inseparable phrasal verb [phrasal verb where the verb and the adverb or preposition cannot be separated, eg **sign for**; to **sign for** goods received]	*vt insep*	verbe transitif à particule inséparable [par exemple : **sign for** (signer un reçu pour); to **sign for** goods received (signer à la réception des marchandises)]
separable phrasal verb [phrasal verb where the verb and the adverb or preposition can be separated, eg **lay off**; **they laid off** the workers]	*vt sep*	verbe transitif à particule séparable [par exemple : **lay off** (licencier); they **laid off** the workers (ils ont licencié les ouvriers)]

Aa

A3 1 *n (paper format)* A3 *m* ; **a sheet of A3** une feuille de format A3
2 *adj* **A3 paper** papier *m* (format) A3

A4 1 *n (paper format)* A4 *m* ; **a sheet of A4** une feuille de format A4
2 *adj* **A4 paper** papier *m* (format) A4

AA¹ *n (abbr* **Advertising Association**) = organisme britannique dont le rôle est de veiller à la qualité des publicités et de défendre les intérêts des annonceurs et des agences de publicité

AA² *n St Exch* (notation *f*) AA *f*

AAA *n St Exch* (notation *f*) AAA *f*

abandon *vt* (**a**) *(idea, project)* abandonner ; **they have had to abandon expansion plans due to a fall in profits** ils ont été contraints d'abandonner leurs projets de développement à la suite d'une baisse des bénéfices (**b**) *Ins (ship, cargo)* abandonner (**to** à) ; **it was decided to abandon the ship to the insurers** il a été décidé d'abandonner le navire aux assureurs (**c**) *Comptr (file, routine)* abandonner

abandonment *n* (**a**) *(of idea, project)* abandon *m* (**b**) *Ins (of ship, cargo)* délaissement *m* ; **the shipping company issued a notice of abandonment to their insurers** la compagnie maritime a donné un avis de délaissement à ses assureurs

ABC *n Banking (abbr* **activity-based costing**) coûts *mpl* par activité

ABC1 *n Mktg* = catégorie sociale allant du cadre supérieur au cadre moyen, au pouvoir d'achat élevé *(dans le cadre du système de classification sociale britannique ABC1)*

> ❝
> *Stuff* had a cover price of £2.50 and was targeted at **ABC1** men aged 25–44 with an average income of around £20,000.
> ❞

abeyance *n (suspense)* **the matter is still in abeyance** la question est toujours pendante *ou* en suspens ; **the final decision on the project is still in abeyance** la décision finale concernant le projet reste en suspens

abort *Comptr* **1** *n (of program)* suspension *f* d'exécution, abandon *m*
2 *vt (program)* suspendre l'exécution de, abandonner

above 1 *n* **the above** *(person)* le (la) susnommé(e) ; *(fact, item)* ce qui se trouve ci-dessus
2 *adj* ci-dessus, précité(e) ; **please contact me at the above address** veuillez me contacter à l'adresse ci-dessus
3 *adv* plus haut ; **mentioned above** cité(e) plus haut *ou* ci-dessus ; **as above** comme ci-dessus

aboveground *adj Am Fin (income, earnings)* déclaré(e)

above-mentioned 1 *n (person)* **the above-mentioned** le (la) susmentionné(e)
2 *adj* sus-mentionné(e), cité(e) plus haut, précité(e) ; **this applies to the above-mentioned employees** ceci concerne les employés susnommés

above-the-line *adj* (**a**) *Mktg* média ❑ *above-the-line advertising* publicité *f* média ; *above-the-line costs* coûts *mpl* média ; *above-the-line expenditure* dépenses *fpl* média ; *above-the-line promotion* promotion *f* média (**b**) *Acct* au-dessus de la ligne ❑ *above-the-line accounts* comptes *mpl* de résultats courants ; *above-the-line costs* coûts *mpl* au-dessus de la ligne ; *above-the-line expenditure* dépenses *fpl* au-dessus de la ligne

> ❝
> British Airways is slashing its **above-the-line** advertising budget – worth an estimated £30m. And it is letting below-the-line agencies go as part of a major cost-cutting exercise.
> ❞

abroad *adv* à l'étranger ; **to be abroad on business** être en voyage d'affaires à l'étranger

absentee *n* absent(e) *m,f*

absenteeism *n* absentéisme *m*

absolute *adj* (**a**) *Mktg* **absolute frequency** fréquence *f* absolue (**b**) *Econ* **absolute advantage** avantage *m* absolu ; **absolute efficiency** efficience *f* absolue, efficacité *f* parfaite (**c**) **absolute majority** majorité *f* absolue

absorb *vt (company)* absorber, incorporer ; *Fin (debts)* absorber ; **the business has been absorbed by a competitor** l'entreprise a été absorbée par un concurrent

absorption *n* (**a**) *(of company)* rachat *m*, absorption *f*, incorporation *f* (**b**) *Acct* **absorption costing** méthode *f* du coût de revient complet

abstract 1 *n (of article)* résumé *m*, abrégé *m*; *Fin* **an abstract of accounts** un extrait de comptes **2** *vt (article)* résumer, abréger

abuse *n* abus *m* ◻ **abuse of authority** abus d'autorité; **abuse of power** abus de pouvoir

.ac *Comptr* = abréviation désignant les universités et les sites éducatifs dans les adresses électroniques britanniques

A/C, a/c *n (abbr* **account***)* c.

ACAS *n (abbr* **Advisory, Conciliation and Arbitration Service***)* = organisme britannique indépendant d'arbitrage des conflits du travail

accelerated depreciation *n Acct* amortissement *m* dégressif, amortissement accéléré

acceleration *n* (**a**) *Fin* **acceleration clause** clause *f* accélératrice (**b**) **acceleration premium** prime *f* de rendement

accelerator *n Comptr* accélérateur *m* ◻ **accelerator card** carte *f* accélératrice

accent *n* accent *m*

accented character *n Comptr* caractère *m* accentué

accept *vt* (**a**) *(sum, offer)* accepter; *Fin* **to accept a bill** accepter un effet; **do you accept credit cards?** est-ce que vous prenez les cartes de crédit? (**b**) **to accept (delivery** *or* **shipment of) goods** réceptionner des marchandises, prendre livraison de marchandises

Acceptable Use Policy *n Comptr* = code de conduite défini par un fournisseur d'accès à l'Internet

acceptance *n* (**a**) *(agreement)* acceptation *f*; *Fin (document)* effet *m* accepté, effet à payer; **to present a bill for acceptance** présenter une traite à l'acceptation ◻ *Am* **acceptance bank** banque *f* d'acceptation, banque d'escompte d'effets étrangers; **acceptance bill** effet contre acceptation, traite contre acceptation; **acceptance fee** commission *f* d'acceptation; *Am* **acceptance house** banque d'acceptation, maison *f* d'acceptation
(**b**) *(of something ordered)* réception *f*
(**c**) **acceptance sampling** échantillonnage *m* pour acceptation; **acceptance test** test *m* d'acceptabilité

accepted *adj Fin (written on accepted bill)* accepté, bon pour acceptation ◻ **accepted bill** effet *m* accepté, acceptation *f*

accepting house *n Br Fin* banque *f* d'acceptation, maison *f* d'acceptation

acceptor *n Fin (of bill)* accepteur *m*, tiré(e) *m,f*

access 1 *n* (**a**) *(right to contact, use)* accès *m*; **to have access to sth** avoir accès à qch; **I don't have access to that information** je n'ai pas accès à ce genre d'informations ◻ **access barrier** barrière *f* d'accès

(**b**) *Comptr* accès *m*; **access denied** *(DOS message)* accès refusé ◻ **access authorization** autorisation *f* d'accès; **access code** code *m* d'accès; **access control** contrôle *m* d'accès; **access level** *(in network)* niveau *m* d'accès; **access number** *(to ISP)* numéro *m* d'accès; **access privileges** droits *mpl* d'accès; **access provider** fournisseur *m* d'accès; **access restriction** restriction *f* d'accès; **access time** temps *m* d'accès **2** *vt Comptr (data)* accéder à; **can you access last year's figures?** est-ce que tu as accès aux chiffres de l'année dernière?

accident *n* accident *m* ◻ *Ins* **accident claim** déclaration *f* d'accident; **accident insurance** assurance *f* (contre les) accidents; **accident policy** police *f* d'assurance accidents

accommodation *n* (**a**) *Fin (of money)* avance *f*, prêt *m* ◻ **accommodation bill** traite *f* ou effet *m* de complaisance (**b**) *(lodging)* logement *m* ◻ **accommodation allowance** indemnité *f* de logement; **accommodation capacity** *(of hotel)* capacité *f* d'hébergement (**c**) *(agreement)* accord *m*; **to come to an accommodation** *(with one's creditors, debtors)* parvenir à un arrangement

accommodations *npl Am (lodging)* logement *m* ◻ **accommodations allowance** indemnité *f* de logement; **accommodations capacity** *(of hotel)* capacité *f* d'hébergement

accord *n Am (agreement)* convention *f*, accord *m*

accordance *n* **in accordance with** en conformité avec, conformément à; **we must work in accordance with current regulations** il nous faut agir conformément à la réglementation en vigueur

according to *prep* (**a**) *(on the evidence of)* selon, d'après; **according to the latest report, profits have risen** selon le dernier rapport, les bénéfices ont augmenté (**b**) *(in accordance with)* suivant, conformément à; **according to instructions** suivant les ordres, conformément aux ordres

account *n* (**a**) *Fin (statement)* compte *m*, note *f*; **to pay a sum on account** payer une somme en acompte; **we bought the car on account** nous avons acheté la voiture à crédit; **payment on account** paiement à compte *ou* à crédit; **I paid £100 on account** j'ai versé un acompte de 100 livres ◻ **account payable** compte créditeur, dette *f* fournisseur; **accounts payable** dettes *fpl* passives *ou* fournisseurs; **accounts payable ledger** livre *m* des créanciers; **account receivable** compte client *ou* débiteur; **accounts receivable** dettes actives, créances *fpl* (clients); **accounts receivable ledger** livre des débiteurs; **account tendered** relevé *m* remis; **as per** *or* **to account tendered** *(on statement)* suivant compte *ou* relevé remis (**b**) *(with shop, company)* compte *m*; *Comptr (with ISP)* abonnement *m* (**with** auprès de); **to have an account with John Lewis** avoir un compte chez John Lewis, être en compte avec John Lewis; **to buy sth on account** acheter qch à crédit; **to settle an account** régler un compte; **to set up an account with sb** s'abonner auprès de qn; **put it on** *or* **charge it to my account** inscrivez-le *ou* mettez-le à mon compte; **cash or account?** vous payez *ou* réglez comptant ou est-ce que vous avez un compte chez nous? ❑ **account card** fiche *f* de facture; **account credit** avoir *m* de compte

(**c**) *Acct* **accounts** *(of company)* comptabilité *f*; **to keep the accounts** tenir les livres *ou* les écritures *ou* la comptabilité; **to enter sth in the accounts** comptabiliser qch ❑ **account balance** *(status)* situation *f* de compte; *(after audit)* reliquat *m* de compte; **account book** livre *m* de comptes, registre *m* de comptabilité; **accounts card** fiche *f* de compte; **accounts clerk** employé(e) *m,f* aux écritures; **accounts department** (service *m* de la) comptabilité; *Comptr* **accounts package** logiciel *m* de comptabilité; *Comptr* **accounts software** logiciel de comptabilité

(**d**) *Banking* compte *m*; **to open an account** (se faire) ouvrir un compte; **to close an account** fermer un compte; **to pay money into one's account** verser de l'argent sur son compte; **to pay sb's salary directly into his/her account** verser le salaire de qn par virement direct sur son compte; **to overdraw an account** mettre un compte à découvert ❑ **account charges** frais *mpl* de tenue de compte; **account fee** commission *f* de compte; **account handling fee** commission de tenue de compte; **account holder** titulaire *mf* d'un compte; **account manager** chargé(e) *m,f* de compte; **account number** numéro *m* de compte; **account statement** relevé *m* ou état *m* ou bordereau *m* de compte

(**e**) *(in advertising, marketing, PR)* budget *m*, compte-client *m*, client(e) *m,f*; **we lost the Guinness account** nous avons perdu le budget Guinness ❑ **account director** directeur(trice) *m,f* des comptes-clients; **account executive** *(in advertising, marketing)* responsable *mf* de budget, chargé(e) *m,f* de budget; *(in PR)* relationniste-conseil *mf*; **account handler** *(in advertising, marketing)* responsable de budget, chargé(e) de budget; *(in PR)* relationniste-conseil; **account manager** *(in advertising, marketing)* responsable de budget, chargé(e) de budget; *(in PR)* relationniste-conseil

(**f**) *St Exch* **the account** la liquidation (mensuelle) ❑ **account day** (jour *m* de) règlement *m*, jour de la liquidation; *Am* **account executive** agent *m* de change

(**g**) *Fin (of expenses)* état *m*, note *f*; *(of transactions)* exposé *m*

(**h**) **to set up in business on one's own ac-** count s'installer à son compte, se mettre à son compte

▸ **account for** *vt insep* (**a**) *(explain)* **to account for sth** comptabiliser qch, justifier qch; **the strong pound accounts for the drop in exports** la solidité de la livre explique la baisse des exportations (**b**) *(make up)* représenter; **wine accounts for five percent of all exports** le vin représente cinq pour cent des exportations totales

accountable *adj (person)* responsable (**to sb** envers qn; **for sth** de qch); *(for sum of money)* redevable (**for** de); **he's directly accountable to the managing director** il rend compte directement au président-directeur général ❑ **accountable receipt** quittance *f* comptable, reçu *m* certifié

accountancy *n Br* comptabilité *f*, expertise *f* comptable ❑ **accountancy firm** cabinet *m* d'expertise comptable

accountant *n* comptable *mf*, agent *m* comptable

accounting *n* comptabilité *f*, expertise *f* comptable ❑ **accounting clerk** commis *m* aux écritures; **accounting control** contrôle *m* de la comptabilité; **accounting day** journée *f* comptable; **accounting entry** écriture *f* comptable, enregistrement *m* comptable; **accounting entry sheet** *or* **form** bordereau *m* de saisie; **accounting firm** cabinet *m* d'expertise comptable; **accounting irregularity** irrégularité *f* comptable; **accounting loophole** échappatoire *f* comptable; **accounting method** méthode *f* de comptabilité; **accounting operation** opération *f* comptable; *Comptr* **accounting package** logiciel *m* de comptabilité; **accounting period** exercice *m* (financier), période *f* comptable; **accounting plan** plan *m* comptable; **accounting policy** politique *f* comptable; **accounting procedure** pratique *f* comptable; **accounting rate of return** taux *m* de rendement comptable; **accounting ratio** ratio *m* comptable; **accounting records** états *mpl* comptables; **accounting rules** règles *fpl* comptables; *Comptr* **accounting software** logiciel de comptabilité; **accounting system** système *m* comptable, plan comptable; **accounting year** exercice (financier *ou* comptable), période comptable

accredit *vt (representative)* accréditer

accreditation *n (of representative)* accréditation *f*

accredited *adj (representative)* accrédité(e)

accrual *n* (**a**) *Fin (of interest, debt, cost)* accumulation *f* ❑ **accrual rate** taux *m* d'accumulation *ou* d'accroissement (**b**) *Acct* **accruals** *(expenses)* charges *fpl* à payer; *(income)* produits *mpl* à recevoir ❑ **accrual accounting**

comptabilité *f* d'engagements; **accruals concept** principe *m* d'indépendance des exercices *ou* de rattachement à l'exercice; **accruals and deferred income** compte *m* de régularisation; *St Exch* **accrual of dividend** échéance *f* de dividende

accrue *Fin* **1** *vt (interest)* produire
  2 *vi (of interest)* s'accumuler, s'accroître, courir; **interest accrues (as) from the 5th of the month** les intérêts courent à partir du 5 du mois; **accruing interest** intérêts *mpl* à échoir

accrued *adj Fin* **accrued benefits** *(under pension scheme)* points *mpl* de retraite; *Acct* **accrued charges** effets *mpl* à payer; *Fin* **accrued dividends** dividendes *mpl* accrus; *Acct* **accrued expenses** frais *mpl* cumulés *ou* accumulés, charges *fpl* à payer; *Acct* **accrued income** effets *ou* produit *m* à recevoir; **accrued interest** intérêts *mpl* courus *ou* échus

> In a separate action, Rare Medium and Motient announced today that Motient repaid approximately $26.2 million, including **accrued interest**, of the $50 million aggregate principal amount of exchangeable notes issued by Motient to Rare Medium by delivering to Rare Medium five million shares of XM Satellite Radio common stock held by Motient.

accumulate **1** *vt (stock)* accumuler ◻ **accumulated depreciation** amortissement *m* cumulé
  2 *vi (capital)* s'accroître; *(interest, stock)* s'accumuler

accumulation *n (of capital)* accroissement *m*; *(of interest)* accumulation *f*

accumulative *adj Fin* cumulatif(ive)

ACH *n Banking (abbr* **automated clearing house)** chambre *f* de compensation automatisée

achieve *vt (aim, goal)* atteindre, parvenir à; **the company achieved all its objectives for the year** la société a atteint tous les objectifs qu'elle s'était fixés pour l'année; **the new marketing strategy achieved very little** la nouvelle stratégie de marketing a été peu efficace

achievement *n* réussite *f*; **the company is proud of its achievements this year** la société est fière des résultats obtenus cette année

acid test ratio *n Acct* ratio *m* de liquidité immédiate

acknowledge *vt* **to acknowledge (receipt of) a letter** accuser réception d'une lettre; **we acknowledge receipt of your letter of 19 April** nous accusons réception de votre lettre du 19 avril, nous avons bien reçu votre lettre du 19 avril

acknowledg(e)ment *n* **(a)** **acknowledgement (of receipt)** *(of letter, e-mail)* accusé *m ou* avis *m* de réception; *(of payment)* reçu *m*, récépissé *m*, quittance *f* ◻ **acknowledgement slip** accusé de réception **(b)** **acknowledgement of debt** reconnaissance *f* de dette

ACORN *n Mktg (abbr* **A Classification of Residential Neighbourhoods)** = classement des différents types de quartiers résidentiels existant en Grande-Bretagne en 39 catégories, utilisé par les entreprises pour mieux cibler leurs clients potentiels lors de campagnes commerciales

acquire *vt (goods, right)* acquérir; *(property)* faire l'acquisition de; *(other company)* prendre le contrôle de, racheter; *(shares)* acheter; **to acquire an interest in a company** prendre une participation dans une société

acquired *adj* acquis(e) ◻ **acquired surplus** surplus *m* acquis

acquisition *n* acquisition *f*, prise *f* de contrôle; **making an acquisition in the software industry will greatly improve the company's future** le rachat d'une société de logiciel améliorera considérablement les perspectives d'avenir de la société ◻ *Acct* **acquisition accounting** = base de préparation des comptes consolidés où une société a pris le contrôle d'une autre; *Acct* **acquisition cost** coût *m* d'acquisition

acquisitive *adj (company)* en (phase de) croissance externe; *(society)* d'acquisition

acquit *vt Fin (debt)* acquitter, s'acquitter de, régler

acquittal, acquittance *n Fin (of debt)* acquittement *m*, décharge *f*, quittance *f*

across-the-board **1** *adj* général(e); **an across-the-board increase** une augmentation générale
  2 *adv* à tous les niveaux; **this applies across-the-board** ceci s'applique à tous les niveaux; **we have had to cut salaries across-the-board** il nous a fallu procéder à une réduction générale des salaires

act **1** *n* **(a)** *Law* **Act (of parliament)** loi *f* **(b)** *Ins* **act of God** (cas *m* de) force *f* majeure
  2 *vi* **to act as secretary/chairperson** exercer les fonctions de secrétaire/président; **to act on behalf of** *or* **for sb** agir au nom de qn, représenter qn

▸ **act on** *vt insep* **to act on a letter** donner suite à une lettre; **to act on sb's instructions** agir selon les instructions de qn

acting *adj (temporary)* suppléant(e), intérimaire, par intérim ◻ **acting manager** directeur(trice) *m,f* intérimaire *ou* par intérim

action **1** *n* **(a)** *(activity)* **to take action** prendre

des mesures ❑ **action plan** plan *m* d'action; **action programme** plan d'action
(**b**) *Law* action *f*, procès *m*; **to bring an action against sb** intenter une action en justice contre qn, poursuivre qn en justice; **action for breach of contract** action contractuelle; **action for libel** procès *ou* plainte *f* en diffamation; **action for damages** action en dommages et intérêts
2 *vt* (*idea, suggestion*) mettre en action; (*decision, plan*) mettre à exécution

activate *vt* activer

active *adj* (**a**) *Banking* (*account*) actif(ive) ❑ **active money** monnaie *f* circulante; **active partner** (*in company*) associé(e) *m,f* gérant(e), (associé(e)) commandité(e) *m,f*
(**b**) (*market*) animé(e), actif(ive); *St Exch* (*shares*) actif; **there is an active demand for oils** les valeurs pétrolières sont très recherchées, il y a une forte demande de valeurs pétrolières
(**c**) *Comptr* **active desktop** bureau *m* actif; **active file** fichier *m* ou dossier *m* actif; **active matrix screen** écran *m* à matrice active; **active program** programme *m* en cours d'exécution; **active window** fenêtre *f* active ou activée

activity *n* (*in business, market, of company*) activité *f*; (*of bank account*) mouvement *m*; **this week has seen a lot of activity on the Stock Market** la Bourse a été très active cette semaine ❑ *Acct* **activity accounting** comptabilité *f* par centres de responsabilité; **activity chart** graphique *m* des activités; **activity ratio** ratio *m* ou coefficient *m* d'activité, ratio de gestion

activity-based costing *n Acct* coûts *mpl* par activité

actual 1 *npl* (**a**) **actuals** (*real figures*) chiffres *mpl* réels; **to compare budgeted amounts with actuals** comparer les prévisions budgétaires et les résultats obtenus (**b**) *St Exch* **actuals** livraisons *fpl* physiques, marchandises *fpl* livrées au comptant
2 *adj* réel(elle) ❑ **actual cost** prix *m* de revient ou d'achat; **actual employment** emploi *m* effectif; **actual figures** chiffres *mpl* réels; *Law* **actual possession** possession *f* de fait; **actual price** prix réel; *St Exch* **actual quotations** cours *mpl* effectifs; **actual tare** tare *f* réelle; *Ins* **actual total loss** perte *f* totale effective; **actual value** valeur *f* réelle

> **"**
> But what we're seeing right now is that we have gotten ahead of the curve, and we are operationally prepared from a systems and billing perspective ... We initially estimated an annual impact of approximately $7 million, and our **actuals** are tracking with this target.
> **"**

actuarial *adj* actuariel(elle) ❑ **actuarial tables** tables *fpl* de mortalité

actuary *n* actuaire *mf*

acute accent *n* accent *m* aigu

ad *n Fam* (*for product, service*) pub *f*; (*classified, for job*) annonce *f*; **to put an ad in the paper** mettre ou insérer une annonce dans le journal ❑ **ad agency** agence *f* publicitaire ou de publicité

adapter *n Comptr* adaptateur *m* ❑ **adapter card** carte-adaptateur *f*

add *vt* ajouter (**to** à); (*figures*) additionner, totaliser; **to add the interest to the capital** ajouter l'intérêt au capital ❑ **added value** valeur *f* ajoutée

▶ **add to** *vt insep* (*increase*) augmenter; **this adds to our expenses** cela augmente (le montant de) nos dépenses; **next year we hope to add to our range of products** nous espérons élargir notre gamme de produits l'année prochaine

▶ **add up 1** *vt sep* (*figures*) additionner, totaliser
2 *vi* (*give correct total*) être juste ou exact(e); **the figures don't add up** les chiffres sont faux; **the accounts won't add up** il y a quelque chose qui ne va pas dans les comptes

▶ **add up to** *vt insep* (*amount to*) s'élever à; **the assets add up to two million** l'actif s'élève à deux millions

add-back *n Acct* réintégration *f*

adding machine *n* machine *f* à additionner

addition *n* (**a**) (*action*) addition *f*; (*thing added*) ajout *m* (**to** à); (*person*) nouveau venu (nouvelle venue) *m,f*; **additions to the staff** adjonction *f* de personnel; **she's the latest addition to the marketing team** c'est la dernière recrue de l'équipe du marketing (**b**) **in addition (to)** en plus (de); **personnel staff in addition to the management will be attending the meeting** la direction ainsi que les employés du service du personnel assisteront à la réunion

additional *adj* (*investment, expenses*) supplémentaire; **this will require additional investment** cela nécessitera un investissement supplémentaire ❑ *Admin* **additional allowance** indemnité *f* complémentaire; **additional charge** supplément *m* (de prix); **at no additional charge** sans supplément; **additional clause** avenant *m*, clause *f* additionnelle; **additional discount** surremise *f*; **additional expenditure** surcroît *m* de dépenses; **additional income** ressources *fpl* d'appoint; *Fin* **additional payment** supplément *m*; **additional session** séance *f* supplémentaire; **additional sources of income** ressources d'appoint; *Admin* **additional tax** impôt *m* additionnel; (*because of underpayment*) supplément d'imposition; **ad-**

ditional tax assessment* redressement *m* fiscal; *additional voluntary contribution* supplément de cotisation retraite *(payé volontairement)*

add-on *n Comptr* produit *m* supplémentaire *ou* complémentaire, extension *f*

address 1 *n* (**a**) *(of person, company)* adresse *f* □ *address book* carnet *m* d'adresses; *address label* étiquette-adresse *f* (**b**) *Comptr* adresse *f* □ *address bus* bus *m* d'adresses; *address file* fichier *m* d'adresses
   2 *vt* (**a**) *(letter, envelope, parcel)* mettre *ou* écrire l'adresse sur; **who's the letter addressed to?** à qui la lettre est-elle adressée?; **the letter was addressed to the personnel manager** la lettre était adressée au directeur du personnel
   (**b**) *(direct)* adresser (**to** à); **please address all enquiries to the personnel department** faire parvenir toute demande de renseignements au service du personnel
   (**c**) *(speak to)* s'adresser à; **to address a meeting** prendre la parole lors d'une réunion
   (**d**) *Comptr* adresser, accéder à

addressable *adj Mktg* utile □ *addressable audience* audience *f* utile; *addressable market* marché *m* utile

addressee *n* destinataire *mf*

adjourn 1 *vt (meeting)* ajourner
   2 *vi (of meeting)* être ajourné(e); **the meeting adjourned at 11 o'clock** on a levé la séance à 11 heures; **to adjourn to another room** passer dans une autre pièce

adjournment *n (of meeting)* ajournement *m*

adjudicate 1 *vt* juger, arbitrer; *Admin (claim)* adjuger; **to adjudicate sb bankrupt** déclarer qn en faillite
   2 *vi (in dispute)* arbitrer

adjudication *n* jugement *m*, décision *f*, arrêt *m*; *Admin (of claim)* adjudication *f* □ *adjudication of or in bankruptcy* jugement déclaratif de faillite; *adjudication order* jugement déclaratif de faillite

adjudicative *adj Law* déclaratif(ive), déclaratoire

adjudicator *n* juge *m*, arbitre *m*

adjust *vt* (**a**) *(prices)* ajuster; *(figures, salaries)* rajuster, réajuster; *(accounts)* régulariser; **the figures have been seasonally adjusted** les chiffres sont les données corrigées des variations saisonnières; **pensions have been adjusted upwards/downwards** les pensions ont été revues à la hausse/à la baisse *ou* ont été augmentées/diminuées; **income adjusted for inflation** revenu réel compte tenu de l'inflation
   (**b**) *(modify)* modifier; **the terms of the contract have been adjusted** les termes du contrat ont été modifiés; **production has been adjusted to meet demand** on a aligné la production sur la demande

   (**c**) *Ins* **to adjust an average** répartir une avarie; **to adjust a claim** régler une demande d'indemnité

adjustable *adj (rate)* variable

adjustable-rate mortgage *n* prêt *m* immobilier à taux variable

adjuster, *Am* **adjustor** *n Ins* inspecteur(trice) *m,f* régleur

adjusting entry *n Acct* écriture *f* de régularisation

adjustment *n* (**a**) *(of prices)* ajustement *m*; *(of figures, salaries)* rajustement *m*, réajustement *m*; **no adjustment was made for seasonal variation** il n'y a pas eu de corrigé des variations saisonnières (**b**) *(modification)* modification *f* □ *Acct adjustment account* compte *m* collectif

adjustor *Am* = **adjuster**

adman *n Fam* publicitaire *m*

admin *n Fam* (**a**) *(work)* travail *m* administratif; **there's a lot of admin in this job** il y a beaucoup de paperasserie dans ce travail (**b**) *(department)* administration *f*; **admin will take care of it** le personnel administratif *ou* l'administration s'en occupera □ *admin building* bâtiment *m* administratif *ou* d'administration; *admin department* service *m* administratif

administer *vt (business, institution, property)* administrer, gérer; *(laws)* appliquer; *(territory, region)* administrer □ *Am administered price* prix *m* imposé

administrate *vt (business, institution, property)* diriger, administrer, gérer; *(finances, fund)* gérer

administration *n* (**a**) *(management) (of business, institution, property)* administration, gestion *f*; *(of territory, region)* administration *f*; **to go into administration** *(receivership)* être placé sous contrôle judiciaire □ *Acct administration costs, administration expenses* frais *mpl* d'administration *ou* de gestion; *Banking administration fee* frais de dossier
   (**b**) *(work)* travail *m* administratif; *(department)* administration *f* □ *administration building* bâtiment *m* administratif *ou* d'administration; *administration department* service *m* administratif
   (**c**) *Am (government)* **the Administration** le gouvernement (fédéral)

administrative *adj (work, skills)* administratif(ive); *(error)* d'administration; **for administrative convenience** pour faciliter le travail administratif □ *administrative building* bâtiment *m* administratif *ou* d'administration; *Acct administrative costs* frais *mpl* d'administration *ou* de gestion; *administrative department* service *m* administratif; *administrative details* détails *mpl* d'ordre administratif; *administra-*

tive expenses frais d'administration *ou* de gestion; ***administrative formalities*** formalités *fpl* administratives; ***administrative headquarters*** siège *m* administratif; ***administrative jargon*** jargon *m* administratif; ***administrative law*** droit *m* administratif; ***administrative machinery*** appareil *m* administratif, mécanisme *m* administratif; ***administrative staff*** personnel *m* administratif; ***administrative unit*** unité *f* administrative

administrator *n* (**a**) *(of company)* administrateur(trice) *m,f*, gérant(e) *m,f*, gestionnaire *mf* (**b**) *(of liquidation of a company's assets)* administrateur(trice) *m,f* judiciaire

admission *n (entry)* admission *f*, entrée *f*; **the admission of Poland into the EU** l'entrée de la Pologne dans l'Union européenne ❑ ***admission requirements*** conditions *fpl* d'admission

admit *vt (allow to enter)* laisser entrer

adopt *vt* (**a**) *(measures, approach, design)* adopter; *(minutes)* approuver; **the company must adopt new working practices for an increase in efficiency** la société doit adopter de nouvelles méthodes de travail de façon à être plus performante (**b**) *Mktg (product)* adopter

adoption *n Mktg (of product)* adoption *f*

ADP *n Comptr (abbr* **automatic data processing)** traitement *m* automatique des données

ADR *n Fin (abbr* **American Depositary Receipt)** certificat *m* américain de dépôt

ADSL *n Comptr, Tel (abbr* **Asynchronous Digital Subscriber Line)** ADSL *f*

adspend *n Fam* dépenses *fpl* de publicité

> ❝ ──────────────────────
> Like most of its competitors, Legal & General's expansion into direct marketing has seen it increase its **adspend**.
> ────────────────────── ❞

ad valorem *adj (duty, tax)* sur la valeur, ad valorem, proportionnel(elle)

advance 1 *n* (**a**) **in advance** *(book, apply, inform)* à l'avance; *(pay)* d'avance; **payable in advance** payable d'avance; **fixed in advance** fixé à l'avance; **thanking you in advance** *(in letter)* en vous remerciant à l'avance, avec mes remerciements anticipés ❑ ***advance booking*** réservation *f* à l'avance; ***advance booking charter*** achat *m* de bloc-sièges; ***advance notice*** préavis *m*; ***advance payment*** *(payment in full)* paiement *m* anticipé *ou* par anticipation; *(part payment)* arrhes *fpl*; ***advance publicity*** publicité *f* d'amorçage; ***advance warning*** préavis (**b**) *Fin (of funds)* avance *f*, acompte *m*; **he asked for an advance of £200 on his salary** il a demandé une avance de 200 livres sur son salaire; **advances on securities** *or* **against collateral** prêts *mpl* sur titres ❑ ***advance account***

compte *m* d'avances; ***advance dividend*** dividende *m* anticipé

2 *vt* (**a**) *Fin (money)* avancer (**to** à); **we will advance him £500 before completion of the contract** nous lui verserons un acompte de 500 livres avant l'achèvement des travaux ❑ ***sum advanced*** avance *f*, acompte *m*

(**b**) *(prices)* augmenter, hausser

(**c**) *(be promoted)* avancer, obtenir de l'avancement

3 *vi (of shares)* augmenter (de prix), monter; **the stocks advanced to their highest point in May** les actions ont atteint leur valeur la plus haute au mois de mai

advantage *n* avantage *m*; **knowledge of French is an advantage** la connaissance du français est un avantage; **to take advantage of sth** *(offer, situation, opportunity)* profiter de qch

adventure *n Fin* spéculation *f* hasardeuse

adverse *adj Fin (balance, budget)* déficitaire; **the stock markets showed an adverse reaction to the Chancellor's budget** les différentes places financières ont mal réagi au budget annoncé par le Chancelier de l'Échiquier

advert *n Fam (for product, service)* publicité *f*, réclame *f*; *(for job)* annonce *f*

advertise 1 *vt (product, service)* faire de la publicité *ou* de la réclame pour; *(job)* mettre une annonce pour; **as advertised on TV** vu(e) à la télé

2 *vi (to sell product, service)* faire de la publicité *ou* de la réclame; *(for job)* mettre une annonce; **to advertise for sb** passer une annonce pour trouver qn

advertisement *n (for product, service)* publicité *f*, réclame *f*; *(for job)* annonce *f*

advertiser *n* annonceur *m*

advertising *n* publicité *f* ❑ ***advertising account*** budget *m* de publicité; ***advertising agency*** agence *f* publicitaire *ou* de publicité; ***advertising agent*** agent *m* publicitaire *ou* de publicité; ***advertising approach*** optique *f* publicitaire; ***Advertising Association*** = organisme britannique dont le rôle est de veiller à la qualité des publicités et de défendre les intérêts des annonceurs et des agences de publicité; ***advertising awareness*** notoriété *f* publicitaire; *Comptr* ***advertising banner*** *(on web page)* bandeau *m* publicitaire; ***advertising budget*** budget de publicité; ***advertising campaign*** campagne *f* publicitaire *ou* de publicité; ***advertising concept*** concept *m* publicitaire; ***advertising consultant*** conseil *m* en publicité; ***advertising copy*** texte *m* publicitaire; ***advertising costs*** frais *mpl* publicitaires; ***advertising density*** densité *f* publicitaire; ***advertising department*** service *m* de publicité; ***advertising director*** directeur(trice) *m,f* de la publicité; ***ad-***

vertising effectiveness efficacité *f* publicitaire; *advertising executive* publicitaire *mf*; *advertising expenses* dépenses *fpl* publicitaires; *advertising gimmick* gadget *m* publicitaire; *advertising insert* encart *m* publicitaire; *advertising jargon* jargon *m* publicitaire; *advertising leaflet* imprimé *m* publicitaire; *advertising manager* directeur(trice) de la publicité; *advertising material* matériel *m* publicitaire; *advertising medium* support *m* de publicité; *advertising potential* potentiel *m* publicitaire; *advertising psychology* psychologie *f* de la publicité; *advertising rates* tarif *m* des insertions *ou* de la publicité; *advertising revenue* recettes *fpl* publicitaires; *advertising sales agency* régie *f* publicitaire; *advertising schedule* programme *m* des annonces; *advertising slogan* slogan *m* publicitaire; *advertising slot* créneau *m* publicitaire; *advertising space* espace *m* ou emplacement *m* publicitaire; *advertising standards* normes *fpl* publicitaires; *Br* **Advertising Standards Authority** ≃ Bureau *m* de vérification de la publicité; *advertising strategy* stratégie *f* publicitaire; *advertising target* cible *f* publicitaire

advertorial *n* publireportage *m*, advertorial *m*

> ❝ ——————————
>
> "The indirect endorsement they offer," says Emap Elan head of research Aida Muirhead, "appears to be a strong factor in generating purchasing interest. And the more an **advertorial** style resembles the writing style and look of the publication carrying it, the better. This prevents interrupting the flow of the reader."
>
> ——————————— ❞

advice *n* (**a**) *(opinion)* conseils *mpl*; **to take legal advice** consulter un avocat (**b**) *(notice)* avis *m*; **as per advice** suivant avis; **until further advice** jusqu'à nouvel avis ◻ *advice note* lettre *f* ou note *f* d'avis

advise *vt* (**a**) *(give advice to)* conseiller; **to advise sb to do sth** conseiller à qn de faire qch; **the company lawyer has advised caution** l'avocat de l'entreprise a recommandé la prudence (**b**) *(inform)* aviser, informer; **we are pleased to advise you that...** nous avons le plaisir de vous informer que...; **we should advise you that you have exceeded your credit limit** nous vous informons que vous avez dépassé votre découvert autorisé (**c**) *Banking, Fin* **to advise a draft** aviser d'une traite, donner avis d'une traite

adviser, *Am* **advisor** *n* conseiller(ère) *m,f*

advising bank *n* banque *f* notificatrice

advisor *Am* = **adviser**

advisory *adj* consultatif(ive) ◻ *advisory board* comité *m* consultatif; *advisory body* comité consultatif; *Banking advisory committee* co-

mité de restructuration; *advisory service* service *m* de renseignements

advocate 1 *n* *(supporter)* défenseur *m*, avocat(e) *m,f*; **a strong advocate of free enterprise** un fervent partisan de la libre entreprise
  2 *vt* prôner, préconiser; **he advocates reducing** *or* **a reduction in spending** il préconise une réduction des dépenses

affair *n* (**a**) *(business, matter)* affaire *f*; **the affair in hand** l'affaire qui nous occupe (**b**) **affairs** *(business, matters)* affaires *fpl*; **her financial affairs** ses finances

affidavit *n Law* affidavit *m*

affiliate 1 *n* *(person)* affilié(e) *m,f*; *Am (company)* société *f* affiliée, filiale *f*
  2 *vt* affilier; **to affiliate oneself to** *or* **with** s'affilier à
  3 *vi* **to affiliate to** *or* **with a society** s'affilier à une société

affiliated *adj (member, organization)* affilié(e) ◻ *affiliated company, affiliated operation* société *f* affiliée, filiale *f*

affiliation *n* société *f* affiliée, filiale *f*

affinity *n affinity (credit) card Br* = carte de crédit émise par un organisme de crédit en collaboration avec une association caritative ou à but non lucratif, de façon à ce qu'une part de chaque transaction revienne à ladite association; *Am* = carte de crédit résultant de la collaboration entre un organisme de crédit et une entreprise commerciale; *affinity marketing* marketing *m* par affinité; *affinity partner* partenaire *m* au sein d'un groupe d'affinité

> ❝ ——————————
>
> Countless other charitable deals exist. Among the most common are **affinity credit card** deals, where a charity gets a certain amount, usually 25p for every £100 spent. ...cause-related marketing, as it is known in the industry, is moving away from just being **affinity marketing** of credit cards and taking on several other guises.
>
> ——————————— ❞

affirmative *adj* (**a**) **to take affirmative action (to do sth)** prendre des mesures (pour faire qch); **we should take affirmative action to make our intentions clear in this marketplace** il nous faut prendre des mesures de façon à faire connaître clairement nos intentions sur ce marché (**b**) *Am* **to take affirmative action** prendre des mesures anti-discriminatoires

affluence *n* richesse *f*; **the affluence of the company's assets is well known** la société est connue pour l'importance de son actif

affluent *adj* riche ◻ *the affluent society* la société d'abondance

afford *vt* (**a**) *(have enough money for)* **to be able**

to afford sth avoir les moyens d'acheter qch; **we can afford to pay all our creditors by the end of the year** nous avons les moyens de payer nos créanciers d'ici la fin de l'année; **the company cannot afford any more new software** la société n'a pas les moyens d'investir davantage dans l'achat de logiciels

(**b**) *(allow oneself)* **we cannot afford to lose these members of staff** on ne peut pas se permettre de perdre ces employés; **we can afford to wait another few days** on peut se permettre d'attendre quelques jours de plus

affordable *adj* abordable

affreightment *n* affrètement *m*

AFL-CIO *n* (*abbr* **American Federation of Labor and Congress of Industrial Organizations**) = la plus grande confédération syndicale américaine

afloat *adv* **to keep sb afloat** renflouer qn; **to keep a business/the economy afloat** maintenir une entreprise/l'économie à flot; *Fin* **to keep bills afloat** faire circuler des effets; **many small businesses are struggling to stay afloat** de nombreuses petites entreprises ont du mal à se maintenir à flot

> **"**
> The chain, which operates the majority of its stores under the Dollar Zone name ... spent the past year converting its variety stores to the dollar format. But the move wasn't enough to **keep the company afloat** despite the recent surge in popularity of dollar stores in the slumping economy.
> **"**

aforementioned *adj* susmentionné(e); **with reference to the aforementioned items,...** en ce qui concerne les articles susmentionnés,...

aforesaid *adj* susmentionné(e), susdit(e)

after-hours *adj St Exch* **after-hours dealing** transactions *fpl* hors bourse; **after-hours market** marché *m* hors bourse

aftermarket *n St Exch* marché *m* secondaire

after-sales *adj* après-vente ❏ **after-sales department** service *m* après-vente; **after-sales marketing** marketing *m* après-vente; **after-sales service** service après-vente

> **"**
> It is difficult enough to entice consumers to buy online without sites blatantly disregarding consumer rights. In the real world, shoppers like stores that carry a wide range of goods at competitive prices. If they have a query, they want it answered promptly and competently, and once they have purchased, they want helpful and efficient **after-sales service**.
> **"**

after-tax *adj* après impôts, net d'impôt ❏ **after-tax profit** bénéfices *mpl* après impôts; **after-tax salary** salaire *m* après impôts *ou* net impôt

against *prep* (**a**) *(in opposition to)* contre; **the workers are against the idea of striking** les travailleurs ne veulent pas se mettre en grève; **to be insured against fire/theft** être assuré(e) contre l'incendie/le vol; *Ins* **against all risks** contre tous les risques (**b**) *(in relation to)* par rapport à; **the pound rose/fell against the dollar** la livre a augmenté/baissé par rapport au dollar; **to get an advance against one's salary** recevoir une avance sur son salaire

age *n* **age bracket** tranche *f* d'âge; **age group** tranche d'âge; **this product is targeted at the 18–24 age group** ce produit vise les 18–24 ans; **age limit** limite *f* d'âge

aged debtors *n Acct* balance *f* âgée

agency *n* agence *f* ❏ **agency account** compte *m* agence; **agency agreement** contrat *m* de mandat, accord *m* de représentation; **agency contract** contrat d'agence; **agency fee** commission *f* de gestion, frais *mpl* d'agence; *Am* **agency shop** = entreprise dans laquelle tous les salariés (qu'ils soient syndiqués ou non) sont représentés par un syndicat qui exige en contrepartie que tous les salariés paient une cotisation; **agency work** travail *m* pour une agence

agenda *n* *(of meeting)* ordre *m* du jour, programme *m*; **to draw up an agenda** dresser l'ordre du jour; **to place a question on the agenda** inscrire une question à l'ordre du jour; **the first item on the agenda** la première question à l'ordre du jour

agent *n* agent *m*, représentant(e) *m,f*; *(for firm)* concessionnaire *mf*; *(for brand)* dépositaire *mf*; **agent for Mercury Ltd** représentant de Mercury Ltd; **he is our agent in the Far East** c'est notre agent pour l'Extrême-Orient

agentry *n Am* fonction *f* d'agent

aggregate 1 *n* somme *f* totale, montant *m* global

2 *adj (amount)* total(e), global(e); *(figure)* global; **for an aggregate period of three years** pendant trois ans en tout ❏ **aggregate demand** demande *f* globale; **aggregate economic activity** ensemble *m* des activités économiques; **aggregate income** revenus *mpl* globaux; **aggregate net increment** accroissement *m* global net; **aggregate output** rendement *m* global *ou* total; **aggregate production** production *f* globale *ou* totale

aggrieved *adj Law* lésé(e) ❏ **aggrieved party** partie *f* lésée

agio *n Fin* (**a**) *(price)* agio *m*, prix *m* du change ❏ **agio account** compte *m* d'agio (**b**) *(business)* commerce *m* du change

agiotage n agiotage m

AGM n (abbr **annual general meeting**) AGA f

agree 1 vt (**a**) (reach agreement on) (price, conditions) s'accorder ou se mettre d'accord sur; **to be agreed** (date) à convenir; (price) à débattre; **unless otherwise agreed** sauf arrangement contraire; **as agreed** comme convenu
(**b**) (approve) **to agree the accounts** or **the books** faire accorder les livres; **the figures were agreed between the accountants** les chiffres ont été acceptés (d'un commun accord) par les experts-comptables
2 vi (**a**) (of books, figures) s'accorder (**b**) Mktg **to agree and counter** approuver et contre-argumenter

▶ **agree on** vt insep (price, date) convenir de

agreed adj (price) convenu(e), forfaitaire ❏ **agreed statement** déclaration f commune

agreement n (**a**) (arrangement, contract) accord m (**on** or **about** sur); **to break an agreement** rompre un accord; **to have an agreement with sb** avoir conclu ou passé un accord avec qn; **to enter into** or **conclude an agreement with sb** passer un accord avec qn; **an agreement has been concluded between the two parties** un accord est intervenu entre les deux parties; **to come to an agreement** parvenir à un accord; **to sign an agreement** signer un accord; **to sign a legal agreement (to do sth)** s'engager (par) devant notaire (à faire qch); **to abide by the agreement** s'en tenir à ce qui a été convenu; **our agreement was that...** nous avions convenu que...
(**b**) (understanding) accord m, entente f; **as per agreement** comme (il a été) convenu; **by mutual agreement** de gré à gré, à l'amiable, d'un commun accord

agribusiness n agrinégoce m

agricultural adj agricole ❏ **agricultural cooperative** coopérative f agricole; EU **agricultural levies** prélèvements mpl agricoles

agriculture n agriculture f

agritourism n agritourisme m

agro-industrial adj agro-industriel(elle)

agro-industry adj agro-industrie f

agrotourism n agritourisme m

aid n aide f, assistance f; **in aid of** au profit de

AIDA n Mktg (abbr **attention-interest-desire-action**) AIDA m

aided recall n Mktg notoriété f assistée

AIM n St Exch (abbr **Alternative Investment Market**) = marché hors cote rattaché à la Bourse de Londres

> ❝
> Several billion pounds have been raised on the Alternative Investment Market (**AIM**) over the last four years, following the billion-plus invested on its predecessor, the Unlisted Securities Market, over a much longer period. Another half billion has flowed into venture capital trusts (VCTs) which offer 20% income tax relief and other incentives to invest in very small companies.
> ❞

AIO n Mktg (abbr **activities, interests and opinions**) AIO mpl ❏ **AIO research** recherche f AIO; **AIO study** étude f AIO

air n **by air** par avion ❏ **air cargo** fret m aérien; **air letter** aérogramme m; **air link** liaison f aérienne; **air miles** = points que l'on peut accumuler lors de certains achats et qui permettent de bénéficier de réductions sur des billets d'avion; **to collect air miles** accumuler des points; **air traffic** trafic m aérien; **air transport** transports mpl aériens; **air waybill** connaissement m aérien, lettre f de transport aérien

aircraft n avion m

airfreight 1 n transport m aérien; (price) fret m, frais mpl (de transport aérien); (cargo) fret aérien ❏ **airfreight company** compagnie f de fret aérien; **airfreight consolidator** groupeur m de fret aérien; **airfreight container** conteneur-avion m; **airfreight services** messageries fpl aériennes
2 vt (goods) expédier par transport aérien

airfreighting n expédition f par avion

airline n compagnie f aérienne

airmail 1 n (service) poste f aérienne; **by airmail** par avion ❏ **airmail letter** aérogramme m
2 adv **to send sth airmail** envoyer qch par avion
3 vt (letter, parcel) envoyer par avion

airport n aéroport m ❏ **airport advertising** publicité f dans les aéroports; **airport hotel** hôtel m d'aéroport; **airport lounge** hall m d'aéroport; **airport shop** boutique f d'aéroport; **airport tax** taxe f d'aéroport; **airport taxi** taxi m desservant l'aéroport; **airport terminal** aérogare f

aisle n (in shop) allée f ❏ **aisle end display** tête f de gondole

alert box n Comptr message m d'alerte

align vt (**a**) Comptr (characters, graphics) aligner, cadrer (**b**) Fin (currency) aligner (**on** sur); **to align two different strategies** harmoniser deux stratégies différentes, rendre deux stratégies différentes compatibles

alignment n (**a**) Comptr (of characters, graphics) alignement m, cadrage m (**b**) Fin (of currencies) alignement m

alimony n Fin, Law pension f alimentaire

allied *adj Econ, Fin (product, industry)* assimilé(e)

all-in 1 *adj (price)* tout compris, forfaitaire ❑ *all-in insurance* assurance *f* tous risques; *Ins* **all-in policy** police *f* tous risques
   2 *adv* tout compris; **the computing system costs £3,000 all-in** le système informatique coûte 3000 livres, tout compris

all-inclusive *adj (price, tariff)* forfaitaire

allocate *vt* (**a**) *(resources, money, capital)* affecter, attribuer (**to** à); *(duties)* assigner (**to** à); *(time)* prévoir (**to** pour); **ten percent of profits were allocated to investment/advertising** dix pour cent des bénéfices ont été affectés aux investissements/à la publicité (**b**) *St Exch (shares)* attribuer, allouer

allocation *n* (**a**) *(of resources, money, capital)* affectation *f*, attribution *f*; *(of duties)* assignation *f*; *(of time)* prévision *f* (**b**) *St Exch (of shares)* attribution *f*, allocation *f*

all-or-none order *n St Exch* ordre *m* tout-ou-rien

allot *vt* (**a**) *(sum of money)* affecter (**to** à); *(job, task)* assigner (**to** à); **the funds have been allotted to the R&D department** les fonds ont été affectés au service recherche et développement (**b**) *St Exch (shares)* attribuer, allouer

allotment *n* (**a**) *(of sum of money)* affectation *f*; *(of job, task)* assignation *f* (**b**) *St Exch (of shares)* attribution *f*, allocation *f* ❑ *allotment letter* avis *m* d'attribution; *allotment right* droit *m* d'attribution

all-out *adj (strike)* tous azimuts; *(effort)* acharné(e); **to make an all-out effort to do sth** faire tout son possible pour faire qch

allow *vt* (**a**) *(give)* **to allow sb a discount** faire un escompte *ou* une remise à qn; **the bank allows five percent interest on deposits** la banque alloue *ou* attribue cinq pour cent d'intérêt sur les dépôts (**b**) *(accept) (claim)* admettre (**c**) *(take into account)* prévoir, compter; **allow a week for delivery** il faut prévoir *ou* compter une semaine pour la livraison

▸ **allow for** *vt insep* tenir compte de; *(difficulties, delay)* prévoir; **after allowing for** *(discount, expenses)* déduction faite de; **to allow for some wastage** prévoir plus large; **we have to allow an extra ten percent for carriage** il faut prévoir un supplément de dix pour cent pour le transport; **has that been allowed for in your figures?** en avez-vous tenu compte dans vos estimations?

allowable *adj* admissible, permis(e); *(claim)* recevable; *(expense)* déductible, remboursable; **expenses allowable against tax** dépenses *fpl* fiscalement déductibles

allowance *n* (**a**) *Admin (grant)* allocation *f*; *(for housing, travel, food)* indemnité *f* (**b**) *Fin (dis-*

count) déduction *f*, concession *f*; *(for tax)* abattement *m*; *(for bad quality)* réfraction *f*

All-Share Index *n Br* = indice du *Financial Times* et de l'Institut des actuaires britanniques

all-time *adj* **unemployment is at an all-time low** le chômage n'a jamais été aussi bas; **sales have reached an all-time high** les ventes ont atteint un niveau record

alphabetical order *n* ordre *m* alphabétique

alphanumeric *adj Comptr* alphanumérique ❑ *alphanumeric keypad* clavier *m* alphanumérique; *alphanumeric numbering* numérotation *f* alphanumérique

alphasort *Comptr* **1** *n* tri *m* alphabétique; **to do an alphasort on sth** trier qch par ordre alphabétique
   2 *vt* trier par ordre alphabétique

alpha stocks *npl St Exch* valeurs *fpl* de père de famille *ou* de premier ordre

alt *n Comptr* **e acute is alt 130** pour e accent aigu, il faut taper Alt 130 ❑ *alt key* touche *f* alt

Alternative Investment Market *n* = marché hors cote rattaché à la Bourse de Londres

AMA *n (abbr American Marketing Association)* = institut américain de marketing

amalgamate 1 *vt (companies)* fusionner; *(industries)* s'unir ❑ *amalgamated union* fédération *f* de syndicats
   2 *vi (of companies)* fusionner

amalgamation *n (of companies)* fusion *f*

amend *vt (resolution, motion, text)* amender; **the report has been amended to include the latest sales figures** le rapport a été modifié de façon à faire figurer le dernier chiffre des ventes

amendment *n (to resolution, motion, text)* amendement *m*

American Express® *n* American Express®; **to pay by American Express®** payer par American Express® ❑ *American Express® card* carte *f* American Express®

American-style option *n St Exch* option *f* américaine

Amex *n* (**a**) *(abbr American Stock Exchange)* = deuxième place boursière des États-Unis (**b**) *(abbr American Express®)* American Express® ❑ *Amex card* carte *f* Amex

amicable settlement *n* règlement *m* à l'amiable

amortizable *adj Fin (debt)* amortissable

amortization *n Fin (of debt)* amortissement *m* ❑ *amortization charges* frais *mpl* d'amortissement

amortize *vt Fin (debt)* amortir

amortizement *n Fin (of debt)* amortissement *m*

amount n (sum of money) somme f; (total) montant m, total m; **amount due** montant dû, somme due; **she billed us for the amount of £50** elle nous a présenté une facture d'un montant de 50 livres; **you're in credit to the amount of £100** vous avez un crédit de 100 livres; **please find enclosed a cheque to the amount of $100** veuillez trouver ci-joint un chèque de 100 dollars □ Acct **amount brought forward** montant à reporter

▶ **amount to** vi s'élever à, se monter à; **profits last year amounted to several million dollars** les bénéfices pour l'année dernière se chiffrent à plusieurs millions de dollars; **the company has debts amounting to over £200,000** les dettes de la société se montent à plus de 200 000 livres

ampersand n esperluette f

analog adj Comptr analogique

analyse vt analyser; (account) dépouiller, décomposer

analysis n analyse f; (of account) dépouillement m, décomposition f □ Acct **analysis ledger** journal m analytique

analyst n analyste mf

anchor store n magasin m phare (d'un centre commercial)

> Located next to the historic Farmer's Market at the corner of 3rd St. and Fairfax in the heart of Los Angeles, The Grove is Southern California's most highly anticipated retail venue. The Grove features over 50 high-end retailers, including **anchor store** Nordstrom, as well as a spectacular 14-screen stadium-seating movie megaplex.

ancillary 1 n (of company) filiale f
2 adj (**a**) (supplementary) auxiliaire; **local services are ancillary to the national programme** les services locaux apportent leur aide ou contribution au programme national (**b**) (subsidiary) (cost, advantage) accessoire □ **ancillary rights** droits mpl dérivés

angel n Fam Fin (investor) commanditaire mf, bailleur(eresse) m,f de fonds

angle bracket n crochet m en chevron

annual adj (holiday, payment, report) annuel(elle) □ **annual accounts** bilan m annuel, comptes mpl de clôture ou de fin d'exercice; **annual budget** budget m annuel; **annual congress** congrès m annuel; **annual contribution** (to pension scheme) cotisation f annuelle; Acct **annual depreciation** dépréciation f annuelle, amortissement m annuel; **annual earnings** (of company) recette(s) f(pl) annuelle(s); (of person) revenu m annuel; **annual general meeting** assemblée f générale (annuelle); **annual guar-**

anteed salary salaire m annuel garanti; **annual income** revenu annuel; Fin **annual instalment** annuité f; **annual leave** congé m annuel; **annual percentage rate** taux m effectif global; Ins **annual premium** prime f annuelle; **annual profit** profit m annuel; **annual report** rapport m annuel de gestion; **annual returns** déclarations fpl annuelles; **annual revenue** recette annuelle; **annual salary** salaire annuel; **he has an annual salary of £50,000** il gagne 50 000 livres par an; **annual sales figures** chiffre m d'affaires annuel; Acct **annual statement of results** déclaration f annuelle de résultats; **annual turnover** chiffre d'affaires annuel; **annual variations** variations fpl annuelles; Acct **annual write-down** dépréciation annuelle, amortissement annuel

annualize vt annualiser; **the annualized figures** le montant total pour un an □ **annualized percentage rate** taux m effectif global

annually adv annuellement, tous les ans

annuitant n rentier m viager

annuity n (regular income) rente f (annuelle); (for life) viager m, rente viagère; (investment) viager m; **to invest money in an annuity, to buy an annuity** placer son argent en viager; **to pay sb an annuity** servir ou faire une rente à qn □ **annuity payment** versement m d'annuité

annul vt (contract) annuler, résilier, résoudre

annulment n (of contract) annulation f, résiliation f, résolution f

anonymous adj Mktg **anonymous buyer** acheteur(euse) m,f anonyme; Comptr **anonymous FTP** protocole m de transfert anonyme; Mktg **anonymous research** recherche f anonyme

ANSI n (abbr **American National Standards Institute**) = association américaine de normalisation

answer 1 n réponse f; **in answer to your letter** en réponse à votre lettre; **there's no answer** (on telephone) ça ne répond pas
2 vt (letter) répondre à; **to answer the telephone** répondre au téléphone

answering adj **answering machine** répondeur m (téléphonique); **answering service** (staffed) permanence f téléphonique; (unstaffed) répondeur téléphonique

answerphone n répondeur m (téléphonique)

anticipate vt (**a**) (expect) prévoir; **we anticipate a good response to our advertisement** nous attendons de bons résultats de notre annonce publicitaire □ **anticipated profit** profit m espéré; **anticipated sales** (taux m de) ventes fpl prévues
(**b**) (be prepared for) anticiper, anticiper sur; **we anticipated our competitors by launching our**

product first nous avons devancé la concurrence en lançant notre produit les premiers; **he anticipated the fall in price and sold early** il a anticipé la baisse des prix et a vendu avant (**c**) *Fin (profit, salary)* anticiper sur

anticipation *n* **in anticipation of** en prévision de; **they raised their prices in anticipation of increased inflation** ils ont augmenté leurs prix en prévision d'une hausse de l'inflation

anti-dumping *adj (laws, legislation)* anti-dumping

anti-glare *adj Comptr (filter, screen)* antireflet

anti-globalization *n* anti-mondialisation *f*

anti-inflationary *adj (measures, policy)* anti-inflationniste

anti-raid *adj Fin (measures, precautions)* anti-raid

anti-takeover *adj (measures, precautions)* anti-OPA

anti-theft tag *n* agrafe *f* anti-vol

antitrust *adj Am Econ* anti-trust ❏ *antitrust law* loi *f* anti-trust

antivirus *n Comptr* antivirus *m* ❏ *antivirus check* vérification *f* antivirale; *antivirus program* programme *m* antivirus

AO(C)B *(abbr* **any other (competent) business***)* divers

APEX *adj (abbr* **advanced purchase excursion***) APEX fare* tarif *m* apex; *APEX ticket* billet *m* apex

apologize *vi* s'excuser; **to apologize to sb for sth** s'excuser de qch auprès de qn, présenter ses excuses à qn pour qch; **we apologize for any inconvenience** veuillez nous excuser pour les désagréments occasionnés

apology *n* excuses *fpl*; **please accept our apologies for the delay** veuillez accepter nos excuses pour ce retard; **the director sends his apologies** le directeur vous prie de l'excuser

apostrophe *n* apostrophe *m*

appeal *Law* **1** *n* appel *m*, pourvoi *m*; **to enter** *or* **to lodge an appeal** interjeter appel, se pourvoir en appel
2 *vi* interjeter appel, se pourvoir en appel; **to appeal against a sentence** appeler d'un jugement, faire appel d'un jugement; **to appeal against a decision** faire opposition à une décision, faire appel (à un tribunal) d'une décision

appellant *Law* **1** *n* partie *f* appelante, appelant(e) *m,f*, demandeur *m* en appel
2 *adj* appelant(e)

append *vt (list, document)* joindre (**to** à); *(signature)* apposer (**to** à); *(notes, comments)* ajouter (**to** à); *Comptr (to database)* ajouter (**to** à); **to append a document to a file** annexer *ou* joindre un document à un dossier; **please refer**

to the lists appended to this document veuillez vous reporter aux listes jointes au présent document

appendix *n (to document, report, book)* appendice *m*

applicant *n (for job)* candidat(e) *m,f*, postulant(e) *m,f* (**for** à); *(for loan, funding, patent)* demandeur(euse) *m,f* (**for** de); *Fin (for shares)* souscripteur(trice) *m,f* (**for** de); *(for trademark)* déposant(e) *m,f* (**for** de)

application *n* (**a**) *(for help, loan, funding, patent)* demande *f* (**for** de); *(for job)* demande (**for** de), candidature *f* (**for** à); **to submit an application** *(for help, loan, funding, patent)* faire une demande; *(for job)* présenter sa candidature; **to make an application for sth** formuler une demande pour obtenir qch; **closing date for applications** date limite de dépôt de candidatures; **full details on application** informations complètes sur demande ❏ *application form (for job)* formulaire *m* de candidature; *(for subscription)* bulletin *m* d'abonnement
(**b**) *St Exch* **application for shares** demande *f* de titres en souscription, souscription *f* d'actions; **to make an application for shares** souscrire (à) des actions; **payable on application** payable à la souscription ❏ *application form (for shares)* bulletin *m* de souscription
(**c**) *Comptr* application *f* ❏ *application software* logiciel *m* d'application

apply *vi* (**a**) **to apply to sb for sth** s'adresser *ou* recourir à qn pour obtenir qch; **apply to the personnel office** adressez-vous au service du personnel; **to apply for a job** faire une demande d'emploi; **she has decided to apply for the job** elle a décidé de poser sa candidature pour cet emploi; **to apply for a grant** faire une demande de bourse; **apply within** *(sign)* s'adresser ici; **to apply in writing** écrire; **to apply in person** se présenter (**b**) *St Exch* **to apply for shares** souscrire (à) des actions

appoint *vt* (**a**) *(person)* nommer; *(committee)* constituer; **to appoint sb to a post** nommer qn à un poste; **Mr Johnston has been appointed general manager** M. Johnston a été nommé directeur général; **he's our newly appointed sales manager** c'est notre nouveau chef de vente, c'est le chef de vente que nous venons de nommer (**b**) *(date, time, place)* fixer; **let's appoint a time for the meeting** fixons une heure pour la réunion

appointed *adj* (**a**) *(date, time, place)* fixé(e) (**b**) *appointed agent* agent *m* attitré

appointee *n* candidat(e) retenu(e) *m,f*

appointment *n* (**a**) *(meeting)* rendez-vous *m*; **to make** *or* **fix an appointment with sb** prendre rendez-vous avec qn; **to break an appointment** ne pas se présenter à un rendez-vous; **to cancel an appointment** annuler un rendez-vous; **please telephone if you cannot make** or **keep your appointment** veuillez téléphoner s'il vous est impossible de venir à votre rendez-vous; **to meet** or **see sb by appointment** recevoir qn sur rendez-vous; **by appointment only** sur rendez-vous; **have you got an appointment?** avez-vous un rendez-vous? ❏ *appointments book* carnet *m* de rendez-vous, agenda *m*; *appointments diary* carnet de rendez-vous, agenda

  (**b**) *(to job)* nomination *f*, désignation *f*; *(posting)* affectation *f*

  (**c**) *(job held)* poste *m*, emploi *m*; **to hold an appointment** être préposé(e) à un emploi; **he's been offered an appointment on the board** on lui a proposé un poste au conseil d'administration

  (**d**) **appointments** *(in newspaper)* offres *fpl* d'emploi

apportion *vt (taxes, expenses)* répartir

apportionment *n (of taxes, expenses)* répartition *f*

appraisal *n (of standards, personnel)* évaluation *f*; *(of object for insurance purposes)* estimation *f*, appréciation *f*; *(before auction)* prisée *f*; **to carry out an appraisal** conduire une expertise

appraise *vt (standards, personnel)* évaluer; *(object for insurance purposes, before auction)* estimer

appreciate *vi (of goods, investment, shares)* prendre de la valeur; *(of value, price)* augmenter; **the euro has appreciated in terms of other currencies** l'euro s'est apprécié vis-à-vis des autres monnaies

appreciation *n (of goods, investment, shares)* augmentation *f* de la valeur; *(of value, price)* augmentation

apprentice 1 *n* apprenti(e) *m,f*
  2 *vt* **to apprentice sb to sb** placer qn en apprentissage chez qn

apprenticeship *n* apprentissage *m*; **to serve one's apprenticeship (with sb)** faire son apprentissage (chez qn); **she did an apprenticeship as a carpenter** elle a fait un apprentissage de charpentier

appro *n Br Fam (abbr* **approval)** **on appro** à l'essai; **to buy sth on appro** acheter qch à l'essai; **to send sth on appro** envoyer qch à titre d'essai

appropriate *vt (funds)* affecter (**to/for** à); **£4,000 has been appropriated to upgrading computers** 4000 livres ont été affectées à l'augmentation de mémoire des ordinateurs

appropriation *n* (**a**) *(of funds)* affectation *f*; *(of payment)* imputation *f*; **appropriation to the reserve** dotation *f* au compte de provisions ❏ *appropriation account* compte *m* d'affectation, compte de pertes et profits (**b**) *Am* crédit *m* budgétaire; **allotment of appropriations** ré-

partition *f* des budgets ❏ *Appropriations Committee* = commission des finances de la Chambre des Représentants qui examine les dépenses

approval *n* (**a**) *(sanction)* approbation *f*; **subject to approval** soumis(e) à l'approbation; **to submit sth for approval (by sb)** soumettre qch à l'approbation (de qn); **for your approval** *(on document)* pour approbation (**b**) *(of document)* ratification *f*, homologation *f* (**c**) **on approval** à l'essai; **to buy sth on approval** acheter qch à l'essai; **to send sth on approval** envoyer qch à titre d'essai; *Am* **approvals** *(goods)* marchandises *fpl* envoyées à l'essai

approve *vt (action, plan, proposal, accounts)* approuver; *(document)* ratifier, homologuer; *(contract)* agréer; *(proposal)* approuver, agréer; **read and approved** *(on document)* lu et approuvé; **the plan must be approved by the committee** il faut que le projet reçoive l'approbation du comité

approved *adj Admin* **(officially) approved** homologué(e) ❏ *approved dealer* concessionnaire *mf* agréé(e)

approx *adv (abbr* **approximately)** env.

approximate *adj* approximatif(ive) ❏ *approximate price* prix *m* indicatif

approximately *adv* environ

approximation *n* approximation *f*

APR *n (abbr* **annual** or **annualized percentage rate)** TEG *m*

APT *n Fin, St Exch (abbr* **arbitrage pricing theory)** théorie *f* de l'évaluation arbitrage

aptitude test *n* test *m* d'aptitude

arb *n Fam Fin, St Exch* arbitragiste *mf*

arbitrage *n Fin, St Exch* arbitrage *m* ❏ *arbitrage pricing theory* théorie *f* de l'évaluation arbitrage

arbitrager, arbitrageur *n Fin, St Exch* arbitragiste *mf*

arbitrate 1 *vt* arbitrer, juger, trancher
  2 *vi* décider en qualité d'arbitre, arbitrer

arbitration *n* arbitrage *m*; **to go to arbitration** recourir à l'arbitrage; **they referred the dispute to arbitration** ils ont soumis le conflit à l'arbitrage; **procedure by arbitration** procédure *f* arbitrale; **settlement by arbitration** règlement *m* par arbitrage ❏ *arbitration board* comité *m* de conciliation, commission *f* paritaire d'arbitrage; *arbitration clause* clause *f* d'arbitrage, clause compromissoire; *arbitration court* tribunal *m* arbitral; *arbitration of exchange* arbitrage de change; *arbitration ruling* décision *f* arbitrale; *arbitration tribunal* tribunal arbitral, instance *f* chargée d'arbitrer les conflits sociaux

arbitrator n arbitre m, médiateur(trice) m,f; **the dispute has been referred to the arbitrator** le conflit a été soumis à l'arbitrage

archive Comptr **1** n archive f
　　2 vt archiver □ **archive copy** copie f archivée; **archive file** fichier m archives; **archive site** site m FTP

archiving n Comptr archivage m

archivist n documentaliste mf

area n (region) région f; **the London area** la région de Londres □ Am Tel **area code** indicatif m; **area manager** directeur(trice) m,f régional(e); **area of operations** branche f d'activité; Mktg **area sample** échantillon m par zone; Mktg **area sampling** échantillonnage m par zone

Ariel n St Exch = système informatique qui rend possible les operations boursières entre souscripteurs sans passer par la Bourse de Londres

arm's-length price n Fin = prix fixé dans les conditions normales de la concurrence

ARR n Acct (abbr **accounting rate of return**) taux m de rendement comptable

arrange **1** vt (meeting, trip) arranger; (time, date) fixer
　　2 vi **to arrange to do sth** s'arranger pour faire qch; (with someone else) convenir ou prévoir de faire qch; **let's arrange a time to meet** fixons une heure pour un rendez-vous; **the meeting is arranged for noon tomorrow** la réunion est prévue pour demain midi

arranged interview n Mktg entretien m organisé

arrangement n (understanding, agreement) arrangement m; Fin (with creditors) accommodement m; **to come to an arrangement with sb** faire un arrangement avec qn; **he came to an arrangement with the bank** il est parvenu à un accord avec la banque; **price by arrangement** prix m à débattre; (after bankruptcy) concordat m; **special designs by arrangement** autres modèles sur demande; **by prior arrangement** sur accord préalable

array n Comptr tableau m, matrice f

arrearage n Am = fait d'avoir des arriérés

arrears npl arriéré m; **we're three months in arrears on the loan payments** nous devons trois mois de traites; **to get into arrears** s'arriérer; **to be paid a month in arrears** être payé(e) en fin du mois; **interest on arrears** intérêts mpl moratoires; **salary with arrears effective as from 1 March** augmentation avec effect rétroactif au 1er mars; **tax in arrears** arriéré d'impôts; **arrears of interest** intérêts non payés; **arrears of work** travail m en retard

arrest vt (growth, development) arrêter; (slow down) entraver, retarder; **in an effort to arrest**

unemployment/inflation pour essayer d'enrayer le chômage/l'inflation

arrival n (of goods) arrivage m; (of person, aeroplane) arrivée f; **to await arrival** (on letter) prière d'attendre l'arrivée □ **arrivals list** liste f des arrivées; **arrival station** gare f d'arrivée; **arrival time** heure f d'arrivée

arrive vi **to arrive at sth** (solution, decision) arriver à qch, parvenir à qch; **to arrive at a price** se mettre d'accord sur un prix

arrow key n Comptr touche f fléchée, touche de direction

article **1** n **(a)** Law (in agreement, treaty) article m, clause f; (in contract) stipulation f □ **articles of apprenticeship** contrat m d'apprentissage; **Articles of Association** statuts mpl (d'une société à responsabilité limitée); **articles and conditions** (of sale, contract) cahier m des charges **(b)** (item) article m
　　2 vt (to trade) mettre en apprentissage; (to profession) mettre en stage; **to article sb to a tradesman** mettre qn en apprentissage chez un commerçant □ Law **articled clerk** clerc m d'avoué (lié par un contrat d'apprentissage)

> ❝
> Shareholders of Royal Ahold, the international food provider, approved all proposed amendments to the company's **Articles of Association** during an Extraordinary General Meeting of Stockholders held today. The par value of Ahold shares will now be expressed in Euro.
> ❞

artificial person n personne f morale

artwork n (for advertisement) illustrations fpl

ASA n **(a)** Br (abbr **Advertising Standards Authority**) ≃ BVP m **(b)** Am (abbr **American Standards Association**) ≃ AFNOR f

asap adv (abbr **as soon as possible**) dès que possible; **we need to reply asap** il faut qu'on réponde dès que possible

ascending adj □ **ascending order** ordre m croissant; **ascending sort** tri m en ordre croissant

ASCII n Comptr (abbr **American Standard Code for Information Interchange**) ASCII m □ **ASCII code** code m ASCII; **ASCII file** fichier m ASCII; **ASCII format** format m ASCII; **ASCII number** chiffre m ASCII

ASE n (abbr **American Stock Exchange**) = deuxième place boursière des États-Unis

ASEAN n (abbr **Association of South East Asian Nations**) ANASE f

A-share n St Exch action f ordinaire sans droit de vote

> Turnover on the local currency **A-share** markets in Shanghai and Shenzhen, which are restricted to Chinese investors, has more than trebled, to a daily $6 billion – 8 billion, and prices have soared … The hard-currency B-share markets, supposedly reserved for foreigners but in fact havens for hot Chinese money, have almost doubled from their all-time lows earlier this year.

asked price, asking price *n* prix *m* demandé, prix de départ; *St Exch* cours *m* offert, cours vendeur

aspirational *adj (product)* qui fait chic; *(consumer)* qui achète des produits de prestige; *(advertising)* qui joue sur le prestige d'un produit ❑ **aspirational group** groupe *m* de référence

> The Fosters Trading Company name is to be dropped and the clothing chain rebranded as a unisex store … The new stores, called d2, will stock male and female clothing and accessories and will be designed to appeal to the **aspirational** consumer.

assembly *n* (**a**) *(meeting)* assemblée *f*, réunion *f* (**b**) *(of machine, furniture)* assemblage *m*, montage *m* ❑ **assembly line** chaîne *f* de montage; **to work on an assembly line** travailler à la chaîne; **assembly line work** travail *m* à la chaîne; **assembly plant** usine *f* d'assemblage; **assembly shop** atelier *m* de montage; **assembly workshop** atelier de montage (**c**) *Comptr* assemblage *m* ❑ **assembly language** langage *m* d'assemblage

assess *vt* (**a**) *(damage)* évaluer; *(value)* estimer; **to assess a property for taxation** évaluer *ou* calculer la valeur imposable d'une propriété; **they assessed the damages at £500** ils ont fixé les dommages et intérêts à 500 livres (**b**) *(tax)* établir; **to assess sb's income** *(for tax purposes)* évaluer les revenus de qn ❑ **assessed income** revenu *m* imposable

assessable 1 *adj* imposable
2 *n Fin* **assessable income** assiette *f* de l'impôt; **assessable profits** assiette de l'impôt

assessment *n* (**a**) *(of damage)* évaluation *f*; *(of value)* estimation *f* (**b**) *(of tax)* calcul *m*; *(of income)* evaluation *f* (**c**) **assessment centre** *(for job candidates)* centre *f* d'évaluation des candidats

assessor *n* expert *m*; *Am* **assessor of taxes** inspecteur(trice) *m,f* des contributions directes

asset *n* (**a**) *Fin* **assets** *(of company)* actif *m*; *(personal)* patrimoine *m*; *(possessions)* avoir *m*, capital *m*; *Law (of inheritance, company)* masse *f*;

(on liquidation after bankruptcy) masse active; **assets and liabilities** actif et passif; **total assets** total *m* de l'actif; **excess of assets over liabilities** excédent *m* de l'actif sur le passif ❑ **asset allocation** répartition *f* des actifs; **asset management** gestion *f* de biens *ou* de capital; *(of individual's wealth)* gestion de patrimoine; **asset stripper** dépeceur *m* d'entreprise; **asset stripping** démantèlement *m* d'entreprise; **asset swap** swap *m* d'actifs; **asset turnover** rotation *f* des capitaux; **asset utilization ratio** taux *m* d'utilisation des actifs; **asset valuation** réserve *f*, provision *f* pour évaluation d'actif; *Acct* **asset value** valeur *f* d'actif

(**b**) *(advantage)* atout *m*; **she's a real asset to the company** elle apporte beaucoup à l'entreprise

assign *vt (task)* assigner (**to** à); *(funds)* affecter (**to** à); *(goods, debts)* céder, transférer (**to** à); *(shares)* attribuer (**to** à); *(appoint)* nommer, désigner; **to assign sb to do sth** charger qn de faire qch; **the property was assigned to his daughter** la propriété fut transférée au nom de sa fille; **she assigned the copyright to the school** elle a fait cession du droit d'auteur à l'école; **Robert has been assigned to the marketing department** Robert a été nommé au marketing

assignable *adj Law* cessible

assigned risk *n Ins* risque *m* cédé

assignee *n Law* cessionnaire *mf*

assignment *n (of task)* attribution *f*; *(of funds)* affectation *f*; *(of goods, debts, property)* cession *f*, transfert *m*; *(of shares)* attribution *f*; *Acct* **assignment of accounts receivable, assignment of debts** transfert de créances; **assignment of contract** = cession des droits et obligations découlant d'un contrat

assignor *n Law* cédant(e) *m,f*

assistant 1 *n* assistant(e) *m,f*
2 *adj* adjoint(e) ❑ **assistant general manager** directeur(trice) *m,f* général(e) adjoint(e); **assistant manager** sous-directeur(trice) *m,f*

associate 1 *n (in business)* associé(e) *m,f*, partenaire *mf*
2 *adj* associé(e) ❑ **associate company** société *f* affiliée, filiale *f*; **associate director** directeur(trice) *m,f* adjoint(e); **associate member** membre *m* associé

associated *adj* associé(e) ❑ **associated company** société *f* affiliée

association *n* association *f*, société *f*; **to form an association** constituer une société

assortment *n (of goods)* assortiment *m*

assume *vt (undertake)* assumer; *(running of company)* prendre en main; *(power, command)* prendre; **he will assume responsibility for**

the new department il sera responsable du nouveau service; *Ins* **to assume all risks** assumer tous les risques; *Law* **to assume ownership** faire acte de propriétaire

assurance *n Br* assurance *f* ▫ *assurance company* compagnie *f* d'assurances; *assurance policy* police *f* d'assurance

assured *n* assuré(e) *m,f*

assurer, assuror *n* assureur *m*

asterisk *n* astérisque *m*

at *prep (in e-mail address)* arrobas, a commercial; **"gwilson at transex, dot, co, dot, uk"** "gwilson, arrobas, transex, point, co, point, uk" ▫ *at sign* arrobas *m*

ATM *n* (**a**) *Banking (abbr* **automated teller machine**) DAB *m* (**b**) *Comptr (abbr* **asynchronous transfer mode**) ATM *m*, commutation *f* temporelle asynchrone

attach *vt* (**a**) *Admin (appendix, document)* joindre; **the attached letter** la lettre ci-jointe; **please find attached...** veuillez trouver ci-joint... (**b**) *(secondment)* affecter; **an official attached to another department** un fonctionnaire détaché à un autre service (**c**) *Comptr (file)* joindre (**to** à); **to attach a file to an e-mail** joindre un fichier à un e-mail (**d**) *Law* saisir

attachment *n* (**a**) *Admin (appendix, document)* pièce *f* jointe (**b**) *(secondment)* détachement *m*; **he's on attachment to the Manchester branch** il est en détachement à l'antenne de Manchester (**c**) *Comptr (of e-mail)* fichier *m* joint (**d**) *Law* saisie *f*, saisie-arrêt *f*; **attachment of property** saisie immobilière

attack 1 *n (on market)* attaque *f* (**on** sur); **they have just launched an attack on the mobile phone market** ils viennent de lancer une offensive sur le marché des téléphones portables **2** *vt (market)* attaquer

attain *vt (goals, results)* réaliser; **to attain a high standard** atteindre un haut niveau

attend *vt (meeting, conference)* assister à; **the conference was well attended this year** la conférence a attiré beaucoup de monde cette année

▶ **attend to** *vt insep (deal with)* s'occuper de; *(client, customer)* s'occuper de; *(order)* exécuter; **I shall attend to it** je m'en occuperai, je m'en chargerai; **are you being attended to?** est-ce qu'on s'occupe de vous?

attendance *n (presence at meeting)* présence *f*; *(people present)* assistance *f*; **there was a good attendance at the meeting** il y avait une assistance nombreuse à la réunion ▫ *attendance sheet (at meeting)* fiche *f* de présence

attention *n* **for the attention of Mr Harvey** *(in letter)* à l'attention de M. Harvey; **it has been brought to our attention that you have**

exceeded your overdraft limit il a été porté à notre connaissance que vous avez dépassé votre autorisation de découvert; **may I have your attention for a moment?** pourriez-vous m'accorder votre attention un instant?

attestation *n* attestation *f* ▫ *attestation of employment* certificat *m* de travail

attested copy *n* copie *f* certifiée conforme

at-the-money option *n St Exch* option *f* au cours, option à la monnaie, option à l'argent

attitude *n Mktg (of consumer to product)* attitude *f* ▫ *attitude research* enquête *f* d'attitudes; *attitude scale* échelle *f* d'attitudes; *attitude survey* enquête d'attitudes

attn *(abbr* **for the attention of**) à l'attention de

attorney *n* (**a**) *(representative)* représentant(e) *m,f*, mandataire *mf* (**b**) *Am (lawyer)* avocat(e) *m,f*

attract *vt* attirer; **the proposal attracted a lot of attention** la proposition a attiré l'attention de beaucoup de gens; **the campaign should attract many new investors** cette campagne devrait attirer un grand nombre de nouveaux investisseurs

attractive *adj (price, offer, proposition)* intéressant(e), attractif(ive)

attributable profit *n Acct* bénéfices *mpl* nets

attribute *n Mktg (of product)* attribut *m* ▫ *attribute list* liste *f* d'attributs

auction 1 *n* **(sale by) auction** (vente *f* aux) enchères *fpl*; **to sell goods** *Br* **by** *or Am* **at auction** vendre des marchandises aux enchères; **to put sth up for auction** mettre qch à l'enchère *ou* aux enchères; **the property was bought at auction** la propriété a été achetée à une vente aux enchères ▫ *auction price* prix *m* d'adjudication; *auction room* salle *f* des ventes; *auction sale* (vente aux) enchères **2** *vt* vendre aux enchères

▶ **auction off** *vt sep* vendre aux enchères

audience *n Mktg (for product, advertisement)* audience *f* ▫ *audience exposure* exposition *f* au public; *audience measurement* mesure *f* d'audience; *audience research* étude *f* d'audience; *audience size* audience cumulée; *audience study* étude d'audience

audioconference *n Tel* audioconférence *f*

audio-typing *n* dactylographie *f* audio-magnéto

audio-typist *n* audiotypiste *mf*

audit 1 *n Fin* vérification *f ou* contrôle *m* des comptes, audit *m* ▫ *Audit Bureau of Circulation* ≃ Bureau *m* de vérification de la publicité; *audit committee* comité *m* d'audit; *audit company* cabinet *m* d'audit; *audit manager* directeur(trice) *m,f* du service d'audit; *Admin* **Audit**

office ≃ Cour *f* des Comptes; ***audit trail*** vérification *f* à rebours
2 *vt Fin (accounts)* vérifier, apurer, examiner

auditing *n Fin* vérification *f* des comptes, audit *m*

auditor *n Fin (of company)* commissaire *m* aux comptes; *Admin (of public body)* vérificateur(trice) *m,f* des comptes, audit *m*, auditeur(trice) *m,f*; **firm of auditors** cabinet *m* d'audit, cabinet comptable ▫ ***auditor's report*** rapport *m* du commissaire aux comptes

auditorship *n Fin* commissariat *m* aux comptes

augmented product *n Mktg* produit *m* augmenté

AUP *n Comptr (abbr* **Acceptable Use Policy)** = code de conduite défini par un fournisseur d'accès à l'Internet

AUR *n (abbr* **asset utilization ratio)** taux *m* d'utilisation des actifs

austerity *n Econ, Fin* **austerity measures** mesures *fpl* d'austérité; **austerity policy** politique *f* d'austérité; **austerity programme** plan *m* d'austérité

autarky *n Econ (system)* autarcie *f*; *(country)* pays *m* en autarcie

authenticate *vt* (**a**) *(document, signature)* authentifier, certifier (**b**) *Comptr* authentifier

authentication *n* (**a**) *(of document, signature)* authentification *f*, certification *f* (**b**) *Comptr* authentification *f*

authority *n* (**a**) *(power)* autorité *f*; **the authorities** les autorités *fpl*; **I'd like to speak to someone in authority** je voudrais parler à un responsable; **she has authority over all the staff** elle a autorité sur tout le personnel (**b**) *(permission)* autorisation *f*; **to give sb authority to do sth** autoriser qn à faire qch

authorization *n* autorisation *f*; **you can't do anything without authorization from the management** vous ne pouvez rien faire sans l'autorisation de la direction

authorize *vt* autoriser; *(loan)* consentir; **to authorize sb to do sth** autoriser qn à faire qch

authorized *adj* autorisé(e); **authorized to sign** habile à signer ▫ ***authorized agent*** mandataire *mf*, agent *m* autorisé *ou* mandataire; *St Exch* **authorized capital** capital *m* autorisé; *Admin* **authorized charges** prix *mpl* homologués; **authorized dealer** concessionnaire *mf* agréé(e), distributeur(trice) *m,f* agréé(e); **authorized distributor** distributeur(trice) agréé(e); **authorized overdraft facility** autorisation *f* de découvert; **authorized price** prix *m* homologué; **authorized representative** *(of company)* mandataire, agent autorisé *ou* mandataire; *St Exch* **authorized share capital** capi-

tal autorisé; **authorized signatory** signataire *mf* autorisé(e) *ou* accrédité(e); **authorized signatory list** liste *f* des signatures autorisées; **authorized stockist** distributeur(trice) agréé(e); *Br St Exch* **authorized unit trust** = sicav autorisée par la commission britannique des opérations de Bourse

autocorrect *vt Comptr* corriger automatiquement

autodial *n Tel* numérotation *f* automatique

automated *adj* automatisé(e) ▫ *Banking* **automated clearing house** chambre *f* de compensation automatisée; **automated reservation** réservation *f* télématique; **automated teller machine** distributeur *m* automatique de billets; **automated ticket** billet *m* informatisé; *Banking* **automated withdrawal** retrait *m* automatique

automatic *adj* automatique ▫ **automatic accounting** comptabilité *f* mécanographique; *Comptr* **automatic backup** sauvegarde *m* automatique; *Tel* **automatic call transfer** transfert *m* d'appel automatique; *Comptr* **automatic data processing** traitement *m* automatique des données; *Tel* **automatic dial, automatic dialling** numérotation *f* automatique; *Comptr* **automatic feed** avance *f* automatique; *Comptr* **automatic input** saisie *f* automatique; **automatic packaging** empaquetage *m* automatique; *Banking* **automatic transfer** virement *m* automatique

automation *n* automatisation *f*

autonomous *adj* autonome

autonomy *n* autonomie *f* (financière); **the department has autonomy in this area** le service a toute liberté d'action dans ce domaine

autoredial *n Tel* renumérotation *f* automatique

autosave *Comptr* **1** *n* sauvegarde *f* automatique
2 *vt* sauvegarder automatiquement

availability *n* disponibilité *f*; **this offer is subject to availability** offre valable dans la limite des stocks disponibles

available *adj* disponible; *(person)* libre; **available at all branches** en vente dans toutes nos succursales; **we regret that this offer is no longer available** nous avons le regret de vous annoncer que cette offre n'est plus valable; **these items are available from stock** nous avons ces articles en magasin; **sum available for dividend** affectation *f* aux actions; **available on CD-ROM** existe en CD-ROM *ou* cédérom; **available for Mac/PC** disponible pour Mac/PC; **available to download from our website** peut être téléchargé à partir de notre site web ▫ *Fin* **available assets** actif *m* disponible *ou* liquide; *Banking* **available balance** solde *m* disponible; *Fin* **available capital** capital *m* disponible; *Fin* **available cash-flow** cash-flow *m* disponible; *Banking, Fin* **available funds** fonds *mpl* liquides *ou* disponibles, disponibilités *fpl*; *Mktg* **available market** marché *m* effectif; *Comptr* **available memory** mémoire *f* disponible

aval *n Banking* aval *m* bancaire

avalize *vt Banking* avaliser

AVC *n* (*abbr* **additional voluntary contribution**) supplément *m* de cotisation retraite (*payé volontairement*)

> **❝**
>
> AVCs are additional voluntary contributions – extra payments made from your salary or other net relevant earnings to top up your company pension. You can pay **AVCs** into a scheme run by your company, known as an in-house **AVC** scheme, or into a free-standing (FSAVC) policy run by another company, or you can pay **AVCs** to buy extra years of service in a final-salary company pension scheme.
>
> **❞**

AVCO *n* (*abbr* **average cost**) coût *m* moyen

average 1 *n* (**a**) (*standard amount*) moyenne *f*; **rough average** moyenne approximative; **sales average** moyenne des ventes (**b**) *Ins* avarie(s) *f(pl)* ❏ **average adjuster** répartiteur(trice) *m,f* d'avaries; **average adjustment** répartition *f* d'avaries; **average bond** compromis *m* d'avarie (**c**) *St Exch* indice *m*
   2 *adj* moyen(enne) ❏ **average cost per unit** coût *m* unitaire moyen; **average due date** échéance *f* moyenne; **average price** prix *m* moyen; **average revenue** produit *m* moyen; **average sample** échantillon *m* normal; **average tare** tare *f* commune, tare moyenne; *Am* **average tax rate** taux *m* d'imposition effectif *ou* moyen; **average unit cost** coût moyen unitaire; **average yield** rendement *m* moyen
   3 *vt* établir *ou* faire la moyenne de; (*perform typical number of*) atteindre la moyenne de;

household spending averages £120 per week les dépenses des ménages sont de *ou* atteignent les 120 livres par semaine en moyenne; **the factory averages ten machines a day** l'usine produit en moyenne dix machines par jour

▸ **average out at** *vi* s'élever en moyenne à; **profits average out at ten percent** les bénéfices s'élèvent en moyenne à dix pour cent; **production averages out at 120 units per day** la production est en moyenne de 120 unités par jour

avoidable costs *npl Acct* coûts *mpl* évitables

avoidance clause *n* clause *f* résolutoire

await *vt* **awaiting your instructions** (*in letter, memo*) dans l'attente de vos instructions; **awaiting delivery** (*of parcel, mail*) en souffrance

award 1 *n* (*damages*) dommages-intérêts *mpl*; (*decision*) arbitrage *m*, adjudication *f*; (*contract*) adjudication
   2 *vt* (*contract*) adjuger; (*pay rise, damages*) accorder

awareness *n* (*of product*) notoriété *f* ❏ **awareness rating** taux *m* de notoriété; **awareness study** étude *f* de notoriété

away *adv* (*absent*) **the boss is away on business this week** le patron est en déplacement cette semaine; **to work away** travailler d'arrache-pied

AWB *n* (*abbr* **air waybill**) LTA *f*

axe, *Am* ax 1 *n* **to get the axe** (*of person*) être licencié(e); (*of project*) être abandonné(e); **to give sb the axe** licencier qn; **to give sth the axe** supprimer qch
   2 *vt* (*person*) licencier; (*project*) supprimer; (*job, position*) supprimer; **the service has been axed for economic reasons** le service a été supprimé pour raisons économiques

AZERTY keyboard *n Comptr* clavier *m* AZERTY

Bb

B2B adj (abbr **business-to-business**) B2B

> Up until March, it had seemed that anyone who had half a business plan and dot.com on the end of their firm's name could raise millions in venture capital in a moment. But even in the early months of the year the mood was shifting. The hottest acronym was no longer B2C – business to consumer – but **B2B**, dot.coms helping business function better with each other.

B2C adj (abbr **business-to-consumer**) B2C

BAA n (abbr **British Airports Authority**) = organisme autonome responsable des aéroports en Grande-Bretagne

baby n Am Fin **baby bond** obligation f de faible montant, mini-obligation f; **baby boomer** enfant mf du baby boom

> They are targeting well-off **baby boomers** who are developing noses for wine and who rate choice and service at least as highly as price and convenience.

back 1 n (of cheque) dos m, verso m
  2 adj (a) (overdue) **back interest** arrérages mpl, intérêts mpl arriérés; Banking **back office** back-office m; Banking **back office staff** personnel m de back-office; **back orders** commandes fpl en souffrance ou en attente; **back pay** rappel m de salaire; **back tax** arriéré m d'impôt
  (b) **to put sth on the back burner** remettre qch à plus tard; **pay increases will have to be put on the back burner** les augmentations de salaire devront attendre
  3 vt (support) soutenir, appuyer; (financially) financer, commanditer; Fin (bill) avaliser, endosser, donner son aval à; (loan) garantir; **to back a winner** bien placer son argent
▶ **back up** Comptr **1** vt sep (data, file) sauvegarder
  2 vi sauvegarder

backdate vt (cheque, document) antidater; **the pay increase is backdated to 1 May** l'augmentation de salaire a un effet rétroactif à compter du 1er mai

back-end load n Am St Exch frais mpl de sortie

backer n (a) Fin (of bill) donneur m d'aval, avaliseur m (b) (financial supporter) bailleur(eresse) m,f de fonds, commanditaire mf; **we need a backer** il nous faut un mécène

background n (a) (of person) (relating to qualifications, experience) expérience f; **what is the candidate's background?** quels sont les antécédents du candidat?; **we need someone with a background in computers** il nous faut quelqu'un qui s'y connaisse en informatique (b) Comptr arrière-plan m □ **background data** données fpl de base; **background job** tâche f d'arrière-plan ou de fond; **background (mode) printing** impression f en arrière-plan; **background task** tâche d'arrière-plan ou de fond

backhander n Br Fam (bribe) pot-de-vin m, dessous-de-table m

backing n (a) (of currency) couverture f, garantie f (b) (support) soutien m, appui m; (financial support) financement m; **to give financial backing to sth** financer qch

backlight n Comptr (of screen) rétroéclairage m

backlit adj Comptr (screen) rétroéclairé(e)

backlog n arriéré m, accumulation f; **to have a backlog of work** avoir du retard dans son travail, avoir du travail en retard; **a backlog of orders** des commandes non exécutées ou en souffrance

backslash n Comptr barre f oblique inversée

backspace n Comptr retour m arrière □ **backspace key** touche f de retour arrière

back-to-back adj Fin **back-to-back credit** crédit m dos-à-dos; **back-to-back loan** prêt m face à face; **back-to-back operation** opération f de face à face

backup n (a) (support) soutien m, appui m □ **backup service** service m après-vente (b) Comptr sauvegarde f; **to do the backup** faire la sauvegarde □ **backup copy** copie f de sauvegarde; **backup file** fichier m de sauvegarde; **backup system** (for saving) système m de sauvegarde; (auxiliary system) système de secours

backward adj Econ **backward integration** intégration f en amont ou ascendante; **backward pricing** rajustement m des prix; Comptr **backward search** recherche f arrière ou vers le haut

backwardation n Fin marché m en déport

❑ *backwardation rate* taux *m* de déport

backward-compatible *adj Comptr* compatible avec les versions antérieures

BACS *n* (*abbr* **Bankers' Automated Clearing System**) = système électronique de paiement; **to pay by BACS** payer par virement électronique

> ❝
> The banks, which have hardly rushed in the past to tackle this issue, now plan to introduce an automated direct debit transfer system through the bank clearing system, **BACS**, – but not until the end of next year.
> ❞

bad 1 *n* **he is £5,000 to the bad** (*overdrawn*) il a un découvert de 5000 livres; (*after a deal*) il a perdu 5000 livres

2 *adj Comptr* **bad command** (*in error messages*) commande *f* erronée; **bad debt** créance *f* irrécouvrable *ou* douteuse; **bad debt insurance** assurance *f* contre les créances irrécouvrables *ou* douteuses; **bad debtor** créance irrécouvrable *ou* douteuse; **bad debt provision** provision *f* pour créances irrécouvrables *ou* douteuses; **bad debts reserve** réserve *f* pour créances irrécouvrables *ou* douteuses; *Comptr* **bad file name** nom *m* de fichier erroné; **bad management** mauvaise gestion *f*; **bad name** mauvaise réputation *f*; **that company has a bad name in the business** la société a mauvaise réputation dans le milieu; **bad payer** mauvais payeur *m*; *Comptr* **bad sector** secteur *m* endommagé

> ❝
> A deterioration in loans to mainland-related companies has forced the Bank of China's local operations to drastically increase **bad debt provisions** in the six months to June 30, causing a 46.74 per cent plunge in pre-tax profit to $3 billion.
> ❞

bail *n Law* caution *f*; **to go** *or* **stand bail for sb** se porter garant(e) de qn

▸ **bail out** *vt sep* (**a**) (*person, company*) renflouer (**b**) *Law* **to bail sb out** se porter garant(e) de qn

bait-and-switch *n Am Mktg* (*for product*) = fait d'appâter le client avec des prix promotionnels pour le fidéliser avant de les augmenter à nouveau; (*for Web site*) = fait d'appâter le visiteur et de le transférer ensuite vers une autre page

balance 1 *n* (**a**) *Fin* (*of account*) solde *m*; *Acct* balance *f*, bilan *m*; **balance in hand** solde en caisse; **balance carried forward** solde à reporter; (*on balance sheet*) report *m* à nouveau; **balance brought forward** solde reporté; (*on*

balance sheet) report; **balance due** solde débiteur, solde dû; **to pay the balance** régler le solde; **off the balance sheet** hors de bilan ❑ **balance book** livre *m* d'inventaire; **balance sheet** bilan; **balance sheet auditing** contrôle *m* du bilan; **balance sheet consolidation** consolidation *f* de bilan; **balance sheet item** poste *m* de bilan; **balance sheet value** valeur *f* bilantielle, valeur d'inventaire

(**b**) (*remainder*) reste *m*; **the balance of your order will be supplied within ten days** le reste de votre commande vous sera livré dans les dix jours

(**c**) *Econ* **balance of payments** balance *f* des paiements; **balance of payments deficit** déficit *m* de la balance des paiements, déficit extérieur; **balance of trade** balance commerciale

2 *vt Fin* (*account*) équilibrer, balancer; (*debt*) compenser; (*budget*) équilibrer; (*settle, pay*) régler, solder; **to balance an account** solder un compte; **to balance the books** dresser *ou* établir le bilan, arrêter les comptes; **to balance one's chequebook** faire ses comptes; **to balance the budget** équilibrer le budget; **to balance an adverse budget** rétablir un budget déficitaire ❑ **balanced budget** budget *m* équilibré, équilibre *m* budgétaire

3 *vi Fin* (*of accounts*) s'équilibrer, balancer; **I can't get the accounts to balance** je n'arrive pas à équilibrer les comptes

▸ **balance out** *vi* (*of figures*) correspondre; **debits and credits should balance out** les débits et les crédits devraient s'équilibrer

balancing *n Fin* (*of accounts*) solde *m*, alignement *m*, arrêté *m*

balloon 1 *n Am Fin* **balloon mortgage** = prêt hypothécaire à court terme comprenant quelques remboursements périodiques et le paiement du plus gros de la somme en une fois à l'échéance du prêt; *Am* **balloon payment** = paiement du solde d'un prêt hypothécaire arrivé à échéance

2 *vi* (*increase dramatically*) monter en flèche; **exports have ballooned in the last twelve months** les exportations ont monté en flèche au cours des douze derniers mois

ballot 1 *n* (**a**) (*vote*) scrutin *m*; **to hold a ballot** organiser des élections; **to take a ballot** procéder à un scrutin *ou* à un vote; **to vote by ballot** voter à bulletin secret (**b**) *St Exch* (*when shares are oversubscribed*) allocation *f* d'actions par tirage au sort

2 *vt* consulter par voie de scrutin; **union members will be ballotted on Tuesday** les membres du syndicat décideront par voie de scrutin mardi

ballpark figure *n* chiffre *m* approximatif; **a ballpark figure of £3,000** une somme qui avoisine les 3000 livres

ballpoint pen n stylo m (à) bille

ban n *(embargo)* embargo m; *(sanction)* sanctions fpl économiques

bancassurance n *Banking* bancassurance f

> **"**
> The term imported from the continent is **bancassurance**. In essence, it is meant to describe the business model that uses a bank's high street branches to sell insurance products.
> **"**

bancassurer n *Banking* bancassureur m

band n *(of ages, tax)* tranche f; *(of salaries)* catégorie f

banded pack n lot m ◻ **banded pack selling** vente f par lot

bandwidth n *Comptr* largeur f de bande

bang vt *St Exch* **to bang the market** faire baisser les prix, écraser le marché

bangtail n *Am Mktg* coupon-réponse m détachable

bank 1 n banque f; **the High Street banks** les grandes banques centrales; **the World Bank** la Banque Mondiale; **the Bank of England/France** la Banque d'Angleterre/de France ◻ **bank acceptance** acceptation f de banque; **bank account** compte m en banque, compte bancaire; **to open/close a bank account** ouvrir/fermer un compte bancaire; **bank advance** avance f bancaire; **bank advice** avis m de la banque; **bank annuity** rente f perpétuelle; **bank balance** solde m (bancaire *ou* en banque); **bank base rate** taux m de base bancaire; **bank bill** effet m *(tiré par une banque sur une autre)*; **bank book** livret m de banque, carnet m de banque; **bank borrowings** emprunts mpl bancaires; **bank branch** agence f bancaire; **bank branch code** code m guichet; **bank buying rate** taux de change à l'achat; **bank card** carte f d'identité bancaire; **bank charges** frais mpl bancaires; **bank clerk** employé(e) m,f de banque; **bank credit** avoir m en banque, crédit m bancaire; **bank debts** dettes fpl bancaires; **bank deposit** dépôt m bancaire *ou* en banque; **bank details** relevé m d'identité bancaire, RIB m; **bank discount** escompte m de banque *ou* en dehors; **bank discount rate** escompte officiel; **bank draft** traite f bancaire; *Am* **bank examiner** inspecteur(trice) m,f de banque; **bank guarantee** garantie f bancaire, caution f de banque; **bank holiday** *(in UK)* jour m férié; *(in US)* jour m de fermeture des banques; **bank interest** intérêt m bancaire; **bank lending** concours bancaire; **bank loan** *(money lent)* prêt m bancaire; *(money borrowed)* emprunt m bancaire; **to take out a bank loan** obtenir un prêt bancaire; **bank manager** direc-

teur(trice) m,f de banque; **bank money** monnaie f de banque; **bank notification** avis m de la banque; **bank overdraft** découvert m bancaire; *Am* **bank paper** *(banknotes)* billets mpl de banque; *(securities, drafts etc)* titres mpl bancaires; **bank rate** taux bancaire, taux d'escompte *ou* de l'escompte; *Acct* **bank reconciliation** rapprochement m bancaire; **bank reserves** réserves fpl bancaires; **bank selling rate** taux de change à la vente; **bank shares** valeurs fpl bancaires; **bank sort code** code guichet; **bank statement** relevé de compte; **bank teller** guichetier(ère) m,f; **bank transaction** transaction f bancaire; **bank transfer** virement m bancaire; **bank transfer advice** avis de virement; **bank treasurer** trésorier(ère) m,f de banque

2 vt *(cheque, money)* mettre *ou* déposer à la banque

3 vi **to bank with sb** avoir un compte (bancaire) chez qn; **where do you bank?, who do you bank with?** à quelle banque êtes-vous *ou* avez-vous votre compte?, quelle est votre banque?

bankable adj bancable, escomptable ◻ **bankable paper** papier m bancable

banker n banquier(ère) m,f ◻ **banker's acceptance** acceptation f bancaire; **Bankers' Automated Clearing System** = système électronique de compensation de chèques; **banker's card** carte f d'identité bancaire; **banker's cheque, banker's draft** traite f bancaire; **banker's order** ordre m de virement bancaire

banking n *(activity)* opérations fpl bancaires; *(profession)* profession f de banquier; **she's in banking** elle travaille dans la banque ◻ *Am* **banking account** compte m en banque, compte bancaire; **banking business** trafic m bancaire; **banking consortium** consortium m de banques; **banking controls** contrôle m bancaire; **banking hours** heures fpl d'ouverture de la banque; **banking house** maison f de banque, établissement m bancaire; **banking law** droit m bancaire; **banking legislation** législation f bancaire; **banking machinery** mécanisme m bancaire; **banking mechanism** mécanisme bancaire; **banking pool** pool m bancaire; **banking product** produit m bancaire; **banking services** services mpl bancaires; **banking system** système m bancaire

banknote n billet m de banque

bankroll *Am* **1** n fonds mpl, finances fpl
2 vt *(deal, project)* financer

bankrupt 1 n failli(e) m,f ◻ **bankrupt's certificate** concordat m
2 adj failli(e); **to go bankrupt** faire faillite; **to be bankrupt** être en faillite; **to adjudicate** *or* **declare sb bankrupt** déclarer qn en faillite
3 vt *(company, person)* mettre en faillite; **the**

deal bankrupted the business la transaction a mis l'entreprise en faillite

bankruptcy *n* faillite *f*; **to present** *or* **file one's petition for bankruptcy** déposer son bilan ❑ *Br* ***bankruptcy court*** ≃ tribunal *m* de commerce; ***bankruptcy proceedings*** procédure *f* de faillite

banner *n* *Comptr (for advertising on Internet)* bandeau *m* publicitaire, bannière *f* publicitaire ❑ ***banner ad, banner advertisement*** bandeau publicitaire, bannière publicitaire; ***banner campaign*** = campagne publicitaire sur Internet utilisant des bandeaux publicitaires

> **❝**
> At group level Unilever has an agreement with service provider America Online to advertise its products to subscribers. Separate from this, its most expensive new-media venture in the UK was a five-week **banner campaign** earlier this year for a new Lynx deodorant fragrance called Apollo.
> **❞**

bar *n* (**a**) ***bar chart*** histogramme *m*, graphique *m* à bâtons *ou* à barres; ***bar code*** code-barre *m* (**b**) *Comptr (menu bar)* barre *f*

bargain 1 *n* (**a**) *(agreement)* marché *m*, affaire *f*; **a bad bargain** une mauvaise affaire; **to strike** *or* **make a bargain with sb** conclure *ou* faire un marché avec qn; **to drive a hard bargain** être dur(e) en affaires (**b**) *(good buy)* affaire *f*, occasion *f* ❑ ***bargain counter*** rayon *m* des soldes; ***bargain offer*** offre *f* exceptionnelle; ***bargain price*** prix *m* de solde *ou* exceptionnel
2 *vi* (**a**) *(negotiate)* négocier (**with** avec); **the unions are bargaining with management for an eight percent pay rise** les syndicats négocient une hausse de salaire de huit pour cent avec la direction (**b**) *(haggle)* **to bargain with sb** marchander avec qn; **to bargain over sth** marchander qch

bargaining *n* marchandage *m* ❑ ***bargaining chip*** monnaie *f* d'échange; **to use sb/sth as a bargaining chip** utiliser qn/qch comme monnaie d'échange; ***bargaining position*** situation *f* permettant de négocier; **we are in a strong bargaining position** nous sommes en position de force pour négocier; ***bargaining power*** pouvoir *m* de négociation; **they have considerable bargaining power** ils ont beaucoup de poids dans les négociations; ***bargaining table*** table *f* des négociations

> **❝**
> As you might expect, larger companies have a distinct negotiating advantage, often using their leverage to qualify for high-volume discounts or get better deals. However, that doesn't mean that small- to medium-sized manufacturers can't beef up their **bargaining power**. For example, by joining or forming a purchasing cooperative, you can mass your company's orders with several other companies' orders, enabling all to receive a better price.
> **❞**

barrier *n* barrière *f*, obstacle *m*; **barrier to entry** barrières *fpl* à l'entrée

barrister *n* *Br Law* **barrister (at law)** ≃ avocat(e) *m,f*

barter 1 *n* échange *m*, troc *m*; **a system of barter** une économie de troc ❑ ***barter economy*** économie *f* de troc; ***barter society*** société *f* vivant du troc; ***barter system*** économie de troc
2 *vt* échanger
3 *vi* faire un échange ou un troc

barterer *n* troqueur(euse) *m,f*

base 1 *n* (**a**) *Banking* ***base date*** date *f* de base; *Banking* ***base lending rate*** taux *m* de base du crédit bancaire; *Am* ***base pay*** salaire *m* de base; *Banking* ***base rate*** taux de base (bancaire); *Am* ***base salary*** salaire de base; ***base year*** année *f* de référence (**b**) *Com* **the company's base** le siège de la société; **an industrial base** une zone industrielle
2 *vt (locate)* **to be based in** être basé(e) à; **where are you based?** où êtes-vous installé?; **the job is based in Tokyo** le poste est basé à Tokyo

baseline *n* (**a**) ***baseline costs*** coûts *mpl* de base; ***baseline sales*** ventes *fpl* de base (**b**) *Comptr (in DTP)* ligne *f* de base

BASIC *n* *Comptr (abbr* **Beginners' All-Purpose Symbolic Instruction Code)** Basic *m*

basic *adj* ***basic commodity*** denrée *f* témoin, denrée de base; ***basic consumer goods*** denrées *fpl* de consommation courante; *Ins* ***basic cover*** assurance *f* de garantie de base; ***basic industry*** industrie *f* de base; ***basic offer*** offre *f* de base; *Br* ***basic pay*** salaire *m* de base; ***basic personal allowance*** abattement *m* à la base; ***basic population*** population *f* mère; *Banking* ***basic rate*** taux *m* de base (bancaire); ***basic rate tax*** impôt *m* forfaitaire; *Br* ***basic salary*** salaire de base; ***basic statistics*** statistiques *fpl* fondamentales; *Br* ***basic wage*** salaire de base

basic-rate *adj* **most people are basic-rate taxpayers** la plupart des gens sont imposés au taux de base ❑ ***basic-rate taxation*** imposition *f* forfaitaire

basis *n* (**a**) *(foundation)* base *f*; **basis of assessment** *(of income tax)* assiette *f* de l'impôt; **basis of calculations** base de calcul; **basis for depreciation** base amortissable; **on the basis of these figures** sur la base de ces chiffres ❑ *Am Fin* ***basis point*** point *m* de base (**b**) *(system)* **employed on a part-time basis** employé(e) à mi-temps; **paid on a weekly basis** payé(e) à la semaine

basket n Econ, Fin **basket clause** clause f fourre-tout; **basket of currencies** panier m de devises, panier de monnaies

batch n (of goods) lot m ◻ Comptr **batch file** fichier m de commandes; **batch number** numéro m de lot; **batch processing** traitement m par lots; **batch production** production f ou fabrication f par lots

baud n Comptr baud m; **at 28,800 baud** à (une vitesse de) 28 800 bauds ◻ **baud rate** débit m en bauds

bay n Comptr baie f

BBB n (abbr **Better Business Bureau**) = organisme américain dont la vocation est de faire respecter la déontologie professionnelle dans le secteur tertiaire

BBS n Comptr (abbr **bulletin board system**) BBS m, serveur m télématique

Bcc Comptr (abbr **blind carbon copy**) copie f cachée

BCE n (abbr **Board of Customs and Excise**) = douane britannique

BD n (abbr **bank draft**) traite f bancaire

BE n (abbr **Bank of England**) Banque f d'Angleterre

b/e n (abbr **bill of exchange**) lettre f de change

bean counter n Am Fam comptable mf

bear 1 n (a) St Exch baissier(ère) m,f, spéculateur(trice) m,f à la baisse; **to go a bear** spéculer à la baisse ◻ **bear closing** arbitrage m à la baisse; **bear market** marché m à la baisse ou baissier; **bear operation** opération f à la baisse; **bear position** position f vendeuse ou baissière; **bear sale** vente f à découvert; **bear speculation** spéculation f à la baisse; **bear trading** spéculation à la baisse; **bear transaction** opération à la baisse (b) Fam **bear hug** = communiqué d'information annonçant une OPA immédiate
2 vt (a) St Exch (prices, shares) pousser à la baisse; **to bear the market** chercher à faire baisser les cours (b) **to bear interest** porter intérêt; **to bear the costs (of sth)** prendre les frais (de qch) à sa charge; **his investment bore eight percent interest** ses investissements lui ont rapporté huit pour cent d'intérêt
3 vi St Exch (of person) spéculer à la baisse; (of stocks) être en baisse

bearer n (of news, letter, cheque) porteur(euse) m,f; (of passport) titulaire mf; **cheque made payable to bearer** chèque m (payable) au porteur ◻ Fin **bearer bill** effet m au porteur; Fin **bearer bond** titre m ou obligation f au porteur; Banking **bearer cheque** chèque au porteur; Fin **bearer paper** papier m au porteur; Fin, St Exch **bearer securities** valeurs fpl au porteur; Fin, St Exch **bearer share** action f au porteur

bearish adj St Exch (market, trend) à la baisse,

baissier(ère); **to be bearish** (of person) spéculer ou jouer à la baisse ◻ **bearish tendency** tendance f à la baisse

bearishness n St Exch tendance f à la baisse

bed n (a) Fam **to get into bed with sb** (form partnership with) travailler en collaboration avec qn (b) St Exch **bed and breakfasting** aller et retour m

before-tax adj brut(e), avant impôts; **before-tax income** revenus mpl bruts

behalf n **to do sth on behalf of sb** (write, phone) faire qch de la part de qn; **to make a payment on behalf of sb** effectuer un versement au nom de qn

behaviour, Am **behavior** n Mktg (of buyer, consumer) comportement m ◻ **behaviour segmentation** segmentation f comportementale

behavioural study, Am **behavioral study** n Mktg étude f du comportement

Belgian franc n Formerly franc m belge

belly n Fam **to go belly up** (of company) faire faillite

below-the-line 1 n Mktg publicité f hors-média
2 adj (a) Mktg hors-média ◻ **below-the-line advertising** publicité f hors-média; **below-the-line costs** coûts mpl hors-média; **below-the-line expenditure** dépenses fpl hors-média; **below-the-line promotion** promotion f hors-média (b) Acct au-dessous de la ligne ◻ **below-the-line accounts** comptes mpl de résultats exceptionnels; **below-the-line costs** coûts mpl au-dessous de la ligne; **below-the-line expenditure** dépenses fpl au-dessous de la ligne

> 66
> Ayres will handle new product development and manage advertising and relationship marketing campaigns. There is likely to be an increased emphasis on **below-the-line** activity because of the high proportion of custom that comes from repeat visitors.
> 99

benchmark 1 n point m de repère, référence f ◻ **benchmark market** marché m de référence; Can Admin **benchmark position** poste-repère m
2 vt comparer

benchmarking n analyse f comparative

benchtest 1 n banc m d'essai
2 vt faire passer au banc d'essai

beneficiary n bénéficiaire mf; **beneficiary under a trust** bénéficiaire d'une fiducie

benefit 1 n (a) Br Admin (state payment) allocation f, prestation f; **to be on benefit** toucher l'aide sociale; **to pay out benefits** verser des prestations ◻ **Benefits Agency** caisse f des allocations sociales (b) (advantage) **benefits** (to *employee)* avantages *mpl* sociaux ❏ **benefits package** avantages sociaux; *Mktg* **benefit segmentation** segmentation *f* par avantages recherchés

2 *vt (person, country)* profiter à; *(trade)* favoriser; **a steady exchange rate benefits trade** un taux d'échange stable est avantageux au commerce *ou* favorise le commerce; **the change will benefit all employees** tous les employés bénéficieront de ce changement

3 *vi* **to benefit from sth** profiter de qch, tirer profit de qch; **to benefit from a rise in prices** profiter de *ou* tirer profit d'une hausse de prix

benevolent *adj* de bienfaisance ❏ **benevolent fund** fonds *m* de prévoyance; **benevolent society** association *f* de bienfaisance

bequeath *vt Law* léguer (**to** à)

bequest *n Law* legs *m*

best-before date *n* date *f* limite de consommation

best-in-class *n Mktg* chef *m* de file

best-of-breed *n Mktg* nec plus ultra *m*

best-perceived *adj Mktg* mieux perçu(e); **the best-perceived product** le produit le mieux perçu

> **"**
> But most important for Adidas is that it has toppled Reebok as the UK's **best-perceived** sports goods brand, knocking Nike into third place. This is a crucial victory for Adidas, which is engaged in a mammoth battle with Nike.
> **"**

best price *n* meilleur prix *m*

best-selling *adj* à grand succès, de grosse vente

better *vt (improve)* améliorer; *(surpass)* faire mieux que; **we must try to better last year's figures** nous devons essayer d'obtenir de meilleurs résultats que l'an dernier; **the company has bettered the competition for the second year running** c'est la deuxième année consécutive que l'entreprise a fait mieux que la concurrence ❏ **Better Business Bureau** = organisme américain dont la vocation est de faire respecter la déontologie professionnelle dans le secteur tertiaire

betterment *n* amélioration *f*; *Law (of property)* plus-value *f*

b/f *Acct (abbr* **brought forward)** reporté(e)

biannual *adj* semestriel(elle)

bid 1 *n* (**a**) *(offer)* offre *f*; *(at auction)* enchère *f*; **to make a bid of £250,000 for a property** faire une offre de 250 000 livres pour une propriété; *(at auction)* mettre une enchère de 250 000 livres sur une propriété; **to make the first** *or*

opening bid faire la première enchère

(**b**) *(tender)* soumission *f*; **the firm made** *or* **put in a bid for the contract** l'entreprise a fait une soumission *ou* a soumissionné pour le contrat

(**c**) *Am St Exch* **the bid and asked** les cours *mpl* d'achat et de vente ❏ **bid bond** caution *f* d'adjudication *ou* de soumission; **bid price** cours acheteur

(**d**) *(attempt)* tentative *f*; **in a bid to reopen negotiations** dans une tentative de relancer les négociations

2 *vt (at auction)* faire une enchère de; **we had to bid another thousand pounds** il nous a fallu surenchérir de mille livres

3 *vi* (**a**) **to bid for sth** faire une offre pour qch; *(at auction)* mettre une enchère sur qch; **to bid a high price** offrir une grosse somme; **to bid over sb** *or* **more than sb** enchérir sur qn

(**b**) *(tender)* faire une soumission, répondre à un appel d'offres; **to bid for** *or* **on a contract** soumissionner à une adjudication; **several firms bid for** *or* **on the project** plusieurs entreprises ont soumissionné pour le projet

▸ **bid up** *vt sep (price, goods)* enchérir sur

bidder *n* (**a**) *(at auction)* enchérisseur(euse) *m,f*; **the lowest bidder** le moins offrant; **the highest bidder** le plus offrant; **there were no bidders** il n'y a pas eu de preneurs (**b**) *(for tender)* soumissionnaire *mf*

bidding *n* (**a**) *(at auction)* enchères *fpl*, mises *fpl*; **the bidding was very brisk** les enchères étaient vives; **to start the bidding for sth at £5,000** mettre qch à prix 5000 livres; **to open the bidding** ouvrir les enchères; **to raise the bidding** monter les enchères; **the bidding is closed** l'enchère est faite, c'est adjugé; **the bidding went against me** on avait enchéri sur mon offre

(**b**) *(tenders)* soumissions *fpl*; **the cheapest** *or* **best bidding** la soumission la plus basse *ou* la plus favorable ❏ *Am St Exch* **bidding price** cours *m* acheteur

biennial *adj* bisannuel(elle)

BIFU *n (abbr* **The Banking, Insurance and Finance Union)** = syndicat britannique des employés du secteur financier

big *adj* **to earn big money** gagner gros ❏ *Br Fam St Exch* **Big Bang** = déréglementation de la Bourse de Londres en octobre 1986; *Am* **the big board** la Bourse de New York; **big business** *(companies)* les grandes entreprises *fpl*; *(trade)* un secteur qui rapporte; *Br* **the Big Four** = les quatre grandes banques anglaises *(Lloyds, National Westminster, Barclays, HSBC)*; *Fam* **Big Idea, big idea** idée-force *f*; **new product development is all about coming up with a Big Idea** le développement de nouveaux produits démarre toujours avec une idée-force

> **"**
> Call centres are **big business**, accounting for roughly one job in 50 in Britain. By 2008, that figure is expected to reach one in 30 as companies try to improve their contact with customers without taking on the expense of local offices or branches.
> **"**

big-budget *adj* à gros budget

bilateral *adj* bilatéral(e) ❑ *bilateral agreement* accord *m* bilatéral

bill 1 *n* (**a**) *(notice of payment due)* facture *f*; *(for gas, electricity)* facture, note *f*; *(in hotel)* note; *Br (in restaurant)* addition *f*; **can we have the bill, please?** *(in restaurant)* l'addition, s'il vous plaît; **to make out a bill** dresser *ou* rédiger une facture; **to pay a bill** payer *ou* régler une facture; **to foot the bill** payer la note *ou* les dépenses
(**b**) *Am (banknote)* billet *m* de banque; **a five-dollar bill** un billet de cinq dollars
(**c**) *Fin (promissory note)* effet *m* (de commerce), traite *f*; **bill made out to bearer** effet au porteur ❑ *bill book* livre *m* d'échéance; *bill broker* courtier(ère) *m,f* de change; *bill for collection* effet à l'encaissement; *bill discounter* courtier(ère) de change; *Customs bill of entry* déclaration *f* d'entrée (en douane); *bill of exchange* lettre *f* de change, effet de commerce; *bills of exchange statement* lettre de change relevé; *bill in foreign currency* effet en devise(s); *bills in hand* portefeuille *m* effets; *bill of lading* connaissement *m*; **through bill of lading** connaissement direct *ou* à forfait; *bills payable* effets à payer; **bill payable at sight** effet payable à vue *ou* à présentation; *Acct bills payable ledger* journal *m ou* livre des effets à payer; *bills receivable* effets à recevoir; *Acct bills receivable ledger* journal *ou* livre des effets à recevoir; *bill of sale* acte *m ou* contrat *m* de vente; *Customs bill of sight* déclaration (en douane) provisoire; *Customs bill of sufferance* lettre d'exemption; *bill without protest* traite sans frais
(**d**) *Law* projet *m* de loi
2 *vt* facturer; **they billed me twice for the spare parts** les pièces de rechange m'ont été facturées deux fois; **he bills his company for his travelling expenses** il se fait rembourser ses frais de voyage par son entreprise

billboard *n* panneau *m* d'affichage, panneau publicitaire ❑ *billboard advertising* publicité *f* sur panneau; *billboard site* emplacement *m* d'affichage

biller *n Am* facturier(ère) *m,f*

billhead *n* en-tête *m* de facture

billing *n* facturation *f* ❑ *billing date* date *f* de

facturation; *billing office* bureau *m* de facturation

billion *n* milliard *m*; **ten billion dollars** dix milliards de dollars

billposter *n* afficheur *m* publicitaire

billposting *n* affichage *m*

billsticker *n* afficheur *m* publicitaire

billsticking *n* affichage *m*

BIM *n* (*abbr* **British Institute of Management**) = organisme britannique dont la fonction est de renseigner et de conseiller les entreprises en matière de gestion, ainsi que de promouvoir l'enseignement de cette discipline

bi-media *adj* bi-média

> **"**
> As it turned out, the introduction of **bi-media** working at BBC News was just a foretaste of what was coming and has now developed into a key part of the survival of the fittest in the media. Back in 1991 at the BBC, it was a practical way of ensuring that the best and brightest from the news ranks were able to report for both the Today programme on Radio 4 and the Nine O'Clock News on BBC TV.
> **"**

bimonthly 1 *adj (twice a month)* bimensuel(elle); *(every two months)* bimestriel(elle)
2 *adv (twice a month)* deux fois par mois; *(every two months)* tous les deux mois

binary *adj Comptr* binaire ❑ *binary code* code *m* binaire

binder *n (for papers)* classeur *m*

binding *adj* obligatoire; *(contract, promise)* qui engage *ou* lie; **the contract is legally binding** ce contrat est juridiquement contraignant; **the agreement is binding on all parties** l'accord engage chaque partie; **it is binding on the buyer to make immediate payment** l'acheteur est tenu de payer immédiatement

bit *n Comptr* bit *m*; **bits per second** bits par seconde

bitmap *Comptr* **1** *n* bitmap *m*
2 *adj* pixélisé(e), bitmap, en mode point ❑ *bitmap font* police *f* pixelisée *ou* bitmap

bitmapped *adj Comptr* pixélisé(e), bitmap, en mode point

biweekly 1 *adj (twice a week)* bihebdomadaire; *(every two weeks)* bimensuel(elle)
2 *adv (twice a week)* deux fois par semaine; *(every two weeks)* tous les quinze jours

B/L, b/l *n (abbr* **bill of lading**) connt.

black 1 *n* **to be in the black** *(of person, company)* être solvable; *(of account)* être créditeur(trice)
2 *adj black book* plan *m* de défense contre une

OPA *ou* anti-OPA; *black economy* économie *f* souterraine *ou* parallèle; *St Exch* **black knight** chevalier *m* noir; *black market* marché *m* noir; **to buy on the black market** acheter au noir; *black marketeer* = personne qui fait du marché noir; *Black Monday* jour *m* du krach (boursier) *(le lundi 19 octobre 1987)*; *black money (earned on black market)* argent *m* du marché noir; *(undeclared)* argent non déclaré au fisc

blackleg *n Fam (strikebreaker)* jaune *m*

blacklist 1 *n* liste *f* noire
  2 *vt* inscrire *ou* mettre sur la liste noire

blank 1 *n (in document)* blanc *m*, (espace *m*) vide *m*; **fill in the blanks** remplissez les blancs *ou* les (espaces) vides
  2 *adj* (**a**) *blank cheque* chèque *m* en blanc; *Fin* *blank credit* crédit *m* en blanc; *Fin* *blank endorsement* endossement *m ou* endos *m* en blanc; *blank form* formulaire *m* (vierge *ou* à remplir), imprimé *m*; *Fin* *blank transfer* cession *f* de parts en blanc
  (**b**) *Comptr (disk, screen)* vide; *(unformatted)* vierge □ *blank unformatted disk* disquette *f* vierge

blanket *adj* général(e), global(e); **a blanket rule for all employees** un règlement qui s'applique à tout le personnel; **our insurance policy guarantees blanket coverage** notre police d'assurance couvre tous les risques □ *blanket agreement* accord-cadre *m*; *Mktg* *blanket family name* = nom de marque unique qui apparaît sur les différents produits commercialisés par une société; *Fin* *blanket mortgage* hypothèque *f* générale; *blanket order* commande *f* globale *ou* d'une portée générale; *Ins* *blanket policy* police *f* globale (tous risques)

blind *adj Am* *blind pool* = fonds d'investissement dans une start-up sans droit de regard de la part des investisseurs; *Mktg* *blind test* test *m* aveugle; *Mktg* *blind testing* tests *mpl* aveugles; *Am* *blind trust* blind trust *m*

blink rate *n Comptr (of cursor)* vitesse *f* de clignotement

blip *n (temporary problem)* contretemps *m*; **the company suffered a blip in February when it lost that contract** l'entreprise a subi un contretemps en février lorsqu'elle a perdu ce contrat

blister pack *n* blister *m*, emballage-bulle *m*

blitz *n Mktg* campagne *f* de marketing intensive; **we are already preparing for the pre-Christmas advertising blitz** nous préparons déjà la campagne de marketing de Noël

> **"**
> "Yes we want sales in Edinburgh but we're not going to launch a billboard **blitz**. It will be gradually, year by year."
> **"**

block 1 *n* (**a**) *(of shares)* paquet *m* □ *block booking* location *f* en bloc; *St Exch* *block issue* émission *f* par série; *block purchase* achat *m* en bloc; *block structure* structure *f* de bloc; *block trading* négociations *fpl* de bloc; *block vote* = mode de scrutin utilisé par les syndicats britanniques par opposition au mode de scrutin "OMOV" (**b**) **to put a block on sth** *(cheque, account, prices, imports)* bloquer qch (**c**) *Comptr* bloc *m* □ *block copy* copie *f* de bloc
  2 *vt* (**a**) *(cheque, account, prices, imports)* bloquer □ *blocked currency* monnaie *f* bloquée *ou* non convertible (**b**) *Comptr (text)* sélectionner

blocking *adj* *blocking majority* majorité *f* de blocage; *blocking minority* minorité *f* de blocage

blue chip *n St Exch* valeur *f* de père de famille *ou* de premier ordre

blue-chip *adj Fin* *blue-chip company* affaire *f* de premier ordre; *blue-chip investment* placement *m* de bon rapport; *St Exch* *blue-chip stocks or shares* valeurs *fpl* de père de famille *ou* de premier ordre

blue-collar *adj* ouvrier(ère) □ *blue-collar union* syndicat *m* ouvrier; *blue-collar worker* col *m* bleu

blue-sky *adj St Exch* *blue-sky law* = loi américaine qui protège le public contre les titres boursiers douteux; *blue-sky security* titre *m* hautement spéculatif *ou* à haut risque

Bluetooth® *n Comptr* technologie *f* Bluetooth®

blurb *n* baratin *m* publicitaire; *(on book jacket)* texte *m* publicitaire

board 1 *n* (**a**) *(of company)* conseil *m* (d'administration); **to be on the board** faire partie *ou* être membre du conseil d'administration; **the bank is represented on the board** la banque fait partie du conseil □ *Board of Customs and Excise* = douane britannique; *board of directors* conseil d'administration; *board of enquiry* commission *f ou* comité *m* d'enquête; *board meeting* réunion *f* du conseil d'administration; *board member* membre *m* du conseil d'administration; *board of referees* commission arbitrale; *Br Formerly* *Board of Trade* ≃ Ministère *m* du Commerce; *board of trustees* conseil de gestion
  (**b**) *Comptr (in PC)* carte *f*; *(in mainframe)* panneau *m*; **on board** installé(e)
  2 *vt Admin (ship) (for inspection)* arraisonner

boarding *n* embarquement *m* □ *boarding card* carte *f* d'embarquement; *boarding pass* carte d'embarquement; *boarding time* heure *f* d'embarquement

boardroom *n* salle *f* de réunion *(du conseil d'administration)*; **to be promoted to the**

boardroom être promu(e) au conseil d'administration; **the decision was taken at boardroom level** le décision à été prise au niveau de la direction

body n (**a**) *(of letter, document, e-mail)* corps m, fond m (**b**) *(organization)* organisme m ❏ **body corporate** personne f morale

bogus company n société f fantôme

boiler room n Am Fam = organisation qui vend illégalement au public des produits financiers très spéculatifs ou sans valeur

bold Comptr **1** n gras m; **in bold** en gras
2 adj gras ❏ **bold face, bold type** caractères mpl gras

► **bolster up** vt sep Fin *(currency, economy)* soutenir

bona fide adj *(genuine)* véritable, authentique; *(offer, agreement)* sérieux(euse)

bonanza adj prospère, favorable; **2001 was a bonanza year for us** nous avons connu une année exceptionnelle en 2001

bond **1** n (**a**) Fin obligation f; **long/medium/short bond** obligation longue/moyenne/courte ❏ **bond equivalent yield** = rendement équivalent à celui d'une obligation; **bond fund manager** gestionnaire mf de fonds obligataire; **bond investment** placement m obligataire; **bond issue** émission f obligataire ou d'obligations; **to make a bond issue** émettre un emprunt; **bond market** marché m obligataire ou des obligations; **bond trading** opérations fpl sur obligations; **bond yield** rendement m de l'obligation
(**b**) Customs **to be in bond** être à l'entrepôt (de la douane); **to put goods in bond** entreposer des marchandises, mettre des marchandises à l'entrepôt; **to take goods out of bond** dédouaner des marchandises, faire sortir des marchandises de l'entrepôt ❏ **bond note** titre m d'obligation
(**c**) Law obligation f, engagement m; **to enter into a bond (with sb)** contracter une obligation ou un engagement (avec qn)
2 vt Customs *(goods)* entreposer, mettre à l'entrepôt

bonded adj Customs *(goods)* entreposé(e), en entrepôt, titré(e) ❏ **bonded warehouse** entrepôt m sous douane, entrepôt réel

bondholder n Fin obligataire mf, détenteur(trice) m,f ou porteur(euse) m,f d'obligations

bond-trading adj des opérations sur obligations ❏ **bond-trading department** service m des opérations sur obligations; **bond-trading ring** corbeille f des obligations

bonus n (**a**) *(on salary)* prime f; **to work on a bonus system** travailler à la prime; **to get a Christmas bonus** toucher une prime de fin

d'année ❏ **bonus pack** prime produit en plus; **bonus scheme** système m de primes (**b**) St Exch *(on shares)* dividende m supplémentaire, bonification f ❏ **bonus issue** émission f d'actions gratuites; **bonus share** action f gratuite ou donnée en prime (**c**) Ins *(to policy holder)* bénéfice m additionnel

book **1** n registre m; **the books** *(of company)* les comptes mpl; **to keep the books** tenir la comptabilité ou les comptes; **he's on our books** *(employee)* il est dans nos fichiers ❏ **book debts** comptes mpl fournisseurs, dettes fpl compte; **book entry** écriture f comptable; **book entry transfer** transfert m de compte à compte; **book value** valeur f comptable, valeur du bilan
2 vt (**a**) *(engage)* embaucher, engager; **we are heavily booked** nous sommes très pris (**b**) *(seat, room, table, ticket)* réserver; **to book sb into a hotel** retenir une chambre d'hôtel pour qn; **fully booked** complet(ète)

► **book up** vt sep **the restaurant/hotel is booked up** le restaurant/l'hôtel est complet

booking n location f, réservation f ❏ **booking agency** agence f de réservation; **booking clerk** préposé(e) m,f à la location; **booking fee** frais mpl de réservation; **booking number** numéro m de réservation; **booking office** guichet m ou bureau m de réservation

bookkeeper n comptable mf

bookkeeping n tenue f de(s) livres, comptabilité f

booklet n livret m, brochure f

bookmark Comptr **1** n signet m
2 vt créer un signet sur

bookwork n tenue f de(s) livres ou des écritures; *(accounts)* comptabilité f; *(secretarial duties)* secrétariat m

Boolean adj Comptr booléen(enne) ❏ **Boolean operator** opérateur m booléen; **Boolean search** recherche f booléenne

boom **1** n boom m, essor m économique; **boom and bust** cycle m expansion-récession ❏ **boom town** *(growing)* ville f champignon; *(prosperous)* ville prospère
2 vt Am *(develop)* développer; *(publicize)* promouvoir
3 vi prospérer, être en plein essor; *(of Stock Market)* être en hausse; **business is booming** les affaires marchent bien ou sont en plein essor; **car sales are booming** les ventes de voitures connaissent une forte progression

boomerang effect n effet m de boomerang

booming adj *(economy, business)* prospère, en plein essor

boomlet n Am Fam mini boom m

boost **1** n **to give sth a boost** *(sales, exports)* faire augmenter qch, doper qch; *(productivity)* développer qch, accroître qch; *(economy)* relancer qch; **the announcement gave the pound a boost on the foreign exchanges** la nouvelle a fait grimper la livre sur le marché des changes; **a boost in sales** une brusque augmentation des ventes

2 *vt (sales)* faire augmenter, doper; *(productivity)* développer, accroître; *(economy)* relancer; **we must do something to boost staff morale** il faut faire quelque chose pour remonter le moral du personnel

▸ **boot up** *Comptr* **1** *vt sep (computer)* amorcer, faire démarrer

2 *vi (of computer)* s'amorcer, démarrer; *(of person)* démarrer

boot disk *n Comptr* disquette *f* de démarrage

booth *n* **(a)** *(at trade fair)* stand *m* (d'exposition) **(b)** *(of interpreter)* cabine *f*

border *n* frontière *f*

borrow *Fin* **1** *vt* emprunter; **to borrow money from sb** emprunter de l'argent à qn; **you can borrow up to three times your salary** vous pouvez emprunter jusqu'à trois fois le montant de votre salaire

2 *vi* emprunter (**from** à); **to borrow on** *or* **at interest** emprunter à intérêt

▸ **borrow against** *vt insep Fin (salary, property)* emprunter sur; **the company borrowed against its assets** l'entreprise a emprunté de l'argent en utilisant son actif comme garantie

borrowed *adj Fin* emprunté(e), d'emprunt ❑ *borrowed capital* capital *m* emprunté *ou* d'emprunt

borrower *n Fin* emprunteur(euse) *m,f*

borrowing *n* emprunts *mpl*; **financed by borrowing** financé(e) par des emprunts ❑ *borrowing capacity* capacité *f ou* facilité *f* d'endettement; *borrowing limit* limite *f* d'endettement; *borrowing power* capacité d'emprunt *ou* d'endettement; *borrowing rate* taux *m* d'emprunt; *borrowing requirements* besoins *mpl* de crédit

> ❝
> A trawl up and down the high street paying a visit to the myriad lenders you will find there can be as good a place as any. This way you will find out how much you are able to borrow, what rates are on offer and which lenders are able to cater to your particular needs. Your own bank might offer its existing customers improved interest rates or increased **borrowing power**.
> ❞

boss *n Fam* patron(onne) *m,f*; **to be one's own boss** être son propre patron

Boston matrix *n Mktg* matrice *f* BCG

bottleneck *n (in production)* goulot *m* d'étranglement

bottom 1 *n* **the bottom has fallen out of the market** le marché s'est effondré

2 *adj Fin* **bottom line** solde *m* final, résultat *m* financier; **black bottom line** solde créditeur; **red bottom line** solde débiteur; **bottom price** prix *m* plancher

▸ **bottom out** *vi (of recession, slump)* atteindre son maximum; *(of price)* atteindre son minimum; **the dollar has bottomed out** le dollar s'est effondré; **sales bottomed out at £40,000** à leur niveau le plus bas, les ventes sont tombées à 40 000 livres

bottom-of-the-range *adj* bas de gamme

bought ledger *n Acct* cahier *m ou* livre *m* des achats

bounce *Fam* **1** *vt* **(a)** *(cheque)* refuser d'honorer **(b)** **to bounce an idea off sb** soumettre une idée à qn **(c)** *Comptr* **bounced message** = message électronique non délivré à l'expéditeur

2 *vi* **(a)** *(of cheque)* être refusé(e) pour nonprovision; **I hope this cheque won't bounce** j'espère que ce chèque ne sera pas refusé **(b)** *Comptr (of e-mail)* revenir à l'expéditeur

▸ **bounce back** *vi (of Stock Exchange)* reprendre, remonter; **the pound has bounced back against the dollar** la livre a regagné du terrain par rapport au dollar

bound *adj (obliged)* obligé(e); **bound by contract** lié(e) par contrat

Bourse *n* Bourse *f* (de valeurs)

boutique *n (shop)* boutique *f*; *(in department store)* rayon *m*

box 1 *n* **(a)** *(container)* boîte *f*; *(crate)* caisse *f* ❑ *box file* boîte de classement, boîte d'archives **(b)** *(postal address)* boîte *f* postale; **PO Box 301** boîte postale 301, BP 301; **Box number 301** *(in advertisements)* Référence 301, Ref. 301 **(c)** *(on form)* case *f*

2 *vt (goods)* mettre en boîte; *(put in crate)* mettre en caisse

boxed *adj (goods)* en boîte; *(in crate)* en caisse

boycott 1 *n* boycottage *m*, boycott *m*
2 *vt* boycotter

BP *n Am Fin (abbr* **basis point)** point *m* de base

bpi *n Comptr (abbr* **bits per inch)** bpp

BPR *n (abbr* **business process reengineering)** réorganisation *f* des processus

bps *n Comptr (abbr* **bits per second)** bps

bracket *n* **(a)** *Admin (of income, tax)* tranche *f*; *(of salaries)* fourchette *f*; **the 15 to 20 age bracket** le groupe *ou* la classe des 15 à 20 ans; **the high/low income bracket** la tranche des gros/petits revenus; **my pay rise put me in the £40,000 bracket** mon augmentation de salaire m'a placé dans la tranche (de revenus) des 40 000 livres annuelles; **what tax bracket are you in?** dans quelle tranche d'imposition es-tu? ❏ *Am Fam* **bracket creep** passage *m* à la tranche d'imposition supérieure

(**b**) *(punctuation mark) (square)* crochet *m*; *(round)* parenthèse *m*; *(curly)* accolade *f*

brain-drain *n* fuite *f* des cerveaux

> **"**
>
> An IT **brain-drain** could hit Tony Blair's plans for Britain to be a leading site for e-commerce, according to e-business consultant Steve Allan. Allan, who has moved to The Netherlands because of the new IR35 tax regulations, said that European businesses are taking advantage of the exodus of British contractors to catch up and overtake the UK.
>
> **"**

brainstorming *n Mktg* remue-méninges *m*, brainstorming *m* ❏ **brainstorming session** réunion *f* de remue-méninges

branch *n* (**a**) *(of shop)* succursale *f*; *(of company)* agence *f*, succursale, filiale *f*; *(of bank)* agence; **this shop has branches all over the country** ce magasin a des succursales dans tout le pays ❏ **branch banking** banque *f* à réseau; **branch manager** directeur(trice) *m,f* de succursale; *(of bank)* directeur(trice) d'agence; **branch office** agence (**b**) *Comptr* branchement *m*

▸ **branch out** *vi* se diversifier, étendre ses activités; **they're branching out into CD-ROMs** ils se lancent dans la production de CD-ROM; **we all agree on the need to branch out into sports equipment** nous sommes tous d'accord sur la nécessité d'étendre nos activités aux équipements de sport

brand *Mktg* **1** *n (of product)* marque *f* ❏ **brand acceptability, brand acceptance** acceptabilité *f* de la marque; **brand advertising** publicité *f* de marque *ou* sur la marque; **brand awareness** notoriété *f* de la marque; **brand bonding** attachement *m* à la marque; **brand building** création *f* de la marque; **brand competition** concurrence *f* entre marques; **brand concept** concept *m* de marque; **brand equity** valeur *f* de la marque; **brand exclusivity** exclusivité *f* à la marque; **brand extension** extension *f* de la marque; **brand familiarity** connaissance *f* de la marque; **brand identifier** identificateur *m* de marque; **brand identity** identité *f* de marque; **brand image** image *f* de marque; **brand imitation** imitation *f* de la marque; **brand leader** marque de tête; **brand lifecycle** cycle *m* de vie de la marque; **brand loyalty** *(of consumer)* fidélité *f* à la marque; **in the war between the major soap-powder manufacturers, brand**

loyalty has been a major factor la fidélité à la marque a joué un rôle majeur dans la guerre entre les grands fabricants de lessives en poudre; **brand management** gestion *f* de (la) marque; **brand manager** chef *m* de marque, directeur(-trice) *m,f* de marque; **brand mapping** carte *f* perceptuelle des marques, carte des positions de marques; **brand mark** emblème *m* de marque; **brand name** marque (de fabrique); **brand name product** produit *m* de marque; **brand name recall** mémomarque *f*; **brand perception** perception *f* de marque; **brand piracy** contrefaçon *f*; **brand policy** politique *f* de marque; **brand portfolio** portefeuille *m* de marque; **brand positioning** positionnement *m* de la marque; **brand preference** préférence *f* pour une marque; **brand recognition** identification *f* de la marque; **brand sensitivity** sensibilité *f* aux marques; **brand strategy** stratégie *f* de la marque; **brand switcher** = personne qui change souvent de marque; **sales promotions are particularly effective in attracting brand switchers** les promotions sont particulièrement efficaces pour attirer ceux qui changent souvent de marque; **brand switching** changement *m* de marque

2 *vt (of product)* marquer

branded *adj Mktg* **branded goods** produits *mpl* de marque; *Mktg* **branded product** produit *m* de marque

branding *n Mktg* marquage *m*, valorisation *f* de la marque; **decisions about branding affect our investment in promotion and packaging** les décisions prises quant à la valorisation de la marque jouent sur le montant investi dans la promotion et le conditionnement ❏ **branding campaign** campagne *f* d'image de marque

brand-led *adj Mktg* conditionné(e) par la marque, piloté(e) par la marque

> **"**
>
> Merloni is hoping to adopt a more **brand-led** approach to its advertising in the white goods market, which is growing by about six per cent year on year.
>
> **"**

brand-loyal *adj Mktg* fidèle à la marque

brand-sensitive *adj Mktg* sensible aux marques

breach **1** *n* **breach of contract** rupture *f* de contrat; **to be in breach of contract** violer un contrat; **breach of discipline** manquement *m* à la discipline; **breach of guarantee** rupture *f* de garantie; **breach of trust** abus *m* de confiance; **breach of warranty** violation *f* de garantie

2 *vt Law (agreement)* violer, rompre

breadwinner *n* soutien *m* de famille

break **1** *n* (**a**) *(in negotiations)* rupture *f* (**b**) *(in-*

terval, rest) pause f; **all employees are entitled to two 15-minute breaks** tous les employés ont droit à deux pauses de 15 minutes (**c**) *Comptr* **break key** touche f d'interruption

 2 *vt (agreement, contract)* rompre

▶ **break down 1** *vt sep Fin (account, figures, expenses)* décomposer, ventiler; *(statistics)* analyser; *(bill, estimate)* détailler; **to break down bulk** ventiler un lot

 2 *vi* (**a**) *(of negotiations, relations)* échouer; **talks between unions and management have broken down** les négociations entre les syndicats et la direction ont échoué (**b**) *(of machine)* tomber en panne

▶ **break even** *vi (of person, company)* rentrer dans ses frais

▶ **break into** *vt insep (market)* percer sur; **many companies are trying to break into the Japanese market** de nombreuses entreprises essaient de percer sur le marché japonais

▶ **break up 1** *vt sep (conglomerate, trust)* scinder, diviser; *(company)* scinder, dissoudre; *(empire)* démembrer; *(coalition)* rompre

 2 *vi (of meeting)* se terminer, prendre fin; *(of partnership)* cesser, prendre fin; *(of talks, negotiations)* cesser

breakage *n (damage)* casse f, avarie f; **to pay for breakages** payer la casse

break-bulk *adj Am* = relatif à des marchandises non unitisées

breakdown *n (of account, figures, expenses)* décomposition f, ventilation f; *(of statistics)* analyse f; *(of bill, estimate)* détail m; *Banking (of charges, interest)* décompte m

break-even 1 *n* seuil *m* de rentabilité; *Acct* point *m* mort, point d'équilibre; **to reach break-even** atteindre le seuil de rentabilité

 2 *adj Fin* **break-even analysis** analyse *f* du point mort; **break-even deal** affaire f blanche; **break-even point** seuil *m* de rentabilité; *Acct* point *m* mort, point d'équilibre; **break-even price** prix *m* minimum rentable; **break-even transaction** opération f blanche

> Certainly, digital TV is costing the two partners a lot of money: more than £800 million has been invested so far and at least £300m more will be needed. But the two companies claim that initiatives such as merging digital's management with the rest of ITV, and introducing new channels such as ITV Sport, will give the impetus needed to get to **break-even point** and beyond.

breakthrough *n (of market)* percée f

break-up *n (of company)* scission f, dissolution f; *(of empire)* démembrement *m* ❏ **break-up bid** = offre d'achat d'une entreprise en difficulté; **break-up price** prix *m* de liquidation; *Acct* **break-up value** valeur f à la casse

bribe 1 *n* pot-de-vin *m*

 2 *vt* offrir un pot-de-vin à

bribery *n* corruption f

bricks-and-mortar *adj* = se dit de commerces traditionnels par opposition aux services en ligne; **a bricks-and-mortar bookstore** une librairie traditionnelle

bridge loan *n Am* prêt-relais *m*

bridging *adj Br* **bridging finance** crédit-relais *m*; *Br* **bridging loan** prêt-relais *m*

brief 1 *n* (**a**) *Law* dossier *m*, affaire f

 (**b**) *(instructions)* brief *m*, mission f; **my brief was to develop sales** la tâche *ou* la mission qui m'a été confiée était de développer les ventes; **the client's brief stated that the advertising should target the 18–34 age group** les instructions du client stipulaient que la campagne devait viser les 18–34 ans

 2 *vt* (**a**) *Law (lawyer)* confier une cause à; *(case)* établir le dossier de

 (**b**) *(inform)* mettre au courant (**on** de); *(instruct)* donner des instructions *ou* des directives à; **have you been briefed?** *(brought up to date)* est-ce que vous avez été mis au courant?; *(given instructions)* est-ce qu'on vous a donné vos instructions?

briefcase *n* serviette f

briefing *n* briefing *m*, réunion f *ou* séance f d'information ❏ **briefing room** salle f de réunion

▶ **bring down** *vt sep (prices, rate of inflation)* faire baisser

▶ **bring forward** *vt sep* (**a**) *Acct (item)* reporter; **brought forward** reporté(e) (**b**) *(date, meeting)* avancer; **the conference has been brought forward to the 28th** la conférence a été avancée au 28

▶ **bring in** *vt sep (of investment, sale)* rapporter; **to bring in interest** rapporter des intérêts; **this investment has brought in six percent** ce placement a rapporté six pour cent d'intérêts; **tourism brings in millions of dollars each year** le tourisme rapporte des millions de dollars tous les ans

▶ **bring out** *vt sep (shares)* émettre; *(product)* lancer, sortir; *(book)* publier

brisk *adj (market, trade)* actif(ive), animé(e); *(competition)* dynamique; **business is brisk** les affaires marchent bien

British Institute of Management *n* = organisme britannique dont la fonction est de renseigner et de conseiller les entreprises en matière de gestion, ainsi que de promouvoir l'enseignement de cette discipline

brochure n brochure f, dépliant m, prospectus m

broker 1 n **(a)** Fin (for insurance, goods) courtier(ère) m,f (de commerce) ❑ **broker's commission** (frais mpl de) courtage m; **broker's contract** courtage; **broker dealer** négociant m courtier **(b)** St Exch agent m de change, courtier(ère) m,f (en Bourse)
 2 vt **to broker an agreement** négocier un accord en tant qu'intermédiaire

brokerage n Fin **(a)** (profession of broker) courtage m ❑ **brokerage house** maison f de courtage **(b)** (fee) (frais mpl de) courtage m

broking n Fin (profession) courtage m

brown goods npl produits mpl électroménagers (tels que télévisions, magnétoscopes)

browse Comptr **1** n **browse mode** mode m survol
 2 vt **to browse the Web** naviguer sur le Web
 3 vi se promener

▶ **browse through** vt insep Comptr se promener dans, survoler

browser n Comptr navigateur m, logiciel m de navigation

browsing n Comptr navigation f; **fast/secure browsing** navigation rapide/sécurisée

BS n (abbr **British Standard**) = indique que le chiffre qui suit renvoie au numéro de la norme fixée par l'association britannique de normalisation

b/s n (abbr **bill of sale**) acte m ou contrat m de vente

B-share n St Exch action f ordinaire avec droit de vote, action à dividende prioritaire

BSI n (abbr **British Standards Institution**) = association britannique de normalisation, ≃ AFNOR f

bt/fwd adj Acct (abbr **brought forward**) reporté(e)

bubble n **bubble economy** = économie dont l'expansion ne repose pas sur des bases solides; **bubble pack, bubble wrap** (for large item) emballage-bulle m

bubble-jet printer n imprimante f à jet d'encre

buck n Fam (dollar) dollar m (américain); **to make a fast** or **quick buck** faire du fric; **bucks** (money) fric m

bucket shop n Fam **(a)** Fin bureau m de courtier marron **(b)** (travel agency) agence f de voyages à prix réduits

budget 1 n **(a)** (financial plan) budget m; (allocated ceiling) enveloppe f budgétaire; **to balance the budget** équilibrer le budget; **to be within budget** être dans les limites du budget; **the project was finished within budget** le

projet a été fini sans dépasser le budget; **we are already well over budget** on a déjà largement dépassé le budget qui était alloué pour le projet ❑ **budget account** compte m crédit; **budget allocation** enveloppe budgétaire; **budget appropriation** affectation f budgétaire; **budget constraint** contrainte f budgétaire; **budget cuts** coupes fpl ou compressions fpl budgétaires; **budget deficit** déficit m budgétaire; **budget estimates** prévisions fpl budgétaires; **budget forecast** prévisions budgétaires; **budget planning** planification f budgétaire; **budget restrictions** restrictions fpl budgétaires; **budget surplus** excédent m budgétaire
 (b) **budget account** (with shop) compte m (crédit); (with bank) compte permanent
 2 adj budgétaire
 3 vt budgétiser; **our main competitor is budgeting a loss this year** notre concurrent principal s'attend à enregistrer une perte pour l'année qui s'achève et prépare son nouveau budget en conséquence
 4 vi dresser ou préparer un budget; **to budget for sth** budgétiser qch

budgetary adj budgétaire ❑ **budgetary control** contrôle m budgétaire; **budgetary limit** plafond m des charges budgétaires; **budgetary mechanism** mécanisme m budgétaire; **budgetary policy** politique f budgétaire; **budgetary resources** ressources fpl du budget; Fin **budgetary speciality** spécialité f budgétaire; **budgetary standards** standards mpl budgétaires; **budgetary strength** effectif m budgétaire; **budgetary variance** écart m budgétaire; **budgetary year** exercice f budgétaire

budgeting n (of person, company) budgétisation f, planification f budgétaire; Acct comptabilité f budgétaire

buffer n **(a)** (protection) **a buffer against inflation** une mesure de protection contre l'inflation ❑ **buffer state** état m tampon; **buffer stock** (of shares) matelas m; (of raw materials) stock m tampon **(b)** Comptr tampon m, mémoire f intermédiaire ❑ **buffer memory** mémoire tampon

bug n Comptr bogue f

bug-ridden adj Comptr bogué(e)

build vt **to build a brand** créer une marque

> "
> It follows the much vaunted launch that month of *The Independent's* first brand building campaign for nearly two years, using cinema and posters. The agency change is the latest in a series of measures by the paper's new management to **build** a stronger **brand** and halt the circulation slide.
> "

▶ **build into** *vt sep* to build sth into a product incorporer qch dans un produit; **the alarm will be built into the system** le système sera doté d'une alarme incorporée

▶ **build up** *vt sep* (**a**) *(develop) (business)* développer, établir; *(reputation)* bâtir, établir; *(production)* accroître, augmenter (**b**) *(advertise)* faire de la publicité pour (**c**) *(stock)* accumuler

building *n* (**a**) *(structure)* bâtiment *m*, immeuble *m* □ **buildings insurance** assurance *f* habitation
  (**b**) *(action)* construction *f* □ **building contract** contrat *m* d'entreprise; **building contractor** entrepreneur(euse) *m,f* en bâtiments; **building industry** industrie *f* du bâtiment; *Am Fin* **building and loan association** ≃ société *f* de crédit immobilier; *Br* **building plot** lotissement *m*; **building sector** secteur *m* du bâtiment; **building site** chantier *m* (de construction); *Br Fin* **building society** ≃ société de crédit immobilier; **building society passbook** ≃ livret *m* d'épargne logement; **the building trade** l'industrie du bâtiment, le bâtiment

build-up *n* (**a**) *(advertising)* publicité *f*; **to give sth a big build-up** faire beaucoup de publicité pour qch (**b**) *(of stock)* accumulation *f*

built-in *adj (incorporated)* incorporé(e) □ **built-in obsolescence** obsolescence *f* programmée *ou* planifiée

bulk 1 *n* (**a**) **in bulk** en gros; **to buy in bulk** acheter en gros *ou* en grande quantité; **to ship sth in bulk** transporter qch en vrac □ **bulk buying** achat *m* en gros; **bulk carrier** vraquier *m*; **bulk discount** remise *f* quantitative; **bulk goods** marchandises *fpl* en vrac; *Mktg* **bulk mailing** mailing *m* à grande diffusion; **bulk order** grosse commande *f*, commande par quantité; **bulk rate** *(for sending letters)* affranchissement *m* à forfait
  (**b**) *Comptr (of information)* volume *m*, masse *f*
  2 *vt (packages)* grouper

bulk-buy *vt* acheter en gros *ou* en grande quantité

bulking *n (of packages)* groupage *m*

bull *St Exch* **1** *n* haussier(ère) *m,f*, spéculateur(trice) *m,f* à la hausse; **to go a bull** spéculer à la hausse □ **bull market** marché *m* à la hausse *ou* haussier; **bull operation** opération *f* à la hausse; **bull position** position *f* acheteur; **bull speculation** spéculation *f* à la hausse; **bull trading** spéculation à la hausse; **bull transaction** opération à la hausse
  2 *vt (prices, shares)* pousser à la hausse; **to bull the market** chercher à faire hausser les cours
  3 *vi (of person)* spéculer à la hausse; *(of stocks)* être en hausse

bulldog bond *n Fin* obligation *f* bulldog *(obligation d'un emprunteur étranger à la Bourse de Londres, libellée en sterling)*

bullet *n* (**a**) *Comptr* puce *f* (**b**) *Am Fin (loan)* emprunt *m* remboursable in fine; *(repayment)* emprunt remboursable in fine □ **bullet bond** obligation *f* remboursable en une seule fois

bulletin board *n Comptr* serveur *m* télématique

bullion *n or m* en barres *ou* en lingots; *Fin* métal *m* □ **bullion reserve** réserve *f* métallique

bullish *adj St Exch (market, trend)* à la hausse, haussier(ère); **to be bullish** *(of person)* spéculer à la hausse □ **bullish tendency** tendance *f* à la hausse

bullishness *n St Exch* tendance *f* à la hausse

bumf *n Fam (documentation)* doc *f*; *(useless papers)* paperasse *f*

bumper *adj (profits, year)* exceptionnel(elle)

bundle *vt Mktg* **to bundle sth with sth** offrir qch en plus de qch; **to come bundled with sth** être vendu(e) avec qch

bundling n (of products) groupage m

buoyancy n St Exch (of market) fermeté f; (of prices, currency) stabilité f

buoyant adj St Exch (market) ferme; (prices, currency) stable

burden vt charger; **burdened with tax/debts** accablé(e) d'impôts/de dettes

bureau n bureau m, agence f ◻ **bureau de change** bureau de change

bureaucracy n bureaucratie f

bureaucratic adj bureaucratique

burn 1 n **burn rate** (of company) point m mort **2** vt Comptr (CD-ROM) graver

bus¹ n (vehicle) (auto)bus m ◻ **bus station** gare f routière

bus² n Comptr bus m ◻ **bus board** carte f bus; **bus controller** contrôleur m de bus

business n (a) (trade) affaires fpl; (commerce) commerce m; **to be in the antiques/restaurant business** être dans les antiquités/la restauration; **what's his line of business?, what business is he in?** qu'est-ce qu'il fait (comme métier)?; **to set up in business** ouvrir un commerce; **to be in/go into business for oneself** être/s'établir ou s'installer à son compte; **she's in business** elle est dans les affaires; **the company has been in business for 20 years** la société existe depuis 20 ans; **they've been in business together for 20 years** ils sont associés depuis 20 ans; **to go out of business** faire faillite; **supermarkets have put many small shops out of business** les supermarchés ont obligé beaucoup de petits magasins à fermer; **business is slow** les affaires ne marchent pas; **I've got some business to discuss with him** il faut que je discute affaires avec lui; **to be away on business** être en déplacement (pour affaires); **to go to London on business** aller à Londres pour affaires; **to lose business** perdre de la clientèle; **to do business with sb** faire affaire ou des affaires avec qn; **to do good business** faire de bonnes affaires; **it's good/bad for business** c'est bon/mauvais pour les affaires; **we have lost business to foreign competitors** nous avons perdu une partie de notre clientèle au profit de concurrents étrangers; **how's business?** comment vont les affaires?; **business is business** les affaires sont les affaires ◻ **business account** compte m professionnel ou commercial; **business accounting** comptabilité f commerciale; **business acquaintance** relation f d'affaires; **business activity** activité f commerciale; **business acumen** sens m des affaires; **business address** (of company) (adresse f du) siège m social; (of person) adresse du bureau; **business administration** gestion f commerciale; **business agent** agent m d'affaires; **business angel** business angel m, investis-

seur m providentiel; **business application** application f bureautique; **business appointment** rendez-vous m d'affaires; **business area** quartier m des affaires; **business associate** associé(e) m,f; **business bank** banque f d'affaires; **business banking** opérations fpl des banques d'affaires; **business buyer** acheteur(euse) m,f industriel(elle); **business call** visite f d'affaires; **business card** carte f (de visite) d'affaires; **business centre** centre m des affaires; **business circles** milieux mpl d'affaires; **business class** (in air travel) classe f affaires; **business college** école f (supérieure) de commerce; **business community** monde m des affaires; **members of the business community are unhappy about government proposals to increase corporation tax** le monde des affaires est opposé au projet gouvernemental d'augmentation de l'impôt sur les sociétés; **business computer** ordinateur m de bureau; **business computing** informatique f de gestion; **business concern** entreprise f commerciale; **business consultancy** cabinet m d'affaires; **business correspondence** correspondance f ou communication f commerciale; **business correspondent** correspondant(e) m,f financier(ère); **business cycle** cycle m des affaires; Comptr **business data processing** informatique d'entreprise; **business economist** économiste mf d'entreprise; **business enterprise** entreprise commerciale; **business ethics** déontologie f ou morale f professionnelle; **business expenses** frais mpl professionnels; **business failure** défaillance f d'entreprise; Comptr **business graphics** graphiques mpl de gestion; **business hotel** hôtel m d'affaires; **business hours** (of office) heures fpl de bureau; (of shop) heures d'ouverture; **business intelligence system** réactique f; **business lawyer** avocat(e) m,f d'affaires; **business letter** lettre f commerciale; **business lounge** (in airport) salon m classe affaires; **business lunch** déjeuner m d'affaires; **business management** gestion d'entreprise; (study) économie f d'entreprise; **business manager** directeur(trice) m,f commercial(e); **business market** marché m des entreprises; **business meeting** rendez-vous d'affaires; Mktg **business mission** mission f d'activité ou de l'entreprise; **business news** chronique f économique; **business operation** opération f commerciale; **business park** parc m ou zone f d'activités; **business partner** partenaire mf commercial(e); **business plan** plan m commercial; **business policy** politique f de gestion; **business portfolio** portefeuille m d'activités; **business premises** locaux mpl commerciaux ou à usage commercial; **business process reengineering** réorganisation f des processus; **business proposition** proposition f d'affaires; **business relations** relations fpl d'affaires ou commerciales; **business school** école (supérieure) de commerce; Econ **business sector** secteur *m* tertiaire *ou* d'affaires; **business ser-vices** services *mpl* du secteur tertiaire, services aux entreprises; *Comptr* **business software** logiciel *m* de bureautique; **business strategy** stratégie *f* d'entreprise *ou* commerciale; **business studies** *(subject)* études *fpl* commerciales **business transaction** transaction *f* commerciale; **business trend** courant *m* d'affaires; **business trip** voyage *m* d'affaires; **business world** monde *m* des affaires

(**b**) *(company, firm)* affaire *f*, entreprise *f*; **to run a business** gérer une entreprise, diriger un commerce; **to have one's own business** travailler à son compte; **business for sale** commerce *m* à vendre; **a profitable business** une entreprise lucrative *ou* rentable; **the small business sector** la petite entreprise

(**c**) *(on agenda)* points *mpl* divers; **any other business** d'autres questions à l'ordre du jour

❝

Nat West is setting up a database of **busi-ness angels** ... experienced business people able and willing to invest in small enterprises. There are also patron angels (people looking for longterm projects to invest in but wanting no personal involvement) and occupational angels (mainly retired or redundant people with up to £50 000 to invest, and looking for day-to-day involvement).

❞

businessman *n* homme *m* d'affaires; **to be a good businessman** s'entendre aux affaires

businesspeople *npl* les femmes *fpl* et les hommes *mpl* d'affaires

businessperson *n* = une femme ou un homme d'affaires

business-to-business *adj* B2B, interentreprise

businesswoman *n* femme *f* d'affaires; **to be a good businesswoman** s'entendre aux affaires

bust *adj Fam* **to go bust** faire faillite; **the company went bust after a year** l'entreprise a fait faillite au bout d'un an

busy *adj* (**a**) *(person)* occupé(e); **the manager is busy with a customer** le directeur est occupé avec *ou* en rendez-vous avec un client (**b**) *(period)* chargé(e); **the summer is our busiest period** c'est en été que nous travaillons le plus (**c**) *Am (telephone line)* occupé(e); **I keep getting the busy signal** ça sonne toujours occupé

button *n Comptr (on mouse)* bouton; *(for menu selection)* case *f*

buy **1** *n* (**a**) *(purchase)* **a good/bad buy** une bonne/mauvaise affaire; **to make a good/bad buy** faire une bonne/mauvaise affaire (**b**) *St Exch* **buy order** ordre *m* d'achat; **to give a buy order** donner un ordre d'achat

2 *vt* acheter; **to buy sth from sb** acheter qch à qn; **to buy earnings** investir en valeurs de croissance

3 *vi Fin* **to buy spot** acheter au comptant; **to buy wholesale** acheter en gros; **to buy stock** acheter des actions; **to buy in bulk** acheter en grande quantité; **to buy on credit** acheter à crédit *ou* à terme

▸ **buy in 1** *vt sep* (**a**) *(goods, commodities)* s'approvisionner de (**b**) *St Exch* acheter, acquérir

2 *vi St Exch* **to buy in against a client** exécuter un client

▸ **buy into** *vt insep (company, sector)* acheter des actions de; **we hope to buy into telecommunications next year** nous espérons pouvoir acheter des parts dans les télécommunications l'an prochain

▸ **buy out** *vt sep (partner)* racheter la part de, désintéresser; **he was bought out for £50,000** on lui a racheté sa part dans l'affaire pour 50 000 livres; **she bought out all the other shareholders** elle a racheté les parts de tous les autres actionnaires

▸ **buy up** *vt sep* (**a**) *(goods, supplies)* acheter en masse (**b**) *Fin (company, shares, stock)* racheter; **the company bought up £50,000 worth of shares** la société a racheté des actions pour une valeur de 50 000 livres

buyback *n* (**a**) *St Exch* rachat *m* d'actions (**b**) *Fin* reprise *f* ❑ **buyback agreement** accord *m* de reprise

❝

Management got the job done, hacking the UK payroll from 17,000 in 1990 to 2,200 today, shutting plants and shovelling cash out of the door. In just nine years, the dividends, special dividends and share **buy-backs** have returned to investors the entire £3.6 billion paid to the government for the assets. And the shareholders still own a company trading at three times the £1.75 price paid at flotation.

❞

buyer *n* (**a**) *(consumer)* acheteur(euse) *m,f*, acquéreur *m*; **first time buyers** *(of property)* = personnes achetant un logement pour la première fois; **buyer beware** = principe selon lequel, lors d'une transaction, il revient à l'acquéreur de s'assurer de la qualité de l'objet acheté; **it's a case of buyer beware if you buy something from a street vendor** c'est au client de se méfier quand il achète quelque chose à un vendeur ambulant ❑ *Mktg* **buyer behaviour** comportement *m* de l'acheteur; *Fin* **buyer credit** crédit-acheteur *m*; *Fin* **buyer credit guarantee** garantie *f* de crédit-acheteur; *Fin* **buyer's market** marché *m* acheteur; *(for house buyers)* marché d'offre, marché offreur; *Fin* **buyer's option** prime *f* acheteur; *Mktg* **buyer readiness** prédisposition *f* à l'achat (**b**) *(for company, shop)* acheteur(euse) *m,f*; **head buyer** acheteur(euse) principal(e)

buy-in *n St Exch* exécution *f*

buying *n* achat *m*; **buying and selling** l'achat et la vente; **buying back** rachat *m*; **buying in** *Mktg* approvisionnement *m*; *St Exch* exécution *f* ❏ *Mktg* **buying behaviour** comportement *m* d'achat; *Mktg* **buying behaviour model** modèle *m* de comportement d'achat; *Mktg* **buying decision** décision *f* d'achat; **buying department** service *m* (des) achats; *Mktg* **buying incentive** incitation *f* à l'achat; *Mktg* **buying inducement** mobile *m* d'achat; *Mktg* **buying motive** motif *m ou* motivation *f* d'achat; **buying order** ordre *m* d'achat; **buying power** pouvoir *m* d'achat; *St Exch* **buying quotation, buying rate** *(of shares)* cours *m* d'achat; *Mktg* **buying situation** situation *f* d'achat

> **❝**
>
> But with economic clouds gathering in America, the strong **buying power** of Europe's consumers is expected to bolster growth. Indeed, even in the German manufacturing sector, growth in foreign orders is nowhere near as bad as in 1992–93, the last recession. Orders for consumer goods are holding up well.
>
> **❞**

buy-out *n (of company)* rachat *m*; *(of partner)* rachat, désintéressement *m*

buy-sell agreement *n* protocole *m ou* accord *m* d'achat et de vente

by-bidder *n* = compère qui fait monter les enchères au cours d'une vente

by-bidding *n* = pratique qui consiste à faire monter les enchères artificiellement au cours d'une vente

bye-laws, by-laws *npl (of company)* statuts *mpl*, règlements *mpl*

by-line *n (on press article)* signature *f*

by-product *n* sous-produit *m*, (produit *m*) dérivé *m*

byte *n Comptr* octet *m*

Cc

CA *n* (**a**) *Br* (*abbr* **chartered accountant**) expert-comptable *mf*, *Can* comptable *mf* agréé(e) (**b**) (*abbr* **Consumers' Association**) = association britannique des consommateurs

C/A, c/a *n* (**a**) *Banking* (*abbr Br* **current** *or* **cheque** *or Am* **checking account**) C/C *m*, CCB *m* (**b**) *Banking* (*abbr* **capital account**) compte *m* de capitaux (**c**) (*abbr* **credit account**) compte *m* créditeur

cable modem *n Comptr* modem-câble *m*

CAC 40 index *n St Exch* indice *m* CAC 40

cache *Comptr* **1** *n* **cache (memory)** antémémoire *f*, mémoire-cache *f*
  2 *vt (data)* mettre en antémémoire *ou* en mémoire-cache

cached *adj Comptr* en antémémoire, en mémoire-cache

cachet *n Mktg* label *m*

CAD *n* (**a**) *Comptr* (*abbr* **computer-assisted design**) CAO *f* (**b**) (*abbr* **cash against documents**) comptant *m* contre documents

CAD/CAM *n Comptr* (*abbr* **computer-assisted design/computer-assisted manufacture**) CFAO *f*

CAE *n Comptr* (*abbr* **computer-assisted engineering**) IAO *f*

CAF *n* (*abbr* **cost and freight**) coût *m* et fret *m*

cafeteria benefit *n* = avantages sociaux à la carte

CAL *n Comptr* (*abbr* **computer-aided learning, computer-assisted learning**) EAO *m*

calculate 1 *vt* calculer
  2 *vi* faire un calcul

calculated risk *n* risque *m* calculé

calculation *n* calcul *m*; **to make a calculation** faire un calcul; **to be out in one's calculations** être loin de son compte

calculator *n* calculatrice *f*

calendar *n* calendrier *m* ❑ *calendar month* mois *m* civil; *calendar year* année *f* civile

call 1 *n* (**a**) *Fin (claim)* demande *f* (d'argent); **call (up)** appel *m* de fonds *ou* de versement; **call for capital** appel de fonds; **payable at call** payable sur demande *ou* à présentation *ou* à vue ❑ *call letter* avis *m* d'appel de fonds; *call loan* prêt *m* à vue, prêt remboursable sur demande; *call*

money argent *m* au jour le jour
  (**b**) *St Exch* option *f* d'achat, call *m*; **call on a hundred shares** option de cent actions; **call of more** option du double ❑ *call feature* = clause de remboursement anticipé au gré de l'émetteur; *call option* option d'achat; *call price* cours *m* du dont; *call warrant* warrant *m* à l'achat
  (**c**) (**telephone**) **call** appel *m*, communication *f* (téléphonique); **to receive a call** recevoir un appel; **to make a call** passer un coup de téléphone; **to give sb a call** téléphoner à qn, appeler qn; **you have a call from Canada** on vous appelle du Canada; **there was a call for you** il y a eu un coup de téléphone *ou* un appel pour toi; **he's on a call** il est en ligne; **will you accept the call?** *(when charges are reversed)* est-ce que vous prenez *ou* acceptez l'appel?; **to put a call through** passer une communication; **to return sb's call** rappeler qn ❑ *call centre* centre *m* d'appels; *call connection* établissement *m* d'appel; *call forwarding* redirection *f* d'appel; *call holding* mise *f* en attente d'appels; *call waiting service* signal *m* d'appel
  (**d**) *(of representative)* visite *f*, passage *m*; **to pay** *or* **make a call on sb** rendre visite à qn
  2 *vt* (**a**) *Fin* **to call a loan** demander le remboursement d'un prêt
  (**b**) *(on telephone)* téléphoner à, appeler
  (**c**) *(order)* **to call a strike** ordonner une grève, lancer un ordre de grève; **to call a meeting** convoquer une réunion
  3 *vi (on telephone)* appeler; **who's calling, please?, may I ask who's calling?** c'est de la part de qui, s'il vous plaît?; **could you call again later?** est-ce que vous pouvez rappeler plus tard?

▶ **call back 1** *vt sep* rappeler; **I'll call you back later** je vous rappellerai plus tard
  2 *vi* rappeler; **could you call back later, please?** est-ce que vous pouvez rappeler plus tard?

▶ **call for** *vt insep (demand)* réclamer; **workers are calling for a wage increase** les travailleurs demandent une augmentation de salaire

▶ **call in** *vt sep* (**a**) *(person)* (*into building, office*) faire entrer; **call Miss Smith in, please** faites entrer Mlle Smith, s'il vous plaît; **an accountant was called in to look at the books** on a fait venir un comptable pour examiner les livres de comptes (**b**) *Fin* **to call in one's money** faire rentrer ses fonds; **to call in a loan** demander le remboursement d'un prêt (**c**) *(currency)* retirer de la circulation

▶ **call off** *vt sep (meeting, strike, deal)* annuler

▶ **call on** *vt insep* (**a**) *(request)* **to call on sb to do sth** demander à qn de faire qch; **they are calling on the government to take action** ils demandent au gouvernement d'agir (**b**) *(visit)* rendre visite à; **the sales reps call on their clients monthly** les représentants de commerce rendent visite à leurs clients une fois par mois

▶ **call up** *vt sep* (**a**) *(on telephone)* téléphoner à, appeler (**b**) *Comptr (help screen, file)* rappeler

callable *adj Fin (debt, bond)* remboursable sur demande *ou* avant échéance; *(loan)* (à terme) révocable

called-up capital *n Fin* capital *m* appelé

calling-in *n* (**a**) *Fin (of debt, loan)* demande *f* de remboursement immédiat (**b**) *(of currency)* retrait *m*

CAM *n Comptr (abbr* **computer-assisted manufacture)** FAO *f*

campaign 1 *n* campagne *f*
2 *vi* faire campagne (**for/against** pour/ contre); **workers are campaigning against the closure of the factory** les travailleurs font campagne contre la fermeture de l'usine □ *campaign plan* plan *m* de campagne

cancel 1 *vt* (**a**) *(order, meeting, reservation, flight)* annuler; *(debt)* faire remise à; *(cheque)* faire opposition à; *(goods)* décommander; *Law (agreement, contract)* annuler, résilier (**b**) *Acct* contrepasser; **to cancel each other** *(of two entries)* s'annuler (**c**) *Comptr* annuler □ *cancel button* case *f* 'annuler'
2 *vi Comptr* s'annuler; **press 'esc' to cancel** appuyez sur 'Echap' pour annuler

cancellation *n (of order, meeting, reservation, flight)* annulation *f*; *(of debt)* règlement *m*; *(of cheque)* opposition *f*; *Law (of agreement, contract)* annulation, résiliation *f* □ *cancellation charge* frais *mpl* d'annulation; *cancellation clause* clause *f* d'annulation *ou* de résiliation; *cancellation fee* frais d'annulation; *cancellation form* bulletin *m ou* bon *m* d'annulation; *cancellation insurance* assurance *f* annulation

C&F, C and F *(abbr* **cost and freight)** coût *m* et fret *m*

C&I, C and I *(abbr* **cost and insurance)** C&A *m*

candidate *n (for job)* candidat(e) *m,f*

cannibalization *n Mktg* cannibalisation *f*, cannibalisme *m*

cannibalize *vt Mktg* cannibaliser

canteen *n* cantine *f*

canvass 1 *vt (person)* démarcher, solliciter des commandes de; *(area)* prospecter
2 *vi* faire du démarchage; **to canvass for customers** prospecter la clientèle

canvasser *n* placier(ère) *m,f*, démarcheur(- euse) *m,f*

canvassing *n (for orders)* sollicitation *f*; *(for custom)* prospection *f*, démarchage *m*

CAP *n EU (abbr* **Common Agricultural Policy)** PAC *f*

cap 1 *n* taux *m* plafond
2 *vt (spending)* plafonner, fixer un plafond à; **these measures have been effective in capping overall expenditure** ces mesures ont permis de limiter les dépenses globales

capacity *n* (**a**) *(of factory, industry)* moyens *mpl* de production; *(output)* rendement *m*; **to work at full capacity** travailler à plein rendement; **the factory has not yet reached capacity** l'usine n'a pas encore atteint son rendement maximum □ *capacity output* rendement *m* maximum
(**b**) *(of container)* capacité *f*
(**c**) *(position)* **in the capacity of** en qualité de; **to act in one's official capacity** agir dans l'exercice de ses fonctions; **he's acting in an advisory capacity** il a un rôle consultatif

capital *n* (**a**) *Fin* capital *m*, capitaux *mpl*, fonds *mpl*; *(assets)* avoir *m*; **to live on one's capital** vivre sur son capital □ *capital account* compte *m* de capitaux; *capital accumulation* accumulation *f* de capital; *capital adequacy ratio* ratio *m* Cooke; *capital allowances* déductions *fpl* (fiscales) sur frais d'établissement; *capital asset pricing model* modèle *m* d'évaluation des actifs; *capital assets* actif *m* immobilisé, immobilisations *fpl* corporelles; *capital bond* obligation *f* à coupon zéro; *capital budget* budget *m* des investissements; *capital budgeting* gestion *f* des investissements; *capital charge* intérêt *m* des capitaux (investis); *capital clause (in memorandum of association)* constitution *f* du capital social; *capital contribution* apport *m* de capitaux; *capital cost* coût *m* du capital; *Acct capital employed* capital engagé, capitaux permanents; *capital equipment* biens *mpl* d'équipement, capitaux fixes; *capital expenditure* mise *f* de fonds, investissements *mpl* (en immobilisations), dépenses *fpl* d'équipement; *capital flight* fuite *f* des capitaux; *capital gains* plus-value *f*; *capital gains distribution* distribution *f* des plus-values; *capital gains tax* impôt *m* sur les plus-values; *capital goods* biens d'équipement *ou* capitaux *ou* production; *capital goods market* marché *m* d'équipement; *capital grant* subvention *f* en capital *capital growth* croissance *m* du capital; *capital income* revenu *m* du capital; *capital inflow* afflux *m* de capitaux *ou* de fonds; *capital injection* injection *f* de capital *ou* de capitaux;

capital investment investissement *m* de capitaux, mise de fonds; *Acct* **capital items** biens capitaux; **capital levy** prélèvement *m* sur le capital; **capital loss** moins-value *f*, perte *f* en capitaux; **capital market** marché financier *ou* des capitaux; **capital movements** mouvements *mpl* des capitaux; **capital outlay** dépenses en capital; **capital profits** plus-value; **capital project evaluation** étude *f* de projet d'investissement; **capital reserves** profits *mpl* mis en réserve, réserves *fpl* non distribuées; *Acct* **capital and reserves** capitaux propres; **capital share** part *f* sociale; *St Exch* **capital shares** actions *fpl* de capitalisation; **capital shortfall** manque *m* de capitaux; **capital stock** capital social, capital-actions *m*, fonds propres; **capital structure** structure *f* financière; **capital tax** impôt *m* sur le capital; **capital transaction** opération *f* en capital; **capital transfer tax** droits *mpl* de mutation; **capital turnover** rotation *f* des capitaux

(b) *(letter)* majuscule *f*, capitale *f* ❏ **capital letter** lettre *f* majuscule

> **❝**
>
> **Capital gains tax** is not a big issue for most people, as few people surpass the CGT allowance each year. In the 1999/2000 tax year, the individual CGT threshold, which applies to children as well as adults, is £6,800. This means a couple would have to realise gains from the sale of investments of more than £14,200 to save tax by putting some of their assets in their child's name.
>
> **❞**

capital-intensive *adj* à forte intensité capitalistique

capitalism *n* capitalisme *m*

capitalist *n & adj* capitaliste *mf*

capitalization *n Fin* capitalisation *f* ❏ **capitalization issue** attribution *f* d'actions gratuites; **capitalization ratio** ratio *m* de capitalisation; **capitalization of reserves** incorporation *f* des réserves au capital

capitalize *vt* (a) *(convert into capital)* capitaliser; *(raise capital from)* constituer le capital social de *(par émission d'actions)*; *(provide with capital)* pourvoir de capital *ou* de fonds ❏ **capitalized value** valeur *f* capitalisée

(b) *(estimate value of)* capitaliser; **they capitalized her investments at £50,000** ils ont capitalisé ses investissements à 50 000 livres; **the company is capitalized at £100,000** la société dispose d'un capital de 100 000 livres

capital-labour ratio *n* ratio *m* capital-travail

capital-output ratio *n* ratio *m* d'intensité de capital

capitation *n Fin* capitation *f* ❏ **capitation tax** capitation

CAPM *n* *(abbr* **capital asset pricing model)** MÉDAF *m*

capped rate *n* taux *m* d'intéret plafonné *ou* capé

capped-rate *adj (mortgage)* à taux d'intérêt plafonné *ou* capé

caps *npl Comptr (abbr* **capital letters)** majuscules *fpl* ❏ **caps lock** verrouillage *m* des majuscules; **caps lock key** touche *f* de verrouillage des majuscules

caption *n (under graph, photo)* légende *f*

captive *adj Mktg* captif(ive) ❏ **captive audience** audience *f* captive; **captive fund** fonds *m* de capital-risque maison; **captive market** clientèle *f* captive, marché *m* captif; **captive product** produit *m* lié

captive-product pricing *n Mktg* fixation *f* du prix des produits liés

capture *vt (market)* accaparer; **in one year they have captured a large part of the mail-order market** en un an ils se sont emparés d'une part importante du marché de la vente par correspondance

car *n* voiture *f* ❏ **car factory** usine *f* d'automobiles; *Br* **car hire** location *f* de voitures; **car industry** industrie *f* automobile; **car manufacturer** constructeur *m* automobile; **car rental** location de voitures

carbon copy *n (copie f au)* carbone *m*

card *n* (a) *(with printed information)* carte *f*; *(for card index)* fiche *f* ❏ **card file** fichier *m*; **card index** fichier; *Banking* **card payment** paiement *m* par carte (b) *Comptr (circuit board)* carte *f* ❏ **card slot** emplacement *m* pour carte

card-index 1 *adj* **card-index file** classeur *m* à fiches

2 *vt* mettre sur fiches

cardphone *n Tel* publiphone *m* *ou* téléphone *m* à carte

career *n* carrière *f*; **a career in banking/engineering** une carrière dans la banque/l'ingénierie; **it was a good/bad career move** ça a été bon/mauvais pour ma/sa/*etc* carrière ❏ **careers adviser** conseiller(ère) *m,f* professionnel(elle); **career break** interruption *f* de carri-ère; **to take a career break** interrompre sa carrière *(pour élever des enfants, reprendre des études etc)*; **career counselling** orientation *f* professionnelle; **careers counsellor** conseiller(ère) *m,f* professionnel(elle); **career development** évolution *f* professionnelle; **Career Development Loan** prêt *m* de formation professionnelle; **careers guidance** orientation professionnelle; **careers office** centre *m* d'orientation professionnelle; **career plan** plan *m* de carrière; **careers service** service *m* d'orientation professionnelle; **career structure** grille *f* d'avancement

care of *prep (in addresses)* **care of Mr McLean**

aux (bons) soins de M. McLean, chez M. McLean

cargo n cargaison f, chargement m; **to take on** or **embark cargo** charger des marchandises; **cargo outward** chargement d'aller; **cargo homeward** chargement de retour □ **cargo boat** cargo m; **cargo plane** avion-cargo m; **cargo ship** cargo

carnet n Customs (pass) passavant m

carriage n (transportation) transport m; (cost of transportation) (frais mpl de) port m, fret m; **to pay the carriage** payer le transport; **carriage forward** (en) port dû, port avancé; **carriage free** franc de port, franco; **carriage insurance paid** port payé, assurance comprise; **carriage paid** (en) port payé □ **carriage charge(s)** frais de port; **carriage costs** frais de port; **carriage trade** clientèle f riche

carrier n (a) (company) entreprise f de transport, transporteur m; **sent by carrier** (by road) expédié par camion ou par transporteur; (by rail) expédié par chemin de fer; (by air) expédié par avion (b) Comptr, Tel (for signal) opérateur m

carry vt (a) (keep in stock) vendre, avoir; **do you carry computer accessories?** est-ce que vous vendez des accessoires pour ordinateurs? (b) (interest) rapporter; **the investment carries ten percent interest over three years** l'investissement rapporte dix pour cent d'intérêts pendant trois ans (c) (proposal, motion) voter; **the motion was carried unanimously** la motion a été votée à l'unanimité (d) (transport) transporter

▸ **carry forward** vt sep Acct (item) reporter; **carried forward** report, à reporter

▸ **carry on** vt sep (trade, business) exercer

▸ **carry out** vt sep (market research) effectuer; (instructions) exécuter; (order) donner suite à

▸ **carry over** vt sep (a) Acct (balance) faire un report de, reporter; **to carry over a loss to the following year** reporter une perte sur l'année suivante
(b) St Exch (shares) reporter, prendre en report; **carried over** (stock) en report
(c) (defer) reporter; **you may carry over your holiday entitlement to the following year** vous avez la possibilité de reporter vos congés sur l'année suivante; **that will have to be carried over to the next meeting** il faudra poursuivre ce point lors de la prochaine réunion

carrying n (a) (transport) transport m □ **carrying capacity** (of vehicle) charge f utile; **carrying charges, carrying costs** frais mpl de port ou de transport (b) Am Acct **carrying cost, carrying value** valeur f comptable (c) Am **carrying charge** supplément m (que l'on paye lorsqu'on achète à crédit)

carry-over n Acct report m

cartage n (transport) transport m, camionnage m; (cost) frais mpl de transport □ **cartage note** bordereau m d'expédition

cartel n cartel m; **to form a cartel** former un cartel; **an oil/steel cartel** un cartel du pétrole/de l'acier □ **cartel laws** lois fpl anti-trust

cartellization n cartellisation f

cart note n (a) (for transporting goods) bordereau m d'expédition (b) (for taking goods from customs) permis m de sortie de marchandises

cartridge n (disk) cartouche f; **ink/toner cartridge** cartouche d'encre/de toner

cascade taxation n imposition f en cascade

CASE n Comptr (abbr **computer-assisted software engineering**) ingénierie f des systèmes assistée par ordinateur

case n (a) (container) **(packing) case** caisse f (b) Law affaire f (c) **case study** étude f de cas (d) Comptr **case insensitive** qui ne distingue pas les majuscules des minuscules; **this URL is case insensitive** le respect de majuscules et des minuscules n'est pas nécessaire pour cette URL; **case sensitive** qui distingue les majuscules des minuscules; **this e-mail address is case sensitive** cette adresse électronique tient compte des majuscules

cash n (coins, banknotes) liquide m, espèces fpl; Fam (money in general) argent m; **to pay (in) cash** (not credit) payer comptant; (money as opposed to cheque) payer en liquide ou en espèces; **to buy/sell sth for cash** acheter/vendre qch comptant; **cash at bank** avoir m en banque; **cash against documents** comptant contre documents; Br Acct **cash on delivery** paiement m à la livraison, livraison f contre remboursement; **cash in hand** argent ou disponibilités fpl en caisse; **cash on shipment** paiement à l'expédition; Acct **cash in till** fonds m de caisse, encaisse f; **cash with order** paiement à la commande, envoi m contre paiement □ **cash account** compte m de caisse; **cash advance** avance m en numéraire, avance de trésorerie; **cash balance** (status) situation f de caisse; (amount remaining) solde m actif, solde de ou en caisse; Acct **cash basis accounting** comptabilité f de caisse ou de gestion; **cash benefits** avantages mpl en espèces; **cash bonus** prime f en espèces; **cash book** livre m ou journal m de caisse; **cash box** caisse f; **cash budget** budget m de trésorerie; **cash and carry** cash and carry m, libre-service m de gros; **cash compensation** indemnité f en argent; Acct **cash contribution** apport m en numéraire ou en espèces; Mktg **cash cow** (product) vache f à lait; **cash crop** culture f de rapport ou commerciale; **cash deal** marché m au comptant; **cash debit** débit m de caisse; **cash deficit** déficit m de caisse ou de tré-

sorerie; *Fin* **cash deposit** versement *m* ou dépôt *m* en espèces; **cash desk** caisse; **cash discount** escompte *m* de caisse, remise *f* sur paiement (au) comptant; **cash dispenser** distributeur *m* (automatique) de billets; **cash dividend** dividende *m* en espèces; **cash equivalents** quasi-espèces *fpl*, actifs *mpl* facilement réalisables; *Acct* **cash expenditure** dépenses *fpl* de caisse; **cash flow** *Fin* cash-flow *m*, trésorerie *f*; *Acct (in cash flow statement)* marge *f* brute d'autofinancement; **cash flow forecast** prévision *f* de trésorerie; **cash flow management** gestion *f* de trésorerie; **cash flow problems** problèmes *mpl* de trésorerie; **cash flow rate** taux *m* d'autofinancement; **cash flow situation** situation de trésorerie; *Acct* **cash flow statement** tableau *m* de financement, tableau des flux de trésorerie; *Fin* **cash incentive** stimulation *f* financière; *Acct* **cash inflow** encaissement *m*; *Acct* **cash item** article *m* de caisse; *Banking* **cash machine** distributeur (automatique) de billets; **cash management** gestion de trésorerie, gestion du cash; **cash nexus** rapports *mpl* d'argent; **cash offer** offre *f* d'achat avec paiement comptant; **they made us a cash offer for the flat** ils nous ont proposé de payer l'appartement (au) comptant; *Acct* **cash order** ordre *m* au comptant; *Acct* **cash outflow** décaissement *m*; **cash outgoings** sorties de trésorerie; *Acct* **cash overs** excédent *m* de caisse; **cash payment** paiement (au) comptant ou en espèces; **cash price** prix *m* au comptant; **cash purchase** achat *m* au comptant, achat contre espèces; *Acct* **cash ratio** ratio *m* ou coefficient *m* de trésorerie; *Acct* **cash receipt** reçu *m* pour paiement en espèces, reçu d'espèces; *Acct* **cash receipts** rentrées *fpl* de caisse; *Acct* **cash receipts and payments** rentrées et sorties de caisse; *Acct* **cash received** *(balance sheet item)* entrée *f* d'argent; **cash register** caisse (enregistreuse); *Acct* **cash report (form)** situation de caisse; **cash requirements** besoins *mpl* de trésorerie; **cash reserves** réserves *fpl* en espèces; **cash return** revenu *m*; **cash sale** vente *f* au comptant; **cash settlement** liquidation *f* en espèces; **cash shortage** insuffisance *f* d'espèces, manquant *m* en caisse; *Acct* **cash statement** état *m* ou bordereau *m* ou relevé *m* de caisse; *Acct* **cash surplus** restant *m* en caisse; **cash terms** conditions *fpl* au comptant; **cash transaction** opération *f* ou transaction *f* au comptant; **cash value** valeur *f* vénale; *Acct* **cash voucher** pièce *f* de caisse, PC *f*; **cash withdrawal** retrait *m* d'espèces
2 *vt (cheque)* toucher, encaisser; *(bill)* encaisser, escompter

▸ **cash in** *vt sep (bond, savings certificate)* se faire rembourser, réaliser

▸ **cash up** *vi Br* faire les comptes, faire la caisse

cashable *adj Fin* encaissable, payable

cash-and-carry arbitrage *n St Exch* arbitrage *m* comptant-terme

cashback *n* (**a**) *(in mortgage lending)* = prime versée par une société de crédit immobilier au souscripteur d'un emprunt (**b**) *(in supermarket)* = espèces retirées à la caisse d'un supermarché lors d'un paiement par carte

cash-based accounting *n* comptabilité *f* de caisse

cashier *n* caissier(ère) *m,f*, préposé(e) *m,f* à la caisse □ *Am* **cashier's check** chèque *m* de banque

cashless society *n* société *f* sans argent *(où toutes les transactions sont effectuées en argent électronique)*

cashpoint *n* point *m* retrait, distributeur *m* (automatique) de billets

cask *n* fût *m*, tonneau *m*

CASM *n Comptr (abbr* **computer-assisted sales and marketing)** vente-marketing *f* assistée par ordinateur

cassette drive *n Comptr* lecteur *m* de cassettes

casting vote *n* voix *f* prépondérante; **the chairman has the casting vote** la voix du président est prépondérante; **to give the casting vote** départager les voix

casual *adj (employment)* occasionnel(elle), temporaire; **to employ sb on a casual basis** employer qn de façon épisodique □ **casual labour** main-d'œuvre *f* occasionnelle; **casual worker** travailleur(euse) *m,f* occasionnel(elle)

casualisation of labour *n Econ* précarisation *f* de l'emploi

catalogue, *Am* **catalog 1** *n* catalogue *m*; **to buy sth by catalogue** acheter qch sur catalogue □ **catalogue number** numéro *m* de catalogue; **catalogue price** prix *m* catalogue
2 *vt* cataloguer

catch *vt Fam St Exch* **to catch a cold** perdre de l'argent lors d'une transaction

category *n* catégorie *f* □ *Mktg* **category leader** chef *m* de file dans sa catégorie

▸ **cater for** *vt insep* (**a**) *(deal with, provide for)* s'occuper de; **we cater for the needs of small companies** nous répondons aux besoins des petites entreprises; **does the building cater for disabled staff?** le bâtiment dispose-t-il de l'équipement nécessaire pour l'accueil d'employés handicapés? (**b**) *(provide meals for)* préparer les repas pour

caveat *n Law* avertissement *m*; **to enter a caveat (against)** former ou mettre opposition (à); **caveat against unfair practices** avertissement contre la concurrence déloyale; **caveat emptor** aux risques de l'acheteur; **caveat sub-**

scriptor aux risques du signataire

CBD n (abbr **cash before delivery**) règlement m avant livraison

CBI n (abbr **Confederation of British Industry**) = patronat britannique, ≃ CNPF m

CBT n (abbr **Chicago Board of Trade**) = Bourse de Chicago

cc vt (abbr **carbon copy**) pcc; **to cc sb sth, to cc sth to sb** envoyer une copie de qch à qn

CCA n Acct (abbr **current cost accounting**) comptabilité f en coûts actuels

CCI n (abbr **Chamber of Commerce and Industry**) CCI f

cd/fwd Acct (abbr **carried forward**) reporté(e)

CD-I, CDI n Comptr (abbr **compact disc interactive**) CD-I m

CDL n (abbr **Career Development Loan**) prêt m de formation professionnelle

CD-R n (**a**) (abbr **compact disc recorder**) graveur m de disque compact (**b**) (abbr **compact disc recordable**) CD-R m

CD-ROM n Comptr (abbr **compact disc-read only memory**) CD-ROM m; **available on CD-ROM** existe en CD-ROM ▫ **CD-ROM burner** graveur m de CD-ROM; **CD-ROM drive** lecteur m de CD-ROM, lecteur de disque optique; **CD-ROM newspaper** journal m sur CD-ROM; **CD-ROM reader** lecteur de CD-ROM; **CD-ROM writer** graveur de CD-ROM

CD-RW n (abbr **compact disc rewritable**) CD m réinscriptible

CD-text n (abbr **compact disc text**) CD-texte m

CDV n (abbr **compact disc video**) CDV m, CD vidéo m

cease vt **to cease trading** cesser ses activités, cesser toute activité commerciale

ceiling n Econ plafond m; **to reach a ceiling** (of prices, interest rates) plafonner; **to have a ceiling of** être plafonné(e) à; **to fix a ceiling to sth** fixer un plafond à qch; **the government has set a three percent ceiling on wage rises** le gouvernement a limité à trois pour cent les augmentations de salaire ▫ **ceiling price** prix m plafond

❝
A rise in global oil prices would not have a direct impact on the Malaysian economy, but higher prices for a sustained period could boost the country's coffers. According to economists, as a net oil exporter, Malaysia will benefit from a rise in oil prices, but the Government's **ceiling price** on retail oil prices will ensure the country's inflation remains in check amid spiralling global oil prices.
❞

cell n Comptr (on spreadsheet) cellule f

cellphone n Am (téléphone m) portable m

cellular phone n téléphone m cellulaire

census n recensement m; **to conduct** or **take a census** faire un recensement ▫ Am **Census Bureau** Bureau m des statistiques; **census of distribution** recensement des distributeurs; **census of production** recensement de la production

center Am = **centre**

central adj **central account** compte m centralisateur; **central bank** banque f centrale; **Central Office of Information** = organisme chargé d'organiser les campagnes d'information du gouvernement britannique; Comptr **central processing unit** unité f centrale (de traitement), processeur m central; **central purchasing** achats mpl centralisés; **central purchasing department** centrale f d'achat(s); **central purchasing group** centrale d'achat(s); **central purchasing office** centrale d'achat(s); **central reservations unit** centrale de réservations; Banking, St Exch **Central Securities Depository** dépositaire m national de titres

centralized adj centralisé(e) ▫ **centralized management** gestion f intégrée; **centralized purchasing** achats mpl centralisés

centre, Am **center** n (**a**) (place, building) centre m (**b**) Comptr centre m

CEO n Am (abbr **chief executive officer**) directeur(trice) m,f général(e); **President and CEO** président-directeur m général, P-DG m

certificate n certificat m ▫ **certificate of airworthiness** certificat de navigabilité; **certificate of approval** certificat d'homologation; **certificate of compliance** certificat de conformité; **certificate of conformity** certificat de conformité; Ins **certificate of damage** certificat d'avarie; **certificate of deposit** certificat de dépôt; Fin **certificate of dishonour** certificat de non-paiement; **certificate of guarantee** certificat de garantie; **certificate of incorporation** certificat d'enregistrement de société; **certificate of insurance** attestation f d'assurance; **certificate of origin** certificat d'origine, label m d'origine; **certificate of proficiency** certificat de capacité; **certificate of quality** certificat de qualité; **certificate of receipt** certificat de chargement; **certificate of registration** (of ship) certificat d'inscription maritime; **certificate of residence** certificat de résidence; **certificat of transfer** acte m de cession; **certificate of value** certificat de valeur

certification n (**a**) (act) certification f, authentification f ▫ **certification mark** marque f de garantie (**b**) (certificate) certificat m

certified adj (**a**) Am **certified public accountant** expert-comptable m (**b**) **certified ac-**

counts comptes *mpl* approuvés; **certified bankrupt** failli *m* concordataire; **certified cheque** chèque *m* certifié; **certified protest** protêt *m* authentique (**c**) *Law* **certified copy** copie *f* certifiée conforme; **certified true copy** *(on document)* pour copie conforme

certify *vt* (**a**) *(confirm)* certifier; **certified by a notary** notarié(e); **this is to certify that Alison Patrick has...** *(on document)* ce document certifie que Alison Patrick a...; **to certify the books** viser les livres de commerce (**b**) *(cheque, invoice)* certifier (**c**) *Am* **certified letter** lettre *f* recommandée; *Am* **certified mail** envoi *m* recommandé; **to send sth by certified mail** envoyer qch en recommandé avec accusé de réception

CET *n EU (abbr* **common external tariff)** tarif *m* externe commun

CF *(abbr* **carriage forward)** (en) port dû, port avancé

c/f *Acct (abbr* **carried forward)** report *m* à nouveau

CFI, *n (abbr* **cost, freight and insurance)** CAF *m*

CFO *n Am (abbr* **Chief Financial Officer)** chef *m* comptable, chef de la comptabilité

CFSP *n EU (abbr* **Common Foreign and Security Policy)** PESC *f*

CFTC *n Am Fin, St Exch (abbr* **Commodity Futures Trading Commission)** = organisme fédéral chargé de réglementer les marchés des options et des contrats à terme de marchandises aux États-Unis

CGI *n Comptr* (**a**) *(abbr* **common gateway interface)** interface *f* commune de passerelle, CGI *f* (**b**) *(abbr* **computer-generated images)** images *fpl* de synthèse

CGT *n (abbr* **capital gains tax)** impôt *m* sur les plus-values

CH *n (abbr* **clearing house)** chambre *f* de compensation *ou* de clearing

chaebol *n Econ* chaebol *m*

> 66
> The Fair Trade Commission (FTC), the nation's antitrust watchdog, has begun to use its scalpel to root out unfair business practices by the nation's five largest business groups in the initial stages of an operation which will later be applied to 24 other groups or **chaebol**. The punitive action by the government agency is expected to serve as a key means to press **chaebol** groups to expedite their restructuring work in compliance with the government call.
> 99

chain *n* (**a**) *(of stores, restaurants)* chaîne *f* ⊐ *Am* **chain bank** banque *f* à succursales multiples; **chain store** magasin *m* à succursales (multi-

ples); *(individual store)* succursale *f* (**b**) **chain of distribution** circuit *m ou* réseau *m* de distribution

chair **1** *n (chairperson)* président(e) *m,f*; **to be in the chair** présider; **to take the chair** prendre la présidence; **to support the chair** se ranger à l'avis du président; **to address the chair** s'adresser au président
2 *vt (meeting)* présider

chairman *n (of meeting)* président(e) *m,f*; *(of company)* président-directeur *m* général, P-DG *m*; **to act as chairman** présider (la séance); **chairman and managing director** président-directeur général, P-DG; **Mr Chairman** Monsieur le Président; **Chairman of the Board** Président du Conseil d'administration ⊐ **chairman's report** rapport *m* (annuel) du président

chairmanship *n* présidence *f*; **under the chairmanship of Mr Greene** sous la présidence de M. Greene

chairperson *n* président(e) *m,f*

chairwoman *n* présidente *f*; **Madam Chairwoman** Madame la Présidente

challenger *n Mktg* challengeur *m*, prétendant(e) *m,f*

chamber *n* **Chamber of Commerce** Chambre *f* de commerce; **Chamber of Commerce and Industry** Chambre de commerce et d'industrie; **Chamber of Trade** Chambre de métiers

Chancellor of the Exchequer *n Br* Chancelier *m* de l'Échiquier, ≃ ministre *m* des finances

change **1** *n* (**a**) **(small) change** (petite) monnaie *f*; **to give change for £20** donner *ou* rendre la monnaie de 20 livres ⊐ **change machine** changeur *m* de monnaie (**b**) **change management** gestion *f* du changement
2 *vt (money)* changer; **to change dollars into euros** changer des dollars en euros

channel *n* (**a**) *(means)* canal *m*, voie *f*; **to go through the official channels** suivre la filière officielle; **to open up new channels for trade** créer de nouveaux débouchés pour le commerce ⊐ **channel of distribution** circuit *m ou* canal de distribution; *Mktg* **channel management** gestion *f* du circuit de distribution (**b**) *Comptr (of communication, data flow, for IRC)* canal *m*

CHAPS *n Br Banking (abbr* **clearing house automated payment system)** = système de télé-compensation interbancaire, ≃ SIT *m*

Chapter 11 *n Am Fin (part of bankruptcy laws)* = ensemble de dispositions légales régissant la procédure de redressement judiciaire; **to file for Chapter 11** faire une demande de redressement judiciaire

character n *Comptr* caractère m; **characters per inch** caractères par pouce; **characters per second** caractères par seconde ❏ *character code* code m de caractère; *character generator* générateur m de caractères; *character insert* insertion f de caractère; *character recognition* reconnaissance f de caractères; *character set* jeu m de caractères; *character smoothing* lissage m de caractères; *character space* espace m; *character spacing* espacement m des caractères; *character string* chaîne f ou séquence f de caractères

charge 1 n *(cost)* frais mpl, prix m; *(to an account)* imputation f; **to make a charge for sth** compter qch, faire payer qch; **there is no extra charge for installation** l'installation est comprise dans le prix; **what's the charge?** combien est-ce que ça coûte?; **at a small charge** moyennant une faible rétribution; *Am* **will that be cash or charge?** vous payez comptant ou vous le portez à votre compte?; **charge to provisions** dotation f aux provisions ❏ *Am* **charge account** compte m crédit d'achats; *charge card* carte f de paiement

2 vt **(a)** *(defer payment of)* **charge it** mettez-le sur mon compte; **charge it to the company's account** mettez-le sur le compte de l'entreprise; **I charged all my expenses to the company** j'ai mis tous mes frais sur le compte de la société

(b) *(person)* faire payer; *(sum)* faire payer, prendre; *(commission)* prélever; **they charged us $50 for delivery** ils nous ont fait payer 50 dollars pour la livraison; **how much will you charge for the lot?** combien demandez-vous pour le tout?; **you will be charged for postage** les frais postaux seront à votre charge

3 vi *(demand payment)* faire payer; **they don't charge for postage and packing** ils ne font pas payer le port et l'emballage

▶ **charge off** vt *Am* *(capital)* amortir, imputer à l'exercice; **we were obliged to charge off the whole operation** il a fallu imputer l'intégralité du coût de l'opération à l'exercice

▶ **charge up** vt sep **to charge sth up to sb's account** mettre qch sur le compte de qn; **could you charge it up?** pourriez-vous le mettre sur mon compte?

chargeable adj **(a)** *(to an account)* imputable; **to be chargeable to sb** *(payable by)* être à la charge de qn, être pris(e) en charge par qn; **who is it chargeable to?** c'est à la charge de qui?; **could you make that chargeable to Crown Ltd?** est-ce que vous pourriez facturer Crown Ltd? ❏ *chargeable expenses* frais mpl facturables; *chargeable weight* poids m de taxation

(b) *Fin* imposable ❏ *chargeable asset* actif m imposable sur les plus-values; *chargeable gain* bénéfice m imposable

chargehand n chef m d'équipe

charitable trust n fondation f d'utilité publique

charity n association f caritative ❏ *charity card* = carte de crédit émise par un organisme de crédit en collaboration avec une association caritative de façon à ce qu'une part de chaque transaction revienne à ladite association; *charity organization* association caritative

chart 1 n *(diagram)* graphique m ❏ *Acct* **chart of accounts** plan m comptable général; *chart analysis* analyse f sur graphiques; *chart analyst* analyste mf sur graphiques

2 vt **(a)** *(on diagram)* faire le graphique ou la courbe de; **this graph charts sales over the last ten years** ce graphique montre l'évolution des ventes au cours des dix dernières années **(b)** *(follow)* *(progress, rise)* retracer; **the director charted a way out of financial collapse** le directeur a établi ou mis au point un plan pour éviter un effondrement financier

charter 1 n **(a)** *(of company)* statuts mpl **(b)** *(of aeroplane, boat)* affrètement m ❏ *charter company* affréteur m; *charter flight* vol m charter; *charter plane* (avion m) charter m

2 vt **(a)** *(company)* accorder une charte à **(b)** *(aeroplane, boat)* affréter

chartered adj **(a)** *Br* *chartered accountant* expert-comptable m, *Can* comptable mf agréé(e); *chartered bank* banque f privilégiée; *chartered company* société f privilégiée ou à charte; *chartered surveyor* expert m immobilier **(b)** *(aeroplane, boat)* affrété(e)

chartist n *St Exch* analyste mf des cours des valeurs boursières, chartiste mf

▶ **chase up** vt sep *(debt)* essayer de se faire rembourser; *(person)* essayer de contacter; **can you chase up the manager for me?** pouvez-vous relancer le directeur à propos de ce que je lui ai demandé?

chat *Comptr* **1** *n* messagerie *f* de dialogue en direct, bavardage *m*, chat *m*

2 *vi* bavarder, chatter ❏ **chat room** site *m* de bavardage, salon *m*

chattel mortgage *n* nantissement *m* de biens meubles

cheap *adj* bon marché, pas cher (chère); **to buy sth cheap** acheter qch (à) bon marché; **it works out cheaper to buy ten kilos** cela revient moins cher d'acheter dix kilos à la fois ❏ **cheap money** argent *m* à bon marché; **cheap rate** tarif *m* réduit

cheaply *adv* (à) bon marché; **they can manufacture more cheaply than we can** ils sont à même de fabriquer à meilleur marché que nous

check 1 *n* (**a**) *(restraint)* frein *m*; **to put a check on production** freiner la production

(**b**) *(verification)* contrôle *m*, vérification *f* ❏ *Mktg* **check question** question *f* de contrôle, question témoin; *Mktg* **check sample** échantillon *m* témoin

(**c**) *Am (bill)* addition *f*, facture *f*

(**d**) *Am (cheque)* chèque *m*

(**e**) *Comptr* **check box** case *f* à cocher

2 *vt* (**a**) *(price increases, inflation)* enrayer; *(production)* freiner

(**b**) *(verify, examine) (accounts, figures)* vérifier; *(document)* examiner; **to check the books** pointer les écritures; **all the sales are checked** toutes les ventes sont contrôlées

(**c**) *Am (baggage)* mettre à la consigne

▶ **check in 1** *vt sep (baggage) (at airport)* (faire) enregistrer; *(at left-luggage)* mettre à la consigne

2 *vi (at hotel)* se présenter à la réception; *(at airport)* se présenter à l'enregistrement

▶ **check off** *vt sep (goods)* recenser; **to check sth off a list** cocher qch dans une liste

▶ **check out** *vi (leave hotel)* quitter l'hôtel

▶ **check over** *vt sep (goods)* examiner, vérifier

checkbook *Am* = **chequebook**

check-in *n (at airport)* **check-in time is 30 minutes prior to departure** les voyageurs sont priés de se présenter à l'enregistrement 30 minutes avant l'heure du départ ❏ **check-in desk** guichet *m* d'enregistrement

checking account *n Am* compte *m* courant

checkless society *Am* = **chequeless society**

check-out *n* (**a**) *(in supermarket)* caisse *f* (**b**) *(in hotel)* **check-out time is at 12 noon** les clients doivent quitter la chambre avant midi (le jour du départ)

cheque, *Am* **check** *n* chèque *m*; **a cheque for**

£10 un chèque de dix livres; **cheque to order** chèque à ordre; **cheque to bearer** chèque au porteur; **to cash a cheque** toucher un chèque; **to endorse a cheque** endosser un chèque; **to make out a cheque (to sb)** établir *ou* faire un chèque (à l'ordre de qn); **who should I make the cheque out to?** à quel ordre dois-je faire *ou* écrire le chèque?; **will you take a cheque?** est-ce que vous acceptez les chèques?; **to pay by cheque** régler par chèque; **to pay a cheque into the bank** déposer un chèque à la banque; **to stop a cheque** faire opposition à un chèque ❏ **cheque account** compte *m* (de) chèques; **cheque counterfoil** talon *m* de chèque, souche *f*; **cheque form** formule *f* de chèque; *Br* **cheque (guarantee) card** carte *f* bancaire *(sans laquelle un chéquier n'est pas valable)*; **cheque number** numéro *m* de chèque; **cheque stub** talon de chèque, souche

chequebook, *Am* **checkbook** *n* carnet *m* de chèques, chéquier *m* ❏ **chequebook account** compte *m* (de) chèques

chequeless society, *Am* **checkless society** *n* société *f* sans chèques

cherry-pick *vt* écrémer

chief *adj Br* **chief accountant** chef *m* comptable, chef de la comptabilité; *Br* **chief executive,** *Am* **Chief Executive Officer** directeur(trice) *m,f* général(e); *Am* **Chief Financial Officer** chef comptable, chef de la comptabilité

Chinese walls *npl* = murs imaginaires qui symbolisent la confidentialité indispensable dans certains milieux financiers et séparent des services qui, par ailleurs, travaillent côte à côte

chip *n Comptr* puce *f*

CHIPS *n Am Banking (abbr* **Clearing House Interbank Payment System)** SIT *m*

choice 1 *n Mktg (selection)* choix *m*; **the product of choice** le premier choix ❏ **choice set** ensemble *m* de considérations, éventail *m* de choix

2 *adj (food, product)* de choix, de première qualité

chooser *n Comptr* sélecteur *m*

Christmas bonus *n* prime *f* de fin d'année

chronic *adj (shortage, unemployment)* chronique

churn 1 *n* = perte de clients passés à la concurrence

2 *vt Fam St Exch (portfolio)* faire tourner

> 〝 ——————————————
>
> The improvements mean that fewer customers are leaving the cable companies than before. Telewest's **churn** has fallen 10% since Singer took over two years ago. NTL's performance has been similar, but both companies say they can still improve. "Do I

still get absolutely legitimate grumps and groans from customers? Yes. We're better but we're not there yet," Singer says. **"**

churning n Fam St Exch (of portfolio) rotation f

CI n (**a**) (abbr **cost and insurance**) C&A m (**b**) (abbr **certificate of insurance**) attestation f d'assurance

CIF, cif n (abbr **cost, insurance and freight**) CAF m

CIM n (**a**) Br (abbr **Chartered Institute of Marketing**) = institut britannique de marketing (**b**) (abbr **Convention internationale concernant le transport des marchandises par chemin de fer**) ▫ **CIM waybill** lettre f de voiture CIM

cinema advertising n publicité f au cinéma

CIO n (abbr **Congress of Industrial Organizations**) CIO m (confédération syndicale américaine)

circular 1 n (**a**) (letter) circulaire f (**b**) (advertisement) prospectus m
    2 adj **circular letter** circulaire f; **circular letter of credit** lettre f de crédit circulaire

circulate 1 vt (**a**) (banknotes) mettre en circulation, émettre (**b**) (document, prospectus) (from person to person) faire circuler; (by mass mailing) diffuser; **please circulate the minutes of this morning's meeting** veuillez faire circuler le compte-rendu de la réunion de ce matin
    2 vi (of money) circuler; **to circulate freely** circuler librement, rouler

circulating adj circulant(e) ▫ Acct **circulating assets** actif m circulant; Fin **circulating capital** capital m circulant

circulation n (**a**) (of capital) roulement m, circulation f (**b**) **to be in circulation** (of money) circuler; **notes in circulation** billets mpl en circulation (**c**) (of newspaper) tirage m; **a newspaper with a large circulation** un journal à grand ou gros tirage ▫ **circulation figures** tirage

circumflex accent n accent m circonflexe

citizen n citoyen(enne) m,f ▫ Admin **Citizens' Advice Bureau** = en Grande-Bretagne, bureau où les citoyens peuvent obtenir des conseils d'ordre juridique, social etc; Admin **Citizens' Charter** = programme lancé par le gouvernement britannique en 1991 et qui vise à améliorer la qualité des services publics

City n **the City** la Cité ou City (de Londres) (centre des affaires); **he's in the City** il est dans la finance (dans la Cité de Londres) ▫ **the City Companies** les corporations fpl de la Cité de Londres

civil adj Law **civil action** action f civile; **Civil Aviation Authority** = organisme de contrôle des compagnies aériennes; **civil engineer** ingénieur m civil; **civil engineering** génie m civil;

civil law droit m civil; **Civil and Public Services Association** = syndicat de la fonction publique; **civil servant** fonctionnaire mf; **civil service** administration f; **Civil Service Union** = syndicat britannique de la fonction publique; Admin **civil status** état m civil

claim 1 n (**a**) (demand) (for damages, compensation) demande f d'indemnisation; (as a right) revendication f, réclamation f; **to put in a claim for sth** demander une indemnité pour qch; **to make a legal claim for sth** revendiquer qch; **they're putting in a claim for better working conditions** ils demandent de meilleures conditions de travail ▫ **claims book** livre m des réclamations; **claims register** cahier m des revendications syndicales
    (**b**) Ins demande f d'indemnité, déclaration f de sinistre; **to make** or **put in a claim (for sth)** demander une indemnité (pour qch) ▫ **claims adjuster** expert m en assurances; **claim form** formulaire m de demande d'indemnité
    (**c**) Mktg promesse f; **they have been making all sorts of claims about their new product** ils ont paré leur nouveau produit de toutes sortes de qualités
    2 vt (**a**) (as a right) réclamer, revendiquer; **to claim damages (from sb)** réclamer des dommages-intérêts (à qn); **workers are claiming the right to strike** les ouvriers revendiquent le droit de (faire) grève
    (**b**) Mktg affirmer; **they claim that their product is the best on the market** ils affirment que leur produit est le meilleur sur le marché

▶ **claim back** vt sep (expenses, cost) se faire rembourser; (VAT) récupérer

claimant n Admin, Ins (for social security, insurance) demandeur(eresse) m,f; Law requérant(e) m,f, partie f requérante

clampdown n répression f, mesures fpl répressives (**on** de); **there has been a clampdown on credit** il y a eu un resserrement du crédit

classified adj (**a**) (secret) classé(e) secret(ète), confidentiel(elle) ▫ **classified information** renseignements mpl classés secrets (**b**) **classified advertisement** (in newspaper) annonce f classée, petite annonce

clause n (of contract, law, treaty) clause f; Ins (of policy) avenant m

claused bill n connaissement m clausé

▶ **claw back** vt sep Fin (expenditure, tax relief) récupérer

clawback n Fin (of expenditure, tax relief) récupération f; (sum) somme f récupérée

clean adj **clean bill** effet m libre ou net, traite f libre ou nette; **clean bill of lading** connaissement m libre ou net

clear 1 adj (**a**) (net) net (nette); **clear of taxes**

net d'impôt ▫ *clear loss* perte *f* sèche; *clear profit* bénéfice *m* net

(**b**) *clear day* jour *m* franc; **three clear days** trois jours francs; **ten clear days' notice** préavis *m* de dix jours francs

(**c**) *(accounts)* en règle

2 *vt* (**a**) *(debt)* liquider, acquitter; *(mortgage)* purger; *(account)* solder

(**b**) *(authorize) (ship)* expédier; *(goods through customs)* dédouaner; **to clear customs** *(of person)* passer la douane; *(of goods)* être dédouané(e)

(**c**) *(make profit of)* **she cleared ten percent on the deal** l'affaire lui a rapporté dix pour cent tous frais payés *ou* dix pour cent net; **I clear a thousand pounds monthly** je fais un bénéfice net de mille livres par mois

(**d**) *Banking (cheque)* compenser, virer; *Fin (bill)* régler

(**e**) *Comptr* **to clear the screen** vider l'écran

3 *vi (of cheque)* être encaissé(e); **it takes three working days for cheques to clear** il y a trois jours ouvrables de délai d'encaissement

► **clear off** *vt sep (debt)* liquider, acquitter; *(stock)* liquider

clearance *n* (**a**) *Customs (of goods)* dédouanement *m*; **to effect customs clearance** procéder aux formalités de la douane ▫ *clearance certificate* lettre *f* de mer; *clearance inward(s)* déclaration *f ou* permis *m* d'entrée; *clearance outward(s)* déclaration *ou* permis de sortie; *clearance papers* papiers *mpl* d'expédition (**b**) *Banking (of cheque)* compensation *f* (**c**) *clearance sale* liquidation *f*, soldes *mpl*

cleared value *n* valeur *f* compensée

clearer *n Banking* = banque appartenant à une chambre de compensation

clearing *n (of cheque)* compensation *f*; *(of account)* liquidation *f*, solde *m*; *(of debt)* acquittement *m*; **general clearing** compensation de chèques en dehors de Londres; **under the clearing procedure** par voie de compensation ▫ *clearing account* compte *m* de compensation; *clearing agreement* accord *m* de clearing; *clearing bank* banque *f* de compensation *ou* de clearing; *clearing house* chambre *f* de compensation *ou* de clearing; **to pass a cheque through the clearing house** compenser un chèque; *clearing member* membre *m* de compensation *ou* de clearing; *clearing system* système *m* de compensation *ou* de clearing; *clearing transaction* opération *f* de compensation *ou* de clearing

clerical *adj clerical error (in document)* faute *f* de copiste; *(in accounting)* erreur *f* d'écriture; *clerical job* emploi *m* de bureau; *clerical staff* personnel *m ou* employés *mpl* de bureau; *clerical work* travail *m* de bureau; *clerical worker* employé(e) *m,f* de bureau

clerk 1 *n* (**a**) *(in office)* employé(e) *m,f* de bureau, commis *m*; *(in bank)* employé(e) de banque (**b**) *Am (in shop)* vendeur(euse) *m,f* (**c**) *Am (receptionist)* réceptionniste *mf* (**d**) *clerk of works* conducteur(trice) *m,f* de travaux

2 *vi Am* travailler comme vendeur(euse)

CLI *n (abbr* **cost-of-living index**) indice *m* du coût de la vie

click *Comptr* **1** *n* clic *m*

2 *vt* cliquer

3 *vi* cliquer (**on** sur); **to click and drag** cliquer et glisser

clickable image *n Comptr* image *f* cliquable

clicks-and-mortar *adj Comptr* clic et mortier *(désigne une entreprise qui existe aussi bien sur l'Internet que dans le réel)*

> **"**
>
> E-tailers once ridiculed traditional traders for the sluggishness with which they set up internet sites. However, these "**clicks-and-mortar**" operations now look best placed to make e-commerce more reliable. They already boast stocked warehouses and supply infrastructure to keep their real world shops in business.
>
> **"**

client *n* (**a**) *(of company, lawyer)* client(e) *m,f* ▫ *Banking client account* compte *m* client; *client base* clientèle *f*; *client confidence* confiance *f* de la clientèle *ou* du client; *client file* dossier *m ou* fichier *m* client; *client list* liste *f* de clients (**b**) *Comptr (part of network)* client *m*

clientele *n* clientèle *f*

client-server database *n Comptr* base *f* de données client-serveur

climb 1 *n* augmentation *f*; **a climb in production costs is expected in the next quarter** une augmentation des coûts de production est prévue au trimestre prochain

2 *vi* augmenter, monter

clinch *vt (deal)* conclure

clip art *n Comptr* clipart *m*

clipboard *n* écritoire *m* à pince; *Comptr* presse-papiers *m*, bloc-notes *m*

clock *n Comptr* horloge *f* ▫ *clock speed* fréquence *f* d'horloge

► **clock in** *vi* pointer (à l'arrivée)

► **clock off** *vi* pointer (à la sortie)

► **clock on** *vi* = **clock in**

► **clock out** *vi* = **clock off**

clocking-in *n* pointage *m* à l'arrivée ▫ *clocking-in card* fiche *f* de pointage

clocking-off *n* pointage *m* à la sortie

clocking-on = **clocking-in**

clocking-out = **clocking-off**

clone n Comptr clone m

close 1 n (**a**) St Exch (on stock market) clôture f; (closing price) cours m de clôture; **at close of business** à la ou en clôture
(**b**) Comptr **close box** case f de fermeture
2 vt (**a**) Acct **to close the books** balancer les comptes, régler les livres; **to close the yearly accounts** arrêter les comptes de l'exercice
(**b**) (meeting) clore; (account) fermer; (deal) conclure, clore
(**c**) St Exch (operation) liquider; **to close a position** couvrir une position
3 vi St Exch clôturer; **the shares closed at 420p** les actions ont clôturé ou terminé à 420 pence; **the share index closed two points down** l'indice (boursier) a clôturé en baisse de deux points

▶ **close down 1** vt sep fermer (définitivement); **the factory was closed down after a drop in orders** l'usine a fermé ses portes à la suite d'une baisse des commandes
2 vi (of factory, business) fermer

▶ **close off** vt sep (account) arrêter

▶ **close out** vt sep Am (goods) solder, liquider (avant fermeture)

▶ **close with** vt insep (finalize agreement with) conclure un marché avec

closed adj (**a**) (shop, factory) fermé(e) (**b**) Am **closed corporation** société f fermée; **closed shop** = entreprise ou usine qui n'embauche que du personnel syndiqué

closed-end adj **closed-end investment fund** société f d'investissement à capital fixe; **closed-end mortgage** prêt m hypothécaire à montant fixe

closed-ended adj Mktg (question) fermé(e)

closedown n fermeture f (définitive)

closeout n Am liquidation f

closing 1 n (**a**) (of shop) fermeture f
(**b**) (of meeting, account) clôture f; (of deal) clôture, conclusion f
(**c**) St Exch (of position) clôture f
2 adj (**a**) (concluding) dernier(ère), final(e) □ **closing speech** discours m de clôture
(**b**) (final) dernier(ère) □ Banking **closing account balance** solde m à la fermeture du compte; **closing bid** dernière enchère f; **closing date** (for application) date f limite; Acct **closing entry** écriture f d'inventaire ou de clôture; **closing stock** stock m à l'inventaire, stock final
(**c**) St Exch **closing price** cours m de clôture; **closing quotations** cotes fpl en clôture; **closing range** fourchette f de cours de clôture; **closing session** séance f de clôture; **closing trade** transactions fpl de clôture; **closing transaction** transaction f de clôture

(**d**) **closing time** (of shop) heure f de fermeture

closing-down n (of factory, business) fermeture f; (of shop) fermeture, liquidation f □ **closing-down costs** frais mpl de liquidation; **closing-down price** prix m de liquidation; **closing-down sale** solde m de fermeture

closing-off n Acct (of accounts) arrêt m

closing-out n Am fermeture f, liquidation f □ **closing-out sale** solde m de fermeture

closure n (of factory, business, shop) fermeture f; St Exch **closure by repurchase** clôture f par rachat

club class n (in air travel) classe f club

cluster n (**a**) Comptr cluster m, bloc m; (of terminals) grappe f (**b**) Mktg **cluster analysis** analyse f par segments; **cluster sample** échantillon m aréolaire ou par grappes; **cluster sampling** échantillonnage m aréolaire ou par grappes

CMO n Am Fin (abbr **collateralized mortgage obligation**) obligation f garantie par une hypothèque

CMR n (abbr **Convention relative au contrat de transport international de marchandises par route**) □ **CMR waybill** lettre f de voiture CMR

Co, co n (abbr **company**) Cie

.co Comptr = abréviation désignant les entreprises commerciales dans les adresses électroniques britanniques

c/o (abbr **care of**) chez, aux bons soins de

coast n côte f

coastal adj côtier(ère) □ **coastal trade** navigation f côtière; **coastal traffic** navigation côtière, cabotage m

coated paper n papier m couché

COBOL n Comptr (abbr **Common Business-Oriented Language**) Cobol m

co-branding n Mktg alliance f de marque, co-branding m

co-chair vt co-présider

co-creditor n Fin cocréancier(ère) m,f

COD, cod adv (abbr Br **cash** or Am **collect on delivery**) livraison contre remboursement, paiement à la livraison; **all goods are sent COD** toutes les marchandises doivent être payées à la livraison

code 1 n (**a**) (Br **dialling** or Am **dialing**) **code** indicatif m (**b**) (rules) code m; **code of ethics** (in profession) déontologie f
2 vt Comptr coder

coded adj Comptr codé(e)

codetermination n Ind = collaboration entre la direction et le personnel pour les prises de décisions

coding n Comptr (providing codes) codage m; (system of codes) codes mpl

co-director n codirecteur(trice) m,f

coefficient tax n impôt m de quotité

coffers npl Fin (funds)(of nation) coffres mpl; (of organization) caisses fpl, coffres

co-founder n (of company) cofondateur(trice) m,f

COGS n Acct (abbr **cost of goods sold**) coût m des produits vendus

COI n (abbr **Central Office of Information**) = organisme chargé d'organiser les campagnes d'information du gouvernement britannique

coin 1 n (**a**) (item of metal currency) pièce f (de monnaie); **a 50p coin** une pièce de 50 pence (**b**) (metal currency) monnaie f; **£50 in coin** 50 livres en espèces
  2 vt **to coin money** battre monnaie

coinage n (**a**) (monetary system) système m monétaire (**b**) (coins) monnaie f

co-insurance n coassurance f

co-insure vt coassurer

co-insurer n coassureur m

COLA n Am Fin (abbr **cost-of-living adjustment**) augmentation f de salaire indexée sur le coût de la vie

cold adj (**a**) Mktg **cold call** visite f à froid; (on phone) appel m à froid; **cold call sales** ventes fpl par approche directe; **cold calling** approche f directe (**b**) Comptr **cold start** démarrage m à froid (**c**) **cold storage** conservation f par le froid; **to put sth into cold storage** mettre qch en chambre froide; **cold storage dock** dock m frigorifique; **cold store** entrepôt m frigorifique

collaborate vi collaborer; **she collaborated with us on the project** elle a collaboré avec nous au projet

collaboration n collaboration f

collapse 1 n (of market, prices) effondrement m; (of currency) dégringolade f
  2 vi (of market, prices) s'effondrer; (of currency) dégringoler

collate vt (documents, data) rassembler

collateral Fin 1 n nantissement m; **what can you provide as collateral?** qu'est-ce que vous pouvez fournir en nantissement?; **to lodge sth as collateral** déposer qch en nantissement; **the bank prefers not to lend without collateral** de préférence, la banque ne prête pas sans nantissement
  2 adj subsidiaire □ **collateral loan** prêt m garanti; **collateral security** nantissement m, garantie f accessoire

> "
> Rapid restructuring is likely to lift asset prices, which buoys economic activity. Rational market participants are aware which assets need to be reallocated – for example, the property held as **collateral** that must be sold when companies are restructured.
> "

collateralize vt Am Fin garantir □ **collateralized mortgage obligation** obligation f garantie par une hypothèque

colleague n collègue mf

collect 1 adj Am **collect call** appel m en PCV; **to make a collect call** faire un appel ou téléphoner en PCV
  2 adv Am (**a**) Tel **to call collect** faire un appel ou téléphoner en PCV (**b**) **to send a parcel collect** envoyer un colis en port dû ou payable à destination
  3 vt (salary) toucher; (debt) recouvrer; (taxes) percevoir, lever; Am **collect on delivery** paiement à la livraison, livraison contre remboursement

collecting adj **collecting agency, collecting bank** banque f de recouvrement; **collecting banker** banquier m encaisseur; **collecting department** service m de recouvrement

collection n (**a**) (of debts) recouvrement m; (of taxes) perception f, levée f (**b**) Fin (of bill) encaissement m; **to hand sth in for collection** donner qch à l'encaissement; **a bill for collection** un effet à l'encaissement □ **collection bank** banque f d'encaissement; **collection charges** frais mpl d'encaissement; **collection fees** frais d'encaissement; **collection period** période f de recouvrement; **collection rate** tarif m d'encaissement

collective 1 n coopérative f
  2 adj collectif(ive) □ **collective bargaining** négociation f de conventions collectives; **collective bargaining agreement** convention f collective; **collective liability** responsabilité f collective; **collective ownership** propriété f collective; **collective responsibility** responsabilité f collective; **collective risk** risque m collectif

> "
> Northwest Airlines, the country's fourth largest airline, and its pilots' union have reached a tentative agreement to extend their current five-year **collective bargaining agreement** by 12 months. The agreement provides for a 4.5% salary increase this September and another 5.5% increase in September 2003.
> "

collectivism n Econ collectivisme m

collectivist n Econ collectiviste mf

collectivity n Econ collectivité f

collector n (a) (of cheque) encaisseur m (b) (of taxes) percepteur m

colon n (punctuation mark) deux-points m

colour, Am **color** n Comptr **colour display** affichage m couleur; **colour graphics** graphisme m en couleur; **colour monitor** moniteur m couleur; **colour printer** imprimante f couleur; **colour printing** impression f couleur; **colour screen** écran m couleur

column n Acct colonne f

.com Comptr = abréviation désignant les entreprises commerciales dans les adresses électroniques

combination n (of lock) combinaison f ❑ **combination lock** serrure f ou fermeture f à combinaison

combine n Fin cartel m, trust m

combined adj **combined transport bill of lading** connaissement m de transport combiné; **combined transport company** entreprise f de transport combiné; **combined transport document** document m de transport combiné

▸ **come out** vi Comptr (exit) sortir; **to come out of a document** sortir d'un document

Comecon n (abbr **Council for Mutual Economic Aid**) Comecon m

comma n (punctuation mark) virgule f

command n (a) Comptr commande f; (from menu options) article m ❑ **command box** boîtier m de commande; **command circuit** circuit m de commande; **command file** fichier m de commande; **command key** touche f Commande (b) Econ **command economy** économie f planifiée

comment card n Mktg fiche f d'observations

commerce n commerce m

commercial 1 n (advertisement) publicité f
  2 adj commercial(e); **a commercial venture** une entreprise commerciale ❑ **commercial agency** agence f commerciale; **commercial aircraft** avion m commercial; **commercial attaché** attaché(e) m,f commercial(e); **commercial bank** banque f commerciale; **commercial bill** effet m de commerce; **commercial break** écran m publicitaire; **commercial broker** courtier(ère) m,f de marchandises; **commercial centre** centre m commercial; **commercial channel** circuit commercial ou de vente; **commercial charter** charte f commerciale; **commercial contract** contrat m commercial; **commercial designer** dessinateur(trice) m,f de publicité; **commercial directory** annuaire m du commerce; **commercial dispute** litige m commercial; **com-mercial district** quartier m des affaires; **com-**

mercial documents papiers mpl d'affaires; **commercial efficiency** rendement m économique; **commercial jurisdiction** juridiction f commerciale; **commercial law** droit m commercial; **commercial lease** bail m commercial; **commercial loan** prêt m commercial; **commercial monopoly** monopole m ou trust m commercial; **commercial paper** billet m de trésorerie; **commercial port** port m marchand ou de commerce; **commercial premises** locaux mpl commerciaux; **commercial process** action f commerciale; **commercial route** route f commerciale; **commercial traveller** VRP m; **commercial tribunal** tribunal m de commerce; **commercial value** valeur f marchande; **commercial vehicle** véhicule m utilitaire

commercialism n (a) (practice of business) commerce m, affaires fpl (b) (profit-seeking) mercantilisme m

commercialization n commercialisation f

commercialize vt (make commercial) commercialiser

commercialized adj (commercial) commercialisé(e)

commercially adv commercialement; **commercially available** disponible dans le commerce

commission 1 n (a) (payment) commission f; **to get three percent commission** toucher trois pour cent de commission; **to work on a commission basis** travailler à la commission; **this post offers a basic salary plus generous commission** ce poste est rémunéré par un salaire de base ainsi qu'un généreux pourcentage sur les ventes ❑ **commission agency** maison f de commission; **commission agent** (agent m) commissionnaire mf; **commission merchant** (agent) commissionnaire; Acct **commission note** note f de commission; **commission sale** vente f à (la) commission
  (b) (committee) commission f ❑ **commission of inquiry** commission d'enquête
  (c) (order) commande f; **work done on commission** travail m fait sur commande; **to carry out a commission** s'acquitter d'une commande
  2 vt (order) commander; **to commission sb to do sth** charger qn de faire qch

Commissioner of the Inland Revenue n Br ≃ Inspecteur m des impôts

commitment n Fin engagement m financier ❑ **commitment fee** commission f d'engagement; **commitment of funds** engagement de dépenses

committed costs npl Acct coûts mpl engagés

committee n comité m, commission f; **to be or sit on a committee** être membre de ou faire partie d'un comité ❑ **committee meeting** réunion f de comité

commodity n (**a**) Econ (product) marchandise f, produit m; (foodstuff) denrée f; **rice is the staple commodity of China** le riz est la ressource principale de la Chine

(**b**) St Exch matière f première; **to trade commodities** spéculer sur les marchés à terme des matières premières; **coffee is considered to be the main agricultural commodity** le café est considéré comme la principale matière négociable □ **commodity broker, commodity dealer** courtier(ère) m,f en matières premières; **commodity exchange** marché m des matières premières; **commodity futures** opérations fpl à terme sur matières premières; **commodity market** marché des matières premières; **commodity money** monnaie f de marchandise; **commodity prices** prix mpl des marchandises, cours mpl des denrées

> **❝**
>
> He says the main reasons why the recovery will continue is to do with **commodity prices** and capital flows, which he says have yet to recover. We are at the bottom of the **commodity price** market – these countries produce raw materials and so it is a very important part of their economy, he says. And people have stopped pulling their money dramatically out of emerging markets.
>
> **❞**

common adj (**a**) EU **Common Agricultural Policy** politique f agricole commune; **common budget** budget m de la Communauté européenne; **common customs tariff** tarif m douanier commun; **common external tariff** tarif externe commun; **Common Fisheries Policy** politique commune de la pêche; **Common Foreign and Security Policy** politique étrangère et de sécurité commune; **the Common Market** le Marché commun

(**b**) (shared) Am **common carrier** (transport company) entreprise f de transports; (telecommunications company) entreprise de télécoms; Fin **common currency** monnaie f commune; Acct **common fixed costs** coûts mpl fixes communs; **common ground** terrain m d'entente; **the two groups need to build on common ground before continuing their discussions** il faut que les deux groupes trouvent un terrain d'entente avant de poursuivre la discussion; **common ownership** copropriété f

(**c**) Am St Exch **common equities, common stock** actions fpl ordinaires

comms n Comptr **comms package** logiciel m de communication; **comms port** port m de communication

communal adj **communal property** biens mpl en commun ou en copropriété; **communal tenure** jouissance f en commun

communicate vi (be in touch) communiquer; (get in touch) prendre contact, se mettre en contact

communication n (**a**) (contact) communication f; **to enter into communication with sb** se mettre en contact avec qn □ **communications channel** canal m de communication; **communications director** directeur(trice) m,f de la communication; **communications expert** expert m en communication; **communications link** liaison f de communications; **communications management** gestion f de la communication; **communications manager** directeur(trice) de la communication; **communication network** réseau m de communication; **communications officer** responsable mf de la communication; Comptr **communications package** logiciel m de communication; **communications sector** secteur m des communications; **communication skills** techniques fpl de communication; **to have good communication skills** savoir communiquer, avoir le sens de la communication; Comptr **communications software** logiciel de communication; **communication strategy** stratégie f de communication; **communications study** étude f de communication

(**b**) (message) communication f, message m

Community n EU **the (European Economic) Community** la Communauté (économique) européenne □ **Community carnet** carnet m communautaire; **Community law** droit m communautaire

community n communauté f; **the business community** le monde des affaires; **the international community** la communauté internationale □ Am Fin **community chest** fonds m commun; **community transit** transit m communautaire

commutation n Am trajets mpl réguliers, migrations fpl quotidiennes (entre le domicile, généralement en banlieue, et le lieu de travail)

commute vi faire la navette; **to commute to work** faire la navette pour se rendre à son travail

commuter n = personne qui fait la navette entre son domicile et son travail □ **commuter belt** banlieue f; **commuter train** train m de banlieue

commuting n trajets mpl réguliers, migrations fpl quotidiennes (entre le domicile, généralement en banlieue, et le lieu de travail)

compact Comptr **1** adj compact(e) □ **compact disc** disque m compact; **compact disc interactive** CD-I m; **compact disc recorder** graveur m de disque compact; **compact disc rewritable** CD m réinscriptible; **compact disc video** CD video m

2 vt (file) comprimer

Companies House, Companies Registration Office *n Br* = institut où sont enregistrées toutes les informations concernant les entreprises du pays

company *n* société *f*, entreprise *f*; **to form** or **incorporate a company** constituer une société; **to liquidate a company** liquider une société; **in company time** pendant les heures de travail; **Richardson and Company** Richardson et Compagnie □ **company accounts** comptes *mpl* sociaux; **Companies Act** loi *f* sur les sociétés; *Am* **company apartment** appartement *m* de fonction; **company car** voiture *f* de fonction; **company census** recensement *m* des entreprises; **company credit card** carte *f* de crédit professionnelle; **company director** directeur(trice) *m,f* général(e); **company doctor** *(doctor)* médecin *m* du travail; *(businessperson)* redresseur *m* d'entreprises; *Br* **company flat** appartement de fonction; **company funds** fonds *m* social; **company law** droit *m* des sociétés; **company lawyer** juriste *mf* d'entreprise; **company manager** chef *m* d'entreprise; **company name** raison *f* sociale, nom *m* commercial; **company planning** planification *f* de l'entreprise; **company policy** politique *f* de la société; **company profile** profil *m* d'entreprise; **company recovery plan** plan *m* de redressement de l'entreprise; **company reserves** épargne *f* des entreprises; **company rules** règlements *mpl* internes; **company savings scheme** plan d'épargne entreprise; **company secretary** secrétaire *mf* général(e); *Am* **company town** = ville dont l'économie tourne autour d'une entreprise unique

comparable worth *n* = principe d'égalité des salaires entre hommes et femmes à travail équivalent

comparative *adj Mktg* **comparative advantage** avantage *m* comparatif; **comparative advertising** publicité *f* comparative; **comparative test** essai *m* comparatif; **comparative testing** essais *mpl* comparatifs

compare 1 *vt* comparer (**with** or **to** avec *ou* à); **we must compare last year's figures with this year's** nous devons comparer les chiffres de l'année dernière avec ceux de cette année
2 *vi* être comparable (**with** à); **how does last month's output compare with this month's?** la production du mois dernier était-elle inférieure ou supérieure à celle de ce mois-ci?; **we compare well with our competitors** nous n'avons rien à envier à la concurrence

comparison *n Mktg* **comparison advertising** publicité *f* comparative; **comparison shopping** achats *mpl* comparatifs

compassionate leave *n* congé *m* pour convenance personnelle

compatibility *n Comptr* compatibilité *f*

compatible *adj Comptr* compatible (**with** avec); **IBM-compatible** compatible IBM □ **com-**

patible computer ordinateur *m* compatible

compensable *adj* indemnisable □ *Acct* **compensable loss** perte *f* indemnisable

compensate *vt (for loss, injury)* dédommager; *(for damage)* indemniser (**for** de)

compensating *adj* compensateur(trice) □ *Fin* **compensating payment** règlement *m* en compensation

compensation *n* (**a**) *(for loss, injury)* dédommagement *m*; *(for damage)* indemnité *f* compensatrice, indemnisation *f*; *Law* réparation *f* civile, composition *f* □ **compensation deal** marché *m* compensatoire; **compensation fund** caisse *f* de garantie (**b**) **compensation package** *Br (for redundancy)* prime *f* de licenciement; *Am (when starting new job)* avantages *mpl* sociaux

compensatory *adj* compensateur(trice), compensatoire □ *EU* **compensatory amounts** montants *mpl* compensatoires; *EU* **compensatory levy** prélèvement *m* compensatoire; *Am* **compensatory time** congé *m* de récupération

compete *vi (of one company)* faire de la concurrence (**with** à); *(of two companies)* se faire concurrence; **they compete with foreign companies for contracts** ils sont en concurrence avec des entreprises étrangères pour obtenir des contrats; **we have to compete on an international level** nous devons être à la hauteur de la concurrence sur le plan international

competence, competency *n* (**a**) *(ability)* compétence *f*; **this lies within his competence** cela rentre dans ses attributions (**b**) **competencies** *(skills)* compétences *fpl*; **her competencies were reassessed at her annual appraisal** ses compétences ont été réexaminées dans le cadre de l'évaluation annuelle du personnel

competent *adj (capable)* compétent(e) (**in** en); *(qualified)* qualifié(e); **is she competent to handle the accounts?** est-elle compétente *ou* qualifiée pour tenir la comptabilité?

competing *adj (companies)* concurrentiel(elle); *(products)* concurrent(e)

competition *n (between companies, candidates)* concurrence *f*; **the competition** *(rivals)* la concurrence; **the company has to stay ahead of the competition** la société doit rester plus compétitive que les autres □ **Competition Commission** Commission *f* de la concurrence

competitive *adj (product)* concurrentiel(elle); *(company, price)* compétitif(ive); **to offer competitive terms** proposer des prix très compétitifs; **industry must become more competitive** l'industrie doit devenir plus compétitive □ **competitive advantage** avantage *m* concurrentiel; **competitive advertising** publicité *f* concurrentielle; **competitive analysis** analyse *f* des concurrents; **competitive awareness** sensibilitéƒcompétitive; **competitive bidding** appel m d'offres; **competitive edge** avance ƒ concurrentielle; **competitive marketplace** marché m de concurrence; **competitive position** positionƒconcurrentielle; **competitive positioning** positionnement m concurrentiel; **competitive pricing** fixationƒdes prix compétitifs; **competitive scope** domaine m concurrentiel, champ m concurrentiel; **competitive strategy** stratégieƒ concurrentielle

> 66
>
> The new, new thing is really serious. The impact of publicity on the Internet is fast and global – instantaneously everywhere. I first noticed it in action three years ago when a client called to complain that its competitor was getting tons of publicity and the client wasn't. I was stunned, because we had just done a **competitive analysis** showing our client had dramatically more publicity.
>
> 99

competitively adv **to be competitively priced** être vendu(e) à un prix compétitif

competitiveness n (of product) concurrence ƒ; (of company, price) competitivité ƒ

competitor n concurrent(e) m,f; **we must keep up with our main competitors** nous ne devons pas nous laisser distancer par la concurrence □ **competitor analysis** analyse ƒ des concurrents

complain vi (make formal protest) formuler une plainte ou une réclamation, se plaindre; **several customers have complained about the quality of service** plusieurs clients se sont plaints du service

complaint n plainte ƒ, réclamation ƒ; **to lodge or make a complaint (against sb/about sth)** déposer une plainte (contre qn/à propos de qch) □ **complaints department, complaints office** service m des réclamations

complete 1 adj complet(ète); **the new software offers a complete service for the business user** le nouveau logiciel répond à tous les besoins de l'homme d'affaires **2** vt (order, contract, work) exécuter

completion n (of work) achèvement m; (of contract, sale) exécution ƒ; **the project is nearing completion** le projet s'achève ou est près de son terme; **payment on completion of contract** paiement à l'exécution du contrat □ **completion date** (of work) dateƒd'achèvement; (of sale) date d'exécution; **completion guarantee** cautionƒde bonne fin

complex n complexe m (industriel)

compliance n (conformity) conformité ƒ; **she acted in compliance with the terms of the contract** elle a agi en accord avec les stipula-

tions du contrat □ **compliance test** test m de conformité

compliant adj conforme (**with** à); Comptr **year 2000 compliant** conforme à l'an 2000

compliments slip n papillon m à en-tête (joint aux envois et portant la mention "avec les compliments de")

comply vi (consent, agree) accepter, consentir; **to comply with sth** (code, specifications) se conformer à qch; (contract) respecter qch; (order) obéir à qch; **cars must comply with existing regulations** les voitures doivent être conformes aux normes en vigueur

component n composant m

composite index n St Exch indice m composé ou composite

composition n (agreement)(with creditors) arrangement m, accommodement m; (on bankruptcy) concordat m préventif

compound 1 adj Acct **compound entry** article m composé; Fin **compound interest** intérêts mpl composés; Fin **compound (net) annual return** annuités ƒpl composées **2** vt (debt) régler à l'amiable

comprehensive adj (insurance) multirisque, tous risques

compress vt Comptr (data, file) comprimer

compression n Comptr compression ƒ □ **compression rate** taux m de compression

comp time n Am Fam congé m de récupération

comptroller n Am contrôleur(euse) m,f; (of accounts) vérificateur(trice) m,f □ **Comptroller General** ≃ président m de la Cour de comptes

compulsorily adv d'office; **to be retired compulsorily** être mis(e) à la retraite d'office

compulsory adj obligatoire □ **compulsory liquidation** liquidation ƒ forcée; Br Admin **compulsory purchase** expropriation ƒ pour cause d'utilité publique; **compulsory purchase order** (ordre m d')expropriationƒ; **compulsory redundancy** licenciement m sec; **compulsory retirement** mise ƒ à la retraite forcée; Law **compulsory sale** adjudication ƒ forcée; **compulsory standards** normes ƒpl d'application obligatoires

computer n ordinateur m; **to be computer literate** avoir des connaissances en informatique; **to put sth on computer** mettre qch sur ordinateur □ **computer analyst** analyste mf; **computer animation** animation ƒ par ordinateur; **computer department** service m informatique; **computer engineer** ingénieur m informaticien; **computer equipment** équipement m informatique; **computer expert** informaticien(enne) m,f; **computer graphics** graphiques mpl; (technique) infographie ƒ; **computer hard-**

ware matériel *m* informatique; **computer literacy** connaissances *fpl* informatiques; **computer manager** directeur(trice) *m,f* (de l') informatique; **computer network** réseau *m* informatique; **computer operator** opérateur(-trice) *m,f* de saisie; **computer population** parc *m* d'ordinateurs; **computer printout** sortie *f* papier; **computer program** programme *m* informatique; **computer programmer** programmeur(euse) *m,f*; **computer programming** programmation *f*; **computer science** informatique *f*; **computer scientist** informaticien(enne); **computer system** système *m* informatique; **computer virus** virus *m* informatique

computer-aided, computer-assisted *adj* assisté(e) par ordinateur □ **computer-aided audit techniques** techniques *fpl* d'audit assistées par ordinateur; **computer-aided design** conception *f* assistée par ordinateur; **computer-aided engineering** ingénierie *f* assistée par ordinateur; **computer-aided interview** entretien *m* assisté par ordinateur; **computer-aided learning** enseignement *m* assisté par ordinateur; **computer-aided manufacture** fabrication *f* assistée par ordinateur; **computer-aided presentation** présentation *f* assistée par ordinateur; **computer-aided trading** commerce *m* assisté par ordinateur; **computer-aided translation** traduction *f* assistée par ordinateur

computer-based training *n* enseignement *m* assisté par ordinateur

computer-enhanced *adj* amélioré(e) par ordinateur

computer-generated *adj* généré(e) par ordinateur □ **computer-generated images** images *fpl* de synthèse

computer-integrated manufacturing *n* fabrication *f* intégrée par ordinateur

computerization *n* informatisation *f*

computerize *vt* informatiser

computerized *adj* informatisé(e) □ *Acct* **computerized accounts** comptabilité *f* informatisée; **computerized banking** informatique *f* bancaire; **computerized data** données *fpl* informatiques; **computerized information system** système *m* informatisé; *St Exch* **computerized trading system** système *m* informatique de cotation

computer-literate *adj* **to be computer-literate** avoir des connaissances en informatique

computing *n* informatique *f*

conceal *vt Fin (assets)* dissimuler

concealed unemployment *n* chômage *m* déguisé

concealment *n Law (of facts)* non-divulgation *f* □ *Fin* **concealment of assets** dissimulation *f* d'actif

concept *n* concept *m* □ *Mktg* **concept development** élaboration *f* de concept; **concept test** test *m* de concept; **concept testing** tests *mpl* de concept

concern **1** *n (business)* entreprise *f*, affaire *f*; *(interest)* intérêt *m*; **a manufacturing concern** une entreprise industrielle; **the whole concern is for sale** toute l'entreprise est à vendre; **we have a concern in the restaurant** nous avons des intérêts dans le restaurant
2 *vt* intéresser; **to whom it may concern** *(on letter)* à qui de droit; **the persons concerned** les intéressés *mpl*; **the department concerned** le service compétent

concert party *n St Exch* action *f* de concert

concession *n* **(a)** *(discount)* réduction *f*; **we offer a ten percent concession to retailers** nous accordons une remise de dix pour cent aux détaillants □ **concession close** *(sales technique)* conclusion *f* de concession **(b)** *(within larger store)* concession *f* **(c)** *(right)* concession *f*; **a mining concession** une concession minière

concessionaire *n* concessionnaire *mf*

concessionary *adj* concessionnaire

concessioner *n* concessionnaire *mf*

conciliation *n* conciliation *f*, arbitrage *m* □ **conciliation board** commission *f* ou comité *m* d'arbitrage; **conciliation magistrate** juge *m* d'instance; **conciliation service** service *m* de conciliation ou de médiation

conciliator *n* conciliateur(trice) *m,f*, médiateur(trice) *m,f*

conclude *vt (meeting, session)* clore, clôturer; *(deal, treaty)* conclure

conclusion *n (of meeting, session)* clôture *f*; *(of deal, treaty)* conclusion *f*

condition *n* **(a)** *(stipulation)* condition *f*; **on condition** sous réserve □ **conditions of application** modalités *fpl* de souscription; **conditions of employment** conditions *fpl* d'embauche; **conditions of sale** conditions de vente **(b)** *(state)* état *m*; **in good/bad condition** *(goods, machine)* en bon/mauvais état

conditional *adj (offer)* conditionnel(elle); **the offer is conditional on your acceptance of our terms of employment** cette offre d'emploi n'est valable que dans la mesure où vous acceptez nos conditions d'embauche □ **conditional acceptance** acceptation *f* sous réserve

confederation *n* confédération *f* □ **Confederation of British Industry** = patronat britannique, ≃ Medef *m*

conference *n* **(a)** *(meeting)* conférence *f*; **to be in conference (with)** *(with several people)* être en conférence (avec); *(with one or two people)* être en réunion (avec) □ *Tel* **conference call** téléconférence *f*; **conference interpreter** interprète *mf* de conférence ; ***conference room*** salle *f* de conférence ; ***conference table*** table *f* de conférence ; **we hope to get management to the conference table** nous espérons réunir la direction en table ronde

(**b**) *(convention)* congrès *m*, colloque *f* ❑ ***conference centre*** centre *m* de congrès ; ***conference coordinator*** responsable *mf* des conférences *ou* des congrès ; ***conference delegate*** congressiste *mf* ; ***conference hall*** salle *f* de conférence ; ***conference organizer*** organisateur(trice) *m,f* de conférences *ou* de congrès ; ***conference pack*** = dossier offert aux conférenciers avec informations générales sur la conférence, petits cadeaux etc

config.sys *n Comptr* fichier *m* config.sys

configuration *n Comptr* configuration *f*, paramétrage *m*

configure *vt Comptr* configurer, paramétrer

confirm 1 *vt* confirmer ; **we confirm receipt of** *or* **that we have received your letter** nous accusons réception de votre lettre

2 *vi* confirmer ; **please confirm in writing** veuillez confirmer par écrit

confirmation *n* confirmation *f* ; **to receive confirmation of sth** recevoir confirmation de qch ; **all bookings subject to confirmation** toute réservation doit être confirmée ❑ ***confirmation of receipt*** accusé *m* de réception

confirmed letter of credit *n* lettre *f* de crédit irrévocable

confirming *adj* ***confirming bank*** banque *f* confirmatrice ; ***confirming house*** organisme *m* confirmateur

conflict *n* conflit *m* ; **the unions are in conflict with the management** les syndicats sont en conflit avec la direction ; **a conflict of interests** un conflit d'intérêts ; **her presence on the boards of two competing companies has led to a conflict of interests** le fait qu'elle siège au conseil d'administration de deux entreprises concurrentes a débouché sur un conflit d'intérêts

conform *vi (of person)* se conformer, s'adapter ; *(of thing)* être en conformité ; **to conform to the law** obéir à la loi ; **all cars must conform to regulations** toute voiture doit être conforme aux normes

conformity *n* conformité *f* ; **in conformity with** conformément à

conglomerate *n* conglomérat *m*

congress *n* congrès *m*

con man *n Fam* escroc *m*

connect 1 *n Comptr* connexion *f* ❑ ***connect time*** durée *f* (d'établissement) de la connexion

2 *vt* (**a**) *Comptr (component, cable)* connecter (**to** à) (**b**) *Tel* mettre en ligne *ou* en communica-

tion (**with** avec) ; **will you connect me with reservations, please?** est-ce que vous pouvez me passer votre service des réservations ?

3 *vi Comptr* (**a**) *(of component, cable)* se raccorder (**to** à) (**b**) *(to Internet)* se connecter (**to** à)

connection *n* (**a**) *(colleague, business contact)* relation *f* (d'affaires) ; **she has some useful connections in the publishing world** elle a des relations utiles dans le monde de l'édition

(**b**) *Tel* communication *f* ; **we had a very bad connection** la communication était très mauvaise

(**c**) *Comptr (to Internet)* connexion *f* ; **to establish a connection** se connecter ; **to have a fast / slow connection** disposer d'une connexion rapide/lente

(**d**) *Comptr (of two components)* connexion *f*, liaison *f* ❑ ***connection kit*** kit *m* d'accès *ou* de connexion

conquer *vt (market, market share)* conquérir

conquest *n (of market, market share)* conquête *f*

consensus *n* consensus *m* ; **there was a consensus of opinion to reject the board's offer** il y avait un consensus en faveur du rejet de la proposition du conseil d'administration ❑ ***consensus management*** gestion *f* par consensus

conservatism concept *n Acct* principe *m* de prudence

consideration *n (payment)* rémunération *f*, finance *f* ; **for a small consideration** moyennant rémunération *ou* finance ; **in consideration of your services** en récompense de vos services

consign *vt (goods)* envoyer, expédier

consignee *n* consignataire *mf*

consigner *n* consignataire *mf*, expéditeur(trice) *m,f*

consignment *n* (**a**) *(goods) (arriving)* arrivage *m*, livraison *f* ; *(being dispatched)* envoi *m* ; **a consignment of machinery** *(arriving)* un arrivage de machines ; *(being dispatched)* un envoi de machines (**b**) *(dispatch)* envoi *m*, expédition *f* ; **on consignment** en consignation, en dépôt (permanent) ; **goods for consignment abroad** marchandises *fpl* à destination de l'étranger ❑ ***consignment invoice*** facture *f* de consignation ; ***consignment note*** bordereau *m* d'expédition

consignor = **consigner**

consistency concept *n Acct* principe *m* de la permanence (des méthodes)

console *n Comptr* pupitre *m* de commande

consolidate *vt* (**a**) *Fin (companies)* fusionner, réunir ; *(shares)* regrouper ; *(debts, funds, loans)* consolider, unifier ; **the company has consolidated its position as the market leader** la société a conforté sa position de leader sur le marché (**b**) *(orders, consignments)* grouper

consolidated *adj* (**a**) *Fin* consolidé(e) ❏ *Fin* **consolidated accounts** comptes *mpl* consolidés *ou* intégrés; *Fin* **consolidated annuities** fonds *mpl* consolidés; *Acct* **consolidated balance sheet** bilan *m* consolidé; *Fin* **consolidated debt** dette *f* consolidée; *Acct* **consolidated entry** écriture *f* consolidée; *Fin* **consolidated funds** fonds consolidés; *Fin* **consolidated loan** emprunt *m* consolidé; *Acct* **consolidated profit and loss account** bilan consolidé; *Acct* **consolidated statement of net income** résultat *m* net consolidé; *Fin* **consolidated stock** fonds consolidés
   (**b**) *(orders, consignments)* groupé(e)
   (**c**) *(in name of company)* = désigne une société née de la fusion de deux entreprises

consolidation *n* (**a**) *Fin (of companies)* fusion *f*; *(of shares)* regroupement *m*; *(of debts, funds, loans)* consolidation *f*, unification *f* (**b**) *(of orders, consignments)* groupage *m*

consolidator *n* groupeur *m*

consols *npl Br Fin* (fonds *mpl*) consolidés *mpl*

consortium *n Fin* consortium *m*

constant *adj (currency)* constant(e); **the dividend of $5 per share paid in 1986 was worth only $2.50 in constant dollars of 1976** le dividende de 5 dollars par action versé en 1986 ne correspondait qu'à 2,5 dollars constants de 1976

constitute *vt (committee)* constituer; *(chairperson)* désigner; **to constitute sb arbitrator** constituer qn arbitre

constructive dismissal *n Ind* = démission provoquée par la conduite de l'employeur

consular *adj* consulaire ❏ **consular fees** frais *mpl* consulaires; **consular invoice** facture *f* consulaire

consult 1 *vt* consulter (**about** sur *ou* au sujet de); **I have to consult my superior before taking a decision** il faut que je consulte mon supérieur hiérarchique avant de prendre une décision
   2 *vi* s'entretenir, discuter (**with** avec); **we have to consult with our supplier about this problem** il faut que l'on discute de ce problème avec notre fournisseur

consultancy *n (company)* cabinet *m* d'experts-conseils; *(advice)* assistance *f* technique ❏ **consultancy fees** frais *mpl* d'expertise; **consultancy service** service *m* d'assistance technique

consultant *n* expert-conseil *m*, consultant(e) *m,f*

consultation *n (discussion)* consultation *f*, délibération *f*; **the matter will be decided in consultation with our colleagues** la décision sera prise en consultation *ou* en concertation avec nos collègues; **he was asked to leave without prior consultation** on l'a renvoyé sans préavis

consumable 1 *n* **consumables** produits *mpl* de consommation, denrées *fpl* alimentaires; *Comptr* consommables *mpl*
   2 *adj* consommable ❏ **consumable goods** produits *mpl* de consommation

consumer *n* consommateur(trice) *m,f* ❏ **consumer acceptance** réceptivité *f* des consommateurs; **consumer adviser** conseiller(ère) *m,f* de clientèle; **Consumers' Assocation** = association britannique de consommateurs; **consumer audit** audit *m* consommateur; **consumer behaviour** comportement *m* du consommateur; **consumer behaviour study** étude *f* du comportement du consommateur; **consumer benefit** bénéfice *m* consommateur; **consumer brand** marque *f* grand public; **consumer confidence** niveau *m* de confiance des consommateurs; **consumer credit** crédit *m* à la consommation; **consumer debt** endettement *m* des consommateurs; **consumer demand** demande *f* des consommateurs; **consumer durables** biens *mpl* de consommation (durables); **consumer expenditure** dépenses *fpl* de consommation; **consumer goods** biens de (grande) consommation; **consumer group** groupe *m* de consommateurs; **consumer industry** industrie *f* de consommation; **consumer journalism** = journalisme dans le cadre de la défense des consommateurs; **consumer loan** prêt *m* à la consommation, prêt personnel; **consumer loyalty** fidélité *f* du consommateur; **consumer magazine** magazine *m* pour les consommateurs; **consumer market** marché *m* de la consommation; **consumer motivation** motivation *f* de consommateur; **consumer organization** organisme *m* de défense des consommateurs; **consumer panel** groupe-témoin *m*, panel *m* de consommateurs; **consumer preference** préférence *f* du consommateur; *Am* **consumer price index** indice *m* des prix à la consommation; **consumer product** bien *m* de consommation; **consumer profile** profil *m* du consommateur; **consumer protection** défense *f* des consommateurs; **consumer protection agency** bureau *m* d'acceuil des consommateurs; **consumer purchasing power** richesse *f* vive; **consumer research** recherche *f* sur les besoins des consommateurs; **consumer resistance** résistance *f ou* réticence *f* des consommateurs; **consumer satisfaction** satisfaction *f* du consommateur; **consumer society** société *f* de consommation; **consumer sovereignty** souveraineté *f* du consommateur; **consumer spending** dépenses de consommation *ou* des ménages; **consumer survey** enquête *f* auprès des consommateurs; **consumer test** test *m* auprès des consommateurs; **consumer test group** groupe test des consommateurs; **consu-**

mer testing tests *mpl* auprès des consomma-teurs; **consumer trends** tendances *fpl* de la consommation

> **"**
>
> That is a bit extreme, but making assump-tions about people can be counter-produc-tive and lead to a puzzling, if not insulting, experience. It is a case of traditional brand-value building competing with the current digital-channels marketing mantra of tailor-ing the retail offering to an audience of one. The Internet has given retailers more direct access to **consumer behaviour** and is ca-pable of producing staggering amounts of "clickstream" and other data for analysis.
>
> **"**

consumerism *n* *(consumer protection)* consu-mérisme *m*; *Econ (consumption)* consommation *f* à outrance

consumption *n* *Econ* consommation *f*

contact 1 *n* (**a**) *(communication)* contact *m*; **to be in contact with sb** être en contact avec qn; **to get in contact with sb** contacter qn, se met-tre en contact avec qn
(**b**) *(acquaintance)* relation *f*; **she has some useful business contacts** elle a quelques bons contacts (professionnels) □ **contact man** agent *m* de liaison
2 *vt* contacter, se mettre en contact avec; **we'll contact you later on this week** nous vous contacterons cette semaine

container *n* *(for storage)* récipient *m*; *(for transport)* conteneur *m*, container *m* □ **contain-er berth** poste *m* à quai pour porte-conteneurs; **container depot** entrepôt *m* de conteneurs; *Br* **container lorry** camion *m* adapté au transport des conteneurs; **container port** port *m* pour conteneurs; **container premium** prime *f* conte-nant; **container ship** (navire *m*) porte-conte-neurs *m*; **container shipping** transports *mpl* maritimes par conteneurs; **container truck** ca-mion adapté au transport des conteneurs

containerization *n* *(of cargo)* transport *m* par conteneurs; *(of port)* conteneurisation *f*, containérisation *f*

containerize *vt* *(cargo)* conteneuriser, contai-nériser, transporter par conteneurs *ou* contai-ners; *(port)* convertir à la conteneurisation *ou* containérisation □ **containerized freight** fret *m* par conteneur *ou* container

contango *St Exch* **1** *n* report *m*; *(percentage)* taux *m* de report; **money on contango** capi-taux *mpl* en report; **contangos are low** les re-ports sont bon marché □ **contango day** jour *m* des reports; **contango rate** taux de report
2 *vt* reporter
3 *vi* reporter une position

contents insurance *n* assurance *f* mobilier

contest *vt* *Law* **to contest a will** contester un testament □ **contested claim** créance *f* liti-gieuse

context-sensitive *adj* *Comptr* contextue-l(elle) □ **context-sensitive help** aide *f* contex-tuelle

contingency *n* éventualité *f*; **to allow for every contingency** parer à toute éventualité □ **contingency fund** fonds *mpl* de prévoyance; **contingency and loss provision** provision *f* pour risques et charges; **contingency plan** plan *m* d'urgence; **contingency reserve** réserve *f* de prévoyance; *Acct* **contingency theory** théorie *f* de la contingence

contingent *adj* (**a**) *(possible)* éventuel(elle) □ **contingent liabilities** *Acct* passif *m* éventuel; *Fin* engagement *m* éventuel; *St Exch* **contin-gent order** ordre *m* conditionnel; *Acct* **contin-gent profit** profit *m* aléatoire; *St Exch* **con-tingent value right** certificat *m* de valeur garantie
(**b**) *(dependent)* contingent(e); **to be contin-gent on** *or* **upon sth** dépendre de qch; **a salary increase is contingent upon group perfor-mance** l'augmentation des salaires dépend des résultats du groupe
(**c**) *Am* **contingent worker** travailleur(euse) *m,f* occasionnel(elle)

continuous *adj* continu(e) □ **continuous bud-get** budget *m* renouvelable; **continuous flow production** production *f* continue; **continuous innovation** innovation *f* continue; **continuous innovator** innovateur(trice) *m,f* continu(e); *Comptr* **continuous input** frappe *f* au kilomè-tre; *Comptr* **continuous mode** mode *m* conti-nu; *Comptr* **continuous paper** papier *m* (en) continu; *Comptr* **continuous processing** trai-tement *m* en temps réel; **continuous produc-tion** production continue; *Mktg* **continuous research** recherche *f* longitudinale; *Comptr* **continuous stationery** papier (en) continu; *St Exch* **continuous trading** cotation *f* en continu

contra *Acct* **1** *n* **per contra** par contre; **as per contra** en contrepartie, porté ci-contre
2 *adj* **contra account** compte *m* de contrepartie *ou* d'autre part; **contra entry** article *m* ou écri-ture *f* inverse, contre-passation *f*
3 *vt* contrepasser

contraband *n* contrebande *f* □ **contraband goods** marchandises *fpl* de contrebande

contract *n* (**a**) *(agreement)* contrat *m*; **to draw up a contract** dresser *ou* rédiger un contrat; **to sign a contract** signer un contrat; **to cancel a contract** résilier *ou* annuler un contrat; **to be bound by contract** être lié(e) par contrat; **to break one's contract** rompre son contrat; **to be under contract (to)** être sous contrat (avec) □ **contract of apprenticeship** contrat d'ap-prentissage; **contract bond** garantie *f* d'exécution; **contract of carriage** contrat de transport; **contract of employment** contrat de travail; **contract law** droit *m* des contrats; **contract note** note *f* ou bordereau *m* de contrat; *St Exch* avis *m* d'exécution ou d'opération sur titre; **contract of service** louage *f* de services

(**b**) *(to supply goods, services)* soumission *f*, adjudication *f*; **to put work out to contract** sous-traiter du travail, faire effectuer un travail en sous-traitance; **to give** or **award a contract to sb** accorder un contrat à qn; **to tender for a contract** soumissionner à une adjudication; **to secure a contract for sth** obtenir un contrat pour qch; **they were given a contract to build the new road** ils se sont vu attribuer le contrat pour construire la nouvelle route; **to enter into a contract** *(of person)* passer un contrat (**with** avec) □ **contract date** date *f* contractuelle; **contract labour** main-d'œuvre *f* contractuelle; **contract price** prix *m* contractuel; **contract staff** personnel *m* en contrat à durée déterminée ou en CDD; **contract work** travail *m* en sous-traitance

2 *vt* **to contract to do sth** s'engager (par contrat) à faire qch, entreprendre de faire qch

3 *vi* **to contract for the supply of sth** s'engager à fournir qch; **to contract for work** entreprendre des travaux à forfait

▶ **contract in** *vi* s'engager par contrat; *(into insurance policy, pension plan)* souscrire

▶ **contract out 1** *vt sep (work)* donner en sous-traitance (**to** à); **the work was contracted out** on a donné le travail à un sous-traitant

2 *vi Br* se dégager d'un contrat; *(out of insurance policy, pension plan)* arrêter de souscrire (**of** à)

contracting party *n* partie *f* contractante

contractor *n* entrepreneur *m*

contractual *adj (agreement, obligations)* contractuel(elle); **on the present contractual basis** selon les stipulations actuelles du contrat □ **contractual agreement** contrat *m*; **contractual allowance** indemnité *f* conventionnelle; **contractual claims** créances *fpl* contractuelles; **contractual cover** garantie *f* conventionnelle; **contractual date** date *f* contractuelle; **contractual guarantee** garantie contractuelle; **contractual labour** main-d'œuvre *f* contractuelle; **contractual liability** responsabilité *f* contractuelle; **contractual price** prix *m* contractuel

contrarian *n* investisseur *m* à contre-courant □ **contrarian investor** investisseur *m* à contre-courant

contribute 1 *vt* donner, verser; **she contributes ten percent of her salary to the pension scheme** elle verse dix pour cent de son salaire dans son plan de retraite

2 *vi* cotiser

contribution *n* (**a**) *(payment)* contribution *f*, cotisation *f*; **employer's and employee's contributions** cotisations *fpl* patronales et ouvrières; **contribution towards costs** participation *f* aux frais (**b**) *Acct (in management accounting)* marge *f* brute; *(made to share capital)* apport *m* □ *Acct* **contribution margin** marge sur les coûts variables; *Acct* **contribution ratio** ratio *m* de marge brute

contributory 1 *n St Exch* = actionnaire qui doit contribuer au paiement des dettes

2 *adj* **contributory insurance** assurance *f* à cotisations; **contributory pension plan** or **scheme** système *m* de retraite par répartition

control 1 *n* (**a**) *(of company, organization)* autorité *f*; **to have control of a business** être à la tête d'une entreprise, diriger une entreprise; **public spending is under the control of our department** le budget national relève de notre département; **the control process showed that objectives were being met** les contrôles effectués montraient que l'on était en train d'atteindre les objectifs fixés

(**b**) *(of exchange rates, prices)* contrôle *m*; **to impose controls on sth** contrôler qch; **there are to be new government controls on financial practices** il y aura de nouvelles réglementations gouvernementales sur les pratiques financières; **inflation must be kept under control** il faut maîtriser l'inflation □ **control account** compte *m* collectif; **control commission** commission *f* de contrôle; *Mktg* **control group** groupe *m* témoin; *Mktg* **control market** marché *m* témoin; *Mktg* **control question** question *f* de contrôle

(**c**) *Comptr* touche *f* contrôle □ **control bus** bus *m* de contrôle; **control key** touche contrôle; **control panel** panneau *m* de configuration

2 *vt* (**a**) *(company, organization)* diriger

(**b**) *(exchange rates, prices)* contrôler; *(inflation)* contrôler, juguler; **to control the rise in the cost of living** enrayer la hausse du coût de la vie

controllable costs *npl* coûts *mpl* maîtrisables

controlled *adj Econ* **controlled economy** économie *f* dirigée; **controlled price** taxe *f*; **to sell sth at the controlled price** vendre qch à la taxe

controller *n Fin* contrôleur(euse) *m,f*; **controller in bankruptcy** contrôleur(euse) aux liquidations

controlling *adj* **controlling factor** facteur *m* déterminant; **controlling interest, controlling share** *(in company)* participation *f* majoritaire; **controlling shareholding** bloc *m* de contrôle

convene 1 *vt (conference, meeting)* convoquer; **to convene a meeting of shareholders** convoquer une assemblée d'actionnaires
2 *vi (of meeting, board, people)* se réunir

convener *n (of trade union)* = secrétaire des délégués syndicaux; *(of meeting)* président(e) *m,f*

convenience *n* **at your earliest convenience** *(in letter)* dans les meilleurs délais; **please reply at your earliest convenience** veuillez répondre dans les meilleurs délais □ *Mktg* **convenience brand** marque *f* pratique; *Mktg* **convenience goods** produits *mpl* de consommation courante; *Mktg* **convenience sample** échantillon *m* de convenance

convenor = **convener**

convention *n* (**a**) *(agreement)* convention *f*; **to sign a convention (on sth)** signer une convention (sur qch) (**b**) *(conference)* convention *f*, congrès *m*

conversational *adj Comptr (mode)* dialogue

conversion *n* (**a**) *Fin (of loan, securities)* conversion *f* □ **conversion cost** coût *m* de conversion; **conversion issue** émission *f* de conversion; **conversion loan** emprunt *m* de conversion; **conversion premium** prime *f* de conversion; **conversion price** prix *m* de conversion; **conversion rate** taux *m* de conversion (**b**) *Comptr* **conversion program** programme *m* de conversion; **conversion software** logiciel *m* de conversion

convert 1 *n Am Fin* obligation *f* convertible (en actions)
2 *vt* (**a**) *Fin* convertir; **to convert pounds into euros** *(as calculation)* convertir des livres en euros; *(by exchanging them)* changer des livres en euros (**b**) *Comptr (file)* convertir (**to/into** en)

convertibility *n Fin (of loan, securities)* convertibilité *f*

convertible *adj Fin (loan, securities)* convertible □ **convertible bond** obligation *f* convertible (en actions); **convertible currency** monnaie *f* ou devise *f* convertible; **convertible loan stock** titres *mpl* de créance convertibles; **convertible money of account** monnaie de compte convertible

convey *vt (goods)* transporter

conveyance *n Law (transfer)* cession *f*, transfert *m*; *(deed)* acte *m* de cession

conveyancing *n Law (procedure)* procédure *f* translative (de propriété); *(drawing up documents)* rédaction *f* des actes translatifs de propriété

cook *vt Fam* **to cook the books** falsifier les comptes

cookie *n Comptr* cookie *m*, cafteur *m*

cooling-off period *n* période *f* de réflexion, délai *m* de réflexion

> **"**
> The directives require suppliers of mail-order goods (as distinct from services) to provide written information about the company and terms of sale, as well as delivering goods promised within a 30-day period. Perhaps more importantly, however, they also give consumers a seven-day **cooling-off period** after the goods are delivered, during which time they can change their mind and receive a full refund.
> **"**

coop *n (abbr* **co-operative**) coop *f*

cooperative 1 *n* coopérative *f*
2 *adj* coopératif(ive) □ **cooperative advertising** publicité *f* coopérative; **cooperative credit society** coopérative *f* de crédit; **cooperative group** coopérative (de consommateurs); **cooperative society** (société *f*) coopérative

co-owner *n* copropriétaire *mf*

co-ownership *n* copropriété *f*

copartner *n* coassocié(e) *m,f*

copartnership *n* coassociation *f*

co-processor *n Comptr* coprocesseur *m*

coproprietor *n* copropriétaire *mf*

copy 1 *n* (**a**) *(of document, letter)* copie *f*; **to make a copy of sth** faire une copie de qch □ **copy typist** dactylo *mf*
(**b**) *(written material)* copie *f*; *(in advertising)* texte *m* □ **copy deadline** date *f* de tombée; *Am* **copy desk** secrétariat *m* de rédaction
(**c**) *Law* expédition *f*
(**d**) *Mktg* **copy test** pré-test *m* publicitaire; **copy testing** pré-tests *mpl* publicitaires
(**e**) *Comptr* **copy and paste** copier-coller *m* □ **copy block** copie *f* de bloc; **copy command** commande *f* de copie; **copy disk** disquette *f* de copie; **copy protection** protection *f* contre la copie
2 *vt* (**a**) *(document, letter)* copier; *(photocopy)* photocopier
(**b**) *Comptr* copier; **to copy sth to disk** copier qch sur disquette; **to copy and paste sth** faire un copier-coller sur qch
3 *vi Comptr* **to copy and paste** faire un copier-coller

copy-protected *adj Comptr* protégé(e) contre la copie

copyright 1 *n* droit *m* de reproduction *ou* d'auteur, copyright *m*; **copyright reserved** tous droits réservés; **to be out of copyright** être

(tombé(e)) dans le domaine public; **it's still subject to copyright** c'est toujours soumis au droit d'auteur; **she has the sole copyright to her invention** elle est seule détentrice du copyright de son invention □ *copyright deposit* dépôt *m* légal; *copyright infringement* violation *f* du droit de reproduction; *copyright notice* mention *f* de réserve
  2 *adj* protégé(e) par les droits d'auteur
  3 *vt* obtenir le copyright de

copywriter *n* rédacteur(trice) *m,f* publicitaire, concepteur(trice) *m,f* rédacteur(trice)

copywriting *n* rédaction *f* publicitaire

cordless *adj* sans fil □ *Comptr* **cordless mouse** souris *f* sans fil; **cordless telephone** téléphone *m* sans fil

core *n* **core assets** actifs *mpl* principaux; **core brand** marque *f* phare; **core business** activité *f* principale; **core competence** noyau *m* de compétences; **core holding** investissement *m* de base *(dans le portefeuille des investisseurs institutionnels)*; **core market** marché *m* principal *ou* de référence; **core message** *(in advertising)* message *m* principal; **core skills** compétences *fpl* de base; **core time** *(in flexitime)* plage *f* fixe

corner 1 *n* monopole *m*; **to make** *or* **have a corner in sth** accaparer qch
  2 *vt (market)* accaparer; **in two years they've cornered the market in software packages** en deux ans, ils ont accaparé le marché du progiciel

cornering *n (of market)* accaparement *m*

Corp, corp *n (abbr* **corporation)** Cie

corpocracy *n* (**a**) *(corporate bureaucracy)* bureaucratie *f* dans l'entreprise (**b**) *(company)* = entreprise monolithique à faible productivité où règne la bureaucratie (**c**) *(corporate power)* = pouvoir exercé par les grandes entreprises

corporate *adj* corporatif(ive), d'entreprise □ *corporate advertising* publicité *f* institutionnelle, publicité d'entreprise; *corporate assets* biens *mpl* sociaux; *corporate banking* banque *f* d'entreprise; *corporate body* personne *f* morale; *corporate bond* obligation *f* de société; *corporate budget* budget *m* de la société; *corporate buy-out* rachat *m* d'entreprise par les salariés; *corporate card* carte *f* de crédit professionnelle; *corporate culture* culture *f* d'entreprise; **their corporate culture emphasizes the need for continuous improvement in customer service** leur culture d'entreprise insiste sur la nécessité d'améliorer constamment le service clientèle; *corporate entertainment* divertissement *m* fourni par la société; *corporate environment* environnement *m* institutionnel; *corporate film* film *m* d'entreprise *ou* institutionnel; *corporate finance* finance *f* d'entreprise; *corporate finance manager* financier(-ère) *m,f* d'entreprise; *corporate governance*

committee groupe *m* de travail interne au Conseil, comité *m* de gouvernement d'entreprise; *corporate hospitality* = réceptions, déjeuners, billets de spectacle *etc* offerts par une entreprise à ses clients; *corporate identity, corporate image* image *f* de marque; **the company cares about its corporate image** la société se préoccupe de son image; *corporate income* revenu *m* de société; *corporate income tax* impôt *m* sur les bénéfices des sociétés; *corporate institution* personne morale; *corporate law* droit *m* des entreprises; *corporate lawyer* juriste *mf* spécialisé(e) en droit des entreprises; *Am* *corporate licensing* cession *f* de licence de marque; *corporate literature* brochures *fpl* décrivant une société; *corporate member (of association)* société-membre *f*; *corporate misery index* = indice de mesure de l'évolution des marges bénéficiaires; *corporate model* modèle *m* d'entreprise; *corporate name* raison *f* sociale; *corporate planning* planification *f* de l'entreprise; *corporate raider* attaquant(e) *m,f*; *corporate responsibility* responsabilité *f* de l'entreprise; **the idea of corporate responsibility is now taken seriously by an increasing number of companies** de plus en plus de sociétés prennent très au sérieux le concept de responsabilité de l'entreprise; *corporate restructuring* restructuration *f*; **two subsidiary companies will be sold off as part of the corporate restructuring plan** deux des filiales seront vendues dans le cadre du plan de restructuration de la société; *corporate sector* secteur *m* des grandes entreprises; *corporate sponsorship* mécénat *m* d'entreprise, parrainage *m* d'entreprises, sponsoring *m*; *corporate strategy* stratégie *f* de l'entreprise; *corporate structure* structure *f* de l'entreprise; *corporate tax* impôt sur les sociétés; *corporate video* film d'entreprise *ou* institutionnel; *Am* *corporate welfare* = aide financière apportée par l'État à des entreprises privées

> **❝**
> As if investors didn't have enough to worry about, a brokerage house has invented a new measure to show that the corporate profit recovery could take longer than the market and some analysts think. A key economic measure in the last decades of the 20th century was the "misery index," which combined inflation and unemployment to show how badly consumers were hurting. But the key gauge for the first decade of the new century could be something called the "**corporate misery index**."
> **❞**

corporation *n Am* société *f*, compagnie *f* □ *Am* *corporation income tax* impôt *m* sur les sociétés; *Br* *corporation tax* impôt sur les sociétés

corporatism *n* corporatisme *m*

corporatist *adj* corporatiste

correct 1 *adj (accurate)* exact(e); **these sales figures are not correct** le chiffre des ventes n'est pas exact
2 *vt (mistake, spelling)* corriger

corrected entry *n Acct* écriture *f* rectificative *ou* d'ajustement

correction *n* **(a)** *(of error, in document)* correction *f* □ **correction fluid** liquide *m* correcteur **(b)** *St Exch (adjustment)* correction *f*

correspond *vi* **(a)** *(be equivalent)* correspondre (**with** *or* **to** à); **the two sets of figures don't correspond** les deux séries de chiffres ne correspondent pas **(b)** *(write letters)* correspondre (**with** avec)

correspondence *n* **(a)** *(letterwriting)* correspondance *f*; **to be in correspondence with sb** être en correspondance avec qn **(b)** *(letters)* correspondance *f*, courrier *m*; **to read one's correspondence** lire son courrier □ **correspondence tray** bac *m* à correspondance *ou* à courrier

correspondent *n* correspondant(e) *m,f*

corresponding entry *n Acct* écriture *f* conforme

corrupt *Comptr* **1** *adj (disk, file)* altéré(e)
2 *vt (disk, file)* altérer

COS *n (abbr* **cash on shipment**) paiement *m* à l'expédition

co-sign *vt* cosigner

co-signatory *n* cosignataire *mf*

cost 1 *n* **(a)** *(price)* coût *m*, frais *mpl*; **cost and freight** coût et fret; **cost, insurance and freight** coût, assurance, fret; **cost per thousand** coût par mille, CPM *m* □ **cost accountant** = comptable *mf* spécialisé(e) en comptabilité analytique *ou* d'exploitation; **cost accounting** comptabilité *f* analytique *ou* d'exploitation; **cost allocation** imputation *f* des charges; **cost analysis** analyse *f* des coûts, analyse du prix de revient; **cost assessment** évaluation *f* du coût; **cost base** prix *m* de base; *Acct* **cost centre** centre *m* de coût *ou* d'analyse; *Acct* **cost curve** courbe *f* des coûts; **cost equation** équation *f* de coût; **cost factor** facteur *m* coût; *Acct* **cost of goods purchased** coût des marchandises achetées; *Acct* **cost of goods sold** coût des marchandises vendues; **cost of living** coût de la vie; **cost management** gestion *f* des coûts; *Acct* **cost overrun** dépassement *m* de coût; **cost price** prix coûtant *ou* de revient; **cost pricing** méthode *f* des coûts marginaux; *Acct* **cost of sales** coût de revient des produits vendus; **cost standard** norme *f* de prix de revient; **cost structure** structure *f* des coûts; **cost unit** unité *f* de coût; **cost variance** écart *m* des coûts
(b) *Law* **costs** frais *mpl* d'instance, dépens *mpl*;

to pay costs payer les frais et dépens
2 *vt* **(a)** *(be priced at)* coûter; **how much does it cost?** combien cela coûte-t-il?; **it costs $25** ça coûte 25 dollars
(b) *(estimate cost of) (article)* établir le prix de revient de; *(job)* évaluer le coût de; **how much was it costed at?** *(of job)* à combien est-ce que le coût a été évalué?
3 *vi Fam (be expensive)* coûter cher, ne pas être donné; **we can do it but it will cost** on peut le faire mais ça ne sera pas donné

cost-benefit *adj* **cost-benefit analysis** analyse *f* coût-profit, analyse des côuts et rendements; **cost-benefit ratio** rapport *m* coût-profit

cost-competitive *adj (product)* à prix compétitif; **we're not cost-competitive** nos prix ne sont pas compétitifs

cost-conscious *adj* qui fait attention aux dépenses

cost-cutter *n* = entreprise qui essaie de réaliser des économies

cost-cutting *adj* d'économie; **the cost-cutting measures that we have implemented should save the company a lot of money** les mesures qui ont été mises en place pour limiter les dépenses devraient faire économiser beaucoup d'argent à l'entreprise

cost-effective *adj* rentable

cost-effectiveness *n* rentabilité *f* □ **cost-effectiveness analysis** analyse *f* de coût et d'efficacité

costing *n* **(a)** *(of article)* estimation *f* du prix de revient; *(of job)* évaluation *f* du coût **(b)** *(document) (of article)* estimation *f* du prix de revient; *(of job)* devis *m*

cost-of-living *adj* **cost-of-living adjustment** *(in salary)* augmentation *f* de salaire indexée sur le coût de la vie; **cost-of-living allowance** indemnité *f* de vie chère; **cost-of-living increase** *(in salary)* augmentation de salaire indexée sur le coût de la vie; **cost-of-living index** indice *m* du coût de la vie

> **"**
> The taxpayer asked the IRS if it was possible to modify his payment plan by adding an annual 4% **cost-of-living adjustment** (COLA) and by including a one-time "catch-up" amount. The IRS denied the request. It held the taxpayer could not modify the annual payment without triggering the 10% penalty for premature distributions.
> **"**

cost-plus 1 *n* taux *m* de marque
2 *adj Fin* à coût majoré; **on a cost-plus basis** sur la base du prix de revient majoré □ **cost-plus pricing** fixation *f* du prix en fonction du coût

cost-push inflation n Econ inflation f par les coûts

cost-reduce vt réduire le coût de

cost-volume-profit analysis n Acct étude f de coût-efficacité

co-trustee n Law coadministrateur(trice) m,f

cottage industry n industrie f artisanale

council n **(a)** (local government) municipalité f; **to be on the council** être au conseil municipal **(b)** (assembly) conseil m ❑ **Council of Europe** Conseil de l'Europe; **Council for Mutual Economic Aid** Comecon m; EU **Council for Security and Cooperation in Europe** Conférence f sur la sécurité et la coopération en Europe

counsel n Law avocat(e)-conseil m,f; **counsel for the defence** avocat(e) m,f de la défense; **counsel for the prosecution** procureur m

counter n (in shop) comptoir m; (in supermarket) rayon m; (in bank) guichet m; Fin **to buy shares over the counter** acheter des actions sur le marché hors cote; **to buy/sell sth under the counter** acheter/vendre qch sous le manteau ❑ **counter cash book** main f courante; Banking **counter services** services mpl (de caisse; Banking **counter staff** employé(e)s mpl,fpl du guichet; **counter transaction** opération f de caisse

counter-appraisal n Am contre-expertise f

counterbid n suroffre f, surenchère f; (during takeover bid) contre-OPA f

> **"**
> There is the possibility of a **counterbid**. Barclays, Aegon, Generali, Allianz and AXA could all be interested. But analysts are sceptical of a serious bidding war. A counterbidder would have to increase the price and at this level it looks hard to justify, says banking analyst John Kirk of broker Fox-Pitt Kelton.
> **"**

counterbidder n surenchérisseur(euse) m,f

counterclaim Law **1** n demande f reconventionnelle; **to make a counterclaim (against sb)** opposer une demande reconventionnelle (à qn)
2 vi opposer une demande reconventionnelle

counterclaimant n Law demandeur(eresse) m,f reconventionnel(elle)

counterfeit 1 n faux m, contrefaçon f
2 adj faux (fausse)
3 vt contrefaire

counterfoil n (of cheque) talon m, souche f ❑ **counterfoil chequebook** carnet m à souche

counter-guarantee n St Exch contre-garantie f

countermand vt (order) annuler

counteroffer n offre f; (higher) surenchère f

counterpart n (document) duplicata m, double m; (person) homologue mf

counterparty risk n Banking risque m de contrepartie

counterproductive adj contre-productif(ive); **closing the factory will be counterproductive to the region's economy** la fermeture de l'usine aura des effets néfastes sur l'économie de la région

countersign vt contresigner

countertrade 1 n commerce m d'échange, troc m
2 vt (goods) échanger, troquer

countertrading n troc m

countervailing adj Fin compensateur(trice), compensatoire

country n pays m ❑ **country of origin** pays m d'origine

coupon n **(a)** Fin (on bearer bond) coupon m ❑ **coupon bond** obligation f au porteur; **coupon yield** rendement m coupon **(b)** (exchangeable voucher) bon m, coupon m; **(money-off) coupon** bon de réduction ❑ **coupon offer** offre f de bon de réduction

courier n coursier(ère) m,f; **to send sth/to arrive by courier** envoyer qch/arriver par coursier

course n (of study) stage m, cours m; **she's doing a course to improve her computer skills** elle fait un stage pour apprendre à mieux se servir d'un ordinateur

court n cour f, tribunal m; **to go to court** aller en justice; **to take sb to court** faire un procès à qn; **to settle out of court** parvenir à un règlement à l'amiable ❑ Br **Court of Appeal** cour d'appel; Am **court of appeals** cour d'appel; **court case** procès m, affaire f; **court of first instance** juridiction f de première instance; EU **Court of Justice of the European Communities** Cour de justice des Communautés européennes; **court order** ordonnance f du tribunal; **court ruling** décision f de justice

courthouse n Am palais m de justice, tribunal m

courtroom n salle f d'audience; (people) tribunal m

covenant Law **1** n **(a)** (promise of money) convention f **(b)** (agreement) engagement m
2 vt s'engager (par contrat) à payer
3 vi **to covenant for a sum** s'engager (par contrat) à payer une somme; **to covenant with sb for sth** convenir (par contrat) de qch avec qn

cover 1 n **(a)** Ins couverture f; **to have cover against sth** être couvert(e) contre qch ❑ **cover**

note lettre *f* de couverture, certificat *m* provisoire d'assurance

(**b**) *Fin* marge *f* de sécurité; **to operate with/without cover** opérer avec couverture/à découvert ❏ *cover ratio* taux *m* de couverture

(**c**) **to send sth under separate cover** faire parvenir qch sous pli séparé ❏ *Am* **cover letter** lettre *f* explicative; *(enclosed with CV)* lettre de motivation; **cover page** *(of fax)* page *f* de garde; **cover sheet** *(of fax)* page de garde

2 *vt* (**a**) *Ins* couvrir (**for** or **against** contre); **to be fully covered** être entièrement couvert(e); **this insurance covers serious illness** cette assurance couvre l'assuré en cas de maladie grave

(**b**) **to be covered** *(of creditor)* être (à) couvert; **to cover a bill** faire la provision d'une lettre de change; *St Exch* **to cover a position** couvrir une position

(**c**) *(be enough for)* couvrir; **to cover one's expenses** rentrer dans ses frais; **to cover a deficit** combler un déficit; *Acct* **to cover a loss** couvrir un déficit

coverage *n Ins* couverture *f*

covered *adj (position)* couvert(e) ❏ *St Exch* **covered (short) position** position *f* (courte) couverte

covering *adj* (**a**) *Br* **covering letter** lettre *f* explicative; *(enclosed with CV)* lettre de motivation (**b**) *St Exch* **covering purchases** rachats *mpl*

co-worker *n Am* collègue *mf*

c/p *(abbr* **carriage paid***)* pp

CPA *n Am (abbr* **certified public accountant***)* ≃ expert-comptable *m*

cpa *n (abbr* **critical path analysis***)* analyse *f* du chemin critique

CPI *n Am (abbr* **Consumer Price Index***)* IPC *m*

cpi *n Comptr (abbr* **characters per inch***)* cpp

cps *n Comptr (abbr* **characters per second***)* cps

CPSA *n Br (abbr* **Civil and Public Services Association***)* = syndicat de la fonction public

CPU *n Comptr (abbr* **central processing unit***)* unité *f* centrale ❏ *CPU board* carte *f* unité centrale

crack *vt (market)* percer sur

▸ **crack open** *vt sep (market)* percer sur

crash 1 *n* (**a**) *(financial)* krach *m* (**b**) *(of computer)* panne *f*

2 *adj* **crash course** cours *m* intensif; **crash programme** programme *m* choc *ou* d'urgence

3 *vi* (**a**) *(of business)* faire faillite; *(of prices, shares, economy)* s'effondrer; **shares crashed from 75p to 11p** le cours des actions s'est effondré: de 75 pence il est passé à 11 pence (**b**) *(of computer network, system)* sauter; *(of computer)* tomber en panne

crate *n (for storage, transport)* caisse *f*

crawler *n Comptr* araignée *f*

crawling peg *n Fin* parité *f* rampante *ou* crémaillère

cream *vt Am* **to cream the market** écrémer le marché

▸ **cream off** *vt sep (money, profits)* écrémer

create *vt* créer; **foreign investment has created many new jobs in the area** les investissements étrangers ont permis la création de nombreux emplois dans la région; **new markets are constantly being created** de nouveaux marchés sont sans cesse en train de se créer

creation *n (of jobs, new markets)* création *f*

creative 1 *n (department, work)* création *f*; *(person)* créatif(ive) *m,f*; **we prefer creative to be handled out of house** nous préférons que tout ce qui est création artistique soit réalisé à l'extérieur

2 *adj* créatif(ive) ❏ *creative copy strategy* copie *f* stratégie créative; *creative department* service *m* de création; *creative director* directeur(trice) *m,f* de la création; *creative marketing* créativité *f* commerciale; *creative team* équipe *f* de création

creativity *n* créativité *f*

credit 1 *n* (**a**) *(for future payment)* crédit *m*; **to give sb credit** faire crédit à qn; **to buy/sell sth on credit** acheter/vendre qch à crédit; **her credit is good** elle a une bonne réputation de solvabilité ❏ *credit account* Banking compte *m* créditeur; *(with shop)* compte client; *credit advice* avis *m* de crédit; *credit agency* agence *f* de crédit; *credit agreement* accord *m* ou convention *f* de crédit; *credit application form* formule *f* de demande de crédit; *credit bank* banque *f* de crédit; *credit broker* courtier(ère) *m,f* en crédits *ou* en prêts; *Am credit bureau* agence de notation; *credit call* = appel téléphonique effectué avec une carte de crédit; *credit card* carte *f* de crédit; *credit card fraud* usage *m* frauduleux de cartes de crédit; *credit card number* numéro *m* de carte de crédit; *credit card transaction* transaction *f* effectuée par carte de crédit; *credit ceiling* plafond *m* de crédit; *credit control* encadrement *m* du crédit; *credit controller* contrôleur(euse) *m,f* du crédit; *credit crunch* resserrement *m* du crédit; *credit enquiry* renseignements *mpl* de crédit, enquête *f* de solvabilité; *credit facilities* facilités *fpl* de crédit; **to give sb credit facilities** accréditer qn (auprès d'une banque); *credit file* dossier *m* crédit; *credit freeze* blocage *m* du crédit, gel *m* des crédits; *credit guarantee fund* caisse *f* de garantie; *credit history* profil *m* crédit; **to obtain information on sb's credit history** établir des renseignements de solvabilité sur qn; *credit institution* établissement *m* de crédit; **credit insurance** assurance-crédit f; **credit limit** limite f de crédit, plafond de crédit; **credit line** Br (loan) autorisation f de crédit; Am (limit) limite ou plafond de crédit; **credit management** direction f des crédits; **credit manager** directeur(trice) m,f des crédits; **credit margin** marge f de crédit; **credit options** formules fpl de crédit; **credit organization** organisme m de crédit; **credit period** délai m de crédit; **credit purchase** achat m à crédit; **credit rating** (of person, company) degré m de solvabilité; Fin (awarded by credit reference agency) notation f; **credit rating agency** agence de notation; **credit restrictions** encadrement du crédit; **credit risk** risque m de crédit; **credit sale** vente f à crédit; **credit scoring** méthode f d'évaluation de la solvabilité, crédit-scoring m; **credit squeeze** encadrement du crédit; **credit terms** modalités fpl du crédit; **credit transaction** transaction à crédit; Am **credit union** société f ou caisse f de crédit

(b) **to be in credit** (of person) avoir un compte créditeur; (of account) être créditeur(trice); Acct **debit and credit** débit m et crédit m □ Acct, Banking **credit balance** solde m créditeur; Acct **credit column** colonne f créditrice; **credit entry** Acct écriture f passée au crédit; Banking article m porté au crédit d'un compte; Acct **credit item** poste m créditeur; **credit memo** bulletin m de versement; **credit note** Acct, Banking note f d'avoir; (in shop) avoir m; Acct **credit side** (of account) avoir; Banking **credit transfer** virement m; **credit voucher** chèque m de caisse

2 vt (account) créditer; **to credit an account with £200, to credit £200 to an account** créditer un compte de 200 livres

" The Money Store, which has 140 employees at branches in Glasgow, Birmingham, Bristol, Manchester, Newcastle and Warrington, is focused on customers such as the self-employed and divorced who can suffer difficulties in getting a **credit rating** from high street lenders. **"**

creditor n créancier(ère) m,f □ Econ **creditor country** pays m créditeur; **creditors' meeting** réunion f des créanciers; Econ **creditor nation** pays créditeur; Acct **creditors' turnover** rotation f des fournisseurs

creditworthiness n solvabilité f

creditworthy adj solvable

creeping adj (inflation) rampant(e)

crisis n crise f; **to take crisis measures** prendre des mesures exceptionnelles □ **crisis management** gestion f des crises

critical adj **critical illness insurance** assurance f longue maladie; **critical path** chemin m critique; **critical path analysis** analyse f du che-

min critique; **critical path method** méthode f du chemin critique; **critical path model** modèle m du chemin critique

CRN n (abbr **customs registered number**) numéro m d'enregistrement douanier

CRO n (abbr **Companies Registration Office**) = institut britannique où sont enregistrées toutes les informations concernant les entreprises du pays

cross vt (cheque) barrer □ **crossed cheque** chèque m barré

cross-border business n commerce m transfrontalier

cross-currency adj Fin **cross-currency interest rate** taux m d'intérêt croisé; St Exch **cross-currency swap** crédit m croisé

cross-hedge n St Exch couverture f croisée

cross-holding n Fin participation f croisée

" This did not satisfy Mr Pébereau, who had made compromises which included BNP retaining its 37% stake in SocGen but reducing its voting rights to less than 20%. He also offered SocGen a **cross-holding** in BNP which would make it his bank's biggest shareholder. **"**

cross-impact analysis n Mktg analyse f d'interférence

cross-media ownership n = contrôle, par un même groupe de journaux, de chaînes de télévision et/ou stations de radio

cross-pricing n fixation f de prix croisés

crown n Br **Crown Agent** = fonctionnaire du ministère britannique du développment outremer chargé des pays étrangers et des organisations internationales; Law **Crown Court** ≃ Cour f d'assises (en Angleterre et au pays de Galles)

crude 1 n (crude oil) brut m
2 adj **crude oil** pétrole m brut

crunch vt Comptr (numbers, data) traiter à grande vitesse

CS n Fin (abbr **capital stock**) capital m social, capital-actions m, fonds mpl propres

CSC n Br Admin (abbr **Civil Service Commission**) = commission de recrutement des fonctionnaires

CSCE n EU (abbr **Council for Security and Co-operation in Europe**) CSCE f

CSD n Banking, St Exch (abbr **Central Securities Depository**) depositaire m national de titres

CUG n Tel (abbr **closed user group**) GFU m

cumulative adj (error) cumulé(e) □ Mktg **cumulative audience** audience f cumulée; **cumulative balance** solde m cumulé; **cumulative**

costs coûts *mpl* cumulés; **cumulative debit** débit *m* cumulé; **cumulative dividend** dividende *m* cumulatif; *Fin* **cumulative interest** intérêts *mpl* cumulatifs; *St Exch* **cumulative preference share** action *f* privilégiée cumulative; **cumulative profit** bénéfice *m* cumulé; **cumulative revenue** revenu *m* cumulé; *St Exch* **cumulative share** action à dividende cumulatif

curb *vt (expenditure, inflation)* contenir; *(imports)* freiner

curly quotes *npl* guillemets *mpl* anglais

currency *n* monnaie *f*; *(foreign)* devise *f* ▫ **currency assets** réserves *fpl* en devises; **currency bloc** bloc *m* monétaire; **currency conversion** conversion *f* de monnaies; **currency dealer** cambiste *mf*; **currency exchange market** marché *m* des changes; **currency expansion** expansion *f* monétaire; **currency exposure** risque *m* de change; **currency fluctuation** mouvement *m* des devises; **currency interest-rate swap** échange *m* d'intérêts et de monnaies; **currency loan** emprunt *m* en devises; **currency manipulation** manipulation *f* monétaire; **currency market** marché monétaire; **currency note** billet *m* de banque; **currency pool** pool *m* de monnaies; **currency risk** risque de change; **currency snake** serpent *m* monétaire; **currency speculation** spéculation *f* sur devises; **currency speculator** spéculateur(trice) *m,f* sur devises; **currency standard** étalon *m* devise; **currency swap** échange de devises; **currency transfer** transfert *m* de devises

current *adj* **current account** *(in bank)* compte *m* courant; *St Exch* liquidation *f* courante; **current affairs** l'actualité *f*, les questions *fpl* d'actualité; **current affairs magazine** magazine *m* d'actualité, news magazine *m*; *Comptr* **current application** application *f* en cours; *Acct* **current assets** actif *m* de roulement; **current cost** prix *m* courant *ou* du marché; *St Exch* cours *m* instantané; **current cost accounting** comptabilité *f* en coûts actuels; **current earnings** bénéfices *mpl* de l'exercice, revenu *m* actuel; **current expenditure** dépenses *fpl* courantes; **current** *Br* **financial** *or Am* **fiscal year** exercice *m* en cours; **current income** *(in accounts)* produits *mpl* courants; *(actual earnings)* revenu actuel; **current liabilities** passif *m* exigible; *Acct* **current net value** valeur *f* actuelle nette; **current rate of exchange** taux *m* de change actuel; *Acct* **current ratio** coefficient *m* de liquidité; *Acct* **current value** valeur actuelle; *Acct* **current value accounting** comptabilité en valeur actuelle; **current year** exercice en cours; *Fin* **current yield** taux de rendement actuel

curriculum vitae *n* curriculum vitae *m*

cursor *n Comptr* curseur *m*; **move the cursor to the right/left** déplacez le curseur vers la droite/gauche; **the word where the cursor is** le mot pointé ▫ **cursor control** contrôle *m* du curseur; **cursor movement key** touche *f* de déplacement du curseur

curve *n* courbe *f*; **the graph shows an upward/downward curve** la courbe accuse une hausse/une baisse; *Am Fam* **to throw sb a curve (ball)** prendre qn à contre-pied; **he threw me a curve (ball) when he accepted their higher offer** il m'a fait un sale coup en acceptant leur surenchère

custodian *n Am St Exch* dépositaire *mf*, conservateur(trice) *m,f* de titres

custody account *n Am* compte *m* de garde

custom *n* **(a)** *(of business)* clientèle *f*; **to lose sb's custom** perdre la clientèle de qn **(b)** *custom house* (poste *m ou* bureau *m* de) douane *f*

customer *n* client(e) *m,f* ▫ **customer account** compte *m* client; **customer appeal** séduction *f* du client; **customer base** base *f* de clientèle, base de consommateurs; **customer care** = qualité du service fourni à la clientèle; **customer code** code *m* client; **customer confidence** confiance *f* de la clientèle, confiance du client; **customer database** base de données de consommateurs; **customer list** liste *f* de clients; **customer loyalty** fidélité *f* de la clientèle; **customer loyalty discount** remise *f* de fidélité; **customer profile** profil *m* de la clientèle; **customer record** fiche *f* client; **customer reference number** code client; **customer relations** relations *fpl* clientèle; **customer relations manager** directeur(trice) *m,f* de la clientèle; **customer satisfaction** satisfaction *f* de la clientèle; **customer satisfaction questionnaire** formulaire *m* d'appréciation; **customer service** service *m* clientèle, service clients; **customer service department** service clientèle, service clients

customer-centred, **customer-driven**, **customer-focused** *adj* tributaire du consommateur

> ❝
> The irony is that, having fragmented in the post-liberalisation world, the UK utilities industry is now beginning to consolidate – this time on a **customer-driven** basis rather than a supply approach. But it is likely to happen under largely foreign ownership, which has nipped in before a new British utilities giant has had time to emerge.
> ❞

customizable *adj* qui peut être personnalisé; **our company offers a customizable package to new employees** notre entreprise propose à ses employés des conditions de travail adaptées à leurs besoins

customize *vt* **we provide a customized service for all our clients** nous fournissons à nos clients un service adapté à leurs besoins ▫ **customized marketing** marketing *m* sur mesure

customs *npl* douane *f*; **to go through customs** passer (à) la douane; **to take sth through customs** faire passer qch à la douane ◻ *customs agency* agence *f* en douane; *customs agent* commissionnaire *mf* en douane; *customs allowance* tolérance *f* ou franchise *f* douanière; *customs barriers* barrières *fpl* douanières; *customs broker* agréé(e) *m,f* en douane, agent *m* en douane; *customs charges* frais *mpl* de douane; *customs classification* nomenclature *f* douanière; *customs clearance* dédouanement *m*; *customs clearance area* aire *f* de dédouanement; *customs clearance authorization* autorisation *f* de dédouanement; *customs control* contrôle *m* douanier; *customs declaration* déclaration *f* de ou en douane; *customs duty* droits *mpl* de douane; *customs examination* vérification *f* en douane; *Br Customs and Excise* ≃ la Régie; *customs formalities* formalités *fpl* douanières; *customs house* (poste *m* ou bureau *m* de) douane; *customs inspection* visite *f* douanière ou de douane; *customs inspector* inspecteur(trice) *m,f* des douanes; *customs invoice* facture *f* douanière; *customs legislation* droit *m* douanier, législation *f* douanière; *customs manifest* manifeste *m* de douane; *customs note* bordereau *m* de douanes; *customs office* bureau de douane; *customs officer* douanier(ère) *m,f*, préposé(e) *m,f* de la douane; *customs papers* dossier *m* de douane; *customs permit* permis *m* de douane; *customs preferential duty* préférences *fpl* douanières; *customs procedure* procédure *f* douanière; *customs receipt* acquit *m* ou quittance *f* ou récépissé *m* de douane; *customs registered number* numéro *m* d'enregistrement douanier; *customs regulations* réglementation *f* douanière; *customs seal* cachet *m* de douane; *customs service* service *m* des douanes; *customs system* régime *m* douanier; *customs tariff* tarif *m* douanier; *customs transit* transit *m* douanier; *customs union* union *f* douanière; *customs value* valeur *f* en douane; *customs visa* visa *m* de la douane; *customs zone* zone *f* sous douane

cut 1 *n* **(a)** *(in wages, prices, costs)* réduction *f*; *(in taxes, production)* baisse *f*, diminution *f*; *(in staff)* compression *f*; **he took a cut in pay** il a été obligé d'accepter une réduction de salaire **(b)** *Comptr* **cut and paste** couper-coller *m*
2 *vt* **(a)** *(wages, prices, costs, staff)* réduire; *(taxes, production)* diminuer, réduire **(b)** *Comptr* couper; **to cut and paste sth** faire un couper-coller sur qch ◻ *cut sheet feed* alimentation *f* feuille à feuille; *cut sheet feeder* dispositif *m* d'alimentation feuille à feuille
3 *vi Comptr* **to cut and paste** faire un couper-coller

▸ **cut back 1** *vt sep (prices)* baisser; *(production)* diminuer; **arms spending has been cut right back** les dépenses d'armement ont été nettement réduites

2 *vi (financially)* économiser, réduire les dépenses

▸ **cut back on** *vt insep* économiser sur; *(time)* réduire; *(production)* diminuer

▸ **cut down** *vt sep (spending)* couper, réduire

▸ **cut down on** *vt insep* réduire

▸ **cut in** *vt sep Fam* **to cut sb in (on a deal)** donner à qn sa part du gâteau; **we could cut him in for £5,000** nous pourrions lui filer 5000 livres

▸ **cut off** *vt sep* **(a)** *(stop)* suspendre; **we are cutting off all overseas investment** nous suspendons tous les investissements à l'étranger **(b)** *(on telephone)* couper; **I was cut off** *(during conversation)* j'ai été coupé; *(disconnected)* on m'a coupé le téléphone

▸ **cut out** *vt sep (oust)* **to cut sb out of a deal** évincer qn dans une affaire

cutback *n (in production, budget)* réduction *f*, diminution *f*

cut-price, *Am* **cut-rate** *adj (goods)* à prix réduit; *(as special offer)* bradé(e)

cut-throat *adj (competition)* acharné(e)

cutting edge *n* **to be at the cutting edge of technology** être à la pointe du progrès

CV *n Br (abbr* **curriculum vitae)** CV *m*

CVP *n Fin (abbr* **cost-volume-profit)** étude *f* de coût-efficacité

CVR *n Fin (abbr* **contingent value right)** CVG *m*

CWO *(abbr* **cash with order)** envoi contre paiement

cyber *n Comptr* cyber *m*

cyberbanking *n Comptr* transactions *fpl* bancaires en ligne

cybernaut *n Comptr* cybernaute *mf*

cyberspace *n Comptr* cyberespace *m*; **in cyberspace** dans le cyberespace

cybersquatting *n Comptr* cybersquatting *m*

> **"**
> Mohamed Al Fayed has been given something to cheer about after winning a landmark **cybersquatting** case. A US district court judge has ruled that Mr Al Fayed's famous London department store, Harrods, can now take possession of 60 Harrods-related internet addresses that were registered in "bad faith".
> **"**

cycle *n (in economy, trade)* cycle *m*

cyclical 1 *n St Exch* **cyclicals** valeurs *fpl* cycliques
2 *adj St Exch* **cyclical stocks** valeurs *fpl* cycliques; **cyclical unemployment** chômage *m* conjoncturel; **cyclical variations** variations *fpl* cycliques

Dd

D/A *npl* (*abbr* **documents against acceptance**) documents *mpl* contre acceptation

DAB *n Comptr* (*abbr* **digital audio broadcasting**) diffusion *f* audionumérique, DAB *f*

dabble *vi* **to dabble on the Stock Exchange** boursicoter

daily *adj* quotidien(enne) ❑ *daily allowance* indemnité *f* journalière; *Acct daily balance interest calculation* méthode *f* par *ou* à échelles; *St Exch Daily Official List* cours *mpl* de clôture quotidiens; *daily takings* recette *f* journalière, rentrées *fpl* journalières; *St Exch daily trading report* rapport *m* de situation journalière

> **"**
> Ordinary Shares will be acquired under the tender offer at a common price that will be set within a specified tender price range. The bottom of the tender price range, which is the lowest price at which tenders will be accepted, will be the average middle market quotation of Ordinary Shares as derived from the **Daily Official List**.
> **"**

daisy-wheel *n* marguerite *f* ❑ *daisy-wheel printer* imprimante *f* à marguerite

damage 1 *n* (**a**) *(to goods)* dommages *mpl*, dégâts *mpl*; *(to ship, cargo)* avaries *fpl*; **the insurance will pay for the damage** l'assurance paiera les dommages ❑ *Ins damage certificate* attestation *f* de sinistre; *damage claim* déclaration *f* de sinistre; *damage report* déclaration de sinistre; *damage survey* expertise *f* des dégâts *ou* d'avarie

(**b**) *Law* **damages** dommages-intérêts *mpl*, dommages *mpl* et intérêts *mpl*; **to award damages to sb for sth** accorder des dommages-intérêts à qn pour qch; **to be awarded damages** obtenir des dommages-intérêts; **to sue sb for damages** poursuivre qn en dommages-intérêts; **to be liable for damages** être tenu(e) des dommages-intérêts; **to claim £1,000 damages** réclamer des dommages-intérêts de 1000 livres

(**c**) *damage limitation* limitation *f* des dégâts; **the redundancies are an exercise in damage limitation** c'est pour essayer de limiter les dégâts qu'ils ont licencié du personnel

2 *vt (goods)* avarier, endommager

damaged *adj (goods)* avarié(e), endomma-

gé(e); **damaged in transit** endommagé en cours de route

▶ **damp down** *vt sep (market)* freiner; *(consumption)* réduire

danger money *n* prime *f* de risque

dash *n (symbol)* tiret *m*; *Comptr* **em-dash** tiret cadratin; *Comptr* **en-dash** tiret demi-cadratin

DAT *n Comptr* (*abbr* **digital audio tape**) DAT *f*, bande *f* audionumérique ❑ *DAT cartridge* cartouche *f* DAT; *DAT drive* lecteur *m* DAT, lecteur de bande audionumérique

data *n* informations *fpl*, données *fpl*; *Comptr* données *fpl*; **an item of data** une information, une donnée; **to collect data on sb/sth** recueillir des données sur qn/qch ❑ *data acquisition* collecte *f ou* saisie *f* de données; *data analysis* analyse *f* de données; *data bank* banque *f* de données; *data bus* bus *m* de données; *data capture* saisie de données; *data carrier* support *m* de données; *data collection* recueil *m ou* collecte de données; *data communications* communication *f ou* transmission *f* de données, télématique *f*; *data compression* compression *f* de données; *data decryption* déchiffrement *m* de données; *data encryption* cryptage *m ou* codage *m* de données; *data entry* entrée *f* de données; *Acct data entry form* fiche *f* d'imputation; *data exchange* échange *m* de données; *data export* export *m* de données; *data import* import *m* de données; *data input* introduction *f* de données; *data link* voie *f* de transmission de données; *data loss* perte *f* de données; *data management* gestion *f* de données; *data manipulation* manipulation *f* de données; *data memory* mémoire *f*; *data network* réseau *m* de données; *data organization* organisation *f* des données; *data path* chemin *m* d'accès aux données; *data privacy* confidentialité *f* des données *ou* de l'information; *data processing* informatique *f*, traitement *m* de l'information *ou* des données; *data processing centre* centre *m* de traitement de l'information; *data processing manager* chef *m* des traitements; *data processing system* système *m* de traitement de l'information; *data processor (machine)* ordinateur *m*; *(person)* informaticien(enne) *m,f*; *data protection* protection *f* de l'information; *Br* **Data Protection Act** = loi sur la protection de l'information; *data recovery* récupération f de données; **data retrieval** recherche f de données; **data security** sécurité f des données; **data set** ensemble m de données; **data sharing** partage m des données; **data source** source f de données; **data storage** stockage m de données; **data throughput** débit m de données; **data transfer** transfert m ou transmission de données

database n Comptr base f de données; **to enter sth into a database** mettre qch dans une base de données □ **database management** gestion f de bases de données; **database management system** système m de gestion de base de données

datacomms n Comptr communication f ou transmission f de données, télématique f □ **datacomms network** réseau m de télématique ou de communication de données; **datacomms software** logiciel m de communication

date 1 n (a) (day) date f; **date as postmark** date de la poste □ **date of birth** date de naissance; **date of delivery** date de livraison; **date of invoice** date de facturation; **date of issue** date d'émission; **date of signature** date de signature; **date stamp** (object) (tampon m) dateur m; (mark) cachet m
(b) **up to date** à jour; (well-informed) au courant (**on** de); **I'm up to date with my work** mon travail est à jour; **to bring/keep sb up to date (on sth)** mettre/tenir qn au courant (de qch); **to bring/keep sth up to date** mettre/tenir qch à jour
(c) **to date** à ce jour; **interest to date** intérêts mpl à ce jour
(d) **out of date** (passport, cheque) périmé(e)
(e) Fin (of bill) terme m, échéance f; **three months after date, at three months' date** à trois mois de date ou d'échéance; **date of maturity** (date f d') échéance
2 vt (letter, cheque) dater; **the cheque is dated 24 March** le chèque est daté du 24 mars

datebook n Am agenda m

daughter company n société f fille

> Splendid Medien AG is the holding company for eight subsidiaries and affiliates, including Splendid Television and former **daughter company** Initial Entertainment Group (IEG) which finances, co-produces and distributes filmed entertainment throughout the world.

dawn n St Exch **dawn raid** raid m (mené dès l'ouverture de la Bourse); **dawn raider** raider m (qui opère dès l'ouverture de la Bourse)

Dax n St Exch **the Dax (index)** l'indice m Dax

day n jour m; (working hours) journée f; **to have/**

take a day off avoir/prendre un jour de congé; **to work an eight-hour day** travailler huit heures par jour; **to be paid by the day** être payé(e) à la journée □ **day of action** jour d'action; **day labour** travail m de jour; **day labourer** ouvrier(ère) m,f journalier(ère) ou à la journée; **day off** jour de congé; St Exch **day order** ordre m valable pour la journée; **day release** formation f continue en alternance; **to be on day release** être en formation continue en alternance; **day shift** (period worked) service m de jour; (workers) équipe f de jour; **to be on day shift, to work the day shift** être de jour; St Exch **day trade** opération f de journée; St Exch **day trader** spéculateur(trice) m,f à la journée; **day work** travail de jour
(b) **we can give you four days' grace** nous pouvons vous accorder un délai de quatre jours □ **day of grace** jour m de grâce; **days of grace** délai m de grâce

day-after recall n Mktg mémorisation f un jour après □ **day-after recall test** test m du lendemain

daybook n Acct brouillard m

dayside n Am personnel m de jour

day-to-day adj courant(e), quotidien(enne); **he is responsible for the day-to-day running of the business** c'est lui qui est chargé d'expédier les affaires courantes; **we can barely afford the day-to-day expenses** on arrive à peine à faire face aux dépenses quotidiennes

DBA n (abbr **Doctor of Business Administration**) (person) docteur m en gestion; (qualification) doctorat m en gestion

dbase n Comptr (abbr **database**) BD f

DBMS n Comptr (abbr **database management system**) SGBD m

DCF n Acct (abbr **discounted cash flow**) cash-flow m actualisé, flux mpl de trésorerie actualisés

DD n Comptr (abbr **double density**) double densité f

D/D n (abbr **direct debit**) prélèvement f automatique

dead adj Fin **dead account** compte m inactif; Fam St Exch **dead cat bounce** = reprise de courte durée lors de l'effondrement des cours de la Bourse; **dead freight** faux fret m; **dead letter** (that cannot be delivered) lettre f non distribuée; (law) loi f tombée en désuétude; Fin **dead loss** perte f sèche; **dead market** marché m mort; **dead money** argent m mort, argent qui dort; **dead period** période f d'inactivité; **dead season** morte-saison f; **dead weight** poids m mort

deadline n (day) date f limite, délai m d'exécution; (time) heure f limite; **to meet/miss a deadline** respecter/laisser passer une date/heure limite; **to work to a deadline** avoir un délai à respecter; **deadline for payment** date limite de paiement

deadlock 1 n impasse f; **to reach a deadlock** aboutir à une impasse; **talks with the union were in deadlock** les négociations avec le syndicat étaient au point mort ou étaient dans l'impasse; **they have succeeded in breaking the deadlock** ils ont réussi à sortir de l'impasse
2 vt **to be deadlocked** (of talks, negotiations) être au point mort

deadweight n chargement m en lourd, port m en lourd ❑ **deadweight cargo** marchandises fpl lourdes

deal 1 n affaire f, marché m; (on Stock Exchange) opération f, transaction f; **to do** or **make a deal with sb** conclure une affaire ou un marché avec qn; **to negotiate a deal** négocier une affaire ou un marché; **to call off a deal** annuler une affaire ou un marché; **it's a deal!** marché conclu!
2 vi négocier, traiter; **our firm has been dealing for over 50 years** notre société est en activité depuis plus de 50 ans; **to deal in leather** faire le commerce des cuirs; **to deal on the Stock Exchange** faire des opérations ou des transactions en Bourse; Fin, St Exch **to deal in options** faire le commerce des primes

▸ **deal with** vt insep (a) (do business with) traiter ou négocier avec (b) (get supplies from) se fournir chez (c) (handle) (problem, query, order, complaint) s'occuper de

dealer n (trader) négociant(e) m,f, marchand(e) m,f (**in** en); (in cars) concessionnaire mf; (on Stock Exchange) courtier(ère) m,f; (in foreign exchange) cambiste mf

dealership n concession f

dealing n (a) St Exch opérations fpl, transactions fpl ❑ **dealing room** salle f des changes, salle de marchés (b) (commerce) commerce m; **dealings** transactions fpl; **to have dealings with sb** faire des affaires avec qn

dealmaker n = homme d'affaires qui négocie des contrats

dealmaking n négociation f de contrats

dear adj (a) (expensive) cher (chère) ❑ **dear money** argent m cher (b) (in letter) **Dear Sir** Monsieur; **Dear Sirs** Messieurs; **Dear Madam** Madame/Mademoiselle; **Dear Sir or Madam** Madame, Monsieur; **Dear Mr Martin** Monsieur; **Dear Ms Carrington** Madame

death n décès m, mort f; **death in service (benefit)** capital-décès m ❑ Fin **death benefit** capital-décès; Br **death duty** droits mpl de succession; Am **death tax** droits de succession

debenture n Fin obligation f ❑ **debenture bond** obligation; **debenture holder** détenteur(trice) m,f d'obligations, obligataire mf; **debenture issue** émission f d'obligations; **debenture loan** emprunt m obligataire; **debenture register** registre m des obligataires; **debenture stock** obligations fpl (sans garantie)

debit 1 n débit m; Acct **debit and credit** débit et crédit m; **your account is in debit** votre compte est débiteur ou déficitaire ❑ **debit account** compte m débiteur; **debit advice** avis m de débit; Acct, Banking **debit balance** solde m débiteur ou déficitaire; **debit card** carte f de paiement à débit immédiat; Acct **debit column** colonne f débitrice ou des débits; **debit entry** Acct écriture f passée au débit; Banking article m porté au débit d'un compte; **debit interest** intérêts mpl débiteurs; Acct **debit item** poste m débiteur; **debit note** facture f ou note f ou bordereau m de débit; Acct **debit side** (of account) débit
2 vt (account) débiter; (person) porter au débit de; **to debit an account with £200, to debit £200 to an account** débiter un compte de 200 livres; **has this cheque been debited to my account?** est-ce que ce chèque a été débité de mon compte?

debrief vt débriefer

debriefing n débriefing m

debt n dette f; (to be recovered) créance f; **to be in debt** être endetté(e), avoir des dettes; **to be £12,000 in debt** avoir 12 000 livres de dettes; **to be in debt to sb** être en dette envers qn; **to pay off a debt** rembourser ou payer une dette; **to be out of debt** n'avoir plus de dettes; **to get** or **run into debt** s'endetter, faire des dettes; **to reschedule** or **restructure a debt** rééchelonner une dette; Fam **to be up to the neck** or **one's ears in debt** être criblé(e) de dettes; **debt owed by us** dette passive; **debt owed to us** dette active ❑ **debt burden** surendettement m, fardeau m de la dette; **debt capacity** capacité f d'endettement; **debt collection** recouvrement m de créances; **debt collection agency** agence f de recouvrements; **debt collector** agent m de recouvrements; **debt due** créance exigible; **debt equity swap** échange m de créances contre actifs; **debt financing** financement m par endettement; **debt of honour** dette d'honneur; **debt instrument** titre m de créance; **debt**

limit limite *f* d'endettement; **debt rating** niveau *m* d'endettement; **debt ratio** ratio *m* d'endettement; **debt reduction programme** désendettement *m*; **debt refinancing** refinancement *m* de dettes; **debt rescheduling, debt restructuring** rééchelonnement *m* des dettes; *Br* **debt service** service *m* de la dette; *Am* **debt servicing** service de la dette; **debt swap** échange de créances

debt-equity ratio *n* ratio *m* capitaux-empruntés-fonds propres

debtor *n* débiteur(trice) *m,f* □ *Acct* **debtor account** compte *m* débiteur; *Econ* **debtor country** pays *m* débiteur; *Econ* **debtor nation** pays débiteur; *Acct* **debtor side** *(of account)* débit *m*, doit *m*; *Acct* **debtors' turnover** rotation *f* des clients

"
Now, of course, the United States is in no position to repeat its midcentury largesse. America has become a **debtor nation** and provides stimulus to the global economy by going deeper into debt as it buys goods from others. And the United States, like other debtors, is beginning to express its enmity toward those from whom it borrows to buy.
"

debug *vt Comptr (program)* déboguer

debugger *n Comptr (program)* débogueur *m*

debugging *n Comptr (of program)* débogage *m*

decasualization *n* the decasualization of labour la régularisation du travail

decasualize *vt (workers)* régulariser le travail de; *(labour)* régulariser

decentralization *n* décentralisation *f*

decentralized *vt* décentralisé(e)

decision *n* décision *f*; **to make a decision** prendre une décision □ **decision model** modèle *m* décisionnel *ou* de décision; **decision table** table *f* décisionnel *ou* de décision; **decision theory** théorie *f* de la décision; **decision tree** arbre *m* décisionnel *ou* de décision

decision-maker *n* décideur(euse) *m,f*, décisionnaire *mf*; **to be a good/bad decision-maker** savoir/ne pas savoir prendre des décisions

decision-making *n* prise *f* de décision(s); **this job calls for a lot of decision-making** ce travail demande qu'on prenne beaucoup de décisions □ **decision-making model** modèle *m* de prise de décision(s); **decision-making power** pouvoir *m* de décision; **the decision-making process** le processus de prise de décision(s); **decision-making tool** outil *m* d'aide à la décision; **decision-making unit** unité *f* de prise de décision(s)

"
But women's international economic and political power is still minimal and much too limited to make the fundamental economic changes especially in accounting and reward systems to recognize women's real economic contributions and thus give women the **decision-making** power they have earned and deserve.
"

decision-tree model *n* modèle *m* de décision en arborescence

declaration *n* déclaration *f* □ **declaration of bankruptcy** jugement *m* déclaratif de faillite; *Fin* **declaration of dividend** déclaration de dividende; **declaration of income** déclaration de revenu; **declaration of intent** déclaration d'intention; **declaration inwards** déclaration d'entrée; *St Exch* **declaration of options** réponse *f* des primes; **declaration outwards** déclaration de sortie; **declaration of solvency** déclaration de solvabilité; *St Exch* **declaration of value** déclaration de valeur

declare *vt* (a) *Customs (goods)* déclarer (b) **to declare sb bankrupt** constater *ou* prononcer l'état de faillite *ou* la faillite de qn; *Fin* **to declare a dividend of ten percent** déclarer un dividende de dix pour cent; *St Exch* **to declare an option** répondre à *ou* donner la réponse à une prime □ **declared value** valeur *f* déclarée

decline 1 *n* déclin *m*; **to be on the decline** être en baisse; *(of industry)* être en déclin □ *Mktg* **decline stage** *(of product)* phase *f* de déclin
2 *vi* (a) *(decrease)* être en baisse; *(of industry)* être en déclin (b) *(refuse)* décliner, refuser

declining *adj* en baisse; *(industry)* déclinant(e) □ *Acct* **declining balance depreciation** amortissement *m* dégressif; *Acct* **declining balance method** méthode *f* de l'amortissement dégressif

decode *vt Comptr* décoder; **the file is automatically decoded when it is received** le fichier est décodé automatiquement à la réception

decoder *n Comptr* décodeur *m*

decoding *n Comptr* décodage *m*

decompress *vt Comptr (file)* décompresser

deconsignment *n* déconsignation *f*

decontrol 1 *n (of prices)* libération *f*
2 *vt* libérer des contraintes du gouvernement; *(prices)* libérer; *(wages)* débloquer

"
She favours the Tobin tax, taxing foreign exchange speculation, but only if it can be made to be practical and thinks that countries have to be careful how to **decontrol** their banks and foreign exchange markets.

Governments may have to step in to stop capital stampeding out of a country in panic with capital controls. **"**

decrease 1 *n* baisse *f*; **sales are on the decrease** les ventes sont en baisse
2 *vi* diminuer, baisser

decreasing *adj* en baisse; *(number, value, strength)* décroissant(e); *(costs)* dégressif(ive) ❑ *Acct* **decreasing rate** taux *m* dégressif

decrypt *vt Comptr* déchiffrer

decryption *n Comptr* déchiffrement *m*

DECT *n Tel (abbr* **digital enhanced cordless telecommunications)** DECT *f*

dedicated *adj (assigned for particular purpose)* spécialisé(e), dédié(e) ❑ *Tel* **dedicated line** ligne *f* spécialisée; *Comptr* **dedicated word processor** machine *f* servant uniquement au traitement de texte

deduct *vt* déduire; *(tax)* prélever; **to deduct £10 from the price** déduire 10 livres du prix; **to be deducted at source** *(of tax)* être prélevé(e) à la source; **after deducting expenses** après déduction des frais

deductible 1 *n Am Ins* franchise *f*
2 *adj* déductible

deduction *n* déduction *f* **(from** sur); *(from salary)* prélèvement *m*, retenue *f*; **after deduction of taxes** après déduction des impôts; **deduction (of income tax) at source** retenue à la source, prélèvement de l'impôt à la source; **after deductions, I'm left with a salary of £20,000** une fois les prélèvements *ou* les retenues décompté(e)s, il me reste un salaire de 20 000 livres

deed *n Law* acte *m* notarié; **to draw up a deed** rédiger un acte ❑ **deed of arrangement, deed of assignment** acte de transfert; **deed of covenant** = déclaration par laquelle on s'engage à verser régulièrement une certaine somme à un particulier, une association caritative, etc; **deed of partnership** acte de société; **deed of sale** acte de vente; **deed of title** titre *m* (constitutif) de propriété; **deed of transfer** acte de cession

"
And at work, are there any expenses you could set against tax such as training fees to professional bodies or travelling costs? Are your donations to charities benefiting from tax relief via the Gift Aid scheme or **deeds of covenant**?
"

deep discount *n* forte remise *f*

deep-discount bond *n* obligation *f* à forte décote

de facto *adj & adv Law* de facto; **de facto possession** possession *f* de fait; **de facto and de jure** de droit et de fait

defalcation *n* détournement *m* de fonds

default 1 *n* **(a)** *Law (failure to appear in court)* défaut *m*, non-comparution *f*
(b) *Fin* **in default of payment** à défaut de paiement ❑ **default interest** intérêts *mpl* moratoires *ou* pour défaut de paiement
(c) *Comptr* défaut *m* ❑ **default drive** lecteur *m* par défaut; **default font** police *f* par défaut; **default setting** configuration *f* par défaut
2 *vi* **(a)** *Law (fail to appear in court)* ne pas comparaître
(b) *Fin* manquer à ses engagements; **to default on a payment** ne pas honorer un paiement
(c) *Comptr* **to default to sth** sélectionner qch par défaut

"
Jenkins told Newsbytes that ZipLink had a total of 99 employees before warning earlier this month that its cash reserves would allow it to operate only until Nov. 17 unless more funds were found. The company said today that, in addition to failing in its bid to raise new cash, it also faced a **default** on payments by its second-largest customer, the free-ISP marketing company Spinway Inc.
"

defaulter *n* débiteur(trice) *m,f* défaillant(e)

defaulting *adj* défaillant(e) ❑ **defaulting party** partie *f* défaillante

defeasance *n Law* abrogation *f*

defect *n* défaut *m*

defective *adj* défectueux(euse)

defend *vt* défendre; **the company must defend its share of the market** l'entreprise doit défendre sa part de marché; **they are defending themselves against the takeover bid** ils essaient de résister à l'OPA

defended takeover bid *n* OPA *f* sauvage

defensive *adj St Exch* **defensive stocks** titres *mpl ou* valeurs *fpl* de placement; **defensive tactics** tactiques *fpl* de défense contre-OPA

defer *vt (decision, meeting)* remettre, reporter; *(payment)* différer, retarder; *(judgement)* suspendre

deferment *n (of decision, meeting)* report *m*; *(of payment)* recul *m*; *(of judgement)* suspension *f*

deferred *adj* différé(e) ❑ **deferred annuity** annuité *f* différée; **deferred assets** actif *m* différé; **deferred charges** frais *mpl* différés; **deferred credit** crédit *m* différé; **deferred debit** débit *m* différé; **deferred income** produit *m* constaté d'avance; **deferred liabilities** passif *m* reporté;

deferred ordinary share action f ordinaire différée; **deferred pay** rappel m de traitement; **deferred payment** paiement m différé; **deferred rebate** rabais m différé; **deferred results** résultats mpl à longue échéance; **deferred share** action différée; **deferred taxation** impôts mpl différés

deficit n Fin déficit m; **to be in deficit** être en déficit ou déficitaire; **the balance of payments shows a deficit of £800 million** la balance des paiements indique un déficit de 800 millions de livres □ **deficit spending** financement m par l'emprunt

definite adj (order, price) ferme

deflate vt Econ, Fin (prices) faire baisser; **to deflate the economy** pratiquer une politique déflationniste; **this measure is intended to deflate the economy** cette mesure est destinée à faire de la déflation

deflation n Econ, Fin déflation f

deflationary adj Econ, Fin (measures) déflationniste; (policy) de désinflation □ **deflationary gap** écart m déflationniste

DEFRA n Br (abbr Department for Environment, Food and Rural Affairs) ≃ ministère m de l'environnement et des affaires rurales

defragmentation n Comptr défragmentation f

defraud vt (the state) frauder; (company, person) escroquer; **he defrauded the government of £15,000 in unemployment benefit** il a frauduleusement perçu 15 000 livres d'allocations chômage

defray vt **to defray sb's expenses** défrayer qn; **to defray the cost of sth** rembourser les frais de qch; **all charges to be defrayed by the purchaser** tous les frais sont à la charge de l'acheteur

defunct adj (company) dissous(oute); (industry) disparu(e)

defund vt cesser de financer

degearing n désendettement m

degressive adj dégressif(ive)

dehire vt Am (dismiss) remercier

deinstall vt Comptr désinstaller

deinstallation n Comptr désinstallation f

deinstaller n Comptr désinstallateur m

deindex vt Fin désindexer

deindexation n Fin désindexation f

deindustrialization n désindustrialisation f

deindustrialize vt désindustrialiser

de jure adj & adv Law de jure

delay 1 n retard m; **we apologize for the delay in dealing with your complaint** veuillez excuser notre retard dans le traitement de votre réclamation; **there will be a 20-minute delay before the meeting** la réunion aura lieu 20 minutes plus tard que prévu; **all flights are subject to delay** tous les vols risquent d'avoir du retard

2 vt (project, decision) retarder; **to be delayed** (of flight, train) avoir du retard

delayering n suppression f d'échelons; **middle management has been cut back through delayering** la suppression d'échelons a réduit la hiérarchie intermédiaire

del credere n ducroire m □ **del credere agent** commissionnaire m ducroire, agent m ducroire; **del credere clause** clause f ducroire; **del credere commission** commission f ducroire

delegate 1 n délégué(e) m,f

2 vt déléguer; **to delegate sb to do sth** déléguer qn pour faire qch; **he must learn to delegate more work to his team** il faut qu'il apprenne à déléguer davantage de travail à son équipe

delegation n (of person, powers) délégation f; **to send a delegation** envoyer une délégation

delete 1 n Comptr effacement m □ **delete command** commande f d'effacement; **delete key** touche f d'effacement

2 vt (**a**) Comptr effacer, supprimer

(**b**) **delete where applicable, delete as appropriate** (on form) rayer la/les mention(s) inutile(s)

(**c**) (from stock, catalogue) **this item has been deleted from our catalogue** cet article ne figure plus dans notre catalogue; **we have decided to delete this item from stock** nous avons décidé de ne plus faire cet article

3 vi Comptr effacer

deleveraging n désendettement m

delinquency n Fin défaillance f, faute f de paiement

delinquent Fin **1** n mauvais payeur m

2 adj (person) défaillant(e); (loan, debt) échu(e), en souffrance

delist vt (**a**) St Exch radier de la cote (**b**) Mktg (product) déréférencer

delisting n (**a**) St Exch radiation f de la cote (**b**) Mktg (of product) déréférencement m

deliver 1 vt (**a**) (letter, parcel) remettre, distribuer (**to** à); (goods) livrer (**to** à); **to have sth delivered** faire livrer qch; **delivered free** livraison franco; **delivered free on board** rendu franco bord; **delivered to domicile** livré à domicile; **delivered at frontier** rendu à la frontière □ **delivered weight** poids m rendu

(**b**) (provide) (service) assurer; Fin **to deliver a profit** rapporter ou faire un profit; Fin **to deliver shares** délivrer des valeurs

2 vi (of supplier) livrer

deliverer *n* livreur *m*

delivery *n (of letter, parcel)* remise *f*, distribution *f; (of goods)* livraison *f;* **to accept** *or* **take delivery of sth** prendre livraison de qch, réceptionner qch; **awaiting delivery** en souffrance; **for immediate delivery** à livrer de suite; **to pay on delivery** payer à *ou* sur livraison; **free delivery** (envoi) livraison franco; **next day delivery** livraison lendemain ◻ *delivery address* adresse *f* de livraison; *delivery charges* frais *mpl* d'expédition *ou* de livraison; *delivery date* date *f ou* jour *m* de livraison; *St Exch delivery month* mois *m* de livraison; *delivery note* bon *m ou* bordereau *m* de livraison; *delivery order* bon de livraison; *delivery point* lieu *m* de livraison; *delivery schedule* planning *m* de livraison; *delivery service* service *m* de livraison; *delivery time* délai *m* de livraison; *delivery van* camion *m* de livraison; *(smaller)* camionnette *f* de livraison

del key *n Comptr* touche *f* d'effacement

de-man *vt* réduire les effectifs de

demand *n* **(a)** *(request)* demande *f*, réclamation *f; (for taxes, rates)* avertissement *m;* **payable on demand** payable au ou sur demande; **there have been demands for the director's resignation** certains ont réclamé la démission du directeur ◻ *Fin demand bill* bon *m* à vue; *Am demand deposit* dépôt *m* à vue; *Am demand deposit account* compte *m* à vue; *Fin demand draft* traite *f* à vue; *Fin demand note* bon à vue **(b)** *Econ* demande *f;* **supply and demand** l'offre *f* et la demande; **to be in (great) demand** être (très) demandé(e) *ou* recherché(e); **there isn't much demand for this product** ce produit n'est pas très demandé ◻ *demand analysis* analyse *f* de la demande; *demand assessment* évaluation *f* de la demande; *demand curve* courbe *f* (d'évolution) de la demande; *demand equation* équation *f* de la demande; *demand factor* facteur *m* de demande; *demand forecasting* prévision *f* de la demande; *demand function* fonction *f* de demande; *demand management* contrôle *m* de la demande

demand-led *adj Econ* tiré(e) par la demande

demand-pull inflation *n Econ* inflation *f* par la demande

demand-side economics *n Econ* économie *f* de la demande

de-man *vt* réduire les effectifs de

de-manning *n* réduction *f* des effectifs

demarcation *n* démarcation *f;* **a clear demarcation of responsibilities is essential in any organization** dans toute organisation, il est essentiel de délimiter les attributions de chacun ◻ *demarcation dispute* conflit *m* d'attributions

demarket *vt* retirer du marché

demarketing *n* démarketing *m*

dematerialization *n Fin* dématérialisation *f*

dematerialize *vt Fin* dématérialiser

demerge *vi* se scinder

demerger *n* scission *f;* **several new companies were formed after the demerger of the holding group** plusieurs entreprises nouvelles ont été créées à la suite de la scission du holding

> 66
> One market minnow is braving the tight IPO climate. In a little-noticed announcement last week, Hay & Robertson, the firm that owns the Admiral and Mountain brands, and markets trendy Kangol gear, is to embark on a three-way **demerger** designed to restore shareholder value.
> 99

demo *n (abbr* **demonstration)** démonstration *f;* **we received a demo of the new software system** quelqu'un est venu nous faire une démonstration du nouveau logiciel ◻ *Comptr demo disk* disquette *f* de démonstration *ou* d'évaluation

demographic 1 *n Fam (segment)* segment *m* démographique
2 *adj* démographique ◻ *demographic analysis* analyse *f* démographique; *demographic data* données *fpl* démographiques; *demographic profile* profil *m* démographique; *demographic segment* segment *m* démographique; *demographic segmentation* segmentation *f* démographique

demographics *npl* statistiques *fpl* démographiques

> 66
> The French, Germans and Italians largely rely on their generous state pension schemes. The British have sensibly moved much faster into private or company schemes; but the **demographics** still mean a pensions crunch everywhere in the developed world.
> 99

demography *n* démographie *f*

demonetarization = **demonetization**

demonetarize = **demonetize**

demonetization *n Fin (of currency)* démonétisation *f*

demonetize *vt Fin (currency)* démonétiser

demonstrate *vt (system, equipment)* faire une démonstration de; **he demonstrated how the new system worked** il nous a montré comment le nouveau système fonctionne

demonstration *n (of system, equipment, product)* démonstration *f;* **they gave us a demon-**

stration of the new model il nous ont fait une démonstration du nouveau modèle ▫ **demonstration model** appareil m ou modèle m de démonstration

demote vt rétrograder; **he was demoted from area manager to sales representative** du poste de directeur régional, il a été rétrogradé au poste de représentant de commerce

demotion n rétrogradation f

demotivate vt démotiver

demotivating adj démotivant(e); **the spate of redundancies has been very demotivating for the workforce** la série de licenciements a eu un effet très démotivant sur le personnel

demurrage n surestarie(s) f(pl)

demutualization n = transformation d'une société mutuelle en société par actions

demutualize vi = passer d'un statut de société mutuelle à un statut de société par actions

> **❝**
>
> However, if the lender is allowed to increase sales arbitrarily, it effectively has a blank cheque to draw on the borrower's money ... People who borrow from a building society which **demutualizes** are particularly vulnerable to this. Building societies, theoretically at least, act solely in their members' interests and have no interest in overcharging.
>
> **❞**

denationalization n dénationalisation f

denationalize vt dénationaliser

denominate vt Fin libeller; **denominated in dollars** libellé en dollars

denomination n Fin valeur f; (of share, banknote) coupure f; **coins of all denominations** pièces fpl de toutes valeurs; **small/large denominations** petites/grosses coupures fpl

department n (in company) service m; (in shop) rayon m; (of government) ministère m; **the sales/personnel department** le service commercial/personnel; **the toy department** le rayon des jouets ▫ Br **Department of Culture, Media and Sport** ministère de la culture, de la communication et des sports; Am **Department of Defense** ministère de la Défense; Br Formerly **Department of Education and Employment**, Am **Department of Education** ≃ ministère de l'Éducation; Br **Department for Education and Skills** ≃ ministère de l'Éducation nationale; Am **Department of Energy** ministère de l'Énergie; Br Formerly **Department of the Environment** ≃ ministère de l'Environnement; Br **Department for Environment, Food and Rural Affairs** ≃ ministère de l'environnement et des affaires rurales; Br **Department of Health**, Am **Department of Health**

and Human Services ministère de la Santé; Am **Department of Housing and Urban Development** ministère du logement et de la ville; Br **Department for International Development** secrétariat m d'État à la Coopération; Am **Department of the Interior** = ministère de l'Intérieur; Am **Department of Justice** ministère de la Justice; Am **Department of Labor** ministère de l'Emploi et de la Solidarité; **department manager** (in company) chef m de service; (in shop) chef de rayon; **department meeting** réunion f de service; Br **Department of Public Works** ≃ ministère de l'Équipement; Br **Department of Social Security** ≃ Sécurité f sociale; Am **Department of State** Département m d'État, ≃ ministère des Affaires étrangères; **department store** grand magasin m; Am **Department of Trade** ministère du Commerce; Br **Department of Trade and Industry** ministère du Commerce et de l'Industrie; Br **Department for Transport**, Am **Department of Transportation** ministère des Transports

departmental adj (in company) de service; (in shop) de rayon; (of government) de ministère ▫ **departmental manager** (in company) chef m de service; (in shop) chef de rayon; **departmental meeting** réunion f de service

departure n (from place) départ m; (from tradition) écart m; (from plan) modification f; **our departure was delayed for three hours** notre départ a été retardé de trois heures; **the introduction of bonuses was a departure from standard company policy** l'introduction de primes représentait une entorse à la politique habituelle de l'entreprise ▫ **departure list** liste f des départs; **departure lounge** (in airport) salle f d'embarquement; **departure time** heure f de départ

dependant n Admin, Law personne f à charge; **do you have any dependants?** avez-vous des personnes à charge?

deplete vt (stock) épuiser

depletion n (of stock) épuisement m

deposit 1 n **(a)** Banking dépôt m; **to make a deposit** déposer de l'argent; **to make a deposit of £500** déposer 500 livres en banque; **on deposit** en dépôt ▫ Br **deposit account** compte m livret, compte de dépôt; (when notice has to be given before withdrawal) compte à terme; **deposit bank** banque f de dépôt; **deposit book** livret m ou carnet m de dépôt; **deposit receipt** récépissé m de dépôt; **deposit slip** bordereau m ou bulletin m de versement

(b) (down payment) acompte m; (not returnable, for contract) arrhes fpl; (against damage) caution f; **to pay** or **put down a deposit on sth** verser un acompte/des arrhes sur qch; **he left £10 as a deposit** il a versé un acompte de 10 livres

2 *vt (money)* déposer; *(document) (with a bank)* mettre en dépôt (**with** dans); *(with a solicitor)* confier (**with** à); *Fin* **to deposit sth as security** nantir qch, gager qch; **you must deposit ten percent of the value of the house** vous devez faire un premier versement correspondant à dix pour cent de la valeur de la maison

depositary *n* dépositaire *mf*

deposition *vt Mktg (product)* dépositionner

depositor *n Banking* déposant(e) *m,f*

depository *n* (**a**) *(warehouse)* dépôt *m*, entrepôt *m* (**b**) *(person)* dépositaire *mf*

depot *n* dépôt *m*, entrepôt *m*

depreciable *adj* (**a**) *Am Fin* amortissable □ *depreciable base* assiette *f* de l'amortissement (**b**) *(liable to depreciation)* dépréciable

depreciate 1 *vt (value)* déprécier, rabaisser; *(goods)* faire perdre de la valeur à; *Acct (property, equipment)* amortir
2 *vi (of goods, money, currency, property, equipment)* se déprécier, se dévaloriser; *(of shares)* baisser; **the pound has depreciated against the dollar** la livre a reculé par rapport au dollar

depreciated *adj Acct* amorti(e); *(currency)* déprécié(e)

depreciation *n (of goods, money, currency, property, equipment)* dépréciation *f*, dévalorisation *f*; *(amount)* moins-value *f*; *(of shares)* moins-value, décote *f* □ *Acct depreciation accounting* comptabilité *f* de la dépréciation; *Acct depreciation charges* frais *mpl* d'amortissement; *Acct depreciation period* durée *f* d'amortissement, période *f* d'amortissement; *Acct depreciation provision* dotation *f* aux amortissements; *Acct depreciation rate* taux *m* d'amortissement; *Acct depreciation schedule* plan *m* d'amortissement

depressed *adj (market, trade)* déprimé(e); *(area, industry)* touché(e) par la crise; *(prices, profits, wages)* en baisse; **this is one of the most depressed sectors of the economy** c'est l'un des secteurs économiques les plus touchés par la crise; **the economy has been in a depressed state for nearly three years** l'économie est dans un état de marasme depuis bientôt trois ans

❝
What makes the difference in the UK is that people are more likely to get on their bikes from **depressed** areas to booming ones such as Cambridge than they are to seek work in Cologne. And if there are serious regional imbalances, the UK government has the power to spend proportionately more money on the needy regions – as it does in Northern Ireland.
❞

depression *n* dépression *f*, crise *f* économique; **the country's economy is in a state of depression** l'économie du pays est en crise

dept *n (abbr* **department)** service *m*

depth *n Mktg (of product)* profondeur *f* □ *depth interview* entretien *m* en profondeur

❝
The **depth interview** is a personal, face-to-face, qualitative interview lasting from 50 to 90 minutes. Usually, **depth interviews** are tape-recorded and transcribed. The **depth interview** is the most powerful and comprehensive of the various qualitative techniques.
❞

deputize 1 *vt* députer; **to deputize sb to do sth** députer qn pour faire qch
2 *vi* assurer l'intérim; **to deputize for sb** remplacer qn, assurer l'intérim de qn

deputy *n (assistant)* adjoint(e) *m,f*; *(temporary replacement)* remplaçant(e) *m,f*; **to act as deputy for sb** suppléer *ou* remplacer qn □ *deputy chairman* vice-président(e) *m,f*; *deputy director* directeur(trice) *m,f* adjoint(e); *deputy manager* sous-directeur(trice) *m,f*, directeur(trice) adjoint(e); *deputy managing director* directeur(trice) général(e) adjoint(e)

DEQ *adj (abbr* **delivered ex quay)** DEQ

deregulate *vt (industry, transport)* déréglementer, déréguler; *(prices, trade, wages)* libérer

deregulation *n (of industry, transport)* déréglementation *f*, dérégulation *f*; *(of prices, trade, wages)* libération *f*

derivative *n St Exch* instrument *m* financier à terme; **to deal in derivatives** faire le commerce des instruments financiers □ *derivative market* marché *m* à terme des instruments financiers

descending *adj Comptr descending order* ordre *m* décroissant; *descending sort* tri *m* en ordre décroissant

description *n (of goods)* désignation *f*

deselect *vt Comptr* désactiver

design 1 *n (composition, structure) (of car, computer etc)* conception *f*, design *m*; *(style)* modèle *m*; **our latest design** notre dernier modèle □ *design agency* agence *f* de design; *design department* bureau *m* d'études; *design engineer* ingénieur *m* d'études; *design engineering* étude *f* de conception; *design team* équipe *f* des concepteurs
2 *vt (plan)* concevoir; **they have designed a product to appeal to younger customers** ils ont conçu un produit ciblé sur le marché de la jeunesse; **this financial package is designed to meet the needs of small businesses** ces produits financiers ont été conçus pour répon-

dre aux besoins des petites entreprises

designer n (in advertising) créatif(ive) m,f; (in engineering, industry) dessinateur(trice) m,f

desire n Mktg (of consumer for product) désir m

desk n (in office) bureau m ❑ **desk calculator** calculatrice f de bureau; **desk diary** agenda m de bureau; **desk job** emploi m de bureau; Mktg **desk research** recherche f documentaire; **desk tray** corbeille f à courrier

deskill vt déqualifier

> Software has already made it easy for managers to do their own admin, and artificial intelligence promises to take over tasks much further up the value chain, eventually replacing large numbers of managerial and professional jobs while **deskilling** many others.

deskilling n déqualification f

desktop n Comptr (screen area) bureau m; **you will find the icon on your desktop** l'icône se trouve sur le bureau ❑ **desktop calculator** calculatrice f; Comptr **desktop computer** ordinateur m de bureau; **desktop publishing** publication f assistée par ordinateur, microédition f; **desktop publishing operator** opérateur(trice) m,f de publication assistée par ordinateur; **desktop publishing package** logiciel m de mise en page

despatch, despatcher etc = **dispatch, dispatcher** etc

destination n destination f ❑ Comptr **destination disk** (hard disk) disque m de destination; (floppy disk) disquette f de destination; Comptr **destination drive** lecteur m de destination; Mktg **destination purchase** achat m prévu

destock vt & vi déstocker

destocking n déstockage m

detail 1 n détail m; **details** (information) renseignements mpl; (name and telephone number) coordonnées fpl; **for further details** pour tous renseignements supplémentaires, pour de plus amples renseignements; **please send me details of your range of products** veuillez me faire parvenir une documentation sur votre gamme de produits; **let me take down your details** laissez-moi vos coordonnées
2 vt (enumerate, specify) détailler

determine vt (date, price) déterminer, fixer; (conditions) fixer

Deutschmark n Formerly (Deutsche) Mark m

devaluation n Econ dévaluation f

devalue vt Econ dévaluer; **the euro has been devalued by three percent** l'euro a été dévalué de trois pour cent

develop 1 vt (a) (skills, idea, market) développer; (product) mettre au point (b) Econ (country, region) mettre en valeur, développer
2 vi (a) (evolve) se développer; **we have developed into one of the leading companies in the field** nous sommes devenus l'une des entreprises les plus importantes dans ce domaine (b) Econ (of country, region) se développer

developer n Econ promoteur(trice) m,f

developing country n Econ pays m en voie de développement

development n (a) (of skills, idea, market) développement m; (of product) mise f au point (b) Econ (of country, region) mise f en valeur, développement m ❑ Br **development area** = zone économiquement sinistrée bénéficiant d'aides publiques en vue de sa conversion; **development assistance** crédits mpl de développement; **development capital** capital-développement m; **development company** société f exploitante ou d'exploitation; **development costs** coûts mpl de développement; **development grant** subvention f pour le développement; **development loan** crédit de développement; **development plan** plan m de développement; **development programme** programme m de développement; **development site** terrain m à lotir; Mktg **development stage** (of product) phase f de développement

device n Comptr (peripheral) unité f périphérique, périphérique m

devolution n (a) (of duty, power) délégation f (b) Law (of property, estate) transmission f, dévolution f (c) (in politics) décentralisation f

devolve vi (a) (of duty, power) incomber; **the responsibility devolves on him** la responsabilité lui incombe (b) Law (of property, estate) passer; **the property devolves on the son** les biens passent ou sont transmis au fils

DG n Admin (abbr **Director General**) directeur(trice) m,f général(e)

DHSS n (a) Br Formerly Admin (abbr **Department of Health and Social Security**) = ministère britannique de la Santé et de la Sécurité sociale (b) Am Admin (abbr **Department of Health and Social Services**) ≃ ministère m de la Santé

diagnostic audit n diagnostic m financier

diagram n schéma m; (graph) diagramme m, schéma

diagrammatic adj schématique

dial 1 n Am **dial code** indicatif m (téléphonique); Am **dial tone** tonalité f
2 vt (number) composer; (operator, country) appeler; **to dial a number** composer ou faire un numéro; **the number you have dialled has not been recognized** ≃ il n'y a pas d'abonné au

numéro que vous avez demandé

3 *vi* composer *ou* faire le numéro ; **to dial direct** obtenir une communication *ou* appeler par l'automatique

dialling, *Am* **dialing** *n Br* **dialling code** indicatif *m* (téléphonique) ; *Br* **dialling tone** tonalité *f*

dialogue, *Am* **dialog** *n* dialogue *m* ❑ *Comptr* **dialogue box** boîte *f* de dialogue ; *Comptr* **dialogue mode** mode *m* de dialogue ; *Comptr* **dialogue window** fenêtre *f* de dialogue

dial-up *n Comptr* **dial-up access** accès *m* commuté ; **dial-up account** compte *m* d'accès par ligne commutée ; **dial-up line** ligne *f* commutée ; **dial-up modem** modem *m* réseau commuté ; **dial-up service** service *m* de télétraitement

diarize *vt* inscrire dans son agenda

diary *n* agenda *m*

Dictaphone® *n* Dictaphone® *m*, appareil *m* à dicter

dictate 1 *vt* (**a**) *(letter)* dicter ; **to dictate sth to sb** dicter qch à qn (**b**) *(determine)* imposer ; **market conditions are dictated by the economic situation** la conjoncture du marché dépend de la situation économique
2 *vi* (**a**) *(dictate text)* dicter (**b**) *(give orders)* **to dictate to sb** donner des ordres à qn

dictating machine *n* appareil *m* à dicter

dictation *n* dictée *f*

differential 1 *n* écart *m*
2 *adj* différentiel(elle) ❑ **differential duties** droits *mpl* différentiels ; **differential pricing** établissement *m* des prix différentiels, tarification *f* différentielle ; **differential rate** taux *m* différentiel ; **differential tariff** tarif *m* différentiel

differentiated marketing *n* marketing *m* de différenciation, marketing différencié

differentiation *n* différenciation *f* ❑ **differentiation strategy** stratégie *f* de différenciation

digicash *n* monnaie *f* électronique

digit *n* chiffre *m*

digital *adj Comptr* numérique ❑ **digital analog(ue) converter** convertisseur *m* analogique numérique ; **digital audio tape** bande *f* numérique ; **digital data** données *fpl* numériques ; **digital display** affichage *m* numérique ; **digital exchange** central *m* numérique ; **digital optical disk** disque *m* optique numérique ; **digital readout** affichage numérique ; **digital signal** signal *m* numérique *ou* électronique ; **digital signature** signature *f* électronique ; **digital versatile disk** disque vidéo numérique ; **digital video disk** disque vidéo numérique

> E-commerce transactions are encrypted, but it is hard to verify that buyers and merchants are who they say they are. That is why Visa is urging a swifter adoption of the Secure Electronic Transaction (SET) protocol and a rapid move towards **digital signatures**.

digitally *adv Comptr* numériquement

digitization *n Comptr* numérisation *f*, digitalisation *f*

digitize *vt Comptr (data)* numériser, digitaliser ❑ **digitized image** image *f* digitalisée

digitizer *n Comptr* numériseur *m*

diluted *adj Fin, St Exch* **fully diluted earnings per share** bénéfice *m* net dilué par action

dilution *n Fin, St Exch* dilution *f* ❑ **dilution of equity** dilution du bénéfice par action ; **dilution of shareholding** dilution des actions

dilutive *adj Fin* à effet de dilution ❑ **dilutive effect** effet *m* de dilution

diminish 1 *vt (price, quality, value)* diminuer, réduire
2 *vi* diminuer, se réduire ; **their profits have diminished** leurs bénéfices ont diminué

diminishing *adj* décroissant(e) ; *(price, quality, value)* en baisse ❑ *Acct* **diminishing balance (method)** amortissement *m* linéaire ; *Econ* **diminishing marginal product** produit *m* marginal décroissant ; *Econ* **diminishing returns** rendements *mpl* décroissants ; **law of diminishing returns** loi *f* des rendements décroissants

> Norman Price, one of the industrialists seconded to the DTI's future and innovation unit, which carried out the survey, said there was a danger that companies invested in their established businesses at the expense of new activities. Increased capital investment in mature business might bring productivity improvements, but such investment was subject to the **law of diminishing returns**.

dinosaur *n Mktg* poids *m* mort, produit *m* dodo

dip 1 *n (in prices, value, figures)* baisse *f* ; **the winter months saw a sharp dip in profits** les bénéfices ont fortement baissé pendant l'hiver
2 *vi (of prices, value, figures)* baisser ; **shares dipped on the London Stock Market yesterday** les actions ont baissé à la Bourse des valeurs de Londres hier

diplex *adj Tel* duplex

dir *n* (**a**) *Admin (abbr* **director***)* directeur(trice) *m,f* (**b**) *Comptr (abbr* **directory***)* répertoire *m*

direct 1 *adj* **direct action** action *f* directe; *Comptr* **direct addressing** adressage *m* direct; **direct advertising** publicité *f* directe; **direct banking** banque *f* à distance; **direct competition** concurrence *f* directe; **direct costs** charges *fpl* directes, frais *mpl* directs; **direct cost accounting** (méthode *f* de) comptabilité *f* des coûts variables; **direct costing** méthode des coûts variables *ou* proportionnels; *Br Banking* **direct debit** prélèvement *m* (bancaire) automatique; **to pay by direct debit** payer par prélèvement automatique; *Br Banking* **direct debit advice** avis *m* de prélèvement; *Br Banking* **direct debit mandate** autorisation *f* de prélèvement; *Am Banking* **direct deposit** prélèvement (bancaire) automatique; **to pay by direct deposit** payer par prélèvement automatique; *Tel* **direct dialling** automatique *m*; **direct expenses** coûts *mpl* directs; **direct fixed costs** charges fixes directes, frais fixes directs; **direct flight** vol *m* direct; **direct investment** investissement *m* direct; **direct labour** main-d'œuvre *f* directe; **direct labour cost** prix *m* de la main-d'œuvre directe; **direct letter of credit** lettre *f* de crédit directe; *Tel* **direct line** ligne *f* directe; *Mktg* **direct mail** publipostage *m*; *Mktg* **direct mail advertising** publicité directe *ou* par publipostage; *Mktg* **direct mail campaign** campagne *f* de publicité directe; **direct marketing** marketing *m* direct; **direct marketing agency** agence *f* de marketing direct; **direct product profitability** rentabilité *f* directe du produit; **direct purchase** achat *m* direct; **direct purchasing** achat direct; **direct response advertising** publicité à réponse directe; **direct sale** vente *f* directe; **direct selling** vente directe; *Fin* **direct tax** impôt *m* direct; *Fin* **direct taxation** contributions *fpl* directes
2 *vt* *(company, work)* diriger; **to direct sb to do sth** ordonner à qn de faire qch

direct-dial *adj Tel* **direct-dial number** numéro *m* direct; **direct-dial telephone** ligne *f* téléphonique directe

direction *n* (**a**) *(of company)* direction *f*; **he will take over the direction of the group** il va prendre la direction du groupe (**b**) **directions** *(instructions)* instructions *fpl*, mode *m* d'emploi □ **directions for use** mode d'emploi

directive *n* directive *f*, instruction *f*

director *n* *(of company)* directeur(trice) *m,f*; *(board member)* administrateur(trice) *m,f* □ **directors' remuneration** rémunération *f* des administrateurs; **directors' report** rapport *m* annuel

directorate *n* (conseil *m* d')administration *f*

director-general *n* directeur(trice) *m,f* général(e)

directorship *n* direction *f*; **during his directorship** pendant sa direction; **he has been of-**

fered a directorship on lui a proposé un poste de directeur

directory *n* *(of telephone numbers)* annuaire *m*; *(of addresses)* répertoire *m* (d'adresses); *Comptr* *(of files)* répertoire □ *Br Tel* **directory enquiries** renseignements *mpl*; *Comptr* **directory structure** structure *f* arborescente

dirigisme *n Econ* dirigisme *m*

dirty *adj* (**a**) *(bill of lading)* clausé(e) (**b**) **dirty money** argent *m* sale *ou* mal acquis *ou* de source douteuse

> **"**
> Despite the strictest anti-money-laundering laws in the world, U.S. banks are still the involuntary custodians of up to $500 billion a year in **dirty money**. Even the $5 billion that drug cartels launder through the receivables departments of U.S. corporations ... passes through a U.S. bank at some point. The United States, says the Brookings Institution's Raymond Baker, is "the largest repository of ill-gotten gains in the world."
> **"**

disability *n* invalidité *f* □ **disability allowance** allocation *f* d'invalidité; **disability benefit** allocation d'invalidité; *Ins* **disability clause** = clause d'une police d'assurance-vie permettant à l'assuré de cesser tout paiement et de recevoir une pension en cas d'invalidité; **disability pension** pension *f* d'invalidité

disbursal *n Am* *(action)* déboursement *m*; *(payment)* debours *m*, dépense *f*

disburse *vt* débourser

disbursement *n* *(action)* déboursement *m*; *(payment)* debours *m*, dépense *f*

discharge 1 *n* (**a**) *Fin* *(of bankrupt)* réhabilitation *f* □ **discharge in bankruptcy** réhabilitation (**b**) *(dismissal)* renvoi *m* (**c**) *Fin* *(of debt)* liquidation *f*, acquittement *m*; *(of account, obligation)* paiement *m*, apurement *m*; **in full discharge** *(on bill)* pour acquit (**d**) *(of cargo)* déchargement *m*; *(of passengers)* débarquement *m*
2 *vt* (**a**) *Fin* *(bankrupt)* réhabiliter, décharger (**b**) *(dismiss)* congédier, renvoyer (**c**) *Fin* *(debt)* liquider, acquitter; *(fine)* payer; *(account, obligation)* apurer, payer, faire l'apurement de (**d**) *(cargo)* décharger; *(passengers)* débarquer

discharged bankrupt *n* failli(e) *m,f* réhabilité(e)

disciplinary *adj* disciplinaire □ **disciplinary action** mesures *fpl* disciplinaires; **to take disciplinary action (against sb)** prendre des mesures disciplinaires (contre qn); **disciplinary board** conseil *m* de discipline; **disciplinary hearing** séance *f* du conseil de discipline; **disci-**

plinary measure mesure *f* disciplinaire; *disciplinary procedure* procédure *f* disciplinaire

disclaimer *n* (**a**) *(denial)* démenti *m*, désaveu *m*; **to issue a disclaimer** publier un démenti (**b**) *Law* désistement *m*, renonciation *f*

disclosure *n St Exch* information *f* aux actionnaires ❑ *Acct* **disclosure of accounts** publication *f* des comptes; *St Exch* **disclosure threshold** seuil *m* d'annonce obligatoire

disconnect *vt (machine)* débrayer, désembrayer

discontinue *vt (production)* abandonner; *(product)* interrompre; **that item has been discontinued** cet article ne se fait plus ❑ *discontinued item* article *m* en fin de série; *discontinued line* fin *f* de série

discount 1 *n* (**a**) *(reduction in price)* remise *f*, rabais *m*; **to give sb a discount** faire une remise à qn; **to buy/sell sth at a discount** acheter/vendre qch au rabais; **to allow a discount of ten percent (on sth)** consentir un rabais de dix pour cent (sur qch) ❑ *discount card* carte *f* de réduction; *Am discount house* solderie *f*, magasin *m* de vente au rabais; *discount price* prix *m* réduit *ou* faible; *discount pricing* politique *f* de prix réduits *ou* faibles; **a large volume of sales is needed to make discount pricing successful** il faut un gros volume de ventes pour qu'une politique de prix réduits soit efficace; *discount rate* taux *m* d'escompte; *discount store* magasin de discount; *discount voucher* bon *m* de réduction
   (**b**) *Fin* escompte *m*; *discounts and allowances* remise, rabais, ristourne, RRR ❑ *discount bank (bank)* banque *f* d'escompte; *(organization)* = organisme qui escompte des traites ou des effets; *discount bond* obligation *f* émise au dessous du pair; *discount house* maison *f ou* comptoir *m* d'escompte; *discount loan* prêt *m* escompté; *discount market* marché *m* de l'escompte; *discount mechanism* mécanisme *m* de l'escompte; *discount operation* opération *f* d'escompte; *discount rate* taux *m* d'escompte
   2 *vt* (**a**) *(price)* baisser; *(goods)* solder
   (**b**) *Fin (bill, banknote)* escompter; *(sum of money)* faire une remise de, escompter

discountable *adj Fin* escomptable

discounted *adj Fin discounted bill* effet *m* escompté; *Acct discounted cash flow* cash-flow *m* actualisé, flux *mpl* de trésorerie actualisés; *Fin discounted rate* taux *m* d'escompte; *Acct discounted value* valeur *f* actualisée

discounter *n (person)* discounter *m*; *(shop)* solderie *f*, magasin *m* de vente au rabais

discounting *n* remise *f*; *Fin* escompte *m* ❑ *discounting bank* banque *f ou* maison *f* d'escompte; *discounting banker* banquier *m* escompteur

discrepancy *n* écart *m*, différence *f*; **there is a discrepancy in the accounts** les comptes ne sont pas justes

discretion *n (judgement)* jugement *m*; **at the manager's discretion** à la discrétion du directeur

discretionary *adj Banking discretionary account* compte *m* avec procuration, compte sous mandat de gestion; *discretionary costs* coûts *mpl* discrétionnaires; *discretionary fund* compte sous mandat de gestion; *Am discretionary income* revenu *m* disponible; *St Exch discretionary order* ordre *m* à appréciation; *discretionary portfolio* portefeuille *m* avec mandat; *discretionary powers* pouvoirs *mpl* discrétionnaires

discriminate *vi* **to discriminate in favour of sb/sth** favoriser qn/qch; **to discriminate against sb/sth** faire de la discrimination envers qn/qch; **to be discriminated against** être victime de discrimination

discriminating *adj Admin (duty, tariff)* différentiel(elle)

discrimination *n (bias)* discrimination *f*

discuss *vt* discuter de; **we can discuss the matter of pay rises at the next meeting** nous pourrons discuter des augmentations de salaires au cours de la prochaine réunion

discussion *n* discussion *f*; **to be under discussion** être en discussion; **to come up for discussion** être discuté(e) ❑ *Comptr discussion group* forum *m* de discussion

diseconomy *n* déséconomie *f*

disemploy *vt Am* remercier, congédier

dishonour, *Am* **dishonor** *vt Fin (bill, cheque)* ne pas accepter, ne pas honorer, refuser de payer; **dishonoured cheque** chèque *m* impayé *ou* non honoré

disincentive *n Econ* facteur *m* décourageant; **heavy taxation is a disincentive to expansion** les taxes élevées découragent toute expansion; **to act as a disincentive to sth** avoir un effet dissuasif sur qch

disincorporate 1 *vt (company)* ôter son statut de société à
   2 *vi (of company)* cesser de fonctionner en tant que société

disinflation *n Econ* désinflation *f*, déflation *f*

disinflationary *adj Econ* désinflationniste

disintermediation *n* désintermédiation *f*

disinvestment *n* désinvestissement *m*

disk *n Comptr* disque *m*; *(floppy)* disquette *f*; **to put sth on disk** enregistrer qch sur disque/disquette ❑ *disk access time* temps *m* d'accès disque; *disk box* boîte *f* à disquettes; *disk capacity* capacité *f* de disque/disquette; *disk con-*

troller contrôleur *m* de disque; *disk controller card* carte *f* contrôleur de disque; *disk copy* copie *f* de disquette; *disk drive* unité *f* ou lecteur *m* de disque/disquette; *disk error* erreur *f* disque; *disk file* fichier *m* disque; *disk fragmentation* fragmentation *f* de disque; *disk mailer* pochette *f* d'expédition de disquette; *disk memory* mémoire *f* à disque; *disk operating system* système *m* d'exploitation de disques; *disk space* espace *m* disque

diskette *n Comptr* disquette *f*; **on diskette** sur disquette ❑ *diskette box* boîte *f* à disquettes

dismiss *vt* (**a**) *(from job)* renvoyer, licencier (**b**) *Law (case)* classer; *(appeal)* rejeter

dismissal *n* (**a**) *(from job)* renvoi *m*, licenciement *m*; **dismissal without notice** licenciement sans préavis ❑ *dismissal procedure* procédure *f* de licenciement (**b**) *Law (of case)* classement *m*; *(of appeal)* rejet *m*

dispatch 1 *n (of letter, parcel, goods)* expédition *f*, envoi *m* ❑ *dispatch department* (service *m* des) expéditions *fpl*; *dispatch note* bulletin *m* ou bordereau *m* ou avis *m* d'expédition; *dispatch rider* coursier(ère) *m,f (à motocyclette)*
2 *vt (letter, parcel, goods)* expédier, envoyer; *(messenger)* envoyer, dépêcher

dispatcher *n* expéditeur(trice) *m,f*

dispatching *n (of letter, parcel, goods)* expédition *f*, envoi *m*

dispenser *n (for cash, drinks)* distributeur *m*

displaced share *n St Exch* action *f* déclassée

displacement *n St Exch* déclassement *m*

display 1 *n* (**a**) *(of goods)* étalage *m*, exposition *f* ❑ *display advertisement* placard *m* publicitaire; *display advertising* étalage publicitaire; *display area* espace *m* d'exposition; *display material* matériel *m* de présentation; *display pack* emballage *m* de présentation *ou* présentoir; *display space* surface *f* d'exposition; *display stand* présentoir *m*; *display unit* présentoir *m*; *display window* vitrine *f*, étalage (**b**) *Comptr (screen)* écran *m*; *(screen, display unit)* afficheur *m*; *(text appearing)* affichage *m* ❑ *display area* surface *f* ou zone *f* d'affichage; *display card* carte *f* d'affichage; *display speed* vitesse *f* d'affichage; *display unit* unité *f* d'affichage ou de visualisation
2 *vt* (**a**) *(goods)* étaler, exposer
(**b**) *Comptr* afficher, visualiser

displayed price *n* prix *m* affiché, prix à la vente

disposable 1 *n* disposables biens *mpl* de consommation non durables
2 *adj* (**a**) *(available)* disponible ❑ *disposable funds* disponibilités *fpl*, fonds *mpl* disponibles; *disposable income* revenu *m* disponible; *disposable personal income* revenu personnel dis-

ponible; *Law disposable portion* quotité *f* disponible (**b**) *(packaging, product)* jetable (**c**) *disposable goods* biens *mpl* de consommation non durables

disposal *n* (**a**) *(of goods, company, assets)* vente *f*; *(of property)* cession *f* (onéreuse), vente; *(of securities)* cession; **for disposal** à vendre, à céder (**b**) *(availability)* **to have sth at one's disposal** disposer de qch, avoir qch à sa disposition

▸ **dispose of** *vt insep (goods, property, securities, company, assets)* vendre

dispute 1 *n* dispute *f*, différend *m*; *(between management and workers)* conflit *m*; *Law* litige *m*; **to be in dispute with sb over sth** être en conflit avec qn sur qch; **in dispute is the right of employees to strike** l'enjeu des discussions est le droit des employés à faire grève
2 *vt (debate)* discuter, débattre; *(call into question)* contester

disruptive strike *n* grève *f* bouchon

dissolution *n (of company, partnership)* dissolution *f*

dissolve *vt (company, partnership)* dissoudre

distress *n Am distress merchandise* = marchandises écoulées à bas prix parce qu'elles sont endommagées ou pour permettre de régler des dettes importantes; *Am distress sale* soldes *fpl* avant fermeture

distressed area *n* quartier *m* défavorisé

distributable *adj (profits, reserves)* distribuable; *(dividend)* répartissable

distribute *vt (goods, work, profits, reserves)* distribuer; *(dividend)* répartir; **Hammond Ltd is the only company allowed to distribute our products** l'entreprise Hammond Ltd est notre distributeur exclusif

distribution *n* distribution *f*, diffusion *f*; *(of dividend)* répartition *f*; **wholesale and retail distribution** commerce *m* de gros et de détail ❑ *distribution agency* agence *f* de distribution; *distribution agent* agent *m* de distribution; *distribution centre* centre *m* de distribution; *distribution chain* chaîne *f* de distribution; *distribution channel* canal *m* de distribution; *distribution contract* contrat *m* de distribution; *distribution costs* frais *mpl* de distribution, coût *m* de la distribution; *distribution cycle* cycle *m* de la distribution; *distribution depot* dépôt *m* de distribution; *distribution market* marché *m* de la distribution; *distribution method* mode *m* de distribution; *distribution network* réseau *m* de distribution, circuit *m* de distribution; *distribution outlet* point *m* de distribution; *distribution planning* planning *m* de distribution; *distribution policy* politique *f* de distribution; *distribution process* processus *m* de distribution; *distribution ratio* ratio *m* de distribution; *distribution rights* droits *mpl* de distribution, droits de diffusion; *distribution system* système *m* de distribution

distributor *n* distributeur(trice) *m,f*; *(of particular make)* concessionnaire *mf* ❏ *distributor's brand* marque *f* de distributeur; *distributor discount* remise *m* du distributeur; *distributor's margin* marge *f* du distributeur; *distributor panel* panel *m* de distributeurs

distributorship *n* to have the distributorship for sth distribuer qch

district *n* région *f* ❏ *Am Law district attorney* ≃ procureur *m* de la République; *Br Admin district council* conseil *m* municipal; *Am Law district court* ≃ tribunal *m* d'instance (fédéral); *district manager* directeur(trice) *m,f* régional(e); *district tax collector* receveur *m* des finances

disturbed *adj St Exch (market)* agité(e)

div *n (abbr* **dividend**) div.

diversification *n* diversification *f*; **the company's recent diversification into cosmetics** la diversification qu'a récemment entreprise la société en pénétrant le marché des cosmétiques ❏ *diversification strategy* stratégie *f* de diversification

diversify 1 *vt (production, portfolio)* diversifier; **we must aim to diversify our product portfolio** il nous faut essayer de diversifier notre portefeuille de produits
  2 *vi (of company)* se diversifier; **the company diversified in the 1960s and started producing food products as well as tobacco** la société s'est diversifiée dans les années 1960 en se lançant dans la production de produits alimentaires en plus de celle du tabac; **to diversify into a new market** se diversifier en pénétrant un nouveau marché; **to diversify into a new product** se diversifier en fabriquant un nouveau produit

> ❝
> First, contrary to popular belief, high yield does not necessarily equate with high risk – as a well-**diversified** portfolio of high yield bonds has shown to deliver higher income with reduced volatility over longer periods of time.
> ❞

divest *vt Am (company)* vendre

divestiture, divestment *n Am* désinvestissement *m*; *Fin (of assets)* scission *f*

dividend *n Fin* dividende *m*; *(from cooperative society)* ristourne *f*; **the company has declared a dividend of ten percent** la société a déclaré un dividende de dix pour cent; **dividend on shares** dividende d'actions; **dividend per share** dividende par action; **cum dividend,** *Am* **dividend on** avec le dividende attaché; **ex divi-dend,** *Am* **dividend off** ex-dividende ❏ *dividend announcement* déclaration *f* de dividende; *dividend cover* taux *m* de couverture du dividende; *dividend mandate* ordonnance *f* de paiement; *dividend policy* politique *f* de dividendes; *dividend share* action *f* de jouissance; *dividend tax* impôt *m* sur les dividendes; *dividend warrant* chèque-dividende *m*, coupon *m* d'arrérages; *dividend yield* taux de rendement des actions *(en dividendes)*

dividend-price ratio *n Am St Exch* ratio *m* cours-bénéfice

division *n (of company, property, inheritance)* division *f* ❏ *division of labour* division du travail

divisional *adj* de division ❏ *divisional director* directeur(trice) *m,f* de la division; *divisional management* gestion *f* cellulaire; *divisional manager* directeur(trice) de la division; *Fin divisional money* monnaie *f* divisionnaire

DJIA *n St Exch (abbr* **Dow Jones Industrial Average**) DJIA *m*

DLO *n (abbr* **dead-letter office**) = bureau où est entreposé le courrier dont les destinataires sont introuvables

DM *n Mktg (abbr* **direct mail**) publipostage *m*

DNS *n Comptr (abbr* **Domain Name System**) système *m* de nom de domaine, DNS *m*

dock 1 *n* dock *m* ❏ *dock dues* droits *mpl* de dock; *dock strike* grève *f* des dockers; *dock warehouse* dock-entrepôt *m*; *Br dock worker* docker *m*
  2 *vt* (**a**) *(ship)* mettre à quai (**b**) *(wages)* faire une retenue sur; **you'll be docked £25** on retiendra 25 livres sur votre salaire
  3 *vi (of ship)* se mettre à quai

docker *n Br* docker *m*

docket 1 *n (on package)* fiche *f*; *(on delivery)* bordereau *m*; *(at customs)* récépissé *m*
  2 *vt (package)* mettre une fiche sur

docking station *n Comptr (for notebook)* station *f* d'accueil

doctor's certificate *n* certificat *m* médical, arrêt *m* de travail

document *n* document *m*; **documents against acceptance** documents contre acceptation; **documents against payment** documents contre paiement ❏ *document case* porte-documents *m*; *document collator* unité *f* de classement de documents; *document cover* pochette *f*; *Comptr document file* fichier *m* document; *document handling* manipulation *f* de documents; *document of payment* titre *m* de paiement; *Comptr document reader* lecteur *m* de documents

documentary *adj* documentaire ❏ *documentary bill* traite *f* documentaire; *documentary charges* frais *mpl* de crédit documentaire; *doc-*

umentary credit crédit *m* documentaire; **documentary credit application** demande *f* d'ouverture de crédit documentaire; **documentary credit department** service *m* des crédits documentaires; **documentary letter of credit** lettre *f* de crédit documentaire; **documentary remittance** remise *f* documentaire

documentation *n* documentation *f*

DoE *n* Br Formerly (abbr **Department of the Environment**) ≃ ministère *m* de l'Environnement

dog *n* Mktg (product) poids *m* mort, gouffre *m* financier

> 66
>
> For the marketing executive guessing the future is more than a routine parlour game to be indulged in at the beginning of each new year. Getting it right or getting it wrong is the difference between being regarded as a star or a **dog**.
>
> 99

DOL *n* Am (abbr **Department of Labor**) ≃ ministère de l'Emploi et de la Solidarité

dole *n* Br Fam Admin (indemnités *fpl* de) chômage *m*; **to be on the dole** être au chômage; **to go on the dole** s'inscrire au chômage □ **dole money** (indemnités de) chômage

dollar *n* dollar *m* □ Econ **dollar area** zone *f* dollar; **dollar balances** soldes *mpl* en dollars; **dollar bill** billet *m* d'un dollar; **dollar crisis** crise *f* du dollar; **dollar diplomacy** diplomatie *f* du dollar; **dollar exchange** change *m* du dollar; **dollar premium** prime *f* sur le dollar; **dollar rate** cours *m* du dollar; **dollar sign** symbole *m* dollar

dollar-cost averaging *n* = calcul du coût moyen en dollars; St Exch coût *m* moyen des actions achetées par sommes fixes

dollarization *n* dollarisation *f*

> 66
>
> The thought of dumping their own yo-yoing currencies for the strong and stable U.S. dollar has made many beleaguered central bankers swoon. And we're not just talking crisis economies such as Ecuador, which in 2000 jilted its inflation-prone sucre in favor of the dollar: Last April, Canada's second-largest bank proclaimed that **dollarization** is the "only viable option" to boost the country's ailing economy.
>
> 99

domain *n* Comptr domaine *m* □ **domain name** nom *m* de domaine; **Domain Name System** système *m* de nom de domaine

domestic *adj* (affairs, policy) intérieur(e); (currency, economy) national(e) □ **domestic airline** ligne *f* intérieure; Am **domestic mail** courrier *m* à destination de l'intérieur; **domestic market**

marché *m* intérieur; **domestic product** produit *m* ménager; **domestic products** denrées *fpl* du pays, produits *mpl* d'origine nationale; **domestic route** (in air travel) ligne intérieure; **domestic sales** ventes *fpl* domestiques; **domestic trade** commerce *m* intérieur

domicile 1 *n* Admin, Fin & Law domicile *m* **2** *vt* (**a**) Admin & Law (person) **domiciled at Leeds** domicilié ou demeurant à Leeds (**b**) Fin **bills domiciled in France** traites *fpl* payables en France □ **domiciled bill** effet *m* domicilié

domiciliation *n* Fin domiciliation *f* □ **domiciliation advice** avis *m* de domiciliation; **domiciliation file** dossier *m* de domiciliation; **domiciliation papers** dossier de domiciliation

dominant brand *n* Mktg marque *f* dominante

donation *n* Law donation *f*

done deal *n* = transaction dans laquelle les invendus ne peuvent être retournés au fournisseur; **the merger is not a done deal yet** (not finalized) la fusion n'est pas encore chose faite

donee *n* Law donataire *mf*

donor *n* Law donateur(trice) *m,f*

door drop *n* Mktg distribution *f* à domicile

door-knocking *n* porte-à-porte *m*

door-to-door *adj* **door-to-door delivery** livraison *f* à domicile; **door-to-door salesman** démarcheur *m*; **door-to-door selling** (vente *f* de) porte-à-porte *m*, vente à domicile

dormant *adj* Banking (account) sans mouvement

DOS *n* Comptr (abbr **disk operating system**) DOS *m* □ **DOS command** commande *f* DOS; **DOS prompt** indicatif *m* (du) DOS, invite *f* du DOS

dosh *n* Br Fam (money) fric *m*

dossier *n* dossier *m*

dot *n* (in e-mail address) point *m*

dotcom *n* (company) start-up *f*

> 66
>
> Having launched his website Teenfront.com from his bedroom aged 14 he had been offered a substantial chunk of cash in return for signing it over to London-based **dotcom** Rools.com. And if you are wondering why anyone would trust a schoolboy to run his own office and hand him a seven-figure cheque remember this was July 2000 – the height of the **dotcom** bubble.
>
> 99

dot-matrix printer *n* Comptr imprimante *f* matricielle

double *adj* (**a**) Comptr **double click** double-clic *m*; **double density** double densité *f*; **double density disk** disquette *f* (à) double densité

(b) *St Exch* **double option** stellage *m*, option *f* du double

(c) *Ins* **double insurance** assurance *f* cumulative; *Fin* **double taxation** double imposition *f*; *Fin* **double taxation agreement** convention *f* de double imposition

(d) **double time** *(pay)* salaire *m* double; **I get double time on Sundays** je suis payé le double le dimanche

(e) **to be in double figures** avoir atteint plus de dix; **inflation is now in double figures** l'inflation a passé la barre des dix pour cent

double-A rating *n St Exch* notation *f* AA

double-click *Comptr* **1** *vt* cliquer deux fois sur, double-cliquer
  2 *vi* cliquer deux fois, faire un double-clic (**on** sur)

double-digit *adj (salary, profit, inflation)* à deux chiffres

double-entry *adj Acct* **double-entry bookkeeping** comptabilité *f* en partie double, digraphie *f*; **double-entry method** principe *m* de la partie double

doubtful *adj Fin* **doubtful debt** créance *f* douteuse; **doubtful loan** prêt *m* douteux

Dow-Jones *n St Exch* **Dow Jones (Industrial) Average** *or* **Index** indice *m* Dow Jones

down 1 *adj* **(a)** *(not working)* **to be down** *(of computer)* être planté; **the network is down/has gone down** le réseau est planté/a planté; **the lines are down** les lignes sont en dérangement □ *Comptr* **down arrow** flèche *f* vers le bas; *Comptr* **down arrow key** touche *f* flèche vers le bas

  (b) **down payment** acompte *m*; **to make a down payment on sth** verser un acompte sur qch; **he made a down payment of £500** il a versé un acompte de 500 livres
  2 *adv (reduced, lower)* **the price of gold is down** le prix de l'or a baissé; **the pound is down two cents against the dollar** la livre a baissé de deux cents par rapport au dollar; **takings are several hundred pounds down on last year** les recettes ont baissé de plusieurs centaines de livres par rapport à l'année dernière; *Fin* **to be down twelve percent as against last year** être en baisse de douze pour cent par rapport à l'année précédente

downgrade *vt (job)* dévaloriser, déclasser; *(person)* rétrograder

download *Comptr* **1** *n* téléchargement *m* □ **download kit** kit *m* de téléchargeur; **download protocol** protocole *m* de téléchargement
  2 *vt* télécharger
  3 *vi* effectuer un téléchargement; **graphic files take a long time to download** le téléchargement de fichiers graphiques est très lent

downloadable *adj Comptr* téléchargeable

downloading *n Comptr* téléchargement *m*

downmarket, *Am* **downscale 1** *adj* bas de gamme
  2 *adv* **to move downmarket** se repositionner à la baisse

downside *n (trend)* **prices have tended to be on the downside** la tendance des prix est plutôt à la baisse □ *St Exch* **downside potential** potentiel *m* de baisse; *St Exch* **downside risk** risque *m* de baisse

downsize *vt (company)* réduire les effectifs de

downsizing *n* réduction *f* des effectifs; **we see downsizing as our only option if the company is to remain competitive** nous considérons qu'une réduction des effectifs est la seule solution possible si nous voulons rester compétitifs

``

> Men who were anxious about changes in the structure of their organisation were also approximately twice as likely to have time off sick. But those working in a company in which **downsizing** was likely were conversely far less likely to take time off – presumably fearing that more sickly workers would be far more likely to be made redundant.

``

downstream *adj (company)* en aval

downswing *n* tendance *f* à la baisse; **the recent downswing in interest rates** la récente tendance à la baisse des taux d'intérêt

downtick *n* **(a)** *(small decrease)* légère diminution *f* **(b)** *St Exch* = négociation d'un titre à un cours inférieur à celui de la négociation précédente

downtime *n* **(a)** *(of machine, factory, worker)* période *f* de non-productivité **(b)** *(time spent on task)* temps *m*; **how much downtime have you spent on this project?** combien de temps est-ce que tu as passé sur ce projet?

downtrend *n* tendance *f* à la baisse

downturn *n* ralentissement *m*; **there has been a recent downturn in profits** depuis peu les bénéfices sont en baisse; **Asian economies have experienced a significant downturn in recent years** l'économie des pays asiatiques a connu un net ralentissement ces dernières années

downward *adj* **the economy is on a downward path** l'économie est sur une mauvaise pente □ **downward market trend** tendance *f* du marché à la baisse; *Fin* **downward movement** mouvement *m* de baisse; **downward trend** tendance à la baisse

downward-compatible *adj Comptr* compatible vers le bas

Dow theory *n St Exch* théorie *f* de Dow

DP *n Comptr* (*abbr* **data processing**) traitement *m* des données, informatique *f*

dpi *Comptr* (*abbr* **dots per inch**) dpi, ppp

drachma *n Formerly* drachme *f*

draft 1 *n* (**a**) (*of letter*) brouillon *m*; (*of law, proposal*) avant-projet *m*; (*of speech*) premier jet *m* ❑ *draft agreement* protocole *m* d'accord; *draft budget* projet *m* de budget; *draft contract* projet de contrat; *draft letter* projet de contrat; *Comptr draft mode* mode *m* rapide *ou* brouillon, mode d'impression rapide, mode liste rapide; *Comptr draft printout* brouillon; *Comptr draft quality* (*of printout*) qualité *f* brouillon *ou* listing, qualité liste rapide; *Comptr draft quality printing* impression *f* en qualité brouillon; *Comptr draft version* version *f* brouillon
(**b**) *Fin* traite *f*, effet *m*; **to make a draft on sb** tirer sur qn
2 *vt* rédiger; (*letter*) faire le brouillon de; (*proposal*) rédiger; (*law, bill, contract*) préparer

draftsman,   draftswoman   *Am* = **draughtsman, draughtswoman**

drag *Comptr* **1** *n* **drag and drop** glisser-lâcher *m*
2 *vt* (*icon*) faire glisser; **to drag and drop sth** faire un glisser-lâcher sur qch
3 *vi* **to drag and drop** faire un glisser-lâcher

dragon bond *n St Exch* = titre émis en Asie mais libellé en dollars américains

drain *n* (*depletion*) perte *f*, épuisement *m*; **a drain on resources** une ponction sur les ressources

DRAM *n Comptr* (*abbr* **dynamic random access memory**) DRAM *f*

draughtsman, *Am* **draftsman** *n* dessinateur *m* industriel

draughtswoman, *Am* **draftswoman** *n* dessinatrice *f* industrielle

draw 1 *n Comptr* **draw program** logiciel *m* de dessin
2 *vt* (**a**) (*salary*) toucher; **to draw money from the bank** retirer de l'argent de la banque (**b**) *Fin* (*cheque, bill*) tirer; **to draw a cheque on one's account** tirer un chèque sur son compte (**c**) (*interest*) produire
3 *vi Fin* **to draw at sight** tirer à vue

▸ **draw out** *vt sep* (*money*) retirer

▸ **draw up** *vt sep* (*document, bill*) dresser, rédiger; (*account, budget, itinerary*) établir; (*programme, procedure*) dresser, établir; (*plan*) élaborer; (*bill of exchange*) créer

drawback *n Customs* rembours *m*

drawdown *n Fin* tirage *m*

"

Until now, anyone wanting to take advantage of **drawdown** had first to make the costly transfer into a personal pension plan. The new rules aim to make this unnecessary by extending **drawdown** to occupational money purchase schemes ... small, self-administered schemes ... executive pension plans ... additional voluntary contributions ... and individual or free-standing AVCs.

"

---

drawee *n Fin* (*of bill*) tiré *m*, payeur *m*

drawer *n Fin* tireur *m*; (*of bill*) souscripteur *m*; **to refer a cheque to drawer** refuser d'honorer un chèque

drawing *n* (**a**) (*of sum*) prélèvement *m*, retrait *m* (**b**) *Fin* (*of cheque, bill*) traite *f* ❑ *drawing account* compte *m* courant, compte de dépôt à vue; *drawing rights* droits *mpl* de tirage

dress-down Friday *n* = fait pour une société d'autoriser ses employés à porter une tenue décontractée le vendredi

---

"

The **dress-down-Friday** policies of various companies are being reversed; London nightclub Annabel's, after a brief fling with relaxing its dress codes, decided to reinstate them ... And Moss Bros is abandoning its casualwear brand, Code, to concentrate on the more formal side of its business.

"

---

drift *n* (*of prices, salaries*) tendance *f* à la hausse

drip advertising *n Mktg* publicité *f* continue, publicité goutte à goutte

drip-feed *vt* (*company*) perfuser

drive *n* (**a**) (*campaign*) campagne *f*; **the company is having a sales drive** la société fait une campagne de vente (**b**) *Comptr* (*for disk*) lecteur *m*, unité *f*; **drive a:/b:** unité de disque a:/b:

▸ **drive down** *vt sep Econ* (*prices, inflation*) faire baisser

▸ **drive up** *vt sep Econ* (*prices, inflation*) faire monter

driver *n Comptr* programme *m* de gestion, pilote *m*, gestionnaire *m* (de périphérique)

drop 1 *n* (**a**) (*in prices, inflation*) chute *f*, baisse *f* (**in** de); **sales show a drop of ten percent** les ventes accusent une baisse de dix pour cent (**b**) (*delivery*) livraison *f*; **I have four drops to make** j'ai quatre livraisons à faire ❑ *drop shipment* = envoi commercial facturé à un grossiste mais expédié directement au détaillant
2 *vt Comptr* (*icon*) lâcher
3 *vi* (*of prices, inflation*) baisser; **sales have dropped by ten percent** les ventes ont baissé

de dix pour cent; *St Exch* **shares dropped a point** les actions ont reculé d'un point; *St Exch* **the pound dropped three points against the dollar** la livre a reculé de *ou* a perdu trois points par rapport au dollar

drop-dead *adj* **drop-dead fee** commission *f* de désintéressement; **drop-dead rate** taux *m* de désintéressement

drop-down menu *n Comptr* menu *m* déroulant

drug *n* **a drug on the market** *(product)* un produit invendable

dry *adj* **dry cargo** cargaison *f* sèche; **dry goods** *Br* marchandises *fpl* sèches; *Am* tissus *mpl* et articles de bonneterie

DSL *n Comptr* (*abbr* **Digital Subscriber Line**) ligne *f* d'abonné numérique, DSL *f*

DSS *n Br Admin* (*abbr* **Department of Social Security**) ≃ Sécurité *f* sociale

DTI *n Br* (*abbr* **Department of Trade and Industry**) ≃ ministère *m* du Commerce et de l'Industrie

DTP *n Comptr* (*abbr* **desktop publishing**) PAO *f* ▫ **DTP operator** opérateur(trice) *m,f* de PAO; **DTP software** logiciel *m* de PAO

dual *adj EU* **dual circulation** *(of currencies)* double circulation *f; EU* **dual circulation period** période *f* de double circulation; **dual currency** deux monnaies *fpl; St Exch* **dual exchange market** double marché *m* des changes; *St Exch* **dual listing** cotation *f* sur deux Bourses; **dual ownership** copropriété *f;* **dual pricing** régime *m* du double prix; *(showing prices in national currency and in euros)* double affichage *m* (des prix)

dual-band *adj Tel* bibande

dual-branded *adj Mktg* sous marque double

dual-currency *adj (system)* bimonétaire

dud *adj (banknote, coin)* faux (fausse); *(debt)* exigible; *(bill)* payable

due 1 *n* **dues** *(membership fees)* cotisation *f*
  2 *adj (owed)* dû (due); *(debt)* exigible; *(bill)* payable; **when is the next instalment due?** quand le prochain versement doit-il être fait?; **I'm due three days' holiday** j'ai trois jours de congé à prendre; **I'm due a rise** j'attends une augmentation de salaire ▫ **due date** date *f* d'échéance, date d'exigibilité

due-date *vt* coter

dull *adj Fin (market)* calme, inactif(ive); **business is dull** les affaires ne marchent pas fort ▫ **dull season** morte-saison *f*

duly *adv (properly)* dûment; *(as expected)* comme prévu; **a duly authorized representative** un(e) représentant(e) dûment accrédité(e); **I duly received your letter of 8 March** j'ai bien reçu votre lettre du 8 mars

dummy 1 *n (product)* objet *m* factice; *(book)* maquette *f*
  2 *adj* factice ▫ **dummy company** société *f* écran *ou* fictive; **dummy pack** emballage *m* factice

dump 1 *n* **dump bin** panier *m* de présentation en vrac, panier présentoir
  2 *vt* **to dump goods** faire du dumping
  3 *vi* faire du dumping

dumper *n (company)* = entreprise pratiquant le dumping

dumping *n (of goods)* dumping *m*

dun *vt* presser, harceler; **to dun sb for money** *or* **payment** presser *ou* harceler qn pour qu'il paye

dunning notice *n* rappel *m*

duopoly *n* duopole *m*

duopsony *n* duopsone *m*

duplex *adj Tel* duplex

duplicate 1 *n (of document, receipt)* duplicata *m*, double *m*; **in duplicate** en double, en deux exemplaires
  2 *adj* double, en double; **a duplicate receipt** un duplicata du reçu ▫ **duplicate copy** duplicata *m*
  3 *vt (document, receipt)* faire un duplicata *ou* un double de; *(on photocopier)* faire une photocopie de

durable 1 *n* **durables** biens *mpl* (de consommation) durables *ou* non périssables
  2 *adj* durable ▫ **durable goods** biens *mpl* (de consommation) durables *ou* non périssables

duration *n (of lease)* durée *f*

Dutch auction *n* vente *f* à la baisse, enchères *fpl* au rabais

dutiable *adj* taxable; *Customs* soumis(e) aux droits de douane

duty *n Customs* droit *m*; **to pay duty on sth** payer un droit *ou* une taxe sur qch; **liable to duty** passible de droits, soumis(e) aux droits; **duty paid** droits acquittés

duty-free *Customs* **1** *n* **(a)** *(goods)* marchandises *fpl* hors taxe, marchandises *fpl* en franchise **(b)** *(shop)* magasin *m* hors taxe
  2 *adj (goods)* hors taxe, en franchise ▫ **duty-free allowance** = quantité de produits hors taxe autorisée; **duty-free entry** admission *f* en franchise; **duty-free import** importation *f* en franchise; **duty-free shop** magasin *m* hors taxe; **duty-free zone** zone *f* franchise

duty-paid *adj Customs (goods)* acquitté(e), dédouané(e)

DVD *n Comptr* (*abbr* **Digital Versatile Disk, Digital Video Disk**) DVD *m*, disque *m* vidéo numérique

dynamic *adj (company, economy)* dynamique ▫ *Comptr* **dynamic data exchange** échange *m* de données dynamiques; *Comptr* **dynamic HTML** HTML *m* dynamique; *Comptr* **dynamic RAM** mémoire *f* RAM dynamique

Ee

E & OE *Br Acct (abbr* **errors and omissions excepted)** SE & O

early *adj* (**a**) **at your earliest convenience** *(in correspondence)* dans les meilleurs délais; **what is your earliest possible delivery date?** quand est-ce que vous pouvez livrer, au plus tôt? ❑ *early closing (of shops)* = jour où l'on ferme tôt; *Fin* **early redemption** amortissement *m* anticipé; *early retirement* retraite *f* anticipée; **to take early retirement** partir en retraite anticipée
(**b**) *Mktg* **early adopter** réceptif *m* précoce; **early majority** majorité *f* innovatrice

earmark *vt (funds)* assigner, affecter (**for** à); **this money has been earmarked for research** cet argent a été affecté à la recherche

earn *vt (money)* gagner; *(interest)* rapporter; **how much do you earn?** combien gagnez-vous?; **to earn a** *or* **one's living** gagner sa vie; **their money is earning a high rate of interest** leur argent est rémunéré à un taux élevé

earned *adj Fin* **earned income** revenus *mpl* salariaux; **earned income allowance** = déduction au titre de revenus salariaux ou professionnels; *Am Admin* **earned income credit** = aide aux foyers à revenu faible, prélevée sur les salaires; **earned interest** revenu *m* des intérêts; *Acct* **earned surplus** bénéfices *mpl* non distribués

earner *n (person)* salarié(e) *m,f;* **one of the biggest earners in the company** un des plus gros salaires de l'entreprise; **this product is the biggest profit earner in our range** de toute notre gamme, ceci est le produit qui rapporte le plus

earning *adj* **earning capacity, earning potential** *(of person)* revenu *m* potentiel; *(of company)* rentabilité *f*, capacité *f* bénéficiaire

earnings *npl (of person)* salaire *m*, revenus *mpl;* *(of company)* revenus; **earnings before interest and tax** bénéfices *mpl* avant impôts et charges; **earnings per share** bénéfice *m* par action ❑ **earnings forecast** résultats *mpl* prévisionnels; **earnings growth** accroissement *m ou* augmentation *f* des bénéfices; **earnings retained** bénéfices non distribués

earnings-related *adj* proportionnel(elle) au revenu ❑ **earnings-related pension** retraite *f* indexée sur le revenu

earnout *n* = supplément de prix payable éventuellement en fonction des bénéfices futurs

(dans le cadre de l'acquisition d'une entreprise)

> ❝
> BTI acquires Atlanta-based Internet solutions firm Max Commerce Inc. for $3 million in cash and stock. The next 18 months may see the facilities-based integrated communications provider pay out an additional **earnout** provision of $9 million based upon certain performance objectives.
> ❞

EAS *n Br (abbr* **Enterprise Allowance Scheme)** fonds *m* d'aide à la création d'entreprise

easy *adj* (**a**) **by easy payments, on easy terms** avec facilités de paiement (**b**) *St Exch (market)* tranquille (**c**) *Fam* **easy money** argent *m* facile

EBIT *npl (abbr* **earnings before interest and tax)** bénéfices *mpl* avant impôts et charges

EBITDA *n (abbr* **earnings before interest, tax, depreciation and amortization)** EBITDA *m*

e-book *n* livre *m* numérique, livre électronique, e-book *m*

EBRD *n (abbr* **European Bank of Reconstruction and Development)** BERD *f*

e-broker *n St Exch* courtier(ère) *m,f* électronique

e-broking *n St Exch* courtage *m* électronique

e-business *n Comptr* commerce *m* électronique

> ❝
> The limited impact of **e-business** on traditional companies was underlined yesterday by a survey showing that more than three-quarters of firms generate less than 5% of their sales from **e-business**. "At the moment the figure is so low because companies are still at the stage between having a website for information purposes and having a website for trading and doing **e-business**", said Nigel Hickson, head of **e-business** for the CBI.
> ❞

EC *n (abbr* **European Community)** CE *f*

e-cash *n Comptr* argent *m* électronique, argent virtuel, e-cash *m*

ECB *n (abbr* **European Central Bank)** BCE *f*

ECGD *n Br (abbr* **Export Credit Guarantee Department)** ≃ COFACE *f*

echelon *n* échelon *m*; **the higher echelons of industry** les échelons supérieurs de l'industrie

ECM *n Am* (*abbr* **European Common Market**) Marché *m* commun européen

ECN *n St Exch* (*abbr* **electronic communications network**) marché *m* électronique privé

ecodevelopment *n* écodéveloppement *m*

ECOFIN *n Fin* (*abbr* **Economic and Financial Council of Ministers**) Conseil *m* Ecofin

e-commerce *n Comptr* commerce *m* électronique; **e-commerce is being recognized as a major on-line service** le commerce électronique devient un service en ligne très important

> **❝**
>
> Suddenly, electronic commerce seems to be everywhere, leaving traditional companies wondering what to do next. Is **e-commerce** yet another fad? ... In "e-Profit," Cohan acknowledges the uncertainties but argues that "**e-commerce** is a force that is not likely to fade ... All companies will eventually be forced to rethink their strategies, management structure and business operations in light of the economic benefits that **e-commerce** enables."
>
> **❞**

econometric *adj* économétrique □ *econometric model* modèle *m* économétrique

econometrician *n* économétricien(enne) *m,f*

econometrics *n* économétrie *f*

economic *adj* (**a**) (*relating to the economy*) économique □ *economic activity tables* tableaux *mpl* d'activité économique; *economic adviser* conseiller(ère) *m,f* économique; *economic agent* acteur *m ou* agent *m* économique; *economic aid* aide *f* économique; *economic analysis* analyse *f* économique; *economic appraisal* évaluation *f* économique; *economic authorities* instances *fpl* économiques; *economic boom* essor *m* économique; *economic climate* climat *m* économique; *economic cost* coût *m* économique; *economic council* conseil *m* économique; *economic crisis* crise *f* économique; *economic cycle* cycle *m* conjoncturel *ou* économique; *economic development* croissance *f* par habitant *ou* per capita; *economic downturn* ralentissement *m* économique; *economic efficiency* efficacité *f* économique; *economic embargo* embargo *m* économique; *economic factor* facteur *m* économique; *economic forces* forces *fpl* économiques; *economic forecast* prévisions *fpl* économiques; *economic growth* croissance *f ou* expansion *f* économique; *economic growth rate* taux *m* de croissance *ou* d'expansion économique; *economic indicator* indicateur *m* économique; *economic integration* intégration *f* économique; *economic interest group* groupement *m* d'intérêt

économique; *economic life* (*of machinery, product*) vie *f* économique, durée *f* de vie utile; *economic lot size* série *f* économique; *economic machinery* mécanismes *mpl* économiques; *economic measure* mesure *f* économique; *EU Economic and Monetary Union* Union *f* économique et monétaire; *economic order quantity* quantité *f* économique de commande; *economic performance* résultats *mpl* économiques; *economic plan* plan *m* économique; *economic planning* planification *f* économique; *economic player* acteur *ou* agent économique; *economic policy* politique *f* économique; *economic principles* principes *mpl* économiques; *economic profit* résultat économique; *economic prospects* prévisions conjoncturelles *ou* économiques; *economic rate of return* taux de rentabilité économique; *economic recession* récession *f* économique; *economic recovery* reprise *f ou* redressement *m* économique; *economic research* étude *f* économique; *economic revival* relance *f* économique; *economic sanctions* sanctions *fpl* économiques; *economic sector* secteur *m* économique; *economic situation* conjoncture *f* économique; *economic slump* dépression *f* économique; *economic stranglehold* mainmise *f* économique; *economic strategy* stratégie *f* conjoncturelle; *economic trend* tendance *f ou* conjoncture économique; *economic union* union économique; *Acct economic value added* valeur *f* ajoutée économique; *economic warfare* guerre *f* économique

(**b**) *Br* (*profitable*) rentable; **to make sth economic** rentabiliser qch □ *economic batch* série *f* économique; *economic batch quantity* effectif *m* de série économique

economical *adj* (*person*) économe; (*machine, method, approach*) économique

economically *adv* (**a**) (*relating to the economy*) économiquement (**b**) (*with economy*) de manière économe; **economically viable** (*campaign, product, project*) économiquement viable

economics **1** *n* (*science*) économie *f*
2 *npl* (*profitability*) rentabilité *f*; (*financial aspects*) aspects *mpl* financiers; **we must consider the economics of the project before making any decisions** nous devons considérer l'aspect financier du projet avant de prendre une décision

economism *n* économisme *m*

economist *n* économiste *mf*

economize *vi* économiser, faire des économies (**on** sur); **the recession has led to a need to economize throughout the company** la récession a conduit au besoin d'économiser dans toute l'entreprise

economy *n* économie *f*; **to practise economy** économiser, épargner; **to make economies**

faire des économies; **it's (a) false economy** ce n'est pas vraiment rentable; **economies of scale** économies *fpl* d'échelle ❑ *economy brand* marque *f* économique; *economy class (in air travel)* classe *f* économique; *economy drive (of company, government)* politique *f* de réduction des dépenses; **I'm on an economy drive at the moment** j'essaie d'économiser en ce moment; *economy measure* mesure *f* de réduction des dépenses; **as an economy measure** par mesure d'économie; *economy pack* paquet *m* économique

ecotax *n* taxe *f* écologique, écotaxe *f*

ecotourism *n* écotourisme *m*

ECP *n EU (abbr* **euro-commercial paper**) billet *m* de trésorerie *(émis sur le marché des eurodevises)*

ECSC *n (abbr* **European Coal and Steel Community**) CECA *f*

ECSDA *n Fin (abbr* **European Central Securities Depositories Association**) association *f* européenne des dépositaires centraux de titres

ECU, ecu *n Formerly EU (abbr* **European Currency Unit**) ÉCU *m*, écu *m*

ed. *n* (**a**) *(abbr* **editor**) éd., édit (**b**) *(abbr* **edited**) sous la dir. de, coll (**c**) *(abbr* **edition**) éd., édit

EDGAR *n Fin (abbr* **electronic data gathering, analysis and retrieval**) = banque de données créée par la commission américaine des opérations de Bourse (le SEC), qui contient toutes sortes d'informations sur de nombreux fonds communs de placement et entreprises publiques

❝ ────────────

VeriSign, Inc., the leading provider of Internet trust services, announced today that it has been selected to provide Internet authentication and payment services for the Securities and Exchange Commission's (SEC) Electronic Data Gathering, Analysis, and Retrieval (**EDGAR**) system. VeriSign will deliver a customized service for digital certificate-based authentication to enable U.S. public companies to digitally sign and securely transmit **EDGAR** filings, in real-time, over the Internet.

──────────── ❞

EDI *n* (**a**) *Fin (abbr* **European Data Interchange**) EED *m* (**b**) *Comptr (abbr* **Electronic Data Interchange**) EDI *m*

edit *vt* (**a**) *(article, text)* corriger, réviser; *(prepare for publication)* éditer (**b**) *Comptr (text)* éditer

editing *n* (**a**) *(of article, text)* correction *f*, révision *f*; *(preparation for publication)* édition *f* (**b**) *Comptr* édition *f* ❑ *editing window* fenêtre *f* d'édition

edition *n (of book, newspaper)* édition *f*

editor *n* (**a**) *(of newspaper, magazine)* rédacteur(trice) *m,f* en chef; *(of article, book)* rédacteur(trice) (**b**) *Comptr (software)* éditeur *m*

editorial 1 *n (article)* éditorial *m*; *(department)* service *m* de la rédaction, rédaction *f*
  2 *adj (decision, comment)* de la rédaction; *(job, skills)* de rédaction ❑ *editorial content* contenu *m* rédactionnel; *editorial freedom* liberté *f* des rédacteurs; *editorial opinion (in press)* avis *m* éditorial; *editorial policy* politique *f* éditoriale; *(in press)* politique de la rédaction

editorialize *vi* émettre des opinions personnelles, être subjectif(ive); **as** *The Times* **editorialized,...** comme l'affirmait l'éditorial du *Times*,...

editorship *n* rédaction *f*; **during her editorship** quand elle dirigeait la rédaction

.edu *Comptr* = abréviation désignant les universités et les sites éducatifs dans les adresses électroniques

EEA *n EU (abbr* **European Economic Area**) EEE *m*

EEB *n EU (abbr* **European Environmental Bureau**) BEE *m*

EEC *n Formerly (abbr* **European Economic Community**) CEE *f*

EEOC *n Am (abbr* **Equal Employment Opportunity Commission**) = commission pour l'égalité des chances d'emploi aux États-Unis

❝ ────────────

Recent large settlements obtained by the **EEOC** include the $18 million settlement of sexual and racial harassment claims with Ford Motor Company in September 1999 and a $28 million settlement of an age discrimination case with Johnson & Higgins, Inc. in July 1999. One year before, the **EEOC** had obtained the largest amount ever paid in the resolution of a sexual harassment case, when Mitsubishi Motor Manufacturing of America agreed to pay $34 million to settle a class action lawsuit filed by the **EEOC** in April 1996.

──────────── ❞

effect 1 *n* (**a**) **to put sth into effect** *(regulation, law)* mettre qch en pratique *ou* en application; **to come into** *or* **take effect** entrer en vigueur; **to remain in effect** demeurer en vigueur; *Br* **with effect from 1 January** applicable à compter du 1er janvier
  (**b**) *(meaning)* sens *m*, teneur *f*; **we have made provisions to this effect** nous avons pris des dispositions dans ce sens
  2 *vt (payment)* effectuer; *(sale, purchase)* réaliser, effectuer

effective *adj* (**a**) *Econ (yield, return, production)* effectif(ive); *(value)* réel(elle) ❑ *effective an-*

nual rate taux *m* annuel effectif; **effective capacity** capacité *f* effective; **effective income** revenu *m* réel; **effective life** *(of product, structure)* durée *f* de vie effective; **effective management** direction *f* *ou* gestion *f* efficace; **effective tax rate** taux d'imposition effectif

   (b) *(regulation, law)* **to become effective** entrer en vigueur; **effective as from 10 October** applicable à compter du 10 octobre ◘ **effective date** date *f* d'entrée en vigueur

efficiency *n* *(of person, company, method)* efficacité *f*; *(of machine)* rendement *m* ◘ **efficiency bonus** prime *f* d'efficacité

efficient *adj* *(person, company, method)* efficace; *(machine)* à haut rendement; **we must make more efficient use of the marketing team** nous devons utiliser notre équipe de marketing de manière plus efficace

efflux, effluxion *n* *(of capital)* exode *m*

EFT *n Comptr* *(abbr* **electronic funds transfer**) transfert *m* de fonds électronique

EFTA *n* *(abbr* **European Free Trade Association**) AELE *f*

EFTPOS *n Comptr* *(abbr* **electronic funds transfer at point of sale**) transfert *m* de fonds électronique sur point de vente

EFTS *n Comptr* *(abbr* **electronic funds transfer system**) = système électronique de transfert de fonds

EGA *n Comptr* *(abbr* **enhanced graphics adapter**) EGA *m*

EGM *n* *(abbr* **extraordinary general meeting**) AGE *f*

e-government *n* administration *f* électronique

> 66
> Departments have raised several concerns about meeting the **e-government** deadline and the report makes several recommendations. Just over half of the 524 services that government departments routinely provide are currently delivered online. But the report pointed out that few are transactional services that allow the public to interact with government.
> 99

EIB *n* *(abbr* **European Investment Bank**) BEI *f*

eighty/twenty rule, 80/20 rule *n Fin* règle *f* 80/20

elastic *adj Econ* *(market, supply, demand)* élastique

elasticity *n Econ* *(of market, supply, demand)* élasticité *f*

electronic *adj Comptr* électronique ◘ **electronic banking** transactions *fpl* bancaires électroniques, bancatique *f*; **electronic billing ma-**

chine caisse *f* électronique; **electronic cash** argent *m* *ou* monnaie *f* électronique; **electronic commerce** commerce *m* électronique; **electronic computer** calculateur *m* électronique; **electronic data interchange** échange *m* de données informatisé; **electronic data processing** traitement *m* électronique de l'information; **electronic directory** annuaire *m* électronique; **electronic funds transfer** transfert *m* de fonds électronique; **electronic funds transfer at point of sale** transfert de fonds électronique au point de vente; **electronic funds transfer system** système *m* électronique de transfert de fonds; **electronic journal** journal *m* électronique; **electronic mail** courrier *m* électronique; **electronic mailbox** boîte *f* à *ou* aux lettres électronique; **electronic mall** galeries *fpl* électroniques; **electronic money** argent électronique, argent virtuel; **electronic newspaper** journal électronique; **electronic office** bureau *m* informatisé; **electronic payment** paiement *m* électronique; **electronic payment terminal** terminal *m* électronique de paiement; **electronic point of sale** point *m* de vente électronique; **electronic purse** porte-monnaie *m* électronique; **electronic shopping** achats *mpl* en ligne *ou* par Internet; *St Exch* **electronic trading** transactions boursières électroniques; **electronic transfer** transfert de fonds électronique

> 66
> Shop globally. Buy locally. That's the message from a number of Nashville merchants who are finding e-Commerce success in a locally-targeted **electronic mall**. GetIt-Nashville.com is an electronic shopping mall that features Nashville businesses and targets local shoppers.
> 99

eligibility *n* *(for job)* admissibilité *f* (**for** à); *(for grant, benefit)* droit *m* (**for** à)

eligible *adj* **(a)** *(for job)* admissible (**for** à); **to be eligible for a pension/a tax rebate** avoir droit à une retraite/un dégrèvement fiscal **(b)** *Br Fin* **eligible bill** effet *m* escomptable; *Am Fin* **eligible paper** effet escomptable

EMA *n* *(abbr* **European Monetary Agreement**) AME *m*

e-mail *Comptr* **1** *n* courrier *m* électronique; **to contact sb by e-mail** contacter qn par courrier électronique; **to send sth by e-mail** envoyer qch par courrier électronique; **to check one's e-mail** consulter sa boîte à lettres électronique ◘ **e-mail account** compte *m* de courrier électronique; **e-mail address** adresse *f* électronique; **e-mail client** client *m* de messagerie électronique; **e-mail software** logiciel *m* de courrier électronique

   2 *vt* *(person)* envoyer un courrier électronique

à; *(document)* envoyer par courrier électronique; **e-mail us at...** envoyez-nous vos messages à l'adresse suivante...

e-marketer *n Comptr* web marketeur *m*, e-marketer *m*

> "
>
> To succeed in the Net Future, an **e-marketer** must harness customer expectations by maximizing the present and future value of customer interactions online and offline, in the virtual mall of the Internet and in the brick-and-mortar walls of a conventional store.
>
> "

e-marketing *n Comptr* marketing *m* électronique

embargo 1 *n* embargo *m*; **to lay** *or* **put an embargo on sth** mettre l'embargo sur qch; **to be under an embargo** *(of ship, goods)* être séquestré(e); **to lift an embargo** lever un embargo
2 *vt* mettre l'embargo sur

embark *vt* prendre à bord, embarquer

embarkation *n* embarquement *m*

embezzle 1 *vt (money, funds)* détourner
2 *vi* commettre des détournements de fonds; **to embezzle from a company** détourner les fonds d'une société

embezzlement *n* embezzlement **(of funds)** détournement *m* de fonds

embezzler *n* auteur *m* d'un détournement de fonds

emergency *n* **emergency fund** fond *m* de secours; **emergency measures** mesures *fpl* d'urgence; **emergency powers** pouvoirs *mpl* extraordinaires; **emergency tax** impôt *m* extraordinaire

emerging market *n* marché *m* émergent

EMI *n (abbr* **European Monetary Institute)** IME *m*

emission *n (of banknotes, currency)* émission *f*

emit *vt (banknotes, currency)* émission *f*

emolument *n* emoluments émoluments *mpl*, rémunération *f*

e-money *n Comptr* argent *m* électronique, argent virtuel

emoticon *n Comptr* émoticon *m*

emotional *adj Mktg (reaction, response)* émotionnel(elle) ❑ **emotional purchase** achat *m* d'émotion

> "
>
> The importance of image in fashion retailing cannot be underestimated: "It is 90% an **emotional purchase**," says Kindleysides. His view is supported by academic re-

search: "Store design in this market ... is crucial in the first place for attracting customers to the store and then for creating the right atmosphere for purchase."

> "

employ 1 *n* **to be in sb's employ** travailler pour qn, être au service de qn
2 *vt* **(a)** *(give work to)* employer; *(new staff)* embaucher; **they employ 20 staff** ils ont 20 employés; **to employ sb as a receptionist** employer qn comme réceptionniste; **he has been employed with the firm for 15 years** il travaille pour cette entreprise depuis 15 ans
(b) *(make use of)* utiliser; **we must employ all our resources to tackle this problem** nous devons utiliser toutes nos ressources pour aborder ce problème

employable *adj (person)* susceptible d'être employé(e); **a good education makes you more employable** une bonne formation donne plus de chances de trouver du travail

employed 1 *npl* personnes *fpl* qui ont un emploi; **the employers and the employed** le patronat et le salariat
2 *adj* employé(e)

employee *n* employé(e) *m,f*; **management and employees** la direction et le personnel ❑ **employee association** comité *m* d'entreprise; **employee benefits** avantages *mpl* accordés aux employés; **employee buy-out** rachat *m* par les employés; **employee's contribution** *(to benefits)* cotisation *f* des salariés, part *f* salariale; **employee incentive scheme** système *m* de rémunération au rendement; **employee profit-sharing scheme** intéressement *m* aux résultats; **to provide an employee profit-sharing scheme** intéresser les employés aux bénéfices; **employee representative** délégué(e) *m,f* du personnel; *Am* **Employee Retirement Income Security Act** = loi américaine sur les pensions de retraite; **employee shareholding** actionnariat *m* ouvrier; *Br* **employee share ownership plan**, *Am* **employee stock ownership plan** plan *m* d'actionnariat des salariés

employer *n* employeur(euse) *m,f*; **employers** *(as a body)* patronat *m* ❑ **employers' association** organisation *f* patronale; **employer's contribution** cotisation *f* patronale; **employers' federation** chambre *f* syndicale, syndicat *m* patronal; **employer's liability** *(for accidents at work)* responsabilité *f* patronale; **employers' liability insurance** assurance *f* des patrons contre les accidents du travail; **employers' organization** organisation patronale

employment *n (occupation)* emploi *m*; *(recruitment)* embauche *f*; **to be without employment** être sans emploi; **to give sb employment** donner un emploi à qn; **to seek employment** chercher un emploi ❑ *Br* **Employment Act** = loi sur l'égalité des chances pour l'emploi; ***employ-ment agency*** agence *f* de placement; ***employ-ment bureau*** bureau *m* de placement; ***employment costs*** coûts *mpl* salariaux; ***em-ployment law*** droit *m* social; ***employment leg-islation*** législation *f* du travail; ***employment policy*** politique *f* de l'emploi; ***employment pro-tection*** protection *f* de l'emploi; ***employment regulations*** code *m* du travail; ***employment and training contract*** contrat *m* de qualifica-tion; ***employment tribunal*** ≃ conseil *m* des prud'hommes

> **"**
>
> Many economists say the Berlusconi gov-ernment's proposals are quite mild because they will end up removing the application of Article 18 in the case of very few workers, and will not even affect those currently em-ployed. However, the unions see Article 18 as the cornerstone of **employment protec-tion** law and believe even a modest change could open the way to a more rigorous set of reforms.
>
> **"**

empower *vt* donner davantage d'autonomie à

empowerment *n* = fait d'accorder davantage d'autonomie (à ses employés)

> **"**
>
> The flexibility to work where and how you want to is another key benefit of **empower-ment**. Again, employers can expect to see an increasingly motivated workforce as a re-sult. Media buyer Kate Parry became Just Media's first teleworker as she became disil-lusioned with working in London. The com-pany set her up with a laptop computer, a fax and a printer. "I am able to speak with my clients and my colleagues efficiently from my home office; communication is the key to our success, so it is very important that I can do this in a suitable environment," she says.
>
> **"**

empty return *n* retour *m* à vide

EMS *n Formerly (abbr* **European Monetary Sys-tem***)* SME *m*

EMU *n (abbr* **Economic and Monetary Union***)* UME *f*

emulation *n Comptr* émulation *f*

enable *vt Comptr (option)* activer

enabled *adj Comptr (option)* activé(e)

enc (**a**) *(abbr* **enclosure***)* PJ (**b**) *(abbr* **enclosed***)* ci-joint

encash *vt Br (cheque)* encaisser

encashable *adj Br (cheque)* encaissable

encashment *n Br (of cheque)* encaissement *m*

enclose *vt (in letter)* joindre; **to enclose sth in a letter** joindre qch à une lettre; **please find en-closed my CV, enclosed please find my CV** veuillez trouver ci-joint *ou* ci-inclus mon CV; **I enclose a cheque for £20** je joins un chèque de 20 livres; **the enclosed cheque** le chèque ci-joint *ou* ci-inclus

enclosure *n (in letter)* pièce *f* jointe

encode *vt Comptr* encoder

encoder *n Comptr* encodeur *m*

encoding *n Comptr* codage *m*, encodage *m*

encrypt *n Comptr* crypter, chiffrer

encryption *n Comptr* chiffrement *m*

end 1 *n (of month, year, meeting)* fin *f*; **to bring sth to an end** *(speech)* conclure qch; *(meeting)* clore qch; **at the end of the month/of the year** à la fin du mois/de l'année □ *Comptr* **end key** touche *f* fin; *Am* **end price** prix *m* de détail; **end product** produit *m* fini
  2 *vt (speech)* conclure; *(meeting)* clore
  3 *vi* finir, se terminer; *(of subscription)* expirer

end-consumer *n* utilisateur(trice) *m,f* final(e)

endgame *n Mktg* objectif *m*

endnote *n Comptr* note *f* de fin de document, NfD *f*

end-of-month *adj* de fin de mois □ **end-of-month balance** solde *m* de fin de mois; **end-of-month payments** échéances *fpl* de fin de mois; **end-of-month settlement** liquidation *f* de fin de mois; **end-of-month statement** relevé *m* de fin de mois

end-of-season sale *n* solde *m* de fin de saison

end-of-year *adj* de fin d'année; *Acct* de fin d'exercice □ *Acct* **end-of-year balance sheet** bilan *m* de l'exercice; **end-of-year bonus** prime *f* de fin d'année

endorse *vt* (**a**) *Fin (document, cheque)* endos-ser; *(bill of exchange)* avaliser, endosser, donner son aval à (**b**) *(approve) (action)* approuver; *(candidacy)* appuyer (**c**) *(product)* faire de la pu-blicité pour; **sportswear endorsed by top ath-letes** des vêtements de sport recommandés par des sportifs de haut niveau

endorsee *n Fin* endossataire *mf*

endorsement *n* (**a**) *Fin (of document, cheque)* endossement *m*, endos *m*; *(of bill of exchange)* aval *m*; *(in insurance policy)* avenant *m*; **en-dorsement in blank** endossement *ou* endos en blanc □ *Fin* **endorsement fee** commission *f* d'endos
  (**b**) *(approval) (of action)* approbation *f*; *(of can-didacy)* appui *m*
  (**c**) *(of product)* **that film star has made a for-tune from her endorsement of cosmetics** cette vedette du cinéma a gagné une fortune en faisant de la publicité pour des cosmetiques

endorser n Fin (of document, cheque) endosseur m, cessionnaire mf ; (of bill of exchange) avaliste mf, avaliseur m

endow vt Fin (person, company) doter (**with** de)

endowment n Fin (action, fund) dotation f □ **endowment fund** fonds m de dotation ; **endowment insurance** assurance f en cas de vie ou à dotation ; **endowment mortgage** prêt-logement m lié à une assurance-vie ; **endowment policy** assurance en cas de vie ou à dotation

> "
>
> The **endowment mortgage** crisis has escalated in the past year with three in five borrowers now told their investment policy will not pay off their home loan. Figures to be published this week by the Association of British Insurers will show that life assurers have issued "red" or "amber" warning letters to 60 per cent of **endowment mortgage** holders telling them to save more. If borrowers do not take action they are likely to face shortfalls of thousands of pounds when their mortgage comes to an end and the **endowment** is not enough to pay off the loan.
>
> "

end-user n utilisateur(trice) m,f final(e) □ **end-user specialist** spécialiste mf du marché utilisateur final

energy n énergie f □ **energy consumption** consommation f d'énergie ; **energy consumption bill** facture f énergétique

enforce vt (policy, decision) mettre en œuvre, appliquer ; (contract) faire exécuter

enforceable adj Law exécutoire □ **enforceable deed** acte m exécutoire ; **enforceable judgement** jugement m exécutoire

engage vt (staff) engager ; **to engage the services of sb** employer les services de qn

engaged adj (a) (busy) occupé(e) ; **I'm otherwise engaged** je suis déjà pris ; **to be engaged in discussions** être engagé(e) dans des discussions (b) Br (telephone) occupé(e) ; **the line or number is engaged** la ligne est occupée ; **I got the engaged tone or signal** ça sonnait occupé

engagement n (a) (meeting, appointment) rendez-vous m ; **to have a previous or prior engagement** être déjà pris(e) (b) (promise, obligation) engagement m ; **to carry out or meet one's engagements** faire face à ses engagements, remplir ses engagements

engineer n ingénieur m

engineering n ingénierie f □ **engineering company** entreprise f de construction mécanique ; **engineering consultancy** société f d'ingénieurs-conseils ; **engineering consultant** ingénieur-conseil m ; **engineering department** service m technique

engross vt Law (make clear copy of) grossoyer

enhance vt (a) Fin (pension, value) augmenter (b) Comptr (image, quality) améliorer

enhanced adj (a) Fin (pension, value) augmenté(e) (b) Comptr (image, quality) amélioré(e) □ **enhanced graphics adapter** carte f EGA ; **enhanced keyboard** clavier m étendu

enhancement n (a) Fin (of pension, value) augmentation f (b) Comptr (of image, quality) amélioration f

enquire, enquiry = **inquire, inquiry**

enter 1 n Comptr touche f (d')entrée □ **enter key** touche (d')entrée
2 vt (a) (market, country) entrer dans ; **all goods entering the market are subject to duty** toutes les marchandises importées sont passibles de droits (b) Acct (item) comptabiliser ; **to enter an item/figures in the ledger** porter un article/des chiffres sur le livre de comptes (c) Comptr (data) entrer, introduire

▸ **enter into** vt insep (business, dispute) entrer dans ; (negotiations) engager ; (contract) passer ; **to enter into partnership with sb** s'associer avec qn ; **to enter into an agreement with sb** conclure un accord avec qn

▸ **enter up** vt sep Acct **to enter up an item/figures in the ledger** porter un article/des chiffres sur le livre de comptes

enterprise n (business) entreprise f □ Br **Enterprise Allowance Scheme** fonds m d'aide à la création d'entreprise ; **enterprise culture** culture f d'entreprise ; **enterprise economy** = type d'économie qui facilite la création d'entreprises ; **enterprise society** = type de société où l'entreprise privée est valorisée ; Br **enterprise zone** = zone d'encouragement à l'implantation d'entreprises dans les régions économiquement défavorisées

> "
>
> We also need to further develop an **enterprise culture**. We're in lockstep with Wal-Mart by being very action-oriented. This applies in our speed to market, streamlined decision making, and empowerment of people down to lower levels.
>
> "

enterprising adj (person) entreprenant(e) ; (idea, project) audacieux(euse)

entertainment n **entertainment allowance** indemnité f de fonction ; **entertainment expenses** frais mpl de représentation ; **entertainment tax** taxe f sur les spectacles

entitle vt **to be entitled to sth** (allowance, benefit) avoir droit à qch ; **his disability entitles**

him to a pension son infirmité lui donne droit à une pension

entitlement n droit m; **entitlement to social security** droit à la sécurité sociale

entrant n (on market) acteur m; **stocks in two new entrants to the market performed well** les actions de deux sociétés nouvellement introduites en Bourse se sont bien comportées

entrepôt n entrepôt m ❑ **entrepôt port** port m franc

entrepreneur n entrepreneur(euse) m,f

entrepreneurial adj (activities, decision) d'entrepreneur; (person, society) qui a l'esprit d'entreprise

entrepreneurship n entreprenariat m

entry n (a) Acct (action) passation f d'écriture, inscription f; (item) article m, écriture f; **to make an entry** passer une écriture, porter un article à compte (b) Comptr (of data) entrée f (c) Customs (of goods into country) entrée f **entry barrier** barrière f à l'entrée; **entry permit** permis m d'entrée; **entry visa** visa m d'entrée (d) (of company on market) entrée f, pénétration f (e) **entry level** (of job) niveau m d'embauche

envelope n enveloppe f; **in a sealed envelope** sous pli cacheté ❑ **envelope file** chemise f (de carton)

environment n Comptr, Econ environnement m; **a pleasant working environment** des conditions fpl de travail agréables

environmental adj **environmental audit** = rapport sur l'impact des activités d'une entreprise sur l'environnement; **environmental damage** dégâts mpl causés à l'environnement; **environmental economics** économie f de l'environnement; **environmental policy** politique f de l'environnement; **environmental protection** protection f de l'environnement

environmentally-friendly adj qui ne nuit pas à l'environnement

EOC n Admin (abbr **Equal Opportunities Commission**) = commission pour l'égalité des chances en matière d'emploi, en Grande-Bretagne

EONIA n St Exch (abbr **Euro Overnight Index Average**) EONIA m, TEMPÉ m

EPOS n Comptr (abbr **electronic point of sale**) point m de vente électronique

EPS n (a) (abbr **earnings per share**) BPA m (b) Comptr (abbr **encapsulated PostScript**) EPS m

equal adj égal(e) ❑ Admin **Equal Employment Opportunities Commission** = commission pour l'égalité des chances en matière d'emploi, aux États-Unis; **equal opportunities** égalité f des chances; Admin **Equal Opportunities Commission** = commission pour l'égalité des chances en matière d'emploi, en Grande-Bretagne;

equal opportunity employer = entreprise s'engageant à respecter la législation sur la non-discrimination dans l'emploi; **equal partners** associé(e)s mpl,fpl à part égale; **equal pay** égalité des salaires; **Equal Pay Act** = loi garantissant l'égalité des chances en matière d'emploi, en Grande-Bretagne; **equal rights** égalité des droits; **equal sign, equals sign** signe m égal

equality n égalité f ❑ **equality of opportunity** égalité des chances

equalization n Fin (of dividends) régularisation f; (of taxes, wealth) péréquation f ❑ **equalization fund** fonds m de parité; **equalization payment** soulte f

equalize vt Fin (dividends) régulariser; (taxes, wealth) faire la péréquation de

equation of payment n Fin échéance f commune

equip vt (factory) outiller, équiper (**with** de); (person) équiper, pourvoir (**with** de); **we must equip our staff with the tools to tackle new technology** nous devons équiper notre personnel des outils nécessaires pour aborder les nouvelles technologies

equipment n équipement m; (in factory) installations fpl, matériel m ❑ **equipment financing** crédit m d'équipement; **equipment leasing** crédit-bail m mobilier; **equipment subsidy** subvention f d'équipement

equity n Fin, St Exch (of shareholders) capitaux mpl ou fonds mpl propres; (of company) capital m actions; **equities** actions fpl ordinaires ❑ **equity capital** capital actions; **equity dilution** dilution f du capital; **equity financing** financement m par actions, financement par capitaux propres; **equity investment** placement m en actions; **equity issue** augmentation f du capital par émission d'actions; **equity leader** valeur f vedette; **equity loan** prêt m participatif; **equity** or **equities market** marché m des actions (ordinaires); **equity risk premium** prime f de risque de variation du prix des actions; **equity share** action ordinaire; **equity share capital** capital en actions ordinaires; **equity switching** rotation f de portefeuille-action; **equities trader** courtier(ère) m,f sur actions; **equity trading** courtage m sur actions; **equity unit trust** sicav f actions; **equity warrant** bon m de souscription d'actions

equity-based unit trust n Fin, St Exch sicav f actions

equity-linked adj Fin, St Exch (policy) libellé(e), investi(e) en actions

equivalences of exchange npl Fin parités fpl de change

equivalent adj équivalent(e); **to be equivalent to sth** être équivalent à qch, équivaloir à qch

erase *vt Comptr, Fin* effacer

ERDF *n Fin* (*abbr* **European Regional Develop-ment Fund**) FEDER *m*

ergonomic *adj* ergonomique

ergonomics *n* ergonomie *f*

ERM *n Formerly Fin* (*abbr* **Exchange Rate Mechanism**) mécanisme *m* de change

error *n* erreur *f*; *Acct* **errors and omissions excepted** sauf erreur ou omission □ *Comptr* **error code** code *m* d'erreur; *Comptr* **error detection** détection *f* d'erreurs; *Comptr* **error message** message *m* d'erreur

escalate *vi* (*of prices*) monter en flèche

escalation clause, escalator clause *n* (*in contract*) clause *f* d'indexation *ou* de révision

escape *n* (**a**) *Comptr* échappement *m* □ **escape key** touche *f* d'échappement (**b**) **escape clause** (*in contract*) clause *f* échappatoire

escrow *n Law* dépôt *m* fiduciaire *ou* conditionnel; **to be held in escrow** être placé(e) en dépôt fiduciaire *ou* en main tierce; **to put sth in escrow** placer qch en dépôt fiduciaire *ou* en main tierce □ *Am* **escrow account** compte *m* bloqué; **escrow agent** dépositaire *mf* légal(e)

escudo *n Formerly* escudo *m*

ESOP *n* (*abbr* **employee** *Br* **share** or *Am* **stock ownership plan**) plan *m* d'actionnariat des salariés

est *adj* (*abbr* **established**) établi(e), fondé(e); **A. Jones, est 1885** A. Jones, établi en 1885

establish *vt* (*system*) établir, édifier; (*business*) fonder; (*agency*) créer; **to establish oneself in business** s'établir dans les affaires

established *adj* (*system, business*) établi(e); **once the company becomes established** quand la société sera bien établie; **established 1890** maison fondée en 1890

establishment *n* (**a**) (*company*) établissement *m*; **a business establishment** un établissement commercial (**b**) (*creation*) (*of system*) établissement *m*; (*of business*) fondation *f*; (*of agency*) création *f* (**c**) **the Establishment** (*dominant group*) l'establishment *m*; **the financial establishment** ceux qui comptent dans le monde financier

estate *n* (**a**) *Law* (*possessions*) biens *mpl* (**b**) (*land*) terre *f*, propriété *f* □ *Br* **estate agency** agence *f* immobilière; *Br* **estate agent** agent *m* immobilier (**c**) (*inheritance*) succession *f* □ *Br* **estate duty**, *Am* **estate tax** droits *mpl* de succession (**d**) (*of bankrupt*) actif *m*

estimate 1 *n* (**a**) (*calculation*) évaluation *f*, calcul *m*; **these figures are only a rough estimate** ces chiffres sont très approximatifs; **give me an estimate of how much you think it will cost** donnez-moi une idée de ce que ça coûtera; **at the lowest estimate it will take three months to complete** au bas mot, cela prendra trois mois pour terminer
 (**b**) (*of cost*) devis *m*; **to put in an estimate (for sth/for doing sth)** établir un devis (pour qch/pour faire qch); **to ask for an estimate (for sth/for doing sth)** demander un devis (pour qch/pour faire qch); **get several estimates before deciding which company to use** faites faire plusieurs devis avant de décider quelle entreprise choisir
 2 *vt* estimer, évaluer; **the cost of the project was estimated at £2,000** le coût du projet était évalué à 2000 livres

estimation *n* estimation *f*, évaluation *f*

estimator *n* expert *m*

e-tail *Comptr* **1** *n* vente *f* en ligne
 2 *vt* vendre en ligne

e-tailer *Comptr n* société *f* de vente en ligne

> **“**
>
> Argos was last night recognised as the country's leading **e-tailer**, winning the most awards at this year's Visa E-tail Awards, as voted for by Visa customers. The 'Bricks to Clicks' award acknowledged Argos' e-tailing expertise, through its successful integration of its High Street, catalogue and Internet operations, and confirmed its position at the forefront of multi-channel retailing in the UK.
>
> **”**

e-tailing *n Comptr* vente *f* en ligne

Ethernet® *n Comptr* Ethernet® *m*

ethical *adj* éthique □ *Fin* **ethical investment** investissement *m* éthique; *Fin* **ethical investment fund** fonds *m* d'investissement éthique, sicav *f* éthique

EU *n* (*abbr* **European Union**) UE *f*

EURIBOR *n Fin, St Exch* (*abbr* **Euro Interbank Offered Rate**) EURIBOR *m*, TIBEUR *m*

euro, Euro *n EU, Fin* euro *m* □ **euro area** zone *f* euro; *St Exch* **Euro Interbank Offered Rate** EURIBOR *m*, TIBEUR *m*; *St Exch* **Euro Overnight Index Average** EONIA *m*, TEMPÉ *m*; *St Exch* **Euro Stoxx** Euro Stoxx *m*; **euro zone** zone euro

Eurobank *n EU* eurobanque *f*

eurobond *n* euro-obligation *f*

eurocard *n* eurocarte *f*

eurocertificate *n* euro-certificat *m*

eurocheque *n* eurochèque *m*

euro-commercial paper *n EU* billet *m* de trésorerie (*émis sur le marché des eurodevises*)

eurocrat *n* eurocrate *mf*

eurocredit *n* eurocrédit *m*

euro-currency *n* eurodevise *f*, euromonnaie *f*

❑ *euro-currency market* marché *m* des eurodevises

> The fund aims to give shareholders access to income at wholesale **euro-currency** market interest rates in the **euro-currency**. The fund invests in a spread of short-term money market instruments with a weighted average maturity of 60 days.

eurodollar *n* eurodollar *m*

Eurofranc *n* eurofranc *m*

Euroloan *n* eurocrédit *m*

euromarket *n* euromarché *m*, marché *m* des eurodevises

Euro-MP *n* député *m* européen

European *adj* européen(enne) ❑ *European Bank of Reconstruction and Development* Banque *f* européenne de reconstruction et de développement; *European Central Bank* Banque centrale européenne; *European Central Securities Depositories Association* Association *f* européenne des dépositaires centraux de titres; *European Coal and Steel Community* Communauté *f* européenne de charbon et de l'acier; *European Commission* Commission *f* européenne; *European commissioner* commissaire *mf* européen(enne); *European Community* Communauté européenne; *European Convention on Human Rights* Convention *f* européenne des droits de l'homme; *European Court of Human Rights* Cour *f* européenne des droits de l'homme; *European Court of Justice* Cour européenne de justice; *European currency snake* serpent *m* monétaire européen; *Formerly European Currency Unit* unité *f* monétaire européenne; *European Development Fund* Fonds *m* européen de développement; *European Economic Area* espace *m* économique européen; *Formerly European Economic Community* Communauté économique européenne; *European Environmental Bureau* Bureau *m* européen de l'environnement; *Formerly European Exchange Rate Mechanism* mécanisme *m* de change européen; *European Free Trade Association* Association européenne de libre-échange; *European Investment Bank* Banque européenne d'investissement; *European Monetary Agreement* Accord *m* monétaire européen; *Formerly European Monetary Cooperation Fund* Fonds européen de coopération monétaire; *European Monetary Institute* Institut *m* monétaire européen; *Formerly European Monetary System* système *m* monétaire européen; *European Monetary Union* Union *f* monétaire européenne; *European Parliament* Parlement *m* européen; *European Regional Development Fund* Fonds européen de développement régional; *European Social Fund* Fonds social européen; *European standards* normes *fpl* européennes; *European Standards Commission* Comité *m* européen de normalisation; *European Union* Union européenne; *European unit of account* unité de compte européenne

European-style option *n St Exch* option *f* européenne

Eurosterling *n* eurosterling *m*

euroyen *n* euroyen *m*

EVA *n* (*abbr* **economic value added**) VAE *f*

evade *vt* **to evade tax** frauder le fisc

evaluate *vt* (*damages, value, cost*) évaluer

evaluation *n* (*of damages, value, cost*) évaluation *f*

event *n* (*corporate activity*) événement *m* ❑ *event advertising* publicité *f* par l'événement; *event(s) management* organisation *f* d'événements publicitaires; *event(s) manager* responsable *mf* de l'organisation d'événements publicitaires; *event promotion* communication *f* événementielle

evergreen *adj Fin* **evergreen facility** possibilité *f* de crédit permanent; **evergreen fund** fonds *m* de crédit permanent non confirmé

evoked set *n Mktg* ensemble *m* évoqué

ex *prep* (**a**) (*out of*) **ex quay** à quai; **ex ship** à bord; **ex warehouse** départ entrepôt, sortie entrepôt; **ex wharf** à quai; **ex works** départ usine, sortie d'usine

(**b**) *Fin, St Exch* (*without*) **ex all, ex allotment** ex-répartition *f*; **ex bonus** ex-capitalisation *f*; **ex cap, ex capitalisation** ex-capitalisation; **ex coupon** ex-coupon *m*, coupon *m* détaché; **this stock goes ex coupon on 1 August** le coupon de cette action se détache le 1er août; **ex dividend** ex-dividende *m*, dividende *m* détaché; **ex interest** sans intérêts; **ex new, ex rights** ex-droit *m*; **ex scrip** ex-répartition

exceed *vt* excéder, dépasser; **demand exceeds supply** la demande excède *ou* dépasse l'offre; **her salary exceeds mine by £4,000 a year** son salaire annuel dépasse le mien de 4000 livres

exceptional *adj Acct* **exceptional item** poste *m* extraordinaire; **exceptional tax** taxe *f* exceptionnelle

excess *n* (*in weight, expenditure*) excédent *m*; *Br Ins* franchise *f*; **there has been an excess of expenditure over revenue** les dépenses ont excédé les recettes ❑ *excess capacity* surcapacité *f*, capacité *f* excédentaire; *excess charges* supplément *m*; *Br Ins* **excess clause** franchise; *excess demand* demande *f* excédentaire; *excess fare* supplément de prix; *excess liquidities* liquidités *fpl* excédentaires; *Br Ins* **excess policy** police *f* complémentaire; *excess profits* surplus *m* des bénéfices; *(unexpected)* bénéfices *mpl* exceptionnels *ou* extraordinaires; **excess profits tax** impôt *m* sur les bénéfices exceptionnels; *Banking* **excess reserves** réserves *fpl* excédentaires; *St Exch* **excess shares** actions *fpl* détenues en surnombre; **excess supply** offre *f* excédentaire; **excess weight** poids *m* excédentaire

exchange 1 *n* **(a)** *Fin (of currency)* change *m*; *Am* **exchanges** *(bills)* lettres *fpl* de change, traites *fpl* □ **exchange adjustments** écarts *mpl* de conversion; **exchange broker** agent *m* de change, cambiste *mf*; **exchange control** contrôle *m ou* réglementation *f* des changes; **exchange cross rate** taux *m* de change entre devises tierces; **exchange dealer** agent de change, cambiste; **exchange equalization account** fonds *m* de stabilisation des changes; **exchange gain** gain *m* de change; **exchange index** indice *m* boursier; **exchange law** droit *m* cambial; **exchange loss** perte *f* de change; **exchange market** marché *m* des changes; **exchange offer** offre *f* publique d'échange; **exchange policy** politique *f* en matière de change; **exchange premium** prime *f* de change; **exchange rate** cours *m ou* taux de change; **at the current exchange rate** au cours du jour; *Formerly EU* **Exchange Rate Mechanism** mécanisme *m* de change; **exchange rate parity** parité *f* du change; **exchange rate stability** stabilité *f* des changes; **exchange rate swap** swap *m* de change; **exchange reserves** réserves *fpl* en devises (étrangères); **exchange restrictions** contrôle *m* des changes; **exchange risk** risque *m* de change; **exchange transaction** opération *f* de change; **exchange value** valeur *f* d'échange, contre-valeur *f*
(b) *(of goods, shares, commodities)* échange *m*
2 *vt* **(a)** *(goods, shares, commodities)* échanger
(b) to exchange contracts *(when buying property)* signer les contrats de vente et d'achat d'une propriété

exchequer *n Br Admin* **the Exchequer** *(money)* le Trésor public; *(government department)* ≃ le ministère des Finances □ *Fin* **exchequer bill** bon *m* du Trésor

excisable *adj Admin* taxable, imposable

excise *n Admin (tax)* contribution *f* indirecte, taxe *f*, *Belg* accise *f*; *Br (department)* service *m* des contributions indirectes, régie *f* □ **excise bond** acquit-à-caution *m*; **excise documents** documents *mpl* administratifs de régie; **excise duty** contribution indirecte; **excise tax** contribution indirecte

exclamation mark, *Am* **exclamation point** *n* point *m* d'exclamation

exclusive 1 *adj* exclusif(ive) □ **exclusive distribution** distribution *f* exclusive; **exclusive distribution agreement** accord *m* de distribution

exclusive; **exclusive economic zone** zone *f* économique exclusive; **exclusive licence** licence *f* exclusive; **exclusive rights** droits *mpl* exclusifs, exclusivité *f*; **exclusive selling rights** droits de vente exclusifs; **exclusive shipment** expédition *f* exclusive; **exclusive territory** territoire *m* exclusif
2 *adv* **exclusive of tax** hors taxe; **exclusive of delivery** frais de livraison non compris

exclusivity *n* exclusivité *f* □ **exclusivity agreement** accord *m* d'exclusivité; **exclusivity clause** clause *f* d'exclusivité

> ❝
> Also, there are five divisions of Kroger representing 514 stores which have contractual conflicts due to an **exclusivity clause** they have in their contracts with News American Marketing In-Store (NAMIS). This **exclusivity clause** is what our counterclaims center on in our legal conflict with NAMIS. If Kroger's contractual conflict remains unresolved, we will lose the 514 stores by mid-September. We are optimistic that we will renew our relationship with these stores when the NAMIS contract expires.
> ❞

ex-directory *adj Br (telephone number)* sur la liste rouge

exec *n Fam (abbr* **executive**) cadre *m*

executable file *n Comptr* fichier *m* exécutable

execute *vt* **(a)** *Fin (transfer)* effectuer **(b)** *Comptr* exécuter □ **execute cycle** cycle *m* d'exécution

execution *n Comptr* exécution *f* □ **execution speed** vitesse *f* d'exécution

executive 1 *n (person)* directeur(trice) *m,f*, cadre *m*; *(board, committee)* bureau *m*, comité *m* central
2 *adj (power)* exécutif(ive); *(ability)* d'exécution; *(job)* de cadre; *(car, plane)* de direction □ **executive board** conseil *m* d'administration; **executive director** directeur(trice) *m,f* administratif(ive); **executive functions** fonctions *fpl* d'encadrement; **executive member** membre *m* du comité de direction; **executive officer** cadre *m* supérieur; **executive pension fund** caisse *f* de retraite des cadres; **executive power** pouvoir *m* exécutif; **executive secretary** secrétaire *mf* de direction; **executive share option scheme** plan *m* d'investissement en actions pour cadres

executor *n Law (of will)* exécuteur(trice) *m,f* testamentaire

exempt 1 *adj* exempté(e), dispensé(e) (**from** de); **exempt from taxes** exonéré(e) *ou* exempt(e) d'impôt
2 *vt* exempter, dispenser (**from** de); *(from taxes)* exonérer, exempter (**from** de)

exemption *n* exemption *f*, dispense *f*; *(from tax)* exonération *f*, exemption □ **exemption clause** clause *f* d'exonération

exercisable *adj St Exch (option)* exerçable

exercise 1 *n* (**a**) *(of one's duties)* exercice *m* (**b**) *St Exch (of option)* levée *f* □ **exercise date** date *f* d'échéance; **exercise notice** assignation *f*; **exercise price** cours *m* de base, prix *m* d'exercice
2 *vt* (**a**) *(duties)* exercer (**b**) *St Exch* **to exercise an option** lever une prime

ex gratia *adj (payment)* à titre de faveur, à titre gracieux

ex-growth *n (decline)* baisse *f*; **to go ex-growth** être en déclin

> "
> Vodafone's performance indicators vindicate neither bulls nor bears. We shall need several more quarters to judge whether the company has or has not gone **ex-growth**. During the long meanwhile the shares will remain volatile.
> "

exhibit 1 *n* objet *m* exposé
2 *vt (object, goods)* exposer, montrer

exhibition *n* (**a**) *(of goods)* étalage *m* (**b**) *(show)* exposition *f* □ **exhibition hall** salon *m* d'exposition; **exhibition stand** stand *m* (d'exposition)

exhibitor *n (at exhibition)* exposant(e) *m,f*

existing *adj Mktg* **existing customer** client(e) *m,f* actuel(elle); **existing market** marché *m* existant *ou* actuel

exit 1 *n* (**a**) **exit barrier** barrière *f* à la sortie; **exit charge(s)** frais *mpl* de sortie; **exit interview** = entretien entre un employeur et son employé lors du départ de ce dernier; **exit permit** permis *m* de sortie; **exit visa** visa *m* de sortie (**b**) *Comptr* sortie *f*
2 *vt Comptr (program, session)* sortir de
3 *vi Comptr* sortir

ex officio *Admin* **1** *adj (member)* de droit
2 *adv (act)* d'office

expand 1 *vt (company, business, staff, market)* agrandir, développer; *Comptr (memory)* étendre; **to expand a company into a multinational** agrandir une société pour en faire une multinationale
2 *vi (of company, business, staff, market)* s'agrandir, se développer; **the mobile phone sector is continuing to expand** le secteur des téléphones portables continue de se développer; **we are looking to expand into the cosmetics industry** nous envisageons de nous diversifier en nous lançant dans l'industrie des cosmétiques; **Texaco expanded into oil production in the later part of last century** Texaco s'est lancée dans la production pétrolière à la fin du siècle dernier

expandable *adj Comptr (memory)* extensible; **4MB expandable to 64MB** 4 Mo extensible à 64 Mo

expanded *adj Comptr* **expanded keyboard** clavier *m* étendu; **expanded memory** mémoire *f* paginée

expanding *adj (company, market)* en expansion

> "
> Waste is the great new growth industry, and as British landfill sites are phased out, in accordance with EU regulations, there will be a need for more and more recycling: "It's an **expanding** market, it's not seasonal, and I could sell exclusively within the UK."
> "

expansion *n* (**a**) *(of company, business, staff, market)* expansion *f*; *(of economy)* relance *f* (**b**) *Comptr (of memory)* extension *f* □ **expansion board** carte *f* d'extension; **expansion card** carte d'extension; **expansion port** port *m* d'extension; **expansion slot** emplacement *m* pour carte d'extension

expansionist *adj* expansionniste

expectation *n* prévision *f*; **performance did not confirm City expectations** les résultats n'ont pas répondu à l'attente de la City; **we have certain expectations of our employees** nous avons certaines exigences envers nos employés

expected *adj* attendu(e) □ **expected monetary value** valeur *f* monétaire escomptée; **expected value** valeur attendue

expend *vt (money)* dépenser (**on** sur)

expenditure *n* (**a**) *(spending)* dépense *f* (**b**) *(amount spent)* dépenses *fpl*; **it entails heavy expenditure** cela entraîne de fortes dépenses

expense *n* (**a**) *(cost)* dépense *f*, frais *mpl*; **at great expense** à grands frais; **it's not worth the expense** c'est trop cher pour ce que c'est □ **expense account** note *f* de frais; **to put sth on the expense account** mettre qch sur la note de frais; **the company gives him an expense account for basic entertaining** l'entreprise lui attribue une allocation pour ses frais de représentation; **expense budget** budget *m* des dépenses
(**b**) **expenses** frais *mpl*; **to meet/cover sb's expenses** rembourser/couvrir les frais de qn; **to put sth on expenses** mettre qch sur la note de frais; **it's on expenses** c'est la société qui paie, ça va sur la note de frais; **to cut down on expenses** réduire les frais; **to incur expenses** faire des dépenses; **to have all expenses paid** être défrayé de tout □ **expenses claim form** note *f* de frais

expensive *adj* coûteux(euse), cher (chère); **to be expensive** coûter cher

experience *n* expérience *f*; **do you have any experience of dealing with the public?** avez-vous déjà travaillé près du public?; **she has considerable management experience** elle a une expérience considérable dans la gestion ❑ *Mktg* ***experience curve*** courbe *f* d'expérience; *Mktg* ***experience effect*** effet *m* d'expérience

expert *n* expert *m*; **he is an expert in this field** il est expert en la matière ❑ ***expert panel*** commission *f* d'experts; ***expert's report*** certificat *m* d'expertise; *Comptr* ***expert system*** système *m* expert

expertise *n* expertise *f*

expiration *n (of options market)* échéance *f*; *(of term)* fin *f*; *(of lease)* expiration *f*; *(of insurance policy)* expiration, échéance

expire *vi (of deadline, lease, insurance policy)* expirer

expiry *n* expiration *f*, fin *f*, échéance *f* ❑ ***expiry date*** date *f* d'échéance

explanatory note *n* note *f* explicative

explore *vt (market)* prospecter

export 1 *n* (**a**) *(product)* article *m* d'exportation; **exports** *(of country)* exportations *fpl*
(**b**) *(activity)* exportation *f*; **for export only** réservé à l'exportation ❑ ***export agent*** commissionnaire *mf* exportateur(trice), agent *m* exportateur; ***export aid*** aide *f* à l'exportation; ***export ban*** interdiction *f* d'exporter *ou* d'exportation; **to impose an export ban on sth** interdire qch d'exportation; ***export company*** société *f* d'exportation; ***export concessionaire*** concessionnaire *mf* export; ***export credit*** crédit *m* à l'exportation; ***export credit guarantee*** garantie *f* de crédit à l'exportation; *Br* ***Export Credit Guarantee Department*** ≃ COFACE *f*; ***export credit rate*** taux *m* de crédit export; ***export declaration*** déclaration *f* d'exportation; ***export department*** service *m* des exportations; ***export director*** directeur(trice) *m,f* export; ***export division*** division *f* des exportations; ***export drive*** campagne *f* visant à stimuler l'exportation; ***export duty*** droit(s) *m(pl)* de sortie; ***export earnings*** revenus *mpl* de l'exportation; ***export gold-point*** point *m* de sortie de l'or; ***export goods*** marchandises *fpl* à l'export; ***export incentive*** prime *f* à l'exportation; ***export label*** label *m* d'exportation; ***export levy*** prélèvement *m* à l'exportation; ***export licence*** licence *f* d'exportation; ***export list*** tarif *m* de sortie; ***export management*** direction *f* export; ***export manager*** directeur(trice) export; ***export market*** marché *m* à l'exportation; ***export office*** bureau *m* d'exportation; ***export order*** commande *f* export *ou* pour l'exportation; ***export permit*** permis *m* d'exportation; ***export potential*** capacité *f* d'exportation; ***export price*** prix *m* à l'export; ***export prohibition*** prohibition *f* de sortie; ***export quota*** quota *m ou* contingent *m* d'exportation; ***export refund*** restitution *f* à l'exportation; ***export reject*** produit *m* impropre à l'exportation; ***export restrictions*** restrictions *fpl* sur les exportations; ***export revenue*** revenus de l'exportation; ***export sales*** ventes *fpl* export *ou* à l'exportation; ***export subsidy*** prime *ou* subvention *f* à l'exportation; ***export tax*** taxe *f* à l'exportation; ***export trade*** commerce *m* d'exportation
2 *vt* (**a**) *(goods)* exporter
(**b**) *Comptr* exporter (**to** vers)
3 *vi* exporter; **the firm exports all over the world** l'entreprise exporte dans le monde entier

exportable *adj* exportable

exportation *n (of goods)* exportation *f*

exporter *n* exportateur(trice) *m,f*; **Britain is now one of the world's biggest exporters of aircraft** la Grande-Bretagne est maintenant l'un des plus grands exportateurs d'avions du monde

exporting *adj* exportateur(trice) ❑ ***exporting country*** pays *m* exportateur

exposé *n* révélations *fpl*; **the newspaper's exposé of the MP's activities** l'enquête du journal sur les activités du parlementaire

exposure *n* (**a**) *(publicity)* couverture *f*; **to get a lot of exposure** *(of company, product)* faire l'objet d'une couverture médiatique importante; **exposure to the media is important for a new product** il est important de bénéficier d'une couverture médiatique pour un nouveau produit (**b**) *Fin* exposition *f* aux risques

express *adj (letter, delivery)* exprès

ext *n* (*abbr* **extension**) poste *m*

extend *vt* (**a**) **to extend credit to sb** accorder un crédit *ou* des facilités de crédit à qn (**b**) *(deadline, contract)* prolonger; *(expiry of bill)* proroger

extended *adj* (**a**) ***extended credit*** accréditif *m* prolongé; ***extended guarantee*** garantie *f* prolongée; ***extended leave*** congé *m* de longue durée; ***extended warranty*** garantie prolongée (**b**) *Comptr* ***extended keyboard*** clavier *m* étendu; ***extended memory*** mémoire *f* étendue

extension *n* (**a**) *Acct (of balance)* transport *m*, report *m* (**b**) *(of credit, deadline, contract)* prolongation *f*; **we need an extension to complete the project** nous avons besoin d'un délai pour terminer le projet (**c**) *(for telephone)* poste *m*; **extension 35** poste 35 ❑ ***extension number*** numéro *m* de poste (**d**) *Comptr (of file)* extension *f* ❑ ***extension slot*** emplacement *m* (pour) périphériques

external *adj* (**a**) *(trade, debt)* extérieur(e) ❑ ***external account*** compte *m* étranger, *Can* compte de non-résident; ***external audit*** audit *m ou* vérification *f* externe; ***external auditing*** vérification externe; ***external auditor*** audi-

teur(trice) *m,f* *ou* vérificateur(trice) *m,f* externe; **external deficit** déficit *m* extérieur; **external financing** fonds *mpl* extérieurs; **external growth** croissance *f* externe
 (**b**) *Comptr* **external cache** cache *m* externe; **external device** dispositif *m* externe, périphérique *m*; *(printer)* imprimante *f*; **external drive** unité *f* (de disque) externe; **external modem** modem *m* externe

extn *n* *(abbr* **extension**) poste *m*

extra 1 *n* *(additional charge)* supplément *m*
 2 *adj* supplémentaire, de plus; **to charge extra** percevoir un supplément □ **extra charge** supplément *m*; **extra cost** surcoût *m*

extract *vt* *Comptr (zipped file)* décompresser

extraordinary *adj* (**a**) *Fin* **extraordinary general meeting** assemblée *f* générale extraordinaire; **to call an extraordinary general meeting of the shareholders** convoquer d'urgence les actionnaires (**b**) *Acct* **extraordinary expenses** frais *mpl* ou dépenses *fpl* extraordinaires; **extraordinary income** produits *mpl* exceptionnels; **extraordinary item** poste *m* extraordinaire; **extraordinary profit or loss** résultat *m* exceptionnel

> **"**
>
> In the first quarter of 2002, Italian energy group Edison reported net consolidated profit of 420m euros which included **extraordinary income** of 425m euros derived from the sale of a 22.2 per cent stake in Italian insurance company Fondiaria.
>
> **"**

extrapolate 1 *vt* extrapoler; **we can extrapolate sales figures of the last ten years to predict future trends** on peut extrapoler les tendances à venir à partir des chiffres de vente de ces dix dernières années
 2 *vi* extrapoler; **to extrapolate from sth** extrapoler à partir de qch

extrapolation *n* extrapolation *f*

extrinsic value *n* *St Exch* valeur *f* extrinsèque

ezine *n* *Comptr* magazine *m* électronique

Ff

faa *adj* (*abbr* **free of all average**) franc de toute avarie

face *n* (**a**) *face value,* *Am* *face amount* (*of bank-note, traveller's cheque*) valeur *f* nominale; (*of stamp, share*) valeur faciale (**b**) (*of document*) recto *m* ❏ *face time* (*meeting*) = rencontre en face à face entre deux personnes (par opposition aux contacts par téléphone ou courrier électronique); (*on TV*) temps *m* de présence à l'écran

America Online executives covered both bases as Chairman-CEO Steve Case and President-COO Bob Pittman hit the Allen dealmaker fest and George Vradenburg, senior vice president-global and strategic policy, accompanied Clinton on his tour of Los Angeles' Watts district. Any **face time** between Vradenburg and the President likely included discussion of AOL's desire to gain access to the cable industry's high-speed broadband pipe.

facilitate *vt* faciliter; **to facilitate a meeting** faciliter une réunion

facilitator *n* auxiliaire *mf*

facility *n* (**a**) (*service*) service *m*; **facilities for payment** facilités *fpl* de paiement; **we offer easy credit facilities** nous offrons des facilités de paiement *ou* de crédit (**b**) **facilities** (*equipment*) installations *fpl*; **we don't have the facilities to hold a conference here** nous ne sommes pas équipés pour organiser une conférence ici

facsimile *n* fac-similé *m*

factor *n* (**a**) (*in multiplication*) indice *m*, coefficient *m*; **the sales increased by a factor of ten** les ventes sont dix fois plus élevées, l'indice des ventes est dix fois plus haut (**b**) *Econ* **factor of production** facteur *m* de production (**c**) (*factoring company*) société *f* d'affacturage

factorage *n* (*charge*) commission *f* d'affacturage

factoring *n* affacturage *m*, factoring *m* ❏ *factoring agent* agent *m* d'affacturage; *factoring charges* commission *f* d'affacturage; *factoring company* société *f* d'affacturage

"A **factoring company** essentially buys your invoices and charges a commission in exchange for rapid settlement," he says. "It is chiefly used by companies with a turnover up to £1m, the kind of organisation that most often depends on a streamlined cashflow. With overseas **factoring**, commission rates are likely to be higher because chasing a debt abroad can be expensive and time consuming."

factory *n* usine *f* ❏ *factory inspection* inspection *f* du travail; *factory inspector* inspecteur(-trice) *m,f* du travail; *factory outlet* magasin *m* d'usine; *factory overheads* frais *mpl* généraux de fabrication; *factory price* prix *m* (sortie) usine; *factory shop* magasin d'usine; *factory unit* unité *f* de fabrication; *factory work* travail *m* d'usine; *factory worker* ouvrier(ère) *m,f* d'usine

fail *vi* (*of project, scheme, negotiations*) échouer; (*of company*) faire faillite

failure *n* (*of project, scheme, negotiations*) échec *m*; (*of company*) faillite *f* ❏ *Am* *failure investment* investissement *m* en valeurs de redressement; *failure rate* taux *m* de panne

fair 1 *n* (*exhibition*) foire *f*
2 *adj* *fair average quality* qualité *f* loyale et marchande; *fair copy* (*of document*) copie *f* au net *ou* au propre; *fair deal* arrangement *m* équitable; *Am* *Fair Employment Practices Commission* = commission dont les membres sont nommés par le Sénat, qui veille à l'application des mesures anti-discriminatoires en matière d'emploi; *fair market value* valeur *f* vénale; *fair trade, fair trading* commerce *m* équitable, pratiques *fpl* loyales; *fair wage* salaire *m* équitable; *fair wear and tear* usure *f* normale

fair-trade *adj* de commerce équitable ❏ *fair-trade agreement* accord *m* de commerce équitable

faith *n* **in good faith** de bonne foi; **to buy sth in good faith** acheter qch de bonne foi

faithfully *adv* **yours faithfully** (*in letter*) veuillez agréer nos meilleures salutations *ou* nos salutations distinguées

fake 1 *n* (*product, document*) faux *m*
2 *adj* faux (fausse)

3 *vt (document)* falsifier; *(signature)* contre-faire

fall 1 *n (of prices, shares, interest rate, value)* baisse *f* (**in** de); *(of currency)* dépréciation *f* (**in** de)
2 *vi (of prices, shares, interest rate, value)* baisser; *(of currency)* se déprécier

▸ **fall back** *vi (of shares)* se replier; **shares fell back one point** les actions se sont repliées d'un point

▸ **fall off** *vi (of profits, takings, sales)* diminuer

fallen angel *n St Exch* ange *m* déchu

falling *adj (prices, shares, interest rate, value)* qui baisse; *(currency)* en baisse; *(market)* baissier(ère), en baisse

falling-off *n* baisse *f*, réduction *f* (**in** de); **there has been a recent falling-off in production** il y a eu récemment une baisse de la production

false *adj* faux (fausse) □ **false bill** fausse facture *f*; **false claim** promesse *f* mensongère; *Acct* **false entry** fausse écriture *f*

falsification *n* falsification *f*

falsify *vt (document)* falsifier; *(balance sheet)* fausser

family *n Br Formerly Admin* **family allowance** allocations *fpl* familiales; *Admin* **family benefits** prestations *fpl* familiales; *Mktg* **family brand** marque *f* générale; **Ford is one of the world's best-known family brands** Ford est l'une des marques générales les plus connues du monde; **family business** entreprise *f* familiale; *Br Admin* **family credit** = prestation complémentaire pour familles à faibles revenus ayant au moins un enfant; *Admin* **family income** revenu *m* familial; *Br Formerly Admin* **family income supplement** ≃ complément *m* familial; *Br Formerly Admin* **family income support** ≃ complément *m* familial; **family leave** congé *m* parental; **family lifecycle** cycle *m* de vie familiale; **family model** modèle *m* familial

family-sized *adj (packet, box)* familial(e)

Fannie Mae *n Am* Fannie Mae *(organisme fédéral de crédit immobilier)*

> ❝
> These government mandated mortgage market "wholesalers", **Fannie Mae** and Freddie Mac – or savings and loan institutions similar to building societies – have been expanding their trillion dollar balance sheets at annualised rates of greater than 20%.
> ❞

FAO 1 *n (abbr* **Food and Agriculture Organization**) FAO *f*
2 *prep (abbr* **for the attention of**) à l'attention de

FAQ 1 *n Comptr (abbr* **frequently asked questions**) FAQ □ **FAQ file** fichier *m* FAQ
2 *adj (abbr* **free alongside quay**) FLQ

faq *n (abbr* **fair average quality**) qualité *f* loyale et marchande

FAS *adj (abbr* **free alongside ship**) FLB

fast mover *n Mktg* article *m* à forte rotation

fast-moving *adj Mktg* à forte rotation □ **fast-moving consumer goods** biens *mpl* de (grande) consommation à forte rotation

fast-track 1 *adj* (**a**) *(executive, graduate, employee)* = qui gravit rapidement les échelons (**b**) *(application, procedure)* accéléré(e)
2 *vt (application, procedure)* accélérer; **he's been fast-tracked for promotion** il a bénéficié d'une promotion accélérée

fast-tracking *n* (**a**) *(of executive, graduate, employee)* avancement *m* rapide (**b**) *(of application)* traitement *m* accéléré; *(of procedure)* accélération *f*

fat cat *n (in industry)* = personne touchant un salaire extrêmement élevé de façon injustifiée

> ❝
> Shell, the self-styled socially responsible oil group, yesterday rekindled the row over boardroom pay by disclosing that its new executive chairman, Phil Watts, won an 82% pay rise to £1.59m last year. The increase in Mr Watts' salary package, including a £455,000 performance bonus, dwarfed the 58% rise given to BP's chief executive Lord Browne which itself retriggered the **fat cat** furore.
> ❞

fault tree *n* arbre *m* de défaillances

faulty *adj* défectueux(euse)

favorable *Am* = **favourable**

favorites *npl Comptr (websites)* favoris *mpl*

favourable, *Am* **favorable** *adj (terms)* bon (bonne), avantageux(euse); **on favourable terms** à des conditions avantageuses, à bon compte

fax 1 *n (machine)* fax *m*, télécopieur *m*; *(document, message)* fax, télécopie *f*; **to send sb a fax** envoyer un fax *ou* une télécopie à qn; **to send sth by fax** envoyer qch par fax *ou* télécopie □ *Comptr* **fax card** carte *f* fax; *Comptr* **fax modem** modem-fax *m*; **fax number** numéro *m* de fax
2 *vt (message, document)* faxer, télécopier, envoyer par fax *ou* télécopie; *(person)* envoyer un fax *ou* une télécopie à

FCFS *(abbr* **first come, first served**) premier arrivé, premier servi

FCL-FCL *(abbr* **full container load-full container load**) FCL-FCL

FCL-LCL (*abbr* **full container load-less than container load**) FCL-LCL

FDI *n* (*abbr* **foreign direct investment**) IDE *m*

feasibility *n* (*of plan*) faisabilité *f* ❑ **feasibility report** rapport *m* de faisabilité; **feasibility stage** phase *f* de faisabilité; **feasibility study** étude *f* de faisabilité; **feasibility test** essai *m* probatoire

featherbed *vt Econ* (*industry, business*) subventionner excessivement

> 〃
>
> Despite US recession, Euro-zone slump, the collapse in American tourists and foot and mouth fears, consumers just keep on spending – so much so that towns in Northern Ireland are reporting a surge in shoppers offloading their punts. Some of this is down to the side effects of the monumental currency switch. At least IR£500 million (£392m) in so-called 'mattress money' is **featherbedding** the economy by boosting consumer spending.
>
> 〃

featherbedding *n Econ* subventionnement *m* excessif

feature 1 *n* (*of product*) caractéristique *f*
 2 *vt* (*of product*) comporter, être équipé(e) de; **all our products feature a money-back guarantee** tous nos produits sont accompagnés d'une garantie de remboursement

Fed *n Am* (**a**) (*abbr* **Federal Reserve Board**) banque *f* centrale (des États-Unis) (**b**) (*abbr* **Federal Reserve (System)**) (système *m* de) Réserve *f* fédérale (**c**) (*abbr* **Federal Reserve (Bank)**) banque *f* membre de la Réserve fédérale (**d**) (*abbr* **Federal**) *Fed Funds* fonds *mpl* fédéraux

> 〃
>
> Hong Kong Monetary Authority interest rates are following the US **Fed Funds** rate in a downward direction, already at 2.0%, and with strong hints by the **Fed**'s Governor Laurence Meyer last week of more monetary easing to come.
>
> 〃

federal *adj Federal Aviation Administration* = direction fédérale de l'aviation civile américaine; *Law* **federal court** cour *f* fédérale; *Federal Debt* dette *f* publique *ou* de l'État; *Federal Deposit Insurance Corporation* = organisme garantissant la sécurité des dépôts dans les banques qui en sont membres; *Federal funds* fonds *mpl* fédéraux; *Federal Housing Administration* = organisme de gestion des logements sociaux aux États-Unis; *Federal Insurance Contributions Act* = loi américaine régissant les cotisations sociales; *Federal Mediation*

and Conciliation Services = organisme américain de conciliation des conflits du travail; *Am Federal National Mortgage Association* FNMA *f* (*organisme fédéral de crédit immobiler*); *Federal Reserve* Réserve *f* fédérale; *Federal Reserve Bank* banque *f* membre de la Réserve fédérale; *Federal Reserve Board* banque centrale (des États-Unis); *Federal Reserve System* système *m* de Réserve *f* fédérale; *Federal Trade Commission* = commission fédérale chargée de veiller au respect de la concurrence sur le marché

> 〃
>
> The **Federal Reserve Board** sets monetary policy, develops banking regulations and examines banks for compliance with laws and regulations. The White House's announcement today that Mr. Olson would serve on the **Federal** board is well received by the Minnesota bankers because Mr. Olson thoroughly understands the issues facing Minnesota banks.
>
> 〃

federation *n* fédération *f*

fee *n* droits *mpl*; (*of lawyer, doctor*) honoraires *mpl*; (*for services*) prestation *f*, redevance *f*; (*for agency*) commission *f*; **to draw one's fees** toucher ses honoraires; **to do sth for a small fee** faire qch contre une somme modique; **to charge a fee** demander une prestation de service; *Law* **property held in fee simple** propriété *f* inconditionnelle

feed *vt Comptr* (*paper*) faire avancer, alimenter; **to feed data into a computer** entrer des données dans un ordinateur

feedback *n* réaction *f*, écho *m*; **we welcome feedback from our customers** nous sommes toujours heureux d'avoir les impressions *ou* les réactions de nos clients; **we need more feedback** nous avons besoin de plus d'informations *ou* d'informations en retour; **this will provide us with much-needed feedback on public opinion** ceci nous fournira des informations dont nous avons grand besoin sur l'opinion publique

feeder *n Comptr* (*for printer, scanner, photocopier*) chargeur *m*

FEPC *adj Am* (*abbr* **Fair Employment Practices Commission**) = commission dont les membres sont nommés par le Sénat, qui veille à l'application des mesures anti-discriminatoires en matière d'emploi

fetch *vt* (*be sold for*) rapporter; (*specific price*) atteindre; **it fetched a high price** cela s'est vendu cher; **it fetched £100,000** cela a atteint les 100 000 livres

FHA *adj* (*abbr* **Federal Housing Administration**) = organisme de gestion des logements sociaux aux États-Unis

fiat (money) n Am monnaie f fiduciaire

❝
And, at the base of the financial system, with the abandonment of gold convertibility in the 1930s, legal tender became backed – if that is the proper term – by the **fiat** of the state. The value of **fiat money** can be inferred only from the values of the present and future goods and services it can command. And that, in turn, has largely rested on the quantity of **fiat money** created relative to demand.
❞

fibre-optic, Am **fiber-optic** adj (technology) de la fibre optique; (system) qui utilise la fibre optique; (components) en fibre optique ◳ **fibre-optic cable** câble m optique, câble en fibres optiques

fibre optics n fibre f optique

FICA n (abbr **Federal Insurance Contributions Act**) = loi américaine régissant les cotisations sociales

fictitious adj **fictitious assets** actif m fictif; **fictitious bill** traite f en l'air; **fictitious cost** charge f fictive; **fictitious person** personne f fictive

fidelity guarantee n Ins assurance f contre les détournements

fiduciary Fin 1 n (trustee) dépositaire mf
2 adj fiduciaire ◳ **fiduciary account** compte m fiduciaire; **fiduciary issue** émission f fiduciaire

field n (a) Mktg (for product) marché m
(b) (sphere of activity, knowledge) domaine m; **what field are you in?, what's your field?** dans quoi travaillez-vous?; **to be an expert in one's field** être expert dans son domaine ◳ **field of activity** sphère f ou secteur m d'activité
(c) (practice as opposed to theory) terrain m; **in the field** sur le terrain ◳ **field engineer** ingénieur m de chantier ou sur le terrain; **field experiment** expérience f sur le terrain; **field marketing** marketing m sur le terrain; **field research** études fpl sur le terrain; **field study** étude sur le terrain; **field test** essai m sur le terrain; **field trial** (for machine) essai sur le terrain; **field work** démarchage m auprès de la clientèle
(d) Comptr (in database) champ m ◳ **field name** nom m de champ

field-test vt soumettre à des essais sur le terrain

FIFO (abbr **first in, first out**) PEPS

fifty-fifty 1 adj **a fifty-fifty venture** un accord d'entreprise en coparticipation à 50%
2 adv **to share the costs fifty-fifty** partager les frais moitié-moitié

figure n chiffre m; **figures** (statistics) statistiques fpl; **the figures for next year look good** les statistiques pour l'année prochaine semblent favorables; **to work out the figures** faire les calculs; **to find a mistake in the figures** trouver une erreur de calcul; **his income runs into six figures** ≃ il a un revenu de plus de 150 000 euros

file 1 n (a) (folder) chemise f; (ring binder) classeur m
(b) (documents) dossier m; **to have/keep sth on file** avoir/garder qch dans ses dossiers; **it's on file** c'est dans les dossiers, c'est classé; **we will keep your name on file** nous garderons votre dossier (de candidature) ◳ Am **file cabinet** classeur m; Am **file clerk** documentaliste mf; **file copy** exemplaire m ou pièce f d'archives
(c) Comptr fichier m ◳ **file compression** compression f de fichiers; **file conversion** conversion f de fichiers; **file extension** extension f du nom de fichier; **file format** format m de fichier; **file lock** verrouillage f de fichiers; **file management** gestion f ou tenue f de fichiers; **file management system** système m de gestion de fichiers; **file manager** gestionnaire m de fichiers; **file menu** menu m fichier; **file merge** fusion f de fichiers; **file name** nom m de fichier; **file name extension** extension de nom de fichier; **file protection** protection f de fichiers; **file server** serveur m de fichiers; **file sharing** partage m de fichiers; **file structure** structure f de fichier; **file transfer** transfert m de fichier; **file transfer protocol** protocole m de transfert de fichier; **file viewer** visualiseur m
2 vt (a) (documents) classer; **file these documents under "sales"** classez ces documents sous la rubrique "ventes"; **what name is it filed under?** sous quel nom est-il classé?
(b) (complaint, claim, request) déposer; Fin **to file one's petition in bankruptcy** déposer son bilan; **to file an application for a patent** déposer une demande de brevet; **to file a claim for damages** intenter un procès en dommages-intérêts; Am **to file one's tax return** remplir sa déclaration d'impôts
3 vi (classify documents) faire du classement

filing n (a) (of documents) classement m; **there is a lot of filing to be done** il y a beaucoup de classement à faire ◳ **filing cabinet** classeur m; Br **filing clerk** documentaliste mf; **filing system** méthode f de classement; **filing tray** corbeille f pour documents à classer (b) (of complaint, claim, request) dépôt m

fill vt (post, vacancy) pourvoir à; **the post has already been filled** le poste est déjà pourvu

▸ **fill in** vt sep (form, cheque stub, application) remplir; (date) insérer

▸ **fill out** vt sep (form, cheque stub, application) remplir

filter n Comptr filtre m

Fimbra n Br (abbr **Financial Intermediaries, Managers and Brokers Regulatory Associa-**

tion) = organisme britannique contrôlant les activités des courtiers d'assurances

final *adj* dernier(ère) ❑ *final acceptance* réception *f* définitive; *final accounts* compte *m* définitif; *final assessment* état *m* récapitulatif; *final copy* copie *f* au net *ou* au propre; *final date (for payment)* date *f* limite; *final demand (for payment)* dernier avis *m*, dernier rappel *m*; *St Exch final dividend* dividende *m* final; *final instalment* dernier versement *m*, versement libératoire; *final offer* dernière proposition *f*; *final payment* dernier paiement *m*; *final product* produit *m* fini; *Fin final settlement* solde *m* de tout compte; *final statement* résultat *m* final

finalization *n (of details, plans, arrangements)* mise *f* au point; *(of deal, decision, arrangement)* conclusion *f*

finalize *vt (details, plans, arrangements)* mettre au point; *(deal, decision, agreement)* mener à bonne fin; *(date)* arrêter

finance **1** *n* **(a)** *(money, field)* finance *f*; **we don't have the necessary finance** nous n'avons pas les fonds nécessaires ❑ *Finance Act* loi *f* de Finances; *finance bill* projet *m* de loi de finances; *finance charges* frais *mpl* financiers; *finance company* société *f* financière, = société britannique de financement pour les achats à crédit; *finance costs* frais financiers; *finance department* direction *f* financière; *finance director* directeur(trice) *m,f* financier(ère); *Br finance house* société financière, = société britannique de financement pour les achats à crédit; *Finance Minister* ministre *m* de l'Économie et des Finances

(b) **finances** *(funds)* finances *fpl*; **the company's finances are a bit low just now** les finances de l'entreprise sont un peu basses en ce moment

2 *vt (project)* financer; *(person, company)* financer, commanditer; **the company has agreed to finance staff training** l'entreprise a donné son accord pour financer la formation du personnel

financial *adj* financier(ère) ❑ *financial accountant* comptable *mf* financier(ère); *financial accounting* comptabilité *f* financière; *financial administration* gestion *f* financière; *financial adviser* conseiller(ère) *m,f* financier(ère); *financial aid* aide *f* financière; *financial analyst* analyste *mf* financier(ère); *financial appraisal* évaluation *f* financière; *financial arrangement* montage *m* financier; *financial assistance* appui *m* financier; *financial authorities* autorités *fpl* financières; *financial backer* bailleur(eresse) *m,f* de fonds; *financial backing* financement *m*, aide *f* financière; *financial centre* place *f* financière; *financial chart* graphique *m* financier; *financial circles* milieux *mpl* financiers; *fi-*

nancial community communauté *f* financière; *financial compensation* contrepartie *f* financière; *financial consultant* conseiller(ère) financier(ère); *financial control* contrôle *m* financier; *financial controller* contrôleur(euse) *m,f* financier(ère); *Acct financial costs* frais *mpl* financiers; *financial crisis* crise *f* financière; *Acct financial deal* opération *f* financière; *financial difficulties* difficultés *fpl* financières, difficultés de trésorerie; *financial director* directeur(trice) *m,f* financier(ère); *financial engineering* ingénierie *f* financière; *financial expenses* charges *fpl* financières; *St Exch financial future* instrument *m* financier à terme; *St Exch financial futures market* marché *m* d'instruments financiers à terme; *financial gearing* effet *m* de levier financier; *financial group* groupe *m* financier; *financial healthcheck* diagnostic *m* financier; *financial imbalance* déséquilibre *m* financier; *financial institution* établissement *m* financier; *financial instrument* instrument financier; *financial intermediary* intermédiaire *mf* financier(ère); *financial journal* revue *f* financière; *financial management* direction *f ou* gestion *f* financière; *financial manager* directeur(trice) financier(ère); *financial market* marché financier; *financial means* moyens *mpl* financiers; *financial news* chronique *f* financière; *financial ombudsman* arbitre *m* financier; *financial partner* partenaire *mf* financier(ère); *financial period* période *f* comptable; *financial plan* plan *m* de financement; *financial planning* planification *f* financière; *financial pool* groupement *m* financier; *financial position* position *f ou* situation *f* financière; *financial press* presse *f* financière; *financial pressure* problèmes *mpl* financiers; *financial product* produit *m* financier; *Acct financial ratio* ratio *m* de gestion; *Acct financial report* rapport *m* financier; *Acct financial reporting* communication *f* de l'information financière; *Br Financial Reporting Council* = commission de contrôle de la qualité de l'information financière publiée par les entreprises; *financial resources* ressources *fpl* financières; *financial review* examen *m* financier; *financial services* services *mpl* financiers; *Financial Services Authority* = organisme gouvernemental britannique chargé de contrôler les activités du secteur financier; *financial situation* situation financière; *financial statement* état *m* financier, déclaration *f* de résultats; *financial strategy* stratégie *f* financière; *financial support* soutien *m* financier; *financial syndicate* syndicat *m* financier; *Financial Times All-Share Index* = indice boursier du *Financial Times* basé sur la valeur de 700 actions cotées à la Bourse de Londres; *Financial Times-(Industrial) Ordinary Share Index* = indice boursier du *Financial Times* basé sur la valeur de 30 actions cotées à la Bourse de Londres; **Financial Times-Stock Exchange 100 Share Index** = principal indice boursier du *Financial Times* basé sur la valeur de 100 actions cotées à la Bourse de Londres; **financial transaction** opération financière; *Br* **financial year** exercice *m* (comptable)

financially *adv* financièrement; **financially sound** solvable

financier *n* financier *m*

financing *n* financement *m* □ **financing capacity** capacité *f* de financement

find *Comptr* 1 *n* **find command** commande *f* de recherche
2 *vt* **to find and replace** trouver et remplacer

finder's fee *n* commission *f* de démarcheur

findings *npl* *(of research, inquiry)* résultats *mpl*; *(of tribunal, committee, report)* conclusion *f*; **as a result of the findings, the R&D department proceeded with their plans for a new model** au vu des résultats de l'étude de marché, le service recherche et développement a poursuivi ses études pour un nouveau modèle

fine *adj Fin* **fine bill** beau papier *m*; *Fin* **fine trade bill** papier de haut commerce *ou* de première catégorie

finish *n St Exch* clôture *f*; **price at the finish** prix *m* de clôture; **trading at the finish** opérations *fpl* de clôture; **shares were up at the finish** les actions étaient en hausse à la clôture

fire *vt (dismiss)* virer; **to get fired** se faire virer

firewall *n Comptr* mur *m* coupe-feu, garde-barrière *f*

“
According to figures from the Department of Trade and Industry (DTI), about 33% of businesses still do not have a **firewall** between their websites and their internal computer systems, leaving them vulnerable to hackers. And 66% do not have intrusion detection systems, which could detect hackers if they penetrated other defences.
”

firm 1 *n* entreprise *f*, firme *f*; *(of lawyers, consultants)* cabinet *m*
2 *adj (offer, sale, deal)* ferme; *(market)* stable; *(contango rates)* tendu(e); **oil shares remain firm at $20** les valeurs pétrolières se maintiennent à 20 dollars; **to place a firm order for sth** passer une commande ferme de qch □ *Fin* **firm currency** devise *f* soutenue; **firm order** commande *f* ferme; **firm sale** vente *f* ferme

firmware *n Comptr* firmware *m*, microprogramme *m*

first 1 *n* (a) *Banking, Fin* **first of exchange** première *f* de change (b) **first in, first out** premier entré, premier sorti; **first in, last out** premier

entré, dernier sorti; **first come, first served** le premier arrivé est le premier servi
2 *adj* premier(ère) □ **first class** *(on train, plane)* première classe *f*; *(for letter, parcel)* tarif *m* normal; **first quarter** *(of year)* premier trimestre *m*; **first refusal** préférence *f*; **to give sb first refusal on sth** donner la préférence à qn pour qch; **the First World** les pays *mpl* industrialisés

first-class *adj* (a) *(seat)* en première classe; *(compartment, ticket)* de première classe (b) *Br (letter, stamp)* au tarif normal; **to send a letter by first-class mail** envoyer une lettre au tarif normal (c) **first-class paper** effet *m* de première catégorie

first-loss *n Ins* premier risque *m* □ **first-loss insurance** assurance *f* au premier risque

first-notice day *n St Exch* premier jour *m* de notification

first-time *adj* **first-time buyer** *(of property)* = personne achetant une propriété pour la première fois; **first-time user** nouvel(elle) utilisateur(trice) *m,f*

“
Leven has the most affordable property market in Britain, according to Halifax, the mortgage bank. The average property bought by a **first-time buyer** costs £34,000. This is less than one-and-a-half times Scottish average earnings for a full-time male employee – a standard measure of house price affordability.
”

fiscal *adj* fiscal(e) □ **fiscal agent** représentant(e) *m,f* fiscal(e); *Econ* **fiscal drag** frein *m* fiscal, érosion *f* fiscale; **fiscal measure** mesure *f* fiscale; *Am Acct* **fiscal period** période *f* comptable; **fiscal policy** politique *f* budgétaire; *Am* **fiscal year** *Fin* exercice *m* (financier), année *f* fiscale *ou* d'exercice; *Admin* année budgétaire

fiscality *n* fiscalité *f*

Five-Year Plan *n Econ* Plan *m* quinquennal

fix *vt (price, interest rate)* fixer; **to fix the budget** déterminer le budget

▶ **fix up** *vt sep* organiser

fixed *adj (price, rate)* fixe □ *Fin* **fixed annuity** rente *f* fixe; *Acct* **fixed asset** actif *m* immobilisé; *Acct* **fixed assets** immobilisations *fpl*, actif immobilisé; *Fin* **fixed capital** capital *m* fixe; **fixed charge** frais *mpl* fixes; **fixed cost** coût *m* fixe *ou* constant; *Fin* **fixed deposit** dépôt *m* à terme (fixe) *ou* à échéance fixe; *Comptr* **fixed disk** disque *m* fixe; *Fin* **fixed exchange rate** taux *m* de change fixe; **fixed income** revenu *m* fixe; *Banking, Fin* **fixed interest** intérêt *m* fixe; *Fin* **fixed investment** immobilisations; *Fin* **fixed maturity** échéance *f* fixe; *Fin* **fixed parity** parité *f* fixe; **fixed property** immeubles *mpl*;

Banking, Fin **fixed rate** taux fixe; **fixed salary** salaire *m* fixe; **fixed savings** épargne *f* mobilière; **fixed wage** salaire fixe; *Fin* **fixed yield** rendement *m* fixe

fixed-income *Am* = **fixed-interest**

fixed-interest *adj Fin (investments, securities)* à intérêt fixe ❏ *fixed-interest market* marché *m* des obligations

fixed-premium *adj (insurance, policy)* forfaitaire

fixed-rate *adj Fin (loan, mortgage)* à taux fixe ❏ *fixed-rate assessment system* régime *m* du forfait; *fixed-rate bond* obligation *f* à revenu fixe; *fixed-rate borrowing* emprunts *mpl* à taux fixe; *fixed-rate financing* financement *m* à taux fixe; *fixed-rate investment* investissement *m* à revenu fixe; *fixed-rate rebate* abattement *m* forfaitaire; *fixed-rate securities* titres *mpl* à revenu fixe

fixed-term *adj* à terme fixe ❏ *Fin fixed-term bill* effet *m* à date fixe; *fixed-term contract* contrat *m* à durée déterminée, CDD *m*; *Fin fixed-term credit* crédit *m* à durée déterminée; *Fin fixed-term deposit* dépôt *m* à terme fixe *ou* à échéance fixe

fixed-yield *adj Fin* à rendement fixe

fixture *n* installation *f* fixe ❏ *fixtures and fittings* reprise *f*; "fixtures and fittings £2,000" "reprise 2000 livres"

flag *n* **flag airline** compagnie *f* aérienne nationale; *flag of convenience* pavillon *m* de complaisance

flagging *adj (economy)* languissant(e)

flagship *n (product)* tête *f* de gamme; **this latest model is the flagship of their new range** ce dernier modèle est le produit vedette de leur nouvelle gamme; **the London store is the flagship of the chain** le magasin de Londres est le plus important de la chaîne ❏ *flagship branch* succursale *f* vedette; *flagship brand* marque *f* étendard, marque fer de lance; *flagship product* produit *m* fer de lance, produit vedette; *flagship store* magasin *m* vitrine

"
The design of Virgin Vie's **flagship store** in Oxford Street – which is based on the principles of Japanese landscape gardening – draws customers into the store via a window water feature.
"

flame *Comptr* **1** *n* message *m* injurieux ❏ *flame war* guerre *f* d'insultes
2 *vt* descendre en flammes, incendier
3 *vi* rédiger des messages injurieux

flamer *n Comptr* auteur *m* d'un message injurieux

flaming *n Comptr* envoi *m* de messages injurieux

flank attack *n Mktg (on market)* attaque *f* latérale

flash pack *n (discounted)* emballage *m* portant une réduction de prix

flat *adj (market)* calme, languissant(e); *(fare, sum)* fixe ❏ *flat bed (of vehicle)* plateau *m*; *flat fee* commission *f* immédiate; *Comptr flat file* fichier *m* de données non structurées; *Comptr flat monitor* écran *m* plat; *flat price* prix *m* unique; *flat rate* tarif *m* fixe; *Comptr flat screen* écran *m* plat

flatbed scanner *n Comptr* scanner *m* ou scanneur *m* à plat

flat-rate *adj* à taux fixe ❏ *Comptr flat-rate connection (to Internet)* connexion *f* à tarif forfaitaire

flat-screen *adj Comptr* à écran plat ❏ *flat-screen monitor* moniteur *m* à écran plat

flaw *n (in product, plan)* défaut *m*

fledgling *adj (company, industry)* naissant(e)

fleet rating *n Ins* tarification *f* flotte, barème *m* des flottes

Fleet Street *n* = rue de Londres, dont le nom sert à désigner les grands journaux britanniques; **the Fleet Street papers** les journaux *mpl* nationaux

"
But Morgan said: "*The Sun* can bluster away about it being a war, and glory in their Lara Logan bazooka exposés selling better than our famine in Malawi investigations, but we're not interested in what they say or what they do. They, like the rest of **Fleet Street**, do not have a clue what we are up to and that's the way I like it."
"

flexcash *n Am* = argent versé par une entreprise à ses employés, le plus souvent pour souscrire une assurance-maladie ou une assurance-vie

flexdollars *npl* = **flexcash**

flexibility *n (of prices, approach)* flexibilité *f*

flexible *adj (prices, approach)* flexible ❏ *flexible budget* budget *m* variable *ou* flexible; *flexible manufacturing system* système *m* de fabrication flexible; *flexible mortgage* emprunt *m* immobilier à échéances variables; *flexible working hours* horaires *mpl* flexibles *ou* à la carte

"
A change in the law to promote **flexible working hours** for parents of young children will help to improve economic effi-

> ciency and save British businesses up to £100m a year in recruitment costs, the trade and industry secretary, Patricia Hewitt, predicted yesterday. 🙶

flexitime, flextime n horaires mpl flexibles ou à la carte

flier n (**a**) Am Fam (speculative venture) entreprise f à risques; **to take a flier** (financial risk) prendre un risque financier (**b**) (leaflet) prospectus m

flight n (**a**) (of plane) vol m ◻ **flight coupon** coupon m de vol; **flight number** numéro m de vol; **flight personnel** personnel m navigant; **flight time** durée f de vol (**b**) **flight capital** capitaux mpl flottants ou fébriles; **flight of capital** évasion f des capitaux, fuite f des capitaux

flip chart n tableau m à feuilles

float 1 n (**a**) Am (petty cash) petite caisse f; Br (in cash register) fonds m de caisse; (cash advance) avance f; (business loan) prêt m de lancement
(**b**) St Exch flottant m ◻ **clean float** taux mpl de change libres ou flottants; **dirty float** taux de change concertés
2 vt (**a**) Fin, St Exch (company) lancer, créer; (onto Stock Market) introduire en Bourse; (loan, bonds, share issue) émettre, lancer
(**b**) Fin (currency) laisser flotter
(**c**) (idea, proposal) émettre

floatation = flotation

floater n effet m à taux flottant

floating 1 n (**a**) Fin, St Exch (of company) proposition f, création f; (onto Stock Market) introduction f en Bourse; (of loan, bonds, share issue) émission f, lancement m
(**b**) Fin (of currency) flottement m
(**c**) (of idea, proposal) lancement m
2 adj (**a**) Fin (currency) flottant(e) ◻ Acct **floating assets** actif m circulant, capital m disponible; Fin **floating capital** capital circulant; Banking **floating charge** nantissement m général; Fin **floating debt** dette f flottante ou courante ou non consolidée; Fin **floating exchange rate** taux m de change flottant; Ins **floating policy** police f d'abonnement ou flottante; Fin **floating rate** taux flottant
(**b**) Comptr **floating accent** accent m flottant; Comptr **floating point** virgule f flottante

floating-rate adj Fin à taux flottant ◻ **floating-rate bond** obligation f à intérêt variable; Banking **floating-rate certificate of deposit** certificat m de dépôt à taux flottant; **floating-rate interest** intérêt m à taux flottant; **floating-rate investment** investissement m à revenu variable; **floating-rate note** effet m à taux flottant; **floating-rate securities** valeurs fpl ou titres mpl à revenu variable

flood vt (market) inonder, encombrer; **the mar-** ket **is flooded with computer games** il y a une surabondance de jeux électroniques sur le marché

floor n (**a**) (in shop) **floor ad** publicité f au sol; **floor display** présentation f au sol; **floor manager** (in department store) chef m de rayon; Am **floor sample** modèle m d'exposition; **floor space** surface f au sol; **floor stand** présentatoir m au sol (**b**) (of Stock Exchange) parquet m ◻ **floor price** prix m seuil; **floor trader** commis m; **floor trading** cotation f à la corbeille

> 🙶
> **Floor price** funds quote three prices ... and a **floor price** (a price below which the bid price cannot fall). This **floor price** is adjusted annually, or after any significant market improvement, to give a new **floor price** which is valid for a year. So no matter what happens to the market, the value of your units will not fall below the **floor price**.
> 🙷

floorwalker n Am (in department store) chef m de rayon

floppy Comptr 1 n disquette f
2 adj **floppy disk** disquette f; **floppy (disk) drive** unité f de disquettes

florin n Formerly florin m

flotation n (**a**) Fin, St Exch (of company) lancement m; (onto Stock Market) introduction f en Bourse; (of loan, bonds, share issue) émission f, lancement (**b**) Fin (of currency) flottement m

flourish vi (of business, economy, trade) prospérer

flourishing adj (business, economy, trade) prospère

flow 1 n Fin (of capital) mouvement m; (of information) circulation f; **flow of money** flux m monétaire ou financier ◻ **flow chart** graphique m d'évolution, organigramme m; **flow diagram** graphique d'évolution, organigramme m; Comptr **flow path** branche f de traitement; Acct **flow sheet** feuille f d'avancement
2 vi (of capital, money) circuler

flow-through method n Am (of accounting) méthode f de l'impôt exigible

fluctuate vi (of market, currency, value) fluctuer; (of price) flotter, varier

fluctuating adj (market, currency, value) fluctuant(e); (price) flottant(e), variable

fluctuation n (of market, currency, value) fluctuation f; (of price) variation f ◻ **fluctuation band, fluctuation margin** marge f de fluctuation

flurry n agitation f; **there has been a late flurry of activity on the Stock Market** à la Bourse on a assisté à une reprise soudaine de l'activité en fin de journée

fly-by-night adj (company) véreux(euse)

flyer n (leaflet) prospectus m

flying picket n Ind piquet m de grève volant

FMCG npl Mktg (abbr **fast-moving consumer goods**) biens mpl de (grande) consommation à forte rotation

FMCS n Am (abbr **Federal Mediation and Conciliation Services**) = organisme de conciliation des conflits du travail

FNMA n Am (abbr **Federal National Mortgage Association**) FNMA f (organisme fédéral de crédit immobilier)

FO n Br Admin (abbr **Foreign Office**) ministère m des Affaires étrangères

FOB, fob adj (abbr **free on board**) FOB, FAB □ **FOB port of embarkation** FAB port m d'embarquement

focus group n Mktg groupe-témoin m □ **focus group interview** entretien m avec les membres du groupe-témoin

> **❝**
> **Focus group** research commissioned for the task force suggests both young and old people regard too many parks as unwelcoming because they are either rundown, poorly maintained or potentially dangerous.
> **❞**

fold vi Fam (of business) fermer ses portes, faire faillite

folder n (**a**) (file, document wallet) chemise f; (ring binder) classeur m (**b**) Comptr (directory) répertoire m

folding money n billets mpl de banque

folio Acct **1** n (sheet) folio m, feuillet m; (book) (livre m) in-folio m
2 vt paginer à livre ouvert

▶ **follow up 1** vt sep (letter) faire suivre d'une seconde lettre; (person) relancer; (advantage) poursuivre; (inquiry, order) donner suite à; (opportunity) saisir; (success) exploiter; **follow up your initial phone call with a letter** confirmez votre coup de téléphone par écrit
2 vi (in selling) faire de la relance

follower n Mktg suiveur m

following 1 adj suivant(e); **the following methods of payment are acceptable** sont acceptés les modes de paiement suivants
2 prep après, suite à; **following our conversation** suite à notre entretien; **following your letter** suite à ou en réponse à votre lettre

follow-me product n Mktg produit m tactique

follow-up n suite f; (of advertising, client) relance f; (of orders) suivi m □ **follow-up letter** lettre f de relance; **follow-up visit** visite f de re-lance; **follow-up work** travail m complémentaire

font n Comptr police f, fonte f

food n aliments mpl □ **the food industry** l'industrie f alimentaire; **food manufacturer** fabricant m de produits comestibles; **food packaging** emballage m des produits alimentaires; **food processing** industrie agro-alimentaire; **food products** produits mpl alimentaires, comestibles mpl, denrées fpl

food-processing adj (industry, sector) agro-alimentaire

foodstuffs npl produits mpl alimentaires, co-mestibles mpl, denrées fpl

footer n Comptr (on document) bas m de page

footfall n Mktg (people entering shop) fréquentation f

> **❝**
> Heathrow Airport, with a **footfall** of 1.2 mil-lion business travellers a month, allows cor-porate advertisers to make use of a medium which reaches business people with lower wastage than standard roadside outdoor sites.
> **❞**

footnote n note f de bas de page

footprint n (of building) surface f au sol

FOOTSIE, Footsie n (abbr **Financial Times-Stock Exchange 100 Index**) = principal indice boursier du Financial Times basé sur la valeur de 100 actions cotées à la Bourse de Londres

> **❝**
> Computer services group Logica is poised to be booted out of the **Footsie** after a profit warning left the shares down 51 pence at 243 pence for a two-day loss of 93 pence, wiping £415 million off its value. The shares peaked at 2724 pence in 2000. The firm, which supplies systems that make text-mes-saging possible, is also axing 700 jobs.
> **❞**

FOR adj (abbr **free on rail**) franco wagon

force n (**a**) (power) force f, puissance f; (of people) force f; **Europe is becoming a powerful economic force** l'Europe devient une grande puissance économique; **our sales force** notre force de vente (**b**) **to be in force** (of law, regula-tion) être en vigueur; **to come into force** entrer en vigueur (**c**) Ins **force majeure** (cas m de) force f majeure; **force majeure clause** clause f de force majeure

▶ **force down** vt sep (prices, inflation) faire baisser

▶ **force up** vt sep (prices, inflation) faire monter

forced adj **forced currency** cours m forcé;

forced loan emprunt *m* forcé; **forced sale** vente *f* forcée; **forced saving** épargne *f* forcée

forecast 1 *n* prévisions *fpl* ❑ *Acct* **forecast balance sheet** bilan *m* prévisionnel; **forecast operating budget** budget *m* d'exploitation prévisionnel; **forecast plan** plan *m* prévisionnel; **forecast sales level** montant *m* prévisionnel des ventes
  2 *vt* prévoir; **he forecasts sales of £2m** il prévoit un chiffre de vente de 2 millions de livres

forecaster *n Econ* expert *m*

foreclose *Law* **1** *vt* saisir; **to foreclose a mortgage** saisir un bien hypothéqué
  2 *vi* saisir le bien hypothéqué; **to foreclose on sb** saisir les biens de qn; **to foreclose on a mortgage** saisir un bien hypothéqué

foreclosure *n Law* forclusion *f*, saisie *f*

foreign *adj* étranger(ère) ❑ **foreign account** compte *m* étranger; **foreign affairs** affaires *fpl* étrangères; **foreign agent** représentant(e) *m,f* à l'étranger; **foreign bill** effet *m* sur l'extérieur *ou* sur l'étranger; *Foreign and Commonwealth Office* ministère *m* britannique des Affaires étrangères; *Foreign and Commonwealth Secretary* ministre *m* britannique des Affaires étrangères; **foreign currency** devises *fpl* étrangères; **foreign currency account** compte en devises étrangères; **foreign currency assets** avoirs *mpl* en devises étrangères; **foreign currency earnings** apport *m* de devises étrangères; **foreign currency holding** avoir *m* en devises étrangères; **foreign currency loan** prêt *m* en devises étrangères; **foreign currency option** option *f* de change; **foreign currency reserves** réserves *fpl* de change, réserves en devises étrangères; **foreign debt** dette *f* extérieure; **foreign direct investment** investissement *m* direct (à l')étranger; **foreign exchange** devises étrangères; **foreign exchange broker** cambiste *mf*, courtier(ère) *m,f* en devises étrangères; **foreign exchange control** contrôle *m* des changes; **foreign exchange dealer** cambiste, courtier(ère) en devises étrangères; **foreign exchange gain** gain *m* de change; **foreign exchange inflow** rentrée *f* de devises étrangères; **foreign exchange loss** perte *f* de change; **foreign exchange market** marché *m* des devises étrangères; **foreign exchange option** option sur devises étrangères; **foreign exchange outflow** sortie *f* de devises étrangères; **foreign exchange rate** cours *m* des devises étrangères; **foreign exchange reserves** réserves de change, réserves en devises étrangères; **foreign exchange risk** risque *m* de change; **foreign exchange transfer** transfert *m* de devises étrangères; **foreign goods** marchandises *fpl* qui viennent de l'étranger; **foreign investments** investissements *mpl* à l'étranger; **foreign investor** investisseur *m* à l'étranger;

foreign labour main-d'œuvre *f* étrangère; **foreign market** marché extérieur; *Br* **Foreign Office** ministère des Affaires étrangères; **foreign policy** politique *f* étrangère *ou* extérieure; **foreign produce** produits *mpl* qui viennent de l'étranger; **foreign rights** droits *mpl* étrangers; **foreign trade** commerce *m* extérieur

> **“**
> These legal reforms are "essential to get credit flowing again and to restore the confidence of domestic and **foreign investors**, without which it will be very difficult to revive investment and growth," she said. Order must also be restored to the **foreign exchange market**, where reports say the central bank plans continued interventions to help support the weak peso.
> **”**

foreman *n* contremaître *m*, chef *m* d'équipe

forementioned *adj Admin, Law* précité(e)

forensic accounting *n* ≃ expertise *f* judiciaire

forex *n* (*abbr* **foreign exchange**) devises *fpl* étrangères ❑ **forex trading** transactions *fpl* en devises étrangères

> **“**
> On the world's adrenaline-charged foreign exchange markets, $1.5 trillion changes hands every day. To set that figure in context, the global trade in merchandise and commercial services last year was $6.5 trillion – or 4.3 days of **forex trading**.
> **”**

forfaiting *n Banking* forfaitage *m*, forfaitisation *f*

forfeit 1 *n* (**a**) *Law (for non-performance of contract)* dédit *m* ❑ **forfeit clause** clause *f* de dédit (**b**) *St Exch* **to relinquish the forfeit** abandonner la prime (**c**) *Law* **to declare goods forfeit** confisquer des marchandises
  2 *vt Law (lose)* perdre par confiscation; *(confiscate)* confisquer; **to forfeit a deposit** perdre les arrhes; **to forfeit a patent** déchoir d'un brevet

forfeiture *n* (**a**) *St Exch (of shares)* déchéance *f*, forfaiture *f* (**b**) *(of sum)* amende *f*, dédit *m*; *(of penalty)* prix *m*, peine *f* (**c**) *Law (loss)* perte *f* par confiscation

forge *vt* contrefaire

forged *adj* faux (fausse)

forgery *n* (**a**) *(activity)* contrefaçon *f*; *(of document, banknote)* falsification *f* (**b**) *(thing forged)* faux *m*; **the signature was a forgery** la signature était contrefaite

form 1 *n* (**a**) *(for applications, orders)* formulaire *m*; **to fill in** *or* **out a form** remplir un formulaire ❑ **form letter** lettre *f* type (**b**) *Comptr (on Inter-*

net) formulaire *m* ❏ *form document* document *m* canevas; *form feed* avancement *m* du papier
2 *vt (company)* fonder, créer; *(committee)* former

formal *adj (official)* officiel(elle) ❏ *formal agreement* accord *m* en bonne et due forme; *formal consent* consentement *m* exprès; *formal demand* demande *f* officielle; *formal notice* mise *f* en demeure

format 1 *n* **(a)** *Comptr* format *m* **(b)** *(of advertisement, publication)* format *m*
2 *vt Comptr (disk)* formater; *(page, text)* mettre en forme, formater

formation *n (of company)* constitution *f*

formatting *n Comptr (of disk)* formatage *m*; *(of page, text)* mise *f* en forme, formatage

for-profit organization *n Am* société *f* à but lucratif

forthcoming *adj* **the funds were not forthcoming** les fonds n'ont pas été débloqués

Fortune 500 *npl* = les cinq cents plus grosses entreprises américaines (dont la liste est établie, chaque année, par le magazine *Fortune*)

> **❝**
> Mr. Stenglein has represented various **Fortune 500** companies, including General Electric, PG& E Corporation, Hughes Electronics, Occidental Chemical Corporation, U.S. Trust Company and General Electric Capital Corporation.
> **❞**

forum *n Comptr* forum *m* (de discussion) ❏ *forum shopping* = fait de rechercher les conditions commerciales les plus favorables

forward 1 *adj* **(a)** *Fin* à terme ❏ *forward account* compte *m* à terme; *forward buying* achat *m* à terme; *forward contract* contrat *m* à terme; *forward dealing* opérations *fpl* à terme; *forward delivery* livraison *f* à terme; *forward exchange market* marché *m* des changes à terme; *forward exchange transaction* opération *f* de change à terme; *forward market* marché à terme; *forward price* prix *m* à terme; *St Exch forward purchase* achat à terme; *forward rate* cours *m* à terme, taux *m* pour les opérations à terme; *forward rate agreement* accord *m* de taux à terme; *St Exch forward sale* vente *f* à terme; *forward trading* opérations *fpl* à terme
(b) *(in direction) Econ forward integration* intégration *f* en aval *ou* descendante; *Comptr forward search* recherche *f* avant, recherche vers le bas; *Comptr forward slash* barre *f* oblique
2 *adv Acct* **to carry the balance forward** reporter le solde à nouveau; **(carried) forward** report *m*
3 *vt* **(a)** *(goods)* expédier, envoyer; **to forward sth to sb** faire parvenir qch à qn; **to forward goods to Paris** acheminer des marchandises sur *ou* vers Paris
(b) *(letter)* faire suivre; **please forward** *(on letter)* (prière de) faire suivre, faire suivre s.v.p.

forwardation *n Fin* report *m*

forwarder *n* transitaire *m*; **forwarder and consolidator** transitaire-groupeur *m*

forwarding *n* expédition *f*, envoi *m* ❏ *forwarding address (for goods)* adresse *f* pour l'expédition; *(for letter)* adresse pour faire suivre le courrier; *forwarding agent* (agent *m*) transitaire *m*, agent de ligne; *forwarding charges* frais *mpl* d'expédition; *forwarding department* service *m* des expéditions; *forwarding house* maison *f* d'expédition; *forwarding instructions* indications *fpl* concernant l'expédition; *forwarding office* bureau *m* d'expédition; *forwarding station* gare *f* d'expédition

FOT *adj (abbr* **free on truck***)* franco camion

foul *adj (bill of lading)* avec réserves

found *vt (company)* fonder, établir

foundation *n* **(a)** *(of company)* fondation *f*, création *f* **(b)** *(institution)* fondation *f*, institution *f* dotée; *(endowment)* dotation *f*, fondation

founder *n (of company)* fondateur(trice) *m,f* ❏ *founder member* membre *m* fondateur; *founder's share* part *f* bénéficiaire *ou* de fondateur

founding *n (of business)* fondation *f*, création *f* ❏ *founding member* membre *m* fondateur; *founding partner* associé(e) *m,f* fondateur(-trice)

fourth *adj* quatrième ❏ *fourth quarter (of year)* quatrième trimestre *m*; **the Fourth World** le quart-monde

FQDN *n Comptr (abbr* **Fully Qualified Domain Name***)* nom *m* de domaine complet

Fr *Formerly (abbr* **franc***)* F

FRA *n Fin (abbr* **Future Rate Agreement, Forward Rate Agreement***)* ATF *m*

fraction *n Fin (of share)* fraction *f*, rompu *m*

fractional *n Fin fractional currency* monnaie *f* divisionnaire; *fractional interest* fraction *f* d'intérêt; *fractional money* monnaie divisionnaire

fragile *adj (goods)* fragile

fragmentation *n Comptr (of hard disk)* fragmentation *f*

framework *n (structure)* cadre *m*; **within the framework of the EU** dans le cadre de l'UE

franc *n* franc *m* ❏ *franc area* zone *f* franc

franchisable *adj* franchisable, qui peut être franchisé(e)

franchise 1 *n* franchise *f*; **several high-street**

shops are run as franchises plusieurs grandes chaînes commerciales fonctionnent selon le système de la franchise ❏ *franchise agreement* accord *m* de franchise; *franchise outlet* boutique *f* franchisée
  2 *vt* franchiser, accorder une franchise à

franchisee *n* franchisé(e) *m,f*

franchiser *n* franchiseur(euse) *m,f*

franchising *n* franchisage *m* ❏ *franchising operation* franchisage

franchisor = **franchiser**

franco 1 *adj* franco ❏ *franco price* prix *m* franco
  2 *adv* franco

frank *vt (letter)* affranchir

franking machine *n Br* machine *f* à affranchir

fraud *n Law* fraude *f*; *Fin* escroquerie *f*; **to obtain sth by fraud** obtenir qch par fraude *ou* frauduleusement

fraudulent *adj* frauduleux(euse) ❏ *fraudulent balance sheet* faux bilan *m*; *fraudulent bankruptcy* faillite *f* frauduleuse; *fraudulent trading* commerce *m* frauduleux; *fraudulent transaction* transaction *f* frauduleuse

fraudulently *adv* frauduleusement

FRB *n Am (abbr* **Federal Reserve Board***)* banque *f* centrale des États-Unis

FRCD *n Banking (abbr* **floating-rate certificate of deposit***)* certificat *m* de dépôt à taux flottant

Freddie Mac *n Am* Freddie Mac *(organisme de crédit américain)*

free 1 *adj* **(a)** *(without charge)* gratuit(e); **free of all average** franc de toute avarie; **free on board** franco à bord; **free carrier** franco transporteur; **free of duty** exempt(e) de droits d'entrée; **free at frontier** franco frontière; **free in and out** bord à bord; **free overside** franco allège; **free at quay** franco long du quai, franco long du bord; **free on rail** franco wagon, franco de rail; **free alongside ship** franco long du quai, franco long du bord; **free of tax** franc d'impôts; **free on truck** franco camion; **free on wharf** franco long du quai, franco long du bord ❏ *free credit* crédit *m* gratuit; *free delivery* livraison *f* gratuite; *St Exch free float* actions *fpl* disponibles (au marché); *free gift* cadeau *m*; *free home delivery* livraison franco à domicile; *Customs free import* entrée *f* en franchise; *St Exch free issue* attribution *f* d'actions gratuites; *Customs free list* liste *f* des marchandises importées en franchise; *free sample* échantillon *m* gratuit; *free trial* essai *m* gratuit; *free trial period* période *f* d'essai gratuit
  (b) *(unrestricted)* libre ❏ *free agent* agent *m* indépendant; *free collective bargaining* négociation *f* des conventions collectives; *free competition* libre concurrence *f*; *free enter-*

prise libre entreprise *f*; *free market* marché *m* libre; *free market economics* libéralisme *m*; *free market economy* économie *f* libérale *ou* de marché; *free marketeer* libéral(e) *m,f*; *free movement (of goods, people, capital)* libre circulation *f*; *Customs free port* port *m* franc; *free trade* libre-échange *m*; *free trade agreement* accord *m* de libre-échange; *free trade area* zone *f* de libre-échange; *free trade association* association *f* de libre-échange; *free trade policy* politique *f* antiprotectionniste, politique de libre-échange; *free trader* libre-échangiste *mf*, antiprotectionniste *mf*; *free trade zone* zone de libre-échange; *free zone* zone franche
  2 *adv* gratuitement; **they will deliver free of charge** ils livreront gratuitement
  3 *vt (prices, trade)* libérer; *(funds)* débloquer

> **"**
> Mr Ralph himself described the sale of Sidex as "the privatisation of the decade" and "hugely important in terms of creating the fully functioning **free market economy** which the European Union has set as a fundamental criterion for Romanian accession to the EU". He recommended the letter be sent since "it would send a strong signal of British government support in the hope that this would stimulate increased British investment in and trade with Romania".
> **"**

freebie *n Fam* cadeau *m*

freedom *n* liberté *f* ❏ *freedom of communication* liberté *f* de communication; *freedom of information* liberté d'information; *Freedom of Information Act* = loi sur la communication aux citoyens des informations de source gouvernementale, en Grande-Bretagne; *freedom of the press* liberté de la presse; *freedom of trade* liberté du commerce

free-flowing *adj (capital)* flottant(e)

Freefone® *n Br Tel* appel *m* gratuit, ≃ numéro *m* vert; **call Freefone® 400** ≃ appelez le numéro vert 400

freehold *n* propriété *f* foncière perpétuelle et libre

freeholder *n* propriétaire *mf* foncier(ère)

freelance 1 *n* travailleur(euse) *m,f* indépendant(e), free-lance *mf*
  2 *adj* indépendant(e), free-lance
  3 *adv* **to work freelance** travailler en indépendant(e) *ou* en free-lance
  4 *vi* travailler en indépendant(e) *ou* en free-lance

freenet *n Comptr* libertel *m*

Freepost® *n Br* franchise *f* postale

freeware *n Comptr* logiciel *m* (du domaine) public, gratuiciel *m*, freeware *m*

freeze 1 n (of credit, wages) blocage m, gel m; (of currency, prices, assets) gel
  2 vt (credit, wages) geler, bloquer; (currency, prices, assets) geler
  3 vi Comptr (of screen, computer) être bloqué(e)

freezing n (of credit, wages) blocage m, gel m; (of currency, prices, assets) gel

freight 1 n (**a**) (transport) fret m, transport m de marchandises; **to send goods by freight** envoyer des marchandises par régime ordinaire
  ❏ **freight price** prix m de transport
  (**b**) (cargo, load) fret m, cargaison f; **to take in freight** prendre du fret
  (**c**) (goods) marchandises fpl (transportées)
  ❏ Am **freight car** wagon m de marchandises; Am **freight depot** gare f de marchandises; **freight forwarder** agent m de fret; **freight insurance** assurance f sur fret; **freight manifest** manifeste m de fret; **freight note** note f de fret; **freight plane** avion m de fret; **freight rate** tarif m marchandises; **freight release** bon m à délivrer; **freight service** service m de marchandises; **freight shipping** messageries fpl maritimes; **freight ton** tonne f d'affrètement; **freight traffic** mouvement m des marchandises; Am **freight train** train m de marchandises; **freight vehicle** véhicule m de transport de marchandises
  (**d**) (cost) (frais mpl de) port m; **freight by weight** fret m au poids; **freight (charges) paid** port payé; **freight forward** port avancé
  2 vt (goods) transporter

freightage n (frais mpl de) port m

freighter n (**a**) (of ship) affréteur m (**b**) (ship) cargo m; (aeroplane) avion m de fret

Freightliner® n train m de marchandises en conteneurs

French franc n Formerly franc m français

frequency n Mktg fréquence f ❏ **frequency rate** taux m de répétition

frequent adj **frequent flyer club** club m de fidélité de compagnie aérienne; **frequent flyer programme** programme m de fidélisation des passagers de compagnies aériennes; **frequent user card** carte f de fidélité

frictional unemployment n chômage m frictionnel ou de mobilité

friction feed n Comptr avancement m par friction

friendly adj Br Fin **friendly society** société f de mutualité; **friendly takeover bid** OPA f amicale

fringe n Am **fringes** avantages mpl accessoires ❏ Br **fringe benefits** avantages accessoires; **fringe market** marché m marginal

FRN n Banking (abbr **floating-rate note**) effet m à taux flottant

front 1 n (**a**) **front desk** réception f; **front man** (spokesman) porte-parole m, réprésentant m; (figurehead) prête-nom m; Am Fam **front money** capital m initial ou de départ; Banking **front office** front-office m
  (**b**) Fam **to pay up front** payer d'avance; **they want £5,000 up front** ils veulent 5000 livres d'avance
  2 vt (**a**) (lead) être à la tête de, diriger (**b**) Am Fam (advance) avancer; **the cashier can front you the money** le caissier peut vous faire une avance

frontage n (of shop) devanture f

front-end adj (**a**) **front-end fee** frais mpl d'entrée; **front-end loading** = système de prélèvement des frais sur les premiers versements (**b**) Comptr **front-end computer** ordinateur m frontal; **front-end processor** processeur m frontal

> **"**
> The charges for buying into a trust are usually at the standard rate. Dunedin, however, has no **front-end fee** for its share plan other than stamp duty.
> **"**

frontier n frontière f ❏ **frontier zone** zone f frontière

front-runner n candidat(e) m,f favori(ite)

front-running n St Exch = type de délit d'initié où un opérateur vend ou achète des valeurs pour son propre compte avant d'effectuer pour un client une grosse opération susceptible d'influencer les cours

frozen adj (**a**) Fin (account) bloqué(e); (credit, wages) gelé(e), bloqué; (currency, prices, assets, debt) gelé (**b**) Comptr bloqué(e)

FRS n Am (abbr **Federal Reserve System**) (système m de) Réserve f fédérale

frustration of contract n Law résolution f de contrat

FSA n (abbr **Financial Services Authority**) = organisme gouvernemental britannique chargé de contrôler les activités du secteur financier

FT n (abbr **Financial Times**) Financial Times m

FTC n Am (abbr **Federal Trade Commission**) = commission fédérale chargée de veiller au respect de la concurrence sur le marché

FT index n (**a**) (abbr **Financial Times-(Industrial) Ordinary Share Index**) = indice boursier du Financial Times basé sur la valeur de 30 actions cotées à la Bourse de Londres (**b**) (abbr **Financial Times-Stock Exchange 100 Index**) = principal indice boursier du Financial Times basé sur la valeur de 100 actions cotées à la Bourse de Londres

FTP n Comptr (abbr **File Transfer Protocol**) protocole *m* de transfert de fichier, FTP *m* ❑ *FTP server* serveur *m* FTP; *FTP site* site *m* FTP

FT-SE index *n* (*abbr* **Financial Times-Stock Exchange 100 Index**) = principal indice boursier du *Financial Times* basé sur la valeur de 100 actions cotées à la Bourse de Londres

fudge *vt* (*figures, results*) truquer

fulfil, *Am* **fulfill** *vt* (*contract, order*) exécuter; (*obligation*) remplir

fulfilment, *Am* **fulfillment** *n* (*of contract, order*) exécution *f*; (*of obligation*) remplissement *m*

full 1 *n* (**a**) (*complete, whole*) **to pay in full** payer intégralement; **we paid the bill in full** nous avons payé la facture dans son intégralité; **they refunded my money in full** ils m'ont entièrement remboursé
 (**b**) (*detailed*) **he gave us a full report** il nous a donné un rapport détaillé; **I asked for full information** j'ai demandé des renseignements complets
 2 *adj* **full assessment system** régime *m* du réel; *Acct* **full consolidation** intégration *f* globale; **full container load** conteneur *m* chargé complètement; **full cost accounting (method)** méthode *f* du coût de revient complet; **full costing** méthode du coût complet; *Ins* **full cover** garantie *f* totale; **full demand** demande *f* soutenue; *Fin* **full discharge** quitus *m*; **full employment** plein emploi *m*; **full fare** (*in air travel*) plein tarif *m*; *St Exch* **full listing** = description d'une société qui apparaît à la cote officielle de la Bourse de Londres; **full load** chargement *m* complet; **full pay** paie *f* entière; **full payment** paiement *m* intégral; *Law* **full power of attorney** procuration *f* générale; **full price** prix *m* fort; **full rate** plein tarif; **full stop** (*punctuation mark*) point *m*; **full time** temps *m* complet; **full warranty** garantie totale; **full weight** poids *m* juste

> ❝
> Tenon Group, the AIM-listed accountancy consolidator, has said it will move up to a **full listing** on the London Stock Exchange – but not until September 2003 at the earliest, writes Philip Smith. The original intention had been for the company to make the switch this year, but chief executive Ian Buckley admitted that would no longer be possible and could be as late as March 2004.
> ❞

full-cost pricing *n Mktg* fixation *f* du prix en fonction du coût

full-employment economy *n* économie *f* de plein emploi

full-line strategy *n Mktg* stratégie *f* de gamme complète

full-time 1 *adj* (*job, employee*) à plein temps, à temps complet; **to be in full-time employment** travailler à plein temps *ou* à temps complet ❑ *full-time contract* contrat *m* à temps plein
 2 *adv* à plein temps, à temps complet

fully *adv Ins* **fully comprehensive** tous risques ❑ *fully diluted earnings per share* bénéfice *m* par action entièrement dilué; *fully paid capital* capital *m* entièrement versé; *fully paid-up security* titre *m* libéré; *fully paid-up share* action *f* entièrement libérée; *fully secured creditor* créancier(ère) *m,f* entièrement nanti(e)

full-year *adj* (*profits, results*) de l'exercice

function *n* (**a**) (*role*) (*of machine*) fonction *f*; (*of person*) fonction, charge *f*; **in his function as a magistrate** en sa qualité de magistrat; **to resign one's functions** se démettre de ses fonctions ❑ *Comptr* **function key** touche *f* de fonction (**b**) (*reception*) réception *f*

functional *adj* fonctionnel(elle); (*approach*) pragmatique ❑ *functional analysis chart* grille *f* d'analyse par fonction; *functional budget* budget *m* fonctionnel; *functional layout* implantation *f* fonctionnelle; *functional organization* organisation *f* fonctionnelle *ou* horizontale; *functional strategy* stratégie *f* fonctionnelle

fund *Fin* **1** *n* (**a**) (*reserve of money*) fonds *m*, caisse *f*; **funds flow statement** tableau *m* des emplois et ressources; **fund of funds** fonds de fonds ❑ *fund accountant* valorisateur(trice) *m,f* de fonds; *fund accounting* valorisation *f* de fonds; *fund management* gestion *f* de fonds; *fund manager* gestionnaire *mf ou* gérant(e) *m,f* de fonds
 (**b**) **funds** (*cash resources*) fonds *mpl*; (*of government*) fonds publics; **to be short of** *or* **low on funds** être à court d'argent; **"insufficient funds"** (*written on cheque*) défaut *m* de provision; *Br* **the Funds** les bons *mpl* du Trésor; **to make a call for funds** faire un appel de fonds
 2 *vt* (*project*) financer; (*company*) pourvoir de fonds; (*public debt*) consolider; **to fund money** placer de l'argent dans les fonds publics; **funded from cashflow** autofinancé(e)

fundable *adj Fin* (*debt*) consolidable

fundamental market analyst *n* analyste *mf* fondamental(e)

funded *adj Fin* (*assets*) en rentes ❑ *funded capital* capital *m* investi; *funded debt* dette *f* consolidée; *funded pension scheme* régime *m* de retraite par capitalisation

fundholder *n* rentier(ère) *m,f*

funding *n* (*of project*) financement *m*; (*of debt*) consolidation *f*; (*of income*) assiette *f*; **BP will put up half of the funding** BP financera le projet à 50% ❑ *funding loan* emprunt *m* de consolidation; *funding operation* opération *f* de financement; **funding plan** plan *m* de financement

fundraiser *n (person)* collecteur(trice) *m,f* de fonds; *(event)* = projet organisé pour collecter des fonds

fundraising *n* collecte *f* de fonds

fungible *St Exch* **1** *n* **fungibles** fongibles *mpl*
  2 *adj* fongible □ **fungible securities** titres *mpl* en suspens

furnish *vt (supply) (provisions)* fournir; *(information, reason)* fournir, donner; **to furnish sb with sth** fournir qch à qn

further 1 *adj* **for further information, phone this number** pour tout renseignement complémentaire, appelez ce numéro; **please send me further information concerning the project** veuillez m'envoyer de plus amples renseignements concernant le projet; **I would like further details of the programme** j'aimerais avoir quelques précisions supplémentaires sur le programme; **until further notice** jusqu'à nouvel ordre
  2 *adv* **further to** *(in letter)* suite à; **further to your letter of 15 June** suite à votre lettre du 15 juin; **further to our telephone call** suite à notre conversation téléphonique
  3 *vt (career)* servir, favoriser; *(cause)* avancer, servir, favoriser

future 1 *n* **(a)** *(of person)* avenir *m*; **a job with a (good) future** une situation pleine d'avenir; **there is a future ahead for bilingual people in publishing** le monde de l'édition offre des possibilités d'avenir pour les personnes bilingues
  (b) *St Exch* **futures** *(financial instruments, contracts)* contrats *mpl* à terme; *(transactions)* opérations *fpl* à terme; *(securities)* titres *mpl* ou valeurs *fpl* à terme □ **futures contract** contrat à terme; **futures exchange** marché *m* à terme; **futures market** marché à terme; **futures option** option *f* sur contrats à terme; **futures and options** contrats à terme et options; **futures and options fund** fonds *mpl* investissant dans les contrats à terme et options; **futures order** ordre *m* à terme; **Future Rate Agreement** accord *m* de taux à terme; **futures trading** négociations *fpl* ou opérations à terme; **futures transaction** opération à terme
  2 *adj Fin* **future delivery** livraison *f* à terme; **goods for future delivery** marchandises *fpl* livrables à terme; **future value** valeur *f* capitalisée

"

The first step consists of a feasibility study for the creation of a regulated **futures market** for categories of fine wines. This innovative project, announced at a conference/debate organized by Paris Europlace at Bordeaux, is based on a finished product – namely homogeneous categories of sought-after fine wines – that is ready to be consumed. The first contract is expected to be a **future** on the top growths of the Bordeaux region, based on a 12-bottle case en primeur for delivery in 32 months' time.

"

FX *n (abbr* **foreign exchange***)* devises *fpl* étrangères □ **FX broker** cambiste *mf*, courtier(ère) *m,f* en devises; **FX dealer** cambiste, courtier(ère) en devises; **FX market** marché *m* des devises étrangères; **FX option** option *f* sur devises; **FX transfer** transfert *m* de devises

FY *n Am (abbr* **fiscal year***)* année *f* fiscale *ou* d'exercice

Gg

G7 n G7 m, groupe m des 7 ❑ **G7 meeting** réunion f du G7; **G7 summit** sommet m du G7

G8 n G8 m, groupe m des 8 ❑ **G8 meeting** réunion f du G8; **G8 summit** sommet m du G8

GA n Ins (abbr **general average**) avarie f commune

GAAP npl Acct (abbr **generally-accepted accounting principles**) PCGR mpl

gag n **gag law** = toute loi limitant la liberté de la presse ou la liberté d'expression; **gag order** = décision de justice visant à interdire à la presse de publier tout article à propos d'une affaire; **to issue a gag order** = interdire à la presse de publier tout article à propos d'une affaire

gagging order n = décision de justice visant à interdire à la presse de publier tout article à propos d'une affaire; **to issue a gagging order** = interdire à la presse de publier tout article à propos d'une affaire

> **“**
>
> Patty Hearst, the newspaper heiress kidnapped by urban guerrillas in California in 1974 and later jailed for participating with them in a bank robbery, could find herself back in court this week for contempt. Despite a **gagging order**, she has given an interview about the pending trial in August of a group member, Kathy Soliah (now Sarah Jane Olsen), captured last year after a quarter of a century on the run.
>
> **”**

gain 1 n (a) (profit) gain m, profit m (b) (increase) accroissement m, augmentation f; Fin **gain in value** plus-value f; **there has been a net gain in profits this year** il y a eu une augmentation nette des bénéfices cette année; **there has been a gain of 100 points on the Dow Jones** l'indice Dow Jones a gagné 100 points; **to gain a share** (of market) gagner des parts de marché 2 vt gagner, bénéficier de; **the share index has gained two points** l'indice des actions a gagné deux points

gain-sharing n participation f aux bénéfices, intéressement m

galloping inflation n Econ inflation f galopante

gamble vi **to gamble on the Stock Exchange** boursicoter, jouer à la Bourse

gameplan n Mktg stratégie f (de marketing)

game theory n Mktg théorie f des jeux

GAO n Am (abbr **General Accounting Office**) = Cour des comptes américaine

gap n écart m, inégalité f; **a gap in the market** un créneau; **there's a technology gap between our two countries** il y a un fossé technologique entre nos deux pays ❑ Mktg **gap analysis** étude f des créneaux; **gap financing** crédit m relais; Mktg **gap level** écart de performance; **gap study** étude des écarts

> **“**
>
> Six insurance companies yesterday formed a European pool to cover damage caused by acts of terror, plugging a **gap in the market** left since the September 11 attacks. Allianz, Zurich, Swiss Re, Hannover Re, XL Capital and Scor said they had established a company called Special Risk Insurance and Reinsurance Luxembourg.
>
> **”**

garnish vt Am Law faire pratiquer une saisie-arrêt à

garnishee n Law tiers m saisi ❑ **garnishee order** ordonnance f de saisie-arrêt

garnishment n Law saisie-arrêt f

gatekeeper n Mktg (in purchasing department) contrôleur m, relais m, filtre m

> **“**
>
> … the supplier's marketing department must try to identify and reach technical specialists, engineers, technical buyers etc. This will depend on how accessible these people are, and on how effective are the **gatekeepers** whose role includes filtering out what they, or the influencer, deem to be undesirable or unnecessary information.
>
> **”**

gateway n Comptr passerelle f (de connexion)

GATT n (abbr **General Agreement on Tariffs and Trade**) GATT m, agétac m

GAW n Am (abbr **guaranteed annual wage**) salaire m annuel garanti

gazump vt = revenir sur une promesse de vente de maison pour accepter l'offre plus élevée d'une tierce personne

gazumping *n* = fait de revenir sur une promesse de vente pour accepter une offre plus élevée

"

Estate agents go around telling people ... that the property from which they are hoping to move is incredibly saleable in the present market conditions ... What if their present home is snapped up in 20 minutes flat, but they can't find what they want? So they don't put their existing property on the market until they have found what they want – which, with thousands of people doing just the same, could be some time ... This encourages **gazumping**, which is, after all, only the market's way of raising prices to the point where demand meets supply. Hence the silly prices.

"

GB *n Comptr (abbr* **gigabyte**) Go *m*

GDP *n Econ (abbr* **gross domestic product**) PIB *m*

gear *vt (link)* indexer; **salaries are geared to the cost of living** les salaires sont indexés au coût de la vie

▸ **gear up** *vt sep* (**a**) *(prepare)* préparer; **the company is geared up for expansion** la société est orientée vers l'expansion (**b**) *(increase)* augmenter; **we must gear up production to meet the demand** il nous faut augmenter la production pour faire face à la demande

gearing *n Fin (leverage)* effet *m* de levier; *(as percentage)* ratio *m* d'endettement □ **gearing adjustment** redressement *m* financier

GEMM *n St Exch (abbr* **gilt-edged market maker**) teneur *m* de marché de premier ordre

general *adj Am Acct* **General Accounting Office** = Cour des comptes américaine; *Banking* **general account manager** chargé(e) *m,f* de clientèle grand public; *Acct* **general accounts** comptabilité *f* générale; **general and administrative expenses** frais *mpl* généraux et frais de gestion; **general agent** agent *m* général; **General Agreement on Tariffs and Trade** accord *m* général sur les tarifs douaniers et le commerce; **general audit** audit *m* général; *Ins* **general average** avarie *f* commune; **general broker** courtier(ère) *m,f* de commerce; **general business** *(on agenda)* questions *fpl* diverses; *Acct* **general cash book** livre *m* de trésorerie générale; **general expenses** frais généraux; **general headquarters** quartier *m* général; *Acct* **general ledger** grand livre; *Law* **general lien** privilège *m* général; **general management** direction *f* générale; **general management committee** comité *m* de direction générale; **general manager** directeur(trice) *m,f* général(e); **general meeting** assemblée *f* générale; *Br* **General**

and Municipal Workers' Union = syndicat britannique des employés des collectivités locales; *Fin* **general obligation bond** emprunt *m* de collectivité locale; *Br* **general overheads**, *Am* **general overhead** frais d'administration générale; **general partnership** société *f* en nom collectif; **general price level** niveau *m* général des prix; **general strike** grève *f* générale; **general tax code** code *m* général des impôts; **general trend** tendance *f* générale; **general wage level** niveau général des salaires

generate *vt* (**a**) *Comptr* créer, générer (**b**) *(income)* créer, produire; **we must try to generate new sources of income** nous devons essayer de créer de nouvelles sources de revenus

generic *Mktg* **1** *n* produit *m* générique
2 *adj* générique □ **generic advertising** publicité *f* générique; **generic brand** marque *f* générique; **generic market** marché *m* générique; **generic name** nom *m* générique; **generic product** produit *m* générique

gentleman's agreement *n* gentleman's agreement *m*

genuine *adj (article)* garanti(e) d'origine; *(diamond, gold, leather)* véritable

geodemographic *adj Mktg* géodémographique □ **geodemographic data** données *fpl* géodémographiques; **geodemographic profile** profil *m* géodémographique; **geodemographic segment** segment *m* géodémographique; **geodemographic segmentation** segmentation *f* géodémographique

geodemography *n Mktg* géodémographie *f*

geographic *adj Mktg* géographique □ **geographic pricing** tarification *f* géographique; **geographic segment** segment *m* géographique; **geographic segmentation** segmentation *f* géographique

geomarketing *n* géomarketing *m*

get *vt* (**a**) *(obtain)* se procurer, obtenir; *(buy)* acheter; **I got this computer cheap** j'ai eu *ou* acheté cet ordinateur bon marché (**b**) *(earn)* gagner; **to get £35,000 a year** gagner 35 000 livres par an (**c**) *(letter, phone call, reply)* recevoir; **I got his answer this morning** j'ai eu *ou* reçu sa réponse ce matin (**d**) *(contact by telephone)* joindre; **I couldn't get her at the office** je n'ai pas pu l'avoir au bureau; **get me Washington 330 330** *(to operator)* appelez-moi Washington 330 330

▸ **get through** *vi* **to get through to sb** *(on telephone)* obtenir la communication avec qn

giant *n (company)* géant *m*; **computer giant Microsoft is in the news this week** Microsoft, le géant de l'informatique, fait la une de l'actualité cette semaine

giant-sized *adj (pack, box)* géant(e)

GIF *n Comptr (abbr* **Graphics Interchange Format**) GIF *m*

gift *n* (**a**) *Law (donation)* don *m*, donation *f*; **as a gift** à titre d'avantage ❑ *gift and inheritance tax* impôt *m* sur les donations et les successions; *gift inter vivos* donation entre vifs (**b**) *(present)* cadeau *m* ❑ *Am gift certificate* bon *m* d'achat, chèque-cadeau *m*; *Br gift token, gift voucher* bon d'achat, chèque-cadeau

gigabyte *n Comptr* gigaoctet *m*

gilt *n St Exch* fonds *m* d'État, valeur *f* de tout repos *ou* de père de famille ❑ *gilts market* marché *m* des valeurs de premier ordre; *gilt switching* rotation *f* de portefeuille-obligation

gilt-edged *adj St Exch* (**a**) *gilt-edged investment* placement *m* de père de famille; *gilt-edged market* marché *m* des valeurs de premier ordre; *gilt-edged market maker* teneur *m* marché des valeurs de premier ordre; *gilt-edged stock, gilt-edged securities* valeurs *fpl* de premier ordre *ou* de père de famille (**b**) *Am gilt-edged bond* valeur *f* du Trésor américain

> 〃
> Five years ago, the prospect of a 10 per cent profit in the course of a year would not have set investors' pulses racing. However, in the context of the dire performance of the UK stock market in the past two years, and the poor prospective returns from **gilt-edged stock** and cash deposits, a 10 per cent return from the FTSE 100 in 2002 takes on a new appeal, and would go some way to restoring two years of capital destruction since the index peaked at 6930 in December 1999.
> 〃

Ginnie Mae *n Am* Ginnie Mae *(organisme gouvernemental de crédit immobilier)*

giro *n Br* (**a**) *(system)* = système de virement interbancaire introduit par la Poste britannique; **to pay by bank giro** payer par virement bancaire ❑ *giro account* compte *m* chèque postal, CCP *m*; *giro cheque* chèque *m* de virement; *giro transfer* transfert *m* par CCP (**b**) *Fam (unemployment benefit)* allocation *f* (de) chômage

Girobank *n Br* service *m* de chèques postaux

give *vt (pay)* donner; **to give a good price for sth** donner *ou* payer un bon prix pour qch; **I'll give you £500 for it** je vous en donnerai 500 livres; **what will you give me for it?** combien m'en offrez-vous?

give-and-take policy *n* politique *f* d'accommodement

giveaway *n Fam (free gift)* prime *f*, cadeau *m* ❑ *giveaway material* cadeaux *mpl* (publicitaires); *giveaway paper* journal *m* gratuit

giveback *n Am* = diminution de salaire des employés négociée avec les syndicats en période de difficultés économiques

given *adj* donné(e); **at a given price** à un cours donné *ou* déterminé

give-up *n Am St Exch* = commission partagée entre plusieurs agents de change lors d'une transaction entre deux firmes

glamour stock *n St Exch* valeur *f* vedette

glare *n Comptr glare filter* filtre *m* antireflet; *glare screen* écran *m* antireflet

glass ceiling *n* = plafond de verre qui désigne métaphoriquement l'ensemble des facteurs qui empêchent les femmes de parvenir aux postes les plus élevés dans le monde professionnel

> 〃
> In the seven years Morag Stuart has been a qualified lawyer, she has seen a marked shift in attitudes towards women in the legal profession which indicate the so-called **glass ceiling** is finally cracking. While in the past some female solicitors would have been held back because of their gender, now Ms Stuart, 29, believes that attitude is simply not tolerated.
> 〃

global *adj* (**a**) *(worldwide)* mondial(e) ❑ *Mktg global audience* audience *f* globale; *Banking global banking* banque *f* universelle; *Fin global bond* obligation *f* multimarchés; *global consumption* consommation *f* mondiale; *global custody* conservation *f* globale; *Fin global equities market* marché *m* mondial des actions; *global finance* la finance internationale; *global market* marché global *ou* international; *global marketing* marketing *m* global *ou* international; *Mktg global marketplace* marché global *ou* international; *global player* acteur *m* international; *global strategy* stratégie *f* globale; *global village* village *m* planétaire (**b**) *(comprehensive)* global(e) ❑ *Comptr global change* changement *m* global; *global finance* financement *m* aux entreprises; *Comptr global search and replace* recherche *f* et remplacement global

> 〃
> British American Tobacco, the world second largest tobacco company, is close to striking a deal with the Ministry of Sound, the nightclub-to-publishing business, that will give BAT a **global strategy** for marketing its cigarettes to young people.
> 〃

globalization *n* globalisation *f*, mondialisation *f* ❑ *globalization strategy* stratégie *f* de globalisation

globalize *vt* globaliser, mondialiser

> Judith Robertson knows a thing or two or three about transitions: She's one of a new breed of people in the investment management business who appear able to glide effortlessly from posting to posting in the **globalized** economy, making the transition from Toronto to Vancouver to San Francisco to London to San Francisco and back to Toronto.

glut 1 n (on market) encombrement m; (of commodity) surabondance f; **there is a glut of oil on the market** il y a une surabondance de pétrole sur le marché; Fin **glut of money** pléthore f de capitaux
2 vt (market, economy) encombrer, inonder; **the market is glutted with luxury goods** il y a une surabondance d'objets de luxe sur le marché

GMC n (abbr **general management committee**) comité m de direction

GMWU n (abbr **General and Municipal Workers' Union**) = syndicat britannique des employés des collectivités locales

GNMA n Am (abbr **Government National Mortgage Association**) GNMA f (organisme gouvernemental de crédit immobilier)

gnome n Fam **the gnomes of Zurich** les grands banquiers mpl suisses

> Who could have suspected that Gordon Brown would realise the aspiration of all his Labour predecessors: to finance a centre-left programme largely out of economic growth? Who could have thought that he would do so after three years without the slightest hint of a financial or economic crisis, without any bother from the **gnomes of Zurich** or bankers' ramps, or other mysterious forces of international capitalism that were always thought certain to undermine a Labour government?

GNP n Econ (abbr **gross national product**) PNB m

go vi **to go live** (of company) entrer en Bourse

▸ **go down** vi (of prices, value) baisser

▸ **go up** vi (of prices, value) monter, augmenter; **the cost of living is going up** le coût de la vie augmente

go-between n intermédiaire mf

gofer n Fam factotum m

go-go stock n St Exch action f hautement spéculative

going adj (a) (profitable) **going concern** affaire f qui marche; **for sale as a going concern** à vendre avec fonds (b) (current) (price) courant(e), actuel(elle); **she's getting the going rate for the job** elle touche le tarif normal pour ce genre de travail

going-concern adj Acct **going-concern concept** principe m de la continuité de l'exploitation; **going-concern status** continuité f d'exploitation

going-rate pricing n Mktg alignement m sur les prix du marché

gold n or m ❑ Fin **gold bond** obligation f or; **gold bullion** encaisse f or, lingots mpl d'or; **gold bullion standard** étalon m or-lingot; **gold card** carte f de crédit illimitée; **gold coin** pièce f d'or; **gold currency** monnaie f d'or; **gold euro** euro m or; **gold exchange standard** étalon de change-or; **gold export point** point m de sortie de l'or; **gold fix, gold fixing** cotation f de l'or; **gold import point** point de sortie de l'or; **gold ingot** lingot d'or; **gold loan** emprunt m or; **gold market** marché m de l'or; **gold mine** mine f d'or; **gold money** monnaie d'or; **gold parachute** prime f de licenciement (versée à certains cadres supérieurs en cas de rachat de l'entreprise); **gold point** point d'or; **gold pool** pool m de l'or; **gold reserve** réserve f d'or; **gold share** valeur f aurifère; **gold standard** étalon-or m

gold-collar worker n col m doré

golden adj **golden handcuffs** primes fpl (versées à un cadre à intervalles réguliers pour le dissuader de partir); **golden handshake** indemnité f de départ; **golden hello** prime d'embauche; **golden parachute** prime de licenciement (versée à certains cadres supérieurs en cas de rachat de l'entreprise); **golden share** participation f majoritaire (souvent détenue par le gouvernement britannique dans les entreprises privatisées); **golden umbrella** prime de licenciement (versée à certains cadres supérieurs en cas de rachat de l'entreprise)

gondola n (for displaying goods) gondole f ❑ **gondola end** tête f de gondole

good adj (cheque, debt) bon (bonne); (investment, securities) sûr(e); (contract, deal) avantageux(euse), favorable; **their credit is good for £5,000** on peut leur faire crédit jusqu'à 5000 livres

goods npl (a) Law (possessions) biens mpl; **goods and chattels** biens et effets mpl (b) (articles) marchandises fpl, articles mpl; **send us the goods by rail** envoyez-nous la marchandise par chemin de fer ❑ **goods depot** dépôt m de marchandises; **goods rate** tarif m marchandises; **goods service** service m de marchandises; **goods station** gare f de marchandises; **goods traffic** mouvement m des marchandises; **goods train** train m de marchandises; **goods in transit** marchandises en transit; **goods vehicle** poids *m* lourd, véhicule *m* utilitaire

good-till-cancelled order *n St Exch* ordre *m* à révocation

goodwill *n* fonds *m* de commerce, biens *mpl* incorporels ❏ **goodwill accounting** comptabilisation *f* de la survaleur

> 66
>
> Accounting convention assumes that **goodwill**, the premium a company pays for an acquisition, is a wasting asset. Why not create an impairment test that would consider market conditions and profitability projections to determine the value of **goodwill**? A 15-person team of accounting firms and investment bankers recently floated such a proposal, which is currently under consideration by the Financial Accounting Standards Board (FASB).
>
> 99

gopher *n* (**a**) *Comptr* (serveur *m*) gopher *m* (**b**) *Fam* (person) factotum *m*

go-slow *Br* **1** *n* grève *f* perlée
2 *adj* **go-slow strike** grève *f* perlée

.gov = abréviation désignant les sites gouvernementaux dans les adresses électroniques

govern *vt* (country, city, bank) gouverner; (company, organization) diriger, gérer

governing *adj* gouvernant(e), dirigeant(e) ❏ **governing body** conseil *m* d'administration

government *n* (of country) gouvernement *m*; (of company, organization) gestion *f* ❏ **government action** action *f* gouvernementale; **government aid** aide *f* gouvernementale ou de l'État; **government auditor** commissaire *mf* aux comptes; **government bond** obligation *f* d'État, bon *m* du Trésor; **government borrowings** emprunts *mpl* de l'État; *Br* **government broker** agent *m* du Trésor; **government developmental grant, government developmental subsidy** prime *f* de développement; **government grant** subvention *f* de l'État; **government loan** emprunt public ou d'État; *Am* **Government National Mortgage Association** GNMA *f* (organisme gouvernemental de crédit immobilier); *Am* **Government Printing Office** = maison d'édition publiant les ouvrages ou documents émanant du gouvernement, ≃ l'Imprimerie *f* nationale; **government property** propriété *f* de l'État; **government resources** ressources *fpl* de l'État; **government revenue** recettes *fpl* publiques; **government securities** effets *mpl* publics, fonds *mpl* publics ou d'État; **government spending** dépenses *fpl* publiques; **government stock** effets publics, fonds publics ou d'État

GPO *n Am* (abbr **Government Printing Office**) = maison d'édition publiant les ouvrages ou documents émanant du gouvernement, ≃ l'Imprimerie *f* nationale

GPRS *n Tel* (abbr **General Packet Radio Service**) GPRS *m*

GPS *n* (abbr **Global Positioning System**) GPS *m*

grace *n* **days of grace** jours *mpl* de grâce ❏ **grace period** délai *m* de grâce

grade 1 *n* (**a**) (in profession) échelon *m*; (on salary scale) indice *m*; **the top grades of the civil service** les échelons supérieurs ou les plus élevés de la fonction publique (**b**) (of product) qualité *f*, catégorie *f* ❏ **grade label** étiquette *f* de calibrage
2 *vt* (products) classer, calibrer

graded *adj* (advertising rates) dégressif(ive); (tax) progressif(ive)

graduate *Br* **1** *n* diplômé(e) *m,f*, licencié(e) *m,f* ❏ **graduate entry** échelon *m* d'entrée pour les diplômés; **graduate training scheme** programme *m* de formation professionnelle pour les diplômés
2 *vi* obtenir sa licence; **she has recently graduated in economics** elle a récemment obtenu sa licence en économie

graduated *adj* (payments, tax) progressif(ive) ❏ **graduated payment mortgage** hypothèque *f* à paiements échelonnés

grain *n* céréales *fpl* ❏ **grain market** marché *m* des céréales

grammar checker *n Comptr* correcteur *m* grammatical

granny bond *n Br Fam Fin* = type d'obligation visant le marché des retraités

grant 1 *n* (**a**) (financial aid) subvention *f*, allocation *f* (**b**) (transfer) (of property) cession *f*; (of land) concession *f*
2 *vt* (subsidy, loan, overdraft) accorder

grant-aided *adj* subventionné(e) par l'État

grant-in-aid *n* subvention *f* de l'État

graph *n* graphique *m*, diagramme *m*; **to plot a graph** tracer un graphique ❏ **graph paper** papier *m* quadrillé

graphic *adj* **graphic artist** graphiste *mf*; **graphic designer** concepteur(trice) *m,f* graphiste; *Comptr* **graphic interface** interface *f* graphique

graphical user interface *n Comptr* interface *f* utilisateur graphique

graphics *npl Comptr* graphismes *mpl*, graphiques *mpl* ❏ **graphics accelerator** accélérateur *m* graphique; **graphics accelerator card** carte *f* accélérateur graphique; **graphics application** application *f* graphique; **graphics card** carte graphique; **graphics display** affichage *m* graphique; **graphics mode** mode *m* graphique; **graphics package** grapheur *m*; **graphics palette** palette *f* graphique; **graphics software** logiciel *m* graphique; ***graphics spreadsheet*** tableur *m* de graphiques; ***graphics tablet*** tablette *f* graphique; ***graphics window*** fenêtre *f* graphique

grass-roots *adj* de base, qui émane de la base; **there is no grass-roots support for their policy** il n'y a pas de soutien de la base pour leur politique; **the grass-roots feeling is that...** le sentiment à la base est que...; **at grass-roots level** à la base ❑ *Mktg* **grass-roots forecasting** prévision *f* de la base

gratis 1 *adj* gratuit(e)
2 *adv* gratis, gratuitement

gratuity *n* (a) *(tip)* pourboire *m*, gratification *f* (b) *Br (payment to employee)* prime *f*

grave (accent) *n* accent *m* grave

graveyard shift *n Fam* équipe *f* de nuit; **I work the graveyard shift** je suis dans l'équipe de nuit

gray *Am* = **grey**

green *adj* **green audit** = rapport sur l'impact des activités d'une entreprise sur l'environnement; ***green card*** *Admin* ≃ permis *m* de travail; *Ins* carte *f* verte, attestation *f* d'assurance; *EU* **green currency** monnaie *f* verte; *Formerly* **green franc** franc *m* vert; ***green marketing*** marketing *m* vert ou écologique; *EU* ***green pound*** livre *f* verte; *Mktg* ***green product*** produit *m* vert ou écologique; ***green rate*** taux *m* vert; *Fin* ***green taxation*** fiscalité *f* écologique; ***green tourism*** tourisme *m* vert

greenback *n Am Fam* billet *m* vert

greenfield site *n* terrain *m* à bâtir *(sur lequel rien n'a jamais été construit)*

> "
> Anyone under the illusion that the British countryside is in safe hands had better think again, and fast. The developers are on the offensive, claiming they need to build on more **greenfield sites**. The government has bowed to the pressure and is proposing an ill-thought-out reform of planning controls, which would guarantee that the south-east would be concreted over. Behind these so-called reforms is the architect of another fiasco, Lord Falconer of the Dome.
> "

greenmail *n Fin* greenmail *m*

grey, *Am* **gray 1** *n Comptr* **shades of grey** niveaux *mpl* de gris
2 *adj* **grey import** importation *f* grise; *St Exch* **grey knight** chevalier *m* gris; **grey market** marché *m* gris; **grey zone** zone *f* grise

greyscale, *Am* **grayscale** *n Comptr* niveau *m* de gris

grievance *n (complaint)* réclamation *f*; **the**

workers put forward a list of grievances les travailleurs ont présenté un cahier de revendications ❑ **grievance procedure** = procédure permettant aux salariés de faire part de leurs revendications

gross 1 *n* douze douzaines *fpl*, grosse *f*
2 *adj (overall, total)* brut(e) ❑ **gross actuarial return** rendement *m* actuariel brut; **gross amount** montant *m* brut; **gross annual interest return** taux *m* de rendement actuariel brut; **gross assets** actif *m* brut; *Ins* **gross average** grosse(s) avarie(s) *f(pl)* commune(s); **gross dividend** dividende *m* brut; **gross domestic product** produit *m* intérieur brut; **gross earnings** recette *f* brute; **gross income** *(in accounts)* produit brut; *(of individual)* revenu *m* brut; **gross loss** perte *f* brute; **gross margin** marge *f* brute; **gross national income** revenu national brut; **gross national product** produit national brut; **gross negligence** négligence *f* grave, faute *f* lourde; **gross operating profit** bénéfice *m* ou résultat *m* brut d'exploitation; **gross proceeds** produit brut; **gross profit** bénéfice brut; **gross profit margin** marge commerciale brute; **gross receipts** recettes *fpl* brutes; **gross redemption yield** rendement actuariel brut; **gross registered tonnage** jauge *f* brute; **gross return** rendement ou résultat brut; **gross salary** salaire *m* brut; **gross value** valeur *f* brute; **gross wage** salaire brut; **gross weight** poids *m* brut; **gross yield** rendement brut
3 *vt (of person, company)* faire ou obtenir une recette brute de; *(of sale)* produire brut; **our firm grossed $800,000 last year** notre société a fait ou obtenu une recette brute de 800 000 dollars l'année dernière

grossed-up *adj Fin* **grossed-up dividend** dividende *m* majoré; *Fin* **grossed-up price** prix *m* fort, plein tarif *m*

ground *n* terrain *m* ❑ **ground handling agent** *(at airport)* agent *m* de réceptif; **ground rent** rente *f* foncière

group *n (of people, companies)* groupe *m*; **the Shell Group** le Groupe Shell; **Group of Seven** groupe des sept; **Group of Eight** groupe des huit ❑ **group advertising** publicité *f* collective; **group booking** réservation *f* de groupe; **group contract** contrat *m* collectif; **group discount** remise *f* pour les groupes, prix *m* de groupe; **group insurance** assurance *f* collective; **group interview** entretien *m* de groupe; **group leader** responsable *mf* de groupe; **group manager** chef *m* de groupe; **group meeting** réunion *f* de groupe; **group subscription** abonnement *m* collectif; *Fin* **group turnover** chiffre *m* d'affaires consolidé ou du groupe

groupage *n* groupage *m* ❑ **groupage bill** connaissement *m* de groupage; **groupage rate** tarif *m* groupage

grouped consignment n envoi m groupé

grow 1 vt **to grow the business** augmenter le chiffre d'affaires; **to grow a company** développer une entreprise

2 vi (increase) augmenter, s'accroître; **our market share has grown by five percent in the last year** notre part du marché a augmenté de cinq pour cent au cours de l'année dernière

> **"**
> He thinks he can **grow the business** into a significant piece of change, much of it coming perhaps from the Microsoft arena where, as much as Lachman is a self-admitted Unix bigot, he knows he has to enter.
> **"**

growing-equity mortgage n Am Fin hypothèque f à capital croissant

growth n (of business, market, industry) croissance f, expansion f; **the experts predict a two percent growth in imports** les experts prédisent une croissance des importations de deux pour cent; **to go for growth** favoriser la croissance; **the recent growth in the number of small businesses** l'augmentation récente du nombre de petites entreprises □ **growth area** secteur m en expansion; **growth company** société f en expansion; **growth curve** courbe f de croissance; **growth developer** stimulateur m de croissance; **growth driver** société en expansion; **growth factor** facteur m de croissance; **growth fund** fonds m commun de placement; **growth index** indice m de croissance; **growth industry** industrie f en plein essor ou en croissance rapide; **growth market** marché m porteur; **growth phase** phase f de croissance; **growth potential** potentiel m de croissance; **growth rate** taux m de croissance; **growth sector** secteur de croissance; St Exch **growth shares, growth stock** actions fpl d'avenir ou de croissance; **growth strategy** stratégie f de croissance; **growth trend** tendance f de croissance

growth-share matrix n Mktg matrice f croissance-part de marché

GST n Austr & Can (abbr **goods and services tax**) TPS f (taxe sur les produits et services)

guarantee 1 n (**a**) (document, promise) garantie f; **this computer has a five-year guarantee** cet ordinateur est garanti cinq ans; **under guarantee** sous garantie □ **guarantee certificate** certificat m de garantie; **guarantee commission** commission f de garantie; **guarantee label** label m de garantie

(**b**) (security) garantie f, caution f, cautionnement m; **to secure all guarantees** s'assurer toutes les garanties nécessaires; **to give sth as a guarantee** donner qch en caution ou en gage □ **guarantee company** société f de sécurité; **guarantee fund** fonds m de garantie

(**c**) (person) garant(e) m,f, caution f; **to act as guarantee (for sb)** se porter garant (de qn)

2 vt (**a**) (product, appliance) garantir; **this computer is guaranteed for five years** cet ordinateur est garanti cinq ans

(**b**) (loan, cheque, debt) garantir, cautionner

guaranteed adj (loan, cheque, debt) garanti(e); **guaranteed by** (on financial document) pour aval, bon pour aval □ Fin **guaranteed bill** traite f avalisée; Fin **guaranteed bond** obligation f garantie; **guaranteed delivery period** délai m garanti de livraison; **guaranteed income** rente f de situation; **guaranteed loan** prêt m garanti; **guaranteed minimum pension** retraite f minimum; **guaranteed minimum wage** salaire m minimum interprofessionnel garanti

guarantor n garant(e) m,f; **to stand as guarantor for sb** se porter garant de qn

guaranty n (**a**) (security) caution f, garantie f (**b**) (guarantor) garant(e) m,f (**c**) (written guarantee) garantie f

guerrilla attack n Mktg guérilla f

guest n (of hotel) client(e) m,f □ **guest worker** travailleur(euse) m,f immigré(e)

GUI n Comptr (abbr **graphical user interface**) interface f utilisateur graphique

guided interview n entretien m directif

guilder n Formerly florin m

guillotine n (for cutting paper) massicot m

gyrations npl (in market) fluctuations fpl

Hh

habitual buying behaviour *n Mktg* comportement *m* d'achat habituel

hack *vi Comptr* **to hack into sth** s'introduire en fraude dans qch

hacker *n Comptr (illegal user)* pirate *m* informatique, hacker *m*; *(expert user)* bidouilleur(euse) *m,f*

haggle *vi* marchander; **to haggle over sth** marchander qch; **to haggle over the price of sth** marchander qch

haircut *n Fam St Exch* marge *f* de sécurité

> *"*
> The stock plunged after the company said that December-quarter earnings will be tiny because of slower-than-expected sales of new products such as the PowerMac Cube. That surely was reason for some decline in the stock — but in my opinion not for a $12 billion **haircut**, which is what the stock got.
> *"*

half-commission man *n* remisier *m*

half-day *n* demi-journée *f*; **tomorrow is my half-day** demain c'est ma demi-journée de congé; **to work half-days** faire des demi-journées

half-yearly **1** *adj* semestriel(elle)
2 *adv* tous les six mois

halo effect *n Mktg* effet *m* de halo

▶ **hammer out** *vt sep (agreement, contract)* élaborer

hammered *adj St Exch (stockbroker)* déclaré(e) insolvable

hammering *n St Exch (of stockbroker)* déclaration *f* d'insolvabilité

hand *n* **to change hands** *(of business)* changer de propriétaire □ **hand baggage, hand luggage** bagages *mpl* à main; **a piece of hand baggage** or **luggage** un bagage à main

▶ **hand in** *vt sep* remettre, déposer; **to hand in one's resignation** démissionner, donner sa démission

handbook *n* manuel *m*

hand-held *adj Comptr* **hand-held computer** ordinateur *m* de poche; **hand-held scanner** scanner *m* ou scanneur *m* à main

handle *vt* **(a)** *(deal with)* s'occuper de; **we can handle orders for overseas** nous prenons des commandes pour l'étranger; **we're too small to handle an order of that size** notre entreprise est trop petite pour traiter une commande de cette importance; **she's good at handling difficult customers** elle sait bien s'occuper des clients difficiles
(b) *(trade in)* faire, vendre; **we don't handle chemical products** nous ne faisons pas de produits chimiques
(c) **handle with care** *(on parcel)* ≃ fragile

handler *n* manutentionnaire *mf*

handling *n* **(a)** *(of goods)* manutention *f*, distribution *f* □ **handling capacity** capacité *f* de traitement; **handling charges** frais *mpl* d'administration; *(for physically shifting goods)* frais de manutention **(b)** *(of order, contract)* traitement *m*, exécution *f*

hand-made *adj* fait(e) à la main

handout *n (brochure)* prospectus *m*; *(sample)* cadeau *m* publicitaire

handset *n Tel* combiné *m*

hands-free *adj Tel* mains libres □ **hands-free device** appareil *m* mains libres

handshake *n Comptr* dialogue *m* d'établissement de liaison

hands-off *adj (approach, manager)* non-interventionniste

hands-on *adj* pratique; **the director has a hands-on style of management** le directeur n'a pas peur de mettre la main à la pâte □ **hands-on training** formation *f* pratique

> *"*
> His departure is a setback for the Business, which was relaunched after Christmas as a joint venture with the Press Association. Sources said Northedge, who had expected to be given a fuller role at the revamped title, felt Neil's **hands-on** approach to editorial would not accommodate him.
> *"*

handwork *n* travail *m* manuel

Hang Seng index *n St Exch* indice *m* Hang Seng, indice Hong Kong

harbour, *Am* **harbor** *n* port *m* □ **harbour dues** droits *mpl* de port; **harbour facilities** équipement *m* portuaire; ***harbour station*** gare *f* maritime

hard *adj* (**a**) ***hard sell*** vente *f* agressive; **to give sb the hard sell** forcer qn à acheter; **to give sth the hard sell** promouvoir qch de façon agressive; ***hard sell techniques*** méthode *f* de vente agressive
(**b**) *Fin (stock, rates)* soutenu(e), ferme ❑ ***hard loan*** prêt *m* aux conditions du marché
(**c**) *Fin* ***hard commodities*** minerais *mpl*; ***hard currency*** devise *f ou* monnaie *f* forte
(**d**) *Comptr* ***hard copy*** copie *f* sur papier, sortie *f* papier; ***hard disk*** disque *m* dur; ***hard drive*** unité *f* de disque dur; ***hard return*** saut *m* de ligne manuel

hard-core *adj Mktg* ***hard-core loyal*** fidèle *mf* absolu(e); ***hard-core loyalty*** fidélité *f* absolue

harden *vi (of prices, market)* s'affermir

hardening *n (of prices, market)* affermissement *m*

hardness *n (of prices, market)* affermissement *m*

hardware *n Comptr* matériel *m*, hardware *m*

hash *n* symbole *m* "#", dièse *m*

hatchet man *n Fam* = personne dont le rôle est de restructurer une entreprise ou une organisation, le plus souvent à l'aide de mesures impopulaires

> Logan is the man on the barricades. When he first arrived at Time Inc. in 1992, some of the older staffers saw it as the ultimate expression of the changes ushered in by the Warner merger. Fears swirled that he would be a financial **hatchet man**. And he imposed unprecedented financial discipline.

haul **1** *n (transport)* transport *m*
2 *vt (transport)* transporter par camion

haulage *n* (**a**) *(transportation)* transport *m* (routier) ❑ ***haulage company*** entreprise *f* de transports, transporteur *m*; ***haulage contractor*** entrepreneur *m* de transports, transporteur
(**b**) *(costs)* frais *mpl* de transport

haulier, *Am* **hauler** *n* entrepreneur *m* de transports, transporteur *m*; *(driver)* routier *m*, camionneur *m*

hazard forecasting *n Mktg* prévision *f* événementielle

HD *Comptr* (**a**) (*abbr* **hard disk**) DD (**b**) (*abbr* **high density**) HD

head *n* (**a**) *(person)* chef *m*; **head of department** chef de service; *(in shop)* chef de rayon ❑ ***head buyer*** acheteur(euse) *m,f* principal(e); ***head cashier*** chef caissier(ère) *m,f*; ***head foreman*** chef d'atelier; ***head office*** siège *m* social
(**b**) ***heads of agreement*** *(draft)* protocole *m* d'accord

headed (note)paper *n* papier *m* à en-tête

header *n (on document)* en-tête *m*

headhunt *vt* recruter; **to be headhunted** être recruté(e) par un chasseur de têtes

> It has also suffered from the loss of key senior staff who were **headhunted** by cross-town rival, Scottish Life, to launch a separate protection specialist which is expected to be operational later this year.

headhunter *n* chasseur *m* de têtes

headhunting *n* chasse *f* aux têtes

heading *n* (**a**) *(of letter, bill)* en-tête *m* (**b**) *(subject)* rubrique *f*; **see under the heading "sales"** voir sous la rubrique "vente"

head-on attack *n Mktg* attaque *f* frontale

headquarter *Am* **1** *vt* **the firm is headquartered in New York** la société a son siège à New York
2 *vi (of company)* **to headquarter in Chicago** établir son siège à Chicago

headquarters *npl* siège *m* social; **the company has its headquarters in Zurich** l'entreprise a son siège social à Zurich

health *n* ***health cover*** couverture *f* santé; ***health inspector*** inspecteur(trice) *m,f* sanitaire; ***health insurance*** assurance *f* maladie; ***health insurance contributions*** cotisations *fpl* maladie; *Am* ***health plan*** assurance maladie; *Br* ***health and safety committee*** comité *m* d'hygiène et de sécurité; *Br* ***Health and Safety Executive*** ≃ inspection *f* du travail; *Br* ***Health and Safety Inspector*** inspecteur(trice) du travail; *Br* ***Health and Safety Officer*** = membre du personnel d'une entreprise chargé de veiller à l'hygiène et à la sécurité; *Br* ***health and safety regulations*** réglementation *f* sur l'hygiène et la sécurité; *Br* ***Health and Safety at Work Act*** loi *f* sur les accidents du travail; ***health sector*** secteur *m* sanitaire; *Br* ***health service*** = système créé en 1946 en Grande-Bretagne et financé par l'État, assurant la gratuité des soins et des services médicaux, ≃ Sécurité *f* sociale

heart share *n Mktg* préférence *f*

heavy *adj (loss, tax)* lourd(e); *(expenditure, payments)* gros (grosse), considérable, important(e); **they expect heavy trading on the Stock Exchange** ils s'attendent à ce que le marché soit très actif; **closures have resulted in heavy job losses** les fermetures ont conduit à des pertes d'emplois élevées ❑ ***heavy equipment*** matériel *m ou* équipement *m* lourd; *Br* ***heavy goods vehicle*** poids *m* lourd; ***heavy industry*** industrie *f* lourde; ***heavy investment***

investissement *m* lourd; *St Exch* **heavy market** marché *m* lourd

hedge *St Exch* **1** *n* **hedge fund** société *f* d'investissement; **hedge ratio** ratio *m* de couverture; **hedge transaction** opération *f* de couverture

2 *vt (shares)* arbitrer; *(transactions)* couvrir

3 *vi* se couvrir; **to hedge against currency fluctuations** se couvrir contre les fluctuations monétaires

> ❝
> ADB [Asian Development Bank] officials argued that developing countries could borrow extremely cheaply by denominating their loans in yen — at interest rates of 0.7 per cent — and **hedging** against the currency risk. But Mr Chino said the bank would review its lending policies following the latest round of international consultations on the subject.
> ❞

hedger *n St Exch* opérateur(trice) *m,f* en couverture

hedging *n St Exch* opérations *fpl* de couverture □ **hedging instrument** instrument *m* de couverture

help *n Comptr* **help button** case *f* d'aide; **help desk** service *m* d'assistance; **help file** fichier *m* d'aide; **help key** touche *f* d'aide; **help line** service d'assistance téléphonique; **help menu** menu *m* d'aide; **help message** message *m* d'aide; **help screen** écran *m* d'aide; **help window** fenêtre *f* d'aide

Helsinki agreement *n* accords *mpl* de Helsinki

hereafter *adv (in legal document)* ci-après

hereby *adv (in legal document)* par la présente; **we hereby declare that...** nous déclarons par la présente que...

heterogeneous *adj (market, goods)* hétérogène

hexadecimal *adj Comptr* hexadécimal(e)

HGV *n Br (abbr* **heavy goods vehicle)** poids *m* lourd □ **HGV licence** permis *m* poids lourd

hidden *adj Fin* **hidden cost** coût *m* caché; **hidden defect** défaut *m ou* vice *m* caché; **hidden extras** dépenses *fpl* supplémentaires inattendues; **hidden price increase** hausse *f* de prix déguisée; **hidden reserve** réserve *f* latente; **hidden tax** impôt *m* déguisé

high 1 *n (peak)* haut *m*, sommet *m*; **the Stock Market reached a new high** la Bourse a atteint un nouveau record *ou* maximum; **prices are at an all-time high** les prix ont atteint un record *ou* leur maximum; *St Exch* **the highs and lows** les hauts et les bas

2 *adj* **(a)** *(cost, price, interest rate)* élevé(e); *(sal-*

ary) élevé, gros (grosse); **to fetch a high price** se vendre cher; **to pay a high price** payer le prix fort; **areas of high unemployment** des régions *fpl* à fort taux de chômage □ **high season** haute saison *f*

(b) *(important)* haut(e); **to hold a high position** être haut placé(e) □ **high finance** haute finance *f*

(c) *Br* **the high street** *(street)* la grand-rue, la rue principale; *(shops)* les commerçants *mpl*, le commerce; **the high street has been badly hit by the recession** les commerçants ont été durement touchés par la récession

3 *adv* **to run high** *(of prices)* être élevé(e); **salaries can go as high as £100,000** les salaires peuvent monter jusqu'à *ou* atteindre 100 000 livres

high-density *adj Comptr (disk, graphics, printing)* haute densité

high-end *adj (goods)* haut de gamme

high-flier *n* **(a)** *(ambitious person)* ambitieux(euse) *m,f*, jeune loup *m* **(b)** *St Exch* valeur *f* en forte hausse

high-grade *adj (goods)* de première qualité, de (premier) choix

high-growth company *n* société *f* en expansion

high-income *adj* à haut revenu □ **high-income group** groupe *m* de contribuables à revenus élevés

high-involvement *adj Mktg* à forte participation des consommateurs

high-level *adj (talks, meeting)* à haut niveau □ **high-level decision** décision *f* prise à un niveau supérieur; **high-level staff** cadres *mpl* supérieurs

highlight *vt (with highlighter pen)* surligner; *Comptr (text)* sélectionner

highlighter *n (pen)* surligneur *m*

highly *adv* **(a)** *(at an important level)* haut; **a highly-placed official** un (une) officiel(elle) de haut rang; *Admin* un (une) haut(e) fonctionnaire **(b)** *(very well)* très bien; **his employees are highly paid** ses employés sont très bien payés *ou* touchent de gros salaires

highly-geared *adj* à ratio d'endettement élevé

> ❝
> EZT invests mostly in zero dividend preference shares — historically the safest form of share in a split, offering a set return over a set period. But the trust is **highly-geared**, which has magnified falls in zero share prices. The trust now has net liabilities of £5.5m.
> ❞

highly-skilled adj (employee, worker) hautement qualifié(e)

high-margin adj à forte marge

high-powered adj (person) qui occupe un poste à hautes responsabilités; (job) à hautes responsabilités

high-quality adj (product) de première qualité, de (premier) choix

high-resolution adj Comptr (à) haute résolution

high-speed adj Comptr de haute vitesse

high-street adj Br **the high-street banks** les grandes banques fpl; **high-street shops** les commerçants mpl, le commerce

high-tech adj (product) perfectionné(e); (industry) de pointe; (approach, solution) qui a recours à une technologie de pointe

high-yield adj (bond, security) à rendement élevé

hire 1 n (**a**) Br (of car, equipment) location f ▫ **hire car** voiture f de location; **hire charges** frais mpl ou prix m de location; **hire company** agence f de location

(**b**) **hire purchase** achat m à crédit ou à tempérament; **to buy sth on hire purchase** acheter qch à crédit ou à tempérament; **hire purchase agreement** contrat m de location-vente

2 vt (**a**) (worker) engager

(**b**) Br (car, equipment) louer, prendre en location; **to hire sb's services** employer les services de qn

3 vi (engage workers) engager du personnel; **the personnel manager has the power to hire and fire** le chef du personnel a tous droits d'embauche et de renvoi

▶ **hire out** vt sep Br (car, equipment) donner en location; **to hire out one's services** offrir ses services

hired adj Br (car, equipment) de location

historical cost n Acct coût m historique ou à l'origine ▫ **historical cost accounting** comptabilité f par coûts historiques

hit Comptr **1** n hit m, accès m; (in search) occurrence f; **this website counted 20,000 hits last week** ce site Web a été consulté 20 000 fois la semaine dernière

2 vt (key) appuyer sur

hi-tech = **high-tech**

▶ **hive off** vt sep (money, profits) séparer; **part of the industry was hived off to private ownership** une partie de cette industrie a été privatisée; **the subsidiary companies will be hived off** les filiales deviendront indépendantes

HMSO n Br (abbr **His/Her Majesty's Stationery Office**) = maison d'édition publiant les ouvrages ou documents approuvés par le Parlement, les ministères et autres organismes officiels, ≃ l'Imprimerie f nationale

HNC n Br (abbr **Higher National Certificate**) = diplôme technique préparé en un an

HND n Br (abbr **Higher National Diploma**) = diplôme technique préparé en deux ans

hoarding n Br (billboard) panneau m d'affichage ▫ **hoarding site** emplacement m d'affichage

hold 1 n **to put sb on hold** (on telephone) mettre qn en attente; **to be on hold** être en attente

2 vt (**a**) (possess) **to hold shares** détenir ou avoir des actions; **to hold five percent of the shares in a company** détenir cinq pour cent du capital d'une société; **to hold office** (of chairperson, deputy) être en fonction, remplir sa fonction; **to hold a seat on the board** avoir un siège au conseil d'administration; **she holds the post of treasurer** elle occupe le poste de trésorière

(**b**) (conversation) avoir; (negotiations) mener; **the meeting will be held at 2 o'clock** la réunion aura lieu à 14 heures; **interviews will be held in early May** les entretiens auront lieu début mai

(**c**) Comptr (store) stocker; **how much data will this disk hold?** quelle quantité de données cette disquette peut-elle stocker?; **the commands are held in the memory** les instructions sont gardées en mémoire

(**d**) (on telephone) **hold the line, please** ne quittez pas, s'il vous plaît; **hold all my calls** ne me passez aucun appel

3 vi (**a**) (on telephone) attendre; **the line's** Br **engaged** or Am **busy, will you hold?** la ligne est occupée, voulez-vous patienter?

(**b**) (remain) se maintenir; **prices held at the same level as last year** les prix se sont maintenus au même niveau que l'année dernière; **the pound held firm against the dollar** la livre s'est maintenue par rapport au dollar

▶ **hold over** vt sep (payment) arriérer, différer; (meeting) remettre, reporter; **payment was held over for six months** le paiement a été différé pendant six mois; **we'll hold these items over until the next meeting** on va remettre ces questions à la prochaine réunion

▶ **hold up 1** vt sep (delay) retarder; **the goods were held up at customs** les marchandises ont été immobilisées à la douane

2 vi se maintenir; **the shares held up well** les actions se sont bien défendues; **the market is holding up well** le marché tient toujours

holder n (of passport, permit, post, account, degree) titulaire mf; (of shares) détenteur(trice) m,f; Fin (of bonds, bill) porteur(euse) m,f, détenteur(trice); (of patent) concessionnaire mf; (of land) propriétaire mf; (of insurance policy) assuré(e) m,f

holding *n Fin (shares in company)* participation *f*; **he has holdings in several companies** il est actionnaire de plusieurs sociétés ❑ ***holding company*** (société *f* en) holding *m*, société à portefeuille; ***holding costs*** coûts *mpl* de détention

❝

The treasury announced that Paolo Scaroni, the Italy-born chief executive of UK glass maker Pilkington, is to take over from Franco Tato as chief executive of state-run electricity giant Enel. Piero Gnudi, chairman of Italian state **holding company** Iri, is to become Enel's chairman.

❞

hole-in-the-wall machine *n Fam Banking* distributeur *m* (de billets)

holiday *n* (**a**) *Br (vacation)* vacances *fpl*; **a month's holiday** un mois de vacances; **to be on/go on holiday** être/aller en vacances; **to get paid holidays** avoir les congés payés ❑ ***holiday entitlement*** congés *mpl* annuels (**b**) *(day off)* (jour *m* de) congé *m* (**c**) *(public)* jour *m* férié

home *n* (**a**) *(house)* maison *f*; *(family unit)* foyer *m*; **to work at** *or* **from home** travailler à domicile ❑ ***home address*** adresse *f* personnelle, domicile *m*; ***home banking*** banque *f* à domicile; ***home computer*** ordinateur *m* familial; ***home computing*** informatique *f* à domicile; ***home delivery*** livraison *f* à domicile; *Am* ***home equity loan*** prêt *m* sur valeur nette de la propriété; ***home improvement loan*** prêt pour travaux de rénovation; ***home loan*** prêt immobilier; ***home owner*** propriétaire *mf*; ***home ownership*** accession *f* à la propriété; **home ownership is increasing** le nombre des personnes propriétaires de leur logement augmente; *Mktg* ***home party selling*** vente *f* domiciliaire; ***home shopping*** téléachat *m*
(**b**) *(country) Econ* ***home consumption*** consommation *f* intérieure; ***home freight*** fret *m* de retour; ***home market*** marché *m* intérieur; *Br* ***Home Office*** ≃ ministère *m* de l'Intérieur; ***home produce*** produits *mpl* nationaux *ou* domestiques; ***home sales*** ventes *fpl* sur le marché intérieur; *Br* ***Home Secretary*** ≃ ministre *m* de l'Intérieur; ***home trade*** commerce *m* intérieur
(**c**) *Comptr* début *m* ❑ ***home key*** touche *f* début; ***home page*** page *f* d'accueil; *(personal page)* page personnelle
(**d**) *Am* ***home office*** *(of company)* siège *m* social

homeowner *n* propriétaire *mf*

homeward *adj* de retour ❑ ***homeward cargo*** cargaison *f* de retour; ***homeward freight*** fret *m* de retour; ***homeward journey*** voyage *m* de retour

homeworker *n* travailleur(euse) *m,f* à domicile

homeworking *n* travail *m* à domicile

homogeneous *adj (market, goods)* homogène

honorarium *n* honoraires *mpl*

honorary *adj (president, chairperson, member)* honoraire

honour, *Am* **honor** *vt (cheque, bill of exchange)* honorer, payer; *(agreement, contract)* honorer

horizontal *adj* ***horizontal communication*** communication *f* horizontale; *Fin* ***horizontal equity*** équité *f* horizontale; ***horizontal integration*** intégration *f* horizontale; *St Exch* ***horizontal spread*** écart *m* horizontal

horse-trading *n Fam* négociations *fpl* acharnées; **a lot of horse-trading was required to clinch the deal** l'accord a été conclu à l'issu de négociations acharnées

❝

AT&T's rejection of Comcast came as no surprise to analysts, but many had expected the **horse-trading** for AT&T Broadband to continue with higher offers for the unit, either from Comcast or other cable companies. "[AT&T] is playing a game of poker at this point," said InfoTech Broadband Analyst Erv Paw. "They're trying to get the price up."

❞

hospitality *n* hospitalité *f* ❑ ***hospitality business*** hôtellerie *f*; ***hospitality industry*** industrie *f* hôtelière; ***hospitality management*** gestion *f* hôtelière; ***hospitality room, hospitality suite*** salon *m* de réception *(où sont offerts des rafraîchissements lors d'une conférence)*

host *Comptr* **1** *n* ***host computer*** ordinateur-serveur *m*; ***host system*** système *m* serveur
2 *vt (website)* héberger

hostile takeover bid *n* OPA *f* hostile

❝

Mr Levy has had a mixed history in the US to date – and that's a considerable understatement. The roots of his satisfaction with the current coup will lie in the acrimonious mid-1990s fall-out with his former business partner, the once venerable FCB (now part of the Interpublic Group), which resulted in a failed **hostile takeover bid**.

❞

hosting *n Comptr (of website)* hébergement *m*

hot *adj* (**a**) *Tel* ***hot line*** numéro *m* d'urgence; ***hot line support*** assistance *f* technique téléphonique, hotline *f* (**b**) *Fin* ***hot money*** capital *m* fébrile *ou* flottant (**c**) *Comptr* ***hot key*** touche *f* personnalisée; ***hot link*** lien *m* hypertexte (**d**) ***hot desking*** = pratique qui consiste à ne pas assigner de bureaux individuels aux employés, ces derniers étant libres de s'installer à n'importe quel poste de travail inoccupé

hotel *n* hôtel *m* ◻ **hotel accommodation** hébergement *m* en hôtel; **the town needs more hotel accommodation** la ville a besoin d'augmenter sa capacité hôtelière *ou* de développer ses ressources hôtelières; **hotel administration** gestion *f* hôtelière; **hotel bill** frais *mpl* de séjour à l'hôtel; **the hotel business** l'hôtellerie *f*; **hotel chain** chaîne *f* d'hôtels; **hotel complex** complexe *m* hôtelier; **hotel desk** réception *f*; **hotel group** groupe *m* hôtelier; **hotel industry** industrie *f* hôtelière; **hotel management** *(training)* gestion hôtelière; *(people)* direction *f* de l'hôtel; **hotel manager** directeur(trice) *m,f* ou gérant(e) *m,f* d'hôtel; **hotel reception** réception d'hôtel; **hotel receptionist** réceptionniste *mf* d'hôtel; **hotel staff** personnel *m* de l'hôtel; **the hotel trade** l'industrie hôtelière; **hotel warrant** warrant *m* hôtelier

hour *n* heure *f*; **to pay sb by the hour** payer qn à l'heure; **to be paid £5 an hour** être payé(e) 5 livres (de) l'heure; **an eight-hour day** une journée (de travail) de huit heures

hourly *adj (rate, pay, output)* à l'heure, horaire; **the hourly wage has been increased** le salaire horaire a été augmenté

house *n* (a) *(company)* maison *f* ◻ *Fin* **house bill** double *m* de connaissement, lettre *f* de change creuse; *Am Mktg* **house brand** marque *f* de distributeur; **house magazine** journal *m* (interne) d'entreprise (b) *St Exch* **the House** la Bourse (de Londres)

household *n* *Econ* ménage *m*; *(for tax purposes)* foyer *m* fiscal ◻ **household budget** budget *m* du ménage; **household consumption** consommation *f* des ménages; **household expenses** dépenses *fpl* du ménage; **household goods** biens *mpl* d'équipement ménagers; **household name** nom *m* de marque connu

householder *n* *(owner)* propriétaire *mf*; *(tenant)* locataire *mf*

house-to-house *adj (selling)* à domicile ◻ **house-to-house canvassing** porte-à-porte *m*, démarchage *m*

housing *n* logement *m*; **the budget allocation for housing has been cut** la part du budget réservée au logement a été réduit ◻ **housing allowance** indemnité *f* de résidence; *Br Admin* **housing association** = association britannique à but non lucratif qui construit ou rénove des logements pour les louer à ses membres; *Br Admin* **housing benefit** = allocation de logement versée par l'État aux individus justifiant de re-

venus faibles; **housing list** = liste d'attente pour bénéficier d'un logement social; **housing market** marché *m* de l'immobilier; **housing shortage** crise *f* du logement

HP *n (abbr* **hire purchase**) achat *m* à crédit *ou* à tempérament

HQ *n (abbr* **headquarters**) QG *m*

HR *npl (abbr* **human resources**) RH *fpl*

HRM *n (abbr* **human resource management**) GRH *f*

HSE *n (abbr* **Health and Safety Executive**) inspection *f* du travail

HTML *n Comptr (abbr* **HyperText Markup Language**) HTML *m* ◻ **HTML editor** éditeur *m* HTML

HTTP *n Comptr (abbr* **HyperText Transfer Protocol**) protocole *m* HTTP ◻ **HTTP server** serveur *m* Web

huckster *n Am Fam* agent *m* de publicité agressif

human *adj* **human engineering** gestion *f* des relations humaines; **human factor** facteur *m* humain; **human resource management** gestion de ressources humaines; **human resources** ressources *fpl* humaines

hurdle rate *n* taux *m* de rendement minimal

❝ ──────────────

In general, three pieces of information form the foundation for analyzing investments: the initial cost, the resulting cash flows, and the discount rate (that is, the required rate of return for a given investment, often referred to as the **hurdle rate** in capital budgeting).

────────────── ❞

hype *Fam* **1** *n (publicity)* battage *m* publicitaire **2** *vt (publicize)* faire du battage publicitaire pour

▸ **hype up** *vt sep Fam (publicize)* faire du battage publicitaire pour

hyperinflation *n* hyperinflation *f*

hyperlink *n Comptr* hyperlien *m*

hypermarket *n* hypermarché *m*

hypermedia *n Comptr* hypermédia *m*

hypersegmentation *n Mktg* hypersegmentation *f*

hypertext *n Comptr* hypertexte *m* ◻ **hypertext link** lien *m* hypertexte

hyphen *n* trait *m* d'union

hyphenate *vt* mettre un trait d'union

hyphenation *n* césure *m*

Ii

IAP n Comptr (abbr **Internet Access Provider**) fournisseur m d'accès à l'Internet, FAI m

IASC n (abbr **International Accounting Standards Committee**) comité m international des normes comptables

IBOR n (abbr **interbank offered rate**) taux m interbancaire offert

IBRD n (abbr **International Bank for Reconstruction and Development**) BIRD f

ICC n (**a**) (abbr **International Chamber of Commerce**) CCI f (**b**) Am (abbr **Interstate Commerce Commission**) = commission fédérale américaine réglementant le commerce entre les États

icon n Comptr icône f □ **icon bar** barre f d'icônes; **icon editor** éditeur m d'icônes

IDB n Fin (abbr **inter-dealer broker**) courtier(-ère) m,f intermédiaire

IDD n Tel (abbr **international direct dialling**) indicatif m du pays

IDE n Comptr (abbr **integrated drive electronics**) IDE m

identification n identification f □ **identification code** (of product) code m d'identification; **identification label** (of product) étiquette f d'identification

identifier n Comptr identificateur m

identity n identité f □ **identity card** carte f d'identité; **identity papers** papiers mpl d'identité

idle 1 adj (**a**) (employee) désœuvré(e); (factory, machine) arrêté(e); St Exch (markets) improductif(ive), dormant(e) (**b**) **to lie idle** (of money) dormir; **to let one's money lie idle** laisser dormir son argent (**c**) **idle time** temps m mort
2 vt Am (make unemployed)(permanently) mettre au chômage; (temporarily) mettre en chômage technique

IFA n (abbr **independent financial adviser**) conseiller(ère) m,f financier(ère) indépendant(e)

IFC n Fin (abbr **International Finance Corporation**) SFI f

ILEC n Tel (abbr **incumbent local exchange carrier**) opérateur m historique

illegal adj illégal(e); Comptr (character, file name, instruction) non autorisé(e)

illegally adv illégalement

illicit adj (trading, profits) illicite

illiquid adj non liquide □ **illiquid assets** actif m non-disponible ou immobilisé

illiquidity n illiquidité f □ **illiquidity premium** prime f d'illiquidité

illustration n Comptr **illustration software** logiciel m graphique

illustrator n illustrateur(trice) m,f

ILO n (abbr **International Labour Organization**) OIT f

ILWU n Ind (abbr **International Longshoremen's and Warehousemen's Union**) = syndicat international de dockers et de magasiniers

image n image f; **their brief is to update the product's image** ils ont pour mission de moderniser l'image du produit; **the company is suffering from an image problem** l'entreprise a un problème d'image □ Comptr **image bank** banque f d'images; Comptr **image digitizer** numériseur m d'image; Comptr **image file** fichier m image; Comptr **image format** format m graphique; Mktg **image pricing** fixation f de prix en fonction de l'image; Comptr **image processing** traitement m d'images; Comptr **image processor** unité f de traitement d'images; Comptr **image refresh rate** taux m de rafraîchissement d'images

imager n Comptr imageur m

IMF n Econ (abbr **International Monetary Fund**) FMI m

imitative product n Mktg produit m d'imitation

immediate adj immédiat(e) □ **immediate**

debit débit *m* immédiat; **immediate delivery** livraison *f* immédiate

immobilization *n* Fin (of capital) immobilisation *f*

immobilize *vt* Fin (capital) immobiliser

immovable Law **1** *n* **immovables** biens *mpl* immobiliers *ou* immeubles
  2 *adj* **immovable property** biens *mpl* immobiliers *ou* immeubles

immunity *n* exemption *f*, exonération *f* (**from** de); **immunity from taxation** exemption *ou* exonération d'impôts

impact *n* impact *m*; **high wages have had a considerable impact on production costs** les salaires élevés ont eu un impact considérable sur les coûts de production □ St Exch **impact day** = jour où l'on annonce une nouvelle émission d'actions; Mktg **impact study** étude *f* d'impact

imperfect *adj* imparfait(e) □ **imperfect competition** concurrence *f* imparfaite

impersonal accounts *npl* Acct comptes *mpl* impersonnels

implement *vt* (plan, strategy, policy) exécuter, mettre en application; (law) appliquer

implementation *n* (of plan, strategy, policy) exécution *f*, application *f*; (of law) application; Mktg (of product) mise *f* en œuvre

implicit *adj* (cost, interest) implicite

import 1 *n* (**a**) (product) article *m* d'importation; **imports** (of country) importations *fpl*
  (**b**) (activity) importation *f*; **import and export** l'importation et l'exportation *f* □ **import agent** commissionnaire *mf* importateur(trice); **import ban** interdiction *f* d'importer *ou* d'importation; **to impose an import ban on sth** interdire qch d'importation; **import controls** contrôles *mpl* à l'importation; **import credit** crédits *mpl* à l'importation; **import declaration** déclaration *f* d'importation; **import duty** droit *m* de douane à l'importation; **import firm** maison *f* d'importation; **import gold-point** point *m* d'entrée de l'or; **import goods** marchandises *fpl* à l'import; **import levy** prélèvement *m* à l'importation; **import licence** licence *f* d'importation; **import list** liste *f* des importations; (of prices) tarif *m* d'entrée; **import permit** permis *m* d'importer *ou* d'importation; **import potential** capacité *f* d'importation; **import price** prix *m* à l'importation; **import prohibition** prohibition *f* à l'importation; **import quotas** contingents *mpl* d'importation; **import restrictions** restrictions *fpl* à l'importation; **import surcharge** surtaxe *f* à l'importation; **import surplus** surplus *m* d'importation; **import tax** taxe *f* à l'importation; **import trade** commerce *m* d'importation; **import wholesaler** grossiste *m* importateur

2 *vt* (**a**) (goods) importer (**from** de)
  (**b**) Comptr importer (**from** depuis)

importation *n* (**a**) (of goods) importation *f*; **for temporary importation** en franchise temporaire (**b**) Am (imported article) article *m* d'importation, importation *f*

importer *n* (person) importateur(trice) *m,f*; (country) pays *m* importateur; **an oil importer** un pays importateur de pétrole; **this country is a big importer of luxury goods** ce pays est un gros importateur de produits de luxe; **Japan is still a net importer of technology** le Japon est toujours un importateur net de technologie □ **importer's margin** marge *f* de l'importateur

import-export *n* import-export *m* □ **import-export company** société *f* d'import-export

importing 1 *n* importation *f*
  2 *adj* importateur(trice) □ **importing country** pays *m* importateur; **importing house** maison *f* d'importation

impose *vt* **to impose a tax on sth** taxer qch; **to impose a ban on sth** interdire qch; **the EU is in favour of imposing a ban on tobacco advertising** l'UE est en faveur d'interdire la publicité pour le tabac

imposition *n* (of tax, ban) imposition *f*

impost *n* impôt *m*

impound *vt* Law (goods) confisquer, saisir; (documents) faire déposer au greffe

imprest *n* avance *f* □ **imprest account** compte *m* d'avances (à montant fixe); **imprest fund** fonds *m* de caisse à montant fixe; **imprest system** comptabilité *f* de prévision

improve *vi* s'améliorer; (of prices, markets) monter, être en hausse; **business is improving** les affaires reprennent; **the pound improved against the dollar** la valeur de la livre a augmenté par rapport à celle du dollar

▶ **improve on, improve upon** *vt insep* **to improve on sb's offer** offrir plus que qn

impulse *n* **impulse buy** achat *m* spontané *ou* d'impulsion *ou* impulsif; **impulse buyer** acheteur(euse) *m,f* impulsif(ive); **impulse buying** achats *mpl* spontanés *ou* d'impulsion *ou* impulsifs; **impulse purchase** achat spontané *ou* d'impulsion *ou* impulsif; **impulse purchaser** acheteur(euse) impulsif(ive); **impulse purchasing** achats spontanés *ou* d'impulsion *ou* impulsifs

inactive *adj* (money, bank account, Stock Market) inactif(ive)

in-box *n* Comptr (for e-mail) boîte *f* de réception, corbeille *f* d'arrivée

Inc *adj* Am (abbr **Incorporated**) ≃ SARL

incapacity *n* incapacité *f*; **his incapacity for work** son incapacité à travailler □ Br **incapacity benefit** prestation *f* d'invalidité

incent vt Am motiver, encourager

incentive n (payment) prime f; Mktg stimulation f; (reduction, free gift) stimulant m, stimulateur m; **the company offers various incentives** la société offre diverses primes □ **incentive bonus** prime d'encouragement ou de rendement; **incentive marketing** marketing m de stimulation; **incentive pay** primes fpl de rendement; **incentive scheme** (for buyers) programme m de stimulation; (for workers) système m de primes; Am **incentive travel** voyage m de récompense

incentivize vt motiver, encourager; **tax breaks will incentivize corporations to invest in their future** les allègements fiscaux encourageront les sociétés à investir dans leur avenir

> ❝
> Such thinking was based on the seminal management book *In Search of Excellence* by former McKinsey employees Tom Peters and Bob Waterman. Enron employees read it avidly. They were also big fans of another book, *The War for Talent*, by McKinsey consultants Ed Michaels, Helen Handfield-Jones and Beth Axelrod, which used Enron as a textbook example of how to **incentivize** staff.
> ❞

incidental 1 n **incidentals** faux frais mpl
  2 adj **incidental costs, incidental expenses** faux frais mpl; **incidental income** revenus mpl accessoires

in-clearing book n Banking livre m du dedans, registre m des chèques à rembourser

include vt comprendre, inclure; (in letter) joindre; **up to and including 31 December** jusqu'au 31 décembre inclusivement; **the price includes VAT** la TVA est comprise (dans le prix)

inclusive adj (price, sum) net (nette); **from 4 to 12 February inclusive** du 4 au 12 février inclus; **inclusive of all taxes** toutes taxes comprises; **inclusive of VAT** TVA comprise

income n (a) (of person) revenu m; **to be on a low/high income** avoir un faible revenu/un revenu élevé; **their combined income totals $200,000** leurs revenus additionnés s'élèvent à 200 000 dollars; **the income from her investments** les revenus provenant de ses placements □ **income bracket, income group** tranche f de salaire ou de revenu; **most people in this area belong to the lower/higher income group** la plupart des habitants de ce quartier sont des économiquement faibles/ont des revenus élevés; **income property** immobilier m de rapport; Br Admin **income support** ≃ RMI m; **income tax** impôt m sur le revenu; **income tax is deducted at source** les impôts sont prélevés à la source; **income tax allowance** dé-

duction f avant impôt, déduction fiscale; **income tax inspector** inspecteur(trice) m,f des contributions directes ou des impôts; **income tax return** déclaration f de revenu; (form) feuille f d'impôt

(**b**) (of company) recettes fpl, revenus mpl; Acct **income from operations** produits mpl de gestion courante ou d'exploitation □ Acct **income account** compte m de produits; **income bond** obligation f à intérêt conditionnel; **income and expenditure account** compte de dépenses et recettes; **income fund** fonds m de placement à revenu fixe; **incomes policy** politique f des revenus; **income smoothing** manipulations fpl comptables; Am Acct **income statement** compte de résultat; **income stock** valeurs fpl de placement; **income stream** flux m de revenus; **income velocity of capital** vitesse f de circulation du capital en revenus; **income velocity of circulation** vitesse de circulation de la monnaie en revenus, vitesse de circulation du capital en revenus

incoming 1 n Fin **incomings** recettes fpl, revenus mpl; **incomings and outgoings** dépenses fpl et recettes
  2 adj (telephone call) de l'extérieur; (fax) en entrée; (mail, e-mail) à l'arrivée □ **incoming inventory** inventaire m d'entrée

in-company adj sur le lieu de travail □ Br **in-company training** formation f sur le lieu de travail; Br **in-company training scheme** stage m organisé par la société

incompatible adj Comptr incompatible (**with** avec)

inconvenience n désagrément m; **we apologize for any inconvenience** veuillez nous excuser pour les désagréments occasionnés

inconvertible adj Fin inconvertible

incorporate 1 vt (company) constituer en société commerciale; (banks) réunir en société
  2 vi (form a corporation) se constituer en société commerciale; (merge) fusionner

incorporated adj Am **Ross and Greene Incorporated** ≃ Ross and Greene SARL □ **incorporated company** ≃ société f à responsabilité limitée; **incorporated sector** ≃ sociétés fpl à responsabilité limitée

incorporation n (of company) constitution f en société commerciale

incoterm n (abbr **international commercial term**) incoterm m, terme m de commerce international

increase 1 n (in price, rate, sales) augmentation f, hausse f (**in** de); (in salary) augmentation (de salaire); **the increase in productivity/in the cost of living** l'augmentation de la productivité/du coût de la vie; **to be on the increase** être en hausse

2 *vt* augmenter; **we must increase output to 500 units a week** il faut augmenter la production à 500 unités par semaine

3 *vi* augmenter; **to increase by ten percent** augmenter de dix pour cent; **to increase in value** augmenter de valeur; **to increase in price** devenir plus cher (chère), augmenter de prix; **the growth rate is likely to increase** le taux de croissance va probablement augmenter

increased *adj* accru(e); **increased demand will lead to increased productivity** un accroissement de la demande entraînera une augmentation de la productivité

increment *n* augmentation *f*; **a salary of £36,000 plus annual increments of £4,000** un salaire de 36 000 livres avec augmentation annuelle de 4000 livres

incremental *adj* croissant(e) ❏ *incremental cash flow* cash-flow *m* marginal; *incremental cost* coût *m* marginal; *incremental increase* augmentation *f* régulière

incur *vt* (*risk*) courir; (*loss*) subir; (*debts*) contracter; (*expenses*) engager; **the expenses incurred amount to several thousand pounds** les dépenses engagées s'élèvent à plusieurs milliers de livres

incurred *adj* Acct **incurred expenditure, incurred expenses** dépenses *fpl* engagées

indebted *adj* endetté(e); **to be heavily indebted to sb** devoir une forte somme à qn

indebtedness *n* endettement *m*

indemnification *n* (**a**) (*act of compensation*) indemnisation *f*, dédommagement *m* (**b**) (*sum reimbursed*) indemnité *f*, dédommagement *m*

indemnify *vt* (**a**) (*compensate*) indemniser, dédommager (**for** de); **you will be indemnified for any losses incurred** vous serez indemnisé *ou* dédommagé de toutes les pertes subies (**b**) (*insure*) assurer, garantir (**against** contre); **to be indemnified against sth** être assuré(e) contre qch

> ❝
> Correctional Properties Trust will receive a total of $18,000,000, including the sale proceeds and lease termination fee. In addition, WCC has agreed to **indemnify** the Company against related liabilities and to pay all of Correctional Properties Trust's expenses associated with the sale of the Facility to the State, whether or not a closing occurs.
> ❞

indemnity *n* (**a**) (*compensation*) indemnité *f*, dédommagement *m* ❏ *Fin* **indemnity bond** obligation *f* indemnitaire (**b**) (*insurance*) assurance *f*, garantie *f*

indent 1 *n* (**a**) *Br* (*order*) commande *f* de marchandises; (*order form*) bordereau *m* de

commande ❏ *closed indent* commande spécifiant le fournisseur; *open indent* commande ne spécifiant pas le fournisseur
(**b**) (*in text*) alinéa *m*
(**c**) (*contract*) contrat *m*; (*of apprentice*) contrat d'apprentissage
2 *vt* (**a**) (*goods*) commander
(**b**) (*line of text*) mettre en retrait; **indent the first line** commencez la première ligne en retrait
3 *vi* (**a**) (*order goods*) passer commande; **to indent on sb for sth** commander qch à qn
(**b**) (*at start of paragraph*) faire un alinéa

independent *adj* indépendant(e) ❏ *independent administration* gestion *f* autonome; *independent financial adviser* conseiller(ère) *m,f* financier(ère) indépendant(e); *independent income* revenus *mpl* indépendants, rentes *fpl*; *independent port* port *m* autonome; *independent retailer* détaillant(e) *m,f* indépendant(e)

index 1 *n* (**a**) (*in book, database*) index *m* (**b**) (*on index cards*) fichier *m* ❏ *index box* boîte *f* à fiches; *index card* fiche *f* (cartonnée) (**c**) *Econ, Fin & St Exch* indice *m* ❏ *index arbitrage* arbitrage *m* sur indice; *index fund* fonds *m* à gestion indicielle, fonds indiciel; *index of growth* indice de croissance; *index option* option *f* sur indice
2 *vt* (**a**) *Comptr* (*database*) indexer (**b**) *Fin* (*salary, pension, payment*) indexer (**to** sur) ❏ *indexed bond* obligation *f* indexée; *indexed loan* emprunt *m* indexé; *indexed portfolio* portefeuille *m* indexé

> ❝
> Trading in the final hour in both Dublin and London was frantic as **index funds** bid the shares up to a close of euro 5.00 (£3.94) with bids for stock at euro 4.98 ... Whether the magical euro 5.00 will trigger more selling by private investors remains to be seen but the shares are well-supported.
> ❞

indexation *n* *Fin* indexation *f* ❏ *indexation clause* clause *f* d'indexation

index-link *n* *Fin* indexer

index-linked *adj* *Fin* indexé(e); **this pension is index-linked to the cost of living** cette retraite est indexée sur le coût de la vie ❏ *index-linked bond* obligation *f* indexée; *index-linked fund* fonds *m* à gestion indicielle, fonds indiciel

index-linking *n* *Fin* indexation *f*

indicator *n* (*sign*) indice *m*

indict *vt* *Law* inculper, mettre en examen

indictment *n* *Law* (*act*) inculpation *f*, mise *f* en examen; (*document*) acte *m* d'accusation; **indictment for fraud** inculpation pour fraude

indigenous company n *(local)* entreprise f locale; *(national)* entreprise nationale

indirect adj indirect(e) ❏ **indirect costs** coûts mpl indirects; **indirect investment** investissement m indirect; **indirect labour** main-d'œuvre f indirecte; Mktg **indirect promotional costs** coûts de promotion indirects; **indirect selling** vente f indirecte; **indirect tax** impôt m indirect; **indirect taxation** contributions fpl indirectes

individual adj individuel(elle) ❏ **individual company accounts** comptes mpl sociaux, comptes d'entreprise individuelle; **individual entity** personne f physique; **individual owner** propriétaire mf individuelle; **individual ownership** propriété f individuelle; Am **individual retirement account** plan m d'épargne retraite personnel; **individual savings account** plan d'épargne en actions

indorse = **endorse**

inducement n *(reward)* incitation f, récompense f; *(bribe)* pot-de-vin m; **he was offered considerable financial inducements to leave his company** on lui a offert des sommes considérables pour l'inciter à quitter son entreprise

induction course n stage m préparatoire ou de formation

industrial 1 adj (a) industriel(elle) ❏ **industrial accident** accident m du travail; **industrial accident insurance** assurance f contre les accidents du travail; **industrial action** grève f; **to take industrial action** se mettre en grève, faire grève; **industrial centre** centre m industriel; **industrial complex** complexe m industriel; **industrial concern** exploitation f industrielle; **industrial design** dessin m industriel; **industrial disease** maladie f professionnelle ou du travail; **industrial dispute** conflit m social; **industrial engineering** génie m industriel; **industrial espionage** espionnage m industriel; Br **industrial estate** zone f industrielle; **industrial goods** biens mpl industriels; **industrial group** groupe m industriel; **industrial injury** accident m du travail; **industrial injuries benefit** indemnité f pour accidents du travail; **industrial insurance** assurance f contre les accidents du travail; **the industrial machine** la machine industrielle; **industrial market** marché m industriel; **industrial marketer** mercaticien(enne) m,f industriel(elle); **industrial marketing** marketing m industriel; Am **industrial park** zone industrielle; **industrial plant** équipement m industriel; **industrial pool** syndicat m industriel; **industrial potential** potentiel m industriel; **industrial product** produit m industriel; **industrial psychology** psychologie f industrielle; **industrial relations** relations fpl entre le patronat et les employés; **industrial town**

ville f industrielle; **industrial trade** échanges mpl industriels; **industrial training** formation f en entreprise; **industrial tribunal** ≃ conseil m des prud'hommes; **industrial union** syndicat d'industrie; **industrial unrest** agitation f sociale; **industrial vehicle** véhicule m industriel; **industrial warrant** warrant m industriel

(b) Econ **industrial unit** atelier m

(c) Fin **industrial bank** banque f industrielle; **industrial monopoly** trust m industriel; St Exch **industrial shares** valeurs fpl industrielles

2 n St Exch **industrials** valeurs fpl industrielles

industrialism n industrialisme m

industrialist n industriel m

industrialization n industrialisation f

industrialize 1 vt industrialiser
2 vi s'industrialiser

industrialized adj industrialisé(e) ❏ **industrialized countries** pays mpl industrialisés

industry n industrie f; **the building industry** l'industrie du bâtiment ❏ **industry expert** expert m de l'industrie; **industry forecast** prévision f de l'industrie; **industry sector** secteur m industriel

inefficiency n inefficacité f

inefficient adj inefficace

inelastic adj *(demand)* fixe

❝

The telcos have one basic advantage over their suffering dot-com cousins: While many Internet firms were built on demand that has yet to materialize (people will love buying groceries over the Internet − right?), the telecom sector is blessed with what economists call **inelastic** demand. In other words, people will always want to make phone calls and transmit data, regardless of how low the market sinks.

❞

inertia selling n Mktg vente f forcée

inexpensive adj bon marché, pas cher (chère)

infect vt Comptr infecter

inferior adj (a) *(goods, quality)* inférieur(e) (b) *(in rank)* subalterne; **she holds an inferior position in the company** elle a un poste subalterne dans la société

inflate 1 vt (a) *(account)* grossir, charger; *(expense account, figures)* gonfler (b) Econ *(prices)* faire monter; **to inflate the currency** provoquer l'inflation monétaire
2 vi *(of prices, money)* subir une inflation; **the government decided to inflate** le gouvernement a décidé d'avoir recours à des mesures inflationnistes

inflated adj Econ *(price)* exagéré(e); *(salaires)*

gonflé(e) ❏ **inflated currency** inflation f monétaire

inflation n Econ inflation f; **inflation is down/up on last year** l'inflation est en baisse/en hausse par rapport à l'année dernière; **inflation now stands at five percent** l'inflation est maintenant à cinq pour cent ❏ **inflation differential** différentiel m d'inflation; **inflation tax** impôt m à la production

inflationary adj Econ inflationniste ❏ **inflationary gap** écart m inflationniste; **inflationary policy** politique f inflationniste; **inflationary pressure** pression f inflationniste; **inflationary spiral** spirale f inflationniste; **inflationary surge** poussée f inflationniste

> ❝
> The same spin comes from the Commission with the European Economic and Monetary Affairs Commissioner, Pedro Solbes, who shares Mr Duisenberg's analysis. A rise in inflation in the Euro zone was not a matter of concern. He indicated in an interview with the French newspaper Liberation that he did not believe this marked the beginning of an **inflationary spiral**.
> ❞

inflationism n Econ inflationnisme m

inflationist 1 n Econ inflationniste mf
  2 adj inflationniste

inflation-proof adj protégé(e) contre les effets de l'inflation

inflight magazine n magazine m inflight

inflow n afflux m; **the inflow of capital/of cheap imports** l'afflux de capitaux/de produits importés de mauvaise qualité

influence peddling n trafic m d'influence

> ❝
> During Bill Clinton's presidency, Republicans were loud in accusing the White House of being too cozy with campaign contributors and lobbyists and relentlessly looking to shape policy to appeal to this or that group of minority voters. **Influence peddling** seemed rife, as did special treatment and access for corporate bigwigs who shelled out for the Democrats.
> ❞

influencer n Mktg préconisateur m, influencer m

influx n afflux m

info n Fam informations fpl, renseignements mpl; **a piece of info** une information, un renseignement

infoaddict n Fam Comptr accro mf de l'Internet

infobahn n Comptr autoroute f de l'information

infohighway n Comptr autoroute f de l'information

infomercial n infomercial m

inform vt (in letter) **I am pleased to inform you that...** j'ai le plaisir ou l'honneur de vous informer que...; **I regret to inform you that...** j'ai le regret de vous faire savoir que...; **we are informed that...** on nous informe que...

informal economy n Econ travail m au noir

> ❝
> The European Commission estimates 7–16 percent of the European economy is **informal**, giving a range of approximately EUR500 billion-1.1 trillion ($448.8 billion to $987 billion) that is effectively a cash economy. The smallest **informal economies** are estimated to be in Scandinavia, Ireland, Austria and the Netherlands, each at around a very honest, and modest, 5 percent of GDP. But that balloons to over 20 percent in Italy and Greece.
> ❞

information n (**a**) (news, facts) informations fpl, renseignements mpl; **a piece of information** une information, un renseignement; **I am sending you this brochure for your information** je vous envoie cette brochure à titre d'information ou de renseignement ❏ **information bureau** bureau m de renseignements; **information card** fiche f de renseignements; **information centre** centre m d'information; Admin **information copy** copie f pour information; **information desk** bureau des renseignements; **information market** marché m de l'information; **information office** bureau des renseignements; **information officer** (press officer) responsable mf de la communication; (archivist) documentaliste mf; **information overload** surinformation f; **information pack** dossier m d'information; St Exch **information prospectus** notice f d'information; **information service** service m de l'information; **information sheet** fiche explicative; **information theory** théorie f de l'information
(**b**) Comptr information f ❏ **information gathering** collecte f d'informations; **information highway** autoroute f de l'information; **information processing** traitement m de l'information; **information retrieval** recherche f docu-mentaire; **information science** informatique f; **information society** société f de l'information; **information storage** mémorisation f des informations; **information superhighway** autoroute de l'information; **information system** système m informatique; **information technology** informatique
(**c**) Am Tel renseignements mpl

informative advertising n Mktg publicité f
informative

infrared adj Comptr infrarouge ❑ **infrared keyboard** clavier m infrarouge; **infrared mouse**
souris f infrarouge

infrastructure n Admin infrastructure f

infringe vt (agreement, rights) violer, enfreindre; **to infringe a copyright** violer les droits
d'auteur; **to infringe a patent** contrefaire un
objet breveté

infringement n (of agreement, rights) violation f; **infringement of copyright** violation des
droits d'auteur; **infringement of a patent**
contrefaçon f d'un objet breveté

ingot n lingot m

inherent vice n Ins vice m inhérent

inherit 1 vt hériter de; **she inherited one million dollars** elle a hérité d'un million de dollars
　　2 vi hériter

inheritable adj dont on peut hériter

inheritance n héritage m; **to come into an inheritance** faire ou toucher un héritage ❑ **inheritance tax** droits mpl de succession

inhibitor n Mktg inhibiteur m

in-home adj Mktg **in-home placement testing**
tests mpl à domicile par des consommateurs-
témoins; **in-home shopping** achats mpl à domicile

in-house 1 adj interne; (staff) qui travaille sur
place ❑ **in-house journal** journal m d'entreprise; **in-house magazine** magazine m d'entreprise; **in-house team** équipe f en interne; **in-
house training** formation f interne
　　2 adv sur place; **we prefer to train our staff
in-house** nous préférons former notre personnel au sein de l'entreprise

initial 1 adj initial(e) ❑ **initial capital** capital m
initial ou d'apport; **initial cost** coût m initial; (of
manufactured product) prix m de revient; **initial
expenditure** frais mpl de premier établissement; **initial investment** investissements mpl
initiaux; St Exch **initial margin** dépôt m initial
ou de marge; Am St Exch **initial public offering**
introduction f en Bourse; **initial stock** stock m
de départ; **initial value** valeur f de départ
　　2 vt (letter, document, changes) parapher

initialization n Comptr initialisation f

initialize vt (a) Comptr initialiser (b) (letter,
document, changes) parapher; **the contract
needs to be initialized** le contrat doit être paraphé

initiate vt (talks, debate) amorcer, engager;
(policy) lancer; (measures) instaurer; Law **to initiate proceedings against sb** entamer des
poursuites contre qn

initiator n Mktg initiateur m

inject vt (money) injecter (**into** dans); **they've
injected billions of dollars into the economy**
ils ont injecté des milliards de dollars dans l'économie

injection n (of money) injection f (**into** dans);
an injection of capital une injection de capitaux

injunction n Law injonction f; **to take out an
injunction against sb** mettre qn en demeure

injured party n Law partie f lésée

ink n encre f ❑ **ink cartridge** cartouche f d'encre; **ink pad** tampon m encreur

inkjet printer n Comptr imprimante f à jet
d'encre

inland adj intérieur(e) ❑ Fin **inland bill** traite f
sur l'intérieur; **inland clearance depot** dépôt
m de dédouanement intérieur; **inland freight**
fret m intérieur; **inland haulage** transport m
routier; **inland mail** courrier m intérieur

Inland Revenue n Br **the Inland Revenue** ≃
le fisc

inner reserve n réserve f latente

innovating company n Mktg entreprise f innovatrice

innovation n innovation f; **innovations in
management techniques** des innovations en
matière de gestion

innovative adj novateur(trice), innovateur(-
trice) ❑ Mktg **innovative product** produit m
(in)novateur

innovator n Mktg (in)novateur(trice) m,f

input 1 n (a) (of production) input m, intrant m
❑ Acct **input tax** TVA f récupérée
　　(b) Comptr (action) entrée f, introduction f;
(data) données fpl (en entrée) ❑ **input box** case
f de saisie; **input device** périphérique m d'entrée; **input form** formulaire m de saisie; **input
grid** grille f de saisie
　　(c) (during meeting, discussion) contribution f;
**we'd like some input from marketing before
committing ourselves** nous aimerions consulter le service marketing avant de nous engager
　　2 vt Comptr (data) entrer

input/output n Comptr entrée/sortie f ❑ **in-
put/output device** périphérique m d'entrée/
sortie

inquire 1 vt demander
   2 vi se renseigner (**about** sur)

inquiry n demande f de renseignements; **to make inquiries (about sth)** se renseigner (sur qch); **with reference to your inquiry of 5 May,...** (in letter) en réponse à votre demande du 5 mai,... ▫ **inquiry office** bureau m de renseignements

inscribed securities npl St Exch titres mpl nominatifs

insert 1 n (**a**) Comptr insertion f ▫ **insert command** commande f d'insertion; **insert key** touche f d'insertion; **insert mode** mode m (d')insertion (**b**) (leaflet) encart m
   2 vt insérer

insertion n Comptr insertion f ▫ **insertion marker** marque f d'insertion; **insertion point** point m d'insertion

insider n Fin, St Exch **the insiders** les initiés mpl ▫ **insider dealing, insider trading** délit m d'initié

❝
Investors should benefit from stronger protection against **insider dealing** and stock market manipulation through the first ever set of Europe-wide rules, under plans agreed yesterday by the European Union. The new legislation, approved yesterday by European finance ministers, is a further step towards the EU's goal of creating a single market for securities by the end of next year.
❞

insolvency n (of person) insolvabilité f; (of company) faillite f; **to declare insolvency** (of person) se déclarer insolvable; (of company) déposer son bilan ▫ **insolvency provision** fonds m de garantie salariale

insolvent adj (person) insolvable; (company) en faillite; **to declare oneself insolvent** (of person) se déclarer insolvable; (of company) déposer son bilan

inspect vt (documents, goods) examiner; (premises, factory, staff) inspecter; (equipment) vérifier, inspecter; (books) contrôler

inspection n (of documents, goods) examen m; (of premises, factory, staff) inspection f; (of equipment) vérification f, inspection; (of books) contrôle m; **to buy goods on inspection** acheter des marchandises sur examen ▫ Customs **inspection order** bon m de visite

inspector n inspecteur(trice) m,f ▫ Am **inspector general** inspecteur général; Br **Inspector of Taxes** inspecteur des impôts

instability n instabilité f (financière)

install, Am **instal** vt (**a**) (machinery, equipment) installer; **to install sb in a post** mettre qn à un poste (**b**) Comptr (software) installer

installation n Comptr installation f ▫ **installation disk** disquette f d'installation

instalment, Am **installment** n (part payment) acompte m, versement m; **to pay in** or **by instalments** payer par versements échelonnés ▫ **instalment loan** prêt m à tempérament ou à remboursements échelonnés; Am **installment plan** vente f à tempérament; **to buy sth on the installment plan** acheter qch à tempérament ou à crédit

installer n Comptr programme m d'installation

installment Am = **instalment**

instant adj (access to savings) immédiat(e)

instant-access adj (bank account) à accès immédiat

❝
The internet-only savings accounts, as usual, offer the best rates to savers prepared to eschew trips to high street branches. Egg offers its internet-only savers 5 per cent, including an introductory offer, which puts it well out in the lead among **instant-access** accounts and is comfortably above official interest rates.
❞

instantaneous audience n Mktg audience f instantanée

institute vt Law **to institute proceedings against sb** intenter un procès contre qn

institution n (organization) institution f; (public, financial) établissement m

institutional adj **institutional advertising** publicité f institutionnelle; Fin **institutional buying** achats mpl institutionnels; **institutional investment** investissement m institutionnel; **institutional investor** investisseur m institutionnel; **institutional savings** épargne f institutionnelle

in-store adj Mktg **in-store advertising** PLV f, publicité f sur le lieu de vente; **in-store advertising space** espace m de PLV, espace de publicité sur le lieu de vente; **in-store demonstration** démonstration f sur le lieu de vente; **in-store promotion** publicité f au point de vente

instruction n Comptr **instructions** (in program) instructions fpl ▫ **instruction manual** guide m de l'utilisateur

instrument n Fin effet m, titre m; Law instrument m, acte m juridique; **an instrument of payment** un moyen de paiement ▫ **instrument of commerce** instrument de commerce; **instrument of incorporation** statut m, acte de constitution; **instrument to order** papier m à ordre

insufficient adj insuffisant(e) ▫ **insufficient capital** insuffisance f de capitaux; Banking **in-**

sufficient funds provision *f* insuffisante, insuffisance de provision; **insufficient resources** insuffisance de ressources

insurable *adj* assurable □ *insurable interest* intérêt *m* pécuniaire; *insurable value* valeur *f* assurable

insurance *n* assurance *f*; *(cover)* garantie *f* (d'assurance), couverture *f*; *(premium)* prime *f* (d'assurance); **to take out insurance (against sth)** prendre *ou* contracter une assurance (contre qch); **how much do you pay in insurance?** combien payez-vous (de prime) d'assurance?; **extend the insurance when you renew the policy** faites augmenter le montant de la garantie quand vous renouvelez le contrat d'assurance; **she got £2,000 in insurance** elle a reçu 2000 livres de l'assurance □ *insurance adviser* assureur-conseil *m*; *insurance agent* agent *m* d'assurance(s); *insurance banker* bancassureur *m*; *insurance broker* courtier(ère) *m,f* d'assurance(s); *insurance certificate* certificat *m ou* attestation *f* d'assurance; *insurance charges* frais *mpl* d'assurance; *insurance claim* demande *f* d'indemnité; *(for more serious damage)* déclaration *f* de sinistre; **to make an insurance claim** faire une demande d'indemnité; *(for more serious damage)* faire une déclaration de sinistre; *insurance company* société *f* d'assurances; *insurance cover* couverture *f*; *insurance form* formulaire *m* d'assurance; *insurance group* groupe *m* d'assurance; *insurance inspector* inspecteur(trice) *m,f* d'une société d'assurances; *insurance money* indemnité *f* d'assurance; *insurance policy* police *f* d'assurance; **to take out an insurance policy** contracter une assurance; *insurance pool* pool *m* d'assurances; *insurance portfolio* portefeuille *m* d'assurances; *insurance premium* prime *f* d'assurance; *insurance proposal* proposition *f* d'assurance; *insurance rate* taux *m* d'assurance; *insurance value* valeur *f* d'assurance

insure 1 *vt* assurer (**against** contre); **to insure one's life** s'assurer sur la vie; **we're insured against flooding** nous sommes assurés contre les inondations
2 *vi* **to insure against sth** s'assurer *ou* se faire assurer contre qch

insured 1 *n* assuré(e) *m,f*
2 *adj* assuré(e) (**against** contre) □ *insured value* valeur *f* assurée

insurer *n* assureur *m*

intangible 1 *n* **intangibles** valeurs *fpl* immatérielles, actif *m* incorporel
2 *adj Acct* **intangible asset** valeur *f* immatérielle, actif *m* incorporel; *intangible fixed assets* immobilisations *fpl* incorporelles; *intangible property* biens *mpl* incorporels

integrated *adj* intégré(e) □ *Comptr* **inte-**

grated circuit board carte *f* à circuit(s) intégré(s); *integrated management system* système *m* intégré de gestion; *Comptr* **integrated package** logiciel *m ou* progiciel *m* intégré; *integrated port facilities* complexe *m* portuaire intégré; *Comptr* **integrated services digital network** réseau *m* numérique à intégration de services; *Comptr* **integrated software** logiciel *m* intégré; *integrated transport network* réseau *m* de transport intégré

integration *n* intégration *f*, concentration *f*

> **"**
> "If Bertelsmann want to pursue their pan-European strategy do they have to go in and bid against the US players for ITV?" said Nicola Stewart, analyst at West LB Panmure ... But she said US companies would take a close look at ITV. "There is a lot of logic in having vertical **integration** between content and distribution assets, especially if there is a common language involved, which has put off the European groups," she said.
> **"**

integrative growth *n* croissance *f* par intégration

intellectual property *n* propriété *f* intellectuelle

intelligent terminal *n Comptr* terminal *m* intelligent

intensive distribution *n* distribution *f* intensive □ *intensive distribution strategy* stratégie *f* de distribution intensive

intention to buy *n* intention *f* d'achat

intention-to-buy-scale *n Mktg* échelle *f* des intentions d'achat

interactive *adj Comptr* interactif(ive) □ *interactive CD* CD-I *m*, disque *m* compact interactif; *interactive digital media* médias *mpl* numériques interactifs; *interactive highway* autoroute *f* interactive; *interactive marketing* marketing *m* interactif

interactivity *n Comptr* interactivité *f*

interbank *adj* interbancaire □ *interbank deposit* dépôt *m* interbancaire; *interbank loan* prêt *m* de banque à banque *ou* entre banques; *interbank market* marché *m* interbancaire; *interbank money* argent *m* de gré à gré entre banques; *interbank offered rate* taux *m* interbancaire offert; *interbank reference rate* taux de référence interbancaire; *interbank transfer* virement *m* interbancaire; *interbank wholesale market* marché de gré à gré entre banques

interbranch *adj* entre succursales *(d'une même entreprise)*

intercept interview *n Mktg* entretien *m* spontané

intercompany *adj* intersociété ❑ *intercompany transactions* transactions *fpl* intersociétés

inter-dealer broker *n St Exch* courtier(ère) *m,f* intermédiaire

interdepartmental *adj* entre services

interest *n* (**a**) *Fin (on loan, investment)* intérêt(s) *m(pl)* (**on** sur); **interest accrued** intérêts courus *ou* échus; **interest on arrears** intérêt de retard; **interest on capital** rémunération *f* de capital; **interest due** intérêts dus; **interest due and payable** intérêts exigibles; **interest paid** intérêts versés; **interest payable** intérêt exigible; **interest received** intérêts perçus; **to bear** *or* **yield interest** porter intérêt, rapporter; **to bear** *or* **yield five percent interest** rapporter du cinq pour cent *ou* un intérêt de cinq pour cent; **to pay interest** payer des intérêts ❑ *interest charges* intérêts (à payer); *(on overdraft)* agios *mpl*; *interest day* jour *m* d'intérêt; *interest and dividend income* produits *mpl* financiers; *interest payment date* date *f* d'échéance des intérêts; *interest rate* taux *m* d'intérêt; **the interest rate is four percent** le taux d'intérêt est de quatre pour cent; *interest rate differential* différentiel *m* de taux d'intérêt; *St Exch* *interest rate swap* échange *m* de taux d'intérêt; *interest table* table *f* des intérêts

(**b**) *(stake)* intérêts *mpl*; **our firm's interests in Europe** les intérêts de notre société en Europe; **to have a financial interest in sth** avoir investi financièrement dans qch; **to have an interest in the profits** participer aux bénéfices; **his interest in the company is £10,000** il a une commandite de 10000 livres

(**c**) *(activity)* activité *f*; **since the late 1980s the firm has had major interests in plastics and engineering** depuis la fin des années 1980 les matières plastiques et l'ingénierie constituent deux des principales activités de la société

interest-bearing *adj* productif(ive) d'intérêts ❑ *interest-bearing account* compte *m* rémunéré; *interest-bearing capital* capital *m* productif d'intérêts; *interest-bearing loan* prêt *m* à intérêt; *interest-bearing securities* titres *mpl* qui produisent des intérêts

interested party *n Law* partie *f* intéressée

interest-free *adj* sans intérêt ❑ *interest-free credit* crédit *m* gratuit; *interest-free loan* prêt *m* sans intérêt

interface *n Comptr* interface *f*

interim *adj* intérimaire ❑ *interim accounts* comptes *mpl* semestriels; *interim budget* budget *m* intérimaire; *Fin* *interim dividend* dividende *m* intérimaire; *Am Acct* *interim income statement* compte *m* de résultat prévisionnel; *interim payment* paiement *m* provisoire; *Br Acct* *interim profit and loss account* compte de résultat prévisionnel; *interim report* rap-

port *m* intérimaire; *Acct* *interim statement* bilan *m* intérimaire

❝ ──────────────────────

Shares in Dixons, the UK retailer, jumped 2.88 per cent to £12.50 after the company declared a special **interim dividend** of 7.5p per ordinary share to be paid on December 13. Sir Stanley Kalms, Dixons' chairman, said total retail sales for the 18 weeks to September 4 were up 20 per cent over the same period last year and 9 per cent higher on a like-for-like basis.

──────────────────────── ❞

intermediary *n* intermédiaire *mf*

intermediate *adj Fin* **intermediate broker** intermédiaire *mf*, remisier *m* (en Bourse); *intermediate credit* crédit *m* à moyen terme; *intermediate goods* biens *mpl* intermédiaires

internal *adj* (**a**) *(within country, company)* intérieur(e) ❑ *internal audit* audit *m* interne; *internal auditing* audit *ou* vérification *f* interne; *internal auditor* audit *ou* auditeur(trice) *m,f* interne; *internal check* contrôle *m* interne; *internal company document* document *m* interne à l'entreprise; *internal debt* endettement *m* intérieur; *internal growth* croissance *f* interne; *internal mail* courrier *m* interne; *internal marketing* marketing *m* interne; *internal memo* note *f* à circulation interne; *internal promotion* promotion *f* interne; *internal rate of return* taux *m* de rentabilité interne; *internal regulations* règlement *m* intérieur; *internal revenue* recettes *fpl* fiscales; *Am* **the Internal Revenue Service** ≃ le fisc, la Direction Générale des Impôts; *internal telephone* téléphone *m* intérieur

(**b**) *Comptr* interne *internal drive* unité *f* (de disque) interne; *internal modem* modem *m* interne; *internal unit* unité interne

international *adj* international(e) ❑ *International Accounting Standards Committee* comité *m* international des normes comptables; *International Bank for Reconstruction and Development* Banque *f* internationale pour la reconstruction et le développement; *Tel* *international call* appel *m* international, communication *f* internationale; *International Chamber of Commerce* Chambre *f* de commerce internationale; *international commodity agreements* accords *mpl* internationaux sur les produits de base; *international community* communauté *f* internationale; *international currency* devise *f* internationale; *Tel* *international* *Br* *dialling code* *or* *Am* *dialing code* indicatif *m* du pays; *international division* division *f* internationale; *International Finance Corporation* Société *f* financière internationale; *International Labour Office* Bureau *m* international du travail; *International Labour Organization* Organisation *f* internationale du travail; *international law* droit *m* international; *Econ* **International Monetary Fund** Fonds *m* monétaire international; *international monetary reserves* réserves *fpl* monétaires internationales; *international money market* marché *m* monétaire international; *international money order* mandat *m* international; *international operations* (of company) opérations *fpl* internationales; *international reply coupon* coupon-réponse *m* international; *international rights* droits *mpl* internationaux; *International Standards Organization* Organisation internationale de normalisation; *international trade* commerce *m* international; *international trademark register* registre *m* international des marques; *international trade organization* organisation professionnelle internationale; *international trading corporation* société de commerce international

❝ ─────────────────────────

The International Federation of Airline Pilots' Associations (IFALPA) has formally requested an investigation by the **International Labour Organisation** (ILO) into the practices of Cathay Pacific Airways management in the ongoing dispute with its pilots. The group charges that Cathay Pacific management has violated international standards of workers protection agreed to by many nations including China.

───────────────────────── ❞

Internet *n Comptr* Internet *m*; **to surf the Internet** naviguer sur l'Internet ❑ *Internet access* accès *m* (à l')Internet; *Internet access provider* fournisseur *m* d'accès Internet; *Internet account* compte *m* Internet; *Internet address* adresse *f* Internet; *Internet banking* opérations *fpl* bancaires par l'Internet; *Internet café* cybercafé *m*; *Internet connection* connexion *f* à l'Internet; *Internet number* numéro *m* Internet; *Internet phone* téléphone *m* Internet; *Internet presence provider* = fournisseur d'accès à l'Internet proposant l'hébergement de sites Web; *Internet protocol* protocole *m* Internet; *Internet Relay Chat* service *m* de bavardage Internet, canal *m* de dialogue en direct; *Internet service provider* fournisseur d'accès à l'Internet; *Internet Society* = organisation non gouvernementale chargée de veiller à l'évolution de l'Internet; *Internet surfer* internaute *mf*; *Internet surfing* navigation *f* sur l'Internet; *Internet telephone* téléphone Internet; *Internet telephony* téléphonie *f* sur l'Internet; *Internet user* internaute

interoffice *adj* interne

interpret 1 *vt* interpréter
2 *vi* faire l'interprète

interpreter *n* interprète *mf*

intervention *n EU* **intervention price** prix *m*

d'intervention; *intervention rate* taux *m* d'intervention

interventionism *n Econ* interventionnisme *m*

interventionist 1 *n* interventionniste *mf*
2 *adj* interventionniste

interview 1 *n* (for job, in market research) entretien *m*; **to give sb an interview** faire passer un entretien à qn; **to invite** *or* **call sb for interview** convoquer qn pour un entretien; **interviews will be held at our London offices** les entretiens se dérouleront dans nos bureaux de Londres
2 *vt* (for job) faire passer un entretien à; (in market research) interroger; **shortlisted candidates will be interviewed in March** les candidats sélectionnés seront convoqués pour un entretien en mars

interviewee *n* (for job) candidat(e) *m,f* (à qui l'on fait passer un entretien); (in market research) enquêté(e) *m,f*, personne *f* interrogée; **the first four interviewees are coming this afternoon** les quatre premières personnes convoquées pour un entretien viennent cet après-midi

interviewer *n* (for job) = personne qui fait passer un entretien; (in market research) enquêteur(trice) *m,f*; **there will be a panel of three interviewers** il y aura trois personnes pour faire passer les entretiens

intestate *adj* **to die intestate** mourir intestat

in-the-money option *n St Exch* option *f* en dedans

intra-Community *adj EU* intracommunautaire

intra-company *adj* intra-entreprise

intra-day *adj St Exch* intrajournalier(ère)

Intranet *n Comptr* Intranet *m*

intrapreneur *n* = personne chargée de lancer de nouveaux projets au sein d'une entreprise

❝ ─────────────────────────

"Steve brings extensive knowledge of business development in health sciences from working as an **intrapreneur** at Monsanto, building several businesses from scratch. His strategic vision will be vital in making Kiva Genetics the leader in the genetics market," said Hugh Rienhoff.

───────────────────────── ❞

in-tray *n* corbeille *f* du courrier à traiter

intrinsic value *n St Exch* valeur *f* intrinsèque

introduce *vt* (product) lancer; *St Exch* (shares) introduire; (laws, legislation) déposer, présenter; (reform, new methods) introduire

introduction *n* (a) *St Exch* introduction *f* au marché hors cote (b) *Mktg* **introduction stage** (of product) phase *f* d'introduction

introductory *adj Mktg* **introductory offer** offre *f* de lancement; **introductory price** prix *m* de lancement

intruder *n Comptr* intrus(e) *m,f*

invalid *adj (argument, objection, document)* non valable; *Comptr (file name)* invalide

invalidate *vt (contract, document)* invalider

invalidity *n* (**a**) *Br Admin* **invalidity benefit** prestation *f* d'invalidité; **invalidity pension** pension *f* d'invalidité (**b**) *(of contract, document)* invalidité *f*

inventory 1 *n* (**a**) *(list)* inventaire *m*; **to draw up** *or* **take an inventory** dresser *ou* faire un inventaire ❑ **inventory book** livre *m* d'inventaire; **inventory of fixtures** état *m* des lieux; **inventory of goods** inventaire des marchandises; **inventory management** gestion *f* de l'inventaire; **inventory method** système *m* d'inventaire; **inventory value** valeur *f* d'inventaire
(**b**) *(stock)* stock(s) *m(pl)* ❑ **inventory account** compte *m* de stock; **inventory control** contrôle *m* des stocks; **inventory level** niveau *m* des stocks; **inventory management** gestion *f* des stocks; **inventory shortage** écart *m* sur stock; **inventory turnaround** rotation *f* des stocks; **inventory valuation** valorisation *f* des stocks
2 *vt* inventorier

inverted commas *n* guillemets *mpl*

invest *Fin* **1** *vt (money)* placer, investir; *(capital)* investir; **to invest money in a business** mettre de l'argent *ou* placer des fonds dans un commerce; **they invested five million dollars in new machinery** ils ont investi cinq millions de dollars dans de nouveaux équipements ❑ **invested capital** capital *m* investi
2 *vi* investir, faire des placements; **to invest in shares/in the oil industry** investir en actions/dans l'industrie pétrolière; **to invest in property** faire des placements dans l'immobilier; **we're going to invest in three new machines** nous allons investir dans trois nouvelles machines; **the company has invested heavily in its Asian subsidiary companies** la société a beaucoup investi dans ses filiales asiatiques; **she's been investing on the Stock Market** elle a investi en Bourse

investment *n Fin* placement *m*, investissement *m*; *(money invested)* investissement, mise *f* de fonds; **are these shares a good investment?** ces actions sont-elles un bon placement?; **property is no longer such a safe investment** l'immobilier n'est plus un placement aussi sûr; **I'd prefer a better return on investment** je préférerais un investissement plus rentable; **the company has investments all over the world** la société a des capitaux investis dans le monde entier ❑ **investment account** compte *m* d'investissement; **investment advice** conseil *m* en placements; **investment adviser** conseiller(ère) *m,f* en placements; **investment analyst** analyste *mf* en placements; **investment appraisal** appréciation *f* des investissements; **investment bank** banque *f* d'affaires; **investment banker** banquier(ère) *m,f* d'affaires; **investment banking** banque d'affaires; **investment boom** boom *m* des investissements; **investment capital** capital-investissement *m*; **investment certificate** certificat *m* d'investissement; **investment company** société *f* d'investissements; **investment consultancy** société de conseil en investissement; **investment curve** courbe *f* d'investissement; **investment fund** fonds *m* commun de placement, fonds d'investissement; **investment grant** subvention *f* d'investissement; **investment house** société de financement; **investment income** revenu *m* provenant d'investissements; **investment institution** société d'investissements; **investment instrument** instrument *m* de placement; **investment management** gestion *f* des investissements; **Investment Management Regulatory Organization** = organisme britannique contrôlant les activités de banques d'affaires et de gestionnaires de fonds de retraite; **investment market** marché *m* des capitaux; **investment objectives** objectifs *mpl* de placement; **investment officer** responsable *mf* des investissements; **investment performance** performance *f* des investissements; **investment plan** plan *m* d'investissement; **investment policy** politique *f* d'investissement; **investment portfolio** portefeuille *m* d'investissements; **investment programme** programme *m* d'investissement; **investment return** retour *m* sur investissements; **investment securities, investment stock** valeurs *fpl* en portefeuille *ou* de placement; **investment subsidy** prime *f* à l'investissement; **investment trust** société de placement

investor *n Fin* investisseur *m*; *(shareholder)* actionnaire *mf*

invisible *Econ* **1** *n* **invisibles** invisibles *mpl*
2 *adj* **invisible assets** actif *m* incorporel, immobilisation *f* (incorporelle); **invisible balance** balance *f* des invisibles; **invisible earnings** gains *mpl* invisibles; **invisible exports** exportations *fpl* invisibles; **invisible imports** importations *fpl* invisibles; **invisible trade** commerce *m* de services

> **"**
> Shell, BAE Systems and HSBC are among the leading British-based firms active in the Middle East either directly or through subsidiaries. They help draw in some £3bn in physical trade a year with a further £3bn estimated to come from **invisibles** such as insurance and shipping.
> **"**

invitation *n invitation to tender* appel *m* d'offres

invite *vt* (**a**) *(ask)* **to invite sb for interview** établir *ou* faire une facture; **we invite applications from all qualified candidates** nous invitons tous les candidats ayant le profil requis à postuler (**b**) *Fin* **to invite bids** *or* **tenders** faire un appel d'offres

invoice 1 *n* facture; **to settle an invoice** régler une facture; **to make out an invoice** établir *ou* faire une facture; **as per invoice** conformément à la facture; **payment should be made within 30 days of invoice** les factures doivent être réglées sous 30 jours; **payable against invoice** à payer à réception de la facture □ *invoice clerk* facturier(ère) *m,f*; *invoice date* date *f* de facturation; *invoice department* service *m* de facturation; *invoice discounting* escompte *m* de créances *ou* de traites; *invoice of origin* facture originale; *invoice price* prix *m* facturé; *invoice value* valeur *f* de facture

2 *vt (goods)* facturer, porter sur une facture; *(person, company)* envoyer la facture à; **to invoice sb for sth** facturer qch à qn

invoicing *n (of goods)* facturation *f* □ *invoicing address* adresse *f* de facturation; *invoicing instructions* instructions *fpl* de facturation; *invoicing machine* machine *f* à facturer; *Comptr invoicing software* logiciel *m* de facturation

inward *adj inward bill of lading* connaissement *m* d'entrée; *inward charges (of ship)* frais *mpl* à l'entrée; *inward customs clearance* entrée *f* en douane; *inward investment* investissement *m* de l'étranger; *inward manifest* manifeste *m* d'entrée; *Acct inward payment* paiement *m* reçu

I/O *n Comptr (abbr input/output)* E/S *f*

IOU *n (abbr I owe you)* reconnaissance *f* de dette

IP *n Comptr (abbr Internet Protocol)* *IP address* adresse *f* IP; *IP number* numéro *m* IP

IPO *n Am St Exch (abbr initial public offering)* introduction *f* en Bourse

IPP *n Comptr (abbr Internet Presence Provider)* = fournisseur d'accès à l'Internet

IRA *n Am (abbr individual retirement account)* plan *m* d'épargne retraite personnel

IRC *n Comptr (abbr Internet Relay Chat)* IRC *m*, service *m* de bavardage Internet, dialogue *m* en direct □ *IRC channel* canal *m* IRC, canal de dialogue en direct

Irish pound *n Formerly* livre *f* irlandaise

iron *n (mineral)* fer *m* □ *iron ore* minerai *m* de fer; *iron and steel industry* sidérurgie *f*; *Iron and Steels Confederation* = syndicat britannique des ouvriers de la sidérurgie

IRR *n (abbr internal rate of return)* taux *m* de rentabilité interne

irrecoverable *adj (debt)* irrécouvrable

irredeemable *Fin* **1** *n* **irredeemables** obligations *fpl* non amortissables
2 *adj (funds, share)* non remboursable; *(bill)* non convertible □ *irredeemable bond* obligation *f* non amortissable

irregularity *n (in accounts)* irrégularité *f*; **there were some irregularities in the paperwork** il y avait quelques irrégularités dans les écritures

irregulars *npl Am* articles *mpl* de deuxième qualité *ou* de qualité moyenne

irrevocable *adj Banking (credit, letter of credit)* irrévocable

IRS *n Am (abbr Internal Revenue Service)* **the IRS** ≃ le fisc

ISA *n Br (abbr individual savings account)* ≃ PEA *m*, plan *m* d'épargne en actions

ISBN *n (abbr International Standard Book Number)* ISBN *m*

ISDN *Comptr* **1** *n (abbr integrated services digital network)* RNIS *m* □ *ISDN card* carte *f* RNIS; *ISDN line* ligne *f* RNIS; *ISDN modem* modem *m* RNIS *ou* Numéris
2 *vt Fam* **to ISDN sth** envoyer qch par RNIS

used **ISDN**, as did 45% of smaller firms with up to 250 employees. Reliability, availability and speed of access were cited as reasons for adoption. ”

island *n Mktg (for displaying goods)* îlot *m*

ISO *n* (*abbr* **International Standards Organization**) ISO *f*

ISOC *n Comptr* (*abbr* **Internet Society**) = organisation non gouvernementale chargée de veiller à l'évolution de l'Internet

ISP *n Comptr* (*abbr* **Internet Service Provider**) fournisseur *m* d'accès à l'Internet

issuable *adj Fin, St Exch* émissible

issue 1 *n* (**a**) *Fin, St Exch (of banknotes, money orders, shares)* émission *f* ❑ ***issue premium*** prime *f* d'émission; ***issue price*** prix *m* d'émission; ***issue value*** valeur *f* d'émission (**b**) *Admin* ***issue card*** carte *f* (de) sortie de stock

2 *vt Fin, St Exch (banknotes, money orders, shares)* émettre; *(bill)* créer; *(new edition, prospectus)* publier; *(letter of credit)* fournir; **to issue a draft on sb** fournir une traite sur qn

issued *adj Fin, St Exch* ***issued capital*** capital *m* émis; ***issued securities*** titres *mpl* émis; ***issued share capital*** capital-actions *m* émis

issuing *adj Fin, St Exch* émetteur(trice) ❑ ***issuing bank*** banque *f* émettrice, banque d'émission; ***issuing company*** société *f* émettrice; ***issuing house*** banque émettrice, banque d'émission; ***issuing monopoly*** monopole *m* d'émission

IT *n Comptr* (*abbr* **information technology**) informatique *f*; **she's our IT expert** c'est notre spécialiste en informatique; **IT has completely revolutionized the way we do business** l'informatique a complètement transformé le monde des affaires

item *n* (**a**) *(article)* article *m*; **please send us the following items** prière de nous envoyer les articles suivants (**b**) *Acct* article *m*, écriture *f*; **item of expenditure** article *m* de dépense (**c**) *(in list, contract)* article *m*; *(on agenda)* question *f*, point *m*; **there are two important items on the agenda** il y a deux points importants à l'ordre du jour

itemize *vt* détailler ❑ ***itemized account*** compte *m* détaillé; ***itemized bill*** facture *f* détaillée; ***itemized billing, itemized invoicing*** facturation *f* détaillée

ITO *n* (*abbr* **International Trade Organization**) organisation *f* professionnelle internationale

Jj

J/A, j/a n Banking (abbr **joint account**) compte m joint

jargon m jargon m

Java n Comptr Java m ❏ **Java script** (langage m) Javascript m

Jaycees npl Am **the Jaycees** = chambre de commerce pour jeunes entrepreneurs

J-curve n Econ courbe f en J

jet lag n fatigue f due au décalage horaire

jet-lagged adj fatigué(e) par le décalage horaire

jingle n Mktg jingle m, sonal m

JIT adj (abbr **just-in-time**) juste à temps, JAT ❏ **JIT distribution** distribution f JAT; **JIT production** production f JAT; **JIT purchasing** achat m JAT

job n (**a**) (employment, post) travail m, emploi m; **to look for a job** chercher du travail ou un emploi; **to lose one's job** perdre son emploi; **to be out of a job** être sans travail ou emploi ❏ Am **job action** action f revendicative; **job advertisement** offre f d'emploi; Admin **job analysis** analyse f des tâches; **job application** demande f d'emploi; **job application form** formulaire m de candidature; **job assignment** assignation f des tâches; **job classification** classification f des emplois; **job creation** création f d'emplois; **job creation scheme** programme m de création d'emplois; **job description** description f de poste; **job enlargement** élargissement m des tâches; **job enrichment** enrichissement m des tâches; **job evaluation** évaluation f des tâches; **job hunter** demandeur m d'emploi; **job hunting** recherche f d'un emploi; **to go/be job hunting** aller/être à la recherche d'un emploi; **job interview** entretien m d'embauche; **job losses** suppressions fpl d'emploi; **job market** marché m de l'emploi; **job offer** offre d'emploi; **job opportunities** débouchés mpl, perspectives fpl d'emploi; **job prospects** perspectives de carrière; **job protection** protection f de l'emploi; **job rotation** rotation f des postes; **job satisfaction** satisfaction f professionnelle; **although the pay is quite low, there is a high level of job satisfaction** bien que le salaire soit assez bas, c'est un poste qui procure une grande satisfaction; **job security** sécurité f d'emploi; **talks of a merger caused speculation about job security** les rumeurs de fusion ont nourri les conjec-tures quant à la sécurité des emplois concer-nés; **job seeker** demandeur(euse) m,f d'emploi; **job sharing** partage m de poste; **job specifica-tion** description f de l'emploi; **job title** fonction f; **job vacancy** poste m à pourvoir

(**b**) (piece of work, task) tâche f, travail m; **to do a job** faire un travail

(**c**) **job lot** lot m; **to buy sth as a job lot** acheter qch en lot; **they sold off the surplus as a job lot** ils ont vendu tout l'excédent en un seul lot

> " Professionals in this program also partici-pate in ongoing **job enrichment** and pro-fessional development activities designed to increase competence and confidence and to provide a forum for group information sharing and problem solving. "

▶ **job out** vt sep sous-traiter; **they jobbed out the work to three different firms** ils ont confié le travail à trois sous-traitants

jobber n (**a**) (piece worker) ouvrier(ère) m,f à la tâche (**b**) St Exch courtier(ère) m,f en Bourse (**c**) (wholesaler) grossiste mf

jobbery n St Exch agiotage m

jobbing n ouvrage m à la tâche

Jobcentre n Br ≃ agence f nationale pour l'emploi, ANPE f

jobholder n salarié(e) m,f

job-hop vi Am = changer d'emploi très sou-vent

jobless 1 npl **the jobless** les sans-emploi mpl
2 adj sans emploi

Jobseekers allowance n Br allocation f (de) chômage

job-share 1 n emploi m partagé
2 vi partager un emploi

join vt (company) entrer dans; (union) devenir membre de

joining fee n Comptr frais mpl d'accès au ser-vice

joint adj (statement, decision, agreement, respon-sibility) commun(e); (contract) (between two parties) bilatéral(e); (between more than two parties) collectif(ive) ❏ Banking **joint account** compte m joint; **joint agreement** accord m commun; Ind convention f collective; **joint**

beneficiary bénéficiaire *mf* conjoint(e); **joint commission** commission *f* mixte *ou* paritaire; **joint committee** commission mixte *ou* paritaire; **joint creditor** cocréancier(ère) *m,f*; **joint debtor** codébiteur(trice) *m,f*; **joint decision** décision *f* collective *ou* commune; **joint enterprise** entreprise *f* en participation; *Law* **joint estate** communauté *f* de biens; *Law* **joint heir** cohéritier(ère) *m,f*; *Law* **joint liability** responsabilité *f* conjointe; **joint management** cogestion *f*; **joint negotiations** négociations *fpl* paritaires; **joint obligation** coobligation *f*; **joint occupancy** colocation *f*; **joint ordering** groupage *m* de commandes; **joint owner** copropriétaire *mf*, propriétaire *mf* indivis(e); **to be joint owners of sth** posséder *ou* détenir qch en commun; **joint ownership** copropriété *f*, propriété *f* indivise; **joint partnership** coassociation *f*; *Ins* **joint policy** police *f* conjointe; **joint production** coproduction *f*; *Law* **joint property** biens *mpl* communs; **joint purchase** coacquisition *f*; **joint report** rapport *m* collectif; **joint representation** démarche *f* collective; *Law* **joint and several debtor** débiteur(trice) *m,f* solidaire et indivise *ou* conjointe et solidaire; *Law* **joint and several guarantor** garant(e) *m,f* solidaire et indivise *ou* conjointe et solidaire; *Law* **joint and several liability** responsabilité *f* solidaire et indivise *ou* conjointe et solidaire; *Law* **joint responsibility** responsabilité conjointe; **joint shares** actions *fpl* indivises; **joint signature** signature *f* collective; **joint statement** déclaration *f* commune; **joint stock** capital *m* social; **joint surety** cautionnement *m* solidaire; **joint tenancy** location *f* commune; **joint tenant** colocataire *mf*; **joint venture** *(undertaking)* opération *f* en commun, entreprise commune; *(agreement)* coentreprise *f*, joint-venture *m*; *(company)* société commune, société en participation; **joint venture agreement** accord de partenariat; **joint venture company** société d'exploitation en commun

jointly *adv* conjointement; **we manage the firm jointly** nous sommes cogérants de la maison; *Law* **jointly liable** conjointement responsable, coresponsable; **jointly and severally liable** responsables conjointement et solidairement

joint-stock *adj Br Fin* **joint-stock bank** banque *f* de dépôt; **joint-stock company** société *f* (anonyme) par actions

journal *n* (**a**) *Acct (for transactions)* livre *m* de comptes, (livre) journal *m* □ **journal entry** écriture *f* comptable, passation *f* d'écriture (**b**) *(magazine)* revue *f*

journalism *n* journalisme *m*

journalist *n* journaliste *mf*

journalistic *adj* journalistique

JPEG *n Comptr* (*abbr* **Joint Photographic Ex-**

perts Group) *(format m)* JPEG *m*

judge *Law* **1** *n* juge *m*
2 *vt* juger; **the case will be judged tomorrow** l'affaire sera jugée demain

judg(e)ment, *Am* **judgment** *n* (**a**) *Law* jugement *m*; **to pass judgement on sb/sth** porter un jugement sur qn/qch; **to sit in judgement** *(of court)* siéger (**b**) *Mktg* **judgement sample** échantillon *m* discrétionnaire; **judgement sampling** échantillonnage *m* discrétionnaire

judg(e)mental, *Am* **judgmental** *adj Mktg* **judgemental forecasting** prévision *f* par estimation; **judgemental method** méthode *f* estimative

judicature *n (judge's authority)* justice *f*; *(court's jurisdiction)* juridiction *f*; *(judge's collectively)* magistrature *f*

judicial *adj* judiciaire; **to bring or take judicial proceedings against sb** attaquer qn en justice □ **judicial enquiry** enquête *f* judiciaire; **judicial power** pouvoir *m* judiciaire; *Am* **judicial review** *(of ruling)* examen *m* d'une décision de justice *(par une juridiction supérieure)*; *(of law)* examen de la constitutionnalité d'une loi

judiciary **1** *n (judicial authority)* pouvoir *m* judiciaire; *(judges collectively)* magistrature *f*
2 *adj* judiciaire

jumbo *adj Fam Fin* **jumbo bond** = obligation de valeur très élevée; *Fam Fin* **jumbo certificate of deposit** certificat *m* de très grand dépôt; *Am Fam Fin* **jumbo loan** prêt *m* géant; *Fam St Exch* **jumbo trade** opération *f* jumbo

> "
> Further, there is now more variety for investors. The previous record for weekly issuance last June was owed entirely to a sole **jumbo bond** offering from Deutsche Telekom AG. By contrast, the recent $15 billion week is the product of a number of issuers, including DaimlerChrysler AG's $7.1 billion deal, as well as deals from Heller Financial Inc., General Motors Corp., and self-issues from Citigroup and Goldman Sachs.
> "

jump **1** *n (rise)* hausse *f* (**in** de); **there has been a sudden jump in house prices** il y a eu une flambée des prix de l'immobilier
2 *vi (rise)* faire un bond, monter en flèche

jumpy *adj St Exch (market)* instable, fluctuant(e)

junior **1** *n (in rank)* subalterne *mf*
2 *adj (in rank)* subalterne; **to be junior to sb** être au-dessous de qn □ *Am* **Junior Chamber of Commerce** = chambre de commerce pour jeunes entrepreneurs; **junior executive** jeune cadre *m*; *Br* **junior partner** jeune associé(e) *m,f*

junk *n Fin, St Exch* **junk bond** obligation *f* à haut rendement mais à haut risque, junk bond *m*; **junk e-mail** messages *mpl* publicitaires; **junk mail** courrier *m* publicitaire

> **"**
> The U.S. **junk bond** market is absorbing a huge amount of new bond supply from corporate "fallen angels," yet analysts aren't fretting that the huge influx is likely to drag down the sector ... Analysts say over the next year they expect tens of billions of dollars of additional bonds to fall into what J.P. Morgan Chase & Co. says is a US$802-billion **junk bond** market.
> **"**

jurisdiction *n* juridiction *f*; **this matter does not come within our jurisdiction** cette affaire n'est pas de notre compétence

juror *n* juré(e) *m,f*

jury *n* jury *m*; **to serve on a jury** faire partie d'un jury

justice *n* justice *f*; **a court of justice** une cour de justice; **to bring sb to justice** traduire qn en justice □ *Am* **the Justice Department** le ministère de la Justice

justification *n Comptr* justification *f* □ **left justification** justification à gauche; **right justification** justification à droite

justified *adj Comptr* justifié(e); **left/right justified** justifié à gauche/droite

justify *vt Comptr* justifier

just-in-time *adj* juste à temps □ **just-in-time distribution** distribution *f* juste à temps; **just-in-time production** production *f* juste à temps; **just-in-time purchasing** achat *m* juste à temps

JV *n* (*abbr* **joint venture**) entreprise *f* commune

Kk

K *n* (**a**) (*abbr* **thousand, thousand pounds**) he **earns 30K** il gagne 30 000 livres (**b**) *Comptr* (*abbr* **kilobyte**) Ko *m*; **how many K are left?** combien de Ko reste-t-il?; **720K diskette** disquette *f* de 720 Ko

kaffir *n Fam St Exch* valeur *f* or sud-africaine

kaizen *n* = optimisation de la rentabilité par un travail d'équipe qui découle d'une confiance partagée entre employeurs et employés

kangaroo *n Fam St Exch* valeur *f* australienne

KB *n Comptr* (*abbr* **kilobyte**) Ko *m*

Kb *n* (*abbr* **kilobit**) Kb *m*

Kbps *Comptr* (*abbr* **kilobits per second**) Kbit/s

keen *adj* (*competition*) acharné(e); (*prices*) compétitif(ive)

keep *vt* (**a**) **to keep the books** tenir la comptabilité *ou* les comptes; **to keep a note of sth** noter qch (**b**) (*have in stock*) vendre; **we don't keep computer accessories** nous ne vendons pas d'accessoires informatiques

▶ **keep down** *vt sep* (*prevent from increasing*) empêcher d'augmenter; **we must keep our expenses down** il faut que nous limitions nos dépenses; **our aim is to keep prices down** notre but est d'empêcher les prix d'augmenter

▶ **keep up** *vt sep* (*prices*) maintenir ferme

keiretsu *n* keiretsu *m*

kerb *n Fam St Exch* **to buy/sell on the kerb** acheter/vendre après la clôture officielle de la Bourse; **business done on the kerb** opérations *fpl* effectuées en coulisse *ou* après clôture de Bourse □ **kerb broker** coulissier *m*, courtier(ère) *m,f* hors Bourse; **kerb market** marché *m* hors cote, coulisse *f*

kerbstone market *n Fam St Exch* marché *m* hors cote, coulisse *f*

key **1** *n Comptr* (*of sort, identification*) indicatif *m*, critère *m*; (*button*) touche *f* □ **key combination** combinaison *f* de touches
2 *adj* (**a**) (*important*) clé □ *Mktg* **key account** compte-clé *m*; *Mktg* **key brand** marque *f* clé; **key factor** facteur *m* clé; **key industry** industrie *f* clé; **key person** pivot *m*; **key position** position *f* clé; **key post** poste *m* clé; **key sector** secteur *m* clé; **key staff** personnel *m* de base (**b**) **key money** pas *m* de porte
3 *vt Comptr* (*data, text*) taper, saisir

▶ **key in, key up** *vt sep Comptr* (*data, text*) taper, saisir

key-account *adj Mktg* **key-account management** gestion *f* de comptes-clés; **key-account sales** ventes *fpl* aux comptes-clés

keyboard **1** *n* (*of typewriter, computer*) clavier *m* □ **keyboard layout** disposition *f* de clavier; **keyboard map** schéma *m* de clavier; **keyboard operator** opérateur(trice) *m,f* de saisie; **keyboard shortcut** raccourci *m* clavier; **keyboard skills** compétences *fpl* de claviste
2 *vt* (*data, text*) taper, saisir
3 *vi* introduire des données par clavier

keyboarder *n Comptr* claviste *mf*, opérateur(trice) *m,f* de saisie

key-escrow *n Comput* système *m* du tiers de confiance (*selon lequel l'utilisateur confie sa clé privée de cryptage à un tiers de confiance agréé*)

find a suitably trustworthy third party, anyway? In some countries where **key-escrow** has been mooted, the banking institutions have been seen as the logical TTP. People trust them with their money, so why not with a crypto key? **"**

keying n Comptr saisie f □ **keying error** faute f de frappe; **keying speed** vitesse f de frappe

Keynesian adj Econ keynésien(enne)

keypad n Comptr pavé m

keystroke n Comptr frappe f (de touche); **keystrokes per minute/hour** vitesse f de frappe à la minute/à l'heure

keyword n Comptr mot m clé □ **keyword advertising** publicité f par mots clés

kick vt Fam **to kick sb upstairs** = donner une promotion à qn dont on veut se débarrasser

kickback n Fam dessous-de-table m, pot-de-vin m

killing n Fam **to make a killing** s'en mettre plein les poches

kilobit n Comptr kilobit m

kilobyte n Comptr kilo-octet m

kindly adv (in letter) **kindly remit by cheque** prière de nous couvrir par chèque; **kindly reply by return of post** prière de répondre par retour de courrier

kite Fam Fin **1** n traite f en l'air, billet m de complaisance; **to fly** or **to send up a kite** tirer en l'air ou à découvert □ **kite flyer** tireur m en l'air ou à découvert
2 vt Am **to kite a cheque** faire un chèque en bois

kiting n Fam Fin (of paper) tirage m en l'air ou à découvert; (of cheque) = fait de faire un chèque en bois

"
The bank holding company will ... more easily identify potential fraud and reduce losses from check **kiting**, a sophisticated scam involving repeated deposits of bad checks through multiple accounts. Check **kiting** scams can cost financial institutions millions of dollars if not detected early in the process.
"

▶ **knock down** vt sep (price) baisser; (salesman) faire baisser; **I managed to knock him down to $500** j'ai réussi à le faire baisser à 500 dollars

knockdown price n Br Fam **for sale at knockdown prices** en vente à des prix imbattables; **I got it for a knockdown price** je l'ai eu pour trois fois rien

knocking copy n Mktg publicité f comparative dénigrante

knock-on effect n répercussions fpl, contre-coup m; **businesses are feeling the knock-on effect of a strong pound** les entreprises subissent le contrecoup d'une livre forte

know-how n savoir-faire m; (technical) know-how m

krona n couronne f (suédoise)

krone n (in Norway) couronne f (norvégienne); (in Denmark) couronne (danoise)

Krugerrand n Krugerrand m

Ll

label 1 n étiquette f ◻ **label of origin** label m d'origine
  2 vt étiqueter

labelling, Am **labeling** n étiquetage m

labor, laborer etc Am = **labour, labourer** etc

labour, Am **labor** n **(a)** (work) travail m **(b)** (manpower) main-d'œuvre f; (workers) ouvriers mpl; **capital and labour** le capital et la main-d'œuvre ◻ Am **labor code** code m du travail; Am **labor contract** contrat m de travail; **labour costs** (coûts mpl de la) main-d'œuvre; Am **Labor Day** fête f du travail (aux États-Unis, célébrée le premier lundi de Septembre); **labour dispute** conflit m du travail; Br Formerly **labour exchange** agence f pour l'emploi; **labour force** effectifs mpl; Econ (of country) population f active; **labour law** droit m du travail; **labour laws** législation f du travail; **labour legislation** législation du travail; **labour market** marché m du travail; **labour regulations** réglementation f du travail; **labour relations** relations fpl sociales; **labour shortage** pénurie f de main-d'œuvre; Am **labor union** syndicat m

labourer, Am **laborer** n ouvrier(ère) m,f

labour-intensive, Am **labor-intensive** adj qui dépend d'une main-d'œuvre considérable

labour-saving, Am **labor-saving** adj qui facilite le travail ◻ **labour-saving device** appareil m facilitant le travail

lack 1 n (of capital, workers) manque m (**of** de)
  2 vt manquer de; **we lack the necessary resources** nous n'avons pas les ressources nécessaires

laddered portfolio n Am Fin portefeuille m d'obligations à rendement échelonné

> **❝**
>
> A **laddered portfolio** of individual bonds has an additional advantage: If you need to sell some of them to raise cash at a time when the bond market is slumping, you can select the more profitable ones for sale and hold the others to maturity. When redeeming bond fund shares, you may be forced to swallow a capital loss if the market is against you.
>
> **❞**

laden adj chargé(e) ◻ **laden weight** poids m en charge

lading n **(a)** (of ship) chargement m **(b)** (of goods) embarquement m, mise f à bord

lag n retard m, décalage m; **there was a lag between completion and publication** il y a eu un décalage entre l'achèvement de l'œuvre et sa publication

laggard n Mktg innovateur(trice) m,f tardif(ive)

laisser-faire, laissez-faire n Econ laisser-faire m ◻ **laisser-faire policy** politique f de laisser-faire

lame duck n (company) canard m boîteux

> **❝**
>
> "Cordiant looks like a **lame duck** to me," the executive said. "It's got some great individual assets but in its current form it's a wounded animal that I don't think anyone will go for."
>
> **❞**

LAN n Comptr (abbr **local area network**) réseau m local

land 1 n **(a)** Law terre(s) f(pl) ◻ **land agent** (administrator) régisseur m, intendant(e) m,f; Br (estate agent) agent m immobilier; **land bank** crédit m foncier; Acct **land charge** dette f foncière; **land ownership** propriété f foncière; **land register** registre m foncier, cadastre m; **land registration** inscription f au cadastre; **land registration certificate** extrait m cadastral; **land registry** cadastre; **land registry (office)** bureau m du cadastre; **land tax** impôt m foncier, contribution f foncière
  (b) Tel **land line** ligne f terrestre
  2 vt (goods) décharger; (passengers) débarquer

landed adj **(a)** Acct **landed costs** coûts mpl fonciers; **landed estate** propriété f foncière; **landed property** propriété foncière, biens mpl fonciers; **landed proprietor** propriétaire mf terrien(enne) **(b)** **landed cost** (of goods) prix m à quai

landing n **(a)** (of goods) déchargement m ◻ **landing certificate** certificat m de déchargement; **landing charges** frais mpl de déchargement; **landing permit** permis m de débarquement **(b)** (of plane) atterrissage m; (of passengers) débarquement m ◻ **landing card** carte f de débarquement; **landing permit** permis *m* de débarquement; **landing and port charges** frais *mpl* de débarquement et de port

land-office business *n Am* entreprise *f* qui monte en flèche

landowner *n* propriétaire *mf* foncier(ère)

landscape *n Comptr* paysage *m*; **to print sth in landscape** imprimer qch en paysage ◻ **landscape mode** mode *m* paysage

lapse 1 *n Law* (**a**) *(of right, patent)* déchéance *f* (**b**) **lapse of time** laps *m* de temps; **after a lapse of three months** au bout de trois mois
2 *vi* (**a**) *Law (of right, patent)* se périmer, tomber en désuétude (**b**) *(of subscription)* prendre fin, expirer; *(of fund, insurance policy)* périmer; **he let his insurance lapse** il a laissé périmer son assurance

lapsed *adj (subscription)* expiré(e); *(fund, insurance policy)* périmé(e) ◻ *St Exch* **lapsed option** option *f* expirée

laptop *n Comptr* portable *m*

large-cap *adj Am (company, corporation)* à grande capitalisation

laser *n Comptr* laser *m* ◻ **laser disc** disque *m* laser; **laser printer** imprimante *f* laser

last *adj* (**a**) *St Exch* **last trading day** dernier jour *m* de cotation (**b**) **last in, first out** dernier entré premier sorti

late *adj* (**a**) *(behind schedule)* en retard ◻ **late delivery** livraison *f* retardée; **late delivery penalty** pénalité *f* de retard; **late payment** retard *m* de paiement; **late payment penalty** pénalité de retard
(**b**) *(in time)* tardif(ive); *Mktg* **late adopter** utilisateur(trice) *m,f* tardif(ive); **late cancellation** annulation *f* tardive; **late entrant** concurrent(e) *m,f* tardif(ive); **late entry** lancement *m* tardif; **late majority** majorité *f* conservatrice
(**c**) *St Exch* **late trading** opérations *fpl* de clôture

latent defect *n* vice *m* caché

launch 1 *n (of product, project)* lancement *m*; **the launch of a new job creation scheme** le lancement d'un nouveau programme de création d'emplois
2 *vt* (**a**) *(product, project)* lancer; **to launch a £3m cash bid** lancer une offre au comptant de 3 millions de livres (**b**) *St Exch (company)* introduire en Bourse; *(shares)* émettre

launching *n (of product, project)* lancement *m*

launder *vt (money)* blanchir

> ❝
> The drug traffickers create links with front companies and people in the United States and Spain from where they draw money from their bank accounts and send interna-

tional money transfers to the Panamanian company. With this great blow, the DAS and the DEA dismembered the largest asset-laundering organization in the world, which managed to **launder** more than 200 million dollars in a single year in Colombia alone
> ❞

laundering *n (of money)* blanchiment *m*

LAUTRO *n Ins (abbr* **Life Assurance and Unit Trust Regulatory Organization**) = organisme britannique chargé d'établir des codes de conduite à l'usage des compagnies d'assurance-vie et des sociétés d'investissement, et de veiller à leur respect

law *n* (**a**) *(rule)* loi *f*; *Econ* **the law of supply and demand** la loi de l'offre et de la demande ◻ **law merchant** droit *m* commercial (**b**) *(system of justice)* droit *m*; *Br* **to go to law** aller en justice ◻ **law court** tribunal *m*, cour *f* de justice; **law department** service *m* du contentieux; **law firm** cabinet *m* juridique; *Br* **the Law Society** = conseil de l'ordre des avocats chargé de faire respecter la déontologie

lawful *adj (legal)* légal(e); *(rightful)* légitime ◻ **lawful currency** cours *m* légal; **lawful owner** possesseur *m* légitime; **lawful trade** commerce *m* licite

lawsuit *n* action *f* en justice; **to bring a lawsuit against sb** intenter une action (en justice) contre qn

lawyer *n* avocat(e) *m,f*; *(for wills, conveyancing)* notaire *m*; *(in company)* conseiller(ère) *m,f* juridique

▶ **lay in** *vt sep (goods, stock)* faire provision de

▶ **lay off** *vt sep* (**a**) *(make redundant)* licencier; *(temporarily)* mettre en chômage technique (**b**) *Ins* **to lay off a risk** effectuer une réassurance

lay-away plan *n Am* vente *f* réservée *ou* à terme

lay-off *n* licenciement *m*; *(temporary)* chômage *m* technique ◻ *Am* **lay-off pay** indemnité *f* de licenciement

layout *n* (**a**) *(of building)* agencement *m* (**b**) *(of plan)* étude *f*, tracé *m* (**c**) *(of advertisement, text)* mise *f* en page, maquette *f*

> ❝
> Analysts argue that M&S has failed to make its store **layouts** help shoppers bring clothing together to make outfits.
> ❞

LBO *n Fin (abbr* **leveraged buy-out**) rachat *m* d'entreprise financé par l'endettement

L/C *n (abbr* **letter of credit**) l/c *f*

LCD *n Comptr (abbr* **liquid crystal display**) affichage *m* à cristaux liquides, LCD *m* ◻ **LCD screen** écran *m* LCD

LCL *n* (*abbr* **less-than-container load**) conteneur *m* chargé en partie

lead *n* (**a**) **leads and lags** termaillage *m* ❑ *lead time* (*for production*) délai *m* de production; (*for delivery*) délai de livraison (**b**) *Mktg* *lead user* utilisateur(trice) *m,f* pilote

leader *n* (**a**) (*head*) chef *m*; (*of association*) dirigeant(e) *m,f* (**b**) *Mktg* (*product*) leader *m*; (*company*) chef *m* de file, leader; *Am* (*loss leader*) produit *m* d'appel (**c**) *St Exch* valeur *f* vedette

leading *adj* principal(e); **a leading shareholder** un des principaux actionnaires; **one of the leading firms in the country** une des plus importantes entreprises du pays ❑ *leading (economic) indicators* principaux indicateurs *mpl* économiques; *Am* *leading price indicator* indice *m* composite des principaux indicateurs; *leading share* valeur *f* vedette

leaflet *n* prospectus *m* ❑ *leaflet drop* distribution *f* de prospectus

learning curve *n* courbe *f* d'assimilation

> **"**
> As a result, the company became an early adopter of Microsoft's recently-launched .NET platform and in just three months, fortified its comprehensive content repository with a technical backbone designed to maximize content delivery and services. Following a short **learning curve**, HealthGate optimized its architecture with the .NET technology and transformed more than 20,000 files into validated, well-formed XML.
> **"**

lease 1 *n* (*of property*) bail *m*; (*of equipment*) location *f*; (*of land*) affermage *m*; (*document*) (contrat *m* de) bail; **the lease runs out in May** le bail expire en mai; **to sign a lease** signer un bail ❑ *lease agreement* contrat *m* de bail; *Acct lease charges* charges *fpl* locatives; *lease contract* (*for property*) contrat de bail; (*for equipment*) contrat de location; *lease financing* leasing *m*, location *f* avec option d'achat; *Acct lease revenue* loyers *mpl*

2 *vt* (**a**) (*of owner*) (*property*) louer *ou* céder à bail; (*equipment*) louer; (*land*) affermer
(**b**) (*of leaseholder*) (*property*) prendre à bail, louer; (*equipment*) louer; (*land*) prendre en fermage

► **lease back** *vt sep* = louer dans le cadre d'une cession-bail

► **lease out** *vt sep* (*property*) louer *ou* céder à bail; (*equipment*) louer; (*land*) affermer

leaseback *n* cession-bail *f*

leased line *n* *Comptr* ligne *f* louée

leasehold 1 *n* (*contract*) bail *m*; (*property*) location *f* à bail
2 *adj* loué(e) à bail

leaseholder *n* locataire *mf*

leasing *n* (*of property*) location *f* à bail; (*of equipment*) location; (*of land*) affermage *m*; (*system*) crédit-bail *m*, leasing *m* ❑ *leasing company* société *f* de leasing

leave *n* (*holiday*) congé *m*; **to be on leave** être en congé; **to take two weeks' leave** prendre deux semaines de congé ❑ *leave of absence* congé exceptionnel; *leave pay* salaire *m* de congé

LED *n* *Comptr* (*abbr* **light-emitting diode**) DEL *f*

ledger *n* *Acct* grand-livre *m*

left *adj* *Comptr* ❑ *left arrow* flèche *f* vers la gauche; *left arrow key* touche *f* de déplacement à gauche; *left justification* justification *f* à gauche

left-click 1 *vt* cliquer avec le bouton gauche de la souris sur
2 *vi* cliquer avec le bouton gauche de la souris (**on** sur)

leftover stock *n* restes *mpl*

legacy *n* *Law* legs *m*; **to leave sb a legacy** faire un legs *ou* laisser un héritage à qn; **to come into a legacy** faire un héritage

legal 1 *adj* (*lawful*) légal(e); (*judicial*) juridique; **to have a legal claim to sth** avoir légalement droit à qch; **this is the legal procedure** c'est la procédure à suivre ❑ *legal action* action *f* en justice; **to take legal action against sb** intenter une action (en justice) contre qn; **to take legal advice** consulter un avocat; *legal adviser* conseiller(ère) *m,f* juridique; *legal aid* aide *f* ou assistance *f* judiciaire; *legal costs* frais *mpl* judiciaires; *legal currency* monnaie *f* courante; *legal department* (*in company*) service *m* du contentieux; *legal director* directeur(trice) *m,f* juridique; *legal dispute* litige *m*; *legal document* acte *m* authentique, document *m* juridique; *legal entity* personne *f* morale; *legal executive* assistant(e) *m,f* (*d'un avocat*); *legal expenses* frais de justice; *legal flaw* vice *m* de forme; *legal guarantee* garantie *f* légale; *Am legal holiday* jour *m* férié, fête *f* légale; *legal owner* propriétaire *mf* légitime; *Am legal pad* bloc-notes *m*; *legal proceedings* poursuites *fpl* judiciaires; **to take legal proceedings against sb** engager des poursuites judiciaires contre qn; *legal rate* taux *m* légal; *legal redress* réparation *f* légale; *legal reserve* réserve *f* légale; *legal secretary* secrétaire *mf* juridique; *legal status* statut *m* légal, statut juridique; *legal system* système *m* juridique; *legal tender* cours *m* légal, monnaie légale; **to be legal tender** avoir cours (légal); *legal value* valeur *f* extrinsèque
2 *n* *Am* (*paper size*) légal *m* (216mm × 356mm)

legality *n* légalité *f*

legalization n légalisation f

legalize vt légaliser

legally adv légalement; **to act legally** agir légalement ou dans la légalité; **to be legally binding** avoir force de loi; **legally responsible** responsable en droit

legal-tender value n Fin valeur f numéraire

legislate vi légiférer; **to legislate in favour of/against sth** légiférer en faveur de/contre qch

legislation n législation f; **the legislation on immigration** la législation sur l'immigration

legislative adj législatif(ive) ❑ **legislative power** pouvoir m législatif

leisure industry n industrie f du temps libre ou des loisirs

> 66
> At present the average person goes out 1.4 times a week. By 2006 Datamonitor estimates this will rise to 1.6 times a week. The **leisure industry** will benefit from a £21bn increase in expenditure on meals and a £5.5bn increase in on-trade drinks expenditure. Three different consumer needs are driving the growth – the desire for experiences, the desire for indulgence and the desire to save time.
> 99

lend 1 vt prêter; **to lend sth to sb, to lend sb sth** prêter qch à qn; **to lend money at interest** prêter de l'argent à l'intérêt; **to lend money against security** prêter de l'argent sur titres
2 vi prêter; **to lend at 12 percent** prêter à 12 pour cent

lender n (person) prêteur(euse) m,f; (institution) organisme m de crédit; **lender of last resort** prêteur m en dernier ressort

lending n prêt m; **bank lending has increased** le volume des prêts bancaires a augmenté ❑ **lending bank** banque f de crédit; **lending banker** banquier m prêteur; **lending country** pays m créancier; **lending limit** plafond m du crédit; **lending policy** (of bank, country) politique f de prêt; **lending rate** taux m de prêt

less prep **the purchase price less ten percent** le prix d'achat moins dix pour cent; **interest less tax amounts to £50** les intérêts nets s'élèvent à 50 livres

lessee n locataire mf (à bail)

lessor n bailleur(eresse) m,f

let Br **1** n location f; **a short/long let** une location de courte/longue durée
2 vt louer; **to let** (sign) à louer

let-out clause n clause f échappatoire

LETS n (abbr **Local Exchange Trading System**) = système d'échange de services dans une communauté donnée, basé sur une monnaie nominale

letter n (**a**) (communication) lettre f; **to notify sb by letter** informer qn par lettre; **your letter of 4 October** votre lettre (en date) du 4 octobre ❑ **letter of acknowledgement** accusé m de réception; St Exch **letter of allotment** avis m d'attribution ou de répartition; **letter of apology** lettre d'excuse; **letter of application** (for job) lettre de demande d'emploi; St Exch (for shares) lettre de souscription; **letter of appointment** lettre de nomination ou d'affectation; **letter of complaint** lettre de réclamation; **letter of confirmation** lettre de confirmation; **letter of consent** lettre d'agrément; **letters of credence** lettres de créance; **letter of dismissal** lettre de licenciement; **letter of guarantee** lettre de garantie; **letter of indemnity** cautionnement m, lettre de garantie; **letter of notification** lettre notificative; **letter opener** coupe-papier m; Comptr **letter quality** qualité f courrier; **near letter quality** qualité quasi-courrier; **letter rate** tarif m lettres; **letter of recommendation** lettre de recommandation; **letter of reference** lettre de recommandation; **letter scales** pèse-lettre m; **letter tray** corbeille f ou panier m à courrier
(**b**) **letters patent** brevet m d'invention, lettres fpl patentes
(**c**) Banking **letter of advice** lettre f d'avis; **letter of credit** lettre de crédit; **letter of exchange** lettre de change; **letter of guaranty** lettre d'aval; **letter of intent** lettre d'intention
(**d**) Am (paper size) lettre f (216mm × 279mm)

letterhead n en-tête m; (paper) papier m à en-tête

letting adj location f ❑ **letting agency** agence f de location; **letting agent** agent m de location

level 1 n (of salaries, prices) niveau m; **to maintain prices at a high level** maintenir les prix à un niveau élevé
2 vt niveler

▸ **level off, level out** vi (of prices, demand, sales) se stabiliser, s'équilibrer

leverage 1 n Fin (gearing) effet m de levier; (as percentage) ratio m d'endettement ou de levier
2 vt tirer profit de

leveraged adj **the company is highly leveraged** la société est fortement endettée ❑ **leveraged buy-out** rachat m d'entreprise financé par l'endettement; **leveraged management buy-out** rachat d'entreprise par les salariés

> 66
> Despite IPC's debt, which stems mostly from its **leveraged buy-out** from Reed two years ago, it is believed the publisher feels Prima and Best are such strong brands that it could not pass up the opportunity to ac-

> quire them. Adding the two titles to its portfolio will substantially increase advertising revenue across the group, IPC believes. **"**

levy 1 n (**a**) *(activity)* prélèvement m; **a capital levy of ten percent** un prélèvement de dix pour cent sur le capital (**b**) *(tax)* impôt m, droit m; **to impose a levy on imports** taxer les importations
  2 vt *(tax)* prélever; **to levy a duty on goods** imposer des marchandises, prélever une taxe sur les marchandises

liability n (**a**) *Law (responsibility)* responsabilité f (**for** de); **to admit liability for sth** endosser la responsabilité de qch □ **liability clause** clause f de responsabilité (**b**) *(eligibility)* assujettisement m (**for** à) (**c**) *Acct, Fin* dette f; **liabilities** *(debts)* passif m; **to meet one's liabilities** rembourser ses dettes

liable adj (**a**) *Law (responsible)* responsable (**for** de); **to be held liable for sth** être tenu(e) (pour) responsable de qch; **to be liable for sb's debts** répondre des dettes de qn; **employers are liable for their staff's mistakes** les employeurs sont responsables des erreurs de leur personnel (**b**) *(eligible)* assujetti(e) (**to** à); **to be liable for tax** *(person)* être assujetti à *ou* redevable de l'impôt; *(goods)* être assujetti à une taxe

liaise vi **to liaise with sb** *(be in contact with)* assurer la liaison avec qn; *(work together with)* collaborer avec qn

liaison n *(contact)* liaison f; *(cooperation)* collaboration f

libel *Law* **1** n *(act of publishing)* diffamation f; *(publication)* écrit m diffamatoire; **to sue for libel** intenter un procès en diffamation □ **libel case** procès m en diffamation; **libel laws** lois fpl contre la diffamation; **libel suit** procès en diffamation
  2 vt diffamer

libellous adj *Law* diffamatoire, diffamateur(-trice)

liberate vt *Fin* libérer

LIBOR n *Br Fin* (abbr **London Inter-Bank Offer Rate**) ≃ TIOP m

licence, *Am* **license¹** n *(to manufacture, sell)* licence f; **to manufacture/sell sth under licence** fabriquer/vendre qch sous licence □ **licence agreement** licence f; **licence holder** titulaire mf d'une licence

license² vt accorder une licence à; **to be licensed to manufacture/sell sth** avoir l'autorisation de fabriquer/vendre qch

licensed adj sous licence □ **licensed brand name** nom m de marque sous licence; **licensed product** produit m sous licence

licensee n titulaire mf d'une licence

licensing n autorisation f □ **licensing agreement** accord m de licence; **licensing requirements** conditions fpl d'autorisation

licensor n concédant(e) m,f

lien n *Law (on property)* privilège m, droit m de retention; **to have a lien on a cargo** avoir un recours sur un chargement; **vendor's lien** privilège du vendeur; **lien on shares** nantissement m d'actions

lieu n **in lieu** à la place; **in lieu of** au lieu de; **take Thursday off in lieu** prenez jeudi à la place; **we get days off in lieu of overtime** on nous accorde des jours de congé en plus pour compenser les heures supplémentaires

life n (**a**) *Fin* **life annuity** rente f ou pension f viagère; *Fin* **life capitalization** capitalisation f viagère; *Fin* **life pension** pension viagère; **life tenancy** location f viagère; **life tenant** usufruitier(ère) m,f
  (**b**) *Ins* **life assurance** assurance f sur la vie, assurance-vie f; **life assurance policy** police f d'assurance sur la vie ou d'assurance-vie; **Life Assurance and Unit Trust Regulatory Organization** = organisme britannique contrôlant les activités de compagnies d'assurance-vie et de sicav; **life expectancy tables** tables fpl d'espérance de vie ou de mortalité; **life insurance** assurance sur la vie, assurance-vie; **life insurance policy** police d'assurance sur la vie ou d'assurance-vie
  (**c**) *Fin (of loan)* durée f □ **life expectancy** *(of product)* durée (utile)

lifecycle n *Mktg (of product)* cycle m de vie □ **lifecycle curve** courbe f du cycle de vie

lifestyle n *Mktg* **lifestyle analysis** analyse f du style de vie; **lifestyle data** données fpl de style de vie; **lifestyle group** socio-style m; **lifestyle segmentation** segmentation f par styles de vie

lifetime n *Fin, St Exch (of option)* durée f de vie

LIFFE n (abbr **London International Financial Futures Exchange**) = marché à terme d'instruments financiers

> **"**
> London robusta coffee futures fell to a seven-week low in late trading on Thursday. Traders said investment funds had been liquidating positions and there had also been some selling from producer countries. The **LIFFE** July contract broke through $495 a tonne, closing $27 down at $488/tonne. This was the lowest for a second-month contract in London since 19 March. **"**

LIFO (abbr **last in, first out**) DEPS

light 1 n *Comptr* **light pen** stylo m optique
  2 adj (**a**) *(market, trading)* faible □ **light indus-**

try industrie *f* légère (**b**) *Mktg* **light user** faible utilisateur(trice) *m,f*

lightning strike *n Ind* grève *f* surprise

limit 1 *n* (**a**) *(restriction)* limitation *f*; **to put** or **set a limit on sth** limiter qch; **the limit on Japanese imports** la limitation des importations japonaises ❑ *Fin* **limit down** limite *f* inférieure *ou* de la baisse; *Fin* **limit up** limite supérieure *ou* de la hausse (**b**) *St Exch* **limit order** ordre *m* limite
2 *vt* limiter; **we're trying to limit costs** nous essayons de limiter les coûts

limitation *n (restriction)* limitation *f*; **limitation of liability** limitation de responsabilité

limited *adj* (**a**) *(market)* étroit(e), restreint(e); *(expenditure)* réduit(e) ❑ **limited edition** (édition *f* à) tirage *m* limité; *Law* **limited liability** responsabilité *f* limitée; **limited warranty** garantie *f* limitée (**b**) **limited company** ≃ société *f* à responsabilité limitée; **limited partner** commanditaire *m*; **limited partnership** société en commandite

limiting clause *n* clause *f* limitative

line *n* (**a**) *(telephone connection)* ligne *f*; **hold the line, please** ne quittez pas; **the line's very bad** la communication est mauvaise; **the line's** *Br* **engaged** or *Am* **busy** la ligne est occupée; **I have Laura Milligan on the line** j'ai Laura Milligan en ligne; **she's on the other line** elle est sur l'autre ligne ❑ **line rental** abonnement *m* (**b**) *(of goods)* ligne *f*, série *f*; **a new line of office furniture** une nouvelle ligne de meubles de bureau ❑ *Mktg* **line addition** ajout *m* à la ligne; **line differentiation** différenciation *f* de ligne; **line extension** extension *f* de ligne; **line filling** consolidation *f* de ligne; **line stretching** extension de ligne (**c**) *(in hierarchy)* **line management** organisation *f* hiérarchique; **line manager** chef *m* hiérarchique; **line organization** organisation hiérarchique; **line and staff management** structure *f* mixte (**d**) *Comptr* **line break** saut *m* de ligne; **line command** commande *f* de ligne; **line end** fin *f* de ligne; **line end hyphen** tiret *m* de fin de ligne; **line feed** changement *m* de ligne; **line printer** imprimante *f* ligne à ligne; **line printout** imprimé *m* ligne à ligne; **line feed** changement *m* de ligne; **line space** interligne *m*; **three line spaces** un triple interligne; **line spacing** interlignage *m*, espacement *m* de lignes; **line width** longueur *f* de ligne (**e**) *(production line)* chaîne *f*; **the new model will be coming off the line in May** le nouveau modèle sortira de l'usine en mai (**f**) **line of credit** ligne *f* de crédit, ligne de découvert

linear *adj* linéaire ❑ **linear metre** mètre *m* linéaire

> **"**
> This form of calculation is very useful to the retailer. It helps him to work out present and expected sales, and to find out how much profit he has made. For example: a unit displaying tins of soup has a total **linear** measurement of 5 metres. From it the retailer sells tins of soup to the value of £200 per month so each **linear metre** of space sells £40.
> **"**

link *n Comptr* lien *m* ❑ **link editor** éditeur *m* de liens

linker *n Comptr* éditeur *m* de liens

liquid *adj* (**a**) *Fin* liquide ❑ **liquid assets** fonds *mpl* liquides; **liquid capital** actif *m* liquide, liquidités *fpl*; **liquid debt** dette *f* liquide; **liquid resources** moyens *mpl* liquides; **liquid securities** valeurs *fpl* liquides (**b**) **liquid crystal display** affichage *m* à cristaux liquides; **liquid crystal screen** écran *m* à cristaux liquides; **liquid paper** *(correction fluid)* liquide *m* correcteur

liquidable *adj Fin* liquidable

liquidate *Fin* **1** *vt (company, debt)* liquider; *(capital)* mobiliser; *St Exch* **to liquidate a position** liquider une position
2 *vi (of company)* entrer en liquidation, déposer son bilan

liquidation *n Fin (of company, debt)* liquidation *f*; *(of capital)* mobilisation *f*; **to go into liquidation** *(of company)* entrer en liquidation, déposer son bilan

liquidator *n Fin (of company)* liquidateur(-trice) *m,f*

liquidity *n Fin (of company, debt)* liquidité *f* ❑ *Banking* **liquidity ratio** ratio *m* de liquidité, coefficient *m* de liquidité

lira *n* lire *f*

LISA *n Br Fin (abbr* **long-term individual savings account)** plan *m* de retraite en actions

list 1 *n* (**a**) *(of bills, assets, liabilities, names)* liste *f*; *Fin, St Exch* **list of applicants** *(for loan, shares)* liste des souscripteurs (**b**) *St Exch* **list of quotations** bulletin *m* des cours (**c**) *Banking* **list of investments** (bordereau *m* de) portefeuille *m*; **list of bills for collection/ for discount** bordereau d'effets à l'encaissement/à l'escompte (**d**) **list price** *(of product)* prix *m* (de) catalogue
2 *vt* (**a**) *(enter in list)* faire une liste de; *(goods)* inventorier; *St Exch* **to be listed on the Stock Exchange** être coté(e) en Bourse (**b**) *(price)* **what are the new laptops listed at?** les nouveaux portables sont vendus combien? (**c**) *Comptr* lister

listed *adj St Exch* **listed company** société *f* cotée en Bourse; **listed securities, listed stock** valeurs *fpl* admises *ou* inscrites à la cote officielle

listing *n* (**a**) *St Exch* admission *f* à la cote officielle; **to have a listing** être coté(e) en Bourse □ **listing agreement** dossier *m* de demande d'introduction en Bourse; **listing particulars** prospectus *m* d'admission à la cote (**b**) *Comptr* listing *m* □ **listing paper** papier *m* continu, papier listing

literature *n* (*information*) documentation *f*

litigant *n Law* partie *f*

litigate *Law* **1** *vt* contester (en justice)
2 *vi* intenter une action en justice

litigation *n Law* action *f* en justice

livelihood *n* moyens *mpl* de subsistance, gagne-pain *m*; **to lose one's livelihood** perdre son gagne-pain

lively *adj Fin* (*market*) animé(e)

living *n* (*livelihood*) vie *f*; **what do you do for a living?** qu'est-ce que vous faites dans la vie?; **to make a living?** gagner sa vie □ **living allowance** indemnité *f* de séjour; **living conditions** conditions *fpl* de vie; **living expenses** indemnité de séjour; **living standards** niveau *m* de vie; **living wage** minimum *m* vital; **£400 a month is not a living wage** on ne peut pas vivre avec 400 livres par mois

Lloyd's Name *n Br Ins* = titre réservé aux membres investissant leur fortune personnelle dans la compagnie d'assurances Lloyd's et s'engageant à avoir une responsabilité illimitée en cas de sinistre

> **"**
> The number of **Lloyd's Names** has fallen from its 35,000 peak to just 12,500 – although only 2,490 of them participated in the last underwriting year. Their numbers dropped off dramatically after 1996 when a rescue package was introduced for Lloyd's at a time when many Names faced personal ruin following £8bn of asbestos-related claims.
> **"**

LMBO *n* (*abbr* **leveraged management buy-out**) rachat *m* d'entreprise par les salariés

LMDS *n Tel* (*abbr* **local multipoint distribution system**) LMDS *m*

load 1 *n* (**a**) (*of ship, lorry*) charge *f*, chargement *m* □ **load bed** (*of lorry*) plateau *m* de chargement; **load factor** facteur *m* de charge; **load limit** charge limite *ou* admise
(**b**) *St Exch* frais *mpl* d'achat *ou* d'acquisition
2 *vt* (**a**) (*ship, lorry*) charger; (*goods*) embarquer; **the ship is loading grain** on est en train de charger le navire de céréales
(**b**) *Ins* (*premium*) majorer

(**c**) *Comptr* charger
3 *vi* (**a**) (*of ship, lorry*) charger; **the ship is loading** le navire est en cours de chargement
(**b**) *Comptr* (*of software, program*) se charger

▶ **load up** *vt sep* (**a**) (*ship, lorry*) charger (**b**) *Comptr* charger

load-carrying capacity *n* charge *f* utile, poids *m* utile

loaded *adj* (**a**) (*ship, lorry*) chargé(e); (*goods*) embarqué(e) □ **loaded net weight** poids *m* net embarqué; **loaded return** retour *m* en charge (**b**) *Ins* **loaded premium** prime *f* majorée, surprime *f*

loading *n* (*of ship, lorry*) chargement *m*; (*of goods*) embarquement *m* □ **loading bay** aire *f* de chargement; **loading dock** embarcadère *m*; **loading permit** permis *m* de chargement; **loading platform** quai *m* de chargement; **loading point** point *m* de chargement; **loading time** délai *m* de chargement

loan 1 *n* (*money lent*) prêt *m*; (*money borrowed*) emprunt *m*; **to take out a loan** faire un emprunt; **to apply for a loan** demander un prêt; **to repay a loan** rembourser un emprunt; *Acct* **loans and advances to customers** créances *fpl* clients; *Acct* **loan at call** prêt remboursable sur demande; **loan at interest** prêt à intérêt; **loan at notice** prêt à terme; **loan on collateral** prêt sur gage *ou* sur nantissement; **loan on mortgage** prêt hypothécaire *ou* sur hypothèque; **loans outstanding** encours *m*; **loan on overdraft** prêt à découvert; **loan repayable on demand** prêt remboursable sur demande; **loan against securities** emprunt sur titres; **loan without security** prêt à fonds perdus; **loan on trust** prêt d'honneur; **loan to value** = rapport entre le capital restant dû et la valeur du bien financé □ *Banking* **loan account** compte *m* de prêt; **loan agreement** contrat *m* de prêt; **loan application** demande *f* de prêt; **loan application form** dossier *m* de demande de prêt; **loan back** cession-bail *f*; *Acct* **loan capital** capital *m* d'emprunt *ou* sur prêt; **loan certificate** titre *m* de prêt; **loan charges** frais *mpl* financiers; **loan company** société *f* de crédit; **loan department** service *m* des crédits; **loan guarantee scheme** = prêts bonifiés d'aide au développement des entreprises; **loan insurance** assurance *f* crédit; **loan market** marché *m* des prêts; **loan maturity** échéance *f* emprunt; *Fin* **loan note** titre *m* d'obligation, titre de créance; **loan office** organisme *m* de crédit; **loan origination fee** commission *f* de montage; **loan repayment insurance** assurance crédit; **loan risk cover** couverture *f* du risque de crédit; *Fam* **loan shark** usurier(ère) *m,f*; **loan stock** emprunt obligataire; **loan transaction** opération *f* de prêt
2 *vt* prêter

loan-back, loanback *n* cession-bail *f* □ **loan-**

back pension retraite *f* par capitalisation

lobby 1 *n* lobby *m*

  2 *vt* faire pression sur; **a group of financiers went to lobby the minister** un groupe de financiers est allé voir le ministre pour faire pression sur lui

  3 *vi* faire campagne; **ecologists are lobbying for the closure of the plant** les écologistes font pression pour obtenir la fermature de la centrale

lobbying *n* lobbying *m*, lobbysme *m*

local *adj* local(e) ❏ *local agent* agent *m* sur le terrain; *Comptr* **local area network** réseau *m* local; *Admin* **local authority** administration *f* locale; *(in town)* municipalité *f*; *Comptr* **local bus** bus *m* local; *Tel* **local call** communication *f* locale; **local council** conseil *m* municipal; **local currency** monnaie *f* locale; **Local Exchange Trading Scheme** = système d'échange de services dans une communauté donnée, basé sur une monnaie nominale; **local tax** impôts *mpl* locaux; **local time** heure *f* locale; **6 a.m. local time** 6 heures du matin heure locale

> **"**
>
> Communities in several countries have also organized indirect exchange systems, most notably using the **Local Exchange Trading System** (LETS), which began in Canada in 1983. LETS is similar to a credit union, but members begin their account balances at zero and exchange with other members. Those who purchase goods incur a debit, while those who sell obtain a credit; debits and credits are denominated in the national currency.
>
> **"**

localization *n Comptr* localisation *f*

localize *vt Comptr* localiser

locate *vi (of company, factory)* s'installer, s'établir, s'implanter

location *n (of company, factory)* emplacement *m*; **the company has moved to a new location** la société a déménagé ❏ *Mktg* **location pricing** fixation *f* des prix selon l'endroit

lock *vt Comptr* verrouiller

► **lock into** *vt sep* **to be locked into sth** *(pension scheme)* ne pas pouvoir changer de qch; *(contract)* être lié(e) par qch; *(company)* être totalement dépendant(e) de qch

► **lock out** *vt sep (workers)* lock-outer

► **lock up** *vt sep (capital)* immobiliser, bloquer

lockout *n (of workers)* lock-out *m*

loco 1 *adj* loco ❏ *loco price* prix *m* loco

  2 *adv* loco; **the prices are loco Hull** les prix incluent le transport jusqu'à Hull

lodge *vt* **(a)** *(claim)* déposer; **to lodge a com-**

plaint porter plainte; **she lodged a formal complaint with the authorities** elle a déposé une plainte officielle auprès de l'administration **(b)** *(money)* consigner, déposer; **to lodge securities with a bank** déposer des titres dans une banque

log 1 *n (record)* journal *m*, registre *m*; *Comptr* fichier *m* compte-rendu; **keep a log of all phone calls** notez tous les appels téléphoniques ❏ *Comptr* **log file** fichier compte-rendu

  2 *vt (information) (on paper)* consigner, inscrire; *(in computer)* entrer

► **log in** = **log on**

► **log off** *Comptr* **1** *vt sep* faire sortir

  2 *vi* sortir

► **log on** *Comptr* **1** *vt sep* faire entrer

  2 *vi (of user)* entrer, ouvrir une session; *(to remote system)* entrer en communication; **to log onto a system** se connecter à un système

► **log out** = **log off**

logical *adj Comptr* logique

logic circuit *n Comptr* circuit *m* logique

logistics *n* logistique *f* ❏ *logistics management* gestion *f* logistique

logo *n* logo *m*

Lombard rate *n Banking* taux *m* Lombard

London *n* Londres *m* ❏ *London Inter-Bank Offer Rate* ≃ TIOP *m*; *London International Financial Futures Exchange* = marché à terme d'instruments financiers; *London School of Economics* = grande école de sciences économiques et politiques à Londres; *London Stock Exchange* Bourse *f* de Londres

long 1 *n St Exch* **longs** titres *mpl* longs, obligations *fpl* longues

  2 *adj* **long credit** crédit *m* à long terme; *Am Fam* **long green** argent *m* liquide; **long lease** bail *m* à long terme; *St Exch* **long position** position *f* acheteur *ou* longue; **to take a long position** acheter à la hausse, prendre une position longue

  3 *adv St Exch* **to go long** acheter à la hausse, prendre une position longue

long-dated *adj Fin* à longue échéance ❏ *long-dated bill* effet *m* ou traite *f* à longue échéance; *long-dated securities* titres *mpl* longs, obligations *fpl* longues

long-distance 1 *adj (telephone call)* longue distance

  2 *adv* **to telephone long-distance** faire un appel longue distance

longitudinal *adj Mktg (research, study)* longitudinal(e)

long-lived assets *npl Acct* actifs *mpl* à long terme, actifs à longue durée de vie

long-range *adj (forecast)* à long terme

longshoreman *n Am* docker *m*

longstanding *adj* de longue date ◻ *long-standing accounts* vieux comptes *mpl*

long-term *adj* à long terme ◻ *Fin* **long-term bond** obligation *f* à long terme; **long-term bond rate** taux *m* long obligataire; *Acct* **long-term borrowings** emprunts *mpl* à long terme; *Acct* **long-term capital** capitaux *mpl* permanents; **long-term credit** crédit *m* à long terme; **long-term debt** dette *f* à long terme; **long-term financing** financement *m* à long terme; **long-term interest rate** taux d'intérêt à long terme; **long-term investments** *Fin* placements *mpl* à long terme; *Acct* immobilisations *fpl* financières; **long-term liabilities** dettes *fpl* ou passif *m* à long terme; **long-term loan** prêt *m* à long terme; **long-term maturity** échéance *f* à long terme; **long-term objective** objectif *m* lointain; **long-term planning** planification *f* à long terme; **long-term unemployment** chômage *m* de longue durée

look-up table *n Comptr* table *f* de recherche *ou* de référence

loophole *n (in law, contract)* vide *m* juridique

loose *adj* (**a**) *(goods)* en vrac (**b**) **loose insert** encart *m* libre

lorry *n Br* camion *m* ◻ **lorry driver** chauffeur *m* de poids lourd

lose 1 *vt (custom, market share, job, money)* perdre; **his shop is losing money** son magasin perd de l'argent; **they are losing their markets to the Koreans** ils perdent leurs marchés au profit des Coréens
2 *vi* perdre; **the dollar is losing in value** le dollar baisse

▶ **lose out** *vi* perdre; **to lose out on a deal** être perdant(e) dans une affaire; **will the Americans lose out to the Japanese in computers?** les Américains vont-ils perdre le marché de l'informatique au profit des Japonais?

loser *n St Exch* valeur *f* en baisse

loss *n* (**a**) *(of custom, market share, job)* perte *f*; **she's seeking compensation for loss of earnings** elle cherche à se faire rembourser le manque à gagner; **the closure will cause the loss of hundreds of jobs** la fermeture provoquera la disparition de centaines d'emplois (**b**) *(financial)* déficit *m*; **to make a loss** perdre de l'argent, être déficitaire; **to run at a loss** *(of business)* tourner à perte; **to sell sth at a loss** vendre qch à perte; **the company announced losses** *or* **a loss of £4m** la société a annoncé un déficit de 4 millions de livres; **we made a loss of ten percent on the deal** nous avons perdu dix pour cent dans l'affaire; *Acct* **loss attributable** perte *f* supportée; *Acct* **loss carry back** report *m* déficitaire sur les exercices précédents; *Acct* **loss carry forward** déficit reportable, report

déficitaire sur les exercices ultérieurs; *Acct* **loss transferred** perte transférée ◻ *Mktg* **loss leader** produit *m* d'appel; *Mktg* **loss leader price** prix *m* d'appel; *Mktg* **loss leader pricing** fixation *f* d'un prix d'appel; *Mktg* **loss pricing** fixation d'un prix d'appel
(**c**) *Ins* sinistre *m*; **to estimate the loss** évaluer le sinistre; **the following losses are not covered by the policy** les sinistres suivants ne sont pas couverts par cette police ◻ **loss adjuster** expert *m* en assurances; **loss assessment** fixation *f* des dommages; **loss ratio** rapport *m* sinistres-primes; **loss risk** risque *m* de perte et d'avaries
(**d**) *(of product being manufactured or transported)* freinte *f* ◻ **loss in transit** freinte de route

loss-making *adj* déficitaire, qui tourne à perte

lot *n* (**a**) *Fin, St Exch (of bonds, shares)* paquet *m*; **in lots** par lots; **to buy/sell in one lot** acheter/vendre en bloc ◻ **lot number** numéro *m* de lot; **lot size** unité *f* de transaction (**b**) *(at auction)* lot *m*; **lot 49 is a set of five paintings** le lot 49 est un ensemble de cinq tableaux (**c**) *Am (piece of land)* terrain *m*

lottery *n* (**a**) *Fin* **lottery bonds** valeurs *fpl* à lot; **lottery loan** emprunt *m* à lots; **lottery loan bond** titre *m* à lots (**b**) *Br* **lottery funding** *(from National Lottery)* = fonds provenant de la loterie nationale

low 1 *n* niveau *m* bas; **the share index has reached a new low** l'indice des actions est descendu à son plus bas niveau; **inflation is at an all-time low** l'inflation est à son niveau le plus bas; *St Exch* **the highs and lows** les hauts et les bas
2 *adj (cost, price, interest rate)* bas (basse), faible; *(salary)* peu élevé(e); **prices are at their lowest** les prix sont au plus bas
3 *adv* **to buy low** acheter à bas prix; *St Exch* acheter quand les cours sont bas

low-ball *vt Am Fam (estimate)* sous-évaluer; **to low-ball a customer** = présenter un devis, dont le total a été délibérément sous-évalué, à un client

low-cost *adj (purchase, purchasing)* à petits prix

low-end *adj Mktg* bas de gamme

lower¹ *vt (prices, interest rate)* baisser

lower² *adj* **lower case** bas *m* de casse, (lettres *fpl*) minuscules *fpl*; **lower limit** plancher *m*

lower-case *adj* en bas de casse, en (lettres) minuscules

lower-income group *n* groupe *m* de contribuables à revenus moyens

low-grade *adj* de qualité inférieure

low-income group *n* groupe *m* de contribuables à faibles revenus

low-interest *adj (credit, loan)* à taux réduit

low-involvement *adj Mktg (purchasing)* à faible participation des consommateurs

low-load fund *n* fonds *m* à faible frais d'entrée

loyal *adj (customer)* fidèle

loyal-customer discount *n Mktg* remise *f* de fidélité

loyalty *n Mktg* **loyalty card** carte *f* de fidélité ; **loyalty discount** remise *f* de fidélité ; **loyalty magazine** = magazine publié par une chaîne de magasins, une banque etc pour ses clients ; **loyalty programme** programme *m* de fidélisation ; **loyalty scheme** programme de fidélisation

> **❝**
>
> In a bid to capitalise on the growth of relationship marketing, AT&T is preparing to launch a managed **loyalty programme** linking the functions of a **loyalty card**, call centre, customer database analysis and campaign management.
>
> **❞**

LSE *n* (**a**) (*abbr* **London School of Economics**) = grande école de sciences économiques et politiques à Londres (**b**) (*abbr* **London Stock Exchange**) Bourse *f* de Londres

Ltd *Br* (*abbr* **limited**) ≃ SARL ; **Dragon Software Ltd** ≃ Dragon Software SARL

lucrative *adj* lucratif(ive)

luggage *n* bagages *mpl* ; **a piece of luggage** un bagage ❑ **luggage allowance** franchise *f* de bagages ; **luggage label** étiquette *f* à bagages

lump sum *n* somme *f* forfaitaire ; **to be paid in a lump sum** être payé(e) en une seule fois

luncheon voucher *n Br* ticket restaurant *m*, ticket-repas *m*

luxury *adj* de luxe ❑ **luxury brand** marque *f* de luxe ; **luxury goods** articles *mpl* de luxe ; **luxury goods industry** industrie *f* de luxe ; **luxury tax** taxe *f* sur les produits de luxe

Mm

MABE n (abbr **Master of Agricultural Business and Economics**) MABE m (diplôme d'agro-économie)

machine 1 n (device, computer) machine f ▫ Comptr **machine code** code m machine; **machine hour** heure f machine; Comptr **machine language** langage m machine; **machine operator** opérateur(trice) m,f à la machine; **machine production** production f en série; **machine shop** atelier m d'usinage; **machine tool** machine-outil f; **machine translation** traduction f assistée par ordinateur; **machine work** travail m à la machine
   2 vt usiner

machine-down time n = durée d'immobilisation d'une machine

machine-produced adj fait(e) à la machine ou en série

machine-readable adj Comptr lisible par ordinateur

machinery n (a) (machines) machines fpl, machinerie f (b) (of organization, government) rouages mpl

machining n usinage m

machinist n opérateur(trice) m,f sur machine

macro n Comptr macro f ▫ **macro language** macrolangage m

macroeconomics n macroéconomie f

macroenvironment n macroenvironnement m

macromarketing n macromarketing m

MACRS n Am Acct (abbr **modified accelerated cost recovery system**) = méthode d'amortissement accéléré

MAD n Acct (abbr **mean absolute deviation**) écart m moyen absolu

mad dog n Fam (company) société f en pleine expansion; **there are several rising mad dogs in the IT sector** il existe plusieurs sociétés en pleine expansion dans le secteur de l'informatique

magnate n magnat m; **he's one of the biggest computer magnates** c'est un des plus grands magnats de l'informatique

magnetic adj Comptr **magnetic card** carte f magnétique; **magnetic card reader** lecteur m de carte magnétique; **magnetic disk** disque m magnétique; (floppy) disquette f magnétique;

magnetic media supports mpl magnétiques; **magnetic strip** (on card) piste f magnétique; **magnetic tape** bande f magnétique

MAI n (abbr **multilateral agreement on investment**) AMI m

maiden name n Admin nom m de jeune fille

mail 1 n (a) (letters, parcels) courrier m; **has the mail arrived?** est-ce que le courrier est arrivé? ▫ Am **mail clerk** employé(e) m,f responsable du courrier; **mail room** service m du courrier
   (b) (postal service) poste f; **to put sth in the mail** mettre qch à la poste; **by mail** par la poste ▫ **mail order** vente f par correspondance; **to buy sth by mail order** acheter qch par correspondance; Mktg **mail survey** enquête f postale; **mail transfer** virement m par courrier
   (c) Comptr courrier m électronique, mél m ▫ **mail address** adresse f électronique; **mail bomb** = messages envoyés en masse pour bloquer une boîte aux lettres; **mail file** fiche f courrier; **mail forwarding** réexpédition f du courrier électronique; **mail gateway** passerelle f (de courrier électronique); **mail path** chemin m du courrier électronique; **mail reader** logiciel m de courrier électronique; **mail server** serveur m de courrier
   2 vt (letter, parcel) poster

mailbox n Comptr boîte f à ou aux lettres

mailer n Mktg mailing m, publipostage m

mailing n Comptr, Mktg (mailshot) publipostage m, mailing m; **to do** or **send a mailing** faire un mailing ▫ **mailing card** carte f de publicité; **mailing list** Mktg liste f de publipostage; Comptr liste de diffusion; **are you on our mailing list?** est-ce que vous êtes dans notre fichier?; **mailing shot** publipostage, mailing; **to do** or **send a mailing shot** faire un mailing

mailmerge n Comptr publipostage m

mail-order adj de vente par correspondance ▫ **mail-order catalogue** catalogue m de vente par correspondance; **mail-order company** maison f de vente par correspondance; **mail-order goods** marchandises fpl achetées par correspondance; **mail-order organization** vépéciste m; **mail-order purchasing** achat m par correspondance; **mail-order retailing, mail-order selling** vente f par correspondance

mailshot Mktg **1** n publipostage m, mailing m; **to do** or **send a mailshot** faire un mailing
   2 vt envoyer un mailing ou un publipostage à

> A common tactic used by unauthorised firms is to use a publicly available share register to **mailshot** a large bulk of UK investors in one go, inviting them to send off for research on a firm whose shares they already own. The small print on the form will then give the company the investor's consent to be contacted directly.

main adj principal(e) ▫ **main branch** (of shop, bank) établissement m principal; **main claim** demande f principale; Acct **main cost centre** centre m d'analyse principal; St Exch **main market** = marché principal de la Bourse de Londres; **main office** bureau m principal; (headquarters) siège m (social); Econ **main product** produit m principal

mainframe n Comptr **mainframe (computer)** ordinateur m central

maintain vt (relations, contact) entretenir; (exchange rate, output) maintenir; **we must maintain our position as market leader** nous devons maintenir notre position de leader sur le marché

maintenance n (a) (of building, equipment) entretien m ▫ **maintenance contract** contrat m d'entretien; **maintenance costs** frais mpl d'entretien; **maintenance department** service m de l'entretien; **maintenance engineer** technicien m d'entretien; **maintenance equipment** matériel m d'entretien; **maintenance programme** programme m d'entretien; **maintenance staff** personnel m d'entretien (b) (financial support) entretien m; Law pension f alimentaire ▫ **maintenance allowance** indemnité f pour frais de déplacement

major 1 n Am (big company) société f de premier ordre; **the oil majors** les grandes compagnies pétrolières
2 adj majeur(e), principal(e) ▫ Br **major shareholder**, Am **major stockholder** actionnaire mf majoritaire

majority n majorité f ▫ **majority decision** décision f prise à la majorité; **majority holding** participation f majoritaire; **majority interest** participation majoritaire; **majority investor** investisseur m majoritaire; Br **majority shareholder**, Am **majority stockholder** actionnaire mf majoritaire; **majority vote** vote f majoritaire

majority-owned subsidiaries npl = filiales dans lesquelles une personne ou une société détient une participation majoritaire

make 1 n (of product) marque f; **what make of computer is it?** c'est quelle marque d'ordinateur?
2 vt (a) (construct) fabriquer, faire; **made in France** (on product) fabriqué en France (b)

(earn) gagner; (profit) gagner, réaliser; **to make £50,000 a year** gagner 50 000 livres par an

▸ **make out** vt sep (list) faire, dresser; (bill) établir, dresser; **to make out a cheque (to sb)** faire un chèque (à l'ordre de qn)

▸ **make over** vt sep céder (**to** à)

▸ **make up** vt sep (a) (deficit, loss) combler (b) (parcel) faire; (order) exécuter, préparer; (list) faire, dresser; (bill) établir, dresser

▸ **make up for** vt insep compenser; **European sales made up for our losses in the UK** les ventes en Europe ont compensé nos pertes au Royaume-Uni

maker n (manufacturer) fabricant(e) m,f; (of machinery, cars) constructeur m ▫ **maker's price** prix m de fabrique; **maker's trademark** cachet m de fabrique

making-up n St Exch **making-up day** jour m de liquidation; **making-up price** cours m de compensation

maladjustment n Econ déséquilibre m

maladministration n (of country, economy) mauvaise administration f; (of business) mauvaise gestion f

mall n **(shopping) mall** galerie f marchande; (with one main shop) centre m commercial

malpractice n faute f professionnelle ▫ **malpractice insurance** = assurance souscrite pour parer à des poursuites judiciaires pour négligence

man vt (organization) fournir du personnel à; (switchboard) assurer le service de; (machine) assurer le fonctionnement de; **to man a nightshift** composer une équipe de nuit; **to man the phone** répondre au téléphone; **the office is manned by a skeleton staff** le bureau tourne à effectif réduit

manage vt (a) (company, factory, project, bank) diriger; (shop, hotel) être le (la) gérant(e) de; (property, estate) gérer (b) (economy, money, resources) gérer; **to manage sb's affairs** gérer les affaires de qn

managed adj Acct **managed costs** coûts mpl maîtrisables; Fin **managed currency** devise f contrôlée ou dirigée; **managed fund** fonds m géré; **managed investment fund** fonds commun de placement géré; **managed mutual fund** fonds commun de placement géré; **managed trade** commerce m dirigé

management n (a) (action) (of company, factory, project) gestion f, direction f; (of economy, money, resources, shop, hotel) gestion; **all their problems are due to bad management** tous leurs problèmes sont dus à une mauvaise gestion; **under Gordon's management sales have increased significantly** depuis que c'est Gordon qui s'en occupe, les ventes ont considéra-blement augmenté ❑ *management accountant* contrôleur *m* de gestion; *management accounting* comptabilité *f* de gestion; *management accounts* comptes *mpl* de gestion; *management audit* contrôle de gestion; *management auditor* contrôleur *m* de gestion; *management chart* graphique de gestion, tableau *m* de bord; *management committee* comité *m ou* conseil *m* de direction; *management company* société *f* de gestion; *management consultancy (activity)* conseil en gestion; *(company)* cabinet *m* (de) conseils; *management consultancy report* audit *m* social; *management consultant* conseiller(ère) *m,f* en gestion; *management control* contrôle de gestion; *management error* erreur *f* de gestion; *management by exception* direction par exceptions; *Am management expenses* frais *mpl* de gestion; *management expert* expert *m* en gestion; *management fees* frais de gestion; *Comptr management information system* système *m* intégré de gestion; *management by objectives* gestion par objectifs; *management operating system* système intégré de gestion; *management report* rapport *m* de gestion; *management science* science *f* de la gestion; *management skills* qualités *fpl* de gestionnaire; *management studies* études *fpl* de gestion; *management style* mode *m* de gestion; *management system* système de direction; *management team* équipe *f* de direction, équipe dirigeante; *management techniques* techniques *fpl* de gestion; *management theory* théorie *f* de la gestion de l'entreprise; *management tool* outil *m* de gestion; *management training* formation *f* des cadres

(b) *(managers, employers)* administration *f*, direction *f*; **negotiations between management and unions have broken down** les négociations entre le patronat et les syndicats ont échoué ❑ *management buy-in* apport *m* de gestion; *management buy-out* rachat *m* d'une société par la direction; **as a result of a management buy-out, the footwear manufacturing business was rescued** suite à son rachat par la direction, l'entreprise de fabrication de chaussures a été sauvée; *management team* équipe *f* dirigeante *ou* de direction

manager *n* (a) *(of company, factory, project, bank)* directeur(trice) *m,f*; *(of shop, hotel)* gérant(e) *m,f*; *(of funds, money)* gestionnaire *mf*; *(of assets)* administrateur(trice) *m,f* (b) *Comptr (of disk)* gestionnaire *m*

manageress *n (of company, bank)* directrice *f*; *(of shop, hotel)* gérante *f*

managerial *adj* directorial(e) ❑ *managerial functions* fonctions *fpl* de direction; *managerial grid* grille *f* de gestion; *managerial position* poste *m* d'encadrement; *managerial skills* qua-

lités *fpl* de gestionnaire; *managerial staff* cadres *mpl*, personnel *m* dirigeant; *managerial structure* hiérarchie *f*

managing director *n* directeur(trice) *m,f* général(e)

M&A *n (abbr* **mergers and acquisitions**) fusions *fpl* et acquisitions *fpl*

> **"**
> Despite a red-hot market for venture-backed initial public offerings, mergers and acquisitions abounded in the first half of 1999, refuting the notion that the rise in **M&A** deals in the past several years was in response to a poor IPO market. … And, as the bull market continues to drive valuations of entrepreneurial companies to record heights, **M&A**s have emerged as a more attractive exit option for venture capitalists.
> **"**

mandate *n* mandat *m* ❑ *Banking* **mandate form** lettre *f* de signatures autorisées

mandatory *adj* obligatoire ❑ *Banking* **mandatory liquid assets** liquidités *fpl* obligatoires; *mandatory powers* pouvoirs *mpl* donnés par mandat; *St Exch* **mandatory quote period** période *f* de quotation obligatoire

man-day *n* jour *m* homme

man-hour *n* heure *f* homme

manifest *n (of ship, aeroplane)* manifeste *m*

manipulate *vt* **to manipulate the accounts** trafiquer les comptes; *St Exch* **to manipulate the market** agir sur le marché

> **"**
> They said there had been speculation that someone may be **manipulating** the market, noting that three-month prices had climbed to $6,200 per tonne last week while tin trading volatility jumped to as high as 25 percent.
> **"**

manpower *n* main-d'œuvre *f*; **we don't have the necessary manpower** nous n'avons pas la main-d'œuvre nécessaire ❑ *manpower forecasting* prévision *f* de l'emploi; *manpower management* gestion *f* de l'emploi; *manpower planning* planification *f* de l'emploi

manual 1 *n (handbook)* manuel *m* (d'utilisation)
2 *adj* manuel(elle) ❑ *Comptr* **manual input** saisie *f* manuelle; *manual labour* travail *m* manuel; *manual operation* fonctionnement *m* manuel; *manual trade* métier *m* manuel; *manual work* travail manuel; *manual worker* travailleur(euse) *m,f* manuel(elle)

manually *adv* manuellement, à la main

manufactory *n Am* manufacture *f*

manufacture 1 *n* fabrication *f*; *(of machinery,*

cars) construction*f*

   2 *vt* fabriquer; *(machinery, cars)* construire ❑ **manufactured goods** biens *mpl* manufacturés; **manufactured products** produits *mpl* manufacturés

manufacturer *n* fabricant(e) *m,f*; *(of machinery, cars)* constructeur *m* ❑ **manufacturer's agent** agent *m* exclusif; **manufacturer brand** marque*f* de fabricant; **manufacturer's liability** responsabilité *f* du fabricant; **manufacturer's price** prix *m* de fabrique; **manufacturer's recommended price** prix conseillé par le fabricant

manufacturing *n* fabrication *f*; **the decline of manufacturing** le déclin de l'industrie manufacturière ❑ *Acct* **manufacturing account** compte *m* de production; **manufacturing capacity** capacité *f* de production; **manufacturing company** entreprise *f* ou société *f* industrielle; **manufacturing costs** frais *mpl* de fabrication; **manufacturing defect** défaut *m* de fabrication; **manufacturing fault** vice *m* de fabrication; **manufacturing industry** industrie *f* de fabrication; **manufacturing licence** brevet *m* ou licence *f* de fabrication; **manufacturing method** méthode *f* de fabrication; **manufacturing monopoly** monopole *m* de fabrication; **manufacturing overheads** frais de fabrication; **manufacturing plant** usine *f* de fabrication; **manufacturing process** procédé *m* ou processus *f* de fabrication; **manufacturing rights** droits *mpl* de fabrication; **manufacturing stage** phase *f* de fabrication; **manufacturing town** ville *f* industrielle

man-year *n* année *f* homme

MAP *n* (*abbr* **maximum average price**) prix *m* moyen maximum

mapping *n* mapping *m*

margin *n* (**a**) *Fin* marge *f*; **to have a low/high margin** avoir une faible/forte marge; **the margins are very tight** les marges sont très réduites ❑ **margin of error** marge d'erreur; **margin of fluctuation** *(of a currency)* marge de fluctuation; **margin of interest** marge d'intérêt
   (**b**) *St Exch* marge *f* de garantie, acompte *m* ❑ **margin call** appel *m* de couverture *ou* de marge *ou* de garantie; **margin dealing** *(method)* cotation *f* par appel de marge; *(high-geared)* arbitrage *m* à la marge *ou* marginal; *(transactions)* arbitrage sur dépôt de titres de garantie; **margin default** défaut *m* de couverture; **margin requirement** couverture *f* obligatoire

> **❝** ───────────────
> Competition in most low- and middle-price lines currently comes from places little expected – China and Germany – where private labeling is being used to crack American markets. In fact, competitors in Black & Decker's consumer lines are suffer-

ing from 1%/year price deflation. Low **margins** also are presenting difficulties in building and protecting brands.
> **❞**

marginal *adj (business, profit)* marginal(e) ❑ **marginal cost** coût *m* marginal; **marginal costing** méthode *f* des coûts marginaux; **marginal cost pricing** méthode des coûts marginaux; **marginal disinvestment** désinvestissement *m* marginal; **marginal profit** bénéfice *m* marginal; **marginal productivity** productivité *f* marginale; **marginal relief** dégrèvement *m* marginal; **marginal return on capital** rendement *m* marginal du capital; **marginal revenue** revenu *m* marginal; **marginal utility** utilité *f* marginale; **marginal value** valeur *f* marginale

marginalism *n* *Econ* marginalisme *m*

marine *adj* maritime ❑ **marine bill of lading** connaissement *m* maritime; **marine insurance** assurance *f* maritime; **marine insurance policy** police *f* d'assurance maritime

marital *adj* *Admin, Law* conjugal(e) ❑ **marital home** domicile *m* conjugal; **marital rights** droits *mpl* conjugaux; **marital status** situation *f* de famille

maritime *adj* maritime ❑ **maritime freight** fret *m* maritime; **maritime freight consolidator** groupeur *m* maritime; **maritime insurance** assurance *f* maritime; **maritime law** droit *m* maritime; **maritime shipment** expédition *f* maritime; **maritime trade** commerce *m* maritime

mark¹ *n* *Formerly (currency)* mark *m*, Deutschmark *m*

mark² **1** *n (level)* niveau *m*; **sales topped the 5 million mark** les ventes ont dépassé la barre des 5 millions
   2 *vt (goods)* marquer

▶ **mark down** *vt sep (price)* baisser; *(goods)* baisser le prix de, démarquer; **everything has been marked down to half price** tout a été réduit à moitié prix; *St Exch* **prices have been marked down** les cours sont en baisse

▶ **mark up** *vt sep (price)* augmenter; *(goods)* augmenter le prix de, majorer; *St Exch* **prices have been marked up** les cours sont en hausse

markdown *n (action)* réduction *f*; *(article)* article *m* démarqué

marked price *n* prix *m* marqué

marker barrel *n* prix *m* du baril de pétrole

market **1** *n* (**a**) *Econ, Mktg* marché *m*; **to be on the market** être en vente; **to come onto the market** arriver sur le marché; **to put sth on the market** mettre qch sur le marché *ou* en vente; **to take sth off the market** retirer qch du marché; **to be in the market for sth** être acheteur de qch, chercher à acheter qch; **to**

find a market for sth trouver un débouché *ou* des acheteurs pour qch; **to corner a market** accaparer un marché; **to find a ready market** trouver à vendre facilement; **there's always a (ready) market for software** il y a toujours une forte demande pour les logiciels; **to price oneself out of the market** perdre sa clientèle en demandant trop cher; **the bottom has fallen out of the market** le marché s'est effondré ❑ **market analysis** analyse *f* du marché; **market analyst** analyste *mf* du marché; **market appeal** attrait *m* commercial; **market appraisal** évaluation *f* du marché; *Am* **market basket** panier *m* de la ménagère; **market challenger** challengeur *m*; **market choice** choix *m* sur le marché; *(product)* choix du marché; **market competition** concurrence *f* du marché; **market conditions** conditions *fpl* du marché; **market correction** correction *f* du marché; **market demand** demande *f* du marché; **market depression** dépression *f* du marché; **market development** développement *m* du marché; **market division** division *f* du marché; **market dynamics** dynamique *f* du marché; **market economy** économie *f* de marché; **market entry** lancement *m* sur le marché; **market expansion** extension *f* du marché; **market exposure** exposition *f* sur le marché; **market fluctuation** mouvement *m* du marché; **market follower** suiveur *m* (sur le marché); **market forces** forces *fpl* du marché; **market forecast** prévisions *fpl* du marché; **market growth** croissance *f* du marché; **market intelligence** information *f* commerciale; **market leader** *(product)* premier produit *m* sur le marché; *(company)* leader *m* du marché; **market maker** teneur *m* de marché; **market manager** directeur(trice) *m,f* de marché; **market mechanism** mécanisme *m* du marché; **market minimum** ventes *fpl* de base; **market orientation** orientation *f* marché; *Formerly Law* **market overt** marché public; **market participant** intervenant(e) *m,f ou* acteur *m* sur le marché; **market penetration** pénétration *f* du marché; **market penetration pricing** tarification *f* de pénétration du marché; **market penetration strategy** stratégie *f* de pénétration; **market pioneer** pionnier *m*; **market positioning** positionnement *m* sur le marché; **market potential** *(of product)* potentiel *m* sur le marché; *(of market)* potentiel du marché; **market price** prix *m* du marché; **market profile** profil *m* du marché; **market prospects** perspectives *fpl* commerciales; **market rate** taux *m* du marché; **market rate of discount** taux d'escompte hors banque; **market report** étude *f* de marché, rapport *m ou* bilan *m* commercial; **market research** étude de marché; **market research has shown that the idea is viable** des études de marché ont montré que l'idée a des chances de réussir; **market research company** société *f* d'études de marché; *Br* **Market Research So-**

ciety = société d'étude de marché britannique; **market researcher** = personne qui fait une étude de marché; **market segment** segment *m* de marché; **market segmentation** segmentation *f* du marché; **market share** part *f* de marché; **market size** *(of product)* part de marché; *(of market)* taille *f* du marché; **market structure** structure *f* du marché; **market study** étude de marché; **market study report** rapport d'étude de marché; **market survey** étude de marché; **market test** test *m* de marché; **market thrust** percée *f* commerciale; **market trends** tendances *fpl* du marché; **market value** valeur *f* marchande

(b) *St Exch* marché *m*; **to play the market** spéculer; **the market has risen ten points** l'indice est en hausse de dix points ❑ **market capitalization** capitalisation *f* boursière; **market commentator** chroniqueur(euse) *m,f* boursier(ère); **market crisis** choc *m* boursier; **market indicator** indicateur *m* de marché; **market maker** intermédiaire *mf*; **market order** ordre *m* au mieux; **market price** cours *m* (de la Bourse); **market price list** mercuriale *f*; **market quotation** cotation *f* au cours du marché; **market rating** cours en Bourse; **market risk** risque *m* du marché; **market size** taille *f* boursière; **market trend** conjoncture *f* boursière; **market value** valeur *f* boursière

2 *vt* commercialiser; *(launch)* lancer

> 66
>
> The primary commodity price index, developed by the economists Enzo R. Grilli and Maw Cheng Yang, takes the international cost of a **market basket** of 24 of the most commonly consumed "renewable and non-renewable resources" – foodstuffs, non-food agricultural goods, and metals – and adjusts for inflation.
>
> 99

marketability *n Mktg* possibilité *f* de commercialisation

marketable *adj* **(a)** *Mktg (goods)* commercialisable **(b)** *St Exch (shares, securities)* négociable

market-driven *adj* déterminé(e) par les contraintes du marché ❑ **market-driven economy** économie *f* de marché

> 66
>
> The nub of it is that the chair must be able to hold the line between the demands of the **market-driven** telecoms industry and the cultural objectives of broadcasting … The great challenge for the chair will be to keep those two objectives in tension, while having the gravitas to lead a review of media ownership rules every three years.
>
> 99

marketer n Mktg mercaticien(enne) m,f, spécialiste mf en marketing

marketing n (study, theory) marketing m, mercatique f; (of product) commercialisation f ❏ **marketing agreement** accord m de commercialisation; **marketing analyst** analyste mf mercaticien(enne); **marketing approach** démarche f marketing; **marketing audit** audit m marketing; **marketing auditor** audit marketing, auditeur(trice) m,f marketing; **marketing budget** budget m marketing; **marketing campaign** campagne f de marketing; **marketing channel** circuit m de commercialisation ou de distribution; **marketing communications channel** canal m de communication commerciale; **marketing company** entreprise f de marketing; **marketing concept** concept m de marketing; **marketing consultancy** (service, activity) conseil m en marketing; (company) société f de conseil en marketing; **marketing consultant** conseiller(ere) m,f commercial(e); **marketing costs** frais mpl de commercialisation; **marketing department** service m du marketing; **marketing efficiency** efficacité f du marketing; **marketing efficiency study** contrôle m d'efficacité du marketing; **marketing environment** environnement m commercial ou marketing; **marketing executive** responsable mf du marketing; **marketing expert** mercaticien(enne) m,f; **marketing fit** ajustement m stratégique; **marketing implementation** mise f en place marketing; Comptr **marketing information system** système m d'information marketing; **marketing intelligence** intelligence f marketing; **marketing intelligence system** système d'intelligence marketing; **marketing management** gestion f du marketing; **marketing manager** directeur (trice) m,f du marketing; **marketing mix** marchéage m, marketing mix m; **marketing myopia** myopie f marketing; **marketing network** réseau m de commercialisation; **marketing orientation** optique f marketing; **marketing plan** plan m marketing; **marketing planner** responsable mf de planification marketing; **marketing planning** planification f marketing; **marketing policy** politique f de commercialisation; **marketing questionnaire** questionnaire f d'étude de marché; **marketing research** recherche f commerciale; **marketing spectrum** marchéage; **marketing spend** dépenses fpl de marketing; **marketing strategy** stratégie f marketing; **marketing study** étude f commerciale ou marketing; **marketing subsidiary** filiale f de distribution; **marketing target** cible f commerciale; **marketing team** équipe f commerciale; **marketing techniques** techniques fpl commerciales; **marketing tool** outil m de marketing

marketization n marchéisation f

market-led adj généré(e) par le marché

marketplace n Econ marché m; **the international/European marketplace** le marché international/européen; **the products in the marketplace** les produits sur le marché

marking n St Exch (of shares) cotation f; **marking to market** comptabilisation f au prix de marché

markka n Formerly mark m finlandais

mark-up n majoration f; **we operate a 2.5 times mark-up** nous appliquons une marge de 2,5 ❏ **mark-up pricing** fixation f du prix au coût moyen majoré; **mark-up ratio** taux m de marge

mart n (a) (market) marché m (b) (auction room) salle f des ventes

marzipan layer n Fam cadres mpl moyens

> **"**
>
> The main grievances inside the firm seem to be coming from what insiders call the **marzipan layer**. This is the group of senior staff who have not been made new partners in the transition to a quoted company. The resentment that comes from people in all sections of the firm, from traders to fund managers, focuses on the 40 new partners, many of whom seem to have leapfrogged their colleagues.
>
> **"**

mass n **mass circulation** diffusion f de masse; **mass consumption** consommation f de masse; **mass dismissal** licenciement m collectif; Mktg **mass display** présentation f en masse; **mass distribution** grande distribution f; **mass distribution sector** secteur m de la grande distribution; **mass mailing** envoi m en nombre; **mass market** marché m de masse; **mass marketing** marketing m de grande consommation, marketing de masse; **mass media** mass médias mpl; **mass production** fabrication f ou production f en série; **it goes into mass production next week** la production en série commence la semaine prochaine; **mass redundancy** licenciement collectif; Comptr **mass storage** mémoire f de masse; **mass unemployment** chômage m sur une grande échelle

mass-produce vt fabriquer en série

master 1 n (expert) maître m, expert m; **master of works** maître d'œuvre
2 adj (a) (expert) maître ❏ **master builder** maître m bâtisseur (b) (main) **master budget** budget m global; **master copy** (of document) original m; Comptr **master disk** disque m maître; **master document** document m maître; Comptr **master file** fichier m maître; **master plan** plan m directeur; **master production schedule** plan de production principal

masterbrand n Mktg marque f vedette

"

As well as Kellogg and Nestlé, Cadbury has made a concerted effort to increase the prominence of its name on all confectionery and spin-off products and spent £870,000 on the **masterbrand** "Tastes Like Heaven" campaign in the year to May.

"

masthead n (of newspaper) cartouche f de titre

matched adj St Exch **matched bargain** mariage m; Am **matched orders** ordres mpl couplés d'achat et de vente (pour stimuler le marché)

matching n (a) Acct rapprochement m, rattachement m □ **matching principle** principe m du rapprochement ou rattachement (b) Am St Exch application f

material n (a) **materials** (equipment) matériel m; **materials and labour** matériel et main-d'œuvre f □ **materials cost** coût m du matériel; **material defect** vice m rédhibitoire; **materials management** gestion f des matières; **material requirements planning** prévision f des besoins matériels (b) Mktg (for marketing, promotion) matériel m

maternity n **maternity benefit** allocation f de maternité; **maternity leave** congé m de maternité

maths co-processor n Comptr coprocesseur m mathématique

matrix n matrice f □ **matrix management** organisation f matricielle; **matrix organization** organisation matricielle; Comptr **matrix printer** imprimante f matricielle

mattress money n Fin argent m thésaurisé

"

Mattress money is fast becoming the el Nino of European economics. The previously dormant stashes of cash, have been jarred into life by their imminent loss of status as legal currency. They can now be invoked to explain any number of bewildering economic phenomena, from rising house prices in France to a building boom in Spain, or even the overall weakness of the euro exchange rate.

"

maturation n Am Fin (of bill, investment, insurance policy) échéance f

mature 1 adj (a) **mature economy** économie f en pleine maturité (b) Fin (bill, investment, insurance policy) échu(e) (c) Mktg (market) arrivé(e) à maturité
2 vi Fin (of bill, investment, insurance policy) échoir, arriver à échéance

maturity n (a) Fin (of bill, investment, insurance policy) échéance f □ **maturity date** date f d'échéance; **maturity value** valeur f à

l'échéance (b) Mktg (of market) maturité f

maximization n maximisation f; **our aim for this year is the maximization of profits** notre but pour cette année est la maximisation des bénéfices

maximize vt maximaliser; Comptr (window) agrandir

maximum 1 n maximum m; **to raise production to a maximum** porter la production au maximum; **the space has been used to the maximum** l'espace a été utilisé au maximum
2 adj maximum, maximal(e) □ **maximum efficiency** rendement m maximum; **maximum fluctuation** variation f maximale autorisée; Ins **maximum foreseeable loss** sinistre m maximum prévisible; **maximum load** charge f maximale; **maximum output** rendement maximum; **maximum price** prix m maximum

MB n Comptr (abbr **megabyte**) Mo

Mb n Comptr (abbr **megabit**) Mb

MBA n (abbr **Master of Business Administration**) MBA m

MBI n (abbr **management buy-in**) apport m de gestion

MBO n (a) (abbr **management buy-out**) rachat m d'une société par la direction (b) (abbr **management by objectives**) gestion f par objectifs

MBps Comptr (abbr **megabytes per second**) mops

Mbps Comptr (abbr **megabits per second**) mbps

MBS n Fin (abbr **mortgage-backed security**) titre m garanti par des créances hypothécaires

m-commerce n m-commerce m

"

The company has predicted that **m-commerce** will become more widespread within the next few years, leading to $25bn generated through mobile payments in 2006 – about 15% of total e-commerce consumer spending. Mobile commerce will comprise of automated payments at vending machines, parking meters, ticket machines, shop counters or taxis as well as mobile Internet payments and transactions between individuals.

"

MD n (abbr **managing director**) directeur(trice) m,f général(e)

mdse n Am (abbr **merchandise**) produit m, marchandise f

meal ticket n Am ticket-restaurant m

mean 1 n (average) moyenne f
2 adj (average) moyen(enne) □ **mean absolute**

deviation écart *m* moyen absolu; **mean price** prix *m* moyen

means 1 *n (method)* moyen *m* □ **means of communication** moyen de communication; **means of payment** moyen de paiement; **means of production** moyen de production; **means of transport** moyen de transport

2 *npl (income, wealth)* moyens *mpl*, ressources *fpl* □ *Admin* **means test** *(for state benefit)* enquête *f* sur les revenus *(d'une personne désirant bénéficier d'une allocation d'État)*; **the grant is subject to a means test** l'allocation est assujettie à des conditions de ressources

means-test *vt Admin* **to means-test sb** = faire une enquête sur les revenus de quelqu'un avant de lui accorder une aide sociale; **all applicants are means-tested** tous les candidats font l'objet d'une enquête sur leurs revenus

> Even though vast chunks of state spending – from university grants to income support – are **means-tested**, the term still carries a real stigma, especially for pensioners. The universal principle – embodied in the welfare state through the state pension, child benefit and NHS – has a binding effect. Poor people feel they are getting something as of right and rich people get something back for their taxes, discouraging them from opting out altogether.

measure *n (action, step)* mesure *f*, démarche *f*; **to take measures to do sth** prendre des mesures pour faire qch

measurement *n* **(a)** *(of performance, productivity)* mesure *f* **(b)** *(of freight)* cubage *m*, encombrement *m* □ **measurement tonnage** jaugeage *m*

mechanical *adj* mécanique □ **mechanical fault** défaut *m* mécanique

mechanism *n* mécanisme *m*

mechanization *n* mécanisation *f*

mechanize *vt* mécaniser

media *n* médias *mpl*; **he works in the media** il travaille dans les médias; **the news media** la presse □ **media advertising** publicité *f* média; **media analysis** analyse *f* des médias; **media analyst** analyste *mf* des médias; **media buyer** acheteur(euse) *m,f* d'espaces (publicitaires); **media buying** achat *m* d'espace; **media consultant** conseil *m* en communication; **media coverage** couverture *f* médiatique; **to get too much media coverage** être surmédiatisé(e); **media event** événement *m* médiatique; **media exposure** couverture médiatique; **media group** groupe *m* de médias; **media hype** battage *m* médiatique; **media mix** mix média *m*; **media plan** plan *m* média; **media planner** mé-

diaplaneur *m*, média planner *m*; **media planning** média planning *m*; **media research** médialogie *f*; **media schedule** calendrier *m* de campagne; **media studies** études *fpl* de communication; **media vehicle** support *m* médiatique

> Carlton will use a wide-ranging **media mix** of radio, posters, press and television … to inform the public, advertising and business communities of its programme and corporate format prior to launch.

media-conscious *adj* médiatique

media-friendly *adj* médiatique

> Over that period, Merrill's merger business had shot to the top of the league tables in 1997 and 1998. Mr. Levy, with his sturdy frame and ready smile, was something of an anomaly within Merrill: a **media-friendly**, larger-than-life banker who stood strikingly apart from his gray, dull-suited peers.

mediagenic *n* médiatique

mediate *vi* servir de médiateur (**for/between** pour/entre)

mediation *n* médiation *f*; **to go to mediation** recourir à une médiation

mediator *n* médiateur(trice) *m,f*

medical *adj* **medical certificate** certificat *m* médical; **medical insurance** assurance *f* médicale; **medical officer** médecin *m* du travail

medium 1 *n (means of communication)* médium *m*, moyen *m* de communication, support *m*; **the choice of media open to us is limited by the budget** le choix de supports qui s'offre à nous est limité par le budget □ *Econ* **medium of exchange** moyen d'échange

2 *adj* moyen(enne); **in the medium term** à moyen terme

medium-dated *adj (gilts, securities)* à échéance moyenne

medium-sized *adj* de taille moyenne

medium-term *adj (forecast, loan)* à moyen terme □ **medium-term credit** crédit *m* à moyen terme; *EU* **medium-term financial assistance** aide *f* financière à moyen terme; **medium-term liabilities** dettes *fpl* à moyen terme; **medium-term maturity** échéance *f* à moyen terme; *Fin* **medium-term note** billet *m* à moyen terme (négociable)

meet 1 *vt* **(a)** *(by arrangement)* rejoindre, retrouver; **to arrange to meet sb** donner rendez-vous à qn, prendre rendez-vous avec qn; **I**

arranged to meet him at 3 o'clock j'ai pris rendez-vous avec lui pour 15 heures

(**b**) *(become acquainted with)* faire la connaissance de; **it was a pleasure to meet you** je suis enchanté d'avoir fait votre connaissance; **I hope to meet you soon** j'espère avoir bientôt le plaisir de faire votre connaissance

(**c**) *(satisfy) (need)* satisfaire à; *(order)* satisfaire, assurer; **to meet sb's requirements** satisfaire aux besoins de qn; **to meet demand** répondre à la demande; **to meet sb's expenses** subvenir aux frais de qn; **the cost will be met by the company** les frais seront pris en charge par la société

2 *vi (assemble)* se réunir; **the delegates will meet in the conference room** les délégués se réuniront dans la salle de conférence; **the committee meets once a month** le comité se réunit une fois par mois

▶ **meet with** *vt insep Am (by arrangement)* rejoindre, retrouver; **I'm meeting with him tomorrow to discuss the budget** je le vois demain pour discuter du budget

meeting *n* réunion *f*; *(of shareholders)* assemblée *f*; **to hold a meeting** tenir une réunion; **the meeting will be held tomorrow at 3 o'clock** la réunion aura lieu demain à 15 heures; **to call a meeting of shareholders/the workforce** convoquer les actionnaires/le personnel; **to open the meeting** déclarer la séance ouverte; **to close the meeting** lever la séance; **to address the meeting** prendre la parole; **to put a resolution to the meeting** mettre une résolution aux voix ◻ **meeting place** lieu *m* de réunion

meg *n Fam Comptr* méga *m*

megabit *n Comptr* mégabit *m*

megabyte *n Comptr* méga-octet *m*; **20 megabyte memory** mémoire *f* de 20 méga-octets

megamerger *n* méga-fusion *f*

melon *n Am Fam (profits)* gros bénéfices *mpl* (à distribuer); **to carve** *or* **cut up the melon** distribuer les bénéfices

member *n* membre *m* ◻ *Am* **member bank** banque *f* membre de la Réserve fédérale; *EU* **member country** pays *m* membre; *St Exch* **member firm** société *f* membre; *EU* **member state** État *m* membre

membership *n* (**a**) *(state)* adhésion *f*; **to apply for membership** faire une demande d'adhésion; **they have applied for membership to the EU** ils ont demandé à entrer dans l'UE; **membership of the union will entitle you to vote in meetings** l'adhésion au syndicat vous donne le droit de voter lors des réunions; **his country's membership of UNESCO is in question** l'adhésion de son pays à l'UNESCO est remise en question ◻ **membership card** carte *f* de

membre *ou* d'adhésion; **membership fee** cotisation *f*, frais *mpl* d'adhésion (**b**) *(members)* membres *mpl*, adhérents *mpl*; **the opinion of the majority of our membership** l'avis de la majorité de nos membres

memo *n* note *f* de service; **I've received a memo from head office** j'ai reçu une note (de service) du siège ◻ *Acct* **memo account** poste *m* de mémoire; *Comptr* **memo field** champ *m* mémo; **memo pad** bloc-notes *m*

memorandum *n* (**a**) *(in office)* note *f* de service (**b**) *(of contract, sale)* mémoire *m* (**c**) *Law* **memorandum and articles of association** statuts *mpl*; **memorandum of association** acte *m* de société; *Banking* **memorandum of satisfaction** = document certifiant le paiement d'une hypothèque

memory *n Comptr* mémoire *f* ◻ **memory access register** registre *m* d'accès mémoire; **memory bank** banc *m* de mémoire; **memory buffer** zone *f* tampon; **memory capacity** capacité *f* de mémoire; **memory card** carte *f* mémoire; **memory chip** puce *f* mémoire; **memory dump** vidage *m* de mémoire; **memory expansion** extension *f* mémoire; **memory expansion card** *or* **board** carte d'extension mémoire; **memory management** gestion *f* de mémoire; **memory manager** gestionnaire *m* de mémoire; **memory space** espace *m* mémoire; **memory upgrade** extension mémoire; **memory variable** variable *f* de mémoire

mentor *n* mentor *m*

mentoring *n* mentoring *m (relation de conseil et de soutien entre un employé expérimenté et un débutant)* ◻ **mentoring scheme** programme *m* de mentoring

> "
> "White people seem to be picked up much earlier and promoted more quickly if they show talent, whereas ethnic minorities often hit a plateau in middle management," says Mitchell. So now there are **mentoring schemes**, in addition to training programmes, to help black and Asian staff move on and up within the corporation.
> "

menu *n Comptr* menu *m* ◻ **menu bar** barre *f* de menu; **menu item** élément *m* de menu; **menu option** option *f* de menu

MEP *n (abbr **Member of the European Parliament**)* député *m* au Parlement européen

mercantile *adj (commercial)* commercial(e); *Econ (concerning mercantilism)* mercantiliste ◻ **mercantile agency** agence *f* commerciale; **mercantile agent** agent *m* commercial; **mercantile agreement** accord *m* commercial; **mercantile bank** banque *f* de commerce; **mercantile broker** agent de change; **mercan-**

tile company société *f* commerciale; ***mercantile law*** droit *m* commercial; ***mercantile nation*** nation *f* commerçante; ***mercantile operation*** opération *f* mercantile; ***mercantile paper*** papier *m* commercial *ou* de commerce; ***mercantile system*** système *m* marchand

mercantilism *n* mercantilisme *m*

merchandise 1 *n* marchandises *fpl*
  2 *vt* marchandiser, commercialiser

merchandiser *n* *(object)* présentoir *m*; *(person)* marchandiseur *m*

merchandising *n* marchandisage *m*, commercialisation *f* ❑ ***merchandising allowance*** remise *f* de marchandisage; ***merchandising techniques*** techniques *fpl* marchandes

merchant *n* *(trader)* négociant(e) *m,f*; *(shopkeeper)* marchand(e) *m,f* ❑ *Br* ***merchant bank*** banque *f* d'affaires *ou* d'investissement; ***merchant banker*** banquier(ère) *m,f* d'affaires; *Am* ***merchant marine,*** *Br* ***merchant navy*** marine *f* marchande; ***merchant ship*** navire *m* marchand *ou* de commerce; ***merchant wholesaler*** grossiste *mf*

merchantable quality *n* qualité *f* marchande; **all goods must be of merchantable quality** tous les articles doivent être vendables

merge 1 *vt* *(banks, companies)* amalgamer, fusionner; *Comptr (files)* fusionner
  2 *vi (of banks, companies)* s'amalgamer, fusionner; **they have merged with their former competitor** ils ont fusionné avec leur ancien concurrent

merger *n* *(of banks, companies)* (absorption-)fusion *f*, unification *f*; *(takeover)* absorption *f* ❑ ***merger accounting*** = base de préparation des comptes consolidés où deux sociétés se sont unifiées; ***mergers and acquisitions*** fusions et acquisitions *fpl*; ***merger premium*** prime *f* de fusion; ***merger talks*** discussions *fpl* en vue d'une fusion

merit *n* mérite *m*; **promotion is on merit alone** l'avancement se fait uniquement au mérite ❑ ***merit bonus*** prime *f* de rendement; ***merit increase*** augmentation *f* au mérite; ***merit rating*** notation *f* du personnel; ***merit system*** système *m* d'avancement fondé sur le mérite

❝
Second, consider the Equal Pay Act, which generally requires that men and women be paid alike for substantially equal work, unless you can justify pay distinctions on the basis of a bona fide **merit system**, seniority system or a factor other than gender. "If the male is paid more than the female, even though you base that on prior salary history, it's going to raise a red flag," Duffie says.
❞

meritocracy *n* méritocratie *f*

message *n* message *m*; **to leave a message (for sb)** laisser un message (pour qn); **would you like to leave a message for him?** voulez-vous (lui) laisser un message?; **can you give her a message?** pouvez-vous lui transmettre un message? ❑ *Comptr* ***message box*** boîte *f* de dialogue; *Comptr* ***message handling*** messagerie *f* (électronique)

messenger *n* messager(ère) *m,f*; **by special messenger** par porteur spécial ❑ ***messenger boy*** garçon *m* de courses

Messrs *nmpl (abbr* **Messieurs**) MM

method *n* méthode *f* ❑ ***methods analysis*** étude *f* des méthodes; ***methods engineer*** ingénieur *m* des méthodes; ***methods engineering*** étude des méthodes; ***methods office*** service *m* des méthodes; ***method of operation*** méthode d'exploitation; ***method of payment*** modalité *f ou* mode *f* de paiement; ***method study*** étude des méthodes

methodical *adj* méthodique

methodology *n* méthodologie *f*

me-too *adj Mktg* ***me-too product*** produit *m* tactique; ***me-too strategy*** stratégie *f* d'imitation

metric *adj* métrique; **to go metric** adopter le système métrique ❑ ***metric hundredweight*** = 50 kilogrammes; ***metric system*** système *m* métrique; ***metric ton*** tonne *f*

mezzanine *n* ***mezzanine debt*** dette *f* subordonnée *ou* mezzanine; ***mezzanine finance*** = méthode de financement d'une partie du capital nécessaire pour acheter une entreprise (utilisée principalement par ses employés)

❝
When it comes to financing mergers, the red-hot market for junk bonds has for years squeezed out **mezzanine debt** as the method of choice. Nowadays, though, as the high-yield market has turned lukewarm to issuers of smaller-sized deals, savvy Wall Street players and financial buyers are quickly moving to capitalize on the newfound role for **mezzanine debt**.
❞

mfd *(abbr* **manufactured**) fabriqué(e)

mgmt *(abbr* **management**) gestion *f*, management *m*

mgr *(abbr* **manager**) directeur(trice) *m,f*, gérant(e) *m,f*

mgt *(abbr* **management**) gestion *f*, management *m*

MHz *Comptr (abbr* **megahertz**) MHz

micro *n Comptr* micro *m*

microcap *adj Fin* microcap

microchip *n Comptr* microprocesseur *m*

microcomputer *n* micro-ordinateur *m*

microcomputing *n* micro-informatique *f*

microcredit *n Fin* microcrédit *m*

microeconomics *n* microéconomie *f*

microfiche *n* microfiche *f*

microfilm *n* microfilm *m*

microlending *n* micro-prêt *m*

microloan *n* micro-prêt *m*

micromanage *vt* **he's got a tendency to micromanage his company** il a tendance à trop s'impliquer dans les détails de la gestion de sa société

> 66
>
> By her own admission, Shapiro was not a good administrator and manager of the staff … That she spent almost as much time out of the office than in attests to how she attempted to run Giants. Her accusation that the board has sought to **micromanage** Giants is inaccurate. In fact, the board only became more involved in management when Ms. Shapiro failed to do so; and in addition, she refused to follow board directions on hiring and compensation.
>
> 99

micromanagement *n* micromanagement *m*

micromarketing *n* micromarketing *m*

microprocessing *n* micro-informatique *f*

microprocessor *n* microprocesseur *m*

microsegment *n Mktg* microsegment *m*

microsegmentation *n Mktg* microsegmentation *f*

mid *adj* **mid June** mi-juin

MidCap *n St Exch* = indice boursier américain composé d'actions de sociétés à moyenne capitalisation, ≃ MidCAC *m*

middle *adj* **middle classes** classes *fpl* moyennes; **middle management** cadres *mpl* moyens; **middle manager** cadre *m* moyen; *St Exch* **middle price** cours *m* moyen

middle-income group *n* groupe *m* de contribuables à revenus moyens

middleman *n* intermédiaire *mf* □ **middleman's business** commerce *m* intermédiaire; **middleman's market** marché *m* intermédiaire

mid-month account *n St Exch* liquidation *f* de quinzaine

mid-range *adj (product)* de milieu de gamme

mileage allowance *n* ≃ indemnité *f* kilométrique

millage *n Am* taux *m* exprimé en millièmes de dollar

millennium bug *n Comptr* bogue *m* de l'an 2000

mind share *n Mktg* part *f* de notoriété

> 66
>
> With personal-video-recording services such as those offered by TiVo Inc. and ReplayTV Inc. capturing more and more **mind share**, supporting time-shifted programming is beginning to show up on the future service lists of video-on-demand vendors. At its most basic level, the concept is simple: Record all programming and make it available on-demand, at any time, with pause, rewind and fast-forward functions.
>
> 99

mine 1 *n* mine *f*, exploitation *f* minière
2 *vt (coal, gold)* extraire; *(coal seam)* exploiter
3 *vi* exploiter une mine

minicomputer *n* mini-ordinateur *m*

MiniDisc® *n Comptr* MiniDisc® *m* □ **MiniDisc® player** lecteur *m* de MiniDiscs

minimal *adj* minimum, minimal(e) □ **minimal value** valeur *f* minimale

minimize *vt* réduire au minimum; **we must try to minimize overheads** nous devons essayer de réduire au minimum les frais généraux

minimum 1 *n* minimum *m*; **to reduce sth to a minimum** réduire qch au minimum; **keep expenses to a minimum** limitez au minimum les dépenses; **a minimum of two years' experience** un minimum de deux ans d'expérience
2 *adj* minimum, minimal(e); **the minimum number of shares** le nombre minimum d'actions □ **minimum charge** tarif *m* minimum; **minimum deposit** acompte *m* minimum; *St Exch* **minimum fluctuation** variation *f* de cours minimale; *Br Formerly Fin* **minimum lending rate** taux *m* de base; **minimum living wage** minimum *m* vital; **minimum output** rendement *m* minimum; **minimum payment** paiement *m* minimum; **minimum price** prix *m* minimum; **minimum rate** taux minimum; **minimum safeguard price** prix minimum de sauvegarde; **minimum stock level** stock *m* d'alerte; **minimum wage** salaire *m* minimum, ≃ SMIC *m*; **minimal weight** poids *m* minimum

minister *n (politician, diplomat)* ministre *m*; **Minister for E-Commerce and Competitiveness** = ministre pour le commerce électronique et la compétitivité; **Minister of State for Energy and Construction** = secrétaire d'État à l'énergie et à l'urbanisme; **Minister of State for Trade and Investment** = secrétaire d'État au commerce et à l'investissement

ministerial *adj (project, crisis)* ministériel(elle); *(post)* de ministre; **to hold ministerial office** être ministre ▫ *ministerial functions* fonctions *fpl* exécutives; *ministerial order* arrêté *m* ministériel; *ministerial responsibility* responsabilité *f* ministérielle

ministry *n (department)* ministère *m*; *(government)* gouvernement *m*

mini tower *n Comptr* mini-tour *f*

minor *adj* mineur(e) ▫ *Br minor shareholder, Am minor stockholder* actionnaire *mf* minoritaire

minority *n* minorité *f* ▫ *minority holding* participation *f* minoritaire; *minority interest* participation minoritaire; *minority investor* investisseur *m* minoritaire; *Br minority shareholder, Am minority stockholder* actionnaire *mf* minoritaire

mint 1 *n Br* **the (Royal) Mint** ≃ (l'hôtel *m* de) la Monnaie ▫ *Fin mint par* pair *m* intrinsèque **2** *vt (coins)* frapper, battre

mintage *n (process of minting)* monnayage *m*, frappe *f* (de monnaie)

minute 1 *n* **minutes** *(of meeting)* procès-verbal *m*, compte-rendu *m*; **to confirm the minutes of the last meeting** approuver le procès-verbal de la dernière réunion; **to take the minutes of a meeting** rédiger le procès-verbal d'une réunion ▫ *minute book* registre *m* des procès-verbaux **2** *vt (facts, comments)* prendre note de; *(meeting)* dresser le procès-verbal *ou* le compte-rendu de

MIP *Ins (abbr* **marine insurance policy**) police *f* d'assurance maritime

mips *Comptr (abbr* **million instructions per second**) MIPS *m*

MIRAS *n Br Formerly (abbr* **Mortgage Interest Relief at Source**) = système par lequel les intérêts dus à une société de crédit immobilier sont déductibles des impôts

mirror site *n Comptr* site *m* miroir

MIS *n* **(a)** *Comptr (abbr* **management information system**) système *m* intégré de gestion **(b)** *Mktg (abbr* **marketing information system**) système *m* d'information marketing

misapplication *n (of money)* détournement *m*

misapply *vt (money)* détourner

misappropriate *vt (money, funds)* détourner; *(property)* voler

misappropriation *n (of money)* détournement *m* ▫ *misappropriation of funds* détournement de fonds, abus *m* de biens sociaux

misbrand *vt* = faire figurer des informations mensongères sur l'emballage de

> **"**
> The president of a "low-fat" baked-goods company went to jail after pleading guilty to **misbranding** products. According to the Food and Drug Administration, the company had simply purchased regular day-old pastries from a Chicago bakery and repackaged them under its "Skinny" line. While all the items were supposed to contain one or two grams of fat and 125 to 165 calories, at least one, a carob doughnut, had 23 1/2 grams of fat and 411 calories.
> **"**

misbranding *n* = fait de faire figurer des informations mensongères sur l'emballage d'un produit

miscalculate *vt* mal calculer

miscalculation *n* erreur *f* de calcul

miscarriage *n Br (of mail, goods)* perte *f*

miscellaneous *adj* divers(es) ▫ *miscellaneous expenses* frais *mpl* divers; *miscellaneous shares* valeurs *fpl* diverses

misconduct *n* **(a)** *(mismanagement)* mauvaise gestion *f*; **they accused her of misconduct of the company's affairs** ils l'ont accusé d'avoir mal géré la société **(b) (professional) misconduct** faute *f* professionnelle

misdate *vt* mal dater

misdirect *vt (letter)* mal adresser

misentry *n Acct* contre-position *f*

misery index *n Am* = indice qui prend en compte les taux de chômage et d'inflation, censé donner un aperçu de l'état de l'économie et du niveau de confiance des consommateurs

> **"**
> One, admittedly artificial, indicator of financial conditions is the **misery index**, which is an average of the depreciation of the currency, the change in the stock market index, and the change in domestic interest rates (in basis points). This index shows that the major developing countries have seen substantial declines in interest rates, exchange rate appreciation, and stock market increases since December 1998.
> **"**

misleading advertising *n* publicité *f* mensongère

mismanage *vt* mal gérer

mismanagement *n* mauvaise gestion *f*

misroute *vt (parcel)* mal acheminer

mission *n* **(a)** *(delegation)* mission *f*; **a Chinese trade mission** une mission commerciale chinoise **(b)** *(of company)* mission *f* ▫ *mission statement* ordre *m* de mission

> **"**
>
> The purpose of the NCC, which was established with government funds in 1975, is to safeguard the interests of consumers – particularly, according to its **mission statement**, "the inarticulate and disadvantaged". It has battled on their behalf against sharp practice, especially in the insurance, banking, supermarket and utilities sectors. Now, however, consumers could be forgiven for wondering whose side it is on.
>
> **"**

missionary selling n Mktg ventes fpl de prospection

mission-critical adj indispensable

> **"**
>
> What you can say about the new economy is that it changes the way we work. Email has long been **mission-critical**, but six months from now you will have to be web-literate to even survive within BP.
>
> **"**

mistake n erreur f; **to make a mistake** faire une erreur

misuse 1 n (of equipment, resources) mauvais emploi m; (of authority) abus m; (of funds) détournement m
  2 vt (equipment, resources) mal employer; (authority) abuser de; (funds) détourner

mixed adj mixte □ **mixed cargo** cargaison f mixte; **mixed costs** frais mpl semi-variables; **mixed economy** économie f mixte; Ins **mixed policy** police f d'assurance mixte; **mixed risks** risques mpl mixtes

mixed-media adj multi-média

MJPEG n Comptr (abbr **Moving Joint Photographic Expert Group**) (format m) MJPEG m

MLM n (abbr **multi-level marketing**) VRC f

MLR n Br Fin (abbr **minimum lending rate**) taux m de base

MMC n Formerly (abbr **Monopolies and Mergers Commission**) = commission britannique veillant au respect de la législation antitrust

MMF n St Exch (abbr **money market fund**) ≃ sicav f monétaire

mobile 1 n (mobile phone) portable m
  2 adj **mobile customs unit** douane f volante; **mobile phone** téléphone m portable

MO n (abbr **money order**) mandat-poste m

mobilization n (of capital) mobilisation f

mobilize vt (capital) mobiliser

mock-up n maquette f

mode n Comptr mode m

model n (**a**) (small version) maquette f (**b**) (ex-

ample) modèle m; **this is our latest model** c'est notre dernier modèle; **we plan to bring out a new model next season** nous projetons de sortir un nouveau modèle la prochaine saison □ **model factory** usine f modèle, usine-pilote f (**c**) Econ modèle m

modem Comptr **1** n modem m; **to send sth to sb by modem** envoyer qch à qn par modem □ **modem cable** câble m modem; **modem card** carte f modem
  2 vt envoyer par modem; **to modem sth to sb** envoyer qch à qn par modem

moderate adj (price, rise) modéré(e); (income) modeste

moderate-income adj aux revenus modestes

moderator n (at meeting) président(e) m,f; (mediator) médiateur(trice) m,f; (of focus group) animateur(trice) m,f

modernization n modernisation f

modernize vt moderniser

modified rebuy n Mktg rachat m modifié

monadic adj Mktg **monadic test** test m monadique; **monadic testing** tests mpl monadiques

monetarism n Econ monétarisme m

monetarist n & adj Econ monétariste mf

monetary adj monétaire □ **monetary adjustment** alignement m monétaire; **monetary aggregate** agrégat m monétaire; **monetary agreement** convention f monétaire; **monetary alignment** alignement monétaire; **monetary area** zone f monétaire; **monetary assets** liquidités fpl; Econ **monetary bloc** bloc m monétaire; **monetary compensatory amounts** montants mpl compensatoires monétaires; **monetary control** contrôle m monétaire; **monetary convention** convention monétaire; **monetary inflation** inflation f monétaire; **monetary parity** parité f des monnaies; **monetary policy** politique f monétaire; Br **Monetary Policy Committee** = comité formé de quatre membres de la Banque d'Angleterre et de quatre économistes nommés par le gouvernement, dont l'un des rôles est de fixer les taux d'intérêt; **monetary reform** réforme f monétaire; **monetary reserves** réserves fpl de change; **monetary standard** étalon m monétaire; **monetary surplus** surplus m monétaire; **monetary system** système m monétaire; **monetary unit** unité f monétaire

monetization n monétisation f

monetize vt monétiser

money n (**a**) (in general) argent m; (currency) monnaie f; **counterfeit money** fausse monnaie; **to make money** (of person) gagner de l'argent; (of business) rapporter de l'argent; **to be worth a lot of money** (thing) valoir cher; (person) être riche; **the deal is worth a lot of money** c'est un contrat qui porte sur de très grosses sommes; **to get one's money back** *(get reimbursed)* se faire rembourser; *(recover one's expenses)* rentrer dans ses fonds ▢ **money of account** monnaie de compte; **money broker** prêteur(euse) *m,f* sur titre; *Banking* **money at call** argent au jour le jour, argent à vue; **money laundering** blanchiment *m* d'argent; *Am* **money manager** gestionnaire *mf* de portefeuille; **money market** marché *m* monétaire *ou* financier; *Am* **money market certificate** instrument *m* de marché monétaire; **money market fund** fonds *m* commun de placement, ≃ sicav *f* monétaire; **money measurement** estimation *f* monétaire; **money order** mandat *m* (postal); **money rate** taux *m* de l'argent; *Banking* **money at short notice** argent à court terme; **money supply** masse *f* monétaire; **money trader** cambiste *mf* **(b)** *St Exch* **to be in the money** être dans les cours; **to be at the money** être à parité; **to be out of the money** être hors des cours

> ❝
> But these problems, together with those seen in the euro switchover, do post a warning. We now know that the far simpler changeover to the euro resulted in large bank payments going astray and a serious liquidity problem in the Euroland **money markets**, which required large injections of cash.
> ❞

money-back *adj* **money-back guarantee** garantie *f* de remboursement; **money-back offer** offre *f* de remboursement

moneychanger *n* **(a)** *(person)* courtier(ère) *m,f* de change **(b)** *Am (machine)* distributeur *m* de monnaie

moneylender *n* prêteur(euse) *m,f*

moneymaker *n* affaire *f* qui rapporte, mine *f* d'or; **to be a moneymaker** *(of shop, business, product)* rapporter

moneymaking *adj* lucratif(ive)

moneyman *n* *Fam* financier *m*

money-off *adj* ▢ **money-off coupon** bon *m* de réduction; **money-off deal** réduction *f* de prix; **money-off voucher** bon de réduction

moneyspinner *n* *Br Fam* affaire *f* qui rapporte, mine *f* d'or

moneyspinning *adj* *Br Fam* lucratif(ive)

monitor 1 *n* *Comptr* moniteur *m*
2 *vt* *Mktg* surveiller

monitoring *n* *Mktg* surveillance *f*, contrôle *m* continu

monometallic *adj* *Fin* monométalliste

monometallism *n* *Fin* monométallisme *m*

Monopolies and Mergers Commission *n* *Formerly* = commission britannique veillant au respect de la législation antitrust

monopolize *vt* monopoliser

monopoly *n* monopole *m*; **to have a monopoly of** *or* **on sth** avoir le monopole de qch; **to form a monopoly** constituer un monopole ▢ **monopoly control** contrôle *m* monopolistique; **monopoly market** marché *m* monopolistique

monopsony *n* monopsone *m*

month *n* mois *m*

monthly 1 *adj* mensuel(elle) ▢ **monthly instalment** mensualité *f*; **monthly payment** mensualité; **monthly repayment** mensualité de remboursement; **monthly statement** relevé *m* de fin de mois
2 *adv* tous les mois; *(pay)* mensuellement

moonlight *vi* *Fam (work illegally)* travailler au noir; *(have second job)* avoir un deuxième emploi

moonlighting *n* *Fam (working illegally)* travail *m* au noir; *(having second job)* cumul *m* d'emplois

moral hazard *n* *Fin, Ins* risque *m* moral

> ❝
> The US Congress is reluctant to fund President Clinton's promise of $210m … for the initiative, and Japan fears that a write off of its $10bn share will create a **moral hazard**. An added condition for indebted countries to fulfil, linking debt relief to poverty reduction, has also caused delays as poor countries struggle to prepare "poverty reduction strategy papers" to the satisfaction of their creditors. The result is that most of the neediest countries are getting nothing from the process.
> ❞

moratorium *n* *Fin* moratoire *m*; *(of debt)* moratoire, suspension *f*; **to declare a moratorium** décréter un moratoire

mortality tables *npl* *Ins* tables *fpl* de mortalité

mortgage 1 *n* *Fin (for house purchase)* crédit *m* *ou* prêt *m* immobilier; *(raised on property)* hypothèque *f*; **a 25-year mortgage at seven percent** un emprunt sur 25 ans à sept pour cent; **to take out a mortgage** prendre un crédit *ou* un prêt immobilier; **to secure a debt by mortgage** hypothéquer une créance; **to pay off a mortgage** rembourser un emprunt; *(raised on property)* purger une hypothèque; **they can't meet their mortgage repayments** ils ne peuvent pas payer les mensualités de leur emprunt ▢ **mortgage bank** banque *f* hypothécaire; **mortgage bond** obligation *f* hypothécaire;

mortgage broker courtier(ère) *m,f* en prêts hypothécaires; **mortgage charge** affectation *f* hypothécaire; **mortgage debenture** obligation hypothécaire; **mortgage deed** acte *m* hypothécaire; **mortgage lender** prêteur(euse) *m,f* hypothécaire; **mortgage loan** prêt hypothécaire, prêt sur hypothèque; **mortgage market** marché *m* hypothécaire; **mortgage rate** taux *m* de crédit immobilier; **mortgage registrar** conservateur(trice) *m,f* des hypothèques; **mortgage repayment** remboursement *m* d'emprunt; **mortgage repossession** mainlevée *f* d'une hypothèque; **mortgage security** garantie *f* hypothécaire
2 *vt (land, building)* hypothéquer, prendre une hypothèque sur; *(title deeds)* engager, mettre en gage

mortgageable *adj* hypothécable

mortgage-backed security *n Fin* titre *m* garanti par des créances hypothécaires

mortgagee *n* créancier(ère) *m,f* hypothécaire

mortgagor *n* débiteur(trice) *m,f* hypothécaire

most-favoured nation, *Am* **most-favored nation** *n* nation *f* la plus favorisée; **this country has most-favoured nation status** ce pays bénéficie de la clause de la nation la plus favorisée

> **"**
> Ukraine's exports would benefit from the proximity of a large single market, said Ms Franey, as well as from demand sparked by economic growth in the candidates. And once they join the EU, the candidates will have to grant Ukraine the same privileges it already enjoys in relations with the EU – notably **most-favoured nation** status, and benefits under the Generalised System of Preferences.
> **"**

motherboard *n Comptr* carte *f* mère

mother company *n* maison *f* mère

motion *n* (a) *(in meeting, debate)* motion *f*; **to propose a motion** proposer une motion; **to carry a motion** faire adopter une motion; **to second a motion** appuyer une motion (b) *(movement)* mouvement *m* ▫ **motion analysis** analyse *f* des mouvements; **motion study** étude *f* des mouvements (c) *Law (request)* demande *f*, requête *f*

motivate *vt* motiver

motivation *n* motivation *f* ▫ *Mktg* **motivation research** recherche *f* de motivation; **motivation study** étude *f* de motivation

motivational *adj* ▫ *Mktg* **motivational research** recherche *f* de motivation; **motivational study** étude *f* de motivation

motive *n (intention)* motif *m*

mount *vt (bid)* lancer; *(campaign, exhibition)* monter, organiser

▶ **mount up** *vi* (a) *(increase)* monter, augmenter; **the bill was mounting up** la facture augmentait (b) *(accumulate)* s'accumuler, s'amonceler

mouse *n Comptr* souris *f* ▫ **mouse button** bouton *m* de souris; **mouse driver** programme *m* de commande de la souris; **mouse mat** tapis *m* de souris; **mouse pad** tapis de souris

mousetrap *n Am* **to build a better mousetrap** élaborer un meilleur produit

> **"**
> The common philosophy among many Southeast Asian executives is that if their products are good – if they **build a better mousetrap** – consumers will know how to get to them. But these executives need to change their focus from achieving short-term sales to building long-term relationships with the key stakeholders in their businesses.
> **"**

movable *Law* 1 *n* **movables** biens *mpl* mobiliers
2 *adj* mobilier(ère) ▫ **movable assets** investissements *mpl* mobiliers; **movable effects** effets *mpl* mobiliers; **movable property** biens *mpl* mobiliers

move 1 *n* (a) *(change of job)* changement *m* d'emploi; *(change of premises)* déménagement *m*
(b) *(step, measure)* pas *m*, démarche *f*; **the new management's first move was to increase all salaries** la première mesure de la nouvelle direction a été de relever tous les salaires; **at one time there was a move to expand** à un moment, on avait envisagé de s'agrandir
2 *vt* (a) *(transfer)* muter; **she's been moved to the New York office/to accounts** elle a été mutée au bureau de New York/affectée à la comptabilité
(b) *(sell)* vendre; **we must move these goods quickly** nous devons vendre ces marchandises rapidement
3 *vi* (a) *(change premises, location)* déménager; **the company has moved to more modern premises** la société s'est installée dans des locaux plus modernes; **he's moved to a job in publishing** il travaille maintenant dans l'édition
(b) *(sell)* se vendre; **the new model isn't moving as quickly as planned** le nouveau modèle ne se vend pas aussi vite que prévu

▶ **move up** *vi St Exch (of shares)* se relever, reprendre; **shares moved up three points today** les actions ont gagné trois points aujourd'hui

moveable = **movable**

movement *n (of capital)* circulation *f*; *(of share prices)* mouvement *m*; *(of market)* activité *f*; **the**

upward/downward movement of interest rates la hausse/baisse des taux d'intérêt

mover n movers and shakers *(key people)* acteurs *mpl*

> 66
>
> The **movers and shakers** of real estate development are among the late arrivals to the great Web party that has revolutionized business practices in almost every sector of our economy. In fact, many in the real estate business are still "arriving" – on their way. As an industry we have not yet tapped even half of the Internet's remarkable potential for advertising and marketing real estate.
>
> 99

moving average n moyenne *f* mobile

MPA n *(abbr Master of Public Administration)* MPA *m (diplôme d'administration publique)*

MPC n *Br (abbr* **monetary policy committee***)* = comité formé de quatre membres de la Banque d'Angleterre et de quatre économistes nommés par le gouvernement, dont l'un des rôles est de fixer les taux d'intérêt

> 66
>
> Most City economists believe the Bank of England monetary policy committee will leave base rates on hold at 5 percent at their two-day meeting tomorrow … It is believed the **MPC** will feel economic indicators show overall inflationary pressures are under control, despite concerns about last week's statement from Halifax, Britain's biggest mortgage lender, that house prices had risen 9.4 percent in the year to August.
>
> 99

MPEG n *Comptr (abbr* **Moving Pictures Expert Group***)* (format *m*) MPEG *m*

mps n *(abbr* **master production schedule***)* plan *m* de production principal

MP3 n *Comptr (abbr* **MPEG1 Audio Layer 3***)* (format *m*) MP3 *m* □ **MP3 player** lecteur *m* MP3

mrp n (a) *(abbr* **manufacturer's recommended price***)* prix *m* conseillé par le fabricant (b) *(abbr* **material requirements planning***)* prévision *f* des besoins matériels

MRS n *(abbr* **Market Research Society***)* = société d'étude de marché britannique

MS-DOS n *Comptr (abbr* **Microsoft Disk Operating System***)* MS-DOS *m*

MTFA n *EU (abbr* **medium-term financial assistance***)* aide *f* financière à moyen terme

MTN n *Fin (abbr* **medium-term note***)* bon *m* à moyen terme (négociable)

multi-access adj *Comptr* à accès multiple

multibrand n *Mktg* marque *f* multiple, multi-marque *f*

multicurrency adj *EU* multidevise

multidiffusion n multidiffusion *f*

multifunctional adj multifonction(s) □ *Banking* **multifunctional card** carte *f* multifonctions; *Comptr* **multifunctional key** touche *f* multifonctions; *Comptr* **multifunctional keyboard** clavier *m* multifonctions

multilateral adj multilatéral(e) □ **multilateral agreement** accord *m* multilatéral; **multilateral trade agreement** accord commercial multilatéral

multi-level marketing n marketing *m* de réseau, vente *f* par réseau coopté

multimedia *Comptr* **1** n multimédia *m*
2 adj multimédia □ **multimedia bus** bus *m* multimédia; **multimedia computer** ordinateur *m* multimédia; **multimedia designer** concepteur(trice) *m,f* multimédia; **multimedia facility** fonction *f* multimédia; **multimedia group** groupe *m* multimédia; **multimedia network** réseau *m* multimédia

multinational **1** n multinationale *f*
2 adj multinational(e) □ **multinational company** société *f* multinationale; **multinational enterprise** entreprise *f* multinationale; **multinational marketing** marketing *m* multinational, mercatique *f* multinationale

multi-part stationery n *Comptr* papier *m* multiple

multiple **1** n *(chain store)* chaîne *f* de magasins
2 adj multiple □ *St Exch* **multiple application** application *f* multiple; **multiple exchange rate** taux *m* de change multiple; *Comptr* **multiple mailboxes** = possibilité d'avoir plusieurs boîtes aux lettres auprès d'un fournisseur d'accès à l'Internet; **multiple management** direction *f* multiple; *St Exch* **multiple options facility** ligne *f* de crédit à options multiples; **multiple ownership** multipropriété *f*; **multiple pricing** = fait d'adapter le prix de vente d'un produit au marché où on le commercialise; *Am* **multiple store** grand magasin *m* à succursales

multiple-choice adj *Mktg (question, questionnaire, survey)* à choix multiples

multiple-use principle n principe *m* de polyvalence

multiplex *Tel* **1** n multiplex *m*
2 vt multiplexer

multiplexer n *Tel* multiplexeur *m*

multiplexing n *Tel* multiplexage *m*

multi-station adj *Comptr* multipostes

multitasking **1** n (a) *(of employee)* = capacité à mener plusieurs tâches de front (b) *Comptr* multitâche *m*

2 adj Comptr multitâche

multi-user adj Comptr pour utilisateurs multiples □ **multi-user software** logiciel m multi-utilisateur; **multi-user system** système m multi-utilisateur

municipal adj municipal(e), de la ville □ Am Fin **municipal bond** obligation f de collectivité locale; **municipal buildings** ≃ mairie f; (in large town) hôtel m de ville

must-have 1 n must m
  2 adj **a must-have product** un must

> We have all talked about customer satisfaction and JD Powers may be measuring it, but being successful in a tight economy requires it. The Consumer Confidence Index does not establish your customers' need for a new home but it does put more pressure on how their money will be spent. Being the builder of a **must-have product** rather than a "choice" is absolutely essential as the willingness to make a major financial investment is now a more difficult commitment for today's consumer.

mutual adj mutuel(elle), réciproque □ **mutual agreement** marché m de gré à gré; **mutual benefit society** société f de secours mutuel(s); Am **mutual fund** fonds m commun de placement; **mutual insurance** assurance f mutuelle; **mutual insurance company** mutuelle f, société f

de mutualité; **mutual status** statut m de mutuelle

> Smaller local institutions claim that they can offer the old-fashioned kind that comes from genuinely knowing your customers. Nationwide made much of its **mutual status** in the recent row over charges for cash machines, setting itself up as the good guy against the shareholder-owned bad guy, Barclays.

mutualization n mutualisation f
mutualize vt mutualiser

mystery n **mystery shopper** client(e) m,f mystère; **mystery shopping** pseudo-achat m

> **Mystery shopping** looks at your operation from the customer's perspective with the advantage of knowing the company's criteria and standards. Researchers, who score your establishment according to a checklist created specifically for your company and tailored to your customer-service goals, make monthly visits. That method can give you great insight into how your business is operating when the manager is not around and whether employees are serving your customers the way you intend.

Nn

N/A, n/a *Admin* *(abbr* **not applicable**) *(on form)* s.o.

NAFTA *n (abbr* **North American Free Trade Agreement**) ALENA *m*

naked *adj* sans garantie □ *Fin* **naked debenture** obligation *f* chirographaire *ou* sans garantie; *St Exch* **naked option** option *f* d'achat vendue à découvert; *St Exch* **naked sale** vente *f* nue

NAM *n Am (abbr* **National Association of Manufacturers**) = organisation patronale américaine

Name *n Br Ins* = titre réservé aux membres investissant leur fortune personnelle dans la compagnie d'assurances Lloyd's et s'engageant à avoir une responsabilité illimitée en cas de sinistre

name 1 *n* (**a**) *(of person)* nom *m*; *(of company)* raison *f* sociale; *(of account)* intitulé *m*; **the shares are in my name** les actions sont à mon nom; **the company trades under the name of Scandia** la société a pour dénomination Scandia □ **name brand** marque *f*; *St Exch* **name day** deuxième jour *m* de liquidation; *Mktg* **name licensing** cession *f* de licence de nom; **name product** marque *f*

(**b**) *(reputation)* réputation *f*; **to have a good/bad name** avoir (une) bonne/ mauvaise réputation; **they have a name for efficiency** ils ont la réputation d'être efficaces

2 *vt (appoint)* nommer, désigner; **she's been named president** elle a été nommée présidente

NAO *n (abbr* **National Audit Office**) ≃ Cour *f* des comptes

narcodollar *n* narcodollar *m*

narration, narrative *n Acct* = note explicative dans un livre de commerce justifiant une écriture

narrow *adj (market)* étroit(e) □ **narrow money** = ensemble des billets et pièces de monnaie en circulation

NASD *n St Exch (abbr* **National Association of Securities Dealers**) = organisme de règlementation du commerce des valeurs boursières

NASDAQ *n St Exch (abbr* **National Association of Securities Dealers Automated Quotation**) le Nasdaq *(Bourse américaine des valeurs technologiques)*

nation *n* nation *f*

national 1 *n (person)* resortissant(e) *m,f*
2 *adj* national(e) □ **national accounting** comptabilité *f* nationale; **national airline** compagnie *f* aérienne nationale; **National Audit Office** ≃ Cour *f* des comptes; **national bank** = banque agréée par le gouvernement américain et qui doit faire partie du système bancaire fédéral; **National Credit Council** Conseil *m* national du crédit; **national debt** dette *f* publique; **National Enterprise Board** ≃ Agence *f* nationale pour le développement industriel; *Banking* **National Giro** = service britannique de chèques postaux; **national government** gouvernement *m* de coalition; *Br* **National Health Service** = système créé en 1946 en Grande-Bretagne et financé par l'État, assurant la gratuité des soins et des services médicaux, ≃ Sécurité *f* sociale; **to get treatment on the National Health (Service)** se faire soigner sous le régime de la Sécurité sociale; **national income** revenu *m* national; *Br* **National Insurance** = système britannique de sécurité sociale (maladie, retraite) et d'assurance chômage; *Br* **National Insurance contributions** cotisations *fpl* à la Sécurité sociale; *Br* **National Insurance number** ≃ numéro de Sécurité sociale; *Am* **National Labor Relations Board** = organisme américain de conciliation et d'arbitrage des conflits du travail, ≃ conseil de prud'hommes; **National Lottery** = loterie nationale britannique; **national market** marché *m* national; **national press** presse *f* nationale; **national product** produit *m* national; *Br* **National Savings Bank** ≃ Caisse *f* nationale d'épargne; *Br* **National Savings Certificate** bon *m* de caisse d'épargne

nationalization *n* nationalisation *f*

nationalize *vt* nationaliser

natural *adj* naturel(elle) ❑ *Ins* **natural disaster** catastrophe *f* naturelle; **natural economy** économie *f* non monétaire; *Comptr* **natural language** langage *m* naturel; **natural life** *(of company)* durée *f* de vie; *(of product)* durée utile; *Law* **natural person** personne *f* physique *ou* naturelle; **natural resources** ressources *fpl* naturelles; **natural wastage** = réduction des effectifs due aux départs d'employés non remplacés

> **"**
> Strong added that the company is looking to cut costs by trimming from 10 percent to 20 percent of staff, although he said it was too early to say where the ax will fall, or how many people will go. "Staff are being offered voluntary redundancy, and we are hoping to achieve some of the reductions by **natural wastage**, but the numbers involved mean that some layoffs may be inevitable," he said.
> **"**

NAV *n* (*abbr* **net asset value**) valeur *f* d'actif net

navigate *Comptr* **1** *vt* naviguer sur; **to navigate the Net** naviguer sur l'Internet
2 *vi* naviguer

navigation *n* navigation *f* ❑ *Comptr* **navigation bar** barre *f* de navigation; **navigation company** compagnie *f* de navigation *ou* de transports maritimes; **navigation dues** droits *mpl* de navigation

NBA *n* *Formerly* (*abbr* **net book agreement**) = accord entre maisons d'édition et libraires stipulant que ces derniers n'ont le droit de vendre aucun ouvrage à un prix inférieur à celui fixé par l'éditeur

NBV *n* *Acct* (*abbr* **net book value**) valeur *f* comptable nette

NDP *n* *Acct* (*abbr* **net domestic product**) produit *m* intérieur net

near *adj* *Comptr* **near letter quality** qualité *f* courrier; *Comptr* **near letter quality printer** imprimante *f* de qualité courrier; *St Exch* **near money** quasi-monnaie *f*; *St Exch* **near month** échéance *f* proche

need *n* *Mktg* besoin *m*; **needs and wants** besoins *mpl* et désirs *mpl* ❑ **needs analysis** analyse *f* des besoins; **needs assessment** estimation *f* des besoins; **need identification** identification *f* des besoins; **need level** niveau *m* des besoins; **need market** marché *m* des besoins; **need recognition** reconnaissance *f* des besoins; **need set** ensemble *m* de besoins; **needs study** étude *f* des besoins

needs-and-wants exploration *n* *Mktg* exploration *f* des besoins et des désirs

needs-based *adj* *Mktg* fondé(e) sur les be-

soins ❑ **needs-based market** marché *m* fondé sur les besoins; **needs-based segmentation** segmentation *f* fondée sur les besoins

negative *adj* négatif(ive) ❑ *Fin* **negative amortization** amortissement *m* négatif; *Fin* **negative amortization loan** prêt *m* à amortissement négatif; *Fin* **negative equity** plus-value *f* immobilière négative, = situation où l'acquéreur d'un bien immobilier reste redevable de l'emprunt contracté alors que son logement enregistre une moins-value; *Fin* **negative income tax** impôt *m* négatif (sur le revenu); *Br Fin* **negative interest** intérêt *m* négatif; *Fin* **negative pledge** clause *f* de nantissement négative; *Fin* **negative prescription** prescription *f* extinctive; *Fin* **negative saving** épargne *f* négative

> **"**
> About 65,000 homeowners in Hong Kong are in **negative equity**, involving loans of HK$127 million (about US$16.3 million), 23% of total outstanding mortgage loans held by banks, the Hong Kong Monetary Authority said Tuesday. The number of people in **negative equity**, whose outstanding loan exceeds the current market value of their property, represents 14% of total mortgage borrowers, the territory's quasi-central bank said in a statement.
> **"**

neglected *adj* *St Exch* (shares) négligé(e)

negligence *n* négligence *f*; **through negligence** par négligence ❑ *Ins* **negligence clause** clause *f* de négligence

negotiability *n* négociabilité *f*

negotiable *adj* (salary, fee) négociable, à débattre; *Fin* (bill, document) négociable; **not negotiable** (on cheque) non à ordre ❑ **negotiable instrument** instrument *m* négociable; **negotiable paper** papier *m* négociable; *Fin* **negotiable stock** titres *mpl* négociables

negotiate **1** *vt* (**a**) (business deal) négocier, traiter; (loan, treaty, salary, fee) négocier; *Fin* (bill, document) négocier, trafiquer; **price to be negotiated** prix à débattre
2 *vi* négocier; **the unions will have to negotiate with the management for higher pay** il faudra que les syndicats négocient une augmentation de salaire auprès de la direction

negotiating table *n* table *m* des négociations; **it's time to sit round the negotiating table and discuss our differences** il est temps de s'asseoir à la table de négociations et de régler nos différends

negotiation *n* négociation *f*; **under negotiation** en négociation; **to be in negotiation with sb** être en pourparlers avec qn; **to enter into negotiations with sb** entamer des négociations avec qn; **to break off/resume negotia-**

tions rompre/reprendre les négociations; **the pay deal is subject to negotiation** l'accord salarial est sujet à négociation

negotiator n négociateur(trice) m,f

nervous adj (market) agité(e), instable

nest egg n bas m de laine, pécule m

> **"**
>
> Nervous about your **nest egg**? If it's loaded with stocks, you should be. Stocks could easily sink further, tread water, or rise slowly. To minimize the damage to your portfolio, you need some holdings that don't move in tandem with equities. The most obvious vehicle is bonds, but you can further protect yourself against market swings by including other alternatives, such as hedge funds, real estate, and oil and gas.
>
> **"**

.net Comptr = abréviation désignant les organismes officiels de l'Internet dans les adresses électroniques

Net n Fam Comptr **the Net** le Net

net 1 adj (weight, price, profit, interest) net (nette) ▫ **net amount** montant m net; **net assets** actif m net; **net asset value** valeur f d'actif net; Formerly **net book agreement** = accord entre maisons d'édition et libraires stipulant que ces derniers n'ont le droit de vendre aucun ouvrage à un prix inférieur à celui fixé par l'éditeur; Acct **net book value** valeur comptable nette; **net capital expenditure** mise f de fonds nette, dépenses fpl nettes d'investissement; Acct **net cash flow** cash-flow m net; St Exch **net change** écart m net; **net contributor** contributeur m net; **net cost** prix m de revient; Acct **net current assets** actif circulant net; **net discounted cash flow** cash-flow actualisé net, flux mpl de trésorerie actualisés net; **net dividend** dividende m net; Econ **net domestic product** produit m intérieur net; **net earnings** (of company) bénéfices mpl nets; (of worker) salaire m net; **net income** (in accounts) produit net; (of individual) revenu m net; **net interest income** net m financier; **net loss** perte f nette; **net margin** marge f nette; **net national income** revenu national net; **net national product** produit national net; **net operating profit** rentabilité f nette d'exploitation; **net present value** valeur actuelle nette; Acct **net present value rate** taux m d'actualisation; **net proceeds** produit net; **net profit** bénéfice m net; **net profit margin** marge commerciale nette; **net profit ratio** ratio m de rentabilité nette; Acct **net realizable value** valeur réalisable nette; **net receipts** recettes fpl nettes; **net registered tonnage** jauge f nette; **net residual value** valeur résiduelle nette; **net result** résultat m final; **net return** rendement m ou résultat net; **net**

salary salaire net; **net tangible assets** actif corporel net; **net tonnage** jauge nette; **net total** montant net; **net value** valeur nette; Acct **net variance** écart net; **net working capital** fonds m de roulement net; **net worth** situation f nette

2 n net m; **net payable** net à payer

3 vt (of person, company) gagner net; (of sale) produire net; (profit) rapporter net; **he nets £20,000 a year** il gagne 20 000 livres net par an

4 adv **net of tax** net d'impôt; **net of VAT** hors TVA

> **"**
>
> **Net asset value** (NAV), worked out by dividing the value of the portfolio, less borrowings, by the number of shares in issue, tells you how much each share can claim of the trust's assets. Discount or premium to NAV, the gap between the share price and the asset value, helps measure a trust's popularity.
>
> **"**

nethead n Fam Comptr accro mf de l'Internet

netiquette n Comptr netiquette f

netizen n Comptr internaute mf

netspeak n Comptr langage m du Net, cyberjargon m

network 1 n réseau m ▫ Comptr **network administrator** administrateur(trice) m,f de réseau; Comptr **network card** carte f réseau; Comptr **network computer** ordinateur m en réseau; Comptr **network driver** gestionnaire m de réseau; Comptr **network management** gestion f de réseau; Comptr **network manager** gestionnaire de réseau; Comptr **network operating system** système m d'exploitation réseau; Comptr **network server** serveur m de réseau; Comptr **network software** logiciel m de réseau; Comptr **network traffic** trafic m de réseau

2 vt Comptr mettre en réseau ▫ **networked system** système m en réseau

3 vi (make contacts) établir un réseau de contacts

networking n (a) Comptr travail m en réseau; (connecting as network) mise f en réseau; **to have networking capabilities** (of terminal) offrir la possibilité d'intégration à un réseau (b) (making contacts) établissement m d'un réseau de contacts

> **"**
>
> Daimler-Chrysler has 13,000 people working in its Auburn Hills, Michigan headquarters. Kathryn Lee, staff labor programs administrator, is proud that her company supports a Women's Network Group and provides a number of opportunities for after-hours **networking**, including guest speakers and presentations.
>
> **"**

neural network n Comptr réseau m neuronal

new adj nouveau(elle); (not used) neuf (neuve) ❑ **new borrowings** nouveaux emprunts mpl; Mktg **new buy situation** situation f de nouvel achat; **new capital** capitaux mpl frais; **new economy** nouvelle économie f; St Exch **new issue** nouvelle émission f; St Exch **new issue market** marché m des nouvelles émissions, marché primaire; **the new media** les nouveaux médias mpl; Fin **new money** crédit m de restructuration, argent m frais; Mktg **new product** nouveau produit m; Mktg **new product development** développement m de nouveaux produits; Mktg **new product marketing** marketing m de nouveaux produits; St Exch **new shares** actions fpl nouvelles

newbie n Fam Comptr internaute mf novice, cybernovice mf

newly industrialized country n nouveau pays m industrialisé

news n (a) (information) nouvelles fpl; (on TV, radio) informations fpl ❑ **news agency** agence f de presse; **news analyst** commentateur m; **news bulletin** bulletin m d'informations; **news conference** conférence f de presse; **news desk** (salle f de) rédaction f; **news editor** rédacteur(-trice) m,f en chef des actualités; **news service** = agence de presse qui publie ses informations par le biais d'un syndicat de distribution

(b) Comptr nouvelles fpl ❑ **news article** article m Usenet; **news reader** logiciel m de lecture de nouvelles; **news server** serveur m de nouvelles

newsgroup n Comptr forum m de discussion, newsgroup m

newsletter n bulletin m (d'informations)

newsocracy n = aux États-Unis, ensemble de la presse et du réseau télévisé à audience nationale

newspaper n journal m ❑ **newspaper advertisement** publicité f presse; **newspaper advertising** publicité presse; **newspaper article** article m de journal; **newspaper clipping** coupure f de presse; **newspaper cutting** coupure de presse; **newspaper report** reportage m (dans un journal)

newssheet n bulletin m

new-to-the-company product n Mktg produit m nouveau dans la société

new-to-the-world product n Mktg produit m nouveau dans le monde

next-day delivery n livraison f lendemain

NF n Banking (abbr **no funds**) manque m de provision

NGO n (abbr **non-governmental organization**) ONG f

NHS n Br (abbr **National Health Service**) = sys-

tème créé en 1946 en Grande-Bretagne et financé par l'État, assurant la gratuité des soins et des services médicaux, ≃ Sécurité f sociale

NI n (abbr **National Insurance**) = système britannique de sécurité sociale (malade, retraite) et d'assurance chômage

NIC n (a) Br (abbr **National Insurance contributions**) cotisations fpl à la Sécurité sociale (b) (abbr **newly industrialized country**) NPI m

niche n Mktg (in market) créneau m, niche f ❑ **niche market** niche; **niche marketing** marketing m ciblé; **niche player** acteur m sur un segment de marché; **niche product** produit m ciblé

❝

Newly launched Bluway.com, a gay- and lesbian-oriented travel site, said it hopes to become an important **niche player** with an assortment of offerings from tour operators, cruise lines and hotels. Company founder Alex Khodorkovsky said the site will enable suppliers and advertisers to reach a gay audience and will ease the travel purchase process for site users.

❞

nickel-and-dime store n Am = magasin à prix unique

NIF n Banking (abbr **note issuance facility**) autorisation f d'émettre les billets de banque

night n nuit f ❑ Banking **night depository** coffre(-fort) m de nuit; **night rate** tarif m de nuit; Banking **night safe** coffre(-fort) de nuit; **night shift** équipe f de nuit; **to be on night shift** être de nuit; **night work** travail m de nuit

Nikkei Index n St Exch indice m Nikkei

nil 1 n néant m, zéro m; **the balance is nil** le solde est nul

2 adj nul (nulle), zéro ❑ **nil balance** solde m nul; **nil growth** croissance f zéro; **nil premium** prime f nulle; **nil profit** bénéfice m nul; **nil return** état m néant

nine-to-five 1 adj (job) routinier(ère); (mentality) de gratte-papier

2 adv **to work nine-to-five** avoir des horaires de bureau

nine-to-fiver n Am = personne qui travaille selon des horaires traditionnels (le plus souvent de 9h à 17h)

❝

Unisys' Schebella is no clock-watcher. "I'm not a **nine-to-fiver**," she says. "I'm available all the time because IT recruiting these days is done on a daily basis and has a sense of urgency to it. So I'm in constant communication with what I call my 'triangle' — the candidates, the customers, and the clients."

❞

NLRB n Am (abbr **National Labor Relations Board**) = organisme américain de conciliation et d'arbitrage des conflits du travail

NNP n (abbr **net national product**) produit m national net

no-claims bonus n Ins bonus m

node n Comptr noyau m

no-fault insurance n Am assurance f non-responsabilité

noise n Comptr bruit m

no-load adj sans frais ❑ St Exch **no-load fund** fonds m sans frais d'acquisition, fonds qui ne prélève pas une commission

nominal adj (**a**) (neglible) nominal(e); (rent) insignifiant(e); **a nominal amount** une somme insignifiante
  (**b**) (token) symbolique; **a nominal contribution of one pound a year** une contribution symbolique d'une livre par an
  (**c**) (in name only) de nom (seulement), nominal(e); **he was the nominal president of the company** il n'était le président de la société que de nom ❑ **nominal partner** associé(e) m,f fictif(ive)
  (**d**) Acct **nominal account** compte m d'exploitation générale; Fin **nominal capital** capital m nominal; Fin **nominal interest rate** taux m d'intérêt nominal; Acct **nominal ledger** grand-livre m général; Fin **nominal price** prix m nominal; St Exch **nominal quote** cours m indicatif; Fin **nominal rate** taux d'intérêt nominal; Fin **nominal value** valeur f nominale; **nominal wages** salaire m nominal; Fin **nominal yield** taux nominal

nominate vt (**a**) (appoint) nommer, désigner; **to nominate sb to a post** désigner qn à un poste; **he was nominated chairman** il a été nommé président (**b**) (propose) proposer; **to nominate sb for a post** proposer la candidature de qn à un poste

nomination n nomination f

nominee n (**a**) (appointed) personne f nommée (**b**) (proposed) candidat(e) m,f ❑ **nominee account** compte m d'intermédiaire; **nominee company** prête-nom m; **nominee name** nom m de l'intermédiaire; St Exch **nominee shareholder** actionnaire mf intermédiaire; St Exch **nominee shareholding** actionnariat m intermédiaire

non-acceptance n Banking (of bill of exchange) non-acceptation f, refus m d'acceptation

non-accruing loan n emprunt m à risques

non-adopter n Mktg = consommateur qui n'essaie jamais de nouveaux produits

nonassessable adj Ins (policy) non imposable

non-bank adj non-banque

non-business marketing n marketing m non-commercial

noncallable adj Fin (bond) qui ne peut être amorti(e) par anticipation

non-competition clause n clause f de non-concurrence

non-contributory pension n caisse f de retraite sans cotisations de la part des bénéficiaires

non-convertible adj (currency) non convertible

non-cumulative adj Fin (shares) non cumulatif(ive) ❑ **non-cumulative quantity discount** remise f sur quantité non cumulable

non-current liabilities npl Acct passif m non exigible

nondeductible adj Fin non déductible

non-delivery n (of goods) non-livraison f; **in the event of non-delivery** dans l'éventualité où les marchandises ne seraient pas livrées

non-durable goods npl produits mpl périssables

non-dutiable adj Customs exempt(e) de droits de douane

non-equity share n St Exch action f sans privilège de participation

non-execution n (of contract) non-exécution f

non-executive director n administrateur(-trice) m,f

nonfood 1 n nonfoods (department, sector) non alimentaire m
  2 adj (department, sector) non alimentaire

non-forfeiture n Law non-déchéance f ❑ Ins **non-forfeiture clause** clause f de reconduction automatique

non-fulfilment n (of contract) non-exécution f

non-governmental organization n organisation f non-gouvernementale

non-interlaced adj Comptr (screen) à balayage progressif

non-liability n Law non-responsabilité f ❑ **non-liability clause** clause f de non-responsabilité

nonmarketable adj Fin, St Exch (assets, bonds, securities) non-négociable

non-negotiable adj non-négociable

non-participating adj Ins (policy) sans participation aux bénéfices; St Exch (share) sans droit de participation

non-payment n non-paiement m; **in case of non-payment** en cas de non-paiement, à défaut de paiement

non-performing loan n Banking prêt m en souffrance

non-probability adj Mktg **non-probability method** (of sampling) méthode f non probabiliste; **non-probability sample** échantillon m non probabiliste; **non-probability sampling** échantillonnage m non probabiliste

non-productive adj Econ improductif(ive)

non-profit-making organization, non-profit organization n Br société f à but non lucratif

non-qualifying policy n régime m de retraite non défiscalisé

non-quoted adj St Exch non côté(e) en Bourse

non-random adj Mktg **non-random sample** échantillon m empirique; **non-random sampling** échantillonnage m empirique

non-recourse finance n Fin financement m sans recours ou à forfait

non-recurring expenditure n frais mpl ou dépenses fpl extraordinaires

non-refundable adj non-remboursable; (packaging) perdu(e)

non-resident account n Banking compte m (de) non-résident

non-returnable adj sans réserve de retour; (bottle, container) non consigné(e); (deposit) non remboursable; (packaging) perdu(e); **sales goods are non-returnable** les articles en solde ne sont pas repris

non-tariff barrier n barrière f non tarifaire

non-taxable adj Admin (revenue) non imposable

non-trading adj **non-trading company** société f civile; **non-trading day** jour m non-ouvrable; **non-trading hours** heures fpl de fermeture

non-union, non-unionized adj (worker) non syndiqué(e)

nonvoting adj Fin, St Exch (share) sans droit de vote

non-warranty n non-garantie f ◻ **non-warranty clause** clause f de non-garantie

no-par adj Fin sans valeur nominale

no-quibble guarantee n garantie f sans conditions

normal adj Mktg **normal distribution curve** courbe f de distribution normale; St Exch **normal market size** taille f normale du marché; **normal retirement age** âge m normal de départ à la retraite

North American Free Trade Agreement n accord m de libre-échange nord-américain

notarial adj Law (functions, procedure) notarial(e); (deed) notarié(e)

notarize vt Law certifier, authentifier ◻ **notarized contract** contrat m notarié; **notarized copy** ≃ copie f certifiée conforme; **notarized deed** acte m notarié

notary n Law **notary (public)** notaire m

note 1 n (a) (information, reminder) note f ◻ Fin **note of hand** billet m à ordre (b) Br (banknote) billet m; **a ten-pound note** un billet de dix livres ◻ Fin **note issue** émission f fiduciaire; **note issue facility** autorisation f d'émettre les billets de banque
2 vt noter, remarquer; (error) relever; (fact) constater; **you will note that there is an error in the account** nous vous faisons remarquer qu'il s'est glissé une erreur dans le compte

notebook n Comptr portable m, notebook m

not-for-profit organization n Am société f à but non lucratif

notice n (a) (notification) avis m, notification f; **until further notice** jusqu'à nouvel ordre ◻ **notice of receipt** accusé m de réception; **notice of withdrawal** avis de retrait de fonds
(b) (warning) avertissement m; (of resignation, redundancy) préavis m; **to give in** or **hand in one's notice** donner sa démission, démissionner; **fifty people have been given their notice** cinquante personnes ont été licenciées; **what notice do you require?** quel est le terme du congé?; **to give sb notice (of sth)** prévenir ou avertir qn (de qch); (of resignation, redundancy) donner un préavis à qn (de qch); **employees must give three months' notice** les employés doivent donner trois mois de préavis; **can be delivered at three days' notice** livrable dans un délai de trois jours; Banking **deposit at seven days' notice** dépôt m à sept jours de préavis ◻ **notice of dismissal** préavis de licenciement
(c) (intent to vacate premises) **notice (to quit)** (avis m de) congé m; **to be under notice (to quit)** avoir reçu son congé; **to give sb notice (to quit)** (of landlord) donner son congé à qn

> ❝
>
> The toughest part came when a meeting that took two months to schedule with a director of e-business for a large manufacturer didn't go the way she hoped it would. The official told Kovacs and York that he had given his **notice to quit** because he was fed up. He'd wasted 18 months setting up a Web storefront only to hear from management that it was being scrapped.
>
> ❞

notification n avis m, notification f; **to give sb notification (of sth)** avertir qn (de qch); **you will receive notification by mail** vous serez averti par courrier

notify *vt* annoncer, notifier; **to notify sb of sth** avertir qn de qch

notional *adj* fictif(ive) ❑ *notional income* revenu *m* fictif; *notional rent* loyer *m* insignifiant

novation *n* Law novation *f*

NOW account *n* Am Banking compte-chèques *m* rémunéré

NPD *n* Mktg (abbr **new product development**) développement *m* de nouveaux produits

NPV *n* Acct (abbr **net present value**) VAN *f* ❑ *NPV rate* taux *m* d'actualisation

NRV *n* Fin (abbr **net realizable value**) valeur *f* réalisable nette

nuisance tax *n* Am impôt *m* vexatoire

> **"**
>
> His most recent bit of mischief is a proposal to put a measure on the November ballot that seeks to impose a nickel-a-bullet tax on every round of ammunition sold in California. Perata's justification for another **nuisance tax** is that it would raise money to offset the costs of emergency and trauma centers that treat people with gunshot wounds.
>
> **"**

null *adj* Law (invalid) nul (nulle); **null and void** nul et non avenu; **to declare a contract null and void** déclarer un contrat nul et non avenu

nullification *n* annulation *f*

nullify *vt* annuler

number 1 *n* nombre *m*; (figure, numeral) chiffre *m* ❑ Comptr **number crunching** calculs *mpl* (rapides); **number key** touche *f* numérique; **numbers lock** verrouillage *m* du clavier numérique; **numbers lock key** touche de verrouillage du clavier numérique
2 *vt* (consecutively) numéroter ❑ **numbered account** compte *m* numéroté

numeric Comptr **1** *n* **numerics** chiffres *mpl* ou caractères *mpl* numériques
2 *adj* numérique ❑ **numeric field** champ *m* numérique; **numeric keypad** clavier *m* ou pavé *m* numérique

numerical *adj* Comptr numérique ❑ *numerical analysis* analyse *f* numérique; *numerical data* données *fpl* numériques; *numerical distribution* distribution *f* numérique; *numerical keypad* pavé *m* numérique

num lock *n* Comptr (abbr **numbers lock**) verr num; **the num lock is on** le pavé numérique est verrouillé ❑ *num lock key* touche *f* de verrouillage du pavé numérique

NYMEX *n* St Exch (abbr **New York Mercantile Exchange**) = marché à terme des produits pétroliers de New York

NYSE *n* St Exch (abbr **New York Stock Exchange**) = la Bourse de New York

Oo

objective n but m, objectif m; **to achieve** or **attain one's objectives** atteindre ses objectifs; **our objective for this year is to increase sales by ten percent** nous avons pour objectif d'augmenter nos ventes de dix pour cent au cours de l'année prochaine

object-orientated, object-oriented adj Comptr orienté(e) objet

obligate vt Am Fin (funds, credits) affecter

obligation n Am Fin obligation f

obligee n Fin (creditor) créancier(ère) m,f; (bondholder) obligataire mf

oblique n (slash) barre f oblique

o.b.o. (abbr **or best offer**) à déb.

observational research n Mktg étude f par observation

obsolescence n obsolescence f □ Ins **obsolescence clause** clause f de vétusté

obsolescent adj obsolescent(e)

obtain 1 vt obtenir; (for oneself) se procurer
2 vi (practice) avoir cours; (rules) être en vigueur; **practices obtaining in British banking** des pratiques courantes dans le système bancaire britannique; **this new system will obtain as from next week** ce nouveau système entrera en vigueur dès la semaine prochaine

obvious defect n vice m apparent

occupancy n (a) (of building) occupation f (b) Law possession f à titre de premier occupant

occupant n (a) (of building) occupant(e) m,f; (tenant) locataire mf (b) Law premier(ère) occupant(e) m,f

occupation n (a) (profession) métier m, emploi m; **what is his occupation?** quel est son métier?; **please state your name and occupation** veuillez indiquer votre nom et votre profession (b) (of building) occupation f; **the offices are ready for occupation** les bureaux sont prêts à être occupés

occupational adj professionnel(elle) □ **occupational accident** accident m du travail; **occupational disease** maladie f professionnelle; **occupational hazard** risque m du métier; **occupational pension fund** caisse f de retraite maison

occupier n occupant(e) m,f

occupy vt occuper

OCR n Comptr (a) (abbr **optical character reader**) lecteur m (à reconnaissance) optique de caractères (b) (abbr **optical character recognition**) OCR f □ **OCR font** fonte f reconnue optiquement; **OCR reader** lecteur m OCR; **OCR software** logiciel m d'OCR

OD Banking 1 n (abbr **overdraft**) découvert m
2 adj (abbr **overdrawn**) à découvert

ODA n Br (abbr **Overseas Development Administration**) = organisme d'aide aux pays en voie de développement

odd-even adj □ **odd-even price** prix m magique; **odd-even pricing** fixation f des prix magiques

odd lot n (a) (of goods) lot m dépareillé (b) St Exch (of shares) lot m de moins de cent actions

odd-lot adj St Exch **odd-lot order** ordre m de moins de cent actions; **odd-lot trading** achats mpl et ventes fpl de lots de moins de cent actions

odd-lotter n Am St Exch petit(e) actionnaire mf

odd-numbers adj □ **odd-numbers price** prix m magique; **odd-numbers pricing** fixation f des prix magiques

OECD n (abbr **Organization for Economic Co-operation and Development**) OCDE f

OEIC n Fin (abbr **open-ended investment company**) ≃ SICAV f, sicav f

OEM n (abbr **original equipment manufacturer**) constructeur m de systèmes originaux, OEM m

OEO n Am (abbr **Office of Equal Opportunity**) = organisme gouvernemental américain qui veille au respect des mesures anti-discriminatoires en matière d'emploi

OFEX n St Exch (abbr **off-exchange**) marché m secondaire

off-balance sheet adj Acct hors bilan □ **off-balance sheet item** poste m ou élément m hors bilan; **off-balance sheet transaction** opération f de hors bilan

off-brand adj sans marque

❝

In 1960 Harry Zimmerman introduced value. He opened his first Service Merchandise catalog showroom, providing consumers an alternative to both discount stores that offered **off-brand** merchandise and traditional retailers who required full retail mark-up.

"

offer 1 *n* offre *f*; **to make sb an offer (for sth)** faire une offre à qn (pour qch); **to be under offer** faire l'objet d'une proposition d'achat; **the house is under offer** on a reçu une offre pour la maison; **what is on offer in the negotiations?** qu'est-ce qui est proposé dans les négociations?; **these goods are on offer this week** ces articles sont en promotion cette semaine; **£500 or nearest offer** 500 livres, à débattre ❑ *Fin* **offer of cover** appel *m* de marge; **offer price** *(of product)* prix *m* vendeur, prix offert; *St Exch* cours *m ou* prix vendeur; **offer by prospectus** offre *f* publique de vente; **offer to purchase** offre publique d'achat; **offer for sale** mise *f* sur le marché

2 *vt* offrir; **he was offered the post** on lui a offert le poste; **to offer goods for sale** mettre des marchandises en vente; **to offer one's services** proposer ses services

offered price *n* prix *m* offert

offeree *n Fin, Law* destinataire *mf* de l'offre

offeror *n Fin, Law* = personne qui fait une offre

offering *n (of new shares)* mise *f* sur le marché ❑ *Am* **offering circular** note *f* d'information

off-exchange *adj St Exch (transaction, contract, market)* hors Bourse, hors cote

office *n* **(a)** *(place)* bureau *m*; *(of lawyer, architect)* cabinet *m*; **he's out of the office at the moment** il n'est pas dans le bureau en ce moment; **for office use only** *(on form)* (cadre) réservé à l'administration ❑ **office account** compte *m* professionnel *ou* commercial; **office address** adresse *f* au bureau; **office automation** bureautique *f*; **office block** immeuble de bureaux; **office building** immeuble de bureaux; **office equipment** matériel *m* de bureau; **office expenses** frais *mpl* de bureau; **office furniture** meubles *mpl ou* mobilier *m* de bureau; **office hours** heures *fpl* de bureau; **office IT** bureautique *f*; **office job** emploi *m* de bureau; **office junior** employé(e) *m,f* de bureau subalterne; **office management** organisation *f* des bureaux; **office manager** chef *m* de bureau; *Am* **office park** parc *m ou* zone *f* d'activités; **office rent** loyer *m* de bureau; **office space** locaux *mpl* pour bureaux; **office staff** personnel *m* de bureau; **office supplies** articles *mpl* de bureau; **office work** travail *m* de bureau; **office worker** employé(e) de bureau

(b) *(position)* fonctions *fpl*; **to be in office, to hold office** être au pouvoir; **to be out of office** ne plus être au pouvoir; **to leave office** quitter ses fonctions

(c) *(government department)* bureau *m*, département *m*; **I have to send this to the tax**

office je dois envoyer ça au centre des impôts ❑ **the Office of Equal Opportunity** = organisme gouvernemental américain qui veille au respect des mesures anti-discriminatoires en matière d'emploi; **the Office of Fair Trading** = organisme britannique de défense des consommateurs et de régulation des pratiques commerciales; **the Office of Management and Budget** = service administratif américain dont le rôle principal est d'aider le président à préparer le budget

officeholder *n* titulaire *mf* d'une fonction

officer *n (in local government)* fonctionnaire *mf*; *(of trade union)* représentant(e) *m,f* permanent(e); *(of company)* membre *m* de la direction; *(of association, institution)* membre du bureau; **the officers of the association meet every month** le bureau de l'association se réunit tous les mois

official 1 *n* fonctionnaire *mf*; **a bank/union official** un(e) représentant(e) de la banque/du syndicat; **a government official** un haut fonctionnaire

2 *adj (statement, visit, strike)* officiel(elle); *(language) (of country)* officiel; *(bureaucratic)* administratif(ive); **his appointment will be made official tomorrow** sa nomination sera rendue officielle demain; **she's here on official business** elle est ici en visite officielle; **to go through the official channels** suivre la filière officielle; **to act in one's official capacity** agir dans l'exercice de ses fonctions; **she was speaking in her official capacity as General Secretary** elle parlait en sa qualité de Secrétaire générale ❑ *St Exch* **official assignee** liquidateur *m* officiel; **official broker** courtier(ère) *m,f* officiel(elle); **official brokerage** courtage *m* officiel; **official document** document *m* officiel; **official exchange rate** cours *m* officiel; **official letter** pli *m* officiel *ou* de service; **official liquidator** liquidateur judiciaire; *Fin* **official list** cote *f* officielle; **official market** marché *m* officiel; *St Exch* **official price** cours en Bourse; **official quotation** cours officiel; *Banking* **official rate** taux *m* officiel d'escompte; *Fin* **official rate of interest** taux d'intérêt légal; **official receiver** administrateur(trice) *m,f* judiciaire; **the official receiver has been called in** on a fait appel à l'administration judiciaire; **official receivership** liquidation *f* judiciaire; **official report** rapport *m* officiel; *Br* **Official Secrets Act** = document relatif au secret-défense, signé par tous les fonctionnaires; **official strike** = grève soutenue par la direction du syndicat

officialese *n Fam* jargon *m* administratif

"

However, five centuries later, it is a matter of debate whether the incomprehensible **officialese** widely used by the French authorities is any easier to understand than Latin – or possibly, double Dutch. Never use one word when half a dozen will do, appears to be the rule of thumb, and make sure as many as possible are archaic and totally incomprehensible without the aid of a dictionary. But help may finally be at hand. A government body has just been set up with the task of simplifying the language of French bureaucracy.

officially *adv* officiellement

off-line 1 *adj* (**a**) *Comptr* non connecté(e); *(processing)* en différé; *(printer)* déconnecté(e); **to be off-line** ne pas être connecté; **to go off-line** se déconnecter □ *off-line mode* mode *m* autonome; *off-line reader* lecteur *m* non connecté (**b**) *Ind (production)* hors ligne
  2 *adv Comptr* hors ligne, hors connexion; **to work off-line** travailler sans se connecter à l'Internet

offload *vt (goods)* débarquer

offloading *n (of goods)* débarquement *m* □ *offloading platform* quai *m* de déchargement

off-peak 1 *adj (consumption, rate)* aux heures creuses □ *off-peak hours* heures *fpl* creuses
  2 *adv* pendant les heures creuses

off-price *adj Am (goods)* à prix réduits; *(store)* d'articles à prix réduits

off-season 1 *n* morte-saison *f*
  2 *adj* hors saison □ *off-season tariff* tarif *m* hors saison
  3 *adv* pendant la morte-saison

offset 1 *n Acct* compensation *f*, dédommagement *m* □ *offset agreement* accord *m* de compensation
  2 *vt (compensate for)* compenser; **to offset sth against tax** déduire le montant de qch de ses impôts; **any wage increase will be offset by inflation** avec l'inflation, les augmentations de salaire n'en seront plus vraiment; **we'll have to offset our research investment against long-term returns** avant de décider de notre budget recherche, il nous faut estimer ce que l'on peut en tirer à long terme

offsetting entry *n Acct* écriture *f* de compensation

offshoot *n (subsidiary)* succursale *f*

offshore 1 *adj* off-shore □ *offshore banking* opérations *fpl* bancaires off-shore; *offshore company* société *f* off-shore; *offshore fund* fonds *m* off-shore; *offshore investment* placement *m* off-shore
  2 *adv* **to keep sth offshore** garder qch offshore

off-the-peg research *n Mktg* = étude de marché utilisant des données déjà rassemblées

off-the-shelf *adj (goods)* prêt(e) à l'usage

□ *off-the-shelf company* société *f* tiroir

OFT *n (abbr* **Office of Fair Trading**) = service britannique de la concurrence et des prix

> ❝
> Following the publication today of a proposed decision by the Office of Fair Trading (**OFT**) that the company has behaved anticompetitively, a British Sky Broadcasting Group plc spokesman said: "BSkyB has not infringed the Competition Act and welcomes its first opportunity to put its case to the **OFT**."
> ❞

OHP *n (abbr* **overhead projector**) rétroprojecteur *m* □ *OHP slide* transparent *m*

OID *n Fin (abbr* **original issue discount bond**) obligation *f* à prime d'émission

oil *n* (**a**) *(petroleum)* pétrole *m* □ *oil company* société *f* pétrolière; *oil crisis* crise *f* pétrolière; *oil field* gisement *m* pétrolifère; *oil industry* industrie *f* pétrolière; *oil magnate* magnat *m* du pétrole; *oil market* marché *m* pétrolier; *oil port* port *m* pétrolier; *oil prices* prix *mpl* pétroliers *ou* du pétrole; *oil products* produits *mpl* pétroliers; *oil revenu* revenu *m* pétrolier; *oil royalty* redevance *f* pétrolière; *oil shares* valeurs *fpl* pétrolières; *oil tycoon* magnat du pétrole (**b**) *St Exch* **oils** (valeurs *fpl*) pétrolières *fpl*

oil-producing country *n* pays *m* producteur de pétrole

old-age pension *n* pension *f* de retraite

oligopolist *n Econ* oligopoliste *mf*

oligopolistic *adj Econ* oligopoliste

oligopoly *n Econ* oligopole *m*

oligopsony *n Econ* oligopsone *m*

OMB *n (abbr* **Office of Management and Budget**) = service administratif américain dont le rôle principal est d'aider le président à préparer le budget

ombudsman *n* ≃ médiateur *m* de la République

omnibus survey *adj Mktg* enquête *f* omnibus

omnium *n St Exch* omnium *m*

on-board surcharge *n Comptr* surcharge *f* "on-board"

oncosts *npl* frais *mpl* généraux

one *n St Exch* unité *f*; **to issue shares in ones** émettre des actions en unités

one-day fall *n St Exch* chute *f* enregistrée en un jour

> ❝
> The FTSE 100 suffered its biggest **one-day fall** since early December as funding worries weighed on telecoms, with Vodafone re-

treating as its revenue figures left investors unimpressed. The index ended down 1.8 percent at 5,131.4, extending losses in late trade as Wall Street sank. Telecoms, banks and oil stocks eroded some 60 index points between them.

"

one-level (distribution) channel *n* canal *m* de distribution court

one-man business *n* entreprise *f* individuelle

one-off *Br* **1** *n (article)* objet *m* unique
2 *adj (article)* spécial(e), hors série; *(order, job)* unique

one-price store *n* magasin *m* à prix unique

one-sided *adj (contract)* unilatéral(e), inégal(e)

one-stop *adj* **one-stop buying** achats *mpl* regroupés; **one-stop shop** magasin *m* où l'on trouve de tout; **one-stop shopping** achats regroupés *(dans un seul magasin)*

one-to-one marketing *n* marketing *m* one to one

one-way *adj (packaging)* perdu(e)

on-line *Comptr* **1** *adj* en ligne; **to be on-line** *(of person)* être connecté(e); **to go on-line** se connecter; **to put the printer on-line** connecter l'imprimante □ **on-line bank** banque *f* en ligne; **on-line banking** transactions *fpl* bancaires en ligne; *St Exch* **on-line broker** courtier(ère) *m,f* électronique; **on-line cash desk terminal** terminal *m* de paiement connecté; **on-line catalogue** catalogue *m* en ligne; **on-line communication** communication *f* en ligne; **on-line help** aide *f* en ligne; *Fin* **on-line investing** investissement *m* en ligne; *Fin* **on-line investor** investisseur *m* en ligne; **on-line marketing** marketing *m* électronique; **on-line mode** mode *m* connecté; **on-line registration** inscription *f* en ligne; **on-line retailer** société *f* de commerce en ligne; **on-line retailing** commerce *m* électronique; **on-line selling** vente *f* en ligne, vente électronique; **on-line service** service *m* en ligne; **on-line shop** magasin *m* électronique; **on-line shopping** achats *mpl* par Internet; **on-line terminal** terminal *m* de paiement connecté; **on-line time** durée *f* de connexion; *St Exch* **on-line trading** transactions boursières électroniques
2 *adv* en ligne; **to buy/order sth on-line** acheter/commander qch en ligne; **to shop on-line** faire un achat/des achats en ligne; **to work on-line** travailler en étant connecté à l'Internet

"
UK-based Interactive Music & Video Shop is an **on-line retailer** selling 230,000 music and video products. As well as selling through its site invs.com, it handles **on-line retailing** for partners that include Sony.
"

ono *adv (abbr **or nearest offer**)* à débattre

on-pack *adj* □ *Mktg* **on-pack offer** prime *f* différée; **on-pack promotion** promotion *f* "on-pack"

on-screen *Comptr* **1** *adj* à l'écran □ **on-screen help** aide *f* en ligne
2 *adv* sur (l')écran; **to work on-screen** travailler sur écran

on-target earnings *npl* salaire *m* de base plus commissions

on-the-job *adj (training, experience)* sur le tas

OPEC *n (abbr **Organization of Petroleum Exporting Countries**)* OPEP *f*

open **1** *adj* ouvert(e) □ *Fin* **open account** compte *m* ouvert; **open cheque** chèque *m* ouvert *ou* non barré; *St Exch* **open contract** position *f* ouverte; *Ins* **open cover** traité *m* facultatif obligatoire; **open credit** crédit *m* à découvert; **open economy** économie *f* ouverte; **open file** dossier *m* ouvert; *Tel* **open line** ligne *f* ouverte; *Econ* **open market** marché *m* libre; *St Exch* **to buy shares on the open market** acheter des actions en Bourse; **open money market** marché libre des capitaux; *St Exch* **open outcry** criée *f*; *Ins* **open policy** police *f* flottante; **open port** port *m* ouvert; *St Exch* **open position** position ouverte; *Mktg* **open question** *(in survey)* question *f* ouverte; *Ind* **open shop** *Br (open to non-union members)* = entreprise ne pratiquant pas le monopole d'embauche; *Am (with no union)* établissement *m* sans syndicat; **open ticket** billet *m* open
2 *vt* ouvrir; *(negotiations, conversation, debate)* entamer; **to open a line of credit** ouvrir un crédit; **to open a loan** ouvrir un emprunt
3 *vi* **(a)** *(of shop, business)* ouvrir **(b)** *St Exch* coter à l'ouverture; **the FTSE opened at 4083** l'indice FTa ouvert à 4083

"
However, Mills recognized that most businesses would still prefer the **open shop**, but argued that sophisticated conservatives, if forced to recognize unions and make concessions on wages and working conditions, would in return try to use labor leaders as a tool to repress rank-and-file discontent.
"

▸ **open up** **1** *vt sep (office, shop)* ouvrir; **to open up a country to trade** ouvrir un pays au commerce
2 *vi (of office, shop)* ouvrir

open-door policy *n (for importing goods)* politique *f* de la porte ouverte

open-ended *adj (agreement, mortgage)* sans date limite □ **open-ended contract** contrat *m* à durée indéterminée; **open-ended credit** crédit *m* à durée indéterminée; **open-ended invest-**

ment company société *f* d'investissement à capital variable, sicav *f*; *Mktg* **open-ended question** question *f* ouverte; **open-ended trust** société d'investissement à capital variable, sicav

opening *n* (**a**) *(of shop, office, account, credit, negotiations)* ouverture *f* ❑ *Acct* **opening balance** solde *m* d'ouverture; *Acct* **opening balance sheet** bilan *m* d'ouverture; *Acct* **opening entry** écriture *f* d'ouverture; **opening hours** heures *fpl* d'ouverture; *Acct* **opening stock** stock *m* initial *ou* d'ouverture

(**b**) *(opportunity)* occasion *f* favorable; *(job)* débouché *m*; *(in market)* débouché; **there are lots of good openings in industry** l'industrie offre de nombreux débouchés intéressants; **we have exploited an opening in the market** nous avons exploité une ouverture sur le marché; **there's an opening with Lakeland Ltd** il y a un poste vacant chez Lakeland Ltd

(**c**) *St Exch* **opening day** jour *m* d'ouverture; **opening price** *(at start of trading)* cours *m* d'ouverture, premier cours; *(of new shares)* cours d'introduction; **opening range** fourchette *f* de cours d'ouverture; **opening session** séance *f* d'ouverture; **opening transaction** opération *f* d'ouverture

open-market *adj* **open-market policy** politique *f* d'open-market; **open-market value** valeur *f* au marché libre

open-plan office *n* bureau *m* paysager

operate 1 *vt* (**a**) *(machine)* faire fonctionner

(**b**) *(business)* gérer, diriger; **she operates her business from home** elle fait marcher son affaire depuis son domicile

2 *vi* (**a**) *(of machine)* fonctionner

(**b**) *(be active)* opérer; **the factory is operating at full capacity** l'usine tourne à plein rendement; **the company operates out of Chicago** le siège de la société est à Chicago; **the company operates in ten countries** la société est implantée dans dix pays

(**c**) *(be in effect)* être en vigueur; **the pay rise will operate from 1 January** l'augmentation des salaires entrera en vigueur le 1er janvier; **the rule doesn't operate in such cases** la règle ne s'applique pas à de tels cas

operating *adj* d'exploitation; **the factory has reached full operating capacity** l'usine a atteint sa pleine capacité de production ❑ *Am* **operating account** compte *m* d'exploitation; **operating assets** actif *m* d'exploitation; **operating budget** budget *m* d'exploitation; *Am* **operating capital** capital *m* d'exploitation *ou* de roulement; **operating cash flow** cash-flow *m* disponible; **operating cost** charge *f* opérationnelle; **operating costs** frais *mpl* *ou* coûts *mpl* d'exploitation; **operating costs analysis** comptabilité *f* analytique d'exploitation; **oper-**

ating cycle cycle *m* d'exploitation; **operating deficit** déficit *m* d'exploitation; **operating expenses** frais d'exploitation; **operating free cash flow** free cash-flow *m* opérationnel; **operating income** résultat *m* d'exploitation; **operating leverage** levier *m* d'exploitation; **operating loss** perte *f* d'exploitation; **operating margin** marge *f* (nette) d'exploitation; **operating monopoly** monopole *m* d'exploitation; **operating officer** agent *m* d'exploitation; **operating process** procédé *m* de travail; **operating profit** bénéfice *m* d'exploitation; **operating ratio** coefficient *m* d'exploitation; **operating rules** règles *fpl* d'exploitation; **operating statement** rapport *m* d'exploitation; **operating subsidy** subvention *f* d'exploitation; *Comptr* **operating system** système *m* d'exploitation; *Comptr* **operating system command** commande *f* système d'exploitation; *Comptr* **operating system software** logiciel *m* de système d'exploitation

operation *n* (**a**) *(functioning)* *(of machine, device)* fonctionnement *m*, marche *f*; *(of process, system)* fonctionnement; *(of market force)* action *f*; **to be in operation** *(of machine)* être en service; *(of company)* être en activité; *(of law, regulation)* être en vigueur; **the plant is in operation round the clock** l'usine fonctionne 24 heures sur 24; **to put sth into operation** *(machine)* mettre qch en service; *(plan)* mettre qch en application; *(law, regulation)* faire entrer qch en vigueur

(**b**) *(act, activity, deal)* opération *f*; **they are to close down their operations in Mexico** ils vont mettre un terme à leurs opérations *ou* activités au Mexique; **the company is moving its soft drinks operation** la société déménage sa branche de boissons non alcoolisées ❑ **operations breakdown** décomposition *f* des tâches; **operations management** gestion *f* d'exploitation; **operations manager** directeur(trice) *m,f* d'exploitation; **operations strategy** stratégie *f* opérationnelle

(**c**) *(running, management)* *(of company)* gestion *f*; *(of machine device)* fonctionnement *m*; *(of process, system)* application *f*

(**d**) *(company)* entreprise *f*, société *f*

(**e**) *Mktg (campaign)* opération *f*

operational *adj* opérationnel(elle); **the design team was operational within six months** en l'espace de six mois, l'équipe de dessinateurs était opérationnelle ❑ **operational audit** audit *m* opérationnel; **operational costs** coûts *mpl* opérationnels *ou* d'exploitation; *Acct* **operational cost accounting** comptabilité *f* analytique d'exploitation; *Acct* **operational cost accounts** comptes *mpl* analytiques d'exploitation; *Acct* **operational cost centre** centre *m* d'analyse opérationnel; **operational efficiency** efficacité *f* opérationnelle; **operational marketing** marketing *m* opérationnel; **operational**

planning planification *f* des opérations; ***operational research*** recherche *f* opérationnelle

operative 1 *n* *(manual worker)* ouvrier(ère) *m,f* **2** *adj* (**a**) *(law, rule, regulation)* en vigueur; **to become operative** entrer en vigueur, prendre effet (**b**) *(system, scheme)* opérationnel(elle); **the system will soon be operative** le système sera bientôt opérationnel

operator *n* (**a**) *Tel* opérateur(trice) *m,f*; **(switchboard) operator** standardiste *mf* (**b**) *(of machine)* opérateur(trice) *m,f* (**c**) *(director)* directeur(trice) *m,f*, dirigeant(e) *m,f*; *(organizer)* organisateur(trice) *m,f*; **there are too many small operators in real estate** l'immobilier compte trop de petites entreprises (**d**) *St Exch* opérateur(trice) *m,f*; **operator for a fall/rise** opérateur à la baisse/hausse

opinion *n* *Mktg* **opinion former, opinion leader** leader *m* d'opinion, préconisateur *m*; **opinion measurement** sondage *m* d'opinion; **opinion measurement technique** technique *f* de sondage d'opinion; **opinion poll** sondage (d'opinion), enquête *f* (d'opinion); **opinion survey** sondage (d'opinion), enquête (d'opinion)

opportunity *n* (**a**) *(chance)* perspective *f*; **the opportunities for advancement are excellent** les perspectives d'avancement sont excellentes (**b**) *Mktg* opportunité *f*; **opportunities and threats** opportunités *fpl* et menaces *fpl*; □ *Econ* **opportunity cost** coût *m* d'opportunité *ou* de renoncement; *Mktg* **opportunity to hear** occasion *f* d'entendre; *Mktg* **opportunity and issue analysis** analyse *f* des attraits et des atouts; *Mktg* **opportunity to see** occasion de voir; *Mktg* **opportunity and threat analysis** analyse des opportunités et des menaces

> ❝
>
> As if economic turmoil, fickle consumers, the rival popularity of computer games and rising music piracy were not enough, the music industry is now faced with **opportunities and threats** presented by the Internet.
>
> ❞

opposite number *n* *(person)* interlocuteur(-trice) *m,f*

opposition *n* *(competitors)* concurrence *f*

▶ **opt in** *vi* décider de participer

▶ **opt into** *vt insep* décider de participer à; **to opt into an association/the EU** entrer dans une association/l'Union européenne

▶ **opt out** *vi* se désengager, se retirer; **many opted out of joining the union** beaucoup ont choisi de ne pas adhérer au syndicat

optical *Comptr adj* optique □ **optical character reader** lecteur *m* optique de caractères; **optical character recognition** reconnaissance *f* op-

tique des caractères; **optical disk** disque *m* optique; **optical drive** lecteur optique; **optical fibres** fibres *fpl* optiques; **optical mouse** souris *f* optique; **optical reader** lecteur optique; **optical reading** lecture *f* optique; **optical scanner** scanneur *m* optique

optimal *adj* optimal(e), optimum □ *Mktg* **optimal price** prix *m* optimum; *Mktg* **optimal psychological price** prix psychologique optimum; **optimal resource allocation** répartition *f* optimale des ressources

optimizer *n* *Comptr* optimiseur *m*

optimum 1 *n* optimum *m*
2 *adj* optimum, optimal(e) □ **optimum conditions** conditions *fpl* optimales; **optimum employment of resources** emploi *m* optimum des ressources

option *n* (**a**) *St Exch* option *f*, (marché *m* à) prime *f*; **to take an option (on sth)** prendre une option (sur qch); **to take up an option** lever une option; **to declare an option** répondre à une option □ **option to buy** option d'achat; **option day** (jour *m* de la) réponse *f* des primes; **option deal** opération *f* à prime; **options desk** desk *m* d'options; **option to double** option du double; **options market** marché *m* à options *ou* à primes; **option money** montant *m* de la prime *f*; **option price** prix de l'option, prime; **option to sell** option de vente; **option on shares** option sur actions; **option spread** écart *m* de prime; **options trading** négociations *fpl* à prime (**b**) *Comptr* option *f* □ **option box** case *f* d'option; **option button** case d'option; **option key** touche *f* Option; **options menu** menu *f* des options

optional *adj* facultatif(ive) □ **optional extra** (accessoire *m* en) option *f*

optional-feature pricing *n* *Mktg* fixation *f* du prix en fonction des options

optionee *n* *St Exch* bénéficiaire *mf* d'options

order 1 *n* (**a**) *(request for goods)* commande *f*; *(goods ordered)* marchandises *fpl* commandées; **to place an order (with sb/for sth)** passer une commande (à qn/de qch); **to make sth to order** faire qch sur commande; **to deliver an order** livrer une commande; **to fill an order** exécuter une commande; **as per order** conformément à votre commande; **another company got the order** ils ont passé la commande auprès d'une autre société; **the goods are on order** les marchandises ont été commandées □ **order book** carnet *m* de commandes; *St Exch* **order to buy** ordre *m* d'achat; **order cycle** cycle *m* de commande; **order cycle time** durée *f* du cycle de commande; **order department** service *m* des commandes; **order flowchart** tableau *m* d'avancement de commandes; **order form** bon *m* de commande; **order number** numéro *m* de commande; *St Exch* **order to sell** ordre de vente (**b**) *(command)* ordre *m*; *(instruction)* instruction *f*; **to give sb orders to do sth** ordonner à qn de faire qch

(**c**) *Fin (document)* mandat *m*; **cheque to order** chèque *m* à ordre; **pay to the order of J. Martin** payez à l'ordre de J. Martin; **pay J. Martin or order** payez à J. Martin ou à son ordre; **by order and for account of J. Martin** d'ordre et pour compte de J. Martin ❑ *order to pay* mandat de paiement

(**d**) *(condition)* **in (good) working order** en (bon) état de fonctionnement *ou* de marche; **out of order** *(telephone)* en dérangement; *(lift, machine)* hors service

(**e**) *Law* ordonnance *f*, arrêté *m*; **he was served with an order for the seizure of his property** il a reçu une ordonnance pour la saisie de ses biens

2 *vt* (**a**) *(goods)* commander

(**b**) *(command)* **to order sb to do sth** commander à qn de faire qch; *Law* **he was ordered to pay costs** il a été condamné aux dépens

order-driven *adj St Exch (market)* dirigé(e) par les ordres

order-to-remittance-cycle *n* cycle *m* commande-livraison-facturation

ordinary *adj Acct* **ordinary activities** *(balance sheet item)* opérations *fpl* courantes; *Fin* **ordinary creditor** créancier(ère) *m,f* ordinaire; **ordinary rate** *(of postage)* tarif *m* normal; *Br Fin, St Exch* **ordinary share** action *f* ordinaire; *Br Fin, St Exch* **ordinary share capital** capital *m* en actions ordinaires

.org *Comptr* = abréviation désignant les organisations à but non lucratif dans les adresses électroniques

organic growth *n* croissance *f* interne

> **❝**
> If Mr Webster manages to resolve the Galileo issue and bind easyJet and Go together, easyJet has a good deal on its hands. It is not paying too much cash, but relying on its high share price to finance the deal. In one fell swoop, easyJet collects more routes and more aircraft, whereas it would have taken much longer to reach the same size through **organic growth**.
> **❞**

---

organigram *n* organigramme *m*

organization *n* (**a**) *(running)* organisation *f*; **we are unhappy with the organization of the company** l'organisation de la société ne nous satisfait pas ❑ *organization chart* organigramme *m*; **organization and methods** méthodes *fpl* et organisation; **organization tree** organigramme en arborescence

(**b**) *(association)* organisation *f*, association *f*; *(official body)* organisme *m*, organisation ❑ *Or-*

ganization for Economic Cooperation and Development Organisation de Coopération et de Développement économiques

(**c**) *Admin (personnel)* cadres *mpl*

(**d**) *Ind (of labour)* syndicalisation *f*

organizational *adj (skills, methods)* organisationnel(elle), d'organisation; *(expenses)* d'organisation ❑ *Econ* **organizational behaviour** comportement *m* de l'individu au sein d'une organisation; **organizational buyer** acheteur(euse) *m,f (pour une organisation)*; **organizational chart** organigramme *m*; **organizational marketer** mercaticien(enne) *m,f* au sein d'une organisation

organize 1 *vt* (**a**) *(put into order)* organiser (**b**) *Ind (workers)* syndiquer ❑ *organized labour* main-d'œuvre *f* syndiquée

2 *vi Ind (of workers)* se syndiquer

organizer *n* organisateur(trice) *m,f*

organizing *n* organisation *f* ❑ *organizing committee* comité *m* d'organisation

origin *n* origine *f*; **country of origin** pays *m* d'origine ❑ *origin of goods label* marque *f* d'origine

original 1 *n (of document)* original *m*; *Fin (of bill of exchange)* primata *m*

2 *adj* original(e) ❑ *Fin* **original capital** capital *m* d'origine; **original cost** coût *m* initial; *Acct* **original document** pièce *f* comptable; **original equipment** constructeur *m* de systèmes originaux; **original invoice** facture *f* originale; *Acct* **original issue discount bond** obligation *f* à prime d'émission; **original packaging** emballage *m* d'origine; **original value** valeur *f* initiale *ou* d'origine

OS *n Comptr (abbr* **operating system***)* système *m* d'exploitation

O/S *adj (abbr* **out of stock***)* épuisé(e)

OSHA *n (abbr* **Occupational Safety and Health Administration***)* = aux États-Unis, direction de la sécurité et de l'hygiène au travail

OTC *adj St Exch (abbr* **over-the-counter***)* hors cote

OTE *npl (abbr* **on-target earnings***)* salaire *m* de base plus commissions

OTH *n Mktg (abbr* **opportunity to hear***)* ODE *f*

OTS *n Mktg (abbr* **opportunity to see***)* ODV *f*

out 1 *adj Acct* **out book** livre *m* du dehors; *Comptr* **out box** *(for e-mail)* boîte *f* d'envoi

2 *adv* **to be out (on strike)** faire grève

outage *n (goods lost)* pertes *fpl*, marchandises *fpl* perdues *(pendant le stockage ou le transport)*

outbid *vt (at auction)* enchérir sur

outbound freight *n* fret *m* de sortie

outflow *n Fin (of gold, currency)* sortie *f*; **outflow per hour** débit *m* par heure

outgoing *adj* (**a**) *(departing) (government, minister, tenant)* sortant(e); *(following resignation)* démissionnaire (**b**) *(train, ship, plane)* en partance; *(mail)* à expédier, au départ; *(telephone call)* sortant(e) ❏ **outgoing inventory** inventaire *m* de sortie; **outgoing shift** équipe *f* sortante

outgoings *npl* dépenses *fpl*, décaissements *mpl*; **the outgoings exceed the incomings** les dépenses excèdent les recettes

outlay 1 *n (expenditure)* frais *mpl*, dépenses *fpl*; *(investment)* investissement *m*; **to get back** *or* **recover one's outlay** rentrer dans ses fonds **2** *vt (spend)* dépenser; *(invest)* investir; **to outlay $10,000 capital** faire une mise de fonds de 10 000 dollars

outlet *n (market)* débouché *m*; *(point of sale)* point *m* de vente; **there are not many sales outlets in Japan** le Japon offre peu de débouchés commerciaux; **our North American outlets** notre réseau (de distribution) en Amérique du Nord ❏ **outlet village** = centre commercial spécialisé dans les marques à prix réduit

outlook *n* horizon *m*, perspectives *fpl* (d'avenir)

>
> She too is concerned about the impact of this upon the **outlook** for the economy – with ABN forecasting GDP growth to decline marginally to 2.4% in 2002, from 2.5% in 2001 – but she notes that this is the first currency crisis that Mboweni has faced in his year of office so far, which could make him particularly susceptible to a knee-jerk reaction.
>

out-of-court settlement *n Law* règlement *m* à l'amiable

out-of-pocket expenses *npl* menues dépenses *fpl*

out-of-the-money option *n St Exch* option *f* en dehors

out-of-town *adj (retail park, development)* = situé à la périphérie d'une ville

outplacement *n* outplacement *m*, = aide à la recherche d'un nouvel emploi, fournie par l'employeur lors d'un licenciement

>
> **Outplacement** services provide a solution to organizational changes that result in the discharge or displacement of employees. E-Cruiter.com's Allen And Associates division provides professional assistance to people seeking to re-enter the job market following corporate downsizing. **Outplacement** services are a key part of the rapidly growing HCM market, which according to leading industry analysts is expected to reach $200 billion by 2003.
>

output 1 *n* (**a**) *(of factory, worker)* production *f*, rendement *m*; *(of machine)* débit *m*, rendement; **this represents 25 percent of the total output** cela représente 25 pour cent de la production totale; **our output is not keeping pace with demand** notre production est insuffisante pour répondre à la demande; **this machine has an output of 6,000 items per hour** cette machine débite 6000 pièces à l'heure; **output per hour** rendement à l'heure, rendement horaire; **output per person** rendement individuel ❏ **output bonus** prime *f* de rendement; **output ceiling** plafond *m* de la production; **output ratio** coefficient *m* de capital; *Acct* **output tax** TVA *f* encaissée, impôt *m* sur la consommation (**b**) *Comptr (of data, information)* sortie *f* ❏ **output buffer** mémoire *f* tampon de sortie; **output device** dispositif *m* ou périphérique *m* de sortie; **output file** fichier *m* de sortie; **output formatting** mise *f* en forme de sortie; **output medium** support *m* de sortie; **output port** port *m* de sortie

2 *vt* (**a**) *(of factory, worker, machine)* produire (**b**) *Comptr (data, information)* sortir (**to** sur)

outreach *n Admin* = recherche des personnes qui ne demandent pas l'aide sociale dont elles pourraient bénéficier ❏ **outreach worker** = employé ou bénévole dans un bureau d'aide sociale

>
> An equalities panel has been appointed to consider issues for the small ethnic minority population in the area, and an equalities officer has begun work. For lone parents, projects are being set up with family centres and there are plans to set up an **outreach** service to help lone parents towards jobs, benefits and better health care.
>

outright *adv* **to buy sth outright** *(for cash)* acheter qch au comptant; *(totally)* acheter qch en bloc

outsell *vt (of goods)* se vendre mieux que; *(of retailer)* vendre plus que; **the brand of cigarettes that outsells all the others** la marque de cigarettes la plus vendue

outside *adj* (**a**) **outside worker** travailleur(euse) *m,f* à domicile (**b**) *St Exch* **outside broker** courtier(ère) *m,f* libre; **outside brokerage** affaires *fpl* de banque; **outside market** marché *m* hors cote *ou* en coulisse; **outside price** prix *m* maximum (**c**) *Tel* **outside line** ligne *f* extérieure

outsider *n St Exch* courtier(ère) *m,f* marron

outsource *vt* externaliser; **computer mainte-nance has been outsourced to another com-pany** l'entretien du matériel informatique a été externalisé

outsourcing *n* externalisation *f*

> **"**
>
> Organizations are increasingly turning to **outsourcing** in an attempt to enhance their competitiveness. Chrysler, for example, out-sources 100% of the manufacture of half of its minicompact and subcompact cars. Furthermore, Chrysler and Ford currently produce less than one-half of the value of all their vehicles in-house. Similarly, Boeing has begun to rely more heavily on **outsour-cing** partners to manufacture its aircraft.
>
> **"**

outstanding *adj (business)* en suspens; *(amount, account)* impayé(e), dû (due); *(pay-ment)* en retard; *(invoice)* en souffrance; *(inter-est)* échu(e) □ *outstanding balance* solde *m* à découvert; *Banking* **outstanding cheque** chèque *m* en circulation; **outstanding credits** encours *m* de crédit; **outstanding debts** créan-ces *fpl* (à recouvrer); **outstanding rent** arriérés *mpl* de loyer; **outstanding shares** actions *fpl* en cours *ou* en circulation

out-supplier *n* fournisseur *m* potentiel

out-tray *n* corbeille *f* du courrier à expédier

outturn *n Fin* rendement *m*

> **"**
>
> Helped mainly by better than expected fis-cal revenues and also lower interest pay-ments, the fiscal **outturn** for 1999 was just below the initial target of 2 percent of GDP.
>
> **"**

outward *adj* **outward bill of lading** connais-sement *m* de sortie; **outward cargo** cargaison *f* d'aller; **outward freight** fret *m* de sortie; *Econ* **outward investment** investissement *m* à l'étranger; **outward mail** courrier *m* (en par-tance) pour l'étranger; **outward manifest** ma-nifeste *m* de sortie; **outward mission** mission *f* à l'étranger; **outward voyage** voyage *m* d'aller

outwork *n* travail *m* fait à domicile

outworker *n* travailleur(euse) *m,f* à domicile

outyear 1 *n* = année suivant l'exercice budgé-taire
2 *adj* = de l'année suivant l'exercice budgétaire

overage *n Am* excédent *m*, surplus *m*

overall *adj* global(e); *(size, area)* total(e); **she has overall responsibility for sales** elle est res-ponsable de l'ensemble du service des ventes □ *overall budget* budget *m* global; *overall con-sumption* consommation *f* totale; *overall de-mand* demande *f* globale; *overall objective*

objectif *m* global; *overall plan* plan *m* d'en-semble

overassess *vt Fin* surimposer

overassessment *n Fin* surimposition *f*

overbid 1 *n* surenchère *f*
2 *vt* enchérir sur
3 *vi* surenchérir

overbook 1 *vt (flight, hotel)* surréserver
2 *vi (of airline, hotel)* surréserver

overbooking *n* surréservation *f*

overborrow *vi (of company)* emprunter de fa-çon excessive

overborrowed *adj (of company)* surendet-té(e)

overborrowing *n (of company)* surendette-ment *m*

overbought *adj St Exch (market)* suréva-lué(e), suracheté(e)

> **"**
>
> Mr Greenspan's dilemma is that he would probably like to raise interest rates – inflation indicators from the labour market are mixed but the productivity miracle cannot continue for ever while signals from the energy sector are less equivocal. He would also like to see the US stock markets down from their cur-rent **overbought** levels. But he must achieve both without causing a nervous market to panic.
>
> **"**

overbuy *vt St Exch (market)* surévaluer, sura-cheter

overcapacity *n Econ* surcapacité *f*

overcapitalization *n Fin* surcapitalisation *f*

overcapitalize *vt Fin* surcapitaliser

overcharge 1 *vt (person)* faire payer trop cher à; *(goods)* survendre; **they overcharged me for the repair** ils m'ont pris trop cher pour la ré-paration
2 *vi* faire payer trop cher

overconsumption *n Econ* surconsommation *f*

overdemand *n* demande *f* excédentaire

overdevelop *vt Econ* surdévelopper

overdevelopment *n Econ* surdéveloppe-ment *m*

overdraft *n Banking* découvert *m*; **to have an overdraft** avoir un découvert; **to allow sb an overdraft** accorder à qn un découvert; **to pay off one's overdraft** rembourser son découvert □ *overdraft facility* autorisation *f* de décou-vert, facilités *fpl* de caisse; *overdraft limit* pla-fond *m* de découvert; *overdraft loan* prêt *m* à découvert

overdraw *Banking* **1** *vt (account)* mettre à découvert; **to be overdrawn** avoir un découvert, être à découvert; **your account is overdrawn** votre compte est débiteur *ou* à découvert; **I'm £100 overdrawn** j'ai un découvert de 100 livres ◻ *overdrawn account* compte *m* à découvert
2 *vi* tirer à découvert

overdue *adj (account)* en retard, impayé(e); *(payment)* en retard, en souffrance; **our repayments are two months overdue** nous avons un retard de deux mois dans nos remboursements ◻ *Fin* **overdue bill** effet *m* en souffrance

overemployment *n Econ* suremploi *m*

overestimate *vt (assets)* majorer; *(item)* surévaluer, surestimer la valeur de

overextend *vt Fin* **to overextend oneself** s'engager au-dessus de ses moyens

overflow *n Comptr (of data)* dépassement *m* de capacité

overfreight *n* poids *m* en excès

overfunding *n* déflation *f* budgétaire

overgear *vt Fin* surendetter; **to be overgeared** être surendetté

overgearing *n Fin* surendettement *m*

overhead **1** *n* charge *f* opérationnelle; *Br* **overheads,** *Am* **overhead** frais *mpl* généraux ◻ *Acct* **overhead absorption rate** taux *m* d'amortissement des frais généraux; **overhead budget** budget *m* des charges; **overhead costs, overhead expenses** frais généraux; *Fin* **overhead variance** variance *f* des frais généraux
2 *adj* **overhead projector** rétroprojecteur *m*

overindustrialization *n* surindustrialisation *f*

overinsurance *n* surassurance *f*

overinsure *vt* surassurer

overinvest *Fin* **1** *vt* trop investir
2 *vi* trop investir, surinvestir (**in** dans)

overinvestment *n Fin* surinvestissement *m*

overissue **1** *n (of paper money)* surémission *f*
2 *vt (paper money)* faire une surémission de

overlap *n Mktg* débordement *m*

overload *vt (market)* surcharger

overmanned *adj* en sureffectif

overmanning *n* sureffectifs *mpl*

overnight *adj Fin* **overnight loan** prêt *m* du jour au lendemain; **overnight rate** taux *m* de l'argent au jour le jour

overpackaging *n Mktg* suremballage *m*

overpay *vt* surpayer, trop payer

overpayment *n (of taxes)* trop-perçu *m*; *(of employee)* rémunération *f* excessive

overperform *vi St Exch (of shares)* avoir un cours anormalement élevé

over-position *vt Mktg* surpositionner

over-positioning *n Mktg* surpositionnement *m*

overprice *vt* vendre trop cher

overpriced *adj* trop cher (chère)

overproduce *vt & vi* surproduire

overproduction *n* surproduction *f*

overrate *vt Admin* surtaxer

override *vt (instruction, authority)* passer outre à, outrepasser; *(decision)* annuler; *(factor)* l'emporter sur

overriding *adj (importance)* primordial(e), capital(e); *(factor)* prépondérant(e) ◻ *Law* **overriding clause** clause *f* dérogatoire; **overriding commission** *(paid to broker)* commission *f* spéciale *ou* d'arrangement

overrun *n* (**a**) *(in cost)* dépassement *m* du budget (**b**) *(in production)* excédent *m*, surplus *m*

overseas **1** *adj* d'outremer, étranger(ère) ◻ *overseas agent* représentant(e) *m,f* à l'étranger; *overseas business* = affaires réalisées avec l'étranger; *overseas debt* dette *f* extérieure; *overseas development* développement *m* outre-mer; *Br* **Overseas Development Administration** = organisme d'aide au pays en voie de développement; *overseas investment* investissement *m* étranger; *overseas market* marché *m* étranger *ou* extérieur *ou* d'outremer; *Am* **Overseas Trade Department** ≃ ministère *m* du Commerce extérieur; *Am* **Overseas Trade Minister** ≃ ministre *m* du Commerce extérieur
2 *adv* à l'étranger

oversold *adj St Exch (market)* sousévalué(e)

overspend **1** *n* dépenses *fpl* excessives
2 *vt (allowance, budget)* dépenser au-delà de, dépasser; *(money)* dépenser trop de
3 *vi* dépenser trop d'argent, dépasser le budget

overspending *n* dépassement *m* budgétaire

overstaffed *adj* en sureffectif

overstaffing *n* sureffectifs *mpl*

overstock **1** *n Am* **overstocks** surplus *m*, excédent *m*
2 *vt (market)* encombrer; *(warehouse)* trop approvisionner (**with** de)

overstocked *adj (market)* encombré(e); *(warehouse)* trop approvisionné(e); **the market is overstocked with foreign goods** le marché regorge de marchandises étrangères

oversubscribe *vt Fin, St Exch (loan, share issue)* sursouscrire; **the share issue was oversubscribed** l'offre d'actions a été sursouscrite

oversubscription *n Fin, St Exch (of loan, share issue)* sursouscription *f*

overtax *vt Fin (goods)* surtaxer; *(person)* surtaxer, surimposer

overtaxation *n Fin* surimposition *f*

over-the-counter *adj Am St Exch* hors cote ❑ *over-the-counter market* marché *m* hors cote

overtime *n* **(a)** *(work)* heures *fpl* supplémentaires; **to do** *or* **work overtime** faire des heures supplémentaires; **an hour's overtime** une heure supplémentaire; **the salary does not include overtime** les heures supplémentaires ne sont pas comprises *ou* comptées dans le salaire ❑ *overtime ban* refus *m* de faire des heures supplémentaires; *overtime pay* rémunération *f* des heures supplémentaires; *overtime rate* tarif *m* des heures supplémentaires

(b) *(pay)* rémunération *f* des heures supplémentaires; **after 6pm we're on overtime** après 18h, on nous paie en heures supplémentaires; **to be paid overtime** être payé en heures supplémentaires

> **"**
>
> National long distance services were hit earlier this week as Indian Telecom Service workers took action because of concern about the Indian Telecom Department's corporatization on October 1. According to local media reports, officials agreed on Thursday to cancel an **overtime ban** – that had seen workers leave their jobs each day at 5pm – and put in extra hours.
>
> **"**

overtrade *vi* avoir une marge d'exploitation trop étroite

overtrading *n* = emballement de l'activité d'une entreprise (au-delà des limites de son capital)

overvaluation *n* surévaluation *f*

overvalue 1 *n (of currency)* survaleur *f*
   2 *vt (assets)* surestimer, majorer; *(object,*

currency) surévaluer

overweight 1 *n* surpoids *m*, poids *m* en excès
   2 *adj (luggage, parcel)* au-dessus du poids réglementaire

overwithhold *vt Am (tax)* retenir trop de

overwrite *Comptr* **1** *n* **overwrite mode** mode *m* de superposition
   2 *vt (file)* écraser

owe *vt* devoir; **to owe sb sth, to owe sth to sb** devoir qch à qn; **the sum owed to her** le montant qui lui est dû

owing *adj* dû (due); **all the money owing to me** tout l'argent qui m'est dû; **to have a lot of money owing** *(to owe)* devoir beaucoup d'argent; *(to be owed)* avoir beaucoup d'argent à récupérer

own *vt* posséder; **50 percent owned company** société détenue à 50 pour cent

own-brand *Mktg* **1** *n* marque *f* de distributeur
   2 *adj* **own-brand label** marque *f* de distributeur; **own-brand product** produit *m* à marque de distributeur

own-branding *n Mktg* apposition *f* de sa propre marque

owner *n* propriétaire *mf* ❑ *Acct* **owner's capital account** compte *m* de l'exploitant

owner-occupied *adj* occupé(e) par le propriétaire

owner-occupier *n* propriétaire *mf* occupant(e)

ownership *n* propriété *f*; **under new ownership** *(sign)* changement de propriétaire; **to be in private/public ownership** appartenir au secteur privé/public

own-label *adj* à marque de distributeur ❑ *own-label brand* marque *f* de distributeur

Pp

P *n* **the four Ps** les quatre P, le marketing mix

> The Marketing Mix may effectively be described and analysed on the basis of the **Four Ps**. These are: PRODUCT PRICE PLACE PROMOTION.

P2P *adj* (*abbr* **peer to peer**) P2P

PA *n* (**a**) (*abbr* **personal assistant**) (*of executive*) assistant(e) *m,f*; (*with secretarial duties*) secrétaire *mf* de direction (**b**) (*abbr* **Press Association**) = agence de presse britannique

p.a. *adv* (*abbr* **per annum**) par an

pack 1 *n* paquet *m*
 2 *vt* (**a**) (*goods*) emballer, empaqueter (**b**) *Comptr* (*database*) condenser, compacter

package 1 *n* (**a**) (*set of proposals*) ensemble *m*; (*contract*) contrat *m* global; **the package includes a company car** l'offre comprend une voiture de société; **the offer is part of a larger package** l'offre fait partie d'un ensemble plus important; **a new package of measures to halt inflation** un nouvel ensemble visant à stopper l'inflation; **we offered them a generous package worth over £100,000** nous leur avons proposé un contrat global très avantageux de plus de 100 000 livres ◻ *package deal* offre *f* globale; **the package deal put forward by the management** l'ensemble des mesures proposées par la direction; **we bought up the lot in a package deal** nous avons tout acheté en un seul lot
 (**b**) *Comptr* (*software*) logiciel *m*
 (**c**) (*parcel*) paquet *m*, colis *m*
 2 *vt* emballer, conditionner; **each item is individually packaged** chaque article est conditionné *ou* emballé séparément

packaged *adj* emballé(e), conditionné(e)

packaging *n* emballage *m* ◻ *packaging charges, packaging costs* frais *mpl* d'emballage

packet *n* (**a**) (*box*) paquet *m*; (*bag, envelope*) sachet *m* (**b**) *Comptr* (*of data*) paquet *m* ◻ *packet switching* commutation *f* de paquets

packing *n* emballage *m*; **postage and packing** frais *mpl* d'emballage et d'envoi ◻ *packing case* caisse *f* *ou* boîte *f* d'emballage; *packing charges, packing costs* frais d'emballage; *packing list* liste *f* de colisage; *packing materials* matériaux *mpl* d'emballage; *packing slip* bon *m* de livraison

Pac Man defense *n Am Fam* contre-OPA *f*

> In a classic **Pac Man defense**, Elf responded to TOTAL FINA's unsolicited offer with a $55 billion counter offer. Jones Day worked with TOTAL FINA to prevent Elf from holding a special shareholders meeting to increase the company's capital to pay for its TOTAL FINA offer — a critical step in defeating the Pac Man offer. Negotiations between the two companies ended when Elf finally accepted an increased offer of $58 billion from TOTAL FINA.

pad *n* (*writing*) **pad** bloc *m*

page[1] *n* (*of book, document, computer file, website*) page *f*; **the business pages** (*in newspaper*) la section économie ◻ *page break* saut *m* de page; *Comptr* *page description language* langage *m* de description de page; *page design* mise *f* en page; *Comptr* *page down* page suivante; *Comptr* *page down key* touche *f* page suivante; *page format* format *m* de page; *Comptr* *page layout* mise en page; *Comptr* *page preview* visualisation *f* de la page à l'écran; *Comptr* *page printer* imprimante *f* page par page, imprimante par pages; *Comptr* *page printer language* langage d'imprimante par pages; *Comptr* *page scanner* lecteur *m* de pages; *Comptr* *page set-up* format de page; *Comptr* *page up* page précédente; *Comptr* *page up key* touche page précédente

▶ **page down** *vi Comptr* feuilleter en avant

▶ **page up** *vi Comptr* feuilleter en arrière

page[2] *vt* (*by loudspeaker*) appeler par haut-parleur; (*by electronic device*) biper; **I'm having her paged** je la fais appeler

pager *n* récepteur *m* d'appels

paginate *vt* paginer

pagination *n* pagination *f*

paid *adj* (**a**) (*person, work*) payé(e), rémunéré(e); **to get paid maternity/sick leave** avoir droit aux congés de maternité/de maladie ◻ *paid holidays* congés *mpl* payés (**b**) (*goods, bill*) payé(e); **paid** (*on bill*) pour acquit ◻ *Acct* *paid cash book* main *f* courante de dépenses

paid-up adj (member) qui a payé sa cotisation ❑ Fin **paid-up capital** capital m versé; **paid-up shares** actions fpl libérées; **paid-up share capital** capital appelé et libéré

paint program n Comptr programme m de dessin bitmap

paired comparison n Mktg comparaison f par paire

palette n Comptr palette f

pallet n palette f ❑ **pallet truck** transpalette f

palletization n palettisation f

palletize vt palettiser ❑ **palletized goods** marchandises fpl sur palette(s)

palletizer n palettiseur m

palmtop n Comptr ordinateur m de poche

pamphlet n brochure f

P & L n (a) (abbr profit and loss) pertes fpl et profits mpl ❑ **P & L account** compte m d'exploitation; **P & L form** compte de résultat; **P & L statement** compte d'exploitation (b) (abbr profit and loss account, profit and loss statement) compte m d'exploitation; **we can see from the P & L that developing the product is not a viable option** le compte d'exploitation montre clairement qu'il ne serait pas rentable de développer ce produit (c) (abbr profit and loss form) compte m de résultat

p & p n Br (abbr postage and packing) frais m de port et d'emballage m

panel n Mktg (for market research) panel m ❑ **panel discussion** table f ronde, débat m; **panel member** panéliste mf; **panel research** recherches fpl par panel

panic n **panic buying** = achats massifs provoqués par la crainte de la pénurie; St Exch achats mpl de précaution; St Exch **panic selling** ventes fpl de précaution

paper n (a) (material) papier m; (document) document m ❑ **paper copy** copie f papier; **paper shredder** déchiqueteuse f
(b) Fin **paper company** société f d'investissement; **paper loss** moins-value f; **paper profit** profit m fictif; **paper securities** titres mpl fiduciaires, papiers mpl valeurs
(c) (banknotes) billets mpl (de banque) ❑ **paper currency** papier-monnaie m; **paper money** papier-monnaie
(d) Comptr **paper advance** (on printer) entraînement m du papier; **paper feed** alimentation f en papier; **paper format** format m de papier; **paper jam** bourrage m de papier; **paper tray** bac m à feuilles

paperless adj électronique ❑ **paperless office** bureau m informatisé; St Exch **paperless trading** marché m ou cotation f électronique

paperwork n travail m administratif

par n Fin (of bills, shares) pair m; **at par** au pair; **to issue shares at par** émettre des actions au pair; **above par** au-dessus du pair; **below par** au-dessous du pair; **close to par** au voisinage de la parité ❑ **par bond** obligation f émise au pair; **par of exchange** pair du change; St Exch **par value** valeur f au pair ou nominale

paragraph n paragraphe m ❑ Comptr **paragraph break** fin f de paragraphe; Comptr **paragraph mark** marque f de paragraphe

parallel adj parallèle ❑ Comptr **parallel cable** câble m parallèle; Comptr **parallel computer** ordinateur m à traitement parallèle; **parallel importing** importations fpl parallèles; **parallel imports** importations parallèles; Comptr **parallel interface** interface f parallèle; **parallel market** marché m parallèle; Comptr **parallel output** sortie f parallèle; Comptr **parallel port** port m parallèle; Comptr **parallel printer** imprimante f parallèle; Comptr **parallel processing** traitement m en parallèle; **parallel rate of exchange** cours m parallèle; Mktg **parallel selling** vente f parallèle

paralysed adj (industry, business) immobilisé(e)

paralysis n (of industry, business) immobilisation f

parameter n Comptr paramètre m

parcel n (a) (package) paquet m, colis m; **to make up a parcel** faire un paquet ❑ **parcel delivery** livraison f de colis à domicile; **parcel delivery company** entreprise f de messageries; **parcel post** service m des colis postaux; **to send sth by parcel post** envoyer qch par colis postal; **parcel rates** tarif m colis postal (b) St Exch (of shares) paquet m

▶ **parcel up** vt sep (goods) empaqueter, emballer

parent company n société f ou maison f mère

Pareto rule n Fin règle f 80/20

pari passu adj Fin, St Exch pari passu (**with** avec)

parity n (a) (equality) parité f; **we have achieved parity of productivity with Japan** nous avons atteint le niveau de productivité du Japon

(b) *Fin* parité *f*; **the two currencies were at parity** les deux monnaies étaient à parité; **euro-dollar parity** parité euro-dollar ❑ *parity of exchange* parité du change; *parity ratio* rapport *m* de parité; *parity table* table *f* des parités; *parity value* valeur *f* au pair

park *vt St Exch* mettre en attente

parking *n St Exch* mise *f* en attente

parlay *vt Am (project)* mener à bien; *(money, investment)* fructifier; **she parlayed the local newspapers into a press empire** elle a bâti un empire de presse à partir des journaux locaux

> 66
> Young & Rubicam **parlayed** a well-received campaign for the National Football League and the United Way into a corporate-image account from the NFL without a review. The New York-based shop will develop ads for the league, its players and its public services efforts, an agency representative said.
> 99

part *n* (a) *(portion)* *part exchange* reprise *f*; **will you take it in part exchange?** voulez-vous le reprendre?; *part load* chargement *m* partiel; *part owner* copropriétaire *mf*; *part ownership* copropriété *f*; *part payment* acompte *m*, paiement *m* partiel; **we received £3,000 in part payment** nous avons reçu un acompte de 3 000 livres; *part shipment* expédition *f* partielle (b) *(for machine)* pièce *f* ❑ *parts and labour warranty* garantie *f* pièces et main-d'œuvre

partial *adj* partiel(elle) ❑ *Banking* *partial acceptance (of bill)* acceptation *f* partielle; *partial exemption (from tax)* exonération *f* partielle; *Ins* *partial loss* perte *f* partielle, sinistre *m* partiel; *partial payment* acompte *m*, paiement *m* partiel

participating interest *n* intérêt *m* de participation; **to hold a participating interest in a company** avoir un intérêt de participation dans une société

participation *n St Exch* ❑ *participation certificate* titre *m* ou bon *m* de participation; *participation rate* taux *m* d'activité

particular lien *n Fin* privilège *m* spécial

partly *adv* partiellement, en partie ❑ *Fin* *partly paid-up capital* capital *m* non entièrement versé; *partly paid-up shares* actions *fpl* non entièrement libérées; *partly secured creditor* créancier(ère) *m,f* partiellement nanti(e)

partner *n* associé(e) *m,f*; **our European partners** nos partenaires européens

partnership *n* (a) *(association)* association *f*; **to enter into** or **go into partnership (with sb)** s'associer (avec qn); **they've gone into partnership together** il se sont associés; **to work**

in partnership with sb/sth travailler en association avec qn/qch; **to dissolve a partnership** dissoudre une association; **they've offered him a partnership** ils lui ont proposé de devenir leur associé ❑ *partnership agreement* accord *m* de partenariat; *partnership share* part *f* d'association; *partnership at will* association de fait (b) *(company)* ≃ société *f* en nom collectif

part-time 1 *adj (contract, job, staff, employee)* à temps partiel; **to be in part-time employment** travailler à temps partiel
  2 *adv* à temps partiel

party *n Law (participant)* partie *f*; **the contracting parties** les parties contractantes

PASCAL *n Comptr* PASCAL *m*

pass 1 *n (permit)* laissez-passer *m* ❑ *pass book* livret *m* de banque
  2 *vt (bill, resolution)* voter; *(invoice)* approuver; **to pass a dividend** conclure un exercice sans payer de dividende

passenger *n (in vehicle, aircraft, ship)* passager(ère) *m,f* ❑ *passenger and cargo plane* avion *m* mixte; *passenger and cargo ship* cargo *m* mixte; *passenger and goods train* train *m* mixte; *passenger list* liste *f* des passagers; *passenger service* service *m* de voyageurs; *passenger ship* navire *m* de passagers; *passenger train* train de voyageurs

passing *adj* *passing customer* client(e) *m,f* de passage; *passing trade* clients *mpl* ou clientèle *f* de passage

passive management *n* gestion *f* passive

passport *n* passeport *m*

pass-through *adj Am* ❑ *pass-through securities* titres *mpl* garantis par des créances hypothécaires; *pass-through tax entity* = société fiscalement opaque

password *n Comptr* mot *m* de passe ❑ *password protection* protection *f* par mot de passe

password-protected *adj Comptr* protégé(e) par mot de passe

paste *vt Comptr* coller (**into/onto** dans)

patch *n* (a) *Comptr (correction)* correction *f* (b) *Mktg (of sales representative)* secteur *m*

patent 1 *n* brevet *m* (d'invention); **to take out a patent (for sth)** prendre un brevet (pour qch); **patent applied for, patent pending** *(on product)* demande de brevet déposée ❑ *patent agent* agent *m* en brevets; *patent law* droit *m* de brevet; *patent office* bureau *m* des brevets; *patent rights* propriété *f* industrielle; *patent specification* description *f* de brevet
  2 *adj (patented)* breveté(e) ❑ *patent goods* articles *mpl* brevetés; *patent medicine* spécialité *f* pharmaceutique
  3 *vt (of authorities)* breveter; *(of inventor)* faire breveter

patented *adj* breveté(e)

patentee *n* titulaire *mf* d'un brevet

paternity leave *n* congé *m* de paternité

> ❝
>
> Ian Swinson worked out a monthlong **paternity leave** before becoming the creative director of eScene Networks, a streaming media applications firm in San Francisco. "If they had said no, there's a good chance I wouldn't have joined," Swinson says. "And I would've left if they hadn't given me the time off [after I started]."
>
> ❞

path *n Comptr* chemin *m* (d'accès)

patron *n* (**a**) *(customer)* client(e) *m,f* (**b**) *(sponsor) (of the arts)* mécène *m*; *(of festival)* parrain *m*, sponsor *m*; **many multinational companies are becoming patrons of the arts** de nombreuses multinationales se lancent dans le mécénat

patronage *n* (**a**) *(custom)* clientèle *f*; *(sponsorship)* mécénat *m* (**b**) *(support)* parrainage *m*

patronize *vt* (**a**) *(shop)* accorder sa clientèle à (**b**) *(support)* parrainer

pattern *n* (**a**) *(sample)* échantillon *m* ❏ *pattern book* livre *m* d'échantillons (**b**) *(standard arrangement)* système *m*, configuration *f*; **research has established that there is a pattern in** *or* **to the data** la recherche a établi que les données ne sont pas aléatoires; **some clear patterns emerge from the statistics** des tendances nettes ressortent des statistiques; **our aim is to achieve economic growth on the Japanese pattern** notre but est d'atteindre un taux de croissance comparable à celui du Japon

pawn 1 *n* **to put sth in pawn** mettre qch en gage; **to take sth out of pawn** dégager qch ❏ *pawn ticket* reconnaissance *f* du mont-de-piété
2 *vt* mettre en gage

pawnbroker *n* prêteur(euse) *m,f* sur gage

pawnshop *n* bureau *m* de prêt sur gage, mont-de-piété *m*

pay 1 *n* *(wages)* salaire *m*, paie *f*; **the pay's good/bad** ça paie bien/mal ❏ *pay advice slip* fiche *f* de paie; *pay agreement* accord *m* salarial; *pay award* augmentation *f* de salaire; *Am pay check* chèque *m* de paie; *Br pay cheque* chèque de paie; *pay day* jour *m* de paie; *Am pay envelope* (envelope) enveloppe *f* de paie; *(money)* paie; *pay equity* équité *f* salariale; *pay freeze* gel *m* ou blocage *m* des salaires; *pay increase* augmentation de salaire; *Acct pay ledger* livre *m* de paie; *pay packet* (envelope) enveloppe de paie; *(money)* paie; *pay policy* politique *f* salariale; *pay rise* augmentation

de salaire; *pay slip* bulletin *m* de paie; *pay talks* négociations *fpl* salariales

2 *vt* (**a**) *(person)* payer; **to pay sb £100** payer 100 livres à qn; **to be paid by the hour/the week** être payé à l'heure/la semaine; **she's paid $5,000 a month** elle est payée *ou* elle touche 5000 dollars par mois
(**b**) *(sum of money)* payer; **you pay £100 now, the rest later** vous payez cent livres maintenant, le solde plus tard; **to pay money into sb's account** verser de l'argent au compte de qn
(**c**) *(bill, debt)* payer, régler; *(dividend)* distribuer; *(fine, taxes)* payer; **to pay cash** payer (argent) comptant, payer en espèces; **to pay a cheque into the bank** déposer un chèque à la banque

3 *vi* payer, régler; **how would you like to pay?** comment souhaitez-vous régler?; **to pay by cheque** payer *ou* régler par chèque; **to pay in cash** payer comptant, payer en liquide *ou* en espèces; **to pay in advance** payer d'avance; **to pay in full** payer intégralement *ou* en totalité; *Fin* **to pay on demand** *or* **on presentation** payer à vue *ou* à présentation; *Fin* **pay to bearer** payez au porteur

▸ **pay back** *vt sep (loan, lender)* rembourser

▸ **pay in** *vt sep (money, cheque)* verser sur un compte

▸ **pay into 1** *vt sep (money, cheque)* **I'd like to pay this cheque into my account** j'aimerais déposer ce chèque sur mon compte
2 *vi* **to pay into a pension scheme** cotiser à un plan de retraite

▸ **pay off 1** *vt sep* (**a**) *(workers)* licencier (**b**) *(debt, loan, mortgage)* rembourser
2 *vi (of work, efforts)* porter ses fruits; **moving the company out of London really paid off** la transfert de la société hors de Londres a été une affaire rentable

▸ **pay out 1** *vt sep* débourser, dépenser
2 *vi* payer

▸ **pay up** *vi* payer

payable 1 *adj* payable; **payable in 24 monthly instalments/in advance** payable en 24 mensualités/d'avance; **to make a cheque payable to sb** faire *ou* libeller un chèque à l'ordre de qn; **please make your cheque payable to Miss Johnston** veuillez libeller votre chèque à l'ordre de Miss Johnston; **payable in cash** payable comptant; **payable at sight** payable à vue; **payable to order** payable à ordre; **payable to bearer** payable au porteur; **payable on delivery/with order** payable à la livraison/à la commande
2 *n Am* **payables** factures *fpl* à payer

pay-as-you-earn, *Am* **pay-as-you-go** *n* prélèvement *m* de l'impôt à la source

payback *n Fin* récupération *f (du capital investi)*

❏ **payback period** délai *m ou* période *f* de remboursement

PAYE *n Br* (*abbr* **pay-as-you-earn**) prélèvement *m* de l'impôt à la source

> ❝
>
> Finally, 5 October is the date for notifying the taxman that you are liable to income or capital gains tax. There's no need to do this if you've been sent a tax return, nor if **PAYE** covers all your income. But if you have new freelance income or have started a new business, you should be putting your hand up to the Revenue by six months after the end of the tax year in which you started – hence 5 October.
>
> ❞

payee *n* (*of postal order, cheque*) bénéficiaire *mf*; (*of bill*) porteur *m*, preneur *m*

payer *n* (**a**) (*in general*) payeur(euse) *m,f*; **a good/bad payer** un bon/mauvais payeur (**b**) (*of cheque*) tireur(euse) *m,f*

paying 1 *n* paiement *m*

2 *adj* (**a**) (*who pays*) payant(e) ❏ **paying bank** domiciliataire *m*, établissement *m* payeur, domiciliation *f* bancaire (**b**) (*profitable*) payant(e), rentable; **it's not a paying proposition** cette proposition n'est pas profitable

paying-in *n Banking* **paying-in book** carnet *m* de versements; **paying-in slip** bordereau *m ou* feuille *f* de versement

payload *n* (*of vehicle*) charge *f* utile

paymaster *n* payeur(euse) *m,f*, intendant(e) *m,f*; (*in administration*) trésorier-payeur *m*; **the World Bank acts as paymaster of the project** la Banque mondiale fait office de bailleur de fonds pour ce projet ❏ **Paymaster General** = le Trésorier-payeur-général britannique

payment *n* paiement *m*, versement *m*; **to make a payment** effectuer un versement; **to stop payment on a cheque** faire opposition à un chèque; **on payment of £100** contre paiement de 100 livres; **on payment of a deposit** moyennant des arrhes; **in easy payments** avec facilités de paiement; **48 monthly payments** 48 versements mensuels, 48 mensualités; **in payment of your invoice** en règlement de votre facture; **to present a bill for payment** présenter un effet au paiement *ou* à l'encaissement; **payment on account** paiement partiel; **payment in advance** paiement d'avance, paiement par anticipation; **payment in arrears** paiement arriéré; **payment in cash** paiement en espèces; **payment by cheque** paiement par chèque; **payment on delivery** livraison *f* contre remboursement; **payment against documents** paiement contre documents; **payment in full** paiement intégral; **payment by instalments** paiement échelonné *ou* par versements; **pay-**

ment in kind paiement en nature ❏ **payment advice** avis *m* de paiement; **payment day** jour *m* de paiement; **payment facilities** facilités *fpl* de paiement; **payment order** ordre *m* de paiement; **payment proposal** proposition *f* de paiement; **payment schedule** échéancier *m* de paiement

payoff *n* (**a**) (*final payment*) paiement *m*, règlement *m* (**b**) (*reward*) indemnité *f*; **executive payoffs are expected to reach £500,000** les indemnités de départ des cadres devraient atteindre 500 000 livres (**c**) (*profit*) rendement *m*

payout *n* (**a**) *Ins* remboursement *m* (**b**) *Am* (*of investment*) récupération *f*

payroll *n* (**a**) (*list of employees*) liste *f* du personnel; **to be on the payroll** faire partie du personnel; **how many do you have on the payroll?** combien d'employés avez-vous?; **she's been on our payroll for over twenty years** elle fait partie de notre personnel depuis plus de vingt ans; **they've added five hundred workers to their payroll** ils ont embauché cinq cents travailleurs supplémentaires; **to be taken off the payroll** (*voluntarily*) quitter l'entreprise; (*get laid off*) être licencié(e); **to do the payroll** faire la paie ❏ *Acct* **payroll ledger** journal *m ou* livre *m* de paie (**b**) (*money paid*) masse *f* salariale ❏ **payroll tax** impôt *m* sur la masse salariale

> ❝
>
> In the 12-month period ending in January 1998, turnover at the Space Coast Credit Union was a horrifying 62 percent. Of 250 employees **on the payroll** that year, the Florida credit union lost 155.
>
> ❞

PB *n Am Banking* (*abbr* **pass book**) livret *m* de banque

PC *n* (*abbr* **personal computer**) PC *m*

p/c *n* (*abbr* **petty cash**) petite caisse *f*

PC-compatible *adj Comptr* compatible PC

PCMCIA *n Comptr* (*abbr* **PC Memory Card International Association**) PCMCIA

PCN *n Tel* (*abbr* **personal communications network**) réseau *m* de téléphonie mobile

PDA *n* (*abbr* **personal digital assistant**) agenda *m* électronique de poche, assistant *m* numérique de poche

PDF *n Comptr* (*abbr* **portable document format**) (format *m*) PDF *m*

PDL *n Comptr* (*abbr* **page description language**) PDL *m*

peak 1 *n* (**a**) (*of price, inflation, demand*) maximum *m*; **production was at its peak** la production était à son maximum ❏ **peak hours** heures *fpl* de pointe; **peak output** rendement *m* optimal; **peak price** prix *m* maximum; **peak rate** tarif *m* heures pleines; **peak season** haute saison *f*; **peak year** année *f* record (**b**) *Br Mktg (on TV)* **peak time** prime time *m*; **peak time advertising** publicité *f* au prime time

2 *vi (of price, inflation, demand)* atteindre un *ou* son maximum; **profits peaked in July** les bénéfices ont atteint un maximum en juillet

peg *vt Fin, St Exch (prices) (fix)* fixer; *(stabilize)* stabiliser; **to peg sth to the rate of inflation** indexer qch sur le taux de l'inflation; **oil was pegged at $20 a barrel** le prix du pétrole était fixé à 20 dollars le baril; **export earnings are pegged to the exchange rate** le revenu des exportations varie en fonction du taux de change

penal *adj* ☐ **penal interest** intérêts *mpl* moratoires; **penal rate** taux *m* d'usure

penalty *n (for late delivery, payment)* amende *f* ☐ **penalty clause** *(in contract)* clause *f* pénale; **penalty interest** pénalité *f* de retard, intérêts *mpl* moratoires; *Am* **penalty rate** *(for overtime)* tarif *m* des heures supplémentaires

pence *npl* pence *mpl*

pending 1 *adj (negotiations)* en cours; *(documents)* en souffrance, en attente; *Law (case)* en instance ☐ **pending tray** corbeille *f* pour les documents en attente

2 *prep* en attendant; **pending your decision** en attendant votre décision

penetrate *vt (market)* pénétrer

penetration *n (of market)* pénétration *f* ☐ **penetration price** prix *m* de pénétration; **penetration rate** taux *m* de pénétration; **penetration strategy** stratégie *f* de pénétration

penny *n Br (coin, unit of currency)* penny *m*; *Am (coin)* cent *m* ☐ *Br* **penny shares** actions *fpl* d'une valeur de moins d'une livre sterling; *Am* **penny stock** actions d'une valeur de moins d'un dollar

pen-pusher *n Fam* gratte-papier *m*

pen-pushing *n Fam* travail *m* de bureau

people-focused *adj* centré(e) sur l'humain

"
Deloitte & Touche's selection for this prestigious list is reflective of the firm's dedication to continuous improvement, the quality of its human resources programs, and its **people-focused** culture, which provides the opportunity for all individuals to realize their full professional and personal potential.
"

pension *n* pension *f*; *(after retirement)* (pension de) retraite *f*; **to be on a pension** toucher une pension; *(after retirement)* toucher une retraite ☐ **pension fund** caisse *f* de retraite; **pension plan** plan *m* de retraite; **pension point** point *m* de retraite; **pension scheme** régime *m* de retraite

▸ **pension off** *vt sep* **to pension sb off** mettre qn à la retraite

pensionable *adj (person)* qui a droit à une pension; *(after retirement)* qui a droit à sa retraite ☐ **pensionable age** âge *m* de la mise à la retraite

pensionary 1 *n (person receiving a pension)* pensionné(e) *m,f*; *(old-age pensioner)* retraité(e) *m,f*

2 *adj (receiving a pension)* pensionné(e); *(receiving an old-age pension)* retraité(e)

pensioner *n* **(old-age) pensioner** retraité(e) *m,f*

PEP *n Formerly Fin (abbr* **personal equity plan**) ≃ PEA *m*

peppercorn rent *n Br* loyer *m* nominal

per *prep* par; **per annum** par an; **per capita** par personne, par tête; **the highest per capita income in Europe** le revenu par habitant le plus élevé d'Europe; **per capita consumption** consommation *f* par tête; **per diem** par jour; *(expenses)* dépenses *fpl* journalières; *Law* **per pro** par procuration; **per pro signature** signature *f* par procuration; **per week** par semaine; **as per invoice** suivant facture; **as per your instructions** conformément à vos instructions; **as per sample** conformément à l'échantillon

p/e ratio *n Acct (abbr* **price/earnings ratio**) ratio *m* cours-bénéfices, rapport *m* cours-bénéfices, PER *m*

perceive *vt Mktg (product, brand)* percevoir

perceived *adj Mktg* **perceived performance** résultats *mpl* perçus; **perceived quality** qualité *f* perçue; **perceived risk** risque *m* perçu; **perceived service** service *m* perçu; **perceived value** valeur *f* perçue; **perceived value pricing** tarification *f* en fonction de la valeur perçue

percent 1 *n* pourcentage *m*

2 *adv* pour cent; **a seven percent interest rate** un taux d'intérêt de sept pour cent; **prices went up ten percent** les prix ont augmenté de dix pour cent

percentage *n* pourcentage *m*; **a high percentage of the staff** une grande partie du personnel; **to get a percentage on sth** *(share of profit, commission)* toucher un pourcentage sur qch

percentile *n* centile *m*

perception *n (of product, brand)* perception *f*

"
Editorial will target women with health and beauty themes harmonised with the Advantage proposition of "treating yourself". The aim is to shift **perception** of the Boots brand from something worthy to something inspirational.
"

perfect competition *n* concurrence *f* parfaite

perforated *adj* ❏ *perforated card* fiche *f* perforée; *perforated paper* papier *m* à bandes perforées

perform *vi* (**a**) *(of company)* fonctionner; *(of shares, investment, currency)* se comporter; **the Manchester branch is performing very well** les résultats de la succursale de Manchester sont très satisfaisants; **how did the company perform in the first quarter?** comment la société a-t-elle fonctionné au premier trimestre?; **shares performed well yesterday** les actions se sont bien comportées hier (**b**) *(of person) (in job, situation)* se débrouiller; **she performs well under pressure** elle se débrouille bien lorsqu'elle est sous pression

performance *n* (**a**) *(of contract, task)* exécution *f* ❏ *performance bond* garantie *f* de bonne fin (**b**) *(of company)* résultats *mpl*, performance *f*; *(of shares, investment, currency)* performance; **the country's poor economic performance** les mauvais résultats économiques du pays; **sterling's performance on the Stock Exchange** le comportement en Bourse de la livre sterling ❏ *performance appraisal (of staff)* évaluation *f*, appréciation *f*; *performance rating* rendement *m* effectif; *Acct performance ratio* ratio *m* d'exploitation; *performance test* test *m* de performance

performance-related *adj performance-related bonus* prime *f* au rendement; *performance-related pay* salaire *m* au rendement

period *n* période *f*; **for a period of three months** pendant une période de trois mois; **within the agreed period** dans les délais convenus ❏ *Fin period bill* effet *m* à terme; *period of grace* délai *m* de grâce

periodic *adj periodic inventory* inventaire *m* périodique; *periodic payments* paiements *mpl* périodiques

periodical *n* périodique *m*

peripheral *Comptr* **1** *n* périphérique *m*
2 *adj* périphérique ❏ *peripheral device, peripheral unit* unité *f* périphérique

perishability *n* périssabilité *f*

perishable **1** *n* perishables denrées *fpl* périssables
2 *adj* périssable ❏ *perishable cargo* chargement *m* périssable; *perishable goods* denrées *fpl* périssables

perk *n (of job)* avantage *m* en nature; **cheap air travel is one of the perks of his job** l'un des avantages de son travail est qu'il bénéficie de billets d'avion à prix réduit

---

❝

When it comes to job **perks**, the average technologist prefers telecommuting tools, according to a survey by Techies.com, an online career network for technology professionals. The online survey of 1,000 tech professionals revealed roughly 30 percent picked discounted or free home PCs as a top **perk**.

❞

---

permanent *adj* permanent(e); *(residence, address)* fixe ❏ *Fin permanent assets* actif *m* immobilisé; *permanent contract* contrat *m* à durée indéterminée; *permanent credit* accréditif *m* permanent; *permanent job* emploi *m* permanent; *(in public service)* poste *m* de titulaire; *permanent member* membre *m* permanent; *permanent post* emploi permanent; *(in public service)* poste de titulaire; *permanent staff* personnel *m* permanent; *(in public service)* personnel titulaire

permatemp **1** *n* = personne employée de façon permanente mais sur la base de contrats à durée déterminée renouvelés
2 *adj* = lié à la pratique consistant à employer des travailleurs sur la base de contrats à durée déterminée renouvelés

---

❝

The right benefit-plan language is the way to avoid costly **permatemp** problems. When the Internal Revenue Service ruled in 1989 that some 600 Microsoft contract workers were actually employees for payroll purposes, little did anyone know that it would start a fire that still rages today across the Redmond campus – and beyond.

❞

---

permissible *adj* permis(e) ❏ *permissible overload* surcharge *f* permise

permission *n* permission *f*, autorisation *f*; **to ask for permission to do sth** demander la permission de faire qch; **to give sb permission to do sth** donner à qn la permission de faire qch, autoriser qn à faire qch ❏ *permission marketing* marketing *m* de permission; *St Exch permission to deal* visa *m* (de la COB)

permit **1** *n* permis *m*; *Customs* acquit-à-caution *m*; *(pass)* laissez-passer *m inv*
2 *vt* permettre; **to permit sb to do sth** permettre à qn de faire qch, autoriser qn à faire qch; **smoking is not permitted** il est interdit de fumer

perpetual *adj* perpétuel(elle) ❏ *perpetual inventory* inventaire *m* permanent, stock *m* stratégique; *perpetual loan* emprunt *m* perpétuel

perpetuity *n* rente *f* perpétuelle

perquisite *n (from job)* avantage *m* en nature; *(advantage)* avantage

personal *adj* personnel(elle); **personal** *(on letter)* personnel ❑ *Ins* **personal accident insurance** assurance *f* contre les accidents corporels; **personal account** *Banking* compte *m* individuel; *St Exch* compte de tiers; *Acct* compte propre; **personal assets** patrimoine *m*; *Banking* **personal assets profile** profil *m* patrimonial; **personal assistant** *(of executive)* assistant(e) *m,f*; *(with secretarial duties)* secrétaire *mf* de direction; *Comptr* **personal computer** ordinateur *m* individuel; *Comptr* **personal computing** informatique *f* individuelle; **personal credit** crédit *m* personnel; *Comptr* **personal digital assistant** agenda *m* électronique de poche, assistant *m* numérique de poche; **personal effects** effets *mpl* personnels; *Formerly Fin* **personal equity plan** ≃ plan *m* d'épargne en actions; **personal estate** propriété *f* mobilière; *Banking* **personal identification number** code *m* confidentiel *(d'une carte bancaire)*; **personal injury** dommage *m* corporel; *Br* **Personal Investment Authority** = organisme chargé de surveiller les activités des conseillers financiers indépendants et de protéger les petits investisseurs; **personal legacy** legs *m* particulier; *Banking* **personal loan** prêt *m* personnel, prêt personnalisé; *Mktg* **personal observation** observation *f* en situation; **personal organizer** *(book)* agenda; *(electronic)* agenda électronique; **personal pension plan** retraite *f* personnelle; **personal property** biens *mpl* personnels; *Mktg* **personal selling** ventes *fpl* personnelles; *Banking* **personal withdrawals** levées *fpl* de compte

personality promotion *n Mktg* promotion *f* par une personnalité

personalty *n Law* biens *mpl* mobiliers; **to convert realty into personalty** ameublir un bien

personnel *n* personnel *m* ❑ **personnel department** service *m* du personnel; **personnel manager** directeur(trice) *m,f* du personnel; **personnel management** direction *f* du personnel; **personnel rating** notation *f* du personnel

person-to-person approach *n Mktg* approche *f* personnalisée

peseta *n Formerly* peseta *f*

PEST *n Mktg (abbr* **political economic sociological technological***)* = facteurs politiques, économiques, sociaux et technologiques (considérés comme les aspects les plus importants lors de l'analyse de l'environnement d'une entreprise)

Peter principle *n* **the Peter principle** le principe de Peter *(théorème humoristique selon lequel chacun finit par atteindre son niveau d'incompétence)*

petition in bankruptcy *n* demande *f* de mise en liquidation judiciaire; **to file a petition in bankruptcy** déposer son bilan

petrochemical 1 *n* **petrochemicals** produits *mpl* pétrochimiques

2 *adj* pétrochimique ❑ **petrochemical industry** industrie *f* pétrochimique

petrocurrency *n* pétromonnaies *fpl*

petrodollar *n* pétrodollar *m*

petroleum *n* pétrole *m* ❑ **petroleum industry** industrie *f* pétrolière; **petroleum products** produits *mpl* pétroliers

petty cash *n* petite caisse *f*; **they'll pay you back out of petty cash** ils vous rembourseront avec la petite caisse ❑ **petty cash book** livre *m* de petite caisse; **petty cash box** petite caisse; **petty cash management** tenue *f* de caisse; **petty cash voucher** bon *m* de petite caisse

pfennig *n Formerly* pfennig *m*

PFI *n (abbr* **private finance initiative***)* partenariat *m* public-privé

phase *n* phase *f*; **the project is going through a critical phase** le projet traverse une phase critique

▸ **phase in** *vt sep (new methods)* adopter *ou* introduire progressivement; *(new installations, equipment)* mettre en place progressivement; **the increases will be phased in over five years** les augmentations seront échelonnées sur cinq ans; **the reforms will have to be phased in** les réformes devront être introduites progressivement

▸ **phase out** *vt sep* éliminer progressivement; **these jobs will be phased out over the next five years** ces postes seront éliminés progressivement au cours des cinq prochaines années

phone 1 *n* téléphone *m*; **to be on the phone** *(speaking)* être au téléphone; *(have a phone)* être abonné(e) au téléphone; **to answer the phone** répondre au téléphone; **you're wanted on the phone** on vous demande au téléphone ❑ **phone bill** facture *f ou* note *f* de téléphone; **phone book** annuaire *m* (téléphonique); **phone call** appel *m* (téléphonique); **phone number** numéro *m* de téléphone

2 *vt* **to phone sb** téléphoner à qn; **I'll phone**

you je vous téléphonerai
  3 vi téléphoner; **to phone for sth** demander qch par téléphone

phonecard n Br Télécarte® f, carte f de téléphone

photocopier n photocopieur m, photocopieuse f

photocopy 1 n photocopie f; **to take** or **make a photocopy of sth** faire une photocopie de qch
  2 vt photocopier

phreaker n pirate m du téléphone

physical adj Fin **physical assets** immobilisations fpl non financières; **physical capital** capital m existant; **physical distribution** distribution f physique; **physical distribution management** gestion f de la distribution physique; Fin **physical fixed assets** immobilisations non financières; **physical inventory** inventaire m physique; **physical property** propriété f physique

PIA n Br (abbr **personal investment authority**) = organisme chargé de surveiller les activités des conseillers financiers indépendants et de protéger les petits investisseurs

PIBOR n (abbr **Paris Interbank Offer Rate**) TIOP m

► **pick up** vi (of business, prices) reprendre; **the market is picking up after a slow start** le marché commence à prendre après avoir démarré doucement

picket 1 n (group) piquet m de grève; (individual) membre m d'un piquet de grève; **there was a picket outside the factory** il y avait un piquet de grève devant l'usine; **twenty pickets stood outside the factory** vingt grévistes se tenaient devant l'usine □ **picket duty** piquet de grève; **to be on picket duty** faire partie d'un piquet de grève; **picket line** piquet de grève; **to stand** or **be on a picket line** faire partie d'un piquet de grève; **to cross a picket line** franchir un piquet de grève
  2 vt **to picket a factory** faire le piquet de grève devant une usine

pick-up point n (for cargo) aire f de chargement; (for passengers) point m de ramassage

piece n pièce f; **to sell sth by the piece** vendre qch à la pièce □ **piece rate** salaire m à la pièce ou à la tache; **to be paid piece rates** être payé(e) à la pièce ou à la tache

piecework n travail m à la pièce ou à la tâche

pieceworker n travailleur(euse) m,f à la pièce ou à la tâche

pie chart n graphique m à secteurs, camembert m

pigeonhole n casier m (à courrier)

piggybacking n (**a**) (in export) exportation f

kangourou (**b**) Banking portage m

pilot 1 n **pilot factory** usine-pilote f; **pilot project** projet-pilote m; **pilot questionnaire** questionnaire-pilote m; **pilot run** présérie f; **pilot scheme** projet-pilote; **pilot series** présérie; **pilot study** étude-pilote f, pré-étude f; **pilot survey** enquête-pilote f
  2 vt (study, scheme) piloter

pilotage n pilotage m

PIMS n Mktg (abbr **profit impact of marketing strategy**) IRSM m

PIN n (abbr **personal identification number**) **PIN (number)** code m personnel

pin n Comptr broche f

pink adj Am **pink dollar** = pouvoir d'achat des homosexuels; Br **pink pound** = pouvoir d'achat des homosexuels; Am Fam **pink slip** lettre f ou avis m de licenciement; **to get a pink slip** se faire virer

> At the outset, analysts argued gay clients might feel reassured that they would not be discriminated against when taking out a loan. However, G&L's problems were not in attracting investors but in finding people who wanted to take out loans, for houses and other purchases, which would bring in the cashflow that banks rely on. Without that, and up against competition from other physical banks, which increasingly recognised that the **pink dollar** was worth the same as any other, it could not survive.

pink-collar adj Am Fam **pink-collar job** = emploi typiquement féminin; **pink-collar worker** employée f de bureau

pipe vt Comptr (commands) chaîner

pipeline n (**a**) (for oil) pipeline f, oléoduc m; (for gas) gazoduc m (**b**) **to be in the pipeline** être en préparation; **they have a new model in the pipeline** ils sont en train de mettre un nouveau modèle au point; **important changes are in the pipeline for next year** d'importants changements sont prévus pour l'année prochaine

piracy n (of copyright) atteinte f au droit d'auteur; (of book, software) piratage m

pirate 1 n (book, software) pirate m □ **pirate edition** édition f pirate
  2 vt (book, software) pirater

pit n St Exch corbeille f

pitch 1 n (of product) promotion f; (of idea) présentation f, soumission f
  2 vt (product) promouvoir; (idea) présenter, soumettre
  3 vi faire une soumission; **to pitch for sth** faire une soumission pour qch

> KFC originally invited five agencies to **pitch**. Apart from Zenith, Initiative and Optimedia, New PHD and Motive were also asked to present but were knocked out after the first round.

pixel n Comptr pixel m

pixellated adj Comptr (image) pixelisé(e), bitmap, en mode point

place 1 n lieu m ❑ **place of birth** lieu de naissance; **place of business** lieu de travail; **place of delivery** lieu de livraison; Fin **place of issue** lieu d'émission; **place of origin** lieu d'origine; **place of payment** lieu de paiement; **place of residence** domicile m; **place of shipment** point m d'expédition; **place of work** lieu de travail
  2 vt (**a**) (order) passer (**with** à); (contract) passer (**with** à); (advertisement) insérer (**in** dans) (**b**) St Exch (shares) placer, disposer

placement n (**a**) (work experience) stage m (en entreprise) (**b**) St Exch (of shares) placement m (**c**) Mktg (of product) placement m

plain paper n papier m non réglé

plaintiff n Law plaignant(e) m,f

plan 1 n (**a**) (strategy) plan m, projet m; **to draw up** or **to make a plan** dresser ou établir un plan; **to put a plan into operation** mettre un plan en œuvre; **plan of action** plan d'action (**b**) (of building, town) plan m
  2 vt (**a**) (arrange) projeter; **to plan to do sth** projeter de faire qch; **an industrial estate is planned for this site** il est prévu d'aménager un parc industriel sur ce site; **they're planning a new venture** ils ont en projet une nouvelle entreprise (**b**) (building, town) faire le plan de (**c**) Econ (economy) planifier

plane n (aeroplane) avion m ❑ **plane ticket** billet m d'avion

planned adj planifié(e) ❑ **planned economy** économie f planifiée; **planned maintenance** entretien m systématique; **planned obsolescence** obsolescence f planifiée; **planned production** production f planifiée; **planned redundancy scheme** plan m social

planner n (**a**) Econ planificateur(trice) m,f (**b**) **(town) planner** urbaniste mf (**c**) (in diary, on wall) planning m

planning n (**a**) (organization) organisation f; **planning and allocation of resources** estimation f des besoins et répartition des moyens ❑ **planning permission** permis m de construire (**b**) Econ (of economy) planification f (**c**) (of building) conception f

planning-programming-budgeting system n Acct système m de planification-programmation-budgétisation, rationalisation f des choix budgétaires

plant n (equipment) matériel m; (factory) usine f; **plant and machinery** matériel et outillage mpl ❑ **plant capacity** capacité f de l'usine; **plant hire** location f d'équipement; **plant layout** schéma m d'installation; **plant manager** directeur(trice) m,f d'usine

plastic Fam **1** n (credit cards) cartes fpl de crédit; **to put sth on the plastic** payer qch avec une carte de crédit; **do they take plastic?** est-ce qu'ils acceptent les cartes de crédit?
  2 adj **plastic money** cartes fpl de crédit

platform n Comptr plate-forme f

player n acteur m; **who are the key players in this market?** qui sont les acteurs principaux sur ce marché?

> But Lexus would be wise to consider the fortunes of Audi. It has taken many years for VW to turn the brand, which already had a long history, into a major **player** in the premium market.

PLC, plc n (**a**) Br (abbr **public limited company**) ≃ SA f; **Scotia Hotels plc** ≃ Scotia Hotels SA (**b**) (abbr **product lifecycle**) cycle m de vie du produit

pledge Fin **1** n gage m, garantie f; **in pledge** en gage ❑ **pledge holder** détenteur(trice) m,f de gage(s)
  2 vt donner en gage ou en garantie; **to pledge one's property** engager son bien; **to pledge securities** déposer des titres en garantie; **pledged securities** valeurs fpl nanties

pledgee n Fin gagiste mf

pledgor n Fin gageur m

plenary 1 n (meeting) réunion f plénière; (session) séance f plénière
  2 adj (meeting, session) plénier(ère)

plotter n Comptr (device) traceur m

▸ **plough back,** Am **plow back** vt sep Fin réinvestir (**into** dans); **to plough the profits back into the company** réinvestir les bénéfices dans la société

▸ **plough in,** Am **plow in** vt sep (money) investir

ploughback, Am **plowback** n bénéfices mpl réinvestis

▸ **plow back, plow in** Am = **plough back, plow in**

▸ **plowback** Am = **ploughback**

plug Fam **1** n (publicity) pub f; **their products got another plug on TV** on a encore fait de la pub pour leurs produits à la télé

2 *vt (product)* faire du battage *ou* de la pub pour

plug-in *n Comptr* module *m* d'extension

plummet *vi (of price, rate, currency)* dégringoler, s'effondrer; **the value of the pound has plummeted** la livre a chuté

plunge *vi* (**a**) *St Exch* risquer de grosses sommes (**b**) *(of price, rate, currency)* chuter, dégringoler; **sales have plunged by 30 percent** les ventes ont chuté de 30 pour cent

PMG *n Br* (**a**) *(abbr Paymaster General)* Trésorier-payeur-général britannique (**b**) *(abbr Postmaster General)* ≃ ministre *m* des Postes et Télécommunications

pmt *n Am (abbr payment)* paiement *m*

P/N *n (abbr promissory note)* billet *m* à ordre, effet *m* à ordre

PO *n* (**a**) *(abbr Post Office)* poste *f* ❑ *PO Box* BP *f* (**b**) *(abbr postal order)* mandat *m* postal

poach *vt (employee)* débaucher; **several of our staff have been poached by a rival company** plusieurs de nos employés ont été débauchés par un de nos concurrents

❝ Highly trained staff are being **poached** from Gateway's Republic of Ireland operation by Internet start-up companies offering inflated salaries, says Gateway's local MD Mike Maloney. The problem is creating shortages in key skill areas, which Maloney has raised with IDA Ireland, the state agency responsible for attracting multinational investment. ❞

pocket *adj* de poche ❑ *pocket calculator* calculatrice *f* de poche; *pocket diary* agenda *m* de poche

pocket-sized *adj* en format de poche

POD *adv Am (abbr pay on delivery)* **to send sth POD** envoyer qch contre remboursement; **all goods are sent POD** touts les marchandises doivent être payées à la livraison

POE *n* (**a**) *(abbr port of embarkation)* port *m* d'embarquement (**b**) *(abbr port of entry)* port *m* d'entrée

point *n* (**a**) *Mktg point of delivery* lieu *m* de livraison; *point of purchase* lieu d'achat, lieu de vente; *point of sale* lieu de vente, point *m* de vente (**b**) *St Exch* point *m*; **the Dow Jones index is up/down two points** l'indice Dow Jones a augmenté/baissé de deux points (**c**) *(for discussion, on agenda)* point *m*; **let's go on to the next point** passons à la question suivante *ou* au point suivant

point-and-click *vt Comptr* pointer et cliquer

pointer *n Comptr* pointeur *m*

point-of-purchase *adj Mktg* sur le lieu de vente ❑ *point-of-purchase advertising* publicité *f* sur le lieu de vente, PLV *f*; *point-of-purchase display* exposition *f* sur le lieu de vente; *point-of-purchase information* informations *fpl* sur le lieu de vente; *point-of-purchase material* matériel *m* de publicité sur le lieu de vente *ou* de PLV; *point-of-purchase promotion* promotion *f* sur le lieu de vente

point-of-sale *adj Mktg* sur le lieu de vente ❑ *point-of-sale advertising* publicité *f* sur le lieu de vente, PLV *f*; *point-of-sale display* exposition *f* sur le lieu de vente; *point-of-sale information* informations *fpl* sur le lieu de vente; *point-of-sale material* matériel *m* de publicité sur le lieu de vente *ou* de PLV; *point-of-sale promotion* promotion *f* sur le lieu de vente *point-of-sale terminal* terminal *m* point de vente

poison pill *n Fam (strategy)* pilule *f* empoisonnée

❝ **Poison-pill** provisions are triggered when a hostile suitor acquires a predetermined percentage of company stock. At that point, all existing shareholders except the suitor are granted options to buy additional stock at a dramatic discount, thus diluting the acquirer's share so as to head off a change in control of the company … According to statistics from Thomson Financial Securities Data, 140 companies adopted **poison pill** provisions in the first half of 2001, up 45 percent from the same period last year. ❞

policy *n* (**a**) *(of company, organization)* politique *f*; **to adopt a policy** adopter une ligne de conduite; **this is in line with company policy** ça va dans le sens de la politique de l'entreprise; **our policy is to hire professionals only** nous avons pour politique de n'engager que des professionnels; **the company's success is essentially down to their inspired marketing policy** le succès de l'entreprise est dû en grande partie à l'intelligence de leur politique de commercialisation ❑ *policy document* document *m* de politique générale; *policy meeting* séance *f* de concertation; *policy position* position *f* de principe; *policy paper* = document énonçant une position de principe; *policy statement* déclaration *f* de principe; *Am policy wonk* conseiller(ère) *m,f* politique (**b**) *Ins* police *f*; **to take out a policy** souscrire une police (d'assurance) ❑ *policy holder* assuré(e) *m,f*

❝ Managing a Mayoral campaign in New York City has to be one of the most stressful jobs in the world and not, under any circumstance, a recommended activity for recovering heart patients. But no one seems to have told that to Richard Schrader, a bearded agitator turned **policy wonk** who's running Mark Green's campaign to succeed Rudolph Giuliani. **"**

policymaker n décideur m

political adj (a) (relating to politics) politique ❑ **political economy** économie f politique; **political editor** rédacteur(trice) m,f en chef politique; **political organization** organisation f politique; **political science** sciences fpl politiques; **political scientist** spécialiste mf en sciences politiques (b) (tactical) (decision, appointment) politique

politician n (man) (homme m) politique m; (woman) (femme f) politique f

politics n politique f; **to go into politics** faire de la politique

poll 1 n (survey) sondage m (d'opinion); **to carry out** or **conduct a poll (on sth)** faire un sondage (sur qch) ❑ **poll tax** (in UK) = impôt aboli en 1993, regroupant taxe d'habitation et impôts locaux, payable par chaque occupant adulte d'une même habitation; (in US) = impôt, aboli en 1964, donnant droit à être inscrit sur les listes électorales
2 vt (person) sonder; **most of those polled were in favour of the plan** la plupart des personnes sondées étaient favorables au projet

polling n sondage m ❑ **polling company** institut m de sondage; **polling method** méthode f de sondage

pollster n enquêteur(trice) m,f

Ponzi scheme n Am = escroquerie dans laquelle l'argent des investisseurs les plus récents sert à payer les premiers investisseurs

"
The investors who have sued Slatkin allege that he used funds collected from new investors to pay returns to older investors, a form of fraud commonly known as a **Ponzi scheme**. Last month, one investor won a court order to freeze Slatkin's brokerage accounts and other assets, including a ranch home in Santa Barbara. **"**

pool 1 n (a) (of companies) groupement m, pool m; (of company cars, computers) parc m (b) (consortium) cartel m; (group of producers) groupement m de producteurs
2 vt (capital, profits, ideas, resources) mettre en commun; (orders) grouper

pooling of interests n Am (absorption-)fusion f, unification f

POP n (a) Comptr (abbr post office protocol) protocole m POP (b) Mktg (abbr point of pur-

chase) lieu m d'achat, lieu de vente

population n population f ❑ **population census** recensement m démographique ou de la population; **population count** dénombrement m de la population; **population explosion** explosion f démographique; **population growth** croissance f démographique; **population statistics** statistiques fpl démographiques

pop-up menu n Comptr menu m local

port n (a) (harbour) port m ❑ **port of arrival** port d'arrivée; **port authority** autorité f ou administration f portuaire; **port of call** port d'escale, escale f; **port charges** droits mpl de port; **port of departure** port de départ; **port of destination** port de destination; **port dues** droits de port; **port of embarkation** port d'embarquement; **port of entry** port d'entrée; **port of loading** port d'embarquement; **port of shipment** port d'expédition; **port of transit** port de passage (b) Comptr port m

portable 1 n (computer) (ordinateur m) portable m
2 adj (a) (computer) portable; (software, program) compatible (b) Fin (pension, mortgage) transférable

portage n (transport) transport m; (cost) (frais mpl de) port m

portal n Comptr portail m

porterage n (of goods, parcels) transport m (par porteurs); (cost) prix m de transport ❑ **porterage facilities** service m de porteurs

portfolio n (a) (for holding documents) porte-documents m (b) Fin, St Exch (of shares) portefeuille m ❑ **portfolio analysis** analyse f de portefeuille; **portfolio diversification** diversification f de portefeuille; **portfolio insurance** assurance f de portefeuille; **portfolio liquidity** liquidité f du portefeuille; **portfolio management** gestion f de portefeuille; **portfolio manager** gestionnaire mf de portefeuille; **portfolio securities** valeurs fpl de portefeuille (c) Mktg portefeuille m ❑ **portfolio mix** portefeuille d'activités (d) **portfolio career** carrière f multiple; **portfolio worker** = travailleur qui cumule les emplois

"
The prototype **portfolio workers** are surely not web designers but women who do night shifts cleaning so that they can rush back to make the kids' breakfast before doing a stint as a barmaid. **Portfolio workers** forfeit security, sick pay, holiday pay and pensions in the name of personal autonomy. They carry the burdens that formerly would have rested on corporate shoulders. **"**

portrait n Comptr portrait m; **to print sth in**

portrait imprimer qch en portrait ◻ *portrait mode* mode *m* portrait

port-to-port *adj* port à port ◻ *port-to-port shipment* expédition *f* port à port

POS *n (abbr* **point of sale)** PDV *m*

position 1 *n* (a) *(circumstances)* état *m*, situation *f*; **the cash position is not good** la situation de la caisse laisse à désirer; **our financial position is improving** notre situation financière s'améliore
(b) *(job)* poste *m*; **it's a position of great responsibility** c'est un poste à haute responsabilité; **there were four candidates for the position of manager** il y avait quatre candidats au poste de directeur; **what was your previous position?** quel était votre poste précédent?
(c) *Mktg (of company, of product on market)* position *f*
(d) *St Exch* position *f*; **to take a long/short position** prendre une position longue/courte ◻ *position limit* limite *f* de position; *position taking* prise *f* de position; *position trader* spéculateur(trice) *m,f* sur plusieurs positions
2 *vt Comptr (cursor, image)* positionner; *Mktg (product)* positionner

positioning *n Mktg* positionnement *m* ◻ *positioning strategy* stratégie *f* de positionnement; *positioning study* étude *f* de positionnement

positive *adj* **positive prescription** prescription *f* acquisitive; **positive vetting** contrôle *m* ou enquête *f* de sécurité *(sur un candidat à un poste touchant à la sécurité nationale)*

possess *vt Law* posséder, avoir

possession *n Law (of property)* possession *f*, jouissance *f*; **to take possession (of sth)** prendre possession (de qch)

possessor *n Law* possesseur *m*, propriétaire *mf*

possessory *adj Law* possessoire ◻ *possessory action* action *f* possessoire; *possessory right* possessoire *m*

post¹ *n Br (mail)* courrier *m*; **by return of post** par retour du courrier; **to send sth by post** envoyer qch par la poste; **it's in the post** c'est parti au courrier; **can you put the cheque in the post?** pouvez-vous poster le chèque? ◻ *post office* (bureau *m* de) poste *f*; **the Post Office** *(organization)* ≃ la Poste; *post office account* compte *m* chèque postal; *post office box* boîte *f* postale; *post office cheque* chèque *m* postal; *Comptr post office protocol* protocole *m* POP; *Br post office savings* ≃ Caisse *f* (nationale) d'épargne; *post office transfer* virement *m* postal
2 *vt* (a) *(letter, parcel)* mettre à la poste, poster; **I'll post it to you** je vous l'enverrai par la poste
(b) *Acct (entry)* passer; **to post an amount** passer un montant; **to post the books** passer les écritures

(c) *(publicize)(results)* annoncer; **they have posted a ten percent increase in profits** ils ont annoncé une augmentation des bénéfices de dix pour cent
(d) *St Exch* **to post security** déposer des garanties

post² **1** *n (job)* poste *m*; **the post is still vacant** nous n'avons pas encore pourvu à ce poste; **he got a post as an economist** il a obtenu un poste d'économiste
2 *vt (assign)* affecter; **to be posted to a different branch** être affecté(e) à une autre succursale

postage *n* affranchissement *m*; **postage and packing** frais *mpl* de port et d'emballage; **postage included** port compris; **postage paid** port payé ◻ *postage receipt* récépissé *m* postal; *postage stamp* timbre-poste *m*

postal *adj* postal(e) ◻ *postal area* zone *f* postale; *postal charges* frais *mpl* d'envoi *ou* de port; *postal delivery* envoi *m* postal; *postal link* liaison *f* postale; *Am postal meter* machine *f* à affranchir; *Br postal order* mandat *m* postal; *postal rates* tarifs *mpl* postaux; *Am* **the Postal Service** ≃ la Poste; *postal services* services *mpl* postaux; *postal survey* enquête *f* postale; *Br postal vote* vote *f* par correspondance

postcode *n Br* code *m* postal

postdate *vt* postdater

posted price *n* prix *m* affiché

poster *n Mktg* affiche ◻ *poster advertising* publicité *f* par affichage, publicité par voie d'affiches; *poster campaign* campagne *f* d'affichage

> Bartle Bogle Hegarty (BBH) has developed a **poster campaign** for the internet-based company that brings modern and contemporary art into mainstream life by portraying it in everyday situations. One poster features a Damien Hirst limited edition print.

poste restante *n* poste *f* restante

post-free 1 *adj (prepaid)* port payé; *(free of postal charges)* dispensé(e) d'affranchissement
2 *adv (prepaid)* en port payé; *(free of postal charges)* en franchise postale

Post-it® *n* note *f* autocollante

postmark 1 *n* cachet *m* de la poste; **date as postmark** le cachet de la poste faisant foi
2 *vt* oblitérer; **the letter is postmarked Phoenix** la lettre vient de *ou* a été postée à Phoenix

postmaster *n Comptr* maître *m* de poste

Postmaster General *n Br* ≃ ministre *m* des Postes et Télécommunications

post-paid 1 *adj* port payé
2 *adv* en port payé

postpone *vt* remettre à plus tard, reporter; *(payment)* différer; **the meeting was postponed until a later date** la réunion a été remise à une date ultérieure

postponement *n* report *m*

post-purchase *adj Mktg* post-achat □ *post-purchase behaviour* comportement *m* post-achat; *post-purchase evaluation* évaluation *f* post-achat

PostScript® *n Comptr* PostScript® *m* □ *PostScript® font* police *f* de caractères PostScript®; *PostScript® printer* imprimante *f* PostScript®

post-test *Mktg* **1** *n* post-test *m*
   2 *vt* post-tester

potential 1 *n* potentiel *m*; **the idea has potential** l'idée a de l'avenir; **there is little potential for development in the firm** l'entreprise offre peu de possibilités de développement; **the scheme has no potential** le projet n'a aucun avenir
   2 *adj* éventuel(elle), potentiel(elle) □ *potential buyer* acheteur(euse) *m,f* éventuel(elle); *potential customer* client *m* potentiel

pound *n (British currency)* livre *f* □ *pound coin* pièce *f* d'une livre; *pound sign* symbole *m* de la livre; *pound sterling* livre sterling

pour *vt (supply in large amounts)* **the government poured money into the industry** le gouvernement a investi des sommes énormes dans cette industrie; **I've already poured a fortune into the company** j'ai déjà investi une fortune dans la société

poverty *n poverty line* seuil *m* de pauvreté; **to live above/on/below the poverty line** vivre en dessus/à la limite/en dessous du seuil de pauvreté; *poverty trap* = situation inextricable de ceux qui dépendent de prestations sociales qu'ils perdent pour peu qu'ils trouvent une activité, même peu rémunérée

power *n* (**a**) *(authority)* pouvoir *m*; **to act with full powers** agir de pleine autorité □ *Mktg power brand* marque *f* forte; *power breakfast* petit déjeuner *m* d'affaires; *power dressing* = façon de s'habiller qu'adoptent certaines femmes cadres dans le but de projeter une image d'autorité; *power lunch* déjeuner *m* d'affaires; *power structure (system)* hiérarchie *f*, répartition *f* des pouvoirs; *(people with power)* = ensemble des personnes qui détiennent le pouvoir; *power struggle* lutte *f* pour le pouvoir
   (**b**) *Law* pouvoir *m* □ *power of attorney* procuration *f*; **to give sb power of attorney** donner procuration à qn
   (**c**) *Comptr power supply* alimentation *f*; *power unit* dispositif *m* d'alimentation; *power user* = personne qui sait utiliser au mieux les ressources de son ordinateur

(**d**) *power station* centrale *f* (électrique)

> ❝
> The **power lunch** is alive and well, according to a recent survey of chief financial officers (CFOs). Nearly half (49 percent) of executives polled said their most successful business meeting outside the office was conducted over a meal.
> ❞

▸ **power down** *Comptr* **1** *vt sep* éteindre
   2 *vi* éteindre

▸ **power up** *Comptr* **1** *vt sep* allumer
   2 *vi* allumer

powerbroker *n* décideur *m* politique

> ❝
> George W Bush scraped to victory in the 2000 presidential election thanks largely to an array of hugely influential rightwing lobbyists and **powerbrokers**. He knows what he owes them – and since September 11 their grip has grown yet tighter.
> ❞

power-down *n Comptr* mise *f* hors tension

power-on *n Comptr* mise *f* sous tension □ *power-on key* touche *f* d'alimentation

power-up *n Comptr* mise *f* sous tension

pp *(abbr per procurationem)* pp

PPB *n (abbr* **planning-programming-budgeting system**) *Acct* système *m* de planification-programmation-budgétisation, rationalisation *f* des choix budgétaires

PPD *adj (abbr* **prepaid**) port payé par le destinataire

ppi *n Comptr (abbr* **pixels per inch**) ppp *m*

PPP *n Comptr (abbr* **point-to-point protocol**) protocole *m* PPP, protocole point à point

PR *n (abbr* **public relations**) RP *f*; **who does their PR?** qui est-ce qui s'occupe de leurs relations publiques? □ *PR agency* agence *f* conseil en communication; *PR company* société *f* conseil en communication; *PR consultancy* agence conseil en communication; *PR consultant* conseil *m* en communication

pre-acquisition *n* acquisition *f* faite au préalable

prebill *vt Acct* préfacturer

prebilling *n Acct* préfacturation *f*

precision *n* précision *f* □ *precision industry* industrie *f* de précision

predate *vt (cheque)* antidater

predator *n (company)* prédateur *m*

predatory *adj* □ *Mktg predatory price* prix *m* prédateur; *predatory pricing* fixation *f* des prix prédateurs

> South African carriers Nationwide and South African Airways (SAA) have appeared before the Competition Tribunal, with Nationwide claiming that the larger airline is using **predatory pricing** techniques to force competitors out of key routes. Nationwide has filed a petition for interim relief, claiming that SAA has maintained prices on the popular Johannesburg to Cape Town and Johannesburg to Durban routes despite increasing fuel prices, yet has raised prices on other routes where it has less competition.

predecessor n prédécesseur m

predictive analysis n analyse f prévisionnelle

pre-empt vt Law (land, property) acquérir par (droit de) préemption

pre-emption n Law préemption f ▫ **pre-emption right** droit m de préemption

pre-emptive adj Law de préemption ▫ St Exch **pre-emptive right** droit m préférentiel de souscription

prefer vt Fin (creditor) privilégier

preference n (a) Econ tarif m ou régime m de faveur; (preferential treatment) traitement m préférentiel ou de faveur (b) St Exch droit m de priorité ▫ Br **preference cumulative dividend** dividende m privilégié ou prioritaire cumulatif; Br **preference dividend** dividende privilégié ou prioritaire; Br **preference share** action f privilégiée ou prioritaire (c) Mktg **preference test** test m de préférence

preferential adj (favourable) préférentiel(elle) ▫ Law **preferential claim** droit m préférentiel ou de préférence; Fin **preferential creditor** créancier(ère) m,f privilégié(e); Fin **preferential debt** créance f privilégiée; Fin **preferential dividend** dividende m privilégié ou prioritaire; Customs **preferential duty** préférences fpl douanières; Fin **preferential investment certificate** certificat m d'investissement privilégié; **preferential price** prix m de faveur; Fin **preferential rate** tarif m préférentiel; Ind **preferential shop** = atelier qui privilégie les travailleurs appartenant à un syndicat; Customs **preferential tariff** tarif préférentiel; **preferential voting** vote m préférentiel

preferred adj (a) **preferred creditor** créancier(ère) m,f privilégié(e); Fin **preferred debt** dette f ou créance f privilégiée (b) Am St Exch **preferred stock** actions fpl privilégiées ou de priorité

prefinancing n Acct préfinancement m

preformatted adj Comptr préformaté(e)

preinstall vt Comptr (software) préinstaller

preinstalled adj Comptr (software) préinstallé(e)

pre-inventory balance n Acct balance f avant inventaire

prejudice 1 n Law (detriment) préjudice m, tort m; **without prejudice to your guarantee** sans préjudice de votre garantie; **to the prejudice of sb's rights** au préjudice des droits de qn **2** vt porter préjudice à, compromettre

preliminary adj préliminaire ▫ **preliminary expenses** frais mpl d'établissement; Law **preliminary investigation** instruction f; **preliminary study** étude f préliminaire

pre-marketing n pré-commercialisation f, pré-marketing m

premises npl locaux mpl, lieux mpl

premium n (a) Ins (payment) prime f; **to pay an additional premium** payer une surprime ▫ **premium discount** ristourne f de prime; **premium rebate** ristourne de prime
(b) (additional sum) (on price) supplément m; (on salary) prime f; St Exch **to pay a premium** verser ou acquitter un premium; **to sell sth at a premium** vendre qch à prime ou à bénéfice; **to issue shares at a premium** émettre des actions au-dessus du pair ou de leur valeur nominale ▫ **premium bonds** ≃ obligations fpl à lots; **premium on redemption** prime de remboursement
(c) Mktg **premium price** prix m de prestige; **premium product** produit m de prestige; **premium selling** vente f à prime; **premium service** service m premier

prepack vt préconditionner, préemballer

prepackage vt préconditionner, préemballer

prepackaged adj préconditionné(e), préemballé(e)

prepacked adj préconditionné(e), préemballé(e)

prepaid adj prépayé(e); Acct payé(e) ou constaté(e) d'avance ▫ **prepaid card** carte f prépayée; **prepaid envelope** enveloppe f affranchie; **prepaid income** produit m constaté d'avance; **prepaid reply** réponse f payée

prepayment n paiement m à l'avance; Acct charge f constatée d'avance ▫ **prepayment clause** clause f de remboursement par anticipation; **prepayment penalty** indemnité f de remboursement par anticipation

preprogram vt Comptr préprogrammer

preprogrammed adj Comptr préprogrammé(e)

prerequisite n condition f préalable

presell vt (customer) prévendre à; (goods) prévendre

present 1 *adj* actuel(elle); **the present year** l'année courante ❑ **present capital** capital *m* appelé; *Acct* **present value** valeur *f* actuelle *ou* actualisée; *Ins* **present value tables** tables *fpl* d'actualisation

2 *vt* (**a**) *(report, information, proposal)* présenter (**b**) *Fin (invoice)* présenter; **to present a cheque for payment** présenter un chèque à l'encaissement; **to present a bill for acceptance** présenter une traite à l'acceptation

presentation *n* (**a**) *(showing)* présentation *f*; **presentation for acceptance** présentation à l'acceptation; **presentation for payment** présentation au paiement; **payable on presentation of the coupon** payable contre remise du coupon; **on presentation of the invoice** au vu de *ou* sur présentation de la facture; **cheque payable on presentation** chèque *m* payable à vue

(**b**) *(formal talk)* présentation *f*; **to give a presentation (on sth)** faire une présentation (de qch) ❑ *Comptr* **presentation graphics** graphiques *mpl* de présentation; *Comptr* **presentation software** logiciel *m* de présentation

(**c**) *Banking* **presentation date** date *f* de présentation

(**d**) *Mktg* **presentation pack** paquet *m* de présentation

presentment *n Fin (of bill of exchange)* présentation *f*

preside *vi* présider; **to preside over a meeting** présider une réunion

presidency *n* présidence *f*

president *n (of country, organization)* président(e) *m,f*; *Am (of company)* président-directeur général *m*, P-DG *m*; *Br* **President of the Board of Trade** Ministre *mf* du Commerce et de l'Industrie

press *n (newspapers)* **the press** la presse; **to get (a) good/bad press** avoir bonne/mauvaise presse ❑ **press agency** agence *f* de presse; **press agent** agent *m* de presse; **the Press Association** = agence de presse britannique; **press attaché** attaché(e) *m,f* de presse; **press badge** macaron *m* de presse; **press baron** magnat *m* de la presse; **press campaign** campagne *f* de presse; **press card** carte *f* de presse; **press clipping** coupure *f* de presse; **the Press Complaints Commission** = organisme britannique de contrôle de la presse; **press conference** confé-

rence *f* de presse; **the Press Council** = organisme indépendant veillant au respect de la déontologie dans la presse britannique; *Br* **press cutting** coupure de presse; **press handout** communiqué *m* de presse; *Mktg* **press insert** encart *m* presse; *Mktg* **press kit** dossier *m* de presse; **press lord** magnat de la presse; **press office** service *m* de presse; **press officer** responsable *mf* des relations avec la presse; *Mktg* **press pack** dossier de presse; **press pass** carte de presse; **press release** communiqué de presse; **press tycoon** magnat de la presse

pressure *n* pression *f*; **copper prices came under renewed pressure** les cours du cuivre ont subi une nouvelle pression ❑ **pressure group** groupe *m* de pression

prestige *n Mktg* **prestige advertising** publicité *f* de prestige; **prestige goods** produits *mpl* de prestige; **prestige model** modèle *m* de prestige; **prestige price** prix *m* de prestige; **prestige product** produit *m* de prestige; **prestige promotion** promotion *f* de prestige

presumptive *adj* **presumptive loss** perte *f* présumée; **presumptive taxation** imposition *f* forfaitaire

pre-tax *adj* brut(e), avant impôts ❑ **pre-tax margin** marge *f* avant impôts; **pre-tax profit** bénéfice *m* brut *ou* avant impôts

pre-test *Mktg* **1** *n* pré-test *m*
2 *vt* pré-tester

prevailing *adj* actuel(elle); **the prevailing economic climate** le climat économique actuel

price 1 *n* prix *m*; *St Exch (of shares)* cours *m*, cote *f*; **to rise** *or* **increase** *or* **go up in price** augmenter; **the price has risen** *or* **increased** *or* **gone up by ten percent** le prix a augmenté de dix pour cent; **to fall** *or* **decrease** *or* **go down in price** baisser; **the price has fallen** *or* **decreased** *or* **gone down by ten percent** le prix a baissé de dix pour cent; **to pay a high price for sth** payer qch cher; **to sell sth at a reduced price** vendre qch à prix réduit; *St Exch* **today's prices** les cours du jour; *St Exch* **what is the price of gold?** quel est le cours de l'or? ❑ **price agreement** accord *m* sur les prix; **price bid** offre *f* de prix; **price bracket** fourchette *f* de prix; **price break** baisse *f* de prix; **price cartel** cartel *m* de prix; **price ceiling** plafond *m* de prix; **price comparison** comparaison *f* des prix; **price competitiveness** compétitivité-prix *f*; **price control** contrôle *m* des prix; **price curve** courbe *f* des prix; **price cut** réduction *f* (des prix), baisse *f* des prix; **price cutting** baisse de prix; **price differential** écart *m* de prix; **price discount** remise *f* sur les prix; **price discrimination** tarif *m* discriminatoire; **price elasticity** élasticité *f* des prix; **price escalation** flambée *f* des prix; **price ex warehouse** prix à la production; **price ex works** prix départ usine; **price fixing** *(control)* contrôle des prix; *(rigging)* entente *f* sur les prix; *St Exch* **price fluctuation** mouvement *m* des cours; **price freeze** gel *m* des prix; **price hike** hausse *f* de prix; **prices and incomes policy** politique *f* des prix et des salaires; **price increase** hausse *ou* augmentation *f* des prix; **price index** indice *m* des prix; **price inflation** inflation *f* des prix; **price label** étiquette *f* de prix; **price labelling** étiquetage *m* de prix; **price leader** prix directeur; **price leadership** = position dominante en matière de fixation des prix; **price level** niveau *m* de prix; **price limit** limite *f* de prix; **price list** tarif, liste *f* des prix; *St Exch* **price maker** fixeur *m* de prix; **price markup** majoration *f* de prix; **price mechanism** mécanisme *m* des prix; *Banking, Fin* **price of money** prix *ou* loyer *m* de l'argent; *Econ* **price pegging** soutien *m* des prix; *Mktg* **price plan** plan *m* prix; *Mktg* **price point** prix (de référence); **price policy** politique des prix; *Mktg* **price positioning** positionnement *m* des prix; **price promotion** promotion *f*; **price proposal** proposition *f* de prix; **price range** échelle *f* des prix, gamme *f* des prix; **price reduction** réduction (des prix); **price regulation** réglementation *f* des prix; **price ring** monopole *m* des prix; **price scale** barème *m* des prix, échelle des prix; *Mktg* **price sensitivity** sensibilité *f* aux prix; **price setting** détermination *f* ou fixation *f* des prix; *St Exch* **price spreads** écarts *mpl* de cours; **price stability** stabilité *f* des prix; *Mktg* **price step** écart de prix; **price structure** structure *f* des prix; **price survey** enquête *f* sur les prix; **price tag** étiquette de prix; **price threshold** seuil *m* de prix; **price ticket** étiquette de prix; **price undercutting** gâchage *m* des prix; **price war** guerre *f* des prix

2 *vt* (**a**) *(decide cost of)* déterminer *ou* fixer le prix de; **the book is priced at £17** le livre coûte 17 livres

(**b**) *(indicate cost of)* mettre le prix sur; **these goods haven't been priced** ces articles n'ont pas reçu de prix *ou* n'ont pas été étiquetés; **all goods must be clearly priced** le prix des marchandises doit être clairement indiqué

(**c**) *(ascertain cost of)* s'informer du prix de; *(estimate value of)* évaluer qch, estimer la valeur de qch; **she priced it in several shops before buying it** elle a vérifié le prix dans plusieurs magasins avant de l'acheter

(**d**) **to price competitors out of the market** éliminer la concurrence en pratiquant des prix déloyaux; **to price oneself out of the market** perdre sa clientèle en pratiquant des prix trop élevés; **we've been priced out of the Japanese market** nous avons perdu le marché japonais à cause de nos prix

(**e**) *Econ (quantity)* valoriser

> **❝**
>
> National Power and its partner in duopoly, PowerGen, are the only game in town. Buy from them or buy candles. They can name their price and they do. One recent Friday, for example, generators raised the **price bid** into the pool at noon by 440 per cent above the sale price at 7am. **❞**

▸ **price down** *vt sep* baisser le prix de; **all items have been priced down by ten percent** tous les articles ont été démarqués de dix pour cent

▸ **price up** *vt sep* augmenter le prix de

price-earnings ratio *n St Exch* ratio *m* cours-bénéfices, rapport *m* cours-bénéfices

price-elastic *adj Mktg* au prix élastique

price-inelastic *adj Mktg* au prix stable

price-sensitive *adj* sensible aux prix

pricing *n* détermination *f* ou fixation *f* du prix ◻ **pricing policy** politique *f* de prix; **pricing research** recherche *f* sur les prix

primary *adj Econ* primaire ◻ **primary data** informations *fpl* primaires; *Fin* **primary dealer** spécialiste *mf* en valeurs du Trésor; *Mktg* **primary demand** demande *f* primaire; *Am St Exch* **primary earnings per share** bénéfices *mpl* premiers par action; **primary industry** industrie *f* primaire; *St Exch* **primary market** marché *m* primaire; **primary product** matière *f* première, produit *m* brut; **primary production** production *f* de matières premières; *Acct* **primary ratio** ratio *m* des bénéfices d'exploitation sur le capital employé; **primary sector** secteur *m* primaire; **the primary sector industries** les industries du secteur primaire

prime *adj Fin* **prime bill** papier *m* commercial de premier ordre; *Fin* **prime bond** obligation *f* de premier ordre; **prime cost** prix *m* de revient; *Fin* **prime lending rate** taux *m* de base bancaire; **Prime Minister** Premier Ministre *m*; *Fin* **prime rate** taux d'escompte bancaire préférentiel; *Mktg* **prime time** *(on TV)* prime time *m*; **prime time advertising** publicité *f* au prime time

principal *n* (**a**) *Law (employer of agent)* mandant *m*, commettant *m*; **principal and agent** mandant et mandataire *m* (**b**) *Fin (capital)* capital *m*; *(of debt)* principal *m*; **principal and interest** capital et intérêts (**c**) *St Exch* donneur(euse) *m,f* d'ordre

print 1 *vt* imprimer

2 *vi (of document)* s'imprimer; *(of printer)* imprimer ◻ **print ad, print advertisement** publicité *f* presse; **print advertising** publicité presse; *Comptr* **print cartridge** cartouche *f*; *Comptr* **print file** fichier *m* d'impression; *Comptr* **print format** format *m* d'impression; *Comptr* **print head** tête *f* d'impression; *Comptr* **print job** fichier à imprimer; *Comptr* **print list** liste *f* de fichiers à imprimer; *Comptr* **print menu** menu *m* d'impression; *Comptr* **print option** option *f* d'impression; *Comptr* **print preview** aperçu *m* avant impression; *Comptr* **print quality** qualité *f* d'impression; *Comptr* **print queue** liste de fichiers à imprimer; *Comptr* **print queuing** mise *f* en attente à l'impression; *Comptr* **print screen** copie *f* d'écran; **to do a print screen** imprimer un écran; *Comptr* **print speed** vitesse *f* d'impression; **print union** syndicat *m* des typographes

▶ **print out** *vt sep Comptr* imprimer

printed *adj* imprimé(e) ❏ **printed form** (état *m*) imprimé *m*; **printed matter** imprimés; **printed paper rate** tarif *m* (des) imprimés

printer *n Comptr* imprimante *f* ❏ **printer cable** câble *m* d'imprimante; **printer driver** programme *m* de commande d'impression; **printer font** fonte *f* imprimante; **printer paper** papier *m* d'impression; **printer peripheral** périphérique *m* d'impression; **printer port** port *m* d'imprimante; **printer sharing** partage *m* d'imprimantes; **printer speed** vitesse *f* d'impression; **printer spooling** mise *f* en attente des fichiers à imprimer

printout *n Comptr* sortie *f* sur papier; *(list, results of calculation)* listing *m*

prior *adj* précédent(e), antérieur(e) (**to** à); **to have a prior engagement** être déjà pris(e); **without prior notice** sans préavis

prioritizing question *n Mktg (in survey)* question *f* par classement

priority *n* priorité *f*; **to have** *or* **take priority (over)** avoir la priorité (sur); **the matter has top priority** l'affaire est prioritaire ❏ *Am* **priority mail** courrier *m* prioritaire; *Law* **priority rights** droits *mpl* de priorité; *St Exch* **priority share** action *f* privilégiée *ou* de priorité

private *adj* (a) *(not state-run)* privé(e) ❏ **private bank** banque *f* privée; **private company** société *f* privée; **private enterprise** entreprise *f* privée; **private finance initiative** partenariat *m* public-privé; **private health insurance** assurance *f* maladie privée; **private industry** privé *m*; **private limited company** société à responsabilité limitée; **private ownership** propriété *f* privée; **private pension** retraite *f* complémentaire; **private sector** secteur *m* privé

(b) *(personal)* personnel(elle) ❏ *Law* **private agreement** accord *m* à l'amiable; *Law* **private contract** acte *m* sous seing privé; **private income** rentes *fpl*; **to live off a private income** vivre de ses rentes; **private investment** investissement *m ou* placement *m* privé; **private investor** investisseur *m* privé; *Tel* **private line** ligne *f* privée; **private means** ressources *fpl* personnelles; **private property** propriété *f* privée; **private secretary** secrétaire *mf* particulier(ère)

(c) *(confidential)* privé(e), confidentiel(elle); **private (and confidential)** *(on letter)* confidentiel

private-label brand *n Mktg* marque *f* de distributeur

privately *adv* **to sell sth privately** vendre qch de gré à gré; **privately owned** *(company)* privé(e)

private-sector *adj (pay, business, management)* privé(e)

privatization *n* privatisation *f*

privatize *vt* privatiser

privileged debt *n* dette *f* privilégiée

privity of contract *n Law* lien *m* contractuel

prize bond *n* obligation *f* à lots, valeur *f* à lots

proactive *adj* qui fait preuve d'initiative ❏ **proactive marketing** marketing *m* proactif; *Admin* **proactive staffing** dotation *f* par anticipation

> **"**
>
> Why is there a need for the director or chairman to attempt secret behind-the-scenes deals? The PCC exists to adjudicate and urge good practice, not to broker compromises. Why indeed wait for a complaint in the first place? One important change the PCC could make is for it to become **proactive** and speak out on abuses before the formality of a complaint.
>
> **"**

probability *n Mktg* **probability method** *(of sampling)* méthode *f* probabiliste; **probability sample** échantillon *m* probabiliste; **probability sampling** échantillonnage *m* probabiliste

probate *Law* **1** *n (of document, will)* validation *f*, homologation *f*; **to value sth for probate** évaluer *ou* expertiser qch pour l'homologation d'un testament ❏ **probate price** prix *m* moyen **2** *vt (document, will)* valider, homologuer

probation *n (trial employment)* période *f* d'essai; **to take sb on probation** prendre qn à l'essai; **to be on probation** être en période d'essai

probationary *adj (period)* d'essai

probationer *n (employee)* employé(e) *m,f* à l'essai *ou* en période d'essai

problem *n* problème *m* ❏ **problem analysis** analyse *f* de problème(s); *Mktg* **problem child** *(company, product)* dilemme *m*; **problem solving** résolution *f* de problèmes

procedure *n* procédure *f*; **what's the correct procedure?** comment doit-on procéder?, quelle est la marche à suivre?; **you must follow the normal procedure** vous devez suivre la procédure normale ❏ *Law* **procedure by arbitration** procédure *f* arbitrale

proceed vi (**a**) (continue) continuer, poursuivre ; **we are now unable to proceed with our plans for expansion** nous sommes maintenant dans l'impossibilité de poursuivre nos projets d'expansion (**b**) (happen) se passer, se dérouler ; **is the meeting proceeding according to plan?** est-ce que la réunion se déroule comme prévu ? (**c**) (act) procéder, agir ; **how should we proceed?** comment doit-on procéder ?, quelle est la marche à suivre ?

proceedings npl (**a**) (meeting) réunion f, séance f ; (record of meeting) compte-rendu m, procès-verbal m (**b**) Law poursuites fpl judiciaires ou en justice ; **to take** or **institute proceedings (against sb)** engager des poursuites (contre qn)

proceeds npl (from sale) recette f

process 1 n (**a**) (method) procédé m, méthode f ; **to develop a process for doing sth** mettre au point un procédé pour faire qch ; **a new manufacturing process** un nouveau procédé de fabrication
(**b**) Comptr procédé m, traitement m
2 vt (**a**) (information, application, order) traiter ; **my insurance claim is still being processed** ma déclaration de sinistre est toujours en cours de règlement ; **we process thousands of applications every week** nous traitons des milliers de demandes chaque semaine
(**b**) Comptr (data) traiter
(**c**) (raw materials) traiter, transformer

processing n (**a**) (of information, application, order) traitement m (**b**) Comptr (of data) traitement m □ **processing language** langage m de traitement ; **processing power** puissance f de traitement ; **processing speed** vitesse f de traitement ; **processing time** temps m de traitement ; **processing unit** unité f de traitement (**c**) (of raw materials) traitement m, transformation f □ **processing industry** industrie f de transformation ; **processing plant** usine f de traitement

processor n Comptr processeur m □ **processor chip** microprocesseur m ; **processor speed** vitesse f du processeur

procuration n Law procuration f

procurator n Law fondé m de pouvoir

produce 1 n produits mpl ; **produce of Spain** produit en Espagne
2 vt (**a**) (manufacture, make) produire, fabriquer ; **we aren't producing enough spare parts** nous ne produisons pas assez de pièces détachées ; **Denmark produces dairy products** le Danemark est un pays producteur de produits laitiers ; **we have produced three new models this year** nous avons sorti trois nouveaux modèles cette année
(**b**) (interest, profit) rapporter ; **my investments produce a fairly good return** mes investissements sont d'un assez bon rapport ; **this ac-**count **produces a high rate of interest** ce compte rapporte des intérêts élevés
(**c**) (raw materials) produire

producer n (of raw materials, goods) producteur(trice) m,f ; **this region is Europe's biggest wine producer** cette région est la plus grande productrice de vin d'Europe □ **producers' association** syndicat m de producteurs ; **producers' co-operative** coopérative f de production ; **producer goods** biens mpl de production

product n produit m □ **product advertising** publicité f de produit ; **product analysis** analyse f de produit ; **product attribute** attribut m du produit ; **product augmentation** amélioration f du produit ; **product awareness** notoriété f ou mémorisation f du produit ; **product awareness level** degré m de mémorisation d'un produit ; **product bundling** groupage m de produits ; **product bundling pricing** fixation f des prix par lot ; **product category** catégorie f de produit ; **product champion** champion m de produit ; **product depth** profondeur f de produit ; **product design** conception f des produits ; **product development** élaboration f de produit ; **product development cost** coût m de l'élaboration du produit ; **product development programme** programme m de mise au point du produit ; **product differentiation** différenciation f du produit ; **product display** présentation f du produit ; **product diversification** diversification f des produits ; **product dynamics** dynamique f des produits ; **product features** caractéristiques fpl du produit ; **product form** type m de produit ; **product group manager** directeur(trice) m,f de groupe de produits ; **product hierarchy** hiérarchie f des produits ; **product image** image f de produit ; **product improvement** amélioration de produit ; **product information sheet** fiche f technique ; **product innovation** innovation f de produit ; **product launch** lancement m de produit ; **product launch file** dossier m de lancement ; EU **product liability** responsabilité f du produit ; **product liability insurance** assurance f de responsabilité du produit ; **product lifecycle** cycle m de vie du produit ; **product lifecycle curve** courbe f du cycle de vie du produit ; **product line** ligne f de produits ; **product line manager** directeur(trice) de ligne de produits ; **product management** gestion f de produits ; **product manager** chef m de produit, directeur(trice) de produit ; **product mapping** carte f perceptuelle de produits ; **product market** marché m de produits ; **product marketing** marketing m du produit ; **product mix** assortiment m ou mix m de produits ; **product mix depth** profondeur de l'assortiment de produits ; **product mix width** largeur f de l'assortiment de produits ; **product orientation** optique f produit ; **product performance test** test m de performance du produit ; *Mktg* **product placement** placement *m* de produit ; **product planning** planification *f* du produit ; **product policy** politique *f* de lancement d'un produit ; **product portfolio** portefeuille *m* de produits ; **product positioning** positionnement *m* du produit ; **product positioning map** carte *f* de positionnement des produits ; **product profile** profil *m* de produit ; **product promotion** communication *f* produit ; **product range** gamme *f* de produits ; **product research** recherche *f* de produits ; **product specialist** spécialiste *mf* produit ; **product test** test de produit ; **product testing** tests *mpl* de produit ; **product testing panel** panel *m* d'essayeurs de produits

production *n* *(process)* production *f*, fabrication *f* ; *(amount produced)* production ; **the workers have halted production** les travailleurs ont arrêté la production ; **to go into/out of production** être/ne plus être fabriqué(e) ; **this model is now in production** le modèle est en cours de production ; **is it in production yet?** est-ce qu'on en a commencé la production ? ; **this model went into/out of production in 2001** on a commencé la fabrication de ce modèle/ce modèle a été retiré de la production en 2001 ; **to cease production** arrêter la production ; **to move** *or* **shift production** relocaliser son unité de production ; **an increase/a fall in production** une hausse/une baisse de la production □ **production budget** budget *m* de production ; **production capacity** capacité *f* de production ; **production control** direction *f* de la production ; **production cost** coût *m* de production ; **production department** service *m* (de) production ; **production engineering** productique *f* ; **production facilities** appareil *m* de production ; **production factor** facteur *m* de production ; **production flowchart** organigramme *m* de production ; **production incentive** prime *f* de rendement ; **production lead time** délai *m* de production ; **production line** chaîne *f* de montage ; **to work on a production line** travailler à la chaîne ; **this model has just come off the production line** ce modèle vient juste de sortir de la chaîne de production ; **production management** gestion *f* de la production ; **production manager** directeur(trice) *m,f* de la production ; *Acct* **production overheads** frais *mpl* généraux de production ; **production planning** planning *m* de la production ; **production plant** usine *f* ; **production schedule** programme *m* de fabrication ; **production scheduling** programmation *f* de la production ; **production target** objectif *m* de production ; **production tool** outil *m* de production ; **production unit** unité *f* de production ; **production worker** agent *m* de fabrication

productive *adj* *Econ* productif(ive) □ **productive forces** forces *fpl* productives ; **productive labour** main-d'œuvre *f* productive ; **productive life** *(of machine)* vie *f* physique

productively *adv* d'une manière productive

productivity *n* productivité *f*, rendement *m* □ **productivity agreement** accord *m* de productivité ; **productivity bargaining** négociation *f* syndicale d'un contrat de productivité ; **productivity bonus** prime *f* de rendement ; **productivity campaign** campagne *f* de productivité ; **productivity deal** contrat *m* de productivité ; **productivity drive** campagne de productivité ; **productivity gains** gains *mpl* de productivité ; **productivity investment** investissement *m* de productivité ; **productivity surplus** surplus *m* de productivité

product/market pair *n* *Mktg* couple *m* produit/marché

product/price policy *n* *Mktg* politique *f* de produit/prix

profession *n* profession *f* ; **by profession** de profession

professional 1 *n* professionnel(elle) *m,f* ; *(executive, lawyer)* membre *m* des professions libérales

2 *adj* (**a**) *(relating to a profession)* professionnel(elle) □ **professional association** association *f* professionnelle ; **professional body** organisme *m* professionnel, organisation *f* professionnelle ; **professional code of ethics** déontologie *f* ; **professional confidentiality** secret *m* professionnel ; **professional fees** frais *mpl* professionnels ; **professional indemnity insurance** assurance *f* de responsabilité professionnelle ; **professional indemnity policy** politique *f* de responsabilité professionnelle ; **professional life** la vie active ; **professional misconduct** faute *f* professionnelle ; **professional negligence** négligence *f* professionnelle ; **professional qualifications** qualifications *fpl* professionnelles ; **professional training** formation *f* professionnelle

(**b**) *(in quality, attitude)* professionnel(elle) ; **he works in a very professional manner** il travaille en professionnel ; **she is very professional in her approach to the problem** elle aborde le problème de façon très professionnelle

proficiency *n* compétence *f* (**in** en) ; **proficiency in a foreign language is essential** la connaissance d'une langue étrangère est indispensable

proficient *adj* compétent(e) (**in** en)

profile *n* *(of candidate, employee, market, product)* profil *m* ; **to have the right profile for the job** avoir le bon profil pour le poste

profit *n* bénéfice *m*, profit *m* ; **profits were down/up this year** les bénéfices ont diminué/augmenté cette année ; **to make a profit** faire un bénéfice *ou* des bénéfices ; **to make a profit**

out of sth faire un bénéfice sur qch; **we made a £1,000 profit on the sale** nous avons réalisé un bénéfice de 1000 livres sur cette vente; **to show a profit** rapporter un bénéfice *ou* des bénéfices; **to be in profit** être bénéficiaire; **to move into profit** *(of business)* devenir rentable; **to sell sth at a profit** faire un bénéfice sur une vente; **profit and loss** pertes *fpl* et profits □ *profit balance* solde *m* bénéficiaire; *Am prof-it center* centre *m* de profit; *Br profit centre* centre de profit; *profit equation* équation *f* de bénéfice; *profit indicator* indice *m* de profit; *profit and loss account, profit and loss statement* compte *m* de résultat; *Formerly* compte de pertes et profits; *profit margin* marge *f* bénéficiaire; *profit motive* motivation *f* par le profit; *profit optimization* optimisation *f* du *ou* des profits; *profit outlook* perspectives *fpl* de profit; *profit target* objectif *m* de profit; *profit tax* impôt *m* sur les bénéfices; *profit warning* = annonce d'une baisse prochaine des bénéfices d'une entreprise

> **"**
> City professionals are naturally wary of a company which has issued three **profit warnings** in the space of two years – the most recent arriving in July. But other market players are more optimistic. They smell more corporate action and they are probably right.
> **"**

profitability *n* rentabilité *f* □ *profitability index* indice *m* de rentabilité; *profitability value (of a company)* valeur *f* de rendement

profitable *adj* rentable; **this factory is no longer profitable** cette usine n'est plus rentable; **it wouldn't be profitable for me to sell** cela ne me rapporterait pas grand-chose de vendre

profitably *adv* avec profit, d'une manière rentable; **we sold it very profitably** on l'a vendu en faisant un bénéfice confortable

profit-centre accounting, *Am* **profit-center accounting** *n Acct* = comptabilité par centres de profits

profit-driven *adj* poussé(e) par les profits

profiteer 1 *n* profiteur(euse) *m,f*
2 *vi* = profiter d'une situation pour faire des bénéfices excessifs

profitless *adj* sans profit; **a profitless deal** une affaire blanche

profit-making *adj* **(a)** *(aiming to make profit)* à but lucratif □ *profit-making organization* association *f* à but lucratif **(b)** *(profitable)* rentable

profit-sharing *n* participation *f* ou intéressement *m* aux bénéfices □ *profit-sharing scheme* système *m* de participation aux bénéfices

profit-taking *n* prise *f* de bénéfices

> **"**
> The question really is whether the activity at SIVB is little more than routine **profit-taking** or whether it reflects a chink in the armor of the super high-tech economy. There are those who insist that any decrease in the bank's IPO/Venture Cap business will be more than offset by an increase in its tradi-tional lending operations.
> **"**

profit-volume ratio *n* rapport *m* profit sur ventes

pro-forma 1 *n (invoice)* facture *f* pro forma
2 *adj pro-forma bill* traite *f* pro forma; *pro-forma invoice* facture *f* pro forma

program *Comptr* **1** *n* programme *m* □ *program disk* disquette *f* programme; *program language* langage *m* de programmation; *program library* bibliothèque *f* de programmes
2 *vt* programmer; **to program a computer to do sth** programmer un ordinateur pour qu'il fasse qch
3 *vi* programmer

programmer *n Comptr* programmeur(euse) *m,f*

programming *n Comptr* programmation *f* □ *programming language* langage *m* de programmation

progress 1 *n* progrès *m*; **to make progress** faire des progrès; **to be in progress** être en cours; **the negotiations in progress** les négociations en cours □ *Ind progress chart* diagramme *m* de l'avancement des travaux; *progress chaser* responsable *mf* du planning; *progress payment* paiement *m* proportionnel (à l'avancement des travaux); *progress report* compte-rendu *m*; *(on work)* rapport *m* sur l'avancement des travaux
2 *vi* progresser; **the talks are progressing well** les pourparlers sont en bonne voie

progressive *adj* progressif(ive) □ *progressive tax* impôt *m* progressif; *progressive taxation* imposition *f* progressive

prohibitive *adj (price)* prohibitif(ive)

project 1 *n* projet *m*; **they're working on a new building project** ils travaillent sur un nouveau projet de construction □ *project analysis* étude *f* de projet; *project management* gestion *f* de projets; *Comptr project management package* gestionnaire *m* de projets; *project manager* directeur(trice) *m,f* de projet; *project milestones* étapes *fpl* principales du projet
2 *vt (forecast)* prévoir; **he's projecting a 40 percent slide in May** il prévoit une baisse de 40 pour cent au mois de mai; **we have at-tempted to project next year's figures/out-**

put nous avons tenté de prévoir les chiffres/la production pour l'année prochaine

> Not only is actual conflict greater today, but even the potential for interpersonal conflicts in the workplace is far greater than at any time in the past. One reason for this is increased time-to-market pressures. The need to rapidly make decisions, establish an engineering direction, and meet **project milestones** adds elements of tension and stress to an already difficult endeavor.

projected adj (forecast) prévu(e), prévisionnel(elle); **the projected growth of the economy** la croissance économique prévue □ **projected demand** demande f prévisionnelle; **projected population** population f prévue; **projected turnover** chiffre m d'affaires prévisionnel

projection n (forecast) projection f, prévision f; **here are my projections for the next ten years** voici mes prévisions pour les dix années à venir

promissory note n Fin billet m ou effet m à ordre

promo n Fam (promotion) promo f

promote vt (**a**) (person) promouvoir, donner de l'avancement à; **to be promoted** être promu(e), recevoir de l'avancement; **she's been promoted to regional manager** elle a été promue au poste de directrice régionale
(**b**) (foster) promouvoir, favoriser; **to promote economic growth** promouvoir ou favoriser la croissance économique
(**c**) (product) promouvoir, faire la promotion de; **to promote a new product** faire la promotion d'un nouveau produit

promoter n promoteur(trice) m,f

promotion n (**a**) (of person) promotion f, avancement m; **to get promotion** être promu(e), recevoir de l'avancement; **there are good prospects of promotion in this company** il y a de réelles possibilités de promotion ou d'avancement dans cette société □ **promotions list** tableau m d'avancement
(**b**) (of product) promotion f; **this week's promotion** la promotion de la semaine □ **promotions agency** agence f de promotion; **promotion budget** budget m promotionnel; **promotion campaign** campagne f de promotion; **promotion team** équipe f promotionnelle

promotional adj promotionnel(elle) □ **promotional campaign** campagne f de promotion; **promotional costs** coûts mpl de promotion; **promotional discount** remise f promotionnelle; **promotional label** étiquette f promotionnelle; **promotional literature** prospectus

mpl promotionnels; **promotional material** matériel m de promotion; **promotional offer** offre f promotionnelle; **promotional policy** politique f de communication, politique de promotion; **promotional price** prix m promotionnel; **promotional sale** vente f promotionnelle; **promotional sample** échantillon m promotionnel; **promotional target** cible f de communication; **promotional video** (cassette f) vidéo f promotionnelle

prompt 1 n (**a**) (for payment) délai m (de paiement) □ **prompt day** jour m de paiement; **prompt note** rappel m d'échéance (**b**) Comptr invite f; (with wording) message m d'invite
2 adj (quick) prompt(e), rapide □ **prompt payment** paiement m dans les délais; **prompt service** service m rapide

proof n (evidence) preuve f □ **proof of credit** titre m de crédit; **proof of delivery** bordereau m de livraison; **proof of identity** pièce f d'identité; **proof of payment** justificatif m de paiement; **proof of postage** certificat m d'expédition; **proof of purchase** reçu m

▶ **prop up** vt sep (business, currency) soutenir; **the government stepped in to prop up the dollar** le gouvernement est intervenu pour soutenir le dollar

propensity n Econ **propensity to consume** propension f à consommer; Econ **propensity to save** propension à épargner

property n (**a**) (land, house) propriété f; (real estate) biens mpl immobilers; **he's investing his money in property** il investit son argent dans l'immobilier; **to get a foot on the property ladder** accéder à la propriété, devenir propriétaire □ Br **property assets** patrimoine m immobilier; **property centre** centre m de vente immobilière; **property charge** dette f foncière; **property developer** promoteur(trice) m,f immobilier(ère); **property development** promotion f immobilière; Br **property loan** prêt m immobilier; **property manager** gérant(e) m,f d'immeubles; **property market** marché m de l'immobilier; **property owner** propriétaire mf; **property shares** valeurs fpl immobilières; **property speculation** spéculations fpl immobilières; **property speculator** spéculateur(trice) m,f immobilier(ère); **property surveyor** (architecte mf) expert(e) m,f; **property tax** impôt m foncier, taxe f foncière (**b**) (possessions) biens mpl; **she left him all her property** elle lui a laissé tous ses biens

proposal n proposition f; **to make a proposal** faire ou formuler une proposition

propose vt proposer; **to propose a motion** présenter ou soumettre une motion

proprietary adj **proprietary article** article m de marque (déposée); **proprietary brand**

marque *f* déposée; **proprietary name** nom *m* déposé

proprietor *n* propriétaire *mf*

pro rata 1 *adj* prorata; **the salary is £21,000 pro rata** le salaire est calculé sur la base de 21 000 livres par an
2 *adv* au prorata

prosecute *vt Law* poursuivre (en justice)

prosecution *n Law* poursuites *fpl* (judiciaires); **to be liable to prosecution** s'exposer à des poursuites judiciaires; **to bring a prosecution against sb** poursuivre qn (en justice)

prospect *n* (**a**) *(chance, likelihood)* perspective *f*; **the prospects for the automobile industry** les perspectives d'avenir de l'industrie automobile; **it's a job without any prospects of promotion** c'est un poste qui n'offre aucune perspective d'avenir
(**b**) *(prospective customer)* client(e) *m,f* éventuel(elle), client(e) potentiel(elle); **he's a good prospect for the manager's job** c'est un candidat potentiel au poste de directeur ▫ **prospect pool** groupe *m* de prospects
2 *vi Mktg* prospecter; **to prospect for new customers** rechercher *ou* démarcher de nouveaux clients

❝
The Internet allows us to inexpensively market, distribute and administer the products and services of several web site/e-commerce products, each with its own market niche and clearly defined customer/**prospect pool**.
❞

prospective *adj (buyer, client)* éventuel(elle), potentiel(elle)

prospectus *n* (**a**) *(about company, product)* prospectus *m* (**b**) *St Exch (about share issue)* appel *m* à la souscription publique

prosperity *n* prospérité *f*

prosperous *adj* prospère

protectionism *n Econ* protectionnisme *m*

protectionist *n & adj Econ* protectionniste *mf* ▫ **protectionist measures** mesures *fpl* protectionnistes

protective *adj Econ (duty, measure)* protecteur(trice)

protest *n* (**a**) *Law* protêt *m* ▫ **protest for non-acceptance** protêt faute d'acceptation; **protest for non-payment** protêt faute de paiement (**b**) *Ins* procès-verbal *m* des avaries

protocol *n Comptr* protocole *m*

prototype *n* prototype *m*

provide *vt* (**a**) *(stipulate)* stipuler; **the contract provides that...** dans le contrat il est stipulé

que... (**b**) *(supply)* fournir; **to provide sb with sth** fournir qch à qn; **the new plant will provide 2,000 jobs** la nouvelle usine créera 2 000 emplois

▸ **provide for** *vt insep* (**a**) *(allow for)* stipuler; **the bill provides for subsidies to be reduced** le projet de loi prévoit une baisse des subventions; *Ins* **this risk is not provided for in the policy** ce risque n'est pas prévu dans la police
(**b**) *(support)* pourvoir aux besoins de; **an insurance policy that will provide for your children's future** une assurance qui subviendra aux besoins de vos enfants
(**c**) *(prepare)* **to provide for sth** se préparer à qch

provident *adj* **provident fund** caisse *f* de prévoyance; **provident society** société *f* de prévoyance

provider *n* (**a**) *(person)* pourvoyeur(euse) *m,f*; **she's the family's sole provider** elle subvient seule aux besoins de la famille (**b**) *(supplier)* fournisseur(euse) *m,f* (**c**) *Comptr* fournisseur *m* d'accès à l'Internet

provision *n* (**a**) *(act of supplying)* approvisionnement *m*; **the provision of new jobs** la création d'emplois; **provision of capital** prestation *f* de capitaux
(**b**) *(allowance)* provision *f*; **to make provision for sth** prévoir qch ▫ *Acct* **provision for bad debts** provision pour créances douteuses; *Acct* **provision for depreciation** provision pour dépréciation; *Acct* **provision for liabilities** provision pour sommes exigibles
(**c**) **provisions** *(supplies)* provisions *fpl*
(**d**) *(in treaty)* disposition *f*; *(in contract)* clause *f*; **under the provisions of the UN charter** selon les dispositions de la charte de l'ONU; **a four percent increase is included in the budget's provisions** une augmentation de quatre pour cent est prévue dans le budget

provisional *adj* provisoire; *(budget)* prévisionnel(elle)

proviso *n* condition *f*, stipulation *f*; **with the proviso that the goods be delivered within one month** à condition que les marchandises soient livrées dans un délai d'un mois; **they accept, with one proviso** ils acceptent, à une condition

proxy *n* (**a**) *Law (power)* procuration *f*; *(person)* mandataire *mf*, fondé(e) *mf* de pouvoir; **by proxy** par procuration; **to vote by proxy** voter par procuration (**b**) *Comptr* mandataire *m*

prudence concept *n Acct* principe *m* de prudence

PSBR *n Br Econ (abbr* **public sector borrowing requirement***)* = besoins d'emprunt du secteur public non couverts par les rentrées fiscales

psychographic adj Mktg (data, profile, segment) psychographique

psychological adj **psychological contract** contrat m psychologique; Mktg **psychological price** prix m psychologique; **psychological profile** profil m psychologique

public 1 n the (general) public le (grand) public; **to issue shares to the public** placer des actions dans le public
2 adj public(ique); St Exch **to go public** être coté(e) en. Bourse □ **public affairs** affaires fpl publiques; Am **public assistance** aide f sociale; **public auction** enchères fpl publiques; **public authorities** pouvoirs mpl publics; **public body** corporation f de droit public; **public company** société f d'État; Br **public corporation** entreprise f publique; **public debt** dette f publique ou de l'État; Banking **public deposits** = avoirs des différents services du gouvernement britannique à la Banque d'Angleterre; **public domain** domaine m public; **to be in the public domain** être dans le domaine public; **public enterprise** (company) entreprise publique; **public expenditure** dépenses fpl publiques; **public finance** finances fpl publiques; **public funds** fonds mpl publics; **public holiday** fête f légale, jour m férié; **public inquiry** enquête f administrative; **public liability** responsabilité f civile; **public liability insurance** assurance f responsabilité civile; **public limited company** ≃ société f anonyme; **public loan** emprunt m public; **public money** fonds publics; **public monies** deniers mpl de l'État; St Exch **public offering** offre f publique; **public opinion** opinion f publique; **public opinion poll** sondage m d'opinion; **public ownership** = fait d'appartenir à l'État; **most airports are under public ownership** la plupart des aéroports appartiennent à l'État; **public property** propriété f publique; **public relations** relations fpl publiques; **giving them a free meal was great public relations** en leur offrant le repas, nous avons fait un excellent travail de relations publiques; **public relations agency** agence f conseil en communication; **public relations consultancy** agence conseil en communication; **public relations consultant** conseil m en relations publiques; **public relations exercise** opération f de relations publiques; **it was a good public relations exercise** ce fut une réussite pour ce qui est des relations publiques; **public relations manager** directeur(trice) m,f des relations publiques; **public relations officer** responsable mf des relations publiques; **public sale** vente f publique; **public sector** secteur m publique; **public sector pay is expected to rise by only three per cent over the next year** on prévoit une hausse d'à peine trois pour cent des salaires du secteur public pour l'année prochaine; **public sector borrowing requirement** = besoins

d'emprunt du secteur public non couverts par les rentrées fiscales; **public sector deficit** déficit m du secteur public; **public sector earnings** revenus mpl du secteur public; **public servant** fonctionnaire mf; **public service** (amenity) service m public ou d'intérêt général; Br (civil service) fonction f publique; **she's in public service** elle est fonctionnaire; **our organization performs a public service** notre association assure un service d'intérêt général; St Exch **public share offer** offre publique de vente; **public spending** dépenses publiques; **public transport** transports mpl en commun; **public utility** Br (amenity) service public; Am (company) = société privée assurant un service public et réglementée par une commission d'État; Br **public utility company** société d'utilité publique; **public works** travaux mpl publics; **public works contractor** entrepreneur m de travaux publics

publication n (activity, published work) publication f

publicity n publicité f; **it'll give us free publicity for the product** ça fera de la publicité gratuite pour notre produit □ **publicity agent** agent m publicitaire ou de publicité; **publicity brochure** brochure f publicitaire; **publicity campaign** campagne f publicitaire ou de publicité; **publicity department** service m de la publicité; **publicity expenses** dépenses fpl publicitaires; **publicity manager** chef m de publicité

publicize vt (product) faire de la publicité pour; **the launch of their new product has been widely publicized** leur nouveau produit a été lancé à grand renfort de publicité

publicly adv publiquement; Econ **publicly owned** à capitaux publics; **the company is 51 percent publicly controlled** la société est contrôlée à 51 pour cent par des capitaux publics

public-service corporation n Am = société privée assurant un service public et réglementée par une commission d'État

publish vt publier

publisher n (person) éditeur(trice) m,f; (company) maison f d'édition

publishing n édition f □ **publishing company, publishing house** maison f d'édition

▸ **pull down** vt sep Comptr (menu) dérouler

▸ **pull out** vi (from deal, arrangement) se désister; **they've pulled out of the deal** ils se sont retirés de l'affaire

pull-down adj Comptr **pull-down menu** menu m déroulant; **pull-down window** fenêtre f déroulante

pull strategy n Mktg stratégie f pull

pump vt Fam (invest) investir; **he pumped a fortune into the business** il a investi une fortune dans cette affaire; **public money is being pumped into the area** la région reçoit d'importantes subventions du gouvernement; **the government has pumped money into the project** le gouvernement a injecté des capitaux dans ce projet

punitive damages npl Law dommages-intérêts mpl punitifs

punt n Formerly livre f irlandaise

punter n Fam (**a**) (customer) client(e) m,f (**b**) St Exch (speculator) boursicoteur(euse) m,f, boursicotier(ère) m,f

> **❝**
> There are few better times to buy a mobile phone than at Christmas. The phone networks and stores always make it a season to be jolly by offering all kinds of deals and promotions. Some entice buyers with extra talk minutes or free text messages. Others are a little less subtle and encourage **punters** to part with their cash in exchange for free games, watches or entry to big money competitions.
> **❞**

purchasable adj achetable

purchase 1 n (act of buying, thing bought) achat m; (of company) rachat m; **to make a purchase** faire un achat □ **purchase account** compte m d'achats; **purchase accounting** = méthode de comptabilité utilisée lors de l'acquisition d'une entreprise, dans laquelle les résultats de la filiale n'apparaissent pas dans le bilan de la société mère; Mktg **purchase behaviour** comportement m d'achat; **purchase budget** budget m des approvisionnements; **purchase cost** coût m d'achat; Acct **purchase of debts** rachat des créances; Mktg **purchase decision** décision f d'achat; Mktg **purchase diary** relevé m d'achat journalier; Acct **purchase entry** écriture f d'achats; Mktg **purchase environment** environnement m d'achat; Mktg **purchase frequency** fréquence f d'achat; Acct **purchase invoice** facture f d'achat; Acct **purchase invoice ledger** journal m factures-fournisseurs; Acct **purchase ledger** (grand-) livre m d'achats; **purchase method** méthode f d'achat; **purchase note** bordereau m d'achat; **purchase order** (for goods, service) bon m de commande; St Exch (for shares) ordre m d'achat; **purchase price** prix m d'achat; **purchase report** relevé d'achat; **purchase return** retour m sur achat; **purchase tax** taxe f à l'achat; **purchase value** valeur f d'achat; **purchase volume** volume m d'achat

2 vt acheter, acquérir; **to purchase sth from sb** acheter qch à qn; **to purchase sth on credit** acheter qch à crédit; Acct **to purchase a**

debt racheter une créance

3 vi acheter; **now is the time to purchase** c'est maintenant qu'il faut acheter

purchaser n acheteur(euse) m,f □ Mktg **purchaser behaviour** comportement m de l'acheteur

purchasing n achat m; (of company) rachat m □ Am **purchasing agent** acheteur(euse) m,f; Mktg **purchasing behaviour** comportement m d'achat; **purchasing behaviour model** modèle m de comportement d'achat; **purchasing costs** frais mpl de passation de commande; **purchasing decision** décision f d'achat; **purchasing department** service m des achats; **purchasing group** groupement m d'achat; **purchasing manager** chef m des achats; **purchasing motivator** mobile m d'achat; Econ **purchasing power** pouvoir m ou capacité f d'achat; **purchasing power parity** parité f du pouvoir d'achat; **purchasing process** processus m d'achat; **purchasing rights** droits mpl d'achat; **purchasing unit** cellule f d'achat

pure adj Econ, Mktg **pure competition** concurrence f pure; Ins **pure premium** prime f pure ou nette

purposive adj Mktg **purposive sample** échantillon m empirique; **purposive sampling** échantillonnage m empirique

push 1 n **push money** prime f au vendeur; Mktg **push strategy** stratégie f push
2 vt St Exch **to push shares** placer des valeurs douteuses

put 1 n St Exch option f de vente, put m □ **put band** période f de validité d'une option de vente; **put bond** emprunt m à fenêtre; **put and call** double option f, stellage m; **put option** option de vente; **put warrant** warrant m à la vente
2 vt (**a**) (invest) placer, investir; **she had put all her savings into property** elle avait placé ou investi toutes ses économies dans l'immobilier (**b**) (present) (suggestion, question) soumettre; (motion) proposer, présenter; **to put a proposal to the board** présenter une proposition au conseil d'administration

► **put back** vt sep (**a**) (postpone) reporter, remettre; **the meeting has been put back to Thursday** la réunion a été reportée ou remise à jeudi (**b**) (delay) retarder; **the strike has put our schedule back at least a month** la grève nous a fait perdre au moins un mois sur notre planning

► **put down** vt sep (**a**) (write) écrire; **to put sth down in writing** remettre qch par écrit (**b**) (pay as deposit) verser; **we've already put £500 down on the computer** nous avons déjà versé un acompte de 500 livres pour l'ordinateur

► **put forward** vt sep (**a**) (bring forward) avancer; **the meeting has been put forward to early next week** la réunion a été avancée au début de la semaine prochaine (**b**) *(suggest)* *(proposal, idea)* avancer; *(candidate)* proposer; **she put her name forward for the post of treasurer** elle a posé sa candidature au poste de trésorière

▸ **put out** *vt sep (sub-contract)* donner en sous-traitance; **we put most of our work out** nous confions la plus grande partie de notre travail à des sous-traitants

▸ **put through** *vt sep (on phone)* **to put sb through to sb** mettre qn en ligne avec qn, passer qn à qn; **put him through, please** mettez-le en ligne *ou* passez-le moi, s'il vous plaît; **I'll put you through to him** je vous le passe

▸ **put up** *vt sep* (**a**) *(money)* fournir; **who's putting up the money for the new business?** qui finance la nouvelle entreprise? (**b**) *(increase)*

faire monter, augmenter; **this will put up the price of oil** ça va faire augmenter le prix du pétrole

P/V *n (abbr* **profit-volume ratio**) rapport *m* profit sur ventes, ratio *m* de volume de bénéfices

pyramid 1 *n* **pyramid scheme** plan *m* commercial en cascade; **pyramid selling** vente *f* pyramidale; **pyramid selling scheme** plan commercial en cascade
  2 *vt (companies)* structurer en pyramide

66

The 1996 Trading Schemes Act outlaws **pyramid selling schemes**, but not investment pyramids. Originators of the investment versions have insured against legal clamp down by requiring that each recruit signs a declaration that her investment is an unconditional gift.

99

Qq

QC n (abbr **quality control**) contrôle m de la qualité

qty n (abbr **quantity**) qté f

qualification n (**a**) (diploma) diplôme m; **list your academic qualifications** indiquez vos diplômes scolaires et universitaires (**b**) (skill, competence) compétence f, aptitude f; **the main qualification we are looking for is a creative mind** ce que nous attendons avant tout du candidat, c'est qu'il fasse preuve d'un esprit créatif

qualified adj (**a**) (having diploma) diplômé(e); **our staff are highly qualified** notre personnel est hautement qualifié; **to be qualified to do sth** avoir les diplômes requis pour faire qch □ **qualified accountant** comptable mf diplômé(e)
(**b**) (skilled, competent) compétent(e); **to be qualified to do sth** avoir les compétences requises pour faire qch
(**c**) (modified) mitigé(e) □ Banking **qualified acceptance** acceptation f conditionnelle ou sous condition; **qualified approval** approbation f avec réserve; Acct **qualified report** rapport m réservé

qualify vt (**a**) (make competent) **to qualify sb to do sth** donner les compétences nécessaires à qn pour faire qch; **her experience qualifies her for the post** son expérience lui permet de prétendre à ce poste (**b**) (modify) mitiger; **they qualified their acceptance of the plan** ils ont accepté le projet sous conditions

qualitative adj qualitatif(ive) □ Mktg **qualitative forecasting** prévisions fpl qualitatives; **qualitative research** études fpl qualitatives; **qualitative study** étude f qualitative

quality n (**a**) (standard) qualité f; **of good/poor quality** de bonne/mauvaise qualité; **we have a reputation for quality** nous sommes réputés pour la qualité de nos produits □ **quality assurance** garantie f de qualité; **quality audit** audit m de qualité; **quality circle** cercle m de qualité; **quality control** contrôle m de la qualité; **quality control department** service m contrôle de la qualité; **quality controller** responsable mf du contrôle de la qualité; **quality goods** marchandises fpl de qualité; **quality improvement** amélioration f de la qualité; **quality label** label m de qualité; **quality management** gestion f qualité; Mktg **quality positioning** positionnement m par la qualité (**b**) (attribute) qualité f; **these are the qualities we are looking for in our candidates** voici les qualités que nous recherchons chez nos candidats

quality-price ratio n rapport m qualité-prix

quango n Br (abbr **quasi-autonomous non-governmental organization**) = organisme crée par le gouvernement et doté de pouvoirs quasi autonomes

> **"**
> Despite the promise of a people's government, the country is increasingly run by unaccountable, secretive crony networks, writes Stuart Weir. Tony Blair and his colleagues have been full of promises to abolish the **quango** state and make "bonfires of **quangos**". But there are no dead **quangos** among the slaughtered sheep and livestock in the funeral pyres and trenches that disfigure the British countryside. No, the **quango** state is alive and well.
> **"**

quantify vt quantifier, évaluer

quantitative adj quantitatif(ive) □ Mktg **quantitative forecasting** prévisions fpl quantitatives; **quantitative research** études fpl quantitatives; **quantitative study** étude f quantitative

quantity n quantité f; **to buy sth in large quantities** acheter qch en grande quantité □ **quantity discount** escompte m sur la quantité ou sur les achats en gros; **quantity rebate** remise f sur la quantité ou sur les achats en gros; **quantity surveying** métrage m; **quantity surveyor** métreur m vérificateur; Econ **quantity theory** théorie f quantitative

quarter n (three-month period) trimestre m; **profits were up during the last quarter** les bénéfices ont augmenté au cours du dernier trimestre □ Br **quarter day** (jour m du) terme m

quarterly 1 n (publication) publication f trimestrielle
2 adj trimestriel(elle)
3 adv tous les trimestres

quartile n quart m

quasi-contract n Law quasi-contrat m

quasi-money n Fin quasi-monnaie f

quay n quai m

quayage n droits mpl de quai

query n Comptr interrogation f ❑ Am **query mark** point m d'interrogation

question mark n (**a**) Br (punctuation mark) point m d'interrogation (**b**) Mktg (product) point m d'interrogation, dilemme m

questionnaire n Mktg questionnaire m ❑ **questionnaire survey** enquête f par questionnaire

queue Comptr **1** n file f d'attente
2 vt (print jobs) mettre en file d'attente

quick adj rapide ❑ Acct **quick assets** actif m liquide; **quick ratio** ratio m de liquidité immédiate; **quick returns** profits mpl rapides; **quick sale** vente f rapide

quid n Br Fam (pound sterling) livre f

quiet adj (market, business, trading) calme; **business is very quiet** les affaires sont très calmes

quit Comptr **1** vt (database, program) sortir de, quitter
2 vi sortir

quittance n Fin quittance f

quorum n quorum m; **to have a quorum** atteindre le quorum; **we don't have a quorum** le quorum n'est pas atteint

quota n (**a**) (limited quantity) quota m; **fishing quotas have been disputed** les quotas pour la pêche ont été contestés (**b**) (share) part f, quota m ❑ Mktg **quota sample** échantillon m par quotas; Mktg **quota sampling** échantillonnage m par quotas; Mktg **quota sampling method** méthode f des quotas

quotable adj St Exch cotable

quotation n (**a**) St Exch cotation f, cours m; **the latest quotations** les derniers cours; **to seek a share quotation** faire une demande d'admission à la cote (**b**) (for work) devis m; **to get a quotation** faire faire un devis; **they gave me a quotation of £500** ils m'ont fait un devis de 500 livres (**c**) **quotation marks** guillemets mpl

quotation-driven adj St Exch (market) à prix affichés

quote 1 n (for work) devis m; **to get a quote** faire faire un devis; **they gave me a quote of £500** ils m'ont fait un devis de 500 livres
2 vt (**a**) St Exch (shares, company) coter; **gold prices were quoted at £500** l'or a été coté à 500 livres; **quoted on the Stock Exchange** coté(e) en Bourse; **to quote an expiry** coter une échéance ❑ **quoted company** société f cotée en Bourse; **quoted investment** valeur f cotée en Bourse; **quoted price** cours m inscrit à la cote officielle; **quoted securities** valeurs fpl de Bourse; **quoted share** action f cotée, action inscrite à la cote officielle
(**b**) (price) indiquer; **to quote sb a price for sth** fixer à qn un prix pour qch; **can you quote me a price?** pouvez-vous m'indiquer un prix?; **they quoted me £500 for the work** ils m'ont fait un devis de 500 livres pour le travail
(**c**) Admin **please quote this number** (in reply) prière de rappeler ce numéro
3 vi **to quote for a job** faire un devis pour un travail

quote-driven adj St Exch (Stock Market) gouverné(e) par les prix

QWERTY keyboard n Comptr clavier m qwerty

Rr

radio n radio f ◻ *radio advertisement* publicité f à la radio; *radio advertising* publicité à la radio; *radio station* station f de radio

radiopager n récepteur m de poche *ou* d'appel

raid *St Exch* **1** n raid m
 2 vt **to raid the bears** chasser le découvert

raider n *St Exch* raider m

rail n *(train system)* chemin m de fer; **to send goods by rail** envoyer des marchandises par chemin de fer ◻ *rail link* liaison f ferroviaire; *rail transport* transport m ferroviaire

rail-air link n liaison f train-aéroport

railroad n *Am (train system)* chemin m de fer

railway n *Br (train system)* chemin m de fer

raise **1** n *Am (pay increase)* augmentation f (de salaire)
 2 vt **(a)** *(price, rate, salary)* augmenter; **to raise interest rates** augmenter les taux d'intérêt **(b)** *(cheque)* faire **(c)** *(capital)* mobiliser, procurer; *(funds)* collecter **(d)** *(taxes)* lever; *(loan)* lancer, émettre

▶ **rake in** vt sep *Fam (money)* amasser; **they must be raking it in** ils s'en mettent plein les poches

▶ **rake off** vt sep *Fam (money, commission)* ramasser

"

The U.S. Department of Labor estimates that administrative costs run somewhere between $100 and $200 per year for each person enrolled in a plan. On top of that, fund managers **rake off** fees – usually 1 to 2% of the balance – to cover costs and leave some profit.

"
---

rake-off n *Fam* pourcentage m, commission f; **to get a rake-off on each sale** toucher un pourcentage *ou* une commission sur chaque vente

rally **1** n *(of prices, shares, business)* reprise f
 2 vi *(of prices, shares, business)* se redresser, reprendre; **the pound rallied in the afternoon** la livre est remontée dans l'après-midi

RAM n *Comptr (abbr* **random access memory)** mémoire f vive

R&D, R and D n *(abbr* **research and develop-**

ment) R-D f ◻ *R&D tax credit* = déductions fiscales pour la recherche et le développement

rand n *(currency)* rand m

random adj (fait(e)) au hasard ◻ *Comptr random access* accès m aléatoire; *Comptr random access memory* mémoire f vive; *random check* contrôle m par sondage(s); *random error* erreur f aléatoire; *random sample* échantillon m aléatoire; *random sampling* échantillonnage m aléatoire; *Mktg random selection* sélection f au hasard; *St Exch random walk* marche f aléatoire

range **1** n **(a)** *(of prices, colours, products)* gamme f; **we stock a wide range of office materials** nous avons en stock une large gamme de matériels de bureau; **this product is the top/bottom of the range** ce produit est le modèle haut/bas de gamme ◻ *Mktg range addition* ajout m à la gamme; *Mktg range stretching* extension f de la gamme
 (b) *St Exch* fourchette f, écart m; **opening/closing range** fourchette de cours d'ouverture/de clôture
 (c) *(of advertising campaign)* rayon m d'action
 2 vi **to range from... to...** aller de... à...; **prices range from £15 to £150** les prix vont de 15 livres à 150 livres

rank 1 n **(a)** *(grade)* rang m, grade m; **to pull rank** abuser de son rang
 (b) *Fin (of debt, mortgage)* rang m
 2 vi **(a)** *(of creditor, claimant)* **to rank after sb** prendre rang *ou* passer après qn; **to rank before sb** prendre rang *ou* passer avant qn; **to rank equally (with sb)** prendre *ou* avoir le même rang (que qn)
 (b) *Law (of share)* **to rank after sth** être primé(e) par qch; **to rank before sth** avoir la priorité sur qch; **to rank equally (with sth)** prendre le même rang (que qch)

ratable = rateable

ratal n *Br (of building)* valeur f locative imposable; *(of site)* évaluation f cadastrale (d'impôts locaux)

rate 1 n **(a)** *(of inflation, tax, interest)* taux m; **the rate is 20p in the pound** le taux est de 20 pence par livre; **to strike for higher rates of pay** faire la grève pour obtenir une augmentation de salaire ◻ *Mktg rate of adoption (of product)* taux d'adoption; *Mktg rate of awareness (of prod-*

uct) taux de notoriété; *rate band* fourchette *f* de taux; *Mktg rate of churn* taux de clients passés à la concurrence; *rate of depreciation* taux d'amortissement; *rate of exchange* cours *m ou* taux du change; *rate of growth* taux d'accroissement *ou* de croissance; *rate of increase* taux d'accroissement *ou* de croissance; *Econ rate of inflation* taux d'inflation; *Mktg rate of penetration* taux de pénétration; *rate of production* taux de production; *Mktg rate of renewal* taux de renouvellement; *rate of return (on investment)* taux de rendement; *rate of return analysis* analyse *f* du rendement; *rate of return pricing* fixation *f* de prix au taux de rendement établi; *rate of taxation* taux d'imposition; *rate of turnover* taux de rotation des stocks; *rate of uptake* taux de succès

(**b**) *(price, charge)* tarif *m*; **the going rate** le tarif courant; **the hourly rate is going to be increased** le taux horaire va être augmenté

(**c**) *Br Formerly* **rates** impôts *mpl* locaux

2 *vt Br (fix rateable value of)* fixer la valeur locative imposable de

> **❝**
> "While most in telecom are quite aware of the high **rate of churn** and the resulting consequences, what is surprising is the increasing rate of this dynamic," says Mary Ellen Smith, Faulkner director of research services. "It is only the expanding number of services and technologies that allow some organizations to remain profitable."
> **❞**

▶ **rate up** *vt sep Ins* **to rate sb up** faire payer à qn une prime plus élevée

rateable *adj Br* **rateable value** valeur *f* locative imposable

rate-cap *vt Br Admin* fixer un taux plafond pour les impôts locaux de

rate-capping *n Br Admin* plafonnement *m* des impôts locaux

ratification *n Law* ratification *f*

ratify *vt Law* ratifier

rating *n* notation *f* ❑ *Mktg* **rating scale** échelle *f* de classement

ratio *n* rapport *m*; *Econ* ratio *m*; **in the ratio of one to three** dans le rapport *ou* la proportion de un à trois

rationalization *n (of industry)* rationalisation *f*

rationalize *vt (industry)* rationaliser

rationing *n (of funds)* rationnement *m*; **banks are warning of mortgage rationing** les banques annoncent qu'elles vont limiter le nombre de prêts immobiliers

rat race *n* foire *f* d'empoigne

> **❝**
> New York is pretty work orientated and the hours can be long. It's less of a **rat race** than London, though, especially the transport. Since September 11, it's like a different city – particularly because my offices are downtown near where the World Trade Center was.
> **❞**

raw *adj (data, statistics)* brut(e) ❑ *raw materials* matières *fpl* premières

RDBMS *n Comptr (abbr* **relational database management system***)* SGBDR *m*

re *prep (abbr* **regarding***)* concernant; **re your letter of 8 March** suite à votre lettre du 8 mars; **re: 2002/2003 sales figures** *(in letter heading)* Réf: les ventes de 2002/2003

reach 1 *n Mktg (of campaign, advertisement)* portée *f*

2 *vt* (**a**) *(extend as far as)* arriver à, atteindre; **inflation has reached record levels** l'inflation a atteint un niveau record (**b**) *(agreement, decision)* arriver à, parvenir à (**c**) *(contact)* joindre; **you can always reach me at this number** vous pouvez toujours me joindre à ce numéro

react *vi (of prices)* réagir

reaction *n (of prices)* réaction *f*

read *vt* lire; *Admin* **read and approved** *(on document)* lu et approuvé; **to take the minutes as read** passer sur la lecture du procès-verbal

▶ **read out** *vt sep Comptr (data)* sortir, extraire de la mémoire

readdress *vt* faire suivre

reader *n* (**a**) *(of book)* lecteur(trice) *m,f*; *Am (company librarian)* documentaliste *mf* (**b**) *Comptr* lecteur *m*

readership *n (of newspaper, magazine)* nombre *m* de lecteurs, lectorat *m*

read-me file *n Comptr* document *m* lisez-moi

read-only *adj Comptr* (à) lecture seule; **that file is read-only** ce fichier est protégé en écriture; **to make a file read-only** mettre un fichier en lecture seule ❑ *read-only disk (hard)* disque *m* en lecture seule; *(floppy)* disquette *f* en lecture seule; *read-only file* fichier *m* en lecture seule; *read-only lock* verrouillage *m* en lecture seule; *read-only memory* mémoire *f* morte; *read-only mode* mode *m* lecture seule

readvertise *vt (job, position)* repasser une annonce pour

read-write head *n Comptr* tête *f* de lecture-écriture

ready *adj* prêt(e); **ready for delivery** livrable; **ready for shipping** sous palan ❑ *ready cash, ready money* argent *m* comptant *ou* liquide; **to pay in ready cash** *or* **money** payer (au) comptant; **ready reckoner** barème *m*

real *adj* (**a**) *(actual)* réel(elle) □ **real accounts** comptes *mpl* de valeur; **real assets** biens *mpl* immobiliers; **real cost** coût *m* réel; **real income** revenu *m* réel; **real profit** profit *m* réel; *Mktg* **real repositioning** repositionnement *m* réel; **real salary** salaire *m* réel; **real terms** termes *mpl* réels; **salaries have fallen in real terms** les salaires ont baissé en termes réels; *Comptr* **real time** temps *m* réel; *Fin* **real value** valeur *f* effective
(**b**) **real estate** *Br Law* biens *mpl* fonciers; *Am (property)* biens immobiliers; *Am* **real estate agency** agence *f* immobilière; *Am* **real estate agent** agent *m* immobilier; *Am* **real estate leasing** crédit-bail *m* immobilier; *Fin* **real estate mortgage investment conduit** obligation *f* garantie par hypothèque; *Am* **real estate office** agence immobilière; **real property** biens immobiliers

realign *vt Fin* réaligner

realignment *n Fin* réalignement *m*; **realignment of currencies** réalignement monétaire

realizable *adj Fin* réalisable □ **realizable assets** actif *m* réalisable; **realizable securities** valeurs *fpl* réalisables

realization *n Fin* réalisation *f*

realize *vt Fin (convert into cash)* réaliser; *(yield financially)* rapporter; **to realize a high price** *(of goods)* atteindre un prix élevé; *(of seller)* obtenir un prix élevé; **how much did they realize on the sale?** combien est-ce qu'ils ont gagné sur la vente?; **these shares cannot be realized** il n'y a pas de marché pour ces titres

reallocate *vt Fin (funds, resources)* réaffecter; *(shares)* attribuer à nouveau, répartir à nouveau

reallocation *n Fin (of funds, resources)* réaffection *f*; *(of shares)* nouvelle attribution *f*, nouvelle répartition *f*

reallot *vt Fin (shares)* attribuer à nouveau, répartir à nouveau

reallotment *n Fin (of shares)* nouvelle attribution *f*, nouvelle répartition *f*

real-time *adj Comptr* en temps réel □ **real-time clock** horloge *f* en temps réel; **real-time graphics** graphiques *mpl* en temps réel; **real-time management** gestion *f* en temps réel; *St Exch* **real-time trading** cotation *f* en temps réel

realtor *n Am* agent *m* immobilier

realty *n Am* biens *mpl* immobiliers

reapply *vi (for job)* poser à nouveau sa candidature (**for** pour); **previous candidates need not reapply** les personnes ayant déjà posé leur candidature n'ont pas besoin de le faire à nouveau

reappoint *vt* **to reappoint sb** réintégrer qn

dans ses fonctions

reappraisal *n* (**a**) *Fin (of property)* réévaluation *f* (**b**) *(of policy)* réexamen *m*

reappraise *vt* (**a**) *Fin (property)* réévaluer (**b**) *(policy)* réexaminer

reasonable *adj (offer, price)* raisonnable

reassess *vt* (**a**) *(policy, situation)* reconsidérer, réexaminer (**b**) *Fin (damages)* réévaluer; *(taxation)* réviser; **you have been reassessed** votre situation fiscale a été réexaminée

reassessment *n* (**a**) *(of policy, situation)* réexamen *m* (**b**) *Fin (of damages)* réévaluation *f*; *(of taxation)* révision *f*

reassign *vt (funds)* réaffecter

reassignment *n (of funds)* réaffectation *f*

rebate *n* (**a**) *(refund)* remboursement *m*; *(of tax)* dégrèvement *m* (**b**) *(discount on purchase)* rabais *m*, ristourne *f*

reboot *Comptr* **1** *vt* réamorcer
2 *vi* se réamorcer

rebrand *vt Mktg (product)* changer la marque de

rebranding *n Mktg (of product)* changement *m* de marque

> 66
>
> We may well see more consolidation in the sector, but a merger between any of the high street banks is a rank outsider. Everyone will be watching closely the **rebranding** of Midland to HSBC.
>
> 99

rebuy *n Mktg* réachat *m* □ **rebuy rate** taux *m* de réachat

recall 1 *n* (**a**) *Mktg (of brand name)* mémorisation *f* □ **recall rate** taux *m* de mémorisation; **recall study** étude *f* de mémorisation; **recall test** test *m* de rappel *ou* de mémorisation (**b**) *(of faulty goods)* rappel *m*
2 *vt (faulty goods)* rappeler

recapitalization *n Fin (of company)* recapitalisation *f*, changement *m* de la structure financière

recapitalize *vt Fin (company)* recapitaliser, changer la structure financière de

> 66
>
> China is still deflating, its banking system needs to be **recapitalized**, but [the] government's ability to raise enough taxes to do it is poor, while consumers save and do not spend to protect their own futures.
>
> 99

recapture *Am Fin* **1** *n* saisie *f*
2 *vt* saisir

receipt 1 *n* (**a**) *(act of receiving)* réception *f*; **to**

be in receipt of sth avoir reçu qch; **we are in receipt of your letter of 9 June** nous avons bien reçu votre lettre du 9 juin; **to pay on receipt** payer à la réception; **to acknowledge receipt (of)** accuser réception (de); **on receipt of this letter** dès réception de cette lettre
 (**b**) *(proof of payment)* reçu *m* (**for** de); *(in supermarket, bar)* ticket *m* de caisse; *(for letter, parcel)* récépissé *m*, accusé *m* de réception; *(for rent, insurance)* quittance *f*; *Customs* récépissé □ **receipt book** carnet *m* de quittances; **receipt in full** quittance finale *ou* libératoire; **receipt stamp** timbre *m* de quittance
 (**c**) **receipts** *(takings)* recettes *fpl*, rentrées *fpl*; **receipts and expenditure** recettes et dépenses *fpl*
 2 *vt* acquitter, quittancer; **to receipt a bill** acquitter une facture

receivable 1 *n* **receivables** *(debts)* comptes *mpl* clients, créances *fpl*; *(bills)* effets *mpl* à recevoir
 2 *adj (account, bill)* à recevoir

receive *vt* recevoir; *(money, salary)* toucher; *St Exch* **to receive a premium** encaisser un premium; **received with thanks** *(on bill)* acquitté, pour acquit □ **received cash book** main *f* courante de recettes

receiver *n* (**a**) *(of goods, consignment)* destinataire *mf*, consignataire *mf* (**b**) *Fin (in bankruptcy)* administrateur(trice) *m,f* judiciaire; **to be in the hands of the receiver(s)** être en règlement judiciaire; **the receivers have been called in at Lawson Trading** Lawson Trading a été placée sous administration judiciare (**c**) *Am* **receiver general** receveur *m* des impôts

"

Leading fresh prepared food firm Geest has announced it has acquired the facilities of Tinsley Foods, which is **in the hands of the receivers**. Geest, which recently revealed an 18% rise in turnover for the interim period, said it planned to continue to invest in capacity to match strong consumer demand for quality fresh products.

"

receivership *n* **to go into receivership** être placé(e) en règlement judiciaire

receiving *n* (**a**) *(of goods)* réception *f* □ **receiving depot** dépôt *m* de réception; **receiving office** bureau *m* de réception; **receiving station** gare *f* d'arrivée (**b**) *Law* **receiving order** ordonnance *f* de mise sous séquestre

reception *n* (**a**) *(at hotel)* réception *f*; *(in office)* accueil *m* □ *Am* **reception clerk** réceptionniste *mf*; **reception desk** réception; **reception room** salle *f* de réception (**b**) *(formal party)* réception *f*

receptionist *n* réceptionniste *mf*

recession *n Econ* récession *f*; **the economy is**

in (a) recession l'économie est en récession

recessionary *adj Econ (conditions, policy)* de récession; **to have a recessionary effect** entraîner une récession

recipient *n (of letter, e-mail message)* destinataire *mf*; *(of cheque, bill)* bénéficiaire *mf*

reciprocal *adj* réciproque, mutuel(elle) □ **reciprocal agreement** accord *m* réciproque; *Mktg* **reciprocal relationships model** modèle *m* de relations réciproques; **reciprocal trading** commerce *m* réciproque

reckon 1 *vt (calculate)* calculer; **to reckon the cost of sth** calculer les frais de qch
 2 *vi (calculate)* calculer

reckoning *n (calculation)* calcul *m*, compte *m*

reclaim *vt (deposit, baggage)* récupérer, réclamer; *(expenses)* se faire rembourser

recognition *n Mktg* reconnaissance *f* □ **recognition score** score *m* de reconnaissance; **recognition test** test *m* de reconnaissance

recognizance *n Law (bond)* engagement *m*; *(money)* caution *f*; **to enter into recognizances for sb** *(with money)* verser une caution pour qn; *(personally)* se porter garant(e) de qn

recognized *adj (agent)* accrédité(e) □ **recognized investment exchange** marché *m* d'investissement agréé; **recognized professional body** = organisme professionnel agréé

recommended retail price *n* prix *m* recommandé *ou* conseillé

recompense *Law* **1** *n (compensation)* dédommagement *m*, compensation *f*
 2 *vt* **to recompense sb for sth** dédommager qn de qch

reconcile *vt (figures, bank statements)* rapprocher; *Acct (accounts, entries)* faire cadrer *ou* accorder

reconciliation *n (of figures, bank statements)* rapprochement *m*; *Acct (of accounts, entries)* ajustement *m* □ **reconciliation account** compte *m* collectif; *Acct* **reconciliation statement** état *m* de rapprochement

reconfigure *vt Comptr* reconfigurer

reconstruction *n (of company)* reconstitution *f*; *(of economy)* restauration *f*

record 1 *n* (**a**) *(account)* rapport *m*; *(file)* dossier *m*; **to make a record of sth** noter qch; **to keep a record of sth** garder une trace écrite de qch; **they keep a record of all deposits** ils enregistrent tous les versements; **do you have any record of the transaction?** avez-vous gardé une trace de la transaction?; **our records show that payment is overdue** nos dossiers font état d'un arriéré de paiement
 (**b**) *(past history)* passé *m*; **his past record with the firm** son passé dans l'entreprise; **the**

makers have an excellent record for high quality les fabricants sont très réputés pour l'excellente qualité de leurs produits (**c**) *Comptr (in database)* article *m*, enregistrement *m*

2 *adj* record; **unemployment is at a record high/low** le chômage a atteint son taux le plus haut/bas

3 *vt (take note of)* enregistrer; **to record the minutes of a meeting** faire le procès-verbal *ou* le compte-rendu d'une réunion

recorded *adj Br* **recorded delivery** recommandé *m*; **to send sth recorded delivery** envoyer qch en recommandé; **recorded message** *(on answering machine)* message *m* enregistré

recoup *vt* (**a**) *(get back) (losses)* récupérer; **to recoup one's investments** rentrer dans ses fonds; **to recoup one's costs** rentrer dans *ou* couvrir ses frais (**b**) *(pay back) (person)* rembourser, dédommager

recourse *n Fin, Law* recours *m*; **to have recourse to sb** avoir recours contre qn; **endorsement without recourse** endossement *m* à forfait

recover **1** *vt* (**a**) *(debt)* recouvrer; *(money, deposit)* récupérer; **to recover one's expenses** rentrer dans ses fonds (**b**) *Law (damages)* obtenir (**c**) *Comptr (file, data)* récupérer

2 *vi (of economy, currency)* se redresser; *(of prices, shares)* se redresser, remonter; *(of market, business)* reprendre

recoverable *adj (debt)* recouvrable; *(packaging)* récupérable

recovery *n* (**a**) *(of debt)* recouvrement *m*; *(of money, deposit)* récupération *f* (**b**) *Law (of damages)* obtention *f* (**c**) *Comptr (of file, data)* récupération *f* (**d**) *(of economy)* relance *f*, redressement *m*; *(of prices, shares)* redressement, remontée *f*; *(of currency)* redressement; *(of market, business)* reprise *f*

recruit **1** *n* recrue *f*
2 *vt* recruter

recruitment *n* recrutement *m* ❏ **recruitment agency** agence *f* de recrutement; **recruitment consultant** conseil *m* en recrutement; **recruitment drive** campagne *f* de recrutement; **recruitment plan** plan *m* de recrutement

rectification *n (of mistake)* rectification *f*, correction *f*; *Acct (of entry)* modification *f*, rectification

rectify *vt (mistake)* rectifier, corriger; *Acct (entry)* modifier, rectifier

recurrent expenses *npl* dépenses *fpl* courantes

recycle *vt (paper, materials)* recycler; *Fin (funds)* remettre en circulation; *(money)* réin-

vestir ❏ *Comptr* **recycle bin** corbeille *f*

recycled *adj (paper, materials)* recyclé(e); *Fin (funds)* remis(e) en circulation

recycling *n (of paper, materials)* recyclage *m*; *Fin (of funds)* remise *f* en circulation; *(of money)* réinvestissement *m* ❏ **recycling facility** installation *f* de recyclage; **recycling plant** usine *f* de recyclage

red **1** *n* **to be in the red** *(of person)* avoir un découvert, être dans le rouge; *(of company)* être en déficit; *(of account)* avoir un solde déficitaire; **to be £5,000 in the red** *(of person)* avoir un découvert de 5 000 livres; *(of company)* avoir un déficit de 5 000 livres; *(of account)* avoir un solde déficitaire de 5 000 livres; **to get out of the red** *(of person)* combler son découvert; *(of company)* sortir du rouge

2 *adj Am Fin* **to go into red ink** *(of person)* être à découvert; *(of company)* être en déficit; *(of account)* avoir un solde déficitaire ❏ **red chip** action *f* de société chinoise; **red tape** *(bureaucracy)* paperasserie *f*

> **❝**
> Otherwise companies will find themselves locked into expensive and time consuming legal battles without any certainty over the timespan or the result. Indeed, such a process could easily be subverted by companies on the receiving end of a hostile bid to stifle the takeover battle with a blanket of legal **red tape**.
> **❞**

redeem *vt Fin* (**a**) *(bond, share)* réaliser; *(coupon)* échanger (**b**) *(annuity, loan, mortgage)* rembourser; *(bill)* honorer; *(debt)* amortir, se libérer de

redeemable *adj Fin (bond, loan, mortgage)* remboursable; *(share)* rachetable

redemption *n Fin* (**a**) *(of bond, share)* remboursement *m*; **redemption before due date** remboursement anticipé ❏ **redemption date** date *f* d'échéance; **redemption fee, redemption premium** prime *f* de remboursement; **redemption price** prix *m* de rachat; **redemption value** valeur *f* de remboursement *ou* de rachat; **redemption yield** rendement *m* à l'échéance (**b**) *(of annuity, loan, mortgage)* remboursement *m*

redeploy *vt (resources)* redéployer; *(workforce)* réaffecter

redeployment *n (of resources)* redéploiement *m*; *(of workforce)* réaffectation *f*

redial *Tel* **1** *n* **redial (feature)** rappel *m* du dernier numéro; **the latest model has automatic redial** le dernier modèle est muni du système de rappel du dernier numéro

2 *vt (number)* refaire

3 *vi* refaire le numéro

redirect *vt (mail)* faire suivre (**to** à)

rediscount 1 *n* réescompte *m*
   2 *vt* réescompter

redline *vt Am* discriminer contre *(dans l'attri-bution de logements ou d'assurances)*

redo *vt* rétablir, refaire

redraft *vt (document, letter, report)* rédiger de nouveau

reduce *vt (rate, expenses, cost, investment)* ré-duire; *(price)* baisser; *(output)* ralentir

reduced *adj* réduit(e); *(goods)* soldé(e), en solde; **to buy sth at a reduced price** acheter qch à prix réduit □ **reduced rate** tarif *m* réduit; **reduced staff** personnel *m* réduit

reduction *n* (**a**) *(of rate, expenses, cost, invest-ment)* réduction *f*; *(of prices)* baisse *f*; *(of taxes)* allègement *m* (**b**) *(discount)* rabais *m*, remise *f*; **to make a reduction (on sth)** faire un rabais *ou* une remise (sur qch); **I'll give you a reduc-tion** je vous fais un prix

redundancy *n Br (dismissal)* licenciement *m*; **the strike caused over three hundred redun-dancies** la grève a causé le licenciement de plus de trois cents personnes □ **redundancy notice** avis *m* de licenciement; **redundancy pay** in-demnité *f* de licenciement; **redundancy pay-ment** indemnité de licenciement

redundant *adj Br (worker)* licencié(e); **to make sb redundant** *(of employer)* licencier qn; **to be made redundant** être licencié, être mis(e) au chômage

reemploy *vt* reprendre, réembaucher

reemployment *n* réembauche *m*

reengineer *vt* réorganiser

reengineering *n* réorganisation *f*

> **❝**
> Investors are growing concerned that the company's customer base is not growing quickly enough while customers themselves are not spending enough. Telewest, which recently claimed it could survive on its cur-rent facilities as long as it executed well, is known to have discussed options with both Liberty Media and Microsoft, two of its major shareholders. It remains silent on whether a financial **reengineering** is under way.
> **❞**

reexport 1 *n (activity)* réexportation *f*; *(prod-uct)* article *m* de réexportation; **reexports** réex-portations *fpl* □ **reexport trade** commerce *m* de réexportation
   2 *vt* réexporter

reexportation *n* réexportation *f*

ref *n (abbr* **reference**) *(at head of letter)* réf; **your**

ref v/réf; **our ref** n/réf

refer *vt* (**a**) *(submit) (matter, proposal)* soumettre; **the dispute has been referred to arbitration** le litige a été soumis à l'arbitrage; **the contract has been referred to us** le contrat nous a été soumis (**b**) *(send, direct)* renvoyer; **to refer a customer to another department** renvoyer un client à un au-tre service (**c**) *Banking* **to refer a cheque to drawer** refuser d'honorer un chèque; **refer to drawer** *(on cheque)* voir le tireur

▶ **refer to** *vt insep (consult) (person, notes)* consulter; *(document)* se reporter à; **I shall have to refer to the board** il faudra que je consulte le conseil de direction

referee *n* (**a**) *(for job)* répondant(e) *m,f*; **please give the names of two referees** veuillez four-nir deux références; **you can give my name as a referee** vous pouvez me citer comme réfé-rence (**b**) *Law* arbitre *m* (**c**) **referee in case of need** *(on bill of exchange)* adresse *f* au besoin

reference *n* (**a**) *(consultation)* référence *f*; **with reference to your letter of 20 March** *(in letter)* suite à votre lettre du 20 mars; **with reference to what was said at the meeting** à propos de *ou* en ce qui concerne ce qui a été dit au cours de la réunion; **reference AB** *(at head of letter)* réfé-rence AB □ **reference number** numéro *m* de ré-férence; **please quote this reference number** *(in reply)* prière de rappeler cette référence
   (**b**) *(testimonial) (from bank)* référence *f*; *(from employer)* référence, recommandation *f*; **to give sb a reference** fournir une référence à qn; **to have good references** avoir de bonnes références; **to take up references** = prendre contact avec les personnes dont un candidat se recommande; **you can use my name as a re-ference** vous pouvez me citer comme réfé-rence
   (**c**) *Mktg* **reference customer** client(e) *m,f* de référence; **reference group** groupe *m* de réfé-rence; **reference price** prix *m* de référence; **re-ference sale** vente *f* de référence
   (**d**) *Banking, Fin* **reference rate** taux *m* de réfé-rence
   (**e**) *(of commission, tribunal)* compétence *f*, pouvoirs *mpl*; **under these terms of reference** aux termes des instructions données; **the ques-tion is outside the tribunal's reference** la question n'est pas de la compétence du tribunal

refinance *Fin* **1** *vt (loan)* refinancer
   2 *vi (of company)* se refinancer

refinancing *n Fin* refinancement *m*

reflate *vt (economy)* relancer

reflation *n* relance *f* (économique)

> **❝**
> In the United States itself, the Bush adminis-tration has unceremoniously shredded the

Washington consensus on the virtues of global free trade by imposing tariffs on imported steel; Alan Greenspan, the chairman of the Federal Reserve, has gone for a hyper-Keynesian policy of **reflation** at any cost; and defence spending, as well as tax cuts, threatens the federal surplus. **"**

reflationary *adj* de relance ❑ *reflationary pressure* pression *f* pour une relance

refloat *vt (economy)* relancer; *Fin (loan)* émettre de nouveau; *(company)* renflouer, remettre à flot

refresh *Comptr* **1** *n* actualisation *f*, rafraîchissement *m* ❑ *refresh rate* taux *m* d'actualisation *ou* de rafraîchissement
2 *vt (screen)* actualiser, rafraîchir

refresher course *n* cours *m* de recyclage

refrigerate *vt* réfrigérer ❑ *Br refrigerated lorry* camion *m* frigorifique; *refrigerated ship* navire *m* frigorifique; *Am refrigerated truck* camion frigorifique

refrigeration *n* réfrigération *f*; **to keep sth under refrigeration** garder qch au réfrigérateur ❑ *refrigeration plant* installation *f* frigorifique

refrigerator *n (storeroom)* chambre *f* frigorifique

refund 1 *n* (a) remboursement *m*; **to get a refund** se faire rembourser (b) *Law (of monies)* restitution *f* (c) *Am (of tax)* bonification *f* de trop-perçu
2 *vt* (a) *(person, money)* rembourser; **to refund sb sth, to refund sth to sb** rembourser qch à qn; **they refunded me the postage** ils m'ont remboursé les frais de port (b) *Law (monies)* restituer
3 *vi Law* faire restitution d'indu

refundable *adj* remboursable

refunding *n* remboursement *m* ❑ *refunding clause* clause *f* de remboursement; *refunding loan* prêt *m* de remboursement

refusal *n* (a) *(of request, proposal, offer)* refus *m*; **to meet with a refusal** essuyer un refus ❑ *Mktg refusal rate* taux *m* de refus (b) *(option to buy)* **to have first refusal (on sth)** avoir la première offre (de qch); **to give sb first refusal (on sth)** donner la priorité à qn (pour qch)

"

As well as bidding to run the station, Innogy is understood to be interested in acquiring a stake in it if Enron's shareholding becomes available. The existing investors in the plant are expected to be offered **first refusal**, but already Western Power has stated that it is not interested in increasing its 15.4 percent holding. **"**

refuse *vt* (a) *(request, proposal, offer)* refuser; **I refused to take delivery of the parcel** j'ai refusé d'accepter le paquet (b) *(permission)* refuser (d'accorder); *(help, visa)* refuser; **he was refused entry** on lui a refusé l'entrée; **they were refused a loan** on leur a refusé un prêt

regard *n* **with regard to** en ce qui concerne; **with regard to your enquiry, I am happy to inform you that…** en ce qui concerne *ou* suite à votre demande, j'ai le plaisir de vous informer que…

regional *adj* régional(e) ❑ *regional council* conseil *m* régional; *Br regional development (of land, buildings)* aménagement *m* du territoire; *(for jobs)* action *f* régionale; *Br regional development corporation* = organisme pour l'aménagement du territoire; *regional director* directeur(trice) *m,f* régional(e); *regional headquarters* direction *f* régionale

register 1 *n* (a) *(book)* registre *m*; *(list)* liste *f*; **to enter sth in a register** inscrire qch dans un registre ❑ *Br Law register of companies* registre du commerce et des sociétés; *St Exch register of shareholders* registre *ou* livre *m* des actionnaires
(b) *Comptr (of memory)* registre *m*
2 *vt* (a) *(record) (name, luggage)* enregistrer; *(company)* immatriculer au registre du commerce; *(shares)* immatriculer; *(trademark)* déposer; *(mortgage)* inscrire; *Comptr (software)* inscrire; **to register a complaint** déposer une plainte
(b) *(indicate)* **the pound has registered a fall** la livre a enregistré une baisse

registered *adj* (a) *(recorded) registered agent* agent *m* agréé; *Fin registered bond* obligation *f* nominative; *registered capital* capital *m* déclaré; *registered charity* organisme *m* de bienfaisance reconnu par l'État; *registered company* = société inscrite au registre de commerce; *Fin registered debenture* obligation nominative; *registered design* modèle *m* déposé; *registered name* nom *m* déposé; *Br registered office* siège *m* social; *Can Fin registered retirement savings plan* régime *m* enregistré d'épargne-retraite; *registered securities* titres *mpl* nominatifs, valeurs *fpl* nominatives; *registered share certificate* certificat *m* nominatif d'action(s); *Br registered shareholder* actionnaire *mf* inscrit(e); *registered stock* titres nominatifs, valeurs nominatives; *Am registered stockholder* actionnaire inscrit(e); *registered tonnage* tonnage *m* net *ou* de jauge; *registered trademark* marque *f* déposée; *Comptr registered user* utilisateur(trice) *m,f* disposant d'une licence; *registered value* valeur *f* enregistrée (b) *(letter, parcel)* recommandé(e); **to send sth by registered post** envoyer qch en recommandé

registrar n (**a**) Br Admin officier m de l'état civil (**b**) Br Law **registrar of companies** directeur(-trice) m,f du registre du commerce et des sociétés

registration n (of name, luggage) enregistrement m; (of shares, company) immatriculation f; (of trademark) dépôt m; (of mortgage) inscription f □ St Exch **registration body** chambre f d'enregistrement; Comptr **registration card** licence f; **registration certificate** matricule f; **registration fees** droits mpl d'inscription; **registration number** Comptr numéro m de licence; (of car) numéro d'immatriculation; Fin **registration and transfer fees** droits d'inscription et de transfert

registry n bureau m d'enregistrement □ **registry fees** droits mpl de greffe; Br Admin **registry office** bureau m d'état civil

regressive adj Fin régressif(ive)

regressively adv Fin régressivement

regular adj (habitual, normal) régulier(ère); **to be in regular employment** avoir un emploi régulier; **to go through the regular channels** suivre la filière normale ou habituelle □ **regular customer** client(e) m,f habitué(e) ou régulier(ère); **regular income** revenu m régulier; **regular price** prix m de règle

regulate vt (control) régler; (with rules) réglementer; **the price is regulated by supply and demand** le prix est déterminé par l'offre et la demande

regulating body n autorité f de régulation

regulation n règlement m; **it's contrary to regulations** c'est contraire au règlement; **it complies with EU regulations** c'est conforme aux dispositions communautaires

regulator n régulateur(trice) m,f

regulatory adj régulateur(trice) □ **regulatory body** organisme m de réglementation

reimburse vt rembourser; **to reimburse sb for sth** rembourser qn de qch

reimport 1 n réimportation f
2 vt réimporter

reimportation n réimportation f

reinitialize vt Comptr réinitialiser

reinstate vt (**a**) (person) réintégrer (**b**) (law, idea, system) rétablir

reinstatement n (**a**) (of person) réintégration f (**b**) (of law, idea, system) rétablissement m

reinsurance n Ins réassurance f

reinsure vt Ins réassurer

reinvest vt Fin réinvestir

reinvestment n Fin réinvestissement m

reissue Fin **1** n (of banknotes, shares) nouvelle émission f

2 vt (banknotes, shares) émettre de nouveau

reject 1 n (object) article m de rebut
2 vt (offer, proposal) rejeter, repousser; (goods, candidate, application) refuser

related to, relating to prep Admin, Law afférent(e) à; **questions related to official procedure** des questions afférentes à la procédure officielle

relational database n Comptr base f de données relationnelle

relationship marketing n Mktg marketing m relationnel

relative adj relatif(ive) □ **relative market share** part f de marché relative

relaunch 1 n (of product) relancement m, relance f
2 vt (product) relancer

release 1 n (**a**) (of debtor) libération f (**b**) Customs (of goods from bond) dédouanement m (**c**) Fin (of credits, funds) déblocage m, dégagement m
2 vt (**a**) (debtor) libérer (**b**) Customs (goods from bond) dédouaner (**c**) Fin (credits, funds) débloquer, dégager

relevant costs npl Acct coûts mpl attribuables

reliability n (of person, company) sérieux m; (of information, account, machine) fiabilité f; (of guarantee) solidité f

reliable adj (person, company) sérieux(euse), à qui on peut faire confiance; (information, account) sûr(e); (machine) fiable; (guarantee) solide

relief n (**a**) (replacement) remplaçant(e) m,f (**b**) Am Admin (state benefit) aide f sociale; **to be on relief** recevoir des aides sociales

reload vt Comptr recharger

relocate 1 vt (company) transférer; (person) muter
2 vi (of company) être transféré(e); (of person) se déplacer

relocation n déménagement m □ **relocation allowance** indemnité f de déménagement; **relocation expenses** frais mpl de déménagement

> ❝
> At Schwab.com, all interns are offered stock options. In addition, college-age interns earn $500 to $600 a week. And graduate students can rake in as much as $5,500 a month for full-time work, plus **relocation expenses** or a housing stipend. The question is, have students become more interested in the money and perks steered their way than in the experience of the internship?
> ❞

remainder 1 n (**a**) (money) solde m; (debt) reliquat m; (supplies) reste m (**b**) (unsold product)

fin f de série; (unsold book) invendu m
   2 vt solder

remarket vt recommercialiser

remarketing n marketing m de relance

REMIC n Am Fin (abbr **real estate mortgage investment conduit**) obligation f garantie par hypothèque

reminder n (lettre f de) rappel m; **reminder of account due** rappel d'échéance ❏ Acct **reminder entry** poste m de mémoire

remit 1 n (area of authority) attributions fpl; **that's outside their remit** cela n'entre pas dans leurs attributions
   2 vt (a) (payment) remettre (b) (cancel) (debt) remettre, faire remise de; **to remit sb's fees** dispenser qn de ses frais; **to remit sb's income tax** dispenser ou exempter qn d'impôt
   3 vi (pay) régler, payer; **please remit by cheque** veuillez régler ou payer par chèque

remittal n Fin (of debt) remise f

remittance n (money) paiement m, règlement m; **return the form with your remittance** renvoyez le formulaire avec votre paiement ou règlement ❏ **remittance advice** avis m de remise; **remittance date** date f de remise; **remittance of funds** remise f de fonds

remittee n destinataire mf (d'un envoi de fonds)

remitter n remettant(e) mf

remortgage vt (house, property) hypothéquer de nouveau, prendre une nouvelle hypothèque sur

remote adj Comptr (user) à distance ❏ **remote access** accès m à distance; **remote banking** banque f à distance; **remote server** serveur m distant; **remote terminal** terminal m distant

removable adj Comptr (disk) amovible, extractible

remunerate vt rémunérer

remuneration n rémunération f (**for** de); **to receive remuneration for sth** être rémunéré(e) pour qch ❏ **remuneration package** = salaire et avantages complémentaires

> "
> … Vodafone pointed out that it has held its focus groups and consulted to show how it has learned from past mistakes of previously over-generous and opaque **remuneration packages**. As shareholders wished, 80 per cent of Gent's package was performance-related; a paltry 20 per cent (£1.192 million) was base pay.
> "

remunerative adj rémunérateur(trice)

rename vt Comptr (file) changer le nom de, renommer

render vt (bill, account) remettre; **as per account rendered** suivant compte remis; **for services rendered** pour services rendus

renegotiate vt renégocier

renegotiation n renégociation f

renew vt (lease, passport, membership, contract) renouveler; (bill) prolonger; **to renew one's subscription (to sth)** se réabonner (à qch)

renewal n (of lease, passport, membership, contract) renouvellement m; (of bill) prolongation f; **renewal of subscription** réabonnement m ❏ Ins **renewal notice** avis m de renouvellement; **renewal premium** prime f de renouvellement

rent 1 n loyer m; **for rent** (sign) à louer ❏ **rent control** contrôle m des loyers; **rent receipt** quittance f de loyer
   2 vt louer; **to rent sth from sb** louer qch à qn
▸ **rent out** vt sep louer; **to rent sth out to sb** louer qch à qn

rental n (a) (hire) location f ❏ **rental agreement** contrat m de location; **rental company** société f de location; **rental market** marché m locatif; **rental property** immeuble m locatif; **rental value** valeur f locative (b) (money) (for house, office) loyer m; (for equipment) location f; (for telephone) abonnement m ❏ Acct **rental charges** charges fpl locatives; **rental income** revenus mpl locatifs

rent-controlled adj (apartment) dont le loyer est contrôlé

rented adj loué(e), locatif(ive), de location ❏ **rented accommodation** logement m locatif; **rented car** voiture f de location; **rented property** immeuble m locatif

rent-free 1 adj exempt(e) de loyer
   2 adv sans payer de loyer

rent-roll n (register) registre m de l'état des loyers; (income) revenu m des loyers

reopen 1 vt rouvrir; (debate, negotiations) reprendre
   2 vi rouvrir; (of debate, negotiations) reprendre

reorder 1 n nouvelle commande f ❏ **reorder level** seuil m de réapprovisionnement
   2 vt faire une nouvelle commande de

reorganization n réorganisation f

reorganize 1 vt réorganiser
   2 vi se réorganiser

rep n Fam (abbr **representative**) VRP m

repackage vt (goods) reconditionner, repenser l'emballage de; (company, image) redorer

repair 1 n (a) (mending) réparation f; **to be under repair** être en réparation; **to carry out repairs on sth** effectuer des réparations sur qch; **closed for repairs** (sign) fermé pour (cause de) travaux (b) (condition) état m; **to be in good/bad repair** être en bon/mauvais état

2 *vt* réparer

repatriate *vt (funds)* rapatrier

repatriation *n (of funds)* rapatriement *m*

repay *vt (person, money, debt)* rembourser

repayable *adj* remboursable; **the amount is repayable in five years** la somme est remboursable en cinq ans

repayment *n* remboursement *m*; **repayments can be spread over 12 months** les remboursements peuvent être échelonnés sur 12 mois ▫ **repayment mortgage** prêt-logement *m (qui n'est pas lié à une assurance-vie)*; **repayment options** formules *fpl* de remboursement; **repayment plan** calendrier *m* des paiements

repeal 1 *n (of law)* abrogation *f*
2 *vt (law)* abroger

repeat 1 *n Comptr* **repeat function** fonction *f* de répétition; **repeat order** commande *f* renouvelée; **repeat purchase** achat *m* renouvelé; **repeat sale** vente *f* répétée
2 *vt (order, offer)* renouveler

repetitive strain injury *n* lésions *fpl* attribuables au travail répétitif

replace *vt* remplacer; *Comptr* **replace all** *(command)* tout remplacer

replacement *n* (**a**) *(person)* remplaçant(e) *m,f*; *(engine or machine part)* pièce *f* de rechange; *(product)* produit *m* de remplacement; **we are looking for a replacement for our secretary** nous cherchons quelqu'un pour remplacer notre secrétaire
(**b**) *(substituting)* remplacement *m* ▫ **replacement cost** coût *m* de remplacement; **replacement sale** vente *f* de remplacement; **replacement staff** personnel *m* de remplacement; *Ins* **replacement value** *(of item)* valeur *f* de remplacement

replenish *vt (stock)* réapprovisionner; **to replenish one's supplies of sth** se réapprovisionner en qch; *Banking* **to replenish an account** approvisionner un compte

reply 1 *n* réponse *f*; **in reply to your letter** en réponse à votre lettre; **reply paid** réponse payée ▫ **reply card** carte-réponse *f*; **reply coupon** coupon-réponse *m*; **reply form** formule *f* de réponse; **reply slip** talon *m* à retourner
2 *vi* répondre (**to** à)

repo *n* (**a**) *(abbr* **repurchase**) rachat *m*; *Banking, St Exch* réméré *m* ▫ *Banking, St Exch* **repo agreement** opération *f* de réméré *ou* de prise en pension, opération repo; *Banking, St Exch* **repo operation** opération de réméré *ou* de prise en pension, opération repo; *Banking, St Exch* **repo rate** taux *m* de réméré *ou* de prise en pension (**b**) *Am Fam St Exch (abbr* **repossession**) réméré *m*

report 1 *n* (**a**) *(account, review)* rapport *m* (**on**

sur); *(of meeting, speech)* compte-rendu *m*; *(official record)* procès-verbal *m*; **to draw up** *or* **make a report on sth** faire *ou* rédiger un rapport sur qch; **to present a report to sb on sth** présenter un rapport à qn sur qch ▫ **report of the board of directors** *(in annual accounts)* rapport de gestion
(**b**) *Acct (balance sheet)* bilan *m*
(**c**) *Comptr (of database)* état *m*
2 *vt* (**a**) *(give account of)* rendre compte de; **to report one's findings (to sb)** faire un rapport (à qn)
(**b**) *Customs* **to report a vessel** déclarer un navire
3 *vi* (**a**) *(present oneself)* se présenter (**to** à); **please report to our branch in Paris** veuillez vous présenter à notre succursale de Paris; **report to my office** présentez-vous à mon bureau
(**b**) *(give account)* faire un rapport (**to sb** à qn; **on sth** sur qch)
(**c**) *(be accountable)* **to report to sb** rendre compte à qn; **I report directly to the sales manager** je dépends directement du chef des ventes

reporting limit *n St Exch* seuil *m* d'annonce obligatoire

reposition *vt Mktg (product)* repositionner

repositioning *n Mktg (of product)* repositionnement *m*

> It has been two years since Baymont Inns & Suites became the name of the brand that had been Budgetel Inns. It was touted then as the largest rebranding and **repositioning** in the history of the lodging industry without a change in ownership.

repossess *vt Law* saisir

represent *vt* représenter; **I represent the agency** je représente l'agence; **he represented the union at the meeting** il a représenté le syndicat à la réunion

representation *n* représentation *f*

representative 1 *n (of group, company, organization)* représentant(e) *m,f*; **he's our company's representative abroad** il représente notre société à l'étranger
2 *adj* représentatif(ive) ▫ *Mktg* **representative sample** échantillon *m* type

reprocess *vt* retraiter

reprocessing *n* retraitement *m*

reprogram *vt Comptr* reprogrammer

reprogrammable *adj Comptr* reprogrammable

repurchase 1 *n* rachat *m*; *Banking, St Exch* réméré *m*; *Mktg* réachat *m*; **sale with option of**

repurchase vente *f* avec faculté de rachat ❏ *Banking, St Exch* **repurchase agreement** opération *f* de réméré *ou* de prise en pension; *Mktg* **repurchase market** marché *m* de renouvellement; **repurchase period** délai *m* de rachat; *Banking, St Exch* **repurchase rate** taux *m* de réméré *ou* de prise en pension; **repurchase right** droit *m* de rachat
2 *vt* racheter; *Mktg* réacheter

request 1 *n* demande *f* (**for** de); **to make a request (for)** faire une demande (de); **samples sent on request** échantillons sur demande
2 *vt* demander; **to request sb to do sth** demander à qn de faire qch; **as requested** (comme) suite à votre demande

require *vt* (**a**) *(qualifications, standard, commitment)* exiger, réclamer; **this job requires skills and experience** ce travail demande *ou* réclame compétence et expérience; **it is required that you begin work at 8 o'clock every morning** on exige de vous que vous commenciez votre travail à 8 heures tous les matins (**b**) *(need)* avoir besoin de; **your presence is urgently required** on vous réclame d'urgence

requirement *n* (**a**) *(need, demand)* exigence *f*; **to meet sb's requirements** satisfaire aux exigences de qn; **this doesn't meet our requirements** ceci ne répond pas à nos exigences (**b**) *(condition, prerequisite)* condition *f* (requise); **she doesn't fulfil the requirements for the job** elle ne remplit pas les conditions requises pour le poste

requisition *n* demande *f*; **to put in a requisition for sth** passer une demande de qch ❏ **requisition number** numéro *m* de référence

resale *n* revente *f* ❏ **resale price maintenance** vente *f* au détail à prix imposé; **resale value** valeur *f* à la revente

resaleable *adj* revendable

reschedule *vt* (**a**) *(appointment, flight, departure)* *(change time of)* modifier l'heure de; *(change date of)* modifier la date de; **the meeting has been rescheduled for next week** la réunion a été reportée à la semaine prochaine (**b**) *Fin (debt)* rééchelonner

rescheduling *n* (**a**) *(of appointment, flight, departure)* *(of time)* modification *f* de l'heure; *(of date)* modification de la date (**b**) *Fin (of debt)* rééchelonnement *m*

rescind *vt* *(agreement)* annuler; *(contract)* résilier; *(law)* abroger

rescission *n* *(of agreement)* annulation *f*; *(of contract)* résiliation *f*; *(of law)* abrogation *f*

research 1 *n* recherche *f*; **to do research (into sth)** faire des recherches (sur qch); **research and development** recherche et développement *m*; **research and engineering** études *fpl* et recherches ❏ **research company** société *f* de recherche; **research department** service *m* de recherche; **research programme** programme *m* de recherches; **research work** travaux *mpl* de recherche
2 *vt* faire des recherches sur
3 *vi* faire des recherches (**into** sur)

researcher *n* chercheur(euse) *m,f*

resell *vt* revendre

reservation *n* *(booking)* réservation *f*; **to make a reservation** faire une réservation ❏ **reservations agent** agent *m* de réservations; **reservations book** agenda *m* de réservation; **reservations desk** bureau *m* des réservations; **reservation form** bon *m* de réservation; **reservation sheet** bordereau *m* de réservations

reserve 1 *n* (**a**) *Fin (of money)* réserve *f*; **to draw on the reserves** puiser dans les réserves ❏ **reserve account** compte *m* de réserve; **reserve bank** banque *f* de réserve; **reserve capital** capital *m* de réserve; **reserve currency** monnaie *f* de réserve; *Acct* **reserve fund** fonds *m* de réserve; **reserve ratio** taux *m* de mise en réserve; **reserve stocks** approvisionnements *mpl* de réserve (**b**) **reserve price** *(at auction)* prix *m* minimum
2 *vt* *(room, table, seat)* réserver

reset *Comptr* **1** *n* réinitialisation *f* ❏ **reset button, reset switch** bouton *m* de réinitialisation
2 *vt* réinitialiser

residence *n* *(stay)* séjour *m*; *(home)* demeure *f* ❏ **residence permit** carte *f* de séjour

resident *n* *(of town, city, in foreign country)* résident(e) *m,f*; *(in hotel)* client(e) *m,f*; **are you a resident of an EU country?** êtes-vous ressortissant d'un pays membre de l'Union européenne?

residual income *n* revenu *m* résiduel

residuary *adj Law* **residuary legacy** legs *m* universel; **residuary legatee** legataire *m* universel

resign 1 *vt* *(job, position)* démissionner de
2 *vi* démissionner; **she resigned from her job/ from the committee** elle a démissionné de son emploi/du comité

resignation *n* démission *f*; **to hand in one's resignation** donner sa démission ❏ **resignation letter** lettre *f* de démission

resolution *n* (**a**) *(formal motion)* résolution *f*; **to put a resolution to the meeting** soumettre *ou* proposer une résolution; **to pass/adopt/reject a resolution (to do sth)** voter/adopter/rejeter une résolution (pour faire qch); **the statutes can only be changed by resolution** les statuts ne peuvent être modifiés que par l'adoption d'une résolution (**b**) *Comptr (of image)* résolution *f*; **high resolution screen** écran *m* à haute résolution *ou* définition

resource n ressource f; **there's a limit to the resources we can invest** il y a une limite à la somme que nous pouvons investir ❑ **resource allocation** allocation f des ressources; **resource management** gestion f des ressources

respect n **with respect to, in respect of** (in letter) en ce qui concerne, concernant

respite n (delay) délai m; **we've been given a week's respite before we need to pay** on nous a accordé un délai d'une semaine pour payer

respond vi répondre; **to respond to a letter** répondre à une lettre

respondent n répondant(e) m,f

response n réponse f; **in reponse to your letter** suite à votre lettre ❑ Comptr **response time** temps m de réponse

responsibility n (a) (control, authority) responsabilité f; **to have responsibility for sth** avoir la charge ou la responsabilité de qch; **the project is their joint responsibility** le projet relève de leur responsabilité à tous les deux; **a position of great responsibility** un poste à haute responsabilité ❑ **responsibility accounting** comptabilité f par centres de responsabilité

(**b**) (task, duty) responsabilité f; **your responsibilities will include product development** vous assurerez entre autres le développement de nouveaux produits; **they have a responsibility to the shareholders** ils ont une responsabilité envers les actionnaires

responsible adj (a) (in control, in authority) responsable; **who's responsible for research?** qui est chargé de la recherche?; **a responsible position** un poste à responsabilité

(**b**) (accountable) responsable; **he is responsible only to the managing director** il n'est responsable que devant le directeur général

(**c**)(serious, trustworthy) responsable; **the chemical industry has become more environmentally responsible** l'industrie chimique se préoccupe davantage de l'environnement; **our bank makes responsible investments** notre banque a une politique d'investissement responsable

restart Comptr **1** n (of system) redémarrage m; (of program) reprise f

2 vt (system) redémarrer; (program) reprendre

3 vi (of system) redémarrer; (of program) reprendre

restitution n (compensation) réparation f; **the company was ordered to make full restitution of the monies** la société a été sommée de restituer l'intégralité de la somme

restock vt (shop) réassortir

restocking n (of shop) réassortiment m

restoration fund n caisse f de restauration

restore Comptr **1** n (of file, text, data) restauration f

2 vt (file, text, data) restaurer

restrict vt (expenses, production) restreindre; **to restrict credits** encadrer le crédit

restricted adj (document, information) secret(ète), confidentiel(elle)

restriction n (of expenses, production) restriction f, limitation f; **to place restrictions on sth** imposer des restrictions sur qch

restrictive adj restrictif(ive) ❑ **restrictive clause** clause f restrictive; **restrictive practices** pratiques fpl restrictives

restructure vt restructurer

restructuring n restructuration f; **the car industry in Europe has undergone massive restructuring in recent years** l'industrie automobile européenne a subi une restructuration en profondeur ces dernières années ❑ **restructuring plan** plan m de restructuration

> **❝**
> The Corporation also announced a comprehensive **restructuring plan** designed to significantly reduce its manufacturing cost base. The plan includes the transfer of production and service operations in the Power Tools and Accessories and Hardware and Home Improvement businesses from facilities in the United States and England to low-cost locations in Mexico, China, and Central Europe as well as actions to reduce selling, general, and administrative expenses.
> **❞**

result 1 n résultat m; **the company's results are down on last year's** les résultats financiers de l'entreprise sont moins bons que l'année dernière; **to yield** or **show results** donner des résultats; **our policy is beginning to show results** notre politique commence à porter ses fruits

2 vi résulter; **to result in sth** avoir qch pour résultat, entraîner qch; **a price rise would inevitably result** il en résulterait inévitablement une augmentation des prix

résumé n (a) (summary) résumé m (b) Am (curriculum vitae) curriculum vitae m

retail 1 n (vente f au) détail m; **a wholesale and retail business** un commerce de gros et de détail ❑ **retail audit** audit m des détaillants; **retail auditor** audit des détaillants, auditeur(trice) m,f des détaillants; **retail bank** banque f de détail; **retail banking** banque de détail; **retail chain** chaîne f de détail; **retail company** maison f de détail; **retail customer** client(e) m,f qui achète au détail; **retail dealer** détaillant(e) m,f; Am **retail elephant** magasin m de grande distribution (qui domine une zone donnée); **retail**

goods marchandises *fpl* au détail; **retail outlet** magasin de (vente au) détail, point *m* de (vente au) détail; **retail panel** panel *m* de détaillants; **retail park** zone *f* commerciale; **retail price** prix *m* de détail; *Br Econ, Fin* **Retail Price Index** indice *m* des prix de détail; **retail price maintenance** prix imposé; **retail sales** vente au détail; **retail shipment** expédition *f* de détail; **retail shop** magasin de (vente au) détail; **retail trade** (commerce *m* de) détail
  2 *vt* vendre au détail
  3 *vi* se vendre (au détail); **they retail at £50 each** ils se vendent à 50 livres la pièce

❝

Located in a mall near P&G's headquarters in suburban Cincinnati, the 4,700-square-foot **retail outlet** is being regarded by the company as a test. However, executives say P&G does not plan on entering the **retail** arena. Instead, the company will use the store to launch new products and refine offerings.

❞

retailer *n* détaillant(e) *m,f* ❑ **retailer co-operative** groupe *m* de détaillants; **retailers' group** groupement *m* de détaillants; **retailer margin** marge *f* du détaillant

retailing *n* vente *f* au détail ❑ **retailing mix** marchéage *m* de distribution

retained *adj Acct* **retained earnings** revenu *m* non distribué; **retained profit** bénéfices *mpl* non distribués

retainer *n* provision *f*; **to pay sb a retainer** verser une provision à qn

retaining fee *n* provision *f*

retire 1 *vt* (**a**) *(person)* mettre à la retraite (**b**) *Fin (bill, bonds, shares)* retirer
  2 *vi* prendre sa retraite; **to retire early** partir en retraite anticipée; **he retired at 65** il a pris sa retraite à 65 ans

retired *adj* (**a**) *(person)* retraité(e), à la retraite (**b**) *Fin (bill, bonds, shares)* retiré(e)

retiree *n Am* retraité(e) *m,f*

retirement *n* (**a**) *(of person)* retraite *f*; **to take early retirement** partir en retraite anticipée ❑ **retirement age** l'âge *m* de la retraite; **retirement benefit** indemnité *f* de départ en retraite; **retirement pay** retraite; **retirement pension** (pension *f* de) retraite; **retirement savings plan** plan *m* d'épargne retraite (**b**) *Fin (of bill, bonds, shares)* retrait *m*

retiring *adj (employee)* qui prend sa retraite ❑ **retiring age** l'âge *m* de la retraite

retool 1 *vt* (**a**) *Ind* rééquiper (**b**) *Am Fam (company)* réorganiser
  2 *vi* (**a**) *Ind* se rééquiper (**b**) *Am Fam (company)* se réorganiser

retrain 1 *vt* recycler
  2 *vi* se recycler

retraining *n* recyclage *m* ❑ **retraining course** stage *m* de recyclage

retrench *Fin* **1** *vt (expenditure, costs)* restreindre
  2 *vi* restreindre ses dépenses, faire des économies

retrenchment *n Fin (of expenditure, costs)* réduction *f*

retrieval *n Comptr (of data, file)* recherche *f*; *(of lost data)* récupération *f*

retrieve *vt Comptr (data, file)* rechercher; *(lost data)* récupérer

retroactive *adj* rétroactif(ive)

retroactively *adv* rétroactivement

retry *vi Comptr* réessayer

return 1 *n* (**a**) *(of goods)* renvoi *m*; **by return of post** par retour du courrier; **on sale or return** *(goods)* vendu(e) avec possibilité de retour; **on return of this coupon** sur renvoi de ce bon ❑ **return address** adresse *f* de l'expéditeur; **return cargo** cargaison *f* de retour; **return freight** fret *m* de retour
  (**b**) *Fin (yield)* rapport *m*, retour *m* (**on** de); **how much return do you get on your investment?** combien est-ce que ton investissement te rapporte?; **to bring a good return** rapporter un bon bénéfice ❑ *Acct* **return on capital** retour sur capital; *Acct* **return on capital employed** retour sur capitaux permanents; **return on capital invested** retour sur capitaux investis; **return on equity** retour sur fonds propres; **return on investment** retour sur investissement; **return on net assets** rendement *m* de l'actif net; **return on sales** retour sur ventes
  (**c**) **returns** *(profit)* bénéfices *mpl*
  (**d**) *(for declaring tax)* (formulaire *m* de) déclaration *f* d'impôts
  (**e**) *Br (round trip)* aller et retour *m* ❑ **return ticket** (billet *m*) aller et retour
  (**f**) *Comptr* retour *m* ❑ **return key** touche *f* retour
  2 *vt* (**a**) *(goods)* renvoyer; **to return sb's call** rappeler qn; **return to sender** *(on letter)* retour à l'expéditeur
  (**b**) *(deposit)* rendre; *(sum paid in excess)* ristourner, rembourser
  (**c**) *Fin (profit, interest)* rapporter

returnable *adj* (**a**) *(container, packaging)* consigné(e); *(purchase)* qui peut être rendu(e) (**b**) *(document)* à retourner; **returnable by 1 July** à renvoyer avant le 1er juillet

revaluation *n Econ, Fin (of currency, property)* réévaluation *f*

revalue *vt Econ, Fin (currency, property)* réévaluer

Revenue *n Br Fam* **the Revenue** ≃ le fisc

revenue *n Fin* revenu *m*; *(from land, property)* revenu, rentes *fpl*; *(from sales)* recettes *fpl* ❑ **revenue account** *(part of ledger)* compte *m* de recettes; *(profit and loss account)* compte d'exploitation; *Am* **revenue bond** obligation *f* à intérêt conditionnel; **revenue budget** budget *m* des recettes; **revenue centre** centre *m* de revenus *ou* de profit; **revenue expenditure** dépenses *fpl* de fonctionnement; **revenue stamp** timbre *m* fiscal; **revenue tariff** tarif *m* douanier fiscal

reverse 1 *adj Acct* **reverse entry** écriture *f* inverse; **reverse mortgage** = contrat où le propriétaire d'une habitation reçoit de l'argent en contrepartie d'un emprunt hypothécaire sur son habitation, celle-ci servant en général de garantie au titre de l'emprunt; *St Exch* **reverse repo operation** opération *f* de mise en pension; *Comptr* **reverse sort** tri *m* en ordre décroissant; *Fin, St Exch* **reverse takeover** contre-OPA *f*
2 *vt* (**a**) *(policy)* inverser; *(decision)* revenir sur (**b**) *Br Tel* **to reverse the charges** appeler en PCV (**c**) *Acct (entry)* contre-passer

reverse-charge call *n Br Tel* communication *f* en PCV

reversionary *adj Ins* **reversionary annuity** rente *f* réversible; *Fin* **reversionary bonus** prime *f* d'intéressement; *Fin* **reversionary owner** nu(e)-propriétaire *mf*; *Fin* **reversionary ownership** nue-propriété *f*

review 1 *n (of policy, salary)* révision *f*; *(of finances, situation)* examen *m*, bilan *m*; **the annual review of expenditure** le bilan annuel des dépenses; **all our prices are subject to review** tous nos prix sont susceptibles d'être révisés; **my salary comes up for review next month** mon salaire doit être révisé le mois prochain
2 *vt (policy, salary)* réviser; *(finances, situation)* examiner; **they should review their security arrangements** ils devraient revoir leurs dispositifs de sécurité

revival *n (in economy)* relance *f*; *(in business, industry)* reprise *f*

revive 1 *vt (economy)* relancer; *(business, industry)* ranimer
2 *vi (of economy, business, industry)* reprendre

revocable *adj Law (contract, law, will)* révocable; *(decision)* sur laquelle on peut revenir; *(order)* que l'on peut annuler ❑ *Fin* **revocable letter of credit** crédit *m* documentaire révocable

revoke *vt (law)* abroger; *(decision)* revenir sur

revolver credit *n Am Fin* crédit *m* renouvelable *ou* revolving

revolving *adj Br Fin* **revolving credit** crédit *m* renouvelable *ou* revolving; **revolving fund**

fonds *m* de roulement; *Br Fin* **revolving letter of credit** crédit documentaire renouvelable *ou* revolving

rewritable *adj Comptr* réinscriptible

rider *n (to document)* annexe *f*

RIE *n (abbr* **recognized investment exchange)** marché *m* d'investissement agréé

rig *St Exch* **1** *n (rise)* hausse *f* factice; *(fall)* baisse *f* factice
2 *vt* **to rig the market** manipuler le marché

> Others, including European ministers and central bankers, charge that the Arabs and their pals in the Organization of the Petroleum Exporting Countries (OPEC) cartel are the spoilsports, accusing them of **rigging the market** and of demanding too much for their product.

rigging *n St Exch* spéculation *f*, agiotage *m*

right 1 *n* (**a**) *(entitlement)* droit *m*; **to have the right to sth** avoir droit à qch; **she has a right to half the profits** elle a droit à la moitié des bénéfices ❑ **right of appeal** droit de recours; **right of entry** droit d'accès; **right of first refusal** droit de préférence; **right to strike** droit de grève (**b**) *St Exch* droit *m* préférentiel de souscription ❑ **rights issue** émission *f* de nouvelles actions à taux préférentiel
2 *adj Comptr* **right arrow** flèche *f* vers la droite; **right arrow key** touche *f* flèche vers la droite; **right justification** justification *f* à droite

right-click *Comptr* **1** *vt* cliquer avec le bouton droit de la souris sur
2 *vi* cliquer avec le bouton droit de la souris (**on** sur)

rightful *adj* légitime ❑ **rightful owner** propriétaire *mf* légitime

rightsize *vt* dégraisser

> "We have made significant strides in **rightsizing** the business, cutting corporate overhead and realigning our product mix with the changing demands of the marketplace," said Marcus Lemonis, chairman and CEO of Recreation USA.

rightsizing *n* dégraissage *m*

rim country *n Am* nouveau pays *m* industrialisé

ring[1] *n* (**a**) *(group)* syndicat *m*, cartel *m* (**b**) **ring binder** classeur *m* à anneaux (**c**) *St Exch* **the Ring** le Parquet

ring[2] *Br* **1** *vt (on telephone)* appeler
2 *vi (on telephone)* appeler

▶ **ring back** *Br* **1** *vt sep* rappeler
2 *vi* rappeler

▶ **ring off** *vi Br (on telephone)* raccrocher

▶ **ring up** *Br* **1** *vt sep* **(a)** *(on telephone)* appeler
(b) *(on cash register)* enregistrer
2 *vi* appeler

ring-fence *vt Fin (funds, resources)* réserver

ringing tone *n Tel* sonnerie*f*, signal *m* d'appel

▶ **rip off** *vt sep Fam* arnaquer

rip-off *n Fam* arnaque*f*

> **"**
>
> We might find ourselves in a similar position in five years' time, when the rest of the world has real broadband access and we are stuck with services that deliver data at one tenth of the speed. This would be a **rip-off** beyond anything seen in the dial-up market, paying over the odds for a service that cannot deliver the benefits we need.
>
> **"**

RISC *n Comptr (abbr* **reduced instruction set chip** *or* **computer)** RISC *m*

rise 1 *n* **(a)** *(in price, cost of living)* hausse*f*; *(in salary, value)* augmentation*f*; *(in bank rates, interest)* relèvement *m*, hausse; **the rise in the price of petrol** la hausse du prix de l'essence; *St Exch* **to speculate on a rise** jouer à la hausse **(b)** *Br (salary increase)* augmentation*f* (de salaire)
2 *vi* monter, augmenter; **prices are rising** les prix montent *ou* sont à la hausse; **the pound has risen against the dollar** la livre s'est appréciée vis-à-vis du dollar; **gold has risen in value by ten percent** la valeur de l'or a augmenté de dix pour cent

rising star *n Mktg* produit *m* d'avenir

risk *n* **(a)** *(possibility)* risque *m*; **to run a risk** courir un risque; **it was a calculated risk** c'était un risque calculé □ *risk analysis* analyse *f* des risques; *Am St Exch* *risk arbitrage* arbitrage *m* risque; *risk assessment* évaluation*f* des risques; *risk asset ratio* coefficient *m* de solvabilité; *Fin risk capital* capital *m* à risque; *risk factor* facteur *m* de risque; *risk management* gestion*f* des risques; *risk management tool* instrument *m* de gestion des risques; *risk manager* gestionnaire *mf* de risques; *risk monitoring* surveillance*f* des risques; *risk premium* prime*f* de risque de marché; *risk spreading* répartition*f* des risques; *risk warning* = avertissement donné aux personnes désirant investir dans les produits dérivés, les renseignant sur les risques inhérents à ce genre d'investissement **(b)** *Ins* risque *m*; **to underwrite a risk** souscrire un risque □ *risk subscribed* risque assuré

risk-averse *adj Fin* = qui n'aime pas prendre de risques

risk-reward ratio *n St Exch* ratio *m* risque-rentabilité

rival *adj & n* rival(e) *m,f*

road *n* route*f*; **to be on the road** *(of salesman)* être sur la route □ *road haulage* transports *mpl* routiers; *road haulage company* entreprise *f* de roulage; *road haulage consolidator* groupeur *m* routier; *road haulage depot* gare*f* routière; *road link* liaison*f* routière; *road traffic* circulation *f* routière; *road transport* transports *mpl* routiers

roadshow *n* tournée*f* de présentation

> **"**
>
> Maritz did not carry out the BA launch in isolation; all staff were briefed face to face on the strategy behind the new identity before it was unveiled to them at a high-tech mobile **roadshow**. Attendance was not compulsory – staff had to feel they were there through choice.
>
> **"**

roam *vi Tel (of mobile phone user)* itinérer

roaming *n Tel (of mobile phone user)* roaming *m*, itinérance*f*; *Comptr (on Internet)* roaming

robber baron *n Fam* requin *m* de l'industrie

> **"**
>
> Ted Turner, for example, used his billion-dollar pledge to the United Nations as public proof that he is on the side of the angels of social justice. Bill Gates has set up a $22 billion foundation, in part to rescue his reputation from the charge that he is a modern-day **robber baron**. CEOs I have talked to often explain their philanthropic involvement by saying, "I am just trying to give back to the community."
>
> **"**

robotics *n* robotique*f*

ROCE *n (abbr* **return on capital employed)** retour *m* sur capitaux permanents

rock bottom *n* **to reach rock bottom** *(of company, finances)* toucher le fond; **prices have reached rock bottom** les prix sont au plus bas

rock-bottom *adj (price)* le plus bas

rocket *vi (of prices, inflation, unemployment)* monter en flèche

rogue trader *n St Exch* opérateur *m* peu scrupuleux

> **"**
>
> The fallout from the Allied Irish Banks scandal began to spread yesterday after it emerged that Citibank had suspended two employees for lavishly indulging the **rogue trader** who lost $691m (£487m) at AIB's subsidiary Allfirst Financial.
>
> **"**

ROI n (abbr **return on investment**) retour m sur investissements

▸ **roll back** vt sep Am (prices, inflation, unemployment) baisser

▸ **roll out** vt sep (launch) (product) lancer; (extend) (production) accroître; **the new scheme will be rolled out nationwide** le nouveau système s'étendra à tout le pays

▸ **roll over** vi Fin renouveler

rollback n Am (in prices, inflation, unemployment) réduction f, baisse f (**in** de)

rollercoaster market n marché m volatile

rolling adj Acct **rolling budget** budget m glissant; Acct **rolling plan** plan m glissant; Ind **rolling strikes** grèves fpl tournantes

roll-on-roll-off n (system) roulage m; (ship) navire m roulier

roll-out n (of product) lancement m

rollover 1 n (in taxation) (disposition f de) roulement m; (of loan) reconduction f
  2 adj (credit, loan) à taux révisable □ **rollover credit** crédit m renouvelable; **rollover loan** prêt m renouvelable

ROM n Comptr (abbr **read only memory**) mémoire f morte, (mémoire) ROM f

root directory n Comptr racine f, répertoire m principal

RORO n (abbr **roll-on-roll-off**) (system) roulage m; (ship) navire m roulier

ROS n (abbr **return on sales**) retour m sur ventes

rota n Br (system) roulement m; (list) tableau m de service

rotation n (of staff, jobs) roulement m

rough 1 n (of design) crayonné m, esquisse f
  2 adj (approximate, not finalized) approximatif(ive) □ **rough calculation** calcul m approximatif; **rough copy** brouillon m; **rough estimate** évaluation f approximative; **rough layout** crayonné m, esquisse f; **rough sketch** ébauche f (de projet)

round 1 n (of talks, visits) série f
  2 adj (**a**) **round brackets** parenthèses fpl; **round figure** chiffre m rond; **in round figures** en chiffres ronds; **round sum** compte m rond; **round table** table f ronde (**b**) Am **round trip** aller et retour m; **round trip ticket** (billet m) aller et retour

▸ **round down** vt sep arrondir au chiffre inférieur

▸ **round up** vt sep arrondir au chiffre supérieur

route 1 n (of traveller) itinéraire m; (of plane, ship) route f
  2 vt (parcel, goods) acheminer

router n Comptr routeur m

routine 1 n Comptr sous-programme m
  2 adj de routine □ **routine business** affaires fpl courantes; **routine maintenance** maintenance f périodique

routing n (**a**) (of parcel, goods) acheminement m (**b**) Comptr routage m

row n Comptr (in spreadsheet) ligne f

Royal Mint n Br Fin **the Royal Mint** ≃ (l'hôtel m de) la Monnaie

royalty n (for invention) redevance f; **royalties** (for author, musician) droits mpl d'auteur

RPI n Br Econ (abbr **Retail Price Index**) indice m des prix de détail

RPM n (abbr **retail price maintenance**) prix m imposé

RRP n (abbr **recommended retail price**) prix m recommandé ou conseillé

RSI n (abbr **repetitive strain injury**) lésions fpl attribuables au travail répétitif

> **"**
> A disabling ailment whose symptoms range from minor pain to loss of function in the affected body part, **RSI** affects millions of people who spend long hours at computers, switchboards and other worksites where repetitive motions are performed – typically hand-intensive exercises such as keyboarding or cutting.
> **"**

RTGS n Banking (abbr **Real-Time Gross Settlement**) RTGS m □ **RTGS system** système m RTGS

RTM n (abbr **registered trade mark**) marque f déposée

rubber cheque, Am **rubber check** n Fam chèque m en bois

rubric n rubrique f

RUF n Fin (abbr **revolving underwriting facility**) facilité f renouvelable de prise ferme

rule 1 n (law, principle) règle f; (regulation) règlement m; **rules and regulations** règles
  2 vi (make decision) statuer (**on** sur); **to rule on a dispute** statuer sur un litige

▸ **rule off** vt sep (account) clore, arrêter

ruler n règle f □ Comptr **ruler line** règle

ruling 1 n (judgement) décision f, jugement m
  2 adj (class) dirigeant(e)

run 1 n Fin (on currency, Stock Exchange) ruée f (**on** sur); (on bank) retrait m massif; **there was a run on the dollar** il y a eu une ruée sur le dollar
  2 vt (**a**) (business, office) diriger; (shop) tenir (**b**) (machinery) faire marcher, faire fonctionner (**c**) Comptr (program) exécuter, faire tourner; **this computer runs most software** on peut utiliser la plupart des logiciels sur cet ordinateur

3 *vi* (**a**) *(of contract, lease, bill of exchange)* courir; **the lease has another year to run** le bail n'expire pas avant un an; **your subscription will run for two years** votre abonnement sera valable deux ans
(**b**) *(of machine)* marcher, fonctionner; **the new assembly line is up and running** la nouvelle chaîne de montage est en service
(**c**) *Comptr* **this software runs on DOS** ce logiciel tourne sous DOS; **do not interrupt the program while it is running** ne pas interrompre le programme en cours d'exécution

▸ **run down** *vt sep (production, stocks)* réduire, diminuer

▸ **run into** *vt insep (amount to)* s'élever à; **the debts run into millions of dollars** la dette s'élève à des millions de dollars

▸ **run out** *vi (of lease, contract)* expirer; *(of money, supplies, resources)* s'épuiser; **to run out of sth** manquer de qch; **to have run out of sth** ne plus avoir de qch

▸ **run up** *vt sep (bill, debt)* laisser accumuler; **I've run up a huge overdraft** j'ai un découvert énorme

runner *n (messenger)* coursier(ère) *m,f*

running 1 *n* (**a**) *(of machine)* marche *f*, fonctionnement *m* ❏ *running costs* frais *mpl* d'entretien (**b**) *(management)* direction *f*; **she leaves the day-to-day running of the depart-ment to her assistant** elle laisse son assistant s'occuper de la gestion quotidienne du service ❏ *running costs* frais *mpl* d'exploitation
2 *adj Banking running account* compte *m* courant

runtime system *n Comptr* système *m* en phase d'exécution

rush *n* (**a**) *rush hour (busy period)* heures *fpl* d'affluence *ou* de pointe (**b**) *(hurry)* hâte *f* ❏ *rush job* travail *m* de première urgence; *rush order* commande *f* urgente

▸ **rush out** *vt sep (new product)* sortir rapidement

▸ **rush through** *vt sep (job)* expédier; *(goods ordered)* envoyer d'urgence; *(order, application)* traiter d'urgence

rust belt *n* = États du Nord des États-Unis (principalement le Michigan et l'Illinois) dont l'industrie (sidérurgie et automobile) a périclité

> **ʻʻ**
>
> The steel dispute threatens to destroy painstaking efforts by the EU and US trade representatives to calm a series of transatlantic trade disputes. European officials believe the US administration is on the brink of sacrificing its free trade credentials to its mid-term electoral prospects in America's **rust belt** states.
>
> **ʼʼ**

Ss

sabbatical 1 *n* congé *m* sabbatique
  2 *adj* sabbatique □ **sabbatical year** année *f* sabbatique

sack *Br Fam* **1** *n* (*dismissal*) renvoi *m*; **to get the sack** se faire virer; **to give sb the sack** virer qn
  2 *vt* (*dismiss*) virer

SAE *n Br* (*abbr* **stamped addressed envelope**) enveloppe *f* timbrée libellée à ses noms et adresse

safe 1 *n* coffre-fort *m*
  2 *adj* (**a**) (*secure*) sûr(e) □ **safe custody** (*of securities, assets*) garde *f* en dépôt; **to place sth in safe custody** mettre qch en dépôt (**b**) (*not dangerous*) sûr(e) □ **safe load** charge *f* admissible

safe-deposit *n* dépôt *m* en coffre-fort □ **safe-deposit box** coffre *m* (*dans une banque*)

safeguard 1 *n* garantie *f* (**against** contre) □ **safeguard clause** clause *f* de sauvegarde
  2 *vt* (*interests, rights*) sauvegarder, protéger
  3 *vi* **to safeguard against sth** se protéger contre qch

safe-keeping *n* garde *f*; **to place securities in the bank for safe-keeping** mettre des valeurs en dépôt à la banque

safety *n* sécurité *f* □ **safety clause** clause *f* de sauvegarde; **safety factor** facteur *m* de sécurité; **safety margin** marge *f* de sécurité; **safety measures** mesures *fpl* de sécurité; **safety precautions** mesures de sécurité; **safety regulations** règles *fpl* de sécurité; **safety standards** normes *fpl* de sécurité; **safety stock** stock *m* tampon *ou* de sécurité; **safety vault** chambre *f* forte

sag 1 *n* (*of shares, prices, demand*) baisse *f*
  2 *vi* (*of shares, prices, demand*) baisser

sagging *adj* (*shares, prices, demand*) en baisse

salaried *adj* (*personnel, job*) salarié(e) □ **salaried employee** salarié(e) *m,f*; **salaried staff** salarié(e)s

salary *n* salaire *m*; **to draw one's salary** toucher son salaire □ **salary advice** bordereau *m* de salaire; **salary curve** courbe *f* de salaire; **salary earner** salarié(e) *m,f*; **salary grade** échelon *m* des salaires; **salary increase** augmentation *f* de salaire; **salary level** échelon salarial; **salary progression curve** courbe d'augmentation de salaire; **salary range** éven-tail *m* des salaires; **salary reduction plan** = réduction des salaires dans le but de payer moins d'impôts, l'argent ainsi épargné étant affecté à d'autres usages; **salary scale** échelle *f* des salaires; **salary structure** structure *f* des salaires

sale *n* (**a**) (*act, event*) vente *f*; **sales** (*turnover*) chiffre *m* d'affaires; (*sector*) la vente; **to work in sales** travailler dans la vente; **for sale** à vendre; **to put sth up for sale** mettre qch en vente; **on sale** en vente; **sale for the account** vente à terme; **sale on approval** vente à l'essai; *St Exch* **sale at arrival** vente à l'arrivée; **sale by auction** vente aux enchères; **sale on CIF basis** vente CAF; **sale at departure** vente au départ; **sale by description** vente sur description; **sale and lease-back** cession-bail *f*; **sale at a loss** vente à perte; **sales and marketing** vente-marketing *f*; **sales and marketing department** service *m* vente-marketing; **sales and marketing director** directeur(trice) *m,f* des ventes et du marketing; **sale with option of repurchase** vente avec faculté de rachat; **sale by order of the court** vente judiciaire; **sale by private agreement** vente à l'amiable; **sales and profit forecast** prévision *f* des ventes et profits; **sale at a reduced price** vente à prix réduit; **sale or return** vente avec faculté de retour; **sale by sample** vente sur échantillon; **sale by sealed tender** vente par soumission cachetée; **sale as seen** vente en l'état □ **sales account** compte *m* des ventes; **sales acumen** sens *m* du commerce; **sale agreement** accord *m ou* protocole *m* de vente; **sales analysis** analyse *f* des ventes; **sales area** (*in store*) surface *f ou* espace *m* de vente; (*district*) région *f* desservie; *Br* **sales assistant** vendeur(euse) *m,f*; **sales audit** audit *m* de vente; **sales budget** budget *m* commercial *ou* des ventes; **sales campaign** campagne *f* de vente; **sales chart** courbe *f* des ventes; *Am* **sales check** ticket *m* de caisse; *Am* **sales clerk** vendeur(euse); **sales commission** commission *f* de vente; **sales consultant** conseiller(ère) *m,f* commercial(e); **sales contract** contrat *m* de vente; **sales counter** comptoir *m* de vente; **sales coverage** couverture *f* du marché; **sales department** service *m* des ventes; **sales director** directeur(trice) commercial(e) *ou* des ventes; **sales drive** campagne de vente; **sales effectiveness** efficacité *f* des ventes; **sales engineer** agent *m* technico-commercial; **sales**

equation équation *f* de vente; **sales executive** cadre *m* commercial; **sales expansion** développement *m* des ventes; *St Exch* **sales fee** frais *mpl* d'achat *ou* d'acquisition; **sales figures** chiffre de vente; **sales floor** surface de vente; **sales force** force *f* de vente; **sales forecast** prévision des ventes; **sales growth** accroissement *m* des ventes; **sales incentive** stimulant *m* de vente; **sales invoice** facture *f* de vente; **sales invoice ledger** journal *m* factures-clients; *Acct* **sales ledger** grand-livre *m* des ventes, journal des ventes; **sales letter** lettre *f* de vente; **sales literature** brochures *fpl* publicitaires; **sales management** direction *f* commerciale *ou* des ventes; **sales manager** directeur(trice) commercial(e) *ou* des ventes; **sales meeting** réunion *f* de représentants; **sales monopoly** monopole *m* de vente; **sales network** réseau *m* commercial *ou* de vente; **sales note** bulletin *m* de vente; **sales objective** objectif *m* de vente; **sales orientation** optique *f* vente; **sales outlet** point *m* de vente; **sales performance** efficacité de vente; **sales personnel** personnel *m* de vente; **sales philosophy** optique vente; **sales pitch** arguments *mpl* de vente; **sales planning** planification *f* des ventes; **sales policy** politique *f* de vente; **sales potential** potentiel *m* de vente; **sale price** *(selling price)* prix *m* de vente; *(reduced price)* prix soldé; **sales programme** programme *m* des ventes; **sales projection** prévision des ventes; **sales promoter** promoteur(trice) *m,f* des ventes; **sales promotion** promotion *f* des ventes; **sales promotion agency** agence *f* de promotion des ventes; **sales quota** quota *m* de ventes; **sales ratio** ratio *m* des ventes; **sales report** rapport *m* *ou* relevé *m* de vente; **sales representative** représentant(e) *m,f* (de commerce), VRP *m*; **sales research** études *fpl* sur les ventes; **sales response** réaction *f* des ventes; **sales room** *(for auction)* salle *f* des ventes; **sales schedule** programme des ventes; *Am* **sales slip** ticket *m* de caisse; **sales staff** personnel de vente; **sales subsidiary** filiale *f* de vente; **sales support** soutien *m* commercial; **sales support staff** personnel de soutien commercial; **sales target** objectif *m* de vente; *Am* **sales tax** TVA *f*, taxe *f* à la valeur ajoutée; **sales team** équipe *f* de vente; **sales technician** agent *m* technico-commercial; **sales technique** technique *f* de vente; **sales territory** territoire *m* de vente; **sales tool** instrument *m* de vente; **sales volume** volume *m* des ventes; *Mktg* **sales wave** vague *f* de vente **(b)** *(at reduced prices)* soldes *mpl*; *Br* **in the sale,** *Am* **on sale** *(article)* en solde; **the sales** les soldes; **I got it in a sale** je l'ai acheté en solde □ **sale price** prix *m* soldé

saleability *n* facilité *f* d'écoulement *ou* de vente

saleable *adj* vendable □ **saleable goods** denrées *fpl* marchandes

saleroom *n (for auction)* salle *f* des ventes

salesman *n (for company)* représentant *m*; *(in shop)* vendeur *m*

salesmanship *n* technique *f* de vente

> "
> While the investment community has been enthralled by Lord Browne's brand of cerebral **salesmanship** at BP, it is far from enamoured by the taciturn style of the 56-year-old Yorkshireman who took over at Shell last July.
> "

salesperson *n (for company)* représentant(e) *m,f*; *(in shop)* vendeur(euse) *m,f*

sales-response function *n* équation *f* de réponse de marché

saleswoman *n (for company)* représentante *f*; *(in shop)* vendeuse *f*

salutation *n (in letter)* titre *m* de civilité

salvage 1 *n (recovery) (of cargo, waste material)* récupération *f*; *(things recovered)* objets *mpl* récupérés □ **salvage company** entreprise *f* de récupération; **salvage money** prime *f* de sauvetage; **salvage value** récupérabilité *f*
2 *vt (cargo, waste material)* récupérer

same-day *adj* **same-day delivery** livraison *f* le jour même; *Banking* **same-day value** valeur *f* jour

sample 1 *n Mktg* échantillon *m*; **up to sample** pareil *ou* conforme à l'échantillon; **to send sth as a sample** envoyer qch à titre d'échantillon; **to buy sth from sample** acheter qch d'après échantillon; **a representative sample of the population** un échantillon représentatif de la population □ **sample base** base *f* de sondage; **sample book** catalogue *m* d'échantillons, livre *m* d'échantillons; **sample card** carte *f* d'échantillons; **sample pack** paquet *m* échantillon; **sample survey** enquête *f* par sondage
2 *vt* **(a)** *(food)* goûter **(b)** *Mktg (public opinion)* sonder

sampler *n Mktg (person)* échantillonneur(euse) *m,f*

sampling *n Mktg* échantillonnage *m* □ **sampling error** erreur *f* d'échantillonnage; **sampling method** méthode *f* de sondage; **sampling offer** offre *f* d'échantillon gratuit; **sampling project** plan *m* d'échantillonnage; **sampling quota** quota *m* d'échantillonnage

Samurai bond *n Fam St Exch* obligation *f* Samouraï

sanction 1 *n* **(a)** *(penalty)* sanction *f*; **to impose (economic) sanctions on a country** prendre des sanctions (économiques) à l'encontre d'un pays **(b)** *(approval)* sanction *f*; **it hasn't yet been given official sanction** ceci n'a pas encore été officiellement approuvé
2 *vt (authorize)* sanctionner, autoriser

sandbag n *(in takeover bid)* = tactique de temporisation utilisée par une entreprise faisant l'objet d'une OPA

sandwich course n *Br* = stage de formation professionnelle en alternance

SASE n *Am (abbr* **self-addressed stamped envelope**) enveloppe *f* timbrée libellée à ses noms et adresse

satcaster n *Fam (abbr* **satellite broadcaster**) satellite *f* de retransmission *ou* de diffusion

> Fuji Television Networks is betting that experience and image matter when its new BS Fuji **satcaster** takes to the air in December. Fuji TV has been in the satcasting business for over three years as one of the main investors in the Sky PerfecTV direct-to-home platform. It has also developed new channels of broadcasting for Sky PerfecTV and worked with the **satcaster** platform to develop data transmission technology.

satcasting n *Fam (abbr* **satellite broadcasting**) retransmission *f* par satellite

satellite n satellite *m*; **(tele)communications satellite** satellite de télécommunications □ **satellite broadcaster** satellite de retransmission *ou* de diffusion; **satellite broadcasting** retransmission *f* par satellite; **satellite channel** chaîne *f* par satellite; **satellite dish** antenne *f* parabolique; **satellite link** liaison *f* par satellite; **satellite network** réseau *m* satellite; **satellite photo** photo *f* satellite; **satellite station** station *f* satellite; **satellite television** télévision *f* par satellite

satisfaction n (**a**) *(of demand, conditions)* satisfaction *f*; *(of contract)* exécution *f*, réalisation *f*; **the satisfaction of the union's demands** la satisfaction des revendications syndicales (**b**) *(of debt)* paiement *m*, liquidation *f*

satisfy vt (**a**) *(demand, conditions)* satisfaire à; *(contract)* remplir (**b**) *(debt)* payer, liquider

saturate vt *(market)* saturer

saturated adj *(market)* saturé(e)

saturation n *(of market)* saturation *f* □ **saturation advertising** publicité *f* intensive; **saturation campaign** campagne *f* intensive *ou* de saturation; **saturation point** point *m* de saturation; **the market has reached saturation point** le marché est saturé

save 1 n *Comptr* sauvegarde *f* □ **save command** commande *f* de sauvegarde; **save function** fonction *f* de sauvegarde; **save option** option *f* de sauvegarde

2 vt (**a**) *(money) (keep for future)* mettre de côté; *(not waste)* économiser; **I save £100 a month in a special account** j'économise 100 li-

vres par mois sur un compte spécial; **how much money have you got saved?** combien d'argent avez-vous mis de côté?; **buying in bulk saves ten percent** l'achat en gros fait économiser dix pour cent

(**b**) *Comptr* sauvegarder; **to save sth to disk** sauvegarder qch sur disquette; **save as...** enregistrer sous...

3 vi (**a**) *(put money aside)* économiser, faire des économies; **to save on sth** économiser sur qch; **you save if you buy in bulk** on fait des économies en achetant en gros

(**b**) *Comptr* sauvegarder; **this file is taking a long time to save** ça prend beaucoup de temps pour sauvegarder ce fichier

save-as-you-earn adj *Br Fin* = plan d'épargne à contributions mensuelles produisant des intérêts exonérés d'impôts

saver n épargnant(e) *m,f*

saving n (**a**) *(thrift, economy)* économie *f*, épargne *f*; **measures to encourage saving** des mesures pour encourager l'épargne

(**b**) *(money saved)* économie *f*; **we made a saving of £500 on the usual price** nous avons fait une économie de 500 livres sur le prix habituel; **savings** économies *fpl*; *Econ* dépôts *mpl* d'épargne □ **savings account** compte *m* d'épargne, compte de caisse d'épargne; **savings bank** caisse *f* d'épargne; **savings bond** ≃ bon *m* d'épargne; *Br* **savings book** livret *m* (de caisse) d'épargne; *Br* **savings certificate** ≃ bon d'épargne; **savings club** club *m* d'épargne; *Am* **savings and loan association** ≃ caisse d'épargne-logement; **savings plan** plan *m* d'épargne; **savings rate** taux *m* d'épargne; *Fin* **savings scheme** plan d'épargne; *Br* **savings stamp** timbre-épargne *m*

SAYE n *Br Fin (abbr* **save-as-you-earn**) = plan d'épargne à contributions mensuelles produisant des intérêts exonérés d'impôts

> **SAYE** was introduced more than 20 years ago as a way to encourage workers to become stakeholders in their own companies and to boost private investment in the stock market. The proceeds of **SAYE** schemes are subject to capital gains tax but the investment is relatively risk free because if the company's share price falls the individual can reclaim the cash they invested rather than taking the price for the shares.

SBA n *Am (abbr* **Small Business Administration**) = organisme fédéral américain d'aide aux petites entreprises

SBU n *(abbr* **strategic business unit**) DAS *m*, UAS *f*

scalage n *Am* remise *f* pour cause de freinte

scale n (of salaries, taxes, prices) échelle f

▸ **scale down** vt sep (reduce) réduire, baisser; **production is being scaled down** on a entrepris de réduire la production

▸ **scale up** vt sep (increase) augmenter; **allowances were scaled up by ten percent** les allocations ont été augmentées de dix pour cent

scaled question n (in market research) question f à échelle de Lickert

scalp Fam **1** n Am petit profit m
2 vt St Exch **to scalp shares** boursicoter

scalper n Fam St Exch spéculateur(trice) m,f à la journée

scalping n Fam St Exch boursicotage m

scan Comptr **1** n lecture f au scanne(u)r
2 vt passer au scanne(u)r, scanner

▸ **scan in** vt sep Comptr (graphics) insérer par scanne(u)r, capturer au scanne(u)r

scanner n Comptr scanner m, scanneur m

scanning n Mktg veille f technologique

scarce adj (commodities) rare, peu abondant(e); **sugar is scarce at the moment** il y a une pénurie de sucre en ce moment □ **scarce currency** devise f forte

scarceness, scarcity n manque m, pénurie f; **there is a scarcity of labour** il y a une pénurie de main-d'œuvre □ **scarcity value** valeur f de rareté

schedule 1 n (a) (plan) programme m, planning m; **a schedule was agreed for the work** on a convenu d'un planning pour le travail; **the work was carried out according to schedule** le travail a été effectué selon les prévisions; **to be on schedule** être dans les temps; **to be behind schedule** être en retard sur le programme; **to be ahead of schedule** être en avance sur le programme; **to go according to schedule** se dérouler comme prévu; **to work to a tight schedule** avoir un emploi du temps chargé
(b) (list) (of items) nomenclature f; (of machines) inventaire m; (of prices) barème m; Admin (of taxes) cédule f; **schedule of charges** tarif m
(c) Law (clause) annexe f
2 vt (a) (plan) prévoir; **the meeting was scheduled for 3 o'clock/Wednesday** la réunion était prévue pour 15 heures/mercredi; **we're scheduled to arrive at 9pm** notre arrivée est prévue à 21 heures
(b) Law (clause) ajouter comme annexe

scheduler n Comptr (package) logiciel m de planification (de projets)

scheme n (a) (system) système m; **the company has a profit-sharing/a pension scheme** l'entreprise a un système de participation aux bénéfices/un régime de retraites complémen-

taires (b) (plan) plan m, projet m; **a scheme for new investment** un plan ou projet pour de nouveaux investissements □ Law **scheme of arrangement** concordat m préventif (à la faillite)

schilling n Formerly schilling m

scoop n (in press) scoop m, exclusivité f; **the paper got a scoop on the story** le journal a publié la nouvelle en exclusivité

scorched earth policy n (against hostile takeover situation) politique f de la terre brûlée

"

Deutsche Börse is believed to be seeking to exercise a penalty clause in the planned iX merger deal which collapsed in September … Financial market sources said Deutsche Börse's claim was unwise and was likely to kill off any co-operation between the two exchanges. Others accused the Deutsche Börse of pursuing a **scorched earth policy** which could put off other potential partners.

"

score n Mktg (in market research) score m

scrambled adj Mktg **scrambled merchandising, scrambled retailing** présentation f d'articles variés

scrap 1 n déchets mpl; **to sell sth for scrap** vendre qch à la casse □ **scrap dealer, scrap merchant** ferrailleur m; **scrap metal** ferraille f; **scrap value** valeur f à la casse, valeur liquidative
2 vt (a) (send to scrap) mettre à la ferraille ou à la casse (b) (abandon) (idea, plans) renoncer à, abandonner; (system) abandonner, mettre au rencart; (machinery) mettre au rebut ou au rencart

scrapbook n Comptr (on Macintosh) album m

scratchpad n Am Comptr bloc-notes m □ **scratchpad memory** mémoire f bloc-notes

screen 1 n Comptr écran m; **on screen** à l'écran; **to work on screen** travailler sur écran; **to bring up the next screen** amener l'écran suivant □ **screen capture** capture f d'écran; **screen display** affichage m; **screen dump** capture d'écran; **screen refresh** actualisation f ou régénération f de l'écran; **screen saver** économiseur m d'écran; **screen shot** capture d'écran; St Exch **screen trader** opérateur(trice) m,f sur écran; St Exch **screen trading** opérations fpl sur écran; St Exch **screen trading system** système m informatisé de transaction
2 vt (candidates, applications) passer au crible; **we screen all our security staff** nous faisons une enquête préalable sur tous les candidats aux postes d'agent de sécurité

screening n (of candidates, applications) sélection f; **after we receive the applications, the screening process can begin** lorsque nous aurons reçu les candidatures, le processus de sélection pourra débuter

scrip *n Fin, St Exch* titre *m* provisoire ❑ *scrip certificate* certificat *m* d'actions provisoire; *Am scrip dividend* certificat de dividende provisoire; *scrip issue* émission *f* d'actions gratuites

scripholder *n Fin, St Exch* détenteur(trice) *m,f* de titres

scroll *Comptr* **1** *n* défilement *m* ❑ *scroll bar* barre *f* de défilement; *scroll box* ascenseur *m*; *scroll button* bouton *m* de défilement; *scroll key* touche *f* de défilement; *scroll lock key* touche d'arrêt de défilement
  2 *vt* faire défiler
  3 *vi* défiler

▶ **scroll down** *Comptr* **1** *vt insep* **to scroll down a document** faire défiler un document vers le bas; **to scroll down a page** passer à la page suivante
  2 *vi (of person)* faire défiler de haut en bas; *(of text)* défiler de haut en bas

▶ **scroll through** *vt insep Comptr (text)* parcourir

▶ **scroll up** *Comptr* **1** *vt insep* **to scroll up a document** faire défiler un document vers le haut; **to scroll up a page** passer à la page précédente
  2 *vi (of person)* faire défiler de bas en haut; *(of text)* défiler de bas en haut

SCSI *n Comptr (abbr small computer systems interface)* SCSI *f* ❑ *SCSI card* carte *f* SCSI

SDR *n (abbr special drawing right)* DTS *m*

SDRAM *n Comptr (abbr synchronous dynamic random access memory)* SDRAM *f*

SEA *n (abbr Single European Act)* AUE *m*

sea *n sea link* liaison *f* maritime; *sea port* port *m* maritime; *sea risk* risque *m* maritime *ou* de mer

seal **1** *n (on deed)* sceau *m*; *(on letter)* cachet *m*; *(on goods for export)* plomb *m*
  2 *vt (deed)* sceller; *(envelope)* cacheter; *(goods for export)* (faire) plomber ❑ *sealed bid, sealed tender* soumission *f* cachetée

sealed-bid pricing *n* fixation *f* d'un prix de soumission

SEAQ *n (abbr Stock Exchange Automated Quotations System)* système *m* de cotation automatisé

search *Comptr* **1** *n* recherche *f*; **to do a search** faire une recherche; **to do a search for sth** rechercher qch; **search and replace** recherche et remplacement *m* ❑ *search engine* moteur *m* de recherche
  2 *vt (file, directory)* rechercher dans; **to search and replace sth** rechercher et remplacer qch
  3 *vi* faire une recherche

season *n* (a) *(for trade)* saison *f*; **it's a busy season for tour operators** c'est une époque très chargée pour les voyagistes; **Christmas is our**

busiest season c'est à Noël que nous travaillons le plus; **in season** en saison; **out of season** hors saison; **the low/high season** la basse/haute saison (b) *season ticket (for public transport)* carte *f* d'abonnement

seasonal *adj (demand, fluctuations)* saisonnier(ère) ❑ *seasonal adjustment* correction *f* des variations saisonnières; *seasonal discount* remise *f* saisonnière; *seasonal index* coefficient *m* saisonnier; *seasonal staff* personnel *m* saisonnier; *seasonal unemployment* chômage *m* saisonnier; *seasonal variations* variations *fpl* saisonnières

seasonally *adv* **seasonally adjusted** *(figures)* corrigé(e) des variations saisonnières ❑ *seasonally adjusted index* indice *m* corrigé des variations saisonnières

> **“**
> Orders for manufactured goods in the US fell in November, pulled down by flagging demand for transportation and defence-related equipment. Factory orders dropped 3.3 per cent in November to a **seasonally adjusted** $321.7bn (£223.4bn). This followed a revised rise of 7.0 per cent in October.
> **”**

SEATO *n (abbr Southeast Asia Treaty Organization)* OTASE *f*

SEC *n (abbr Securities and Exchange Commission)* = commission américaine des opérations de Bourse, ≃ COB *f*

second¹ **1** *n* **seconds** articles *mpl* défectueux ❑ *second of exchange* deuxième *m* de change
  2 *adj* second(e), deuxième ❑ *Fin second debenture* obligation *f* de deuxième rang; *Fin second endorser* tierce porteur *m*; *Fin second mortgage* deuxième hypothèque *f*; *second quarter (of year)* deuxième trimestre *m*

second² *vt (motion)* appuyer; *(speaker)* appuyer la motion de

second³ *vt (employee)* détacher, envoyer en détachement; **she's been seconded to head office** elle a été détachée au siège social

secondary *adj* secondaire ❑ *Acct secondary cost centre* centre *m* d'analyse auxiliaire; *secondary data* informations *fpl* secondaires, données *fpl* secondaires; *St Exch secondary distribution* revente *f* de titres; *secondary industry* industrie *f* secondaire; *St Exch secondary market* marché *m* secondaire; *St Exch secondary offering* revente *f* de titres; *Br secondary picketing* piquets *mpl* de grève de solidarité; *secondary product* sous-produit *m*; *secondary production* production *f* manufacturée; *secondary sector* secteur *m* secondaire; *secondary supplier* fournisseur *m* secondaire

second-hand 1 *adj (goods)* d'occasion □ *second-hand dealer* brocanteur(euse) *m,f,* revendeur(euse) *m,f*; *second-hand market* marché *m* de revente; *second-hand shop* magasin *m* d'occasions; *second-hand trade* brocante *f* *(commerce)*
2 *adv (buy)* d'occasion

secondment *n* détachement *m*; **to be on secondment** être en détachement

second-rate *adj (goods)* de qualité inférieure

secret *adj* secret(ète) □ *secret ballot* vote *m* à bulletin secret; *secret funds* caisse *f* noire; *Am* *secret partner* associé(e) *m,f* commanditaire, bailleur(eresse) *m,f* de fonds; *secret reserve* réserve *f* occulte

secretarial *adj (tasks)* de secrétaire, de secrétariat; **to have a secretarial job** avoir un travail de secrétaire □ *secretarial course* cours *m* de secrétariat; *secretarial pool* pool *m* de secrétaires; *secretarial school* école *f* de secrétariat; *secretarial skills* notions *fpl* de secrétariat; *secretarial work* travail *m* de secrétaire

secretary *n* secrétaire *mf*

section *n* (**a**) *(sector)* section *f*; **the business section of the community** les commerçants et les hommes d'affaires de notre communauté (**b**) *(of document)* section *f*; *(of law)* article *m*

sector *n* (**a**) *(area)* secteur *m*; **the banking sector** le secteur bancaire; **he works in the advertising sector** il travaille dans la publicité; **whole sectors of society live below the poverty line** des catégories sociales entières vivent en dessous du seuil de pauvreté (**b**) *Comptr (of screen, disk)* secteur *m*

sectorization *n* sectorisation *f*

secure 1 *adj* (**a**) *(investment, job)* sûr(e) (**b**) *Comptr secure electronic transaction* protocole *m* SET; *secure HTTP* protocole *m* HTTP sécurisé; *secure server* serveur *m* sécurisé; *secure sockets layer* protocole SSL
2 *vt* (**a**) *(obtain) (agreement, loan)* obtenir (**b**) *(guarantee) (debt, loan)* garantir; **the loan is secured by mortgages on several properties** le prêt est garanti par plusieurs hypothèques

secured *adj Fin secured bond* obligation *f* cautionnée; *secured credit card* = type de carte de crédit dont le détenteur doit posséder des fonds servant de garantie de paiement; *secured creditor* créancier(ère) *m,f* privilégié(e); *secured debenture* obligation cautionnée; *secured debt* créance *f* garantie; *secured loan (from lender's point of view)* prêt *m* garanti; *(from borrower's point of view)* emprunt *m* garanti; *secured note* billet *m* garanti

securitization *n St Exch* titrisation *f*

securitize *vt St Exch* titriser

security *n* (**a**) *(financial guarantee)* garantie *f*; *(for payment of debt)* caution *f*, cautionnement *m*; *(collateral)* nantissement *m*; *(person)* garant(e) *m,f*; **to give sth as security** donner qch en cautionnement; **to stand security for sb** se porter garant *ou* caution pour qn; **to lend money on security** prêter de l'argent sur nantissement *ou* sur garantie; **to lend money without security** prêter de l'argent à découvert; **what security do you have for the loan?** quelle garantie avez-vous pour couvrir ce prêt? □ *security deposit* dépôt *m* de garantie; *security of tenure (of property)* bail *m* assuré; *(of job)* sécurité *f* de l'emploi
(**b**) *St Exch* **securities** titres *mpl,* valeurs *fpl*; *securities in portfolio* titres en portefeuille □ *securities department* service *m* des titres; *Securities and Exchange Commission* = commission américaine des opérations de Bourse, ≃ COB *f*; *securities firm* maison *f* de titres; *securities house* société *f* de Bourse; *security interest* privilège *m*; *Securities and Investment Board* = commission britannique des opérations de Bourse, ≃ COB *f*; *securities market* marché *m* des titres, marché des valeurs (mobilières); *securities portfolio* portefeuille *m* de titres;
(**c**) *(safety, confidentiality)* sécurité *f* □ *security certificate* certificat *m* de sécurité; *security code* code *m* confidentiel; *Security Council* Conseil *m* de sécurité; *security level* niveau *m* de sécurité; *security officer* agent *m* de sécurité; *security tag* étiquette *f* magnétique

seed capital, seed money *n Fin* capital *m* initial

seek time *n Comptr* temps *m* d'accès

see-saw effect *n* effet *m* balançoire

segment 1 *n Mktg (customer base, market)* segment *m* □ *Acct segment margin* marge *f* sectorielle; *segment reporting* analyse *f* par secteur d'activité
2 *vt Mktg (customer base, market)* segmenter

segmentation *n Mktg (of customer base, market)* segmentation *f*

seize *vt Law (goods)* saisir, opérer la saisie de

seizure *n Law (of goods)* saisie *f*

select *vt* (**a**) *(candidate)* sélectionner, choisir (**b**) *Comptr* sélectionner; **select 'enter'** tapez 'entrée'; **to select an option** activer une option (**c**) *Mktg* sélectionner

selection *n* (**a**) *(of candidate, team, product)* sélection *f* □ *selection committee* comité *m* de sélection; *selection criterion* critère *f* de sélection (**b**) *Comptr* sélection *f* □ *selection box* rectangle *m* de sélection (**c**) *Mktg* sélection *f* □ *selection error* erreur *f* d'echantillonnage *(dans le cadre d'une étude de marché)*; *selection method* méthode *f* de sélection

selective *adj Mktg* sélectif(ive) □ *selective dis-*

tortion distorsion ƒ sélective; **selective distribution** distribution ƒ sélective; **selective marketing** marketing *m* sélectif; **selective perception** perception ƒ sélective; **selective retention** rétention ƒ sélective; **selective selling** distribution sélective

self-assessment *n Br (for tax purposes)* = système de déclaration des revenus pour le paiement des impôts, par opposition au prélèvement à la source □ **self-assessment form** formulaire *m* de déclaration de revenus

> A leading professional body yesterday called for an inquiry into the Government's tax **self-assessment** system after official figures showed one in 10 taxpayers had failed to hit the deadline. The Chartered Institute of Taxation said more research was urgently needed. According to Inland Revenue figures only 8.25 million tax returns, or 90.6 per cent of the total 9.11 million due, were filed ahead of the 31 January deadline.

self-employed 1 *npl* **the self-employed** les travailleurs *mpl* indépendants
  2 *adj* indépendant(e), qui travaille à son (propre) compte □ **self-employed person** travailleur(euse) *m,f* indépendant(e)

self-financing 1 *n* autofinancement *m*
  2 *adj* autofinancé(e)

self-insurance *n* auto-assurance ƒ

> Looking for a way to manage costs and have greater control over the health benefits you provide your employees? **Self-insurance** may be a workable alternative. Self-insuring means you pay health benefits with corporate assets rather than paying a premium to transfer that responsibility to a third party, says James Kinder, CEO of the Self-Insurance Institute of America in Santa Ana, California.

self-insure *vi* s'auto-assurer

self-liquidating *adj* auto-amortissable □ **self-liquidating premium** prime ƒ auto-payante

self-mailer *n Mktg* carte ƒ de publicité directe *(qui est mise à la poste sans enveloppe)*

self-management *n* autogestion ƒ

self-regulation *n* autorégulation ƒ

self-regulatory organization *n Br* organisme *m* autoréglementé *ou* autonome

self-service 1 *n (shop)* libre-service *m*
  2 *adj* en self-service, en libre-service

self-sufficiency *n (of nation, resources)* autosuffisance ƒ; *Econ* autarcie ƒ

self-sufficient *adj* autosuffisant(e); *Econ* autarcique; **self-sufficient in oil** autosuffisant en pétrole

self-tender *n Fin* = proposition de rachat présentée par une entreprise à ses actionnaires

self-test *Comptr* **1** *n* autotest *m*
  2 *vi* s'autotester

sell 1 *n Am* **sell date** date ƒ limite de vente; *St Exch* **sell order** injonction ƒ à la vente; **sell price** prix *m* (du) comptant
  2 *vt* vendre; *St Exch (shares)* vendre, réaliser; **to sell sth to sb, to sell sb sth** vendre qch à qn; **to sell sth for cash** vendre qch (au) comptant; **to sell sth at a loss** vendre qch à perte; **he sells computers for a living** il gagne sa vie en vendant des ordinateurs
  3 *vi (of product)* se vendre; *(of person)* vendre; *St Exch* **to sell short** vendre à découvert; **to sell at best** vendre au mieux
▸ **sell forward** *vt sep St Exch* vendre à terme
▸ **sell off** *vt sep* **(a)** *(goods) (at reduced price)* solder; *(to clear)* liquider; **the house was sold off to pay debts** la maison a été vendue pour régler des créances **(b)** *(shares)* vendre
▸ **sell out 1** *vt sep* **(a)** *St Exch* vendre, réaliser **(b) to be sold out** *(of book, item)* être épuisé(e)
  2 *vi* **(a)** *(sell business)* vendre son commerce; *(sell stock)* liquider (son stock); **he sold out to some Japanese investors** il a vendu à des investisseurs japonais **(b)** *(run out)* vendre tout le stock; **to sell out of sth** ne plus avoir de qch
▸ **sell up 1** *vt sep (business)* vendre, liquider; *(goods)* procéder à la liquidation de
  2 *vi (sell business)* vendre son commerce

sellable *adj* vendable

sell-by date *n* date ƒ limite de vente

seller *n* **(a)** *(person)* vendeur(euse) *m,f* □ **seller's market** *St Exch* marché *m* à la hausse; *(for buying property)* marché vendeur; *St Exch* **seller's option** prime ƒ vendeur **(b)** *(article)* **to be a good/bad seller** se vendre bien/mal; **it's one of our biggest sellers** c'est un de nos articles qui se vend le mieux

selling *n (of goods)* vente ƒ; *St Exch (of shares)* vente, réalisation ƒ □ *St Exch* **selling climax** = forte baisse du prix des actions dû à des ventes massives; **selling costs** frais *mpl* commerciaux; **selling licence** licence *m* de vente; **selling point** argument *m* de vente; **selling power** puissance ƒ de vente; **selling price** prix *m* de vente; *Acct* **selling price variance** variance ƒ du prix de vente; **selling rate** *(of currency)* taux *m* de vente

sell-off *n* **(a)** *(of goods) (at reduced price)* solde *m*; *(to clear)* liquidation ƒ **(b)** *(of shares)* dégagement *m*

sell-out *n (to clear)* liquidation ƒ

semantic differential *n Mktg* différentiel *m* sémantique

semi-automated *adj* semi-automatisé(e)

semi-colon *n (punctuation mark)* point-virgule *m*

semi-finished *adj* semi-fini(e) ❑ *semi-finished product* produit *m* semi-fini

semi-manufactured *adj* semi-manufacturé(e) ❑ *semi-manufactured product* produit *m* semi-manufacturé

semi-public company *n* société *f* d'économie mixte

semi-retired *adj* en préretraite progressive

semi-retirement *n* préretraite *f* progressive

semi-skilled *adj* spécialisé(e) ❑ *semi-skilled labour* main-d'œuvre *f* spécialisée; *semi-skilled worker* ouvrier(ère) *m,f* spécialisé(e)

semi-variable *adj (costs)* semi-variable

send *vt (person)* envoyer; *(letter, parcel, money)* envoyer, expédier; **to send sb sth, to send sth to sb** envoyer qch à qn; **all customers on our mailing list will be sent a catalogue** tous les clients qui figurent sur notre liste d'adresses recevront un catalogue

▶ **send away** *vi* **to send away for sth** se faire envoyer qch; *(by mail order)* commander qch par correspondance

▶ **send back** *vt sep (goods)* renvoyer

▶ **send for** *vt insep* **to send for sth** se faire envoyer qch; *(by mail order)* commander qch par correspondance

▶ **send in** *vt sep* envoyer; **please send in a written application** veuillez envoyer une demande écrite; *(for job)* veuillez poser votre candidature par écrit

▶ **send off** 1 *vt sep (letter, parcel, money)* envoyer, expédier
2 *vi* **to send off for sth** se faire envoyer qch; *(by mail order)* commander qch par correspondance

▶ **send on** *vt sep (mail)* faire suivre

▶ **send out** *vt sep* envoyer, expédier

sender *n* expéditeur(trice) *m,f*

senior 1 *n (in rank)* supérieur(e) *m,f*
2 *adj (in rank)* supérieur(e); **to be senior to sb** être le supérieur de qn ❑ *Fin senior debt* dette *f* senior; *senior executive* cadre *m* supérieur; *senior management team* équipe *f* dirigeante; *senior partner* associé(e) *m,f* principal(e)

seniority *n (in age)* priorité *f* d'âge; *(in length of service)* ancienneté *f*; *(in rank)* supériorité *f*

sensitive *adj Fin (market)* sensible

separator *n Comptr* séparateur *m*

sequence *n Comptr* séquence *f*

sequential *adj Comptr* séquentiel(elle) ❑ *sequential access* accès *m* séquentiel; *sequential processing* traitement *m* séquentiel

sequester, sequestrate *vt Law (goods)* séquestrer, mettre sous séquestre

sequestration *n Law* mise *f* sous séquestre ❑ *sequestration order* ordonnance *f* de mise sous séquestre

serial *adj* (a) *Comptr* série ❑ *serial cable* câble *m* série; *serial interface* interface *f* série; *serial output* sortie *f* série; *serial port* port *m* série; *serial printer* imprimante *f* série (b) *serial number (of product)* numéro *m* de série (c) *St Exch serial bond* obligation *f* échéant en série

Serious Fraud Office *n Br* ≃ Service *m* de la répression des fraudes

SERPS *n Br Fin (abbr* **State Earnings-Related Pension Scheme**) = retraite versée par l'État, calculée sur le salaire

> ❝
> To get a maximum (but still small) Basic Pension, workers must contribute into the program for nearly fifty years. Originally enacted in 1975, **SERPS** was designed to significantly supplement the minimal and inadequate Basic Pension. At the same time, however, employers were allowed to "contract out" of **SERPS** if their private pension plans met or exceeded the **SERPS** provisions.
> ❞

serve *vt (customer)* servir

server *n Comptr* serveur *m* ❑ *server administrator* administrateur *m* de serveur; *server software* logiciel *m* de télémaintenance

service *n* (a) *(employment)* service *m*; **ten years' service** dix années de service; **promotion according to length of service** avancement *m* à l'ancienneté; **bonuses depend on length of service** les primes sont versées en fonction de l'ancienneté ❑ *service agreement, service contract* contrat *m* de service
(b) *(in shop, restaurant)* service *m*; **service included** service compris ❑ *service charge* service
(c) *(facility provided) service charge* frais *mpl* administratifs; *(paid by tenants)* prestations *fpl* locatives; *service provider (for Internet)* fournisseur *m* d'accès
(d) *(working order)* service *m*; **to bring sth into service** *(machine, vehicle)* mettre qch en service; **the cash dispenser isn't in service at the moment** le distributeur est hors service *ou* n'est pas en service en ce moment ❑ *service life* durée *f* de vie; *service manual* manuel *m* d'entretien; *service record* fiche *f* d'entretien
(e) *Econ* **services** services *mpl*; **goods and services** biens *mpl* et services ❑ *service bureau* so-

ciété *f* de services; *Comptr* société de traitement à façon; **service company** société de services; **service fee** prestation *f* de service; **service industry** industrie *f* tertiaire; *Am* **service mark** marque *f* de service; **service sector** secteur *m* des services; **analysts predict continued growth in the service sector** les analystes prédisent une croissance soutenue dans le secteur des services

(**f**) *Am* **service center** ville *f* commerciale *(qui dessert toute une région)*

2 *vt* (**a**) *(machine)* entretenir

(**b**) *Fin (loan, debt)* assurer le service de

session *n (period of activity, meeting)* séance *f*; **to hold a session** se réunir

SET® *n Comptr (abbr* **secure electronic transaction**) SET® *f*

set 1 *n* (**a**) *Comptr (of characters, instructions)* jeu *m*, ensemble *m* (**b**) *Fin (of bills of exchange)* jeu *m*

2 *adj (price)* fixe

3 *vt (fix) (date, limit, price, schedule)* fixer, déterminer; *(rule, guideline, objective)* établir; *Comptr (tabs, format)* poser; **to set a value on sth** évaluer qch, estimer la valeur de qch; **it's up to them to set their own production targets** c'est à eux d'établir leurs propres objectifs de production; **a deficit ceiling has been set** un plafonnement du déficit a été imposé *ou* fixé; **the price was set at $500** le prix a été fixé à 500 dollars; **how are exchange rates set?** comment les taux de change sont-ils déterminés?

▸ **set against** *vt sep (deduct, offset)* déduire; **to set losses against tax** déduire les pertes des impôts

▸ **set aside** *vt sep (money)* mettre de côté; *(time, place)* réserver; **this room is set aside for meetings** cette pièce est réservée aux réunions

▸ **set off** *vt sep (deduct, offset)* déduire; **some of these expenses can be set off against tax** certaines de ces dépenses peuvent être déduites des impôts

▸ **set up 1** *vt sep* (**a**) *(company)* créer, fonder; *(system, programme)* mettre en place; *(computer)* configurer; *(committee)* constituer; **you'll be in charge of setting up training programmes** vous serez responsable de la mise en place des programmes de formation

(**b**) *(financially, in business)* installer, établir; **he set his son up in a dry-cleaning business** il a acheté à son fils une entreprise de nettoyage à sec; **she can finally set herself up as an accountant** elle peut enfin s'installer comme comptable

2 *vi (in business)* s'installer, s'établir; **he's setting up in the fast-food business** il se lance dans la restauration rapide; **to set up on one's own** s'installer à son compte

set-aside *n EU* gel *m* des terres

>   **❝**
>
> Non-food oilseed production will evolve together with the level of **set-aside** and stabilise around 2.2 million tonnes over the medium term.
>
>   **❞**

setback *n Fin, St Exch* tassement *m*, repli *m*

settings *n Comptr* paramètres *mpl*, réglages *mpl*

setting-up *n (of company, organization)* lancement *m*, création *f*

settle 1 *vt* (**a**) *(day, date, place)* fixer, déterminer; *(terms)* convenir (**b**) *(question, problem, dispute)* régler; *Law* **to settle a matter out of court** régler une affaire à l'amiable; **lawyers were called in to settle the remaining differences** on a fait appel aux avocats pour régler les derniers différends (**c**) *(account)* régler; *(bill)* acquitter, régler; *(debt, fine)* payer (**d**) *(money, allowance, estate)* constituer; **to settle an annuity on sb** constituer une rente à qn

2 *vi Law* **to settle out of court** régler l'affaire à l'amiable

▸ **settle up** *vi (pay bill)* régler; **I must settle up with the plumber** il faut que je règle le plombier

settlement *n* (**a**) *(of question, problem, dispute)* règlement *m* ❑ **settlement by arbitration** règlement arbitral *ou* par arbitrage; **settlement in kind** règlement en nature

(**b**) *(of account)* règlement *m*; *(of bill)* acquittement *m*, règlement; *(of debt, fine)* paiement *m*; **I enclose a cheque in settlement of your account** veuillez trouver ci-joint un chèque en règlement de votre compte ❑ **settlement discount** remise *f* pour règlement rapide; **settlement period** délai *m* de règlement, terme *m* de liquidation; **settlement value** valeur *f* transactionnelle

(**c**) *St Exch* liquidation *f* ❑ **settlement day** jour *m* de (la) liquidation; **settlement note** feuille *f* de liquidation; **settlement price** cours *m* de liquidation; **settlement value** valeur *f* liquidative

(**d**) *(agreement)* accord *m*; **to reach a settlement** parvenir à un accord

set-up *n (arrangement, system)* organisation *f*, système *m*; **the project manager explained the set-up to me** le chef de projet m'a expliqué comment les choses fonctionnaient *ou* étaient organisées; **this is the set-up** voici comment ça se passe; **what's the economic set-up in these countries?** quel est le système économique de ces pays? ❑ *Comptr* **set-up charge** frais *mpl* d'inscription; *Acct* **set-up costs** frais de lancement; *Acct* **set-up fee** *(for account)* frais de constitution; *Comptr* **set-up program** programme *m* d'installation

sever *vt (contract)* résilier

several liability n Law responsabilité f individuelle

severally adv Law **severally liable** responsable individuellement

severance pay n indemnité f de licenciement

sexual adj **sexual discrimination** discrimination f sexuelle; **sexual harrassment** harcèlement m sexuel

sexy adj Fam Mktg (product) branché(e)

> Major appliance brands have never been **sexy**, but lately a couple have expanded their horizons to become more exciting and relevant. Riding a wave of strong economic growth and low interest rates, appliance makers are on a tear, with the consumer remodeling frenzy showing no signs of slowing.

SF n (abbr **sinking fund**) fonds mpl ou caisse f d'amortissement

SFO n Br (abbr **Serious Fraud Office**) ≃ Service m de la répression des fraudes

SGML n Comptr (abbr **Standard Generated Markup Language**) SGML m

shade 1 n Comptr **shades of grey** niveaux mpl ou tons mpl de gris
2 vt Am **to shade prices** établir des prix dégressifs; **prices shaded for quantities** tarif dégressif pour le gros

shadow printing n Comptr impression f ombrée

shake-out n Econ dégraissage m

shake-up n Fam (of company, organization) remaniement m, restructuration f

> User companies must speak out to safeguard their interests ahead of an expected **shake-up** in the software industry, an analyst has warned. Research published last week by UK research firm Xephon predicts a wave of acquisitions over the next few months. This will see larger IT suppliers fighting to acquire small, innovative software companies in a bid to boost flagging revenues.

sham adj (dividend) fictif(ive)

share 1 n (a) Fin, St Exch action f, titre m; **to allot shares** attribuer des actions; **to issue shares** émettre des actions; **to transfer shares** transférer des actions; **to hold** or **have shares (in)** détenir des actions (dans); **to own 51 percent of the shares** détenir 51 pour cent du capital ◽ **share account** compte-titres m; **share application form** bulletin m de souscription d'actions; **share capital** capital-actions m; **share certificate** titre d'actions, certificat m d'actions; **share dealing** opérations fpl de Bourse; **share dividend** dividende m d'action; **share economy** économie f d'actionnariat populaire; **share fluctuation** mouvement m des valeurs; **share index** indice m boursier; **share issue** émission f d'actions; **share ledger** registre m des actionnaires; **share market** marché m des actions; **share option** stock-option f; **share portfolio** portefeuille m d'actions; **share premium** prime f d'émission; **share prices** cours m des actions; **share price index** indice m des cours d'actions; **share register** registre des actions; **share splitting** division f ou fractionnement m des actions; **share subscription form** bulletin de souscription d'actions; **share swap** échange m d'actions
(b) (portion) part f; **to give sb a share of the profits** donner à qn une part des bénéfices; **to have a share in a business** avoir des intérêts dans une affaire ◽ Mktg **share point** point m de part de marché; **share of voice** part de voix
2 vt partager; **to share an office with sb** partager un bureau avec qn; **responsibility is shared between the manager and his assistant** la responsabilité est partagée entre le directeur et son assistant
3 vi **to share in the profits** avoir part aux bénéfices

shareholder n Fin, St Exch actionnaire mf ◽ **shareholders' equity** capitaux mpl ou fonds mpl propres, avoir m des actionnaires; Acct **shareholders' funds** haut m de bilan; **shareholders' meeting** réunion f d'actionnaires; **shareholders' register** registre m des actionnaires

shareholding n Fin, St Exch actionnariat m; **he has a major shareholding in the company** il est un des principaux actionnaires de la société

share-out n partage m, répartition f

shareowner = **shareholder**

sharepicker n Fin, St Exch = personne qui sélectionne des actions pour établir un portefeuille

sharepicking n Fin, St Exch sélection f d'actions

shareware n Comptr shareware m, partagiciel m, logiciel m contributif

shark n Fam (in business) raider m, requin m ◽ **shark watcher** détecteur m de requin

sharp adj (rise, fall, change) brusque, soudain(e)

shed vt perdre; **oil stocks shed 1.4 percent yesterday** les valeurs pétrolières ont perdu 1,4 pour cent hier

sheet n (of paper) feuille f ◽ Comptr **sheet feeder** bac m d'alimentation papier

sheet-fed printer n Comptr imprimante f feuille à feuille

sheet-feed n Comptr avancement m du papier

shelf n (in shop) rayon m, étagère f ▫ **shelf depreciation** usure f en magasin; **shelf facing** facing m, frontale f; **shelf impact** impact m en linéaire; **shelf life** (of product) durée f de vie; **shelf space** linéaire m, capacité f linéaire; **shelf yield** vente f par mètre linéaire

> **❝**
> In Australia, Patak's largest foreign market, it found that, although there was little Indian food around when its first shipment arrived in 1988, familiarity with Far Eastern food and many Australians' British roots helped open up supermarket **shelf space**.
> **❞**

shell company n société f fictive

shelving n rayonnage m

shift 1 n (**a**) (period worked) poste m, équipe f; (workers) équipe; **to work shifts, to be on shifts** avoir un travail posté; **what shift are you on this week?** à quel poste avez-vous été affecté cette semaine?; **to be on eight-hour shifts** faire les trois-huit; **I'm on the night/morning shift** je suis dans l'équipe de nuit/du matin; **she works long shifts** elle fait de longues journées ▫ **shift work** travail posté ou en équipe; **she does shift work** elle fait les trois-huit; **shift worker** travailleur(euse) m,f posté(e) ou en équipe
(**b**) (change) changement m ▫ Comptr **shift key** touche f (des) majuscules
2 vt Fam (sell) écouler; **how can we shift this old stock?** comment écouler ces vieilles marchandises?
3 vi Fam (sell) se vendre; **those TVs just aren't shifting at all** ces télés ne se vendent pas du tout

ship 1 n navire m ▫ **ship's certificate of registry** certificat m d'immatriculation d'un navire; **ship's papers** papiers mpl de bord; **ship's protest** déclaration f d'avarie
2 vt (**a**) (send by ship) expédier (par mer); (carry by ship) transporter (par mer); **we're having our luggage shipped** nous expédions nos bagages par mer
(**b**) (send by any means) expédier; (carry by any means) transporter; **the goods will be shipped by train** (sent) les marchandises seront expédiées par le train; (transported) les marchandises seront transportées par chemin de fer
(**c**) (embark) (passengers, cargo) embarquer

shipbroker n courtier m maritime

shipbrokerage n courtage m maritime

shipment n (**a**) (sending of goods) expédition f
(**b**) (cargo, goods shipped) chargement m, cargaison f

shipped adj embarqué(e) ▫ **shipped bill** connaissement m embarqué; **shipped weight** poids m embarqué

shipper n (of goods) expéditeur(trice) m,f

shipping n (by any means) expédition f, transport m; (by ship) expédition maritime ▫ **shipping address** adresse f de livraison; **shipping agency** agence f maritime; **shipping agent** agent m maritime; **shipping bill** connaissement m embarqué; **shipping charges** frais mpl de transport ou d'expédition; **shipping clerk** expéditionnaire mf; **shipping company** entreprise f de transports (routiers); **shipping costs** frais d'expédition; **shipping depot** dépôt m d'expédition; **shipping document** document m d'expédition; **shipping dues** droits mpl de navigation; **shipping line** ligne f maritime, ligne de navigation; **shipping note** permis m d'embarquement; **shipping office** bureau m d'expédition; (maritime) agence maritime

shipyard n chantier m naval

▶ **shoot up** vi (of prices, inflation, demand) monter en flèche

shop 1 n (**a**) (for goods) magasin m; **to keep a shop** tenir un magasin; **to talk shop** parler boutique; **to set up shop** (open a shop) ouvrir un magasin; (start a business) s'établir, s'installer ▫ **shop assistant** vendeur(euse) m,f; **shop front** devanture f (de magasin); **shop window** vitrine f
(**b**) (workshop) atelier m ▫ **the shop floor** (place) l'atelier; (workers) les ouvriers mpl; **shop foreman** chef m d'atelier; **shop steward** délégué(e) m,f syndical(e)
2 vi faire ses courses; **to shop around** comparer les prix; **I shopped around before opening a bank account** j'ai comparé plusieurs banques avant d'ouvrir un compte; **our company is shopping around for new premises** notre société est à la recherche de nouveaux locaux

shopkeeper n commerçant(e) m,f, détaillant(e) m,f

shopping n courses fpl; **to do one's/the shopping** faire ses/les courses ▫ **shopping area** quartier m commerçant; **shopping basket** Econ panier m de la ménagère; Br Comptr (for on-line purchases) caddie® m; Am Comptr **shopping cart** (for on-line purchases) caddie®; **shopping centre** centre m commercial; **shopping complex** complexe m commercial; **shopping mall** galerie f marchande

▶ **shore up** vt sep (currency) soutenir; **Brazil started selling off its foreign currency reserves in an attempt to shore up its currency** le Brésil a vendu une partie de ses réserves de change afin de soutenir sa monnaie

short 1 n St Exch **shorts** titres mpl courts
2 adj (**a**) (lacking, insufficient) insuffisant(e); **to**

be short of staff/money manquer de personnel/d'argent; **to give short weight** ne pas donner le poids; **the weight is 50 grams short** il manque 50 grammes au poids □ *short delivery* livraison *f* partielle, manque *m* à la livraison; *short ton* tonne *f* courte; *short weight* poids *m* insuffisant

(b) *Fin short bill* traite *f* à courte échéance; *short payment* moins-perçu *m*; *short rate* taux *m* à court terme

(c) *St Exch short account* opérations *fpl* à découvert; *short covering* couverture *f* de position; *short hedge* couverture courte *ou* de vente; *short interest* opérations à découvert; *short position* position *f* vendeur *ou* baissière; *short sale* vente *f* à découvert; *short seller* vendeur(euse) *m,f* à découvert; *short selling* vente à découvert; *short squeeze* short squeeze *m*

3 *adv St Exch* **to sell short** vendre à découvert; **to buy short** acheter à court terme

> **“**
>
> A **short squeeze** occurs when institutional investors take large positions in already heavily shorted stocks and then request delivery of the shares. This transaction reduces the liquidity of the shares and forces a premature closing out of the short position.
>
> **”**

shortage *n (of labour, resources, materials, staff)* manque *m*, pénurie *f*; *(of money)* manque

shortcut *n Comptr* raccourci *m* □ *shortcut key* touche *f* de raccourci

short-dated *adj Fin (bill)* à courte échéance; *(paper)* court(e)

shortfall *n* insuffisance *f*, manque *m*; **there's a shortfall of $100** il manque 100 dollars

> **“**
>
> Companies are declining to provide pensions themselves because they can no longer afford the guarantee. Iceland, for instance, found that it had to pay £78m into a scheme valued at just over £500m to make good a **shortfall** that had appeared. Nationwide explained the problem in a different way. To maintain benefits at their promised level, it would have had to raise its contribution from 12.6 per cent of salaries to 19 per cent.
>
> **”**

shorthand *n* sténographie *f*, sténo *f*; **to take notes in shorthand** prendre des notes en sténo □ *shorthand typist* sténodactylo *mf*

shorthanded *adj* à court de personnel; **we're very shorthanded at the moment** nous sommes vraiment à court de personnel en ce moment

shortlist *Br* **1** *n* liste *f* des candidats présélec-

tionnés *ou* retenus; **eight candidates are on the shortlist and have been contacted** huit candidats ont été présélectionnés et contactés

2 *vt (candidate)* présélectionner, retenir; **to be shortlisted for sth** être parmi les candidats retenus à qch

short-staffed *adj* à court de personnel; **we're very short-staffed at the moment** nous sommes vraiment à court de personnel en ce moment

short-term *adj* à court terme □ *short-term bond* obligation *f* à court terme; *short-term borrowings* emprunts *mpl* à court terme; *short-term capital* capital *m* à court terme; *short-term contract* contrat *m* à durée déterminée, CDD *m*; *short-term credit* crédit *m* (à) court terme; *short-term credit facilities* crédits *mpl* de trésorerie; *short-term debt* dette *f* à court terme; *short-term financing* financement *m* à court terme; *short-term interest rate* taux *m* d'intérêt à court terme; *short-term investment* investissement *m ou* placement *m* à court terme; *short-term liabilities* passif *m* à court terme; *short-term loan (from borrower's point of view)* emprunt *m* à court terme; *(from lender's point of view)* prêt *m* à court terme; *short-term maturity* échéance *f* à court terme; *short-term planning* planification *f* à court terme

short-termism *n* politique *f* du court terme

short-time *adj short-time worker* chômeur(euse) *m,f* partiel(le); *short-time working* chômage *m* partiel

show **1** *n (exhibition)* exposition *f* □ *show house* maison *f* témoin

2 *vt (profit, loss, records)* afficher; **prices show a ten percent increase on last year** les prix ont augmenté de dix pour cent par rapport à l'an dernier

showcard *n (in shop)* pancarte *f*; *(of samples)* carte *f* d'échantillons

showcase **1** *n* vitrine *f*; **a showcase for British exports** une vitrine pour les exportations britanniques

2 *vt* exposer, présenter; **the exhibition will showcase our new product range** nous présenterons notre nouvelle gamme de produits dans le cadre de l'exposition

> **“**
>
> Springboard 2001: New York is one of a series of forums designed to accelerate investments in high-growth women-led businesses and facilitate new deal flow to investors. The forum will **showcase** 30 women seeking seed, early and later stage funding. Selected entrepreneurs will present their business plans to the tri-state area's venture capital, angel and corporate investors.
>
> **”**

showroom n salle f ou salon m d'exposition

shpt n (abbr **shipment**) envoi m

shred vt (documents) détruire

shredder n déchiqueteuse f

shrink vi (of profits, savings, income, budget) diminuer, se réduire ; (of economy) se contracter

shrinkage n (through theft) coulage m ; (through damage) casse f ; (while in transit) pertes fpl

> 〞
> According to Hollinger, results of the survey should serve as a wake-up call to the retail industry that **shrinkage** continues to be a significant source of revenue loss amounting to billions of dollars.
> 〞

shrink-wrap vt emballer sous film plastique

shrink-wrapped adj emballé(e) sous film plastique

shut vi (of shop, business) fermer

▸ **shut down** 1 vt sep (a) (shop, business) fermer ; (production) arrêter (b) Comptr (system) arrêter ; (computer) éteindre
2 vi (a) (of shop, business) fermer (b) Comptr (of system) s'arrêter

shutdown n (a) (of shop, business) fermeture f (b) Comptr fermeture f, arrêt m de fin de session

shut-out n lock-out m

SIB n (abbr **Securities and Investment Board**) = commission britannique des opérations de Bourse, ≃ COB f

sick adj **sick building syndrome** = maladie qu'on retrouve chez des personnes travaillant dans des bâtiments équipés de la climatisation ; **sick day** = jour d'absence pour cause de maladie ; **sick leave** congé m (de) maladie ; **to be on sick leave** être en congé (de) maladie ; **sick pay** indemnité f de maladie

> 〞
> Further, the agency agrees with an estimate from the World Health Organization that up to 30 percent of all new and remodeled buildings worldwide have excessive air-quality problems that can lead to **sick building syndrome** or building-related illness.
> 〞

sickness benefit n Br Admin prestations fpl de l'assurance maladie

sickout n Am Ind = grève où tous les employés prétendent être malades le même jour

sideline n (a) (product) ligne f de produits secondaires ; **they've made recycling a profitable sideline** ils ont fait du recyclage une activité secondaire rentable ; **it's only a sideline**

for us ce n'est pas notre spécialité (b) (job) occupation f ou travail m secondaire

sight n (a) Fin **sight bill** effet m à vue ; **sight deposit** dépôt m à vue ; **sight draft** traite f à vue ; **sight letter of credit** crédit m utilisable à vue ; **sight maturity** échéance f à vue ; **sight paper** papier m à vue ; **sight quotation** cotation f à vue (b) **to sell sth sight unseen** vendre qch sans inspection ; **to buy sth sight unseen** acheter qch sans l'avoir vu

> 〞
> The notion of store returns or exchanges is a fairly foreign one to these shoppers, and Latin Americans are even more skeptical about security and satisfaction with products bought **sight unseen**.
> 〞

sighting n Fin (of bill) présentation f

sign 1 vt (one's name, document, cheque) signer ; (bill of exchange) accepter ; **to sign a deal** passer un marché ; **the deal will be signed and sealed tomorrow** l'affaire sera définitivement conclue demain
2 vi (write one's name) signer

▸ **sign for** vt insep (delivery, parcel) signer un reçu pour ; **to sign for goods received** signer à la réception de marchandises ; **the files have to be signed for** il faut signer pour retirer les dossiers

▸ **sign on** vi Br Fam (register as unemployed) s'inscrire au chômage ; **you have to sign on every two weeks** il faut pointer (au chômage) toutes les deux semaines

▸ **sign out** vt sep **to sign sth out** (file, equipment) signer un registre pour emprunter qch

signatory n & adj signataire mf □ **signatory countries** pays mpl signataires

signature n signature f ; **to put one's signature to sth** apposer sa signature sur qch ; **his signature was on the letter** la lettre portait sa signature ; **the signature of the company** la signature sociale ; **for signature** (on document) pour signature

silent partner n Am associé(e) m,f commanditaire, bailleur(eresse) m,f de fonds

silver n argent m □ **silver certificate** papier-monnaie m (garanti par les réserves métalliques en argent) ; **silver export point** silver-point m de sortie ; **silver import point** silver-point d'entrée ; **silver money** monnaie f d'argent ; **silver parachute** = indemnité versée à un employé lorsque son emploi est supprimé suite à une fusion ; **silver standard** étalon m argent

SIM n Tel (abbr **subscriber identity module**) **SIM card** carte f SIM

SIMM n Comptr (abbr **single in-line memory module**) SIMM m

simple adj Law **simple contract** convention f verbale, acte m sous seing privé; Fin **simple debenture** obligation f chirographaire; Fin **simple interest** intérêt(s) m(pl) simple(s); **simple majority** majorité f simple; St Exch **simple position** position f élémentaire

simplex adj Tel simplex, unidirectionnel(elle)

simulate vt Comptr simuler

simulation n Comptr simulation f

simulator n Comptr simulateur m

simultaneous adj Mktg **simultaneous product development** développement m simultané de produits; **simultaneous translation** traduction f simultanée

sincerely adv Br **yours sincerely,** Am **sincerely** (in letter) veuillez agréer, Monsieur/Madame, l'expression de mes sentiments distingués

single 1 n Br (ticket) aller m simple
2 adj (**a**) (one only) EU **single currency** monnaie f unique; **Single European Act** acte m unique européen; **Single (European) Market** marché m unique (européen); Ins **single premium** prime f unique; **single tax** impôt m unique; Comptr **single user licence** licence f individuelle d'utilisation
(**b**) (not double) **to be in single figures** être inférieur(e) à dix; **inflation is now in single figures** l'inflation est descendue à moins de dix pour cent □ Comptr **single density** simple densité f; Comptr **single density disk** disquette f (à) simple densité; Acct **single entry** partie f simple

single-entry adj Acct **single-entry bookkeeping** comptabilité f en partie simple; **single-entry method** principe f de la partie simple

singletasking Comptr **1** n monotâche m
2 adj monotâche

singly adv (packaged) individuellement; **to be sold singly** se vendre à la pièce

sink 1 vt (**a**) (debt, loan) amortir (**b**) (invest) investir; **we sank a fortune into this company** nous avons englouti une fortune dans cette société
2 vi (of prices, currency, rate, profits) baisser, diminuer; **the dollar has sunk to half its normal value** le dollar a perdu la moitié de sa valeur; **profits have sunk to an all-time low** les bénéfices sont au plus bas

sinking fund n fonds mpl ou caisse f d'amortissement

sister company n société f sœur

sit-down strike n grève f sur le tas

site 1 n (**a**) (piece of land) terrain m; **the development project includes sites for small businesses** le projet immobilier prévoit des terrains pour de petites entreprises (**b**) (building) site chantier m (de construction) □ **site foreman**

chef m de chantier; **site manager** directeur(-trice) m,f de chantier (**c**) Comptr site m (**d**) Mktg (for advertising) emplacement m
2 vt situer

sit-in n (grève f avec) occupation f des lieux

sitting tenant n locataire mf dans les lieux ou en place

situation n (**a**) (state of affairs) situation f; **the firm's financial situation isn't good** la situation financière de la société n'est pas bonne; **the skills needed in an interview situation** les compétences dont on a besoin pour faire face à un entretien (**b**) (job) emploi m, situation f; **situations vacant/wanted** (in advertisements) offres fpl/demandes fpl d'emplois

size n taille f; Comptr (of font) corps m, taille □ Comptr **size box** case f de dimensionnement

skeleton n **skeleton organization** organisation f squelettique; **skeleton staff** personnel m réduit

skill n aptitude f, compétence f; **computer technology requires us to learn new skills** l'informatique nous oblige à acquérir de nouvelles compétences

skilled adj (worker) qualifié(e); (task) de spécialiste □ **skilled labour** main-d'œuvre f qualifiée

skim vt Mktg (market) écrémer

skimming n Mktg (of market) écrémage m □ **skimming price** prix m d'écrémage

skip vt Comptr (command) sauter

slack adj (business) calme; **the slack season for tourists** la période creuse pour le tourisme; **business is slack at the moment** les affaires marchent au ralenti en ce moment

slacken vi (of business) ralentir

slash 1 n (punctuation mark) barre f oblique
2 vt (prices) casser; (cost, taxes) réduire considérablement; **prices have been slashed by 40 percent** les prix ont été réduits de 40 pour cent

sleep vi Comptr être en veille □ **sleep mode** veille f

sleeping adj **sleeping economy** économie f à ressources sous-exploitées; Br **sleeping partner** associé(e) m,f commanditaire, bailleur(eresse) m,f de fonds

slide n (for presentation) diapositive f, diapo f □ **slide show** projection f de diapositives

sliding adj **sliding peg** parité f à crémaillère; **sliding scale** (for tax) barème m; (for prices, salaries) échelle f mobile

sliding-scale adj **sliding-scale depreciation** amortissement m dégressif; **sliding-scale tariff** tarif m dégressif; **sliding-scale taxation** impôt m dégressif

slip 1 n (printed paper) bordereau m

2 vi (of prices) glisser; **shares slipped to 125p** le prix des actions a baissé jusqu'à 125 pence

slogan n slogan m (publicitaire), accroche f

slot n (**a**) Comptr emplacement m (**b**) (opening) créneau m

slow 1 adj (business, market) calme; **business is slow** les affaires ne marchent pas fort
2 adv **to go slow** faire une grève perlée

▸ **slow down 1** vt sep ralentir; **production is slowed down during the winter** pendant l'hiver, la production tourne au ralenti
2 vi ralentir; **growth slowed down in the second quarter** il y a eu un ralentissement de la croissance au cours du deuxième trimestre

slowdown n Am grève f perlée

sluggish adj (market, business, economy) calme, stagnant(e); **trading is always rather sluggish on Mondays** les affaires ne marchent jamais très fort le lundi

slump 1 n (in prices, sales, market) effondrement m; (economic depression) crise f (économique); **there has been a slump in investment** les investissements sont en forte baisse; **a slump in prices/demand** une forte baisse des prix/de la demande
2 vi (of prices, currency, economy) s'effondrer

slush fund n caisse f noire

> **"**
> They discussed a plan to create a **slush fund** in the administrative affairs section so they could entertain central government officials who made business trips to Okinawa. They filed for bogus business trips and used the pooled expense money whenever necessary.
> **"**

small adj (**a**) (in size) **small ad** petite annonce f; Comptr **small caps, small capitals** petites capitales fpl; **small letters** lettres fpl minuscules; **the small print** (in contract) ce qui est écrit en petits caractères; **make sure you read the small print before you sign** lisez bien ce qui est écrit en petits caractères avant de signer (**b**) (in scale, range) **small business** petite entreprise f; **small businessman** petit entrepreneur m; **small change** petite ou menue monnaie f; **small firm** petite entreprise; **small investor** petit(e) porteur(euse) m,f; **small and medium-sized businesses** petites et moyennes entreprises; **small and medium-sized enterprise** petite et moyenne entreprise; **small and medium-sized industry** petite et moyenne industrie f; **small saver** petit(e) épargnant(e) m,f; **small shareholder** petit(e) porteur(euse); **small shopkeeper** petit(e) commerçant(e) m,f; **small trader** petit(e)

commerçant(e); **small wholesale selling** vente f en semi-gros

SmallCap n St Exch = indice boursier américain composé d'actions de sociétés à petite et moyenne capitalisation

small-claims court n Br Law tribunal m d'instance

small-scale adj (model) à taille réduite □ **small-scale industry** la petite industrie

smart adj **smart card** carte f à puce; **smart card reader** lecteur m de carte à puce; **smart money** placement m astucieux; **smart terminal** terminal m intelligent

SME n (abbr **small and medium-sized enterprise**) PME f

smear campaign n (in press) campagne f de diffamation

> **"**
> Significantly, Downing Street refused to endorse Mr Byers's claim that he did not veto the compromise plan. But it rejected Mr Sixsmith's allegation that "sources close to No 10" had launched a **smear campaign** against him by urging journalists to investigate how many properties he owns.
> **"**

SMI n (abbr **small and medium-sized industry**) PMI f

smiley n Comptr souriant m, émoticon m

SMS Tel (abbr **short message service**) **1** n (service) texte m; (message) message m texte
2 vt envoyer un message texte à

SMTP n Comptr (abbr **Simple Mail Transfer Protocol**) protocole m SMTP

smuggle 1 vt passer en contrebande; **to smuggle sth through customs** passer qch en fraude à la douane
2 vi faire de la contrebande

▸ **smuggle in** vt sep (goods) faire entrer en contrebande

▸ **smuggle out** vt sep (goods) faire sortir en contrebande

smuggler n contrebandier(ère) m,f

smuggling n contrebande f

snail mail n Fam courrier m escargot, courrier postal

> **"**
> E-mail is putting the squeeze on **snail mail** as computer users opt for the faster, cheaper and more convenient method of writing to friends, family and business associates. Feeling the pinch is the Communications Authority of Thailand (CAT), the country's postal service operator. The CAT has suf-

fered decreasing mail volume for the past several years as more and more Thais become Internet users and discover the benefits of e-mail.

"

snake n Econ serpent m (monétaire)

SNG n (abbr **satellite news gathering**) SNG m

snowball effect n effet m boule de neige

soar vi (of prices, profits, inflation) monter en flèche; **sales have soared since the advertising campaign** les ventes ont monté en flèche depuis la campagne publicitaire

soaring adj (prices, profits, inflation) qui monte en flèche

social adj **social assets** patrimoine m social; **social benefits** acquis mpl sociaux; **social charges** (levied on employers) charges fpl sociales; **social contract** contrat m social, convention f sociale; **social cost** coût m social; **social dumping** dumping m social; **social entitlements** acquis sociaux; Br Admin **social fund** caisse f d'aide sociale; **social integration** insertion f sociale; **social ownership** propriété f collective; **social report** bilan m social; **social security** prestations fpl sociales; **to be on social security** toucher une aide sociale; **social security benefits** prestations sociales; **social security contribution** prélèvement m social; **social security office** caisse de la Sécurité sociale; **social security provisions** prévoyance f sociale; **social security system** régime m de Sécurité sociale; **social welfare (system)** protection f sociale

sociodemographic adj socio-démographique □ **sociodemographic data** données fpl socio-démographiques; **sociodemographic profile** profil m socio-démographique; **sociodemographic segment** segment m socio-démographique; **sociodemographic segmentation** segmentation f socio-démographique

socio-economic adj socio-économique □ **socio-economic classification** classification f socio-professionnelle; **socio-economic group** groupe m socio-économique

sociological adj sociologique □ **sociological survey** enquête f sociologique

sociology n sociologie f

socio-professional adj socio-professionnel(elle) □ **socio-professional group** catégorie f socio-professionnelle

socket n (a) (slot) prise f (femelle) (b) Comptr socket f, port m

SOFFEX n St Exch (abbr **Swiss Options and Financial Futures Exchange**) SOFFEX f (bourse suisse pour le négoce des options et des contrats à terme)

soft 1 n softs biens mpl non durables

2 adj **soft commodities** biens mpl non durables; Comptr **soft copy** visualisation f sur écran; **soft currency** devise f ou monnaie f faible; **soft goods** biens non durables; Br tissus mpl, textiles mpl; **soft loan** prêt m bonifié; Am Pol **soft money** = sommes employées pour le financement d'une campagne électorale en utilisant divers stratagèmes afin de rester dans la légalité; Comptr **soft return** saut m de ligne automatique; **soft sell** méthode f de vente non agressive

"

The result has been to introduce advertising material that marketers describe as relevant to, as an extension of, or as "contextual" to the content – less intrusive and in-your-face than flashy, oversized banners or pop-up ads. The **soft sell** in other words.

"

software n Comptr logiciel m, software m □ **software bug** bogue m de logiciel; **software company** éditeur m de logiciels; **software developer** développeur(euse) m,f; **software error** erreur f de logiciel; **software failure** panne f logicielle; **software package** logiciel; **software piracy** piratage m de logiciels; **software pirate** pirate m de logiciels; **software problem** problème m de logiciel; **software producer** éditeur de logiciels

sola of exchange n Fin seule f de change

sold out adj (goods) épuisé(e); **we're sold out of that product** nous n'avons plus cet article en stock, nous avons tout vendu

sole adj unique □ **sole agency** représentation f exclusive; **sole agency contract** contrat m de représentation exclusive; **sole agent** agent m exclusif; (for particular brand) concessionnaire m exclusif; **to be sole agent for Rover** avoir la représentation exclusive de Rover; **sole contract** contrat exclusif; **sole dealer** concessionnaire exclusif; **sole owner** propriétaire mf unique; **sole representative** agent exclusif; **sole right** droit m exclusif; **sole supplier** fournisseur m exclusif; **sole trader** entreprise f unipersonnelle

solicitor n Br (in court cases) avocat(e) m,f; (for wills, property) notaire m □ **solicitor general** (in UK) conseil m juridique de la Couronne; (in US) représentant(e) m,f du gouvernement (auprès de la Cour suprême)

solus adj Mktg (position, site) isolé(e) □ **solus advertisement** publicité f isolée; **solus position** emplacement m isolé; **solus site** emplacement isolé

solvency n solvabilité f □ **solvency ratio** ratio m ou taux m de solvabilité

solvent adj solvable; **in such cases the directors must declare that the company is solvent**

dans de tels cas, l'entreprise doit déclarer être solvable

SOP n (abbr **standard operating procedure**) = marche à suivre normale

sort 1 n (**a**) (putting in order) tri m; **the program will do an alphabetical sort** le programme exécutera un tri alphabétique ❑ **sort routine** routine f de tri (**b**) Banking **sort code** code m guichet
  2 vt (put in order) trier; **to sort sth in ascending/descending order** trier qch par ordre croissant/décroissant
  3 vi trier; (of file, data) se trier

sorting n Banking **sorting code** code m guichet; **sorting office** centre m de tri

sound¹ n Comptr **sound card** carte f son

sound² adj (investment) sûr(e); (business, financial position) solide

soundbite n petite phrase f (prononcée à la radio ou à la télévision pour frapper les esprits)

> **"**
>
> Yesterday's plan for the railways was launched on the trite **soundbite** that the Government wants to see a "safer, better and bigger" railway … the aims are inherently contradictory, which demonstrates not only the huge task the Government faces in trying to improve the railways but also the wider lack of coherence on transport that has dogged New Labour ever since it was elected in 1997.
>
> **"**

source n (**a**) (of revenue) source f; (of goods) provenance f; **income is taxed at source** les impôts sont prélevés à la source ❑ Acct **source and application of funds** état m de flux de trésorerie; **sources and use of funds statement** état de mouvements de trésorerie (**b**) Comptr **source disk** disque m source; (floppy) disquette f source; **source document** document m de base, document source; **source file** fichier m source; **source language** langage m source; **source text** texte m de départ

space n (in text) espace m ou f ❑ **space bar** (on keyboard) barre f d'espacement

spacing n (in text) (horizontal) espacement m; (vertical) interligne m ou f

spam Comptr **1** n messages mpl publicitaires
  2 vt spammer, envoyer des messages publicitaires en masse à
  3 vi spammer, envoyer des messages publicitaires en masse

> **"**
>
> An Australian man has been given a two-year suspended jail sentence for his part in sending mass commercial e-mail, or **spam**,

and bulletin board postings to millions of Internet users. Wayne John Loughnan of Noosa Heads, Queensland, was sentenced to two years in jail on Tuesday after pleading guilty to charges of securities fraud and unlawful interference with third-party computer systems.
>
> **"**

spammer n Comptr = personne qui envoie des messages publicitaires en masse

spamming n Comptr spamming m, envoi m de messages publicitaires en masse

spare 1 n (spare part) pièce f de rechange, pièce détachée
  2 adj (funds, capital) disponible ❑ **spare part** pièce f de rechange, pièce détachée

speak vi (on telephone) **who's speaking?** qui est à l'appareil?; (before transferring call) c'est de la part de qui?; **Mr Thomas? – yes, speaking** Mr Thomas? – lui-même

spec n (abbr **specification**) spécifications fpl

special adj Br **special delivery** (of mail) envoi m en exprès; **special delivery parcel** colis m exprès; Fin **special drawing rights** droits mpl de tirage spéciaux; **special offer** offre f spéciale; **on special offer** en promotion; **special permit** autorisation f spéciale; **special price** prix m spécial; **special promotion** promotion f spéciale; **special provision** stipulation f particulière; **special rate** taux m de faveur; **special rate of taxation** taxation f d'office; **special savings account** plan m d'épargne populaire

specialist 1 n spécialiste mf
  2 adj (skills, equipment) de spécialiste ❑ **specialist press** presse f spécialisée; **specialist retailer** détaillant(e) m,f spécialisé(e)

speciality, Am **specialty** n spécialité f; **our speciality is electronic components** nous nous spécialisons dans les composants électroniques ❑ **speciality goods** produits mpl spécialisés

specialization n spécialisation f; **his specialization is computers** il est spécialisé en informatique

specialize vi se spécialiser (**in** dans); **we specialize in electronics** nous nous spécialisons dans l'électronique

specialty Am = **speciality**

specie n Fin (coins) espèces fpl; **to pay in specie** payer en espèces

specification n (**a**) (of contract) stipulation f (**b**) **specifications** (of machine, building materials etc) spécifications fpl; (for technical project, schedule) cahier m des charges ❑ **specifications sheet** fiche f technique (**c**) Mktg **specification buying** achats mpl spécifiés

specify vt spécifier, préciser; **unless otherwise**

specified sauf indication contraire; **the rules specify a five-minute break** le règlement spécifie une pause de cinq minutes ❑ **specified load** charge *f* prescrite

specimen *n* spécimen *m* ❑ **specimen invoice** modèle *m* de facture; **specimen signature** spécimen de signature

speculate *vi Fin, St Exch* spéculer; **to speculate on the Stock Market** spéculer *ou* jouer en Bourse; **to speculate in oils** spéculer sur les valeurs pétrolières; **to speculate for a fall** spéculer à la baisse; **to speculate for a rise** spéculer à la hausse

speculation *n Fin, St Exch* spéculation *f*; **speculation in oil** spéculation sur le pétrole

speculative *adj Fin, St Exch* spéculatif(ive) ❑ **speculative buying** achats *mpl* spéculatifs; **speculative securities** valeurs *fpl* spéculatives *ou* de spéculation; **speculative selling** vente *f* spéculative; **speculative shares** valeurs spéculatives

speculator *n Fin, St Exch* spéculateur(trice) *m,f*

speech recognition *n Comptr* reconnaissance *f* de la parole

speed dial *n Tel* numérotation *f* abrégée

speedwriting *n* écriture *f* abrégée

spellcheck *n Comptr* correction *f* orthographique *ou* d'orthographe; **to do** *or* **run a spellcheck on a document** effectuer une correction orthographique *ou* d'orthographe sur un document

spellchecker *n Comptr* correcteur *m* orthographique *ou* d'orthographe

spend 1 *n* dépenses *fpl*; **we must increase our marketing spend** nous devons augmenter le budget marketing; **this year's spend has exceeded the budget by 10 percent** nous avons dépassé de 10 pour cent les dépenses prévues au budget de l'année écoulée
2 *vt* (**a**) *(money)* dépenser; **to spend money on sth** dépenser de l'argent en qch (**b**) *(time)* passer; **to spend time on sth/doing sth** passer du temps sur qch/à faire qch

> "
> Pernod Ricard, the French drinks group which recently bought part of Seagram, has announced that it will increase its marketing **spend** in Central and South America by around 20%. The move by the makers of Clan Campbell and Havana Club comes despite the region's economic instability.
> "

spending *n* dépenses *fpl* ❑ **spending cuts** réductions *fpl* des dépenses; **spending limit** plafond *m* budgétaire; **spending money** argent *m*

de poche; *Econ* **spending power** pouvoir *m* d'achat

sphere *n (of interest, activity)* sphère *f*, domaine *m*; **sphere of activity** domaine d'activité; **it's not my sphere** ce n'est pas de mon domaine, ce n'est pas dans mes compétences; **the question is outside the committee's sphere** la question ne relève pas des compétences du comité

spin *Fam* **1** *n (on information)* **to put the right spin on a story** présenter une affaire sous un angle favorable; **the government has been criticized for indulging in too much spin** on a reproché au gouvernement de trop manipuler les informations fournies au public ❑ **spin doctor** = chargé des relations publiques d'un parti politique
2 *vi (of spin doctor)* présenter les choses sous un angle favorable

> "
> Meanwhile, the former royal **spin doctor**, Simon Lewis, has been reflecting on his time trying to cast Britain's leading dysfunctional family in a better light. On his first day he turned up at the Buckingham Palace gates … and was asked by a policeman who he was. "I'm the Queen's new director of communications," said Lewis proudly. The reply: "Does that mean you're here to fix the telephones?"
> "

spinner *n Mktg (for displaying goods)* tourniquet *m*

spin-off *n (product)* produit *m* dérivé, retombée *f* ❑ **spin-off company** entreprise *f* dérivée; **spin-off product** produit dérivé

> "
> Southampton Innovations was set up as an autonomous limited company to give Ashby the freedom to hunt for winning technology within the university, patent it and then find outside chief executives to run **spin-off companies** to develop it commercially.
> "

spiral 1 *n* spirale *f*; **an inflationary spiral** une spirale inflationniste
2 *vi (of prices)* monter en flèche, s'envoler

split 1 *n Fin, St Exch (of shares)* division *f*, fractionnement *m*
2 *adj* (**a**) *Fin* **split capital investment trust** sicav *f* mixte; *Fin* **split coupon bond** obligation *f* à coupon partagé; *Comptr* **split screen** écran *m* divisé, multi-écran *m* (**b**) **he works a split shift** sa journée de travail est divisée en deux tranches horaires
3 *vt Fin, St Exch* **to split shares** diviser *ou* fractionner des actions; **the shares were split 50**

percent, one new share for each two shares held les actions ont été fractionnées à raison d'une action nouvelle pour deux anciennes

SPOC n (abbr **single point of contact**) = personne unique à qui l'on doit s'adresser pour certains types de renseignements dans l'entreprise

spoil 1 vt (goods) avarier
2 vi (of goods) s'avarier

spoilage n déchets mpl

spoiler campaign n Mktg = campagne lancée par une entreprise pour minimiser l'impact d'une campagne publicitaire menée par une société concurrente

spokesman n porte-parole m

spokesperson n porte-parole m

spokeswoman n porte-parole m (femme)

sponsor 1 n (of sportsman, team, tournament) sponsor m; (of film, TV programme) sponsor, commanditaire m
2 vt sponsoriser

sponsorship n (of sportsman, team, tournament) sponsoring m, parrainage m; (of film, TV programme) parrainage □ **sponsorship agreement** contrat m de sponsoring; **sponsorship budget** budget m alloué au sponsoring; **sponsorship deal** contrat de sponsoring

spontaneous recall n Mktg notoriété f spontanée

spooler n Comptr (for printing) spouleur m, pilote m de mise en file d'attente

spot n (a) Fin **spot buying** achats mpl au comptant; **spot cash** argent m comptant; **to pay spot cash** payer comptant; **spot credit** crédit m ponctuel ou à court terme; St Exch **spot deal** opération f au comptant; St Exch **spot delivery** livraison f au comptant ou immédiate; St Exch **spot exchange rate** cours m au comptant; **spot goods** marchandises fpl livrables au comptant; St Exch **spot market** marché m au comptant; St Exch **spot price** prix m au comptant; St Exch **spot quotation** cotation f à vue; St Exch **spot rate** cours au comptant; St Exch **spot trading** négociations fpl au comptant; St Exch **spot transaction** opération ou transaction f au comptant (**b**) (in advertising) message m publicitaire, spot m

spread 1 n (**a**) (between two rates) différence f; St Exch (between buying and selling prices) différence, écart m (**b**) St Exch (range of investments) diversification f
2 vt (payments) échelonner, étaler
3 vi St Exch spéculer sur les différentiels de cours

spreadsheet n Comptr feuille f de calcul; (software) tableur m

square 1 n Fam **the Square Mile** = la City de Londres, dont la superficie fait environ un mile carré
2 adj **square brackets** crochets mpl
3 vt (account, bill) régler; (debt) acquitter; (books) balancer

> **❝**
> The more solemn atmosphere reflects financial reality in the **Square Mile**. HSBC's full-year financial results tomorrow are expected to predict a difficult year ahead. The Bank Of England's Monetary Policy Committee is likely to announce on Thursday that interest rates will stay at their current low levels.
> **❞**

squeeze 1 n (on credit) resserrement m
2 vt (profits, budget) réduire

SRO n Br St Exch (abbr **self-regulatory organization**) organisme m auto-réglementé ou autonome

SSP n Br Admin (abbr **statutory sick pay**) = indemnité de maladie versée par l'employeur

stability n (of prices, market, economy) stabilité f

stabilization n (of prices, market, economy) stabilisation f □ **stabilization plan** plan m d'assainissement

stabilize 1 vt (prices, market, economy) stabiliser
2 vi (of prices, market, economy) se stabiliser

stabilizing adj stabilisateur(trice); **to have a stabilizing influence on prices** exercer une influence stabilisatrice sur les prix □ **stabilizing policy** politique f de stabilité

stable adj (prices, market, economy) stable

staff 1 n personnel m, employés mpl; **to be on the staff** faire partie du personnel; **staff only** (sign) réservé au personnel □ **staff appraisal** évaluation f du personnel; **staff cutbacks** compression f du personnel; **staff increase** dotation f en effectifs; **staff management** direction f du personnel; **staff manager** chef m du personnel; **staff motivation** motivation f du personnel; **staff organization** organisation f fonctionnelle ou horizontale; **staff representative** délégué(e) m,f ou représentant(e) m,f du personnel; **staff shortage** insuffisance f de personnel; **staff training** formation f du personnel; **staff turnover** roulement m du personnel
2 vt **the office is staffed by volunteers** le personnel du bureau est composé de volontaires; **the desk is staffed at all times** il y a toujours quelqu'un au bureau

staffing n recrutement m; **the delay is due to staffing difficulties** le retard est dû à des problèmes de recrutement □ **staffing policy** politique f de recrutement du personnel

stag n St Exch loup m

stage n (phase) stade m; Mktg (of product) phase f; **the next stage in computer technology** le stade suivant du développement de l'informatique; **the changes were instituted in stages** les changements ont été introduits progressivement

stagflation n Econ stagflation f

stagger vt (payments) échelonner, répartir; (holidays) étaler; **they plan to bring in staggered working hours** ils ont l'intention de mettre en place un système d'échelonnement des heures de travail; **employees' vacation times are staggered over the summer months** les vacances du personnel sont étalées sur tout l'été

staggered adj **staggered delivery** livraison f échelonnée; **staggered payments** paiements mpl échelonnés, paiement m par versements échelonnés; **staggered strike** grève f tournante

stagnant adj (economy, prices, trade) stagnant(e)

stagnate vi (of economy, prices, trade) stagner

stagnation n (of economy, prices, trade) stagnation f

stake 1 n (a) (interest, share) intérêt m, part f; (investment) investissement m; (shareholding) participation f; **she has a ten percent stake in the company** elle a une participation de dix pour cent dans la société; **the company has a big stake in nuclear energy** la société a fait de gros investissements dans le nucléaire (b) Am (savings) (petite) pécule f, bas m de laine
2 vt Am (aid financially) financer; **he is staking the newspaper for half a million dollars** il investit un demi-million de dollars dans le journal

stakeholder n partie f prenante ▫ Br **stakeholder pension** = plan de retraite à coût réduit conçu pour les travailleurs indépendants ou à temps partiel

stale adj (cheque) périmé(e), prescrit(e)

stall vi **to stall (for time)** essayer de gagner du temps; **I think they're stalling on the loan until we make more concessions** je crois qu'ils vont retarder le prêt jusqu'à ce que nous leur fassions davantage de concessions

stamp 1 n (a) (for letter, parcel) timbre m (b) (device) tampon m; (mark) cachet m (c) **stamp duty** droit m de timbre
2 vt (a) (document) tamponner; **he stamped the firm's name on each document** il a tamponné le nom de la société sur chaque document; **incoming mail is stamped with the date received** le courrier qui arrive est tamponné à la date de réception (b) (letter, parcel) timbrer, affranchir ▫ Br **stamped addressed envelope** enveloppe f timbrée libellée à ses noms et adresse

stand 1 n (at exhibition) stand m (d'exposition)
2 vi (a) (be valid) tenir; **the agreement stands** le contrat tient toujours; **even with this new plan, our objection still stands** ce nouveau plan ne remet pas en cause notre objection première (b) (of statistics) **inflation/unemployment stands at five percent** le taux d'inflation/de chômage est à cinq pour cent; **their turnover now stands at three million pounds** leur chiffre d'affaires atteint désormais les trois millions de livres

▸ **stand down** vi (resign) démissionner

▸ **stand off** vt sep Br (workers) faire chômer

stand-alone n Comptr poste m autonome ▫ **stand-alone computer** ordinateur m autonome

standard 1 n (a) (level) niveau m; **to be up to/below standard** être du/en dessous du niveau requis; **most of the goods are up to standard** la plupart de marchandises sont de qualité satisfaisante ▫ **standard of living** niveau m de vie (b) (set requirements) norme f; (for weights, measures, currency) étalon m; **to make a product comply with standards** adapter un produit aux normes; **to set standards for a product** fixer des normes pour un produit ▫ **standards commission** commission f de normalisation
2 adj (design, size) standard ▫ **standard allowance** (in taxation) déduction f forfaitaire; **standard assessment system** régime m du forfait; **standard cost** coût m standard; **standard cost accounting** méthode f des coûts standards; **standard costing** méthode des coûts standards; **standard deviation** écart m type; **stan-**

dard document document *m* type; **standard ending** *(of letter)* formule *f* de politesse; **standard letter** lettre *f* type; **standard opening** *(of letter)* formule de politesse; **standard operating procedure** = marche à suivre normale; *Ins* **standard policy** police *f* (d'assurance) type; **standard practice** pratique *f* courante; **standard price** prix *m* standard; **standard rate** *(of tax)* taux *m* standard; **standard sample** échantillon *m* modèle; **standard weight** poids *m* normal

standardization *n* standardisation *f*; *(of methods, products, production)* normalisation *f*

standardize *vt* standardiser; *(methods, products, production)* normaliser

standby *n* (a) *Fin* ligne *f* de crédit ◻ **standby agreement** accord *m* d'aide en réserve; **standby credit** crédit *m* stand-by *ou* de soutien; **standby letter of credit** caution *f* bancaire; **standby loan** prêt *m* conditionnel (b) *(for flight)* **to be on standby** être en stand-by ◻ **standby passenger** passager(ère) *m,f* (en) stand-by; **standby ticket** billet *m* en stand-by (c) *Comptr* **standby mode** *(of printer)* veille *f*

standing 1 *n (status)* réputation *f*; **enquiries were made into his financial standing** on a enquêté sur sa situation financière; **the scandal has damaged the company's standing** le scandale a nui à la réputation de la société
2 *adj* **standing charges** *(on bill)* frais *mpl* d'abonnement; *Br Fin* **standing order** virement *m* automatique; **I get paid by standing order** je reçois mon salaire par virement bancaire

standstill *n* **to be at a standstill** *(of economy, production)* être paralysé(e) ◻ **standstill agreement** moratoire *m*

❝
The major shareholders in Anaconda Nickel … have come to a **standstill agreement** regarding their stakes. In the hectic hours before today's extraordinary general meeting, they agreed not to increase their stakes above 30 percent in the period up to Dec. 31 2001, or 90 days after the publication of key recommendations of a strategic review, whichever is the later.
❞

staple¹ 1 *n (for paper)* agrafe *f* ◻ **staple gun** agrafeuse *f*
2 *vt* agrafer (**to** à)

staple² 1 *n (basic foodstuff)* aliment *m* de base; *(basic product)* article *m* de base
2 *adj (foodstuffs, products)* de base; *(export, crop)* principal(e) ◻ **staple commodity** produit *m* de base; **their staple commodity is cotton** le coton est leur produit de base

stapler *n* agrafeuse *f*

star *n* (a) *Mktg (product)* vedette *f* (b) *St Exch* **star analyst** analyste *mf* de choc (c) *Comptr* **star network** réseau *m* connecté en étoile; *Comptr* **star structure** structure *f* en étoile

start 1 *n* début *m* ◻ *Comptr* **start button** bouton *m* Démarrer
2 *vt* (a) *(machine, device)* mettre en marche; **to start the printer again, press this key** pour remettre en marche l'imprimante, appuyez sur cette touche (b) *(business)* fonder, créer; *(project, campaign)* lancer
3 *vi* commencer; **she started on $500 a week** elle a débuté à 500 dollars par semaine

▸ **start up** *vt sep (business)* fonder, créer; *(project, campaign)* lancer; *(computer)* mettre en route

starting *n* **starting date** date *f* d'entrée en vigueur; **starting price** prix *m* initial; *(at auction)* prix d'appel; **starting salary** salaire *m* de départ

start-up *n* (a) *(of new business)* lancement *m*; **there have been 500 start-ups this year** il y a eu 500 créations d'entreprises cette année ◻ **start-up capital** capital *m* initial *ou* de départ; **start-up costs** frais *mpl* de lancement *ou* d'établissement; **start-up loan** prêt *m* initial (b) *(Internet company)* start-up *f*, jeune pousse *f* (c) *Comptr* démarrage *m* ◻ **start-up disk** disquette *f* de démarrage; **start-up mode** mode *m* démarrer; **start-up screen** écran *m* d'accueil

state¹ *n (country, administrative region)* État *m* ◻ *Am* **state bank** banque *f* de dépôts *(agréée par un État)*; **state budget** budget *m* de l'État; **state control** contrôle *m* étatique; **to be placed under state control** être nationalisé(e); **state monopoly** monopole *m* d'État; **state pension** pension *f* de l'État

state² *vt (conditions, demands, reasons)* déclarer; **please state salary expectations** veuillez indiquer le salaire souhaité

state-aided *adj* subventionné(e) par l'État

state-controlled *adj (industry)* nationalisé(e); *(economy)* étatisé(e); **the oil company is 51 percent state-controlled** l'État détient 51 pour cent des actions de la compagnie pétrolière

stated *adj (amount, date, price)* fixé(e); *(limit)* prescrit(e); **it will be finished within the stated time** cela va être terminé dans les délais prescrits

statement *n* (a) *(of facts, situation)* exposé *m*, compte-rendu *m*; *(to press)* communiqué *m* ◻ **statement of intent** protocole *m* d'intention; **statement of principle** déclaration *f* de principe (b) *(of expenses, sales figures)* état *m*; *(from bank)* relevé *m* de compte (bancaire) ◻ *Acct* **statement of account** état *ou* relevé de compte; **statement of affairs** bilan *m* de liquidation; *Acct* **statement of assets and liabil-**

ities relevé des dettes actives et passives; **statement of changes in financial position** état des mouvements de trésorerie; **statement of expenditure, statement of expenses** état ou relevé des dépenses; *Am Acct* **statement of financial position** bilan; **statement of invoices** relevé de factures; *Ins* **statement of loss** certificat *m* d'avarie; *Acct* **statement of results** déclaration de résultats; **statement of sales figures** état des ventes; *Acct* **statement of sources and applications of funds** tableau *m* de financement

state-of-the-art *adj* avancé(e); **the method incorporates state-of-the-art technology** la méthode utilise des technologies de pointe

> 66
> "Seats on any given flight can be sold in many different markets. The idea of investing in **state-of-the-art** technology is to better match supply with demand and ensure that each market is allocated an appropriate number of seats, especially when traffic mix and seasonal travel have to be factored in. Ultimately, we want to minimize seat wastage."
> 99

state-owned *adj* nationalisé(e) ❑ **state-owned company** société *f* d'État, entreprise *f* publique

stationery *n* papeterie *f*; *(writing paper)* papier *m* à lettres ❑ *Admin* **the Stationery Office** = maison d'édition britannique publiant les documents approuvés par le Parlement, les ministères et autres organismes officiels, ≃ l'Imprimerie *f* nationale

statistic *n* chiffre *m*, statistique *f*

statistical *adj* statistique ❑ **statistical analysis** analyse *f* statistique; **statistical data** données *fpl* statistiques; **statistical indicator** indicateur *m* statistique; **statistical table** tableau *m* statistique

statistician *n* statisticien(enne) *m,f*

statistics 1 *n (science)* statistique *f* **2** *npl (figures)* statistiques *fpl*

status *n (position)* position *f*, statut *m*; **what's your status in the company?** quelle est votre position dans l'entreprise? ❑ *Comptr* **status bar** barre *f* d'état; *Comptr* **status box** zone *f* d'état; **status enquiry** enquête *f* de solvabilité; **status enquiry department** service *m* des renseignements commerciaux; *Comptr* **status line** ligne *f* d'état; **status report** état *m* de situation

statute *n Law* loi *f*, ordonnance *f*; **statutes** *(of company)* statuts *mpl*, règlements *mpl* ❑ **statute book** recueil *m* des lois; **statute law** droit *m* écrit

statutory *adj (price controls, income policy)* ob-

ligatoire; *(rights, duties, regulations)* statutaire; *(holiday)* légal(e) ❑ **statutory company** société *f* concessionnaire; **statutory maternity pay** indemnité *f* de maternité à charge de l'État; **statutory report** = rapport annuel sur l'état de l'entreprise *(obligatoire dans le cadre de la loi sur les sociétés)*; **statutory reserve** réserve *f* statutaire; **statutory rights** droits *mpl* statutaires; **statutory sick pay** = indemnité de maladie versée par l'employeur

steady 1 *adj (growth, increase, decline)* régulier(ère), progressif(ive); *(price, rate, Stock Market)* stable; **inflation remains at a steady five percent** l'inflation s'est stabilisée à cinq pour cent
2 *vi (of growth, increase, decline)* devenir régulier(ère); *(of price, rate, Stock Market)* se stabiliser

steep *adj (price)* élevé(e); *(rise, fall)* considérable; **a steep drop in share prices** une forte chute des prix des actions

steering committee *n* comité *m* de restructuration

> 66
> He said France could not "take refuge" behind the views of its own national scientific body – the food safety agency – to oppose a commission decision resuming British beef exports which itself had been based on the opinion of an EU scientific body, the scientific **steering committee** of veterinary experts.
> 99

step costs *npl Acct* frais *mpl* progressifs

sterling *n* sterling *m*; **in sterling** en livres sterling; **five thousand pounds sterling** cinq mille livres sterling ❑ **sterling area** zone *f* sterling; **sterling balances** soldes *mpl* ou balances *fpl* en sterling; **sterling bloc** bloc *m* sterling

stevedore *n* docker *m*, débardeur *m*

sticker price *n* prix *m* affiché *ou* à la vente

stimulate *vt (production)* encourager, activer; *(growth, trade)* stimuler

stimulation marketing *n* marketing *m* de stimulation

stimulus *n Mktg* stimulant *m* ❑ **stimulus response** réponse *f* stimulée

stipend *n* traitement *m*, appointements *mpl*

stipendiary *adj* rémunéré(e)

stipulate *vt* stipuler; **it is stipulated that construction shall start next month** il est stipulé que la construction doit commencer le mois prochain; **please stipulate the quantity on your order form** veuillez stipuler la quantité sur votre commande ❑ **stipulated quality** qualité *f* prescrite

stipulation *n* stipulation *f*; **they accepted, but**

with the stipulation that the time limit be extended ils ont accepté sous réserve que les délais soient prolongés

stock 1 n (**a**) *(of goods)* stock m; **stocks are low** il y a peu de marchandises en stock; **while stocks last** jusqu'à épuisement des stocks; **to be in stock** être en stock; **to be out of stock** être épuisé(e); **we're out of stock** nous sommes en rupture de stock ❑ *stock book* livre m des inventaires; *stock clearance* liquidation f de stock; *stock control* gestion f ou contrôle m des stocks; *stock control system* système m de contrôle de stocks; *stock in hand* marchandises fpl en stock ou en magasin; *stock holding distribution* distribution f numérique; *stock issued form* bon m de sortie; *stock level* niveau m des stocks; *stock outage* rupture f de stock; *stock received form* bon d'entrée; *stock sheet* fiche f de stock; *stock shortage* manquant en stock; *stock transfer* cession f de parts; *stock turnover* mouvement m des stocks; *stock turnover ratio* coefficient m de rotation; *stock valuation* évaluation f des stocks

(**b**) St Exch *(in UK)* valeurs fpl, actions fpl, titres mpl; *(in US)* actions ordinaires; **stocks and shares** valeurs boursières ou mobilières, titres ❑ Am *stock average* indice m des titres; Am *stock certificate* titre m; Am *stock company* société f anonyme par actions; *stock dividend* dividende m (en) action; *the Stock Exchange* la Bourse; *stock exchange* bourse f des valeurs; *stock exchange committee* chambre f syndicale des agents de change; *Stock Exchange crash* krach m boursier; *Stock Exchange Daily Official List* ≃ Bulletin de la Cote Officielle; *stock exchange dealer* opérateur(trice) m,f boursier(ère); *stock exchange order* ordre m de Bourse; *stock exchange transaction* transaction f ou opération f boursière; *stock index* indice de la Bourse; *stock list* cours mpl de la Bourse; *the Stock Market* la Bourse; *stock market* marché m boursier; *stock market boom* envolée f du marché boursier; *stock market bubble* bulle f boursière; *stock market fluctuation* mouvement m boursier; *stock market forecast* prévision f boursière; *stock market investment* placement m financier; *stock market manipulation* manœuvre f boursière; *stock market price* cours m de la Bourse; *stock market report* bulletin m des cours de la Bourse; *stock market value* valeur f en Bourse; *stock option* stock-option f, option f de titres; *stock option plan* plan m d'option sur titres; *stock price level* niveau m de cours des actions; *stock purchase plan* plan d'option sur titres

2 vt (**a**) *(supply)* approvisionner (**with** de); **this shop is well stocked** ce magasin est bien approvisionné

(**b**) *(have in stock)* avoir en stock; **we don't stock that item any more** nous ne vendons ou faisons plus cet article

stockbroker n St Exch *(person)* agent m de change; *(company)* société f de Bourse ❑ *stockbroker belt* = partie de la banlieue sud de Londres où habitent les agents de change et autres personnes du même milieu socio-professionnel; *stockbroker's clerk* commis m d'agent de change

> **"**
> A farmer killed in a shooting accident had acquired squatter's rights over 57 acres of prime development land in Berkshire, a high court judge ruled yesterday. The four fields, which would be worth millions with planning consent, are on the outskirts of Henwick, near Thatcham, in one of the most desirable parts of the county's **stockbroker belt**.
> **"**

stockbroking n St Exch commerce m des valeurs en Bourse ❑ *stockbroking firm* société f de Bourse

stockholder n St Exch actionnaire mf ❑ *stockholder's equity* capitaux mpl ou fonds mpl propres, avoir m des actionnaires

stock-in-trade n marchandises fpl en stock ou en magasin

stockist n stockiste mf

stockjobber n St Exch (**a**) Br Formerly = avant 1986, intermédiaire en Bourse qui traitait directement avec les agents de change et non avec le public (**b**) Am agent m de change

stockkeeper n Am magasinier(ère) m,f

stockkeeping n tenue f des stocks

stockless purchase plan n plan m d'achat sans stock

stocklist n (**a**) *(inventory)* inventaire m; **to make a stocklist of goods** inventorier des marchandises (**b**) St Exch cote f de la Bourse

stockman n magasinier m

stockpicker n Fin, St Exch = personne qui sélectionne des actions pour établir un portefeuille

stockpicking n Fin, St Exch sélection f d'actions

stockpile 1 n stocks mpl de réserve
2 vt stocker

stockroom n magasin m, réserve f

stocktake vi faire ou dresser un inventaire

stocktaking n inventaire m (des stocks); **to do the stocktaking** faire l'inventaire; **stocktaking is in February** on fait l'inventaire en février ❑ *stocktaking sale* solde m après inventaire

stop 1 n St Exch *stop order* ordre m stop; *stop payment* opposition f (à un chèque)
2 vt Br *(withhold)* **to stop payment** suspendre des paiements; **to stop a cheque** faire opposition à un chèque; **to stop sb's wages** retenir le

salaire de qn; **the money will be stopped out of your wages** la somme sera retenue sur votre salaire

stop-go policy n Br Econ politique f économique en dents de scie, politique du stop-and-go

stop-loss adj St Exch **stop-loss order** ordre m stop; **stop-loss selling** ordre de vente stop

stoppage n (**a**) (strike) grève f, arrêt m de travail (**b**) Br (sum deducted) retenue f; **my wages are a lot less after stoppages** après les retenues, il ne reste plus grand-chose de mon salaire

storage n (**a**) (action) entreposage m, emmagasinage m; (space available) (espace m de) rangement m; (state) stockage m; **to put sth into storage** entreposer qch □ **storage capacity** capacité f d'entreposage ou d'emmagasinage; **storage charges** frais mpl d'entreposage ou d'emmagasinage; **storage facilities** entrepôt m (**b**) Comptr mémoire f □ **storage capacity** capacité f de stockage; **storage device** dispositif m de stockage; **storage medium** support m de stockage

store 1 n (**a**) (supply) provision f, stock m, réserve f (**b**) (warehouse) entrepôt m (**c**) (large shop) grand magasin m; Am (shop) magasin □ Mktg **store audit** contrôle m des points de vente; Mktg **store brand** marque f de magasin; **store card** carte f de crédit (d'un magasin) (**d**) Comptr mémoire f
2 vt (**a**) (goods) mettre en magasin, entreposer (**b**) Comptr stocker

stored production n Acct production f stockée

storefront n Am devanture f de magasin

storehouse n entrepôt m

storekeeper n (**a**) (in warehouse) magasinier(ère) m,f (**b**) Am (shopkeeper) commerçant(e) m,f, détaillant(e) m,f

storeroom n réserve f

straddle n St Exch ordre m lié, opération f à cheval; **to take a straddle position** = jumeler simultanément un achat sur une époque avec une vente sur une autre

straight-line adj Acct **straight-line depreciation** amortissement m linéaire; **straight-line depreciation method** mode m ou méthode f d'amortissement linéaire; **straight-line method** mode ou méthode linéaire; **straight-line rate** taux m linéaire

strapline n Mktg signature f, base line f

❝
Gone is the exuberant "It Could Be You" slogan that carried the Lottery through its first five years. The new "Maybe. Just Maybe" **strapline** stresses the enjoyment of anticipation as much as the prospect of winning.
❞

strategic adj stratégique □ **strategic business plan** plan m stratégique d'entreprise; **strategic business unit** domaine m d'activité stratégique, unité f d'activité stratégique; **strategic fit** ajustement m stratégique; **strategic group** groupe m stratégique; **strategic management** gestion f stratégique; **strategic marketing** marketing m stratégique; **strategic planning** planification f stratégique; **strategic position** position f stratégique; **strategic positioning** positionnement m stratégique; **strategic review** revue f stratégique; **strategic segmentation** segmentation f stratégique; **strategic targeting** ciblage m stratégique; **strategic withdrawal** (of product, campaign) repli m stratégique

strategically adv stratégiquement

strategy n stratégie f

stratified adj Mktg **stratified sample** échantillon m stratifié; **stratified sampling** échantillonnage m stratifié

straw boss n Am Fam chef m d'équipe

stream vt Comptr transmettre en continu (sur l'Internet)

streaming n Comptr streaming m, transmission f en continu (sur l'Internet)

streamline vt (production, methods) rationaliser; (company, department, industry) dégraisser

❝
The sweeping restructuring, including plans to scrap the second delivery, **streamline** the transport network and outsource some non-core operations is expected to cost £2.4bn. The plan is being underpinned by a package of measures announced yesterday by the government.
❞

streamlined adj (production, methods) rationalisé(e); (company, department, industry) dégraissé(e)

streamlining n (of production, methods) rationalisation f; (of company, department) dégraissement m

street n St Exch **street dealing** transactions fpl hors Bourse; **street market** marché m hors Bourse; **street price** cours m hors Bourse

strength n (of product, company) force f □ Mktg **strengths, weaknesses, opportunities and threats** forces, faiblesses, opportunités et menaces fpl

strengthen 1 vt (financial position, currency, economy) consolider
2 vi (of financial position, currency, economy) se consolider

stress-related illness n maladie f due au stress

strike 1 *n* (**a**) *(of workers)* grève *f*; **to be on strike** faire (la) grève, être en grève; **to come out** *or* **go on strike** se mettre en grève ❑ **strike ballot** = vote avant que les syndicats ne décident d'une grève; *Ins* **strike clause** clause *f* pour cas de grève; **strike fund** = caisse de prévoyance permettant d'aider les grévistes; **strike leader** meneur *m* de grève; **strike notice** préavis *m* de grève; **strike pay** allocation *f* de grève (**b**) *St Exch* **strike price** prix *m* d'exercice **2** *vt (bargain, deal, agreement)* conclure **3** *vi (of workers)* faire grève; **they're striking for more pay** ils font grève pour obtenir une augmentation de salaire

strikebound *adj (factory, department)* paralysé(e) par une *ou* la grève; *(industry, country)* paralysé par des grèves

strikebreaker *n* briseur(euse) *m,f* de grève

striker *n* gréviste *mf*

striking price *n St Exch* prix *m* d'exercice

string *n* (**a**) *Comptr (of characters)* chaîne *f* (**b**) **to pull strings** faire jouer ses relations; **somebody pulled strings to get him the job** il a eu le poste par piston; **with no strings attached** sans conditions

strip mall *n Am* = centre commercial qui longe une route

> ❝
> Naturally, you have to feel comfortable making transactions over the Internet. Although an online broker-banker is likely to have branches for times when you crave a tete-a-tete transaction, chances are it won't be as convenient as the bank at your local **strip mall**.
> ❞

stripped bond *n St Exch* félin *m*, obligation *f* à coupon zéro

strong *adj (market)* ferme; *(currency, price)* solide; **the pound is getting stronger** la livre se raffermit

strongroom *n* chambre *f* forte

struck *adj Am (industry)* bloqué(e) pour cause de grève; *(factory)* fermé(e) pour cause de grève

structural *adj Econ* **structural change** changement *m* stucturel; **structural unemployment** chômage *m* structurel

structure 1 *n* structure *f* **2** *vt* structurer ❑ *Mktg* **structured interview** entretien *m* structuré

stub *n (of cheque)* souche *f*, talon *m*

study *n (of market, feasibility)* étude *f* ❑ **study group** groupe *m* d'étude

stuffer *n Mktg* encart *m*

► **stump up** *Br Fam* **1** *vt sep* casquer **2** *vi* casquer (**for** pour)

stumpage *n Am* valeur *f* de bois d'œuvre

style *n Comptr* **style bar** barre *f* de style; **style sheet** feuille *f* de style

subaccount *n Acct* sous-compte *m*

subagency *n* sous-agence *f*

subagent *n* sous-agent *m*

subcommittee *n* sous-comité *m*

subcontract 1 *n* contrat *m* de sous-traitance **2** *vt (work, order)* sous-traiter; **they subcontract some of the work out to local firms** ils sous-traitent une partie du travail à des entreprises locales **3** *vi* travailler en sous-traitance; **they have a lot of small companies who subcontract for them** beaucoup de petites sociétés travaillent pour eux en sous-traitance

subcontracting *n* sous-traitance *f* ❑ **subcontracting agreement** accord *m* de sous-traitance

subcontractor *n* sous-traitant *m*

subdirectory *n Comptr* sous-répertoire *m*

subheading *n* intertitre *m*

subject *adj (liable)* **to be subject to sth** *(fine, taxation, commission)* être passible de qch; **the terms are subject to alteration without notice** les termes peuvent être modifiés sans préavis; **the price is subject to a handling charge** les frais de manutention sont en sus

sublease 1 *n* sous-location *f* **2** *vt* sous-louer

subledger *n Acct* grand livre *m* auxiliaire

sublessee *n* sous-locataire *mf*

sublessor *n* sous-bailleur(eresse) *m,f*

sublet 1 *n* sous-location *f* **2** *vt* sous-louer

subletter *n* sous-bailleur(eresse) *m,f*

subletting *n* sous-location *f*

subliminal advertising *n* publicité *f* subliminale

submarket *n* sous-marché *m*

submenu *n Comptr* sous-menu *m*

subordinate 1 *n* subordonné(e) *m,f* **2** *adj (job, position)* subalterne; **to be subordinate to sb** être subordonné(e) à qn

subordinated debt *n* dette *f* subordonnée

subrogation *n Law* subrogation *f*

subroutine *n Comptr* sous-programme *m*

subscribe 1 *vt Fin (shares)* souscrire ❑ **subscribed capital** capital *m* souscrit **2** *vi* (**a**) *(to newspaper, magazine, ISP)* s'abonner (**to** à); **to subscribe to the Internet** s'abonner à l'Internet (**b**) *Fin (to loan, share issue)* souscrire (**to** à)

subscriber n (**a**) *(to newspaper, magazine, Internet)* abonné(e) *m,f* (**b**) *Fin (to loan, share issue)* souscripteur(trice) *m,f* (**c**) *(of new company)* signataire *mf* des statuts

subscription n (**a**) *(to newspaper, magazine, Internet)* abonnement *m*; **to take out a subscription to sth** s'abonner à qch □ *subscription form* bulletin *m* d'abonnement; *subscription rate* prix *m* de l'abonnement (**b**) *Fin (to loan, share issue)* souscription *f* □ *subscription list* liste *f* de souscriptions; *subscription right* droit *m* de souscription (d'actions)

subsidiarity n subsidiarité *f*

subsidiary 1 n *(company)* filiale *f*
2 *adj* subsidiaire, auxiliaire □ *subsidiary account* sous-compte *m*; *subsidiary claim* demande *f* subsidiaire; *subsidiary company* filiale *f*

subsidize *vt* subventionner; **the company was subsidized to the tune of £3 million** l'entreprise a reçu trois millions de livres de subventions □ *subsidized industry* industrie *f* subventionnée

subsidy n subvention *f*

sub-standard *adj (goods)* de qualité inférieure

substitute n *(product)* produit *m* de substitution □ *substitute product* produit de substitution

substitution n substitution *f* □ *Fin substitution of debt* novation *f* de créance; *substitution market* marché *m* de substitution *ou* environnant

subtenancy n sous-location *f*

subtenant n sous-locataire *mf*

subvention n *Am* subvention *f*

success fee n prime *f* de rendement

successor n successeur *m*

sue *Law* 1 *vt* poursuivre (en justice), intenter un procès à; **to sue sb for sth** poursuivre qn en justice pour qch; **he sued the factory for damages** il a poursuivi l'usine pour obtenir des dommages-intérêts
2 *vi* intenter un procès, engager des poursuites

suicide pill n *(defensive tactics in takeover)* clause *f* de suicide

suit n *Law* action *m*, procès *m*; **to bring** *or* **file a suit against sb** poursuivre qn en justice, intenter un procès à qn

suite n *Comptr (of software)* suite *f* logicielle, ensemble *m* logiciel

sum n *(amount of money)* somme *f*; *(total)* total *m* □ *sum advanced* mise *f* hors; *sum in excess*

somme en excédent; *sum payable* somme payable, charge *f* à payer

summary n résumé *m* □ *Acct summary balance sheet* bilan *m* condensé; *summary dismissal* renvoi *m* sommaire; *summary report* rapport *m* récapitulatif

summit n *(meeting)* sommet *m*; **to hold a summit** tenir un sommet □ *summit conference* conférence *f* au sommet

summon *vt (person, meeting)* convoquer; *Law (witness)* assigner *ou* citer à comparaître

summons *Law* 1 n assignation *f* *ou* citation *f* à comparaître
2 *vt* assigner *ou* citer à comparaître

sundry 1 n sundries *(items)* articles *mpl* divers; *(costs)* frais *mpl* divers
2 *adj* divers(e) □ *sundry charges* frais *mpl* divers; *sundry expenses* frais divers; *sundry income* produits *mpl* accessoires

sunk costs npl coûts *mpl* irrécupérables

sunrise industry n industrie *f* naissante

> **"**
> The war against terrorism has left corporate America in a cleft stick. On the one hand, the kneejerk reaction of business is to retrench – rapidly – after the terrorist attacks. After all, the renaissance of US industry in the 1990s has been a story not just of American dominance in **sunrise industries**, but also ruthless cost-cutting to make firms more efficient.
> **"**

sunset industry n industrie *f* déclinante

superannuate *vt* (**a**) *(person)* mettre à la retraite (**b**) *(object)* mettre au rebut

superannuated *adj* (**a**) *(person)* à la retraite (**b**) *(object)* suranné(e), désuet(ète)

superannuation n *(act of retiring)* mise *f* à la retraite; *(pension)* pension *f* de retraite; *(contribution)* cotisation *f* pour la retraite □ *superannuation fund* caisse *f* de retraite

supercomputer n *Comptr* super-ordinateur *m*

superhighway n *Comptr* autoroute *f*

supermajority n majorité *f* qualifiée

supermarket n supermarché *m* □ *supermarket bank* = banque qui appartient à une chaîne de supermarchés

superstock n *Am St Exch* actions *fpl* à droit de vote double

superstore n hypermarché *m*, grande surface *f*

supertax n impôt *m* sur les grandes fortunes

supervise *vt* superviser, surveiller

supervision n supervision *f*, surveillance *f*

supervisor n (in office) chef m de service; (in factory) chef d'équipe

supervisory board n conseil m de surveillance

supplement 1 n (a) (additional amount) supplément m; **a supplement is charged for occupying a single room** il y a un supplément à payer pour les chambres à un lit (b) (to newspaper, magazine) supplément m
  2 vt compléter

supplementary adj Acct **supplementary entry** écriture f complémentaire; **supplementary pension** complément m (de) retraite

supplier n fournisseur(euse) m,f □ **supplier code** code m fournisseur; Acct **supplier credit** crédit-fournisseur m, avoir-fournisseur m; **supplier file** fiche f fournisseur

supply 1 n (a) Econ offre f; **supply and demand** l'offre et la demande □ **supply curve** courbe f de l'offre; **supply and demand mechanism** mécanisme m de l'offre et de la demande; **supply price** prix m de l'offre (b) (stock) provision f, réserve f; (act of supplying) approvisionnement m; **supplies** provisions fpl; **we are expecting a new supply of microchips** nous espérons recevoir bientôt un nouveau stock de microprocesseurs; **this paper is in short supply** nous sommes à court de ce papier
  2 vt (goods, services) fournir; **to supply sb with sth, to supply sth to sb** fournir qn de qch, fournir qch à qn; **they supply all the local retailers** ils fournissent tous les détaillants du coin

supply-side economics n économie f de l'offre

support 1 n (a) (funding) soutien m; **they depend on the government for financial support** ils sont subventionnés par le gouvernement; **what are your means of support?** quelles sont vos sources de revenus? □ EU **support price** prix m de soutien
  (b) (backing) soutien m, appui m; **to give** or **lend one's support to sth** accorder son appui à qch □ **support activities** fonctions fpl complémentaires; **support services** services mpl de soutien; **support staff** personnel m de soutien ou des services généraux
  (c) Comptr assistance f technique □ **support line** assistance technique téléphonique
  2 vt (a) (financially) subvenir aux besoins de
  (b) (back) soutenir, appuyer
  (c) Comptr permettre l'utilisation de, supporter; **this package is supported by all workstations** ce progiciel peut être utilisé sur tous les postes de travail
  (d) Fin (price, currency) maintenir

supporting document n pièce f justificative

surcharge 1 n (extra duty, tax) surtaxe f; (on price) supplément m; (on tax) majoration f (fiscale), majoration (d'impôt); **a seven percent import surcharge** une surtaxe de sept pour cent sur les importations
  2 vt (charge extra duty or tax on) surtaxer; (charge a supplement to) faire payer un supplément à

surety n (person) caution f, garant(e) m,f; (collateral) caution, sûreté f; **to stand surety (for sb)** se porter caution (pour qn)

surf vt Comptr **to surf the Net** naviguer sur l'Internet

surface n **surface mail** courrier m par voie de terre; **by surface mail** par voie de terre; **surface transport** transport m terrestre

surfeit n surabondance f; **there is a surfeit of imported goods** il y a trop d'importations

surge 1 n forte augmentation f
  2 vi augmenter brusquement; **stock markets surged on news of interest rate cuts in the US** les marchés boursiers ont connue une hausse soudaine à l'annonce de la baisse des taux d'intérêt aux États-Unis

surname n nom m de famille

surplus 1 n (a) (of product, stock, commodity) surplus m, excédent m; **EU grain surpluses** excédents de céréales de l'UE; **Japan's trade surplus** l'excédent commercial du Japon (b) Acct plus-value f; **surplus of assets over liablilities** excédent m de l'actif sur le passif
  2 adj en surplus, excédentaire; **they export their surplus agricultural produce** ils exportent leurs surplus agricoles □ **surplus production** production f excédentaire; **surplus stock** surplus mpl

surrender 1 n Ins (of policy) rachat m □ **surrender value** valeur f de rachat
  2 vt (right) céder; Ins (policy) racheter

surtax 1 n surtaxe f
  2 vt surtaxer

survey 1 n (a) Br (of building) expertise f
  (b) (study, investigation) étude f, enquête f; **they carried out a survey of retail prices** ils ont fait une enquête sur les prix au détail
  (c) (opinion poll) sondage m □ **survey research** recherche f par sondage
  2 vt (a) Br (building) expertiser, faire une expertise de
  (b) (study, investigate) faire une étude de, étudier; **the report surveys the current state of the manufacturing industry** le rapport étudie l'état actuel de l'industrie manufacturière
  (c) (poll) sonder; **65 percent of women surveyed were opposed to the measure** 65 pour cent des femmes interrogées étaient contre cette mesure

surveyor n Br (of building) expert m

survivor's pension n pension f de réversion

suspect n Mktg client(e) m,f potentiel(elle) ❏ **suspect pool** clients potentiels

suspend vt (a) (payment) suspendre; **the government has suspended the repayment of foreign debts** le gouvernement a suspendu le remboursement de sa dette extérieure (b) (employee) suspendre

suspense account n compte m d'ordre

suspension n (a) (of payment) suspension f (b) (of employee) suspension f, mise f à pied (c) **suspension file** dossier m suspendu

sustainability n (of development, agriculture, resource, environment) viabilité f, durabilité f

sustainable adj (development, agriculture, resource, environment) viable, durable

sustained yield n Econ rendement m soutenu

SVGA n Comptr (abbr **Super Video Graphics Array**) SVGA m ❏ **SVGA monitor** moniteur m SVGA

swap 1 n Banking, St Exch échange m financier, swap m ❏ **swap agreements** accords mpl d'échanges; **swap facilities** facilités fpl de crédits réciproques; **swap option** option f sur swap de taux d'intérêt
2 vt St Exch swaper

swaption n St Exch option f sur swap de taux d'intérêt

> **"**
> In addition to buying the gilts, Scottish Widows has been trying to peg its interest rate exposure by arranging deals to borrow from big companies or buy complex derivatives instruments known as **swaptions.**
> **"**

sweat equity n Am plus-value f (acquise grâce à des améliorations, au travail fourni etc)

> **"**
> While the terms of these two deals were not disclosed, it is generally believed that agencies can go for 1.5 times their revenue. In Burrell's case, that could amount to $32.7 million, according to Advertising Age. "These mergers are good because they recognize the **sweat equity** that multicultural agencies have put into the business," says the AA's Donahue.
> **"**

sweatshop n atelier m clandestin

SWIFT n (abbr **Society for Worldwide Interbank Financial Telecommunication**) = société internationale de télécommunications financières interbanques

swingline adj (loan, credit) immédiatement disponible

swing shift n Am (work period) = poste de 16

heures à minuit; (team) = équipe qui travaille de 16 heures à minuit

swipe 1 n **swipe card** badge m
2 vt (card) passer dans un lecteur de cartes

Swiss franc n franc m suisse

switch 1 n (a) Br **Switch**® = société de cartes de paiement britannique ❏ **Switch® card** = carte de paiement utilisée en Grande-Bretagne (b) Comptr (in DOS) clé f (c) St Exch **switch trading** arbitrage m
2 vt St Exch **to switch a position** = reporter une position d'une échéance à une autre plus éloignée

switchboard n standard m ❏ **switchboard operator** standardiste mf

switching n St Exch arbitrage m de portefeuille

sworn statement n déclaration f ou déposition f faite sous serment

SWOT n Mktg (abbr **strengths, weaknesses, opportunities, threats**) forces, faiblesses, opportunités et menaces fpl ❏ **SWOT analysis** analyse f des forces, faiblesses, opportunités et menaces

> **"**
> ... a **SWOT** (Strength, Weakness, Opportunity and Threat) **analysis** is a fundamental tool in corporate strategic planning. Once planners have conducted a **SWOT analysis**, they are in a position to articulate the mission, strategy, and objectives of the organization.
> **"**

symbol n symbole m

sympathy n **to come out in sympathy** se mettre en grève par solidarité ❏ **sympathy strike** grève f de solidarité

syndicate 1 n syndicat m, groupement m; **to form a syndicate** se syndiquer; **the loan was underwritten by a syndicate of banks** le prêt était garanti par un consortium bancaire; **a syndicate of British and French companies** un groupement de sociétés françaises et britanniques
2 vt (a) (industry) syndiquer (b) Fin **syndicated credit** crédit m consortial; **syndicated loan** prêt m en participation; **syndicated shares** actions fpl syndiquées

syntax n Comptr syntaxe f ❏ **syntax error** erreur f de syntaxe

SYSOP n Comptr (abbr **Systems Operator**) sysop m, opérateur m système

system n (a) (structure, method) système m; **a new system of sorting mail** un nouveau système pour trier le courrier ❏ **systems and procedures** méthodes fpl administratives
(b) Comptr système m ❏ **systems analysis** ana-

lyse *f* des systèmes; ***systems analyst*** analyste-programmeur(euse) *m,f*; ***system clock*** horloge *f* du système; ***system crash*** panne *f* du système; ***system disk*** disque *f* système; ***systems engineering*** planification *f* des systèmes; ***system error*** erreur *f* système; ***system failure*** panne *f* du système; ***system file*** fichier *m* système; ***system folder*** dossier *m* système; ***systems management*** direction *f* systématisée; ***system prompt*** message *m* d'attente du système; ***system software*** logiciel *m* d'exploitation, logiciel système

systematic *adj* systématique

Tt

tab 1 *n (on typewriter, word processor)* tabulation *f*; **to set tabs (at)** régler *ou* positionner les tabulateurs (à) ❑ *tab key* tabulateur *m*, touche *f* de tabulation; *tab points* points *mpl* de tabulation; *tab setting* tabulation; *tab stop* taquet *m* de tabulation
 2 *vt (text)* mettre en colonnes (avec des tabulations)

table 1 *n* **(a)** *(chart)* table *f*, tableau *m*; *(of prices)* barème *m*; **the results are set out in the following table** les résultats sont donnés dans le tableau suivant ❑ *table of account codes* grille *f* d'imputation; *table of contents* table *f* des matières **(b)** *(furniture)* table *f*; **to get round the negotiating table** s'asseoir à la table des négociations
 2 *vt* **to table a motion/proposal** *Br (present)* présenter une motion/une proposition; *Am (postpone)* ajourner une motion/une proposition

tabloid *n (paper size, format)* tabloïd *m (279mm × 432mm)*; *(newspaper)* tabloïde *m*

tabular *adj (statistics, figures)* tabulaire; **in tabular form** sous forme de tableau

tabulate *vt* **(a)** *(present in table form)* mettre sous forme de tableau **(b)** *(classify)* classifier

tabulator *n* tabulateur *m*

tag 1 *n* **(a)** *(showing price)* étiquette *f* (de prix) **(b)** *Comptr (code)* balise *f*
 2 *vt Comptr* baliser

take 1 *n Fam (takings)* recette *f*; *(share)* part *f*
 2 *vt* **(a)** *(remove)* **to take an amount out of one's income** prélever une somme sur son revenu; **to take sth off the market** retirer qch du marché
 (b) *(receive) (money)* **she takes home £3,000 a month** son salaire net est de 3000 livres par mois
 (c) *(accept) (cheque, credit card)* accepter; **he won't take less** il refuse d'accepter un prix moins élevé; **does the machine take pound coins?** est-ce que la machine accepte les pièces d'une livre?
 (d) *(write down) (letter, name and address, notes)* prendre; **to take the minutes** rédiger le procès-verbal

▸ **take back** *vt sep* **(a)** *(employee)* reprendre; **the factory took back the workers** l'usine a repris les ouvriers **(b)** *(goods)* rapporter; **take it back to the shop** rapporte-le au magasin

▸ **take off** *vt sep* **(a)** *(deduct)* déduire, rabattre; **he took ten percent off the price** il a réduit le prix de dix pour cent, il a déduit dix pour cent du prix **(b)** *(time)* **to take a day off** prendre un jour de congé; **she takes Thursdays off** elle ne travaille pas le jeudi

▸ **take on** *vt sep* **(a)** *(worker)* engager, embaucher **(b)** *(responsibility, task)* se charger de; *(new contract, customer)* accepter

▸ **take out** *vt sep (permit, licence, patent)* prendre, obtenir; *(insurance policy)* souscrire à; *(subscription)* prendre; **to take out a mortgage** prendre un emprunt-logement

▸ **take over 1** *vt sep (company) (become responsible for)* prendre la direction de; *(buy out)* racheter; **they were taken over by a Japanese firm** ils ont été rachetés par une entreprise japonaise; *St Exch* **to take over an issue** absorber une émission
 2 *vi (of new manager)* prendre la direction; **to take over from sb** *(replace)* relever qn dans ses fonctions

▸ **take up** *vt sep* **(a)** *(offer)* accepter; **to take sb up on an offer** accepter l'offre de qn **(b)** *Fin (bill)* honorer, retirer; *St Exch (option)* lever, consolider; *(shares)* souscrire à **(c)** *(position, post)* prendre; **to take up one's duties** entrer en fonctions

take-home pay *n* salaire *m* net

takeover *n (of company)* rachat *m*, prise *f* de contrôle ❑ *takeover bid* offre *f* publique d'achat, OPA *f*; **to be the subject of a takeover bid** être l'objet d'une OPA; *St Exch* *takeover stock* titres *mpl* ramassés

taker *n (buyer)* preneur(euse) *m,f*, acheteur(euse) *m,f*; **there were no takers** personne n'en voulait

takings *npl* recette *f*; **the day's takings** la recette de la journée

talks *npl* *(negotiations)* négociations *fpl*, pourparlers *mpl*

tally 1 *n* *(record)* pointage *m*; **to keep a tally of goods** pointer des marchandises ❑ *tally file* classeur *m* des entrées et sorties
  2 *vt* *(goods)* pointer
  3 *vi* *(of figures, accounts)* correspondre (**with** à), s'accorder, concorder (**with** avec); **these accounts do not tally** ces comptes ne s'accordent pas

tangible *Acct* **1** *n* **tangibles** actif *m* corporel, valeurs *fpl* matérielles
  2 *adj* *tangible assets* actif *m* corporel, valeurs *fpl* matérielles; *tangible fixed assets* immobilisations *fpl* corporelles; *tangible movables* meubles *mpl* corporels

tankage *n* *(storing in tanks)* stockage *ou* mise *f* en réservoir; *(storage fee)* frais *mpl* de stockage *ou* de mise en réservoir; *(capacity)* contenance *f* *ou* capacité *f* des réservoirs

tap *n* *Fin* valeur *f* du Trésor mise aux enchères; **long/medium/short tap** valeurs *fpl* émises à un prix déterminé par l'État à long/moyen/court terme ❑ *tap issue* émission *f* des valeurs du Trésor; *tap stock* valeur du Trésor mise aux enchères

tape *n* *Comptr* bande *f* ❑ *tape backup* sauvegarde *f* sur bande; *tape backup system* système *m* de sauvegarde sur bande; *tape backup unit* unité *f* de sauvegarde sur bande; *tape unit* unité de bande

tapering *adj* *Fin* *(rate)* dégressif(ive) ❑ *tapering charge* tarif *m* dégressif

taper relief *n* *Br* = réduction progressive des impôts sur les plus-values en fonction du nombre d'années pendant lequel on détient un bien avant de le vendre

> ❝
> Everyone has this £3,000 limit and, if it's not used up in one year, the amount can be carried forward to the next. After three years, the tax payable on a gift starts reducing until it reaches nil at year seven. Small gifts of up to £250 can be made to any number of people. This is known as **taper relief**.
> ❞

tare *n* tare *f*; *(of lorry)* poids *m* net; **to allow for the tare** faire la tare

TARGET *n* *Banking, EU* (*abbr* **Trans-European Automated Real-Time Gross Settlement Transfer System**) TARGET *m*

target 1 *n* *(objective)* but *m*, objectif *m*; **to meet production targets** atteindre les objectifs de production; **to be on target** *(of plans)* se dérouler comme prévu; *(of productivity)* atteindre les objectifs prévus
  2 *adj* *Mktg* *target audience* audience *f* cible;

Mktg *target buyer* acheteur(euse) *m,f* cible; *target company* société *f* cible; *Mktg* *target consumer* consommateur(trice) *m,f* cible; *target cost* coût *m* ciblé; *target date* date *f* ciblée *ou* visée; *Comptr* *target disk* *(hard)* disque *m* cible; *(floppy)* disquette *f* cible; *Mktg* *target group* groupe *m* cible; *Mktg* **Target Group Index** indice *m* des groupes cibles; *Mktg* *target market* marché *m* cible; *target marketing* marketing *m* ciblé; *target population* population *f* cible; *target price* prix *m* d'équilibre; *target pricing* fixation *f* du prix en fonction de l'objectif
  3 *vt* *(market)* cibler; *(advertising campaign)* diriger; **the benefits are targeted at one-parent families** les allocations visent les familles monoparentales

targetting *n* *Mktg* ciblage *m*

tariff *n* (**a**) *(list of prices)* tableau *m* des prix, tarif *m* (**b**) *(tax)* tarif *m*, droit *m* de douane ❑ *tariff agreement* accord *m* tarifaire; *tariff barrier* barrière *f* tarifaire; *tariff laws* lois *fpl* tarifaires; *tariff level indices* taux *mpl* indices des tarifs

task *n* tâche *f* ❑ *task force* groupe *m* d'intervention; *task sheet* fiche *f* de poste

taskbar *n* *Comptr* barre *f* des tâches

tax 1 *n* *(on income)* impôt *m*, contributions *fpl*; *(on goods, services, imports)* taxe *f*; **most of my income goes on tax** la plus grande partie de mes revenus va aux impôts; **I paid over $5,000 in tax** j'ai payé plus de 5000 dollars d'impôts; **there is a high tax on whisky** le whisky est fortement taxé; **to put a ten percent tax on sth** imposer *ou* taxer qch à dix pour cent; **to levy a tax on sth** frapper qch d'une taxe; **to be liable to tax** être assujetti(e) à l'impôt; **before tax** hors taxe; *(income)* avant impôt; **after tax** après impôt; **exclusive of tax** hors taxe; **tax and spend** = politique alliant une fiscalité élevée et de fortes dépenses publiques ❑ *tax adjustment* redressement *m* fiscal *ou* d'impôt; *tax allowance* abattement *m* fiscal, déduction *f* fiscale; *tax assessment* avis *m* d'imposition, fixation *f* de l'impôt; *tax audit* vérification *f* fiscale; *tax authorities* administration *f* fiscale; *tax avoidance* évasion *f* fiscale; *tax band* tranche *f* d'imposition; *tax base* assiette *f* fiscale; *tax benefit* avantage *m* fiscal; *tax bite* proportion *f* du revenu pris par l'impôt; *tax bracket* tranche *ou* fourchette *f* d'imposition; *tax break* allègement *m* fiscal; *tax burden* pression *f* fiscale, poids *m* de la fiscalité; *tax ceiling* plafond *m* fiscal *ou* de l'impôt; *tax centre* centre *m* des impôts; *tax code* barème *m* fiscal; *tax collector* percepteur *m* d'impôt, receveur *m* des contributions; *tax consultant* conseiller(ère) *m,f* fiscal(e); *tax credit* aide *f* fiscale, avoir *m* fiscal; *tax cut* baisse *f* *ou* réduction *f* des impôts; *tax cutting* baisse *ou* réduction des impôts; *tax de-*

ducted at source impôt retenu à la base *ou* à la source; **tax deduction** déduction fiscale; **tax deduction at source** perception *f* à la source; *Am* **tax dollars** impôts *mpl (payés par la population)*; **tax domicile** domicile *m* fiscal; **tax evasion** fraude *f ou* évasion fiscale; **tax exemption** exemption *f* d'impôt; **tax exile** = personne qui réside à l'étranger pour minimiser la responsabilité fiscale; **tax form** déclaration *f* d'impôts; **tax fraud** fraude fiscale; *EU* **tax harmonization** harmonisation *f* fiscale; **tax haven** paradis *m* fiscal; **tax holiday** = période de grâce accordée pour le paiement des impôts; **tax incentive** incitation *f* fiscale, avantage fiscal; **tax inspection** contrôle *m* fiscal; **tax inspector** inspecteur(trice) *m,f* des contributions directes *ou* des impôts; **tax law** droit *m* fiscal; **tax laws** législation *f* fiscale; **tax liability** *(of person)* assujetissement *m* à l'impôt; *(of goods, product)* exigibilité *f* de taxe; **tax loophole** échappatoire *f* fiscale; **tax loss** déficit *m* fiscal reportable; **tax on luxury goods** taxe de luxe; **tax office** centre des impôts; **tax official** agent *m* du fisc; **tax privilege** privilège *m* fiscal; **tax provision** disposition *f* fiscale; **tax resources** ressources *fpl* fiscales; **tax rate** taux *m* d'imposition; **tax rebate** dégrèvement *m* fiscal; **tax reduction** abattement fiscal; **tax refund** *(on goods)* détaxe *f*; *(of income tax)* restitution *f* d'impôts; **tax regime** régime *m* fiscal; **tax relief** dégrèvement fiscal; **tax return** déclaration de revenu, feuille *f* d'impôt; **tax revenue** recettes *fpl ou* rentrées *fpl* fiscales; **tax roll** rôle *m* d'impôt *ou* des contributions; **tax rules** réglementation *f* fiscale; **tax schedule** barème d'imposition; **tax shelter** avantage fiscal; **tax shield** protection *f* fiscale; **tax survey** enquête *f* fiscale; **tax system** régime fiscal *ou* d'imposition; **tax threshold** minimum *m* imposable, seuil *m* d'imposition; **tax on value** taxation *f* à la valeur; **tax on weight** taxation au poids; **tax year** année *f* fiscale *ou* d'imposition

2 *vt (person, company)* imposer, frapper d'un impôt; *(goods, services, imports)* taxer, frapper d'un taxe; **the rich will be more heavily taxed** les riches seront plus lourdement imposés; **luxury goods are taxed at 28 percent** les articles de luxe sont taxés à 28 pour cent; **small businesses are being taxed out of existence** accablées d'impôts, les petites entreprises disparaissent

> ❝
> **Tax cutting** can encourage people to do the right thing. **Tax relief** for charitable giving, and a **tax holiday** for charities, is accepted by both major parties, and does help increase the amount of charitable money.
> ❞

taxable *adj* imposable ❑ **taxable base** base *f*

d'imposition; **taxable income** revenu *m* imposable, assiette *f* fiscale *ou* de l'impôt; **taxable profit** bénéfice *m* fiscal *ou* imposable; **taxable transaction** opération *f* imposable

taxation *n* **(a)** *(of person, company)* imposition *f*; *(of goods)* taxation *f* ❑ **taxation at source** prélèvement *m* de l'impôt à la source, imposition à la source **(b)** *(taxes)* impôts *mpl*, contributions *fpl*

tax-deductible *adj* déductible des impôts

tax-deferred *adj Am* à impôt différé

tax-exempt *adj (income)* exonéré(e) d'impôts; *(goods)* exonéré de taxes

tax-free *adj (income)* exonéré(e) d'impôts; *(goods)* exonéré de taxes ❑ **tax-free shopping** achats *mpl* hors taxes

taxman *n Br Fam* **the taxman** le fisc

> ❝
> David Clowes will earn £60,000 this tax year – but he will not pay the **taxman** a penny. Mr Clowes, 54, left, who runs the London Keyholding Company, has used every tax shelter he can lay his hands on to stay out of the tax collector's hands.
> ❞

taxpayer *n* contribuable *mf*

tax-sensible *adj* = caractérisé par une approche pragmatique concernant la fiscalité

T-bill *n Am (treasury bill)* bon *m* du trésor

TCP/IP *n Comptr (abbr* **transmission control protocol/Internet protocol)** TCP-IP

TD *n Am (abbr* **Treasury Department)** ministère *m* des Finances

team *n* équipe *f*; **she's a team player** elle a l'esprit d'équipe ❑ **team building** création *f* d'un esprit d'équipe; **team dynamics** dynamique *f* d'équipe; **team leader** chef *m* d'équipe; **team spirit** esprit *m* d'équipe

teamster *n Am* camionneur *m*, routier(ère) *m,f*; **the Teamsters** *(union)* = syndicat américain des camionneurs

teamwork *n* travail *m* d'équipe

teaser *n Mktg* **teaser ad** aguiche *f*; **teaser campaign** campagne *f* teasing

techie *n Fam Comptr* = terme péjoratif ou humoristique désignant les informaticiens

technical *adj* technique ❑ **technical adviser** conseiller(ère) *m,f* technique; **technical analysis** analyse *f* sur graphiques; **technical assistance, technical backup** assistance *f* technique; *St Exch* **technical correction** correction *f* d'un cours en Bourse; **technical department** service *m* technique; **technical director** directeur(trice) *m,f* des services techniques; **technical equipment** capital *m* technique; **technical handbook, technical instructions** notice f technique; **technical manager** directeur(trice) technique; **technical skill** compétence f technique; **technical standard** norme f technique; Comptr **technical support** support m technique

technician n technicien(enne) m,f

technique n technique f

technology n technologie f ❑ **technology park** parc m technologique

teething troubles npl difficultés fpl initiales ou de départ; **we're having teething troubles with the new computer** nous avons des problèmes de mise en route avec le nouvel ordinateur

> **❛❛**
> Who'd have thought you could make supermarket shopping work online? Top marks to Tesco for having the vision to go ahead and do it. Despite early **teething troubles**, since its revamp this service has become simple and efficient.
> **❜❜**

telebanking n banque f à domicile

telecomms npl (abbr **telecommunications**) télécommunications fpl

telecommunications npl télécommunications fpl ❑ **telecommunications network** réseau m de télécommunications; **telecommunications satellite** satellite m de télécommunications

telecommute vi faire du télétravail, télétravailler

telecommuter n télétravailleur(euse) m,f

telecommuting n télétravail m

> **❛❛**
> For employees, **telecommuting** can be a huge boon, allowing them to live anywhere they choose and forgo the frustrations usually associated with a good job in a crowded city. For the company, the promise of a **telecommuting** program is equally grand. The company can be sure its current work force will be happier and more productive, and it can look forward to hiring the best people for the job, regardless of their locations.
> **❜❜**

teleconference n téléconférence f

teleconferencing n téléconférence f

telegenic adj télégénique

telegram n télégramme m; **to send sb a telegram** envoyer un télégramme à qn

telegraph 1 n télégraphe m ❑ **telegraph service** service m télégraphique

2 vt (news) télégraphier; (person) envoyer un télégramme à
3 vi télégraphier

telegraphic adj télégraphique ❑ **telegraphic address** adresse f télégraphique; Fin **telegraphic transfer** transfert m télégraphique

telemarketing n télémarketing m

telematics n télématique f

teleorder 1 n commande f par ordinateur
2 vt commander par ordinateur

telephone 1 n téléphone m; **to be on the telephone** (have a telephone) être abonné(e) au téléphone; (talking) être au téléphone; **to have a good telephone manner** savoir bien parler au téléphone; **to order sth by telephone** commander qch par téléphone; **the boss is on the telephone for you** le patron te demande au téléphone; **you're wanted on the telephone** on vous demande au téléphone ❑ **telephone banking** opérations fpl bancaires par téléphone; **telephone bill** facture f de téléphone; **telephone book** annuaire m (téléphonique); **telephone call** appel m téléphonique, coup m de téléphone; **telephone canvassing** prospection f téléphonique, démarchage m à distance, télédémarchage m; **telephone code area** circonscription f téléphonique; **telephone communications** liaison f téléphonique; **telephone dealing** cotation f par téléphone; **telephone directory** annuaire (téléphonique); **telephone exchange** central m téléphonique; **telephone follow-up** relance f téléphonique; Mktg **telephone interview** entretien m téléphonique, entretien par telephone; **telephone line** ligne f téléphonique; **telephone link** liaison téléphonique; **telephone marketing** prospection téléphonique; **telephone message** message m téléphonique; **telephone network** réseau m téléphonique; **telephone number** numéro m de téléphone; **telephone order** commande f téléphonique ou par téléphone; **telephone prospecting** démarchage à distance; **telephone sales** ventes fpl par téléphone; **telephone selling** vente par téléphone; **telephone subscriber** abonné(e) m,f du téléphone; **telephone survey** enquête f téléphonique, enquête par téléphone; **telephone system** réseau téléphonique
2 vt téléphoner à; **to telephone New York** appeler New York
3 vi téléphoner

telephonist n Br téléphoniste mf

telephony n téléphonie f

teleprinter n Br téléscripteur m, téléimprimeur m

teleprocessing n télétraitement m, télégestion f

telesales n phoning m, téléventes fpl ❑ **telesales person** vendeur(euse) m,f par téléphone

teleshopping n téléachat m, achats mpl à domicile

teletex n Comptr télétex m

teletypewriter n Am téléscripteur m, téléimprimeur m

television n télévision f ❏ **television advertisement** publicité f télévisée; **television advertising** publicité télévisée; **television audience** (reached by advertising) audience f télévisuelle; **television campaign** campagne f télévisuelle; **television channel** chaîne f de télévision; **television commercial** spot m; Br **television licence** redevance f; **television sponsoring** parrainage-télévision m; **television tie-in** partenariat m télévision; **television viewer** téléspectateur(trice) m,f; **television viewing panel** panel m de téléspectateurs

teleworker n télétravailleur(euse) m,f

teleworking n télétravail m

> ❝
> The mass adoption of **teleworking** and the death of the City worker is still some way off. Moreover, though **teleworking** projects typically result in 20% better productivity from employees, too many fail because of inflexible management.
> ❞

telex 1 n télex m; **to send sth by telex** envoyer qch par télex ❏ **telex message** message m télex; **telex transfer** virement m par télex
2 vt envoyer par télex, télexer

teller n caissier(ère) m,f, guichetier(ère) m,f

Telnet n Comptr Telnet m

temp 1 n intérimaire mf ❏ **temp agency** agence f d'intérim
2 vi faire de l'intérim

temping n intérim m ❏ **temping agency** agence f d'intérim

template n Comptr (for keyboard) réglette f; (for program) modèle m

temporary adj (work, employee) intérimaire, temporaire; (measures) temporaire, provisoire ❏ **temporary contract** (for employment) contrat m temporaire; Customs **temporary entry** admission f temporaire; Comptr **temporary file** fichier m temporaire; Customs **temporary importation** importation f temporaire; **temporary labour** main-d'œuvre f temporaire; **temporary measures** mesures fpl provisoires; **temporary staff** personnel m intérimaire

tenable adj (company) défendable

tenancy n location f; (period) occupation f; **to take up the tenancy on a house** prendre une maison en location; **during my tenancy of the house** pendant que j'étais locataire de la maison ❏ **tenancy agreement** bail m (de location)

tenant n locataire mf

ten-cent store n Am bazar m

tendency n tendance f (**to** à); **an upward/downward tendency** (in prices) une tendance à la hausse/à la baisse

tender 1 n (bid) offre f, soumission f; **to make or put in a tender for sth** soumissionner ou faire une soumission pour qch; **to invite tenders for a job, to put a job out to tender** mettre un travail en adjudication; **by tender** par voie d'adjudication ❏ **tender document** document m d'offre; **tender form** formule f de soumission; **tender pool** syndicat m d'enchères; **tender proposal** soumission f d'offre
2 vt (**a**) (services) offrir; (bid, offer) faire; (resignation) donner (**b**) (money) tendre
3 vi faire une soumission; **to tender for a contract** soumissionner à un appel d'offres

tenor n Fin (of bill) (terme m d')échéance f

tentative adj (provisional) provisoire

tenure n (of post) occupation f; (of property) bail m; (of land) fermage m; **during his tenure as chairman** pendant qu'il occupait le poste de président

term n (**a**) **terms** (conditions) conditions fpl; (of agreement, contract) termes mpl; (rates, tariffs) conditions, tarifs mpl; **terms and conditions** cahier m des charges; **under the terms of the agreement** selon les termes de l'accord; **on easy terms** avec facilités de paiement ❏ **terms of credit** conditions de crédit; **terms of delivery** conditions de livraison; **terms of exchange** termes d'échange; **terms of payment** conditions ou termes de paiement; **terms of reference** (of commission) attributions fpl, mandat m; Econ **terms of trade** termes de l'échange
(**b**) Fin (of bill of exchange) (terme m d')échéance f; **to set or put a term to sth** mettre fin ou un terme à qch ❏ **term bill** effet m à terme; **term day** (jour m du) terme; **term deposit** dépôt m à terme; **term draft** traite f à terme; Ins **term insurance** assurance f à terme; **term loan** (from borrower's point of view) emprunt m à terme; (from lender's point of view) prêt m à terme
(**c**) (duration) terme m, période f; **the loan shall be for a term of ten years** l'emprunt sera conclu pour dix ans ❏ **term of notice** délai m de préavis; **term of office** mandat m

terminable annuity n rente f à terme

terminal 1 n (**a**) (at airport) terminal m; (for goods) terminus m (**b**) Comptr (poste m) terminal m
2 adj Ins **terminal bonus** = bonus versé au titulaire d'une assurance-vie, au terme de celle-ci; Fin **terminal charges** charges fpl terminales; Acct **terminal loss** perte f finale; St Exch **terminal market** marché m à terme; **terminal**

price cours *m* du livrable

terminate *vt (employment, project)* mettre fin à; *(contract)* résilier

termination *n (of employment, project)* fin *f*; *(of contract)* résiliation *f* ❑ **termination of business** cessation *f* d'activités; **termination clause** clause *f* de résiliation

terminator *n Comptr* terminateur *m*

territorial waters *npl* eaux *fpl* territoriales

territory *n* territoire *m*; *(of salesperson)* territoire, région *f*

tertiary *adj (industry, market)* tertiaire ❑ **tertiary sector** secteur *m* des services

TESSA *n Br Formerly (abbr* **tax-exempt special savings account)** = plan d'épargne exonéré d'impôts

test 1 *n* (**a**) *(of machine, product, equipment)* essai *m*, épreuve *f*, test *m*; *(of quality)* contrôle *m*; **to carry out tests on sth** effectuer des tests sur qch ❑ **test certificate** certificat *m* d'essai (**b**) *(of reaction, popularity)* évaluation *f* ❑ *Mktg* **test area** zone *f* ou région *f* test; *Mktg* **test city** ville-test *f*; *Mktg* **test market** marché *m* témoin, marché test; *Mktg* **test shop** magasin *m* laboratoire; *Mktg* **test site** site-témoin *m*
   2 *vt* (**a**) *(machine, product, equipment)* essayer; *(quality)* contrôler (**b**) *(reaction, popularity)* mesurer, évaluer

tester *n (person)* contrôleur(euse) *m,f*, vérificateur(trice) *m,f*; *(machine)* appareil *m* de contrôle *ou* de vérification

testimonial *n (certificate)* attestation *f*; *(reference)* recommandation *f* ❑ *Mktg* **testimonial advertising** témoignage *m*, publicité *f* testimoniale

testing *n (of machine, product)* essai *m*, épreuve *f*; *(of quality)* contrôle *m*

test-market *vt Mktg* tester sur le marché

text 1 *n Comptr* texte *m* ❑ **text block** bloc *m* de texte; **text buffer** mémoire *f* tampon de texte; **text editor** éditeur *m* de texte; **text field** champ *m* de texte; **text file** fichier *m* texte; **text layout** disposition *f* de texte; *Tel* **text message** message texte *m*, mini-message *m*; **text mode** mode *m* texte; **text processing** traitement *m* de texte; **text processor** (unité *f* de) traitement de texte; **text wrap** habillage *m* du texte
   2 *vt Tel* envoyer un message texte *ou* un mini-message à

text-message *vt Tel* envoyer un message texte *ou* un mini-message à

theoretical inventory *n* inventaire *m* théorique

thermal *adj Comptr* **thermal paper** papier *m* thermique *ou* thermosensible; **thermal printer** imprimante *f* thermique *ou* thermoélectrique

think tank *n* groupe *m* d'experts

third *adj* troisième ❑ *Am* **third class** *(for mail)* ≃ tarif *m* lent; **third party, third person** tierce personne *f*, tiers *m*; **third quarter** *(of year)* troisième trimestre *m*; **the Third World** le tiers-monde

third-class *adj Am* ≃ au tarif lent

third-generation, 3G *adj Comptr, Tel* de troisième génération, 3G

third-party *adj Ins* **third-party holder** tierce détenteur(trice) *m,f*; **third-party insurance** assurance *f* au tiers; **third-party liability** responsabilité *f* au tiers; **third-party owner** tiers possesseur *m*; **third-party risk** risque *m* de recours de tiers; **third-party subscriber** tiers souscripteur(trice) *m,f*

three-button mouse *n Comptr* souris *f* à trois boutons

three-level channel *n* canal *m* de distribution long

threshold *n* seuil *m*; **the government has raised tax thresholds in line with inflation** le gouvernement a relevé les tranches de l'impôt pour tenir compte de l'inflation ❑ **threshold agreement** accord *m* d'indexation des salaires sur les prix; *EU* **threshold price** prix *m* du seuil

thrift *n Am* caisse *f* d'épargne ❑ **thrift institution** caisse d'épargne; **thrift shop** = magasin vendant des articles d'occasion au profit d'œuvres charitables

thrive *vi (company, industry)* prospérer

thriving *adj (company, industry)* prospère, florissant(e)

through 1 *prep Am* **Monday through Friday** de lundi à vendredi
   2 *adj Fin* **through bill** connaissement *m* direct; **through freight** marchandises *fpl* en transit
   3 *adv (on telephone)* **to get through to sb** joindre qn; **to put sb through to sb** mettre qn en ligne avec qn, passer qn à qn

throughput *n* débit *m*, rendement *m*; *Comptr* capacité *f* de traitement

thumbnail *n Comptr* vignette *f*

thumbtack *n Am* punaise *f*

tick *Br* **1** *n* (**a**) *Fam (credit)* crédit *m*; **to buy sth on tick** acheter qch à crédit (**b**) *(mark)* coche *f*; **to put a tick against sth** cocher qch (**c**) *St Exch* **tick size** échelon *m* de cotation
   2 *vt (on form)* cocher; **tick the appropriate box** cocher la case correspondante

ticket n (**a**) *(for plane, train)* billet m; *(for underground, bus)* billet, ticket m (**b**) *(label)* étiquette f (de prix) (**c**) *St Exch* **ticket day** jour m de la déclaration des noms

▸ **tie up** vt sep *(money)* immobiliser; **their money is all tied up in shares** leur argent est entièrement investi dans des actions

tied adj **tied agent** agent m lié; **tied loan** prêt m conditionnel *ou* à condition; **tied outlet** magasin m sous franchise exclusive, concession f exclusive

tied-up capital n *Fin* capital m engagé

tie-in n *Mktg* = livre, cassette, vidéo etc lié à un film, une émission ou un concert ❑ **tie-in promotion** promotion f collective; **tie-in sale** vente f jumelée

> “
> Burger King Corp. won exclusive sponsorship rights to the Backstreet Boys' fall tour and will launch a CD and video **tie-in** in August … This is the first national music **tie-in** for Burger King, which is targeting teens and tweens with the promotion. Although the chain did not disclose how it would distribute the CD and video, a **tie-in** with its Big Kids Meal is expected.
> ”

tie-up n *(merger)* (absorption-)fusion f, unification f

TIFF n *Comptr* *(abbr* **Tagged Image File Format)** (format m) TIFF m

tiger economy n = pays à l'économie très performante; **the (Asian) tiger economies** les dragons mpl *ou* les tigres mpl asiatiques

tight adj (**a**) *(schedule, deadline)* serré(e) (**b**) *(budget, credit, discount)* serré(e), resserré(e); **to work on a tight budget** travailler avec un budget serré

tighten vt *(budget, credit)* resserrer

tile vt *Comptr (windows)* afficher en mosaïque

till n caisse f; **to do the till** faire la caisse ❑ **till receipt** ticket m de caisse, reçu m de caisse

time n (**a**) *(in general)* temps m ❑ **time frame** délai m; **time limit** délai; **the work must be completed within the time limit** le travail doit être terminé avant la date limite; **time management** gestion f du temps de travail; **time to market** temps m d'accès au marché; **time and methods study** étude des temps et des méthodes; **time and motion consultant** expert m en productivité, spécialiste mf de l'organisation scientifique du travail; **time and motion studies** organisation f scientifique du travail, OST f; **time and motion study** étude de productivité *(qui porte sur l'organisation scientifique du travail)*; *Mktg* **time pricing** fixation f des prix en fonction du moment; *Comptr* **time sharing** partage m de temps; **time slot** créneau m horaire; *St Exch*

time value valeur f temporelle (**b**) *(by clock)* heure f; **time of arrival/departure** heure d'arrivée/de départ ❑ **time card** feuille f de présence; **time clock** pointeuse f; **time difference** décalage m horaire; **time rate** rémunération f au temps passé; **time sheet** fiche f horaire; **time work** travail m à l'heure; **time worker** *(paid hourly)* horaire mf; *(paid daily)* journalier(ère) m,f (**c**) *(credit)* terme m; *Am* **to buy sth on time** acheter qch à tempérament *ou* à terme ❑ *St Exch* **time bargain** marché m à terme; *Fin* **time bill** traite f à terme; *Am* **time deposit** dépôt m à terme; **time draft** traite à terme; **time loan** emprunt m à terme; *Ins* **time policy** police f à terme; **time value** valeur f temporelle (**d**) *(hourly wages)* **we pay time and a half on weekends** nous payons les heures du week-end une fois et demie le tarif normal; **overtime is paid at double time** les heures supplémentaires sont payées *ou* comptées double

> “
> Avnet Applied Computing (AAC) … officially opened a new engineering laboratory built to provide a resource-rich environment where original equipment manufacturer customers and AAC engineers can work side-by-side to cut the **time to market** of their designs.
> ”

timekeeper n (**a**) *(supervisor)* pointeau m (**b**) *(employee)* **he's a good timekeeper** il est toujours à l'heure, il est toujours très ponctuel; **he's a bad timekeeper** il n'est jamais à l'heure

timekeeping n *Br (of employee)* ponctualité f; **he was sacked for bad timekeeping** il a été renvoyé pour manque de ponctualité *ou* non-respect des horaires

timetable **1** n (**a**) *(for transport)* horaire m (**b**) *(schedule)* emploi m du temps **2** vt *(talks, meeting)* *(fix time of)* fixer une heure pour; *(fix date of)* fixer une date pour

tin parachute n = indemnité versée à un employé lorsque son poste est supprimé suite à une fusion

> “
> Even less common than gold or silver parachutes are **tin parachutes** – severance plans that cover all of the employees of a company in the event it undergoes a change in control. The value of a tin parachute will vary significantly from company to company, says Siske, but will typically provide a severance payment linked to the recipients' years of service and/or their age, often with a cap, such as 1.5 times annual compensation.
> ”

tip 1 n (cash) pourboire m
   2 vt donner un pourboire à

Tipp-Ex® **1** n correcteur m liquide, Tipp-Ex®
m
   2 vt **to Tipp-Ex® sth out** effacer qch (avec du
Tipp-Ex®)

TIR n (abbr **Transport International Routier**)
TIR m

title n (**a**) Law droit m, titre m □ **title deed** titre
(constitutif) de propriété (**b**) Comptr **title bar**
barre f de titre

TL n (**a**) (abbr **time loan**) emprunt m à terme (**b**)
(abbr **total loss**) perte f totale

TM n (abbr **trademark**) marque f (de fabrique)

TMT (abbr **technology, media and telecommunications**) TMT □ **TMT company** entreprise f
du secteur TMT; **TMT sector** secteur m TMT

> ❝
> The company's story is typical of many of
> the transformations that took place in the
> so-called **TMT sector** during the internet
> frenzy in that it decided to move away from
> its old defence electronics business to focus
> on supplying telecoms equipment.
> ❞

Tobin tax n Fin taxe f Tobin

toggle Comptr **1** n **toggle key** touche f à bascule; **toggle switch** commande f à bascule
   2 vi basculer; **to toggle between two applications** alterner entre deux applications

token adj (payment, rent) symbolique □ Comptr
token ring network réseau m en anneau à jeton; Ind **token strike** grève f symbolique ou
d'avertissement

tolerance n tolérance f (permise) □ **tolerance
margin** marge f de tolérance

toll n (**a**) (on bridge, road) péage m □ **toll bridge**
pont m à péage; **toll road** route f à péage (**b**) Am
Tel frais mpl d'interurbain □ **toll call** communication f interurbaine

toll-free Am **1** adj **toll-free number** ≃ numéro
m vert
   2 adv (call) gratuitement

tone n Tel tonalité f; **leave a message after the
tone** (on answering machine) laissez votre message après le bip sonore

toner n (for printer, fax) toner m, encre f □ **toner
cartridge** cartouche f de toner ou d'encre; **toner cassette** cassette f de toner ou d'encre

tonnage n (of ship) tonnage m, jauge f; (of port)
tonnage □ **tonnage certificate** certificat m de
jaugeage

tonne n tonne f métrique

tool n (implement) outil m; (set of) **tools** outillage m; **the computer has become an essential
tool for most businesses** l'ordinateur est devenu un outil essentiel pour la plupart des entreprises; **to down tools** (stop working) cesser de
travailler; (go on strike) se mettre en grève
□ Comptr **tool bar** barre f d'outils; **tool palette**
palette f d'outils

toolbox n Comptr boîte f à outils

top 1 n St Exch **to buy at the top and sell at the
bottom** acheter au plus haut et vendre au plus
bas; **the top of the range** le haut de gamme
   2 adj **this job should be given top priority** ce
travail doit être fait en priorité □ **top copy** (of
document) original m; **top management** cadres
mpl supérieurs; **top price** prix m fort; **top quality** qualité f supérieure; **top rate** (of tax) taux m
maximum
   3 vt (exceed) dépasser; **production topped
five tons last month** la production a dépassé
les cinq tonnes le mois dernier; **to top sb's offer**
renchérir sur l'offre de qn

top-down adj hiérarchisé(e) □ Mktg **top-
down forecasting** prévisions fpl hiérarchisées;
top-down management gestion f par le haut

> ❝
> Forget capital; it's relatively easy to obtain
> nowadays. Today's scarce, sought-after
> strategic resource is expertise, which
> comes in the form of employees. Although
> organizations have changed mightily from
> the days of hierarchical, **top-down man-
> agement**, they still have a long way to go.
> ❞

top-heavy adj (company, structure) (with too
many senior staff) trop lourd(e) du haut; (overcapitalized) surcapitalisé(e)

top-of-the-range adj haut de gamme □ **top-
of-the-range item** article m haut de gamme

top-up card n Tel recharge f

▶ **tot up** vt sep Br additionner

total 1 n total m; **the total comes to $389** cela
fait au total 389 dollars
   2 adj (amount, cost, output etc) total(e); **marketing the product accounts for 20 percent of
the total costs** le coût de commercialisation
du produit revient à 20 pour cent du coût total
□ **total annual expenses** consommations fpl de
l'exercice; **total assets** total m de l'actif; **total
asset value** valeur f de bilan; **total constructive
loss** perte f totale; **total contract value** valeur
totale du contrat; **total distribution cost** coût
m total de distribution; **total exemption** exonération f totale; **total export sales** chiffre m
d'affaires à l'exportation; **total fixed cost** coût
fixe total; **total gross income** revenu m brut
global; **total insured value** valeur totale assurée; **total liabilities** total du passif; **total loss**
perte totale; **total loss settlement** règlement
m en perte totale; **total net income** revenu net

global; **total payable** total à payer; **total quality control** contrôle *m* de la qualité globale; **total quality management** gestion *f* de la qualité globale; **total sales** chiffre d'affaires global; **total unit cost** coût complet unitaire

3 *vt* (**a**) *(add up)* additionner (**b**) *(amount to)* s'élever à

totalize *vt* totaliser, additionner

touch *n* (**a**) *(communication)* **to be in touch with sb** être en contact avec qn; **to get in touch with sb** se mettre en contact avec qn (**b**) *Comptr* **touch screen** écran *m* tactile; **touch screen computer** ordinateur *m* à écran tactile

touchpad mouse *n* *Comptr* souris *f* tactile

touch-sensitive *adj* *Comptr (screen)* tactile; *(key, switch)* à effleurement

touch-tone telephone *n* téléphone *m* à touches

touch-type *vi* taper au toucher

tour *n* *(by tourist)* voyage *m* ❏ **tour operator** voyagiste *m*, tour-opérateur *m*

tourism *n* tourisme *m*

tourist *n* touriste *mf* ❏ **tourist attraction** centre *m* d'intérêt touristique; **tourist board** office *m* du tourisme; **tourist centre** centre de tourisme; **tourist class** *(in air travel)* classe *f* touriste; **tourist facilities** installations *fpl* touristiques; **tourist (information) office** bureau *m* de tourisme, syndicat *m* d'initiative; **tourist season** saison *f* touristique; **the tourist trade** le tourisme

tower *n* *Comptr* boîtier *m* vertical, tour *f* ❏ **tower system** système *m* à boîtier vertical *ou* à tour

town *n* **town and country planning** aménagement *m* urbain et rural; **town hall** hôtel *m* de ville; **town planner** urbaniste *mf*; **town planning** urbanisme *m*

TQC *n* *(abbr* **total quality control**) QG *f*

TQM *n* *(abbr* **total quality management**) gestion *f* de la QG

trackball *n* *Comptr* boule *f* de commande, trackball *m ou f*

tracker fund *n* *St Exch* fonds *m* indiciel *ou* à gestion indicielle

trackpad *n* *Comptr* tablette *f* tactile

trade 1 *n* (**a**) *(commerce)* commerce *m*, affaires *fpl*; **it's good for trade** cela fait marcher le commerce; **to do a roaring trade** faire des affaires en or ❏ **trade acceptance** acceptation *f* commerciale; **trade agreement** accord *m* commercial; **trade association** association *f* professionnelle; **trade balance** balance *f* commerciale; **trade ban** interdiction *f* de commerce; **trade barrier** barrière *f* commerciale; **trade bills** effets *mpl* de commerce; **trade**

bloc union *f* douanière; *Acct* **trade credit** crédit *m* fournisseur *ou* commercial; *Acct* **trade creditor** créancier(ère) *m,f* d'exploitation; **trade cycle** cycle *m* de commercialisation; *Acct* **trade debt** dettes *fpl* d'exploitation; *Acct* **trade debtor** compte *m ou* créance *f* client; **trade deficit** balance commerciale déficitaire, déficit *m* commercial; **trade delegation** délégation *f* commerciale; *Br* **Trade Descriptions Act** = loi qui empêche la publicité mensongère; **trade embargo** embargo *m* commercial; **trade exhibition** foire-exposition *f*, exposition *f* commerciale; **trade fair** foire *f* commerciale; **trade figures** chiffre *m* d'affaires; **trade gap** déficit commercial; **trade marketing** marketing *m* commercial, trade marketing *m*; **trade name** *(of product)* nom *m* de marque; *(of company)* raison *f* commerciale; **trade negotiations** négociations *fpl* commerciales; **trade policy** politique *f* commerciale; **trade practices** usages *mpl* commerciaux; **trade price** *(of stock)* prix *m* de négociation; *(of product)* prix marchand; **trade restraint** restriction *f* de concurrence; *St Exch* **trade ticket** avis *m* d'opéré, avis d'opération sur titres

(**b**) *(profession)* métier *m*; **to be in the trade** être du métier; **he's a plumber by trade** il est plombier de son état *ou* métier ❏ **trade body** syndicat *m* professionnel; **trade directory** répertoire *m* des métiers; **trade discount** remise *f* professionnelle; **trade journal** journal *m* professionnel; *Br* **trade press** presse *f* spécialisée *ou* professionnelle; **trade register** registre *m* du commerce; **trade representative** délégué(e) *m,f* commercial(e); **trade secret** secret *m* professionnel *ou* de fabrication; *Br* **trade union** syndicat *m*; **Trades Union Congress** = confédération des syndicats britanniques; **trade union council** conseil *m* syndical; **trade unionism** syndicalisme *m*; **trade unionist** syndicaliste *mf*; **trade union tariff** tarif *m* syndical

(**c**) *Am (transaction)* marché *m*, affaire *f*

2 *vt St Exch* négocier ❏ **traded option** option *f* négociable *ou* cotée

3 *vi* (**a**) *(do business)* faire du commerce, commercer; **he trades in clothing** il est négociant en confection; **the company trades under the name of Prism Ltd** l'entreprise opère sous le nom de Prism Ltd; **to trade at a loss** vendre à perte; **to trade with sb** avoir des relations commerciales avec qn

(**b**) *St Exch (of shares, commodity, currency)* s'échanger (**at** à); **corn is trading at $2.20** le maïs se négocie à 2,20 dollars

▸ **trade down** *vi St Exch* acheter des valeurs basses

▸ **trade in** *vt sep* faire reprendre

▸ **trade up** *vi St Exch* acheter des valeurs hautes

trade-in *n* reprise *f* ❏ **trade-in allowance** valeur *f* de reprise; ***trade-in facility*** facilité *f* de reprise; ***trade-in price*** prix *m* à la reprise; ***trade-in value*** valeur de reprise

trademark *n* marque *f* (de fabrique)

trade-off analysis *n* Mktg analyse *f* conjointe

trader *n* commerçant(e) *m,f*, marchand(e) *m,f* (**in** en); *(on large scale)* négociant(e) *m,f* (**in** en); *St Exch* opérateur(trice) *m,f*

tradesman *n* (**a**) *(tradesman)* commerçant *m*, marchand *m* (**b**) *(skilled workman)* ouvrier *m* qualifié

trading *n* commerce *m*, négoce *m*; **trading on the Stock Exchange was heavy** le volume de transactions à la Bourse était important □ *Acct* ***trading account*** compte *m* d'exploitation; ***trading bank*** banque *f* commerciale; ***trading capital*** capital *m* de roulement; ***trading company*** entreprise *f* commerciale; *St Exch* ***trading day*** jour *m* de Bourse; *Br* ***trading estate*** zone *f* industrielle; *St Exch* ***trading floor*** parquet *m*, corbeille *f*; ***trading hours*** *Fin* heures *fpl* d'ouverture; *St Exch* horaires *fpl* des criées; *St Exch* ***trading instrument*** instrument *m* de négociation, outil *m* de spéculation; ***trading licence*** carte *f* de commerce; ***trading loss*** perte *f*; *St Exch* ***trading member*** intermédiaire *m* négociateur; *St Exch* ***trading month*** mois *m* d'échéance; ***trading nation*** nation *f* commerçante; *St Exch* ***trading order*** ordre *m* de négociation; ***trading partner*** partenaire *m* commercial; *Am St Exch* ***trading post*** parquet, corbeille; ***trading profit*** bénéfice *m* d'exploitation; *Acct* ***trading and profit and loss account*** compte de résultat; *St Exch* ***trading range*** écart *m* de prix, fourchette *f* de cotation; **prices are stuck in a trading range** les prix ne varient pas beaucoup; ***trading results*** résultats *mpl* de l'exercice; *St Exch* ***trading room*** salle *f* des changes *ou* des marchés; *St Exch* ***trading session*** séance *f* boursière; ***trading stamp*** timbre-prime *m*, vignette-épargne *f*; ***trading standards*** normes *fpl* de conformité; *Br* ***Trading Standards Office*** ≃ Direction *f* de la consommation et de la représentation des fraudes; ***trading volume*** volume *m* d'affaires; ***trading year*** exercice *m* comptable

> **❝**
> The platinum price moved higher Thursday with one analyst from Merrill Lynch & Co. New York, observing that the price is meandering in the **trading range** with a slight phasing out of physical metal on the market.
> **❞**

traffic 1 *n (trade)* commerce *m*; *(illegal)* trafic *m* □ *Mktg* ***traffic builder*** article *m* d'appel
2 *vi* **to traffic in sth** faire le commerce de qch; *(illegally)* faire le trafic de qch

train 1 *vt (employee)* former; **he's training**

somebody to take over from him il forme son successeur; **she was trained in economics** elle a reçu une formation d'économiste
2 *vi* recevoir une formation; **to train as an accountant** recevoir une formation de comptable; **where did you train?** où avez-vous reçu votre formation?

trained *adj* qualifié(e); *(engineer, translator)* diplômé(e)

trainee *n* stagiaire *mf*; ***trainee computer programmer*** élève *mf* programmeur

traineeship *n* stage *f*

training *n* formation *f*; **I've had business training** j'ai suivi une formation commerciale □ ***training centre*** centre *m* de formation; ***training course*** stage *m* (de formation); ***training division*** division *f* de formation; ***training officer*** directeur(trice) *m,f* de formation; ***training programme*** programme *m* de formation; ***training scheme*** plan *m* de formation; ***training time*** temps *m* de formation

tranche *n (of loan, payment, shares)* tranche *f*

transact *vt (deal, purchase, sale)* traiter, négocier; **to transact business (with sb)** faire des affaires (avec qn)

transaction *n* (**a**) *(deal)* opération *f* (commerciale), affaire *f*; *Fin, St Exch* transaction *f*; **cash transactions have increased** les mouvements d'espèces ont augmenté □ ***transaction costs*** frais *mpl* de Bourse (**b**) *(act of transacting)* conduite *f*, gestion *f*; **transaction of business will continue as normal** la conduite des affaires se poursuivra comme à l'accoutumé

transfer 1 *n* (**a**) *(of employee)* mutation *f*; *(of goods)* transfert *m*, transport *m*; *(of air passenger)* transfert; *Fin, St Exch (of shares, funds, capital)* transfert; *Banking (of money from one account to another)* virement *m* □ ***transfer advice*** avis *m* de virement; ***transfer of bonded goods*** mutation *f* d'entrepôt; ***transfer certificate*** certificat *m* de transfert; ***transfer cheque*** chèque *m* de virement; *St Exch* ***transfer duty*** droits *mpl* de transfert; *St Exch* ***transfer by endorsement*** transmission *f* par endossement; *St Exch* ***transfer fee*** frais *mpl* de transfert; *St Exch* ***transfer form*** formule *f* de transfert; *Fin* ***transfer order*** ordre *m* de virement; ***transfer passenger*** *(between flights)* voyageur(euse) *m,f* en transit; ***transfer payment*** paiement *m* de transfert; *St Exch* ***transfer register*** registre *m* des transferts; ***transfer restrictions*** restrictions *fpl* de transfert
(**b**) *Acct (of debt)* transport *m*; *(of entry)* contre-passation *f* □ ***transfer entry*** article *m* de contre-passation
(**c**) *Law (of property, ownership, rights)* cession *f* □ ***transfer deed*** acte *m* de cession; *Br* ***transfer tax*** droits *mpl* de succession; *(between living*

persons) droit de mutation
   (d) *Comptr (of data)* transfert *m* ❏ **transfer rate** taux *m* de transfert; **transfer speed** vitesse *f* de transfert
   2 *vt* **(a)** *(employee)* muter; *(goods)* transférer, transporter; *Fin (shares, funds, capital)* transférer; *Banking (money)* virer
   (b) *Acct (debt)* transporter; *(entry)* contrepasser
   (c) *Law (property, ownership, rights)* céder, faire cession de; **she will transfer the rights over to him** elle va lui céder les droits
   (d) *Tel (call)* transférer; **I'm transferring you now** je vous mets en communication ❏ *Br* **transfer charge call** communication *f* en PCV
   (e) *Comptr (data)* transférer
   3 *vi* **(a)** *(of employee)* être muté(e); **to transfer to a different department** être transféré(e) dans un autre service
   (b) *(of air passenger)* changer

transferable *adj (document)* transmissible; *Law (property, ownership, rights)* cessible ❏ **transferable bond** obligation *f* transmissible ou transférable; **transferable credit** crédit *m* transférable; **transferable letter of credit** lettre *f* de crédit transférable; **transferable securities** valeurs *fpl* négociables; **transferable share** action *f* au porteur

transferee *n Fin, St Exch (of shares, funds, capital)* bénéficiaire *mf*; *Law (of property, ownership, rights)* cessionnaire *mf*

transferor *n Fin, St Exch (of shares, funds, capital)* vendeur(euse) *m,f*; *Law (of property, ownership, rights)* cédant(e) *m,f*

tranship, transhipment = **transship, transshipment**

transit *n* transit *m*; **in transit** en transit; **goods lost in transit** marchandises perdues en cours de route ❏ **transit entry** déclaration *f* de transit; **transit permit** permis *m* de transit; **transit port** port *m* de transit; **transit system** régime *m* de transit; **transit visa** visa *m* de transit

translate 1 *vt* traduire
   2 *vi* traduire; **she translates for the EU** elle fait des traductions pour l'Union européenne

translation *n* traduction *f* ❏ **translation agency** agence *f* ou bureau *m* de traduction

translator *n* traducteur(trice) *m,f*

transmission *n Comptr (of data)* transmission ❏ **transmission protocol** protocole *m* de transmission

transparency *n (for overhead projector)* transparent *m*

transport 1 *n* transport *m*; **means of transport** moyen *m* de transport ❏ **transport advertising** affichage *m* transport; **transport allowance** indemnité *f* de déplacement; **trans-**

port charges frais *mpl* de transport; **transport company** société *f* de transport; **transport costs** frais de transport; **transport facilities** moyens *mpl* de transport
   2 *vt* transporter

transportation *n* transport *m*

transship *vt* transborder

transshipment *n* transbordement *m* ❏ **transshipment bill of lading** connaissement *m* de transbordement;

trash *n Am Comptr* poubelle *f*

travel 1 *n* voyages *mpl* ❏ **travel agency** agence *f* de voyages; **travel agent** agent *m* de voyages; **travel agent's** agence de voyages; **travel allowance** indemnité *f* de déplacement; **travel documents** documents *mpl* de voyage; **travel expenses** frais *mpl* de déplacement; **travel goods** articles *mpl* de voyage
   2 *vi* voyager; **to travel on business** voyager pour affaires

traveler, traveling *Am* = **traveller, travelling**

traveller, *Am* **traveler** *n* voyageur(euse) *m,f* ❏ **traveller's cheque,** *Am* **traveler's check** chèque *m* de voyage

travelling, *Am* **traveling 1** *n* voyages *mpl* ❏ **travelling allowance** indemnité *f* de déplacement; **travelling expenses** frais *mpl* de déplacement
   2 *adj* **travelling salesman** voyageur *m* de commerce

treasurer *n* trésorier(ère) *m,f* ❏ **treasurer's report** rapport *m* financier

treasury *n Fin (funds)* trésor *m* (public); *(place)* trésorerie *f*; **the Treasury** *(government department)* ≃ le ministère des finances ❏ **Treasury bill** ≃ bon *m* du Trésor; **Treasury bond** ≃ bon du Trésor (à long terme); **Treasury note** billet *m* de trésorerie; **treasury savings** économies *fpl* de financement; **Treasury scrip** inscription *f* sur le grand-livre; *Am* **Treasury Secretary** ≃ ministre *m* des finances; **treasury swap** échange *m* cambiste; **Treasury warrant** mandat *m* du Trésor

❝
Goldman Sachs has been notified that the Securities and Exchange Commission plans to pursue a case against it for allegedly trading US **Treasury bonds** based on inside information … The $3,000bn **Treasury** market rallied, with 30-year bonds seeing the biggest one-day gain in 14 years.
                                                          ❞

treaty *n (international)* traité *m*; *(between individuals)* contrat *m*, accord *m*; **they sold the property by private treaty** ils ont vendu la propriété par accord privé

treble *vt* tripler

tree *n (of data)* arbre *m* ❑ *tree diagram, tree structure* arborescence *f*

trend *n* tendance *f*; **the general trend of the market** les tendances du marché; **house prices are on an upward/downward trend** le prix des maisons est à la hausse/baisse ❑ *Mktg trend analysis* analyse *f* des tendances; *trend reversal* renversement *m* de tendance

triad market *n Mktg* marché *m* de la triade

trial 1 *n* **(a)** *(test)* essai *m*; **to give sth a trial** faire l'essai de qch; **on trial** à l'essai; **give her a month's trial before you take her on** prenez-la un mois à l'essai avant de l'embaucher ❑ *trial lot* envoi *m* à titre d'essai; *trial offer* offre *f* d'essai; *trial order* commande *f* d'essai; *trial period* période *f* d'essai; *trial subscription* abonnement *m* à l'essai
(b) *Acct trial balance* balance *f* d'inventaire
(c) *Law* procès *m*; **to stand trial (for sth)** passer en justice (pour qch); **to bring sb to trial (for sth)** faire passer qn en justice (pour qch)
2 *vt* tester

tri-band *adj Tel* tri-bande

tribunal *n* tribunal *m*

trickle-down theory *n Econ* = théorie selon laquelle les richesses accumulées par un petit nombre bénéficieront à tous les membres de la société

❝
In retirement Galbraith has continued in articles, speeches, and books to argue for strong government, progressive taxes and public spending. He is not a "Third Way" man. He ridiculed the Reaganite **trickle-down theory** of wealth distribution, preferring the earthier phrase "the horse-and-sparrow theory" – "If you feed the horse enough oats, some will pass through to the road for the sparrows."
❞

trigger 1 *n (of change, decision)* déclenchement *m*; **the strike was the trigger for nationwide protests** la grève a donné le signal d'un mouvement de contestation dans tous le pays
2 *vt* déclencher; **the crisis has triggered huge numbers of closures** la crise a déclenché un grand nombre de fermetures

▸ **trigger off** *vt sep* déclencher

triple-A rating *n St Exch* notation *f* AAA

triple witching hour *n Am Fam St Exch* = heure d'avant la fermeture de la Bourse le troisième vendredi des mois de mars, juin, septembre et décembre, caractérisée par une activité intense

❝
Note that a trade can be put in by a trader to be executed at the market closing price for a given stock. Regardless of what the price is, the trade will be executed. The deluge of orders on the **triple witching hour** at the market closing price often caused the ticker to be delayed up to a half hour at the closing.
❞

triplicate 1 *n* triplicata *m*; **in triplicate** en trois exemplaires
2 *vt (document)* rédiger en trois exemplaires

troubleshoot *vi* régler un problème

troubleshooter *n (in conflict)* médiateur(-trice) *m,f*; *(in crisis)* expert *m (appelé en cas de crise)*

❝
Mr James has a reputation as a corporate **troubleshooter** capable of reviving the fortunes of struggling companies like Railtrack, a record that has earned him the nickname of the Red Adair of the business world. As well as the Dome, his talents have been turned to Dan-Air, the airline, and the British Shoe Corporation.
❞

troubleshooting *n (in conflict)* médiation *f*; *Comptr* dépannage *m*

trough *n Econ (of wave, graph, cycle)* creux *m*

truck 1 *n* camion *m* ❑ *truck driver* camionneur *m*
2 *vt* camionner, transporter par camion

truckage *n Am* camionnage *m*

trucker *n Am* camionneur *m*

true *adj true copy (of document)* copie *f* conforme; *true discount* escompte *f* en dedans; *Acct true and fair view (of accounts)* image *f* fidèle; *true sample* échantillon *m* représentatif

trust *n* **(a)** *Law (investment)* fidéicommis *m*; **to set up a trust for sb** instituer un fidéicommis pour qn ❑ *trust account* compte *m* en fidéicommis; *trust deed* acte *m* de fidéicommis; *trust fund* fonds *m* en fidéicommis **(b)** *Fin (cartel)* trust *m*, cartel *m* ❑ *trust bank* banque *f* de gestion de patrimoine; *trust company* société *f* fiduciaire

trustbuster *n Am Fam* briseur *m* de trusts

trusted third party *n Comptr (for Internet transactions)* tierce partie *f* de confiance

trustee *n Law (of fund, property)* fidéicommissaire *m*; *(of charity)* administrateur(trice) *m,f* ❑ *trustee in bankruptcy* syndic *m* de faillite

try *vt (product)* essayer

TTP n Comptr (abbr **trusted third party**) (for Internet transactions) TPC f

TUC n Br (abbr **Trades Union Congress**) = confédération des syndicats britanniques

turbomarketing n Mktg turbo-marketing m

▶ **turn down** vt sep (applicant, job) refuser; (offer) rejeter

▶ **turn out** vt sep (goods) produire, fabriquer

▶ **turn over** vt sep (capital) faire rouler; **he turns over £1,000 a week** son chiffre d'affaires est de 1000 livres par semaine

▶ **turn round** vt sep (process, deal with) traiter, s'occuper de; **the stocks are turned round every four months** le délai de rotation (des stocks) est de quatre mois

turnaround n (of order) traitement m; **they offer a faster turnaround** leurs délais sont plus courts □ **turnaround time** délai m d'exécution

turnkey adj (project, operation, system) clés en main

turnover n (**a**) Fin (of company) chiffre m d'affaires; **his turnover is £100,000 per annum** il fait 100 000 livres d'affaires par an □ **turnover tax** impôt m ou taxe f sur le chiffre d'affaires (**b**) (of stock) écoulement m, rotation f; (of capital) roulement m; **the staff turnover there is very high** le taux de renouvellement du personnel y est très élevé □ **turnover rate** taux m de rotation

turnround n (**a**) (of stock) rotation f (**b**) (of passenger ship, plane) = temps nécessaire au débarquement et à l'embarquement de nouveaux passagers; (for freight) = temps nécessaire au déchargement et au chargement d'une nouvelle cargaison (**c**) (time taken to complete round trip) temps m de rotation □ **turnround rate** vitesse f de rotation (**d**) Comptr temps m de rotation

tutorial n Comptr didacticiel m □ **tutorial program** didacticiel

twin-pack selling n Mktg vente f jumelée

2G adj Comptr, Tel 2G

2.5G adj Comptr, Tel 2.5G

two-level channel n canal m de distribution long

tycoon n magnat m; **an oil tycoon** un magnat du pétrole

type 1 n (text) caractères mpl
2 vt taper (à la machine)
3 vi taper (à la machine)

▶ **type out** vt sep taper (à la machine)

▶ **type up** vt sep taper (à la machine)

typeface n police f (de caractères)

typewriter n machine f à écrire

typing n dactylographie f □ **typing error** faute f de frappe; **typing paper** papier m machine; **typing pool** équipe f de dactylos; **typing skills** compétences fpl en dactylographie; **typing speed** vitesse f de frappe

typist n dactylographe mf

Uu

UAW n *(abbr* **United Automobile Workers**) = syndicat américain de l'industrie automobile

UBR n *Br Fin (abbr* **uniform business rate**) = taxe assise sur la valeur des locaux commerciaux, ≃ taxe *f* professionnelle

UCATT n *(abbr* **Union of Construction, Allied Trades and Technicians**) = syndicat britannique des employés du bâtiment

UCITS n *Fin (abbr* **undertakings for collective investment in transferables**) OPCVM *m*

UCW n *(abbr* **Union of Communication Workers**) = syndicat britannique des communications

UDC n *Br Admin (abbr* **Urban District Council**) = conseil d'une communauté urbaine

UDM n *(abbr* **Union of Democratic Mineworkers**) = syndicat britannique de mineurs

ullage n = quantité de liquide perdue par l'évaporation ou par des fuites au cours du transport

ultimate *adj* **ultimate consumer** utilisateur(-trice) *m,f* final(e); **ultimate holding company** holding *m* tête de groupe *(dont certaines filiales sont également des holdings)*

umbrella n **umbrella committee** comité *m* de coordination; **umbrella fund** fonds *m* de consolidation; **umbrella organization** organisme *m* de tutelle; **umbrella trademark** marque *f* ombrelle

> ❝ ————————————
> Other so-called advantages they were supposed to offer, such as **umbrella funds** that allowed cheap or free switching between sub-funds, lower charges because of the need for only one set of administration for the **umbrella fund**, have failed to transpire.
> ————————————— ❞

UMTS n *Tel (abbr* **Universal Mobile Telecommunications Services**) UMTS *m*

UMW n *(abbr* **United Mineworkers of America**) = syndicat américain de mineurs

UN n *(abbr* **United Nations**) ONU *f*

unabsorbed cost n coût *m* non-absorbé

unaccounted for *adj (money)* qui manque; **these £60 are unaccounted for in the balance sheet** ces 60 livres ne figurent pas au bilan; **there is still a lot of money unaccounted for** il manque toujours beaucoup d'argent

unadvertised *adj (job)* non affiché(e); *(meeting, visit)* discret(ète), sans publicité

unallocated *adj* non affecté(e), non alloué(e) ❑ **unallocated cash** argent *m* non alloué

unallotted *adj Fin, St Exch (shares)* non réparti(e)

unanimous *adj (consent, decision)* unanime ❑ **unanimous vote** vote *m* à l'unanimité

unappropriated *adj (money)* inutilisé(e), disponible ❑ **unappropriated profits** bénéfices *mpl* non distribués

unassigned revenue n recettes *fpl* non gagées

unaudited *adj (figures)* non certifié(e); *(accounts)* non verifié(e)

unauthorized *adj* non autorisé(e) ❑ *Comptr* **unauthorized access** accès *m* non autorisé

unavailable *adj (person)* indisponible, non disponible; *(goods, resources)* qu'on ne peut se procurer; **the manager is unavailable** le directeur n'est pas disponible

unavoidable costs npl *Acct* coûts *mpl* induits

unbalanced *adj* **(a)** *Acct (account)* non soldé(e) **(b)** *Fin (economy)* déséquilibré(e)

unbankable *adj Fin* non bancable ❑ **unbankable bill** effet *m* non bancable; **unbankable paper** papier *m* non bancable

unbonded warehouse n entrepôt *m* fictif

unbranded *adj Mktg* sans marque ❑ **unbranded product** produit *m* sans marque

unbundle vt *(company)* dégrouper

unbundling n *(of company)* dégroupage *m*

uncallable *adj (bond)* non remboursable

uncalled *adj Fin (capital)* non appelé(e)

uncashed *adj (cheque)* non encaissé(e)

unclaimed *adj (dividend)* non réclamé(e) ❑ **unclaimed goods** marchandises *fpl* en souffrance

uncommercial *adj* peu commercial(e)

unconditional *adj (acceptance, offer)* sans condition ❑ *Fin* **unconditional order** ordre *m* (de payer) pur et simple

unconfirmed letter of credit n *Fin* lettre *f* de crédit révocable

unconscionable bargain *n Law* contrat *m* léonin

unconsolidated *adj Fin (debt)* non consolidé(e)

uncovered *adj Fin (purchase, sale)* à découvert; *(cheque)* sans provision ◻ **uncovered advance** avance *f* à découvert; **uncovered balance** découvert *m*; *St Exch* **uncovered position** position *f* non couverte

uncrossed *adj (cheque)* non barré(e)

UNCTAD *n (abbr* **United Nations Conference on Trade and Development)** CNUCED *f*

undated *adj* non daté(e), sans date

underbid *vt* **to underbid sb** *(for tender)* faire des soumissions plus avantageuses que qn

underborrow *vi (of company)* ne pas emprunter assez

underborrowed *adj (company)* sous-endetté(e)

underborrowing *n (of company)* sous-endettement *m*

underbuy *vt (goods)* payer moins cher que

undercapitalization *n* sous-capitalisation *f*

undercapitalize *vt* sous-capitaliser

undercapitalized *adj* sous-capitalisé(e)

undercharge *vt (customer)* faire payer insuffisamment *ou* moins cher à; **I was undercharged** on m'a fait payer moins cher, on ne m'a pas fait payer le prix indiqué; **she undercharged him by £60** elle lui a fait payer 60 livres de moins que le prix

undercut *vt (competitor)* vendre moins cher que; *(prices)* casser

> **"**
> Mr O'Leary claimed Ryanair was "Europe's only low-cost airline", with fares **undercutting** its rivals by up to a third. He insisted EasyJet's takeover of Go represented little threat, dismissing that company's chairman, Stelios Haji-Ioannou, as "the son of a billionaire", adding: "He's Greek, I'm Irish. The Greeks have never beaten the Irish at anything. Not even drinking."
> **"**

underdeveloped *adj Econ (country)* sous-développé(e)

underemployed *adj Econ* sous-employé(e)

underemployment *n Econ* sous-emploi *m*

underequipped *adj* sous-équipé(e)

underfund *vt* sous-capitaliser

underfunded *adj* sous-capitalisé(e)

underground economy *n* économie *f* souterraine

underinsure *vt* sous-assurer

underinsured *adj* sous-assuré(e)

underinvestment *n* insuffisance *f* d'investissement

underlying *adj* sous-jacent(e) ◻ **underlying asset** actif *m* sous-jacent; *St Exch* **underlying futures contract** contrat *m* à terme sous option; **underlying mortgage** hypothèque *f* sous-jacente; *St Exch* **underlying security** titre *m* sous-jacent

undermanned *adj* à court de personnel

undermanning *n* manque *m* de main-d'œuvre

underpaid *adj* sous-payé(e)

underperform *vi (of shares)* avoir un cours trop bas

underpin *vt (market)* soutenir

underpriced *adj* très bon marché (par rapport à sa valeur réelle)

underproduce 1 *vt* produire insuffisamment de
2 *vi* produire insuffisamment

underquote *vt (goods, securities, services)* = proposer à un prix inférieur à celui du marché; *(competitor)* vendre moins cher que

undersell *vt (person, company)* vendre moins cher que; *(goods)* vendre au-dessous de la valeur de

undersigned 1 *n* **the undersigned** le (la) soussigné(e); **I, the undersigned, declare that...** je soussigné déclare que...
2 *adj* soussigné(e)

understaffed *adj* qui manque de personnel; **to be understaffed** manquer de personnel

understaffing *n* manque *m* de personnel

understanding *n (agreement)* accord *m*, entente *f*; **to come to an understanding with sb (about sth)** s'entendre avec qn (sur qch)

undersubscribed *adj St Exch (issue, share)* non-souscrit(e)

undertake *vt (job, project)* se charger de, entreprendre; *(responsibility)* assumer; **to undertake to do sth** entreprendre de faire qch

undertaking *n* **(a)** *(enterprise)* entreprise *f* **(b)** *(promise)* engagement *m*; **to give an undertaking to do sth** s'engager à faire qch ◻ **undertaking to purchase** promesse *f* d'achat; **undertaking to sell** promesse de vente

undertax *vt (goods, product)* taxer insuffisamment; *(person)* ne pas faire payer assez d'impôts à

undervaluation *n (of goods)* sous-évaluation *f*

undervalue *vt (goods)* sous-évaluer

underwater *adj Am (share prices)* décoté(e) ❏ ***underwater option*** option *f* à prix glissant à la baisse

> **"**
> This provides employees with a guaranteed return within a specified time period, but assures the company that the bonus is paid only if the stock options remain **underwater**.
> **"**

underwrite *vt* (**a**) *Ins (policy, risk)* garantir (**b**) *St Exch (new issue)* garantir, souscrire

underwriter *n* (**a**) *Ins (of policy, risk)* assureur *m* (**b**) *St Exch (of new issue)* syndicataire *mf* ❏ ***underwriter agent*** agent *m* souscripteur

underwriting *n* (**a**) *Ins (of policy, risk)* garantie *f* (**b**) *St Exch (of new issue)* garantie *f*, souscription *f* ❏ ***underwriting agent*** agent *m* souscripteur; ***underwriting commission*** commission *f* de garantie; ***underwriting contract*** contrat *m* de garantie; ***underwriting fee*** commission de placement; ***underwriting share*** part *f* syndicataire; ***underwriting syndicate*** syndicat *m* de garantie

undifferentiated marketing *n* marketing *m* indifférencié

undischarged *adj* (**a**) *Law (bankrupt)* non réhabilité(e), non déchargé(e) (**b**) *Fin (debt)* non liquidé(e)

undisclosed *adj (sum)* non révélé(e) ❏ ***undisclosed principal*** acheteur(euse) *m,f* non identifié(e) *ou* anonyme

undiscountable *adj Fin* inescomptable

undistributed *adj (money, earnings)* non distribué(e) ❏ ***undistributed profit*** bénéfice *m* non distribué

undo *vt Comptr (command)* annuler, défaire; **undo changes** annuler dernière opération ❏ ***undo command*** commande *f* d'annulation

unearned *adj* non gagné(e) en travaillant *ou* par le travail ❏ ***unearned income*** revenus *mpl* non professionnels, rentes *fpl*; *Fin* ***unearned increment*** plus-value *f*

uneconomic *adj Br (unprofitable)* peu rentable

uneconomical *adj (person)* peu économe; *(machine, method, approach)* peu économique

unedited *adj Comptr (text)* non édité(e)

unemployed 1 *npl* **the unemployed** les chômeurs *mpl*, les sans-emploi *mpl*
2 *adj* (**a**) *(person)* en chômage, sans emploi (**b**) *(capital, funds)* inemployé(e)

unemployment *n* chômage *m* ❏ *Br Formerly* ***unemployment benefit*** allocation *f* chômage, indemnité *f* de chômage; *Am* ***unemployment compensation*** allocation chômage, indemnité

de chômage; ***unemployment crisis*** crise *f* de l'emploi; ***unemployment fund*** caisse *f* de chômage; ***unemployment insurance*** assurance *f* chômage; ***unemployment level, unemployment rate*** taux *m* de chômage

unendorsed *adj Banking (cheque)* non endossé(e)

unenforceable *adj (contract)* non exécutoire

unexchangeable *adj Fin (securities)* impermutable, inéchangeable

unfair *adj* ***unfair competition*** concurrence *f* déloyale; ***unfair dismissal*** licenciement *m* abusif; ***unfair trading*** pratiques *fpl* déloyales

unfavourable, *Am* **unfavorable** *adj (balance of trade, exchange rate)* défavorable

unforeseen expenses *npl* dépenses *fpl* non prévues au budget

unformatted *adj Comptr (disk)* non formaté(e)

unfunded *adj Fin* sans capitaux suffisants ❏ ***unfunded debt*** dette *f* flottante *ou* non consolidée

ungeared *adj Fin* sans endettement ❏ ***ungeared balance sheet*** bilan *m* sans emprunts *ou* à faible endettement

UNIDO *n (abbr* **United Nations Industrial Development Organization)** UNIDO *f*

uniform *adj* ***uniform accounting*** comptabilité *f* uniforme; *Br Fin* ***uniform business rate*** = taxe assise sur la valeur des locaux commerciaux, ≃ taxe *f* professionnelle; ***uniform rate*** taux *m* uniforme

unilateral *adj (action, decision, contract)* unilatéral(e)

unincorporated *adj* non enregistré(e)

uninitialized *adj Comptr* non initialisé(e)

uninstall, *Am* **uninstal** *vt Comptr* désinstaller, supprimer

uninsured *adj* non assuré(e)

union *n (trade union)* syndicat *m* ❏ ***union agreement*** convention *f* collective; ***union card*** carte *f* syndicale; ***union claims*** revendications *fpl* syndicales; ***union demands*** revendications syndicales; ***union dues*** cotisation *f* syndicale; *Am* ***union label*** label *m* syndical *(étiquette stipulant qu'un article a été fabriqué par de la main-d'œuvre syndiquée)*; ***union leader*** dirigeant(e) *m,f* syndical(e); ***union meeting*** réunion *f* syndicale; ***union member*** syndiqué(e) *m,f*; ***union official*** responsable *mf* syndical(e); ***union representative*** délégué(e) *m,f* syndical(e); *Am* ***union shop*** atelier *m* d'ouvriers syndiqués, union shop *m*

unionism *n* syndicalisme *m*

unionist *n* syndicaliste *mf*

unionize *vt* syndiquer

unique *adj Mktg* **unique proposition** proposition *f* unique ; **unique selling point** *or* **proposition** proposition unique de vente

UNISON *n* = "super-syndicat" de la fonction publique en Grande-Bretagne

unissued *adj (shares, share capital)* non encore émis(e)

unit *n* unité *f* ; **each lot contains a hundred units** chaque lot contient cent unités ❑ **unit of account** unité de compte ; **unit of consumption** unité de consommation ; **unit cost** coût *m* unitaire ; **unit of currency** unité monétaire ; **unit of labour** unité de travail ; **unit labour cost** coût unitaire de travail ; **unit price** prix *m* unitaire *ou* à l'unité ; **unit of production** unité de production ; *Br St Exch* **unit trust** sicav *f*, fonds *m* commun de placement ; **unit of weight** unité de poids

unitary *adj* unitaire

United Nations *npl* **the United Nations** les Nations *fpl* Unies ❑ **United Nations Organization** Organisation *f* des Nations unies

universal *n Am* **universal product code** code *m* barres ; *Comptr* **universal serial bus** norme *f* USB, port *m* série universel

universe *n Mktg (number of people in group or segment)* univers *m*

Unix *n Comptr* UNIX *m*

unlawful *adj* illégal(e)

unlimited *adj (funds)* inépuisable ; *Ins (cover)* sans limitation de somme ❑ **unlimited company** société *f* à responsabilité illimitée ; **unlimited liability** responsabilité *f* illimitée ; **unlimited warranty** garantie *f* illimitée

unlisted *adj* (**a**) *St Exch (share, company)* non coté(e), non inscrit(e) à la cote ❑ **unlisted market** Bourse *f* coulisse ; **unlisted securities** valeurs *fpl* du second marché ; **unlisted securities market** second marché *m*, marché hors cote (**b**) *Am (telephone number)* sur la liste rouge

unload 1 *vt (ship, truck, goods)* décharger ❑ **unloading place, unloading point** point *m* de déchargement ; **unloading port** port *m* de déchargement
2 *vi* (**a**) *(of ship, truck)* décharger (**b**) *Am (flood market)* inonder le marché

unlock *vt (assets)* débloquer

unmarketable *adj (goods)* invendable ; *(assets)* non réalisable

unmortgaged *adj* libre d'hypothèques

unnegotiable *adj (cheque, bill)* non négociable

UNO *n (abbr* **United Nations Organization)** ONU *f*

unofficial *adj (appointment, meeting)* non officiel(elle) ❑ **unofficial price** cours *m* hors Bourse *ou* hors cote ; **unofficial strike** grève *f* sauvage

unorganized *adj Ind* non-syndiqué(e)

unpack *vt (goods)* déballer

unpaid *adj* (**a**) *(person)* non salarié(e) ; *(post)* non rétribué(e) ❑ **unpaid leave** congé *m* sans solde (**b**) *(account, bill, debt, salary)* impayé(e)

unpledged revenue *n Fin* recettes *fpl* non gagées

unpriced *adj* non étiqueté(e), qui n'a pas d'étiquette de prix

unprocessed *adj (material, data)* brut(e)

unproductive *adj (capital, work)* improductif(ive) ❑ **unproductive land** terres *fpl* en non-valeur

unproductiveness *n (of capital, work)* improductivité *f*

unprofessional *adj* peu professionnel(elle)

unprofitable *adj (business)* peu rentable ; *(discussions)* peu profitable

unquoted *adj St Exch (share)* non coté(e) ❑ **unquoted company** société *f* non cotée ; **unquoted securities** valeurs *fpl* non cotées

unreadable *adj Comptr* illisible

unrealizable *adj Fin (capital, assets)* non réalisable

unrealized *adj Fin (capital, assets)* non réalisé(e) ; *(gain, loss)* latent(e)

unrecoverable *adj (debt)* inexigible

unredeemed *adj Fin (loan)* non amorti(e), non remboursé(e) ; *(draft)* non honoré(e) ; *(mortgage)* non purgé(e)

unrefined material *n* matière *f* non travaillé(e)

unrest *n* agitation *f*

unsaleable *adj (goods)* invendable

unsecured *adj (loan, overdraft)* non garanti(e), à découvert ; *(debt)* sans garantie ❑ **unsecured advance** avance *f* à découvert ; **unsecured credit card** = carte de crédit dont le détenteur n'est pas tenu de fournir de garantie ; **unsecured creditor** créancier(ère) *m,f* ordinaire *ou* chirographaire ; **unsecured debenture** obligation *f* non garantie ; **unsecured debt** créance *f* chirographaire *ou* sans garantie ; **unsecured loan** prêt *m* non garanti ; **unsecured overdraft** découvert *m* en blanc

unsettled *adj* (**a**) *(market)* instable (**b**) *(account, bill, debt)* impayé(e)

unskilled *adj (worker)* non qualifié(e), non spécialisé(e) ; *(job, work)* qui ne nécessite pas de connaissances professionnelles ❑ **unskilled la-**

bour main-d'œuvre *f* non spécialisée ; **unskilled labourer** ouvrier(ère) *m,f* non spécialisé(e)

unsocial *adj* **to work unsocial hours** travailler en dehors des heures normales

unsold *adj* invendu(e)

unsolicited application *n* candidature *f* spontanée

unsound *adj* *(enterprise, investment)* peu sûr(e), risqué(e) ; *(business)* peu sûr, précaire ; **the project is economically unsound** le projet n'est pas sain *ou* viable sur le plan économique

unspent *adj* *(sum, balance)* non dépensé(e)

unstable *adj* *(market, prices)* instable

unstamped *adj* *(letter)* sans timbre, non affranchi(e) ; *(document)* non estampillé(e)

unsteady *adj* *(prices)* variable ; *(market)* agité(e)

unstructured interview *n* entretien *m* libre, entretien non structuré

unsubscribe *vi* se désabonner

unsubscribed *adj* *Fin (capital)* non souscrit(e)

untaxed *adj* *(income)* exempt(e) *ou* exonéré(e) d'impôt ; *(goods)* non imposé(e), non taxé(e)

untradable *adj* *St Exch* incotable

unweighted *adj* *Econ (index)* non pondéré(e) ❑ **unweighted figures** chiffres *mpl* bruts

unzip *vt* *Comptr* dézipper

UP *n* *(abbr* **unit price**) PU *m*

up 1 *adj* *Comptr* **up arrow** flèche *f* vers le haut ; **up arrow key** touche *f* de déplacement vers le haut
  2 *adv* **(a)** *(higher)* **the price of gold is up** le prix de l'or a augmenté ; **the pound is up ten cents against the dollar** la livre a gagné dix cents par rapport au dollar ; **profits are up 25 percent on last year** les profits ont augmenté de 25 pour cent par rapport à l'année dernière **(b)** **up front** *(pay)* d'avance

UPC *n* *Am (abbr* **universal product code**) code *m* barres

update *Comptr* **1** *n* *(of software package)* mise *f* à jour, actualisation *f*
  2 *vt* mettre à jour, actualiser

upgradability *n* *Comptr* possibilités *fpl* d'extension

upgradable *adj* *Comptr (hardware, system)* évolutif(ive) ; *(memory)* extensible

upgrade *Comptr* **1** *n* *(of hardware, system)* augmentation *f* de puissance ; *(of software)* mise *f* à jour *ou* à niveau, actualisation *f* ❑ **upgrade kit** kit *m* d'évolution *ou* d'extension ; **upgrade slot** emplacement *m* d'évolutivité
  2 *vt* *(hardware, system)* optimiser ; *(software)* améliorer, perfectionner

upgradeability, upgradeable = **upgra-**

dability, upgradable

upkeep *n* *(maintenance)* entretien *m* ; *(cost)* frais *mpl* d'entretien

upload *vt* *Comptr* télécharger *(vers le serveur)*

upmarket 1 *adj* *(goods, service)* haut de gamme ; *(customer, client)* au pouvoir d'achat élevé
  2 *adv* **to move upmarket** se repositionner à la hausse

upper *adj* **upper case** haut *m* de casse, (lettres *fpl*) majuscules *fpl* ; **upper classes** classes *fpl* supérieures ; **upper limit** plafond *m* ; **upper price limit** prix *m* limite

upper-case *adj* en haut de casse, en (lettres) majuscules ❑ **upper-case character** caractère *m* majuscule

UPS *n* *Comptr (abbr* **uninterruptible power supply**) onduleur *m*

upscale *adj* *Am (goods, service)* haut de gamme ; *(customer, client)* au pouvoir d'achat élevé

> 66
>
> The **upscale** client is demanding more, and tour operators seeking to capitalize are ripe for the challenge … "There is an increasing emphasis on experience," says Tauck, echoing what many industry leaders in the **upscale** market are saying about leisure travel. "While they do want service and the finest amenities, **upscale** clients are increasingly sophisticated and want to learn about and engage in a destination," says Tauck.
>
> 99

upset price *n* *(at auction)* mise *f* à prix

upside *n* *(trend)* **prices have been on the upside** les prix ont été à la hausse ❑ *St Exch* **upside potential** potentiel *m* de hausse ; *St Exch* **upside risk** risque *m* de hausse

upstream *adj* *(company)* en amont

upswing *n* mouvement *m* vers la hausse ; **the Stock Market is on the upswing** la Bourse est en hausse ; **there has been an upswing in sales** il y a eu une progression des ventes

uptick *n* **(a)** *(small increase)* légère augmentation *f* ; **last week's uptick in interest rates** la légère augmentation des taux d'intérêt de la semaine dernière **(b)** *St Exch* = négociation d'un titre à un cours supérieur à celui de la négociation précédente

> 66
>
> Although the trading statement did not look so far out, analysts also have hopes for an **uptick** in business for the private sector in the Far East and the US later this year. Profits, around £114m in 2001 according to the consensus of forecasts, look set to increase to £130m this year.
>
> 99

up-to-date *adj* (**a**) *(most recent)* à jour; **to bring sb up-to-date on sth** mettre qn au courant de qch (**b**) *(modern) (machinery, methods)* moderne

uptrend *n* tendance *f* à la hausse

upturn *n (in economy)* redressement *m*; *(in production, sales)* reprise *f*, progression *f*; **there has been an upturn in the market** il y a eu une progression du marché

upward *adj* **upward market trend** orientation *f* du marché à la hausse; **upward mobility** mobilité *f* sociale; *Fin* **upward movement** mouvement *m* de hausse; **upward tendency, upward trend** tendance *f* à la hausse

upward-compatible *adj Comptr* compatible vers le haut

urban *adj* urbain(e) ◦ *Br* **urban district** district *m* urbain; *Br Admin* **urban district council** conseil *m* de district urbain; **urban planner** urbaniste *mf*; **urban renewal** rénovations *fpl* urbaines; **urban transport** transport *m* urbain; **urban unemployment** chômage *m* en zones urbaines

> ❝ The panel is tasked with crafting an **urban renewal** plan as part of the government's economic stimulus measures by considering issues including the construction of waste disposal and recycling plants, international airports and disaster refuge areas, as well as making use of vacant lots. ❞

urgent *adj* urgent(e); **it's not urgent** ce n'est pas urgent

URL *n Comptr (abbr* **uniform resource locator)** (adresse *f*) URL *m*

US *(abbr* **United States) 1** *n* **the US** les USA *mpl*, les États-Unis *mpl*
2 *adj* des États-Unis, américain(e) ◦ *US dollar* dollar *m* américain

usance *n Banking, Fin (time limit)* usance *f*; **at thirty days' usance** à usance de trente jours ◦ *usance bill* effet *m* à usance

USB *n Comptr (abbr* **universal serial bus)** norme *f* USB, port *m* série universel

use *vt (product)* utiliser

use-by date *n* date *f* de péremption

used *adj (product, car)* d'occasion

Usenet *n Comptr* Usenet *m*

user *n (of machine, computer, product)* utilisateur(trice) *m,f*; *(of telephone)* abonné(e) *m,f* ◦ *Comptr* **user ID, user identification** identification *f* de l'utilisateur; *Comptr* **user interface** interface *f* utilisateur; *Comptr* **user language** langage *m* utilisateur; *Comptr* **user manual** manuel *m* d'utilisation; *Comptr* **user name** nom *m* de l'utilisateur; *Comptr* **user network** réseau *m* d'utilisateurs; *Mktg* **user panel** panel *m* d'utilisateurs; *Comptr* **user software** logiciel *m* utilisateur; *Comptr* **user support** assistance *f* à l'utilisateur

user-definable *adj Comptr (characters, keys)* définissable par l'utilisateur

user-friendliness *n* convivialité *f*

user-friendly *adj* convivial(e)

> ❝ El Al's frequent-flyer clubs, Matmid and Loyal Club, are more **user-friendly** now that the carrier has introduced several advantages for its members. Members can now access their account statement via the carrier's Web site by entering their seven-digit membership number along with a PIN code. ❞

USM *n St Exch (abbr* **unlisted securities market)** second marché *m*

USP *n Mktg (abbr* **unique selling point** *or* **position)** proposition *f* unique de vente

USPHS *n (abbr* **United States Public Health Service)** = direction américaine des Affaires sanitaires et sociales

usufruct *n Law* usufruit *m*

usufructary *Law* **1** *n* usufruitier(ère) *m,f* **2** *adj* usufruitier(ère)

usurer *n* usurier(ère) *m,f*

usurious *adj (interest)* usuraire

usury *n* usure *f*

utility *n* (**a**) *(service)* **(public) utility** service *m* public ◦ *Am* **utility stocks** valeurs *fpl* de services publics (**b**) *Comptr* utilitaire *m* ◦ *utility program* (logiciel *m*) utilitaire

utilization *n* utilisation *f*

utilize *vt (use)* utiliser, se servir de; *(make best use of)* exploiter

Vv

vacancy n poste m vacant; **to fill a vacancy** pourvoir à un emploi; **the vacancy has been filled** le poste a été pourvu; **we have a vacancy for a sales assistant** nous avons un poste de vendeur à pourvoir, nous cherchons un vendeur; **do you have any vacancies?** avez-vous des postes à pourvoir?

vacant adj (**a**) (job, position) à pourvoir, vacant(e); **there are several vacant places to be filled** il y a plusieurs postes à pourvoir; **a secretarial job has become vacant** un poste de secrétaire est devenu disponible ou vacant (**b**) (room, apartment) libre ❑ **vacant possession** libre possession f; **apartments sold with vacant possession** appartements libres à la vente

vacate vt (hotel room) quitter, libérer; (house, property) quitter; (job) démissionner de; Law **to vacate the premises** vider les lieux

vacation n (**a**) Am (holiday) vacances fpl; **a month's vacation** un mois de vacances; **to be on/go on vacation** être/aller en vacances; **to get vacation with pay** avoir les congés payés ❑ **vacation leave** congés mpl annuels (**b**) Br Law (of courts) vacations fpl, vacances fpl judiciaires

vacuum pack n emballage m sous vide

vacuum-packed adj emballé(e) sous vide

valid adj (contract, passport) valide, valable; **valid for six months** valable six mois

validate vt valider

validation n validation f

validity n validité f

valorization n Fin valorisation f

valorize vt Fin valoriser

valuable 1 n **valuables** objets mpl de valeur
  2 adj de valeur

valuate vt Am Fin estimer, expertiser; **the house was valuated at $100,000** la maison a été expertisée ou estimée ou évaluée à 100 000 dollars

valuation n Fin (**a**) (act) évaluation f, estimation f, expertise f; **to get a valuation of sth** faire évaluer ou estimer ou expertiser qch; **to make a valuation of sth** évaluer ou estimer ou expertiser qch ❑ **valuation charge** taxation f à la valeur (**b**) (price) évaluation f; **the valuation put on the business is £100,000** l'affaire a été

évaluée ou estimée ou expertisée à 100 000 livres

valuator n expert m (en expertise de biens)

value 1 n valeur f; **to be of value** avoir de la valeur; **to be of no value** être sans valeur; **to be good/poor value (for money)** être d'un bon/mauvais rapport qualité-prix; **to go up/down in value** prendre/perdre de la valeur; **to set** or **put a value on sth** estimer la valeur de qch; **they put a value of £150,000 on the property** ils ont estimé ou expertisé la propriété à 150 000 livres; **of no commercial value** sans valeur commerciale; **value as a going concern** valeur d'usage; **to the value of** pour une valeur de; **what will this do to the value of property?** quel effet est-ce que ça va avoir sur le prix de l'immobilier? ❑ Banking **value in account** valeur en compte; Fin **value added** valeur ajoutée; Fin **value analysis** analyse f de valeur; Mktg **value brand** marque f de valeur; Mktg **value chain** chaîne f de valeur; Fin **value for collection** valeur à l'encaissement; Fin **value date** date f de valeur; Fin **value day** jour m de valeur; **value engineering** analyse f de valeur; **value in exchange** valeur d'échange, contre-valeur f; Banking **value in gold currency** valeur-or f; **value at liquidation** valeur liquidative ou de liquidation; **value at maturity** valeur à l'échéance; Fin **value for money audit** = estimation des performances d'une société à but non lucratif ou d'un service gouvernemental; Fin **value below rate** décote f; **value in use** valeur d'usage
  2 vt (goods, damage) évaluer, estimer, expertiser; **to have sth valued** faire évaluer ou estimer ou expertiser qch; **they valued the company at $10 billion** ils ont estimé la valeur de la société à 10 milliards de dollars

value-add n Mktg valeur f ajoutée

value-added adj (product, service) à valeur ajoutée ❑ Br **value-added tax** taxe f à la valeur ajoutée

valued policy n Ins assurance f forfaitaire

valueless adj sans valeur

valuer n expert m (en expertise de biens)

variability n variabilité f

variable 1 n variable f
  2 adj variable ❑ **variable cost** coût m variable; **variable expenses** frais mpl variables; EU **variable import levy** prélèvement m à l'importa-

tion; **variable income** revenu(s) *m(pl)* variable(s); *Banking* **variable interest rate** taux *m* d'intérêt variable; *Banking* **variable rate** taux variable; **variable yield** revenu variable

variable-income *adj (bond, investment)* à revenu(s) variable(s)

variable-rate *adj* **variable-rate interest** intérêt *m* variable; **variable-rate mortgage** prêt *m* immobilier à taux variable; *Fin* **variable-rate security** valeur *f* à revenu variable

variable-yield *adj Fin (investments, securities)* à revenu variable

variance *n Acct* variance *f*, écart *m* □ **variance analysis** analyse *f* des écarts

variation *n* variation *f*; **the level of demand is subject to considerable variation** le niveau de la demande peut varier considérablement □ *Ins* **variation of risk** modification *f* de risque

variety store *n Am* grand magasin *m*

VAT *n Br (abbr* **value-added tax**) TVA *f*; **exclusive of** *or* **excluding VAT** hors TVA; **subject to VAT** soumis(e) à la TVA; **to be VAT registered** être assujetti(e) à la TVA □ **VAT credit** crédit *m* de TVA; **VAT exempt amount** montant *m* exonéré de TVA; *Fam* **VAT man** = inspecteur de la TVA; **VAT rate** taux *m* de TVA; **VAT registration number** code *m* assujetti TVA; **VAT return** déclaration *f* de TVA; **VAT statement** état *m* TVA

> ❝
>
> A High Court judge ruled yesterday that the **VAT man** is perfectly entitled to pursue prostitutes. Mr Justice Jacob decided that members of the world's oldest profession should not be allowed to exploit a loophole because of their illegal activities and avoid paying value-added tax. The ruling, while difficult to enforce, raises the prospect of pimps and procurers having to keep accounts for inspection by Customs and Excise, just like any other business.
>
> ❞

vault *n Banking* salle *f* des coffres

VCR *n (abbr* **video cassette recorder**) magnétoscope *m*

VCT *n (abbr* **venture capital trust**) FCPR *m*

VDU *n Comptr (abbr* **visual display unit**) moniteur *m* □ **VDU operator** personne *f* travaillant sur écran

veep *n Am Fam* vice-président(e) *m,f*

vend *vt Law* vendre

vendee *n Law* acquéreur *m*

vendible *adj* commercialisable, vendable

vending machine *n* distributeur *m* automatique

vendor *n Law* vendeur(euse) *m,f*; *Comptr* fournisseur *m* □ **vendor's lien** privilège *m* du vendeur; *St Exch* **vendor placing** = opération par laquelle une société s'engage à vendre de nouvelles actions à un investisseur en échange d'un apport en espèces; *St Exch* **vendor's shares** actions *fpl* d'apport *ou* de fondation

vendue *n Am* vente *f* aux enchères

venture *n* entreprise *f* □ **venture capital** capital-risque *m*; **venture capital company** société *f* à capital-risque; **venture capitalist** spécialiste *mf* de la prise de risques *(dans la finance)*; **venture capital trust** fonds *m* commun de placement à risques; **venture team** équipe *f* commando

> ❝
>
> 3i, the UK's largest **venture capital** provider, is pulling back from funding smaller companies that are not involved in technology or other growth areas … The **venture capitalist** is setting up a special team to manage investments of less than £2m in non-technology companies to "maximise value". This could involve sales and mergers but not a flood of disposals.
>
> ❞

verbal *adj (agreement, offer, promise)* verbal(e)

verdict *n* verdict *m*

verification *n* vérification *f*

verify *vt* vérifier

vertical *adj* vertical(e) □ **vertical concentration** concentration *f* verticale; **vertical equity** équité *f* verticale; **vertical integration** intégration *f* verticale; **vertical merger** concentration verticale; *St Exch* **vertical spread** écart *m* vertical; **vertical trust** trust *m* vertical; *Am* **vertical union** confédération *f* syndicale

vessel *n (ship)* vaisseau *m*

vested interest *n* **to have a vested interest in a business** avoir des capitaux investis dans une entreprise, être intéressé(e) dans une entreprise; **vested interests** *(rights)* droits *mpl* acquis; *(investments)* capitaux *mpl* investis; *(advantages)* intérêts *mpl*; **there are vested interests in industry opposed to trade union reform** ceux qui ont des intérêts dans l'industrie s'opposent à la réforme des syndicats

vet *vt (person)* enquêter sur; *(application)* examiner minutieusement; *(facts, figures)* vérifier soigneusement; **she was thoroughly vetted for the job** ils ont soigneusement examiné sa candidature avant de l'embaucher; **the committee has to vet any expenditure exceeding £100** le comité doit approuver toute dépense au-delà de 100 livres

veto 1 *n* veto *m*; **right of veto** droit *m* de veto; **to use one's veto** exercer son droit de veto; **to**

impose *or* **put a veto on sth** mettre *ou* opposer son véto à qch
   2 *vt* mettre *ou* opposer son veto à

VGA *n Comptr* (*abbr* **video graphics array**) VGA *m*

viability *n* viabilité *f*

viable *adj* viable; **it's not a viable proposition** cette proposition n'est pas viable

vice-chairman *n* vice-président(e) *m,f*

vice-chairmanship *n* vice-présidence *f*

vice-presidency *n* vice-présidence *f*

vice-president *n* vice-président(e) *m,f*

video *n* vidéo *f* ▫ *Comptr* **video accelerator card** carte *f* vidéo accélératrice; *Comptr* **video board** carte vidéo; *Comptr* **video card** carte vidéo; **video clip** clip *m* (vidéo); **video compact disc** disque *m* compact vidéo; **video link** liaison *f* vidéo; **video recorder** magnétoscope *m*

videoconference *n* vidéoconférence *f*

videoconferencing *n* vidéoconférence *f*

videophone *n* visiophone *m* ▫ **videophone conference** visioconférence *f*

videotex *n Comptr* vidéotex *m*

view *vt Comptr* (*codes, document*) visualiser

Viewdata® *n* vidéotex *m*

viewer *n Comptr* (*program*) visualiseur *m*

viewphone *n Tel* vidéophone *m*

violate *vt* (*law*) violer, enfreindre; (*agreement*) violer

VIP *n* (*abbr* **very important person**) VIP *mf*, personnage *m* de marque ▫ **VIP lounge** = salon d'accueil dans un aéroport réservé aux personnages de marque

viral marketing *n* marketing *m* viral

> "
> Persuasion works best when it's invisible. The most effective marketing worms its way into our consciousness, leaving intact the perception that we have reached our opinions and made our choices independently. As old as humankind itself, over the past few years this approach has been refined, with the help of the internet, into a technique called **viral marketing**.
> "

virtual *adj Comptr* virtuel(elle) ▫ **virtual reality** réalité *f* virtuelle

virus *n Comptr* virus *m*; **to disable a virus** désactiver un virus ▫ **virus check** détection *f* de virus; **to run a virus check on a disk** faire tourner le programme détecteur de virus sur une disquette; **virus detection** détection de virus; **virus detector** détecteur *m* de virus; **virus program** programme *m* virus

virus-checked *adj Comptr* qui a été passé(e) au détecteur de virus

virus-free *adj Comptr* dépourvu(e) de virus

Visa® *n* Visa® *f*; **to pay by Visa®** payer par Visa® ▫ **Visa® card** carte *f* Visa®

visa 1 *n* visa *m*
   2 *vt* viser, apposer un visa à

visible 1 *n Econ* **visibles** biens *mpl* visibles
   2 *adj* **visible balance** balance *f* visible; **visible defect** défaut *m* apparent; **visible exports** exportations *fpl* visibles; **visible imports** importations *fpl* visibles; **visible reserve** réserve *f* visible; **visible trade** commerce *m* de biens

visit 1 *vt* (*person*) rendre visite à; (*place*) visiter
   2 *vi* **to be visiting** être de passage; *Am* **to visit with sb** rendre visite à qn

visiting fireman *n Fam* visiteur *m* de marque

> "
> Although Kenyan head of state Daniel Arap Moi kept his cool while on camera, he was reported to be furious on February 7 when he said goodbye to International Monetary Fund **visiting fireman** Jose Fajgenbaum, leaving after a two-week mission in Nairobi.
> "

visitor *n* visiteur(euse) *m,f*; **all visitors must report to reception** tous les visiteurs doivent se présenter à l'accueil ▫ **visitor attraction** centre *m* d'intérêt touristique; **visitor centre** centre d'accueil

visual display unit *n Comptr* écran *m ou* console *f* de visualisation

vocational *adj* professionnel(elle) ▫ **vocational guidance** orientation *f* professionnelle; **vocational training** formation *f* professionnelle

voice *n Tel* **voice mail** messagerie *f* vocale; *Comptr* **voice recognition software** logiciel *m* de reconnaissance vocale; *Comptr* **voice synthesizer** synthétiseur *m* de paroles

voice-activated *adj Comptr* à commande vocale

void 1 *adj* (*deed, contract*) nul (nulle); **null and void** nul et non avenu; **to make sth void** annuler qch, rendre qch nul
   2 *vt* (*deed, contract*) annuler, rendre nul (nulle)

voidable *adj* annulable

voidance *n* annulation *f*

volatile *adj* volatil(e)

volatility *n* volatilité *f*

volume *n* volume *m* ▫ **volume of activity** volume d'activité; **volume of business** volume d'affaires; **volume of current output** volume de la production courante; **volume of exports** volume des exportations; **volume of imports** volume des importations; *Comptr* **volume**

label label *m* de volume; *Mktg* **volume mailing** multipostage *m*, publipostage *m* groupé; *volume of output* volume de la production; *volume of purchases* volume d'achats; *volume of sales* volume de ventes, chiffre *m* d'affaires; *volume of trade* volume des échanges commerciaux

voluntary *adj* (**a**) *(unpaid)* *(work, worker)* bénévole; **the shop is run on a voluntary basis** le magasin est tenu par des bénévoles; **many people like to include voluntary work on their CV** beaucoup de gens mentionnent leur expérience du bénévolat sur leur CV

(**b**) *(optional)* facultatif(ive) ❑ *Fin* *voluntary arrangement* = arrangement entre une entreprise et ses créanciers de façon à éviter la mise en liquidation; *voluntary chain* chaîne *f* volontaire; *voluntary export restraint* quotas *mpl* volontaires à l'export; *voluntary group* groupe *m* volontaire; *voluntary insurance* assurance *f* facultative; *voluntary liquidation* liquidation *f* volontaire; *voluntary redundancy* départ *m* volontaire; *voluntary retailer chain* chaîne volontaire de détaillants

vote **1** *n* (**a**) *(ballot)* vote *m*, scrutin *m*; **to put sth to the vote** soumettre qch au vote; **to take a vote on sth** voter sur qch; **to take the vote** procéder au scrutin ❑ *vote of confidence* vote de confiance; *vote of no confidence* motion *f* de censure; *vote of thanks* discours *m* de remerciement; **to propose a vote of thanks to sb** voter des remerciements à qn (**b**) *(individual vote)* voix *f*, vote *m*; **to give one's vote to sb** voter pour qn; **to cast one's vote** voter

2 *vt* voter; **to vote to do sth** voter pour faire qch; **to vote sb in** élire qn; **to vote sb out** ne pas réélire qn

3 *vi* voter (**for/against** pour/contre); **most of the delegates voted against the chairman** la plupart des délégués ont voté contre le président; **to vote by a show of hands** voter à main levée; **to vote by proxy** voter par procuration

voter *n* électeur(trice) *m,f*

voting **1** *n* vote *m*, scrutin *m* ❑ *voting paper* bulletin *m* de vote; *St Exch* **voting rights** *(of shareholders)* droit *m* de vote; *Br St Exch* **voting shares** actions *fpl* donnant droit au vote; *Am St Exch* **voting stock** actions donnant droit au vote

2 *adj (assembly, member)* votant(e)

voucher *n* (**a**) *(for purchase)* bon *m* (**b**) *(receipt)* reçu *m*, récépissé *m* (**c**) *Acct* pièce *f* comptable

VP *n* *(abbr* **vice-president***)* vice-président(e) *m,f*

VRAM *n* *Comptr* *(abbr* **video random access memory***)* VRAM *f*

VRM *n* *(abbr* **variable-rate mortgage***)* prêt *m* immobilier à taux variable

VSAT *n* *Tel* *(abbr* **very small aperture terminal***)* VSAT *m*, microstation *f* (terrienne)

Ww

W3 n Comptr (abbr **World Wide Web**) W3 m, le Web m

wage n **wage(s)** salaire m, paie f □ **wage(s) agreement** accord m salarial; **wage(s) bill** masse f salariale, charges fpl salariales; **wage bracket** fourchette f de salaire; **wage ceiling** salaire plafonné; **wage claim** revendication f salariale; **wage cut** réduction f de salaire; **wage differential** écart m salarial ou de salaire; **wage earner** salarié(e) m,f; **wage economy** économie f salariale; **wage floor** plancher m des salaires; **wage freeze** gel m ou blocage m des salaires; **wage increase** augmentation f de salaire; **wage inflation** inflation f des salaires; Acct **wages ledger** journal m de paie; **wage packet** (envelope) enveloppe f de paie; (money) paie; **wage policy** politique f salariale ou des salaires; **wage and price index** indice m des prix et des salaires; **wage pyramid** pyramide f des salaires; **wage rate** taux m des salaires; **wage restraint** restriction f salariale; **wage scale** échelle f des salaires; **wages sheet** bordereau m de salaire; **wage slip** bordereau de salaire; **wage structure** structure f des salaires; **wage zone** zone f de salaires

wage-price spiral n spirale f inflationniste prix-salaires

wageworker n Am salarié(e) m,f

WAIS n Comptr (abbr **wide area information service system**) WAIS m

waiter n St Exch coursier m

waiting n **waiting list** liste f d'attente; **waiting period** délai m d'attente; **waiting room** salle f d'attente; **waiting time** temps m mort

waive vt (condition, requirement) abandonner; (law, rule) déroger à; (claim, right) renoncer à

waiver n (of condition, requirement) abandon m; (of law, rule) dérogation f; (of claim, right) renonciation f

wake-up call n Tel appel m de réveil

▶ **walk out** vi (a) (strike) se mettre en grève (b) (leave) partir

walkout n grève f (surprise); **to stage a walk-out** se mettre en grève

wallpaper n Comptr papier m peint

Wall Street n Wall Street (quartier de la Bourse de New York) □ **the Wall Street Crash** le krach de Wall Street

WAN n Comptr (abbr **wide area network**) réseau m longue distance

want ad n Am petite annonce f

WAP n Tel (abbr **wireless applications protocol**) WAP m □ **WAP phone** téléphone m WAP

war chest n caisse f spéciale; (of trade union) caisse de grève

warehouse 1 n entrepôt m, dépôt m de marchandises □ **warehouse book** livre m de magasin; **warehouse charges** frais mpl d'entreposage ou de magasinage; **warehouse keeper** magasinier m; **warehouse manager** responsable mf d'entrepôt; **warehouse receipt** récépissé m d'entrepôt; **warehouse warrant** certificat m d'entrepôt
2 vt entreposer, mettre en entrepôt □ **warehoused goods** marchandises fpl en entrepôt

warehouseman n magasinier m

warehousing n (a) (of goods) entreposage m, magasinage m □ **warehousing charges** frais mpl d'entreposage ou de magasinage; **warehousing company** société f d'entrepôts; **warehousing costs** frais d'entreposage ou de magasinage; **warehousing entry** déclaration f d'entrée en entrepôt; **warehousing system** système m d'entrepôt (b) St Exch (of shares) parcage m d'actions

warm adj Comptr **warm boot** redémarrage m à chaud; Comptr **warm start** redémarrage à chaud

warning n (a) (caution) avertissement m □ Comptr **warning message** message m d'avertissement; **warning strike** grève f d'avertissement (b) (advance notice) avis m; **we only received a few days' warning** nous n'avons été prévenus que quelques jours à l'avance (c) (alarm, signal) alerte f

warrant 1 n (a) Law (written order) mandat m (b) (for goods) certificat m d'entrepôt (c) St Exch bon m de souscription d'actions (d) (for payment) bon m; (guarantee) garantie f
2 vt (a) (justify) justifier; **costs are too high to warrant further investment** les frais sont trop élevés pour justifier d'autres investissements (b) (guarantee) garantir

warranted adj garanti(e)

warrantee n Law porteur(euse) m,f d'une garantie

warrantor n Law répondant(e) m,f, garant(e) m,f

warranty n garantie f; Law (in contract) clause f pénale; **this computer has a five-year warranty** cet ordinateur est garanti cinq ans; **under warranty** sous garantie; **extended warranty** extension f de la garantie; **on-site warranty** garantie sur site; **return-to-base warranty** garantie retour atelier ❏ **warranty certificate** certificat m de garantie; **warranty clause** clause de garantie

wastage n (**a**) (of materials, money) gaspillage m; (wasted material) déchets mpl; **to allow for wastage** tenir compte du gaspillage (**b**) (reduction of workforce) départ m d'employés

waste 1 n (**a**) (of materials, money, resources) gaspillage m; (of time) perte f (**b**) (refuse) déchets mpl ❏ **waste disposal** élimination f des déchets; **waste material** déchets; **waste products** produits mpl de rejet
2 vt (materials, money, resources) gaspiller; (time) perdre

wastebasket n Comptr corbeille f

wasting asset n Acct actif m qui se déprécie

watchdog n (organization) organisme m de contrôle ❏ Comptr **watchdog program** programme m sentinelle

❝
THE US accountancy **watchdog**, the Financial Accounting Standards Board, has proposed toughening the so-called 3 per cent rule that allowed Enron to keep special purpose entities, such as partnerships, off its books by ensuring third-party investors held at least 3 per cent of the entities.
❞

watered stock n titres mpl dilués

waybill n feuille f de route, connaissement m, lettre f de voiture

WB n (abbr **waybill**) feuille f de route, connaissement m, lettre f de voiture

weak adj (currency) faible; (market) en baisse, baissier(ère) ❏ **weak point** point m faible

weaken 1 vt (currency) affaiblir, faire baisser; (market, prices) faire fléchir
2 vi (of currency) s'affaiblir, baisser; (of market, prices) fléchir

wealth n richesse(s) f(pl) ❏ **wealth tax** impôt m de solidarité sur la fortune

wealthy 1 npl **the wealthy** les riches mpl
2 adj riche

wear n usure f ❏ **wear and tear** usure; **fair wear and tear** usure normale

Web n Comptr **the Web** le Web, la Toile ❏ **Web authoring** création f de pages Web; **Web authoring program** programme m de création

de pages Web; **Web authoring tool** outil m de création de pages Web; **Web browser** navigateur m, logiciel m de navigation; **Web cam** caméra f Internet; **Web consultancy** = société conseil pour la création et l'administration de sites Web; **Web design agency** = société spécialisée dans la conception de sites Web; **Web designer** concepteur(trice) m,f de sites Web; **Web hosting** hébergement m de sites Web; **Web master** Webmaster m, Webmaître m, Webmestre m, responsable mf de site Web; **Web page** page f Web; **Web server** serveur m Web; **Web site** site m Web; **Web space** espace m Web

webcast Comptr **1** n webcast m
2 vt diffuser sur l'Internet

webcasting n Comptr webcasting m

website n Comptr site m Web

webzine n webzine m

week n semaine f

weekday n jour m de semaine; Admin jour ouvrable

weekly 1 adj hebdomadaire ❏ **weekly paper** hebdomadaire m; **weekly pay** salaire m hebdomadaire; **weekly trading report** bilan m hebdomadaire; **weekly wage** salaire hebdomadaire
2 adv chaque semaine

weight 1 n poids m; **weight when empty** poids à vide; **to sell sth by weight** vendre qch au poids ❏ **weight limit** limite f de poids; **weights and measures** poids mpl et mesures fpl; **weight note** note f de poids
2 vt Econ (index, average) pondérer

weighted adj Econ (index, average) pondéré(e) ❏ Acct **weighted average cost** coût m moyen pondéré; **weighted distribution** distribution f valeur

weighting n Econ (of index, average) pondération f, coefficient m; Admin **London weighting** (in salary) indemnité f de résidence à Londres

❝
The weekend starts two days early for many of the capital's pupils today, as NUT members take a day of strike action to campaign for a one-third increase in **London weighting**. Far from "being held hostage", as some have put it, pupils will probably feel the opposite.
❞

welcome n Comptr **welcome message** message m d'accueil; **welcome pack** (at conference, in hotel) documentation f

welfare n Am (state aid) aide f sociale; **to live on welfare** vivre de l'aide sociale; **people on welfare** les personnes ou ceux qui touchent l'aide sociale; **the welfare lines are lengthen-**

ing la masse des gens qui touchent le chômage augmente; **to stand in the welfare line** recevoir les allocations chômage ▫ *Am* **welfare benefits** avantages *mpl* sociaux; *Am* **welfare centre** ≃ centre *m* d'assistance sociale; *Am* **welfare check** (chèque *m* d')allocations *fpl*; **welfare economics** économie *f* du bien-être; **the welfare economy** l'économie du bien-être; *Am* **welfare office** bureau *m* d'aide sociale; *Am* **welfare payments** prestations *fpl* sociales; *Am* **welfare service** ≃ service *m* d'assistance sociale; **the Welfare State** *(concept)* l'État *m* providence; **the government wants to cut back on the Welfare State** le gouvernement veut réduire les dépenses de sécurité sociale; **welfare work** travail *m* social; **welfare worker** assistant(e) *m,f* social(e)

WFTU *n* (*abbr* **World Federation of Trade Unions**) FSM *m*

wharf 1 *n* quai *m* ▫ **wharf dues** droits *mpl* de quai
  2 *vt* (**a**) *(goods)(store)* entreposer sur le quai; *(unload)* débarquer (**b**) *(ship)* amarrer à quai
  3 *vi* venir à quai, amarrer à quai

wharfage *n* droits *mpl* de quai

wharfinger *n* gardien(enne) *m,f* de quai

wheeler-dealer *n Fam* brasseur *m* d'affaires *(plus ou moins en marge de la loi)*

wheeling and dealing *n Fam* magouilles *fpl*

❝
The languishing gold price has not dampened the amount of **wheeling and dealing** going on among local producers. Junior mining company Harmony Ltd., for example, is still solidly in the market to raise 1 billion rand ($128 million) to buy two mines from industry giant AngloGold.
❞

white *adj* **white goods** appareils *mpl* ménagers; *St Exch* **white knight** chevalier *m* blanc; **white paper** livre *m* blanc; *Am* **white sale** promotion *f* sur le blanc; *St Exch* **white squire** actionnaire *mf* loyal(e)

whiteboard *n* tableau *m* blanc

white-collar *adj* d'employé de bureau ▫ **white-collar crime** délinquance *f* économique et financière; **white-collar union** syndicat *m* d'employés de bureau; **white-collar worker** col *m* blanc

whizz-kid *n Fam* jeune prodige *m*; **she's a computer whizz-kid** c'est un vrai génie de l'informatique

❝
This seemingly lottery-like sector is famous for being over-crowded by poorly equipped entrepreneurs attracted by well publicised

"get-megarich-quick" tales of Internet businesses started by **whizz-kid** teenagers in their parents' garages who then float their companies a couple of years later.
❞

whole-life insurance, whole-of-life insurance *n Ins* assurance-décès *f*

wholesale 1 *n* (vente *f* en) gros *m*; **wholesale and retail** le gros et le détail
  2 *adj* de gros ▫ **wholesale bank** banque *f* de gros; **wholesale co-operative** coopérative *f* d'achats; **wholesale customer** client(e) *m,f* qui achète en gros; **wholesale dealer** grossiste *mf*; **wholesale distribution** distribution *f* en gros; **wholesale firm** maison *f* de gros; **wholesale goods** marchandises *fpl* en gros; **wholesale manufacture** fabrication *f* en série; *Banking* **wholesale market** marché *m* de gré à gré entre banques; **wholesale price** prix *m* de gros; **wholesale price index** indice *m* des prix de gros; **wholesale trade** commerce *m* de gros
  3 *adv* *(buy, sell)* en gros; **I can get it for you wholesale** je peux vous le procurer au prix de gros

wholesaler *n* grossiste *mf*, marchand(e) *m,f* ou commerçant(e) *m,f* en gros ▫ **wholesaler dealer** grossiste, marchand(e) en gros; **wholesaler margin** marge *f* du grossiste

wholesaling *n* vente *f* en gros

wholly-owned subsidiary *n* filiale *f* à cent pour cent

wide area network *n Comptr* réseau *m* longue distance

widow's pension *n* allocation *f* veuvage

wildcard *n Comptr* joker *m* ▫ **wildcard character** caractère *m* joker

wildcat *n* (**a**) **wildcat strike** grève *f* sauvage (**b**) *Am Mktg (product, company)* dilemme *m*

will *n* testament *m*; **to make a will** faire un testament

▸ **wind up** *(company)* liquider, dissoudre; *(account)* régler, clôturer; *(speech, meeting)* terminer; **the business will be wound up by the end of the year** l'entreprise sera liquidée avant la fin de l'année

windbill *n Fin* billet *m* ou effet *m* de complaisance

windfall *n (unexpected gain)* aubaine *f* ▫ **windfall dividends** dividendes *mpl* exceptionnels; **windfall payment** paiement *m* exceptionnel; **windfall profits** bénéfices *mpl* exceptionnels; **windfall revenues** revenus *mpl* exceptionnels; **windfall tax** impôt *m* sur les bénéfices exceptionnels

winding-up *n (of company)* liquidation *f*; *(of account)* clôture *f* ▫ **winding-up order** ordre *m* de mise en règlement judiciaire

window n (**a**) *(of shop)* vitrine f □ **window display** étalage m; **window dressing** *(in shop)* présentation f de l'étalage; *Acct* habillage m de bilan (**b**) *Comptr* fenêtre f (**c**) *Fam (in schedule)* créneau m, moment m libre; **I've got a window at 10.30** j'ai un trou à 10h30; **a window of opportunity** de nouvelles possibilités fpl (**d**) **window envelope** enveloppe f à fenêtre

> Airlines are tricky businesses, as British Airways has unhappily proven. A few delays or technical problems and the wheels could come off. EasyJet clearly sees a **window of opportunity** – it wants to buy big quickly, while traditional carriers struggle to cope with the fallout from September 11.

win-win adj **a win-win situation** = une solution qui convient à tout le monde

> Ariba's Glynn agrees that constant pressure on suppliers is limiting the potential of online trade exchanges. "We've got to change from that single-sided view where we just beat the supplier to death," Glynn says. "We've got to get to that **win-win situation** where both sides feel they are getting better deals."

WIP n *(abbr* **work in progress**) travail m en cours

▶ **wipe off** vt sep *(debt)* annuler; **several millions of pounds were wiped off the value of shares** la valeur des actions a baissé de plusieurs millions de livres

wireless mouse n *Comptr* souris f sans fil

wire service n *Am* agence f de presse

withdraw vt (**a**) *(money)* retirer; **I need to withdraw £500 from my account** il faut que je retire 500 livres de mon compte (**b**) *(order)* annuler

withdrawal n *(of money)* retrait m; **to make a withdrawal** faire un retrait □ **withdrawal limit** plafond m de retrait; **withdrawal notice** avis m de retrait; **withdrawal slip** bordereau m de retrait

withhold vt *(rent, tax)* refuser de payer; **to withhold payment** refuser de payer

withholding n **the withholding of payments** le refus de payer; **the withholding of taxes** le refus de payer les impôts □ *Am* **withholding tax** impôt m retenu à la source, retenue f fiscale

without prep *Law* **without prejudice** *(on document)* sous toutes réserves; **without recourse** *(on bill of exchange)* sans recours

with-pack premium n *Mktg* prime f directe

word n *Comptr* **word count** nombre m de mots;

to do a word count compter les mots; **word count facility** fonction f de comptage de mots; **word processing** traitement m de texte; **word processor** machine f de traitement de texte

word-of-mouth advertising n publicité f de bouche à oreille

word-process vt *Comptr* réaliser par traitement de texte

word-processing adj *Comptr* de traitement de texte □ **word-processing package** logiciel m de traitement de texte; **word-processing software** logiciel de traitement de texte

wordwrap n *Comptr* passage m automatique à la ligne suivante

work 1 n (**a**) *(labour)* travail m; **this report needs more work** il y a encore du travail à faire sur ce rapport; **to start work, to set to work** se mettre au travail; **she set to work on the contract** elle a commencé à travailler sur le contrat □ *Comptr* **work area** zone f de travail; **work flow** rhythme m de travail; **work flow schedule** plan m de travail; **work in progress** travail en cours; *(sign)* travaux; **work progress** avancement m des travaux; **work rate** cadence f de travail; **work to rule** grève f du zèle; **work standard** norme f de travail; **work study engineer** ingénieur m en organisation
(**b**) *(employment)* travail m, emploi m; **to look for work** chercher du travail; **to be out of work** être sans travail *ou* sans emploi; **to take time off work** prendre des congés; **she's off work today** elle ne travaille pas aujourd'hui □ **work colleague** collègue mf de travail; **work experience** expérience f professionnelle; **work permit** permis m de travail
(**c**) *(task)* travail m; **to take work home** ramener du travail à la maison; **he's trying to get some work done** il essaie de travailler un peu □ **work group** groupe m de travail
(**d**) **works** *(construction)* travaux mpl; *(factory)* usine f □ **works committee, works council** comité m d'entreprise; **works manager** chef m d'établissement; **works owner** maître m d'ouvrage
2 vt *(employee)* faire travailler; **the boss works his staff hard** le patron exige beaucoup de travail de ses employés
3 vi (**a**) *(of person)* travailler; **he works in advertising** il travaille dans la publicité; **we have to work to a budget** nous devons travailler avec un certain budget; **to work to rule** faire la grève du zèle
(**b**) *(of machine)* fonctionner
(**c**) *(of plan, idea, method)* marcher

> Flights to France were worst affected as an all day walkout interrupted more than 7,000 flights. Shorter stoppages in Greece, Portu-

gal, Hungary and Italy brought airports to a standstill, and in Switzerland, Belgium, Luxembourg and Austria staff **worked to rule**. ,,

▸ **work out 1** vt sep (**a**) (plan) élaborer (**b**) (account) examiner; (price) établir, calculer
2 vi (total) **to work out at** s'élever à; **the total works out at £9,000** le montant s'élève à 9000 livres

▸ **work up** vt sep **to work one's way up** faire son chemin; **she worked her way up from secretary to managing director** elle a commencé comme secrétaire et a fait son chemin jusqu'au poste de P-DG

workable adj (project, plan) réalisable

workaholic n Fam bourreau m de travail

workday n (day's work) journée f de travail; (working day) jour m ouvrable

worker n travailleur(euse) m,f; (in industry) ouvrier(ère) m,f; **workers and management** partenaires mpl sociaux □ **workers' co-operative** coopérative f ouvrière; **worker director** = ouvrier qui fait partie du conseil d'administration; **worker participation** participation f ouvrière; **worker representation** représentation f du personnel

workforce n main-d'œuvre f, personnel m

work-in n Ind = occupation d'une entreprise par le personnel (avec poursuite du travail)

working adj (person) qui travaille; (population) actif(ive) □ Fin **working account** compte m d'exploitation; **working agreement** accord m, entente f; Acct **working assets** actif m circulant; Fin **working capital** fonds mpl de roulement; Fin **working capital cycle** cycle m du besoin en fonds de roulement; Fin **working capital fund** compte d'avances; Fin **working capital requirements** besoins mpl en fonds de roulement; **working class** classe f ouvrière; **working conditions** conditions fpl de travail; **working copy** (of document) copie f de travail; **working day** journée f (de travail); Admin jour m ouvrable; **during a normal working day** pendant la journée de travail; **Sunday is not a working day** le dimanche est chômé; **working document** document m de travail; **working environment** environnement m professionnel; **working expenses** frais mpl généraux, frais d'exploitation; **working hours** heures fpl de travail; **working interest** participation f d'exploitation; **working lunch** déjeuner m d'affaires ou de travail; **working man** ouvrier m; **working party** groupe m de travail; **working week** semaine f de travail; **working woman** ouvrière f; (woman who works) femme f qui travaille

workload n travail m à effectuer, charge f de travail; **to have a heavy workload** être sur-

chargé(e) de travail; **my workload has eased off a bit** j'ai un peu moins de travail en ce moment

workman n (manual worker) ouvrier m; (craftsman) artisan m

workmanlike adj (efficient) professionnel(elle); (well made) bien fait(e)

workmanship n exécution f; **a good/shoddy piece of workmanship** du travail bien/mal fait

workplace n lieu m de travail; **in the workplace** sur le lieu de travail

workshare n travail m en temps partagé; (person) travailleur(euse) m,f en temps partagé; **workshares are becoming more common** le partage du travail devient de plus en plus courant

worksharing n partage m du travail; **we have a worksharing arrangement** nous avons un système de partage du travail; **worksharing is becoming more and more popular** le partage du travail est de plus en plus courant

worksheet n feuille f de travail

workshop n atelier m

workstation n Comptr station f ou poste m de travail

work-to-rule n grève f du zèle

workweek n Am semaine f de travail

world n (**a**) (earth) monde m □ **World Bank** Banque f mondiale; **world economy** conjoncture f économique mondiale; **the World Fair** l'Exposition f universelle; **world markets** marchés mpl mondiaux ou internationaux; **world reserves** réserves fpl mondiales; **world trade** commerce m international; **World Trade Organization** Organisation f mondiale du commerce; Comptr **the World Wide Web** le World Wide Web (**b**) (domain) monde m, milieu m; **the business world** le monde des affaires; **the financial world** le monde de la finance

worldwide 1 adj mondial(e), global(e) □ Ins **worldwide policy** police f universelle; **worldwide rights** droits mpl d'exploitation pour le monde entier
2 adv partout dans le monde, dans le monde entier; **this product is now sold worldwide** ce produit se vend maintenant dans le monde entier

WORM Comptr (abbr write once read many times) WORM

worth 1 n valeur f; **£500 worth of damage** pour 500 livres de dégâts, des dégâts qui se montent à 500 livres; **a week's worth of supplies** suffisament de provisions pour une semaine
2 prep **to be worth sth** valoir qch; **how much is it worth?** combien est-ce que cela vaut?; **what is the euro worth?** combient vaut l'euro?

worthless *adj (object, advice, suggestion)* sans valeur

WP *n Comptr* (**a**) (*abbr* **word processing**) traitement *m* de texte, TTX *m* (**b**) (*abbr* **word processor**) machine *f* de traitement de texte

wrap 1 *vt (goods)* emballer
2 *vi Comptr (of text)* se boucler

wrist rest *n Comptr* repose-poignets *m*

writ *n Law* ordonnance *f*; **to serve a writ on sb** assigner qn en justice ❑ **writ of execution** ordonnance *f* de saisie

write 1 *n Comptr* **write access** accès *m* en écriture; **write area** zone *f* d'écriture; **write density** densité *f* d'écriture; **write protection** protection *f* contre l'écriture *ou* en écriture; **write speed** vitesse *f* d'écriture
2 *vt (letter, name, address)* écrire; *(cheque)* faire; *(CD-ROM)* graver, enregistrer; *Am* **to write sb** écrire à qn; *Comptr* **to write sth to disk** écrire qch sur disque
3 *vi* écrire; **to write to sb** écrire à qn

▶ **write away for** *vt insep (order by post)* commander par lettre, écrire pour commander; **I wrote away for a catalogue** j'ai écrit pour commander un catalogue; **I had to write away for spare parts** j'ai dû écrire pour commander des pièces

▶ **write down** *vt sep* (**a**) *(note)* noter; *(put in writing)* mettre par écrit (**b**) *Fin (capital, stock)* réduire; *Acct (asset)* déprécier

▶ **write off** *vt sep* (**a**) *Fin (capital, stock)* amortir (**b**) *Acct (bad debt, asset)* passer par profits et pertes

▶ **write up** *vt sep Fin (capital, stock)* augmenter; *Acct (asset)* revaloriser

write-down *n Acct* dépréciation *f* ❑ **write-down of accounts receivable** dépréciation de créances

write-off *n Acct* annulation *f* par écrit, passa-

tion *f* par pertes et profits

write-protect *vt Comptr* protéger contre l'écriture *ou* en écriture

write-protected *adj Comptr* protégé(e) contre l'écriture *ou* en écriture

write-up *n Acct* augmentation *f*

written *n* **written agreement** convention *f* écrite; **written offer of employment** lettre *f* d'embauche; **written proof** pièce *f* justificative; **written undertaking** promesse *f* écrite, engagement *m* écrit

written-down cost, written-down value *n Acct* valeur *f* amortie

wrongful *adj* **wrongful dismissal** licenciement *m* abusif; **wrongful trading** = situation dans laquelle une société poursuit ses opérations en dépit du fait que la mise en liquidation est inévitable

> **"**
> ───
> Under UK insolvency legislation, if a company goes into insolvent liquidation, a director will be liable for **wrongful trading** (and liable to contribute personally to the company's losses) if, at some time before the commencement of the winding up, the director knew or, perhaps more significantly, ought to have concluded that there was no reasonable prospect that the company would avoid going into insolvent liquidation but continued to trade in any event.
> ─── **"**

WTO *n* (*abbr* **World Trade Organization**) OMC *f*

WWW *n Comptr* (*abbr* **World Wide Web**) WWW, W3

WYSIWYG *n Comptr* (*abbr* **what you see is what you get**) tel écran-tel écrit *m*, tel-tel *m*, Wysiwyg *m* ❑ **WYSIWYG display** affichage *m* tel écran-tel écrit *ou* tel-tel *ou* Wysiwyg

Xx Yy

XD *adj (abbr* **ex dividend**) ex-dividende

X-Dax *n St Exch* **the X-Dax (index)** le X-Dax, l'indice *m* X-Dax

xerography *n* xérographie *f*

Xerox® **1** *n (machine)* photocopieur *m*, photocopieuse *f; (copy)* photocopie *f* ▫ *Xerox® copy* photocopie; *Xerox® machine* photocopieur, photocopieuse
2 *vt* photocopier

Xetra-Dax *n St Exch* **the Xetra-Dax index** l'indice *m* Xetra-dax

XMCL *n Comptr (abbr* **Extensible Media Commerce Language**) XMCL *m*

XML *n Comptr (abbr* **Extensible Markup Language**) XML *m*

Yankee bond *n Am Fin* obligation *f* Yankee

year *n (twelve-month period)* an *m; (referring to duration)* année *f;* **to earn £40,000 a year** gagner 40 000 livres par an; **the year under review** l'exercice *m* écoulé; *Acct* **year ended 31 December 2002** exercice clos le 31 décembre 2002; *Comptr* **year 2000 compliant** protégé(e) contre le bogue de l'an 2000 ▫ *year of assessment* année *f* d'imposition; *year's profits* profits *mpl* de l'exercice; *year's purchase* taux *m* de capitalisation des bénéfices

yearbook *n* annuaire *m*

year-end *adj Acct* de fin d'exercice ▫ *year-end accounts* compte *m* de résultats; *year-end audit* vérification *f* comptable de fin d'exercice; *year-end closing of accounts* clôture *f* annuelle des livres; *year-end loss* perte *f* de fin d'exercice; *year-end profits* bénéfices *mpl* de fin d'exercice

yearly **1** *adj* annuel(elle) ▫ *yearly accounts* comptes *mpl* annuels; *yearly payment* annuité *f*, versement *m* annuel; *yearly premium* prime *f* annuelle
2 *adv* annuellement

year-on-year *adj* sur un an ▫ *year-on-year growth* la croissance sur un an; *year-on-year results* les résultats *mpl* sur un an

yellow *adj the Yellow Pages®* les Pages *fpl* jaunes®; *yellow sticker (Post-it®)* note *f* autocollante

yen *n* yen *m*

yes/no question *n Mktg (in survey)* question *f* fermée

yield **1** *n (from investments)* rapport *m*, rendement *m; (from tax)* recette *f*, rapport ▫ *yield capacity* productivité *f; yield curve* courbe *f* des taux; *yield gap* prime *f* de risque
2 *vt (dividend, interest)* rapporter; *(income)* créer; **the investment bond will yield five percent** le bon d'épargne rapportera cinq pour cent

youth *n youth market* marché *m* de la jeunesse; *youth marketing* marketing *m* de la classe des jeunes, marketing des juniors

yuppie *n* yuppie *mf*

Z z

zap vt Comptr (file) écraser

ZBB n Acct (abbr **zero base budgeting**) BBZ m

Z chart n diagramme m en Z

zero n zéro m □ Acct **zero base budgeting** budget m base zéro, budgétisation f base zéro ; **zero coupon bond** obligation f émise à coupon zéro ; Mktg **zero defects** zéro défaut m ; Mktg **zero defects purchasing** achats mpl de qualité à 100%, achats zéro défaut ; Econ **zero growth** croissance f zéro, croissance économique nulle ; **zero rating** taux m zéro

zero-rated adj (for VAT) exempt(e) ou exonéré(e) de TVA ; **in Britain, books are zero-rated** en Grande-Bretagne, les livres sont exempts ou exonérés de TVA

zero-rating n franchise f de TVA, taux m zéro

Zip® n Comptr **Zip® disk** cartouche f Zip® ; **Zip® drive** lecteur m Zip®

zip 1 n Am **zip code** code m postal
2 vt Comptr zipper, compresser

zone 1 n (area) zone f
2 vt (classify) désigner ; **to zone an area as industrial/residential** classer un secteur zone industrielle/résidentielle

zoning n zonage m

zoom box n Comptr case f zoom

SUPPLÉMENT

Table des matières

GUIDE DE COMMUNICATION EN ANGLAIS

Table des matières

La présentation de la lettre

La correspondance administrative ou commerciale, influencée par le fax et le courrier électronique, exige l'emploi d'un style direct et concis. On emploiera de préférence un ton amical mais respectueux en évitant les abréviations ou les contractions telles que "don't", "I've" et "she'd" pour "do not", "I have" et "she had/would" qui doivent être réservées au courrier privé ou à la communication orale.

Chaque paragraphe doit comporter un maximum de trois ou quatre phrases et traiter d'un seul sujet. On veillera à ne pas mélanger passé et présent à l'intérieur d'une même phrase et à respecter les règles de la concordance des temps.

L'orthographe et la grammaire doivent être impeccables.

Dans les pays anglo-saxons, la lettre d'affaires est toujours dactylographiée. Les paragraphes sont alignés à gauche, sans retrait, et séparés par une ligne de blanc. En anglais britannique, la date, les adresses, les formules d'appel et de politesse ne comportent aucun signe de ponctuation. En anglais américain, on insère une virgule avant l'année dans la date, un point après les abréviations Mr., Ms., etc., deux-points après la formule d'appel et une virgule après la formule de politesse.

Formules d'appel et formules de politesse

La formule de politesse varie en fonction de la formule d'appel utilisée. Voir le tableau au verso.

- **formule d'appel**
- **formule de politesse**

Lorsqu'on ne connaît pas le nom de la personne à qui l'on s'adresse :

Dear Sir
Dear Madam

Yours faithfully (Br)

En anglais américain, la formule de politesse est toujours inversée :

Faithfully yours (Am)

Lorsqu'on ne sait pas s'il s'agit d'un homme ou d'une femme :

Dear Sir or Madam
ou **Dear Sir/Madam**

Lorsqu'on s'adresse à une société ou à un organisme sans préciser le nom du destinataire :

Dear Sirs (Br)
Gentlemen (Am)

Lorsqu'on connaît le nom de la personne à qui l'on s'adresse :

Dear Mr Jameson
Dear Mrs Lucas
Dear Miss Crookshaw
Dear Ms Greening

Yours sincerely (Br)
Sincerely yours (Am)
Sincerely (Am)

(L'abréviation Ms est de plus en plus employée lorsqu'on s'adresse à une femme car elle permet de ne pas préciser s'il s'agit d'une femme mariée (Mrs) ou non (Miss).)

Dear Dr Illingworth

Ton plus amical :
Yours very sincerely (Br)

Style moins soutenu :
With best wishes
With kind regards
Kindest regards

Aux États-Unis, l'abréviation est généralement suivie d'un point :

Mr., Mrs., Ms., Dr.

Plus rare:
Yours respectfully
Respectfully yours (Am)
Respectfully (Am)

Lorsqu'on s'adresse au rédacteur en chef d'un journal :
Sir

à un conseiller :
Dear Councillor Henderson
Dear Councillor Mr/Mrs/Ms Adams

à un député :
Dear Mr/Mrs Brown

à un gouverneur :
Dear Governor Almanza

à un représentant ou membre du Congrès :
Sir/Madam
Dear Congressman/Congresswoman Fox
Dear Senator Mitcham

au Premier ministre :
Dear Sir/Madam
Dear Prime Minister

au président des États-Unis :
Sir/Madam
Dear Mr/Madam President

Presentation d'une lettre dactylographiée

Les paragraphes sont alignés à gauche, sans retrait, et séparés par une ligne de blanc.

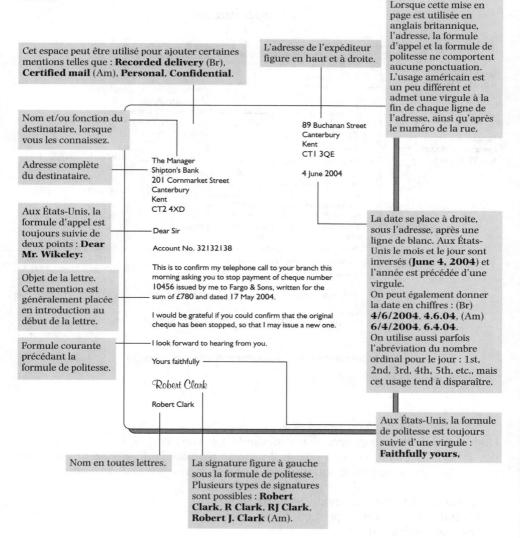

Lorsque cette mise en page est utilisée en anglais britannique, l'adresse, la formule d'appel et la formule de politesse ne comportent aucune ponctuation. L'usage américain est un peu différent et admet une virgule à la fin de chaque ligne de l'adresse, ainsi qu'après le numéro de la rue.

Cet espace peut être utilisé pour ajouter certaines mentions telles que : **Recorded delivery** (Br), **Certified mail** (Am), **Personal**, **Confidential**.

L'adresse de l'expéditeur figure en haut et à droite.

Nom et/ou fonction du destinataire, lorsque vous les connaissez.

Adresse complète du destinataire.

Aux États-Unis, la formule d'appel est toujours suivie de deux points : **Dear Mr. Wikeley:**

Objet de la lettre. Cette mention est généralement placée en introduction au début de la lettre.

Formule courante précédant la formule de politesse.

La date se place à droite, sous l'adresse, après une ligne de blanc. Aux États-Unis le mois et le jour sont inversés (**June 4, 2004**) et l'année est précédée d'une virgule.
On peut également donner la date en chiffres : (Br) **4/6/2004, 4.6.04**, (Am) **6/4/2004, 6.4.04**.
On utilise aussi parfois l'abréviation du nombre ordinal pour le jour : 1st, 2nd, 3rd, 4th, 5th, etc., mais cet usage tend à disparaître.

Aux États-Unis, la formule de politesse est toujours suivie d'une virgule : **Faithfully yours,**

Nom en toutes lettres.

La signature figure à gauche sous la formule de politesse. Plusieurs types de signatures sont possibles : **Robert Clark, R Clark, RJ Clark, Robert J. Clark** (Am).

Contents of the letter image:

89 Buchanan Street
Canterbury
Kent
CT1 3QE

4 June 2004

The Manager
Shipton's Bank
201 Cornmarket Street
Canterbury
Kent
CT2 4XD

Dear Sir

Account No. 32132138

This is to confirm my telephone call to your branch this morning asking you to stop payment of cheque number 10456 issued by me to Fargo & Sons, written for the sum of £780 and dated 17 May 2004.

I would be grateful if you could confirm that the original cheque has been stopped, so that I may issue a new one.

I look forward to hearing from you.

Yours faithfully

Robert Clark

Robert Clark

Presentation d'une lettre sur papier à en-tête

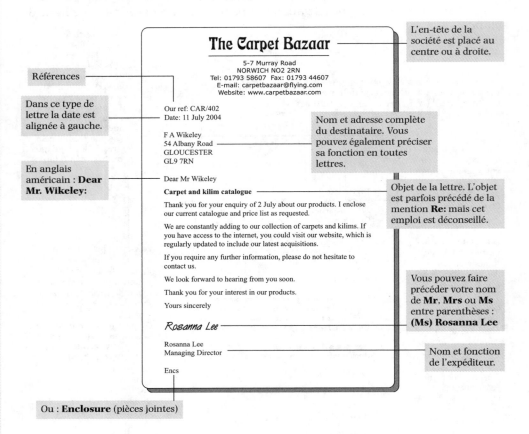

L'en-tête de la société est placé au centre ou à droite.

Références

Dans ce type de lettre la date est alignée à gauche.

En anglais américain : **Dear Mr. Wikeley:**

The Carpet Bazaar

5-7 Murray Road
NORWICH NO2 2RN
Tel: 01793 58607 Fax: 01793 44607
E-mail: carpetbazaar@flying.com
Website: www.carpetbazaar.com

Our ref: CAR/402
Date: 11 July 2004

F A Wikeley
54 Albany Road
GLOUCESTER
GL9 7RN

Dear Mr Wikeley

Carpet and kilim catalogue

Thank you for your enquiry of 2 July about our products. I enclose our current catalogue and price list as requested.

We are constantly adding to our collection of carpets and kilims. If you have access to the internet, you could visit our website, which is regularly updated to include our latest acquisitions.

If you require any further information, please do not hesitate to contact us.

We look forward to hearing from you soon.

Thank you for your interest in our products.

Yours sincerely

Rosanna Lee

Rosanna Lee
Managing Director

Encs

Nom et adresse complète du destinataire. Vous pouvez également préciser sa fonction en toutes lettres.

Objet de la lettre. L'objet est parfois précédé de la mention **Re:** mais cet emploi est déconseillé.

Vous pouvez faire précéder votre nom de **Mr**, **Mrs** ou **Ms** entre parenthèses : **(Ms) Rosanna Lee**

Nom et fonction de l'expéditeur.

Ou : **Enclosure** (pièces jointes)

Enveloppes et adresses

L'adresse doit être aussi précise que possible. Les sites Web des services postaux des différents pays peuvent être utiles pour trouver l'adresse complète d'un particulier, d'un organisme ou d'une entreprise, y compris le code postal précis.

Royaume-Uni : www.royalmail.com
Canada : www.canadapost.ca
Irlande : www.anpost.ie
États-Unis : www.usps.gov
Australie : www.auspost.com.au
Nouvelle-Zélande : www.nzpost.co.nz

Il est recommandé de n'inclure aucun signe de ponctuation et, surtout aux États-Unis et au Canada, de rédiger l'adresse en majuscules (voir les modèles ci-dessous).

- **Au Royaume- Uni :**

  Mr (Mrs, Ms, Dr, etc.), prénom (ou initiale), nom de famille
  (Dénomination du lieu et/ou) Numéro, nom de la rue
  Localité (ville, village)
  COMTÉ ou GRANDE VILLE
  CODE POSTAL

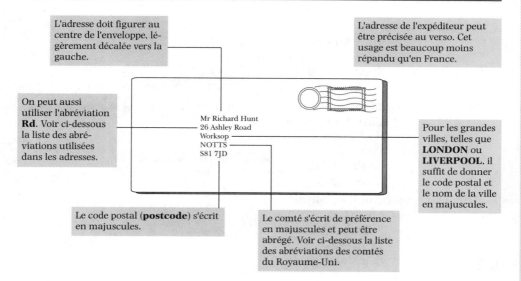

L'adresse doit figurer au centre de l'enveloppe, légèrement décalée vers la gauche.

L'adresse de l'expéditeur peut être précisée au verso. Cet usage est beaucoup moins répandu qu'en France.

On peut aussi utiliser l'abréviation **Rd**. Voir ci-dessous la liste des abréviations utilisées dans les adresses.

Mr Richard Hunt
26 Ashley Road
Worksop
NOTTS
S81 7JD

Pour les grandes villes, telles que **LONDON** ou **LIVERPOOL**, il suffit de donner le code postal et le nom de la ville en majuscules.

Le code postal (**postcode**) s'écrit en majuscules.

Le comté s'écrit de préférence en majuscules et peut être abrégé. Voir ci-dessous la liste des abréviations des comtés du Royaume-Uni.

- **Aux États-Unis :**

  Mr. (Mrs., Ms., Dr., etc.), PRÉNOM (et/ou INITIALE), NOM (DÉNOMINATION DU LIEU et/ou) NUMÉRO, NOM DE LA RUE LOCALITÉ (ville, village), ÉTAT et CODE POSTAL

  La ville, l'abréviation de l'Etat et le code postal (**ZIP code**) se suivant sur la même ligne.

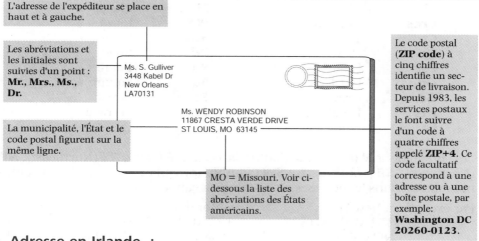

L'adresse de l'expéditeur se place en haut et à gauche.

Les abréviations et les initiales sont suivies d'un point : **Mr., Mrs., Ms., Dr.**

Ms. S. Gulliver
3448 Kabel Dr
New Orleans
LA70131

Ms. WENDY ROBINSON
11867 CRESTA VERDE DRIVE
ST LOUIS, MO 63145

La municipalité, l'État et le code postal figurent sur la même ligne.

Le code postal (**ZIP code**) à cinq chiffres identifie un secteur de livraison. Depuis 1983, les services postaux le font suivre d'un code à quatre chiffres appelé **ZIP+4**. Ce code facultatif correspond à une adresse ou à une boîte postale, par exemple: **Washington DC 20260-0123**.

MO = Missouri. Voir ci-dessous la liste des abréviations des États américains.

- **Adresse en Irlande :**

  Mrs Kathleen Ryan
  48 The Glen
  Roden Park
  Rathfarnham
  Dublin 14
  (Ireland)

  Il n'y a pas de code postal en Irlande, sauf à Dublin où l'on utilise un chiffre entre 1 et 18 pour désigner les différents secteurs de la ville. Pour les adresses rurales, on emploie l'abréviation Co. pour désigner le comté où le destinataire est domicilié : par exemple, Co. Clare pour le comté de Clare.

  Ou : **Republic of Ireland**.

- **Adresse au Canada :**

      Mr & Mrs Fitzgerald
      28 Alpine Boulevard
      St Albert AB T8N 2M7
      (Canada) └──────── AB = Alberta. Les deux premières lettres du code postal canadien représente la province ou le territoire. Voir ci-dessous la liste des abréviations des provinces et des territoires du Canada.

- **Adresse en Australie :**

      Gareth Connolly
      55 Elizabeth Street
      Potts Point
      NSW 2020 ── Abréviation de l'État ou du territoire (voir la liste ci-dessous).
      (Australia)

- **Adresse en Nouvelle-Zélande :**

      Mr J Hall
      3 Bridge Avenue
      Te Atatu
      Auckland 8

- **Abréviations utilisées dans les adresses**

Les abréviations suivantes s'emploient couramment dans les adresses. Elles peuvent figurer aussi bien dans l'en-tête de la lettre que sur l'enveloppe.

Apt	Apartment	**Mtn**	Mountain
Av ou **Ave**	Avenue	**Pde**	Parade
Blvd	Boulevard	**Pk**	Park
Cl	Close	**Pl**	Place
Cres	Crescent	**Plz**	Plaza
Ct	Court	**Rdg**	Ridge
Dr	Drive	**Rd**	Road
Est	Estate	**Rm**	Room
Gdns	Gardens	**Sq**	Square
Gr	Grove	**St**	Street
Hts	Heights	**Ter**	Terrace
La	Lane		

Les abréviations **N** (North), **S** (South), **W** (West), **E** (East), **NE** (Northeast), **NW** (Northwest), **SE** (Southeast) et **SW** (Southwest) sont également très courantes, notamment dans les adresses américaines et canadiennes.

Par exemple, à New York :   à Montréal :

      351 W 32ND ST   123 MAIN ST NW ─────┐
      NEW YORK, │   MONTREAL QC H3Z 2Y7 │
      NY 10001 │

Cette adresse se lit : **three hundred and fifty-one West Thirty-second Street**

Cette adresse se lit : **one hundred and twenty-three Main Street Northwest**

- **Abréviations des comtés au Royaume-Uni**

En règle générale, pour les noms des comtés se terminant en **-shire**, on ne garde que la première syllabe à laquelle on ajoute un '**s**' : **Beds** = **Bedfordshire, Berks** = **Berkshire, Bucks** = **Buckinghamshire, Cambs** = **Cambridgeshire, Gloucs** = **Gloucester, Herts** = **Hertfordshire, Lancs** = **Lancashire, Lincs** = **Lincolnshire, Notts** = **Nottinghamshire, Staffs** = **Staffordshire, Wilts** = **Wiltshire.**

Exceptions : **Northants = Northamptonshire, Oxon = Oxfordshire**
Les comtés suivants ne s'abrègent pas : **Avon, Cleveland, Greater Manchester, Humberside, Kent, Merseyside, Tyne and Wear**.

- **Abréviations des États américains**

AL	Alabama	MT	Montana
AK	Alaska	NE	Nebraska
AZ	Arizona	NV	Nevada
AR	Arkansas	NH	New Hampshire
CA	California	NJ	New Jersey
CO	Colorado	NM	New Mexico
CT	Connecticut	NY	New York
DE	Delaware	NC	North Carolina
DC	District of Columbia	ND	North Dakota
FL	Florida	OH	Ohio
GA	Georgia	OK	Oklahoma
HI	Hawaii	OR	Oregon
ID	Idaho	PA	Pennsylvania
IL	Illinois	RI	Rhode Island
IN	Indiana	SC	South Carolina
IA	Iowa	SD	South Dakota
KS	Kansas	TN	Tennessee
KY	Kentucky	TX	Texas
LA	Louisiana	UT	Utah
ME	Maine	VT	Vermont
MD	Maryland	VA	Virginia
MA	Massachusetts	WA	Washington
MI	Michigan	WV	West Virginia
MN	Minnesota	WI	Wisconsin
MS	Mississippi	WY	Wyoming
MO	Missouri		

- **Abréviations des provinces et des territoires du Canada**

AB	Alberta	NU	Nunavut
BC	British Columbia	ON	Ontario
MB	Manitoba	PE	Prince Edward Island
NB	New Brunswick		
NF	Newfoundland	QC	Quebec
NT	Northwest Territories	SK	Saskatchewan
NS	Nova Scotia	YT	Yukon

- **Abréviations des États et territoires australiens**

ACT	Australian Capital Territory
NSW	New South Wales
NT	Northern Territory
QLD	Queensland
SA	South Australia
TAS	Tasmania
VIC	Victoria
WA	Western Australia

Modèles de lettres

• Pour prendre rendez-vous

Références. Ou :
Our reference: ...
Your reference: ...

En-tête centré ou à gauche.

Ou : **I refer to your letter of 12 September enclosing/ proposing ...**
Further to our telephone conversation yesterday, ...

Ou : **September 29, 2004** (Am)

Ou : **Mr. Patrick Meers** (Am)

Ou : **Dear Mr Meers:** (Am)

Ou : **should like** (plus soutenu)

Ou : **Could you please confirm the dates at your earliest convenience/as soon as possible...**
I would appreciate confirm- ation (of the dates) ...

Ou : **I am very interested in your proposals/products/ programme...**
I confirm my interest in your company's products/in meeting with you

Ou : **I could possibly come to your office/the UK early next week.**
Would it be possible for you to come/could you possibly come to our Paris office on 4 October/next week for a meeting with ...?

Ou : **If you have any questions/ queries, please ...**
Should you have any questions/ Should you require any further information, ...
Please do not hesitate to get in touch, if you have/require...

Ou : **Sincerely (yours),** (Am)

Ou : **(Mrs) Susanne Valat**

Ou : **I look forward to seeing you at the end of the month/ to doing business with you.**
Looking forward to hearing from you, I remain, (suivi de la formule de politesse)

LOOK NOW
14-16 avenue de Belleville
75020 Paris
E-mail: looknow@mode.fr
Tel: (00 33) (0)1 49 00 4900
Fax: (00 33) (0)1 49 00 4901

Our Ref: S901R3
Your Ref: s/02P

29 September 2004

Mr Patrick Meers
Distribution Manager
Meers Ltd
16 Roehampton Road
London
SW15 5LU

Dear Mr Meers

Thank you for your letter dated 12 September. I was extremely interested to read your proposals and would like to arrange a meeting with you to discuss them further.

I would be available to come to London during the last week of February, if that is convenient for you. I would be accompanied by my personal assistant, Martine Barry, and can arrange to bring samples of both our winter and spring lines.

I would be grateful if you could confirm the dates as soon as possible . If you require any further details, please do not hesitate to contact me.

I look forward to meeting you.

Yours sincerely

Susanne Valat

Susanne Valat
Managing Director

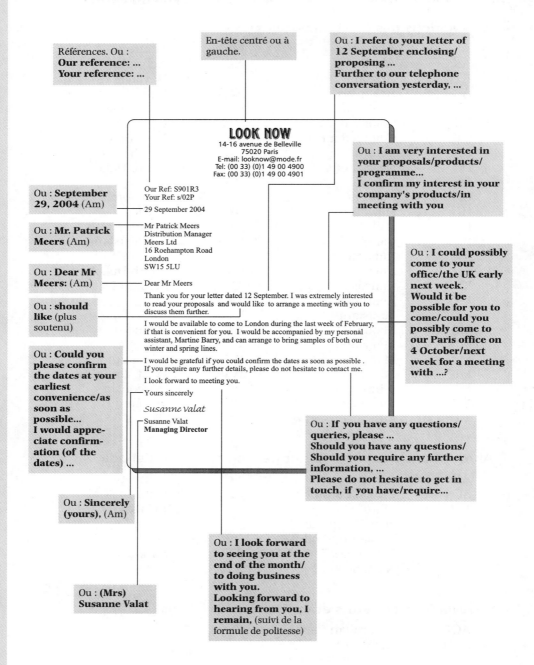

• Suite à un rendez-vous

Dans les pays anglo-saxons, après un premier contact, on préfère souvent appeler les personnes par leur prénom. Vous pouvez dans ce cas commencer votre lettre par **Dear Susanne.**

Ou :
**There are several points that were raised that I would like to discuss further. Firstly, ...
Secondly, ...
I agree fully with your proposal to ..., and would like to confirm ...**
Ou : **As we agreed/discussed on Wednesday, ...**

Ou : **I would like to thank you for affording me the opportunity to meet with you and your staff.**

Ou : **I would like to arrange another meeting with you to discuss matters/the proposal/details further, and suggest next Friday/you come to our Paris office on ...
I should like to discuss matters further and will phone you early next week/write to you again.**

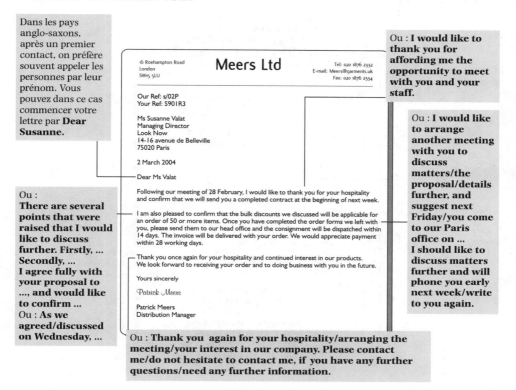

16 Roehampton Road
London
SW15 5LU

Meers Ltd

Tel: 020 1876 2332
E-mail: Meers@garments.uk
Fax: 020 1876 2334

Our Ref: s/02P
Your Ref: S901R3

Ms Susanne Valat
Managing Director
Look Now
14-16 avenue de Belleville
75020 Paris

2 March 2004

Dear Ms Valat

Following our meeting of 28 February, I would like to thank you for your hospitality and confirm that we will send you a completed contract at the beginning of next week.

I am also pleased to confirm that the bulk discounts we discussed will be applicable for an order of 50 or more items. Once you have completed the order forms we left with you, please send them to our head office and the consignment will be dispatched within 14 days. The invoice will be delivered with your order. We would appreciate payment within 28 working days.

Thank you once again for your hospitality and continued interest in our products. We look forward to receiving your order and to doing business with you in the future.

Yours sincerely

Patrick Meers

Patrick Meers
Distribution Manager

Ou : **Thank you again for your hospitality/arranging the meeting/your interest in our company. Please contact me/do not hesitate to contact me, if you have any further questions/need any further information.**

• Réponse à une demande de renseignements

Ou : **Thank you for your enquiry of 13 March about our equipment/services/products ...
In response to your enquiry of 7 April, we have pleasure in enclosing full details of..., together with our price list.**

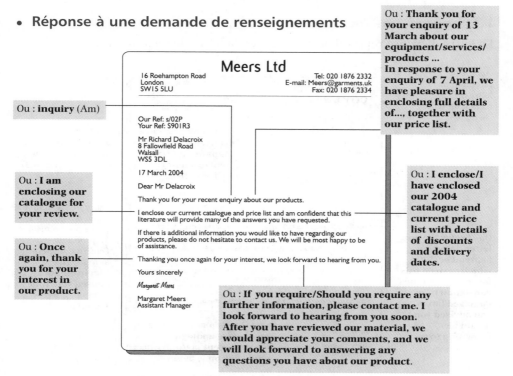

Meers Ltd

16 Roehampton Road
London
SW15 5LU

Tel: 020 1876 2332
E-mail: Meers@garments.uk
Fax: 020 1876 2334

Ou : **inquiry** (Am)

Our Ref: s/02P
Your Ref: S901R3

Mr Richard Delacroix
8 Fallowfield Road
Walsall
WS5 3DL

17 March 2004

Dear Mr Delacroix

Thank you for your recent enquiry about our products.

I enclose our current catalogue and price list and am confident that this literature will provide many of the answers you have requested.

If there is additional information you would like to have regarding our products, please do not hesitate to contact us. We will be most happy to be of assistance.

Thanking you once again for your interest, we look forward to hearing from you.

Yours sincerely

Margaret Meers

Margaret Meers
Assistant Manager

Ou : **I am enclosing our catalogue for your review.**

Ou : **Once again, thank you for your interest in our product.**

Ou : **I enclose/I have enclosed our 2004 catalogue and current price list with details of discounts and delivery dates.**

Ou : **If you require/Should you require any further information, please contact me. I look forward to hearing from you soon. After you have reviewed our material, we would appreciate your comments, and we will look forward to answering any questions you have about our product.**

- ## Lettre de réclamation

note: une lettre de réclamation doit être ferme mais polie, autoritaire sans être personnelle dans les reproches ni vindicative dans le ton

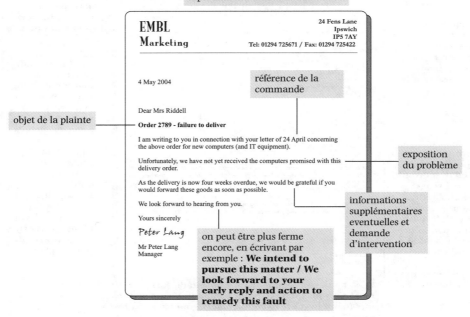

objet de la plainte

référence de la commande

exposition du problème

informations supplémentaires eventuelles et demande d'intervention

on peut être plus ferme encore, en écrivant par exemple : **We intend to pursue this matter / We look forward to your early reply and action to remedy this fault**

- ## Réponse à une réclamation

La lettre d'excuse reprend la structure de la lettre de réclamation.

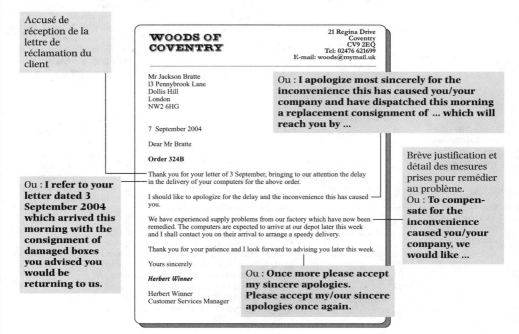

Accusé de réception de la lettre de réclamation du client

Ou : **I apologize most sincerely for the inconvenience this has caused you/your company and have dispatched this morning a replacement consignment of ... which will reach you by ...**

Brève justification et détail des mesures prises pour remédier au problème.
Ou : **To compensate for the inconvenience caused you/your company, we would like ...**

Ou : **I refer to your letter dated 3 September 2004 which arrived this morning with the consignment of damaged boxes you advised you would be returning to us.**

Ou : **Once more please accept my sincere apologies. Please accept my/our sincere apologies once again.**

- ## Publipostage

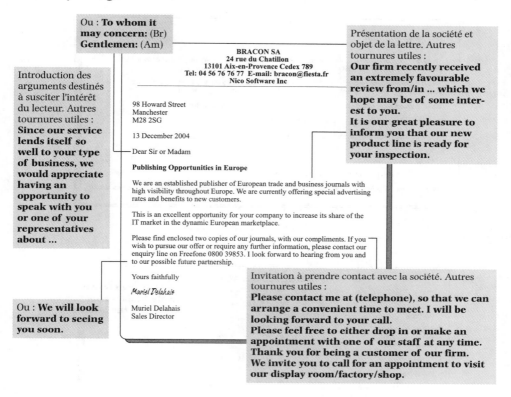

Ou : **To whom it may concern:** (Br) **Gentlemen:** (Am)

Présentation de la société et objet de la lettre. Autres tournures utiles :
Our firm recently received an extremely favourable review from/in ... which we hope may be of some interest to you.
It is our great pleasure to inform you that our new product line is ready for your inspection.

Introduction des arguments destinés à susciter l'intérêt du lecteur. Autres tournures utiles :
Since our service lends itself so well to your type of business, we would appreciate having an opportunity to speak with you or one of your representatives about ...

BRACON SA
24 rue du Chatillon
13101 Aix-en-Provence Cedex 789
Tel: 04 56 76 76 77 E-mail: bracon@fiesta.fr
Nico Software Inc

98 Howard Street
Manchester
M28 2SG

13 December 2004

Dear Sir or Madam

Publishing Opportunities in Europe

We are an established publisher of European trade and business journals with high visibility throughout Europe. We are currently offering special advertising rates and benefits to new customers.

This is an excellent opportunity for your company to increase its share of the IT market in the dynamic European marketplace.

Please find enclosed two copies of our journals, with our compliments. If you wish to pursue our offer or require any further information, please contact our enquiry line on Freefone 0800 39853. I look forward to hearing from you and to our possible future partnership.

Yours faithfully

Muriel Delahais

Muriel Delahais
Sales Director

Ou : **We will look forward to seeing you soon.**

Invitation à prendre contact avec la société. Autres tournures utiles :
Please contact me at (telephone), so that we can arrange a convenient time to meet. I will be looking forward to your call.
Please feel free to either drop in or make an appointment with one of our staff at any time.
Thank you for being a customer of our firm.
We invite you to call for an appointment to visit our display room/factory/shop.

- ## Commande

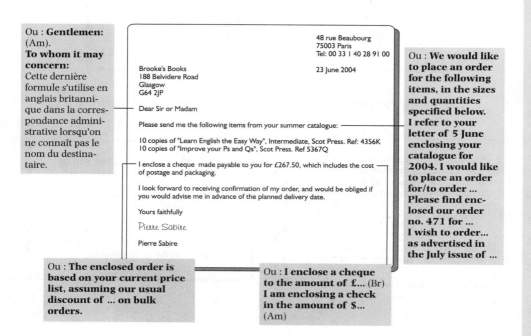

Ou : **Gentlemen:** (Am).
To whom it may concern:
Cette dernière formule s'utilise en anglais britannique dans la correspondance administrative lorsqu'on ne connaît pas le nom du destinataire.

48 rue Beaubourg
75003 Paris
Tel: 00 33 1 40 28 91 00

Brooke's Books
188 Belvidere Road
Glasgow
G64 2JP

23 June 2004

Dear Sir or Madam

Please send me the following items from your summer catalogue:

10 copies of "Learn English the Easy Way", Intermediate, Scot Press. Ref: 4356K
10 copies of "Improve your Ps and Qs", Scot Press. Ref 5367Q

I enclose a cheque made payable to you for £267.50, which includes the cost of postage and packaging.

I look forward to receiving confirmation of my order, and would be obliged if you would advise me in advance of the planned delivery date.

Yours faithfully

Pierre Sabire

Pierre Sabire

Ou : **We would like to place an order for the following items, in the sizes and quantities specified below.**
I refer to your letter of 5 June enclosing your catalogue for 2004. I would like to place an order for/to order ...
Please find enclosed our order no. 471 for ...
I wish to order...
as advertised in the July issue of ...

Ou : **The enclosed order is based on your current price list, assuming our usual discount of ... on bulk orders.**

Ou : **I enclose a cheque to the amount of £...** (Br)
I am enclosing a check in the amount of $... (Am)

- ## Réponse

> Dear Mr Sabire
> Dear Customer
>
> Thank you for your order no ... It is receiving our immediate attention and will be dispatched to you by ... Please allow 28 days for delivery.
>
> This is to acknowledge receipt of your order no ... dated ..., and to advise you that the goods will be dispatched within 7 working days.
>
> We acknowledge receipt of your order of 12 July, which will be dispatched within 14 days.
>
> We cannot accept responsibility for goods damaged in transit.
>
> I hope we may continue to receive your valued custom.
>
> **Ou** :
>
> We regret that we will be unable to fulfil your order for ...
>
> We regret that the goods you ordered are temporarily out of stock/we no longer stock the goods you ordered.

- ## Facture

> **BROOKE'S BOOKS**
> 188 Belvidere Road
> Glasgow G64 2JP
> Tel: 0141 762 0854
>
> **INVOICE**
>
> **Invoice No**: I459
> **Date**: 9 July 2004
> **Order No**: 321SB
>
> **To**: Pierre Sabire
> 48 rue Beaubourg
> 75003 Paris
>
> | | |
> |---|---|
> | 10 copies of "Learn English the Easy Way", Intermediate, Scot Press. Ref: 4356K @ £12.25 each | £122.50 |
> | 10 copies of "Improve your Ps and Qs", Scot Press. Ref 5367Q @ £13.50 each | £135.00 |
> | Postage and packaging | £ 10.00 |
> | Total due: | **£267.50** (incl. VAT) |
>
> Payment would be appreciated within 14 days of receipt.
>
> Thanking you in advance.

Ou : **Payment is to be made 14 days after receipt of the invoice**.

- ## Lettre de rappel

> Our records indicate that payment on your account is overdue to the amount of £ ... If the amount has already been paid, please disregard this notice. If you have not yet posted your payment, please use the enclosed envelope to send payment in full.
>
> Thank you in advance for your anticipated co-operation in this matter.

Ou :
mailed (Am)

Ou : **in the amount of** ... (Am)

- ## Deuxième rappel

> On 12 July 2004 we notified you of your overdue account for order no. ...
>
> To date we still have not received payment for the above order.
>
> Please give this matter your most urgent attention. Payment must be made within the next ten days.

- **Envoi du règlement**

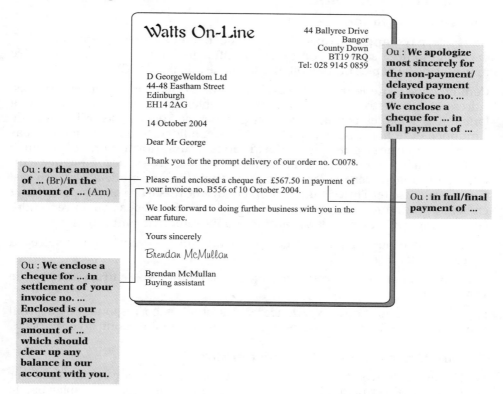

Watts On-Line

44 Ballyree Drive
Bangor
County Down
BT19 7RQ
Tel: 028 9145 0859

Ou : **We apologize most sincerely for the non-payment/ delayed payment of invoice no. ... We enclose a cheque for ... in full payment of ...**

D GeorgeWeldom Ltd
44-48 Eastham Street
Edinburgh
EH14 2AG

14 October 2004

Dear Mr George

Thank you for the prompt delivery of our order no. C0078.

Ou : **to the amount of ... (Br)/in the amount of ... (Am)**

Please find enclosed a cheque for £567.50 in payment of your invoice no. B556 of 10 October 2004.

We look forward to doing further business with you in the near future.

Ou : **in full/final payment of ...**

Yours sincerely

Brendan McMullan

Brendan McMullan
Buying assistant

Ou : **We enclose a cheque for ... in settlement of your invoice no. ... Enclosed is our payment to the amount of ... which should clear up any balance in our account with you.**

Recherche d'emploi

Lettre de motivation

Dans les pays anglo-saxons, la lettre de candidature doit toujours être dactylographiée, sauf si l'annonce spécifie qu'il faut envoyer une lettre manuscrite. Le papier utilisé doit être le même que pour le CV.

Comme pour toute lettre d'affaires, le style doit être clair, concis et courtois. Adressez votre lettre à la personne responsable, en précisant son nom et sa fonction si vous les connaissez. N'oubliez pas de rappeler les références de l'annonce et le poste pour lequel vous êtes candidat. Si vous ne joignez pas votre CV, donnez toutes les informations utiles (formation, expérience professionnelle, compétences, diplômes). Si votre lettre est accompagnée d'un CV, il est inutile de répéter les informations qui s'y trouvent déjà. Dans ce cas, vous devez susciter l'intérêt du lecteur, en faisant ressortir vos compétences et en démontrant que vous possédez les qualités requises. Vous pouvez reprendre certains mots clés utilisés dans l'annonce pour retenir son attention.

L'expérience et les diplômes que vous mentionnez doivent correspondre au poste proposé.

Vous devez montrer dans votre lettre que vous connaissez l'entreprise et qu'elle vous intéresse.

Expliquez en quoi votre expérience et vos qualités correspondent au profil demandé. N'oubliez pas d'ajouter que vous êtes disponible pour un entretien.

Candidature envoyée par courrier électronique

Le CV et la lettre de candidature peuvent être envoyés par courrier électronique. Il est préférable d'envoyer également une version papier par la poste.

- **Demande de stage**

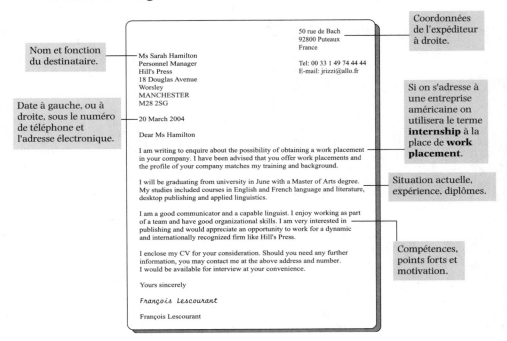

- ## Candidature spontanée

29 Bletchley Road
Worthing
West Sussex
BN14 7QY

Tel: 01903 990092

Alexander Maxwell
Personnel Manager
Kingsway Ltd
24-28 Finchley Rd
London
N2 0TT

13 December 2004

Dear Mr Maxwell

I wish to enquire about any vacancy you may have in your Sales Department. Your customer services manager, Don Griffiths, suggested I wrote to you.

As you can see from the enclosed CV, I have a good educational background and twelve years' experience in sales, both as sales representative and sales executive.

I am currently working for a software company in Kent, where I have acquired essential IT skills. I believe this combined experience in sales and computing would be ideal for the job profile.

Should you consider my application favourably, I should be pleased to attend an interview at any time.

Yours sincerely

William Brownston

Enclosure

Si vous connaissez quelqu'un travaillant déjà dans l'entreprise, signalez-le.

Ou : **As you will note from the enclosed CV** (Br)/ **résumé** (Am), **I have specialized in/ majored in** (Am) **physics and have participated in significant research.**

Ou : **I would like to/I wish to inquire about the possibility of becoming a ... at your factory/ facility/in your company.**

Ou : **I have been/I was given your address by a colleague of mine/of yours,** (nom de la personne), **who has reason to believe you may be recruiting staff (for your sales team).**
I am seeking a position in sales/ publishing at a (high technology) company such as yours.

Ou : **at your convenience.
I would like to learn more about ..., and I will contact your office early next week to arrange an appointment at your convenience.**

Tournures utiles :

**I know how to/I can operate a cash register/a computer/power equipment
I am computer literate/a good communicator/a good organizer
I am a capable linguist/can speak fluent English and German
I have good computer/IT/language/editing/communication/organizational skills
I can learn new tasks and enjoy/can accept a challenge
I enjoy working/can work with a variety of people
I work well in a team, and can also work under pressure
I perform well under stress/am good with difficult customers
I can handle multiple tasks simultaneously**

- ## Réponse à une annonce

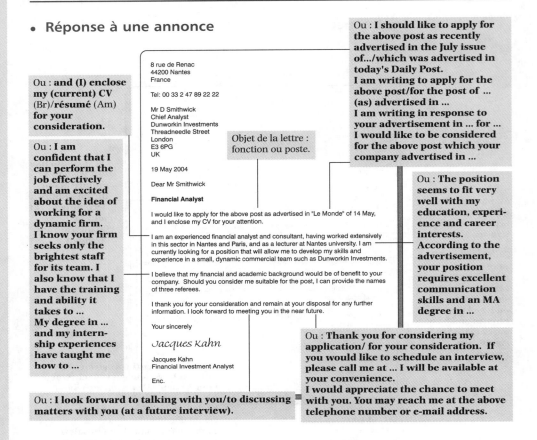

Ou : I should like to apply for the above post as recently advertised in the July issue of.../which was advertised in today's Daily Post.
I am writing to apply for the above post/for the post of ... (as) advertised in ...
I am writing in response to your advertisement in ... for ...
I would like to be considered for the above post which your company advertised in ...

Ou : and (I) enclose my (current) CV (Br)/résumé (Am) for your consideration.

Ou : I am confident that I can perform the job effectively and am excited about the idea of working for a dynamic firm. I know your firm seeks only the brightest staff for its team. I also know that I have the training and ability it takes to ... My degree in ... and my internship experiences have taught me how to ...

Objet de la lettre : fonction ou poste.

Ou : The position seems to fit very well with my education, experience and career interests. According to the advertisement, your position requires excellent communication skills and an MA degree in ...

8 rue de Renac
44200 Nantes
France

Tel: 00 33 2 47 89 22 22

Mr D Smithwick
Chief Analyst
Dunworkin Investments
Threadneedle Street
London
E3 6PG
UK

19 May 2004

Dear Mr Smithwick

Financial Analyst

I would like to apply for the above post as advertised in "Le Monde" of 14 May, and I enclose my CV for your attention.

I am an experienced financial analyst and consultant, having worked extensively in this sector in Nantes and Paris, and as a lecturer at Nantes university. I am currently looking for a position that will allow me to develop my skills and experience in a small, dynamic commercial team such as Dunworkin Investments.

I believe that my financial and academic background would be of benefit to your company. Should you consider me suitable for the post, I can provide the names of three referees.

I thank you for your consideration and remain at your disposal for any further information. I look forward to meeting you in the near future.

Your sincerely

Jacques Kahn

Jacques Kahn
Financial Investment Analyst

Enc.

Ou : Thank you for considering my application/ for your consideration. If you would like to schedule an interview, please call me at ... I will be available at your convenience.
I would appreciate the chance to meet with you. You may reach me at the above telephone number or e-mail address.

Ou : I look forward to talking with you/to discussing matters with you (at a future interview).

Curriculum vitae

Un bon CV se distingue aujourd'hui par sa concision (deux pages au maximum). Il est conseillé de mentionner l'expérience professionnelle et les diplômes en fonction du poste et de l'entreprise visés.

Le CV peut respecter l'ordre chronologique ou adopter l'ordre chronologique inversé, où l'on commence par l'emploi le plus récent et termine par le plus ancien. Ce format est le plus courant. Il est également possible de rédiger un CV ciblé, dans le cadre d'une candidature à une fonction ou à un secteur professionnel précis, en insistant plus sur les compétences et les résultats que sur le parcours.

Les articles (**a**, **an** et **the**) sont généralement omis. Vous pouvez utiliser des verbes pour décrire vos expériences, par exemple : **managed**, **organized**, **supervised**, **designed**, **co-ordinated**, **developed**, etc. Dans un CV envoyé par courrier électronique, ou susceptible d'être scanné, il est préférable d'utiliser des substantifs et des mots clés que le logiciel pourra reconnaître, par exemple : **management**, **organization**, **supervision**, **design**, **co-ordination**, **development of**, etc.

Ne mentionnez pas les références sur le CV. Si l'employeur les demande, imprimez-les sur une feuille séparée.

Si vous envoyez votre CV par courrier électronique, choisissez une police ordinaire et un corps moyen, entre 10 et 14 points. N'insérez pas de tableaux ni de graphiques et évitez d'utiliser des caractères italiques ou soulignés.

- ## Diplômé anglais ayant une première expérience

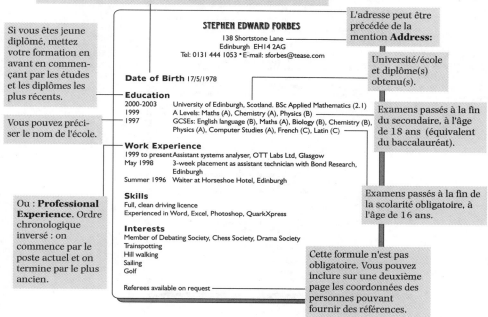

Vous n'êtes pas obligé d'indiquer votre date de naissance. Si vous le souhaitez, vous pouvez préciser votre nationalité, **Nationality:**, et votre situation de famille, **Single** ou **Married**, précédée ou non de la mention : **Status:** ou **Marital Status:**

L'adresse peut être précédée de la mention **Address:**

Si vous êtes jeune diplômé, mettez votre formation en avant en commençant par les études et les diplômes les plus récents.

Université/école et diplôme(s) obtenu(s).

Vous pouvez préciser le nom de l'école.

Examens passés à la fin du secondaire, à l'âge de 18 ans (équivalent du baccalauréat).

Ou : **Professional Experience**. Ordre chronologique inversé : on commence par le poste actuel et on termine par le plus ancien.

Examens passés à la fin de la scolarité obligatoire, à l'âge de 16 ans.

Cette formule n'est pas obligatoire. Vous pouvez inclure sur une deuxième page les coordonnées des personnes pouvant fournir des références.

STEPHEN EDWARD FORBES
138 Shortstone Lane
Edinburgh EH14 2AG
Tel: 0131 444 1053 • E-mail: sforbes@tease.com

Date of Birth 17/5/1978

Education
2000-2003   University of Edinburgh, Scotland. BSc Applied Mathematics (2.1)
1999   A Levels: Maths (A), Chemistry (A), Physics (B)
1997   GCSEs: English language (B), Maths (A), Biology (B), Chemistry (B), Physics (A), Computer Studies (A), French (C), Latin (C)

Work Experience
1999 to present   Assistant systems analyser, OTT Labs Ltd, Glasgow
May 1998   3-week placement as assistant technician with Bond Research, Edinburgh
Summer 1996   Waiter at Horseshoe Hotel, Edinburgh

Skills
Full, clean driving licence
Experienced in Word, Excel, Photoshop, QuarkXpress

Interests
Member of Debating Society, Chess Society, Drama Society
Trainspotting
Hill walking
Sailing
Golf

Referees available on request

- ## Cadre anglais

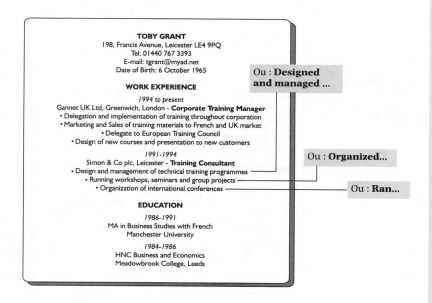

TOBY GRANT
198, Francis Avenue, Leicester LE4 9PQ
Tel: 01440 767 3393
E-mail: tgrant@myad.net
Date of Birth: 6 October 1965

WORK EXPERIENCE

1994 to present
Gannet UK Ltd, Greenwich, London - **Corporate Training Manager**
• Delegation and implementation of training throughout corporation
• Marketing and Sales of training materials to French and UK market
• Delegate to European Training Council
• Design of new courses and presentation to new customers

1991-1994
Simon & Co plc, Leicester - **Training Consultant**
• Design and management of technical training programmes
• Running workshops, seminars and group projects
• Organization of international conferences

EDUCATION

1986-1991
MA in Business Studies with French
Manchester University

1984-1986
HNC Business and Economics
Meadowbrook College, Leeds

Ou : **Designed and managed ...**

Ou : **Organized...**

Ou : **Ran...**

- ## Diplômé américain ayant une première expérience

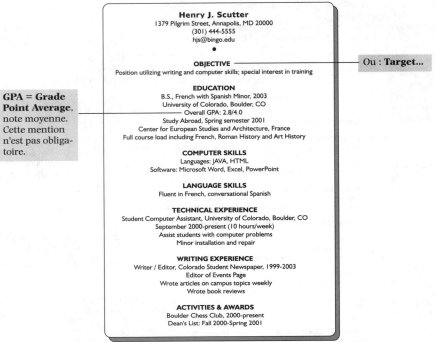

Henry J. Scutter
1379 Pilgrim Street, Annapolis, MD 20000
(301) 444-5555
hjs@bingo.edu
•

OBJECTIVE ——————— Ou : **Target...**
Position utilizing writing and computer skills; special interest in training

EDUCATION
B.S., French with Spanish Minor, 2003
University of Colorado, Boulder, CO
—— Overall GPA: 2.8/4.0
Study Abroad, Spring semester 2001
Center for European Studies and Architecture, France
Full course load including French, Roman History and Art History

COMPUTER SKILLS
Languages: JAVA, HTML
Software: Microsoft Word, Excel, PowerPoint

LANGUAGE SKILLS
Fluent in French, conversational Spanish

TECHNICAL EXPERIENCE
Student Computer Assistant, University of Colorado, Boulder, CO
September 2000-present (10 hours/week)
Assist students with computer problems
Minor installation and repair

WRITING EXPERIENCE
Writer / Editor, Colorado Student Newspaper, 1999-2003
Editor of Events Page
Wrote articles on campus topics weekly
Wrote book reviews

ACTIVITIES & AWARDS
Boulder Chess Club, 2000-present
Dean's List: Fall 2000-Spring 2001

GPA = Grade Point Average, note moyenne. Cette mention n'est pas obligatoire.

- ## Cadre américain

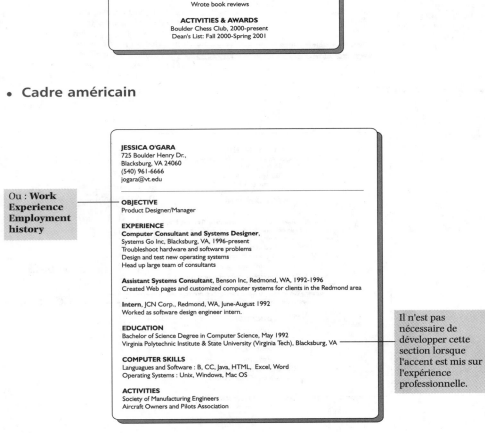

JESSICA O'GARA
725 Boulder Henry Dr.,
Blacksburg, VA 24060
(540) 961-6666
jogara@vt.edu

OBJECTIVE
Product Designer/Manager

EXPERIENCE
Computer Consultant and Systems Designer,
Systems Go Inc, Blacksburg, VA, 1996-present
Troubleshoot hardware and software problems
Design and test new operating systems
Head up large team of consultants

Assistant Systems Consultant, Benson Inc, Redmond, WA, 1992-1996
Created Web pages and customized computer systems for clients in the Redmond area

Intern, JCN Corp., Redmond, WA, June-August 1992
Worked as software design engineer intern.

EDUCATION
Bachelor of Science Degree in Computer Science, May 1992
Virginia Polytechnic Institute & State University (Virginia Tech), Blacksburg, VA

COMPUTER SKILLS
Languagues and Software : B, CC, Java, HTML, Excel, Word
Operating Systems : Unix, Windows, Mac OS

ACTIVITIES
Society of Manufacturing Engineers
Aircraft Owners and Pilots Association

Ou : **Work Experience Employment history**

Il n'est pas nécessaire de développer cette section lorsque l'accent est mis sur l'expérience professionnelle.

- ## Diplômé français ayant une première expérience

Vous n'êtes pas obligé de préciser votre nationalité ou votre âge. Ces informations, tout comme la situation de famille, sont souvent omises.

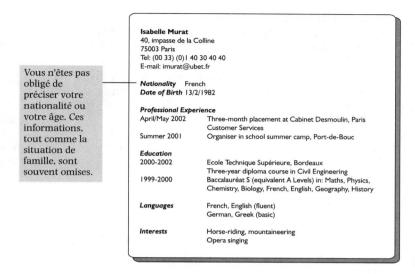

Isabelle Murat
40, impasse de la Colline
75003 Paris
Tel: (00 33) (0)1 40 30 40 40
E-mail: imurat@ubet.fr

Nationality   French
Date of Birth 13/2/1982

Professional Experience

April/May 2002	Three-month placement at Cabinet Desmoulin, Paris
	Customer Services
Summer 2001	Organiser in school summer camp, Port-de-Bouc

Education

2000-2002	Ecole Technique Supérieure, Bordeaux
	Three-year diploma course in Civil Engineering
1999-2000	Baccalauréat S (equivalent A Levels) in: Maths, Physics, Chemistry, Biology, French, English, Geography, History

Languages	French, English (fluent)
	German, Greek (basic)

Interests	Horse-riding, mountaineering
	Opera singing

- ## Cadre français

Laurent Marie
25, rue des Arquebusiers   Tel: 02 24 24 45 73
76000 Rouen   E-mail: mariel@battisto.com.fr

Human Resources Consultant

Work Experience

1993 - present	Human Resources Consultant, Cabinet Battisto-Langlade, Rouen
	Advising companies on accounting, recruitment strategies
1989 - 1992	Personnel Manager, Conseil général, Le Havre
	Recruiting, planning of training programmes, staff follow-up
1987 - 1988	Assistant to Personnel Manager, Société Pierre et Fils, Le Havre

Education

1985	Master of Business Administration, Boston University
1983 - 1984	DEA 'Langage et Médias' - Paris X
1982	Master's Degree in History - Paris IV
1978	Baccalauréat (equivalent A Levels), specialising in Maths, Académie de Paris.

Other Experience
Year spent in Africa (1986/7) as part of a mission with the voluntary medical aid organisation, "Médecins sans frontières"
Member of a voluntary association promoting adult literacy

Languages	Fluent English and Spanish

Computer Skills	Mac OS, Word, Excel

La télécopie

Quelques conseils pour la rédaction de documents transmis par télécopieur ou fax :
- Ne mentionnez que les informations essentielles.
- Vous pouvez adopter un style télégraphique et utiliser des abréviations et des acronymes pour remplacer des mots, voire des expressions entières. Seules les abréviations reconnues doivent être employées (voir p. 27)
- Veillez au ton général du message : les messages courts et factuels peuvent sembler froids. Il est donc conseillé de terminer par une formule de politesse amicale, telle que "Best Wishes".

- **Dans une entreprise**

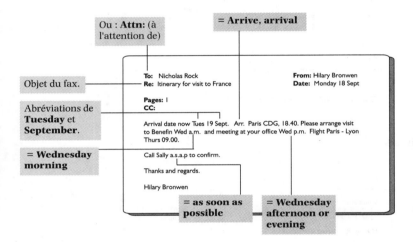

- **Pour confirmer une réservation**

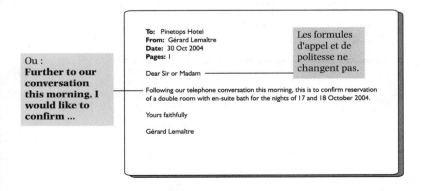

Le courrier électronique

Le courrier électronique étant un moyen de communication rapide, le style des messages est souvent familier et télégraphique et l'emploi des abréviations et des acronymes est très courant. Selon la netiquette, ou code de conduite sur le réseau, il est déconseillé d'écrire un message tout en majuscules car cela pourrait être interprété comme un signe de mauvaise humeur.

Les formules d'appel traditionnelles (**Dear ...**) sont généralement omises. Si vous connaissez bien votre correspondant, vous pouvez commencer par une formule familière telle que **Hello** ou **Hi**, suivie du prénom de la personne.

- **Message interne**

Formule d'appel familière, sans ponctuation, pouvant être omise.

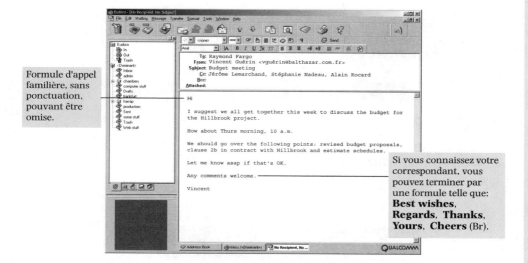

Si vous connaissez votre correspondant, vous pouvez terminer par une formule telle que: **Best wishes**, **Regards**, **Thanks**, **Yours**, **Cheers** (Br).

- **Message d'une entreprise à une autre**

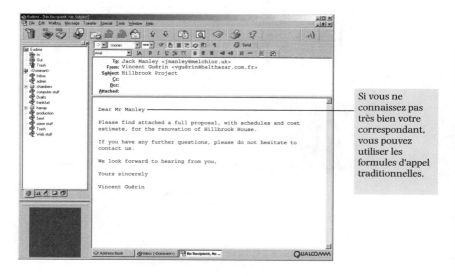

Si vous ne connaissez pas très bien votre correspondant, vous pouvez utiliser les formules d'appel traditionnelles.

- **Réservation**

- **Message au fournisseur d'accès**

= as soon as possible

Abréviations et acronymes : correspondance générale

a/c	account (compte)	**eg**	for example (par exemple)
ack.	acknowledge	**EGM**	extraordinary general meeting
add.	addendum (addenda)		(assemblée générale
AGM	annual general meeting		extraordinaire)
	(assemblée générale annuelle)	**enc(s)**	enclosure(s) (pièce(s) jointe(s))
am, a.m.	ante meridiem, morning (du	**ETA**	estimated time of arrival (heure
	matin)		d'arrivée prévue)
AOB	any other business (questions	**FAO**	for the attention of (à l'attention
	diverses)		de)
approx.	approximately	**ff**	following (suite à)
	(approximativement)	**HM**	His/Her Majesty (eg: HMC = Her
APR	annual percentage rate (taux		Majesty's Customs) (Sa Majesté le
	effectif global)		Roi/la Reine)
asap, a.s.a.p.	as soon as possible (dès que	**ie, i.e.**	in other words (c'est-à-dire)
	possible)	**Inc., Incorp**	incorporated (SA)
av.	average (moyenne)	**incl.**	included, including (joint(e), y
bal.	balance (solde)		compris)
b/d	banker's draft (chèque bancaire)	**infm., info**	information
bc., bcc.	blind (carbon) copy (copie cachée	**inst**	of this month (courant, de ce mois)
	d'une note de service, d'une lettre)	**L/C**	letter of credit (lettre de crédit)
b/e	bill of exchange (lettre de change)	**Ltd**	limited company (SARL)
bk	bank; book (banque; livre)	**MD**	managing director (PDG)
bkcy, bkpt	bankruptcy, bankrupt (faillite, en	**mgr.**	manager (directeur, dirigeant,
	faillite)		responsable)
B/L, bl	bill of lading (connaissement)	**mtg.**	meeting (réunion)
b/s	bill of sale (acte de vente, contrat	**NB**	nota bene
	de vente)	**OD**	overdraft (découvert, solde
BST	British Summer Time (heure d'été		débiteur)
en	Grande-Bretagne)	**OHP**	overhead projector
c.	circa (environ)		(rétroprojecteur)
CB	cash book (livre de caisse)	**ono**	or nearest offer (prix à débattre)
cc	carbon copy (copie à)	**p.a.**	per annum (par an)
CEO	chief executive officer (PDG)	**p&p**	postage and packing (frais
CET	Central European Time (heure de		d'emballage et d'expédition)
	l'Europe centrale)	**PAYE**	pay as you earn (retenue de l'impôt
CFO	chief financial officer (chef		sur le revenu à la base ou à la
	comptable)		source)
chq	cheque (chèque)	**P&L**	profit and loss (pertes et profits)
c.i.f., CIF	cost, insurance, freight (coût,	**PLC**	public limited company (SA)
	assurance et fret)	**pm, p.m.**	post meridiem (de l'après-midi/du
C/O	care of; carried over; cash order		soir)
	(aux bons soins de; reporté; ordre	**p.o.**	postal order (mandat postal)
	au comptant)	**pp**	post procurationem, on behalf of
Co	company; county (entreprise;		(au nom de)
	comté)	**pps**	additional postscript (post
COD	cash on delivery (paiement à la		postscriptum)
	livraison)	**Pres.**	president
Conf	confirm; conference (confirmez;	**Prof.**	professor
	conférence)	**ps**	postscript (postscriptum)
contd, cont'd	continued (suite)	**PTO**	please turn over (tournez la page
CV	curriculum vitae		svp)
DD	direct debit (prélèvement	**rc'd**	received (reçu)
	automatique)	**re**	with reference to (objet, à propos
del.	delivery; delivered (livraison; livré)		de, en référence à)
Dir	director (directeur)	**Ref**	reference (référence)
Dr	Doctor (docteur, médecin)	**req, reqd**	required (requis)
E&O	errors and omissions excepted	**retd**	retired (retraité)
	(sauf erreur ou omission)	**sae**	stamped addressed envelope

	(enveloppe timbrée)	**tbc**	to be confirmed (à confirmer)
sase	self-addressed stamped envelope	**ult.**	ultimo, last (dernier)
	(enveloppe timbrée à son propre	**viz**	namely (à savoir, c'est-à-dire)
	nom)	**VP**	vice-president
SO	standing order (virement	**yf**	Yours faithfully (cordialement)
	automatique)	**ys**	Yours sincerely (cordialement)

Abréviations et acronymes : courrier électronique et forums

Adv	advice (conseil)	**IIRC** *Fam*	if I recall correctly (si mes souvenirs sont bons)
AFAICT *Fam*	as far as I can tell (pour autant que je sache)	**IMO, IMHO** *Fam*	in my (humble) opinion (à mon (humble) avis)
AFAIK *Fam*	as far as I know (pour autant que je sache)	**IOW** *Fam*	in other words (autrement dit)
AFK	away from keyboard (indique que l'on va quitter son poste)	**ISTM** *Fam*	it seems to me (il me semble que)
		ITRO *Fam*	in the region of (environ)
AIUI *Fam*	as far as I understand (si j'ai bien compris)	**NRN** *Fam*	no reply necessary (réponse facultative)
B4 *Fam*	before (avant)	**NW!** *Fam*	no way! (sûrement pas!)
BAK	back at keyboard (de retour devant l'écran)	**OTOH** *Fam*	on the other hand (d'un autre côté)
BBL *Fam*	be back later (je reviens)	**OTT** *Fam*	over the top (excessif)
BTW *Fam*	by the way (à propos)	**PD**	public domain (domaine public)
cld	could	**POV**	point of view (point de vue)
Doc	document	**prhps**	perhaps (peut-être)
EOF	end of file (fin de fichier)	**RTFM** *très Fam*	read the f***ing manual (regarde dans le manuel, nom de Dieu!)
F2F *Fam*	face to face (en face, face à face)		
FAQ	frequently asked questions (foire aux questions)	**RUOK** *Fam*	are you OK? (ça va?)
		TIA *Fam*	thanks in advance (merci d'avance)
FOC	free of charge (gratuit, gratuitement)	**TNX** *Fam*	thanks (merci)
Foll	following, to follow (suivant, à suivre)	**TVM** *Fam*	thanks very much (merci beaucoup)
FYI	for your information (pour ton information)	**VR**	virtual reality (réalité virtuelle)
		WRT *Fam*	with regard to (en ce qui concerne)
HTH *Fam*	hope this helps (j'espère que cela te sera utile)	**urgt**	urgent

Le téléphone

• Prononciation des numéros de téléphone

20995   Two oh double nine five (Br)
               Two zero double nine five (Am)

• Pour obtenir un renseignement

- Can I have directory enquiries (Br) *or* directory assistance (Am) please?
- I'm trying to get through to a London number.
- What is the (country) code for Canada?
- How do I get an outside line?

• **Pour demander un interlocuteur**

Hello,
- could I speak to ...?
- can I speak to ...?
- I'd like to speak to ...
- (could I have) extension 593 please?

• **Pour répondre à un appel**

- Robert McQueen speaking, can I help you?
- Hello, this is ...
- Yes, speaking (pour confirmer que l'on est bien la personne demandée).
- Hold on/hold please, I'll (just) get him/her.
- I'm sorry, he's/she's not here. Can I take a message?
- I'm afraid he's away on business/out of the office/off sick/on holiday/on vacation (Am).

• **Pour laisser un message**

Sur un répondeur :
- I'm returning your call....
- I'll be in London next week, perhaps we can ...
- I'd like to talk to you about ...
- Could you call me back, so we can discuss ...?

À une autre personne :
- Could you ask him/her to call me on ...?
- Could you tell him/her I won't be able to ...?
- I'll call back later.
- I need to speak to him/her urgently.
- Please ask him/her to confirm. Thank you.

• **Pour demander une confirmation**

- Could you spell that, please?
- Could you speak a bit more slowly, please?
- I'm sorry, I didn't catch that. Could you repeat that, please?
- Let me check, 11 a.m. Wednesday 10th. Yes, that's fine.

• **Pour conclure un appel**

- Thank you, I look forward to seeing you on Wednesday. Goodbye.
- Thank you for your help.

• **Message de répondeur téléphonique**

- We are unable to take your call at the moment/I am not here at the moment. Please leave a message after the tone.

LES RÉUNIONS D'AFFAIRES DANS LES PAYS ANGLO-SAXONS

par Maddy Glas

Maddy Glas, Docteur de la Sorbonne, après avoir travaillé dans plusieurs pays de l'Union européenne, enseigne le français des affaires au département de langues de l'INSEAD en France.

Table des matières

Considérations générales

Les réunions tiennent une place essentielle dans l'organisation de la vie de l'entreprise. Une réunion formelle présente certaines, ou toutes les caractéristiques suivantes:

- Un horaire spécifique lui est réservé (habituellement hebdomadaire ou mensuel)
- Généralement, le même groupe de personnes est concerné par la réunion.
- La réunion ne doit pas déranger le cours normal des activités.

Lexique:

une réunion	**meeting**
la réunion du conseil d'administration	**board meeting**
la salle de direction	**boardroom**
la salle de réunion	**meeting room**
une réunion de la direction	**management meeting**
une réunion de vente	**sales meeting**
une réunion informelle	**informal meeting**
le brainstorming	**brainstorming session**
un comité d'orientation	**planning committee**
le compte-rendu	**minutes**

Chacune des caractéristiques mentionnées ci-dessus implique certains accords tacites:

- La réunion est prioritaire sur toute autre activité d'ordre professionnel ou personnel.
- Les liens créés entre les participants dans le cadre de réunions régulières font naître des réseaux de communication informels entre ceux-ci (le café ou "pub", le club de golf, le country club). Cela n'autorise pas pour autant les familiarités entre les participants; à titre d'exemple, il est exclu de téléphoner à un collègue à son domicile sans y avoir été préalablement invité par celui-ci. En outre, c'est au cours des réunions que doivent être prises les décisions concernant la vie de l'entreprise, et nulle part ailleurs.
- Les réunions doivent être efficaces et permettre d'atteindre le but fixé.
- La réunion doit durer aussi peu de temps que possible.
- Arriver en retard à une réunion d'affaires en Grande-Bretagne est impensable.

1. La préparation de la réunion

L'ordre du jour ("the agenda") est préparé à l'avance et envoyé aux personnes dont la présence est requise. Il comporte la liste numérotée des points à l'ordre du jour ("items"). Y figurent les points incrits à l'ordre du jour de la réunion précédente qui n'avaient pas pu être abordés, ainsi que différents points soulevés mais laissés en suspens. Le président de la réunion et les participants ont également la possibilité de faire inscrire à l'ordre du jour tout point qui leur semble devoir être discuté. La personne qui préside la réunion ("chair") est la personne la plus haut placée dans la hiérarchie de l'entreprise, c'est généralement le PDG ("managing director") ou le Directeur des ventes ("sales manager"). En son absence, la fonction de président revient à son adjoint ou à son subordonné immédiat.

Agenda

Meeting held at Transex offices, Milton Keynes

Date:	24 April 2004, 10.00 am
Attending:	DG, JEK, PN, IR, HG, FMcP, MM, Philippe Lebrun, Marie-Hélène Vouvay
Minutes:	EF

1. Minutes of last meeting
2. Report on sales year to date   PN
3. Report on Web site activity and on-line sales   HG
4. Update on French market   Philippe Lebrun
5. Discussion of 2005 projects
6. Staff recruitment   MM
7. Date of next meeting
8. AOB

NB: Le mot "chairman" est considéré comme sexiste. Il est préférable de dire "chairperson" ou encore "chair". Par ailleurs, on utilise souvent les expressions "Mister chairman" ou "Madam chairman" pour s'adresser à la personne qui préside la réunion. Aux États-Unis, les adresses formelles comme celles précédemment mentionnées sont rarement utilisées. S'il s'agit d'une réunion vraiment officielle, comme lors d'un conseil d'administration, on peut utiliser Monsieur/Madame ("Mr/Mrs") suivi du nom propre.

Dans la plupart des entreprises, l'usage est d'appeler ses collègues par leur prénom. Puisqu'en anglais la forme unique "you" ne permet pas la distinction entre tutoiement et vouvoiement si familière aux francophones, et que les prénoms sont utilisés presque systématiquement, c'est par le degré d'intimité que l'on montre en public que se manifeste le respect. Être respectueux envers son supérieur ne signifie pas qu'il faille nécessairement épouser les vues de ce dernier.

C'est à l'assistant(e) personnel(le) du président qu'il incombe de préparer la réunion. C'est à cette personne que revient la tâche de taper les convocations ainsi que l'ordre du jour et de les envoyer aux participants au moins 24 heures avant la date prévue pour la réunion. Les participants qui désirent faire inscrire un ou plusieurs points à l'ordre du jour doivent le faire au moins 48 heures avant la réunion. Il n'est pas nécessaire d'avoir l'accord préalable du président pour faire inscrire un point à l'ordre du jour. Le premier et le dernier point abordés sont immuables: toute réunion débute avec la lecture du compte-rendu de la séance précédente ("minutes of last meeting"), et se termine avec l'AOB ("Any Other Business") qui regroupe divers points annexes à traiter. Lorsque la discussion en cours s'écarte du sujet ou traîne en longueur, le président a la possibilité de l'interrompre en demandant aux participants d'intervenir en fin de séance (dans le cadre de la partie Any Other Business"), de façon à pouvoir traiter en priorité les points les plus importants. Il dit alors:

Bring that up at the end	Mentionnez cela à la fin de la réunion

Toute absence doit être annoncée à l'avance et justifiée. Seul un rendez-vous d'affaires d'une extrême urgence constitue un motif valable (et encore convient-il d'en discuter avec le président au préalable).

Les décisions prises lors d'une réunion sont immédiatement applicables et toutes les informations utilisées lors des débats sont confidentielles.

2. Le déroulement de la réunion

Dans une réunion de travail à la française, la notion de temps n'est pas primordiale. Le rôle du président est de faire la synthèse des différents points de vue présentés. Dans les pays anglo-saxons, les réunions d'affaires sont très fonctionnelles: les points à discuter sont inscrits à l'ordre du jour à l'avance, et les participants doivent arriver préparés. Les longs discours et les digressions ne sont pas tolérés. Il faut savoir s'en tenir au sujet ("stick to the point") et être le plus concis possible.

Le rôle du président est de permettre à tous ceux qui veulent participer de pouvoir le faire. Il doit interrompre toute discussion qui n'est pas directement liée au sujet à traiter. Il doit également s'assurer que les débats mènent bien à une décision et à une conclusion. Au Royaume-Uni, il est déconseillé de faire signe au président pour lui demander l'autorisation d'intervenir: ce serait faire preuve de faiblesse dans la mesure où le rôle du président est de faire respecter l'ordre du jour et non de donner ou de refuser la parole aux participants. Cependant, la situation est différente aux États-Unis où le rôle du président est précisément de veiller à ce que la réunion se déroule dans la discipline.

Pour signifier son approbation, on peut utiliser des expressions comme:

I agree	Je suis d'accord/j'approuve
Hear! Hear!	Très bien! très bien!
I think you are absolutely right when you say ...	Je suis totalement de votre avis lorsque vous dites que ...
Good point	C'est tout à fait vrai
Why didn't I think of that?	Comment n'y ai-je pas pensé?

Les expressions suivantes sont couramment utilisées au cours des discussions pour exprimer le désaccord:

With all due respect	Soit dit sans vouloir vous offenser
Allow me to disagree	Permettez-moi de ne pas être de votre avis
If I might be so bold ...	Si je peux avoir la hardiesse de ...

La désapprobation est exprimée par des phrases comme:

That's nonsense	C'est complètement absurde
I beg to differ	Permettez-moi d'être d'un autre avis
I don't understand why you say ...	Je ne comprends pas pourquoi vous dites que ...

L'un des mots les plus importants en anglais est sorry (je suis désolé), qui est rarement utilisé pour exprimer un regret sincère mais qui constitue plutôt une façon d'exprimer poliment un désaccord. Ainsi on peut dire:

I'm sorry to disagree with you	Je ne suis pas de votre avis

"I'm sorry" est la manière la plus commune d'interrompre quelqu'un. On peut également utiliser:

Sorry to interrupt you, but ...	Désolé(e) de vous interrompre, mais ...

Refuser net d'être interrompu est impoli, mais des expressions comme celles qui suivent sont souvent utilisées:

Can I just finish what I want to say and then you can make your point	Je termine ce que je veux dire puis vous pourrez vous exprimer
Just a moment	Un instant, s'il vous plâit
I've almost finished	J'ai presque terminé

En ce qui concerne l'organisation du plan de table, au Royaume-Uni, la seule place fixe appartient au président/à la présidente de la réunion, son ou sa secrétaire à ses côtés. Cependant, il se crée des habitudes et il vaut mieux les respecter. Aux États-Unis en particulier, les places ne sont pas fixes et les gens choisissent leur place en fonction des rapports qu'ils entretiennent avec leurs collègues, de l'ordre du jour, etc.

On peut "tomber la veste" et desserrer son nœud de cravate, mais le degré d'informalité dans la manière de s'habiller est déterminé par le président et la politique de l'entreprise. Il est parfois possible de fumer mais ce n'est pas toujours le cas. Des boissons non alcoolisées ou chaudes sont à la disposition des participants mais manger est considéré comme incorrect au Royaume-Uni. Aux États-Unis, il n'est pas rare de manger pendant les réunions. Cette pratique est même courante dans certaines entreprises où une personne se charge de commander le déjeuner que les participants prennent pendant la réunion. Le plus simple est de "suivre le mouvement" ou de demander aux anciens quelles sont les habitudes de l'entreprise.

Encore une fois, la règle d'or est d'être rapide et précis. Seul le président, en tant que personne la plus haut placée dans la hiérarchie, peut se permettre de ne pas suivre les strictes conventions d'une réunion d'affaires. Les discussions ne doivent jamais dégénérer en disputes: il faut éviter les situations d'hostilité ouverte. L'accent est toujours mis sur "l'esprit d'équipe". On utilise rarement le vote à main levée. Le rôle du président est de clarifier les différents points de vue et de dégager le point de vue majoritaire. La répétition d'un même argument n'est pas acceptable. Pour faire pencher la balance du côté d'une minorité, il est nécessaire d'introduire de nouveaux arguments et de nouveaux faits.

Le président clôt la discussion concernant un point particulier et ouvre la discussion sur le point suivant de l'ordre du jour. Une fois le débat clos sur un point, le rouvrir est considéré comme incorrect. Au Royaume-Uni, la réunion est un forum qui appuie la politique de l'entreprise. L'utilisation d'une réunion pour faire avancer ses propres projets est un art. Il est inopportun de solliciter l'appui d'autres membres du groupe sur un point particulier avant une réunion. La situation est toute autre aux États-Unis, où le contraire se passe. Il est courant de chercher à connaître les participants et d'essayer de les influencer si nécessaire; de nombreux directeurs considéreraient comme dangereux d'assister à une réunion importante sans avoir auparavant "vendu" leur point de vue et sans s'être assurés de l'appui d'un certain nombre de membres du groupe.

3. Le compte-rendu de la réunion

Le compte-rendu est tapé et envoyé aux participants en précisant habituellement la date, l'heure et le lieu de la réunion suivante. L'ordre du jour de la réunion suivante inclut la possibilité d'introduire toute correction jugée nécessaire.

Minutes of meeting held at Transex offices, Milton Keynes

Date: 24 April 2004, 10.00 am
Chair: DG
Attending: JEK, PN, IR, HG, FMcP, MM, Philippe Lebrun, Marie-Hélène
              Vouvay
Apologies: IR
Minutes: EF

1. **Minutes of last meeting**
   Approved without alteration
2. **Report on sales, year to date**
   PN distributed sales figures for year to date and explained that the fall from last year's sales is due to several outstanding invoices.
   ACTION: PN to ask Accounts department to chase invoices
3. **Report on Web site activity and on-line sales**
   HG reported that there were 2045 hits on the company Web site last week and 56 on-line orders were placed. Redesign of the home page interface is being considered.

---

4. Pour conclure

A. *La présentation d'arguments*

Puisqu'il n'y a pas de manière standard de présenter des arguments en Grande-Bretagne, il n'y a aucune raison qu'un homme d'affaires français utilise une autre logique que le système de la thèse, antithèse, synthèse. Dans la mesure où les réunions sont courtes, et que l'on rappelle constamment aux participants de ne pas s'écarter du sujet, la personne qui réussit à parler la dernière, soit au moment où un nouveau sujet va être abordé, soit à la fin de la réunion, détient un certain avantage à condition de ne pas trop en profiter.

B. *La notion de responsabilité*

Les hommes d'affaires anglo-saxons assument les conséquences de leurs erreurs. Il serait inacceptable de chercher à se décharger de ses responsabilités sur quelqu'un d'autre. De même, on attend des autres qu'ils admettent franchement leurs erreurs. On considère comme un signe de faiblesse le fait de chercher des excuses, même lorsque certaines de ces excuses sont fondées. Celui qui assume ses décisions et sait tirer les leçons de ses erreurs fait preuve d'intelligence et gagne le respect de ses collègues. On peut dire calmement et sans aucune honte:

I'm sorry, but I made a mistake. It won't happen again.	Je suis désolé mais j'ai fait une erreur. Cela ne se reproduira pas.

C. *L'humour*

L'humour est un moyen efficace de désamorcer les situations de crise au cours d'une réunion. Ce serait se méprendre sur la fonction de l'humour dans la culture britannique que de s'imaginer être la cible des moqueries des autres participants lorsqu'ils plaisantent. La fonction du rire est de faciliter la communication et de détendre l'atmosphère en créant une certaine complicité entre les participants. Il est plus facile de travailler avec des gens avec qui on peut également plaisanter. Très souvent, le contenu d'une remarque peut paraître proche de l'insulte comme par exemple la phrase suivante: "What can you expect from a man/a woman who eats snails?" (Que peut-on attendre d'une personne qui mange des escargots?). Mais l'utilisation de l'insulte dans un contexte qui demande une coopération amicale est l'essence de cet humour. L'utilisation de clichés tels que "N'oubliez jamais qui a gagné la bataille de Waterloo" (Don't forget who won the Battle of Waterloo) est une manière de rire de soi-même, pour commencer, puis de la vie en général.

LE TRAVAIL AVEC UN INTERPRÈTE

Avec la mondialisation des échanges économiques et commerciaux, l'interprétation est un moyen de plus en plus fréquemment utilisé pour faciliter la communication entre les gens parlant des langues différentes. Pour se faire comprendre du plus grand nombre, il est indispensable de savoir comment travailler avec un interprète de façon efficace.

Il existe trois sortes d'interprétation:

- L'interprétation simultanée
- L'interprétation consécutive
- Le chuchotage

L'**interprétation simultanée** est la forme d'interprétation la plus couramment utilisée dans les conférences et les réunions d'affaires. L'intervenant parle dans un micro et sa voix est transmise aux interprètes qui sont installés dans des cabines insonorisées où ils disposent d'écouteurs et d'un micro. Ils interprètent directement dans la langue adéquate et les auditeurs, assis à des pupitres spécialement équipés, écoutent la traduction au moyen d'un casque.

On utilise l'**interprétation consécutive** lorsque l'interprétation simultanée est impossible pour des raisons pratiques, lors de la visite d'une usine ou au cours d'un dîner, par exemple. L'interprète se tient debout ou assis auprès du locuteur et interprète ce que dit celui-ci quand il marque une pause, en s'aidant parfois de notes.

Le **chuchotage** est la forme d'interprétation la plus rarement utilisée. L'interprète est assis à côté des délégués et traduit simultanément ce qui est dit en chuchotant.

Comment présenter un exposé à un public multilingue

Si vous savez que votre exposé doit être interprété dans d'autres langues, il est important de se souvenir des points suivants:

- Il faut tenir compte du fait que des gens de cultures différentes écouteront votre exposé. Souvenez-vous que plaisanteries et mots d'esprit sont difficilement traduisibles et que tous les peuples n'ont pas le même sens de l'humour. Les références culturelles très spécifiques sont souvent incompréhensibles pour les auditeurs venant d'autres pays que le vôtre, et sont donc à éviter. Essayez dans la mesure du possible de vous exprimer dans une langue simple car les termes familiers ou très techniques posent parfois des problèmes de traduction.

- Si vous avez rédigé votre texte à l'avance, fournissez-en un exemplaire aux interprètes. Il est préférable de le leur faire parvenir deux semaines avant la date de votre exposé, mais si cela s'avère impossible, il est impératif de le leur distribuer avant de prendre la parole, accompagné de copies de tous les documents dont vous vous servirez pendant votre exposé. Il est également utile de fournir à l'avance aux interprètes des informations d'ordre général sur le sujet traité.

- Si vous intervenez dans une conférence où l'on utilise l'interprétation simultanée, vous devrez parler dans un micro. N'oubliez pas que l'interprète se trouve dans une cabine insonorisée et qu'il ne vous entend que grâce au micro. Assurez-vous que votre micro est allumé et que les interprètes vous entendent. Parlez dans la direction du micro sans trop vous en rapprocher. Maintenez une distance constante entre votre bouche et l'appareil de façon à éviter les écarts de volume. Rappelez-vous que si vous tournez le dos au micro pour consulter un tableau ou un écran situé derrière vous, l'interprète n'entendra rien de ce que vous direz. Pour éviter ce genre de problème, la plupart des conférenciers qui utilisent un rétro-projecteur portent un micro-cravate. Si c'est votre cas, sachez qu'à chaque fois que vous frôlerez le micro avec la main ou avec votre veste, seuls des grésillements parviendront aux oreilles des interprètes.

- Lorsque vous vous servez d'un rétro-projecteur, assurez-vous que les interprètes peuvent voir l'écran. Il est important de commenter les documents projetés, sans quoi seuls les gens qui connaissent la langue dans laquelle ils sont rédigés pourront suivre.

- Le défaut le plus courant des conférenciers qui s'adressent à un public multilingue est de parler trop vite. Les interprètes ne se contentent pas de répéter ce que vous dites, ils doivent d'abord traduire vos paroles et il ont donc besoin de plus de temps que vous. D'autre part, il se peut que certains délégués dont la langue maternelle n'est pas celle que vous utilisez vous écoutent sans passer par les interprètes. Il est donc indispensable de ne pas adopter un rythme trop rapide. Plus vous parlerez vite, moins l'on vous comprendra.

- Pour garder un rythme adéquat, il est recommandé de marquer une pause après chaque phrase. Cela permet aux auditeurs d'assimiler ce que vous venez de dire et aux interprètes de finir de traduire. Tout bon conférencier attend que les interprètes aient fini de parler pour continuer son exposé.

- Il est essentiel de s'exprimer distinctement. Si vous marmonnez, les interprètes seront dans l'impossibilité de traduire quoi que ce soit.

- En observant ces consignes la prochaine fois que vous participerez à une conférence internationale ou à une réunion d'affaires, vous contribuerez à l'amélioration de la communication et de la compréhension entre les peuples.

Les choses à faire et à ne pas faire lorsqu'on travaille avec un interprète

✓ À faire:

- fournir à l'avance un exemplaire de votre exposé aux interprètes, accompagné de copies de tous les documents dont ils auront besoin, et notamment de ceux qui seront projetés sur écran.

- Allumer votre micro et l'utiliser convenablement.

- Parler lentement et distinctement.

✗ À ne pas faire:

- Inclure de trop nombreuses plaisanteries et références culturelles spécifiques dans votre exposé.

- Tourner le dos au micro lorsque vous commentez des documents projetés sur écran.

- Passer d'une langue à une autre au milieu d'une phrase.

ÉTATS DU MONDE

On trouvera le nom anglais des pays dans la deuxième colonne. Pour la traduction anglaise des monnaies et des langues officielles, se reporter au tableau correspondant dans le supplément anglais.

On notera également que les abréviations des monnaies qui figurent dans la cinquième colonne sont les abréviations standard internationales, telles qu'elles ont été définies par l'ISO. Elles diffèrent des abréviations locales et sont utilisées lors des opérations financières internationales.

Nom français	Nom anglais	Nom local	Langue(s) officielle(s)	Monnaie
Afghanistan	Afghanistan	Afghānestān	dari, pachto	1 afghani (AFA) = 100 puls
Afrique du Sud	South Africa	South Africa	anglais, afrikaans	1 rand (ZAR) = 100 cents
Albanie	Albania	Shqīpëri	albanais	1 lek (ALL) = 100 qindarka
Algérie	Algeria	Al-Jazā'ir (arabe), Algérie (français)	arabe	1 dinar algérien (DZD) = 100 centimes
Allemagne	Germany	Bundesrepublik Deutschland	allemand	1 euro (EUR) = 100 cents
Andorre	Andorra	Andorra	catalan, français, espagnol	1 euro (EUR) = 100 cents
Angola	Angola	Angola	portugais	1 nouveau kwanza (AOK) = 100 iwei
Arabie Saoudite	Saudi Arabia	Al-'Arabīyah as Sa'udīyah	arabe	1 riyal (SAR) = 20 qirshes = 100 halalas
Argentine	Argentina	Argentina	espagnol	1 peso argentin (ARS) = 100 centavos
Arménie	Armenia	Hayastani Hanrapetut'yun	arménien	1 dram (AMD) =100 louma
Australie	Australia	Australia	anglais	1 dollar australien (AUD) = 100 cents
Autriche	Austria	Österreich	allemand	1 euro (EUR) = 100 cents
Azerbaïdjan	Azerbaijan	Azarbaijan	azéri	1 manat (AZM) =100 kepik
Bahamas	The Bahamas	Bahamas	anglais	1 dollar des Bahamas (BSD) = 100 cents
Bahreïn	Bahrain	Dawlat al-Bahrayn	arabe	1 dinar de Bahreïn (BHD) = 1000 fils
Bangladesh	Bangladesh	Gana Prajatantri Bangladesh	bengali	1 taka (BDT) = 100 paisa
Barbade	Barbados	Barbados	anglais	1 dollar de la Barbade (BBD) = 100 cents
Belgique	Belgium	Belgique (français), België (flamand)	flamand, français, allemand	1 euro (EUR) = 100 cents
Belize	Belize	Belize	anglais	1 dollar de Belize (BZD) = 100 cents
Bénin	Benin	Bénin	français	1 franc CFA (XOF) = 100 centimes

Nom français	Nom anglais	Nom local	Langue(s) officielle(s)	Monnaie
Bhoutan	Bhutan	Druk-Yul	tibétain	1 ngultrum (BTN) = 100 roupies
Biélorussie	Belarus	Belarus	biélorusse	1 rouble biélorusse (BYB) =100 kopeks
Birmanie ▸ Myanmar	Burma			
Bolivie	Bolivia	Bolivia	espagnol	1 boliviano (BOB) = 100 centavos
Bosnie Herzégovine	Bosnia-Herzegovina	Bosnia-Herzegovina	serbo-croate	1 dinar (BAD) = 100 paras
Botswana	Botswana	Botswana	anglais	1 pula (BWP) = 100 thebe
Brésil	Brazil	Brasil	portugais	1 real brésilien (BRL) = 100 centavos
Brunei	Brunei	Brunei	malais	1 dollar de Brunei (BND) = 100 cents
Bulgarie	Bulgaria	Bălgarija	bulgare	1 lev (BGL) (*pl* leva) = 100 stotinki (*sing* stotinka)
Burkina	Burkina Faso	Burkina Faso	français	1 franc CFA (XOF) = 100 centimes
Burundi	Burundi	Burundi	français, kirundi	1 franc du Burundi (BIF) = 100 centimes
Cambodge	Cambodia	Preah Reach Ana Pak Kampuchea	khmer	1 riel (KHR) = 100 sen
Cameroun	Cameroon	Cameroon	français, anglais	1 franc CFA (XAF) = 100 centimes
Canada	Canada	Canada	français, anglais	1 dollar canadien (CAD) = 100 cents
Cap-Vert	Cape Verde	Cabo Verde	portugais	1 escudo du Cap-Vert (CVE) = 100 centavos
Centrafricaine, République	Central African Republic	République Centrafricaine	français, sango	1 franc CFA (XAF) = 100 centimes
Chili	Chile	Chile	espagnol	1 peso chilien (CLP) = 100 centavos
Chine	China	Zhongguo	chinois	1 yuan (CNY) = 10 jiao = 100 fen
Chypre	Cyprus	Kipros (grec), Kibris (turc)	grec, turc	1 livre chypriote (CYP) = 1000 mils
Colombie	Colombia	Colombia	espagnole	1 peso colombien (COP) = 100 centavos
Comores	Comoros	Comores	français, comorien	1 franc des Comores (KMF) = 100 centimes
Congo	Congo	Congo	français	1 franc CFA (XAF) = 100 centimes
Congo, République démocratique du	Democratic Republic of Congo	Congo	français, lingala	1 nouveau zaïre (ZRN) = 100 makuta (*sing* likuta)
Corée du Nord	Korea, North	Choson Minjujuüi In'min Konghwaguk	coréen	1 won (NKW) = 100 chon

Nom français	Nom anglais	Nom local	Langue(s) officielle(s)	Monnaie
Corée du Sud	Korea, South	Taehan-Min'guk	coréen	1 won (KRW) = 100 chon
Costa Rica	Costa Rica	Costa Rica	espagnol	1 colón [Fr colon] (CRC) (pl colones) = 100 céntimos
Côte d'Ivoire	Côte d'Ivoire (Ivory Coast)	Côte d'Ivoire	français	1 franc CFA (XOF) = 100 centimes
Croatie	Croatia	Hrvatska	serbo-croate	1 kuna (HRK) = 100 lipas
Cuba	Cuba	Cuba	espagnol	1 peso cubain (CUP) = 100 centavos
Danemark	Denmark	Danmark	danois	1 krone [Fr couronne danoise] (DKK) (pl kroner) = 100 øre
Djibouti	Djibouti	Djibouti	arabe, français	1 franc de Djibouti (DJF) = 100 centimes
Dominicaine, République	Dominican Republic	República Dominicana	espagnol	1 peso dominicain (DOP) = 100 centavos
Dominique	Dominica	Dominica	anglais, français créole	1 dollar des Caraïbes orientales (XCD) = 100 cents
Égypte	Egypt	Jumhuriyat Misr al-Arabiya	arabe	1 livre égyptienne (EGP) = 100 piastres
Émirats Arabes Unis	United Arab Emirates	Ittihād al-Imārāt al-'Arabīyah	arabe, anglais	1 dirham (AED) = 100 fils
Équateur	Ecuador	Ecuador	espagnol	1 sucre (ECS) = 100 centavos
Érythrée	Eritrea	Eritrea	tigrinya, arabe	1 birr (ETB) = 100 cents
Espagne	Spain	España	espagnol	1 euro (EUR) = 100 cents
Estonie	Estonia	Eesti Vabariik	estonien	1 kroon [Fr couronne estonienne] (EEK) = 100 senti
États-Unis	United States of America	United States of America	anglais	1 dollar US (USD) = 100 cents
Éthiopie	Ethiopia	Ityopiya	amharique	1 birr (ETB) = 100 cents
Féroé, îles	Faroe Islands	Faroyar/ Faeroerne	féroïen, danois	1 krone [Fr couronne danoise] (DKK) (pl kroner) = 100 øre
Fidji, îles	Fiji	Matanitu Ko Viti	anglais	1 dollar fidjien (FJD) = 100 cents
Finlande	Finland	Suomen Tasavalta	finnois, suédois	1 euro (EUR) = 100 cents
France	France	République française	français	1 euro (EUR) = 100 cents
Gabon	Gabon	République gabonaise	français	1 franc CFA (XAF) = 100 centimes
Gambie	The Gambia	Gambia	anglais	1 dalasi (GMD) = 100 bututs
Géorgie	Georgia	Sakartvelos Respublica	géorgien, russe	1 lari (GEL) = 100 tetri
Ghana	Ghana	Ghana	anglais	1 cedi (GHC) = 100 pesewas

Nom français	Nom anglais	Nom local	Langue(s) officielle(s)	Monnaie
Grèce	Greece	Elliniki Dimokratia	grec	1 euro (EUR) = 100 cents
Groenland	Greenland	Grønland (danois), Kalaallit Nunaat	danois, groenlandais	1 krone [*Fr* couronne danoise] (DKK) (*pl* kroner) = 100 øre
Guatemala	Guatemala	Guatemala	espagnol	1 quetzal (GTQ) (*pl* quetzales) = 100 centavos
Guinée	Guinea	République de Guinée	français	1 franc guinéen (GNF) = 100 centimes
Guinée-Bissau	Guinea-Bissau	Republica da Guiné-Bissau	portugais	1 franc CFA (GWP) = 100 centimes
Guinée Équatoriale	Equatorial Guinea	Guinea Ecuatorial	espagnol	1 franc CFA (XAF) = 100 centimes
Guyana	Guyana	Guyana	anglais	1 dollar de la Guyana (GYD) = 100 cents
Guyane	French Guyane	Guyane	français	1 euro (EUR) = 100 cents
Haïti	Haiti	République d'Haïti	français	1 gourde (HTG) = 100 centimes
Hollande ▸ Pays-Bas	Holland			
Honduras	Honduras	Honduras	espagnol	1 lempira (HNL) = 100 centavos
Hongrie	Hungary	Magyar Koztarsasag	hongrois	1 forint (HUF) = 100 fillér
Inde	India	Bhārat (hindi)	hindi, anglais	1 roupie indienne (INR) = 100 paise
Indonésie	Indonesia	Republik Indonesia	indonésien	1 rupiah (IDR) = 100 sen
Irak	Iraq	Jumhouriya al Iraquia	arabe	1 dinar irakien (IQD) = 1000 fils
Iran	Iran	Jomhoori-e-Islami-e-Iran	persan	1 rial (IRR) = 100 dinars
Irlande	Ireland	Poblacht na hEireann	irlandais, anglais	1 euro (EUR) = 100 cents
Islande	Iceland	Ísland	islandais	1 couronne islandaise (ISK) = 100 aurar (*sing* eyrir)
Israël	Israel	Medinat Israel	hébreu, arabe	1 shekel (ILS) = 100 agorot
Italie	Italy	Repubblica Italiana	italien	1 euro (EUR) = 100 cents
Jamaïque	Jamaica	Jamaica	anglais	1 dollar jamaïcain (JMD) = 100 cents
Japon	Japan	Nihon	japonais	1 yen (JPY) = 100 sen
Jordanie	Jordan	Al'Urdun	arabe	1 dinar jordanien (JOD) = 1 000 fils
Kazakhstan	Kazakhstan	Kazak Respublikasy	kazakh, russe	1 Tenge (KZT) = 100 tiyn
Kenya	Kenya	Jamhuri ya Kenya	swahili, anglais	1 shilling du Kenya (KES) = 100 cents
Kirghizistan	Kyrgyzstan	Kyrgyz Respublikasy	kirghiz	1 som (KGS) = 100 tiyin

Nom français	Nom anglais	Nom local	Langue(s) officielle(s)	Monnaie
Koweït	Kuwait	Dowlat al-Kuwayt	arabe	1 dinar koweïtien (KWD) = 1 000 fils
Laos	Laos	Lao	laotien	1 kip (LAK) = 100 att
Lesotho	Lesotho	Lesotho	anglais, sotho	1 loti (LSL) (*pl* maloti) = 100 lisente
Lettonie	Latvia	Latvijas Republika	letton	1 lats (LVL) (*pl* lati) = 100 santimi (*sing* santims)
Liban	Lebanon	Al-Lubnān	arabe	1 livre libanaise (LBP) = 100 piastres
Liberia	Liberia	Liberia	anglais	1 dollar libérien (LRD) = 100 cents
Libye	Libya	Lībyā	arabe	1 dinar libyen (LYD) = 1000 dirhams
Liechtenstein	Liechtenstein	Furstentum Liechtenstein	allemand	1 franc suisse (CHF) = 100 centimes/rappen
Lituanie	Lithuania	Lietuva	lituanien	1 litas (LTL) (*pl* litai)= 100 centai (*sing* centas)
Luxembourg	Luxembourg	Lëtzebuerg (Letz), Luxembourg (français), Luxemburg (allemand)	français, allemand	1 euro (EUR) = 100 cents
Macédoine	Macedonia	Republika Makedonija	macédonien	1 denar (MKD) = 100 paras
Madagascar	Madagascar	Repoblikan'i Madagasikara	malgache, français	1 franc malgache (MGF) = 100 centimes
Malaisie	Malaysia	Federation of Malaysia	malais	1 ringgit [*Fr* dollar malaisien] (MYR) = 100 cents
Malawi	Malawi	Dziko la Malaŵi	chichewa, anglais	1 kwacha (MWK) = 100 tambalas
Maldives	Maldives	Maldives Divehi Jumhuriya	divehi	1 rufiyaa (MVR) = 100 laari
Mali	Mali	Mali	français	1 franc CFA (XOF) = 100 centimes
Malte	Malta	Malta	anglais, maltais	1 livre maltaise (MTL) = 100 cents = 1000 miles
Maroc	Morocco	Mamlaka al-Maghrebia	arabe	1 dirham (MAD) = 100 centimes
Martinique	Martinique	Martinique	français, créole	1 euro (EUR) = 100 cents
Maurice, île	Mauritius	Mauritius	anglais	1 roupie mauricienne (MUR) = 100 cents
Mauritanie	Mauritania	Mauritanie (français), Mūrītāniyā (arabe)	arabe	1 ouguiya (MRO) = 5 khoums
Mexique	Mexico	México	espagnol	1 peso mexicain (MXN) = 100 centavos
Micronésie	Micronesia	Micronesia	anglais	1 dollar US (USD) = 100 cents

Nom français	Nom anglais	Nom local	Langue(s) officielle(s)	Monnaie
Moldavie	Moldova	Republica Moldovenească	roumain	1 leu (MDL) (*pl* lei) = 100 bani (*sing* ban)
Mongolie	Mongolia	Mongol Ard Uls	khalkha	1 tugrik (MNT) = 100 mongo
Mozambique	Mozambique	República de Moçambique	portugais	1 metical (MZM) = 100 kobo
Myanmar	Myanmar	Myanmar	birman	1 kyat (MMK) = 100 pyas
Namibie	Namibia	Namibia	anglais	1 dollar namibien (NAD) = 100 cents
Nauru	Nauru	Naeoro (nauruan), Nauru (anglais)	nauruan, anglais	1 dollar australien (AUD) = 100 cents
Népal	Nepal	Nepal Adhirajya	népalais	1 roupie népalaise (NPR) = 100 paisa
Nicaragua	Nicaragua	Nicaragua	espagnol	1 cordoba oro (NIO) = 100 centavos
Niger	Niger	Niger	français	1 franc CFA (XOF) = 100 centimes
Nigéria	Nigeria	Nigeria	anglais, français	1 naira (NGN) = 100 kobo
Norvège	Norway	Kongeriket Norge	norvégien	1 couronne norvégienne (NOK) = 100 øre
Nouvelle-Zélande	New Zealand	New Zealand	anglais	1 dollar néo-zélandais (NZD) = 100 cents
Oman	Oman	Saltanat 'Uman	arabe	1 rial omanais (OMR) = 1 000 baizas
Ouganda	Uganda	Uganda	anglais, swahili	1 shilling ougandais (UGX) = 100 cents
Ouzbékistan	Uzbekistan	Uzbekistan	ouzbek	1 soum (UZS) = 100 tiyin
Pakistan	Pakistan	Pākistān	urdu, anglais	1 roupie pakistanaise (PKR) = 100 paisa
Panamá	Panama	Panamá	espagnol	1 balboa (PAB) = 100 centésimos
Papouasie-Nouvelle-Guinée	Papua New Guinea	Papua New Guinea	anglais, néo-mélanaisien	1 kina (PGK) = 100 tosa
Paraguay	Paraguay	Paraguay	espagnol	1 guaraní (PYG) = 100 céntimos
Pays-Bas	The Netherlands	Koninkrijk der Nederlanden	néerlandais	1 euro (EUR) = 100 cents
Pérou	Peru	Perú	espagnol	1 nouveau sol (PEN) = 100 centavos
Philippines	Philippines	Pilipinas	tagalog, anglais	1 peso philippin (PHP) = 100 centavos
Pologne	Poland	Rzeczpospolita Polska	polonais	1 zloty (PLN) = 100 groszy (*sing* grosz)
Polynésie française	French Polynesia	Territoire de la Polynésie française	polynésien, français	1 Franc CFP (XPF) = 100 centimes
Porto Rico	Puerto Rico	Puerto Rico	espagnol, anglais	1 dollar US (USD) = 100 cents

Nom français	Nom anglais	Nom local	Langue(s) officielle(s)	Monnaie
Portugal	Portugal	Portugal	portugais	1 euro (EUR) = 100 cents
Principauté de Monaco	Monaco	Monaco	français	1 euro (EUR) = 100 cents
Qatar	Qatar	Dowlat Qatar	arabe	1 riyal (QAR) = 100 dirhams
Roumanie	Romania	Romānia	roumain	1 leu (ROL) (*pl* lei) = 100 bani (*sing* ban)
Royaume-Uni	United Kingdom	United Kingdom	anglais	1 pound sterling [*Fr* livre sterling] (GBP) = 100 pence (*sing* penny)
Russie	Russia	Rossiya	russe	1 rouble (RUR) = 100 kopeks
Rwanda	Rwanda	Rwanda	kinyarwanda, français, anglais	1 franc rwandais (RWF) = 100 centimes
Saint-Marin	San Marino	San Marino	italien	1 euro (EUR) = 100 cents
Salomon, îles	Solomon Islands	Solomon Islands	anglais	1 dollar des îles Salomon (SBD) = 100 cents
Salvador	El Salvador	El Salvador	espagnol	1 colón [*Fr* colon salvadorien] (SVC) (*pl* colones) = 100 centavos
Samoa	Samoa	Samoa	samoan, anglais	1 tala (WST) = 100 sene
Sénégal	Senegal	Sénégal	français, ouolof	1 franc CFA (XOF) = 100 centimes
Seychelles	Seychelles	Seychelles	français, anglais, créole	1 roupie des Seychelles (SCR) = 100 cents
Sierra Leone	Sierra Leone	Sierra Leone	anglais	1 leone (SLL) = 100 cents
Singapour	Singapore	Singapore	chinois, anglais, malais, tamoul	1 dollar de Singapour (SGD) = 100 cents
Slovaquie	Slovakia	Slovenska Republika	slovaque	1 couronne slovaque (CSK) = 100 haleriov
Slovénie	Slovenia	Republika Slovenija	slovène	1 tolar (SIT) =100 stotins
Somalie	Somalia	Somaliya	arabe, somali	1 shilling somalien (SOS) = 100 cents
Soudan	The Sudan	As-Sūdān	arabe	1 dinar soudanais (SDD) = 100 piastres
Sri Lanka	Sri Lanka	Sri Lanka	cinghalais, tamoul	1 roupie de Sri Lanka (LKR) = 100 cents
Suède	Sweden	Konungariket Sverige	suédois	1 couronne suédoise (SEK) = 100 öre
Suisse	Switzerland	Schweiz (allemand), Suisse (français), Svizzera (italien)	français, allemand, italien, romanche	1 franc suisse (CHF) = 100 centimes/rappen
Surinam	Surinam	Suriname	néerlandais	1 gulden [*Fr* florin] de Surinam (SRG) = 100 cents
Swaziland	Swaziland	Umbouso we Swatini	swazi, anglais	1 lilangeni (SZL) (*pl* emalangeni) = 100 cents

Nom français	Nom anglais	Nom local	Langue(s) officielle(s)	Monnaie
Syrie	Syria	As-Sūrīyah	arabe	1 livre syrienne (SYP) = 100 piastres
Tadjikistan	Tajikistan	Jumkhurii Tojikistan	tadjik	1 rouble tadjik (TJR) = 100 tanga
Taïwan	Taiwan	T'aiwan	chinois	1 dollar de Taïwan (TWD) = 100 cents
Tanzanie	Tanzania	Tanzania	swahili, anglais	1 shilling tanzanien (TZS) = 100 cents
Tchad	Chad	Tchad	français, arabe	1 Franc CFA (XAF) = 100 centimes
Tchèque, République	Czech Republic	Česká Republika	tchèque	1 couronne tchèque (CZK) = 100 haleru
Thaïlande	Thailand	Prathet Thai	thaï	1 baht (THB) = 100 satang
Togo	Togo	Togo	français	1 franc CFA (XOF) = 100 centimes
Tonga	Tonga	Tonga	anglais, tongan	1 pa'anga (TOP) = 100 seniti
Trinité-et-Tobago	Trinidad and Tobago	Trinidad and Tobago	anglais	1 dollar de Trinité-et-Tobago (TTD) = 100 cents
Tunisie	Tunisia	Tunisiya	arabe, français	1 dinar tunisien (TND) = 1000 millimes
Turkménistan	Turkmenistan	Turkmenostan	turkmène	1 manat (TMM) = 100 tenesi
Turquie	Turkey	Tūrkiye	turc	1 livre turque (TRL) = 100 kurus
Ukraine	Ukraine	Ukraina	ukrainien, russe	1 hrivna (UAK) = 100 kopiykas
Uruguay	Uruguay	Uruguay	espagnol	1 peso uruguayen (UYU) = 100 centésimos
Vanuatu	Vanuatu	Vanuatu	bichlamar, anglais, français	1 vatu (VUV) = 100 centimes
Vatican, cité du	Vatican City	Citta' del Vaticano	italien	1 euro (EUR) = 100 cents
Venezuela	Venezuela	Venezuela	espagnol	1 bolívar (VEB) (pl bolívares) = 100 céntimos
Vietnam	Vietnam	Viêt-nam	vietnamien	1 dông (VND) = 10 hao = 100 xu
Yémen	Yemen	Al-Yamaniya	arabe	1 riyal yéménite (YER) = 100 fils
Yougoslavie	Yugoslavia	Jugoslavija	serbo-croate (serbe)	1 dinar yougoslave (YUN) = 100 paras
Zaïre	Zaire	▶ Congo, République démocratique du		
Zambie	Zambia	Zambia	anglais	1 kwacha (ZMK) = 100 ngwee
Zimbabwe	Zimbabwe	Zimbabwe	anglais	1 dollar du Zimbabwe (ZWD) = 100 cents

DIVISIONS ADMINISTRATIVES

Comtés anglais

Comté	Centre administratif	Abréviation
Avon[1]	Bristol	
Bedfordshire	Bedford	Beds
Berkshire	Reading	Berks
Buckinghamshire	Aylesbury	Bucks
Cambridgeshire	Cambridge	Cambs
Cheshire	Chester	Ches
Cleveland[1]	Middlesbrough	
Cornwall	Truro	Corn
Cumbria[1]	Carlisle	
Derbyshire	Matlock	Derby
Devon	Exeter	
Dorset	Dorchester	
Durham	Durham	Dur
Essex	Chelmsford	
Gloucestershire	Gloucester	Glos
Greater London[1]	-	
Greater Manchester[1]	-	
Hampshire	Winchester	Hants
Hereford and	Worcester[1]	Worcester
Hertfordshire	Hertford	Herts
Humberside[1]	Hull	
Isle of Wight	Newport	IOW
Kent	Maidstone	
Lancashire	Preston	Lancs
Leicestershire	Leicester	Leics
Lincolnshire	Lincoln	Lincs
Merseyside[1]	Liverpool	
Norfolk	Norwich	
Northamptonshire	Northampton	Northants
Northumberland	Newcastle upon Tyne	Northumb
Nottinghamshire	Nottingham	Notts
Oxfordshire	Oxford	Oxon
Shropshire	Shrewsbury	
Somerset	Taunton	Som
Staffordshire	Stafford	Staffs
Suffolk	Ipswich	
Surrey	Kingston upon Thames	
Sussex, East	Lewes	
Sussex, West	Chichester	
Tyne and Wear[1]	Newcastle	
Warwickshire	Warwick	War
West Midlands[1]	Birmingham	W Midlands
Wiltshire	Trowbridge	Wilts
Yorkshire, North	Northallerton	N Yorks
Yorkshire, South	Barnsley	S Yorks
Yorkshire, West	Wakefield	W Yorks

[1] Les comtés créés en 1974 ont été formés de la façon suivante: **Avon**: une partie du Somerset et du Gloucestershire **Cleveland**: une partie du comté de Durham et du Yorkshire **Cumbria**: Cumberland, Westmoreland, et une partie du Lancashire et du Yorkshire **Greater London**: Londres et la plus grande partie du Middlesex **Greater Manchester**: une partie du Lancashire, du Cheshire et du Yorkshire **Hereford and Worcester**: Hereford et la plus grande partie du Worcestershire **Humberside**: une partie du Yorkshire et du Lincolnshire **Merseyside**: une partie du Lancashire et du Cheshire **Tyne and Wear**: une partie du Northumberland et du comté de Durham **West Midlands**: une partie du Staffordshire, du Warwickshire et du Worcestershire

Écosse

Division administrative[1]	Centre administratif
Aberdeen City	Aberdeen
Aberdeenshire	Aberdeen
Angus	Forfar
Argyll and Bute	Lochgilphead
Clackmannanshire	Alloa
Dumfries and Galloway	Dumfries
Dundee City	Dundee
East Ayrshire	Kilmarnock
East Dunbartonshire	Kirkintilloch
East Lothian	Haddington
East Renfrewshire	Giffnock
Edinburgh, City of	Edinburgh
Falkirk	Falkirk
Fife	Glenrothes
Glasgow City	Glasgow
Highland	Inverness
Inverclyde	Greenock
Midlothian	Dalkeith
Moray	Elgin
North Ayrshire	Irvine
North Lanarkshire	Motherwell
Orkney Islands	Kirkwall
Perth and Kinross	Perth
Renfrewshire	Paisley
Scottish Borders	Newton St Boswells
Shetland Islands	Lerwick
South Ayrshire	Ayr
South Lanarkshire	Hamilton
Stirling	Stirling
West Dunbartonshire	Dumbarton
Western Isles (Eilean Siar, Comhairle nan)	Stornoway
West Lothian	Livingston

Comtés irlandais

Comté	Centre administratif
Carlow	Carlow
Cavan	Cavan
Clare	Ennis
Cork	Cork
Donegal	Lifford
Dublin	Dublin
Galway	Galway
Kerry	Tralee
Kildare	Naas
Kilkenny	Kilkenny
Laoighis (Leix)	Portlaoise
Leitrim	Carrick
Limerick	Limerick
Longford	Longford
Louth	Dundalk
Mayo	Castlebar
Meath	Trim
Monaghan	Monaghan
Offaly	Tullamore
Roscommon	Roscommon
Sligo	Sligo
Tipperary	Clonmel
Waterford	Waterford
Westmeath	Mullingar
Wexford	Wexford
Wicklow	Wicklow

[1] Les comtés d'Écosse ont été remplacés par neuf "regional councils" et 53 "district councils" en 1975, qui furent eux-mêmes remplacés par 29 "unitary authorities" ou "council areas" (divisions administratives) en avril 1996, les trois "islands councils" (pour l'ouest de l'Écosse) restant inchangés.

Pays de Galles

Division administrative	Centre administratif
Anglesey, Isle of	Llangefni
Blaenau Gwent	Ebbw Vale
Bridgend	Bridgend
Caerphilly	Hengoed
Cardiff	Cardiff
Carmarthenshire	Carmarthen
Ceredigion	Aberaeron
Conwy	Conwy
Denbighshire	Ruthin
Flintshire	Mold
Gwynedd	Caernarfon
Merthyr Tydfil	Merthyr Tydfil
Monmouthshire	Cwmbran
Neath Port Talbot	Port Talbot
Newport	Newport
Pembrokeshire	Haverfordwest
Powys	Llandrindod Wells
Rhondda, Cynon, Taff	Clydach Vale
Swansea	Swansea
Torfaen	Pontypool
Vale of Glamorgan	Barry
Wrexham	Wrexham

Irlande du Nord

Division administrative	Centre administratif
Antrim	Antrim
Ards	Newtownards
Armagh	Armagh
Ballymena	Ballymena
Ballymoney	Balleymoney
Banbridge	Banbridge
Belfast	
Carrickfergus	Carrickfergus
Castlereagh	Belfast
Coleraine	Coleraine
Cookstown	Cookstown
Craigavon	Craigavon
Derry	
Down	Downpatrick
Dungannon	Dungannon
Fermanagh	Enniskillen
Larne	Larne
Limavady	Limavady
Lisburn	Lisburn
Magherafelt	Magherafelt
Moyle	Ballycastle
Newry and Mourne	Newry
Newtownabbey	Newtownabbey
North Down	Bangor
Omagh	Omagh
Strabane	Strabane

États-Unis: liste des États

Abréviations : la première abréviation indique la forme la plus couramment utilisée, la seconde correspond au code postal de l'État (ZIP code).

État	Abréviations	Surnom	Habitants	Capitale
Alabama	Ala; AL	Camellia State, Heart of Dixie	Alabamians	Montgomery
Alaska	AK	Mainland State, The Last Frontier	Alaskans	Juneau
Arizona	Ariz; AZ	Apache State, Grand Canyon State	Arizonans	Phoenix
Arkansas	Ark; AR	Bear State, Land of Opportunity	Arkansans	Little Rock
Californie (California)	Calif; CA	Golden State	Californians	Sacramento
Caroline du Nord (North Carolina)	NC	Old North State, Tar Heel State	North Carolinians	Raleigh
Caroline du Sud (South Carolina)	SC	Palmetto State	South Carolinians	Columbia

État	Abréviations	Surnom	Habitants	Capitale
Colorado	Colo; CO	Centennial State	Coloradans	Denver
Connecticut	Conn; CT	Nutmeg State, Constitution State	Nutmeggers	Hartford
Dakota du Nord (North Dakota)	N Dak; ND	Flickertail State, Sioux State, Peace Garden State	North Dakotans	Bismarck
Dakota du Sud (South Dakota)	S Dak; SD	Sunshine State, Coyote State	South Dakotans	Pierre
Delaware	Del; DE	Diamond State, First State	Delawareans	Dover
District de Columbia (District of Columbia)	DC	DC, the District	Washingtonians	Washington
Floride (Florida)	Fla; FL	Everglade State, Sunshine State	Floridians	Tallahassee
Géorgie (Georgia)	Ga; GA	Empire State of the South, Peach State	Georgians	Atlanta
Hawaï (Hawaii)	HI	Aloha State	Hawaiians	Honolulu
Idaho	ID	Gem State	Idahoans	Boise
Illinois	Ill; IL	Prairie State, Land of Lincoln	Illinoisans	Springfield
Indiana	Ind; IN	Hoosier State	Hoosiers	Indianapolis
Iowa	IA	Hawkeye State, Corn State	Iowans	Des Moines
Kansas	Kans; KS	Sunflower State, Jayhawker State	Kansans	Topeka
Kentucky	Ky; KY	Bluegrass State	Kentuckians	Frankfort
Louisiane (Louisiana)	La; LA	Pelican State, Sugar State, Creole State	Louisianians	Baton Rouge
Maine	ME	Pine Tree State	Downeasters	Augusta
Maryland	Md; MD	Old Line State,	Marylanders	Annapolis
Massachusetts	Mass; MA	Bay State, Old ColonyBay	Staters	Boston
Michigan	Mich; MI	Wolverine State, Great Lake State	Michiganders	Lansing
Minnesota	Minn; MN	Gopher State, North Star State	Minnesotans	St Paul
Mississippi	Miss; MS	Magnolia State	Mississippians	Jackson
Missouri	Mo; MO	Bullion State, Show Me State	Missourians	Jefferson City
Montana	Mont; MT	Treasure State, Big Sky Country	Montanans	Helena
Nebraska	Nebr; NE	Cornhusker State, Beef State	Nebraskans	Lincoln
Nevada	Nev; NV	Silver State, Sagebrush State, Battle Born State	Nevadans	Carson City
New Hampshire	NH	Granite State	New Hampshirites	Concord

État	Abréviations	Surnom	Habitants	Capitale
New Jersey	NJ	Garden State	New Jerseyites	Trenton
New Mexico	N Mex; NM	Sunshine State, Land of Enchantment	New Mexicans	Santa Fe
New York	NY	Empire State	New Yorkers	Albany
Ohio	OH	Buckeye State	Ohioans	Columbus
Oklahoma	Okla; OK	Sooner State	Oklahomans	Oklahoma City
Oregon	Oreg; OR	Sunset State, Beaver State	Oregonians	Salem
Pennsylvanie (Pennsylvania)	Pa; PA	Keystone State	Pennsylvanians	Harrisburg
Rhode Island	RI	Little Rhody, Plantation State	Rhode Islanders	Providence
Tennessee	Tenn; TN	Volunteer State	Tennesseans	Nashville
Texas	Tex; TX	Lone Star State	Texans	Austin
Utah	Utah; UT	Mormon State, Beehive State	Utahans	Salt Lake City
Vermont	Vt; VT	Green Mountain State	Vermonters	Montpelier
Virginie Occidentale (West Virginia)	W Va; WV	Panhandle State, Mountain State	West Virginians	Charleston
Virginie (Virginia)	Va; VA	Old Dominion State, Mother of Presidents	Virginians	Richmond
Washington	Wash; WA	Evergreen State, Chinook State	Washingtonians	Olympia
Wisconsin	Wis; WI	Badger State, America's Dairyland	Wisconsinites	Madison
Wyoming	Wyo; WY	Equality State	Wyomingites	Cheyenne

États et territoires australiens

Nom	Capitale
Australian Capital Territory	Canberra
New South Wales	Sydney
Northern Territory	Darwin
Queensland	Brisbane
South Australia	Adelaide
Tasmania	Hobart
Victoria	Melbourne
Western Australia	Perth

Provinces canadiennes

Nom	Capitale
Alberta	Edmonton
British Columbia	Victoria
Manitoba	Winnipeg
New Brunswick	Fredericton
Newfoundland	St John's
Northwest Territories and Nunavut	Yellowknife
Nova Scotia	Halifax
Ontario	Toronto
Prince Edward Island	Charlottetown
Quebec	Quebec City
Saskatchewan	Regina
Yukon Territory	Whitehorse

RAPPORTS FINANCIERS BRITANNIQUES ET AMÉRICAINS

En ce qui concerne la présentation et le calcul des données financières, les différences entre les pays dans le monde se sont réduites avec le temps, mais les bases historiques n'en sont pas moins différentes.

- La comptabilité française est réglementée par l'État depuis le XVIIᵉ siècle, et avec pour objectif d'aider au calcul de l'impôt et à la gestion de l'économie.
- À l'intérieur d'un cadre statutaire, les comptabilités britannique et américaine ont été réglementées en détail par la profession comptable; elles tirent leur origine de la révolution industrielle, époque à laquelle il devint nécessaire de réunir des fonds pour financer et contrôler les programmes industriels.

Historiquement, le bilan est le plus ancien rapport financier. Il s'agissait à l'origine pour l'entreprise d'établir un inventaire annuel de tous ses biens tout en décomptant les dettes afin d'estimer la valeur de son patrimoine. La différence de la valeur entre deux inventaires annuels représente la perte ou le gain sur l'année écoulée.

La comptabilité moderne, elle, se passe de la réévaluation annuelle, mais elle garde une base de données des transactions financières dans le grand livre, base qui sert à établir les états financiers. Il s'agit (a) du bilan, (b) du compte de résultat, (c) du tableau des flux de trésorerie, et (d) de l'annexe.

- Le **bilan** ("balance sheet") montre d'une part, les modes de financement de l'entreprise, lesquels se répartissent entre le capital non remboursable (les fonds souscrits par les actionnaires), et la dette ou emprunt qui doit être remboursé; d'autre part, l'actif – les équipements de production et les éléments courants d'exploitation que le passif a financés. L'actif est normalement divisé entre l'actif immobilisé (la capacité de production à long terme) et l'actif circulant (éléments d'exploitation tels que le stock de marchandises et les montants dus par les clients, ainsi que les liquidités).
- Le **compte de résultat** ("profit and loss account") donne une présentation détaillée des produits et des dépenses de l'année.
- Le **tableau des flux de trésorerie** ("cash flow statement") analyse les changements dans la structure financière de l'entreprise au cours d'une même année, c'est-à-dire les sommes rapportées par les différentes opérations, la part des fonds investis et les conséquences de ces deux flux sur l'endettement de l'entreprise.
- L'**annexe** ("notes to the accounts") a le même statut réglementaire que les états financiers et sert en principe d'outil pour une analyse complémentaire.

La comptabilité s'établit sur une base qu'on appelle "comptabilité d'engagement". Elle essaie de saisir toutes les opérations contractuelles (par exemple la livraison de produits aux clients), plutôt que de se limiter à un traitement des flux de trésorerie. En conséquence le compte d'exploitation est une estimation économique, ce qui explique l'intérêt d'un tableau des flux de trésorerie qui examine ceux-ci séparément.

Si les rapports financiers de différents pays donnent à peu près les mêmes informations, la présentation diverge quelque peu. Cependant les éléments fondamentaux du bilan que représentent le capital, la dette, l'actif immobilisé, l'actif circulant, existent bien et sont facilement identifiables. Le bilan fonctionne sur le fait que la totalité des sources de financement (dettes et capital, le passif) est toujours égal à la globalité de l'utilisation du financement (actifs immobilisé et circulant).

- Si l'Union européenne a été une force majeure d'harmonisation dans la présentation des états financiers, elle en admet encore plusieurs formats différents. La France et le Royaume-Uni ont fait un choix différent, leurs états financiers ne se ressemblent donc pas dans tous les détails.
- La France permet aux grandes entreprises d'utiliser un format international, par conséquent tous les bilans ne sont pas faits de façon identique.
- En Europe, la tradition veut que bien que les entreprises doivent respecter les formats admis, elles peuvent néanmoins fournir des renseignements complémentaires.
- Aux États-Unis, bien qu'il n'y ait pas de formats spécifiques, il y a un minimum de catégories d'informations à respecter. Si les pratiques des entreprises américaines varient, le format utilisé par une majorité d'entre elles est celui donné dans l'exemple.
- En général les autorités ne limitent pas l'utilisation de l'annexe. Les entreprises américaines et britanniques ont donc tendance à offrir une présentation très simple du bilan, en utilisant des chiffres en agrégat, et à garder le détail pour l'annexe.

Modèles de rapports financiers britanniques

Présentation reconnue par le 4ème Directive de l'UE

Profit and loss account

for the year ended 30 June	20X2	20X1
(in thousands of pounds)		
Turnover	50,925	46,543
Costs		
Cost of Sales	15,342	13,467
Marketing expenses	8,843	6,923
Administration costs	18,261	18,236
Exceptional items	30	38
Operating profit before finance costs	8,449	7,879
Finance costs (net)	(3,054)	(2,652)
Profit on ordinary activities before taxation	5,395	5,227
Tax on profit on ordinary activities	(1,356)	(1,369)

Charges analysées par fonction

Faux ami: catégorie de charge courante qui est anormale mais pas "exceptionnelle"

Détails des charges et produits en annexe

	4,039	3,858
Profit attributable to shareholders	4,039	3,858
Dividends	(1,903)	(1,808)
Retained profit	2,136	2,050
Earnings per ordinary share	2.1p	2.0p

Balance sheet ← Formule utilisée parfois par des sociétés américaines

at 30 June

(in thousands of pounds)

	20X2	20X1
Fixed assets		
Tangible assets ← Analyse des immobilisations dans l'annexe	109,703	102,805
Investments	5,000	5,000
	114,703	107,805
Current assets		
Stocks	276	298
Debtors	4,087	4,592
Cash at bank and in hand	3,086	6,818
	7,449	11,708
Creditors		
Amounts falling due within one year	14,006	13,870
Net current liabilities	(6,557)	(2,162)
Total assets less current liabilities	108,146	105,643
Creditors		
Amounts falling due after more than one year	(41,199)	(40,792)
Provision for liabilities and charges	(,236)	(,306)
Net assets ← La présentation montre: actif moins dettes = capitaux propres	66,711	64,545
Capital and reserves		
Share Capital	19,032	19,032
Share premium	43,321	43,321
Revenue reserves	4,358	2,192
	£66,711	£64,545

Cash flow statement
for the year ended 30 June ← L'exercice comptable n'est pas forcément l'année civile

(in thousands of pounds)

	20X2	20X1
Operating profit	8,479	7,917
Depreciation	3,136	2,870
Movement on stock	22	219
Movement on debtors	558	(537)
Movement on creditors	(150)	(556)
Provisions	(70)	(360)
Net cash flow from operating activities	11,975	9,553
Interest received	303	429
Interest paid	(4,029)	(3,417)
Dividends paid	(1,827)	(1,693)
Net cash flow from returns on investments and servicing finance	(5,553)	(4,681)
Tax paid	(1,166)	(1,465)
Investing activities		
Purchase of tangible fixed assets	(9,543)	(11,373)
Sale of tangible fixed assets	210	783
Investment in shares	(1,000)	(1,395)
Net cash flow from investing activities	(10,333)	(11,985)
Financing activities		
Issue of shares	—	22
Increase in debt	1,345	9,610
Net cash flow from financing activities	1,345	9,632
Net increase (decrease) in cash	(3,732)	1,054
Cash at beginning of period	£6,818	£5,764
Cash at end of period	£3,086	£6,818

(Net cash flow from returns on investments and servicing finance / Tax paid) ← Catégories spécifiques à la version britannique

Modèles de rapports financiers américains

Statement of earnings
for the year ended March 31

Deux exercices précédents doivent être montrés

(in millions of dollars except per share amounts)	20X2	20X1	20X0
Net revenue			
Sales	24,991	20,317	16,410
Costs and expenses			
Cost of goods sold	15,490	12,123	9,158
Research and development	2,027	1,761	1,620
Selling, general and administrative	4,925	4,554	4,228
	22,442	18,438	15,006
Earnings from operations	2,549	1,879	1,404
Interest income and other, net	029	025	017
Interest expense	155	121	096
Earnings before taxes	2,423	1,783	1,325
Provision for taxes	824	606	444
Net Earnings	1,599	1,177	881
Earnings per share (in dollars)	$6.14	$4.65	$3.49

Les charges sont ventilées par destination plutôt que par nature

Les charges de recherche sont souvent mises en évidence

Information obligatoire

Balance sheet

March 31 (in millions of dollars)	20X2	20X1
Assets		
Current assets		
Cash and cash equivalents	1,357	890
Short-term investments	1,121	755
Accounts & notes receivable	5,028	4,208
Inventories		
Finished goods	2,466	2,121
Purchased parts and fabricated assemblies	1,807	1,570
Other current assets	730	693
Total current assets	12,509	10,237
Property, plant & equipment		
Land	508	504
Buildings & leasehold improvements	3,472	3,264
Machinery & equipment	3,958	3,759

L'actif est présenté avec les éléments à court terme en tête

Accumulated depreciation	*Détails fournis dans l'annexe*	7,938 (3,610) 4,328	7,527 (3,347) 4,180
Long-term receivables and other assets		2,730 19,567	2,320 16,736

Liabilities and shareholders' equity

Current liabilities:

Notes payable and short-term borrowings	2,469	2,190
Accounts payable	1,466	1,223
Employee compensation and benefits	1,256	1,048
Taxes on earnings	1,245	922
Deferred revenues	598	507
Other accrued liabilities	1,196	978
Total current liabilities	8,230	6,868

Long-term debt	*Détails fournis dans l'annexe*	547	667
Other liabilities		864	690

Shareholders' equity

Common stock	*Sociétés américaines peuvent racheter leurs propres actions*	1,186	1,090
less Treasury stock		(153)	(153)
Retained earnings		8,893	7,574
Total shareholders' equity		9,926	8,511

Total liabilities and equity	$19,567	$16,736

Consolidated statement of cash flows ← *Présentation américaine ressemble beaucoup aux autres pays*

for the years ended March 31
(in millions of dollars)

	20X2	20X1	20X0
Cash flows from operating activities:			
Net earnings	$1,599	$1,177	$881
Adjustments to reconcile net earnings to cash provided by operating activities:			
Depreciation and amortization	1,006	846	573
Deferred taxes on earnings	(156)	(137)	(35)
Changes in assets & liabilities:			
Accounts and notes receivable	(848)	(709)	(380)
Inventories	(582)	(1,056)	(399)
Accounts payable	243	283	226
Taxes on earnings	320	452	163
Other current assets and liabilities	585	200	328
Other, net	57	86	(69)
	2,224	1,142	1,288
Cash flows from investing activities:	(1,257)	(1,405)	(1,032)
Investment in property, plant & equipment			
Disposal of property plant & equipment	291	215	183
Purchase of short-term investments	(2,758)	(1,634)	(782)
Maturities of short-term investments	2,392	1,283	883
Purchase of long-term investments	(332)	(22)	(53)

Maturities of long-term investments	47	22	4
Acquisitions, net of cash	(62)	(86)	(411)
Other, net	69	23	(58)
	(1,610)	(1,604)	(1,266)
Cash flows from financing activities:			
Increase in notes payable and short-term borrowings	250	815	186
Issuance of long-term debt	64	387	309
Payment of current maturities of long-term debt	(159)	(228)	(79)
Dividends	(305)	(242)	(213)
Other, net	4	(22)	(209)
	(146)	710	(6)
Increase in cash and cash equivalents	468	248	16
Cash and cash equivalents at beginning of year	889	641	625
Cash and cash equivalents at end of year	$1,357	$889	$641

Aa

A3 nm *(format de papier)* A3

A4 nm *(format de papier)* A4

abaissement nm *(des prix, des taux, d'un impôt)* lowering, reduction; *(des barrières douanières)* lowering; *(d'une monnaie)* weakening

abaisser vt *(prix, taux, impôt)* to lower, to reduce; *(barrières douanières)* to lower

abandon nm **(a)** *(de marchandises, de droits)* renunciation ❑ *Bourse* **abandon de l'option, abandon de prime** relinquishment *or* abandonment of the option **(b)** *(d'un projet)* shelving **(c)** *Ordinat (de programme)* abort

abandonner vt **(a)** *(marchandises, droits)* to abandon, to give up; **abandonner ses biens à ses créanciers** to surrender one's goods to one's creditors; **il a abandonné son poste de directeur** he gave up his post of director **(b)** *(projet)* to abandon, to shelve **(c)** *Ordinat (fichier, sous-programme)* to abort

abattage nm **à l'abattage** *(vente)* at knockdown prices

abattement nm *Fin (rabais)* reduction; *(d'impôts)* allowance ❑ **abattement à la base** basic personal allowance; **abattement fiscal** tax allowance, tax reduction; **abattement forfaitaire** fixed-rate rebate

abîmé, -e adj *(articles, marchandises)* damaged

abîmer 1 vt *(articles, marchandises)* to damage, to spoil
  2 **s'abîmer** vpr *(articles, marchandises)* to get damaged

abolir vt *(loi, impôt)* to abolish

abonné, -e 1 adj *(à un journal, à une revue)* subscribing; **être abonné à une revue/au Minitel®** to subscribe to a magazine/to Minitel®
  2 nm,f **(a)** *(à un journal, à une revue)* subscriber **(b)** *Tél* **un abonné du téléphone/d'Internet** a telephone/an Internet subscriber; **il n'y a pas d'abonné au numéro que vous avez demandé** ≃ the number you have dialled has not been recognized ❑ **abonné numérique** digital subscriber

abonnement nm **(a)** *(à un journal, à une revue)* subscription; **prendre** *ou* **souscrire un abonnement à qch** to take out a subscription to sth; **sur abonnement** on subscription ❑ **abonnement collectif** group subscription; **abonnement à l'essai** trial subscription **(b)** *Tél (au téléphone)* line rental **(c)** *Ordinat (à un fournisseur d'accès)* account, subscription (**auprès de** with); **abonnement à un service en ligne** on-line subscription ❑ **abonnement à forfait** flat-rate subscription *(to Internet)*

abonner 1 vt **abonner qn à un journal/une revue** to take out a subscription to a newspaper/magazine for sb
  2 **s'abonner** vpr **(a)** *(à un journal, à une revue)* to take out a subscription (**à** to) **(b)** *Tél* **s'abonner au téléphone** to have a telephone installed **(c)** *Ordinat (à un fournisseur d'accès)* to subscribe; **s'abonner auprès de qn** to set up an account with sb

abordable adj affordable, reasonable

aboutir vi *(réussir)* to be successful; **aboutir à un compromis/à un accord/à un échec** to end *or* result in compromise/agreement/failure; **l'entreprise n'a pas abouti** the venture fell through

aboutissement nm *(conclusion)* result, outcome; *(résultat positif)* success

above the line adj inv *(coûts, dépenses)* above-the-line

abrogatif, -ive adj *Jur (clause)* annulling, rescinding

abrogation nf *Jur* abrogation, repeal

abrogatoire adj *Jur (clause)* annulling, rescinding

abroger vt *Jur (loi)* to abrogate, to repeal, to rescind

absence nf absence; **la réunion commencera en l'absence du directeur** the meeting will begin without the director; **en l'absence du directeur, c'est à M. Dufour qu'il faut s'adresser** while the director is away *or* during the director's absence, you should speak to Mr Dufour

absent, -e 1 adj absent
  2 nm,f absentee

absentéisme nm absenteeism

absenter **s'absenter** vpr to go away; **s'absenter pour affaires** to go away on business

absorber vt *Écon (entreprise)* to take over, to absorb; **la multinationale va absorber cette entreprise** the multinational is going to take over *or* absorb this company

absorption *nf Écon* takeover, absorption; **l'absorption d'une petite société par une grosse** the takeover *or* absorption of a small company by a large one

absorption-fusion *nf* merger

abus *nm Jur* **abus de biens sociaux** misappropriation of funds; **abus de confiance** breach of trust; **abus de pouvoir** abuse of power

> " ——————
>
> Le garde des Sceaux a déclaré qu'il ne "souhaite pas que, dans le cadre de la loi d'amnistie, il puisse y avoir une amnistie politico-financière". En revanche, le ministre n'a pas exclu la possibilité de modifier la loi sur la délinquance financière. Il a affirmé en effet qu'il existait des "problèmes" concernant la durée des instructions et l'imprescriptibilité des **abus de biens sociaux**.
>
> —————— "

abuser abuser de *vt ind* **abuser de son autorité** to abuse one's power

abusif, -ive *adj (prix)* excessive

AC *nf Mktg (abrév* **audience cumulée)** cumulative audience

ac (**a**) *(abrév* **argent comptant)** cash (**b**) *(abrév* **année courante)** current year

accabler *vt* **accabler la population d'impôts** to overtax the population; **être accablé de dettes** to be burdened with debt

accalmie *nf* slack period, lull; **le marché financier traverse une période d'accalmie** the financial market is going through a slack period *or* a lull

accaparement *nm (du marché)* cornering; *(du pouvoir)* seizing

accaparer *vt (marché)* to corner; *(pouvoir)* to seize; *Écon* **accaparer des marchandises** *(pour contrôler le marché)* to withhold goods from the market

accéder accéder à *vt ind Ordinat (programme)* to access

accélérateur *nm Ordinat* accelerator ❏ **accélérateur graphique** graphic(s) accelerator

accent *nm* accent ❏ **accent aigu** acute accent; **accent circonflexe** circumflex accent; *(utilisé seul)* caret; **accent grave** grave accent

acceptabilité de la marque *nf Mktg* brand acceptability *or* acceptance

acceptable *adj (prix, conditions)* acceptable

acceptant, -e 1 *adj* acceptant
2 *nm,f* acceptant, acceptor

acceptation *nf (d'un chèque, d'un effet, d'un contrat, de marchandises)* acceptance; **sous réserve d'acceptation du dossier** subject to a favourable report; **bon pour acceptation** *(sur* *effet)* accepted bill; **présenter un effet à l'acceptation** to present a bill for acceptance; **refus d'acceptation** non-acceptance; **acceptation par intervention** acceptance for honour ❏ **acceptation bancaire** banker's acceptance; *Banque* **acceptation conditionnelle, acceptation sous condition** qualified acceptance; *Banque* **acceptation partielle** partial acceptance *(of bill)*

accepté, -e *adj (chèque, effet, contrat, marchandises)* accepted; **accepté** *(sur effet)* accepted bill

accepter *vt (contrat, marchandises)* to accept; *(chèque, effet)* to accept, to sign, to honour

accepteur, -euse *nm,f (d'une facture)* acceptor, drawee

Acces *nf (abrév* **Association des chaînes du câble et du satellite)** = association of French cable and satellite channels

accès *nm* (**a**) *(entrée)* access; **avoir accès à qch** to have access to sth; **des marchandises en libre accès** freely available goods; **accès réservé au personnel** *(sur panneau)* staff only; **accès interdit** *(sur panneau)* no entry, no admittance; **l'accès au statut de membre de l'Union européenne** entry into the European Union
(**b**) *Ordinat, Tél* access; *(à une page Web)* hit; **avoir accès à qch** to be able to access sth; **à accès multiple** multi-access; **accès refusé** access denied ❏ **accès aléatoire** random access; **accès commuté** dial-up access; **accès à distance** remote access; **accès par ligne commutée** dial-up access; **accès non autorisé** unauthorized access; **accès sécurisé par mot de passe** password-protected access; **accès séquentiel** sequential access

accessibilité *nf (à un produit, à un marché)* accessibility; *(d'un prix)* affordability

accessible *adj (produit, marché)* accessible; *(prix)* affordable

accession *nf* **accession à la propriété** home ownership; **faciliter l'accession à la propriété** to make it easier for people to become home owners; **accession à la monnaie unique** entry into the single currency; **accession au statut de membre de l'Union européenne** entry into the European Union

> " ——————
>
> Les prix des logements privés, en location comme en **accession à la propriété**, remontent aussi à cause de cette pénurie de logements sociaux. Il faut que baisse le coût du foncier, celui de la construction.
>
> —————— "

accessoire de bureau *nm Ordinat* desk accessory

accident *nm* accident ❏ **accident du travail** industrial accident, occupational accident

accidenté, -e *nm,f* accident victim □ *accidenté du travail* victim of an industrial accident

accise *nf Can & Belg* excise (duty)

accolade *nf* (curly) bracket

accommodant, -e *adj* **être accommodant en affaires** to be easy to do business with

accommodement *nm* arrangement, agreement; *(avec ses créanciers)* composition; **parvenir à un accommodement (avec qn)** to come to an arrangement *or* agreement (with sb)

accommoder *vt* to adapt; **accommoder un produit aux désirs des clients** to adapt *or* tailor a product to the clients' wishes

accompagnateur, -trice *nm,f* tour guide, courier

accomplir *vt (tâche)* to perform, to carry out; *(formalités)* to go through

accord *nm* (**a**) *(convention)* agreement; **signer un accord** to sign an agreement; **conclure un accord** to come to *or* reach an agreement □ *accord à l'amiable* private agreement; *(sans procès)* out-of-court settlement; *accord bilatéral* bilateral agreement; *accord de clearing* clearing agreement; *accord commercial* trade agreement; *accord de commercialisation* marketing agreement; *accord commercial multilatéral* multilateral trade agreement; *accord de compensation* offset agreement; *accord de distribution exclusive* exclusive distribution agreement; *accords d'échanges* swap agreements; *accord d'exclusivité* exclusivity agreement; *accord de franchise* franchise agreement; *Accord général sur les tarifs douaniers et le commerce* General Agreement on Tariffs and Trade; *accords de Helsinki* Helsinki Agreement; *accord d'indexation des salaires sur les prix* threshold agreement; *accords internationaux sur les produits de base* international commodity agreements; *accord de libre-échange* Free Trade Agreement; *accord de licence* licensing agreement; *Accord monétaire européen* European monetary agreement; *accord multilatéral* multilateral agreement; *accord de partenariat* partnership agreement, joint venture agreement; *accord de productivité* productivity agreement; *accord réciproque* reciprocal agreement; *accord de représentation* agency agreement; *accord de reprise* buyback arrangement; *accord salarial* pay *or* wage agreement; *accord de sous-traitance* subcontracting agreement; *accord tarifaire* tariff agreement; *Bourse accord de taux futur* future rate agreement; *Bourse accord de taux à terme* forward rate agreement; *accord verbal* verbal agreement

(**b**) *(entente)* **être d'accord avec qn/qch** to agree with sb/sth; **d'un commun accord** by common consent, by mutual agreement

(**c**) *(assentiment)* agreement, consent; **avoir l'accord de qn** to have sb's agreement *or* consent; **donner son accord** to agree, to consent

> «
> Sitôt réélu pour un mandat de trois ans, Jean-Paul Cluzel, Pdg de RF1, ambitionne de réaliser une seconde implantation à Marseille. Le 15 janvier, il prévoit de se rendre dans cette ville pour présenter un **accord de partenariat** avec deux stations associatives.
> »

accord-cadre *nm* outline agreement, blanket agreement

accorder **1** *vt (découvert bancaire, remise)* to allow, to give; *(dommages-intérêts)* to award; *(prêt)* to authorize, to extend; *(subventions)* to give, to grant; **accorder une licence à qn** to license sb

2 s'accorder *vpr (se mettre d'accord)* to agree, to come to an agreement (**avec qn** with sb; **sur qch** on sth); **s'accorder sur le prix** to agree on the price; *Compta* **faire s'accorder les livres** to agree the books

accréditation *nf* **l'accréditation d'un produit/d'un service à une norme de qualité** the awarding of a quality standard to a product/service

accrédité, -e **1** *adj* accredited; **notre représentant dûment accrédité** our duly authorized representative

2 *nm,f* (**a**) *Admin* agent (**b**) *Fin* holder of a letter of credit (**c**) *Compta* beneficiary, payee

accréditer *vt* (**a**) *(représentant)* to accredit (**b**) *Fin (client)* to open an account for, to open credit facilities for; **être accrédité auprès d'une banque** to have credit facilities at a bank

accréditeur *nm Fin* surety, guarantor

accréditif *nm* (**a**) *(lettre de crédit)* letter of credit; *Compta* credential (**b**) *(crédit)* credit; **loger un accréditif sur une banque** to open credit facilities with a bank □ *accréditif permanent* permanent credit; *accréditif prolongé* extended credit

accroche *nf Mktg* slogan

accrocheur, -euse *adj Fam (slogan)* catchy

accroissement *nm* growth, increase (**de** in); **les nouveaux équipements ont permis un accroissement de la productivité** the new equipment has led to an increase in productivity □ *accroissement des bénéfices* earnings growth; *Compta, Fin accroissement global net* aggregate net increment; *accroissement des ventes* sales growth

accroître **1** *vt* to increase; *(productivité)* to increase, to raise

2 s'accroître *vpr* to increase, to rise, to grow

accueil nm (**a**) *(lieu)* reception; **passez à l'accueil** go to the reception desk, go to reception; **tenir l'accueil** to be on reception (**b**) *(façon d'accueillir)* reception, welcome; **cérémonie d'accueil** welcoming ceremony; **discours d'accueil** welcoming speech (**c**) *Fin* **faire (bon) accueil à une traite** to meet *or* honour a bill

accueillir vt (**a**) *(loger)* to accommodate; **cet hôtel peut accueillir jusqu'à 500 visiteurs** this hotel can accommodate up to 500 guests (**b**) *(recevoir)* *(personne, décision, proposition)* to greet; **accueillir qch favorablement/défavorablement** *(idée, projet, décision)* to give sth a favourable/an unfavourable reception; **le projet a été très mal accueilli par la direction** the project got a very cool reception from the management (**c**) *Fin (traite)* to meet, to honour

accumulation nf *(de marchandises) (action)* stockpiling; *(résultat)* stockpile; *(de stocks)* accumulation, build-up; *(de dettes)* accumulation ❑ **accumulation de capital** capital accumulation; **accumulation des intérêts** accrual of interest

accumulé, -e adj *(marchandises)* stockpiled; *(stocks, dettes)* accumulated; *Fin (intérêts)* accrued

accumuler 1 vt *(marchandises)* to stockpile; *(stocks)* to accumulate, to build up; *(dettes)* to accumulate
2 s'accumuler vpr to accumulate; *Fin (intérêts)* to accrue

accusé, -e 1 adj *(baisse, hausse)* sharp
2 nm **accusé de réception** *(d'une lettre)* acknowledgement (of receipt), acknowledgement slip; *(d'un colis)* receipt; *Ordinat* acknowledgement; **envoyer un accusé de réception (à qn)** to send (sb) an acknowledgement

accuser vt (**a**) *(bénéfice, perte, baisse, hausse)* to show, to indicate; **la Bourse accuse une forte baisse** the Stock Market is registering big losses (**b**) **accuser réception de qch** to acknowledge (receipt of) sth; **nous accusons réception de votre lettre du 20 juin** we acknowledge receipt of your letter of 20 June

achalandage nm (**a**) *(fonds de commerce)* goodwill; **l'achalandage se vend avec l'établissement** the goodwill is to be sold with the business (**b**) *(clientèle)* custom, clientele

achalandé, -e adj **bien achalandé** *(qui compte de nombreux clients)* with a large clientele; *(bien approvisionné)* well-stocked; **mal achalandé** *(qui compte peu de clients)* with a small clientele; *(mal approvisionné)* poorly-stocked

achat nm *(action)* purchase, purchasing; *(chose achetée)* purchase; **faire un achat** to make a purchase; **faire l'achat de qch** to purchase sth; **un bon/mauvais achat** a good/bad buy; **la livre vaut 2,5 francs suisses à l'achat** the buying rate for sterling is 2.5 Swiss francs ❑ **achat en bloc** block purchase; **achat sur catalogue** mail-order purchasing; **achats centralisés** centralized purchasing; *Mktg* **achats comparatifs** comparison shopping; **achat au comptant** cash purchase; **achat à crédit** credit purchase; *(location-achat)* hire purchase, *Am* installment plan; **achats directs** direct purchasing; **achats à domicile** teleshopping; **achat de droits** rights buying; *Mktg* **achat d'émotion** emotional purchase; **achat d'espace** media buying; **achat en espèces** cash purchase; **achats hors taxes** duty-free shopping; *Mktg* **achat impulsif, achat d'impulsion** impulse purchase; *Fin* **achats institutionnels** institutional buying; *Ordinat* **achat par Internet** on-line purchase; *Mktg* **achats juste à temps** just-in-time purchasing; *Ordinat* **achat en ligne** on-line purchase; **achat à petits prix** low-cost purchase; **achats de précaution** panic buying; *Mktg* **achat prévu** destination purchase; *Mktg* **achats de qualité à 100%** zero defects purchasing; **achats regroupés** one-stop buying; *Mktg* **achat renouvelé** repeat purchase; *Mktg* **achats spécifiés** specification buying; **achats spéculatifs** speculative buying; *Mktg* **achat spontané** impulse purchase; **achat de système** systems buying; **achat à tempérament** hire purchase, *Am* installment plan; *Bourse* **achat à terme** forward purchase; *Mktg* **achats zéro défaut** zero defects purchasing

> **"**
> En 1997, les ventes de bonbons en sachet reculent, la confiserie de chocolat aussi. Tous les fabricants se plaignent d'une organisation du linéaire trop floue, parfois désordonnée, ce qui limiterait la découverte de nouveaux produits et les **achats d'impulsion**.
> **"**

acheminement nm *(de marchandises) (itinéraire)* flow, routing; *(expédition)* sending, shipping (**sur** *ou* **vers** to); **l'acheminement des marchandises se fait par Calais** the goods are routed through Calais; **acheminement du courrier** mail handling

acheminer 1 vt *(marchandises)* to send, to ship (**sur** *ou* **vers** to)
2 s'acheminer vpr **s'acheminer vers qch** *(décision, accord)* to move towards sth; **les syndicats s'acheminent vers une décision en faveur d'une grève** the unions are moving towards a decision to strike

achetable adj purchasable

acheter vt (**a**) *(acquérir)* to buy, to purchase; **acheter qch à qn** *(faire une transaction)* to buy sth from sb; *(en cadeau)* to buy sth for sb; **acheter qch en gros/au détail** to buy sth wholesale/retail; **acheter qch à crédit/(au) comptant** to buy sth on credit/for cash; **acheter qch à tempérament** to buy sth on hire purchase or Am on the installment plan; *Bourse* **acheter à terme** to buy forward (**b**) *Fam* **acheter qn** *(soudoyer)* to buy sb off

acheteur, -euse *nm,f* (**a**) *(acquéreur)* buyer, purchaser; *Jur* vendee; **on n'a pas pu trouver acheteur pour ce produit** there are no buyers for or there is no market for this product ❏ *Mktg* **acheteur anonyme** anonymous buyer; *Mktg* **acheteur cible** target buyer; *Mktg* **acheteur éventuel** potential buyer; *Mktg* **acheteur impulsif** impulsive buyer, impulse buyer; **acheteur industriel** business buyer; *Mktg* **acheteur non-identifié** anonymous buyer; *Mktg* **acheteur potentiel** potential buyer (**b**) *(pour un magasin)* buyer ❏ **acheteur principal** head buyer

achèvement *nm (d'un travail, d'un projet)* completion

achever *vt (travail, projet)* to complete

acompte *nm (versement régulier)* instalment; *(avance, premier versement)* down payment, deposit; *(sur salaire)* advance; **payer par acomptes** to pay by or in instalments; **payer** *ou* **verser un acompte de 4000 euros** *ou* **4000 euros en acompte (sur qch)** to make a down payment of 4,000 euros (on sth), to pay a deposit of 4,000 euros (on sth); **recevoir un acompte sur son salaire** to receive an advance on one's salary ❏ **acompte de** *ou* **sur dividende** interim dividend; **acompte minimum** minimum deposit; *Fin* **acompte provisionnel** interim payment, advance payment

à-côté *nm Fam (gain d'appoint)* extra; **avoir de petits à-côtés** to make a bit of extra money, to make some money on the side

acquéreur, -euse *nm,f* purchaser, buyer; *Jur* vendee

acquérir *vt* (**a**) *(acheter)* to buy, to purchase (**b**) *(obtenir) (expérience, responsabilités)* to gain, to acquire; **acquérir de la valeur** to go up in value; **l'expérience qu'il a acquise sur le terrain lui a été utile** the experience he gained on the job has been useful

acquis, -e 1 *adj (droits)* acquired, established **2** *nmpl* **acquis sociaux** social benefits, entitlements

❝
Le cabinet a décidé hier que le taux de la taxe sur la valeur ajoutée sera augmenté pour garder le déficit budgétaire à 6,5%. Les **acquis sociaux** seront toutefois maintenus.
❞

acquisition *nf* (**a**) *(action)* acquisition; **faire**

l'acquisition de qch *(acheter)* to purchase sth; *(entreprise)* to acquire sth (**b**) *(chose acquise)* acquisition; *(chose achetée)* purchase (**c**) *Ordinat* **acquisition de données** data acquisition

acquit *nm* receipt; **donner acquit de qch** to give a receipt for sth; **pour acquit** *(sur facture, quittance)* received (with thanks), paid ❏ *Douanes* **acquit (de douane)** customs receipt; **acquit de paiement** receipt

acquit-à-caution *nm Douanes* bond note, excise bond

acquittement *nm (d'une dette)* payment, discharge; *(d'une facture, des droits)* payment

acquitter 1 *vt* (**a**) *(payer) (dette)* to pay off, to discharge; *(facture, droits)* to pay (**b**) *(comme preuve de paiement)* to receipt (**c**) *(chèque)* to endorse **2 s'acquitter** *vpr* **s'acquitter de qch** *(dette)* to pay sth off, to discharge sth; *(facture, droits)* to pay sth

acte *nm* (**a**) *Jur (document officiel)* act, deed; **rédiger** *ou* **dresser un acte** to draw up an act or a deed ❏ **acte authentique** legal document; **acte de cession** deed of transfer, transfer deed; **acte de constitution, acte constitutif** *(d'une société)* memorandum of association; **acte déclaratif d'association** statement of intent to work together; **acte de fidéicommis** trust deed; **acte hypothécaire** mortgage deed; **acte notarié, acte sur papier timbré** deed executed and authenticated by a notary; **acte de propriété** title deed; *Jur* **acte sous seing privé** private agreement; **acte de société** deed of partnership; **acte de transfert** deed of assignment; **acte translatif (de propriété)** deed of transfer, transfer deed; *UE* **Acte unique européen** Single European Act; **acte de vente** bill of sale (**b**) **actes** *(d'une conférence)* records, proceedings

acteur *nm (participant)* participant, party; *(dans un secteur, d'un marché)* player; **les différents acteurs de la négociation** the different participants in or parties involved in the negotiations ❏ **acteur économique** economic agent or player; **acteur international** global player; **acteur du marché, acteur sur le marché** market player; **les acteurs sociaux** = employers, workers and trade unions

❝
Le Web est devenu un autre canal de vente qui va bouleverser la manière de travailler des **acteurs** de la communication et du marketing.
❞

actif, -ive 1 *adj* (**a**) *(marché)* active; *Écon (population)* working ❏ **la vie active** professional life; **entrer dans la vie active** to start working (**b**) *Ordinat (fichier, fenêtre)* active **2** *nm Compta* assets; **excédent de l'actif sur le**

passif excess of assets over liabilities □ *actif cir-culant* circulating *or* floating *or* current assets; *actif circulant net* net current assets; *actif corporel* tangible assets; *actif corporel net* net tangible assets; *actif différé* deferred assets; *actif disponible* available assets; *actif fictif* fictitious assets; *actif immobilisé* fixed *or* capital *or* permanent assets; *actif incorporel* invisible assets; *actif liquide* available assets, quick assets; *actif net* net assets; *actif réalisable* realizable assets; *actif réel* real assets; *actif de roulement* current assets

action *nf* (**a**) *Bourse, Fin* share; *(document)* share certificate; **actions** shares, equity, *Am* stock; **avoir des actions dans une société, détenir des actions d'une société** to have shares *or* a shareholding in a company; **émettre des actions sur un marché** to issue shares on a market; **les actions ont augmenté/baissé** shares rose/fell □ *action d'apport* *(délivrée au fondateur d'une société)* founder's share; *(émise par une société en contrepartie d'un apport en nature)* vendor's share; *action d'attribution* bonus share; *actions d'avenir* growth shares, growth stock; *action de capitalisation* capital share; *actions en circulation* outstanding shares; *action cotée (en Bourse)* quoted share; *actions en cours* outstanding shares; *actions de croissance* growth shares, growth stock; *action différée* deferred share; *action de distribution* income share; *action à dividende cumulatif* cumulative share; *action donnée en prime* bonus share; *action entièrement libérée* fully paid-up share; *action gratuite* bonus share; *actions indivises* joint shares; *action libérée* paid-up share; *action non entièrement libérée* partly paid-up share; *actions nouvelles* new shares; *action ordinaire* *Br* ordinary share, *Am* common stock; *action ordinaire différée* deferred *Br* ordinary share *or* *Am* common stock; *action au porteur* bearer share, transferable share; *action de premier rang, action de priorité, action privilégiée* *Br* preference share, *Am* preferred stock; *action privilégiée cumulative* cumulative preference share; *action syndiquée* syndicated share

(**b**) *Jur* action, lawsuit; **intenter une action contre qn** to take legal action against sb, to institute proceedings against sb, to take sb to court □ *action civile* civil action; *action contractuelle* action for breach of contract; *action en contrefaçon* action for infringement of patent; *action en dommages et intérêts* action *or* claim for damages; *action judiciaire, action en justice* action, lawsuit

(**c**) *Mktg (campagne)* campaign □ *action commerciale* marketing campaign; *action promotionnelle* promotional campaign; *action de vente* sales campaign *or* drive

(**d**)*(acte)* action □ *action de conversion* exchange

actionnaire *nmf Bourse, Fin Br* shareholder, *Am* stockholder □ *actionnaire majoritaire* majority *Br* shareholder *or* *Am* stockholder; *actionnaire minoritaire* minority *Br* shareholder *or* *Am* stockholder; *actionnaire de référence* major *Br* shareholder *or* *Am* stockholder

actionnariat *nm Bourse, Fin* shareholding □ *actionnariat intermédiaire* nominee shareholding; *actionnariat ouvrier* employee shareholding

> **"**
> D'un autre côté se profile la possibilité d'une démocratisation de la propriété des entreprises avec la généralisation et la mutualisation de l'**actionnariat** (notamment par les fonds de pension) qui pourrait entraîner la véritable mort de Marx ... L'économie ouverte pourrait achever la mutation du capitalisme prédateur en un capitalisme redistributif en faisant des salariés les premiers actionnaires.
> **"**

activé, -e *adj Ordinat (fichier, fenêtre)* active; *(option)* enabled

activer *vt* (**a**) *(processus, projet)* to speed up (**b**) *Ordinat* to activate; **activer une option** to select an option

activité *nf* (**a**) *(occupation)* activity; **activités** *(d'une entreprise)* operations, activities □ *activité bancaire* banking; *l'activité commerciale* business activities; *l'activité industrielle* industrial activities; *l'activité professionnelle* professional life (**b**) **en activité** *(entreprise)* in action, in operation; *(usine)* in production; *(personne)* working; **il est toujours/n'est plus en activité** he's still/no longer working; **en pleine activité** in full operation (**c**) *(du marché)* activity; **sans activité** dull, slack; **en pleine activité** active, brisk

actuaire *nmf Assur, Fin* actuary

actualisation *nf* (**a**) *Ordinat (d'écran)* refresh; *(d'un logiciel)* update (**b**) *Écon* discounting

actualisé, -e *adj* (**a**) *Ordinat (écran)* refreshed; *(logiciel)* updated (**b**) *Écon* discounted

actualiser *vt* (**a**) *Ordinat (écran)* to refresh; *(logiciel, informations)* to update (**b**) *Écon* to discount

actuariat *nm Assur, Fin (profession)* actuarial profession

actuariel, -elle *adj Assur, Fin* actuarial

actuel, -elle *adj* present, current; **à l'heure actuelle** currently; **le cours actuel du dollar** the current exchange rate for the dollar

actuellement *adv* at present, at the present time, currently

adaptabilité *nf (d'une entreprise, de la main-d'œuvre)* adaptability

adaptateur nm Ordinat adapter

adapter 1 vt to adapt; **adapter la main-d'œuvre aux nouvelles technologies** to adapt the workforce to new technology; **adapté aux besoins du client** adapted or tailored to the needs of the customer

　2 s'adapter vpr to adapt; **s'adapter au marché/à la demande** to adapt to the market/to demand

addendum nm addendum

addition nf (**a**) (calcul) adding up, addition; **faire l'addition des chiffres** to add up the figures (**b**) **en addition au paragraphe 2,...** further to paragraph 2,... (**c**) (au restaurant) Br bill, Am check

additionnel, -elle adj (**a**) (coût, frais) additional, extra (**b**) Ordinat (option, extension) add-on

additionner vt to add (up)

adéquation nf balance; **l'adéquation entre l'offre et la demande favorise la stabilité des prix** the balance between supply and demand encourages stable prices; **il n'y a pas adéquation entre l'offre et la demande** there is an imbalance between supply and demand; **mettre en adéquation** to balance □ **adéquation des fonds propres** capital adequacy

> **“**
> Au total, cette année-là, le budget du PCF devra tenir compte d'un différentiel de 27 millions de francs (4,2 millions d'euros). **Mettre en adéquation** les dépenses et les recettes nécessite la mise en place d'un "plan de sauvegarde de l'emploi" actuellement à l'étude en liaison avec le comité d'entreprise de la place du Colonel-Fabien: 44 postes sur 104 doivent être supprimés.
> **”**

adjoindre 1 vt (**a**) (associer) **adjoindre qn à qn** to give sb to sb; **on lui a adjoint un collaborateur** he was given an assistant (**b**) (ajouter) **adjoindre qch à qch** to add sth to sth; **adjoindre des équipements à un ordinateur** to upgrade a computer with add-ons; **adjoindre une pièce à une lettre** to include or enclose a document with a letter

　2 s'adjoindre vpr **s'adjoindre qn** to take sb on; **il s'est adjoint un collaborateur** he's taken on an assistant

adjoint, -e 1 adj assistant, deputy

　2 nm,f assistant, deputy □ **adjoint au directeur** assistant manager, deputy manager

adjudicataire nmf (**a**) (pour l'obtention d'un contrat) successful tenderer; **être déclaré adjudicataire de qch** to secure the contract for sth (**b**) (dans une vente aux enchères) highest or successful bidder

adjudication nf (**a**) (d'un contrat) (appel d'offres) invitation to tender; (attribution) award; **obtenir l'adjudication d'un contrat public** to be awarded a public contract; **mettre qch en adjudication** to invite tenders for sth, to put sth out to tender; **par voie d'adjudication** (pour l'obtention d'un contrat) by tender (**b**) (de biens) (attribution) auctioning off; (vente aux enchères) (sale by) auction; **mettre qch en adjudication** to put sth up for (sale by) auction; **par voie d'adjudication** by auction

adjuger vt **adjuger qch à qn** (contrat) to award or give sth to sb; (aux enchères) to knock sth down to sb; **ils ont adjugé les fournitures de bureau à Corbier** they have awarded or given the contract for office supplies to Corbier

admettre vt (**a**) (autoriser) to allow; **admettre un recours** to allow a claim (**b**) (accueillir) to admit; **admettre qn au conseil d'administration** to admit sb to the board of directors; Bourse **admettre une société à la cote** to list a company

administrateur, -trice nm,f (**a**) (d'une société, d'une banque) (non-executive) director; (d'un journal) business manager □ **administrateur délégué** managing director; Jur **administrateur judiciaire** (de biens, d'une entreprise) (official) receiver (**b**) Ordinat **administrateur de réseau** network administrator, network manager; **administrateur de serveur** server administrator

administratif, -ive 1 adj administrative; **détails d'ordre administratif** administrative details

　2 nm,f administrative worker; **les administratifs** the administrative staff

administration nf (**a**) (gestion) administration, direction, management; (ensemble des directeurs) board of directors □ **administration du personnel** personnel management; **administration des ventes** sales management

　(**b**) (service) **l'Administration** the Civil Service; **entrer dans l'Administration** to enter the Civil Service, to become a civil servant □ **administration des Douanes** Br Customs and Excise, Am Customs Service; **administration fiscale** tax authorities; **administration locale** local authority; **administration portuaire** port authorities

　(**c**) Jur trusteeship

　(**d**) Ordinat **administration de réseau** network management

administrer vt (société, biens) to manage

admissible adj (à un concours) eligible; **il a été admissible au concours d'HEC** he qualified for the oral HEC exam

admission nf (**a**) Douanes (de marchandises) entry □ **admission en douane** entry; **admission en franchise** duty-free entry; **admission temporaire** temporary entry (of products destined for re-export after processing) (**b**) Bourse

admission à la cote admission to quotation, listing; **faire une demande d'admission à la cote** to seek admission to quotation (c) *(accueil)* entry, admission; **l'admission des pays de l'Est dans l'Union européenne** the entry *or* admission of Eastern European countries into the European Union

adopter *vt (résolution, méthode)* to adopt; *(rapport)* to accept; *(projet de loi)* to pass; *Mktg (produit)* to adopt; **adopté à l'unanimité** carried unanimously

adopteur *nm Mktg (d'un produit)* adopter □ *adopteur précoce* early adopter; **les adopteurs précoces de notre nouveau produit représentent cinq pour cent du marché potentiel** the early adopters of our new product make up five percent of the potential market

adoption *nf (d'une résolution, d'une méthode)* adoption; *(d'un rapport)* acceptance; *(d'un projet de loi)* passing; *Mktg (d'un produit)* adoption

adressable *adj Ordinat* addressable

adressage *nm Ordinat* addressing; **mode d'adressage** address mode □ *adressage direct* direct addressing

adresse *nf* address; **changer d'adresse** to change one's address; **faire son changement d'adresse** to have one's mail redirected; **inconnu à cette adresse** *(sur lettre)* not known at this address □ *Fin* **adresse au besoin** *(sur lettre de change)* referee in case of need; *adresse au bureau* office address, business address; *Ordinat* *adresse électronique* e-mail address; *adresse de facturation* invoicing address, address for invoicing; *Ordinat* **adresse Internet** Internet address; *Ordinat* **adresse IP** IP address; *adresse de livraison* delivery address; *(d'objets volumineux)* shipping address; *adresse personnelle* home address; *adresse professionnelle* business address; *adresse télégraphique* telegraphic address; *adresse URL* URL

adresser 1 *vt* (a) *(courrier, colis)* to address; **adresser qch à qn** to send sth to sb; **cette lettre ne m'est pas adressée** this letter isn't addressed to me (b) *Ordinat* to address **2 s'adresser** *vpr* **s'adresser à qn** *(parler à)* to speak to sb; **veuillez vous adresser au service après-vente** please contact the after-sales department

ADSL *nf Ordinat (abrév **Asynchronous** or **Asymmetric Digital Subscriber Line**)* ADSL

ad valorem *adj inv Jur (droit, taxe)* ad valorem

advertorial *nm* advertorial

AELE *nf (abrév **Association européenne de libre-échange**)* EFTA

aérogare *nf* (air) terminal

aérogramme *nm* airmail letter

AFB *n (abrév **Association française des banques**)* French Bankers' Association

affacturage *nm* factoring

affactureur *nm* factor

affaire *nf* (a) **affaires** *(activités commerciales)* business; **entrer dans les affaires** to go into business; **être dans les affaires** to be in business; **faire des affaires avec qn** to do business with sb, to deal with sb; **faire de bonnes affaires** to be successful, to do good business; **faire de mauvaises affaires** to be doing badly, to be in difficulties; **faire des affaires importantes** to do business on a large scale, to have a big turnover; **parler affaires** to talk business; **comment vont les affaires?** how's business?; **les affaires vont mal** business is bad; **je vais à Londres pour affaires** I'm going to London on business □ *affaires courantes* routine business (b) *(transaction)* deal, transaction; **faire affaire (avec qn)** to do a deal (with sb); **conclure une affaire (avec qn)** to clinch a deal (with sb) □ *affaire blanche* profitless *or* break-even deal; *affaire en or* deal of the century (c) *(entreprise)* business, firm; **être à la tête d'une grosse affaire** to be at the head of a large business *or* firm; **son usine est une grande affaire** his factory is a large concern; **administrer** *ou* **gérer** *ou* **diriger une affaire** to run a business; **lancer** *ou* **démarrer une affaire** to start a business □ *Fin* **affaire de premier ordre** blue-chip company (d) *(achat à bon marché)* bargain; **faire une (bonne) affaire** to get a (good) bargain (e) *Jur* case, lawsuit (f) *Admin* **affaires** affairs □ *affaires publiques* public affairs

affairisme *nm* wheeling and dealing, money-making

“

En lui et par lui, la conduite des affaires publiques n'est plus que le service du dividende. Le règne du nouveau capital – et c'est presque une première sur notre continent – est ainsi porté à son comble : l'**affairisme** est au pouvoir et le pouvoir se confond avec l'**affairisme**.

”

affairiste *nmf* wheeler-dealer

affectation *nf* (a) *(d'une somme, de crédits)* assignment, allocation; **affectation aux dividendes** sum available for dividend □ *affectations budgétaires* budget appropriations; *affectation de fonds* appropriation of funds; *affectation hypothécaire* mortgage charge (b) *(des tâches)* assignment (c) *(d'un employé)* appointment

affecter *vt* (a) *(somme, crédits)* to assign, to allocate (b) *(employé)* to appoint (à to); **être af-**

fecté à un poste to be appointed to a post

afférent, -e *adj Jur* **afférent à** relating to, pertaining to; **la part afférente à** the portion accruing to

affermage *nm (d'un emplacement publicitaire)* contracting

affermer *vt (emplacement publicitaire)* to contract for

affichage *nm* (a) *(publicitaire)* bill-sticking, bill-posting; *(ensemble d'affiches)* posters; *(publicité)* poster advertising, display advertising □ **affichage transport** transport advertising (b) *Ordinat* display □ **affichage couleur** colour display; **affichage à cristaux liquides** liquid crystal display; **affichage graphique** graphics display; **affichage numérique** digital display; **affichage tel écran-tel écrit** *ou* **tel-tel** *ou* **Wysiwyg** WYSIWYG

affiche *nf (annonce officielle)* public notice; *(publicitaire)* poster, advertisement □ **affiche publicitaire** poster, advertisement

afficher 1 *vt* (a) *(présenter)* to show; **afficher un déficit/un excédent** to show a deficit/a surplus; **afficher des résultats encourageants** to show encouraging results
(b) *Ordinat (message)* to display; *(fichiers, articles)* to show; **l'écran affiche...** the on-screen message reads..., the screen displays the message...
(c) *(mettre en évidence)* to put up, to display; **afficher une vente** to advertise a sale, *Am* to post a sale
2 s'afficher *vpr Ordinat (sur un écran)* to be displayed

afficheur *nm* (a) *(personne)* bill-sticker, bill-poster □ **afficheur publicitaire** bill-sticker, bill-poster (b) *Ordinat* visual display unit, VDU □ **afficheur LCD** LCD display

affidavit *nm Jur* affidavit

affiliation *nf* affiliation

affilié, -e 1 *adj* affiliated
2 *nm,f* (affiliated) member, associate

afflux *nm (de marchandises, d'or)* inflow, influx □ *Compta* **afflux de capitaux, afflux de fonds** capital inflow

affranchir *vt (à la main)* to put a stamp/stamps on; *(à la machine)* to frank; **une lettre insuffisamment affranchie** a letter with insufficient postage

affranchissement *nm* (a) *(à la main)* stamping; *(à la machine)* franking (b) *(coût)* postage; □ **affranchissement à forfait** bulk rate *(for sending letters)*

affrètement *nm (d'un avion, d'un navire)* charter, chartering

affréter *vt (avion, navire)* to charter

affréteur *nm (d'un avion, d'un navire)* charterer

AFNOR *nf (abrév* **Association française de normalisation)** = French industrial standards authority, *Br* ≃ BSI, *Am* ≃ ASA

AF-P *nf (abrév* **Agence France-Presse)** = French international news agency

AG *nf (abrév* **assemblée générale)** GM

AGE *nf (abrév* **assemblée générale extraordinaire)** EGM

agence *nf* (a) *(bureau)* agency, bureau □ **agence d'affaires** (general) business agency; **agence commerciale** commercial agency, mercantile agency; **agence conseil en communication** public relations *or* PR agency; **agence de design** design agency; **agence de distribution** distribution agency; **agence en douane** customs agency; **Agence France-Presse** = French international news agency; **agence immobilière** *Br* estate agent's *or* agency, *Am* real estate agency; **agence d'intérim** temping agency; **agence locale d'aide aux entreprises** regional business development agency; **agence de location** *(de locaux)* letting agency; *(d'équipements)* hire *or* rental company; **agence maritime** shipping agency; **agence de marketing direct** direct marketing agency; **Agence nationale pour l'emploi** = French national employment bureau, *Br* ≃ Jobcentre; **agence de notation** *Br* credit (rating) agency, *Am* credit bureau; **agence de placement** employment agency *or* bureau; **agence de presse** press *or* news agency; **agence de promotion** promotions agency; **agence de promotion des ventes** sales promotion agency; **agence de publicité** advertising agency; **agence de recouvrements** debt collection agency; **agence de recrutement** recruitment agency; **agence de renseignement(s)** information bureau; **agence de réservation** booking agency; **agence de tourisme** travel agency *or* agent's; **agence de travail intérimaire** temping agency; **agence de voyages** travel agency *or* agent's
(b) *(d'une banque, d'une société)* branch (office); **la maison a plusieurs agences à l'étranger** the company has several branches overseas □ **agence bancaire** bank branch

agencement *nm (d'un magasin)* layout

agenda *nm* (a) *(livre)* diary □ **agenda de bureau** desk diary; **agenda électronique** personal organizer; **agenda électronique de poche** personal digital assistant; **agenda numérique**

de poche personal digital assistant; *agenda organisateur* personal organizer, Filofax®; *agenda de poche* pocket diary; *agenda de réservation* reservations book (**b**) *Ordinat (ordinateur portable)* notebook

agent *nm* agent □ *agent d'affacturage* factoring agent; *agent d'affaires* business agent, general agent; *agent agréé* registered agent; *agent d'assurance(s)* insurance broker *or* agent; *agent attitré* appointed agent; *agent autorisé* authorized representative; *agent en brevets* patent agent; *Bourse, Fin agent de change* stockbroker; *agent commercial* sales representative; *agent commercial exclusif* sole agent *or* representative; *agent commissionnaire* commission agent; *agent comptable* accountant; *agent de contact* contact; *agent à demeure* agent on the spot; *agent direct* commission agent; *agent de distribution* distribution agent; *agent en douanes* customs agent *or* broker; *agent économique* economic agent *or* player; *agent exclusif* sole agent; *agent exportateur* export agent; *agent de fabrication* production worker; *agent du fisc* tax official; *agent de fret* freight forwarder, forwarding agent; *agent général* general agent; *agent immobilier* Br estate agent, Am realtor, real estate agent; *agent importateur* import agent; *agent indépendant* free agent; *agent intermédiaire* middleman; *agent de liaison* contact; *agent de ligne* forwarding agent; *agent de location* letting agent; *agent de maîtrise* foreman, supervisor; *agent mandataire* authorized agent; *agent maritime* shipping agent; *agent publicitaire, agent de publicité* advertising agent, publicity agent; *agent de réceptif* ground handling agent; *agent de recouvrement(s)* debt collector; *agent de réservation* reservation agent; *agent de sécurité* security officer; *agent souscripteur* underwriting *or* underwriter agent; *agent technico-commercial* sales technician, sales engineer; *agent de transmission* runner, messenger; *agent du trésor* government broker; *agent de voyages* travel agent

AGÉTAC, agétac *nm (abrév* **accord général sur les tarifs douaniers et le commerce)** GATT

agio *nm* (**a**) *Fin (dans un échange de devises)* agio (**b**) *Banque* **agios** *(quand on est à découvert)* bank charges, interest charges; *(d'un emprunt)* interest payments

agiotage *nm Bourse* speculating, gambling

agioter *vi Bourse* to speculate, to gamble

agioteur, -euse *nm,f Bourse* speculator, gambler

agir *vi Bourse* **agir sur le marché** to manipulate the market

agitation *nf* (**a**) *(troubles)* unrest □ *agitation*

sociale industrial unrest (**b**) *(sur le marché de la Bourse)* activity

agrafe *nf* staple □ *agrafe antivol* anti-theft *or* security tag

agrafer *vt* to staple

agrafeuse *nf* stapler

agrandir 1 *vt* (**a**) *(entreprise, usine, locaux)* to expand (**b**) *Ordinat* to enlarge, to magnify; *(fenêtre)* to maximize
2 s'agrandir *vpr (entreprise, marché)* to expand; **le marché des logiciels s'agrandit** the software market is expanding

agréé, -e 1 *adj* recognized, authorized; *(échantillon)* approved
2 *nm Jur* lawyer *(before a "tribunal de commerce")*

agréer *vt (fournisseur, équipement, contrat)* to approve; **veuillez agréer** *ou* **je vous prie d'agréer l'expression de mes sentiments distingués, veuillez agréer l'assurance de ma haute considération** *(dans une lettre)* *(à une personne dont on ne connaît pas le nom)* Br Yours faithfully, Am Sincerely *(à une personne dont on connaît le nom)* Br Yours sincerely, Am Sincerely

agrégat *nm Écon* aggregate □ *agrégat monétaire* monetary aggregate

agrément *nm* (**a**) *(accord)* approval; **agir avec l'agrément de ses supérieurs** to act with the approval of one's superiors (**b**) *(d'agence de voyages)* agency appointment (**c**) *(garantie financière)* bonding scheme

agricole *adj* agricultural

agriculteur, -trice *nm,f* farmer

agriculture *nf* agriculture, farming

agritourisme *nm* agritourism, agrotourism

agroalimentaire 1 *adj (industrie, secteur)* food
2 *nm* **l'agroalimentaire** the food-processing industry

> **"**
> Dans la matinée, une centaine d'agriculteurs du Vaucluse avaient manifesté pour les mêmes motifs, s'emparant notamment des chariots de deux supermarchés à Avignon. ... Quelque 700 personnes, majoritairement des salariés de l'**agroalimentaire**, ont manifesté à l'appel de la CFDT et de la CGT samedi à Briec (Finistère), pour protester contre la fermeture d'un abattoir du groupe avicole Doux.
> **"**

agro-industrie *nf* agro-industry

agro-industriel, -elle *adj* agro-industrial

agro-monétaire *adj* agri-monetary

aguiche *nf Mktg* teaser (ad)

AIDA *nm Mktg* (*abrév* **attention-intérêt-désir-action**) AIDA

aide *nf* (**a**) *(assistance)* assistance, help; *(sous forme d'argent)* aid □ *Écon* **aide au développement** foreign aid (to developing countries); **aide économique** economic aid; **aide de l'État** government aid; **aide à l'exportation** export aid; **aide financière** financial aid *or* assistance; *Compta* **aide fiscale** tax credit; **aide gouvernementale** government aid; **aide judiciaire** legal aid; **aide personnalisée au logement** ≃ housing benefit; **aide publique au développement** official development assistance; **aide à la réinsertion professionnelle** help to re-enter the job market; **aide au retour** = voluntary repatriation allowances for immigrant workers leaving France; **aide sociale** *Br* social security, *Am* welfare (**b**) *Ordinat* help □ **aide contextuelle** context-sensitive help; **aide en ligne** on-line help

aide-comptable *nmf* bookkeeper

aile *nf* **battre de l'aile** *(entreprise)* to be struggling

AIO *nm Mktg* (*abrév* **activités, intérêts et opinions**) AIO

aire *nf* area □ **aire de chargement** loading bay; **aire de dédouanement** customs clearance area; **aire d'embarquement** departure lounge

ajournement *nm* *(d'une décision, d'une réunion, d'un voyage)* postponement; *(après le début d'une séance)* adjournment

ajourner *vt* *(décision, réunion, voyage)* to postpone; *(après le début d'une séance)* to adjourn

ajout *nm* (**a**) *Mktg* **ajout à la gamme** range addition; **ajout à la ligne** line addition (**b**) *Ordinat* **ajout de mémoire** memory upgrade

ajouté *nm* *(à un contrat)* rider, addition

ajouter **1** *vt* (**a**) *(additionner)* to add (**à** to) (**b**) *Ordinat* to append
2 s'ajouter *vpr* **s'ajouter à** to be added to; **à cela viennent s'ajouter les frais de transport** on top of this there are travel expenses (to be added)

ajustement *nm* *(des salaires, d'une monnaie, des prix)* adjustment □ **ajustement fret** bunker adjustment factor; **ajustement saisonnier** seasonal adjustment; *Mktg* **ajustement stratégique** strategic *or* marketing fit

ajuster *vt* *(salaires, prix, monnaie)* to adjust

ALE *nf* (*abrév* **Association de libre-échange**) FTA

aléatoire *adj* *(contrat)* aleatory; *(sondage, échantillon, échantillonnage)* random; *(marché, spéculation)* risky

ALENA *nm* (*abrév* **Accord de libre-échange nord-américain**) NAFTA

aliénation *nf Jur* *(de droits, d'une propriété)* transfer

aliéner *vt Jur* *(droits, propriété)* to transfer

alignement *nm* (**a**) *Compta (d'un compte)* making up, balancing (**b**) *Fin* alignment (**sur** with); **alignement des prix** alignment of prices, price alignment; **l'alignement des salaires sur le coût de la vie** bringing salaries into line with the cost of living (**c**) *Écon (d'une monnaie, d'une économie)* alignment □ **alignement monétaire** monetary alignment *or* adjustment (**d**) *Ordinat* alignment

aligner *vt* (**a**) *Compta (compte)* to make up, to balance (**b**) *Fin* to align, to bring into line (**sur** with); **les petits commerçants doivent aligner leurs prix sur ceux des grandes surfaces** small shopkeepers have to bring their prices into line with those of hypermarkets (**c**) *Écon (monnaie, économie)* to align (**d**) *Ordinat* to align

aliment *nm* (**a**) *(nourriture)* food (**b**) *Assur* interest *or* risk value

alimentaire *adj* food; **l'industrie alimentaire** the food industry; **produits alimentaires** foodstuffs, food products

alimentation *nf* (**a**) *(aliments)* **produits d'alimentation** foodstuffs, food products (**b**) *Ordinat* **alimentation feuille à feuille** cut sheet feed, single sheet feed; **alimentation page par page** cut sheet feed, single sheet feed; **alimentation papier** sheet feed, paper feed

alimenter *vt* (**a**) *(compte bancaire)* to pay money into (**b**) *Ordinat (imprimante)* to feed

alinéa *nm* *(renfoncement)* indent; *(texte)* paragraph; **faire un alinéa** to indent

allègement, allégement *nm* *(d'impôts, de charges, de dépenses)* reduction □ **allègement fiscal** tax relief

> **"**
> En proposant un **allégement** de 30% de l'impôt sur le revenu en cinq ans, soit un manque à gagner pour l'État de quelque 15 milliards d'euros … le candidat Chirac a frappé fort.
> **"**

alléger *vt* *(impôts, charges, dépenses)* to reduce

aller *nm* outward journey; **un aller (simple)** *Br* a single (ticket), *Am* a one-way ticket; **un aller (et) retour** *Br* a return (ticket), *Am* a round trip ticket

alliance *nf* alliance □ *Mktg* **alliance de marque** co-branding

allier s'allier *vpr* to join, to unite (**avec** with)

allocataire *nmf* beneficiary

allocation *nf* (**a**) *Admin (prestation financière)* allowance, *Br* benefit, *Am* welfare □ **allocation chômage** unemployment benefit, *Br* ≃ Job

Seekers Allowance; **allocation de déplacement** mobility allowance; **allocations familiales** Br child benefit, Am dependents' allowances; **allocation de grève** strike pay; **allocation d'invalidité** disability benefit; **allocation logement** housing benefit; **allocation de maternité** maternity benefit; **allocation vieillesse** old-age pension
(**b**) *(attribution) (d'argent)* allocation; *(de dommages-intérêts, d'une indemnité)* awarding
(**c**) *Bourse (de titres)* allocation, allotment

allouer *vt* (**a**) *Admin (salaire, pension)* to grant, to award (**b**) *(attribuer) (argent)* to allocate; *(dommages-intérêts, indemnité)* to award; *(dépense, budget)* to allow, to pass (**c**) *Bourse (titres)* to allocate, to allot

allumer *vt & vi Ordinat* to power up

alourdir 1 *vt (charges, impôts)* to increase
2 s'alourdir *vpr (charges, impôts)* to increase

alphabétique *adj* **par ordre** *ou* **dans l'ordre alphabétique** in alphabetical order; **classer qch par ordre alphabétique** to put sth in alphabetical order, to alphabetize sth

alphanumérique *adj* alphanumeric

alt *Ordinat* alt; **pour e accent aigu, il faut taper alt 130** e acute is alt 130

altération *nf Ordinat (d'un disque, d'un fichier)* corruption

altéré, -e *adj Ordinat (disque, fichier)* corrupt

altérer *Ordinat* **1** *vt (disque, fichier)* to corrupt
2 s'altérer *vpr (disque, fichier)* to go corrupt

alternance *nf (en politique)* change of government

alterner *vi* to alternate, to take turns; **les différents pays alternent à la présidence de l'Union européenne** the different countries alternate the presidency of the European Union

AM *nf Assur (abrév* **Assurance maladie**) health insurance

amalgamation *nf (d'entreprises)* merger; *(de fonctions; de postes)* merge

amalgamer *vt (entreprises, fonctions, postes)* to merge; **amalgamer une entreprise à une autre** to merge one company with another

amateurisme *nm (incompétence)* amateurism

ambulant, -e *adj* itinerant, travelling

AME *nm (abrév* **Accord monétaire européen**) EMA

amélioration *nf* (**a**) improvement (**de** in); *Fin (de fonds de retraite)* enhancement □ *Mktg* **amélioration du produit** product augmentation *or* improvement (**b**) *Ordinat (d'image, de qualité)* enhancement

améliorer 1 *vt* (**a**) *(produit, service)* to improve; *(image, qualité)* to enhance (**b**) *Fin (fonds de re-*

traite) to enhance (**c**) *(logiciel)* to upgrade;
2 s'améliorer *vpr* to improve

> **"**
> Au-delà de 65 ans, les Espagnols peuvent à la fois toucher leur pension et travailler (et donc cotiser)! Avantage pour le salarié: la pension est **améliorée** de 2% pour chaque année supplémentaire de travail.
> **"**

aménagement *nm* (**a**) *Admin, Écon* planning, development □ **aménagement du territoire** regional development, town and country planning; **aménagement urbain** town planning; **aménagement urbain et rural** town and country planning (**b**) *(du temps de travail)* flexibility (**c**) *(amendement)* adjustment □ **aménagement fiscal** tax adjustment

aménager *vt* (**a**) *(magasin)* to fit out (**b**) *(horaire)* to plan, to work out

amende *nf* fine; *(pour retard de livraison)* penalty; **infliger une amende à qn** to fine sb; *(pour retard de livraison)* to penalize sb

amendement *nm* amendment

amender *vt (proposition, loi, texte)* to amend

AMI *nm Écon (abrév* **Accord multilatéral sur l'investissement**) MAI

amiable *Jur* **1** *adj (accord)* conciliatory □ **amiable compositeur** arbitrator
2 à l'amiable *adv* out of court; **régler qch à l'amiable** to reach a private *or* an amicable agreement about sth; *(sans procès)* to settle sth out of court

AMM *nf (abrév* **autorisation de mise sur le marché**) = official authorization for marketing a pharmaceutical product

amont *nm Écon, Mktg* upside; **d'amont** *(activités)* upstream; **en amont** *(société)* upstream

amorçage *nm Ordinat* booting

amorce *nf (début)* beginning; **on assiste à une amorce de reprise économique** we are witnessing the beginnings of economic recovery

amorcer 1 *vt Ordinat* to boot (up); **amorcer de nouveau** to reboot
2 s'amorcer *vpr* (**a**) *Ordinat* to boot (up) (**b**) *(commencer)* to begin; **la reprise économique s'amorce** economic recovery has begun

amorti, -e *adj Fin (bien)* depreciated; *(frais, investissement, capital)* amortized

amortir 1 *vt* (**a**) *Fin (rentabiliser)* **le matériel a été amorti dès la première année** the equipment had paid for itself by the end of the first year; **il a loué la machine pour en amortir le coût** he rented out the machine to make it pay *or* to recoup the cost (**b**) *Fin (dette)* to pay off, to amortize; *(prêt)* to repay; *(obligation)* to redeem (**c**) *Compta (équipement)* to write off,

to amortize, to depreciate
2 s'amortir *vpr (dépenses, investissement)* to pay for itself

amortissable *adj Fin (dette)* redeemable

amortissement *nm* **(a)** *(rentabilité)* profitability; **l'amortissement d'un équipement est plus rapide si on emprunte à court terme** equipment pays for itself faster if it's paid for with a short-term loan **(b)** *Fin (d'une dette)* repayment, amortization ◻ **amortissement anticipé** redemption before due date **(c)** *Compta (perte de valeur)* depreciation ◻ **amortissement accéléré** accelerated depreciation; **amortissement annuel** annual depreciation; **amortissement dégressif** sliding scale depreciation; **amortissement linéaire** diminishing balance (method)

> "
> Il s'agit des écarts entre les prix d'acquisition et l'actif net des sociétés acquises, écarts énormes au moment de la bulle technologique, et qui n'ont pas été amortis. On estime ainsi que l'**amortissement** nécessaire des survaleurs aux États-Unis représente deux années de résultats des entreprises!
> "

amovible *adj* **(a)** *Ordinat (disque dur)* removable **(b)** *(personnel)* transferable, mobile

ample *adj (ressources, provisions)* extensive, ample; **pour de plus amples renseignements, veuillez contacter...** for further information, please contact...; **jusqu'à plus ample informé** until further information is available

ampleur *nf (d'un problème, des dégâts, d'une crise)* scale, extent; *(des ressources, des provisions)* abundance ◻ *Mktg* **ampleur de gamme** breadth of range

an *nm* year; **par an** yearly, per year; *Fin* per annum; **un prêt sur 20 ans** a loan over 20 years

analogique 1 *adj Ordinat* analogue
2 *nf* analogue (broadcasting)

analyse *nf* analysis ◻ **analyse des attraits et des atouts** opportunity and issue analysis; **analyse des besoins** needs analysis; **analyse du chemin critique** critical path analysis; **analyse des concurrents** competitor analysis; **analyse conjointe** conjoint *or* trade-off analysis; **analyse des coûts** cost analysis; **analyse coûts-bénéfices** cost-benefit analysis; **analyse de coût et d'efficacité** cost-effectiveness analysis; **analyse coût-profit** cost-benefit analysis; **analyse des coûts et rendements** cost-benefit analysis; **analyse de la demande** demand analysis; **analyse démographique** demographic analysis; **analyse de données** data analysis; **analyse des écarts** variance analysis; **analyse économique** economic analysis; **analyse des**

forces et faiblesses strengths and weaknesses analysis; **analyse des forces, faiblesses, opportunités et menaces** SWOT analysis; **analyse sur graphiques** chart analysis; **analyse du marché** market analysis; **analyse des marchés** market research; **analyse des médias** media analysis; **analyse des mouvements** motion analysis; *Ordinat* **analyse numérique** numerical analysis; **analyse des opportunités et des menaces** opportunity and threat analysis; **analyse du point-mort** break-even analysis; **analyse de portefeuille** portfolio analysis; **analyse prévisionnelle** predictive analysis; **analyse du prix de revient** cost analysis; **analyse de produit** product analysis; **analyse du rendement** rate-of-return analysis; **analyse des risques** risk analysis; **analyse par segment** cluster analysis; **analyse statistique** statistical analysis; **analyse du style de vie** lifestyle analysis; *Ordinat* **analyse de système, analyse systémique** systems analysis; **analyse des tâches** job analysis; **analyse des tendances** trend analysis; **analyse de valeur** value analysis *or* engineering; **analyse des ventes** sales analysis

analyser *vt (résultats, chiffres)* to analyse

analyste *nmf* analyst ◻ **analyste financier** financial analyst; **analyste sur graphiques** chart analyst; *Mktg* **analyste du marché** market analyst; **analyste des médias** media analyst; **analyste en placements** investment analyst

analyste-programmeur, -euse *nm,f Ordinat* systems analyst

analytique *adj* analytical

ancien, -enne *adj* **(a)** *(d'autrefois) (emploi, directeur)* former, old **(b)** *(vieux)* old; **je suis plus ancien que vous dans la profession** I've been in the profession longer than you; **il n'est pas assez ancien dans l'entreprise** he hasn't worked for the company for long enough

ancienneté *nf* seniority; **être promu à l'ancienneté** to be promoted by seniority

> "
> Les banques prennent ensuite d'autres paramètres en considération, tels que l'**ancienneté** dans l'entreprise ou dans la fonction ainsi qu'un certain nombre de données socioprofessionnelles.
> "

ancrage *nm Ordinat* justification ◻ **ancrage à droite** right justification; **ancrage à gauche** left justification

animateur, -trice *nm,f Mktg (d'une réunion de groupe)* leader, moderator ◻ **animateur des ventes** marketing executive

animation *nf* **(a)** *Fin (du marché)* briskness, buoyancy **(b)** *Mktg* promotion; **faire des animations dans les supermarchés** to promote products in supermarkets ❏ **animation commerciale** marketing campaign; **animation des ventes** sales drive or promotion

animé, -e adj Fin (marché) brisk, buoyant

anneau à jeton nm Ordinat token ring

année nf year ❏ **année budgétaire** Br financial year, Am fiscal year; Compta **année civile** calendar year; **année comptable** accounting year; **année en cours** current year; **année d'exercice** Br financial year, Am fiscal year; **année fiscale** tax year; **année d'imposition** year of assessment; **année record** peak year; **année de référence** base year; **année sabbatique** sabbatical year

annexe 1 adj (document, pièce) attached; (industries) subsidiary; (revenus) supplementary
2 nf (**a**) (de contrat) annexe; (de projet de loi) rider; (de loi) schedule; (de livre, de rapport) appendix; (de lettre) enclosure; (document joint) attached document; **en annexe à ma lettre** enclosed with my letter; **en annexe veuillez trouver...** please find enclosed... (**b**) Compta **annexes** notes to the accounts

annexer vt (document, pièce) to append, to attach

annonce nf advert, advertisement; **demander qch par voie d'annonces** to advertise for sth; **insérer ou mettre une annonce dans un journal** to put an advertisement in a newspaper ❏ **annonces classées** classified ads; **annonce publicitaire** advert, advertisement

annonceur nm (de publicité) advertiser

annoncier, -ère nm,f (personne) publicity editor

annuaire nm (d'un organisme) yearbook; (liste d'adresses) directory ❏ **annuaire du commerce** commercial directory; **annuaire électronique** electronic telephone directory (on Minitel®); **annuaire du téléphone, annuaire téléphonique** telephone directory

annualisation nf annualization; **l'annualisation du temps de travail permettra de répondre à une demande saisonnière** calculating working hours across the year will enable us to meet seasonal demand

annualiser vt to annualize

annualité nf yearly recurrence ❏ **annualité budgétaire** yearly or annual voting of the budget

annuel, -elle 1 adj annual, yearly
2 nm annual publication

annuellement adv annually, yearly

annuitaire adj (dette) redeemable by yearly payments

annuité nf (**a**) Fin (dans le remboursement d'un emprunt) annual instalment or repayment ❏ Compta **annuité d'amortissement** annual

depreciation or writedown; **annuités composées** compound (net) annual return; Compta **annuité constante** (de remboursement) fixed annual payment (**b**) (année de service) year of service (**c**) (rente) annuity ❏ **annuité différée** deferred annuity

annulable adj (contrat) voidable, revocable

annulation nf (**a**) (d'une réservation, d'une commande, d'un projet) cancellation; (d'une dette) cancellation, writing off; (d'un marché, d'une grève) calling off ❏ **annulation de dernière minute** late cancellation; **annulation rétroactive** retroactive cancellation (**b**) Ordinat cancel ❏ **annulation d'entrée** (commande) cancel entry; **annulation des révisions** (commande) undo changes (**c**) Jur (d'un jugement) quashing; (d'un contrat) annulment, invalidation

annuler vt (**a**) (réservation, commande, projet) to cancel; (dette) to cancel, to write off; (marché, grève) to call off (**b**) Ordinat to cancel; (opération) to undo; **annuler les révisions** (commande) undo changes (**c**) Banque (chèque) to cancel (**d**) (remplacer) to supersede, to cancel; **ce catalogue annule les précédents** this catalogue supersedes all previous issues (**e**) Jur (jugement) to quash; (contrat) to annul, to invalidate

ANP nm Ordinat (abrév **assistant numérique personnel**) PDA

ANPE nf (abrév **Agence nationale pour l'emploi**) = French national employment bureau, Br ≃ Jobcentre

antécédents nmpl (d'un employé, d'une société) previous history, track record

antémémoire nf Ordinat cache (memory); **mettre en antémémoire** to cache

anticipation nf **payer par anticipation** to pay in advance ❏ **paiement par anticipation** advance payment, prepayment

anticipé, -e adj (remboursement) before due date; (dividende, paiement) advance; (ventes) expected; (retraite) early; **avec mes remerciements anticipés** (dans une lettre) thanking you in advance

anticiper vt **anticiper un paiement** to pay in advance; **anticiper un paiement de dix jours** to pay ten days early

anticommercial, -e adj (attitude) unbusinesslike

antidater vt to backdate, to antedate

anti-discriminatoire adj (mesures, politique) anti-discriminatory

antidumping adj (loi, législation) anti-dumping

antiéconomique adj contrary to economic principles, uneconomic

antigrève *adj (loi, législation)* antistrike

anti-inflationniste *adj Écon* anti-inflationary

anti-mondialisation *nf* antiglobalization

antiprotectionniste 1 *adj* anti-protectionist, free-trade
   2 *nmf* anti-protectionist, free-trader

antireflet *adj Ordinat* non-reflecting, antiglare

antitrust *adj (loi) Br* anti-monopoly, *Am* antitrust

antivirus *nm Ordinat* antivirus *m*

AOC *nf (abrév* **appellation d'origine contrôlée)** = guarantee of quality

apaisement *nm (du marché)* calming down

apaiser s'apaiser *vpr (marché)* to calm down

APE *nf (abrév* **Assemblée parlementaire européenne)** EP

APEC *nf (abrév* **Association pour l'emploi des cadres)** = employment agency for executives and graduates

aperçu avant impression *nm Ordinat* print preview

apériteur *nm Assur* leading underwriter

APL *nf (abrév* **aide personnalisée au logement)** ≃ housing benefit

apostrophe *nf* apostrophe

appareil *nm* (a) *(machine)* apparatus, appliance □ *appareil de démonstration* demonstration model; *appareil à dicter* Dictaphone®; *appareil mains libres* hands-free device; *appareils ménagers* white goods
   (b) *(téléphone)* telephone; **qui est à l'appareil?** who's speaking?
   (c) *(système)* apparatus, machinery □ *l'appareil administratif* administrative machinery; *l'appareil législatif* the machinery of the law; *appareil de production* production facilities

appartement *nm Br* flat, *Am* apartment □ *appartement de fonction* company *Br* flat *or Am* apartment; *appartement témoin Br* show flat, *Am* model apartment

appartenir appartenir à *vt ind (être la propriété de)* to belong to; *(être membre de)* to belong to, to be a member of

appauvrir 1 *vt* to impoverish
   2 s'appauvrir *vpr* to become impoverished, to grow poorer

appauvrissement *nm* impoverishment

appel *nm* (a) *Fin* call; **faire un appel de fonds** to call up capital □ *Bourse* **appel de couverture, appel de garantie, appel de marge** margin call; *appel d'offres* invitation to tender; **faire un appel d'offres** to invite bids *or* tenders
   (b) **appel (téléphonique)** (telephone) call, phone call; **prendre un appel** to take a (telephone) call; **recevoir un appel** to receive a (telephone) call; **il y a eu un appel pour vous** there was a (telephone) call for you □ *appel automatique* automatic dial; *Mktg* **appel à froid** cold call; *appel gratuit Br* Freefone® call, *Am* toll-free call; *appel en PCV Br* reverse-charge call, *Am* collect call; *appel de réveil* wake-up *or* alarm call
   (c) *(demande)* call, demand; **appel à la grève** call to strike; **faire appel aux services de qn** to call on sb's services
   (d) *Ordinat* call; *(de commande)* selection

appelé, -e *adj Fin (capital)* called-up

appeler 1 *vt* (a) **appeler qn (au téléphone)** to ring sb (up), to call sb (b) *(inciter)* **appeler les salariés à un arrêt de travail/à la grève** to call a stoppage/a strike (c) *Jur* **appeler qn à comparaître devant un tribunal** to summon sb to appear before a court (d) *Ordinat (fichier)* to call up
   2 *vi (inciter)* **appeler à un arrêt de travail/à la grève** to call a stoppage/a strike

appellation d'origine contrôlée *nf* = guarantee of quality

applicable *adj* applicable; **le règlement est applicable immédiatement** the ruling will take effect immediately

application *nf* (a) *(des sanctions, d'un règlement, des mesures)* application; **entrer en application** to take effect, to come into force; **mettre qch en application** to enforce sth, to apply sth (b) *Ordinat* application □ *application bureautique* business application; *application graphique* graphics application; *application en service* current application

appliquer 1 *vt (sanctions, règlement, mesures)* to enforce, to apply
   2 s'appliquer *vpr (sanctions, règlement, mesures)* to apply (**à** to)

appoint *nm (revenu supplémentaire)* additional income

appointements *nmpl* salary; **toucher ses appointements** to draw one's salary

appointer *vt* **appointer qn** to pay sb a salary

apport *nm* (a) *(fait d'apporter)* contribution; *Écon* inflow, influx; **cette région bénéficie de l'apport (en devises) du tourisme** this area benefits from the financial contribution made by tourism; **sans apport extérieur nous étions perdus** without outside financial help we'd have been ruined □ *apport d'argent frais* injection of new money; *Compta* *apport en capital* capital contribution; *apport en espèces (dans un investissement)* cash contribution; *apport en gestion* management buy-in; *Compta* *apport en nature* contribution in kind; *Compta* *apport en numéraire* cash contribution (b)

Fin (dans une entreprise) initial share

> Il est vrai qu'au Cetelem, la fourchette de taux pour l'achat d'une voiture neuve, avec 25% d'**apport**, qui allait encore de 11,88% à 15% en avril, est passé en septembre de 9% à 13,92%.

apporter *vt (capitaux)* to contribute

apposer *vt (sceau, cachet, scellés)* to affix (**à** to); **apposer sa signature au bas d'une lettre** to put one's signature to a letter

apposition *nf (d'un sceau, d'un cachet, de scellés, d'une signature)* affixing

appréciateur, -trice *nm,f* appraiser, valuer

appréciatif, -ive *adj* evaluative

appréciation *nf* (**a**) *(estimation)* valuation, estimation; *(d'un préjudice)* estimation, assessment; **faire l'appréciation de qch** to value sth □ *appréciation des investissements* investment appraisal; *appréciation du personnel* staff appraisal; *appréciation des risques* risk assessment
(**b**) *(augmentation)* appreciation; **l'appréciation de la livre par rapport au dollar freine les exportations britanniques** the rise of the pound against the dollar is curbing British exports □ *appréciation monétaire* currency appreciation

apprécier 1 *vt (estimer)* to value, to estimate; *(préjudice)* to estimate, to assess
2 **s'apprécier** *vpr (augmenter)* to rise; **l'euro s'est apprécié par rapport au dollar** the euro has risen against the dollar

apprenti, -e *nm,f* apprentice

apprentissage *nm* apprenticeship; **mettre qn en apprentissage chez qn** to apprentice sb to sb; **faire son apprentissage chez qn** to serve one's apprenticeship with sb

approbation *nf (d'un document, des comptes, de comptes-rendus)* approval; **pour approbation** *(sur document administratif)* for approval, subject to approval; **soumettre qch à l'approbation (de qn)** to submit sth for approval (by sb); **donner son approbation (à qch)** to give (sth) one's approval

approche *nf Mktg* **approche directe** cold calling; *approche personnalisée* person-to-person approach

appropriation *nf* appropriation □ *appropriation de fonds* embezzlement, misappropriation of funds

approuver *vt (document, comptes, comptes-rendus)* to approve; *(appel)* to endorse; *(décision)* to approve of; *Admin (nomination)* to confirm; **approuver et contre-argumenter** to

agree and counter; **lu et approuvé** *(sur document)* read and approved

approvisionnement *nm* (**a**) *(action)* supplying (**en** with); *(d'un magasin)* stocking (**en** with); **l'approvisionnement du pays en pétrole/en matières premières est compromis par l'embargo** the supply of oil/raw materials to the country has been jeopardized by the embargo (**b**) *(réserve)* supply, stock; **faire un approvisionnement de qch** to stock up with sth, to lay in a supply of sth □ *approvisionnements de réserve* reserve stocks (**c**) *(dans l'industrie de transformation)* raw materials and component parts

> Automne 2000 : la Californie expérimente une pénurie d'électricité digne d'un pays en développement. Le marché, dérégulé deux ans plus tôt, se révèle incapable d'assurer l'**approvisionnement** de la région la plus riche du monde.

approvisionner 1 *vt* (**a**) *Banque (compte)* to pay money into; **son compte en banque n'est plus approvisionné** his bank account is no longer in credit (**b**) *(fournir)* to supply (**en** with); **cette entreprise nous approvisionne en pièces détachées** this company supplies us with spare parts
2 **s'approvisionner** *vpr* to get in supplies (**en** of); **s'approvisionner chez qn** to get one's supplies from sb

approvisionneur, -euse *nm,f* supplier

approximatif, -ive *adj (calcul, devis, estimation)* approximate, rough; **ce chiffre est très approximatif** this figure is only a rough estimate

approximation *nf* approximation

appui *nm (soutien)* backing, support; **il a apporté son appui à notre projet** he backed *or* supported our project □ *appui financier* (financial) backing; **la société ne bénéficie pas d'un appui financier suffisant** the company does not have sufficient financial backing

appuyer 1 *vt* to back, to support; **appuyer qn financièrement** to back sb (financially), to give sb financial backing; **appuyer la candidature de qn** to back *or* support sb's application
2 *vi Ordinat* **appuyer sur** *(touche)* to hit, to press

après-vente *adj inv* after-sales

aptitude professionnelle *nf* ability, aptitude

apurement *nm* (**a**) *(des comptes)* auditing (**b**) *(d'une dette, du passif)* discharge

apurer *vt* (**a**) *(comptes)* to audit (**b**) *(dette, passif)* to discharge

AR nm (abrév **accusé de réception**) acknowledgement (of receipt)

araignée nf Ordinat crawler

arbitrage nm (**a**) Jur (dans un conflit social) arbitration; **recourir à l'arbitrage** to go to arbitration; **soumettre une question à un arbitrage** to refer a question to arbitration; **soumettre un litige à l'arbitrage d'un tiers** to take a dispute to arbitration by a third party ❏ **arbitrage à l'amiable** out-of-court settlement
(**b**) Bourse, Fin arbitrage, switch trading ❏ **arbitrage à la baisse** bear closing; **arbitrage de change** arbitration of exchange; **arbitrage comptant-terme** cash and carry arbitrage; **arbitrage sur indice** index arbitrage; **arbitrage à la marge, arbitrage marginal** (high-gear dealing) margin dealing; **arbitrage risque** risk arbitrage

arbitragiste nmf Bourse, Fin arbitrageur

arbitral, -e adj Jur arbitral; **procédure arbitrale** procedure by arbitration; **solution arbitrale** settlement by arbitration

arbitralement adv Jur by arbitration

arbitre nm Jur arbitrator, adjudicator ❏ **arbitre financier** financial ombudsman; **arbitre rapporteur** referee

arbitrer vt Jur to arbitrate

arborescence nf Ordinat (structure) tree diagram; (chemin) directory path

arbre nm (diagramme) tree ❏ **arbre de décision** decision tree

archivage nm filing

archive nf (**a**) Ordinat archive (**b**) **archives** archives, records

archiver vt (documents officiels) to archive; (dossiers, factures) to file

archiviste nmf (fonction publique) keeper of public records; (employé de bureau) filing clerk

ardoise électronique nf Ordinat notepad computer

argent nm (**a**) (richesse) money; **payer en argent** to pay (in) cash; **placer son argent** to invest one's money; **trouver de l'argent** to raise money ❏ **argent à bon marché** cheap money; Compta **argent en caisse** cash in hand; (recettes) takings; **argent comptant** cash; Banque **argent à court terme** money at short notice; Ordinat **argent électronique** e-cash; Fam **argent facile** easy money; **argent frais** new money; **argent au jour le jour** call money, day-to-day money; **argent liquide** cash (in hand); **argent mal acquis** dirty money; **argent mort** dead money; **argent sale** dirty money; Ordinat **argent virtuel** e-cash; **argent à vue** call money
(**b**) (métal) silver

"
Après l'annonce d'une éventuelle privatisation d'Air France, voici donc un nouveau projet qui confirme la volonté de la droite au pouvoir de récupérer au plus vite de l'**argent frais**, en bradant les entreprises nationales les plus rentables.
"

argentier nm financier

"
Après avois admis que les attentats "pourraient retarder la reprise de la croissance solide de nos économies", les grands **argentiers** se sont déclarés fermement attachés à prendre les mesures nécessaires "pour accroître la croissance économique et préserver la santé de nos marchés financiers".
"

argumentaire nm promotion leaflet; **l'argumentaire est très convaincant** the sales pitch is very convincing

argument de vente nm selling point; **arguments de vente** (d'un vendeur) sales pitch

argus nm = guide to used car prices; **acheter/vendre qch à l'argus** to buy/sell sth for the book price; **valeur à l'argus** book price

armateur nm shipowner

armement nm (profession) merchant shipping

arr. nm (abrév **arrondissement**) = administrative subdivision of Paris, Lyons and Marseilles

arrangement nm agreement, settlement; (avec ses créanciers) composition; **parvenir à un arrangement** to come to an agreement; **sauf arrangement contraire** unless otherwise agreed

arranger s'arranger vpr to come to an agreement (**avec** with); **s'arranger à l'amiable avec ses créanciers** to come to an amicable agreement with one's creditors

arrérager 1 vi to be in arrears
2 s'arrérager vpr to fall into arrears

arrérages nmpl arrears

arrêt nm (**a**) (interruption) stoppage ❏ **arrêt maladie** sick leave; **être en arrêt maladie** to be on sick leave; **arrêt de paiement** (d'un chèque) stopping; **arrêt de travail** (grève) stoppage; (congé) sick leave; (certificat) doctor's or medical certificate; **être en arrêt de travail** to be on sick leave (**b**) Ordinat **arrêt de fin de session** shutdown

arrêté nm (**a**) Admin, Jur order, decree ❏ **arrêté d'exécution** decree providing for the enforcement of a law; **arrêté ministériel** ministerial order; **arrêté municipal** bylaw; **arrêté préfec-**

toral bylaw (**b**) *Banque* **arrêté de compte** *(fermeture)* settlement of account; *(bilan)* statement of account

arrêter 1 *vt* (**a**) *(cesser) (production, fabrication)* to stop (**b**) *Banque (compte)* to close, to settle; *Compta (comptes de l'exercice)* to close (**c**) *(décider de) (date, prix)* to fix; *(plan, procédure, marché)* to decide on, to settle on
 2 s'arrêter *vpr* (**a**) *(cesser)* to stop; **l'entreprise s'est arrêtée de fonctionner** the company has closed down; **il s'est arrêté de travailler l'an dernier** he stopped work last year (**b**) *Ordinat (système)* to shut down

arrhes *nfpl* deposit; **verser des arrhes** to pay a deposit

arriéré, -e 1 *adj* (**a**) *(dû)* late, behind, in arrears; *(paiement)* overdue, outstanding; *(intérêts)* outstanding, in arrears (**b**) *Écon (pays)* underdeveloped, backward
 2 *nm* (**a**) *(dette)* arrears; **avoir des arriérés** to be in arrears; **arriéré de loyer** rent arrears, back rent; **arriéré d'impôts** tax arrears, back taxes
 (**b**) *(retard) (de commandes, de correspondance, de travail)* backlog; **j'ai beaucoup d'arriéré dans mon travail** I have a large backlog of work

arrière-plan *nm Ordinat* background

arriérer *vt (paiement)* to postpone, to delay, to defer

arrière-saison *nf (dans le domaine du tourisme)* low season

arrivage *nm (de marchandises)* consignment, delivery; *Fin (de fonds)* accession; **nous attendons un arrivage venant de France** we're expecting a consignment *or* delivery from France

arrivant, -e *nm,f* arrival; **un nouvel arrivant sur le marché de l'informatique** a new arrival on the IT market

arrivée *nf (de marchandises, d'un avion, d'une personne)* arrival

arriver *vi* (**a**) *(venir)* to arrive; **arriver à échéance** *(paiement)* to fall due; *(contrat)* to expire (**b**) *(parvenir)* **arriver à faire qch** to manage to do sth

arrobas *nm Ordinat* at sign; **"gdurand, arrobas, transex, point, fr"** "gdurand at transex, dot, fr"

arrondir *vt (somme)(vers le haut)* to round up; *(vers le bas)* to round down; **vous pouvez arrondir à deux cents euros** you can round it up to two hundred euros; **arrondir à l'euro supérieur/inférieur** to round up/down to the nearest euro; *Fam* **arrondir ses fins de mois** to supplement one's income, to make a bit extra on the side

arrondissement *nm* = administrative subdi-

vision of Paris, Lyons and Marseilles

ART *nm (abrév* **Autorité de régulation des télécommunications**) = French telecommunications and Internet watchdog, *Br* ≃ Oftel

art. *nm (abrév* **article**) article

article *nm* (**a**) *(produit)* article, item; **faire l'article (pour qch)** to make a sales pitch (for sth); **nous ne suivons** *ou* **faisons plus cet article** we don't stock that item any more □ *Mktg* **article d'appel** loss leader; **article bas de gamme** bottom-of-the-range item; **article breveté** patented item; **articles de bureau** office supplies; **articles de consommation courante** consumer goods; **article démarqué** markdown; **articles d'exportation** export goods, exports; **article en fin de série** discontinued item; **article à forte rotation** fast mover; **articles de grande consommation** consumables, consumer goods; **article haut de gamme** top-of-the-range item; **articles de luxe** luxury goods; **article de marque** branded article; **article de première nécessité** basic commodity; **article de rebut** reject; **article en réclame** special offer; **articles de voyage** travel goods
 (**b**) *(d'une facture)* item; *(d'un compte)* entry; *(d'un loi, d'un contrat)* article □ *Compta* **article de contre-passation** contra entry, transfer entry; **article au débit** debit entry; **articles de dépense** items of expenditure; **articles divers** sundries; **article inverse** contra entry, transfer entry
 (**c**) *Ordinat (d'un menu)* command; *(dans une base de données)* record; *(dans des groupes de discussion)* article

artisan, -e *nm,f* craftsman, *f* craftswoman

artisanal, -e *adj (activité, travaux)* traditional; *(à la main)* hand-made

artisanat *nm* craft industry

ASBL *nf (abrév* **association sans but lucratif**) *Br* non-profit-making *or Am* not-for-profit organization

ascenseur *nm Ordinat* scroll box

ASCII *nm Ordinat (abrév* **American Standard Code for Information Interchange**) ASCII

ASE *nf (abrév* **Agence spatiale européenne**) ESA

asile *nm (document publicitaire)* stuffer, insert

assainir *vt (budget, monnaie, économie)* to stabilize; *(bilan)* to balance; **assainir ses finances** to put one's finances in order

assainissement *nm (d'une monnaie, de l'économie)* stabilization; *(d'un bilan)* balancing; *(des finances)* putting in order □ **assainissement budgétaire** budgetary stabilization; **assainissement monétaire** stabilization of the currency

> **"**
> ... le président de la Banque centrale européenne n'a pas tort de rappeler que "la poursuite de la voie de l'**assainissement budgétaire** est essentielle, tout comme la vigilance pour assurer une stricte adhésion aux plans à moyen terme et une mise en œuvre rigoureuse des procédures du Pacte de stabilité de croissance".
>   **"**

ASSEDIC nf (abrév **Association pour l'emploi dans l'industrie et le commerce**) = French unemployment benefit department, Br ≃ Jobcentre, Am ≃ Unemployment Office; **toucher les ASSEDIC** ≃ to get Br Job Seekers Allowance or Am welfare

assemblage nm (dans l'industrie) assembly

assemblée nf (**a**) (réunion) meeting ❑ **assemblée extraordinaire** extraordinary meeting; **assemblée générale** general meeting; **assemblée générale d'actionnaires** general meeting of shareholders; **assemblée générale annuelle** annual general meeting; **assemblée générale extraordinaire** extraordinary general meeting (**b**) (élus) **Assemblée parlementaire européenne** European Parliament

assentiment nm assent; **donner/refuser son assentiment (à qch)** to give/withhold one's assent (to sth)

asseoir vt Fin **asseoir un impôt** to calculate the basis for a tax; **asseoir l'impôt sur le revenu** to base taxation on income

assesseur nm Jur assessor

assiduité nf (**a**) (application) assiduity (**b**) (ponctualité) regularity

assiette nf (d'un impôt, d'un taux) base; (d'une hypothèque) = property or funds on which a mortgage is secured ❑ **assiette de l'amortissement** depreciation, depreciable base; **assiette fiscale, assiette de l'impôt** taxable income

assignation nf (**a**) Fin (de parts, de fonds) allotment, allocation (**à** to) (**b**) (d'une tâche, d'un poste) assignment (**à** to) (**c**) Bourse exercise notice

assigner vt (**a**) Fin (parts, fonds) to allot, to allocate (**à** to) (**b**) (tâche, poste) to assign (**à** to)

assistance nf assistance ❑ **assistance judiciaire** legal aid; **assistance maritime** salvage; **assistance technique** technical assistance or support; **assistance technique téléphonique** support line; Ordinat **assistance à l'utilisateur** user support

assistant, -e nm,f assistant ❑ **assistant de direction** personal assistant, PA

assisté, -e 1 adj (**a**) Admin (personne) on Br social security or Am welfare (**b**) Ordinat **assisté par ordinateur** (conception, enseignement, fabrication, production) computer-aided, computer-assisted
2 nm,f Admin person on Br social security or Am welfare

assister 1 vt (soutenir financièrement) to help (financially)
2 assister à vt ind to be present at, to attend

association nf (**a**) (organisation) association ❑ **association à but lucratif** profit-making organization; **association sans but lucratif, association à but non lucratif** Br non-profit-making or Am not-for-profit organization; **association capital-travail** profit-sharing scheme; **association de consommateurs** consumer association; **Association européenne de libre-échange** European Free Trade Association; **Association française des banques** French Bankers' Association; **Association de libre-échange** Free Trade Agreement; **association loi 1901** = type of non-profit-making organization; **association professionnelle** professional association, trade association (**b**) (collaboration) partnership; **entrer en association avec qn** to enter into partnership with sb ❑ **association de fait** partnership at will

associé, -e 1 adj joint, associate
2 nm,f associate, partner; **prendre qn comme associé** to take sb into partnership ❑ **associé commanditaire** sleeping partner; **associé commandité** active partner; **associé fictif** nominal partner; **associé fondateur** founding partner; **associé gérant** managing partner; **associé majoritaire** senior partner; **associé minoritaire** junior partner; **associés à part égale** equal partners; **associé passif** sleeping partner; **associé principal** senior partner; **associé en second** junior partner

associer 1 vt (joindre, lier) to associate; **associer les travailleurs aux profits de leur entreprise** to allow workers to share in their company's profits; **son entreprise est associée au projet** his company is taking part in the project
2 s'associer vpr to enter or go into partnership; **s'associer à** ou **avec qn** to enter or go into partnership with sb; **s'associer qn** to take sb on as a partner

assorti, -e adj **bien/mal assorti** (magasin) well-/poorly-stocked

assortiment nm (de marchandises) assortment, selection, range ❑ Mktg **assortiment de produits** product mix

assortir 1 vt (magasin) to stock, to supply
2 s'assortir vpr to buy one's stock; **il s'assortit dans les magasins de gros** he buys his stock wholesale

assouplir vt (réglementation, contrôle, conditions, crédit) to relax

assouplissement *nm (de la réglementation, du contrôle, des conditions, du crédit)* relaxing

assujetti, -e 1 *adj* **être assujetti à l'impôt/aux droits de douane** to be liable for tax/customs duty
2 *nm,f* = person liable for tax

assujettir *vt* **assujettir qn à qch** *(taxe, impôt, règlement)* to subject sb to sth

assujettissement *nm (à l'impôt)* liability

assumer *vt (risque)* to take; *(responsabilité)* to take on; *(dépenses)* to meet

assurable *adj Assur* insurable

assurance *nf* (a) *Assur* insurance; **contracter une assurance** to take out insurance, to take out an insurance policy; **il est dans les assurances** he's in insurance; *Fam* **je vais écrire à mon assurance** I'm going to write to my insurance company ❑ **assurance (contre les) accidents** accident insurance; **assurance contre les accidents corporels** personal accident insurance; **assurance contre les accidents du travail** industrial accident insurance; **assurance annulation** cancellation insurance; **assurance à capital différée** endowment insurance; *Suisse* **assurance casco** comprehensive insurance, all-risks insurance; **assurance en cas de vie** endowment insurance; **assurance chômage** *(payé par le patron et le salarié)* unemployment insurance; **assurance coface** = standard export guarantee insurance; **assurance collective** group insurance; **assurance à cotisations** contributory insurance; **assurance crédit** loan repayment insurance; **assurance cumulative** double insurance; **assurance décès-invalidité** whole life and disability insurance; **assurance à dotation** endowment insurance; **assurance facultative** voluntary insurance; **assurance forfaitaire** fixed-premium insurance; **assurance sur fret** freight insurance; **assurance habitation** buildings insurance; **assurance insolvabilité** insurance against bankruptcy; **assurance invalidité** critical illness cover; **assurance longue maladie** critical illness insurance; **assurance maladie** health insurance; **assurance maladie privée** private health insurance; **assurance maritime** marine insurance; **assurance contre les mauvaises créances** bad debt insurance; **assurance médicale** medical insurance; **assurance multirisque** comprehensive insurance; **assurance mutuelle** mutual insurance; **assurance de portefeuille** portfolio insurance; **assurance au premier risque** first-loss insurance; **assurance responsabilité civile** public liability insurance; **assurance de responsabilité du produit** product liability insurance; **assurance au tiers** third party insurance; **assurance tous risques** comprehensive insurance, all-risks insurance; **assurance sur la vie** life insurance, life assurance (b) *Admin* **assu-**

rance chômage unemployment benefit; **assurance invalidité** disability pension; **assurance maladie** sickness benefit; **assurance maternité** maternity benefit; **assurances sociales** *Br* ≃ National Insurance, *Am* ≃ welfare

assurance-vie *nf Assur* life insurance, life assurance; **prendre une assurance-vie** to take out life insurance *or* assurance

assuré, -e 1 *adj Assur* insured
2 *nm,f* (a) *Assur* policyholder, insured person; **les assurés** the insured (b) *Admin* **assuré social** ≃ member of *Br* the National Insurance scheme *or Am* the Social Security scheme

assurer 1 *vt* (a) *Assur* **assurer qn** to insure sb; **la Compagnie n'assure pas contre les dégâts causés par la pluie** the Company will not insure against damage caused by rain; **assurer un immeuble contre l'incendie** to insure a building against fire; **assurer qch pour deux millions d'euros** to insure sth for two million euros (b) *(garantir)* to ensure, to guarantee; **assurer une rente à qn** to settle an annuity on sb (c) *(se charger de)* to be in charge of; **assurer un service** to provide a service; **une permanence est assurée le samedi après-midi** there is someone on duty on Saturday afternoons
2 **s'assurer** *vpr* to take out insurance *or* an insurance policy (**contre** against); **s'assurer sur la vie** to take out life insurance *or* assurance

assureur *nm* underwriter; *(agent)* insurance agent; *(compagnie)* insurance company; *(courtier)* insurance broker

assureur-conseil *nm* insurance adviser

astérisque *nm* asterisk

astreinte *nf Jur* = daily fine for delay in payment of debt

atelier *nm* (a) *(lieu)* (work)shop; **il est devenu contremaître après cinq ans d'atelier** he became a foreman after five years on the shopfloor ❑ **atelier de montage** assembly (work)shop; **atelier d'usinage** machine shop (b) *(personnel)* workshop staff (c) *(groupe de travail)* work group

atermoiement *nm (délai de paiement)* = arrangement with creditors for extension of time for payment; *(d'une lettre de change)* renewal

ATF *nm Bourse (abrév* **accord de taux futur***)* forward rate agreement, future rate agreement

ATM *nm Ordinat (abrév* **asynchronous transfer mode***)* ATM

atout *nm* asset, advantage; **la connaissance d'une langue étrangère est un atout** knowledge of a foreign language is an asset *or* an advantage; **l'abondance des ressources naturelles est un atout pour la région** the abundance of natural resources is an asset to the area

attaché, -e *nm,f* attaché ◻ *attaché commercial (d'une ambassade)* commercial attaché; *(d'une entreprise)* sales representative; *attaché de presse* press attaché

attaché-case *nm* attaché case

attachement à la marque *nm Mktg* brand bonding

attaque *nf Mktg (sur un marché)* attack ◻ *attaque frontale* head-on attack; *attaque latérale* flank attack

attaquer *vt* (a) *Mktg (marché)* to attack (b) *Jur (décision)* to contest, to appeal against; *attaquer qn en justice* to bring an action against sb

atteindre *vt (objectifs)* to attain, to achieve; **le nombre des chômeurs a atteint la barre des deux millions** unemployment has reached the two million mark

atteinte *nf (à un droit, une liberté)* violation; **cette nouvelle mesure constitue une atteinte au droit des salariés** this new measure violates employees' rights

attente *nf* (a) *Tél* **mettre qn en attente** *(au téléphone)* to put sb on hold; **être en attente** *(au téléphone)* to be on hold (b) *Ordinat* **liste de fichiers à imprimer en attente** print queue (c) **dans l'attente de votre réponse** *ou* **d'une réponse de votre part** *(dans une lettre)* I look forward to receiving your reply

attention *nf* **à l'attention de** *(sur un document)* for the attention of

attentisme *nm* wait-and-see policy; **l'attentisme des investisseurs explique le ralentissement du marché boursier** the wariness of investors explains why the stock market is so sluggish

attentiste 1 *adj (attitude, politique)* wait-and-see
   2 *nmf* = person who adopts a wait-and-see policy

attestation *nf* certificate ◻ *attestation d'assurance* insurance certificate; *attestation de conformité* certificate of conformity; *attestation médicale* medical certificate; *Assur* **attestation de sinistre** damage certificate

attirer *vt (investissements, acheteurs)* to attract

attitré, -e *adj (fournisseur, représentant)* appointed

attitude *nf Mktg (du consommateur)* attitude; **l'attitude du consommateur à l'égard du produit est décevante** the consumer attitude towards the product is disappointing

attractif, -ive *adj (prix)* attractive

attraction *nf (pour un produit)* attraction; **les automobiles allemandes suscitent une attraction très marquée chez les Britanniques** German cars are very popular with the British

attrait commercial *nm Mktg* market appeal; **ce produit présente un attrait commercial certain** this product has definite market appeal

attribuer *vt (salaire, prime)* to assign, to allocate (**à** to); *Bourse (actions, dividendes)* to allocate, to allot; **l'entreprise a attribué une part de ses actions au personnel** the company has allocated *or* allotted some of its shares to its employees

attribut *nm Mktg (d'un produit)* attribute

attributaire *nmf Jur* beneficiary; *Bourse (d'actions, de dividendes)* allottee

attribution *nf* (a) *(d'un salaire, d'une prime)* assigning, allocation; *Bourse (d'actions, de dividendes)* allocation, allotment (b) *Mktg* attribution

aubaine *nf Can (achat avantageux)* bargain

audience *nf Mktg* audience ◻ *audience captive* captive audience; *audience cible* target audience; *audience cumulée* cumulative audience; *audience globale* global audience; *audience instantanée* instantaneous audience; *audience télévisuelle* television audience; *audience utile* addressable audience

audioconférence *nf* audioconference

audionumérique *adj* digital audio

audiotypiste *nmf* audio-typist

audit *nm* (a) *(service)* audit; **être chargé de l'audit d'une société** to audit a company ◻ *audit consommateur* consumer audit; *audit des détaillants* retail audit; *audit externe* external audit; *audit général* general audit; *audit interne* internal audit; *audit marketing* marketing audit; *audit opérationnel* operational audit; *audit social* management consultancy report; *audit de vente* sales audit (b) *(personne)* auditor ◻ *audit des détaillants* retail auditor; *audit externe* external auditor; *audit interne* internal auditor; *audit marketing* marketing auditor

auditeur, -trice *nm,f* (a) *(chargé de l'audit)* auditor ◻ *auditeur des détaillants* retail auditor; *auditeur externe* external auditor; *auditeur interne* internal auditor; *auditeur marketing* marketing auditor (b) *Admin* **auditeur à la Cour des comptes** = junior official at the French Audit Office

augmentation *nf* (a) *(des dépenses, du chômage, des effectifs, de la consommation, de l'inflation)* increase (**de** in); **une augmentation de trois pour cent** a three percent increase; **être en augmentation** to be on the increase, to be rising; **le chiffre d'affaires est en augmentation sur l'année dernière** the turnover is showing an increase *or* is up on last year's; **demander une augmentation** to ask for *Br* a (pay) rise *or* *Am* a raise ◻ *augmentation des béné-*

fices earnings growth; **augmentation du capital** increase in capital; **augmentation de prix** price increase; **augmentation du prix de vente** mark-up; **augmentation de salaire, augmentation salariale** *Br* (pay) rise, *Am* raise (**b**) *Ordinat* **augmentation de puissance** upgrade, upgrading

augmenter 1 *vt (impôts, taux d'intérêt, prix)* to increase, to put up, to raise; *(dépenses)* to increase; **augmenter qn** to raise *or* increase sb's salary, to give sb *Br* a (pay) rise *or Am* a raise; **augmenter les ventes de dix pour cent** to increase sales by ten percent

2 *vi (impôts, taux d'intérêt, prix)* to increase, to go up, to rise; *(dépenses)* to increase; **augmenter de valeur** to increase in value; **tout a augmenté de prix** everything has gone up in price; **le chiffre d'affaires a augmenté de dix pour cent par rapport à l'année dernière** the turnover has increased by ten percent *or* is ten percent up on last year

aujourd'hui *adv* today; **aujourd'hui en huit** a week today; **à compter** *ou* **à dater d'aujourd'hui** from today

austérité *nf Écon* austerity; **politique d'austérité** austerity policy

autarcie *nf* autarky □ **autarcie économique** direct production

autarcique *adj* autarkic

authenticité *nf (d'une signature, d'un document)* authenticity

authentification *nf* (**a**) *(d'une signature, d'un document)* authentication (**b**) *Ordinat* authentication

authentifier *vt (signature, document)* to authenticate

authentique *adj (signature, document)* authentic, genuine

autocorrecteur, -trice *adj Ordinat* self-correcting

autofinancé, -e *adj Fin* self-financed; **8 milliards d'euros autofinancés à un tiers seulement** 8 billion euros, only a third of which was self-financed

autofinancement *nm Fin* self-financing

> "
> Il y a donc nécessité impérieuse d'investir rapidement. Mais la SNCF ne peut dégager à elle seule les marges de son **autofinancement**, sauf à augmenter ses tarifs au détriment de sa mission de service public.
> "

autofinancer s'autofinancer *vpr Fin* to be self-financing

autogérer 1 *vt (entreprise, usine)* to self-manage

2 s'autogérer *vpr (entreprise, usine)* to be self-managing

autogestion *nf* self-management

autogestionnaire *adj* = based on workers' self-management

autolimitation *nf* setting of voluntary limits

autolimiter *vt* to set voluntary limits to; **les Japonais autolimitent leurs exportations de voitures** the Japanese set voluntary limits to their car exports

automation *nf* automation

automatique *adj* automatic

automatisation *nf* automation

automatiser *vt* to automate

autonome *adj (organisme, gestion)* autonomous; *(syndicat)* independent

autonomie *nf* autonomy

autorégulation *nf* self-regulation

autorisation *nf* (**a**) *(permission)* authorization, permission; **donner à qn l'autorisation de faire qch** to authorize sb to do sth, to give sb permission to do sth; **demander l'autorisation de faire qch** to ask permission to do sth; **avoir l'autorisation de vendre qch** to be licensed to sell sth □ *Ordinat* **autorisation d'accès** access authorization; *Banque* **autorisation de crédit** line of credit; *Banque* **autorisation de découvert** overdraft facility; **autorisation de dédouanement** customs clearance authorization; *Fin* **autorisation d'émettre des billets de banque** note issuance facility; *Banque* **autorisation de prélèvement** direct debit mandate (**b**) *(document)* licence, permit □ **autorisation d'exporter** export permit; **autorisation spéciale** special permit

autorisé, -e *adj (transfert, découvert, dépenses, transaction)* authorized; **les milieux autorisés** official circles; **de source autorisée, le ministre aurait déjà signé l'accord** sources close to the minister say that he's already signed the agreement

autoriser *vt (transfert, découvert, dépenses, transaction)* to authorize; **autoriser qn à faire qch** to authorize sb to do sth, to give sb permission to do sth

autorité *nf* (**a**) *(pouvoir)* authority; **agir de pleine autorité** to act with full powers (**b**) *(organisation)* **les autorités** the authorities □ **autorités financières** financial authorities; **l'autorité fiscale** the (income) tax authorities; **autorité portuaire** port authority; **autorité de régulation** regulating body

autoroute *nf Ordinat* **autoroute de l'information** information superhighway; **autoroute interactive** interactive highway

autosuffisance *nf Écon* self-sufficiency

autosuffisant, -e *adj Écon* self-sufficient

autotest *nm Ordinat* self-test

autotester s'autotester *vpr Ordinat* to self-test

auxiliaire *nmf* (**a**) *(aide)* auxiliary, assistant (**b**) *Admin (employé temporaire)* temporary worker

AV *nm Banque (abrév* **avis de virement**) (bank) transfer advice

aval *nm* (**a**) *Fin (d'un effet de commerce)* endorsement, guarantee; **donner son aval à un billet** to endorse *or* guarantee *or* back a bill ❑ **aval bancaire** bank guarantee (**b**) *(accord)* approval; **donner son aval à qn/qch** to give sb/sth one's approval; **pour aval** *(sur document)* for approval (**c**) *Écon, Mktg* downside; **d'aval** *(activités)* downstream; **en aval** *(société)* downstream

avaliser *vt Fin (effet de commerce)* to endorse, to guarantee, to back

avaliseur, -euse *nm,f Fin* endorser, guarantor, backer

avaliste *nmf Fin* endorser, guarantor, backer

à-valoir *nm* advance (payment)

avance *nf* (**a**) *Fin (d'argent)* **avance (de fonds)** advance; **par avance, à titre d'avance** as an advance; **faire** *ou* **accorder une avance de mille euros à qn** to give sb an advance of a thousand euros, to advance sb a thousand euros; **demander une avance sur son salaire** to ask for an advance on one's salary ❑ **avance bancaire** bank advance; **avance à découvert** unsecured *or* uncovered advance; **avances en devises** foreign currency loan; **avance en numéraire, avance de trésorerie** cash advance (**b**) *(avantage)* lead; **conserver son avance sur ses concurrents** to retain one's lead over one's competitors; **être en avance sur la concurrence** to be ahead of the competition (**c**) **d'avance** in advance; **payé d'avance** paid in advance, prepaid; **payable à l'avance** payable in advance (**d**) *Ordinat* feed ❑ **avance automatique** automatic feed

avancé, -e *adj (économie, technologie)* advanced

avancement *nm* (**a**) *(d'un projet, des travaux)* progress; **compte-rendu de l'avancement des travaux** progress report; **paiements proportionnels à l'avancement des travaux** progress payments (**b**) *(promotion)* promotion; **obtenir de l'avancement** to be promoted (**c**) *Ordinat* **avancement par friction** friction feed; **avancement du papier** sheet feed

avancer *vt* (**a**) *(dans le temps)* to advance, to bring forward; **la réunion a été avancée du 14 au 7** the meeting has been brought forward from the 14th to the 7th (**b**) *(financièrement)* **avancer de l'argent à qn** to advance money to sb; *(prêter)* to lend sb money; **avancer un mois**

d'appointements à qn to advance sb a month's salary, to pay sb a month's salary in advance

avantage *nm* advantage ❑ *Écon* **avantage absolu** absolute advantage; **avantages accessoires** fringe benefits; **avantage comparatif** comparative advantage; **avantage concurrentiel** competitive advantage; **l'avantage concurrentiel de notre offre réside dans l'excellence de notre service** the competitive advantage of what we have to offer lies in the excellence of our service; **avantages en espèces** cash benefits; **avantage fiscal** tax benefit, tax incentive; **avantages en nature** payments in kind; **avantages sociaux** financial benefits

avantager *vt* to advantage, to favour; **la faiblesse de la livre avantage les exportateurs britanniques** the weak pound gives British exporters an advantage

avantageux, -euse *adj (contrat, affaire)* profitable; *(prix)* reasonable, attractive; *(conditions)* favourable

avant-contrat *nm* preliminary contract

avant-projet *nm* draft

avarie *nf Assur* average, damage *(sustained by a ship)* ❑ **avaries communes** general average

avarié, -e *adj (marchandises)* damaged

avarier *vt (marchandises)* to damage

avenant *nm (de police d'assurance)* endorsement, additional clause

avenir *nm* future; **d'avenir** *(métier, secteur, marché)* up-and-coming; **les nouveaux procédés techniques ont de l'avenir** the new technical processes have a promising future

avertissement *nm* (**a**) *(avis préalable)* warning; *Bourse, Fin* profit warning; **renvoyer qn sans avertissement préalable** to dismiss sb without notice (**b**) *Ordinat* **avertissement de réception** *(de message)* acknowledgement; **avertissement à réception d'un courrier** mail received message

> "
> Ainsi, l'**avertissement** sur résultats d'IBM, suivi de celui du canadien Nortel, et les craintes concernant les comptes de Cisco ont entraîné cette semaine les valeurs techno à la baisse sur toutes les places financières.
> "

avili, -e *adj (biens)* depreciated

avilir 1 *vt (monnaie)* to depreciate, to devalue; *(prix)* to bring down
2 s'avilir *vpr (biens)* to depreciate, to decrease in value

avilissement *nm (d'une monnaie)* depreciation, devaluation; *(des biens)* depreciation; *(de prix)* fall, drop

avion *nm* aircraft, *Br* aeroplane, *Am* airplane; **en avion** by air, by plane; **par avion** *(sur lettre)* (by) airmail ◻ *avion charter* charter plane; *avion commercial* commercial aircraft; *avion de transport de marchandises* freighter, *Am* freight plane

avion-cargo *nm* cargo plane, freighter, *Am* freight plane

avis *nm* *(pour informer)* notice, notification; **jusqu'à nouvel avis** until further notice; **suivant avis** as per advice; **avis par écrit** notice in writing; **donner avis de qch** to give notice of sth; **donner avis que...** to give notice that... ◻ *Bourse avis d'appel de fonds* call letter; *Bourse avis d'attribution* letter of allotment; *avis de la banque* bank notification *or* advice; *avis de crédit* credit advice; *avis de débit* debit advice; *avis de domiciliation* domiciliation advice; *avis éditorial (dans la presse)* editorial opinion; *Bourse avis d'exécution* contract note; *avis d'expédition* dispatch *or* consignment note; *avis d'imposition* tax assessment; *avis de licenciement* redundancy notice; *avis de livraison* delivery note; *avis de paiement* payment advice; *avis de prélèvement* direct debit advice; *avis de réception* acknowledgement (of receipt); *avis de rejet* notice of returned cheque; *avis de remise* remittance advice; *Assur avis de renouvellement* renewal notice; *Bourse avis de répartition* letter of allotment; *avis de retrait* withdrawal notice; *Banque avis de virement* (bank) transfer advice

aviser *vt* to inform, to notify; **aviser qn de qch** to advise *or* inform sb of sth; **aviser qn de faire qch** to give sb notice to do sth

avocat, -e *nm,f Jur* lawyer, *Am* attorney; **consulter un avocat** to take legal advice ◻ *avocat d'affaires* business lawyer

avocat-conseil *nm Jur* counsel

avoir *nm* (**a**) *(bien)* property, possessions; *(capital)* capital; *(sur compte)* credit; **doit et avoir** debit and credit; **obtenir un avoir** to be given credit, to obtain *or* to get credit ◻ *avoir en banque* bank credit; *avoir en devises* foreign currency holding, foreign currency assets; *avoir fiscal* tax credit (**b**) **avoirs** assets ◻ *avoirs disponibles* liquid assets (**c**) *(attestation de crédit)* credit note

> **"** Qu'est-ce que l'**avoir fiscal**? Comme son nom l'indique, l'**avoir fiscal** est un avoir qui revient à l'actionnaire, afin d'éviter à ce dernier de subir une double imposition. Pourquoi cela? ... Sans l'**avoir fiscal**, il y aurait bien une double imposition: au niveau de la société, puis au niveau de l'actionnaire. **"**

avoir-client *nm Compta* customer credit

avoir-fournisseur *nm Compta* supplier credit

avoué *nm Jur Br* ≃ solicitor, *Am* ≃ attorney

ayant-compte *nm Banque* account holder

ayant droit *nm* beneficiary (**à** of)

Bb

B2B *adj* (*abrév* **business to business**) B2B

B2C *adj* (*abrév* **business to consumer**) B2C

babillard *nm Ordinat* bulletin board system, BBS

bac¹ *nm* (**a**) *Ordinat* **bac d'alimentation** sheet feed; *bac d'alimentation papier* sheet feeder; *bac à feuilles* paper tray; *bac à papier* paper tray (**b**) *bac à correspondance, bac à courrier* correspondence tray

bac² *nm* (*abrév* **baccalauréat**) = secondary school examination qualifying for entry to university, *Br* ≃ A-levels, *Am* ≃ high-school diploma; **bac + 3** *(dans une annonce)* = three years of higher education required

baccalauréat *nm* = secondary school examination qualifying for entry to university, *Br* ≃ A-levels, *Am* ≃ high-school diploma

backbone *nm Ordinat* backbone

back-office *nm Banque* back office

badge *nm* (**a**) *(d'identité)* name badge (**b**) *(d'accès)* swipe card, key card

baie *nf Ordinat* bay

bail *nm* lease; **prendre une maison à bail** to take out a lease on a house; **céder** *ou* **donner une maison à bail** to lease (out) a house, to let a house; **bail à céder** *(sur panneau)* lease for sale; **signer un bail** to sign a lease; **renouveler un bail** to renew a lease; **résilier un bail** to cancel a lease □ *bail assuré* security of tenure; *bail commercial* commercial lease; *bail emphytéotique* 99-year lease; *bail à long terme* long lease; *bail à loyer* rental agreement, lease

bailleur, -eresse *nm,f* (**a**) *bailleur de fonds* *(investisseur)* (financial) backer; *(associé passif)* *Br* sleeping partner, *Am* silent partner (**b**) *Jur* lessor

baisse *nf* (**a**) *(des prix, du chômage, du taux de l'inflation)* fall, drop (**de** in); **la baisse de l'euro** the fall in the value of the euro; **le marché des obligations a connu une baisse sensible** the bond market has dropped considerably; **être en baisse** *ou* **à la baisse** to be falling; **revoir** *ou* **reviser les chiffres à la baisse** to revise figures downwards □ *baisse des impôts* tax cut

(**b**) *Bourse (des cours, des valeurs)* fall; **être orienté à la baisse** to be falling; **spéculations à la baisse** bear speculations; **jouer** *ou* **spéculer à la baisse** to bear, to go a bear, to speculate for a fall; **acheter en baisse** to buy on a falling market; **les actions sont en baisse** shares are falling

baisser 1 *vt* *(prix, loyer)* to lower, to reduce, to bring down; **faire baisser le coût de la vie** to lower *or* reduce *or* bring down the cost of living; **la concurrence fait baisser les prix** competition brings prices down

2 *vi* *(prix, actions)* to fall; *(stocks)* to be running low; **le dollar a baissé** the dollar has weakened

baissier, -ère *Bourse* **1** *adj* *(marché)* bearish

2 *nm,f* bear

balance *nf Compta (d'un compte)* balance; **la balance est en excédent** there is a surplus; **faire la balance** to make up the balance sheet; **balance de l'actif et du passif** credit and debit balance, balance of assets and liabilities □ *balance agée* aged debtors; *balance de caisse* cash balance; *Écon balance du commerce, balance commerciale* balance of trade; *balance générale des comptes* balance of payments; *balance d'inventaire* trial balance; *balance des paiements* balance of payments; *balance visible* visible balance

balancer *vt (compte)* to balance; **balancer les comptes** to balance *or* make up the books

balise *nf Ordinat* tag □ *balise de début* opening tag; *balise de fin* closing tag

baliser *vt Ordinat* to tag

banc *nm* (a) *banc d'essai* benchtest; **mettre une idée au banc d'essai** to test out an idea (b) *Ordinat* **banc de mémoire** memory bank

bancable *adj Fin* bankable

bancaire *adj (chèque, commission, crédit, dépôt, frais, prêt)* bank; *(opération)* banking

bancarisation *nf* **la bancarisation de l'économie** the growing role of banks in the economy; **la bancarisation de la population française** the spread of the use of banking services among the French population

bancarisé, -e *adj* **être bancarisé** to have a bank account, to use the banking system; **presque toutes les PME sont bancarisées** almost all small businesses have a bank account *or* use the banking system

bancassurance *nf* bancassurance

> Le "Lion de Trieste", comme l'appellent les Italiens, pouvait difficilement laisser passer sans réagir la création d'un groupe de **bancassurance** San Paolo IMI-INA, capable de talonner dans nombre de secteurs, notamment l'assurance-vie. Generali veut aussi échapper à l'appétit d'éventuels groupes étrangers.

bancatique *nf Banque* electronic banking

bande *nf* (a) *Ordinat* tape □ **bande audionumérique** digital audio tape, DAT; **bande de défilement** scroll bar; **bande magnétique** magnetic tape (b) *Fin* **bande de fluctuation** *(d'une monnaie)* fluctuation band

bandeau *nm (espace publicitaire)* advertising space *(in the shape of a band around a vehicle)*; *Ordinat (dans un site Web)* banner

bannière *nf Ordinat* banner

banquable = **bancable**

banque *nf* (a) *(établissement, organisation)* bank □ **banque d'acceptation** *Br* accepting *or* *Am* acceptance house *or* bank; **banque d'affaires** *Br* merchant bank, *Am* investment bank; **banque centrale** central bank; **Banque centrale européenne** European central bank; **banque de clearing** clearing bank; **banque commerciale** commercial bank, trading bank; **banque compensatrice** clearing bank; **banque confirmatrice** confirming bank; **banque de crédit** credit bank, lending bank; **banque de dépôt** deposit bank, *Br* joint-stock bank; **banque de détail** retail bank; **banque émettrice, banque d'émission** issuing bank *or* house; **banque d'encaissement** collection bank; **banque d'épargne** savings bank; **banque d'escompte** discount house *or* bank, discounting house *or* bank; **Banque européenne d'investissement** European Investment Bank; **Banque europé-** enne de reconstruction et de développement European Bank of Reconstruction and Development; **la Banque de France** the Bank of France; **banque de gestion de patrimoine** trust bank; **banque de gros** wholesale bank; **banque hypothécaire** mortgage bank; **banque industrielle** industrial bank; **Banque internationale pour la reconstruction et le développement** International Bank for Reconstruction and Development; **banque d'investissement** *Br* merchant bank, *Am* investment bank; **banque en ligne** on-line bank, Internet bank; **la Banque mondiale** the World Bank; **banque notificatrice** advising bank; **banque de placement** issuing bank *or* house; **banque privée** private bank; **banque privilégiée** chartered bank; **banque de recouvrement** collecting agency, collecting bank

(b) *(activité)* banking □ **banque à distance** remote banking; **banque à domicile** telebanking, home banking; **banque d'entreprise** corporate banking; **banque en ligne** on-line banking; **banque à réseau** branch banking; **banque universelle** global banking

(c) *(secteur)* banking; **elle travaille dans la banque** she works in banking; **la haute banque** high finance

(d) *Ordinat* **banque de données** data bank; **banque d'images** image bank

> Aux observateurs qui ont pu s'étonner, pendant le long feuilleton bancaire français, que le tabou d'une intervention étrangère soit demeuré si pesant et si efficace, les responsables gouvernementaux ou bancaires français avaient la réponse prête: "Peut-être, mais avez-vous déjà essayé d"acheter une banque allemande?" Les pratiques européennes dans la **banque de dépôt** (la banque d'affaires, en général, est déjà internationalisée) demeurent nationales.

banqueroute *nf Jur* bankruptcy; **faire banqueroute** to go bankrupt □ **banqueroute frauduleuse** fraudulent bankruptcy; **banqueroute simple** bankruptcy *(with irregularities amounting to a breach of the law)*

banqueroutier, -ère *adj & nm,f* bankrupt

banquier, -ère *nm,f* banker □ **banquier d'affaires** investment banker, *Br* merchant banker; **banquier encaisseur** collecting banker; **banquier escompteur** discounting banker; **banquier prêteur** lending banker

baratin *nm Fam* sales pitch □ **baratin publicitaire** sales pitch

barème *nm* (a) *(tableau)* ready reckoner (b) *(tarification)* scale; *(de prix)* list □ **barème fiscal, barème d'imposition** tax rate schedule *or* structure; **barème des salaires** salary scale

> **❝**
> Selon un **barème** simple: plus on part tôt, moins on touche (de 45 à 75% du revenu moyen de la carrière). Et à l'opposé, chaque mois de labeur supplémentaire se traduit par 0,6% de plus sur sa pension après 65 ans.
> **❞**

baril nm (de pétrole) barrel

barre nf (**a**) (niveau) level; **en dessous de la barre des trois pour cent** below the three percent mark (**b**) Ordinat bar ❏ **barre de défilement** scroll bar; **barre d'espacement** space bar; **barre d'état** status bar; **barre d'icônes** icon bar; **barre de lancement rapide** quick launch bar; **barre de menu** menu bar; **barre de navigation** navigation bar; **barre oblique** oblique, slash; **barre oblique inversée** backslash; **barre d'outils** tool bar; **barre de sélection** menu bar; **barre de style** style bar; **barre de titre** title bar

> **❝**
> À 47 euros, le cours reste cependant bien en deçà du plafond d'août, qui avait atteint la **barre** des 60 euros.
> **❞**

barré, -e adj (chèque) crossed

barrer vt (chèque) to cross

barrière nf barrier ❏ **barrière d'accès** access barrier; **barrière commerciale** trade barrier; **barrières douanières** trade barriers; **barrière à l'entrée** entry barrier; **barrière non tarifaire** non-tariff barrier; **barrière à la sortie** exit barrier; **barrière tarifaire** tariff barrier

BAS nm (abrév **Bureau d'aide sociale**) welfare office

bas¹, basse 1 adj (prix, taux de change, taux d'intérêt) low; **acheter/vendre qch à bas prix** to buy/sell sth cheap; **leurs actions sont au niveau le plus bas** their shares have reached an all-time low

2 nm (**a**) (du marché) low end (**b**) Ordinat **bas de casse** lower-case; **en bas-de-casse** lower-case, in lower case; **bas de page** footer (**c**) Bourse **les hauts et les bas** the highs and lows **3** adv low; Bourse **les cours sont tombés très bas** prices have fallen very low

bas² nm **bas de laine** nest egg; **le bas de laine des Français** the savings of small-time French investors

> **❝**
> Au-delà des cas France Télécom et Alcatel, la baisse de la Bourse a bel et bien eu un impact négatif sur le **bas de laine** des actionnaires salariés.
> **❞**

bascule nf Ordinat toggle

basculer vi Ordinat to toggle

basculeur nm Ordinat toggle (key)

base nf (**a**) (fondement) basis; **sur une base nette** on a net basis; **de base** (prix, salaire) basic ❏ Compta **base amortissable** basis for depreciation; Compta **base de calcul** basis of calculations; **base hors taxe** amount exclusive of VAT; **base d'imposition** taxable base (**b**) (dans une entreprise) shop floor; **le patron ne sait pas communiquer avec la base** the boss can't communicate with the shop floor (**c**) Ordinat (d'imprimante laser) engine ❏ **base de données** database; **mettre qch dans une base de données** to enter sth into a database; **base de données client- serveur** client-server database; **base de données de consommateurs** customer database; **base de données relationnelle** relational database (**d**) Mktg base ❏ **base de clientèle** customer base; **base de consommateurs** customer base; **base de sondage** sample base

basé, -e adj **être basé à** to be based in; **leur entreprise est basée à Sophia Antipolis** their company is based in Sophia Antipolis

Basic nm Ordinat BASIC

bâtiment nm (**a**) (édifice) building; **nous avons une cantine dans le bâtiment** we have a canteen in the building or on the premises ❏ **bâtiment administratif** administration building (**b**) (secteur) **le bâtiment, l'industrie du bâtiment** the building trade or industry

battage nm (publicité) hype; **faire du battage autour de qn/qch** to hype sb/sth up ❏ **battage médiatique** media hype; **battage publicitaire** hype

baud nm Ordinat baud; **à (une vitesse de) 1 200 bauds** at 1,200 baud

bavarder vi Ordinat to chat

BBS nm Ordinat (abrév **bulletin board system**) BBS

BBZ nm Compta (abrév **budget base zéro**) ZBB

BCE nf (abrév **Banque centrale européenne**) European central bank

BD nf Ordinat (abrév **base de données**) dbase

beau papier nm Fin fine bill

BEI nf (abrév **Banque européenne d'investissement**) EIB

bénef nm Fam (abrév **bénéfice**) profit

bénéfice nm (**a**) (gain) profit; **bénéfice de ou pour l'exercice 2002** profits for the year 2002; **rapporter des bénéfices** to yield a profit; **donner ou enregistrer un bénéfice** to show a profit; **réaliser ou dégager un bénéfice** to make a profit; **vendre qch à bénéfice** to sell sth at a profit ❏ **bénéfice par action** earnings per share;

bénéfice après impôts after-tax profit; **bénéfice avant l'impôt** pre-tax profit; **bénéfice brut** gross profit; **bénéfice cumulé** cumulative profit; **bénéfices distribuables** distributable profits; **bénéfice escompté** desired profit; **bénéfices exceptionnels** excess profits; **bénéfices de l'exercice** current earnings; **bénéfice d'exploitation** operating *or* trading profit; **bénéfices extraordinaires** excess profits; **bénéfices financiers** interest received; **bénéfices de fin d'exercice** year-end profits; **bénéfice fiscal** taxable profit; **bénéfice imposable** taxable profit; **bénéfice marginal** marginal profit; **bénéfice net** after-tax profit, net profit; **bénéfice net dilué par action** fully diluted earnings per share; **bénéfices non distribués** undistributed profits, retained earnings, earnings retained; **bénéfices premiers par action** primary earnings per share; **bénéfice transféré** profit transferred (**b**) *(avantage)* benefit; **petits bénéfices** perks ❑ *Mktg* **bénéfice consommateur** *(d'un produit)* consumer benefit

bénéficiaire 1 *adj (entreprise)* profit-making; *(compte)* in credit; *(bilan)* showing a profit
 2 *nmf* (**a**) *Assur, Jur* beneficiary (**b**) *(d'un chèque)* payee ❑ **bénéficiaire conjoint** joint beneficiary

bénéficier *vt ind* **bénéficier de qch** to benefit by *or* from sth; **ils bénéficient de la nouvelle politique fiscale du gouvernement** they are benefiting from the government's new tax policy

bénévole 1 *adj (travail)* voluntary; **être employé à titre bénévole** to do voluntary work
 2 *nmf* volunteer, voluntary worker

BEP *nm* *(abrév* **brevet d'études professionnelles***)* = vocational diploma

Bercy *nm (ministère)* = the French Ministry of Finance

besoin *nm* need, requirement; **notre produit répond au besoin fondamental du consommateur** our product meets the consumer's basic need ❑ *Compta* **besoins de crédit** borrowing requirements; *Compta* **besoins en fonds de roulement** working capital requirements; *Compta* **besoins de trésorerie** cash requirements

BF *nf (abrév* **Banque de France***)* Bank of France

bibande *Tél* **1** *adj* dual-band
 2 *nm* dual-band mobile phone

bibliothèque *nf Ordinat* library ❑ **bibliothèque de programmes** program library

biclic *nm Ordinat* double click

bicliquer *vi Ordinat* to double-click

bidirectionnel, -elle *adj Ordinat* bidirectional

bidon *adj Fam (société)* phoney; *(chèque)* dud

bidouilleur, -euse *nm,f Ordinat* hacker, expert user

bien *nm* possession; *Jur* assets; **biens** possessions, property; **biens et services** goods and services ❑ *Compta* **biens capitaux** capital goods *or* items; **bien de consommation** consumer product *or* good; **bien de consommation durable** consumer durable; **biens de consommation à forte rotation** fast-moving consumer goods; **biens de consommation non durables** disposable goods; *Compta* **biens corporels** tangible assets; **biens durables** (consumer) durables, durable goods; **biens non durables** soft commodities; **biens d'équipement** capital goods; **biens d'équipement ménagers** household goods; **biens fonciers** landed property; **biens immeubles, biens immobiliers** real assets, real estate, immovable property; **biens industriels** industrial goods; **biens intermédiaires** semi-finished goods, intermediate goods; **biens manufacturés** manufactured goods; **biens meubles, biens mobiliers** personal property *or* estate, movable property; **biens personnels** personal property; **biens de première nécessité** staples; **biens de production** capital goods, producer goods; *Compta* **biens sociaux** corporate assets *or* funds

> ❝
> Au dernier trimestre 2001, déjà, l'investissement avait reculé de 12%! Et l'indicateur avancé de l'investissement – les commandes de **biens d'équipement** – est ressorti en baisse de plus de 15% en janvier. Pourtant, les analystes expliquent que, en tenant compte de la volatilité, ce chiffre annonce un rebond et l'enclenchement d'une dynamique positive.
> ❞

bien-être *nm* (material) well-being ❑ **l'économie du bien-être** the welfare economy

bien-fonds *nm* real estate

bilan *nm* (**a**) *Compta* statement; **bilan (comptable)** balance sheet; **dresser** *ou* **établir** *ou* **faire un bilan** to draw up a balance sheet ❑ **bilan annuel** annual accounts; **bilan condensé** summary balance sheet; **bilan consolidé** consolidated balance sheet; **bilan de l'exercice** end-of-year balance sheet; **bilan financier** financial statement; **bilan de fin d'exercice** end-of-year balance sheet; **bilan de groupe** consolidated balance sheet; **bilan intérimaire** interim statement; **bilan de liquidation** statement of affairs; **bilan d'ouverture** opening balance sheet; **bilan prévisionnel** forecast balance sheet
 (**b**) *(appréciation)* appraisal, assessment; **dresser le bilan de ses pertes** to add up one's losses; **faire le bilan de santé d'une entreprise** to as-

sess *or* evaluate the state of a company ❏ *bilan de carrière* = summary of one's employment record; *bilan de compétence* = summary of one's skills

　(c) *(rapport)* report ❏ *Mktg bilan commercial* market report; *Fin bilan hebdomadaire* weekly trading report; *Fin bilan social* social report

　(d) *Fin (de l'actif, des responsabilités)* schedule; *déposer son bilan* to file one's petition (in bankruptcy)

　(e) *Banque (d'un compte)* balance

bilatéral, -e *adj (accord, contrat)* bilateral

bilatéralisme *nm* bilateralism

billet *nm* (a) *(pour voyager)* ticket ❏ *billet d'abonnement* season ticket; *billet d'aller Br* single *or Am* one-way ticket; *billet d'aller (et) retour Br* return *or Am* round-trip ticket; *billet apex* APEX ticket; *billet d'avion* plane ticket; *billet circulaire Br* return *or Am* round-trip ticket; *billet informatisé* automated ticket; *billet open* open ticket; *billet de retour Br* return *or Am* round-trip ticket; *billet simple Br* single *or Am* one-way ticket; *billet en stand-by* standby ticket; *billet de transport* ticket

　(b) *Fin (effet)* note, bill ❏ *billet de complaisance* accommodation bill; *billet à longue échéance* long-term bill; *billet à moyen terme* medium-term bill; *billet à ordre* note of hand, promissory note; *billet au porteur* bearer bill; *billet de reconnaissance de dettes* IOU; *billet du Trésor* Treasury bill; *billet de trésorerie* commercial paper

　(c) *(argent)* **billet (de banque)** *Br* (bank)note, *Am* bill; *un billet de cent euros* a hundred-euro *Br* note *or Am* bill ❏ *billet vert* dollar

billétique *nf Banque, Ordinat* cash dispenser technology

billion *nm* trillion

bi-média *adj* bi-media

binaire *adj Ordinat* binary

BIOS *nm Ordinat (abrév Basic Input/Output System)* BIOS

bip *nm (appareil)* pager, beeper

BIPE *nm (abrév Bureau d'informations et de prévisions économiques)* = autonomous organization which forecasts economic trends and provides a consultation service for businesses

biper *vt* to page

BIRD *nf (abrév Banque internationale pour la reconstruction et le développement)* IBRD

bisynchrone *adj* bisynchronous, bisync

BIT *nm (abrév Bureau international du travail)* ILO

bit *nm Ordinat* bit; *bits par seconde* bits per second

bitmap *adj & nm Ordinat* bitmap

blâme *nm Admin (sanction)* reprimand; *donner un blâme à qn* to reprimand sb; *recevoir un blâme* to be reprimanded

blâmer *vt Admin* to reprimand

blanc, blanche 1 *adj Ordinat* blank
　2 *nm (dans un document)* blank (space)

blanchiment *nm (de l'argent)* laundering

blanchir *vt (argent)* to launder

blindage *nm Ordinat* shield

blister *nm* blister pack; *être vendu sous blister* to be sold in blister packs

bloc *nm* (a) *(ensemble) (de marchandises)* job lot; *(de titres)* parcel; *acheter qch en bloc* to buy the whole stock of sth (b) *(zone)* bloc ❏ *bloc monétaire* currency bloc; *bloc sterling* sterling bloc (c) *(groupe d'actionnaires)* shareholding ❏ *bloc de contrôle* controlling shareholding (d) *(au sein d'une entreprise)* department (e) *Ordinat (de texte)* block

blocage *nm* (a) *Écon (des tarifs, des fonds, des crédits)* freeze; *blocage des prix et des salaires* price and wage freeze (b) *Ordinat blocage majuscule* caps lock

bloc-notes *nm* notepad, memo pad ❏ *Ordinat bloc-notes électronique* electronic notepad

blocus *nm (economic)* blockade

bloqué, -e *adj Ordinat (écran)* frozen

bloquer *vt (chèque)* to stop; *(compte)* to freeze, to block; *(prix, salaires, crédits)* to freeze

blue chip *nm* blue chip

BO *nm (abrév Bulletin officiel)* = official listing of all new laws and decrees

BOCE *nm (abrév Bulletin officiel des Communautés européennes)* = official listing of all new EC directives

bogue *nm Ordinat* bug ❏ *bogue de l'an 2000* millennium bug; *bogue de logiciel* software bug

bogué, -e *adj Ordinat* bug-ridden

boîte *nf* (a) *(pour ranger)* box ❏ *boîte archive* archive file; *boîte de classement* box file (b) *(pour le courrier)* *boîte à ou aux lettres Br* post box, *Am* mailbox; *boîte postale* post office box (c) *Ordinat boîte de dialogue* dialogue box; *boîte à disquettes* diskette box; *boîte à ou aux lettres électronique* mailbox ; *boîte à outils* toolbox (d) *Fam (entreprise)* firm

boîtier *nm Ordinat* case ❏ *boîtier de commande* command box; *boîtier vertical* tower

bon¹, bonne *adj* (a) *(investissement, crédit)* good; *acheter qch à bon marché* to buy sth cheap (b) *(valable)* valid; *ce billet est bon pour trois mois* this ticket is valid for three months

bon² *nm* (a) *(papier)* voucher, coupon ❏ *bon d'achat* discount voucher *(for future purchases)*; *bon d'annulation* cancellation form; *bon de* *caisse (justifiant sortie de fonds)* cash voucher; *Compta* interest-bearing note; **bon de commande** order form, purchase order; **bon à délivrer** freight release; **bon d'entrée** stock received form; **bon d'épargne** savings certificate; **bon d'expédition** dispatch note, consignment note; *Fin* **bon pour euros** *(sur chèque)* = letters printed on cheque before amount to be written in figures; **bon de garantie** guarantee, guarantee slip; **bon de livraison** delivery note; **bon à moyen terme négociable** medium term note; **bon de petite caisse** petty cash voucher; **bon de réception des marchandises** receipt note; **bon de réduction** money-off coupon *or* voucher; **bon de remboursement** money-off voucher; **bon de réservation** reservation form; **bon de sortie** stock issued form; *Douanes* **bon de visite** inspection order

(b) *Fin* bond ❏ **bon d'épargne** savings bond *or* certificate; **bon nominatif** registered bond; **bon au porteur** bearer bond; **bon de souscription d'actions** equity *or* subscription warrant; *Bourse* **bon de souscription de parts de créateurs d'entreprise** = stock option in start-up company with tax privileges; **bon du Trésor** Treasury bill; *(obligation à long terme)* Treasury bond

> **"**
> À l'automne 1997, les **bons de souscription de parts de créateurs d'entreprise** (BSPCE) sont créés : il s'agit de stock-options à la fiscalité allégée pour les entreprises de moins de sept ans, non cotées et évoluant dans des secteurs innovants, à l'exclusion des activités bancaires, financières, d'assurances, de gestion ou de location d'immeuble ...
> **"**

bonification *nf* (a) *(rabais)* reduction (b) *(prime)* bonus ❏ *Assur* **bonification pour non sinistre** no-claims bonus

bonifié, -e *adj Fin (prêt)* soft, at a reduced rate of interest

bonus *nm* (a) *(avantage)* bonus ❏ *Mktg* **bonus produit** product bonus (b) *Assur* no-claims bonus; **j'ai un bonus de 35 pour cent sur mon assurance** I have a 35 percent no-claims bonus on my insurance

bonus-malus *nm Assur* no-claims bonus system

> **"**
> La France est le dernier pays – avec le Luxembourg – à pratiquer une réduction automatique du coût de l'assurance quand il y a absence de sinistres. Or, selon Bruxelles, ce **bonus-malus** empêche les compagnies étrangères de pénétrer le marché français, et coûte, finalement, plus cher à l'assuré.
> **"**

bookmark *nm Ordinat* bookmark

booléen, -enne *adj Ordinat* Boolean

boom *nm Fin* boom

boomerang *nm* **faire boomerang** to boomerang

bordereau *nm* note, slip; *(formulaire)* form; *(de marchandises)* invoice, account; *(dans un devis)* list, schedule; **suivant bordereau ci-inclus** as per enclosed statement ❏ **bordereau d'achat** *(dans le commerce)* purchase note; *Bourse* bought note; *Compta* **bordereau de caisse** cash statement; *Compta* **bordereau de compte** statement of account; **bordereau de débit** debit note; *Banque* **bordereau de dépôt** paying-in slip; **bordereau de douanes** customs note; *Banque* **bordereau d'encaissement** paying-in slip; **bordereau d'envoi** dispatch note, consignment note, waybill; *Fin* **bordereau d'escompte** list of bills for discount; **bordereau d'expédition** dispatch note, consignment note, waybill; **bordereau de livraison** delivery note; **bordereau (des) prix** price list; *Banque* **bordereau de remboursement** withdrawal slip; *Banque* **bordereau de remise (d'espèces** *ou* **de chèques)** paying-in slip; **bordereau de réservations** reservation sheet; *Banque* **bordereau de retrait** withdrawal slip; *Compta* **bordereau de saisie** accounting entry sheet; **bordereau de salaire** wage slip, salary advice; *(liste des salaires payés)* wages sheet; **bordereau de vente** list of sales; *Banque* **bordereau de versement** paying-in slip, deposit slip

bordure *nf Ordinat (d'un paragraphe, d'une cellule)* border

bouché, -e *adj (marché)* clogged

bouche à oreille *nm Mktg* word-of-mouth advertising

boucler 1 *vt Bourse (position)* to close (out) **2 se boucler** *vpr Ordinat (lignes)* to wrap

bouder *vt (produits)* to refuse to buy, to boycott

bouillon *nm Fam* **boire le bouillon** *(faire faillite)* to go under

boule de commande *nf Ordinat* trackball

bourgeois, -e *adj* middle-class

bourgeoisement *adv Admin* **occuper bourgeoisement un local** to occupy premises for residential purposes only

bourgeoisie *nf* middle class

bourrage (de) papier *nm Ordinat* paper jam

bourse *nf* (a) **la Bourse (des valeurs)** the Stock Exchange, the Stock Market; **la Bourse de Londres** the London Stock Exchange; **la Bourse monte/est calme** the market is rising/is quiet; **en** *ou* **à la Bourse** on the Stock Exchange *or* Stock Market; **jouer à la Bourse** to play the market, to speculate on the Stock Market; **coup de Bourse** deal on the Stock Exchange ❑ *Bourse de commerce* commodities exchange; *Bourse coulisse* unlisted market; *Bourse d'instruments financiers à terme* financial futures exchange; *Bourse de(s) marchandises* commodities exchange

(b) *(lieu) bourse de l'emploi* = employment exchange; *bourse du travail (réunion)* = meeting of local trade unions for the purpose of reaching agreement on how best to defend their interests and provide community services; *(lieu)* = local trade union centre

boursicotage *nm Bourse* dabbling *or* speculating on the Stock Market

boursicoter *vi Bourse* to dabble *or* speculate on the Stock Market

> "
> En dehors du cadre de l'actionnariat salarié, la baisse de la Bourse a eu d'autant plus d'effet qu'il n'existait aucun élément pour l'amortir. Certains cadres se disent "calmés" de leur envie de **boursicoter**.
> "

boursicoteur, -euse, boursicotier, -ère *nm,f Bourse* small-time speculator

boursier, -ère *Bourse* 1 *adj (opérations)* Stock Exchange, Stock Market
   2 *nm,f* (Stock Exchange) operator

boutique *nf Br* shop, *Am* store; **tenir boutique** to run a shop; **fermer boutique** to close down, to shut up shop; **parler boutique** to talk shop ❑ *boutique franchisée* franchise outlet; *boutique hors taxe* duty-free shop

boutiquier, -ère *nm,f Br* shopkeeper, *Am* storekeeper

bouton *nm Ordinat* button ❑ *bouton de défilement* scroll button; *bouton Démarrer* start button; *bouton de navigation* navigation button; *bouton de réinitialisation* reset button; *bouton de souris* mouse button

boycott, boycottage *nm* boycott

boycotter *vt* to boycott

BP *nm (abrév* **boîte postale)** PO Box

BPA *nm (abrév* **bénéfice par action)** EPS

BPE *nm Fin (abrév* **bon pour euros)** *(sur chèque)* = letters printed on cheque before amount to be written in figures

bpp *nmpl Ordinat (abrév* **bits par pouce)** bpi

bps *nmpl Ordinat (abrév* **bits par seconde)** bps

brader *vt* to sell off, to sell cheaply

braderie *nf* clearance sale

brainstorming *nm (activité)* brainstorming; *(séance)* brainstorming session

branche *nf (de l'industrie)* branch, sector

branchement *nm Ordinat* connection

bras droit *nm (personne)* right-hand man

brevet *nm* (a) *(d'invention)* patent; **demande de brevet déposée** *(sur produit)* patent pending; **prendre un brevet** to take out a patent ❑ *brevet de fabrication* manufacturing licence; *brevet d'inventeur, brevet d'invention* (letters) patent (b) *(diplôme)* diploma ❑ *brevet d'études professionnelles* = vocational diploma; *brevet de technicien supérieur* = advanced vocational training certificate

breveté, -e *adj (invention)* patented; *(personne)* holding letters patent

breveter *vt (invention)* to patent; **faire breveter qch** to take out a patent for sth

brief *nm* brief

briefing *nm* briefing

briseur, -euse *nm,f briseur de grève* strikebreaker

broche *nf Ordinat* pin

brochure *nf* brochure ❑ *brochure publicitaire* publicity brochure

brouillard *nm* day book ❑ *Compta brouillard de caisse* cash book

brouillon *nm* (a) *(ébauche)* (rough) draft, rough copy ❑ *(papier) brouillon* *Br* scrap *or* *Am* scratch paper (b) *Ordinat* **version brouillon** draft version

brouteur *nm Ordinat* browser

brut, -e 1 *adj* (a) *(pétrole, minerai)* crude (b) *(bénéfice, valeur, poids)* gross (c) *(données, chiffres, statistiques)* raw
   2 *adv* gross; **gagner 20 000 euros brut** to earn 20,000 euros gross, to gross 20,000 euros
   3 *nm* crude (oil)

BSPCE *nm Bourse (abrév* **bon de souscription de parts de créateurs d'entreprise)** = stock option in a start-up company with tax privileges

BTP *nm (abrév* **bâtiment et travaux publics)** construction industry

BTS *nm (abrév* **brevet de technicien supérieur)** = advanced vocational training certificate

Buba *nf (abrév* **Bundesbank) la Buba** the Bundesbank

budget *nm* (a) *(plan financier)* budget; **inscrire qch au budget** to budget for sth; **tenir le budget** to keep within budget ❑ *budget annuel* annual budget; *budget des approvisionnements* purchase budget; *Compta budget base zéro* zero-base budgeting; *budget des charges* overhead budget, cost budget; *budget commercial* sales budget; *budget des dépenses* expense budget; *budget équilibré* balanced budget; *Écon budget de l'État* state budget; *budget d'exploitation* operating budget; *budget d'exploitation prévisionnel* forecast operating budget; **budget familial** household budget; **budget de fonctionnement** operating budget; **budget glissant** rolling budget; **budget global** master budget, overall budget; *Compta* **budget d'investissement** *ou* **des investissements** capital budget; **budget marketing** marketing budget; **budget du ménage** household budget; **budget mensuel** monthly budget; **budget prévisionnel** provisional budget; **budget de production** production budget; **budget promotionnel** promotion budget; **budget publicitaire, budget de publicité** advertising *or* publicity budget; **budget des recettes** revenue budget; *Compta* **budget renouvelable** continuous budget; **budget de trésorerie** cash budget; **budget des ventes** sales budget (**b**) *(dans la publicité, dans le marketing)* account; **l'agence s'est assuré le budget Brook** the agency has secured the Brook account

budgétaire *adj (année) Br* financial, *Am* fiscal; *(contrainte, contrôle, gestion)* budgetary

budgétisation *nf* budgeting ❑ *Compta* **budgétisation base zéro** zero-base budgeting

budgétiser *vt* to include in the budget, to budget for

bug *nm Ordinat* bug

bulle *nf Bourse* **bulle boursière** Stock Market bubble, surge on the Stock Market; **bulle spéculative** speculative bubble

> **"**
>
> Bien sûr, la **bulle boursière** a en partie éclaté, de façon relativement bénigne. Mais d'énormes déséquilibres subsistent. Au Japon d'abord, où la dette totale … atteint désormais trois fois le PIB annuel du pays.
>
> **"**

bulletin *nm (communiqué)* bulletin; *(d'entreprise)* newsletter; *(formulaire)* form ❑ **bulletin d'abonnement** subscription form; **bulletin d'annulation** cancellation form; **bulletin de bagages** *Br* luggage ticket, *Am* baggage check; **bulletin de commande** order form; *Bourse* **Bulletin de la cote officielle** Stock Exchange Daily Official List; *Bourse* **bulletin des cours** official (Stock Exchange) price list; **bulletin d'expédition** dispatch note, consignment note, waybill; **bulletin de garantie** (certificate of) guarantee; **bulletin d'inscription** registration form; **Bulletin officiel** = official listing of all new laws and decrees; **Bulletin officiel des Communautés européennes** = official listing of all new EC directives; **bulletin de paie** pay (advice) slip, salary advice note; **bulletin de salaire** pay (advice) slip, salary advice note; *Bourse* **bulletin de souscription d'actions** share subscription form, share application form; **bulletin de vente** sales note; **bulletin**

de versement paying-in *or* deposit slip; **bulletin de vote** voting paper

bulletin-réponse *nm* reply form

bureau *nm* (**a**) *(agence)* office ❑ **bureau d'affaires** business centre; **Bureau d'aide sociale** welfare office; **bureau des brevets** patent office; **bureau du cadastre** Land Registry Office; **bureau de change** bureau de change; *Can* **Bureau du Contrôleur Général** Office of the Controller General; **bureau de cotation** credit *Br* agency *or* *Am* bureau; **bureau de douane** custom(s) house, customs office; **bureau d'enregistrement** registration office; **bureau d'évaluation** credit *Br* agency *or* *Am* bureau; **bureau d'expédition** forwarding office, shipping office; **bureau d'exportation** export office; **bureau d'information** information office; **Bureau international du travail** International Labour Organization; **bureau de perception** tax office; **bureau de placement** employment agency *or* bureau; **bureau de poste** post office; **bureau de publicité** advertising agency; **bureau de renseignements** information office; **bureau de tourisme** tourist office; **bureau de traduction** translation agency; **Bureau de vérification de la publicité** = French advertising standards authority, *Br* ≃ ASA

(**b**) *(lieu)* office ❑ **bureau central** head office; **bureau informatisé** electronic office, paperless office; **bureau paysager** open-plan office; **bureau principal** head office

(**c**) *(meuble)* desk ❑ **bureau d'inscriptions** registration desk; **bureau de renseignements** enquiry *or* information desk; **bureau des réservations** reservation desk

(**d**) *(personnel)* (office) staff

(**e**) *(commission)* committee; **constituer le bureau** *(d'une société)* to set up a committee

(**f**) *(service)* department ❑ **bureau d'achat** purchase department; **bureau d'études** design *or* planning department; *(de recherche)* R&D department; **bureau d'étude technique** engineering and design department

(**g**) *(port)* port ❑ **bureau de départ** port of departure; **bureau de destination** port of destination; **bureau d'entrée** port of entry; **bureau de passage** port of transit

(**h**) *Ordinat (écran)* desktop ❑ **bureau actif** active desktop; **bureau électronique** electronic desktop

bureaucrate *nmf* bureaucrat

bureaucratie *nf (système)* bureaucracy; *(ensemble des fonctionnaires)* bureaucrats

bureaucratique *adj* bureaucratic

bureaucratiser *vt* to bureaucratize

Bureautique® *nf* office automation

bus *nm Ordinat* bus ❑ **bus d'adresses** address bus; **bus de contrôle** control bus; **bus de don-**

nées data bus; **bus multimédia** multimedia bus

business nm Fam business; **faire du business** to be in business; **il est dans le business** he's in the business □ **business angel** (commanditaire) angel

> **"**
>
> Ils ont été (ou sont encore) chef d'entreprise ou cadre dirigeant, et ils ont de l'argent. La création d'entreprise les titille et ils sont prêts à investir dans de jeunes sociétés en panne de capitaux. Ce sont les **business angels**:

des investisseurs privés qui font aussi profiter l'entreprise de leurs conseils, de leur savoir-faire et de leurs relations.

"

but nm goal, aim; **à but lucratif** profit-making; **à but non lucratif** Br non-profit-making, Am not-for-profit

butineur nm Ordinat browser

BVP nm (abrév **Bureau de vérification de la publicité**) = French advertising standards authority, Br ≃ ASA

Cc

c *n Anciennement (abrév* **centime**) centime

CA *nm* (**a**) *(abrév* **chiffre d'affaires**) turnover (**b**) *Can (abrév* **comptable agréé**) *Br* ≃ CA, *Am* ≃ CPA

cabinet *nm* office; *(de juge)* chambers □ *cabinet d'affaires* business consultancy; *cabinet d'assurances* insurance firm; *cabinet d'audit* audit company; *cabinet conseil* consultancy; *cabinet de conseil en gestion* management consultancy; *Mktg* *cabinet d'études* market research firm; *cabinet d'expertise comptable* accounting firm; *cabinet d'experts-conseils* consultancy; *cabinet juridique* law firm; *cabinet de recrutement* recruitment agency; *cabinet de traduction* translation agency

câble *nm Ordinat* cable; *câbles* cabling, cables □ *câble d'imprimante* printer cable; *câble parallèle* parallel cable; *câble série* serial cable

câblé, -e *adj Ordinat* hard-wired

CAC *nf (abrév* **Compagnie des agents de change**) = French stockbrokers' association; *l'indice CAC 40, le CAC 40* the CAC 40 (index) *(main Paris Stock Exchange Index)*

> **"**
> Le **CAC 40** n'est pas l'indice de la production industrielle en France, mais l'indice qui traduit le tonus, la vitalité, les résultats des sociétés, choisies parmi les principales capitalisations, dont Paris est le principal marché de cotation.
> **"**

cache *nm Ordinat* cache □ *cache du disque dur* hard disk cache; *cache externe* external cache

caché, -e *adj (fonds)* hidden

cachet *nm (sceau)* seal; *(tampon)* stamp □ *cachet de douane* customs seal; *cachet de fabrique* maker's trademark; *cachet de la poste* postmark; *le cachet de la poste faisant foi* date of postmark will be taken as proof of postage

cacheter *vt* to seal; *envoyer qch sous pli cacheté* to send sth in a sealed envelope

CAD *nm (abrév* **Comité d'aide au développement**) DAC

c.-à-d. *(abrév* **c'est-à-dire**) ie

cadastrage *nm Admin* land registration

cadastral, -e *adj Admin* cadastral

cadastre *nm Admin (registre)* land register, cadastre; *(administration)* cadastral survey office, ≃ land registry

cadastrer *vt Admin* to enter in the land register

caddie® *nm Ordinat (pour achats en ligne) Br* shopping basket, *Am* shopping cart

cadeau *nm Mktg* **cadeau (publicitaire)** free gift, freebie

cadence *nf* rate □ *cadence de production* rate of production; *cadence de travail* work rate

cadencé, -e *adj Ordinat* **cadencé à** running at

cadrage *nm Ordinat (d'objets)* positioning; *(de caractères)* alignment

cadre *nm* (**a**) *(dans une entreprise)* executive, manager; **les cadres** the managerial staff, the management; **jeune cadre** junior executive; **passer cadre** to become an executive, to be promoted to management □ *cadre commercial* sales executive; *cadres dirigeants* senior executives, top management; *cadre d'entreprise* company executive, company manager; *cadres moyens* middle management; *cadres supérieurs* senior executives, top management
(**b**) *(registre)* list of staff; **rayé des cadres** dismissed; **hors cadre** seconded, on secondment (**c**) *(dans un formulaire)* space, box; *Ordinat (pour graphique)* box; **cadre réservé à l'administration** *(sur formulaire)* for official *or* office use only
(**d**) *(domaine)* framework; **dans le cadre de ce programme d'expansion** as part of this expansion programme; **cela n'entre pas dans le cadre de mes fonctions** it falls outside the scope of my responsibilities, it's outside my remit
(**e**) *(environnement)* environment □ *cadre de travail* working environment

cadrer 1 *vt Ordinat* to position
2 *vi* to be consistent (**avec** with); **les chiffres que vous nous avez communiqués ne cadrent pas avec les nôtres** the figures you gave us don't tally with *or* are not consistent with ours

caduc, caduque *adj Jur (legs)* null and void; *(accord, contrat)* lapsed; *(dette)* barred by the Statute of Limitations

caducité *nf Jur* lapsing

CAF 1 adj (abrév **coût, assurance, fret**) CIF
   2 nf (abrév **Caisse d'allocations familiales**) = child benefit office

cafteur nm Ordinat cookie

cage nf Ordinat scroll box

cahier nm (**a**) (livre) notebook ❏ Compta **cahier des achats** purchase ledger (**b**) (liste) **cahier des charges** (d'un contrat) terms and conditions; (d'une vente) specifications; **cahier des revendications syndicales** claims register

CAHT nm (abrév **chiffre d'affaires hors taxes**) pre-tax turnover

caisse nf (**a**) Fin (coffre) cash box; (dans un magasin, un garage) cash desk; (dans un supermarché) checkout; **les caisses de l'État** the coffers of the State; **payez à la caisse** pay at the (cash) desk or at the till; **tenir la caisse** to be in charge of the cash; **passer à la caisse** to go to the cash desk; (dans un supermarché) to go through the checkout; (payer) to pay; (se faire payer) to be paid; (se faire licencier) to be paid off ❏ **caisse comptable** cash register, till; **caisse électronique** electronic billing machine, electric service till; **caisse enregistreuse** cash register, till
   (**b**) (argent) cash (in hand); (recette) takings; **faire la** ou **sa caisse** to balance the cash, to do the till, Br to cash up; **avoir 4000 euros en caisse** to have 4,000 euros in hand ❏ **caisse d'amortissement** sinking fund; **caisse noire** slush fund
   (**c**) (pour marchandises) case, box; **mettre des marchandises en caisse** to case or crate goods ❏ **caisse** ou **boîte d'emballage** packing case
   (**d**) (organisme) fund ❏ **caisse de chômage** unemployment fund; **caisse de compensation** = equalization fund for payments such as child benefit, sickness benefit, pensions; **caisse de garantie** credit guarantee fund, compensation fund; Can **caisse populaire** credit union; **caisse de prévoyance** provident fund; **caisse de retraite** pension fund; **caisse de retraite des cadres** executive pension fund; **caisse de retraite maison** occupational pension fund
   (**e**) Banque **Caisse des dépôts et consignations** = public financial institution which manages National Savings Bank funds and local community funds; **caisse d'épargne** savings bank; **caisse d'épargne-logement** Br ≃ building society, Am ≃ savings and loan association; **Caisse nationale d'épargne** ≃ National Savings Bank; **caisse régionale** ≃ local (bank) branch
   (**f**) Admin **caisse d'allocations familiales** = child benefit office; **Caisse nationale d'assurance vieillesse** = French government department dealing with benefit payments relating to old age; **caisse primaire d'assurance maladie** = French government department dealing with

health insurance; **caisse de la Sécurité sociale** social security office

> **"**
> "C'est assez simple. S'il n'y avait pas 2,5 millions de chômeurs, il y aurait de l'argent qui rentrerait dans les **caisses de retraite**. Et si ça ne suffisait pas, on pourrait peut-être ponctionner un petit peu sur les profits des grandes entreprises pour compenser."
> **"**

caissier, -ère nm,f (dans un restaurant, un magasin) cashier; (dans un supermarché) checkout operator; (dans une banque) cashier, teller ❏ **caissier de nuit** (dans un hôtel) night auditor; **caissier principal** chief or head cashier

calcul nm calculation; **faire** ou **effectuer un calcul** to make a calculation; **faire une erreur de calcul** to miscalculate

calculable adj (prix) calculable; (dégâts) estimable

calculateur, -trice 1 nm Ordinat (desktop) calculator ❏ **calculateur électronique** electronic computer
   2 nf **calculatrice** calculator ❏ **calculatrice de bureau** desk calculator; **calculatrice imprimante** print-out calculator; **calculatrice de poche** pocket calculator

calculer 1 vt to calculate, to work out
   2 se calculer vpr to be calculated (**sur** on)

calculette nf (pocket) calculator

calendrier nm (**a**) (tableau) calendar (**b**) (emploi du temps) timetable, schedule; **établir un calendrier** to draw up a timetable or schedule; **mon calendrier ne le permet pas** my timetable or schedule does not allow it ❏ **calendrier de campagne** media schedule; **calendrier de remboursement** repayment schedule

calibrage nm (de vis, de boulons) grading

calibrer vt (vis, boulons) to grade

calme adj (marché, Bourse) quiet, calm; **nos affaires sont calmes en août** business is quiet in August

cambial, -e adj Fin exchange

cambiste Fin **1** adj (marché) foreign exchange
   2 nmf foreign exchange dealer or broker

camembert nm Fam pie chart

camion nm Br lorry, Am truck ❏ **camion frigorifique** refrigerated Br lorry or Am truck; **camion semi-remorque** Br articulated lorry, Am trailer truck

camion-citerne nm tanker

camionnage nm (prix, service) haulage, carriage, Am truckage; **une entreprise de camionnage** a haulage firm, Am a trucking business

camionner *vt* to carry, to haul, *Am* to truck

camionnette *nf Br* van, *Am* panel truck

camionneur *nm* (**a**) *(entrepreneur) Br* haulier, *Am* trucker (**b**) *(chauffeur) Br* lorry driver, *Am* truck driver

camoufler *vt Compta* **camoufler un bilan** to window-dress the accounts

campagne *nf* campaign; **lancer une campagne** to launch a campaign ❑ *campagne d'affichage* poster campaign; *campagne commerciale* marketing campaign; *campagne de dénigrement* countermarketing; *campagne de diffamation* smear campaign; *campagne intensive* saturation campaign; *campagne de presse* press campaign; *campagne de productivité* productivity campaign *or* drive; *campagne de promotion* promotion(al) campaign; *campagne publicitaire, campagne de publicité* advertising *or* publicity campaign; *campagne de publicité directe* direct mail campaign; *campagne de recrutement* recruitment campaign *or* drive; *campagne de saturation* saturation campaign; *campagne teasing* teaser campaign; *campagne télévisuelle* television campaign; *campagne de vente* sales campaign *or* drive

canal *nm Écon, Mktg* channel ❑ *canal de communication* communications channel; *canal de communication commerciale* marketing communications channel; *canal de distribution* distribution channel; *canal de distribution court* one-level channel; *canal de distribution long* two-level/three-level channel, conventional marketing channel

> **"**
> Certains doutent cependant que le Net devienne un jour un **canal de distribution** privilégié. "L'immédiateté est un atout de fidélisation, pas de vente," estime ainsi Henri Debruyne, directeur général de Capa Conseil.
> **"**

candidat, -e *nm,f* candidate, applicant (**à** for); **se porter candidat à un poste** to apply for a job

candidature *nf* application (**à** for); **faire acte de candidature** *ou* **poser sa candidature à un poste** to apply for a post; **retirer sa candidature** to withdraw one's application; **date limite de dépôt de candidatures** closing date for applications ❑ *candidature en ligne* e-mail application; *candidature spontanée* unsolicited application

> **"**
> Certaines entreprises d'ailleurs, tel Procter & Gamble, n'acceptent plus que les **candidatures** sur le web ... A ceux qui envoient des courriers papier, on téléphone gentiment en

leur demandant de refaire une **candidature en ligne**: cela ne prend qu'une vingtaine de minutes.
> **"**

cannibalisation *nf (d'un produit)* cannibalization

cannibaliser *vt (produit)* to cannibalize

cannibalisme *nm (d'un produit)* cannibalization

CAO *nf Ordinat (abrév* **conception assistée par ordinateur**) CAD

CAP *nm (abrév* **certificat d'aptitude professionnelle**) = vocational training certificate

cap *nm (étape)* mark; **notre usine a passé le cap des mille employés** our factory has passed the thousand-employee mark

capacité *nf* (**a**) *(possibilité)* capacity ❑ *capacité d'achat* purchasing power; *capacité de crédit* borrowing power *or* capacity; *capacité effective* effective capacity; *capacité d'emprunter* borrowing power *or* capacity; *capacité d'endettement* borrowing capacity; *capacité d'exportation* export potential; *capacité de financement* financing capacity; *capacité d'hébergement (d'un hôtel)* accommodation capacity; *capacité d'importation* import potential; *capacité d'imposition* ability to pay tax; *capacité de production* manufacturing *or* production capacity; *capacité de traitement* handling capacity
(**b**) *(aptitude)* capacity; **la survie de l'entreprise dépendra de sa capacité à innover** this company's survival will depend on its capacity for innovation
(**c**) *(d'un tonneau)* content, capacity ❑ *capacité d'emmagasinage* storage capacity; *capacité linéaire* shelf space
(**d**) *Ordinat* capacity ❑ *capacité de disque* disk capacity; *capacité de disquette* disk capacity; *capacité de mémoire* memory capacity; *capacité de stockage* storage capacity; *capacité de traitement* throughput

capé, -e *adj Fin (taux)* capped

> **"**
> Les adeptes du variable peuvent aussi opter pour un taux **capé** (bloqué à la hausse), qui permet de se garantir contre une hausse inconsidérée du taux à la hausse, tout en se réservant la possibilité de profiter des baisses.
> **"**

caper *vt Fin (taux)* to cap

capitaine d'industrie *nm* captain of industry

capital *nm Fin* capital, assets; **une société au capital de cinq millions d'euros** a company with a capital of *or* capitalized at five million euros; **avoir des capitaux dans une affaire** to have vested interests in a business; **fournir les capitaux pour un projet** to fund or finance a project; **investir** ou **mettre des capitaux dans une affaire** to invest or put capital into a business; **posséder un capital** to have some capital; **les capitaux qui circulent** the capital in circulation; **capital et intérêt** capital and interest ❑ **capital actions** share capital, equity (capital); **capital en actions ordinaires** equity or ordinary share capital; **capital appelé** called-up or present capital; **capital d'apport** initial or start-up capital; **capital autorisé** authorized (share) capital; **capital circulant** circulating or floating capital; **capital déclaré** registered capital; **capital de départ** start-up capital; **capital disponible** available capital; **capital émis** issued (share) capital; **capital d'emprunt, capital emprunté** loan capital; **capital engagé** tied-up capital or trading capital, capital employed; **capital entièrement versé** fully paid capital; **capital d'établissement** invested capital; **capital exigible** current liabilities; **capital existant** physical capital; **capital d'exploitation** Br working capital, Am operating capital; **capitaux fébriles** hot money, floating capital; **capital fixe** fixed capital; **capitaux flottants** hot money, floating capital; **capitaux frais** new capital; **capitaux gelés** frozen assets; **capital humain** (d'une entreprise) manpower; **capital improductif** idle or unproductive capital; **capital initial** initial or start-up capital; **capitaux investis** invested or funded capital; **capital libéré** fully paid capital; **capital nominal** nominal capital; **capital non entièrement versé** partly paid-up capital; **capital d'origine** original capital; **capitaux permanents** capital employed, long-term capital; **capital sur prêt** loan capital; **capital productif d'intérêts** interest-bearing capital; **capitaux propres** Br shareholders' or Am stockholders' equity; **capital de réserve** reserve capital; **capital à risque** risk capital; **capital roulant** circulating capital; **capital de roulement** Br working capital, Am operating capital; **capital social** (issued) share capital, Am capital stock; **capital souscrit** subscribed capital; **capital technique** (technical) equipment; **capital versé** paid-up capital

capital-décès nm Fin death benefit

capitale nf capital (letter)

capitalisable adj capitalizable

capitalisation nf (des intérêts, des revenus) capitalization ❑ **capitalisation boursière** market capitalization

"

Air France, qui joue pourtant dans une autre catégorie (42 millions de voyageurs par an), prend très au sérieux ce petit concurrent. Le géant français n'a pas tort : la **capitalisa-tion boursière** du trublion irlandais dépasse la sienne ! En France, il est déjà numéro 1 sur les vols Paris-Dublin et ne compte pas en rester là.

"

capitaliser vt to capitalize

capitalisme nm capitalism ❑ **capitalisme sauvage** ruthless capitalism

"

"C'est pourquoi le **capitalisme** européen, son Etat providence, son respect des individus qu'ils produisent ou non au sens marchand du terme, me paraît plus moderne et plus facteur de progrès que le **capitalisme sauvage**."

"

capitaliste adj & nmf capitalist

capitalistique adj capital-intensive

capital-marque nm Mktg brand equity; **le succès de notre produit s'explique par la valeur de son capital-marque** the success of our product is down to the value of its brand equity

capital-risque nm venture capital, risk capital

capital-risqueur nm venture capitalist

"

Directeur des pépinières du Nord-Pas-de-Calais et ancien banquier, Dominique Delzenne ne manque jamais de le rappeler : "Les créateurs d'entreprise oublient trop souvent que les banquiers ne sont pas des **capital-risqueurs** et qu'ils n'assurent pas un service public. Ils doivent prendre un minimum de risques avec l'argent que leur confie leurs clients."

"

captif, -ive adj (marché) captive

caractère nm (signe) character, letter; Ordinat character; **écrivez en caractères d'imprimerie** please write in block letters ❑ **caractère accentué** accented or accent character; **caractère alphanumérique** alphanumeric character; **caractère de contrôle** control character; **caractère gras** bold character; **caractère italique** italic character; **caractère joker** wildcard character; **caractère majuscule** upper-case character; **caractère minuscule** lower-case character; **caractères par pouce** characters per inch; **caractères par seconde** characters per second; **caractère spécial** special character

caractéristique nf (d'un produit) characteristic, feature ❑ **caractéristiques techniques** specifications

carence nf Écon insolvency

cargaison nf cargo ❑ **cargaison d'aller** outward cargo; **cargaison mixte** mixed cargo; **car-**

gaison de retour homeward cargo; ***cargaison sèche*** dry cargo

cargo *nm (navire)* cargo ship, freighter □ ***cargo mixte*** passenger and cargo ship

carnet *nm* (a) *(petit cahier)* notebook □ ***carnet d'adresses*** address book; ***carnet ATA*** ATA carnet; *Banque* ***carnet de banque*** pass book, bank book; ***carnet de commandes*** order book; ***carnet communautaire*** community carnet; ***carnet de dépenses*** account book; *Banque* ***carnet de dépôt*** deposit book; ***carnet de passage en douanes*** carnet; ***carnet de quittances*** receipt book; ***carnet de rendez-vous*** appointments book; ***carnet à souche*** counterfoil book; *Banque* ***carnet de versements*** paying-in book (b) *(ensemble)* ***carnet de chèques*** chequebook; ***carnet de voyage*** travel documents

carrière *nf* career; **faire carrière dans qch** to pursue a career in sth

carriérisme *nm* careerism

carriériste *nmf* careerist

carte *nf* (a) *(document officiel)* card □ ***carte d'abonnement*** *(pour les transports)* season ticket; ***carte accréditive*** charge card; ***carte d'adhérent*** membership card; ***carte American Express®*** American Express® card; ***carte Amex®*** Amex card; ***carte bancaire*** bank card; ***carte bancaire à puce*** smart card *(used as a bank card)*; ***carte Bleue®*** = bank card with which purchases are debited directly from the customer's bank account; *Admin* ***carte de commerce*** trading licence; ***carte de crédit*** credit card; ***carte de crédit professionnelle*** company credit card; ***carte de débarquement*** landing card; ***carte de débit*** debit card; ***carte d'échantillons*** sample card; ***carte d'embarquement*** boarding pass; ***carte de fidélité*** loyalty card; ***carte d'identité*** identity card; ***carte d'identité bancaire*** bank card; ***carte Mastercard®*** Mastercard®; ***carte de membre*** membership card; ***carte à mémoire*** smart card; ***carte de paiement*** debit *or* charge card; *Tél* ***carte Pastel*** phonecard *(use of which is debited to one's own phone number)*; *Mktg* ***carte perceptuelle*** perceptual map; ***carte perforée*** punch card; ***carte de presse*** press card; ***carte de publicité*** mailing card; ***carte de publicité directe*** self-mailer; ***carte à puce*** smart card; ***carte de réduction*** discount card; ***carte de représentant*** sales representative's official identity card; ***carte de retrait*** bank card; ***carte de Sécurité sociale*** ≃ National Insurance Card; ***carte de séjour*** residence permit; ***carte syndicale*** union card; ***carte T*** reply-paid card; ***carte de téléphone*** phonecard; *Assur* ***carte verte*** green card; ***carte Visa®*** Visa® card; ***carte de visite*** *(d'une entreprise)* business card

(b) *Ordinat* card □ ***carte accélérateur graphique*** graphics accelerator card; ***carte accélératrice*** accelerator card *or* board; ***carte d'affichage*** display card; ***carte bus*** bus board; ***carte à circuit(s) intégré(s)*** integrated circuit board, IC board; ***carte contrôleur de disque*** disk controller card; ***carte d'extension*** expansion card *or* board; ***carte d'extension mémoire*** memory expansion card *or* board; ***carte fax*** fax card; ***carte graphique*** graphics card; ***carte magnétique*** magnetic card; ***carte mémoire*** memory card; ***carte mère*** motherboard; ***carte modem*** modem card; ***carte réseau*** network card; ***carte RNIS*** ISDN card; ***carte SCSI*** SCSI card; ***carte son*** sound card; ***carte de télécopie*** fax card; ***carte unité centrale*** CPU board; ***carte vidéo*** video card; ***carte vidéo accélératrice*** video accelerator card

(c) **avoir carte blanche (pour faire qch)** to have carte blanche (to do sth); **donner carte blanche à qn** to give sb carte blanche

carte-adaptateur *nf Ordinat* adapter card

cartel *nm Écon* cartel □ ***cartel de l'acier*** steel cartel; ***cartel de prix*** price cartel

cartellisation *nf Écon* cartelization

carte-réponse *nf* reply card

carton *nm (boîte)* cardboard box

cartouche *nf* cartridge □ ***cartouche d'encre*** ink cartridge; *Ordinat* ***cartouche d'enregistrement sur bande audionumérique*** DAT cartridge; ***cartouche de toner*** toner cartridge; *Ordinat* ***cartouche Zip®*** Zip® disk

case *nf* (a) *(sur un formulaire)* box; **cocher la case correspondante** tick the appropriate box (b) *Ordinat* button; *(en forme de boîte)* box □ ***case d'aide*** help button; ***case "annuler"*** cancel button; ***case de dimensionnement*** size box; ***case de fermeture*** close box; ***case d'option*** option box *or* button; ***case de pointage*** check box; ***case de redimensionnement*** size box; ***case de saisie*** input box; ***case zoom*** zoom box (c) *Suisse* ***case postale*** post office box

cash and carry 1 *adj* cash-and-carry **2** *nm* cash-and-carry (store)

cash-flow *nm* cash flow □ ***cash-flow actualisé*** discounted cash flow; ***cash-flow courant*** current cash flow; ***cash-flow marginal*** incremental cash flow; ***cash-flow net*** net cash flow

> ❝
> L'activité de location simple, qui bénéficie d'un environnement particulièrement favorable, devrait contribuer à hauteur de 60% au **cash-flow courant** (résultat courant plus montant des amortissements) en 1999.
> ❞

cassation *nf Jur* annulment, cassation

casse *nf* (a) *(objets cassés)* breakages; **payer la casse** to pay for breakages (b) **mettre qch à la**

casse to scrap sth; **vendre qch à la casse** to sell sth for scrap

casser *vt* **casser les prix** to slash prices

cassette *nf* cassette ❑ *cassette d'alimentation (de copieuse)* paper tray; *cassette audio* audio cassette; *cassette compacte numérique* digital compact cassette; *cassette numérique* digital audio tape; *cassette de toner (d'imprimante)* toner cassette; *cassette vidéo* video (cassette)

catalogage *nm* cataloguing

catalogue *nm* catalogue; **acheter qch sur catalogue** to buy sth from a catalogue ❑ *catalogue d'échantillons* sample book; *catalogue illustré* illustrated catalogue; *catalogue en ligne* on-line catalogue; *catalogue des prix* price list; *catalogue de vente par correspondance* mail-order catalogue

cataloguer *vt (produits)* to catalogue

catégorie *nf* category ❑ *catégorie de produit* product category; *catégorie socio-professionnelle* socio-professional group

cause *nf* **pour cause de** owing to, because of; **fermé pour cause d'inventaire** closed for stocktaking; **absent pour cause de maladie** absent due to ill-health; **bail à céder pour cause de départ** for sale due to relocation

caution *nf Fin* (a) *(gage)* security, guarantee; **demander une caution** to ask for security; **fournir caution** to give security ❑ *caution d'adjudication* bid bond; *caution bancaire, caution de banque* bank guarantee; *caution de soumission* bid bond
(b) *(garant)* surety, guarantor; **être caution de qn, se porter caution pour qn** to stand surety *or* security for sb
(c) *(pour appartement)* deposit; **verser une caution** to pay a deposit; **il faut verser 1000 euros de caution** a deposit of 1,000 euros must be paid

cautionnement *nm Fin* (a) *(garantie)* surety, bond, guarantee ❑ *cautionnement solidaire* joint surety (b) *(somme)* security, caution money

cautionner *vt Fin (personne)* to stand surety for, to act as guarantor for

CB® *nf (abrév* **Carte Bleue®)** = bank card with which purchases are debited directly from the customer's bank account

CBV *nm Bourse (abrév* **Conseil des Bourses de valeurs)** = regulatory body of the Paris Stock Exchange

CC *nm Banque (abrév* **compte courant)** CA

CCI *nf* (a) *(abrév* **Chambre de commerce et d'industrie)** Chamber of Commerce and Industry (b) *(abrév* **Chambre de commerce internationale)** ICC

CCP *nm (abrév* **compte chèque postal)** = post office account, *Br* ≃ Giro account, *Am* ≃ Post Office checking account

CCR *nm Fin (abrév* **coefficient de capitalisation des résultats)** p/e ratio

CD *nm* (a) *(abrév* **comité directeur)** board of directors (b) *(abrév* **corps diplomatique)** CD (c) *Ordinat (abrév* **compact disc)** CD ❑ *CD réinscriptible* CD-RW; *CD vidéo* CD video

CDD *nm (abrév* **contrat à durée déterminée)** fixed-term contract

CDI *nm (abrév* **contrat à durée indéterminée)** permanent contract

> "
> Du côté des employeurs, les entreprises d'intérim, soucieuses de gommer l'image de précarité qui leur colle à la peau, ont multiplié les initiatives: accès à une mutuelle, à la formation continue, et même caution pour convaincre les propriétaires de louer un appartement à un salarié sans **CDI**.
> "

CD-I *nm Ordinat (abrév* **Compact Disc Interactif)** CDI

CD-R *nm Ordinat (abrév* **compact disc recordable)** CD-R

CD-ROM *nm Ordinat (abrév* **Compact Disc read-only memory)** CD-ROM ❑ *CD-ROM d'installation* installation CD-ROM

CD-RW *nm Ordinat (abrév* **compact disc rewritable)** CD-RW

CDV *nm Ordinat (abrév* **compact disc video)** CDV

CE 1 *nm* (a) *(abrév* **Conseil de l'Europe)** Council of Europe (b) *(abrév* **comité d'entreprise)** works council
2 *nf (abrév* **Communauté européenne)** EC

cédant, -e 1 *adj (partie)* granting, assigning
2 *nm,f (d'actions)* grantor, assignor

céder *vt* (a) *(droit)* to give up, to surrender; **les droits à eux cédés** the rights granted to them (b) *(commerce)* to sell; *(bail)* to dispose of, to sell; **céder qch à bail** to lease sth

cédérom *nm* CD-ROM ❑ *cédérom d'installation* installation CD-ROM

cédétiste *nmf* = member of the CFDT trade union

Cedex *nm (abrév* **courrier d'entreprise à distribution exceptionnelle)** = postal code ensuring rapid delivery of business mail

cédille *nf* cedilla

CEE *nf Anciennement (abrév* **Communauté économique européenne)** EEC

cégétiste *nmf* = member of the CGT trade union

CEL nm (abrév **compte épargne logement**) savings account (for purchasing a property)

cellulaire adj (gestion) divisional

cellule nf (a) Ordinat (dans un tableur) cell (b) **cellule d'achat** purchasing unit

CEN nm (abrév **Comité européen de normalisation**) European Standards Commission

cent¹ nm hundred; **pour cent** percent; **intérêt de sept pour cent** seven percent interest; **cent pour cent** one hundred percent

cent² nm (unité divisionnaire de l'euro) cent

centime nm Anciennement centime

central, -e 1 adj (banque) central; (bureau) head, main
  2 nm **central (téléphonique)** (telephone) exchange ❑ **central numérique** digital exchange
  3 nf **centrale d'achat(s)** central purchasing office or group; (au sein d'une entreprise) central purchasing department; **centrale électrique** power station; **centrale de réservations** central reservations unit or office; **centrale syndicale** group of affiliated trade unions

centralisateur, -trice adj centralizing

centralisation nf centralization

centraliser vt to centralize

centre nm centre ❑ **centre d'accueil** (pour touristes) visitor centre; **centre administratif** administrative building; **centre d'affaires** business centre; (dans aéroport, hôtel) business lounge; Compta **centre d'analyse** cost centre; Compta **centre d'analyse auxiliaire** secondary cost centre; Compta **centre d'analyse opérationnel** operational cost centre; Compta **centre d'analyse principal** main cost centre; **centre d'appels** call centre; **centre de calcul** computing centre; **centre de chèques postaux** PO cheque account centre; **centre commercial** shopping centre; **centre de conférences** conference centre; Compta **centre de coût** cost centre; **centre de distribution** distribution centre; **Centre d'études sur les revenus et les coûts** = government body carrying out research into salaries and the cost of living; **centre des impôts** tax centre or office; **centre industriel** industrial centre; **centre d'information** information centre; **centre d'intérêt touristique** tourist or visitor attraction; Compta **centre de profit** profit centre; **centre de revenus** revenue centre; **centre de tourisme** tourist centre; **centre de traitement de l'information** data processing centre; **centre de tri** sorting office

CERC nm (abrév **Centre d'études sur les revenus et les coûts**) = government body carrying out research into salaries and the cost of living

cercle de qualité nm Écon quality circle

CERN nm (abrév **Conseil européen pour la recherche nucléaire**) CERN

certain, -e 1 adj (prix, date) definite, fixed
  2 nm Fin fixed or direct rate of exchange; **le certain de la livre est de 1,66 euros** the rate of exchange for the pound is 1.66 euros

certificat nm certificate ❑ Bourse **certificat d'actions** share certificate; Bourse **certificat d'actions provisoire** scrip certificate; **certificat d'aptitude professionnelle** = vocational training certificate; Assur **certificat d'assurance** insurance certificate; Assur **certificat d'avarie** certificate of damage; **certificat de capacité** (d'employé) certificate of proficiency; **certificat de chargement** certificate of receipt; **certificat de conformité** certificate of compliance, clear report of findings; **certificat de déchargement** landing certificate; **certificat de dépôt** (de marchandises) warehouse warrant; Banque certificate of deposit; Banque **certificat de dépôt à taux flottant** floating-rate certificate of deposit; Bourse **certificat de dividende provisoire** scrip dividend; **certificat d'enregistrement de société** certificate of incorporation; Douanes **certificat d'entrepôt** ou **d'entreposage** warehouse warrant; **certificat d'essai** test certificate; **certificat d'expertise** expert's report; **certificat de garantie** guarantee; **certificat d'homologation** certificate of approval; **certificat d'inscription maritime** certificate of registration; **certificat d'investissement** investment certificate; **certificat d'investissement privilégié** preferential investment certificate; **certificat médical** medical certificate; Bourse **certificat nominatif d'actions** registered share certificate; **certificat de non-paiement** (de chèque) notification of unpaid cheque; (de lettre de change) certificate of dishonour; **certificat d'origine** certificate of origin; Assur **certificat provisoire d'assurance** cover note; **certificat de qualité** certificate of quality; **certificat de résidence** certificate of residence; **certificat de titres** share certificate; **certificat de transfert** transfer certificate; **certificat de travail** (pour certifier qu'on est employé) attestation of employment; (pour certifier qu'on a été employé) employer's reference; Fin **certificat de trésorerie** treasury bond; **certificat de valeur** certificate of value; Bourse **certificat de valeur garantie** contingent value right

certification nf Jur certification, authentication; (d'une signature) witnessing

certifier vt Jur to certify, to attest; (signature) to witness; **une copie certifiée conforme (à l'original)** a certified copy of the original document

cessation nf stoppage, termination; (d'un contrat) termination ❑ **cessation d'activité** termination of business; *(d'une personne)* retirement; **cessation de paiements** suspension of payments; **être en état de cessation de paiements** to have suspended all payments; **cessation de travail** stoppage

"

Si personne ne songe à repousser l'âge légal de la retraite, symbole de la lutte sociale, de plus en plus de salariés partiront bien au-delà de leurs 60 ans. L'âge moyen de **cessation d'activité** devrait passer de 58 à … 67 ans d'ici 2040 simplement pour préserver l'équilibre des régimes de retraite!

"

cesser *vt (activité, paiement)* to stop

cessibilité *nf Jur (de biens)* transferability, assignability; *(d'une traite, d'une pension retraite)* negotiability

cessible *adj Jur (biens)* transferable, assignable; *(traite, pension retraite)* negotiable

cession *nf Jur* cession, transfer; *(document)* deed of transfer □ **cession d'actifs** sale of assets; **cession de bail** leaseback; **cession de biens** assignment of property; **cession de licence** licensing; **cession de licence de marque** corporate licensing; **cession de licence de nom** name licensing; *Fin* **cession de parts** stock transfer; *Fin* **cession de parts en blanc** blank transfer; **cession en pleine propriété** renunciation; *Fin* **cession de titres** stock transfer

"

Le titre De Dietrich chutait de 4,6%, à 60,10 euros, vendredi. Le groupe a annoncé un bénéfice net … de 21,9 millions d'euros au premier semestre, contre 13,5 millions d'euros l'année précédente. Le groupe a réalisé une plus-value exceptionnelle de 10,21 millions d'euros à la faveur d'une **cession de titres**.

"

cession-bail *nf* leaseback

cessionnaire **1** *adj Jur* cessionary
2 *nmf* **(a)** *Jur (de biens)* transferee, assignee; *(d'un effet de commerce, d'une créance)* holder **(b)** *(d'un chèque)* endorser

césure *nf Ordinat* break, hyphenation

C&A *(abrév* **coût et assurance**) C&I

cf. *(abrév* **confer**) cf

CFAO *nf Ordinat (abrév* **conception et fabrication assistées par ordinateur**) CAD/CAM

CFDT *nf (abrév* **Confédération française et démocratique du travail**) = French trade union

CFTC *nf (abrév* **Confédération française des travailleurs chrétiens**) = French trade union

CGC *nf (abrév* **Confédération générale des cadres**) = French trade union for managerial staff

CGI *nf Ordinat (abrév* **common gateway interface**) CGI

CGT *nf (abrév* **Confédération générale du travail**) = French trade union *(linked to the French Communist Party)*

chaebol *nm Écon* chaebol

"

Le sommet pourrait être l'occasion d'engager avec le Sud une coopération économique que souhaitent Séoul et ses milieux d'affaires. La délégation accompagnant Kim Dae-jung à Pyongyang compte dans ses rangs les hauts responsables des quatre **chaebols** (conglomérats industriels) les plus importants de Corée du Sud.

"

chaînage *nm Ordinat* chaining; *(de commandes)* piping

chaîne *nf* **(a)** *(de magasins, de restaurants)* chain □ **chaîne de détail** retail chain; **chaîne de distribution** distribution chain; *Mktg* **chaîne de valeur** value chain; **chaîne volontaire de détaillants** voluntary retailer chain **(b)** *(dans l'industrie)* **chaîne de fabrication** production line; **chaîne de montage** assembly line **(c)** *Ordinat* string □ **chaîne de caractères** character string

chaîner *vt Ordinat* to chain; *(commandes)* to pipe

challengeur *nm* (market) challenger

chambre *nf* **(a)** *(organisation)* Banque **chambre de clearing** clearing house; **Chambre de commerce** Chamber of Commerce; **Chambre de commerce et d'industrie** Chamber of Commerce and Industry; **Chambre de commerce internationale** International Chamber of Commerce; *Banque* **chambre de compensation** clearing house; *Banque* **chambre de compensation automatisée** automated clearing house; *Bourse* **chambre d'enregistrement** registration body; **Chambre des métiers** Chamber of Trade; **chambre syndicale** employers' federation; **chambre syndicale des agents de change** Stock Exchange committee **(b)** *(local)* **chambre des criées** auction room, *Br* saleroom, *Am* salesroom; **chambre forte** strongroom

chambrier *nm* = journalist who reports on events in the French National Assembly, *Br* ≃ Parliamentary correspondent

champ *nm* **(a)** *(portée)* **champ d'action** field or sphere of activity; *Mktg* **champ concurrentiel** competitive scope **(b)** *Ordinat* field □ **champ mémo** memo field; **champ numérique** numeric field; **champ de texte** text field

champion de produit *nm Mktg* product champion

change *nm Fin* exchange; **le change est avantageux/défavorable** the exchange rate is good/bad; **au change du jour** at the current rate of exchange ❑ *change du dollar* dollar exchange

changement *nm* (**a**) *(modification, substitution)* change ❑ *changement d'adresse* change of address; *changement d'hypothèque* transfer of mortgage; *Mktg changement de marque* brand switching; *changement de propriétaire (sur panneau)* under new ownership; *changement stucturel* structural change (**b**) *Ordinat changement de ligne* line feed; *changement de page* page break

changer *vt Fin (argent)* to change, to exchange; **changer un billet de banque** to change a banknote; **changer des dollars contre des euros** to change dollars into euros

changeur *nm* (**a**) *(personne)* money changer (**b**) *changeur de monnaie (machine)* change machine

chantier *nm* (**a**) *(pour entreposer)* depot (**b**) building site ❑ *chantier de construction* building site; *chantier de construction navale, chantier naval* shipyard

charge *nf* (**a**) *(obligation financière)* charge, expense; *(impôt)* tax; **le loyer plus les charges** rent plus service charge; **être à la charge de qn** *(personne)* to be dependent on sb; *(transport, réparations)* to be chargeable to sb; **les frais de transport sont à notre charge** the cost of transport is chargeable to us; **les réparations sont à la charge du locataire** the repairs are to be paid for by the tenant ❑ *Compta charges courantes* current expenses; *charges directes* direct costs; *Compta charges d'exploitation* running costs; *Compta charge fictive* fictitious cost; *charges financières* financial expenses; *charges fiscales* tax (burden); *Compta charges fixes* fixed costs; *Compta charges locatives* rental charges *or* expenses; *charges de main-d'œuvre* labour cost; *charges de main-d'œuvre directes* direct labour cost; *charges nettes* net costs; *Compta charge opérationnelle* overhead, operating cost; *charges patronales* employer's contributions; *Compta charge à payer* sum payable; *Compta charges à payer* accrued expenses, accruals; *charges publiques* public expenditure; *charges sociales* *Br* National Insurance contributions *(paid by the employer)*, *Am* Social Security charges *(paid by the employer)*; *charges sociales salariales* employee's contributions; *charges terminales* terminal charges; *charges variables* variable costs (**b**) *(cargaison) (d'un camion)* load; *(d'un navire)* cargo; **prendre charge d'une cargaison** to load (up), to take in cargo ❑ *charge admise* load limit; *charge admissible* safe load; *charge complète* *Br* lorry load, *Am* truck load; *charge incomplète* part load; *charge limite* load limit;

charge maximale maximum load; *charge prescrite* specified load; *charge utile* capacity (load)

(**c**) *(responsabilité)* charge, responsibility; **avoir la charge de qch** to be in charge of sth

(**d**) *(fonction)* office ❑ *charge d'avoué* solicitor's practice

chargé, -e 1 *adj* (**a**) *(véhicule, navire)* loaded, laden; *(emploi du temps)* busy (**b**) *(responsable)* **être chargé de qch/de faire qch** to be responsible for sth/for doing sth

2 *nm chargé de budget* account executive; *chargé de clientèle* account manager; *chargé de comptes* account manager; *chargé de dossier* project manager; *Mktg chargé d'étude* market researcher; *chargé de mission* project manager; *chargé de relations clients* customer relations manager; *charge de travail* wordload

chargement *nm* (**a**) *(action) (de camion)* loading; *(de cargaison)* shipping, loading (**b**) *(marchandises)* load, consignment; **prendre chargement** to take on cargo ❑ *chargement complet* full load; *chargement périssable* perishable cargo; *chargement réglementaire* regulation load (**c**) *(de lettre, colis)* registration; *(lettre)* registered letter; *(colis)* registered parcel

charger 1 *vt* (**a**) *(donner la responsabilité à)* **charger qn de qch/de faire qch** to put sb in charge of sth/of doing sth (**b**) *(camion, navire)* to load (up); **charger des marchandises sur un train** to load goods onto a train (**c**) *Banque (compte)* to overcharge (on)

2 *vi Ordinat (disque, programme)* to load up

3 se charger *vpr* (**a**) *(prendre la responsabilité)* **se charger de qch** to take sth on; **se charger de faire qch** to undertake to do sth (**b**) *Ordinat (disque, programme)* to load; **se charger automatiquement** to load automatically, to autoload

chargeur *nm (pour imprimante, scanner, photocopieuse)* feeder

charte *nf* charter ❑ *charte commerciale* commercial charter

charte-partie *nf* charter party

charter *nm (avion)* charter plane; *(vol)* charter flight

chartiste *nmf Écon* chartist

chasser *vt Bourse* **chasser le découvert** to raid the bears

chasseur de têtes *nm* headhunter

chat *nm Ordinat* chat

chatter *vi Ordinat* to chat

chef *nm (responsable)* head ❑ *chef des achats* purchasing manager; *chef d'atelier* shop foreman; *chef de bureau* office manager; *chef de* *chantier* site foreman; **chef comptable, chef de la comptabilité** chief accountant; **chef d'entreprise** company manager; **chef d'équipe** team leader; **chef d'établissement** works manager; **chef de fabrication** production manager; **chef de file** *Banque, Bourse* lead manager; *Mktg (produit)* leader; **chef du groupe** group leader; **chef hiérarchique** line manager; **chef de marque** brand manager; **chef du personnel** personnel manager; **chef de produit** product manager; **chef de projet** project manager; **chef de (la) publicité** publicity manager; **chef de rayon** *(d'un magasin)* department manager; **chef de service** department manager; **chef des traitements** data processing manager; **chef des ventes** sales manager; **chef de zone** area manager

chemin *nm* (a) *(moyen de transport)* **chemin de fer** *Br* railway, *Am* railroad; **envoyer des marchandises par chemin de fer** to send goods by rail (b) *Ordinat* path ❑ **chemin d'accès** path; **chemin d'accès aux données** data path; **chemin du courrier électronique** mail path

chemise *nf* **chemise (cartonnée)** folder

chèque *nm Br* cheque, *Am* check; **émettre** *ou* **faire un chèque** to write a cheque; **encaisser** *ou* **tirer** *ou* **toucher un chèque** to cash a cheque; **établir** *ou* **libeller un chèque à l'ordre de qn** to make a cheque out to sb; **faire opposition à un chèque** to stop a cheque; **payer** *ou* **régler par chèque** to pay by cheque; **refuser d'honorer un chèque** to refer a cheque to drawer; **remettre** *ou* **déposer un chèque à la banque** to pay a cheque into the bank; **un chèque de 600 euros** a cheque for 600 euros ❑ **chèque bancaire** cheque; **chèque de banque** *Br* banker's cheque, banker's draft, *Am* cashier's check; **chèque barré** crossed cheque; **chèque en blanc** blank cheque; *Fam* **chèque en bois** *Br* rubber cheque, *Am* dud check; **chèque de caisse** credit voucher; **chèque certifié** certified cheque; **chèque en circulation** outstanding cheque; **chèque non barré** uncrossed cheque; **chèque à ordre** cheque to order; **chèque ouvert** open cheque; **chèque périmé** out-of-date cheque; **chèque au porteur** cheque made payable to bearer, bearer cheque; **chèque postal** = cheque drawn on the postal banking system, *Br* ≃ Giro (cheque); **chèque postdaté** post-dated cheque; **chèque sans provision** bad cheque; **chèque de virement** transfer cheque; **chèque de voyage** traveller's cheque

> ❝
> Limiter les pénalités pour les petits **chèques sans provision**, créer une somme insaisissable sur un compte bancaire : le ministère de l'Economie Laurent Fabius doit signer cette semaine deux décrets pour adoucir les relations entre les banques et les personnes disposant de faibles ressources.
> ❞

chèque-cadeau *nm* gift token

chèque-dividende *nm Fin* dividend warrant

chèque-repas, chèque-restaurant *nm Br* luncheon voucher, *Am* meal ticket

chéquier *nm Br* chequebook, *Am* checkbook

cher, chère 1 *adj* (a) *(onéreux)* dear, expensive; **ce magasin est trop cher** this shop is too expensive; **c'est trop cher pour moi** I can't afford it (b) *(dans une lettre)* **Cher client** Dear customer; **Cher Monsieur** Dear Mr X; *(officiel)* Dear Sir
2 *adv* **acheter qch cher** to pay a high price for sth; **se vendre cher** to fetch a high price; **ça ne vaut pas cher** it's not worth much

cherté de la vie *nf* high cost of living

chevalier *nm (dans une OPA)* **chevalier blanc** white knight; **chevalier gris** grey knight; **chevalier noir** black knight

> ❝
> Côté Elf, c'est un choc, et la riposte a du mal à s'organiser. Trois scénarios sont envisagés: contraindre l'agresseur à relever son offre, trouver un **chevalier blanc** pouvant venir à la rescousse – le nom de l'italien ENI est alors évoqué – ou lancer une offre publique d'échange sur l'assaillant. Cette dernière réplique sera préférée.
> ❞

chiffre *nm* (a) *(nombre)* figure, number; **en chiffres ronds** in round figures ❑ *Ordinat* **chiffre ASCII** ASCII number; *Écon* **chiffres bruts** unweighted figures; **chiffres réels** actual figures
(b) *(total)* amount, total; **les dépenses de la société atteignent un chiffre de quatre millions d'euros** the company's spending has reached a figure of four million euros ❑ **chiffre d'affaires** sales figures, turnover; **la société a** *ou* **fait un chiffre d'affaires d'un million d'euros** the company has a turnover of a million euros; **chiffre d'affaires annuel** annual sales figures *or* turnover; **chiffre d'affaires consolidé** group sales figures *or* turnover; **chiffre d'affaires critique** break-even point; **chiffre d'affaires à l'exportation** total export sales; **chiffre d'affaires global** total sales; **chiffre d'affaires prévisionnel** projected sales figures *or* turnover; **chiffre de vente** sales figures; **ils ont augmenté leur chiffre de vente** they have increased their sales

chiffrement *nm Ordinat (de message)* encoding, encryption ❑ **chiffrement de données** data encryption

chiffrer 1 *vt (coût, dégâts, dommages)* to estimate, to assess; **chiffrer des travaux** to draw up an estimate of the cost of work; **il est trop tôt pour chiffrer le montant des dégâts** it's too early to put a figure to the damage

2 se chiffrer *vpr* **se chiffrer à** to add up to, to amount to; **leurs pertes se chiffrent en centaines de millions d'euros** their losses add up to *or* amount to hundreds of millions of euros

chiffreur *nm Ordinat* encoder, encrypter

chiffrier *nm* counter cash book

chirographaire *adj Fin (créance, créancier)* unsecured

choc *nm* crisis ❑ *Bourse* **choc boursier** market crisis; *Écon* **choc pétrolier** oil crisis

choix *nm* (a) *(gamme, sélection)* choice, selection; **au choix de l'acheteur** at the buyer's option; **à choix multiples** *(question, questionnaire, enquête)* multiple choice (b) *(qualité)* **de choix** choice, selected; **de tout premier choix** first-class, high-grade; **de second choix** second grade

chômage *nm* unemployment; **au chômage** out of work, unemployed; **s'inscrire au chômage** to sign on; **mettre qn au chômage** to put sb out of work ❑ **chômage conjoncturel** cyclical unemployment; **chômage déguisé** concealed unemployment; **chômage de longue durée** long-term unemployment; **chômage de mobilité** frictional unemployment; **chômage partiel** short-time working; **être en chômage partiel** to work short time; **chômage résiduel** frictional unemployment; **chômage saisonnier** seasonal unemployment; **chômage structurel** structural unemployment; **chômage technique** lay-off; **être en chômage technique** to have been laid off

chômer *vi (personne)* to be unemployed; *(entreprise, machine)* to stand idle, to be at a standstill; **les usines chôment** the factories are at a standstill; **laisser chômer son argent** to let one's money lie idle

chômeur, -euse *nm,f* unemployed person; **les chômeurs** the unemployed; **le nombre des chômeurs est très important** the unemployment figures are very high; **les chômeurs de longue durée** the long-term unemployed ❑ **chômeur partiel** short-time worker

chronique[1] *adj (chômage, déficit)* chronic

chronique[2] *nf (dans la presse)* (regular) column ❑ **chronique boursière** markets column; **chronique financière** financial news

chroniqueur, -euse *nm,f* columnist ❑ **chroniqueur boursier** market commentator; **chroniqueur financier** financial columnist

chronomètre *nm Ordinat* timer

chute *nf (d'une monnaie, des exportations, des ventes)* fall, drop (**de** in); **être en chute libre** to be in freefall

> Avec une perte pour le groupe de 8,28 milliards d'euros en 2001, une dette de 65 milliards, un cours de Bourse **en chute libre**, des acquisitions payées au prix fort (Orange, Mobilcom), son sort est des plus incertains.

chuter *vi* to fall, to drop; **faire chuter les cours** to cause a heavy fall *or* drop in prices

CI *nm (abrév* **certificat d'investissement)** investment certificate

ci-après *adv* below; *Jur* hereinafter; **les dispositions ci-après** the provisions set out below; **ci-après dénommé l'acheteur** hereinafter referred to as the Buyer

ciblage *nm Mktg* targeting ❑ **ciblage stratégique** strategic targeting

cible *nf Mktg* target ❑ **cible commerciale** marketing target; **cible de communication** promotional target; **cible marketing** marketing target; **cible média** media target; **cible publicitaire** advertising target

cibler *vt Mktg* to target; **notre campagne publicitaire cible en priorité les jeunes** our advertising campaign is targeted principally at young people

ci-contre *adv* opposite; *Compta* **porté ci-contre** as per contra

ci-dessous *adv* below; **voir le tableau ci-dessous** see the table below

ci-dessus *adv* above; **voir le graphique ci-dessus** see the above diagram

CIDEX *nm (abrév* **courrier individuel à distribution exceptionnelle)** = system grouping letter boxes in country areas

Cie *(abrév* **compagnie)** Co

ci-inclus, -e 1 *adj* enclosed; **la copie ci-incluse** the enclosed copy

2 *adv* **(vous trouverez) ci-inclus copie de votre lettre** (please find) enclosed a copy of your letter

ci-joint, -e 1 *adj* enclosed; *(fichier)* attached; **les pièces ci-jointes** the enclosed documents

2 *adv* **(veuillez trouver) ci-joint mon chèque** please find enclosed my cheque; **(veuillez trouver) ci-joint mon CV** please find attached my CV

circonscription *nf Admin* division, district ❑ **circonscription téléphonique** telephone code area

circuit *nm* (a) *Écon* channel ❑ **circuit commercial** commercial channel; **circuit de commercialisation** marketing channel; **circuit de distribution** distribution network; **circuits de vente** commercial channels (b) *Ordinat* circuit

❑ *circuit de commande* command circuit

circulaire 1 *adj (lettre)* circular
  2 *nf* circular

circulant, -e *adj Fin (billets, devises)* in circulation; *(capitaux)* circulating

circulation *nf* (a) *Fin (des billets, des capitaux, des devises)* circulation ❑ *circulation monétaire* circulation of money, money in circulation (b) *Écon* movement, circulation; **la libre circulation des personnes/des biens/des capitaux** the free movement of people/goods/capital

circuler *vi Fin (billets, devises)* to be in circulation; *(capitaux)* to be circulating; **faire circuler des effets** to keep bills afloat

citoyen, -enne *nm,f* citizen

classe *nf* (a) *(rang)* class; *Admin* rank, grade; **de première classe** *(produits)* top-quality; *(hôtel)* first-class
  (b) *(dans la hiérarchie sociale)* class ❑ *classes dirigeantes* ruling classes; *classes moyennes* middle classes; *classes ouvrières* working classes; *classes supérieures* upper classes
  (c) *(dans les transports)* class ❑ *classe affaires* business class; **voyager en classe affaires** to travel business class; *classe club* club class; *classe économique* economy class; *classe touriste* tourist class
  (d) *Compta* group of accounts ❑ *classe de revenu* income bracket

classement *nm (de documents)* filing

classer *vt* (a) *(ordonner)* to class, to classify (b) *(documents)* to file; **classer qch par ordre alphabétique** to file sth in alphabetical order (c) *Jur* **classer une affaire** to close a case

classeur *nm (meuble)* filing cabinet; *(dossier)* folder; *Ordinat* filer ❑ *classeur à anneaux* ring binder; *Admin classeur des entrées et sorties* tally file; *classeur à fiches* card-index file

classification *nf* classification ❑ *classification d'emplois* job classification; *classification de fonctions* job classification

clause *nf Jur* clause ❑ *Fin clause accélératrice* acceleration clause; *clause additionnelle* additional clause, rider; *clause d'annulation* cancellation clause; *clause d'arbitrage* arbitration clause; *clause compromissoire* arbitration clause; *clause conditionnelle* proviso; *clause contractuelle* = clause in a contract; *clause de dédit* penalty *or* forfeit clause; *Jur clause dérogatoire* overriding clause; *clause ducroire* del credere clause; *clause échappatoire* escape clause; *clause d'exclusivité* exclusivity clause; *clause d'exonération* exemption clause; *clause de force majeure* force majeure clause; *clause de franchise* excess clause; *clause de garantie* warranty clause; *Compta clause d'indexation* escalation clause, indexation clause; *clause limitative* limiting clause; *Assur clause de né-*

gligence negligence clause; *clause de non-concurrence* non-competition clause; *clause de non-garantie* non-warranty clause; *clause pénale* penalty clause; *Fin clause au porteur* pay to bearer clause; *Assur clause de reconduction automatique* non-forfeiture clause; *Assur clause de régularisation* = clause stating that insurance starts after payment of the first premium; *clause de remboursement* refunding clause; *clause de remboursement par anticipation* prepayment clause; *clause de réserve de propriété* retention of title clause; *clause de résiliation* termination clause, cancellation clause; *clause résolutoire* avoidance clause; *clause restrictive* restrictive clause; *clause de sauvegarde* safety clause; *Assur clause de vétusté* obsolescence clause

clausé, -e *adj (connaissement)* dirty

clavier *nm (d'ordinateur, de machine à écrire)* keyboard; **introduire des données par clavier** to key (in) data ❑ *clavier alphanumérique* alphanumeric keypad; *clavier AZERTY* AZERTY keyboard; *clavier élargi, clavier étendu* enhanced keyboard; *clavier multi-fonction* multifunctional keyboard; *clavier numérique* numeric keypad; *clavier QWERTY* QWERTY keyboard

claviste *nmf Ordinat* keyboarder

clé 1 *adj (industrie, poste, secteur)* key
  2 *nf* (a) *Ordinat* key; *(du DOS)* switch ❑ *clé de chiffrement* encryption key; *clé gigogne* dongle (b) *Banque clé RIB* = two-digit security number allocated to account-holders

clearing *nm Fin* clearing

clef = clé

clic *nm Ordinat* click; **double clic** double click; **faire un clic (sur)** to click (on)

client, -e *nm,f* client, customer; *(d'un hôtel)* guest; *(dans la publicité)* account; **c'est un bon client** he's a good customer; **la France est un gros client du Japon pour la robotique** France is one of Japan's big customers for robotics ❑ *client actuel* existing customer; *Compta client douteux* doubtful debt, possible bad debt; *client éventuel* prospective customer, prospect; *client habitué* regular customer; *client imprévu* chance customer; *Ordinat client de messagerie électronique* e-mail client, mail reader; *client mystère* mystery shopper; *client de passage* passing customer; *client potentiel* potential customer; *client de référence* reference customer; *client régulier* regular customer; *client sans réservation (dans un hôtel)* chance guest, walk-in

clientèle *nf (clients)* customers; *(fait d'acheter)* custom; **attirer la clientèle** to attract custom; **avoir une grosse clientèle** to have a large clientele; **accorder sa clientèle à qn** to patronize sb, to give sb one's custom □ *clientèle de passage* passing trade

clignotant *nm Écon* signal, indicator; **le clignotant de la hausse des prix** the warning light *or* signal that prices are rising

climat *nm (économique, social)* climate

clip *nm* video □ *clip vidéo* video

clipart *nm Ordinat* clip art

cliquer *vi Ordinat* to click (**sur** on); **cliquer deux fois** to double-click; **cliquer avec le bouton gauche/droit de la souris (sur)** to left-click/right-click (on); **cliquer et glisser** to click and drag

clone *nm Ordinat* clone

clore *vt (séance, réunion)* to close; *Ordinat* **clore une session** to log off, to log out

clos, -e *adj (achevé)* finished, concluded; **les inscriptions seront closes le 3 mars** the closing date for applications is 3 March; *Compta* **exercice clos le 31 déc 2002** year ended 31 Dec 2002

clôture *nf* (**a**) *(d'une réunion)* conclusion, end; *(d'un débat)* closure; **clôture des inscriptions le 3 mars** closing date for applications is 3 March; **prononcer la clôture des débats** to end the discussion, to bring the discussion to a close
(**b**) *Bourse* close; **être ferme en clôture** to close firm; **la valeur de l'euro en clôture** the closing value of the euro, the value of the euro at the close
(**c**) *Ordinat* close □ *clôture de session* logging off
(**d**) *(d'un compte)* closing □ *Compta* **clôture annuelle des livres** year-end closing of accounts; *Compta* **clôture de l'exercice** end of the financial year

clôturer **1** *vt* (**a**) *(séance, débat)* to close, to end, to conclude; *Jur* **clôturer une faillite** to close a bankruptcy (**b**) *Compta (comptes, livres)* to close
2 *vi Bourse (valeur, indice)* to close; **le CAC 40 a clôturé en baisse/hausse de 9 points** the CAC 40 closed 9 points down/up; **le dollar a clôturé à 75 pence** the dollar closed at 75 pence

club d'investissement *nm* investment club

CM *nf (abrév* **Chambre des métiers**) Guild Chamber

CMP *nm (abrév* **coût moyen pondéré**) weighted average cost

CNAM *nf (abrév* **Caisse nationale d'assurance maladie**) = French government department dealing with health insurance and sickness benefit

CNAV *nf (abrév* **Caisse nationale d'assurance vieillesse**) = French government department dealing with benefit payments relating to old age

CNC *nm (abrév* **Conseil national de la consommation**) = consumer protection organization

CNCE *nm (abrév* **Centre national du commerce extérieur**) = national export organization

CNE *nm (abrév* **Caisse nationale d'épargne**) ≃ National Savings Bank

CNPF *nm Aciennement (abrév* **Conseil national du patronat français**) = national council of French employers, *Br* ≃ CBI

CNRS *nm (abrév* **Centre national de la recherche scientifique**) = national organization for scientific research, *Br* ≃ SRC

CNUCED *nf (abrév* **Conférence des Nations Unies pour le commerce et l'industrie**) UNCTAD

coacquéreur, -euse *nm,f* joint purchaser

coacquisition *nf* joint purchase

coadministrateur, -trice *nm,f* co-director

coalition *nf* coalition

coassociation *nf* joint partnership

coassocié, -e *nm,f* joint partner

coassurance *nf* coinsurance

coassurer *vt* to coinsure

COB *nf Bourse (abrév* **Commission des opérations de Bourse**) = French Stock Exchange watchdog

cobol *nm Ordinat* COBOL

co-branding *nm Mktg* co-branding

coche *nf Br* tick, *Am* checkmark

cocher *vt Br* to tick, *Am* to check; **cocher la case correspondante** *(sur formulaire) Br* tick *or Am* check the appropriate box

cocontractant, -e *Jur* **1** *adj* contracting
2 *nm,f* contracting partner

cocréancier, -ère *nm,f* joint creditor

codage *nm Ordinat* encoding, coding □ *codage de données* data encryption

code *nm* (**a**) *(symboles)* code □ *code assujetti TVA* VAT registration number; *code client* customer code, customer reference number; *code confidentiel* security code; *(pour carte bancaire)* personal identification number, PIN (number); *code fournisseur* supplier code; *code général des impôts* general tax code; *Banque code guichet* sort code, bank branch code; *Banque code personnel (pour carte bancaire)* personal identification number, PIN number; *Banque code porteur* personal identification number, PIN number; *code postal Br* postcode, postal code, *Am* zip code; *code SICOVAM* = 5-digit code allocated to French securities by the central securities depository
(**b**) *Ordinat* code □ *code d'accès* access code; *code ASCII* ASCII code; *code binaire* binary

code; **code de caractère** character code; **code de commande** command code; **code d'identification** identification code; **code machine** machine code
  (**c**) *(ensemble de lois)* code □ **code de commerce** commercial law; **code du travail** employment regulations

code-barres *nm* bar code

codébiteur, -trice *nm,f* joint debtor

codemandeur, -eresse *nm,f Jur* joint plaintiff

coder *vt Ordinat* to encode, to code

codétenteur, -trice *nm,f Jur* joint holder

CODEVI, codevi *nm (abrév* **Compte pour le développement industriel)** = type of instant-access government savings account

> **"**
>
> Plafonnés à 30 000 francs de dépôts et rémunérés à 2,25%, les **codevi** (comptes pour le développement industriel) doivent être considérés comme des outils de trésorerie complémentaires. Permettant tous les allers et retours possibles, ils tiennent office, dans la plupart des cas, de comptes rémunérés à des conditions de taux nettement plus avantageuses que celles couramment offertes sur le marché.
>
> **"**

codification *nf Jur (des lois)* codification, classification

codifier *vt Jur (lois)* to codify, to classify

codirecteur, -trice *nm,f* joint manager

codirection *nf* joint management

coefficient *nm (proportion)* ratio □ **coefficient d'activité** activity ratio; **coefficient de capital** output ratio; **coefficient de capitalisation des résultats** price-earnings ratio; **coefficient d'erreur** margin of error; *Compta* **coefficient d'exploitation** performance *or* operating ratio; **coefficient de liquidité** liquidity ratio, current ratio; **coefficient de rotation** stock turnover ratio; **coefficient saisonnier** seasonal index; **coefficient de solvabilité** risk asset ratio, solvency coefficient; **coefficient de trésorerie** cash ratio

coentrepreneur, -euse *nm,f* joint venturer

coentreprise *nf* joint venture

coéquation *nf Admin* proportional assessment

cœur de cible *nm Mktg* core market, core audience

> **"**
>
> ... Avec ce reformatage, la station s'inscrit pleinement dans le pôle radio de la CLT, en totale complémentarité commerciale avec RTL2, également dirigée par Axel Duroux dont le **cœur de cible** est les 25–34 ans.
>
> **"**

COFACE *nf (abrév* **Compagnie française d'assurances pour le commerce extérieur)** = export insurance company, ≃ ECGD

coffre *nm Banque* safe-deposit box; **les coffres de l'État** the coffers of the State □ **coffre de nuit** night safe

coffre-fort *nm* safe □ **coffre-fort de nuit** night safe

cofinancement *nm* joint venture

cofinancer *vt* to finance jointly

cofondateur, -trice *nm,f* co-founder

cogérance *nf* joint management

cogérant, -e *nm,f* joint manager

cogérer *vt* to manage jointly

cogestion *nf* joint management

col *nm* **col blanc** white-collar worker; **col bleu** blue-collar worker; **col doré** gold-collar worker

colicitant, -e *nm,f Jur* co-vendor

colis *nm* parcel, package; **envoyer qch par colis postal** to send sth by parcel post □ **colis contre remboursement** *Br* cash on delivery parcel, *Am* collect on delivery parcel; **colis exprès** special delivery parcel

collaborateur, -trice *nm,f* assistant; *(dans la presse)* contributor

collaboration *nf* collaboration; **travailler en étroite collaboration (avec qn)** to work in close collaboration (with sb)

collaborer *vi (entreprises)* to collaborate; **collaborer à qch** *(projet)* to take part in sth; *(journal)* to contribute to sth; **les deux services collaborent étroitement** the two departments work closely together

collecte *nf* **collecte de données** data collection, data acquisition; **collecte de fonds** fundraising; **collecte d'informations** news gathering

collecter *vi* to raise funds

collectif, -ive 1 *adj (action, travail, responsabilité)* collective; *(licenciements)* mass
  2 *nm* (**a**) *Fin* **collectif budgétaire** interim budget (**b**) *(association)* collective

collection *nf (d'échantillons)* line

collectivisme *nm Écon* collectivism

collectivité *nf* group □ **collectivités locales** local authorities

collègue *nmf* colleague, *Am* co-worker □ **collègue de travail** work colleague, *Am* co-worker

coller *vt Ordinat* to paste

collusion d'intérêts *nf* merging of interests

colocataire *nmf* joint tenant, co-tenant

colonne *nf (de chiffres, dans la presse)* column

❑ *Compta* **colonne créditrice** credit column; *Compta* **colonne débitrice** debit column

combiné *nm Tél* handset

combler *vt (perte)* to make good; *(découvert)* to pay off

comestible **1** *adj (aliments, denrées)* consumable
2 *nm* **comestibles** consumables

comité *nm* committee ❑ *comité de conciliation* arbitration *or* conciliation board; *comité consultatif* advisory board; *comité de coordination* umbrella committee; *comité directeur*, *comité de direction* board of directors; *comité d'enquête* board of inquiry; *comité d'entreprise* works council *or* committee; *Comité européen de normalisation* European Standards Commission; *comité d'hygiène et de sécurité* health and safety committee; *comité d'organisation* organizing committee; *comité de restructuration* steering committee, advisory committee; *comité de sélection* selection committee; *Mktg* *comité synectique* idea committee

commande *nf* **(a)** *(de produit)* order; **faire** *ou* **passer une commande (à qn/de qch)** to put in *or* place an order (with sb/for sth); **exécuter une commande** to fill an order; **livrer une commande** to deliver an order; **fait sur commande** made to order; **payable à la commande** payment with order, cash with order; **conformément à votre commande** as per (your) order ❑ *commande en attente* back order; *commande d'essai* trial order; *commande export*, *commande pour l'exportation* export order; *commande ferme* firm order; *commande par ordinateur* teleorder; *commandes par quantités* bulk orders; *commande renouvelée* repeat order; *commande en souffrance* back order; *commande téléphonique*, *commande par téléphone* telephone order; *commande urgente* rush order
(b) *Ordinat* command ❑ *commande d'annulation* undo command; *commande à bascule* toggle switch; *commande binaire* bit command; *commande de copie* copy command; *commande DOS* DOS command; *commande d'effacement* delete command; *commande erronée (message d'erreur)* bad command; *commande d'insertion* insert command; *commande de recherche* find command; *commande système d'exploitation* operating system command; *à commande vocale* voice-activated

commander *vt* **(a)** *(marchandises)* to order; **commander qch chez qn** to order sth from sb; **commander ferme** to place a firm order; **commander qch par téléphone** to order sth by telephone; **commander qch par ordinateur** to teleorder sth **(b)** *Ordinat* to drive; **commandé**

par menu menu-driven; **commandé à la voix** voice-activated

commanditaire *nmf* **(a)** *(d'une entreprise) Br* sleeping *or Am* silent partner **(b)** *Mktg (d'un tournoi, d'un spectacle)* sponsor

commandite *nf* **(a)** *commandite par actions* partnership limited by shares; *commandite simple* limited partnership, mixed liability company **(b)** *(fonds)* = capital invested by sleeping partner(s)

commandité, -e **1** *adj* **(a)** *(associé)* active partner; *(entreprise)* financed *(as a limited partner)* **(b)** *Mktg (tournoi, spectacle)* sponsored
2 *nm,f* active partner

commanditer *vt* **(a)** *(entreprise)* to finance *(as a limited partner)* **(b)** *Mktg (tournoi, spectacle)* to sponsor

commerçant, -e **1** *adj (quartier)* commercial, business; **être commerçant** *(personne)* to have business acumen
2 *nm,f* trader; *(qui tient un magasin)* shopkeeper; **petit commerçant** small trader ❑ *commerçant de détail* retailer; *commerçant en gros* wholesaler

commerce *nm* **(a)** *(activité, secteur)* commerce, trade; **le petit commerce** *(petits commerçants)* small traders; **être dans le commerce, faire du commerce** to be in trade, to run a business; **faire du commerce avec qn/un pays** to do business with sb/a country; **faire le commerce de qch** to trade in sth ❑ *commerce de biens* visible trade; *commerce de demi-gros* cash and carry; *commerce de détail* retail trade; *Ordinat* *commerce électronique* electronic commerce, e-commerce; *commerce d'exportation* export trade; *commerce extérieur* foreign trade; *commerce frauduleux* fraudulent trading; *commerce de gros* wholesale trade; *commerce d'importation* import trade; *commerce intérieur* domestic trade, home trade; *commerce intermédiaire* middleman's business; *commerce international* international trade, world trade; *commerce maritime* maritime trade; *commerce réciproque* reciprocal trading; *commerce de réexportation* re-export trade; *commerce de services* invisible trade
(b) *(circuit de distribution)* market; **on ne trouve pas encore ce produit dans le commerce** this item is not yet available on the market; **cela ne se trouve plus dans le commerce** this item has gone off the market
(c) *(magasin) Br* shop, *Am* store; **commerce à céder** *(sur panneau)* business for sale; **tenir un commerce** to run a business

commercer *vi* to trade, to deal (**avec** with)

commercial, -e **1** *adj (activité, attaché, droit, effet)* commercial; *(balance, embargo, tribunal)* trade; *(délégué, direction, service)* sales; **avoir**

des contacts commerciaux avec qn to have trading links with sb
2 *nm,f (personne)* salesman, *f* saleswoman

commercialement *adv* commercially

commercialisable *adj* marketable

commercialisation *nf* marketing

commercialiser *vt* **(a)** *(mettre dans le commerce)* to market; **le produit sera commercialisé en janvier** the product will be coming onto the market in January **(b)** *Fin (effet)* to negotiate

commettant *nm Jur* principal; **commettant et mandataire** principal and agent

commis *nm* **(a)** *(dans un magasin) Br* sales assistant, *Am* sales clerk **(b)** *(dans une banque, une administration)* clerk; *Bourse* floor trader; **premier commis** chief clerk □ **commis d'agent de change** stockbroker's clerk; *Fin* **commis aux comptes** government auditor; **commis aux écritures** accounting clerk; **commis principal** chief clerk

commissaire *nm* **(a)** *(membre d'une commission)* commissioner □ **commissaire européen** European commissioner **(b)** *Fin* **commissaire aux comptes** government auditor **(c)** *(d'une exposition)* organizer

> ❝
> Le naufrage d'Enron, alors même qu'Arthur Andersen, l'auditeur en charge de vérifier les comptes, n'a jamais tiré le signal d'alarme, pose une nouvelle fois la question de l'indépendance des **commissaires aux comptes**.
> ❞

commissaire-priseur *nm* auctioneer

commissariat *nm* commissionership □ **commissariat aux comptes** auditorship

commission *nf* **(a)** *(comité)* commission, committee □ **commission administrative** management committee; **commission arbitrale, commission d'arbitrage** conciliation board; **commission de comptabilité** audit committee; **commission de contrôle** control commission; **commission d'enquête** board of inquiry; **Commission européenne** European Commission; **commission mixte** joint commission; **commission de normalisation** standards commission; **Commission des opérations de Bourse** = French Stock Exchange watchdog; **commission paritaire** joint commission
(b) *(pourcentage)* commission, percentage; *Fin* brokerage; **trois pour cent de commission** three percent commission; **il reçoit** *ou* **touche une commission de cinq pour cent sur chaque vente** he gets a commission of five percent on each sale; **être payé à la commission** to be paid on a commission basis □ **commission d'accep-**

tation acceptance fee; **commission d'affacturage** factoring charges; **commission d'arrangement** overriding commission; **commission de bourse** transaction costs; **commission de change** agio; **commission de chef de file** management fee; **commission de compte** account fee; **commission de désintéressement** drop dead fee; **commission ducroire** del credere commission; **commission d'endos** endorsement fee; **commission d'engagement** commitment fee; **commission de garantie** underwriting fee; **commission de gestion** agency fee; **commission de montage** loan origination fee; **commission de placement** underwriting fee; *Bourse* **commission de rachat** redemption fee; *Bourse* **commission de souscription** front load; **commission spéciale** overriding commission; *Banque* **commission de tenue de compte** account handling fee; **commission de vente** sales commission

commissionnaire *nmf* (commission) agent, broker □ **commissionnaire d'achat** buyer; *Fin* **commissionnaire en banque** outside broker; **commissionnaire en douane** customs agent or broker; **commissionnaire ducroire** del credere agent; **commissionnaire expéditeur** forwarding agent, carrier; **commissionnaire à l'export, commissionnaire exportateur** export agent; **commissionnaire en gros** factor; **commissionnaire à l'import, commissionnaire importateur** import agent; **commissionnaire de transport** forwarding agent, carrier

commissionner *vt (projet)* to commission

commun, -e *adj* common; **faire bourse commune** to pool resources; **créer une société en commun avec qn** to start a company in partnership with sb

communautaire *adj UE (de la Communauté européenne)* Community

communauté *nf* **(a)** *UE* **la Communauté européenne** the European Community **(b)** *(collectivité)* community □ *Admin* **Communauté européenne de charbon et de l'acier** European Coal and Steel Community; **communauté financière** financial community; **communauté internationale** international community **(c)** *Jur* **communauté de biens** joint estate

commune *nf Admin* commune *(smallest territorial division)*

communication *nf* **(a)** *(échange)* communication; **se mettre en communication avec qn** to get in touch with sb; **avoir communication d'un dossier** to get hold of a file, to have had a file passed on to one; **demander communication d'un dossier** to ask for a file □ **communication commerciale** business correspondence; **communication horizontale** horizontal communication; **communication**

interne internal company document
  (**b**) *Ordinat* communication ▫ *communication de données* data communications, data-comms; *communication en ligne* on-line communication; *communication télématique* datacommunications, datacomms
  (**c**) *Tél* communication (téléphonique) telephone call; **mettez-moi en communication avec M. Martin** put me through to Mr Martin; **je vous passe la communication** I'll put you through; **vous avez la communication** you're through; **la communication est mauvaise** the line is bad ▫ *communication internationale* international call; *communication interurbaine* toll call; *communication locale* local call; *communication longue distance* long-distance call; *communication en PCV Br* reverse-charge call, *Am* collect call;
  (**d**) *Mktg (publicité)* promotion ▫ *communication événementielle* event promotion; *communication institutionnelle* corporate promotion; *communication sur le lieu de vente* point-of-sale promotion; *communication produit* product promotion
  (**e**) *(message)* communication, message; *(dans la presse)* statement; **transmettre une communication à qn** to pass on a message to sb
  (**f**) *(dans un congrès, une conférence)* paper; **faire une communication** to give a paper

communiqué *nm* communiqué ▫ *communiqué de presse* press release

communiquer 1 *vt (renseignements, statistiques, données)* to communicate, to give
  2 *vi* to communicate (**avec** with); **communiquer par téléphone/fax/courrier électronique** to communicate by telephone/fax/e-mail

commutatif, -ive *adj Jur* commutative

commutation temporelle asynchrone *nf Ordinat* asynchronous transfer mode

compacter *vt Ordinat (base de données)* to pack

compagnie *nf* company; **Thomas et Compagnie** Thomas and Company ▫ *compagnie par actions* joint-stock company; *compagnie aérienne* airline; *compagnie d'assurances* insurance company; *compagnie bancaire* bank; *compagnie captive* daughter company, subsidiary company; *compagnie à charte* chartered company; *compagnie mère* parent company; *compagnie de navigation* shipping line; *compagnie privilégiée* chartered company; *compagnie de transports maritimes* navigation company

comparabilité *nf* comparability

comparaison par paire *nf Mktg* paired comparison

comparatif, -ive *adj (tests, publicité, étude)* comparative

compatibilité *nf Ordinat* compatibility

compatible 1 *adj* (**a**) *(non contraire)* compatible (**avec** with); **cela n'est pas compatible avec mon emploi du temps** that won't fit into my schedule
  (**b**) *Ordinat* compatible; **ces deux applications ne sont pas compatibles** these two functions are incompatible *or* not compatible; **compatible vers le haut/vers le bas** upward/downward compatible; **compatible avec les versions antérieures** backward compatible; **compatible IBM** IBM-compatible; **compatible Mac** Mac-compatible
  2 *nm Ordinat* **compatible (PC)** (PC) compatible

compensable *adj Fin (chèque)* clearable, payable; **être compensable à Paris** to be cleared at Paris, to be domiciled in Paris

compensateur, -trice *adj Fin* compensatory

compensation *nf Fin* compensation; *(de chèque)* clearing

compensatoire *adj Fin* compensatory

compenser *vt (perte)* to make up for, to offset; *Fin (chèque)* to clear

compétence *nf* (**a**) *(capacité)* competence; **ses compétences en informatique font de lui le candidat idéal** his computing skills make him the ideal candidate ▫ *compétences de base* core skills; *compétences de claviste* keyboard skills; *compétence technique* technical skill (**b**) *Jur* area of jurisdiction

compétent, -e *adj* (**a**) *(capable) (personne)* competent (**b**) *(approprié)* appropriate, relevant; **adressez-vous au service compétent** apply to the appropriate *or* relevant department, apply to the department concerned (**c**) *Jur (tribunal, autorité)* competent; **seul le maire est compétent en la matière** only the mayor is competent in this matter

compétiteur, -trice *nm,f* competitor

compétitif, -ive *adj (prix)* competitive; **leurs produits sont très compétitifs** *ou* **sont à des prix très compétitifs** their products are very competitively priced

compétition *nf* competition; **il existe une compétition féroce sur le marché de l'informatique** there is fierce competition within the IT market

compétitivité *nf (d'une entreprise, d'une économie)* competitiveness

compiler *vt* to compile

complément *nm* **un complément d'information est nécessaire** further information is required; **demander un complément d'enquête** to order a more extensive inquiry ▫ *complément (de) retraite* supplementary pension

complémentaire *adj* (**a**) *(supplémentaire)* additional, further; **pour tout renseignement complémentaire s'adresser à...** for further information apply to... (**b**) *Compta (écriture)* supplementary

compléter *vt* (**a**) *(remplir) (formulaire)* to complete (**b**) *(ajouter à)* to add to; **compléter une gamme de produits** to add to a range of products

complexe *nm Écon* complex; **le complexe industriel de la vallée du Rhône** the Rhone valley industrial complex □ **complexe commercial** shopping centre *or* complex; **complexe hôtelier** hotel complex; **complexe industriel** industrial complex

comportement *nm* (**a**) *Mktg* behaviour □ **comportement d'achat** buying *or* purchasing behaviour; **comportement d'achat habituel** habitual buying *or* purchasing behaviour; **comportement de l'acheteur** buyer *or* purchaser behaviour; **comportement du consommateur** consumer behaviour; **comportement post-achat** post-purchase behaviour (**b**) *Bourse, Fin (du marché, des cours, des actions)* performance

comporter se comporter *vpr (fonctionner)* to perform; **ses actions se sont bien comportées** his/her shares have performed well

composé, -e *adj Fin (intérêts)* compound

composer *vt (numéro de téléphone)* to dial

composition *nf* (**a**) *(d'un portefeuille)* building up (**b**) *Tél* dialling □ **composition automatique** automatic dialling

compostage *nm (d'un billet de transport)* punching

composter *nm (billet de transport)* to punch

comprendre *vt (englober)* to include; **le prix comprend les frais d'envoi** the price includes postage; **la TVA est-elle comprise dans le total?** does the total include VAT?

compresser *vt Ordinat (fichier)* to compact, to compress, to zip

compresseur de données *nm Ordinat* data compressor

compression *nf* (**a**) *(réduction)* reduction □ **compressions budgétaires** budget cuts; **compression des dépenses** spending cuts; **compression des dépenses budgétaires** budget cuts; **compression du personnel** staff cutbacks (**b**) *Ordinat (de données)* compression; *(d'un fichier)* compacting, compression

comprimer *vt* (**a**) *(réduire)* to cut down, to reduce (**b**) *Ordinat (données)* to compress; *(fichier)* to compact, to compress

compris, -e *adj (inclus)* included; **service compris/non compris** service included/not included; **six mille euros par mois tout compris** six thousand euros a month all inclusive *or* all in

compromis *nm* compromise, arrangement; **mettre une affaire en compromis** to submit a case to arbitration; **obtenir** *ou* **arriver à un compromis avec ses créanciers** to compound with one's creditors □ *Assur* **compromis d'avarie** average bond; **compromis de vente** sale agreement

compta *nf Fam (abrév* **comptabilité***)* accounts, accounting

comptabilisation *nf Compta* posting, entering in the accounts; *(dénombrement)* counting; **faire la comptabilisation de qch** to enter sth in the accounts

comptabiliser *vt Compta* to post, to enter in the accounts; *(dénombrer)* to count

comptabilité *nf* (**a**) *(livres)* accounts; *(technique)* bookkeeping, accounting; **passer qch en comptabilité** to put sth through the books *or* accounts; **tenir la comptabilité** to keep the books *or* the accounts □ **comptabilité analytique** cost accounting; **comptabilité analytique d'exploitation** operational cost accounting; **comptabilité budgétaire** budgeting; **comptabilité de caisse** cash basis accounting; **comptabilité commerciale** business accounting; **comptabilité en coûts actuels** current cost accounting; **comptabilité par coûts historiques** historical cost accounting; **comptabilité des coûts variables** direct cost accounting; **comptabilité de la dépréciation** depreciation accounting; **comptabilité d'engagements** accrual accounting; **comptabilité financière** financial accounting; **comptabilité générale** general accounts; *(système)* financial accounting; **comptabilité de gestion** management accounting; **comptabilité informatisée** computerized accounts; **comptabilité mécanographique** automatic accounting; **comptabilité en partie double** double-entry bookkeeping; **comptabilité en partie simple** single-entry bookkeeping; **comptabilité de prévision** imprest system; **comptabilité de prix de revient** cost accounting; **comptabilité publique** public finance; **comptabilité uniforme** uniform accounting (**b**) *(service)* accounts department; **adressez-vous à la comptabilité** apply to the accounts department

comptable 1 *adj (travail)* accounting, bookkeeping; *(machine, méthode, plan)* accounting **2** *nmf* accountant □ *Can* **comptable agréé** *Br* chartered accountant, *Am* certified public accountant; **comptable financier** financial accountant

comptant 1 *adv* **payer comptant** to pay (in) cash; **payer cent euros comptant** to pay a hundred euros in cash; **acheter/vendre qch comptant** to buy/sell sth for cash

2 *nm* cash; **acheter/vendre qch au comptant** to buy/sell sth for cash; **payable au comptant** *(lors d'un achat) Br* cash *or Am* collect on delivery; *(sur présentation de titre, de connaissement)* payable on presentation; **comptant contre documents** cash against documents

compte *nm* **(a)** *Compta* account; **comptes** *(comptabilité)* accounts; **tenir les comptes** to keep the accounts *or* the books; **faire ses comptes** to make up *or* do one's accounts; **vérifier les comptes** to audit the books □ **compte accréditif** charge account; **compte des achats** purchase account; **compte d'affectation** appropriation account; **compte d'agence** agency account; **comptes analytiques d'exploitation** operational cost accounts; **comptes annuels** annual accounts; **comptes approuvés** certified accounts; **compte de capital** capital account; **compte centralisateur** central account; **compte de charges** expense account; **comptes clients** accounts receivable, *Am* receivables; **compte collectif** reconciliation account, adjustment account; **comptes consolidés** consolidated accounts; **compte de contrepartie** contra account; **compte à crédit** credit account; **compte créditeur** account in credit, credit account; **compte débiteur** debit account, debtor account; **compte définitif** final accounts; **compte des dépenses et recettes** income and expenditure account; **compte détaillé** itemized account; **compte d'exploitation** *Br* trading account, working account, *Am* operating account; **compte d'exploitation générale** nominal account; **comptes fournisseurs** book debts; **comptes de gestion** management accounts; **comptes intégrés** consolidated accounts; **compte de pertes et profits** profit and loss account; **compte de prêt** loan account; **compte de production** manufacturing account; **compte des recettes et des dépenses** revenue account; **compte de régularisation** *(de l'actif)* prepayments and accrued income; *(du passif)* accruals and deferred income; **compte de résultat** profit and loss account, *Am* income statement; **comptes de résultat courants** above-the-line accounts; **comptes de résultat exceptionnels** below-the-line accounts; **compte de résultat prévisionnel** interim profit and loss account, *Am* interim income statement; **comptes semestriels** interim accounts; **comptes sociaux** company accounts; **compte de stock** inventory account; **comptes trimestriels** interim accounts; **comptes de valeur** real accounts; **compte des ventes** sales account

(b) *(chez un commerçant)* account; **avoir un compte chez qn** to have an account with sb; **(se faire) ouvrir un compte chez qn** to open an account with sb; **mettre** *ou* **inscrire qch sur le compte de qn** to enter sth to sb's account; **mettez-le** *ou* **inscrivez-le à mon compte** charge it to my account; **régler un compte** to settle an account; **pour règlement de tout compte** *(sur facture)* in full settlement □ **compte d'abonnement** budget account; **compte d'accès par ligne commutée** dial-up account; **compte agence** agency account; **compte client** customer account; **compte de courrier électronique** e-mail account; **compte crédit (d'achats)** budget account, credit account; **compte Internet** Internet account; **compte permanent** *Br* credit account, *Am* charge account

(c) *Banque, Bourse* account; **ouvrir un compte (en banque)** to open a bank account; **verser de l'argent à son compte, alimenter son compte** to pay money into one's account □ **compte d'affectation** appropriation account; **compte d'agio** agio account; **compte d'avances** imprest account, advance account; **compte bancaire, compte en banque** *Br* bank account, *Am* banking account; **compte bloqué** frozen account, *Am* escrow account; **compte (de) caisse** cash account; **compte de caisse d'épargne** savings account; **compte chèques** *Br* current account, *Am* checking account; **compte chèque postal** = account held at the Post Office, *Br* ≃ Giro account, *Am* ≃ Post Office checking account; **compte client** client account; **compte commercial** office *or* business account; **compte de compensation** clearing account; **compte conjoint** joint account; **compte courant** *Br* current account, *Am* checking account; **compte créditeur** account in credit, credit balance; **compte débiteur** account in debit, debit balance; **compte à découvert** overdrawn account; **compte de dépôt** deposit account; **compte de dépôt à vue** drawing account; **compte en devises étrangères** foreign currency account; **compte d'épargne** savings account; **compte épargne logement** savings account *(for purchasing a property)*; **compte étranger** non-resident *or* foreign account; **compte inactif** dead account; **compte individuel** personal account; **compte d'intermédiaire** nominee account; **compte d'investissement** investment account; **compte joint** joint account; **compte (sur) livret** savings account; *Can* **compte de non-résident** non-resident *or* foreign account; **compte numéroté** numbered account; **compte ouvert** open account; **compte de prêt** loan account; **compte prête-nom** nominee account; **compte de produits** income account; **compte professionnel** business account; *Bourse* **compte propre** personal account; **compte rémunéré** interest-bearing account; **compte de réserve** reserve account; **compte à terme** *Bourse* forward account; *Banque* deposit account

(d) **être** *ou* **travailler à son compte** to have one's own business; **s'installer** *ou* **se mettre à son compte** to start one's own business (**e**) *(calcul)* calculation; **faire le compte de qch** to add sth up, to calculate sth; **le compte y est** the amount is correct ❑ *compte rond* round sum

(**f**) *(fonds)* fund❑ *compte sous mandat de gestion* discretionary fund

compte-clé *nm* key account

compter 1 *vt* (**a**) *(calculer)* to count, to add up (**b**) *(faire payer)* to charge; **compter qch à qn** to charge sb for sth; **je vous compterai cent euros pour cet article** I'll charge you a hundred euros for this article

2 *vi (calculer)* to count; **à compter de** as from or of; **à compter du 1er janvier** as from 1 January, with effect from 1 January

compte-rendu *nm* report; *(d'une réunion)* minutes

compte-titres *nm Fin* share account

❝

Avec le **compte-titres** ordinaire, vous disposez d'une totale liberté. Tant sur le choix des placements (actions françaises ou internationales, fonds profilés ...), que sur les possibilités de retrait.

❞

compteur *nm Ordinat* counter

comptoir *nm* (**a**) *(bureau)* desk ❑ *comptoir d'enregistrement* check-in desk; *comptoir d'information* information desk; *comptoir de réception* reception desk; *comptoir de vente* sales counter (**b**) *Écon (cartel)* trading syndicate (**c**) *Banque* bank branch ❑ *comptoir d'escompte* discount house

comptoir-caisse *nm* cash desk

concaténé, -e *adj Ordinat* concatenated

concédant *nm Fin* grantor

concéder *vt (délai, réduction)* to grant

concentration *nf Écon* integration ❑ *concentration horizontale* horizontal integration; *concentration verticale* vertical integration

concept *nm* concept ❑ *concept de marketing* marketing concept; *concept de marque* brand concept; *concept publicitaire* advertising concept

concepteur, -trice *nm,f* designer ❑ *concepteur graphique* graphic designer; *concepteur multimédia* multimedia designer; *concepteur rédacteur* copywriter; *concepteur de sites Web* Web designer

conception *nf* design; **un produit de conception française** a French-designed product ❑ *conception assistée par ordinateur* computer-aided or computer-assisted design; *conception des produits* product design

concerner *vt* to concern; **en ce qui concerne** as regards, concerning; **les salariés concernés**

par cette mesure the employees concerned or affected by this measure

concerté, -e *adj (action, développement)* concerted

concession *nf* concession, franchise ❑ *concession exclusive et réciproque* tied outlet

concessionnaire 1 *adj (société)* concessionary

2 *nmf* agent, dealer; *(de licence)* licensee; *(de brevet)* patentee; *(de contrat de franchisage)* franchisee ❑ *concessionnaire agréé* approved dealer; *concessionnaire exclusif* sole agent or dealer; *concessionnaire export* export concessionaire

concevoir *vt (produit)* to design

conciliation *nf* arbitration, conciliation

conclure *vt* (**a**) *(discours, réunion)* to conclude, to end (**par** with) (**b**) *(accord, pacte)* to finalize; *(marché)* to clinch; *(vente)* to close; *(entente)* to reach

conclusion *nf (d'un accord, d'un pacte)* finalizing

concordat *nm* composition ❑ *concordat préventif (à la faillite)* composition, legal settlement *(between owners and creditors)*

concordataire *adj (failli)* certified

concours *nm* (**a**) *(pour obtenir un poste)* competitive examination ❑ *concours externe* external competitive examination; *concours interne* internal competitive examination (**b**) *(participation)* participation; **ce projet a été réalisé avec le concours d'Air France** this project was realized with the participation of or in association with Air France (**c**) *Banque* **concours bancaire** bank lending

concurrence *nf* (**a**) *Écon (concept)* competition; **la concurrence** *(les entreprises concurrentes)* the competition; **faire (de la) concurrence à qn/qch** to compete with sb/sth; **être en concurrence avec qn** to be in competition with sb; **entrer en concurrence avec qn** to compete with sb; **faire jouer la concurrence** to shop around; **nos prix défient toute concurrence** our prices are unbeatable; **la libre concurrence** free or open competition ❑ *concurrence acharnée* cut-throat competition; *concurrence déloyale* unfair competition; *concurrence directe* direct competition; *concurrence entre marques* brand competition; *concurrence imparfaite* imperfect competition; *concurrence parfaite* perfect competition; *concurrence pure* pure competition

(**b**) **à concurrence de, jusqu'à concurrence de** up to, up to the limit of; **vous pouvez être à découvert jusqu'à concurrence de 5000 euros** your overdraft limit is 5,000 euros

concurrencer *vt* to compete with; **leur nouvelle gamme ne peut concurrencer la nôtre** their new line can't compete with ours; **ils nous concurrencent dangereusement** they're very dangerous *or* serious competitors for us

concurrent, -e 1 *adj (industries, produits)* competing, rival
   2 *nm,f* competitor, rival; *(pour un poste)* candidate □ **concurrent principal** major competitor; *Mktg* **concurrent tardif** late entrant

concurrentiel, -elle *adj* competitive; **ces marchandises sont vendues à des prix concurrentiels** these goods are competitively priced

condenser *vt* Ordinat *(base de données)* to pack

condition *nf* **(a)** *(stipulation)* condition, stipulation; **sans condition** *(offre)* unconditional; **acheter des marchandises sous condition** to buy goods on sale or return; **signer qch sans condition/sous condition** to sign sth unconditionally/conditionally *or* provisionally; **envoyer des marchandises à condition** to send goods on approval; **conditions** *(d'une vente, d'un accord, d'un contrat)* terms; **faire de meilleures conditions** to give sb better terms □ **conditions d'admission** admission requirements; **conditions d'autorisation** licensing requirements; **conditions de crédit** terms of credit; **conditions d'embauche** conditions of employment; **conditions d'emploi** conditions of employment; **conditions de livraison** terms of delivery; **conditions du marché** market conditions; **conditions de paiement** terms (of payment); **condition préalable** prerequisite; **condition provisionnelle** proviso; **conditions de vente** conditions of sale
   (b) conditions *(circonstances)* conditions □ **conditions économiques (du marché)** economic situation; **conditions de travail** working conditions; **conditions de vie** living conditions
   (c) *(état)* condition; **les marchandises nous sont parvenues en bonne condition** the goods arrived in good condition

conditionné, -e *adj* prepacked, prepackaged

conditionnel, -elle *adj (vente, offre)* conditional; *(acceptation, endos)* qualified; *(clause)* provisory

conditionnement *nm (fait d'emballer, emballage)* packaging

conditionner *vt* to package

conditionneur, -euse *nm,f* packer

confectionner *vt* to manufacture; **confectionné sur demande** made up to order

conférence *nf (congrès)* conference; *(réunion)* meeting; **il est en conférence** he's in a meeting □ **conférence de presse** press conference; **conférence au sommet** summit (conference)

conférencier, -ère *nm,f* speaker

confiance de la clientèle, confiance du client *nf Mktg* client confidence

confidentialité *nf* confidentiality □ *Ordinat* **confidentialité des données** data privacy

confidentiel, -elle *adj (dossier, rapport, information)* confidential; **confidentiel** *(sur document)* private and confidential

confier *vt* **confier qch à qn** *(mission, tâche, dossier)* to entrust sth to sb, to entrust sb with sth

configurable *adj Ordinat* configurable

configuration *nf Ordinat* configuration □ **configuration par défaut** default setting; **configuration matérielle** hardware configuration

configurer *vt Ordinat* to configure

confirmation *nf* confirmation

confirmer *vt* to confirm; **les derniers chiffres confirment cette tendance** the latest figures confirm this trend; **confirmer qch par écrit** to confirm sth in writing

confisquer *vt* to confiscate, to seize

conflit *nm* dispute □ **conflit d'attributions** demarcation dispute; **conflits sociaux, conflits du travail** industrial *or* labour disputes

conforme *adj* compliant (**à** with); **conforme à l'an 2000** year 2000 compliant; **conforme à la demande** as per order; **conforme à la description** as represented; **conforme à l'échantillon** true to sample

conformément à *prép* in accordance with; **conformément à votre demande du 13 avril** in accordance with *or* as per your request of 13 April

conformer se conformer *vpr* **se conformer à qch** *(décision, règlement)* to abide by sth, to comply with sth

conformité *nf (d'un produit aux normes)* compliance (**à** with); **en conformité avec** in accordance with

conforter *vt* **conforter ses positions** to consolidate one's position

confrère *nm (de profession)* colleague; *(d'association)* fellow member

❝

Le deuxième constructeur d'automobiles japonais, Honda, a signé un accord de même nature avec un **confrère** chinois. Ces partenariats s'inscrivent dans une complémentarité entre les capacités productives des entreprises chinoises et les compétences technologiques des japonaises.

❞

congé *nm* **(a)** *(arrêt de travail)* leave (of absence) □ **congé pour convenance personnelle**

compassionate leave; **congé exceptionnel** leave of absence; **congé de longue durée** extended leave; **congé (de) maladie** sick leave; **congé (de) maternité** maternity leave; **congé de naissance** paternity leave; **congé parental d'éducation** = unpaid maternity or paternity leave; **congé (de) paternité** paternity leave; **congé sabbatique** sabbatical

(b) *(vacances)* Br holiday, Am vacation; **être en congé** to be on Br holiday or Am vacation; **prendre un congé d'une semaine** to take a week off; **un après-midi de congé** an afternoon off ◻ **congé annuel** Br annual leave, Am vacation leave; **congés payés** Br paid leave or holidays, Am paid vacation; **congé sans solde** Br unpaid leave or holidays, Am unpaid vacation

(c) *(avis de renvoi)* notice; **demander son congé** to hand in one's resignation, to give in one's notice; **donner (son) congé à qn** *(à un employé)* to give sb his/her notice, to dismiss sb; **donner congé à qn** *(à un locataire)* to give sb notice to quit; *(à un propriétaire)* to give sb notice of leaving

> **❝**
> A défaut d'accord, le salarié peut imposer son choix. Durant le **congé paternité**, le père reçoit les indemnités journalières de la Sécurité sociale, calculées comme celles de la mère. Elles sont à peu près égales à son salaire net, limitées au plafond Sécurité sociale.
> **❞**

congédiement *nm* dismissal

congédier *vt* to dismiss

conglomérat *nm Écon* conglomerate

congrès *nm* congress ◻ **congrès annuel** annual congress

congressiste *nmf* conference delegate

conjoint, -e 1 *adj (dette, compte, responsabilité)* joint

2 *nm,f Admin* spouse; **il faut l'accord des deux conjoints** the agreement of both husband and wife is necessary

conjointement *adv* jointly; **conjointement et solidairement** jointly and severally

conjoncture *nf Écon* **conjoncture (économique)** economic situation, economic circumstances; **on assiste à une dégradation de la conjoncture économique** a deterioration in the economic situation is taking place ◻ *Bourse* **conjoncture boursière** market trend

> **❝**
> La reprise économique allemande est là, mais avec un peu de retard ... L'indice de confiance ZEW – établi sur les opinions des analystes et des investisseurs sur la **conjoncture** – a grimpé, d'un coup, de plus de 21 points.
> **❞**

conjoncturel, -elle *adj Écon (chômage, fluctuations)* cyclical; *(prévisions, stratégie, politique)* economic

conjoncturiste *nmf Écon* economic analyst or planner

connaissance *nf* (a) **prendre connaissance de qch** *(dossier, rapport)* to acquaint oneself with sth (b) *Mktg* **connaissance de la marque** brand familiarity, brand awareness (c) *Ordinat* **connaissances informatiques** computer literacy; **avoir des connaissances informatiques** to be computer-literate

connaissement *nm* bill of lading, waybill ◻ **connaissement aérien** air waybill; **connaissement clausé** dirty bill of lading; **connaissement direct** through bill; **connaissement embarqué** shipped bill, shipping bill; **connaissement d'entrée** inward bill of lading; **connaissement maritime** marine bill of lading; **connaissement net** clean bill of lading; **connaissement de sortie** outward bill of lading; **connaissement de transbordement** transshipment bill of lading

connecté, -e *adj Ordinat* **être connecté** to be connected

connecter *Ordinat* **1** *vt* to connect; **connecté en anneau/bus/étoile** in a ring/bus/star configuration; **connecté en série** series-connected; **connecter en boucle** to daisy-chain

2 se connecter *vpr* **se connecter à un système** to log on to a system

connecteur *nm Ordinat* connector

connectivité *nf Ordinat* connectivity

connexion *nf Ordinat* connection

conquérir *vt (marché, part de marché)* to conquer; **l'entreprise a réussi à conquérir de nouvelles parts de marché en dépit de la récession** the company has managed to conquer new market shares despite the recession

conquête *nf (d'un marché, d'une part de marché)* conquest; **la conquête de nouveaux marchés en Asie est une des priorités de l'entreprise** conquering new Asian markets is one of the company's priorities

consacrer *vt (budget, fonds)* to devote (**à** to); **avez-vous dix minutes à me consacrer?** can you spare me ten minutes?

conseil *nm* (a) *(personne)* consultant ◻ **conseil en communication** media consultant; **conseil financier** financial consultant or adviser; **conseil fiscal** tax consultant; **conseil en gestion** management consultant; **conseil juridique** legal adviser; **conseil en marketing** marketing consultant; **conseil de presse** press adviser; **conseil en promotion** advertising consultant; **conseil en publicité** advertising consultant; **conseil en recrutement** recruitment consultant (**b**) *(assemblée)* council, committee; *(d'une entreprise)* board; *(réunion)* meeting; **la banque fait partie du conseil** the bank is represented on the board ❑ *conseil d'administration* board of directors; *conseil d'arbitrage* conciliation *or* arbitration board; *Conseil des Bourses de valeurs* = regulatory body of the Paris Stock Exchange; *conseil de direction* management committee; *conseil de discipline* disciplinary board; *conseil Ecofin* ECOFIN; *conseil économique* economic council; *conseil d'entreprise* works committee; *Conseil de l'Europe* Council of Europe; *conseil général* regional council; *conseil de gestion* board of trustees; *Conseil national du crédit* National Credit Council; *conseil des prud'hommes* industrial tribunal; *conseil régional* regional council; *Conseil de sécurité (de l'ONU)* Security Council; *conseil de surveillance* supervisory board; *conseil syndical* trade union council

(**c**) *(pour aider)* advice ❑ *conseil en placements* investment advice

conseiller¹, -ère *nm,f* (**a**) *(spécialiste)* adviser, consultant ❑ *conseiller de clientèle* consumer adviser; *conseiller commercial* marketing *or* sales consultant; *conseiller de direction* management consultant; *conseiller économique* economic adviser; *conseiller financier* financial adviser *or* consultant; *conseiller financier indépendant* independent financial adviser; *conseiller fiscal* tax consultant; *conseiller en gestion (d'entreprise)* management consultant; *conseiller juridique* legal adviser; *conseiller en marketing, conseiller en mercatique* marketing consultant; *conseiller en placements* investment adviser; *conseiller professionnel* careers adviser *or* counsellor; *conseiller technique* technical adviser (**b**) *(membre d'un conseil)* councillor ❑ *conseiller municipal* local councillor

conseiller² *vt* to advise; **conseiller qch à qn** to recommend sth to sb; **conseiller à qn de faire qch** to advise sb to do sth

consentement *nm* consent; **donner son consentement à qch** to consent to sth ❑ *consentement exprès* formal consent

consentir 1 *vt (prêt)* to grant; *(remise)* to allow; **on m'a consenti une remise de dix pour cent/un délai supplémentaire de quinze jours** I was allowed a ten percent discount/another two weeks

2 *vi* to consent, to agree (**à** to)

conservateur, -trice *nm,f conservateur des hypothèques* mortgage registrar; *Bourse conservateur de titres* custodian

conservation *nf Bourse* custody ❑ *conservation globale, conservation internationale (d'actions)* global custody; *conservation nationale (d'actions)* local custody; subcustody

consignataire *nmf* (**a**) *(dépositaire)* depositary (**b**) *(destinataire)* consignee

consignateur, -trice *nm,f* consigner, shipper

consignation *nf* (**a**) *(d'argent)* deposit (**b**) *(de marchandises)* consignment; **en consignation** on consignment; **envoyer qch à qn en consignation** to consign sth to sb, to send sth to sb on consignment

consigne *nf* (**a**) *(pour les bagages) Br* left-luggage office, *Am* checkroom ❑ *consigne automatique* lockers (**b**) *Douanes* **laisser des marchandises en consigne** to consign goods; **il a dû laisser des marchandises en consigne à la douane** his goods were held up at customs (**c**) *(d'emballage)* deposit (**d**) *(ordres)* orders, instructions; **suivre les consignes** to follow orders

consigné, -e *adj (emballage)* returnable

consigner *vt* (**a**) *(bagages) Br* to leave at the left-luggage office, *Am* to check (**b**) *Douanes (marchandises)* to consign (**à** to); **ses marchandises ont été consignées par la douane car il n'avait pas les documents requis** his goods were held up at customs because he didn't have the necessary papers (**c**) *(emballage)* to charge a deposit on (**d**) *(argent)* to deposit (**e**) *(noter)* to record, to put down

console *nf Ordinat* console ❑ *console de visualisation* visual display unit, VDU

consolidation *nf Fin (d'une dette)* funding, financing; *(des bénéfices, des fonds, d'un bilan)* consolidation ❑ *Mktg* **consolidation de ligne** line filling

consolidé, -e *Fin* **1** *adj (dette)* funded, financed; *(bénéfices, fonds, bilan)* consolidated

2 *nm* **consolidés** consols

consolider *vt Fin (dette)* to fund, to finance; *(bénéfices, fonds, bilan)* to consolidate; **l'euro a consolidé son avance à la Bourse** the euro has strengthened its lead on the Stock Exchange

consommable 1 *adj* consumable

2 *nm Ordinat* **consommables** consumables

consommateur, -trice *nm,f Écon* consumer; **producteurs et consommateurs** producers and consumers ❑ *Mktg* **consommateur cible** target consumer; *Mktg* **consommateur final** end-user

consommation *nf Écon* consumption ❑ *consommation d'énergie* energy consumption; *Compta* **consommations de l'exercice** total annual expenses; *consommation intérieure* home consumption; *consommation de masse* mass consumption; *consommation des ménages* household consumption; *consommation mondiale* world consumption; *consommation par tête* per capita consumption; *consommation totale* overall consumption

> **"**
> Une situation que la Bourse n'apprécie pas à l'heure où l'inflation menace et où la reprise s'amorce sans que les composantes principales de la demande (**consommation des ménages** et investissements des entreprises) soient suffisamment solides.
> **"**

consommatique *nf* consumer research

consommatisme *nm* consumerism

consommer *vt* to consume

consomptible *adj* consumable

consortial, -e *adj* consortium, syndicated

consortium *nm* consortium, syndicate ❑ *consortium de banques* banking consortium

constant, -e *adj Fin* constant; **en euros/dollars constants** in constant euros/dollars

constat *nm Jur* certified statement *or* report; **dresser** *ou* **faire un constat** to draw up a report ❑ *constat amiable* = report of road accident agreed by the parties involved

constatation *nf* (**a**) *Assur* **constatation des dommages** assessment of damages (**b**) *Compta* **constatation de stock** stocktake

constaté, -e *adj Fin (valeur)* registered; **constaté d'avance** *(charge)* prepaid

constater *vt* (**a**) *(observer) (augmentation, hausse, baisse)* to note (**b**) *Assur (dommages)* to assess

constituer 1 *vt* (**a**) *(créer) (société, comité, association)* to form, to set up; *(capital, stocks)* to build up (**b**) *(représenter)* to constitute, to represent; **ceci constitue une faute professionnelle grave** this constitutes serious professional misconduct; **ceci constitue un excellent résultat pour l'entreprise** this represents an excellent result for the company
  2 se constituer *vpr* **se constituer en SARL** to form a limited company; **se constituer un portefeuille de clients** to build up a client portfolio

constitutif, -ive *adj Jur* constitutive

constitution *nf (d'une société, d'un comité, d'une association)* formation, setting up; *(du capital, des stocks)* building up

constructeur *nm* builder ❑ *constructeur automobile* car manufacturer

constructeur-promoteur *nm* property developer

constructible *adj (terrain)* suitable for building on

construction *nf* building, construction; **être en construction** to be under construction

construire *vt* to build, to construct

consultant, -e *nm,f* consultant

consultatif, -ive *adj (comité, conseil, document)* consultative, advisory; **avoir une voix consultative** to be present in an advisory capacity; **à titre consultatif** in an advisory capacity

consulter *vt* to consult

consumérisme *nm* consumerism

consumer magazine *nm* = free leaflet advertising the products of a shop or other company, usually promoting particular products and/or special offers

contact *nm* (**a**) *(personne)* contact; **il a de nombreux contacts dans la profession** he has a lot of contacts in the industry (**b**) *(lien)* contact; **prendre contact** *ou* **se mettre en contact avec qn** to get in touch *or* in contact with sb (**c**) *Ordinat* **contact de page** hit

contacter *vt (personne)* to contact; **ils l'ont contacté pour un entretien** they contacted him to arrange an interview; **on peut me contacter par téléphone au bureau** I can be reached by phone at the office

container = **conteneur**

contaminé, -e *adj Ordinat* **contaminé par un virus** virus-infected

conteneur *nm* container

conteneurisation *nf* containerization

conteneuriser *vt* to containerize

contenir *vt (inflation)* to control, to check

contentieux *nm (conflit)* dispute; *Jur* litigation; *(service)* legal department; **avoir un contentieux avec qn** to be in dispute with sb; **les contentieux en cours** the claims being disputed

contenu *nm (d'un colis)* contents; *(d'une lettre, d'un document)* content

contestation *nf* (**a**) *(d'une loi, d'un testament, d'un document)* contesting; *(d'un droit)* contesting, questioning (**b**) *(litige)* dispute

contester *vt (loi, testament, document)* to contest; *(droit)* to contest, to question

contingent *nm* quota ❑ *contingents d'exportation* export quotas; *contingents d'importation* import quotas

contingentement *nm* (**a**) *(imposition de quotas)* fixing of quotas; **le contingentement des importations** the fixing of import quotas (**b**) *(système)* quota system of distribution

contingenter *vt (importations, exportations)* to fix quotas on, to limit ❑ *produits contingentés* fixed quota products

continuité d'exploitation *nf Fin* going-concern status

contractant, -e *Jur* **1** *adj* contracting
  2 *nm,f* contracting party

contracter *vt (dette)* to incur, to contract; *(emprunt)* to contract; **contracter une assurance**

to take out insurance *or* an insurance policy

contraction *nf (de l'activité, de la demande, du crédit)* reduction (**de** in)

contractuel, -elle **1** *adj (main-d'œuvre, garantie)* contractual; *(droits)* granted by contract **2** *nm,f* contract worker

> **"**
>
> Et France Télécom, qu'en pense-t-il ? Des milliers d'emplois supprimés en quelques années, des **contractuels** surexploités, des militants syndicalistes traînés en conseil de discipline ou devant la justice, la casse de tout le système social, la remise en cause des droits les plus élémentaires, le harcèlement moral, 24 milliards de francs de bénéfices ... C'est ça la réalité quotidienne d'une ex-entreprise publique où l'Etat est encore majoritaire.
>
> **"**

contrat *nm (accord)* contract; **être lié par contrat** to be bound by contract; **passer un contrat (avec qn)** to enter into a contract (with sb); **rédiger** *ou* **dresser un contrat** to draw up a contract; **résilier un contrat** to cancel a contract ▫ *contrat d'agence* agency contract; *Admin* **contrat aidé** = employment contract whereby part of an employee's salary is paid by the state; *contrat d'apprentissage* contract of apprenticeship; *contrat d'assurance* insurance policy; *contrat d'assurance-vie* life insurance policy; *contrat de bail* lease agreement; *contrat de base* principal contract; *contrat collectif* group contract; *contrat commercial* commercial contract; *contrat de concession* licence agreement; *contrat à courte durée* short-term contract; *contrat à durée déterminée* fixed-term contract; *contrat à durée indéterminée* permanent contract; *contrat d'embauche* *Br* employment contract, contract of employment, *Am* labor contract; *contrat d'emploi-solidarité* = short-term contract subsidized by the government; *contrat d'entreprise* building contract; *contrat exclusif* sole contract; *contrat de garantie* underwriting contract; *contrat de licence* licensing agreement; *contrat de location* rental agreement; *contrat de location-vente* *Br* hire-purchase agreement, *Am* installment plan agreement; *contrat de mandat* agency agreement; *contrat de mission d'intérim* temporary contract; *contrat notarié* notarized contract; *contrat à plein temps* full-time contract; *contrat de prêt* loan agreement; *contrat de productivité* productivity deal; *contrat psychologique* psychological contract; *contrat de qualification* employment and training contract; *contrat de représentation exclusive* sole agency contract; *contrat de service* service contract; *contrat social* social contract;

contrat de sponsoring sponsorship deal; *contrat temporaire* temporary contract; *contrat à temps partiel* part-time contract; *contrat à temps plein* full-time contract; *Bourse, Fin* **contrat à terme** forward contract, futures contract; *Bourse, Fin* **contrat à terme d'instruments financiers** financial futures contract; *Bourse, Fin* **contrat à terme sous option** underlying futures contract; *contrat de transport* contract of carriage; *contrat de travail* *Br* employment contract, contract of employment, *Am* labor contract; *contrat de travail temporaire* temporary contract; *contrat de vente* bill of sale, sales contract, sales agreement

contre-analyse *nf* check analysis

contre-assurance *nf* reinsurance

contre-attaque *nf* countermove

contrebalancer *vt* to offset; **les bénéfices ne contrebalancent plus les pertes** profits are no longer balancing losses

contrebande *nf (activité)* smuggling; *(marchandises)* contraband; **faire de la contrebande** to smuggle goods; **faire entrer des marchandises en contrebande** to smuggle in goods; **de contrebande** smuggled

contre-écriture *nf Compta* contra-entry

contre-épreuve *nf* cross-check

contre-expertise *nf* second valuation

contrefaçon *nf* (a) *(d'une marque)* counterfeiting; *(d'un brevet, d'un droit de reproduction)* infringement (b) *(d'un billet de banque, de monnaie)* forgery; *(d'un produit)* imitation

contrefacteur, -trice *nm,f* (a) *(d'une marque)* counterfeiter; *(d'un brevet, d'un droit de reproduction)* infringer (b) *(d'un billet de banque, de monnaie)* forger; *(d'un produit)* imitator

contrefaire *vt* (a) *(marque)* to counterfeit; *(brevet, droit de reproduction)* to infringe (b) *(billet de banque, monnaie)* to forge; **contrefaire des produits de luxe** to manufacture imitation luxury goods

contremaître, -esse *nm,f* foreman, *f* forewoman

contremarché *nm* countermove

contre-offensive *nf* counteroffer

contre-offre *nf* counteroffer

> **"**
>
> Pour arriver à une solution rapide, le patron de TotalFina suggère même aux actionnaires d'Elf de refuser l'augmentation de capital nécessaire pour financer la **contre-offre**, qui sera proposée à l'assemblée générale le 3 septembre.
>
> **"**

contre-OPA *nf* counterbid

contre-ordre *nm* counterorder; **sauf contre-ordre de votre part** unless we hear from you to the contrary

contrepartie *nf* (**a**) *(compensation)* compensation; **en contrepartie** in return (**de** for) ❏ **contrepartie financière** financial compensation; **vous aurez la contrepartie financière de la perte subie** you will be financially compensated for the loss incurred (**b**) *Fin (dans une transaction)* other party (**c**) *Compta* contra; *(d'une inscription)* counterpart; *(d'un registre)* duplicate; **en contrepartie** per contra (**d**) *(de document)* counterpart, duplicate (**e**) *Bourse* hedging, market making; **faire (de) la contrepartie** to operate against one's client

contre-passation *nf* (**a**) *Compta* journal entry, contra-entry; *(d'un article, d'une entrée)* reversing, transferring (**b**) *Fin (d'un effet)* return, endorsement, backing

contre-passer *vt* (**a**) *Compta (article, entrée)* to reverse, to transfer (**b**) *Fin (effet)* to return, to endorse, to back

contreseing *nm* countersignature

contresigner *vt* to countersign

contretemps *nm* hitch, mishap; **nous vous prions de nous excuser de ce contretemps** please excuse us for this unexpected inconvenience

contre-valeur *nf Fin* exchange value; **pour la contre-valeur de 300 euros** in exchange for 300 euros

contribuable *nmf* taxpayer

❝

La crise des années 30, et plus récemment celle du Japon, sont censées nous avoir enseigné, il faut que l'argent ne coûte rien et que l'État apparaisse comme "prêteur en dernier ressort". Or il paraît difficile d'imaginer, qu'au final, le **contribuable** américain assume des pertes consécutives à tous les dépôts de bilan.

❞

contribuer contribuer à *vt ind* to contribute to; **ceci a contribué à faire baisser l'inflation** this helped to bring down inflation

contributeur *nm UE* contributor ❏ **contributeur net** net contributor

contribution *nf Admin (impôt)* tax; **contributions** *(à l'État)* taxes; *(à la collectivité locale) Br* ≃ council tax, *Am* ≃ local taxes; **(bureau des) contributions** tax office, *Br* ≃ Inland Revenue, *Am* ≃ Internal Revenue; **lever** *ou* **percevoir une contribution** to collect *or* levy a tax; **payer ses contributions** to pay one's taxes ❏ **contributions directes** direct taxation; **contribution**

foncière land tax; **contributions indirectes** indirect taxation; **contribution sociale généralisée** = income-based tax deducted at source as a contribution to paying off the French social security budget deficit

contrôlable *adj (inflation, chômage)* controllable

contrôle *nm* (**a**) *(de l'information, de déclarations)* checking, verification; *(des employés, du travail, des marchandises)* inspection; *Compta (des comptes)* checking, auditing ❏ **contrôle bancaire** banking controls; *Compta* **contrôle du bilan** audit; **contrôle budgétaire** budgetary control; *Fin* **contrôle des changes** (foreign) exchange control; **contrôle de la comptabilité** accounting control; *Fin* **contrôle de comptes** audit; *Mktg* **contrôle continu** monitoring; **contrôle de douanes, contrôle douanier** customs control; **contrôle d'efficacité du marketing** *ou* **mercatique** marketing efficiency study; **contrôle financier** financial control; *Fin* **contrôle fiscal** tax inspection; **contrôle de gestion** management audit; **contrôles à l'importation** import controls; **contrôle monétaire** monetary control; **contrôle monopolistique** monopoly control; **contrôle des points de ventes** store audit; **contrôle de présence** timekeeping; **contrôle des prix** price control; **contrôle de (la) qualité** quality control; **contrôle de la qualité globale** *ou* **totale** total quality control; **contrôle par sondage(s)** random check; **contrôle des stocks** *Br* stock *or Am* inventory control (**b**) *(maîtrise)* control; **prendre le contrôle d'une entreprise** to take over a company (**c**) *Ordinat* control ❏ **contrôle d'accès** access control; **contrôle du curseur** cursor control

contrôler *vt* (**a**) *(information, déclarations)* to check, to verify; *(employés, travail, marchandises)* to inspect; *Compta (comptes)* to check, to audit; **contrôler les livres** to check the books (**b**) *(prix, inflation, chômage)* to control (**c**) *(entreprise)* to control; **ce groupe contrôle dix pour cent de notre entreprise** this group controls ten percent of our company (**d**) *Ordinat* **contrôlé par le logiciel** software-controlled; **contrôlé par menu** menu-driven, menu-controlled; **contrôlé par ordinateur** computer-controlled

contrôleur, -euse 1 *nm,f* (**a**) *(des comptes)* auditor ❏ **contrôleur des contributions** tax inspector, inspector of taxes; **contrôleur du crédit** credit controller; **contrôleur des douanes** customs inspector; **contrôleur financier** financial controller; **contrôleur de gestion** management accountant; **contrôleur des impôts** tax inspector, inspector of taxes; **contrôleur aux liquidations** controller in bankruptcy (**b**) *(du travail)* supervisor **2** *nm Ordinat* **contrôleur d'affichage** display *or* screen controller; **contrôleur de bus** bus controller; **contrôleur de disque** disk controller

convenir convenir de *vt ind* to agree on, to come to an agreement on; **convenir d'un prix/ d'une date (avec qn)** to agree on a price/date (with sb)

convention *nf* agreement; *Jur (d'un contrat)* article, clause ◻ **convention collective** collective (bargaining) agreement; **convention de crédit** credit agreement; **convention de double imposition** double taxation agreement; **convention écrite** written agreement; **convention monétaire** monetary agreement; **convention sociale** social contract; **convention verbale** verbal agreement

conventionné, -e *adj* (**a**) *(médecin, clinique)* registered with the health system, *Br* ≃ NHS (**b**) *(prix, honoraires)* agreed, set

convenu, -e *adj (prix, honoraires)* agreed, set; **comme convenu, les marchandises commandées seront livrées le 22 courant** as agreed, the goods ordered will be delivered on the 22nd

conversion *nf* (**a**) *Fin (d'argent, de devises étrangères, de titres, d'un emprunt)* conversion ◻ **taux de conversion** rate of exchange, exchange rate (**b**) *Ordinat (de données)* conversion ◻ **conversion de fichier** file conversion

convertibilité *nf Fin* convertibility

convertible *Fin* **1** *adj (obligation, monnaie)* convertible (**en** into)
2 *nf* convertible

convertir *vt* (**a**) *Fin (argent, devises étrangères, titres, emprunt)* to convert (**en** into); **convertir des valeurs en espèces** to convert securities into cash; **convertir des rentes** to convert stock (**b**) *Ordinat (données)* to convert; **convertir un système en numérique** to digitize a system

convertissement *nm Fin (de valeurs en espèces)* conversion (**en** into)

convertisseur analogique numérique *nm Ordinat* digitizer

convivial, -e *adj (ordinateur, machine)* user-friendly

convivialité *nf (d'un ordinateur, d'une machine)* user-friendliness

convocation *nf* (**a**) *(d'une assemblée)* convening (**b**) *(d'un employé, d'un candidat)* summoning

convoquer *vt* (**a**) *(assemblée)* to call together, to convene; **convoquer les actionnaires** to call *or* summon the shareholders to a meeting; **convoquer une assemblée générale** to call a general meeting (**b**) *(employé, candidat)* to call in; **le directeur m'a convoqué** the manager called me in; **elle m'a convoqué dans son bureau** she called me into her office; **ils m'ont convoqué pour passer un entretien** they've called me in for an interview

coobligation *nf* joint obligation

cookie *nm Ordinat* cookie

coopératif, -ive *Écon* **1** *adj (société, banque)* co-operative
2 *nf* **coopérative** co-operative, co-op ◻ **coopérative d'achats** wholesale co-operative; **coopérative agricole** agricultural co-operative; **coopérative ouvrière** workers' co-operative; **coopérative de production** producers' co-operative; **coopérative vinicole** wine co-operative

coopération *nf Écon* co-operation ◻ **société de coopération** co-operative society

coopératisme *nm Écon* co-operation, co-operative system

cooptation *nf* co-option

coopter *vt* to co-opt

coordinateur, -trice **1** *adj* co-ordinating
2 *nm,f* co-ordinator

coordination *nf (d'ouvriers)* committee

coordonnées *nfpl* name, address and telephone number; **laissez-moi vos coordonnées et je vous contacterai** leave me your details and I'll contact you

coparticipant, -e *nm,f Jur* copartner

coparticipation *nf Jur* copartnership; **coparticipation des employés dans les bénéfices** profit-sharing

copatronage *nm* co-sponsoring, cosponsorship

copie *nf* (**a**) *(d'un document, d'une lettre)* copy; **faire une copie de qch** to copy sth, to make a copy of sth ◻ **copie archivée** archive (copy); *Admin, Jur* **copie authentique** certified copy; **copie au carbone** carbon copy; *Admin, Jur* **copie certifiée conforme** certified copy; **copie conforme (à l'original)** true *or* exact copy; **pour copie conforme** *(sur document)* certified true copy; **copie pour information** information copy; **copie au net** fair copy, final copy; **copie papier** paper copy; **copie au propre** fair copy, final copy; *Mktg* **copie stratégie (créative)** (creative) copy strategy; **copie de travail** working copy
(**b**) *Ordinat* copy ◻ **copie de bloc** copy block; **copie en clair** hard copy, printout; **copie de disquette** *(commande DOS)* disk copy; **copie d'écran** print screen; **copie sur papier** hard copy, printout; **copie de sauvegarde** backup copy; **copie de sûreté** backup copy

copier *vt (document, lettre)* to copy; *Ordinat* **copier qch sur le disque dur** to copy sth onto hard disk; **copier qch sur disquette** to copy sth to disk

copier-coller *nm Ordinat* copy-and-paste; **faire un copier-coller (sur qch)** to copy and paste (sth)

copieur *nm* (photo)copier

coporteur *nm Fin* joint holder

coposséder *vt Jur* to own jointly, to have joint ownership of

copossesseur *nm Jur* joint owner

copossession *nf Jur* joint ownership

copreneur, -euse *nm,f Jur* co-lessee, co-tenant

coprésidence *nf* co-chairmanship

coprésident, -e *nm,f* co-chairman, *f* co-chairwoman

coprocesseur *nm Ordinat* co-processor ❏ **co-processeur arithmétique** maths co-processor

coproducteur, -trice *nm,f* coproducer, joint producer

coproduction *nf* coproduction

copropriétaire *nmf Jur* joint owner, co-owner

copropriété *nf Jur* joint ownership, co-ownership

copyright *nm* copyright

copyrighter *vt* to copyright

copy stratégie *nf Mktg* copy strategy ❏ **copy stratégie créative** creative copy strategy

coquille vide *nf* shell company (exempt from taxes)

> **"**
> Créer, pour le compte d'une connaissance, une société offshore afin d'acheter un bien immobilier à l'étranger en évitant les impôts? Rien de plus simple, il suffit que l'acheteur vienne, dès lendemain, prendre possession d'une **coquille vide** – une société-écran exemptée d'impôts – pour 650 dollars, payables par carte Visa® ou par virement.
> **"**

corbeille *nf* (a) *Bourse* trading floor ❏ **corbeille des obligations** bond-trading ring (b) *Ordinat* (de Mac) wastebasket, *Am* trash; (dans Windows®) recycle bin ❏ **corbeille d'arrivée** (pour courrier électronique) in box; **corbeille de départ** (pour courrier électronique) out box (c) (panier) **corbeille à courrier** desk tray; **corbeille à papier** paper tray

corporatif, -ive *adj* (institution, système) corporative; (image, esprit) corporate

corporation *nf* corporate body ❏ **corporation professionnelle** professional body

corps *nm* (a) (d'un document, d'un courrier électronique) body (b) *Ordinat* (de police de caractères) point size, type size, font size (c) (groupe) body ❏ **corps constitué** corporate body; **corps de métier** trade

correcteur *nm* (a) *Ordinat* checker ❏ **cor-**

recteur grammatical grammar checker; **correcteur d'orthographe, correcteur orthographique** spellchecker (b) **correcteur liquide** correcting fluid, *Br* Tipp-Ex®, *Am* whiteout

correction *nf* correction ❏ **correction du marché** market correction; *Ordinat* **correction d'orthographe, correction orthographique** spellcheck; **correction des variations saisonnières** seasonal adjustment

correspondance *nf* correspondence; **être en correspondance avec qn** to be in correspondence with sb; **référence à rappeler dans toutes les correspondances** please quote this reference number in all correspondence ❏ **correspondance commerciale** business correspondence

correspondant, -e *nm,f* (dans la presse) correspondent ❏ **correspondant financier** financial correspondent

corriger *vt* to correct; **corriger qch à la hausse/à la baisse** (chiffre) to round sth up/down; **en données corrigées des variations saisonnières** seasonally adjusted; *Ordinat* **corriger automatiquement** to autocorrect

cosignataire *nmf* co-signatory

cosignature *nf* co-signature

cosigner *vt* to co-sign

cotation *nf Bourse* quotation, listing ❏ **cotation en continu** continuous *or* all-day trading; **cotation à la corbeille** floor trading; **cotation au cours du marché** market quotation; **cotation à la criée** open-outcry trading; **cotation de l'or** gold fixing; **cotation par téléphone** telephone dealing; **cotation à vue** spot quotation, sight quotation

cote *nf* (a) *Bourse* (valeur) quotation; (liste) share index; **inscrit** *ou* **admis à la cote** listed *or* quoted on the Stock Exchange; **retirer qch de la cote** (société, actions) to delist sth; **hors cote** (actions) unlisted; (marché) *Br* unofficial, *Am* over-the-counter ❏ **cote à la clôture, côte de clôture** closing price; **cote officielle** official list; **cote des prix** official list, official share list (b) *Jur* (d'un document) (classification) mark (c) *Admin* assessment ❏ **cote foncière** assessment on land; **cote mobilière** property assessment (d) (de dépenses, d'impôts) quote, share, proportion

coté, -e *adj Bourse* listed, quoted; **non coté** unlisted, unquoted; **être coté à 100 euros** to be trading at 100 euros

coter *vt* (a) *Bourse* to list, to quote; **des valeurs qui seront cotées en Bourse demain** shares which will go on the Stock Exchange tomorrow; **coter à l'ouverture/à la clôture** to open/close (b) *Jur* (documents) to classify; **coté, daté et paraphé** numbered, dated and signed

cotisant, -e *nm,f* (**a**) *(à une organisation)* subscribing member (**b**) *(à une caisse, à une mutuelle)* contributor

cotisation *nf* (**a**) *(à une organisation)* subscription (**b**) *(à une caisse, à une mutuelle)* contribution ▫ **cotisation annuelle** annual contribution; **cotisations maladie** health insurance contributions; **cotisation ouvrière** employee's contribution; **cotisation patronale** employer's contribution; **cotisation des salariés** employee's contribution; **cotisations à la Sécurité sociale** ≃ National Insurance contributions; **cotisations sociales** ≃ National Insurance and National Health contributions; **cotisation syndicale** union dues

❝

Elle compromet la compétitivité de la France, et, surtout, son indispensable spécialisation vers les activités à haute valeur ajoutée. Ces activités exigent des cadres et employés dits à "valeur internationale de marché", les VIM, que la fiscalité et les **cotisations sociales** rendent trop chers pour des entreprises installées en France.

❞

cotiser *vi* (**a**) *(à une organisation)* to subscribe (**à** to) (**b**) *(à une caisse de retraite, à une mutuelle)* to contribute, to pay one's contributions (**à** to); **cotiser à la Sécurité sociale** ≃ to pay one's National Insurance (contributions)

coulage *nm (perte)* wastage; *(vol)* petty theft; *(fuite)* leakage

couler 1 *vt (affaire, entreprise)* to bring down, to cause to go under
2 *vi (affaire, entreprise)* to go under

coulisse *nf Bourse* outside market, kerb market

coulissier *nm Bourse* outside broker, kerb broker

coupe *nf* cut ▫ **coupes budgétaires** budget cuts; **coupe claire** drastic cut; **coupe sombre** drastic cut

❝

D'autant que le renouveau économique s'est opéré sur fond de **coupes claires** dans les effectifs du secteur public : 140 000 fonctionnaires ont été jetés au chômage depuis 1998 et les chaebols (conglomérats) ont licencié massivement. Ultime chiffre éclairant : 89 000 des 831 000 chômeurs, démoralisés par la situation actuelle, ont arrêté leur recherche de travail.

❞

coupe-papier *nm* letter opener

couper *vt (texte)* to cut

couper-coller *nm Ordinat* cut-and-paste; **faire un couper-coller (sur qch)** to cut and paste (sth)

couple produit/marché *nm Mktg* product/market pair

coupon *nm Fin* coupon ▫ **coupon d'action** coupon; **coupon attaché** cum dividend *or* coupon; **coupon détaché, coupon échu** ex dividend *or* coupon; **coupon de vol** flight coupon

couponing, couponnage *nm Fin* couponing

coupon-prime *nm* gift voucher

coupon-réponse *nm* reply coupon ▫ **coupon-réponse international** international reply coupon

coupure *nf Fin* denomination; **coupure de 50 euros** 50-euro note; **50 000 euros en petites coupures** 50,000 euros in small notes *or* denominations; **en coupures usagées** in used notes

❝

Cette activité historique de "grossiste" en devises étrangères vient de connaître un gonflement artificiel avec le passage à l'euro : CPR-Billets a recueilli avant le 17 février des tombereaux de **coupures** diverses que les Français avaient ramenées de leurs voyages dans les pays de l'Euroland.

❞

cour *nf (tribunal)* court ▫ **Cour d'appel** *Br* ≃ Court of Appeal, *Am* ≃ appelate court; **Cour de cassation** ≃ Supreme Court of Appeal; **la Cour des comptes** ≃ the Audit Office; **Cour européenne des droits de l'homme** European Court of Human Rights; **Cour européenne de justice** European Court of Justice; **cour de justice** law court

courant, -e 1 *adj* (**a**) *(en cours)* current; **l'année courante** the current year; **le cinq (du mois) courant** the fifth of this month; **fin courant** at the end of this month (**b**) *(marque, taille)* standard
2 *nm* trend; **le courant économique actuel** the present economic situation ▫ **courant d'affaires** business trend

courbe *nf* curve; *(graphe)* graph ▫ **courbe d'augmentation de salaire** salary progression curve; *Compta* **courbe des coûts** cost curve; *Écon* **courbe de croissance** growth curve; *Mktg* **courbe du cycle de vie (du produit)** (product) lifecycle curve; *Mktg* **courbe de la demande** demand curve; *Mktg* **courbe de distribution** distribution curve; *Mktg* **courbe de distribution normale** normal distribution curve; *Mktg* **courbe d'expérience** experience curve; **courbe d'investissement** investment curve; *Mktg* **courbe de l'offre** supply curve; **courbe des prix** price curve; **courbe des salaires** salary curve; **courbe des taux** yield curve; **courbe des ventes** sales chart

courir *vi (intérêts)* to accrue; *(bail)* to run; **les**

intérêts qui courent the accruing interest; **le bail n'a plus qu'un an à courir** the lease has only one more year to run; **le mois qui court** the current month

courrier nm mail, Br post; **par retour du courrier** by return of post; **dépouiller son courrier** to go through or open one's mail ◽ **courrier de départ** outgoing mail; **courrier électronique** e-mail, electronic mail; **envoyer un courrier électronique à qn** to e-mail sb; **envoyer qch par courrier électronique** to send sth by e-mail; **contacter qn par courrier électronique** to contact sb by e-mail; Fam **courrier escargot** snail mail; **courrier interne** internal mail; **courrier publicitaire** junk mail

courriériste nmf (dans la presse) columnist

cours nm (a) (d'argent) currency; **avoir cours** to be legal tender ◽ **cours forcé** forced currency; **cours légal** legal tender; **avoir cours légal** to be legal tender

(b) Bourse, Fin (d'une action) price, quotation; (de devises) rate; **au cours (du jour)** at the current daily price; **quel est le cours du sucre?** what is the price or quotation for sugar?; **premier cours** opening price ◽ **cours acheteur** bid price; **cours des actions** share prices; **cours de base** exercise price; **cours de la Bourse** market price; **cours en Bourse** official price; **cours du change** rate of exchange, exchange rate; **cours de clôture** closing price; **cours de compensation** settlement price, making-up price; **cours des devises** foreign exchange rate; **cours du disponible** spot rate; **cours du dollar** dollar rate; **cours du dont** call price; **cours effectifs** actual quotations; **cours étranger** foreign exchange; **cours hors Bourse, cours hors cote** unofficial price, street price; **cours d'introduction** opening price; **cours de liquidation** settlement price; **cours du livrable** terminal price; **cours du marché** market price or rate; **cours du marché au comptant** current market spot rate; **cours moyen** middle price; **cours officiel** official exchange rate, official quotation; **cours d'ouverture** opening price; **cours parallèle** parallel rate of exchange; **cours de rachat** buying-in price; **cours spot** spot price; (de devises) spot rate; **cours à terme** forward rate; **cours vendeur** offer price; **cours à vue** spot rate

(c) **en cours** (affaires) in hand, outstanding; (travaux, négociations) in progress; (année) current; **en cours de production** in production

courses nfpl shopping; **faire ses/les courses** to do one's/the shopping

coursier, -ère nm,f (d'une entreprise quelconque) messenger; (de messageries) courier

court, -e adj Fin (titres, obligations) short-dated; **à court terme** short-term; **à courte échéance** short-dated

courtage nm (profession) brokerage, broking; (commission) brokerage, commission; (contrat) broker's contract; **être vendu par courtage** to be sold on commission; **faire le courtage** to be a broker ◽ **courtage sur actions** equity trading; **courtage électronique** e-broking, on-line broking; **courtage en immeubles** real estate agency; **courtage officiel** official brokerage

courtier, -ère nm,f broker ◽ **courtier sur actions** equities trader; **courtier d'assurances** insurance broker; **courtier de Bourse** stockbroker; **courtier de change** exchange broker or dealer, bill broker; **courtier de commerce** general broker; **courtier à la commission** commission agent; **courtier électronique** e-broker, on-line broker; **courtier intermédiaire** inter-dealer broker; **courtier libre** outside broker; **courtier de marchandises** commercial broker; **courtier maritime** ship broker; **courtier marron** outside broker; **courtier en matières premières** commodity broker or dealer; **courtier en valeurs mobilières** stockbroker

coût nm cost; **coût par mille** cost per thousand ◽ **coût d'accroissement** incremental cost; **coût d'achat** purchase cost; (sur bilan) cost of goods purchased; **coût d'acquisition** acquisition cost; **coûts administratifs** administrative costs; **coût assurance fret** cost insurance freight; **coûts attribuables** relevant costs; **coûts de base** baseline costs; **coûts cachés** hidden costs; **coût du capital** capital cost; **coût ciblé** target cost; **coût complet unitaire** total unit cost; **coûts constants** fixed costs or expenses; **coûts cumulés** cumulative costs; **coûts de détention** holding costs; **coûts de développement** development costs; **coûts directs** direct costs; **coûts discrétionnaires** discretionary costs; **coût (total) de distribution** (total) distribution cost; **coût économique** economic cost; **coût de l'élaboration du produit** product development cost; **coûts engagés** committed costs; **coût d'entretien** maintenance cost; **coûts évitables** avoidable costs; **coûts d'exploitation** operational costs; **coût fixe** fixed cost; **coûts fixes communs** common fixed costs; **coût fixe total** total fixed cost; **coûts fonciers** landed costs; **coût de fonctionnement** operating or running cost; **coût de fret** freight cost; **coût et fret** cost and freight; **coût global** total cost; **coûts hors-médias** below-the-line costs; **coûts indirects** indirect costs; **coûts induits** unavoidable costs; **coût initial** initial cost, original cost; **coûts irrécupérables** sunk costs; **coût kilométrique** cost per kilometre; **coût de main-d'œuvre** labour cost; **coût marginal** marginal cost, incremental cost; **coûts média** above-the-line costs; **coût moyen unitaire** average unit cost; **coûts opérationnels** operational costs; **coûts opératoires** operating costs; **coûts prévisionnels** estimated costs; **coût de production** production cost; **coût réel** real cost; **coût de remplacement** replacement cost; **coût de revient** cost price; **coût salarial** labour cost; **coût social** social cost; **coût standard** standard cost; **coût unitaire** unit cost; **coût unitaire moyen** average cost per unit, average unit cost; **coût unitaire de travail** unit labour cost; **coût variable** variable cost; **le coût de la vie** the cost of living

coûtant adj au ou à prix coûtant at cost price

coût-efficacité nf cost-effectiveness

coûter vi to cost; **combien ça coûte?** how much is it?, how much does it cost?; **cela coûte mille euros** it costs a thousand euros; **coûter cher** to be expensive

coûteux, -euse adj costly, expensive; **peu coûteux** inexpensive

couvert, -e adj (a) Assur (risque, personne) covered; **je suis couvert contre l'incendie** I'm covered against fire (b) Fin **être à couvert** (pour un crédit) to be covered; Bourse **vendre à couvert** to hedge, to sell for futures

couverture nf (a) Fin cover; Bourse margin, hedge; **une commande sans couverture** an order without security or cover; **exiger une couverture de 20 pour cent en espèces** to claim a margin of 20 percent in cash; **opérer avec couverture** to hedge □ Bourse **couverture boursière obligatoire** margin requirement; Bourse **couverture courte** short hedge; Bourse **couverture longue** long hedge; Bourse **couverture obligatoire** margin requirement; Bourse **couverture de position** short covering
(b) Assur cover □ **couverture d'assurance** insurance cover; **couverture du risque de crédit** loan risk cover; **couverture santé** health cover
(c) Mktg coverage □ **couverture du marché** sales coverage; **couverture médiatique** media coverage

couvrir 1 vt (a) (frais, dépenses) to cover; **le prix de vente couvre à peine les frais** the selling price barely covers the cost; **prière de nous couvrir par chèque** (sur facture) kindly remit by cheque
(b) Assur (risque, personne) to cover; **cette assurance ne couvre pas les risques de vol** this insurance doesn't cover us/you against theft
(c) Fin (emprunt) to cover, to secure
(d) (enchère) to bid higher than, to outbid
2 se couvrir vpr Bourse to cover (oneself), to hedge; **se couvrir en achetant à long terme** to hedge by buying at long date; **se couvrir en rachetant** to cover oneself by buying back

covendeur, -euse nm,f co-vendor, joint seller

CPAM nf Admin (abrév **caisse primaire d'assurance maladie**) = French government department dealing with health insurance

CPM nm (abrév **coût par mille**) cost per thousand

cpp Ordinat (abrév **caractères par pouce**) cpi

cps Ordinat (abrév **caractères par seconde**) cps

cpt (abrév **comptant**) cash

CR nm (abrév **compte-rendu**) (d'une réunion) minutes

crayon nm (a) (pour écrire) pencil (b) Ordinat **crayon lumineux, crayon optique** light pen

crayonné nm rough (layout)

CRDS nf (abrév **contribution au remboursement de la dette sociale**) = income-based tax deducted at source as a contribution to paying off the French social security budget deficit

créance nf debt; Jur claim; **amortir une créance** to write off a debt □ **créance chirographaire** unsecured debt; **créance contractuelle** contractual claim; **créance douteuse** doubtful debt; **créance exigible** debt due; **créance garantie** secured debt; **créances gelées** frozen credits; **créance hypothécaire** debt secured by a mortgage; **créance irrécouvrable** bad debt; **créance litigieuse** contested claim; **créance privilégiée** preferential or preferred debt

> **"**
>
> Ce clivage idéologique s'accompagne d'autres dangers. Avec des **créances douteuses** estimées à au moins 30% de leurs prêts, les banques chinoises ne sont pas à l'abri d'un séisme financier.
>
> **"**

créancier, -ère nm,f creditor □ **créancier chirographaire** unsecured creditor; **créancier entièrement nanti** fully secured creditor; **créancier d'exploitation** trade creditor; **créancier hypothécaire** mortgagee; **créancier ordinaire** unsecured or ordinary creditor; **créancier partiellement nanti** partly secured creditor; **créancier privilégié** secured or preferential or preferred creditor

créateur, -trice 1 adj créateur d'emplois (industrie, secteur) job-creating
2 nm,f (d'un nouveau produit) designer □ **créateur d'entreprise(s)** entrepreneur

> **"**
>
> L'espèce d'Europhorie actuelle cache sans aucun doute le désir d'Europe unie pour la paix, la coopération, mais aussi l'aspiration à ce que la monnaie européenne serve avant tout à des projets communs de développement durable, solidaire, **créateur d'emplois**.
>
> **"**

créatif, -ive *nm,f Mktg (de publicité)* designer

création *nf* (**a**) *(d'un nouveau produit)* creation, designing; *(d'une société)* founding, establishment □ **création d'emplois** job creation; **il y a eu 3000 créations d'emplois en mai** 3,000 new jobs were created in May (**b**) *(chose créée)* new product; **nos dernières créations** our latest creations (**c**) **création de pages Web** Web authoring

crédirentier, -ère *nm,f Jur* recipient of an allowance

crédit *nm* (**a**) *(prêt)* credit; **acheter/vendre qch à crédit** to buy/to sell sth on credit *or* on hire purchase *or Am* on the installment plan; **faire crédit à qn** to give sb credit; **ouvrir un crédit à qn** to open a credit account in sb's favour *or* in sb's name; **ouvrir un crédit chez qn** to open a credit account with sb □ **crédit back to back** back-to-back credit; **crédit bancaire, crédit en banque** bank credit; **crédit en blanc** blank credit; **crédit bloqué** frozen credit; **crédit commercial** trade credit; **crédit à la consommation, crédit au consommateur** consumer credit; **crédit consortial** syndicated credit; **crédit (à) court terme** short-term credit; *Bourse* **crédit croisé** cross-currency swap; **crédit à découvert** open credit; **crédits de développement** development loans; **crédit différé** deferred credit; **crédit documentaire** documentary credit, letter of credit; **crédit dos à dos** back-to-back credit; **crédit de droits** = delay in payment of indirect taxes; **crédits d'équipement** equipment financing; **crédits à l'exportation** export credit; **crédit foncier** = government-controlled building society; **crédit fournisseur** supplier's credit, trade credit; **crédit gratuit** interest-free credit; **crédit immobilier** mortgage, home loan; **crédits à l'importation** import credit; **crédit d'impôt** *(abattement)* tax rebate; *(report)* tax credit; **crédit irrévocable** irrevocable letter of credit; **crédit (à) long terme** long-term credit; **crédit (à) moyen terme** medium-term credit; **crédit permanent** *Br* revolving *or Am* revolver credit; **crédit personnel** personal credit; **crédit ponctuel** spot credit; **crédit renouvelable** *Br* revolving *or Am* revolver credit; **crédit de réserve** standby credit; **crédit de restructuration** new money; **crédit révocable** revocable letter of credit; **crédit revolving** *Br* revolving *or Am* revolver credit; **crédit de sécurité** swing line; **crédit de soutien** standby credit; **crédit à taux réduit** low-interest loan; **crédit à taux révisable** rollover credit; **crédit à terme** term loan; **crédit transférable** transferable credit; **crédits de trésorerie** (short-term) credit facilities; **crédit de TVA** VAT credit; **crédit utilisable à vue** sight credit (**b**) *(en comptabilité)* credit side; **porter une somme au crédit de qn** to credit sb with a sum

crédit-acheteur *nm* buyer credit

crédit-bail *nm* leasing □ **crédit-bail immobilier** real estate leasing; **crédit-bail mobilier** equipment leasing

> " Le secteur du **crédit-bail** se réduit comme peau de chagrin en Bourse. Cette semaine encore, la restructuration s'est accélérée avec l'annonce de l'OPA de PHRV sur Bail Saint-Honoré. La crise de l'immobilier et la fin du statut fiscal privilégié des Sicomi sont passées par là. De plus, la concurrence s'est intensifiée avec l'arrivée des banques sur le marché du **crédit-bail**. "

créditer *vt (compte)* to credit (**de** with); **créditer qn de 4000 euros** to credit sb *or* sb's account with 4,000 euros; **faire créditer son compte d'une somme** to pay a sum into one's account

créditeur, -trice 1 *adj (compte, solde)* credit **2** *nm,f* person whose account is in credit

crédit-fournisseur *nm* supplier credit

crédit-relais *nm Br* bridging loan, *Am* bridge loan

crédit-scoring *nm* credit scoring

crédoc *nm (abrév* **crédit documentaire**) documentary credit, letter of credit

créer 1 *vt (emplois, nouveau produit, hypothèque)* to create; *(entreprise)* to set up **2 se créer** *vpr* (**a**) *(emplois, nouveau produit, hypothèque)* to be created; *(entreprise)* to be set up (**b**) *(pour soi-même)* **se créer une clientèle** to build up a clientele

créneau *nm* (market) niche, gap in the market; **exploiter un nouveau créneau** to fill a new gap *or* niche in the market; **trouver un bon créneau** to find a good gap *or* niche in the market □ **créneau horaire** time slot; **créneau porteur** big gap in the market

> " D'où l'abandon de certaines lignes hexagonales et le basculement de celles restantes sur le **créneau** du petit prix. Seule solution, selon Jean-Charles Corbet, pour remplir au moins 70% de ces vols. Et pour devancer – de peu – l'arrivée des spécialistes du genre. "

creux, -euse 1 *adj (période, marché)* slack; *(heures)* off-peak **2** *nm* **une période de creux, un creux** a slack period

criée *nf (vente)* auction; *(salle)* auction room

crier *vt* to put up for auction, to auction

crise *nf* crisis, slump; **traverser une période de**

crise to go through a crisis (period) ❑ *crise du dollar* dollar crisis; *crise économique* economic crisis; *crise de l'emploi* unemployment crisis; *crise financière* financial crisis; *crise du logement* housing shortage; *crise pétrolière* oil crisis

critère *nm* criterion ❑ *critères de sélection* selection criteria

crochet *nm* square bracket; **entre crochets** in square brackets

croissance *nf* growth; **notre entreprise est en pleine croissance** our company is growing rapidly ❑ *croissance du capital* capital growth; *croissance démographique* demographic growth, population growth; *croissance économique* economic growth; *croissance externe* external growth; *croissance par habitant* per capita economic development; *croissance interne* internal growth; *croissance du marché* market growth; *croissance négative* negative growth; *croissance par tête* per capita economic development; *croissance zéro* zero growth, nil growth

> **"**Les conjoncturistes ont tendance à dire qu'un pays est en récession lorsqu'il connaît deux trimestres consécutifs de **croissance négative**," explique Cyril Blesson, du Bipe (Bureau d'informations et de prévisions économiques). **"**

croissant, -e *adj (chiffre d'affaires, production, chômage)* increasing

croître *vi (chiffre d'affaires, production, chômage)* to grow, to increase

cryptage *nm Ordinat* encryption

crypter *vt & vi Ordinat* to encrypt

cryptographie *nf Ordinat* encryption

CSG *nf (abrév* **contribution sociale généralisée**) = income-based tax deducted at source as a contribution to paying off the French social security budget deficit

culbute *nf Fam* **faire la culbute** *(entreprise) (échouer)* to go bust *or* belly up; *(faire un bénéfice)* to make a huge profit

culminer *vi Bourse (cours)* to peak

culture d'entreprise *nf Écon* enterprise culture, corporate culture

cumul *nm (de fonctions, de mandats, de pouvoirs)* concurrent holding; *(de salaires)* concurrent drawing

cumulard, -e *nm,f Fam (directeur)* = person making money as the head of several companies; *(employé)* holder of several jobs

cumulatif, -ive *adj (actions, dividende)* cumulative

cumulé, -e *adj (intérêts)* accrued

cumuler *vt* **(a)** *(fonctions, mandats, pouvoirs)* to hold concurrently; *(salaires)* to draw concurrently **(b)** *(intérêts)* to accrue

curriculum vitae *nm Br* curriculum vitae, *Am* résumé

curseur *nm Ordinat* cursor

CV *nm (abrév* **curriculum vitae**) *Br* CV, *Am* résumé

CVG *nm Bourse (abrév* **certificat de valeur garantie**) CVR

CVS *adj (abrév* **corrigé des variations saisonnières**) seasonally adjusted

cyberbanque *nf Ordinat* on-line bank, Internet bank

cybercommerce *nm Ordinat* e-commerce

cyberculture *nf Ordinat* cyberculture

cyberespace *nm Ordinat* cyberspace; **dans le cyberespace** in cyberspace

cyberjargon *nm Ordinat* netspeak

cyberlibraire *nm Ordinat* Internet bookshop

cybermonde *nm Ordinat* cyberspace; **dans le cybermonde** in cyberspace

cybernaute *nmf Ordinat* Internet surfer, cybernaut

cyber-recrutement *nm Ordinat* e-recruitment, online recruitment

> **"**La France apparaît néanmoins plus traditionnelle que la Grande-Bretagne, où la plupart des grandes sociétés n'acceptent déjà plus les candidatures papier. Seule consolation pour les webphobiques: certaines entreprises choisissent délibérément de ne pas se cantonner au seul **cyber-recrutement**. **"**

cybersquatting *nm Ordinat* cybersquatting

cybertexte *nm Ordinat* cybertext

cycle *nm* **(a)** cycle ❑ *cycle des affaires* business cycle; *Mktg cycle commande-livraison-facturation* order-to-remittance cycle; *Mktg cycle de commercialisation* trade cycle; *cycle conjoncturel* economic *or* business cycle; *Mktg cycle de la distribution* distribution cycle; *cycle économique* economic *or* business cycle; *cycle d'exploitation* operating cycle; *cycle des taux* interest-rate cycle; *Mktg cycle de vie* lifecycle; *Mktg cycle de vie familiale* family lifecycle; *Mktg cycle de vie de la marque* brand lifecycle; *Mktg cycle de vie du produit* product lifecycle, PLC **(b)** *Ordinat* **cycle d'exécution** execute cycle

cyclique *adj (économie, crise)* cyclical

> **"**
>
> Les secteurs qui auraient dû être favorisés (les pétrolières et les sociétés les moins sensibles au **cycle économique** et au **cycle des taux**, telles que la distribution alimentaire et les biens de consommation non cycliques) ont peu monté, TotalFinaElf subissant paradoxalement des prises de bénéfices cette semaine.
>
> **"**

Dd

DAB[1] *nm* *Banque* *(abrév* **distributeur automatique de billets)** *Br* cash dispenser, cashpoint, *Am* ATM

DAB[2] *nf (abrév* **digital audio broadcasting)** DAB

dactylo 1 *nmf (abrév* **dactylographe)** typist □ **dactylo intérimaire** temp
2 *nf (abrév* **dactylographie)** typing

dactylographie *nf* typing

dactylographié, -e *adj (lettre, document)* typed, typewritten

dactylographier *vt (lettre, document)* to type

DAS *nm Mktg (abrév* **domaine d'activité stratégique)** SBU

DAT *nm (abrév* **digital audio tape)** DAT

datation *nf (d'un contrat)* dating

date *nf* date; **sans date** *(lettre)* undated; **la lettre porte la date du 5 mai** the letter is dated 5 May; **mettre la date sur une lettre** to date a letter; **à date fixe** on a fixed date; **à trente jours de date** thirty days after date; **la facture n'a pas été payée à la date prévue** the bill wasn't paid on time; **prendre date** *ou* **fixer une date pour qch** to fix a date for sth □ **date d'achèvement** completion date, date of completion; *Banque* **date de base** base date; **date butoir** deadline, cutoff date; **date ciblée** target date; **date de clôture** closing date; **date contractuelle** date of agreement, contract date; *Fin* **date d'échéance** *(de dû)* maturity date, due date; *(de terme)* expiry date; *Bourse, Fin* **date d'émission** date of issue; **date d'entrée en vigueur** effective date, starting date; **date d'exécution** completion date; **date d'exigibilité** due date; **date d'expiration** expiry date; **date de facturation** invoice date, date of invoice; *Fin* **date de jouissance** date from which interest begins to run; **date limite** deadline; **date limite de consommation** best-before date; **date limite de paiement** deadline for payment; **date limite de remise de documents** copy deadline; **date limite de vente** sell-by date; **date de livraison** delivery date; **date de naissance** date of birth; *Fin* **date d'ouverture de l'exercice** first day of the financial year; **date de péremption** use-by date; **date de la poste** date as postmark; *Banque* **date de présentation** presentation date; **date prévue d'achèvement** target date; **date de remise** remittance date; **date de signature** date of signature; *Banque* **date de valeur** value date; **date de validité** expiry date; **date visée** target date

dater 1 *vt (lettre)* to date; **votre lettre datée d'hier/du 13 mars** your letter dated yesterday/ 13 March
2 *vi* to date (**de** from); **à dater de ce jour** *(d'aujourd'hui)* from today; *(de ce jour-là)* from that day; **à dater du 15** on and after the 15th

dation *nf Jur* gift *(made to an heir in the course of one's lifetime to avoid inheritance tax)* □ **dation en paiement** payment in kind

DC *nm Fam (abrév* **directeur de la création)** creative director

DD *Ordinat* **1** *adj (abrév* **double densité)** DD
2 *nm (abrév* **disque dur)** HD

DDE *nm Ordinat (abrév* **dynamic data exchange)** DDE

DEA *nm (abrév* **diplôme d'études approfondies)** = postgraduate qualification which is a prerequisite for PhD candidates

débâcle *nf Fin* **débâcle (financière)** crash

déballage *nm (de marchandises)* unpacking; *(exposition)* display

déballer *vt (marchandises)* to unpack; *(exposer)* to display

débarquer 1 *vt (marchandises)* to unload; *(passagers)* to land, to disembark
2 *vi (passagers)* to land, to disembark

débat *nm* debate; *Jur* **débats** proceedings

débattre *vt* to discuss; **à débattre** *(prix)* to be agreed; *(salaire)* negotiable

débauchage *nm* **(a)** *(licenciement)* laying off **(b)** *(embauche d'employés d'autres entreprises)* poaching

débaucher *vt* **(a)** *(licencier)* to lay off, to make redundant **(b)** *(employés d'autres entreprises)* to poach

débit *nm* **(a)** *Compta* debit; *(sur un compte)* debit side; **inscrire** *ou* **porter un article au débit** to debit an entry; **porter une somme au débit de qn** to debit sb *or* sb's account with an amount □ **débit de caisse** cash debit; **débit cumulé** cumulative debit; **débit différé** deferred debit; **débit immédiat** immediate debit
(b) *(ventes)* sale; **des marchandises de bon débit** marketable *or* saleable goods; **ces mar-**

chandises ont peu de débit there is little demand for these goods
(**c**) *(commerce)* shop
(**d**) *Ordinat* rate; **à haut débit** broadband ❏ **débit en bauds** baud rate; **débit binaire** bit rate; **débit de données** data throughput
(**e**) *(d'une machine)* output ❏ **débit horaire** hourly output

> " ──────
>
> "France Télécom mène une stratégie de retardement. En France, les opérateurs alternatifs ont seulement 0,1% du marché de l'Internet **à haut débit**. France Télécom est en train d'établir un nouveau monopole."
>
> ──────── "

débitant, -e *nm,f* retailer

débiter *vt* (**a**) *Compta (compte)* to debit; **débiter une somme à qn, débiter qn d'une somme** to debit sb with an amount; **débiter une somme d'un compte** to debit an account with an amount, to debit an amount to an account; **débiter les frais de poste au client** to charge the postage to the customer (**b**) *(vendre)* to sell (**c**) *(produire)* to yield; **cette usine débite 250 voitures par jour** this factory produces 250 cars a day

débiteur, -trice **1** *adj (compte, solde)* debit; **mon compte est débiteur de plusieurs milliers d'euros** my account is several thousand euros overdrawn
2 *nm,f* debtor ❏ **débiteur hypothécaire** mortgagor

déblocage *nm Fin (de crédits, de capitaux)* unfreezing; *(des prix, des salaires)* decontrolling; *(de fonds)* releasing, making available

débloquer *vt Fin (crédits, capitaux)* to unfreeze; *(prix, salaires)* to decontrol; *(fonds)* to release, to make available

> " ──────
>
> Le directeur général du FMI, Michel Camdessus, a rendu public un communiqué insistant sur la nécessité de mener à bien les réformes économiques afin que le fonds puisse **débloquer** en septembre la seconde tranche de son aide financière de 11,2 milliards de dollars.
>
> ──────── "

débogage *nm Ordinat* debugging

déboguer *vt Ordinat* to debug

débogueur *nm Ordinat* debugger

débouché *nm* (**a**) *Mktg* outlet, market, opening; **créer de nouveaux débouchés pour un produit** to open up new markets *or* to create new outlets for a product (**b**) *(de carrière)* job opportunity; **cette formation n'offre aucun débouché** this training does not lead to any career openings

> " ──────
>
> Elle pilote depuis dix ans une étonnante manifestation – "Futurallia" – au cours de laquelle des entreprises venues de toute la planète rencontrent à Poitiers des PME françaises en quête de **débouchés**. Malgré une mise de fonds très modeste, 150 000 euros, le succès a été tel que "Futurallia" s'est délocalisée au Québec en 2000 et est en passe de devenir une rencontre à vocation nationale.
>
> ──────── "

déboursement *nm* outlay, expenditure

débourser *vt (somme, argent)* to spend, to lay out

débrayer *vt Ordinat* to disconnect

debriefing *nm* debriefing

début *nm (commencement)* beginning, start; **être en début de carrière** to be at the start of one's career; **être à ses débuts** *(société)* to be in its infancy

décaissement *nm* (**a**) *(retrait)* cash withdrawal; **faire un décaissement** to make a withdrawal (**b**) *(somme)* sum withdrawn; *Compta* **décaissements** outgoings

décaisser *vt* (**a**) *(marchandises)* to unpack (**b**) *(somme)* to withdraw

décalage *nm* (**a**) *(écart)* gap; **il existe un décalage entre l'évolution des prix et celle des salaires** there is a delay between price and salary increases; **le décalage entre l'offre et la demande fait évoluer les prix à la baisse** the gap between supply and demand lowers prices (**b**) *décalage horaire* time difference; **tenez compte du décalage horaire si vous leur téléphonez** remember the time difference if you're phoning them; **souffrir du décalage horaire** to suffer from jet lag

décentralisation *nf* (**a**) *Admin* decentralization ❏ *décentralisation administrative* devolution (**b**) *(des bureaux, des services)* relocation *(away from large towns)*

décentraliser *vt* (**a**) *Admin* to decentralize (**b**) *(bureaux, services)* to relocate *(away from large towns)*

décharge *nf* (**a**) *Jur (d'une obligation)* discharge (**b**) *(attestation)* receipt; **il faut signer une décharge avant de prendre livraison** you have to sign a receipt before accepting delivery (**c**) *Fin* (tax) rebate; **porter une somme en décharge** to mark a sum as paid

déchargement *nm (d'un navire, de marchandises)* unloading

décharger *vt* (**a**) *Fin (compte)* to discharge; **décharger qn de qch** *(dette)* to discharge sb from sth; *(impôt)* to exempt sb from sth (**b**) *(navire, marchandises)* to unload

déchéance nf (**a**) Fin (de droits, de titres, d'un brevet) forfeiture; (d'une police) expiry (**b**) Compta **tomber en déchéance** to lapse ▫ **déchéance du terme** event of default

déchet nm (de poids, valeur) loss, decrease; **il y a du déchet** there is some wastage ▫ **déchet de route** loss in transit

déchiffrement nm Ordinat decryption ▫ **déchiffrement de données** data decryption

déchiffrer vt Ordinat to decrypt

décideur, -euse 1 adj decision-making
2 nm,f decision-maker

décision nf (choix) decision; Jur ruling; **prendre/arriver à une décision (quant à** ou **au sujet de)** to make/to reach a decision (about); **prise de décision** decision-making; **soumettre une question à la décision de qn** to submit a matter for sb's decision ▫ **décision d'achat** buying decision, purchasing decision; **décision arbitrale** arbitration ruling; **décision autonome** autonomous decision; **décision collective, décision commune** joint decision; Jur **décision de justice** court ruling

déclarant, -e nm,f Admin, Jur declarant ▫ **déclarant de TVA** VAT-registered person

déclaratif, -ive adj Jur declaratory

déclaration nf (**a**) (annonce) declaration, announcement; **faire une déclaration** to make an announcement ▫ **déclaration de changement de domicile** notification of change of address; **déclaration commune** agreed statement; **déclaration d'intention** declaration of intent; **déclaration de principe** statement or declaration of principle; **déclaration sous serment** sworn statement, affidavit
(**b**) Compta return ▫ **déclarations annuelles** annual returns; **déclaration annuelle de résultats** annual statement of results; **déclaration de cessation de paiement** declaration of bankruptcy; **déclaration de faillite** declaration of bankruptcy; **déclaration fiscale** income tax return; **déclaration d'impôts** tax return; **remplir sa déclaration d'impôts** to Br make or Am file one's tax return; **déclaration de résultats** statement of results, financial statement; **déclaration de revenu** income tax return; **déclaration de solvabilité** declaration of solvency; **déclaration de TVA** VAT return
(**c**) Douanes declaration ▫ **déclaration de** ou **en douane** customs declaration, bill of entry; **déclaration d'entrée** declaration or clearance inwards; **déclaration d'entrée en entrepôt** warehousing entry; **déclaration d'exportation** export declaration; **déclaration d'importation** import declaration; **déclaration provisoire** bill of sight; **déclaration de sortie** declaration or clearance outwards; **déclaration de transit** transit entry
(**d**) Assur **déclaration d'accident** accident claim; **déclaration d'avarie** (ship's) protest; **déclaration d'incendie** fire claim; **déclaration de sinistre** (d'une assurance) damage report; (réclamation) notice of claim, insurance claim
(**e**) Bourse **déclaration de dividende** dividend announcement, declaration of dividend; **déclaration de valeur** declaration of value
(**f**) Admin **déclaration d'utilité publique** = government decision that a large public works project is vital and should therefore go ahead despite public protest

déclaré, -e adj (**a**) (valeur) declared; (transferts) certified (**b**) Admin **déclaré d'utilité publique** (entreprise) declared vital by the government

déclarer 1 vt (**a**) (annoncer) to declare; (employé) to register; **je déclare la séance levée** I declare the meeting closed
(**b**) Douanes to declare; **marchandises à déclarer** goods to declare; **avez-vous quelque chose à déclarer?** have you anything to declare?; **rien à déclarer** nothing to declare
(**c**) Compta (dividende) to declare; **déclarer ses revenus au fisc** to Br make or Am file one's tax return
(**d**) Ordinat (valeur) to define
2 se déclarer vpr (**a**) (se prononcer) **se déclarer pour** ou **en faveur de/contre qch** to declare oneself in favour of/against sth
(**b**) Bourse **se déclarer acheteur** to call the shares; **se déclarer vendeur** to put the shares

déclassé, -e adj (**a**) Bourse (valeurs) displaced (**b**) (emploi, produit, hôtel) downgraded

déclassement nm (**a**) Bourse (de valeurs) displacement (**b**) (d'emploi, de produit, d'hôtel) downgrading

déclin nm decline; **être en déclin** to be on the decline

décliner 1 vt (**a**) (refuser) (offre, invitation) to decline; **décliner toute responsabilité** to accept no liability; **décliner une juridiction** to refuse to acknowledge a jurisdiction (**b**) Mktg to produce; **notre produit est décliné dans une large gamme de couleurs** our product is available in a wide range of colours
2 se décliner vpr Mktg to be available

décodage nm Ordinat decoding

décoder vt Ordinat to decode

décodeur nm Ordinat decoder

décommander 1 vt (commande, livraison) to cancel; (réunion) to cancel, to call off
2 se décommander vpr to cancel

décomposer vt (**a**) Compta (compte, résultats) to analyse, to break down; (dépenses) to break down (**b**) (tâches) to break down

décomposition nf (**a**) Compta (d'un compte, des résultats) analysis, breakdown; (des dé-

penses) breakdown (**b**) *(des tâches)* breakdown

décompresser *vt Ordinat (fichier)* to decompress

décompte *nm* (**a**) *(déduction)* deduction; *(calcul)* calculation; **j'ai fait le décompte de ce que vous m'avez payé et de ce que vous me devez** I've deducted what you've paid from what you owe me (**b**) *(solde)* balance; **payer le décompte** to pay the balance due *(on an account)* (**c**) *(relevé d'une opération)* detailed account, breakdown

décompter *vt* to deduct

déconcentration *nf (de bureaux, d'entreprises)* relocation *(away from large towns)*

déconcentrer *vt (bureaux, entreprises)* to relocate *(away from large towns)*

déconfiture *nf* financial collapse; *Jur* insolvency

> **"**
> En 1995, un trader fou détourne 860 millions de livres, provoquant la **déconfiture** de la Banque Barings, fondée en 1762. Mais le coup de grâce sera porté, en décembre dernier, par Kenneth Lay.
> **"**

déconnecté, -e *adj Ordinat (imprimante)* off-line

déconnecter se déconnecter *vpr Ordinat (imprimante)* to go off-line

déconsignation *nf* deconsignment

déconsigner *vt* (**a**) *(emballage)* to return (**b**) *(bagages)* to collect from the *Br* left-luggage office *or Am* checkroom

décote *nf* (**a**) *(d'impôt)* tax relief (**b**) *Fin* below par rating, value below rate; **une société qui souffre d'une décote** an undervalued company □ **décote en Bourse** *(d'une action)* discount (**c**) *(baisse)* depreciation, loss in value

> **"**
> De plus, le fisc suivra son dossier de près après le redressement … La valeur de votre résidence principale, estimée, en général, par comparaison avec des transactions effectuées alentour, subit une **décote** de 20% dans votre déclaration. Si vous avez beaucoup de "meubles meublants", vous pouvez leur appliquer une valeur forfaitaire de 5% du montant de votre patrimoine.
> **"**

découpage *nm* (**a**) *Mktg* breakdown; **découpage des ventes par pays** breakdown of sales by country (**b**) *Ordinat (de fichier, d'image)* splitting

découper *vt Ordinat (fichier, image)* to split

découvert *nm* (**a**) *Banque* **découvert (bancaire)** overdraft; **demander une autorisation**

de découvert to apply for an overdraft; **accorder à qn un découvert** to allow sb an overdraft; **avoir un découvert** *ou* **être à découvert de 2000 euros** *(autorisé)* to have a 2,000-euro overdraft; *(non autorisé)* to be overdrawn by 2,000 euros; **mettre un compte à découvert** to overdraw an account □ *découvert de la balance commerciale* trade gap; *découvert en blanc* unsecured overdraft (**b**) *Assur* things not covered by insurance (**c**) *Bourse* **acheter à découvert** to buy short; **vendre à découvert** to go a bear, to sell short

décret *nm* decree; **promulguer un décret** to issue a decree □ *Admin* **décret présidentiel** *Br* ≃ order in council, *Am* ≃ executive order

décréter *vt (mesure, nomination)* to decree, to order; *(loi)* to enact; *(grève)* to call, to order; *Jur (moratoire)* to declare

décrocher *vt* (**a**) *(combiné téléphonique)* to pick or lift up; **décrocher le téléphone** *(pour ne pas être dérangé)* to take the phone off the hook; *(pour répondre)* to pick up the phone (**b**) *(contrat, commande, emploi)* to land

DECS *nm (abrév* **diplôme d'études comptables supérieures**) = postgraduate qualification in accounting

DECT *nf Tél (abrév* **digital enhanced cordless telecommunications**) DECT

dédié, -e *adj (serveur, ligne téléphonique)* dedicated

dédit *nm* forfeit, penalty; **dédit en cas d'inexécution du contrat** penalty for breaking a contract

dédommagement *nm* compensation, damages; **réclamer un dédommagement** to claim compensation; **recevoir une somme en dédommagement** *ou* **à titre de dédommagement** to receive a sum in *or* by way of compensation

dédommager 1 *vt* to indemnify, to compensate (**de** for); **dédommager qn d'une perte** to compensate sb for a loss
2 se dédommager *vpr* **se dédommager de ses pertes** to recoup one's losses

dédouanage *nm Douanes (à la douane)* customs clearance; *(de l'entrepôt)* taking out of bond

dédouané, -e *adj Douanes (marchandises)* duty-paid

dédouanement = **dédouanage**

dédouaner *vt Douanes (faire passer à la douane)* to clear through customs; *(récupérer de l'entrepôt)* to take out of bond

déductible *adj (dépense)* deductible; **déductible de l'impôt** tax-deductible

déduction *nf* deduction, allowance; **après dé-**

duction des impôts after deduction of tax; **sous déduction de dix pour cent** less ten percent, minus ten percent; **entrer en déduction de qch** to be deductible from sth; **sans déduction** terms net cash; **déduction faite des frais d'essence** after deduction of petrol costs ❑ *déduction avant impôt* (income) tax allowance *déduction pour dons* deduction for donations; *déduction fiscale* (income) tax allowances; *déduction forfaitaire* (d'impôts) standard allowance; *déductions sur frais d'établissement* capital allowances

déduire *vt* to deduct; **déduire cinq pour cent** to deduct five percent; **les frais de poste sont à déduire du prix total** the postage is to be deducted from the total price; **tous frais déduits** after deduction of expenses

défaillance *nf* (**a**) (d'entreprise) failure (**b**) *Jur* (d'une créance, d'un emprunteur) default

> ❝
>
> Des taux moins élevés, sans surcoût, c'est déjà beaucoup. Mais ce n'est pas tout. Les courtiers permettent aussi de réaliser des économies sur les primes d'assurance. Car un crédit est toujours assorti d'une assurance, qui couvre le prêteur en cas de **défaillance** (décès, invalidité, incapacité temporaire) de l'emprunteur.
>
> ❞

défaillant, -e *Jur* **1** *adj* defaulting **2** *nm,f* defaulter, absconder

défaire *vt Ordinat* (opération) to undo

défalcation *nf* deduction; (d'une mauvaise créance) writing off; **défalcation faite des frais** after deducting the expenses

défalquer *vt* to deduct (**de** from); (mauvaise créance) to write off

défaut *nm* (**a**) (imperfection) defect ❑ *défaut apparent* visible defect; *défaut caché* hidden defect; *défaut de fabrication* manufacturing fault *or* defect; *défaut de fonctionnement* malfunction

(**b**) (manque) lack ❑ *défaut de provision* (sur chèque) refer to drawer, insufficient funds; **le chèque a été refusé pour cause de défaut de provision** the cheque was refused because of insufficient funds

(**c**) *Jur* default; **faire défaut** to fail to appear, to default; **jugement par défaut** judgement by default ❑ *défaut de comparution* failure to appear; *défaut de livraison* non-delivery; *défaut de paiement* failure to pay, non-payment

(**d**) *Ordinat* default; **par défaut** by default; **sélectionner qch par défaut** to default to sth; **clavier par défaut** default keyboard; **lecteur par défaut** default drive

défavorable *adj* (balance commerciale) adverse; (change) unfavourable

défectueux, -euse *adj* imperfect, faulty

défendeur, -eresse *nm,f Jur* defendant

défendre *vt* (**a**) *Jur* (accusé) to defend; (cause) to defend, to champion; (droit, opinion) to defend, to uphold (**b**) (protéger) to defend, to guard (**contre** against *or* from); **défendre ses intérêts** to protect one's interests

défense *nf* défense des consommateurs consumer protection, consumerism; *Mktg* **défense contre-offensive** counteroffensive defence; *Mktg* **défense mobile** mobile defence; *Mktg* **défense préventive** pre-emptive defence

déficit *nm Fin* deficit; **être en déficit** to be in deficit; **accuser un déficit** to show a deficit; **combler un déficit** to make up a deficit ❑ *déficit de la balance commerciale* trade deficit; *déficit budgétaire* budget deficit; *déficit de caisse* cash deficit; *déficit commercial* trade deficit *or* gap; *déficit d'exploitation* operating deficit; *déficit extérieur* external deficit, balance of payments deficit; *déficit fiscal remboursable* negative income tax; *déficit fiscal reportable* tax loss; *Compta* **déficit reportable** loss carry forward; *Écon* **déficit du secteur publique** public sector deficit; *déficit de trésorerie* cash deficit

déficitaire *adj* (entreprise) loss-making; (compte) in debit; (budget) in deficit, adverse; (balance, solde) adverse; (bilan) showing a loss; **être déficitaire** to show a deficit

> ❝
>
> Autrefois un modèle, elle est arrivée au terme du processus de libéralisation, les coûts se sont alourdis, la séparation radicale des activités et le manque d'investissement ont été catastrophiques. Des rachats au prix fort, un secteur "colis" **déficitaire** mais surtout des bureaux de poste, franchisés pour la plupart, non rentables, car ils ne s'appuient pas sur le placement de produits financiers.
>
> ❞

défilement *nm Ordinat* scrolling

défiler *vi Ordinat* **faire défiler un document** to scroll through a document; **défiler vers le bas, faire défiler de haut en bas** to scroll down; **défiler vers le haut, faire défiler de bas en haut** to scroll up

défini, -e *adj Ordinat* **défini par l'utilisateur** user-defined

définissable *adj Ordinat* **définissable par l'utilisateur** user-definable

définition *nf* **définition de fonction** job description; **définition de mission** mission statement

défiscalisé, -e *adj* tax free

défiscaliser *vt* to exempt from tax

déflation nf Écon deflation

déflationniste adj Écon deflationary

défragmentation nf Ordinat defragmentation

défrayer vt **défrayer qn** to pay sb's expenses

dégagement nm Fin (de fonds, de crédits) release

dégager 1 vt Fin (**a**) (fonds, crédits) to release (**b**) (bénéfices, excédent) to show
2 se dégager vpr **se dégager d'une dette** to discharge or pay off a debt

dégât nm damage; **les dégâts occasionnés au matériel se chiffrent en millions d'euros** the damage to the equipment amounts to several million euros; **limiter les dégâts** to limit the damage

dégeler vt Fin (avoir, crédits) to unfreeze, to unblock

dégonflement nm (des dépenses) cutback (**de** in); (du marché) collapse (**de** of)

dégrader 1 vt (matériel, outil de production) to damage
2 se dégrader vpr (situation économique, relations) to deteriorate, to get worse; **les relations entre les salariés et le patronat se dégradent** relations between management and staff are deteriorating or getting worse

degré nm degree □ **degré de liquidité** degree of liquidity, liquidity ratio; **degré de solvabilité** credit rating

dégressif, -ive 1 adj (impôt, amortissement) graded, graduated; (tarif) tapering
2 nm discount □ **dégressif sur le volume** bulk discount

dégrèvement nm (remise) reduction □ **dégrèvement fiscal** tax relief; **dégrèvement marginal** marginal relief

dégrever vt (produits) to reduce tax on; (contribuable) to grant tax relief to; (industrie) to derate; (propriété) to reduce the assessment on

dégriffé, -e 1 adj = with its designer label removed and reduced in price
2 nm = reduced-price designer item with its label removed

dégringolade nf (d'une entreprise, d'une monnaie) collapse; (des prix, des valeurs) slump (**de** in)

dégringoler vi (entreprise, monnaie) to collapse; (prix, valeurs) to slump

dégroupage n Tél unbundling

❝

Les opérateurs alternatifs espèrent un changement radical des conditions du **dégroupage**, cette possibilité qui leur est offerte de louer les lignes téléphoniques de France Télécom pour offrir des services Internet haut débit au grand public et aux entreprises.

❞

déguisé, -e adj (impôt, chômage) hidden

déjeuner d'affaires nm business lunch, working lunch

DEL nf (abrév **diode émettrice de lueur**) LED

délai nm time limit, time allowed; **dans un délai de trois ans** within three years, within a three year limit; **dans les plus brefs délais, dans le plus court délai, dans les meilleurs délais** as soon as possible; **un délai franc de cinq jours** five clear days' grace; **sans délai** without delay; **dans les délais prescrits** ou **impartis** within the required time □ **délai d'attente** waiting period; **délai de carence** waiting period; **délai de chargement** loading time; **délai de commercialisation** (d'un produit) launching period; **délai de congé** term of notice; **délai de crédit** credit period; **délai d'embarquement** loading time; **délai d'exécution** deadline; (de livraison, de production) lead time, turnaround time; **délai de garantie** guarantee period, term of guarantee; **délai garanti de livraison** guaranteed delivery period; **délai de grâce** extension, period of grace; **délai de livraison** delivery time, lead time; **délai de paiement** (fixé par contrat) term of payment; **demander un délai de paiement** to request a postponement of payment; **délai de préavis** term of notice; **délai de production** lead time; **délai de rachat** repurchase period; **délai de recouvrement des sommes** period for debt recovery; **délai de récupération** payback period; **délai de réflexion** cooling-off period; **délai de règlement** settlement period; **délai de remboursement** payback period; **délai de rigueur** strict deadline; **avant le 20 février, délai de rigueur** by 20 February at the very latest; **délai de validité** period of validity

délai-congé nm term of notice

délaissé, -e adj Bourse (valeurs) neglected

délaissement nm (**a**) Jur (d'un droit, d'une succession) relinquishment (**b**) Assur abandonment

délaisser vt (**a**) Jur (droit, succession) to relinquish, to forego (**b**) Assur (à l'assureur) to abandon

délégation nf (**a**) (de pouvoirs, d'autorité) delegation; **agir par délégation** to act on the authority invested in one □ **délégation de signature** power of attorney (**b**) Jur (d'une créance) assignment, transfer (**c**) (groupe de personnes) delegation; **une délégation commerciale japonaise** a Japanese trade delegation

délégué, -e 1 adj acting
2 nm,f delegate, representative □ **délégué d'atelier** shop steward; **délégué commercial** sales representative; **délégué général** man-

aging director; **délégué du personnel** staff representative; **délégué syndical** union representative

déléguer vt (**a**) *(personne, pouvoir, autorité)* to delegate (**b**) *Jur (créance)* to assign, to transfer

délimiter vt *Ordinat (champ)* to delimit

délimiteur nm *Ordinat (d'un champ)* delimiter

délit nm *Jur Br* offence, *Am* misdemeanor; **en flagrant délit** red-handed; *Jur* in flagrante delicto; **prendre qn en flagrant délit** to catch sb red-handed *or* in the act ❏ *Fin* **délit d'initié** insider dealing *or* trading; **délit de presse** press offence

> **"**
> Michel Conin est à l'origine d'une plainte pour **délit d'initié** et manipulation de cours, dont l'instruction a été confiée au juge Philippe Courroye en février dernier. "Pour faciliter la souscription des salariés à la fin de l'année 2000, Carrefour et sa banque BNP-Paribas ont fait chuter le cours de l'action, à un moment où ils auraient dû s'abstenir de toute transaction", précise Conin, statistiques en main.
> **"**

délivrance nf *(d'un certificat, d'un reçu)* delivery, issue; *(d'un brevet)* granting

délivrer vt *(certificat, reçu)* to deliver, to issue; *(brevet)* to grant

délocalisation nf *(d'une entreprise, de la production)* relocation; *(des capitaux)* expatriation

délocaliser 1 vt *(entreprise, production)* to relocate; *(capitaux)* to expatriate
2 se délocaliser vpr to relocate

> **"**
> L'externalisation et la délocalisation répondent à des objectifs différents. En **délocalisant** une activité en Inde ou aux Philippines, une entreprise cherche d'abord à profiter d'une main-d'œuvre de trois à sept fois moins chère.
> **"**

déloyal, -e adj *(procédé, concurrence, pratique commerciale)* unfair

demande nf (**a**) *(requête)* request (**de** for); **faire la demande de qch** to ask for sth; **faire qch à** *ou* **sur la demande de qn** to do sth at sb's request; **travailler à la demande** to work to order; **adresser une demande** to apply in writing; **faire une demande de qch par écrit** to write off for sth, to send for sth; **il faut remplir une demande** you must fill in an application form; **faire une demande de remboursement** to request repayment; **suite à votre demande** as requested, further to your request; **sur demande** on application, on request; **payable**

sur demande *(chèque)* payable on demand *or* at sight ❏ **demande d'emploi** job application; **demandes d'emploi** *(dans un journal)* situations wanted; *Assur* **demande d'indemnité** claim; **demande officielle** formal demand; **demande de prêt** loan application; **demande de renseignements** inquiry, request for information

(**b**) *Écon* demand; **l'offre et la demande** supply and demand; **répondre à la demande** to meet demand; **la demande est en hausse/en baisse** demand is up/down; **la demande croissante de produits biologiques** the increasing demand for organic products ❏ **demande des consommateurs** consumer demand; **demande excédentaire** overdemand, excess demand; **demande globale** global demand; **demande du marché** market demand; **demande prévisionnelle** projected demand; **demande primaire** primary demand; **demande soutenue** full demand

(**c**) *Jur* claim ❏ **demande accessoire** related claim; **demande compensatoire** counterclaim; **demande de dommages-intérêts** claim for damages; **demande principale** main claim; **demande en renvoi** request for referral to another court; **demande subsidiaire** subsidiary claim

demander vt (**a**) *(réclamer)* to ask for; *(dommages-intérêts)* to claim; *(emploi)* to apply for; **combien demandez-vous de l'heure?** how much do you charge per hour?; **demandez notre catalogue** send for our catalogue; **on vous demande au téléphone** you're wanted on the phone, there's a call for you (**b**) *(chercher)* to want; **être très demandé** *(produit, article)* to be in great demand

demandeur¹, -eresse nm,f *Jur* plaintiff, claimant ❏ **demandeur en appel** appellant

demandeur², -euse nm,f (**a**) **demandeur d'emploi** job seeker (**b**) *(d'un produit, d'un service)* customer

démantèlement nm *(des barrières douanières)* removal, lowering; *(du marché)* breaking up; *(d'une entreprise, d'un service)* dismantling ❏ **démantèlement d'entreprise** asset stripping

démanteler vt *(barrières douanières)* to remove, to lower; *(marché)* to break up; *(entreprise, service)* to dismantle

> **"**
> Il faudra attendre la venue ... de Bernd Zevens, P-DG de Ruwel Bayonne, pour que soit rétabli le service ingénierie chargé d'optimiser le processus de fabrication **démantelé** deux ans plus tôt.
> **"**

démarchage nm *(porte-à-porte)* door-to-door selling; *(prospection)* canvassing; **faire du dé-**

marchage to do door-to-door selling, to sell door-to-door ❑ *démarchage à distance* telephone prospecting

démarche *nf* (**a**) *(initiative)* step; **faire une démarche auprès de qn** to approach sb; **faire les démarches nécessaires pour faire qch** to take the necessary steps to do sth ❑ *démarche collective* joint representation (**b**) *(approche)* approach ❑ *démarche marketing* marketing approach

démarcher 1 *vt (client, entreprise)* to visit **2** *vi (faire du porte-à-porte)* to do door-to-door selling, to sell door-to-door

démarcheur, -euse *nm,f* (**a**) *(représentant)* door-to-door salesman, *f* saleswoman ❑ *démarcheur en assurances* insurance agent (**b**) *(prospecteur)* canvasser ❑ *démarcheur en publicité* advertisement canvasser

démarketing *nm* demarketing; **la consommation d'alcool requiert la mise en œuvre d'une politique de démarketing** alcohol consumption requires a policy of demarketing to be implemented

démarque *nf* marking down, markdown ❑ *démarque inconnue* shrinkage

démarqué, -e *adj* marked down

démarquer *vt* to mark down

démarrage *nm* (**a**) *(d'une entreprise)* start-up; *(d'une affaire, d'une campagne publicitaire, d'un projet)* start (**b**) *Ordinat* start-up ❑ *démarrage automatique* autostart; *démarrage à chaud* warm start; *démarrage à froid* cold start

démarrer 1 *vt* (**a**) *(affaire, campagne publicitaire, projet)* to start up (**b**) *Ordinat* to boot (up), to start up **2** *vi (débuter) (affaire, campagne publicitaire, projet)* to start up; *(dans une progression)* to take off, to get off the ground; **les ventes ont bien démarré** sales have got off to a good start

démembrement *nm (d'une entreprise)* breaking up ❑ *démembrement de propriété* division of inherited property *(between heirs)*

> ❝
> D'après le Code général des impôts, les biens en usufruit sont inclus dans le patrimoine de l'usufruitier pour leur valeur en pleine propriété. Cela signifie que si vous pratiquez un **démembrement de propriété** sur un ou plusieurs de vos biens immobiliers, en conservant l'usufruit, la base taxable au titre de l'ISF restera identique.
> ❞

démembrer *vt (entreprise)* to break up

démenti *nm* disclaimer; **publier un démenti** to publish a disclaimer

démettre 1 *vt* (**a**) *(renvoyer)* **démettre qn de ses fonctions** to remove sb from his/her post (**b**) *Jur (débouter)* **démettre qn de son appel** to dismiss sb's appeal **2 se démettre** *vpr (démissionner)* to resign; **se démettre de ses fonctions** to resign one's post

demeure *nf Jur* **mettre qn en demeure de payer** to give sb notice to pay

demi-gros *nm* cash and carry

demi-produit *nm* semi-finished product

demi-salaire *nm* half-pay

démission *nf* resignation; **donner sa démission** to hand in one's resignation

démissionner *vi* to resign (**de** from)

démodulateur *nm Ordinat* demodulator

démographie *nf* demography

démographique *adj* demographic; **statistiques démographiques** demographics

démonétisation *nf Fin* demonetization

démonétiser *vt Fin* to demonetize

démonstrateur, -trice *nm,f* demonstrator

démonstration *nf (d'article)* demonstration ❑ *démonstration sur le lieu de vente* in-store demonstration

dénationalisation *nf* denationalization

dénationaliser *vt* to denationalize

déni *nm Jur* denial, refusal ❑ *déni de justice* denial of justice

dénier *vt Jur* to deny, to refuse

deniers *nmpl* money, funds ❑ *deniers de l'État, deniers publics* public funds

> ❝
> Poursuivie pendant deux mandatures, dépassant les clivages gauche-droite, la nouvelle procédure budgétaire donne à l'Etat les moyens d'une gestion moderne des **deniers publics**.
> ❞

dénombrement *nm* counting ❑ *dénombrement de la population* population count

dénombrer *vt* to count

dénomination *nf (d'une société)* name ❑ *dénomination sociale* corporate name

dénommer *vt* to name; **ci-après dénommé…** *(dans un contrat)* hereinafter referred to as…

denrée *nf* commodity; *(aliment)* foodstuff ❑ *denrées alimentaires* food products, foodstuffs; *denrées de base* basic commodities; *denrées de consommation courante* basic consumer goods; *denrées marchandes* saleable goods; *denrées du pays* home produce; *denrées périssables* perishable goods; *denrées de première nécessité* staple commodities; *denrée témoin* basic commodity

densité *nf* (**a**) *Ordinat* **à double densité** double-density (**b**) *Mktg* **densité publicitaire** advertising density

déontologie (professionnelle) *nf* professional code of ethics

dépannage *nm Ordinat* troubleshooting

dépareillé, -e *adj (articles)* odd

départ *nm* (**a**) **départ entrepôt** ex warehouse; **départ usine** ex works (**b**) *(du travail)* departure ▫ **départ anticipé** early retirement; **départ en préretraite** early retirement; **départ en retraite** retirement; **départ volontaire** voluntary redundancy (**c**) *(d'un compte)* opening date

> "
>
> En Espagne, les **départs anticipés** passent par la case chômage. La *jubilación* hispanique, réformée en décembre, énonce un principe original: la retraite n'est plus incompatible avec une activité salariée.
>
> "

département *nm Admin* (**a**) *(dans un ministère)* department (**b**) *(de la France)* department *(division of local government)* ▫ **départements et territoires d'outre-mer** = French overseas departments and territories

dépassement *nm* exceeding, excess; **il y a un dépassement de crédit de plusieurs millions** the budget has been exceeded by several million ▫ **dépassement budgétaire** overspending; *Ordinat* **dépassement de capacité** overflow; *Compta* **dépassement de coût** cost overrun

dépasser *vt (excéder)* to exceed; **la demande dépasse l'offre** demand exceeds supply; **les ventes ont dépassé le chiffre de l'an dernier** sales figures have overtaken last year's; *Fin* **dépasser un crédit** to exceed a credit limit

dépeceur d'entreprise *nm* asset stripper

dépens *nmpl* cost, expenses; *Jur* costs; **être condamné aux dépens** to be ordered to pay costs

dépense *nf* expenditure, expense; **dépenses** expenses; **contrôler les dépenses** to check expenditure; **faire des dépenses** to incur expenses; **faire trop de dépenses** to overspend ▫ *Compta* **dépenses de caisse** cash expenditure; *Compta* **dépenses en capital** capital expenditure *or* outlay; *Écon* **dépenses de consommation** consumer expenditure; *Compta* **dépenses courantes** current expenditure; *Compta* **dépenses de création** above-the-line costs; *Compta* **dépenses diverses** sundry expenses; *Compta* **dépenses d'équipement** capital expenditure; *Compta* **dépenses d'exploitation** operating costs; **dépenses extraordinaires** extras; *Compta* **dépenses de fonctionnement** operating costs; *Compta* **dépenses d'investissement** capital expenditure; *Écon* **dépenses des ménages** household expenditure; *Écon* **dépense nationale** national expenditure, government spending; **dépenses non prévues au budget** unforeseen expenses; **dépenses prévues au budget** foreseen expenses; **dépenses publicitaires** advertising expenses, publicity expenses; *Écon* **dépenses publiques** public spending, government spending

dépenser *vt* to spend; **dépenser de l'argent en qch** to spend money on sth; **dépenser de l'argent inutilement** to waste money

déplacement *nm* (**a**) *(d'un fonctionnaire, d'un service)* transfer (**b**) *(voyage)* trip, journey; **déplacements** travel; **être en déplacement** to be on a (business) trip; **le directeur est en déplacement à l'étranger** the manager is abroad on business (**c**) *Écon* **un déplacement de l'offre et de la demande** a shift *or* swing in supply and demand (**d**) *Fin (de fonds)* movement (**e**) *Ordinat (de curseur)* movement

déplacer *vt* (**a**) *(fonctionnaire, service)* to transfer (**b**) *Fin (fonds)* to move

déplafonnement *nm (d'un prix)* removal of the upper limit *or* the ceiling

déplafonner *vt (prix)* to remove the upper limit *or* the ceiling on; *Fin* **déplafonner un crédit** to raise the ceiling on a credit, to raise a credit limit

dépliant *nm* leaflet ▫ **dépliant publicitaire** advertising leaflet

déplombage *nm Ordinat* decoding, decrypting

déplomber *vt Ordinat* to decode, to decrypt

déposant, -e *nm,f* (**a**) *Fin* depositor (**b**) *Jur* deponent

déposer *vt* (**a**) *(faire enregistrer) (marque, brevet)* to register; **déposer une demande de brevet** to file an application for a patent; **déposer son bilan** to file for bankruptcy (**b**) *(verser)* **déposer une caution** to leave a deposit; **déposer de l'argent (à la banque)** to deposit *or* lodge money (at the bank) (**c**) *Jur* **déposer une plainte (contre qn)** to lodge a complaint (against sb)

> "
>
> Le numéro 2 allemand du BTP, plombé par des pertes récurrentes (240 millions d'euros en 2001) et par un endettement de plus de 1,5 milliard d'euros, a **déposé son bilan**. Déjà en 1999 Gerhard Schröder était monté en créneau pour convaincre les banques de sauver Philipp Holzmann, au bord de la faillite.
>
> "

deposit *nm Fin* initial margin

dépositaire 1 adj (établissement) which holds securities on trust
  2 nmf (**a**) (de papiers confidentiels) trustee, depositary ❑ Admin **dépositaire de l'autorité publique** = officer of the state; Jur **dépositaire légal** escrow agent; Admin **dépositaire public** = government official with responsibility for the management of public funds; Jur **dépositaire de valeurs** holder of securities on trust (**b**) (de produits) agent ❑ **dépositaire agréé** authorized agent; **dépositaire exclusif** sole agent (**c**) (d'un fonds de placement) custodian

déposition nf Jur statement, deposition (made by witness); **faire/recueillir une déposition** to make/take a statement

dépositionner vt Mktg to deposition

dépôt nm (**a**) Banque deposit; **faire un dépôt** (d'argent) to make a deposit; **mettre qch en dépôt dans une banque** to deposit sth with a bank; **un dépôt à sept jours de préavis** a deposit at seven days' notice ❑ **dépôt bancaire, dépôt en banque** bank deposit; **dépôt en coffre-fort** safe-deposit; **dépôt à court terme** short-term deposit; **dépôt à échéance fixe** fixed deposit; **dépôt d'espèces** cash deposit; **dépôt de garantie** margin deposit; **dépôt initial** initial margin; **dépôt interbancaire** interbank deposit; **dépôt de marge** initial margin; **dépôt à terme** (short-)term deposit, Am time deposit; **dépôt à terme fixe** fixed deposit; **dépôt à vue** demand deposit, sight deposit
  (**b**) (d'une marque, d'un brevet) registration; **effectuer le dépôt d'une marque** to register a trademark ❑ **dépôt légal** copyright deposit
  (**c**) (entrepôt) depot; Douanes **être en dépôt** to be in bond ❑ **dépôt de distribution** distribution depot; **dépôt d'expédition** shipping depot; **dépôt de marchandises** goods depot, warehouse; **dépôt de réception** receiving depot
  (**d**) Fin **en dépôt** (argent, document, marchandises) in trust; **avoir qch en dépôt** to hold sth in trust
  (**e**) Compta **dépôt de bilan** (d'une entreprise) (filing of petition in) bankruptcy

dépouillement nm (d'un compte, d'un rapport) breakdown, analysis; (du courrier) opening; (des données) processing; (d'appels d'offres) checking

dépouiller vt (**a**) (compte, rapport) to break down, to analyse; (courrier) to open; (données) to process; (appels d'offres) to check (**b**) Jur **dépouiller qn de ses droits** to strip sb of his/her rights

dépréciation nf (**a**) (dévaluation) depreciation, fall in value ❑ Compta **dépréciation annuelle** annual depreciation; Compta **dépréciation de créances** write-down of accounts receivable; Compta **dépréciation fonctionnelle** (du matériel) wear and tear (**b**) (mauvaise évaluation) underrating, undervaluing

déprécier 1 vt (**a**) (dévaluer) to depreciate (**b**) (mal évaluer) to undervalue
  2 se déprécier vpr to depreciate, to fall in value

déprédateur, -trice nm,f Fin (de fonds) embezzler

déprédation nf Fin (de fonds) embezzlement

dépression nf Bourse depression ❑ **dépression économique** economic slump; **dépression du marché** market depression

déprimé, -e adj Bourse (marché) depressed

déprogrammer vt (**a**) (rendez-vous) to cancel (**b**) Ordinat to remove from a program

DEPS nm (abrév **dernier entré, premier sorti**) LIFO

dérangement nm (**a**) Tél (panne) **la ligne est en dérangement** the line is out of order, there's a fault on the line (**b**) (gêne) disturbance, trouble; **excusez-moi pour le dérangement** I'm sorry to disturb or trouble you; **je vous envoie un coursier, cela vous évitera un dérangement** I'll send a courier so as not to put you to any trouble

déranger vt (gêner) to disturb; **ne pas déranger** (sur panneau) do not disturb; **excusez-moi de vous déranger** I'm sorry to disturb or trouble you; **si cela ne vous dérange pas** if it's no trouble to you

dérapage nm **le dérapage des prix** the uncontrolled increase in prices; **le dérapage de l'économie** the downward spiral of the economy ❑ **dérapage budgétaire** uncontrolled overspending

> ❝
> En Europe, parler de "reflation" est une solution élégante pour emballer un **dérapage** éventuel des prix dû au passage à l'euro. Mais c'est aussi une façon commode pour les experts de tenter de dissuader une banque centrale de continuer de mener une politique trop musclée contre l'inflation.
> ❞

déréférencement nm Mktg (d'un produit) delisting

déréférencer vt Mktg (produit) to delist; **certains produits ont été déréférencés par le distributeur** some products have been delisted by the distributor

déréglementation nf deregulation

déréglementer vt to deregulate

dérégulation nf deregulation

déréguler vt to deregulate

dérivé, -e 1 adj **produit dérivé** by-product
  2 nm by-product

dernier, -ère adj (ultime) last, final ❑ **dernier**

avis final demand; *Bourse* ***dernier cours*** closing price; ***dernier délai*** deadline; ***dernière enchère*** closing bid; *Bourse* ***dernier jour de cotation*** last trading day; ***dernier paiement*** final payment; ***dernier prix*** final offer; *Bourse* ***dernière proposition*** final offer; ***dernier rappel*** *(de facture)* final demand; ***dernier versement*** final instalment

dérogation *nf* exemption (**à** from); *Jur* waiver; *(à une loi)* derogation, impairment (**à** of); **dérogation à un règlement** departure from a rule, exception to a rule; **par dérogation au règlement** notwithstanding the rules

dérogatoire *adj Jur* derogatory

dérouler 1 *vt Ordinat (menu)* to pull down **2 se dérouler** *vpr (avoir lieu)* to take place; **la réunion du conseil d'administration s'est déroulée au siège social du groupe** the board meeting took place at the company's headquarters; **les événements qui se déroulent à Paris risquent d'affoler les investisseurs** the events that are unfolding *or* taking place in Paris are likely to scare off investors

désactivation *nf Ordinat* deactivation

désactivé, -e *adj Ordinat* disabled

désactiver *vt Ordinat* to deactivate, to disable

désaisonnalisé, -e *adj* seasonally adjusted

désaisonnaliser *vt* to seasonally adjust

descendre *vi (prix)* to come down, to fall; *Bourse (actions)* to drop, to fall; **descendre en flèche** to plummet

descripteur *nm Ordinat* descriptor

description *nf* description ❑ ***description de brevet*** patent specification; ***description de poste*** job description

désembrayer *vt Ordinat* to disconnect

désencadrement *nm (des crédits)* unblocking

désencadrer *vt (crédits)* to unblock

désendettement *nm* degearing, clearing of debts

> **❝**
> Une chose est sûre: dans une conjoncture boursière qui s'annonce déprimée pour le premier semestre, voire toute l'année 2002, France Télécom aura du mal à tenir ses objectifs de **désendettement** ... A moins de céder certaines filiales, et de procéder à de nouvelles augmentations de capital.
> **❞**

désendetter se désendetter *vpr* to clear one's debts

déséquilibre *nm* imbalance; **il existe dans ce pays un déséquilibre très important entre les secteurs secondaire et tertiaire** there is a considerable imbalance between the secondary and tertiary sectors in this country; **déséquilibre de la balance commerciale** unfavourable *or* adverse trade balance ❑ ***déséquilibre financier*** financial imbalance

désescalade *nf (de prix, des actions)* downturn

désétatiser *vt (industrie)* to denationalize

déshypothéquer *vt* to free from mortgage

désignation *nf* (a) *(de marchandises)* description (b) *(nomination)* appointment; **la désignation de qn à un poste** the appointment of sb to a post

designer *nm* designer

désigner *vt* (a) *(marchandises)* to describe (b) *(nommer)* to appoint; *(représentant, fondé de pouvoir)* to nominate; **désigner qn à un poste** to appoint sb to a post

désindexation *nf* removal of index-linking

désindexer *vt* to stop index-linking; **ces pensions ont été désindexées** these retirement schemes are no longer index-linked

désinflation *nf Écon* disinflation

désinflationniste *adj Écon* deflationary

désinstallateur *n Ordinat* deinstaller

désinstallation *n Ordinat* deinstallation

désinstaller *vt Ordinat* to deinstall

désintéressement *nm (de partenaire)* buying out; *(de créditeur)* paying off

désintéresser *vt (partenaire)* to buy out; *(créditeur)* to pay off

> **❝**
> Dans l'hypothèse d'une liquidation judiciaire (entraînant une cessation d'activité automatique), le liquidateur désigné par le tribunal pourra décider la mise en vente du domicile principal pour **désintéresser** vos créanciers. Si, en revanche, vous faites l'objet d'une procédure de redressement judiciaire, le tribunal saisi pourra décider de vous accorder un plan de remboursement et échelonner vos dettes sur dix ans au maximum.
> **❞**

désinvestir *vt Fin* to disinvest in

désinvestissement *nm Fin* disinvestment ❑ ***désinvestissement marginal*** marginal disinvestment

désir *nm (de l'acheteur)* desire

désistement *nm Jur (d'une demande)* waiver; *(d'une poursuite)* withdrawal

désister se désister *vpr Jur* **se désister d'une demande** to waive a claim; **se désister d'une poursuite** to withdraw an action

DESS *nm (abrév* **diplôme d'études supérieures spécialisées)** = postgraduate diploma

dessaisir 1 *vt* (a) *Jur* **dessaisir un tribunal d'une affaire** to remove a case from a court (b) *Admin* **dessaisir qn d'un dossier** to remove sb from a project
 2 se dessaisir *vpr* **se dessaisir de qch** to relinquish sth, to part with sth

dessaisissement *nm* (a) *Jur* **le dessaisissement d'un tribunal d'une affaire** the removal of a case from a court (b) *Admin* relinquishment

dessin *nm* design; *(représentation)* drawing □ **dessin assisté par ordinateur** computeraided design; **dessin industriel** industrial design; **dessin du produit** product design

dessinateur, -trice *nm,f* designer □ **dessinateur de publicité** commercial designer

déstabilisant, -e, déstabilisateur, -trice *adj* destabilizing

déstabilisation *nf* destabilization

déstabiliser *vt* to destabilize

destinataire *nmf (de courrier)* addressee, recipient; *(de marchandises)* consignee; *(d'un message électronique)* recipient

destination *nf* (a) *(lieu)* destination; **marchandises à destination de la province et de l'étranger** goods for consignment to the provinces and abroad; **un navire à destination de Bordeaux** a ship bound for Bordeaux (b) *(usage) (de capitaux, de fonds)* use

destiner *vt* (a) *(affecter)* **destiner des fonds à qch** to allot or assign funds to sth; **cet argent est destiné à la recherche** this money is earmarked for or is going towards research (b) *(réserver)* **des marchandises destinées à l'exportation** goods intended for export (c) *(concevoir pour)* **ces mesures sont destinées à réduire le chômage** these measures are designed to reduce unemployment

déstockage *nm* destocking, reduction in stocks □ *Compta* **déstockage de production** *(poste de bilan)* decrease in stocks

déstocker *vt* to destock, to reduce stocks of

destructeur de documents *nm* shredder

désuet, -ète *adj* obsolete

désuétude *nf* disuse; **tomber en désuétude** to fall into disuse; *Jur (droit)* to lapse; *(loi)* to fall into abeyance □ **désuétude calculée** planned or built-in obsolescence

détacher 1 *vt* (a) *Bourse* **détacher un coupon d'une action** to detach a coupon from a share (b) *(employé)* to second; **c'est un cadre détaché dans le secteur public** he's a manager who has been assigned or seconded to the civil service
 2 se détacher *vpr Bourse* **le coupon de ces actions se détache le 1er août** this stock goes ex-coupon on 1 August

détail *nm* (a) *(élément)* detail; **donner tous les**

détails to go into all the details, to give full details; **pour de plus amples détails, s'adresser à…** for more details, please contact… (b) *(énumération) (d'un compte, d'un inventaire)* items; *(d'une facture)* breakdown; **faire le détail de qch** to itemize sth, to break sth down (c) *(dans la vente)* retail; **vendre qch au détail** to sell sth retail

détaillant, -e *nm,f* retailer, shopkeeper □ **détaillant indépendant** independent retailer; **détaillant spécialisé** specialist retailer

détaillé, -e *adj (facture, relevé de compte)* itemized

détailler *vt* (a) *(marchandises)* to retail, to sell retail (b) *(facture, relevé de compte)* to itemize

détaxe *nf* (a) *(suppression)* lifting of tax or duty; *(diminution)* reduction of tax or duty; **vendus en détaxe** duty-free; **la détaxe des marchandises à l'exportation** the lifting of duty on exports (b) *(remboursement)* tax refund; **cela m'a fait 500 euros de détaxe** the reduction of duty saved me 500 euros □ **détaxe postale** refund on postage paid in error

détaxé, -e *adj (produits, articles)* duty-free

détaxer *vt (supprimer)* to lift the tax or duty on; *(diminuer)* to reduce the tax or duty on

> "
> Une révolution: c'est ce qu'avait provoqué dans le capitalisme allemand la décision du gouvernement Schröder de **détaxer** les plus-values sur les ventes de sociétés. D'un coup, banquiers et assureurs se sont mis à vendre avec frénésie leurs participations industrielles, auparavant gelées par une fiscalité dissuasive.
> "

détecteur *nm* **détecteur de faux billets** forged banknote detector; *Ordinat* **détecteur de virus** virus detector

détection *nf Ordinat* **détection d'erreurs** error detection; **détection virale** virus detection

détenir *vt (valeurs, titres, compte)* to hold; **société détenue à 50 pour cent** 50 percent-owned company; **ils détiennent 30 pour cent des parts de la société/des parts de marché** they have a 30 percent shareholding in the company/a 30 percent market share; **détenu par des intérêts privés** privately held

détente *nf (des taux d'intérêt)* lowering, easing

détenteur, -trice *nm,f (d'argent, d'un compte)* holder □ **détenteur d'actions** *Br* shareholder, *Am* stockholder; **détenteur de gage(s)** pledge holder; **détenteur de titres** *Br* shareholder, *Am* stockholder

détérioration *nf* deterioration

détériorer 1 *vt* to damage

2 se détériorer *vpr* to deteriorate

détermination *nf* fixing, setting ❑ *détermination des prix* price fixing, price setting

déterminer *vt* to determine, to ascertain; **déterminer le revenu imposable** to assess taxable income; **déterminer les conditions d'un contrat** to fix the conditions of a contract

détournement *nm Fin* **détournement d'actif** embezzlement of assets; **détournement de fonds** misappropriation of funds, embezzlement

détourner *vt (fonds)* to misappropriate, to embezzle

dette *nf* debt; **avoir des dettes** to be in debt (envers to); **faire des dettes** to run into debt; **avoir 10 000 euros de dettes** to be 10,000 euros in debt; **s'acquitter d'une dette** to pay off a debt; **assurer le service d'une dette** to service a debt ❑ *Compta* **dettes actives** accounts receivable; **dettes bancaires** bank debts; **dette caduque** debt barred by the Statute of Limitations; **dettes compte** book debts; **dette consolidée** consolidated *or* funded debt; **dette courante** floating debt; *Compta* **dette à court terme** short-term debt; *Compta* **dettes à court terme** current liabilities; **la dette de l'État** *Br* the national debt, *Am* the public debt; **dette exigible** debt due for (re)payment; **dettes d'exploitation** trade debt; **dette extérieure** foreign debt, overseas debt; **dette flottante** floating debt; **dette foncière** property charge; *Compta* **dettes fournisseurs** accounts payable; **dette d'honneur** debt of honour; *(hypothécaire)* mortgage debt; **dette inexigible** unrecoverable debt; **dette inscrite** consolidated debt; **dette liquide** liquid debt; *Compta* **dettes à long terme** long-term liabilities; **dette mezzanine** mezzanine debt; *Compta* **dettes à moyen terme** medium-term liabilities; **dette non consolidée** unfunded debt, floating debt; *Compta* **dettes passives** accounts payable, liabilities; **dette privilégiée** preferred *or* privileged debt; **la dette publique** *Br* the national debt, *Am* the public debt; **dette subordonnée** mezzanine debt; **dette véreuse** bad debt

DEUG *nm (abrév* **diplôme d'études universitaires générales)** = degree gained after a two-year course

DEUST *nm (abrév* **diplôme d'études universitaires scientifiques et techniques)** = university degree awarded after a two-year course of study in science and/or technical subjects

Deutsche Mark *nm Anciennement* Deutschmark

deuxième 1 *adj* second; **de deuxième choix, de deuxième qualité** *(marchandises, articles)* inferior ❑ *deuxième hypothèque* second mortgage; *Bourse* **deuxième jour de liquidation** name day; **deuxième trimestre** second quarter

2 *nm Fin* **deuxième de change** second of exchange

deux-points *nm* colon

dévalorisation *nf* **(a)** *(action) (de la monnaie)* devaluation; *(de marchandises)* marking down **(b)** *(résultat) (de la monnaie)* fall in value, depreciation; *(de marchandises)* mark-down

dévaloriser 1 *vt (monnaie)* to devalue; *(marchandises)* to mark down; **dévaloriser une monnaie de dix pour cent** to devalue a currency by ten percent

2 se dévaloriser *vpr (monnaie)* to depreciate; *(marchandises)* to lose value

dévaluation *nf (de la monnaie)* devaluation

dévaluer 1 *vt (monnaie)* to devalue
2 se dévaluer *vpr (monnaie)* to drop in value

devancement *nm Fin (d'une échéance)* payment before the due date, prepayment

devancer *vt* **(a)** *Fin* **devancer une échéance** to settle an account early, to pay a bill before the due date **(b)** *(concurrence)* to overtake; **sur ce marché, nous ne sommes plus devancés que par les Japonais** now only the Japanese are ahead of us in this market

> **❝**
>
> En Malaisie, avec plus de 7 milliards de dollars d'investissements industriels en 2001, les entrprises chinoises ont **devancé** les japonaises.
>
> **❞**

devanture *nf* **(a)** *(vitrine) Br* shop window, *Am* store window **(b)** *(façade) Br* shop front, *Am* store front **(c)** *(étalage)* window display

développement *nm (d'une entreprise, de l'économie)* development, growth; *(d'un produit)* development; **être en plein développement** to be growing fast; **ce produit n'est qu'au stade de son développement** this product is only at the development stage ❑ *développement durable (d'une économie)* sustainable development; **développement du marché** market development; **développement de nouveaux produits** new product development; **développement régional** regional development; **développement des ventes** sales expansion

développer 1 *vt (entreprise, économie, produit)* to develop
2 se développer *vpr (entreprise, économie)* to develop, to grow; *(produit)* to develop; **les usines Viaut cherchent à se développer** Viaut are seeking to expand

développeur, -euse *nm,f* software developer

déverrouiller *vt Ordinat* to unlock; *(majus-*

cules) to lock off; **déverrouiller un fichier en écriture** to unlock a file, to remove the read-only lock on a file

devis *nm* estimate, quotation; **établir un devis** to draw up an estimate *or* a quotation; **faire faire un devis pour qch** to get an estimate *or* a quotation for sth; **le devis des réparations s'élève à trois mille euros** the estimate *or* quotation for the repairs comes to three thousand euros ▫ *devis appréciatif* estimate, quotation; *devis descriptif* specification; *devis estimatif* estimate, quotation

devise *nf Fin* currency ▫ *devise contrôlée* managed currency; *devise convertible* convertible currency; *devise(s) étrangère(s)* foreign currency; *devise faible* soft *or* weak currency; *devise forte* hard *or* strong currency; *devise internationale* international currency; *devise non convertible* non-convertible currency; *devise soutenue* firm currency

devise-titre *nf Fin* foreign security, exchange currency

devoir *vt* **devoir qch à qn** to owe sb sth; **il me doit mille euros** he owes me a thousand euros; **la somme qui m'est due** the amount owing to me *or* due to me; **reste à devoir** *(sur facture)* balance due

dézipper *vt Ordinat (fichier)* to unzip

diagnostic *nm Ordinat* **diagnostic d'autotest** self-test diagnosis; *Fin* **diagnostic financier** financial healthcheck, diagnostic audit

diagramme *nm* diagram; *(graphique)* graph ▫ *diagramme à bâtons* bar chart; *diagramme de circulation* flow chart; *diagramme à secteurs* pie chart

dialogue *nm* **(a)** *(négociations)* dialogue, talks ▫ *dialogue Nord-Sud* dialogue *or* talks between North and South **(b)** *Ordinat* **dialogue d'établissement de liaison** handshaking

dialoguer *vi* **(a)** *(négocier)* to hold talks; **les syndicats vont de nouveau dialoguer avec le ministre** the unions are to resume talks with the minister **(b)** *Ordinat* to interact

diaporama *nm* slide show

Dictaphone® *nm* Dictaphone®

dictée *nf* dictation; **écrire qch sous la dictée de qn** to write sth at sb's dictation

dicter *vt* **(a)** *(courrier, lettre)* to dictate **(à** to) **(b)** *(imposer)* to dictate; **ces mesures ont été dictées par la conjoncture économique** these measures were dictated by the economic situation

didacthèque *nf Ordinat* set of educational software *or Am* teachware

didacticiel *nm Ordinat* piece of educational software *or Am* teachware

dièse *nm* hash

diffamateur, -trice *Jur* **1** *adj (texte)* libellous **2** *nm,f (par écrit)* libeller

diffamation *nf Jur (par un texte)* libel

diffamatoire *adj Jur (texte)* libellous

diffamer *vt Jur (par un texte)* to libel

différé, -e 1 *adj (paiement, crédit)* deferred **2** *nm Ordinat* **en différé** *(traitement)* off-line

différence *nf (entre deux prix)* difference; *Bourse (entre le cours offert et le cours demandé)* spread

différenciation *nf Mktg* differentiation ▫ *différenciation de ligne* line differentiation; *différenciation du produit* product differentiation

différencié, -e *adj (marketing)* differentiated

différend *nm* difference of opinion, disagreement (**entre** between); *Jur* dispute

différentiel, -elle 1 *adj* differential **2** *nm* differential ▫ *différentiel d'inflation* inflation differential; *différentiel de prix* price differential; *différentiel sémantique* semantic differential; *différentiel de taux* interest rate differential

différer *vt (jugement, paiement, réunion)* to defer, to postpone; **différer l'échéance d'un effet** to let a bill lie over

difficulté *nf* difficulty; **être en difficulté** *(entreprise, économie, secteur)* to be in difficulties *or* trouble ▫ *difficultés financières, difficultés de trésorerie* financial difficulties; **nous connaissons actuellement quelques difficultés financières** we are currently experiencing some financial difficulties

diffuser *vt (produits, livres)* to distribute; *(rapport)* to circulate; **leurs produits sont diffusés sur une grande échelle** their products are widely available

diffusion *nf (de produits, de livres)* distribution; *(d'un journal)* circulation; *(publicité, émission)* to broadcast; **ce sont des articles de grande diffusion** they are widely available products ▫ *diffusion de masse (d'un journal)* mass circulation

digital, -e *adj Ordinat* digital

digitalisation *nf Ordinat* digitization

digitaliser *vt Ordinat* to digitize

digitaliseur *nm Ordinat* digitizer

digraphie *nf Compta* double-entry bookkeeping

dilapider *vt (fortune)* to waste, to squander; *(fonds publics)* to embezzle

dilemme *nm Mktg (produit)* problem child

diluer *vt Fin (capital, actions)* to dilute; **diluer le bénéfice par action** to dilute equity; **diluer en-**

tièrement des actions to fully dilute shares

dilution nf Fin (du capital, des actions) dilution ❑ **dilution du bénéfice par action** dilution of equity

dimensionner vt (objets) to size

diminuer 1 vt to cut, to reduce; **montant net diminué du prix de vente** net amount less purchase price
2 vi to fall, to drop

diminution nf reduction, decrease (**de** in); **la diminution des charges patronales est censée encourager l'embauche** it is hoped that the reduction of employer's contributions will stimulate employment; **faire une diminution sur un compte** to allow a rebate on an account

dire nm Jur allegation; **au dire de l'expert** according to expert opinion or to the experts

direct, -e adj (impôts, ligne téléphonique) direct; **être en rapport** ou **contact direct** ou **en relations directes avec qn** to be in direct contact with sb

directeur, -trice 1 adj (équipe, instances) management, executive; (force) directing, managing
2 nm,f (qui fait partie du conseil d'administration) director; (d'un magasin, d'un service) manager ❑ **directeur des achats** purchasing manager; **directeur adjoint** deputy director/manager; **directeur administratif** executive director; **directeur administratif et financier** administrative and financial manager; **directeur d'agence** branch manager; **directeur de banque** bank manager; **directeur de chantier** site manager; **directeur de la clientèle** customer relations manager; **directeur commercial** sales director/manager; **directeur de la communication** communications director/manager; **directeur des comptes-clients** account director/manager; **directeur de la création** creative director; **directeur du crédit** credit manager; **directeur de division** (au siège) divisional director; **directeur exécutif** executive director; **directeur d'exploitation** operations director/manager; **directeur export** export director/manager; **directeur des exportations** export manager; **directeur financier** financial director/manager; **directeur de formation** training officer; **directeur général** (d'une entreprise) Br managing director, Am chief executive officer; (d'une organisation internationale) director general, general manager; **directeur général adjoint** Br deputy managing director, Am vice-president; **directeur gérant** executive director; **directeur hiérarchique** line manager; **directeur d'hôtel** hotel manager; **directeur (de l')informatique** computer manager; **directeur intérimaire, directeur par intérim** acting manager; **directeur juridique** legal director; **directeur de marché** market manager; **directeur du marketing** marketing director/manager; **directeur de marque** brand manager; **directeur du personnel** personnel director/manager; **directeur de production** production manager; **directeur de produit** product manager; **directeur de projet** project director/manager; **directeur de la promotion des ventes** sales promotion manager; **directeur de la publicité** advertising director/manager; **directeur de recherche et développement** director of research and development, R&D director; **directeur de recherche mercatique, directeur de recherche marketing** marketing research director/manager; **directeur régional** regional director/manager, area director/manager; **directeur des relations publiques** public relations director/manager; **directeur des ressources humaines** human resources manager; **directeur de service** head of department; **directeur du service d'audit** audit manager; **directeur des services techniques** technical director; **directeur de succursale** branch manager; **directeur technique** technical manager; **directeur d'usine** plant manager; **directeur de la vente-marketing** sales and marketing director/manager; **directeur des ventes** sales director/manager; **directeur de zone** regional manager

direction nf (a) (d'une entreprise, d'un magasin, d'un service) management; **la direction** (bureau) the director's office; (locaux) head office; **avoir la direction d'une entreprise** to manage a company; **il a confié la direction du service clientèle à son fils** he put his son in charge of the customer services department ❑ **direction commerciale** sales management; **direction des crédits** credit management; **direction des entreprises** business management; **direction par exceptions** management by exception; **direction de l'exploitation** operations management; **direction export** export management; **direction financière** financial management; **direction générale** general management, senior management; **Direction générale des impôts** Br ≃ Inland Revenue, Am ≃ Internal Revenue; **direction multiple** multiple management; **direction par objectifs** management by objectives; **direction du personnel** personnel management; **direction de la production** production control; **direction de projet** project management; **direction régionale** regional headquarters; **direction des ressources humaines** human resources management; **direction des ventes** sales management
(b) (service) department ❑ **direction du contentieux** legal department; Admin **Direction départementale de l'action sanitaire et sociale** = office administering health and social services at regional level; **direction de l'exploitation** operations department; **direction financière** finance department; Admin **Direc-**

tion générale de la santé = central administrative body for health and social services; *Admin* **Direction des hôpitaux** = central government office for hospital administration; **direction marketing, direction mercatique** marketing department; **direction du personnel** personnel department; **direction du trésor** finance department

(c) *(ensemble des cadres)* management; *(conseil d'administration)* board (of directors)

(d) *Ordinat* **direction systématisée** systems management

directoire *nm* board of directors

directorial, -e *adj* directorial, managerial

dirigé, -e *adj (économie)* controlled, planned; *(monnaie)* managed, controlled

dirigeant, -e 1 *adj (cadres)* managing; *(classes)* ruling

2 *nm,f* manager; **les dirigeants** management
❏ **dirigeant syndical** union leader

diriger 1 *vt (entreprise, équipe)* to manage, to run; *(production)* to control; *(investissements, fonds)* to channel (**vers** to)

2 se diriger *vpr* **se diriger vers** to head for, to move towards; **l'économie se dirige vers la reprise/la récession** the economy is picking up/heading for recession

dirigisme *nm Écon* state control

> **❝** ————————————————
>
> Par rapport aux autres continents, notamment américain, l'Europe se caractérise par la recherche d'un équilibre entre l'individu et le collectif, entre la performance économique et le développement des normes sociales, par la mise en place d'une régulation qui évite l'ultra-libéralisme destructeur et le **dirigisme** étouffant.
>
> ———————————————— **❞**

dirigiste *Écon* **1** *adj* interventionist
2 *nmf* advocate of state control

discount *nm* discount; **un discount de 20 pour cent** a 20 percent discount

discounter¹ *nm* discounter

discounter² *vt & vi* to sell at a discount

discours *nm* speech ❏ **discours de clôture** closing speech; **discours de remerciement** vote of thanks

discrimination *nf* discrimination ❏ **discrimination raciale** racial discrimination; **discrimination sexuelle** sexual discrimination

disparaître *vi* **tout doit disparaître** *(sur panneau)* everything must go

disponibilité *nf* (a) *Admin* leave of absence; **mettre qn en disponibilité** *(au chômage)* to lay sb off; **prendre une disponibilité** to take leave of absence; **demander une mise en disponibi-**

lité to ask for leave of absence (b) *Fin* **disponibilités** available funds, liquid assets ❏ **disponibilités en caisse** cash in hand; **disponibilités monétaires** money supply (c) **disponibilités du stock** items available in stock

disponible 1 *adj* (a) *Admin (fonctionnaire)* on leave of absence (b) *Fin (fonds, capital, solde)* available (c) *(article)* available; **ces articles sont disponibles en magasin** these items can be supplied from stock

2 *nm* (a) *Fin* **le disponible** available assets, liquid assets (b) **le disponible** *(articles)* items available in stock; *Ordinat* **disponible pour Mac/PC** available for the Mac/PC

disposer disposer de *vt ind* to have at one's disposal; **disposer de capitaux importants** to have a large capital at one's disposal; **nous disposons d'une large gamme de produits** we offer a wide range of products; **le directeur va vous recevoir, mais sachez qu'il ne dispose que de trente minutes** the manager can see you now, but he only has half an hour

dispositif *nm* (a) *(mesures)* system, plan; **il s'agit d'un dispositif gouvernemental pour favoriser l'emploi des jeunes** it's a government plan to stimulate youth employment

(b) *Ordinat* **dispositif d'alimentation** power unit; *(pour papier)* sheet feed; **dispositif d'alimentation feuille à feuille** cut sheet feed, stacker; **dispositif d'alimentation papier** sheet feed, paper feed; **dispositif externe** external device; **dispositif de sortie** output device; **dispositif de stockage** storage device

(c) *(appareil)* device ❏ *Tél* **dispositif de redirection d'appel** call-forwarding device

disposition *nf* (a) *(disponibilité)* **avoir qch à sa disposition** to have sth at one's disposal; **mettre qch à la disposition de qn** to put *or* place sth at sb's disposal, to make sth available to sb; **je suis à votre disposition** I am at your disposal; **ils ont mis une secrétaire à la disposition du directeur** a secretary has been made available for the manager ❏ **disposition fiscale** tax provision

(b) **dispositions** *(préparatifs)* arrangements; **prendre des dispositions pour faire qch** to make the necessary arrangements to do sth

(c) *(d'un texte, d'un clavier)* layout

(d) *(tendance)* tendency; *(du marché)* tone, trend

(e) *Jur* clause, stipulation

disque *nm (enregistrement)* disc; *Ordinat* disk ❏ **disque amovible** removable disk; **disque audionumérique** compact disc; **disque cible** target disk; **disque compact** compact disc; **disque compact audionumérique** digital compact disc; **disque compact interactif** interactive CD, CDI; **disque compact vidéo** video compact disc; **disque de démarrage** boot disk;

disque de destination destination disk; *disque dur* hard disk; *disque fixe* fixed disk; *disque laser* laser disc; *disque magnétique* magnetic disk; *disque optique* optical disk; *disque optique compact* CD-ROM; *disque optique numérique* digital optical disk; *disque souple* floppy disk; *disque source* source disk; *disque système* system disk; *disque vidéo numérique* digital video disk

disquette *nf Ordinat* diskette, floppy (disk); **sur disquette** on diskette, on floppy ◻ *disquette cible* target disk; *disquette de copie* copy disk; *disquette de démarrage* boot disk, start-up disk; *disquette de démonstration* demo disk; *disquette de destination* destination disk; *disquette de diagnostic* diagnostic disk; *disquette (à) double densité* double density disk; *disquette d'évaluation* demo disk; *disquette d'installation* installation disk, installer; *disquette magnétique* magnetic disk; *disquette optique* optical disk, floptical disk; *disquette pour PC* PC disk; *disquette programme* program disk; *disquette (à) simple densité* single density disk; *disquette source* source disk; *disquette système* system disk; *disquette vierge* blank unformatted disk

dissimulation d'actif *nf Jur* (fraudulent) concealment of assets

dissolution *nf Jur (d'un contrat)* dissolution, termination; *(d'une entreprise)* winding up

dissoudre *vt Jur (contrat)* to dissolve, to terminate; *(entreprise)* to wind up

distance *nf Ordinat* **à distance** remote

distorsion sélective *nf Mktg* selective distortion

distribuable *adj (bénéfice)* distributable

distribuer *vt* (a) *Mktg (produits, marchandises)* to distribute (b) *(fonctions, tâches)* to allocate, to allot (c) *(actions, bénéfices)* to distribute; *(dividendes)* to pay (d) *(courrier)* to deliver

distributaire *nmf Jur* distributee

distributeur, -trice 1 *nm,f (vendeur)* distributor, dealer ◻ *distributeur agréé* authorized stockist *or* distributor; *distributeur en gros* wholesaler
2 *nm (machine) distributeur automatique de billets Br* cash dispenser, cashpoint, *Am* ATM; *distributeur de monnaie* change machine

distribution *nf* (a) *(de produits)* distribution; **la grande distribution** large-scale distribution ◻ *distribution à domicile* door drop; *distribution d'échantillons* sampling; *distribution exclusive* exclusive distribution; *distribution à flux tendus* just-in-time distribution; *distribution en gros* wholesale distribution; *distribution de masse* mass distribution; *distribution numérique* numerical distribution; *distribution physique* physical distribution; *distri-bution sélective* selective distribution; *distribution valeur* weighted distribution
(b) *(de fonctions, de tâches)* allocation, allotment
(c) *(de bénéfices)* distribution; *(de dividendes)* payment ◻ *Bourse* **distribution d'actions** share allotment *or* allocation; *distribution des richesses* distribution of wealth
(d) *(du courrier)* delivery

divers, -e 1 *adj* sundry, miscellaneous
2 *nmpl* sundries

diversification *nf* diversification; **l'entreprise a adopté une stratégie de diversification** the company has adopted a policy of diversification; **la diversification de l'entreprise est la condition de sa survie** the company must diversify if it is to survive ◻ *diversification industrielle* diversification, lateral integration of industry; *diversification de portefeuille* portfolio diversification; *diversification des produits* product diversification

> **"**
> Didier Mathus joue la **diversification industrielle** – "l'histoire nous a montré que la mono-industrie n'est pas la panacée" – et sectorielle, pour développer le tertiaire et résorber le chômage féminin (60% des chômeurs). Sans oublier la carte de l'action culturelle: "C'est en jouant sur tous ces tableaux qu'on aide la population à passer ce cap psychologique difficile."
> **"**

diversifier 1 *vt (production, activités, économie)* to diversify
2 **se diversifier** *vpr (entreprise)* to diversify; *(produits, activités, économie)* to become diversified

dividende *nm Fin* dividend; **toucher un dividende** to draw a dividend; **déclarer** *ou* **annoncer un dividende** to declare *or* announce a dividend; **avec dividende** cum div(idend), *Am* dividend on; **sans dividende** ex div(idend), *Am* dividend off ◻ *dividendes accrus* accrued dividends; *dividende d'action* share *or* stock dividend, dividend on shares; *dividende par action* dividend per share; *dividende anticipé* advance dividend; *dividende brut* gross dividend; *dividende cumulatif* cumulative dividend; *dividende définitif* final dividend; *dividende en espèces* cash dividend; *dividende fictif* sham dividend; *dividende final* final dividend; *dividende intérimaire, dividende par intérim* interim dividend; *dividende net* net dividend; *dividende prioritaire, dividende de priorité* preference dividend; *dividende prioritaire cumulatif* preference cumulative dividend; *dividende privilégié* preference dividend

diviser *vt (répartir)* to divide; *Bourse, Fin (actions)* to split

division *nf* (**a**) *(répartition)* division; *Bourse, Fin (des actions)* splitting ❑ **division du marché** market division; **division du travail** division of labour (**b**) *(partie)* division, department ❑ **division des exportations** export division; **division de formation professionnelle** training division; **division internationale** international division

DLC *nf* (*abrév* **date limite de consommation**) best-before date

DN *nf* (*abrév* **distribution numérique**) numerical distribution

DNS *nm Ordinat* (*abrév* **Domain Name System**) DNS

DOC *nm Ordinat* (*abrév* **disque optique compact**) CD-ROM

dock *nm* (**a**) *(bassin)* dock, dockyard (**b**) *(entrepôt)* warehouse ❑ **dock entrepôt** dock-warehouse; **dock frigorifique** cold storage dock

docker *nm Br* docker, *Am* longshoreman

document *nm* document; **rédiger un document** to draw up a document ❑ *UE* **document administratif unique** unique data folder; *Ordinat* **document de base** source document; **documents contre acceptation** documents against acceptance; **documents contre paiement** documents against payment; **document d'embarquement** shipping document; **document d'expédition** shipping document; **document interne à l'entreprise** internal company document; **document maître** master document; **documents maritimes** shipping documents; **document officiel** official document; **document d'offre** tender document; *Mktg* **document de publicité directe** direct mailing; **document source** source document; *Compta* **document de synthèse** financial statement; **document transmissible** transferable document; **document de transport combiné** combined transport document; **document de travail** working document; **document type** standard document; **documents de voyage** travel documents

documentaire *adj* documentary; **ce rapport vous est fourni à titre documentaire** this report is supplied for information only

documentaliste *nmf* information officer, *Am* file clerk ❑ **documentaliste iconographique** picture researcher

documentation *nf* (**a**) *(technique)* documentation ❑ **documentation iconographique** picture research (**b**) *(publicités)* literature, documentation; **voulez-vous recevoir notre documentation?** would you like us to send you our literature? ❑ **documentation de presse** press kit

documenter 1 *vt* to document; **bien documenté** *(rapport)* well-documented; *(personne)* well-informed

2 se documenter *vpr* to gather information *or* material (**sur** on)

doit *nm Compta, Fin* debit, liability; *(d'un compte)* debit side; **doit et avoir** debits and credits; *(personnes)* debtors and creditors

dollar *nm* dollar; **un billet de cinq dollars** a five-dollar *Br* note *or Am* bill ❑ **dollar américain** US *or* American dollar

domaine *nm* (**a**) *(propriété)* estate, property; **Domaine (de l'État)** State property ❑ **domaine public** public ownership; **être dans le domaine public** to be out of copyright; **tomber dans le domaine public** to come into the public domain (**b**) *(secteur d'activité)* field, domain; **c'est du domaine du service commercial** that's for the marketing department to deal with ❑ *Mktg* **domaine d'activité stratégique** strategic business unit; **domaine concurrentiel** competitive scope

> **"**
>
> Il y a, depuis quelques années, c'est certain, une rupture des habitudes d'achat. En tout cas pour les classiques, qui sont dans le **domaine public**. On a beau faire des éditions bien préfacées, bien annotées, avec un texte sûr, le prix … nous a souvent fait du tort. Nous, ce qu'on cherche, ce n'est pas à baisser le prix au maximum.
>
> **"**

domicile *nm* (place of) residence, home; **sans domicile fixe** of no fixed abode; **travailler à domicile** to work from home; **le chéquier sera renvoyé à votre domicile** the chequebook will be sent to your home address; **ils livrent à domicile** they have a delivery service ❑ *Jur* **domicile conjugal** marital *or* matrimonial home; **domicile fiscal** tax domicile

domiciliataire *nmf* paying agent

domiciliation *nf* domiciliation ❑ **domiciliation bancaire** payment *(by banker's order)*

domicilié, -e *adj* (**a**) *(personne)* resident, domiciled (**à** at); **être domicilié à Londres** to be domiciled in London (**b**) *(salaire)* paid directly into one's bank account

domicilier *vt* to domicile

dominer *vt* *(secteur, marché)* to dominate

dommage *nm* (**a**) *(dégâts matériels)* damage; **subir un dommage** to suffer damage; **réparer les dommages** to repair *or* to make good the damage (**b**) *Jur (préjudice)* harm ❑ **dommage corporel** personal *or* physical injury; **dommages et intérêts** damages; **dommage matériel** damage to property, material damage; **dommages punitifs** punitive damages

dommages-intérêts *nmpl Jur* damages; **fixer les dommages-intérêts** to fix damages; **poursuivre qn en dommages-intérêts** to sue sb for damages, to bring an action for damages against sb; **verser/obtenir des dommages-intérêts** to pay/to be awarded damages ❑ *dommages-intérêts compensatoires* compensation

domotique *nf Ordinat* home automation

DOM-TOM *nmpl* (*abrév* **Départements et territoires d'outre-mer**) = French overseas departments and territories

donation *nf Jur* donation ❑ *donation inter vivos* gift inter vivos; *donations parents-enfants* donations from parents to children

donnée *nf* piece of information; *Ordinat* piece of data; **données** information; *Ordinat* data; **je n'ai pas toutes les données du problème** I don't have all the information on the problem; **en données corrigées des variations saisonnières** seasonally adjusted ❑ *données de base* background data; *données brutes* raw data; *données démographiques* demographic data; *Ordinat* **données numériques** digital data; *données primaires* primary data; *données secondaires* secondary data; *données de style de vie* lifestyle data

donneur, -euse *nm,f Fin* **donneur d'aval** guarantor *or* backer of bill; *donneur de caution* guarantor; *donneur d'ordre* principal

doper *vt* (*exportations, ventes*) to boost; **la dépréciation du dollar a dopé les ventes à l'étranger** the depreciation in the value of the dollar has boosted export sales

---
“

A l'avenir, la montée en puissance des mobiles (Orange), de l'Internet (Wanadoo) et des transmissions de données (Equant) devrait **doper** l'excédent brut d'exploitation et accroître les liquidités.

”

---

dormant, -e *adj Fin* (*compte*) dormant; (*marché, capital*) unproductive, lying idle

DOS *nm Ordinat* (*abrév* **disk operating system**) DOS

dos *nm Fin* (*d'un effet, d'un chèque*) back; **signer au dos d'un chèque** to endorse a cheque, to sign the back of a cheque; **voir au dos** see over *or* overleaf

dossier *nm* (**a**) (*pièces, documents*) file, dossier; (*chemise*) folder, file; **verser une pièce au dossier** to file a document; **constituer un dossier sur qn/qch** to build up a file on sb/sth ❑ *dossier d'appel d'offres* tender documents; *dossier de candidature* application; *dossier client* client file; *dossier crédit* credit file; *dossier de crédit immobilier* mortgage application; *Bourse dossier de demande d'introduction en Bourse* listing agreement; *Banque dossier de demande de prêt* loan application form; *dossier de do-*

miciliation domiciliation papers, domiciliation file; *dossier de douane* customs papers, customs file; *dossier de lancement* (*d'un produit*) product launch file; *dossier de presse* book of press cuttings; *Mktg* press pack, press kit; *dossier suspendu* suspension file; *dossier de voyage* travel documents

(**b**) (*sujet*) question, matter; **le dossier du GATT** the GATT question; **s'occuper du dossier de l'environnement** to be responsible for environmental matters

(**c**) *Ordinat* (*répertoire*) folder; (*fichier*) file ❑ *dossier actif* active file; *dossier archivé* archive file; *dossier clos* closed file; *dossier ouvert* open file; *dossier sauvegardé* saved file; *dossier système* system file

---
“

Pour bien négocier un **dossier de crédit immobilier**, il est indispensable de collecter le maximum d'épargne et de présenter son meilleur profil d'emprunteur aux banquiers, qui l'apprécient prioritairement en fonction de sept critères (endettement, emploi, revenus, âge …).

”

---

dotation *nf* (**a**) (*fonds*) (*d'hôpital, de collège*) endowment, foundation; (*à un chef d'État*) allowance (**b**) (*subvention*) grant (**c**) *Can Admin* **dotation en effectifs** staff increase (**d**) *Compta* provision ❑ *dotation aux amortissements* depreciation provision, allowance for depreciation; *dotation en capital* capital contribution; *dotation au compte de provisions* appropriation to the reserve; *dotation aux provisions* charge to provisions

doter *vt* (**a**) (*hôpital, collège*) to endow (**b**) (*équiper*) to equip (**de** with)

douane *nf Douanes* (**a**) (*à la frontière*) customs; **passer à la douane** *ou* **au bureau de douane** to go through customs; **passer qch en douane** to clear sth through customs; **passer qch en fraude à la douane** to smuggle sth through customs; **marchandises en douane** bonded goods; **soumis aux droits de douane** dutiable ❑ *douane volante* mobile customs unit (**b**) (*administration*) **la douane** *Br* ≃ Customs and Excise, *Am* the Customs Service (**c**) (*taxe*) customs duty; **exempté de douane** duty-free

douanier, -ère 1 *adj* customs
2 *nm,f* customs officer

double 1 *adj* double; **à double revenu** (*foyer, ménage*) two-income; **en double exemplaire** in duplicate ❑ *double affichage des prix* dual pricing; *double circulation (de monnaies)* dual circulation; *Ordinat* **double densité** double density; *Compta* **double emploi** duplication (of entry); *double imposition* double taxation; *Bourse* **double marché des changes** dual exchange market; *Bourse* **double option** double option, put and call option

2 *nm (exemplaire)* duplicate, copy; *Ordinat* backup; **veuillez nous adresser un double de la facture** please send us a copy of the bill; **j'ai tous mes papiers en double** I have duplicates *or* copies of all my papers ❑ *double de connaissement* house bill

double-clic *nm Ordinat* double click; **faire un double-clic (sur)** to double-click (on)

double-cliquer *vi Ordinat* to double-click

DPE *nf (abrév* **direction par exceptions)** management by exception

dpi *Ordinat (abrév* **dots per inch)** dpi

DPO *nf (abrév* **direction par objectifs)** management by objectives

drachme *nf Anciennement* drachma

drainage *nm (de capital, de ressources)* tapping

drainer *vt (capital, ressources)* to tap

DRAM *nf Ordinat (abrév* **dynamic random access memory)** DRAM

dresser *vt (plan, contrat, bilan, liste)* to prepare, to draw up; *(facture)* to make out

DRH 1 *nm (abrév* **directeur des ressources humaines)** human resources manager

2 *nf (abrév* **direction des ressources humaines)** human resources management

droit *nm* **(a)** *(prérogative)* right; **tous droits (de reproduction) réservés** *(sur livre)* all rights reserved; **avoir droit à qch** to have a right to sth, to be entitled to sth; **avoir des droits sur qn/qch** to have rights over sb/sth; *Jur* **de droit et de fait** de facto and de jure; **à qui de droit** *(sur lettre)* to whom it may concern; **s'adresser à qui de droit** to apply to an authorized person; **faire droit à une demande** to comply with *or* accede to a request ❑ *droit d'accès* right of entry; *droits d'achat* purchasing rights; *Bourse droit d'attribution* allotment right; *droit d'auteur* copyright; *droit au bail* right to a lease; *droits contractuels* rights granted by contract; *droits de distribution, droits de diffusion (d'un produit)* distribution rights; *droits étrangers* foreign rights; *droits exclusifs* sole rights, exclusive rights; *droits d'exclusivité* sole rights, exclusive rights; *droits d'exploitation pour le monde entier* worldwide rights; *droits de fabrication* manufacturing rights; *droit de grève* right to strike; *droits internationaux* international rights; *droit de licenciement* right to dismiss; *droit de préemption* right of first refusal, pre-emptive right; *droit de préférence* right of first refusal; *droit préférentiel de souscription* rights issue; *droit de rachat* repurchase right, buyback right; *droit de recours* right of appeal; *droits de reproduction* reproduction rights; *droit de sortie* export duty; *droit de souscription (d'actions)* subscription

right; *droits statutaires* statutory rights; *Fin droits de tirage* drawing rights; *Fin droits de tirage spéciaux* special drawing rights; *droits de vente exclusifs* exclusive selling rights; *Bourse droits de vote (des actionnaires)* voting rights

(b) *(en argent)* fee; *(imposition)* duty; *(taxe)* tax; **droits à la charge du vendeur/de l'acheteur** duty to be paid by the seller/purchaser ❑ *droits ad valorem* ad valorem duty; *droits d'auteur* royalties; **recevoir des droits d'auteur de 10 pour cent** to receive royalties of 10 percent; *droit de courtage* brokerage (fee); *droits différentiels* differential duties; *droits de dock* dock dues; *droits de douane* customs duty; *droit de douane à l'importation* import duty; *droits d'enregistrement* registration fees; *droit d'entrée* import duty; *droit d'exportation* export duty; *Compta droit fixe* fixed rate of duty; *Banque droits de garde* custody account charges; *droits de greffe* registry dues; *droit d'immatriculation* registration fee; *droit d'importation* import duty; *droits d'inscription* registration fees; *droits d'inscription et de transfert* registration and transfer fees; *droits de mutation* capital transfer tax; *droits de navigation* shipping dues, navigation dues; *droits de port* harbour dues, port dues; *droits de quai* wharf dues; *droit de sortie* export duty; *droits de succession* inheritance tax, death duties, *Am* death tax; *droit de timbre* stamp duty; *droits de transfert* transfer duty

(c) *Jur* law ❑ *droit administratif* administrative law; *droit bancaire* banking law; *droit de brevet* patent law; *droit cambial* exchange law; *droit civil* civil law; *droit commercial* commercial law; *droit communautaire* Community law; *droit constitutionnel* constitutional law; *droit des contrats* contract law; *droit douanier* customs legislation; *droit écrit* statute law; *droit fiscal* tax law; *droit international* international law; *droit maritime* maritime law; *droit des obligations* contract law; *droit social* employment law; *droit des sociétés* corporate law, company law; *droit du travail* labour law

DSL *nf Ordinat (abrév* **Digital Subscriber Line)** DSL

DTS *nmpl Fin (abrév* **droits de tirage spéciaux)** special drawing rights

dû, due 1 *adj (que l'on doit)* due, owing; **en port dû** carriage forward

2 *nm* due; **payer son dû** to pay the amount owed

dual-band *adj Tél* dual-band

ducroire *nm* del credere; *(agent)* del credere agent

dûment *adv* duly; **dûment expédié/reçu** duly dispatched/received; **dûment accrédité** *(re-*

présentant) duly authorized

dumping *nm Écon* dumping; **faire du dumping** to dump ❑ *dumping social* social dumping

"

On les accuse aussi de se livrer à un **dumping social** en confiant leur fabrication à des imprimeries de labeur qui crachent brochures et magazines à des coûts 35% inférieurs à ceux des presses des quotidiens payants, peuplées d'ouvriers du Livre au statut en béton.

"

duopole *nm* duopoly

duplicata *nm* duplicate (copy) ❑ *duplicata de reçu* duplicate receipt

duplication *nf (d'un document, d'un logiciel)* copying ❑ *Mktg* **duplication d'audience** audience duplication

dupliquer *vt (document, logiciel)* to copy, to make a copy of

durée *nf (d'un bail)* duration, term; *(de crédit)* term; *(d'un prêt)* life; **les syndicats essaient de faire baisser la durée hebdomadaire de travail** the unions are trying to have the working week shortened ❑ *Compta* **durée d'amortissement** depreciation period; *Ordinat* **durée de connexion** on-line time; *Mktg* **durée du cycle de commande** order cycle time; **durée (utile) de vie** *(d'un produit)* life expectancy, shelf life

DUT *nm (abrév* **diplôme universitaire de technologie)** = qualification awarded after a two-year course of study in technology

DV *nf Mktg (abrév* **distribution valeur)** weighted distribution

DVD *nm Ordinat (abrév* **Digital Video Disk, Digital Versatile Disk)** DVD

dynamique 1 *adj (concurrence)* brisk
  2 *nf* dynamics ❑ *dynamique d'équipe* team dynamics; *dynamique du marché* market dynamics; *dynamique des produits* product dynamics

Ee

EAO *nm (abrév* **enseignement assisté par ordinateur**) CAL

EBITDA *nm (abrév* **earnings before interest, tax, depreciation and amortization**) EBITDA

e-book *nm Ordinat* e-book

écart *nm (entre deux chiffres)* difference; *Compta* spread, variance; *Bourse* spread; *Mktg* gap; **il y a un écart de cent euros entre les deux comptes** there is a discrepancy of a hundred euros between the two accounts; *Bourse* **l'écart entre le prix d'achat et le prix de vente** the spread between bid and asked prices; **l'écart se creuse entre les pays riches et les pays pauvres** there is a growing gap between the rich and poor countries □ *Bourse* **écart d'acquisition** goodwill; **écart budgétaire** budgetary variance; **écart de caisse** cash shortage; *Fin* **écarts de conversion** exchange adjustments; **écarts de cours** price spreads; **écart des coûts** cost variance; **écart déflationniste** deflationary gap; *Bourse* **écart horizontal** horizontal spread; **écart inflationniste** inflationary gap; **écart moyen absolu** mean absolute deviation; **écart net** net variance; *Mktg* **écart de performance** gap level; *Bourse* **écart de prime** option spread; **écart de prix** price differential; **écart salarial** *ou* **de salaire** wage differential; **écart sur stock** inventory shortage; **écart type** standard deviation; *Bourse* **écart vertical** vertical spread

> "
> Par exemple, les pertes sur les sicav en 2001 se sont échelonnées en moyenne entre -18 et -25%. Cette différence de performance s'explique par les légers **écarts** que s'autorisent les gérants par rapport à l'indice.
> "

e-cash *nm Ordinat* e-cash

échange *nm* (**a**) *Fin* exchange; *(commerce)* trade; **les échanges entre la France et l'Allemagne ont connu une progression spectaculaire** trade between France and Germany has increased spectacularly □ **échanges commerciaux** trade; **échanges industriels** industrial trade; **échanges internationaux** international trade; **échanges en valeurs** turnover *(on a securities trading account)*; **échanges en volume** tonnage

(**b**) *Banque, Bourse* swap □ **échange d'actions** share swap; **échange cambiste** treasury swap; **échange de créances** debt swap; **échange de créances contre actifs** debt equity swap; **échange de dette** debt swap; **échange de devises** currency swap; **échange financier** swap; **échange d'intérêts et de monnaies** currency interest-rate swap; **échange de taux d'intérêt** interest-rate swap; **échange à terme** forward swap

(**c**) *Mktg* **échange standard** *(de produit)* replacement

(**d**) *Ordinat* **échange de données** data exchange; **échange dynamique de données** dynamic data exchange; **échange de données informatisé, échange électronique de données** electronic data exchange

échangeable *adj* exchangeable (**contre** for)

échanger 1 *vt* to exchange; **les marchandises ne sont ni reprises ni échangées** goods cannot be returned or exchanged

2 s'échanger *vpr Bourse* to trade; **ces titres s'échangent à 70 euros** these securities are trading at 70 euros

échantillon *nm* (**a**) *Mktg (pour un sondage)* sample □ **échantillon aléatoire** random sample; **échantillon aréolaire** cluster sample; **échantillon de convenance** convenience sample; **échantillon discrétionnaire** judgement sample; **échantillon empirique** purposive sample, non-random sample; **échantillon modèle** standard sample; **échantillon non probabiliste** non-probability sample; **échantillon normal** average sample; **échantillon probabiliste** probability sample; **échantillon par quotas** quota sample; **échantillon représentatif** true or fair sample; **échantillon stratifié** stratified sample; **échantillon témoin** check sample; **échantillon type** representative sample

(**b**) *(d'un produit)* sample; **pareil** *ou* **conforme à l'échantillon** up to sample; **envoyer qch à titre d'échantillon** to send sth as a sample □ **échantillon gratuit** free sample; **échantillon publicitaire** free sample; **échantillon promotionnel** promotional sample

échantillonnage *nm* (**a**) *Mktg (action)* sampling; *(groupe de personnes)* sample; **l'échantillonnage se fait sur un produit sur cent** one product in a hundred is sampled *or* tested □ **échantillonnage aléatoire** random sampling; *échantillonnage aréolaire* cluster sampling; *échantillonnage empirique* purposive or non-random sampling; *échantillonnage non probabiliste* non-probability sampling; *échantillonnage probabiliste* probability sampling; *échantillonnage par quotas* quota sampling; *échantillonnage par zone* area sampling (**b**) *(série d'échantillons)* range of samples

échantillonner vt (**a**) *Mktg (population)* to sample (**b**) *(préparer des échantillons de)* to prepare samples of (**c**) *(comparer)* to verify or to check by the samples

échantillonneur, -euse nm,f *Mktg (personne)* sampler

échappatoire nf loophole □ *échappatoire comptabilité* accounting loophole; *échappatoire fiscale* tax loophole

échappement nm *Ordinat* escape

échauffement nm *Fin (de l'économie)* overheating

échéance nf (**a**) *Fin (de dû)* maturity date, due date; *(de terme)* expiry date; **avant échéance** *(paiement, règlement)* before the due date; **à trois mois d'échéance** at three months' date; **emprunter à longue/à courte échéance** to borrow long/short; **prêter à longue/à courte échéance** to lend long/short; **venir à échéance** to fall due, to mature; **faire face à ses échéances** to meet one's financial commitments; **avoir de lourdes échéances** to have heavy financial commitments; **l'intérêt n'a pas été payé à l'échéance** the interest is overdue □ *échéance commune* equation of payment; *échéance à court terme* short-term maturity; *Banque échéance emprunt* loan maturity; *Compta échéances de fin de mois* end-of-month payments; *échéance fixe* fixed maturity; *échéance à long terme* long-term maturity; *échéance moyenne* average due date; *échéance à moyen terme* medium-term maturity; *Bourse échéance proche* near month; *échéance à vue* sight bill or maturity (**b**) *(d'un bail, d'un contrat)* expiration

échéancier nm *Fin* bill book; *Compta* due date file □ *échéancier de paiement* payment schedule

échelle nf scale; **à l'échelle mondiale/nationale** on a world/national scale; **de grande échelle** large-scale □ *Mktg échelle d'attitudes* attitude scale; *Mktg échelle de classement* rating scale; *Mktg échelle d'importance* importance scale; *échelle mobile (des prix, salaires)* sliding scale; *échelle des prix* price range; *échelle des salaires* salary scale; *échelle des traitements* salary scale

échelon nm (**a**) *(degré d'une hiérarchie, d'une organisation)* grade; **monter/descendre d'un échelon** to go up/down a grade; **le dernier/premier échelon** the bottom/top grade; **il a gravi rapidement tous les échelons** he quickly climbed to the top of the ladder □ *échelon salarial, échelon des salaires* salary grade (**b**) *(niveau)* level; **à l'échelon ministériel/directorial** at ministerial/managerial level; **à l'échelon régional/national** on a regional/national level; **à tous les échelons** on every level □ *Bourse échelon de cotation* tick size

> **"**
>
> En outre, chaque région choisit un jour chômé supplémentaire … L'Espagne délègue aux régions. Les Espagnols disposent de 14 jours fériés, mais échappent à la concentration sur le mois de mai. Deux jours sont décidés **à l'échelon régional**: cette décision, prise en 1983, a été vécue comme une grande victoire des régionalistes.
>
> **"**

échelonnement nm (**a**) *(de paiements)* spreading (**b**) *(de vacances)* staggering

échelonner vt (**a**) *(paiements)* to spread (out); **les versements sont échelonnés sur dix ans** the instalments are spread (out) over ten years (**b**) *(vacances)* to stagger

échoir vi (**a**) *Fin (dette)* to fall due; *(investissement)* to mature; **le terme échoit le 20 de ce mois** the date for payment is the 20th of this month; **le délai est échu** the deadline has expired (**b**) *(bail)* to expire

échos nmpl *(des clients, des consommateurs)* feedback

échu, -e adj *Fin* due; *(intérêts)* outstanding

écluse nf *Ordinat* firewall

école nf school □ *école de commerce* business college, business school; *École nationale d'administration* = prestigious university-level college preparing students for senior posts in the civil service and public management; *école de secrétariat* secretarial school; *École supérieure de commerce de Paris* = prestigious business and management school

e-commerce nm *Ordinat* e-commerce

économat nm (**a**) *(magasin)* staff (discount) store (**b**) *(fonction d'économe)* bursarship; *(bureau)* bursar's office

économe nmf bursar

économétrique adj econometric

économie nf (**a**) *(système)* economy; **l'économie de la France** the French economy □ *économie d'actionnariat populaire* share economy; *économie capitaliste* capitalist economy; *économie de la connaissance* knowledge economy; *économie de dimension* economy of scale; *économie dirigée* controlled or planned economy; *économie d'échelle* economy of scale; *économie libérale* free-market economy; **économie de marché** market economy; **économie mixte** mixed economy; **économie non monétaire** natural economy; **économie ouverte** open economy; **économie parallèle** black economy; **économie planifiée** planned economy; **économie en pleine maturité** mature economy; **économie de plein emploi** full-employment economy; **économie politique** political economy; **économie à ressources sous-exploitées** sleeping economy; **économie salariale** wage economy; **économie souterraine** black economy; **économie de troc** barter economy

(**b**) *(discipline)* economics ❑ **économie d'entreprise** business management; **économie de l'environnement** environmental economics

(**c**) *(gain)* saving; **faire une économie de temps** to save time; **vous faites une économie de 20 pour cent** you make a saving of 20 percent ❑ **économie de main-d'œuvre** labour saving

(**d**) **économies** *(épargne)* savings; **faire des économies** to save money

> ❝
> Croissance forte, inflation maîtrisée à 6,8% fin 2001, chômage le plus bas d'Europe centrale … la Hongrie a tiré profit d'une décennie de transition vers l'**économie de marché**. Sa recette? Miser sur les investissements étrangers.
> ❞

économique *adj* (**a**) *(relatif à l'économie)* economic (**b**) *(avantageux)* economical

économiquement *adv* (**a**) *(du point de vue de l'économie)* economically; **les économiquement faibles** the lower-income groups (**b**) *(à moindre frais)* inexpensively; **économiquement viable** economically viable

économiser 1 *vt (argent, temps)* to economize, to save; **économiser sur qch** to economize on sth

2 *vi* **économiser sur qch** to economize on sth

économiseur d'écran *nm Ordinat* screen saver

économiste *nmf* (political) economist ❑ **économiste d'entreprise** business economist

écotaxe *nf* ecotax

> ❝
> Pour d'autres en revanche, ce mouvement pourrait buter son incapacité à proposer, au-delà de la taxe Tobin et autres **écotaxes**, des solutions alternatives à l'économie de marché.
> ❞

écoulé, -e *adj* (**a**) *(du mois dernier)* of last month; **votre lettre du 25 écoulé** your letter of the 25th of last month; **payable fin écoulé** due at the end of last month (**b**) *(passé)* **l'exer-**

cice écoulé the last financial year

écoulement *nm (de marchandises, d'un surplus, des stocks)* sale; **d'écoulement facile/difficile** fast-/slow-moving

écouler 1 *vt (marchandises, surplus, stocks)* to sell (off); **écouler qch à bas prix** to sell sth off cheaply; **écouler qch à perte** to sell sth at a loss; **facile/difficile à écouler** easy/difficult to sell; **écouler entièrement son stock** to clear one's stock

2 **s'écouler** *vpr* (**a**) *(marchandises, surplus, stocks)* to sell; **notre stock s'écoule rapidement** our stock is selling fast (**b**) *(délai)* to expire; **le délai de grâce que nous vous avions consenti s'est écoulé** the extension we agreed to has expired

écran *nm* (**a**) *Ordinat* screen; **à l'écran** on screen; **travailler sur écran** to work on screen ❑ **écran d'accueil** start-up screen; **écran d'aide** help screen; **écran antireflet** antiglare screen; **écran couleur** colour screen *or* display; **écran à cristaux liquides** liquid crystal screen; **écran divisé** split screen; **écran à haute définition, écran haute résolution** high-resolution screen; **écran LCD** LCD screen; **écran à matrice active** active matrix screen; **écran plat** flat screen; **écran pleine page** full page display; **écran tactile** touch *or* touch-sensitive screen; **écran de visualisation** visual display unit, VDU (**b**) **écran publicitaire, écran de publicité, écran de pub** commercial break

écraser *vt* (**a**) *(accabler)* **écraser qn d'impôts** to overburden sb with taxes; **écraser le marché** to glut *or* flood the market; **écraser les prix** to slash prices (**b**) *Ordinat (fichier)* to zap, to overwrite

écrémage *nm Mktg (du marché)* skimming

écrémer *vt Mktg (marché)* to skim

écrire *vt* to write; *(noter)* to write down; **écrire à qn** to write to sb; **écrire une lettre à la machine** to type a letter; *Ordinat* **écrire qch sur un disque** to write sth to disk; *Compta* **écrire la comptabilité** to write up the books

écrit, -e 1 *adj (convention, déclaration)* written; **écrit à la main** handwritten; **écrit à la machine** typewritten, typed

2 *nm* (**a**) **par écrit** in writing; **consigner** *ou* **coucher qch par écrit** to put sth down in writing; **confirmez-le nous par écrit** give us written confirmation, confirm it to us in writing (**b**) *(document)* (written) document; **signer un écrit** to sign a document

écriture *nf* (**a**) *Compta (opération)* entry, item; **passer une écriture** to make an entry ❑ **écriture d'achats** purchase entry; **écriture d'ajustement** corrected entry; **écriture de clôture** closing entry; **écriture complémentaire** supplementary entry; **écriture comptable** accounting entry, journal entry; *écriture con-forme* corresponding entry; *écriture d'inventaire* closing entry; *écriture inverse* reverse entry; *écriture d'ouverture* opening entry; *écriture rectificative* corrected entry; *écriture regroupement* consolidated entry; *écriture de régularisation* adjusting entry; *écriture de virement* transfer entry

(**b**) *Compta* **écritures** *(comptes)* accounts; **tenir les écritures** to keep the accounts *or* the books; **arrêter les écritures** to close the accounts; **passer les écritures** to post (up) the books ▫ *écritures en partie double* double-entry bookkeeping; *écritures en partie simple* single-entry bookkeeping

(**c**) *écriture abrégée* speedwriting

ÉCU, écu *nm Anciennement Fin (abrév* **European currency unit**) ECU, ecu

EDI *nm Ordinat (abrév* **échange de données informatisé**) EDE

éditer *vt Ordinat* to edit; **non édité** unedited

éditeur, -trice 1 *nm,f (qui publie)* (book) publisher

2 *nm Ordinat (de programme)* editor ▫ *éditeur d'icônes* icon editor; *éditeur de liens* linker, link editor; *éditeur de logiciel* software company; *éditeur de texte* text editor

édition *nf* (**a**) *(activité)* (book) publishing (**b**) *(exemplaire)* edition ▫ *édition pirate* pirate edition; *édition à tirage limité* limited edition (**c**) *Ordinat (de données)* editing; *(de menu)* edit

éditique *nf Ordinat* electronic publishing

EED *nm Ordinat (abrév* **échange électronique de données**) EDI

effaçable *adj Ordinat (mémoire)* erasable

effacement *nm Ordinat* deletion

effacer 1 *vt Ordinat (données)* to erase, to delete; *(écran)* to clear

2 *vi* to delete

effectif, -ive 1 *adj* (**a**) *Fin (coût, monnaie, taux)* effective; *(valeur, revenu)* real; *(circulation)* active; *(rendement)* actual

(**b**) *(règlement, mesures)* in effect; **cette loi sera effective au 1ᵉʳ janvier** this law will come into effect on 1 January

2 *nm* (**a**) *(employés)* staff; **l'usine emploie un effectif de 49 personnes** the factory employs 49 people *or* has a staff of 49; **à effectif réduit** short-staffed

(**b**) *Fin* **effectif budgétaire** budgetary strength, *Am* authorized strength

(**c**) *effectif de série économique* economic batch quantity

effectuer 1 *vt (paiement, calculs, réservation)* to make; *(dépenses)* to incur; *(étude)* to carry out; *(commande)* to place

2 s'effectuer *vpr (paiement, voyage)* to be made

effet *nm* (**a**) *(résultat, conséquence)* effect; **les effets de la crise économique** the effects of the economic crisis; **facture avec effet rétroactif** backdated bill; **nul et sans effet** null and void; **prendre effet** to take effect ▫ *Fin* **effet balançoire** see-saw effect; *effet boomerang* boomerang effect; **avoir un effet boomerang** to boomerang; *effet boule de neige* snowball effect; **les analystes craignent l'effet boule de neige de la crise asiatique** the analysts are afraid of the snowball effect of the Asian crisis; *Fin* **effet de dilution** dilutive effect; *Fin* **effet de levier** leverage, *Br* gearing; *Fin* **effet de levier financier** financial leverage, *Br* financial gearing; *Ordinat* **effet de transition** transition

(**b**) *Fin* bill ▫ *effet accepté* accepted bill; *effet bancable* bankable bill, eligible paper; *effet bancaire* bill, draft; *effet de cavalerie* kite; *effet de commerce, effet commercial* bill of exchange, commercial paper; *effet de complaisance* accommodation bill; *effet contre acceptation* acceptance bill; *effet à courte échéance* short, short-dated bill; *effet à date fixe* fixed-term bill; *effet en devise(s)* bill in foreign currency; *effet domicilié* domiciled bill; *effet à l'encaissement* bill for collection; *effets à encaisser* accounts receivable; *effet endossé* endorsed bill; *effet escomptable* eligible bill; *effet escompté* discounted bill; *effet sur l'extérieur* foreign bill; *effet libre* clean bill; *effet à longue échéance* long, long-dated bill; *effets nominatifs* registered stock; *effet à ordre* promissory note; *effet payable à vue* sight bill; *effets à payer* bills payable; *effet au porteur* bearer bill, bill made out to bearer; *effets publics* government stock *or* securities; *effets à recevoir* bills receivable; *effet en souffrance* overdue bill; *effet à taux flottant* floating rate note, FRN; *effet à terme* period *or* term bill; *effet à usance* usance bill; *effet à vue* sight bill *or* draft

(**c**) *Assur* commencement

(**d**) *Jur* **effets mobiliers** personal effects, movable effects; *effets personnels* personal effects

efficace *adj (méthode)* effective; *(personne)* efficient

efficacement *adv (avec succès)* effectively; *(de façon productive)* efficiently

efficacité *nf (d'une méthode)* effectiveness; *(d'une personne)* efficiency ▫ *efficacité du coût* cost effectiveness; *efficacité économique* economic efficiency; *efficacité opérationnelle* operational efficiency; *efficacité parfaite* absolute efficiency; *efficacité promotionnelle* promotional effectiveness; *efficacité publicitaire* advertising effectiveness; *efficacité relative* relative efficiency; *efficacité de vente* sales performance

efficience *nf (d'une entreprise)* efficiency ▫ *efficience absolue* absolute efficiency

effleurement *nm Ordinat* **à effleurement** *(clavier)* touch-sensitive

effondrement *nm (des prix, des marchés, des cours, des bénéfices)* slump (**de** in); *(d'une monnaie)* collapse

> **"**
> Fortement ébranlées par l'**effondrement** des marchés en septembre, les valeurs des services aux entreprises profitent de perspectives 2002 plus favorables pour regagner du terrain perdu.
> **"**

effondrer s'effondrer *vpr (prix, marchés, cours, bénéfices)* to slump; *(monnaie)* to collapse; **le marché s'est effondré** the bottom has fallen out of the market

effort *nm* effort □ *Mktg* **effort de commercialisation** marketing effort; **effort financier** financial outlay; **effort de marketing, effort de mercatique** marketing effort; **effort de promotion** promotional campaign; **effort publicitaire** advertising campaign

effritement *nm Bourse (des cours)* crumbling

effriter s'effriter *vpr Bourse (cours)* to crumble

EGA *nm Ordinat (abrév* **enhanced graphics adapter)** EGA

égalité *nf* equality; **égalité devant l'emploi** equal opportunities for employment □ **égalité des chances** equal opportunities; **égalité des salaires** equal pay

élaboration *nf (d'un plan, d'une idée, d'une stratégie)* working out, development; *(d'une constitution, d'une loi, d'un budget)* drawing up □ **élaboration de concept** concept development; *Mktg* **élaboration de produit** product development

élaborer *vt (plan, idée, stratégie)* to work out, to develop; *(constitution, loi, budget)* to draw up

élargir 1 *vt (gamme de produits, activités, clientèle)* to expand; *(marché)* to expand, to broaden
　2 s'élargir *vpr (entreprise, marché, organisation)* to expand

élargissement *nm (d'une gamme de produits, d'activités, de clientèle)* expansion; *(du marché)* expansion, broadening

élasticité *nf (de l'offre, de la demande, du marché, des prix)* elasticity; **quelle est l'élasticité de la demande par rapport au prix du produit?** how elastic is the demand in relation to the price of the product?

élastique *adj (offre, demande, marché, prix)* elastic

électrocopie *nf* xerography

électronique 1 *adj (réservation, traitement de données, point de vente, argent)* electronic
　2 *nf* electronics

élément *nm* (**a**) *Ordinat (d'un menu)* item □ **élément ET** AND element (**b**) *(donnée)* factor; **éléments** data, information □ **élément du prix de revient** cost factor (**c**) *Compta (d'un compte)* item

élevé, -e *adj (prix, taux)* high; **les dépenses sont élevées** expenditure is running high

élever 1 *vt (prix, taux)* to raise, to put up; **élever qn à un rang supérieur** to promote sb
　2 s'élever *vpr* **s'élever à** to come to, to amount to; **la facture s'élève à mille euros** the bill comes to *or* amounts to a thousand euros

éluder *vt (loi, règlement)* to elude; **éluder le paiement de l'impôt** to evade payment of tax

e-mail *nm Ordinat* e-mail

émargement *nm (d'un document, d'un compte)* initialling *(in the margin)*

émarger 1 *vt (document, compte)* to initial *(in the margin)*; *(signer)* to sign; *(courrier)* to sign for
　2 *vi* to draw one's salary; **il émarge aux fonds secrets** he's paid out of the secret funds

emballage *nm* (**a**) *(contenant)* packaging; **l'emballage est consigné** there is a deposit on the packaging; **emballage compris** packaging included; **emballage gratuit** packaging free of charge □ **emballage factice** dummy pack; **emballage géant** giant pack; **emballage d'origine** original packaging; **emballage perdu** non-returnable packaging; **emballage de présentation** *ou* **présentoir** display pack; **emballage réutilisable** recyclable packaging; **emballage transparent** blister pack; **emballage sous vide** vacuum pack (**b**) *(action)* packing, packaging

emballage-bulle *nm* blister pack

emballement *nm (des cours, du marché)* boom (**de** in); **on a assisté à l'emballement de la demande pour ce genre de produits** we have witnessed the boom in demand for this type of product

> **"**
> L'impact est réel, et les entrepreneurs américains songent à réinvestir, y compris dans le secteur high-tech, que l'on disait sinistré voilà encore quelques semaines. Ensuite, il y a l'**emballement** des indicateurs censés anticiper la conjoncture. La batterie des indices – Conference Board, ISM (ex-NAPM), NAHB et Michigan – s'affole, et la quasi-totalité est repassée dans le vert.
> **"**

emballer 1 *vt (dans une boîte)* to pack; *(dans du papier)* to wrap up; **emballé sous vide** vacuum-packed
　2 s'emballer *vpr (cours, marché)* to spiral out of control

embarcadère *nm* loading dock

embargo *nm* embargo; **lever l'embargo** to lift

the embargo; **mettre l'embargo sur qch** to put an embargo on sth ◻ *embargo commercial* trade embargo; *embargo économique* economic embargo

embarquement *nm* (**a**) *(de marchandises)* loading (**b**) *(de personnes)* boarding

embarquer 1 *vt* (**a**) *(marchandises)* to load (**b**) *(personnes)* to board
  2 s'embarquer *vpr (aller à bord)* to go on board, to board

embarras *nm* difficulty, trouble; **l'entreprise connaît des embarras financiers** the company is in financial difficulty

embauchage, embauche *nf* taking on, hiring

embaucher *vt* to take on, to hire

emblème de marque *nm Mktg* brand mark

émergent, -e *adj (marché)* emerging

émetteur, -trice *Fin* **1** *adj (banque, organisme)* issuing
  2 *nm,f (de billets, d'actions, d'une carte)* issuer; *(d'un chèque)* drawer

émettre *vt Fin (chèque, actions, billets de banque, timbres)* to issue; *(emprunt)* to float; *(lettre de crédit)* to open

émission *nf Fin (d'un chèque, d'actions, de billets de banque, de timbres)* issue; *(d'un emprunt)* flotation; *(d'une lettre de crédit)* opening ◻ *Bourse* **émission d'actions** share issue; *Bourse* **émission d'actions gratuites** scrip issue, bonus issue; *Bourse* **émission boursière** share issue; *Bourse* **émission de conversion** conversion issue; *Banque* **émission fiduciaire** fiduciary or note issue; *Bourse* **émission obligataire, émission d'obligations** bond issue, debenture issue; *Bourse* **émission par série** block issue; *Bourse* **émission des valeurs du Trésor** tap issue

emmagasinage *nm* (**a**) *(de marchandises)* storage (**b**) *(frais)* storage charges

emmagasiner *vt (marchandises)* to store

émoluments *nmpl (d'un employé)* salary, pay; **percevoir des émoluments** to receive payment

émoticon *nm Ordinat* emoticon, smiley

empaquetage *nm (action)* packing, packaging; *(emballage)* packaging; **poids net à l'empaquetage 250g** net weight when packed, 250g ◻ *empaquetage automatique* automatic packaging

empaqueter *vt* to pack, to package

emplacement *nm* (**a**) *(site)* site, location; **ce serait l'emplacement idéal pour notre nouvelle usine** that would be the ideal site or location for our new factory ◻ *emplacement d'affichage* billboard site, *Br* hoarding site; *emplacement isolé* solus position, solus site; *emplacement publicitaire* advertising space

(**b**) *Ordinat* slot ◻ *emplacement pour carte* card slot; *emplacement pour carte d'extension* expansion slot; *emplacement d'évolutivité* upgrade slot; *emplacement (pour) périphériques* extension slot

> De nouvelles boutiques ouvrent à Beverly Hills (Los Angeles), à SoHo (New York), à Tokyo et à Barcelone. En France, le magasin parisien de la rue de Rennes a été re-looké, et le groupe est à la recherche d'un troisième **emplacement**, mieux situé.

emploi *nm* (**a**) *(situation)* job; *(embauche)* employment, work; **être sans emploi** to be out of work or unemployed; **chercher un emploi, être à la recherche d'un emploi** to be looking for work or a job; **solliciter un emploi** to apply for a job; **créer de nouveaux emplois** to create new jobs ◻ *emploi de bureau* desk job, office job; *emplois jeunes* = state-subsidized jobs created specifically for young people as part of the French government's drive to combat unemployment; *emploi à mi-temps* part-time job; *emploi permanent* permanent job; *emploi à plein temps* full-time job; *emplois de proximité* = jobs created at local community level, typically involving childminding, caring for the elderly etc; *emploi à temps partiel* part-time job (**b**) *(utilisation)* use; *(des capitaux)* deployment ◻ *emploi du temps* timetable, schedule

employé, -e *nm,f* employee ◻ *employé d'administration* government employee; *employé de banque* bank clerk; *employé de bureau* office worker; *employé aux écritures* accounts clerk; *employé de l'expédition* shipping clerk; *employé de magasin Br* sales assistant, *Am* clerk; *employé occasionnel* casual worker; *employé de la Régie Br* ≃ Customs and Excise officer, *Am* ≃ Customs Service officer

employer *vt* (**a**) *(faire travailler) (personne)* to employ; **employer qn comme secrétaire** to employ sb as a secretary; **employé à plein temps/à temps partiel** employed full-time/part-time (**b**) *(utiliser)* to use; **employer les grands moyens** to take drastic measures (**c**) *Compta* to enter; **employer qch en recette** to enter sth in the receipts

employeur, -euse *nm,f* employer

emporter *vt (marché)* to close; *(contrat)* to land

emprunt *nm Banque, Fin* (**a**) *(somme)* loan; **faire un emprunt** *(auprès d'une banque)* to take out a loan; **emprunt à huit pour cent** loan at eight percent; **procéder à un nouvel emprunt** to make a new loan issue; **amortir un emprunt** to redeem a loan; **contracter un emprunt** to raise a loan; **couvrir un emprunt** to cover a loan; **émettre un emprunt** to float a loan; **placer un emprunt** to place a loan; **rembourser un emprunt** to repay a loan; **souscrire un emprunt** to subscribe a loan ◻ *emprunt consolidé, emprunt de consolidation* consolidated loan, funding loan; *emprunt de conversion* conversion loan; *emprunt à court terme* short-term loan; *emprunt à découvert* unsecured loan; *emprunt en devises* currency loan; *emprunt d'État* government loan; *Bourse emprunt à fenêtre* put bond; *emprunt forcé* forced loan; *emprunt sur gage* loan against security; *emprunt garanti* secured loan; *emprunt indexé* indexed loan; *emprunt à long terme* long-term loan; *emprunt à lots* lottery loan; *emprunt obligataire* bond issue, loan stock; *(titre)* debenture bond; *emprunt obligataire convertible* convertible loan stock; *emprunt or* gold loan; *emprunt perpétuel* perpetual loan; *emprunt personnel* personal loan; *emprunt public* government loan, public loan; *emprunt remboursable sur demande* call loan, loan repayable on demand; *emprunt de remboursement* refunding loan; *emprunt à risques* non-accruing loan; *emprunt à terme (fixe)* term loan, time loan; *emprunt sur titres* loan on securities *or* stock **(b)** *(action)* borrowing

emprunter *vt* to borrow; **emprunter qch à qn** to borrow sth from sb; **la société a dû emprunter pour s'acquitter de ses dettes** the company had to borrow to pay off its debts; **emprunter sur hypothèque** to borrow on mortgage; **emprunter sur titres** to borrow on securities; **emprunter à long/à court terme** to borrow long/short; **emprunter à intérêt** to borrow at interest

emprunteur, -euse 1 *adj* borrowing
  2 *nm,f* borrower

émulateur de terminal *nm Ordinat* terminal emulator

émulation *nf Ordinat* emulation ◻ *émulation de terminal* terminal emulation

émuler *vt Ordinat* to emulate

ENA *nf* (*abrév* **École nationale d'administration**) = prestigious university-level college preparing students for senior posts in the civil service and in public management

encadrement *nm* **(a)** *Admin (fonction)* management; *(cadres)* executives **(b)** *Écon* control ◻ *encadrement du crédit* credit control *or* restrictions; *encadrement des loyers* rent control; *encadrement des prix* price control

encadrer *vt* **(a)** *Admin (personnel, équipe)* to manage; **nous sommes bien encadrés** we have a good management team **(b)** *Écon (prix, loyers, crédit)* to control

encaissable *adj Fin (chèque)* cashable; *(argent, traite)* collectable, receivable; **ce chèque est**

encaissable à la banque this cheque can be cashed at the bank

encaisse *nf* cash (in hand), cash balance; *(d'un magasin)* money in the till ◻ *encaisse disponible* cash in hand; *encaisse métallique* gold and silver reserves, bullion; *encaisse or* gold bullion; *encaisse or et argent* gold and silver reserves, bullion

encaissement *nm Fin (d'un chèque)* cashing; *(d'argent, d'une traite)* collection, receipt ◻ *encaissements et décaissements* cash inflows and outflows

encaisser *vt* **(a)** *Fin (chèque)* to cash; *(argent, traite)* to collect, to receive **(b)** *(marchandises)* to pack (in boxes)

encaisseur, -euse *Fin* **1** *adj (banque, établissement)* collecting
  2 *nm (d'un chèque)* payee; *(de l'argent, d'une traite)* collector, receiver

encart *nm* insert ◻ *encart publicitaire* advertising insert

enchaînement *nm Ordinat* concatenation

enchère *nf* bid; **les enchères** bidding; **mettre** *ou* **porter une enchère** to make a bid; **mettre qch aux enchères** to put sth up for auction; **couvrir une enchère** to make a higher bid; **faire monter les enchères** to up *or* raise the bidding; **l'enchère a monté jusqu'à deux cents euros** the bidding rose to two hundred euros ◻ *enchères publiques* public auction; *enchères au rabais* Dutch auction

enchérir *vi* to make a higher bid; **enchérir de mille euros** to bid another thousand euros; **enchérir sur qn** to outbid sb

enchérisseur, -euse *nm,f* bidder; **vendre au (plus offrant et) dernier enchérisseur** to sell to the highest bidder

encodage *nm Ordinat* encoding

encoder *vt Ordinat* to encode

encodeur *nm Ordinat* encoder

encombré, -e *adj (marché)* glutted, flooded

encombrement *nm* **(a)** *Ordinat* **faible encombrement sur le disque dur** low use of hard disk space **(b)** *(de marchandises)* glut, surplus

encombrer *vt (marché)* to glut, to flood; **les logiciels encombrent le marché** there is a glut *or* surplus of software packages on the market

encouragements *nmpl* incentives ◻ *encouragements à l'exportation* export incentives; *encouragements à la production* production incentives

encourir *vt (frais)* to incur

encours, en-cours *nm* **(a)** *Banque* loans outstanding; **l'encours de la dette** the outstanding debt ◻ *encours de crédit* outstanding credits; *encours débiteur autorisé* authorized overdraft facility (**b**) *Compta* **encours de production de biens** work-in-progress (**c**) **encours de fabrication** material undergoing processing; **encours de route** stock awaiting transfer *(to another department)*

> "Zebank est un succès. En moins d'un an, nous avons déjà attiré 70 000 clients et avons ainsi dépassé nos objectifs de départ de 25%", affirme un de ses représentants. L'encours moyen des comptes serait même de 3000 euros: un niveau élevé.

endetté, -e *adj (pays, personne, entreprise)* in debt

endettement *nm* (**a**) *(action)* running *or* getting into debt; *(état)* debt ❏ **endettement des consommateurs** consumer debt; **endettement extérieur** foreign debt; **endettement intérieur** internal debt (**b**) *Compta* indebtedness, gearing

> ... en Europe, où les ménages du Nord (en Allemagne, aux Pays-Bas, au Danemark notamment) ont accumulé un **endettement** sans aucun précédent, adossé à des actifs immobiliers dangereusement survalorisés.

endetter 1 *vt* **endetter qn** to get sb into debt; **l'acquisition de nouvelles machines a endetté la société** the purchase of new machinery has got the company into debt
2 s'endetter *vpr* to get into debt

endiguement *nm Bourse, Fin* hedging

endiguer *vt (montée des prix, inflation, chômage)* to contain

endommager *vt* (**a**) *(abîmer)* to damage (**b**) *Ordinat* to corrupt

endos *nm (sur effet, chèque)* endorsement ❏ **endos en blanc** blank endorsement

endossataire *nmf* endorsee

endossement *nm (sur effet, chèque)* endorsement ❏ **endossement en blanc** blank endorsement

endosser *vt (effet, chèque)* to endorse

endosseur, -euse *nm,f (d'effet, de chèque)* endorser

énergétique *adj (ressources, besoins)* energy

engagement *nm* (**a**) *(promesse)* undertaking, commitment; **contracter** *ou* **prendre un engagement** to enter into an undertaking *or* a commitment; **prendre l'engagement de faire qch** to undertake to do sth; **rompre ses engagements** to fail to honour one's commit-

ments; **sans engagement (de votre part)** with no obligation (on your part) ❏ **engagement écrit** written undertaking
(**b**) *Fin (de capital, d'investissements)* locking up, tying up; *(de dépenses, de frais)* incurring ❏ **engagement bancaire** (bank) commitment; **engagement de dépenses** commitment of funds; **engagement hors bilan** contingent liabilities
(**c**) *(mise en gage) (au mont-de-piété)* pawning; *(auprès de créanciers)* pledging; *(d'une propriété)* mortgaging
(**d**) *(embauche)* appointment
(**e**) *(de négociations)* beginning, start; *Jur (de poursuites)* institution

engager 1 *vt* (**a**) *Fin (capital, investissements)* to lock up, to tie up; *(dépenses, frais)* to incur
(**b**) *(mettre en gage) (au mont-de-piété)* to pawn; *(auprès de créanciers)* to pledge; *(propriété)* to mortgage
(**c**) *(embaucher)* to hire, to take on
(**d**) *(négociations)* to begin, to start; *Jur* **engager des poursuites (contre)** to take legal action (against), to institute proceedings (against)
(**e**) *(lier)* to bind, to commit; **votre signature vous engage à respecter les termes du contrat** signature of the contract obliges you to respect its terms; **cela n'engage à rien** it doesn't commit you to anything
2 s'engager *vpr* (**a**) *(promettre)* **s'engager à faire qch** to undertake to do sth; **s'engager par contrat à faire qch** to contract to do sth; **s'engager vis-à-vis de qn** to contract with sb
(**b**) *(se lancer)* **s'engager dans une affaire** to get involved in a deal

engorgement *nm (du marché)* flooding, glutting

engorger *vt (marché)* to flood, to glut

enlèvement *nm (de marchandises)* collection; **enlèvement et livraison** collection and delivery

enlever 1 *vt* (**a**) *(marchandises, actions)* to snap up (**b**) *(contrat, affaire)* to get, to land
2 s'enlever *vpr (marchandises)* to sell quickly, to get snapped up

énoncé *nm (d'un contrat, d'une loi)* text, wording

enquête *nf* (**a**) *Mktg* survey ❏ **enquête d'attitude** attitude survey; **enquête auprès des consommateurs** consumer survey; **enquête fiscale** tax survey; **enquête sur les lieux** field study; **enquête de marché** market survey; **enquête omnibus** omnibus survey; **enquête d'opinion** opinion poll; **enquête pilote** pilot survey; **enquête postale** mail survey, *Br* postal survey; **enquête sur les prix** price survey; **enquête par questionnaire** questionnaire survey; **enquête sociologique** sociological survey; **enquête de solvabilité** credit inquiry, status inquiry; **enquête par sondage** opinion poll; **enquête téléphonique** telephone interview *or* survey; **enquête sur le terrain** field study (**b**) *Jur* inquiry, investigation ◻ **enquête administrative** public inquiry; **enquête judiciaire** judicial inquiry

enquêté, -e *nm,f Mktg* interviewee

enquêter *vi Mktg (faire un sondage)* to conduct a survey (**sur** into)

enquêteur, -trice *nm,f Mktg* pollster

enrayer *vt (montée des prix, inflation, chômage)* to curb

enregistrement *nm* (**a**) *(d'une société)* registration, incorporation; **faire l'enregistrement d'une société** to register a company (**b**) *(d'une commande)* booking, entering (up) ◻ *Compta* **enregistrement comptable** accounting entry (**c**) *Admin* **l'Enregistrement** the Registration department (**d**) *Ordinat (de données)* logging, recording; *(article de base de données)* record (**e**) *(dans un aéroport)* check-in; **se présenter à l'enregistrement** to check in

enregistrer *vt* (**a**) *(commande)* to book, to enter (up); *(bénéfice)* to show; **les meilleures ventes enregistrées depuis des mois** the best recorded sales for months
 (**b**) *(afficher)* to show; **enregistrer le courrier** to log the mail
 (**c**) *Ordinat (données, programme)* to store; *(sauvegarder) (changements, ajouts)* to save; *(CD-ROM)* to write; **voulez-vous enregistrer les modifications?** do you want to save changes?; **enregistrer sous...** save as ...
 (**d**) *(dans un aéroport)* **(faire) enregistrer ses bagages** to check in one's baggage

enseigne *nf (d'un produit)* brand name; *(d'un magasin, d'une société)* name

> " ─────────────────
>
> L'euro, avait-on dit, allait révolutionner les produits des grandes **enseignes** alimentaires. Les paquets de gâteaux, les yaourts? Ils seraient plus grands, ou plus petits, pour établir de nouveaux prix faciles à retenir.
>
> ───────────────── "

enseignement assisté par ordinateur *nm* computer-aided *or* computer assisted-learning

ensemble *nm* (**a**) *(totalité)* **ces mesures concernent l'ensemble du personnel** these measures concern the entire staff (**b**) *(groupe)* set ◻ *Mktg* **ensemble de besoins** need set; *Mktg* **ensemble de considérations** consideration set, product choice set; *Mktg* **ensemble évoqué** evoked set (**c**) *Ordinat (de caractères, d'informations)* set ◻ **ensemble de données** data set; **ensemble logiciel** software suite

entamer *vt* (**a**) *(travail, recherche, négociations)*

to begin, to start; *(démarches)* to initiate; **entamer une vente** to open a sale; *Jur* **entamer des poursuites (contre)** to take legal action (against), to institute proceedings (against) (**b**) *(capital, profits)* to eat into

entente *nf (accord)* agreement, understanding (**entre** between) ◻ **entente industrielle** combine, cartel

en-tête *nm (d'une lettre, d'un document)* heading; *(papier)* letterhead; *Ordinat* header ◻ **en-tête de facture** billhead

entièrement *adv* entirely, completely; **entièrement versé** *(capital)* fully paid-up

entité *nf Compta* item

entraînement du papier *nm (d'une imprimante)* paper advance

entrée *nf* (**a**) *(action)* entry, entrance; **l'entrée de l'Autriche dans l'Union européenne** Austria's entry into the European Union ◻ **entrée en fonction** assumption of one's duties; **l'entrée en fonction du nouveau directeur est prévue pour le 1ᵉʳ mai** the new director is scheduled to take up his post on 1 May; **entrée en jouissance** taking possession; **entrée en séance** opening of a meeting; **entrée en vigueur** coming into force
 (**b**) *(de marchandises)* import ◻ **entrée de capitaux** capital inflow; **entrée en douane** inward customs clearance, clearance inward; **entrée en franchise** free import
 (**c**) *Ordinat (processus)* input, entry; *(information)* entry; *(touche)* enter (key) ◻ **entrée de données** data entry
 (**d**) *(voie d'accès)* way in, entrance
 (**e**) *Compta (dans un livre de comptes)* entry

entrée/sortie *nf Ordinat* input/output

entreposage *nm* warehousing, storing; *Douanes* bonding

entreposer *vt* to warehouse, to store; *Douanes* to bond, to put in bond

entreposeur *nm* (**a**) *(qui tient un entrepôt)* warehouseman; *Douanes* officer in charge of a bonded store (**b**) *(commerçant)* = wholesaler selling goods under a government monopoly

entrepositaire *nmf* warehousekeeper

entrepôt *nm* (**a**) *(bâtiment)* warehouse; *Douanes* bonded warehouse; *Douanes* **mettre des marchandises en entrepôt** to bond goods, to put goods in bond; **à prendre à l'entrepôt** *ou* **en entrepôt** at warehouse ◻ **entrepôt de** *ou* **en douane** bonded warehouse; **entrepôt fictif** unbonded warehouse; **entrepôt frigorifique** cold store; **entrepôt maritime** wharf; **entrepôt réel** bonded warehouse (**b**) *(port)* entrepôt; **Londres est un grand centre d'entrepôt** London has a large entrepôt trade

entreprendre *vt* to undertake; **entreprendre**

de faire qch to undertake to do sth

entrepreneur, -euse *nm,f* (**a**) *(de travaux)* contractor ❑ *entrepreneur (en bâtiments)* building contractor; *entrepreneur de roulage, entrepreneur de transport* haulage contractor; *entrepreneur de travaux publics* public works contractor (**b**) *(chef d'entreprise)* entrepreneur

entreprise *nf* (**a**) *(firme)* company, business; **les grandes entreprises** big business ❑ *entreprise artisanale* small-scale enterprise; *entreprise commerciale* business enterprise, business concern; *entreprise commune* joint venture; *Mktg entreprise défendable* tenable firm; *Mktg entreprise dominante* dominant firm; *entreprise exportatrice* export company; *entreprise de factage* delivery service; *entreprise familiale* family business; *entreprise individuelle* sole trader; *entreprise industrielle* manufacturing company; *Mktg entreprise innovatrice* innovator, market pioneer company; *entreprise d'investissement* investment company; *entreprise marginale* firm with only a marginal profit; *entreprise de messageries* parcel delivery company; *entreprise multinationale* multinational company *or* enterprise; *entreprise nationale* national business; *entreprise en participation* joint venture *or* enterprise; *entreprise phare* leading company; *entreprise prestataire de services* service company; *entreprise privée* private company *or* enterprise; *entreprise publique* state-owned company *or* enterprise, public corporation *or* enterprise; *entreprise de récupération* salvage company; *entreprise de roulage* road haulage company; *entreprise de service public* public utility company; *entreprise de transports (routiers)* haulage *or* carrying company; *entreprise de travail intérimaire* temp agency; *entreprise de travaux publics* civil engineering company; *entreprise unipersonnelle* one-man business, sole trader; *entreprise unipersonnelle à responsabilité limitée* sole trader with limited liability; *entreprise de vente par correspondance* mail-order company (**b**) *(action, initiative)* enterprise, undertaking, venture (**c**) *Jur (louage)* contracting; **mettre qch à l'entreprise** to put sth out to contract; **prendre qch à l'entreprise** to contract for sth

entrer 1 *vt* (**a**) *(introduire)* **entrer des marchandises en contrebande** *ou* **en fraude** to smuggle in goods
(**b**) *Ordinat (données)* to enter, to input; *(au clavier)* to key in
2 *vi* (**a**) *(marchandises)* to enter, to be imported; **entrer dans un marché** to enter a market; **les marchandises qui entrent en France sont soumises à des droits de douane** goods entering France are subject to customs duty; **ces marchandises sont entrées en fraude sur le**

territoire these goods were smuggled into the country
(**b**) *(commencer)* **entrer en association avec qn** to form a partnership with sb; **entrer en concurrence avec qn** to go into competition with sb; **entrer en fonction** to take up one's duties; **entrer en liquidation** to go into liquidation; **entrer en relation avec qn** to get in contact with sb; **entrer dans la vie active** to start one's working life; **entrer en vigueur** to come into force, to take effect
(**c**) *Ordinat (utilisateur)* to log in *or* on

entretenir *vt* (**a**) *Compta (comptes)* to keep in order (**b**) *(garder en bon état)* to maintain; **entretenir de bonnes relations avec qn** to remain on friendly *or* good terms with sb

entretien *nm* (**a**) *(conversation)* conversation, talk; *(entre employeur et candidat)* interview; **avoir des entretiens avec le patronat** to hold talks *or* discussions with the employers; **convoquer qn à un entretien** to call sb for interview ❑ *entretien d'embauche* job interview
(**b**) *Mktg* interview ❑ *entretien assisté par ordinateur* computer-assisted interview; *entretien directif* guided interview; *entretien de groupe* group interview; *entretien libre* unstructured interview; *entretien non directif* unguided interview; *entretien non structuré* unstructured interview; *entretien organisé* arranged interview; *entretien en profondeur* depth interview; *entretien spontané* intercept interview; *entretien structuré* structured interview; *entretien par téléphone, entretien téléphonique* telephone interview
(**c**) *(de matériel)* maintenance; **entretien et réparations** servicing and repairs ❑ *entretien systématique* planned maintenance

entrevue *nf* interview ❑ *entrevue de départ* exit interview

envahir *vt (marché)* to flood

enveloppe *nf* (**a**) *(pour le courrier)* envelope; **mettre une lettre sous enveloppe** to put a letter in an envelope ❑ *enveloppe affranchie* prepaid envelope; *enveloppe à fenêtre* window envelope; *enveloppe timbrée* stamped addressed envelope
(**b**) *Fin (somme)* sum; *(budget)* budget; **nous disposons d'une enveloppe de 70 000 euros pour la commercialisation du produit** we have a budget of 70,000 euros to market the product ❑ *enveloppe budgétaire* budget (allocation); *enveloppe fiscale* = tax-sheltered savings scheme; *enveloppe salariale* wages bill

❝

Première précaution à prendre: choisir l'**enveloppe fiscale** la plus adaptée à vos besoins (compte-titres ordinaire, plan d'épargne en actions ou assurance-vie).

❞

envelopper *vt* to wrap (up)

enveloppe-réponse *nf* reply-paid envelope

environnement *nm* (**a**) *(milieu)* environment
❑ **environnement d'achat** purchase environment; **environnement commercial** marketing
environment; **environnement institutionnel**
corporate environment; **environnement du
marché** market environment; **environnement
marketing, environnement mercatique** marketing environment (**b**) *Ordinat* environment

envoi *nm* (**a**) *(action)* sending; **faire un envoi
tous les mois** to send goods every month ❑ **envoi exprès** express delivery, *Br* special delivery;
envoi de fonds remittance (of funds); **faire un
envoi de fonds à qn** to send *or* remit funds to
sb; **envoi en groupage, envoi groupé** grouped
consignment; **envoi par mer** shipment; **envoi
en nombre** mass mailing; **envoi contre paiement** cash with order; **envoi postal** postal delivery; **envoi recommandé** recorded delivery;
envoi contre remboursement *Br* cash on delivery, *Am* collect on delivery; **envoi à titre d'essai** sent on approval
(**b**) *(ce qui est envoyé)* *(colis)* parcel; *(lettre)* letter; *(marchandises)* consignment (**de** of); **j'ai
bien reçu votre envoi du 10 octobre** I acknowledge receipt of your consignment of 10 October
(**c**) *Ordinat* **envoi multiple** crossposting;
faire un envoi multiple de qch to cross-post
sth

envolée *nf (hausse rapide)* rapid rise; **l'envolée
du dollar** the rapid rise in the dollar

> Comme le fait remarquer en effet le secré-
> taire général de l'OPEP, Ali Rodriguez, c'est
> la spéculation qui est responsable de l'**en-
> volée** des cours du brut car la demande,
> toujours faible, ne justifie pas le niveau de
> prix atteint.

envoler s'envoler *vpr (cours, prix)* to soar

envoyer *vt* to send; *(fonds, mandat)* to send, to
remit; **envoyer une lettre à qn** to send sb a letter; **envoyer qch par fax/par télex** to send sth
by fax/by telex; **envoyer qch par chemin de fer**
to send sth by rail; **envoyer qch par la poste** *ou*
par courrier to mail sth, *Br* to post sth; **je lui ai
envoyé un chèque par la poste** I sent him/her
a cheque by post

envoyeur, -euse *nm,f (de lettre, de marchandises)* sender

EONIA *nm (abrév* **Euro Overnight Index Average)** EONIA

épargnant, -e *nm,f* saver, investor

épargne *nf (action)* saving; *(sommes)* savings;
(épargnants) savers, investors ❑ **épargne com-**

plément de retraite pension fund savings;
épargne des entreprises company reserves;
épargne forcée forced saving; **épargne institutionnelle** institutional savings; **épargne in-
vestie** investments; **épargne liquide** on-hand
savings; **épargne mobilière** fixed savings;
épargne négative negative saving; **l'épargne
privée** private investors; **l'épargne productive**
re-invested savings

épargne-logement *nm* **plan d'épargne-
logement** home savings plan, *Br* ≃ building society account, *Am* ≃ savings and loan association account; **prêt d'épargne-logement** home
loan

épargner 1 *vt* to save
   2 *vi* to save (money)

épargne-retraite *nf* pension fund, retirement fund

épine dorsale *nf Ordinat* backbone

éponger *vt Fin (déficit, dette)* to mop up, to absorb; **éponger le pouvoir d'achat excédentaire** to mop up excess purchasing power

> En cause, le refus du conseil d'administra-
> tion de Napster d'accepter une offre du
> géant allemand des médias Bertelsmann,
> déjà actionnaire majoritaire du site : les
> pleins pouvoirs sur Napster contre 18 mil-
> lions d'euros et la promesse d'**éponger** la
> dette de 78 millions. Bertelsmann stoppe
> d'un coup ses versements nécessaires à la
> survie de la start-up, et les deux dirigeants
> claquent la porte.

EPS *nf Ordinat (abrév* **encapsulated Post-
Script®)** EPS

épuisé, -e *adj* (**a**) *(marchandises)* sold out, out
of stock; *(ressources, réserves, stocks)* exhaus-
ted (**b**) *(lettre de crédit)* invalid

épuisement *nm (de marchandises)* selling out;
(de ressources, de réserves, de stocks) exhaus-
tion; **jusqu'à épuisement des stocks** while
stocks last

épuiser 1 *vt (marchandises)* to sell out of; *(ressources, réserves, stocks)* to exhaust
   2 s'épuiser *vpr* to run out

équation *nf* (**a**) *Compta* equation ❑ **équation
de bénéfice** profit equation; **équation de coût**
cost equation (**b**) *Mktg* equation ❑ **équation de
la demande** demand equation; **équation de réponse de marché** sales-response function;
équation de vente sales equation

équilibration *nf (d'un budget)* balancing

équilibre *nm* **en équilibre** *(budget)* balanced
❑ **équilibre budgétaire** balanced budget

équilibrer *vt (budget)* to balance

équipe *nf* team; **travailler par équipes** to work in shifts; **faire équipe avec qn** to team up with sb □ *Mktg* **équipe commando** venture team; **équipe commerciale** marketing team; **équipe de création** creative team; **équipe de direction, équipe dirigeante** management team; **équipe dirigeante** senior management team; **équipe de jour** day shift; **équipe de nuit** night shift; **équipe promotionnelle** promotion team; **équipe de vente** sales team

équipement *nm (machines)* equipment; *(installations)* facilities □ **équipements collectifs** public facilities *or* amenities; **équipement industriel** industrial plant; *Ordinat* **équipement informatique** computer equipment; **équipement lourd** heavy equipment; **équipement portuaire** harbour facilities

équipementier *nm* manufacturer of components

e-recrutement *nm Ordinat* e-recruitment, online recruitment

ergonomie *nf* ergonomics

ergonomique *adj* ergonomic

érosion monétaire *nf* depreciation of money

erreur *nf* (a) *(faute)* error, mistake; **faire** *ou* **commettre une erreur** to make a mistake; **par erreur** by mistake; **induire qn en erreur** to mislead sb; **il y a une erreur dans votre compte** there is a mistake in your account; **sauf erreur ou omission** errors and omissions excepted; **sauf erreur de notre part** unless we are mistaken □ **erreur de calcul** miscalculation; *Mktg* **erreur d'échantillonnage** sampling error; *Compta* **erreur d'écriture** clerical error; **erreur de gestion** management error; **erreur typographique** printing error

(b) *Ordinat* error □ **erreur aléatoire** random error; **erreur de codage** coding error; **erreur disque** disk error; **erreur fatale** fatal error; **er-**

reur de logiciel software error; **erreur de syntaxe** syntax error; **erreur système** system error

E/S *nf Ordinat (abrév* **entrée/sortie)** I/O

escalade *nf (des prix, des taux d'intérêt)* escalation

escomptable *adj Compta* discountable

escompte *nm* (a) *(de commerce)* discount; **accorder** *ou* **faire un escompte sur qch** to allow or give a discount on sth; **à escompte** at a discount; *Can* **50 pour cent d'escompte sur toute la marchandise** 50 percent discount on all goods □ **escompte sur les achats en gros** bulk discount, quantity discount; **escompte de caisse** cash discount; **escompte commercial** trade discount; **escompte au comptant** cash discount; **escompte à forfait** forfaiting; **escompte professionnel** *(au détaillant)* trade discount; **escompte d'usage** trade discount

(b) *Fin* discount; **prendre à l'escompte un effet de commerce** to discount a bill of exchange; **présenter une traite à l'escompte** to have a bill discounted □ **escompte de banque** bank discount; **escompte de créances** invoice discounting; **escompte en dedans** true discount; **escompte en dehors** bank discount; **escompte officiel** *Br* bank discount rate, *Am* prime rate; **escompte de règlement** discount for early payment; **escompte de traites** invoice discounting

(c) *Bourse (de valeurs)* call for delivery before settlement

escompter *vt* (a) *Fin (traite)* to discount (b) *Bourse (valeurs)* to call for delivery of before settlement

escompteur *nm Fin* discount broker

ESCP *nf (abrév* **École supérieure de commerce de Paris)** = prestigious business and management school

escroc *nm* crook, swindler

escroquer *vt* to swindle; **escroquer qch à qn, escroquer qn de qch** to swindle *or* cheat sb out of sth

escroquerie *nf (action)* swindling; *(résultat)* swindle; *(délit)* fraud

escudo *nm Anciennement* escudo

espace *nm* (a) *Ordinat* space □ **espace disque** disk space; **espace insécable** hard space; **espace mémoire** memory space; **espace Web** Web space (b) *Mktg* **espace d'exposition** display area; **espace de PLV** in-store advertising space; **espace publicitaire** advertising space; **espace de vente** sales area (c) **espace économique** economic area; *UE* **Espace économique européen** European Economic Area; *UE* **espace judiciaire européen** common European legal framework; *UE* **espace social européen** common European social legislation

espacement *nm Ordinat (interligne)* spacing ▫ **espacement arrière** backspace; **espacement des caractères** character spacing; **espacement des colonnes** column spacing; **espacement des lignes** line spacing

espacer *vt Ordinat* to interspace

espèces *nfpl (argent)* cash; **payer en espèces** to pay in cash ▫ *Compta* **espèces en caisse** cash in hand

espérance de vie *nf (d'un produit)* life expectancy, shelf life

esperluette *nf* ampersand

espionnage industriel *nm* industrial espionage

esprit *nm* **esprit d'entreprise** entrepreneurship; **esprit d'équipe** team spirit

> **“**
>
> Faut-il plus d'efficacité ou plus d'équité? Le conflit entre l'efficience économique et la redistribution des richesses peut se nouer, par exemple, autour de l'impôt sur le revenu: faut-il moins taxer les hauts revenus pour encourager l'**esprit d'entreprise**, au détriment de la recherche de l'équité?
>
> **”**

essai *nm* (**a**) *(de produit)* trial, test; **à l'essai** on a trial basis; **à titre d'essai** subject to approval; **acheter qch à l'essai** to buy sth on approval; **faire l'essai de qch** to test sth; **essais** *(procédure)* testing ▫ **essai à banc** benchtest; **essais comparatifs** comparative tests; **essai gratuit** free trial; *Ordinat* **essai de performance** benchmark; **essai probatoire** feasibility test; **essais de produit** product testing (**b**) *(d'employé)* trial; **prendre** *ou* **engager qn à l'essai** to take sb on for a trial *or* probationary period

essayer *vt (produit, méthode)* to try (out), to test; **essayer une nouvelle marque** to try out a new brand

ESSEC *nf (abrév* **École supérieure des sciences économiques et commerciales**) = university-level business school

essor *nm (d'un secteur, de l'économie)* rapid growth; **en plein essor** *(secteur, économie)* booming ▫ **essor économique** economic boom

estampillage *nm (d'un document)* stamping; *(de marchandises)* marking

estampille *nf (sur document)* (official) stamp; *(sur marchandises)* mark

estampiller *vt (document)* to stamp; *(marchandises)* to mark

estimateur, -trice *nm,f* appraiser, valuer

estimatif, -ive *adj (valeur, état)* estimated

estimation *nf* (**a**) *(détermination) (d'un prix)* estimation; *(de marchandises, d'une propriété)* valuation; *(de dommages)* assessment ▫ **estimation des besoins** needs assessment; *Compta* **estimation des frais** estimate of costs (**b**) *(valeur, quantité estimée)* estimate

estimer *vt (prix)* to estimate; *(marchandises, propriété)* to value; *(dommages, besoins)* to assess

établir 1 *vt* (**a**) *(entreprise)* to establish, to set up (**b**) *(budget)* to draw up, to establish; *(compte, contrat)* to draw up; *(prix)* to fix; *(objectifs)* to determine
2 s'établir *vpr* to set up in business; **s'établir à son compte** to start one's own business, to become self-employed

établissement *nm* (**a**) *(d'une entreprise)* establishing, setting up
(**b**) *(d'un budget)* drawing up, establishing; *(d'un compte, d'un contrat)* drawing up; *(des prix)* fixing; *(d'objectifs)* determining ▫ *Tél* **établissement d'appel** call connection; **établissement des prix différentiels** differential pricing; **établissement des prix de revient** costing
(**c**) *(institution)* establishment, institution ▫ **établissement bancaire** bank; **établissement de crédit** credit institution; *Compta* **établissement déclarant** company making the return; **établissement dépositaire** financial institution holding securities on trust; **établissement financier** financial institution; *Fin* **établissement payeur** paying bank
(**d**) *(entreprise)* business, firm; **les établissements Martin** Martin & Co ▫ **établissement affilié** affiliated company, *Am* affiliate; **établissement commercial** commercial premises; **établissement industriel** factory, manufacturing company; **établissement principal** main branch *or* office; **établissement d'utilité public** public utility

étalage *nm* (**a**) *(de marchandises)* display; *(dans une vitrine)* window display; **faire l'étalage** to put goods on display; *(dans une vitrine)* to dress the window(s); **mettre qch à l'étalage** to display sth in the window ▫ **étalage publicitaire** display advertising (**b**) *(impôt)* tax paid by street trader

étalager *vt* to display, to put on display

étalagiste *nmf* (**a**) *(marchand)* street trader (**b**) *(dans un magasin)* window dresser

étalement *nm* (**a**) *(de marchandises)* displaying (**b**) *(de paiements)* spreading (out); *(de vacances)* staggering

étaler *vt* (**a**) *(marchandises)* to display (**b**) *(paiements)* to spread (out); *(vacances)* to stagger; **étalez vos versements sur deux ans** spread your payments out over two years

étalon *nm (de poids et mesures)* standard ▫ *Fin* **étalon de change-or** gold exchange standard; **étalon devise** currency standard; *Fin* **étalon**

monétaire monetary standard

étalonnage, étalonnement *nm* standardization

étalonner *vt* to standardize

étalon-or *nm* gold standard ❏ *étalon-or lingot* gold bullion standard

état *nm* (**a**) *(rapport)* form; *(des ventes)* statement, list; *(des paiements, marchandises)* schedule, list ❏ *état appréciatif* evaluation, estimation; *état des dépenses* statement of expenses; *état financier* financial statement; *Jur état de frais* bill of costs; *état imprimé* printed statement *or* form; *état des lieux* inventory of fixtures *(in rented premises)*; **faire l'état des lieux** to inspect the premises; *état nominatif* list of names; *état périodique* progress report; *état de rapprochement* reconciliation statement; *Admin états de service* service record; *état de situation* status *or* state-of-play report; *état des ventes* statement of sales figures

(**b**) *(condition)* state, condition; **en bon/mauvais état** *(marchandises)* in good/bad condition ❏ *état financier, état de fortune* financial standing *or* situation

(**c**) *Compta état de caisse* cash statement; *états comptables* accounting records; *états comptables et commerciaux* internal company records; *état de compte* bank statement, statement of account; *Compta* position on an account; *état détaillé (d'un compte)* breakdown; *état de flux de trésorerie* source and application of funds; *état néant* nil return; *état de rapprochement* reconciliation statement; *état récapitulatif* final assessment, adjustment account; *état TVA* VAT statement *or* return

(**d**) *(autorité centrale)* **l'État** the State

(**e**) *(nation, territoire aux États-Unis)* state ❏ *UE État membre* member state; *état tampon* buffer state

(**f**) *Admin état civil (d'une personne)* (civil) status; *(lieu)* registry office

(**g**) *Ordinat (d'une base de données)* report ❏ *état du projet* status report

étatisation *nf* state control

étatisé, -e *adj* state-controlled

étatiser *vt* to bring under state control

état-major *nm* *(d'entreprise, d'usine)* top management

❝
L'**état-major** français n'a pas apprécié les leçons de management de son actionnaire britannique. "Nous avions inventé des structures, on nous a envoyé à grands frais des consultants: des gamins de 30 ans qui apprennent à ceux qui ont trente ans de métier

comment on fait des magasins", a déclaré Loyez. ❞

État-patron *nm* **l'État-patron** the State as an employer

État-providence *nm* **l'État-providence** the welfare state

éteindre *vt Ordinat* to power down, to shut down

étendre 1 *vt Ordinat (mémoire)* to upgrade, to expand
2 s'étendre *vpr (grève)* to spread; *(fortune, entreprise)* to expand, to grow larger

étiquetage *nm (de bagages, de marchandises)* labelling ❏ *étiquetage du prix* price labelling

étiqueter *vt (bagages, marchandises)* to label

étiquette *nf* label ❏ *étiquette à bagages* luggage label; *étiquette de calibrage (d'un produit)* grade label; *étiquette d'identification (d'un produit)* identification label; *étiquette magnétique* security tag; *étiquette porte-prix* price label; *étiquette de prix* price label *or* tag; *étiquette d'un produit* product label; *étiquette promotionnelle* promotional label; *étiquette de qualité* quality label

étiquette-adresse *nf* address label

étranger, -ère 1 *adj (d'un autre pays)* foreign
2 *nm,f (d'un autre pays)* foreigner; *Admin* alien
3 *nm* **l'étranger** *(pays étrangers)* foreign countries; **à l'étranger** abroad; **aller/vivre à l'étranger** to go/live abroad

Ets *nmpl (abrév* **établissements)** Ets Legrand Legrand

ETSI *nm (abrév* **European Telecommunications Standards Institute)** ETSI

étude *nf* study; **le projet est encore à l'étude** the project is still at the development stage ❏ *Mktg étude ad hoc* ad hoc survey; *Mktg étude AIO* AIO research; *Mktg étude d'audience* audience research; *étude des besoins* needs study *or* analysis; *étude de cas* case study; *étude des charges* cost analysis; *Mktg étude client* customer survey; *Mktg étude commerciale* marketing study; *études commerciales (dans école de commerce)* business studies; *étude de communication* communications study; *étude comparative* comparative study; *étude du comportement* behavioural study *or* analysis; *Mktg étude du comportement du consommateur* consumer behaviour study; *étude de conception* design engineering; *étude de coût-efficacité* cost-volume-profit analysis; *Mktg étude des créneaux* gap analysis; *Mktg étude auprès des consommateurs* consumer *or* customer survey; *étude documentaire* desk research; *étude économique* economic research; *étude de faisabilité* feasibility study; *étude d'impact*

impact study; **étude longitudinale** longitudinal study; *Mktg* **étude de marché** market study; **faire une étude de marché** to do market research; *Mktg* **étude de marché standard** omnibus survey; *Mktg* **étude marketing** marketing study; *Mktg* **étude de mémorisation** recall study; *Mktg* **étude mercatique** marketing study; **étude des méthodes** methods analysis; **études de motivation** motivational research; *Mktg* **étude de notoriété** awareness study; *Mktg* **étude de positionnement** positioning study; **étude préliminaire** preliminary *or* pilot study; **étude de produit** product analysis; **étude de projet** project analysis; **étude de projet d'investissement** capital project evaluation; *Mktg* **étude prospective du marché** market study; **études qualitatives** qualitative research; **études quantitatives** quantitative research; **études et recherches** research and engineering; *Mktg* **étude de satisfaction de la clientèle** customer satisfaction survey; **étude des temps et des méthodes** time and methods study; **étude des temps et des mouvements** time and motion study; **étude sur le terrain** field study; *Mktg* **études sur les ventes** sales research

étude-pilote *nf* pilot study

EURIBOR *nm* (*abrév* **Euro Interbank Offered Rate**) EURIBOR

EURL *nf* (*abrév* **entreprise unipersonnelle à responsabilité limitée**) trader with limited liability

euro *nm UE* (*monnaie*) euro; **en euros** in euros

euro-certificat *nm Bourse* euro-certificate

eurochèque *nm* Eurocheque

eurocrate *nmf* eurocrat

eurodevise *nf* euro-currency

eurodollar *nm* eurodollar

euromarché *nm* euromarket

euromonnaie *nf* euro-currency

euro-obligation *nf* eurobond

Europe *nf* Europe □ **l'Europe des quinze** = the fifteen member states of the European Union; **l'Europe sociale** social Europe (*a united Europe committed to a progressive social and welfare policy*); **l'Europe Verte** (European) Community agriculture *or* farming

---
❝

Parallèlement, l'Europe doit se retrouver une politique économique commune. Le pacte de stabilité budgétaire doit être redéfini, le chantier de l'harmonisation fiscale enfin relancé, et l'**Europe sociale** abordée de façon empirique en trouvant des solutions à des problèmes tels que la "transférabilité" effective des retraites.

❞

Euro Stoxx *nm Bourse* Euro Stoxx; **l'Euro Stoxx 50** the Euro Stoxx 50 index

évaluable *adj* (*marchandises, propriété*) appraisable, assessable

évaluation *nf* (**a**) (*action*) evaluation; (*d'une propriété, de biens*) valuation, appraisal; (*des dommages*) assessment; (*de risques, d'une quantité*) estimation; **une évaluation en gros** a rough estimate □ **évaluation approximative** rough estimate; **évaluation du coût** cost assessment; **évaluation des coûts** cost analysis; **évaluation de la demande** demand assessment; **évaluation économique** economic appraisal; **évaluation d'un emploi** job evaluation; **évaluation financière** financial appraisal; **évaluation du marché** market appraisal; **évaluation des performances** (*d'un employé*) performance appraisal; *Mktg* **évaluation post-achat** post-purchase evaluation (**b**) (*quantité, valeur*) (*d'une propriété, de biens, des stocks*) valuation; (*des dommages*) assessment; (*d'une quantité*) estimate □ **évaluation des risques** risk assessment; **évaluation des stocks** stock control

évaluer *vt* to evaluate; (*propriété, biens*) to value, to appraise; (*dommages*) to assess (**à** at); (*risques, quantité*) to estimate; *Fin* **évaluer les coûts de qch** to cost sth

évasion *nf* **évasion des capitaux** flight of capital; **évasion fiscale** tax avoidance

---
❝

Les mesures anti-**évasion fiscale** viennent contrarier ceux qui voudraient les imiter. Les possibilités redeviennent restreintes. De plus, la traque à "l'argent sale" menée par l'OCDE laisse prévoir la mise en place de mesures qui viendront aussi gêner les candidats à l'évasion fiscale.

❞

éventail *nm* range □ **éventail des prix** price range; **éventail de produits** range of products; **éventail des salaires** salary range

éventuel, -elle *adj* possible; (*client*) potential, prospective

évolué, -e *adj* (**a**) (*marché, économie, demande*) developed (**b**) *Ordinat* (*langage*) high-level

évoluer *vi* (**a**) (*marché, économie, demande*) to develop (**b**) *Ordinat* **faire évoluer qch** to upgrade sth

évolutif, -ive *adj* (**a**) *Ordinat* upgradeable (**b**) (*poste*) with prospects (for promotion)

évolution *nf* (*du marché, de l'économie, de la demande*) development

évolutivité *nf Ordinat* upgradeability

examen *nm* examination; (*des comptes*) inspection; **la question est à l'examen** the question is under consideration □ **examen**

financier financial review

examiner *vt* to examine; *(comptes)* to go through, to inspect; *(question)* to look into, to consider

excédent *nm (d'un budget, d'une balance)* surplus; **dégager un excédent** to show a surplus; **la balance commerciale est en excédent** the trade balance shows a surplus; **il y a un excédent des exportations sur les importations** there is an excess of exports over imports □ ***excédent budgétaire*** budget surplus; *Compta* ***excédent de caisse*** cash overs; ***excédents et déficits*** overs and shorts; ***excédent de dépenses*** deficit; **nous avons un excédent de dépenses** we are overspending; *Compta* ***excédent d'exploitation*** operating profit; ***excédent de main-d'œuvre*** overmanning; ***excédent de production*** surplus produce

excédentaire *adj (production)* excess; *(budget)* surplus; **écouler la production excédentaire sur les marchés extérieurs** to dump excess production on foreign markets

excéder *vt* to exceed; **excéder le montant de son compte** to overdraw one's account; **nos pertes excèdent nos bénéfices** our losses are greater than our profits

exceptionnel, -elle *adj* (**a**) *(taxe)* exceptional (**b**) *(année)* exceptional; *(prix)* special

excès *nm* excess; **un excès des dépenses sur les recettes** an excess of expenditure over revenue; **un excès de l'offre sur la demande** an excess of supply over demand

exclusif, -ive *adj (droit, produit, distributeur)* exclusive

exclusivité *nf (droit)* sole *or* exclusive rights (**de** to); **avoir un contrat d'exclusivité** to have an exclusive contract; **nous avons l'exclusivité de la vente de ce produit** we have the (sole) rights for this product □ ***exclusivité à la marque*** brand exclusivity

ex-coupon *adv Fin* ex coupon

ex-dividende *adv Fin* ex dividend

ex-droit *adv Fin* ex rights

exécutable *adj* feasible; *Ordinat (programme)* executable

exécuter *vt* (**a**) *(effectuer) (travail, plan)* to execute, to carry out; *(ordres, décision, opération comptable, commande)* to carry out (**b**) *Ordinat (programme)* to execute, to run; *(commande)* to execute, to carry out (**c**) *Jur (débiteur)* to distrain upon; *(jugement, mandat)* to enforce; *(contrat)* to fulfil the terms of (**d**) *Bourse (spéculateur)* to hammer; *(client)* to sell out against

exécuteur, -trice *nm,f (d'un ordre)* executor □ ***exécuteur testamentaire*** executor

exécutif, -ive 1 *adj (comité, pouvoir)* executive

2 *nm (comité exécutif)* executive committee; **un exécutif de cinq membres** an executive of five

exécution *nf* (**a**) *(d'un travail, d'un plan)* execution, carrying out; *(d'ordres, d'une décision, d'une opération comptable, d'une commande)* carrying out; **en voie d'exécution** in progress (**b**) *Ordinat (d'un programme)* execution, running; *(d'une commande)* execution, carrying out (**c**) *Jur (d'un jugement, d'un mandat)* enforcement; *(d'un contrat)* fulfilment (**d**) *Bourse (d'un spéculateur)* hammering; **exécution au prix du marché** execution at market

exécutoire *Jur* **1** *adj (contrat, jugement, mandat)* enforceable

2 *nm* writ of execution □ ***exécutoire des dépens*** order to pay costs

exemplaire *nm (unité)* copy; **le livre a été tiré à 10 000 exemplaires** 10,000 copies of the book were published; **le journal tire à 150 000 exemplaires** the newspaper has a circulation of 150,000; **en double exemplaire** in duplicate; **en triple exemplaire** in triplicate □ *Admin* ***exemplaire d'archives*** file copy; ***exemplaire gratuit*** presentation copy; ***exemplaire de lancement*** advance copy

exempt, -e *adj* **exempt d'impôts** tax-exempt; *Douanes* **exempt de droits** duty-free; **exempt de frais** free of charge

exempter *vt* to exempt sb (**de** from)

exemption *nf* exemption (**de** from) □ ***exemption fiscale, exemption d'impôt*** tax exemption

exercer *vt* (**a**) *Bourse (option)* to exercise; **exercer par anticipation** to exercise in advance (**b**) *Jur* **exercer des poursuites (contre)** to take legal action (against) (**c**) *(profession)* to practise; **exercer ses fonctions** to carry out one's duties

exercice *nm* (**a**) *Compta Br* financial year, *Am* fiscal year; **l'exercice de ce mois** this month's trading □ ***exercice budgétaire*** budgetary year; ***exercice comptable*** accounting year; ***exercice en cours*** current *Br* financial *or Am* fiscal year; ***exercice financier*** *Br* financial *or Am* fiscal year; ***exercice fiscal*** tax year (**b**) *(d'une profession)* practice; **dans l'exercice de ses fonctions** in the exercise of one's duties

> ❝
>
> Et les espoirs du PDG danois, Ebbe Pelle Jacobson, précipité au chevet de l'entreprise moribonde en 1998, risquent fort d'être déçus. En novembre 2001, il affirmait: "Nous attendons l'équilibre pour l'**exercice** 2001-2002." Pour 2001, c'est raté, avec une perte de plus de 10 millions d'euros. Et 2002 ne se présente pas mieux.
>
> ❞

exhiber *vt (objet, marchandises)* to exhibit

exigence nf demand, requirement; **il n'est pas à la hauteur des exigences du poste** he is not up to the requirements of the job; **la marchandise répond à toutes les exigences** the goods are up to standard in every way; **satisfaire aux exigences de ses clients** to meet one's customers' requirements

exiger vt to demand, to require (**de** from)

exigibilité nf **exigibilités** current liabilities; **exigibilité immédiate** immediately due ❑ Fin **exigibilité de taxe** tax liability

exigible adj (paiement) due; (dette, impôt) due for payment, payable; **exigible à vue** payable at sight

existant, -e 1 adj existing; **majorer les tarifs existants** to increase existing tariffs
   2 nm **les existants** stock (in hand) ❑ Compta **existant en caisse** cash in hand; **existant en magasin** stock (in hand)

existence nf Compta **existences en caisse** cash in hand; **existence en magasin** stock (in hand)

exister vi (article) to be available; **ce modèle existe aussi en bleu** this model is also available in blue

ex-navire adv ex ship

exonération nf exemption (**de** from) ❑ **exonération des droits** exemption from duty; **exonération fiscale** tax exemption; **exonération partielle** partial exemption; **exonération totale** total exemption

exonérer vt (**a**) (personne, entreprise) to exempt (**de** from); **exonérer qn de l'impôt sur le revenu** to exempt sb from income tax (**b**) (marchandises) to exempt from import duty

expansion nf (d'une ville, d'une industrie) expansion; **être en pleine expansion** to be booming ❑ **expansion économique** economic growth; **expansion monétaire** currency expansion

expansionnisme nm expansionism

expansionniste adj & nmf expansionist

expatriation nf Fin (d'argent, de capitaux) movement abroad

expatrier vt Fin (argent, capitaux) to invest abroad

expédier vt (**a**) (envoyer) (marchandises) to dispatch, to ship; (lettre, colis) to send; Douanes **expédier des marchandises en douane** to clear goods through customs; **expédier des marchandises par navire** to send goods by sea, to ship goods; **expédier des marchandises par fret aérien** to airfreight goods; **expédiez ceci par le premier courrier** get this off by the first post; **expédier un colis par la poste** to mail or Br to post a parcel (**b**) (s'occuper de) to deal with; **expédier les affaires courantes** to deal with the day-to-day matters (**c**) Jur (contrat, acte) to draw up

expéditeur, -trice 1 adj (bureau, compagnie, gare) shipping, dispatching
   2 nm,f (**a**) (de courrier) sender (**b**) (de marchandises) shipper, consignee; (par bateau) shipper

expédition nf (**a**) (envoi) (de marchandises) dispatch, shipment; **expéditions** (service) dispatch department, shipping department; **expédition franco à partir de 1000 euros** orders of 1,000 euro and over delivered free ❑ **expédition par avion** airfreighting; **expédition par bateau** shipping; **expédition par chemin de fer** sending by rail, railfreighting; **expédition par courrier** mailing, Br posting; **expédition de détail** retail shipment; **expédition exclusive** exclusive shipment; **expédition maritime** maritime shipment; **expédition par mer** shipping, shipment; **expédition partielle** part shipment or consignment; **expédition port à port** port to port shipment; **expédition par la poste** mailing, Br posting (**b**) (marchandises) consignment, shipment (**c**) Jur (de contrat, d'acte) copy; **première expédition** first authentic copy; **en double expédition** in duplicate

expéditionnaire nmf shipping clerk

expérience nf (**a**) (connaissance, apprentissage) experience ❑ **expérience professionnelle** work experience (**b**) (test) experiment ❑ **expérience sur le terrain** field experiment

expert, -e 1 adj expert, skilled (**en/dans** in); **la main-d'œuvre la plus experte** the most highly-skilled labour
   2 nm (**a**) (chargé d'expertise) expert ❑ **expert en communication** communications expert; **expert en gestion** management expert (**b**) Assur loss adjuster, claims adjuster; (en bâtiment) surveyor ❑ **expert en assurances** loss adjuster, claims adjuster

expert-comptable nm Br ≃ chartered accountant, Am ≃ certified public accountant

expert-conseil nm consultant

expertise nf (**a**) Assur (des dégâts) (expert) assessment; **faire l'expertise de qch** to appraise or value sth; (dégâts) to assess sth ❑ **expertise d'avarie, expertise des dégâts** damage survey (**b**) (rapport) expert's report

expertiser vt Assur (dégâts) to assess; **faire expertiser qch** to have sth appraised or valued; (dégâts) to have sth assessed

expert-répétiteur nm Assur loss adjuster

expiration nf (de bail, de contrat) expiry, expiration; **arriver à expiration** to expire

expirer vi (bail, contrat) to expire

exploit nm Jur writ

exploitant, -e *nm,f* exploitant **(agricole)** farmer; **les petits exploitants** small farmers

exploitation *nf* **(a)** *(d'une entreprise)* running, operation **(b)** *(d'un brevet)* commercialization; *(d'une invention)* utilization **(c)** *(entreprise)* concern; **petite exploitation** smallholding ❑ *exploitation agricole* farm; *exploitation commerciale* business (concern); *exploitation familiale* family business; *exploitation industrielle* industrial concern; *exploitation minière* mine

exploiter *vt* **(a)** *(entreprise)* to run **(b)** *(brevet)* to commercialize; *(invention)* to utilize

exploration des besoins et des désirs *nf* *Mktg* needs-and-wants exploration

expomarché *nm* trade mart

export *nm* export, exportation ❑ *Ordinat* **export de données** data export

exportable *adj* exportable

exportateur, -trice 1 *adj (pays)* exporting; *(secteur)* export; **être exportateur de qch** to export sth; **les pays exportateurs de pétrole** the oil-exporting countries
   2 *nm,f* exporter

exportation *nf* **(a)** *(action)* export, exportation; *(produit)* export; **faire de l'exportation** to export; **le montant des exportations a augmenté de 10 pour cent cette année** exports have risen by 10 percent this year; **ce produit marche très fort à l'exportation** this product is doing very well on the export market; **réservé à l'exportation** reserved for export, for export only ❑ *exportation de capitaux* export of capital; *exportations invisibles* invisible exports; *exportation kangourou* piggybacking; *exportations visibles* visible exports **(b)** *Ordinat (d'un fichier)* exporting; *(données exportées)* exported data

exporter 1 *vt* **(a)** *(marchandises)* to export (**vers** to) **(b)** *Ordinat* to export (**vers** to)
   2 s'exporter *vpr (marchandises)* to be exported (**vers** to); **ce genre de produit s'exporte mal** this type of product is not good for exporting

exposant, -e *nm,f* **(a)** *(dans une foire)* exhibitor **(b)** *Jur* petitioner, deponent

exposé *nm* account, statement ❑ *exposé verbal (de mission)* briefing

exposer *vt (produits, marchandises)* to display; **exposer des marchandises en vente** to display goods for sale

exposition *nf* **(a)** *(foire)* exhibition, show ❑ *exposition commerciale* trade exhibition; *exposition interprofessionnelle* trade exhibition; *l'Exposition universelle* the World Fair **(b)** *(de marchandises)* display ❑ *Mktg* **exposition sur le lieu de vente** point of sale display; *Mktg* **exposition sur le marché** market exposure; **exposi-tion au public** audience exposure **(c)** *Fin* **exposition aux risques** exposure

exposition-vente *nf* display *(where the items are for sale)*

exprès *adj* express; **par exprès** by special delivery; **envoyer qch en exprès** to send sth special delivery

expression *nf* **veuillez agréer l'expression de nos sentiments les meilleurs** *(à quelqu'un dont on connaît le nom)* *Br* yours sincerely, *Am* sincerely; *(à quelqu'un dont on ne connaît pas le nom)* *Br* yours faithfully, *Am* sincerely

expropriation *nf Jur (d'une personne)* expropriation; *(d'une propriété)* compulsory purchase

exproprier *vt Jur (personne)* to expropriate; *(propriété)* to place a compulsory purchase order on

expulser *vt (locataire)* to evict

expulsion *nf (d'un locataire)* eviction

ex-répartition *adv Fin* ex allotment

extensible *adj Ordinat (matériel, système)* upgradeable; *(mémoire)* expandable, upgradeable

extension *nf* **(a)** *Ordinat (augmentation)* expansion; *(dispositif)* add-on ❑ *extension mémoire* memory expansion *or* upgrade; *extension du nom de fichier* file name extension **(b)** *Mktg* expansion, extension ❑ *extension de la gamme* range stretching; *extension de la ligne* line stretching, line extension; *extension de marché* market expansion; *extension de la marque* brand extension

extérieur 1 *adj* **(a)** *(étranger) (échanges, commerce)* foreign, external **(b)** *(étranger à la chose considérée)* **le travail a été accompli par des personnes extérieures à l'entreprise** the work was done out of house
   2 *nm* **l'extérieur** foreign countries; **à l'extérieur** abroad; **de l'extérieur** from abroad

externalisation *nf* outsourcing

externaliser *vt* to outsource

> **"**
> Parallèlement, les entreprises occidentales **externalisent** des fonctions de plus en plus de leur cœur de métier. Pour le transport, l'entretien ou la maintenance, la pratique s'est systématisée et sophistiquée. "Il y a dix ans, des sociétés possédaient encore des wagons pour acheminer leur production ... Aujourd'hui, leurs prestataires se chargent de tout, jusqu'au tracé des itinéraires!"
> **"**

extinction *nf Jur (d'un droit)* extinguishment; *(d'un contrat)* termination; *(d'une hypothèque)* redemption; *Compta (d'une dette)* discharge

extrabudgétaire *adj Fin* extra-budgetary

extra-comptable *adj Compta (ajustement)* off-balance sheet

extractible *adj (disque)* removable

extrait *nm Fin, Jur (d'un acte, d'un compte-rendu, d'un titre, d'un bilan)* abstract ❑ **extrait cadastral** land registration certificate; **extrait de compte** *Compta* statement of account; *Banque* bank statement

extraordinaire *adj (assemblée, réunion)* extraordinary

extrapolation *nf* extrapolation

extrapoler 1 *vt* to extrapolate
   2 *vi* to extrapolate; **extrapoler à partir de qch** to extrapolate from sth

e-zine, ezine *nm Ordinat* e-zine, ezine

Ff

FAB *adj (abrév* **franco à bord)** FOB

fabricant, -e *nm,f* maker, manufacturer

fabrication *nf (construction)* manufacture, production; *(qualité)* workmanship; **de fabrication française** made in France, French-made □ *fabrication assistée par ordinateur* computer-aided *or* computer-assisted manufacture; *fabrication à la chaîne* mass production; *fabrication intégrée par ordinateur* computer-integrated manufacturing; *fabrication par lots* batch production; *fabrication en série* mass production

fabrique *nf* factory, works □ *fabrique de vêtements* clothing factory

fabriquer *vt* to manufacture; **fabriquer qch à la chaîne** to mass-produce sth; **fabriqué en France** made in France; **fabriquer qch en grande série** to mass-produce sth; **fabriqué sur commande** made to order; **fabriqué sur mesure(s)** made to measure

FAC *adj Assur (abrév* **franc d'avarie commune)** FGA

façade *nf Assur* fronting

facilité *nf* **(a)** *(possibilité)* facility □ *Banque* *facilités de caisse* overdraft facilities; *facilités de crédit* credit facilities; *facilités de crédits réciproques* swap facilities; *facilité d'endettement* borrowing capacity; *facilités de paiement* payment facilities, easy terms; *facilité de reprise (d'un produit)* trade-in facility **(b)** *(simplicité) Mktg* **facilité d'écoulement** saleability; *facilité d'emploi (d'un ordinateur)* user-friendliness; *facilité de vente* saleability

facing *nm Mktg* shelf facing

facob *nm Assur (abrév* **facultatif obligatoire)** open cover

façon *nf (qualité de travail)* workmanship; *(main-d'œuvre)* labour; **façon et fournitures** labour and material

fac-similé *nm* facsimile, exact copy; *Ordinat* hard copy

factage *nm* **(a)** *(livraison)* carriage and delivery, transport; **payer le factage** to pay the carriage **(b)** *(du courrier)* delivery

facteur *nm* factor □ *facteur de charge* load factor; *facteur clé* key factor; *facteur de consommation* demand factor; *facteur coût* cost factor; *facteur de demande* demand factor;

facteur de déséquilibre destabilizing factor; *facteur déterminant* controlling factor; *facteur économique* economic factor; *facteur humain* human factor; *facteur de production* production factor; *facteur de risque* risk factor; *facteur de sécurité* safety factor; *Mktg* *facteur de situation* situational factor

factoring *nm* factoring

facturation *nf Compta* invoicing, billing □ *facturation détaillée* itemized invoicing *or* billing

facture *nf* invoice, bill; **faire** *ou* **dresser** *ou* **établir une facture** to make out an invoice; **payer** *ou* **régler une facture** to settle an invoice, to pay a bill; **selon** *ou* **suivant facture, conformément à la facture** as per invoice; *Écon* **la facture pétrolière de la France** France's oil bill □ *facture d'achat* purchase invoice; *facture de consignation* consignment invoice; *facture détaillée* itemized invoice *or* bill; *facture douanière* customs invoice; *facture énergétique* energy consumption bill; *facture fiscale* tax bill; *facture originale* original invoice; *facture pro forma, facture provisoire* pro forma invoice; *facture de téléphone* telephone bill; *facture de vente* sales invoice

> **"**
> En incluant les mesures annoncées pour 2003, les ménages auront vu leur **facture fiscale** diminuer de plus de 20 milliards d'euros depuis 2000.
> **"**

facturer *vt (personne)* to invoice, to bill; *(produit, service)* to charge for; **facturer qch à qn** to invoice sb for sth, to bill sb for sth; **le papier nous a été facturé 60 euros** we were charged 60 euro for the paper; **je ne vous ai pas facturé les pièces détachées** I haven't invoiced you for the spare parts

facturette *nf* credit card sales voucher

facturier, -ère 1 *nm,f* invoice clerk
2 *nm* sales book
3 *nf* **facturière** invoicing machine

faculté *nf* **(a)** *(droit)* option, right; **louer un immeuble avec faculté d'achat** to rent a building with the option of purchase □ *Bourse* **faculté du double** call of more; *Bourse* **faculté de rachat** repo *or* repurchase agreement **(b)** *Assur* **facultés** cargo □ *facultés assurées* insured cargo (**c**) *(capacité)* ability ❑ **facultés contributives** ability to pay

FAI *nm Ordinat (abrév* **fournisseur d'accès à l'Internet)** IAP

faible *adj (demande, prix, revenu, marge)* low; *(monnaie)* weak, *(quantité)* small; *Mktg (utilisateur)* light

faiblesse *nf (d'un concurrent, d'un produit)* weakness

failli, -e 1 *adj (commerçant)* bankrupt
   2 *nm* (adjudicated) bankrupt ❑ **failli concordataire** certified bankrupt; **failli déchargé** discharged bankrupt; **failli non déchargé** undischarged bankrupt; **failli réhabilité** discharged bankrupt

faillite *nf* bankruptcy, insolvency; **être en (état de) faillite** to be bankrupt *or* insolvent; **faire faillite** to go bankrupt, to fail; **déclarer** *ou* **mettre qn en faillite, prononcer la faillite de qn** to declare sb bankrupt; **se mettre en faillite** to file a petition in bankruptcy ❑ **faillite frauduleuse** fraudulent bankruptcy; **faillite simple** bankruptcy

> **❝**
> En 1992, premier coup de semonce avec la faillite frauduleuse du tycoon Robert Maxwell. Pour maintenir à flot son empire de papier … le rival de Rupert Murdoch puisait dans les fonds de pension. Coopers, qui auditait les comptes du groupe, paiera très cher de n'avoir rien vu.
> **❞**

faire *vt* (**a**) *(paiement, versement)* to make; *(chèque)* to make out; **faire un chèque de 100 euros** to make out a cheque for 100 euros (**b**) *(vendre)* to sell; **nous ne faisons que le gros** we only deal wholesale; **nous ne faisons plus cet article** we no longer sell this article (**c**) *(s'élever à)* to come to; **combien cela fait-il?** how much does that come to?

faisabilité *nf (d'un projet)* feasibility

falsification *nf (de documents, de comptes)* falsification; *(d'une signature)* forgery

falsifier *vt (documents, comptes)* to falsify; *(signature)* to forge, to fake

familial, -e *adj* (**a**) *(entreprise)* family-run, family-owned (**b**) *Mktg (paquet, emballage, format)* family-size(d)

famille *nf* (**a**) *(ménage)* household (**b**) *Mktg (de produits)* family, line

FAO *nf (abrév* **fabrication assistée par ordinateur)** CAM

FAQ *Ordinat (abrév* **frequently asked questions, foire aux questions)** FAQ

faussaire *nmf* counterfeiter, forger

faute *nf* (**a**) *(erreur)* mistake, error ❑ *Ordinat*

faute de copiste clerical error; *Ordinat* **faute de frappe** keying *or* typing error; **faute d'impression** misprint; **faute professionnelle** professional misconduct (**b**) *(manque)* **faute de** for lack of; **faute de paiement sous quinzaine, nous serons dans l'obligation de majorer notre facture de 10 pour cent** should payment not be made within fourteen days, we shall be obliged to add a 10 percent surcharge to your bill

faux, fausse 1 *adj (chèque)* forged; *(argent)* counterfeit; *(billet, pièce)* dud; *(déclaration)* false ❑ **faux bilan** fraudulent balance sheet; **fausse écriture** false entry; **fausse facture** false bill; **faux frais** incidental expenses; **faux fret** dead freight
   2 *nm Jur (objet, activité)* forgery; **s'inscrire en faux contre qch** to dispute the validity of sth; **inculper qn pour faux et usage de faux** to prosecute sb for forgery ❑ *Compta* **faux en écritures** forgery

faveur *nf* **en faveur de qn** *(à l'avantage de)* in favour of sb; **le solde est en votre faveur** the balance is in your favour

favorable *adj (balance commerciale, taux de change)* favourable; **à des conditions favorables** on favourable terms; **notre demande a reçu un accueil favorable** our request was favourably received

favoris *nmpl Ordinat* favorites

favoriser *vt (croissance, emploi, exportations)* to encourage, to promote

fax *nm (appareil)* fax (machine); *(message)* fax; **envoyer qch par fax** to send sth by fax, to fax sth ❑ *Ordinat* **fax modem** fax modem

faxer *vt* to fax

fco *adv (abrév* **franco)** franco

FCP *nm Fin (abrév* **fonds commun de placement)** investment trust, mutual fund

FCPR *nm Fin (abrév* **fonds commun de placement à risques)** VCT

FDR *nm (abrév* **fonds de roulement)** working capital

FECOM *nm (abrév* **Fonds européen de coopération monétaire)** EMCF

FED *nm (abrév* **Fonds européen de développement)** EDF

FEDER *nm (abrév* **Fonds européen de développement régional)** ERDF

fédération *nf* federation ❑ **fédération syndicale** *Br* trade *or* *Am* labor union; **fédération de syndicats** amalgamated union

félin *nm Bourse* stripped bond

femme d'affaires *nf* businesswoman

fenêtre *nf Ordinat* window ❑ **fenêtre active, fenêtre activée** active window; **fenêtre d'aide**

help window; **fenêtre déroulante** pull-down window; **fenêtre de dialogue** dialogue window; **fenêtre d'édition** editing window; **fenêtre graphique** graphics window

ferraille *nf* scrap metal

ferrailleur *nm* scrap dealer, scrap merchant

férié, -e *adj* **lundi prochain est férié** next Monday is a (public) holiday

ferme¹ **1** *adj* (**a**) *(stable)* firm, steady; **maintenir les prix fermes** to keep prices steady; **le marché reste très ferme** the market remains very steady (**b**) *(acheteur, commande, offre, valeur)* firm
 2 *adv* **vendre/acheter ferme** to sell/buy firm

ferme² *nf Jur* farming lease; **prendre une terre à ferme** to rent a piece of land; **donner qch à ferme** to farm sth out

fermer 1 *vt* (**a**) *(compte)* to close; *(usine, entreprise)* to close down; **fermer ses portes** to close down (**b**) *Ordinat (fichier, fenêtre)* to close; *(commande)* to end
 2 *vi* (**a**) *(usine, entreprise) (temporairement)* to close, to shut; *(définitivement)* to close down (**b**) *Bourse (actions)* to close; **les actions ont fermé à 55 euros** shares closed at 55 euros

fermeté *nf* steadiness

fermeture *nf* (**a**) *(d'un compte)* closing; *(d'une usine, d'une entreprise)* closure; **fermeture pour travaux** *(sur panneau)* closed for repairs (**b**) *Ordinat (d'un fichier, d'une fenêtre)* closing; *(d'une commande)* ending; *(d'un ordinateur)* shutdown

ferret *nm* tag

ferroviaire *adj (réseau, ligne)* railway; *(transports)* rail

fête *nf* **fête légale** public holiday, *Br* bank holiday, *Am* legal holiday; **la fête du Travail** Labour Day

feuille *nf (imprimé)* form ❏ **feuille d'accompagnement** covering document; *Compta* **feuille d'avancement** flow sheet; *Ordinat* **feuille de calcul** spreadsheet; **feuille d'émargement** payroll; **feuille d'impôt** tax return; *Compta* **feuille de liquidation** settlement note; **feuille de maladie** = medical expense claim form; **feuille de paie** payslip; **feuille de présence** *(d'un employé)* time card; **feuille de réservation** reservation form, booking form; **feuille de route** waybill; **feuille de service** (duty) roster; **feuille de soins** medical expense claim form; *Ordinat* **feuille de style** style sheet; **feuille de transfert** deed of transfer; **feuille de travail** worksheet; *Banque* **feuille de versement** paying-in slip

feuille-à-feuille *adj Ordinat (imprimante)* sheet-fed

feuilleter *vi Ordinat* **feuilleter en arrière** page down; **feuilleter en avant** page up

FF *nm Anciennement (abrév* **franc français**) French Franc

fibre *nf* **câble en fibres optiques** fibre-optic cable

fibre optique *nf* fibre optics; **fibres optiques** optical fibres

fiche *nf* (**a**) *(formulaire)* form; *(papier)* sheet, slip; **remplir une fiche** to fill in *or* fill out a form ❏ **fiche d'accueil** registration form; **fiche d'appréciation** customer satisfaction questionnaire; **fiche d'arrivée** registration form; **fiche client** customer record; *(d'un hôtel)* guest file; **fiche de compte** accounts card; **fiche de contrôle** docket; **fiche courrier** mail checklist *or* file; **fiche d'entretien** service record; **fiche de facture** account card; **fiche fournisseur** supplier file; **fiche gigogne** dongle; **fiche horaire** time sheet; *Compta* **fiche d'imputation** data entry form; **fiche d'inscription** registration form; **fiche d'observations** *(questionnaire d'évaluation)* comment card; **fiche de paie** payslip; **fiche perforée** perforated card; **fiche de pointage** clocking-in card; **fiche de poste** task sheet; **fiche de présence** *(de salarié)* attendance sheet; **fiche prospect** potential-customer file; **fiche de renseignements** information card; **fiche de stock** stock sheet; **fiche technique** specifications sheet, data sheet, product information sheet; **fiche voyageur** *(d'un hôtel)* registration card for foreign guests (**b**) *(carte)* (index) card; **mettre qch sur fiches** to card-index sth ❏ **fiche cartonnée** index card

fichier *nm* (**a**) *(boîte)* card-index file; *(meuble)* card-index cabinet (**b**) *(ensemble de fiches)* card-index file (**c**) *Ordinat* file ❏ **fichier actif** active file; **fichier d'adresses** mailing list, address file; **fichier ASCII** ASCII file; **fichier binaire** binary file; **fichier client** client file; **fichier de commande** command file; **fichier compte-rendu** log file; **fichier disque** disk file; **fichier document** document file; **fichier exécutable** executable file; **fichier FAQ** FAQ file; **fichier à imprimer** print job; **fichier joint** *(de courrier électronique)* attachment; **fichier lisez-moi** read-me file; **fichier maître** master file; **fichier principal** master file; **fichier de sauvegarde** backup file; **fichier source** source file; **fichier système** system file; **fichier temporaire** temporary file; **fichier texte** text file

fictif, -ive *adj (compte)* impersonal; *(société)* fictitious

fidéicommis *nm Jur* trust

fidéicommissaire *nm Jur* trustee

fidèle 1 *adj (client)* loyal; **rester fidèle à un produit** to stick with a product; *Mktg* **fidèle à la marque** brand-loyal
 2 *nmf* regular *or* loyal customer ❏ *Mktg* **fidèle absolu** hard-core loyal

fidélisation *nf Mktg* = building up of customer loyalty

fidéliser *vt Mktg* to win the loyalty of; **fidéliser la clientèle** to develop customer loyalty

> **"**
>
> Chez nous, les nouveaux venus ont cherché à copier Air France en pensant **fidéliser** la clientèle avec davantage de services et une image différente. Pour créer une compagnie low cost aujourd'hui, il leur faudrait faire table rase du passé, repenser complètement l'organisation et les coûts.
>
> **"**

fidélité *nf Mktg (d'un client)* loyalty ❑ **fidélité absolue** hard-core loyalty; **fidélité du client** customer loyalty; **fidélité du consommateur** consumer loyalty; **fidélité à la marque** brand loyalty

fiduciaire **1** *adj (prêt, devise)* fiduciary; **en dépôt fiduciaire** in escrow, in trust; **avoirs en monnaie fiduciaire** *(d'une banque)* cash holdings; **une circulation fiduciaire excessive entraîne l'inflation** too much paper money in circulation leads to inflation
  2 *nm Jur* fiduciary, trustee

fiduciairement *adv Jur* in trust

fiducie *nf Jur* trust

figer *vt (salaires)* to freeze

figurer *vi* to appear, to figure; **ces articles figurent dans le catalogue** these articles appear or are listed in the catalogue

fil *nm* **sans fil** *(téléphone, souris)* cordless

file d'attente *nf Ordinat* print queue *or* list; **mettre en file d'attente** to spool, to queue

filiale *nf* subsidiary (company) ❑ **filiale commune** jointly-owned subsidiary; **filiale consolidée** consolidated subsidiary; **filiale de distribution** marketing subsidiary; **filiale étrangère** foreign subsidiary; **filiale de vente** sales subsidiary

filialiser *vt* to affiliate

filière *nf* **(a)** *(procédures)* channels; **passer par** *ou* **suivre la filière** *(pour obtenir quelque chose)* to go through official channels; *(comme employé)* to work one's way up ❑ **la filière administrative** the official channels **(b)** *Fin* **filière électronique** electronic transfer **(c)** *Bourse* **établir la filière** to trace the succession of previous shareholders **(d)** *(secteur)* sector ❑ **filière agro-alimentaire** food-processing sector

film publicitaire *nm (à la télévision)* commercial; *(au cinéma)* cinema advertisement

filtre anti-reflet *nm Ordinat* glare filter

fin *nf* **(a)** *(de contrat, de bail)* expiry, expiration; **mettre fin à un contrat** to terminate a contract; **être en fin de droits** = to be nearing the end of the period in which one is entitled to benefits; **fin courant** at the end of the current month; **fin prochain** at the end of next month ❑ **fin d'année** year end; **fin d'exercice** year end **(b)** **fin de série** *(d'articles)* discontinued line **(c)** *Banque* **sauf bonne fin** under reserve **(d)** *Ordinat* **fin de ligne** line end; **fin de page** page break; **fin de page obligatoire** hard page break; **fin de paragraphe** paragraph break; **fin de session** logoff

final, -e *adj (règlement, solde)* final

finance *nf* **(a)** *(domaine)* finance; **le monde de la finance** the financial world; **la haute finance** *(milieu)* high finance; *(personnes)* the top bankers ❑ **finance d'entreprise** corporate finance **(b)** **finances** *(argent)* finances; **les finances de la compagnie vont mal** the company's finances are in a bad state ❑ **finances publiques** public funds

financement *nm* financing, funding; **le financement du projet sera assuré par la compagnie** the company will finance *or* fund the project ❑ **financement déguisé** back-door financing; **financement par emprunt, financement par l'endettement** debt financing; **financement aux entreprises** global finance; **financement initial** start-up capital; **financement à long terme** long-term financing; **financement à taux fixe** fixed-rate financing

financement-relais *nm* bridge financing

financer *vt (projet)* to finance, to fund; *(personne)* to back; **l'opération a été entièrement financée par emprunt** the transaction was financed entirely through borrowing; **BP financera le projet à 50 pour cent** BP will put up 50 percent of the funding for the project

financier, -ère **1** *adj* financial; **solide au point de vue financier** financially sound
  2 *nm,f* financier ❑ **financier d'entreprise** corporate finance manager

financièrement *adv* financially

finaud, -e *nm,f Ordinat* hacker

firme *nf* business, firm, concern

firmware *nm Ordinat* firmware

fisc *nm Br* ≃ Inland Revenue, *Am* ≃ Internal Revenue, IRS; **les employés du fisc** tax officials; **frauder le fisc** to evade tax

> **"**
>
> Ces grosses entreprises n'ont aucun intérêt à **frauder le fisc** en dissimulant une partie des rentrées en liquide : elles opèrent dans un circuit comptable précis où ce genre de pratique est très difficile à cacher.
>
> **"**

fiscal, -e *adj* fiscal, tax; **dans un but fiscal** for tax purposes

fiscalement *adv* fiscally, from the point of view of taxation; **dans quel pays êtes-vous fiscalement domicilié?** in which country do you pay tax?

fiscaliser *vt* to tax

fiscaliste *nmf* tax consultant

fiscalité *nf* tax system □ *fiscalité écologique* green taxation; *fiscalité excessive* excessive taxation; *fiscalité indirecte* indirect taxation

"

Derrière la volonté affichée de protéger l'environnement à travers une **fiscalité écologique**, les mesures sont maigres … l'idée de taxer les activités polluantes, nuisibles au développement durable, pour alléger en revanche les charges sociales qui pèsent sur l'emploi, restera encore l'an prochain assez théorique.

"

fixage *nm Bourse* fixing

fixation *nf (d'une date, d'une heure, d'un rendez-vous)* fixing, arranging; *(des impôts, des dommages-intérêts)* assessment; *(d'un prix, d'un taux, d'un salaire)* fixing, setting; *(des conditions, des objectifs)* setting; *(des indemnités)* determination

fixe 1 *adj (capital, actif, prix, coûts, traitement)* fixed; *(adresse)* permanent
2 *nm* fixed salary; **toucher un fixe** to be on a fixed salary

fixer *vt (date, heure, rendez-vous)* to fix, to arrange; *(impôts, dommages-intérêts)* to assess; *(prix, taux, salaire)* to fix, to set (**à** at); *(conditions, objectifs)* to set; *(indemnités)* to determine; *Bourse* **fixer un cours** to make a price

fixeur de prix *nm Bourse* price maker

flambée *nf (des prix, des cours)* leap

"

La **flambée** des cours est spectaculaire. Avec l'intensification du conflit au Proche-Orient, le prix du baril de pétrole est monté la semaine dernière jusqu'à 28 dollars, son plus haut niveau depuis six mois.

"

FLB *adv (abrév* **franco long du bord)** FAS

flèche *nf (a)* **monter en flèche** *(prix)* to shoot up, to rocket **(b)** *Ordinat* arrow □ *flèche vers le bas* down arrow; *flèche vers la droite* right arrow; *flèche vers la gauche* left arrow; *flèche vers le haut* up arrow

fléchir *vi (marché, devises)* to weaken; *(prix, cours, demande)* to fall, to drop; **les prix des actions fléchissent** share prices are down

fléchissement *nm (du marché, des devises)* weakening; *(des prix, des cours, de la demande)* fall, drop

flexibilité *nf Fin (d'une entreprise, de la main-d'œuvre)* flexibility

flexible *adj Fin (entreprise, main-d'œuvre)* flexible

florin *nm Anciennement* florin

flottaison *nf (d'une monnaie)* floating, fluctuation

flottant, -e 1 *adj* **(a)** *(dette, capitaux, taux de change, police d'assurance)* floating **(b)** *Ordinat (accent)* floating
2 *nm Bourse* float

flottement *nm (d'une monnaie)* floating, fluctuation

flotter *vi (prix)* to fluctuate; *(monnaie)* to float; **faire flotter la livre** to float the pound

flouze *nm Fam* cash

fluctuation *nf Fin (du marché, des cours)* fluctuation (**de** in) □ *fluctuations saisonnières* seasonal fluctuations

fluctuer *vi Fin (marché, cours)* to fluctuate

fluidité *nf* fluidity

flux *nm (de fonds)* flow; **à flux tendus** *(transport, distribution, production)* just-in-time □ *flux financier* flow of money, monetary flow; *flux monétaire* flow of money, monetary flow; *flux réel* flow of goods; *flux de trésorerie* cash flow

FMI *nm (abrév* **Fonds monétaire international)** IMF

FNE *nm (abrév* **Fonds national de l'emploi)** = French national employment fund

FO *nf (abrév* **Force Ouvrière)** = French trade union

FOB *adj (abrév* **free on board)** FOB

focalisation *nf Mktg* targeting □ *focalisation stratégique* strategic targeting

focaliser *vt Mktg* to target

foi *nf* **(a)** **un texte qui fait foi** an authentic text; **la lettre doit partir avant le 29, le cachet de la poste faisant foi** the letter must be postmarked no later than the 28th **(b)** *Jur* **en foi de quoi** in witness whereof; **de bonne foi** bona fide; **de mauvaise foi** mala fide

foire *nf (trade)* fair □ *foire commerciale* trade fair; *foire du livre* book fair; *Ordinat* **foire aux questions** FAQ

foire-échantillon, foire-exposition *nf* trade fair

foncier, -ère 1 *adj (impôt, rente)* land
2 *nm* land tax □ *foncier bâti* landed property; *foncier non bâti* land for development

fonction *nf* **(a)** *(poste)* office; *(titre)* job title; **entrer en fonction, prendre ses fonctions** to take up one's duties; **être en fonction** to be in office; **démettre qn de ses fonctions** to fire sb; **se démettre de ses fonctions** to resign one's post; **cela ne fait pas partie de mes fonctions** that's not part of my duties ❑ *la fonction publique* the public or civil service

(**b**) *(rôle)* function; **les fonctions de président** the functions of a chairman; **faire fonction de gérant** to act as manager ❑ *fonctions complémentaires* support activities; *Écon fonction de demande* demand function; *fonctions de direction* managerial functions; *fonctions d'encadrement* executive functions

(**c**) *Ordinat fonction de comptage de mots* word count facility; *fonction copier-coller* copy-and-paste facility; *fonction couper-coller* cut-and-paste facility; *fonction multimédia* multimedia facility; *fonction de répétition* repeat function; *fonction de sauvegarde* save function

(**d**) **en fonction de** according to, with respect to; **les salaires offerts seront en fonction de l'expérience** the salary offered will be commensurate with experience

> ❝
>
> François Bayrou ne supporte plus le soutien affiché de l'ancien ministre centriste Jacques Barrot à Jacques Chirac. Le président de l'UDF a donc décidé de sévir. Il veut convoquer, avant le congrès de décembre, une commission de discipline pour **démettre** Barrot **de ses fonctions** de président de la fédération UDF de Haute-Loire.
>
> ❞

fonctionnaire *nmf* government official, *Br* civil servant; **haut fonctionnaire** senior government official or *Br* civil servant; **petit fonctionnaire** junior government official or *Br* civil servant; **un fonctionnaire de l'Union européenne** a European Union official

fonctionnariser *vt* to make part of the civil service

fonctionnarisme *nm* officialdom, red tape

fonctionnel, -elle *adj (organisation, responsabilité)* functional

fonctionnement *nm* (**a**) *(d'une entreprise)* running, functioning; **pour le bon fonctionnement du service, il est préférable que tous les employés aient les mêmes horaires** if the department is to run efficiently it is preferable that all staff have the same working hours (**b**) *(d'une machine)* running, working; **en (bon) état de fonctionnement** in (good) working order ❑ *fonctionnement manuel* manual operation (**c**) *Ordinat fonctionnement en réseau* networking

fonctionner *vi* (**a**) *(entreprise)* to run, to function; **cette entreprise fonctionne 24 heures** sur 24 the company functions round the clock (**b**) *(machine)* to run, to work (**c**) *Ordinat* to run

fondateur, -trice *nm,f* founder

fondé, -e de pouvoir *nm,f Jur* agent *(holding power of attorney)*; *(mandant)* proxy; *(directeur de banque)* manager with signing authority; **il est le fondé de pouvoir (de)** he holds power of attorney (for)

fonder *vt* (**a**) *(commerce)* to start, to set up; **fondé en 1928** established in 1928 (**b**) *Fin (dette)* to fund

fondre **1** *vt (compagnies)* to amalgamate, to merge

2 se fondre *vpr (compagnies)* to amalgamate, to merge

fonds 1 *nm* (**a**) *(organisme)* fund ❑ *Fonds européen de coopération monétaire* European Monetary Cooperation Fund; *Fonds européen de développement* European Development Fund; *Fonds européen de développement régional* European Regional Development Fund; *Fonds monétaire international* International Monetary Fund; *Fonds national de l'emploi* = French national employment fund; *Fonds national de garantie des salaires* national guarantee fund for the payment of salaries; *Fonds social européen* European Social Fund

(**b**) *(capital)* fund, funds ❑ *fonds d'amortissement* sinking fund; *fonds de capital-risque maison* captive fund; *fonds commun de placement* investment fund, mutual fund; *fonds commun de placement d'entreprise* company investment fund or mutual fund; *fonds commun de placement géré* managed investment fund or mutual fund; *fonds commun de placement à risques* venture capital trust; *fonds de consolidation* umbrella fund; *fonds dédié* captive fund; *fonds de dotation* endowment fund; *fonds à faible frais d'entrée* low-load fund; *fonds fédéraux* federal funds; *fonds en fidéicommis* trust fund; *fonds de garantie (d'un emprunt)* guarantee fund; *fonds géré* managed fund; *fonds à gestion indicielle* index or tracker fund; *fonds d'indemnisation* compensation fund; *fonds indiciel* index or tracker fund; *fonds d'investissement* investment fund; *fonds monétaire* money market fund; *Can fonds de parité* equalization fund; *fonds de pension(s)* pension fund; *fonds de placement sur le marché monétaire* money market fund; *fonds de prévoyance* contingency fund; *fonds de réserve* reserve fund; *fonds de retraite maison ou d'entreprise ou de groupe* occupational pension scheme; *fonds pour risques bancaires généraux* fund for general banking risks; *fonds de roulement* working capital, revolving fund; *fonds de roulement net* net working capital; *fonds de stabilisation des* *changes* exchange equalization account (**c**) *Bourse* stocks, securities □ ***fonds consolidés*** consolidated stock *or* annuities, *Br* consols (**d**) ***fonds de commerce*** goodwill; ***fonds (de commerce) à vendre*** business for sale *(as a going concern)* **2** *nmpl (ressources)* funds; **réunir des fonds** to raise funds; **je n'ai pas les fonds suffisants pour ouvrir un magasin** I don't have the (necessary) funds *or* capital to open a shop; **rentrer dans ses fonds** to get one's money back; **être en fonds** to be in funds; **faire** *ou* **fournir les fonds de qch** to put up the funds for sth; **mettre des fonds dans qch** to invest money in sth □ ***fonds de caisse*** cash in hand; ***fonds communs*** pool; ***fonds disponibles*** liquid assets, available funds; ***fonds d'État*** Government stocks; ***fonds liquides*** liquid assets, available funds; ***fonds off-shore*** offshore funds; ***fonds perdus*** annuity; **placer son argent à fonds perdus** to purchase an annuity; ***fonds propres*** shareholders' equity, equity (capital); ***fonds publics*** public funds; ***fonds social*** company funds

> 66
> La France ne fait que s'engager dans une voie ouverte par les États-Unis et le Canada. Les employeurs ne vont d'ailleurs pas être les seuls à payer. Le **fonds d'indemnisation** des victimes de l'amiante portera sa contribution.
> 99

fonte *nf Ordinat* font □ ***fonte de caractère*** character font; ***fonte écran*** screen font; ***fonte imprimante*** printer font; ***fonte reconnue optiquement*** OCR font

force *nf* (**a**) *Assur (puissance)* **(cas de) force majeure** force majeure, act of God; ***forces économiques*** economic forces; *Écon* **les forces du marché** market forces; ***forces productives*** productive forces; ***force de vente*** sales force (**b**) *Mktg (d'un produit, d'un concurrent)* strength □ ***forces, faiblesses, opportunités et menaces*** strengths, weaknesses, opportunities and threats, SWOT

forcé, -e *adj (emprunt)* forced, compulsory; *(cours, vente)* forced; *(liquidation)* compulsory

forclore *vt Jur* to foreclose

forclusion *nf Jur* foreclosure

forfait *nm (contrat)* fixed-rate contract; *(somme)* lump sum; **être au forfait** to be taxed on estimated income; **travailler au forfait** to work for a flat rate; **payer qn au forfait** to pay sb a flat rate; **verser un forfait** to pay a fixed sum □ ***forfait de port*** carriage forward

forfaitaire *adj (prix)* inclusive, fixed; *(indemnités)* basic

forfaitairement *adv* in a lump sum; *(facturer)* in a lump sum, in one amount

formalité *nf* formality □ ***formalités administratives*** administrative formalities; ***formalités douanières*** customs formalities

format *nm* (**a**) *(dimension)* format, size; **papier format A4** A4 paper; **grand format** large-sized; **petit format** small-sized □ ***format de poche*** pocket size (**b**) *Ordinat* format □ ***format ASCII*** ASCII format; ***format de fichier*** file format; ***format graphique*** image format; ***format d'impression*** print format; ***format de page*** page format *or* layout; ***format de papier*** paper format; ***format de paragraphe*** paragraph format; ***format TIFF*** TIFF

formatage *nm Ordinat* formatting

formater *vt Ordinat* to format; **non formaté** unformatted

formation *nf* (**a**) *(constitution)* development, formation; **la formation des prix sur le marché** market pricing; **en voie de formation** *(société)* developing □ ***formation de réserves*** building up of reserves (**b**) *(des employés)* training; **suivre une formation** to get training, to take a training course; **être en formation** to be undergoing training □ ***formation continue*** = day release or night school education for employees provided by companies; ***formation en entreprise*** in-house training; ***formation interne*** in-house training; ***formation du personnel*** staff training; ***formation pratique*** practical training, hands-on training; ***formation professionnelle*** professional *or* vocational training; ***formation sur le tas*** on-the-job training

forme *nf* **en bonne et due forme** *(reçu, contrat)* bona fide; **faire une réclamation en bonne et due forme** to use the correct procedure in making a complaint

> 66
> Quant à l'initiative gouvernementale de validation des acquis professionnels par un diplôme **en bonne et due forme**, elle est encore balbutiante.
> 99

former *vt* (**a**) *(constituer)* to form (**b**) *(donner une formation à)* to train; **former qn à qch** to train sb in sth; **formé à la gestion** trained in management techniques

formulaire *nm (imprimé)* form; **remplir un formulaire** to fill in *or* out a form □ ***formulaire d'appréciation*** customer satisfaction questionnaire; ***formulaire d'assurance*** insurance form; ***formulaire de candidature*** (job) application form; ***formulaire de demande*** application form; ***formulaire de demande d'indemnité*** claim form; ***formulaire de détaxe*** tax-free shopping form; *Ordinat* ***formulaire de saisie*** input form; *Bourse* ***formule de transfert*** transfer form

formule nf (**a**) (texte) (d'un contrat) wording ❑ **formule de politesse** (au début d'une lettre) standard opening; (à la fin) standard ending (**b**) (méthode) option; **nous avons aussi une formule à 1000 euros** we also have a 1,000 euro option ❑ **formules de crédit** credit options; **formules de paiement** methods of payment; **formules de remboursement** repayment options (**c**) Admin (formulaire) form; **remplir une formule** to fill in or out a form ❑ **formule de chèque** cheque form, Am blank check; **formule de demande de crédit** credit application form; **formule d'effet de commerce** form for bill of exchange; **formule de réponse** reply form; **formule de soumission** tender form

formuler vt (réclamation, demande) to formulate; (acte) to draw up

fort, -e adj (**a**) (important) (hausse, baisse) sharp, big; (perte, consommation, demande) heavy; (somme) large; **avoir un fort salaire** to have a high salary, to be highly paid; **payer le prix fort pour qch** to pay the full price for sth; **les prix sont en forte hausse** prices are soaring ❑ Mktg **forte remise** deep discount (**b**) Fin (devise) strong

fortement adv (rémunéré) highly; (taxé) heavily

fortune nf fortune, wealth; **faire fortune** to make one's fortune; **avoir une fortune personnelle** to have independent means

forum de discussion nm (sur l'Internet) forum

fourchette nf (écart) bracket, range; **une fourchette de 10 à 20 pour cent** a 10 to 20 percent band; **une fourchette comprise entre 1000 et 1500 euros** prices ranging from 1,000 to 1,500 euros ❑ Bourse **fourchette de cotation** trading range; Bourse **fourchette de cours de clôture** closing range; Bourse **fourchette de cours d'ouverture** opening range; **fourchette d'imposition** tax bracket; **fourchette de prix** price bracket or range; **fourchette de salaire** wage bracket; **fourchette de taux** rate band

fourni, -e adj (approvisionné) **bien/mal fourni** well-/poorly-stocked

fournir 1 vt (**a**) (approvisionner) to supply; **fournir qch à qn** to supply sb with sth; **ce magasin nous fournit tout le matériel de bureau** this shop supplies us with all our office equipment (**b**) Fin (lettre de crédit) to issue (**sur** on); (traite, chèque) to draw (**sur** on); **fournir qch en nantissement** to lodge sth as collateral
2 vi **fournir aux dépenses** to contribute to the expenses
3 se fournir vpr **il se fournit chez nous** he is a customer of ours, he's one of our customers

fournisseur, -euse 1 adj **les pays fournisseurs de la France** the countries that supply France (with goods)
2 nm,f supplier; **quel est votre fournisseur habituel?** who's your usual supplier? ❑ Fin **fournisseur en capitaux** funder, supplier of capital; **fournisseur exclusif** sole supplier; **fournisseur principal** prime supplier; **fournisseur secondaire** secondary supplier
3 nm ❑ Ordinat **fournisseur d'accès** access provider; **fournisseur d'accès Internet** Internet access provider; **fournisseur de contenu** content provider; **fournisseur de services Internet** Internet service provider

fourniture nf (**a**) (action) supplying, providing (**b**) **fournitures** (choses fournies) supplies ❑ **fournitures de bureau** office supplies

foyer nm (domicile) home, household; Mktg household unit ❑ Fin **foyer fiscal** household (as a tax unit)

❝

La question de savoir comment partager l'effort dans le cas où plusieurs salaires coexistent dans le **foyer fiscal** n'est pas tout à fait résolue; mais il y a des solutions. L'idée: récupérer la totalité par petits bouts ou casser le système du **foyer fiscal** en individualisant l'imposition.

❞

fraction nf fraction; **par 10 euros ou fraction de 10 euros** for each 10 euros or fraction thereof ❑ Compta **fraction imposable** part subject to tax; **fraction d'intérêt** interest accrued

fractionnement nm dividing up; (des paiements) spreading (out); Bourse, Fin (des actions) split

fractionner vt to divide up; (paiements) to spread (out); Bourse, Fin (actions) to split

fragmentation nf fragmentation ❑ **fragmentation de disque** disk fragmentation

frais nmpl expenses, costs; Jur costs; **tous frais payés** all expenses paid; **tous frais déduits** all expenses deducted; Jur **être condamné aux frais** to be ordered to pay costs; **sans frais** free of charge; (sur une lettre de change) no expenses; **à grands frais** at great cost, expensively; **à peu de frais** at little cost, inexpensively; **couvrir ses frais, rentrer dans ses frais** to get one's money back, to recover one's expenses, to break even; **menus frais** petty or incidental expenses ❑ **frais d'abonnement** standing charges; **frais accessoires** incidental costs or expenses; Compta **frais accumulés** accrued expenses; **frais d'achat** purchase costs; **frais d'adhésion** membership charge; **frais administratifs, frais d'administration** administrative or administration costs; (en échange d'un service) handling charge; **frais d'administration générale** Br general overheads, Am general overhead; **frais d'agence** agency fee; **frais**

d'amortissement amortization or depreciation charges; **frais d'annulation** cancellation charge or fee; **frais d'assurance** insurance charges; **frais bancaires, frais de banque** bank charges; **frais de Bourse** transaction costs; **frais de bureau** office expenses; **frais de camionnage** haulage charges; **frais de commercialisation** marketing costs; **frais commerciaux** selling costs; **frais de constitution** *(de société)* start-up costs; *(de compte)* set-up fee; **frais consulaires** consular fees; **frais de courtage** brokerage, broker's commission; *Compta* **frais cumulés** accrued expenses; **frais de déchargement** landing charges; **frais dégressifs** decreasing costs; **frais de déménagement** relocation expenses; **frais de déplacement** travelling or travel expenses; **frais de désistement** rupture of contract costs; **frais différés** deferred charges; **frais directs** direct costs; **frais de distribution** distribution costs; **frais divers** sundry charges, sundries; **frais de dossier** administrative costs; **frais de douane** customs charges or duties; **frais d'emballage** packaging costs; **frais d'encaissement** collection charges or fees; **frais à l'entrée** *(d'un navire)* inward charges; **frais d'entrée** *(d'une sicav)* front-end or front-load fee; *Bourse* commission on purchase of shares; **frais d'entreposage** storage or warehouse or warehousing charges; **frais d'entretien** *(de matériel)* maintenance costs or expenses; **frais d'envoi** carriage costs; **frais d'établissement** start-up costs, preliminary costs; **frais d'expédition** shipping costs or charges; **frais d'expertise** consultancy fees; **frais d'exploitation** operating costs or expenses; **frais extraordinaires** extraordinary expenses; **frais de fabrication** manufacturing or production costs; **frais facturables** chargeable expenses; **frais financiers** interest charges, financial costs; **frais fixes** fixed charges; **frais de fonctionnement** operating costs; **frais généraux** *Br* overheads, *Am* overhead; **frais généraux de fabrication** factory *Br* overheads or *Am* overhead; **frais généraux et frais de gestion** general and administrative expenses; **frais de gestion** administration costs; **frais d'inscription** membership fee; **frais d'installation** initial expenses; **frais d'interurbain** toll; **frais judiciaires, frais de justice** legal costs or expenses; **frais de lancement** set-up or start-up costs; **frais de liquidation** closing-down costs; **frais de livraison** delivery costs or charges; **frais de magasinage** warehouse or storage charges; **frais de main-d'œuvre** labour costs; **frais de manutention** handling charges or costs; **frais de pilotage** pilotage; **frais de port** *(de marchandises)* carriage (costs), carrying charges; *(de lettres, de colis)* postal charges; **frais de portage** porterage; **frais de port et d'emballage** postage and packing; **frais portuaires** port charges;

frais de premier établissement initial expenditure; **frais professionnels** business charges or expenses; **frais de publicité** advertising costs; **frais de recouvrement** collection charges; **frais de représentation** expense account, entertainment allowance; **frais de réservation** booking fee, reservation charge; **frais de séjour** living expenses; **frais semi-variables** mixed costs; **frais de sortie** exit charges, back-end load; **frais de tenue de compte** account charges; *(de compte bancaire)* bank charges; **frais de transfert** transfer fee; **frais de transport** transport or shipping charges, carriage; **frais de trésorerie** finance costs; **frais variables** variable costs

franc[1] *nm* franc; **pièce de cinq francs** five-franc coin □ *Anciennement* **franc belge** Belgian franc; *Anciennement* **franc français** French franc; *Anciennement* **franc lourd** new franc; *Anciennement* **franc luxembourgeois** Luxembourg franc; *Anciennement* **franc or** gold franc; **franc suisse** Swiss franc; *Anciennement* **franc symbolique** *(lors d'un rachat d'entreprise)* nominal sum; **franc vert** green franc

franc[2], **franche** *adj* (a) *(gratuit)* free; **franc d'avaries** free of average; **franc de douane** duty paid; **franc de tout droit** duty-free, free of duty; **franc d'impôts** tax-exempt; **franc de port** carriage paid (b) *(complet)* complete, whole; **huit jours francs** eight clear days

franchisage *nm* franchising

franchise *nf* (a) *(exonération)* exemption; **importer** *ou* **faire entrer qch en franchise** to import sth duty-free; **en franchise d'impôt** exempt from tax, tax free; **(en) franchise postale** postage paid □ *franchise de bagages* luggage or baggage allowance; **franchise fiscale** tax exemption (b) *(d'assurance)* *Br* excess, *Am* deductible □ *franchise d'assurance* *Br* excess or *Am* deductible clause (c) *(de commerce)* franchise; **ouvrir un magasin en franchise** to open a franchise

franchisé, -e *nm,f* franchisee

franchiser *vt* to franchise

franchiseur, -euse *nm,f* franchisor

franco *adv* franco (de port) free, carriage paid; **livré franco** delivered free; **livraison franco frontière française** delivered free as far as the French frontier; **franco (à) domicile** delivery free, carriage paid; **échantillons franco sur demande** free samples available on request; **franco allège** free over side; **franco (de ou à) bord** free on board; **franco de douane** free of customs duty; **franco d'emballage** free of packing charges; **franco frontière** free at frontier; **franco gare** free on rail; **franco gare de réception** free on rail; **franco long du bord** free alongside ship; **franco long du navire** free alongside ship; **franco long du quai** free alongside ship, free on quay or wharf; **franco de port et d'emballage** postage and packing paid; **franco rendu** free delivered; **franco de tous frais** free of all charges; **franco transporteur** free carrier; **franco wagon** free on rail

frappe nf (dactylographie) typing; (sur un clavier d'ordinateur) keying □ Ordinat **frappe en continu** type-ahead; Ordinat **frappe au kilomètre** continuous input; Ordinat **frappe de touche** keystroke

frapper vt (affecter) to hit; **la crise frappe surtout les PME** small businesses are particularly badly hit by the crisis; **frapper un produit d'une taxe** to impose a duty on a product

fraude nf fraud; **faire entrer** ou **introduire qch en fraude** to smuggle sth through customs □ **fraude civile** fraud, wilful misrepresentation; **fraude douanière** illegal importation, smuggling; **fraude fiscale** tax fraud, tax evasion

> ❝
> Les documents produits révèlent une énorme **fraude fiscale** qui peut être évaluée à 1 milliard de francs de l'époque (5 milliards de baths) au détriment de la Thaïlande. Bouygues-Thaï a cumulé toutes les conditions pour que son chantier soit hyper bénéficiaire tout en parvenant à se déclarer déficitaire afin d'échapper à l'impôt de l'administration thaïlandaise : fausses factures, travail clandestin, montages fiscaux …
> ❞

frauder vt (État, douane) to defraud; **frauder le fisc** to evade tax

fraudeur, -euse nm,f (a) (escroc) defrauder (b) (à la douane) smuggler (c) (du fisc) tax dodger

frauduleusement adv fraudulently

frauduleux, -euse adj fraudulent

FRBG nm (abrév **fonds pour risques bancaires généraux**) FGBR

free-lance 1 adj (travail) freelance
  2 nmf (personne) freelancer, freelance
  3 nm (travail) freelance work; **elle travaille en free-lance** she's a freelancer, she works on a freelance basis

freeware nm Ordinat freeware; **freewares** freeware programs

freinage nm (de l'inflation) curbing; (de production) cutting back; (des importations, des salaires) reduction

freiner vt (inflation) to curb; (production) to cut back; (importations, salaires) to reduce

freinte nf wastage, loss in volume or weight (during transit or manufacture)

fréquence nf frequency □ Mktg **fréquence ab-**

solue absolute frequency; Mktg **fréquence d'achat** purchase frequency; Ordinat **fréquence d'horloge** clock speed; **fréquence de rafraîchissement** refresh rate; **fréquence d'utilisation** usage frequency

fret nm (a) (cargaison) freight; **prendre du fret** to take in freight □ **fret aérien** airfreight, air cargo; **fret d'aller** outward freight; **fret payé** freight paid; **fret au poids** freight by weight; **fret de retour** homeward freight, return freight; **fret de sortie** outward freight (b) (location) chartering; **donner un navire à fret** to freight (out) a ship; **prendre un navire à fret** to charter a ship (c) (coût du transport) freight (charges); **payer le fret** to pay the freight (charges) □ **fret forfaitaire** lump-sum freight (charges)

fréter vt (navire) to freight (out); (voiture, camion) to hire; (avion) to charter

fréteur nm shipowner; **fréteur et affréteur** owner and charterer

fric nm Fam cash

frontale nf Mktg shelf facing

front-office nm Banque front office

fructifier vi (capital) to yield a profit; **faire fructifier son argent** to make one's money yield a profit

> ❝
> Le rôle de ces investisseurs en private equity (capital privé), qui interviennent loin des traditionnelles salles de marché, est de choisir au cœur du tissu économique français les meilleurs placements. Leurs clients? Les fameux fonds de pension qui sont chargés de **faire fructifier** au mieux les intérêts de la plupart des retraités anglo-saxons et qui, en moyenne, investissent entre 5 et 8% de leurs gigantesques portefeuilles dans les entreprises non cotées, soit l'équivalent de 1450 milliards de francs (221 milliards d'euros) en 2000.
> ❞

FS nm (abrév **franc suisse**) Swiss franc

FSE nm (abrév **Fonds social européen**) ESF

FTP nm Ordinat (abrév **File Transfer Protocol**) FTP

fuite nf **fuite des capitaux** flight of capital; **fuite des cerveaux** brain drain

> ❝
> La lutte de la banque centrale de Russie contre les **fuites de capitaux** porte ses fruits – ces fuites ont été réduites de moitié – et devrait se concrétiser par l'adoption d'une réglementation bancaire cohérente et efficace.
> ❞

fusion *nf* (**a**) *(de sociétés)* merger; **opérer une fusion** to merge; **fusions et acquisitions** mergers and acquisitions (**b**) *Ordinat* **fusion de fichiers** file merge

> **"**
>
> Envisagée depuis bientôt un an, la **fusion** entre les deux opérateurs scandinaves a été officialisée: le suédois Telia achète le finlandais Sonera par échange d'actions.

Cette opération de près de 10 milliards d'euros est le premier rapprochement entre deux anciens monopoles nationalisés.
> **"**

fusionnement *nm (de sociétés)* merger, amalgamation

fusionner 1 *vt* (**a**) *(sociétés)* to merge, to amalgamate (**b**) *Ordinat (fichiers)* to merge
2 *vi (sociétés)* to merge, to amalgamate

Gg

G7 *nm* (*abrév* **Groupe des Sept**) G7

G8 *nm* (*abrév* **Groupe des Huit**) G8

gadget publicitaire *nm* advertising gimmick

gage *nm* security; *(chez le prêteur sur gages)* pledge; **laisser qch en gage** to leave sth as security; **mettre qch en gage** to pawn *or* pledge sth; **rester en gage** to remain as security ❑ *Jur* **gage mobilier** mortgage over assets *or* over property

gagé, -e *adj* (*emprunt*) guaranteed, secured

gager *vt* (*emprunt*) to guarantee, to secure

gagiste *nmf* secured creditor, pledgee

gagner 1 *vt* (**a**) (*acquérir*) to earn; **gagner de l'argent** to earn money; **gagner dix mille euros par mois** to earn ten thousand euros a month; **il gagne bien sa vie** he earns a good salary, he makes good money (**b**) (*part de marché*) to capture; **nos concurrents gagnent du terrain** our competitors are gaining ground (**c**) *Bourse* to gain; **l'indice a gagné deux points** the index has gained two points

2 *vi* to increase; **notre production gagne en qualité** the quality of our product is improving

gain *nm* (**a**) (*profit*) gain, profit; **les gains et les pertes** the profits and the losses ❑ *Compta* **gain latent** unrealized gain (**b**) (*rémunération*) gains, earnings ❑ *gains invisibles* invisible earnings (**c**) (*économie*) saving; **un gain de temps** a saving of time ❑ *gains de productivité* productivity gains

> ❝
> Tirant les leçons de l'échec du WAP, les opérateurs insistent désormais sur les **gains de productivité** induits plus que sur la technologie elle-même.
> ❞

galerie marchande *nf* shopping centre, *Am* shopping mall

gamme *nf* (*de produits*) range, series; (*de prix*) range; **étendre sa gamme de produits** to widen one's product range; **bas de gamme** (*de qualité inférieure*) bottom-of-the-range; (*peu prestigieux*) downmarket; **haut de gamme** (*de qualité supérieure*) top-of-the-range; (*prestigieux*) upmarket; **milieu de gamme** middle-of-the-range; **un ordinateur d'entrée de gamme** an entry-level computer

garant, -e *nm,f* guarantor, warrantor, surety; **se porter garant pour qn, servir de garant à qn** to stand surety *or* guarantor for sb; **se porter garant de qch** to stand guarantor for sth, to guarantee sth

> ❝
> Par ailleurs, il est trop tôt pour exclure totalement l'idée que France Télécom – c'était la principale inquiétude de la Bourse – soit obligé de **se porter garant** d'une partie des 6,5 milliards de dettes de l'opérateur allemand.
> ❞

garantie *nf* (**a**) (*d'un produit*) guarantee, warranty; **sous garantie** under guarantee ❑ *garantie illimitée* unlimited warranty; *garantie légale* legal guarantee; *garantie limitée* limited warranty; *garantie pièces et main-d'œuvre* parts and labour warranty; *garantie prolongée* extended warranty; *garantie de remboursement intégral* money-back guarantee; *garantie totale* full warranty; *Assur* full cover

(**b**) *Fin* (*d'une émission d'actions, d'un contrat*) underwriting; (*d'un emprunt*) backing, security ❑ *garantie accessoire* collateral security; *garantie bancaire* bank guarantee; *garantie de bonne exécution, garantie de bonne fin* performance bond; *garantie contractuelle* contractual guarantee; *garantie conventionnelle* contractual cover; *garantie de crédit acheteur* buyer credit guarantee; *garantie de crédit à l'exportation* export credit guarantee; *garantie d'exécution* contract bond; *garantie hypothécaire* mortgage security; *garantie offre* bid bond

(**c**) (*de l'exécution d'un contrat*) guarantee, pledge; (*d'un paiement*) security, guarantee

garantir *vt* (**a**) (*produit, service*) to guarantee; **nous garantissons un délai de livraison d'une semaine** we guarantee delivery within seven days; **cet ordinateur est garanti cinq ans** this computer is guaranteed for five years

(**b**) (*dette*) to guarantee; **garantir le paiement d'une dette** to guarantee a debt

(**c**) *Fin* (*émission d'actions, contrat*) to underwrite; (*emprunt*) to back, to secure

(**d**) *Assur* to cover; **son assurance le garantit contre le vol** his insurance covers him against theft

garde *nf* **déposer qch en garde** to place sth in

safe custody ❑ **garde en dépôt** safe custody

garde-barrière *nm Ordinat* firewall

Garde des Sceaux *nm* French Minister of Justice

gare *nf (de chemin de fer)* (*Br* railway *or Am* railroad) station ❑ **gare d'arrivée** *(pour passagers)* arrival station; *(pour marchandises)* receiving station; **gare de départ** *(pour passagers)* departure station; **gare expéditrice, gare d'expédition** forwarding station, dispatch station; **gare de marchandises** goods station, *Am* freight depot; **gare maritime** harbour station; **gare routière** *(pour passagers)* bus station; *(de camions)* road haulage depot

gaspillage *nm* waste

gaspiller *vt* to waste

gâter *vt* to spoil, to damage

GATT *nm Écon (abrév* **General Agreement on Tariffs and Trade**) GATT

géant, -e 1 *adj (carton, paquet)* giant-size

2 *nm* giant; **un géant de l'informatique** a computer giant; **un géant de l'électroménager** a major player *or* giant in the household appliances business

> **"**
> Le **géant** de l'informatique a jeté un froid sur les places boursières en annonçant des résultats pour son premier trimestre fiscal 2002 largement en recul par rapport à l'an dernier et en deçà des prévisions des analystes financiers.
> **"**

gel *nm Fin (blocage)* freeze ❑ **gel des crédits** credit freeze; **gel des prix** price freeze; **gel des salaires** wage freeze

gelé, -e *adj Fin (bloqué)* frozen

geler *vt Fin (bloquer)* to freeze

générateur, -trice 1 *adj* **un secteur générateur d'emplois/de capitaux** a job-creation/capital growth sector

2 *nm Ordinat* generator ❑ **générateur de caractères** character generator

génération *nf Ordinat* generation

générer *vt* (**a**) *(profits, emplois)* to generate (**b**) *Ordinat* **généré par ordinateur** computer-generated

générique *adj (publicité, marché, produit)* generic

génie *nm* engineering ❑ **génie civil** civil engineering; **génie électronique** electronic engineering; **génie industriel** industrial engineering

géodémographique *adj* geodemographic

géomarketing *nm* geomarketing

gérance *nf* (**a**) *(fonction)* management; **donner**

la gérance d'un commerce à qn to appoint sb manager of a business ❑ *Fin* **gérance de portefeuille** portfolio management (**b**) *(période)* managership; **pendant sa gérance** during his time as manager

gérant, -e *nm,f* manager ❑ **gérant de fonds** fund manager; **gérant d'immeubles** property manager; **gérant de portefeuille** portfolio manager

gérer *vt (entreprise)* to manage, to run; *(finances)* to manage

gestion *nf* (**a**) *Fin (d'une entreprise, de travaux, des comptes)* management; *(d'affaires)* conduct; **mauvaise gestion** bad management, mismanagement ❑ **gestion actif-passif** assets and liabilities management; **gestion administrative** administration; **gestion des affaires** business management; **gestion autonome** independent administration; **gestion budgétaire** budgetary control; **gestion de capital** asset management; **gestion cellulaire** divisional management; **gestion du circuit de distribution** distribution channel management; **gestion commerciale** business management; **gestion de la communication** communications management; **gestion de comptes-clés** key-account management; **gestion par consensus** consensus management; **gestion des coûts** cost management; **gestion des crises** crisis management; **gestion par département** divisional management; **gestion de la distribution physique** physical distribution management; **gestion de division** divisional management; **gestion des effectifs** manpower management; **gestion de l'emploi** manpower management; **gestion d'entreprise** business management; **gestion financière** financial management, financial administration; **gestion de fonds** fund management; **gestion indicielle** index fund management; **gestion indicielle répliquée** passive management; **gestion intégrée** centralized management; **gestion de l'inventaire** inventory management; **gestion des investissements** investment management; **gestion logistique** logistics management; **gestion du marketing** marketing management; **gestion de la marque** brand management; **gestion des matières, gestion du matériel** materials management; **gestion mercatique** marketing management; **gestion par objectifs** management by objectives; **gestion des opérations** operations management; **gestion paritaire, gestion participative** participative management; **gestion passive** passive management; **gestion du personnel** personnel management; **gestion de portefeuille** portfolio management; **gestion prévisionnelle** budgetary control; **gestion de la production** production control; **gestion de produits** product management; **gestion de projets** project management; **gestion qualité** quality control, quality management; **gestion de la qualité globale** *ou* **totale** total quality management; **gestion des ressources** resource management; **gestion des ressources humaines** human resource management; **gestion des risques** risk management; **gestion des sociétés** business management; **gestion des stocks** inventory management, inventory *or* stock control; **gestion stratégique** strategic management; **gestion du temps de travail** time management; **gestion de trésorerie** cash (flow) management; **gestion zéro-défaut** total quality management

(**b**) *Ordinat* management ◻ **gestion de bases de données** database management; **gestion de données** data management; **gestion des fichiers** file management; **gestion de parc réseau** network management; **gestion des systèmes d'information** informations systems management

gestionnaire 1 *adj* administrative

2 *nmf (dirigeant)* administrator; *(d'un service)* manager ◻ **gestionnaire de fonds** fund manager; **gestionnaire de portefeuille** portfolio manager; **gestionnaire de(s) stock(s)** *Br* stock controller, *Am* inventory controller

3 *Ordinat* manager, driver ◻ **gestionnaire de fichiers** file manager; **gestionnaire de fichiers et de répertoires** filer; **gestionnaire de mémoire** memory manager; **gestionnaire de projets** project management package; **gestionnaire de réseau** network manager, network driver

GFU *nm Tél (abrév* **groupe fermé d'utilisateurs)** CUG

GIE *nm (abrév* **groupement d'intérêt économique)** economic interest group

GIF *nm Ordinat (abrév* **Graphics Interchange Format)** GIF

gigaoctet *nm Ordinat* gigabyte

gisement *nm* ◻ **gisement de clientèle** pool of customers, potential customer pool; **gisement pétrolifère** oil field

glissement *nm (d'une monnaie, des salaires)* slide

glisser 1 *nm Ordinat* **glisser d'icônes** icon drag

2 *vi* (**a**) *Ordinat* **faire glisser** *(pointeur)* to drag (**b**) *(salaires, monnaie)* to slip, to slide; **le pays glisse vers la crise économique** the country is heading towards recession

glisser-lâcher *nm Ordinat* drag and drop ◻ **glisser-lâcher d'icônes** icon drag and drop

global, -e *adj (montant, somme, budget, demande)* total; *(résultat)* overall; *(production)* aggregate; *(revenu)* gross; **le budget global de publicité excède les coûts de production** the total publicity budget is higher than the produc-

tion costs; **la société propose une offre globale à ses clients** the company offers a complete package to all its clients

globalisation *nf* globalization

globaliser *vt* to globalize

GM *nm (abrév* **grand magasin)** department store

GMS *nfpl (abrév* **grandes et moyennes surfaces)** large and medium commercial outlets

❝
Lentement mais sûrement, hypermarchés et supermarchés accentuent leur poids sur la distribution de carburants. À ce titre, l'année qui vient de se terminer leur a permis de franchir un cap symbolique, les **GMS** vendant désormais plus d'un litre d'essence sur deux.
❞

Go *nm Ordinat (abrév* **gigaoctet)** GB

gondole *nf Mktg (présentoir)* gondola

gonfler *vt (prix, chiffres)* to inflate; *(résultats)* to exaggerate

gopher *nm Ordinat* gopher

gouffre financier *nm Mktg (produit)* financial disaster, dog

goulot d'étranglement *nm* bottleneck

❝
BMW a été en effet l'un des premiers à négocier des horaires flexibles, autour d'une moyenne hebdomadaire de 35 heures. De quoi éliminer les **goulots d'étranglement** et répondre à la demande avec des lignes de production qui tournent à plus de 110% de leur capacité!
❞

gouvernement *nm* government

gouverner *vt* to govern, to rule

gouverneur *nm* governor

GPAO *nf Ordinat (abrév* **gestion de production assistée par ordinateur)** computer-aided production management

GPRS *nm Tél (abrév* **General Packet Radio Service)** GPRS

GPS *nm Tél (abrév* **Global Positioning System)** GPS

grâce *nf (dans un délai)* grace; **une semaine de grâce** a week's grace

gracieux, -euse *adj* free (of charge); **à titre gracieux** gratis, free of charge

grade *nm Admin* rank; **monter en grade** to be promoted; **il a été promu au grade de chef de service** he was promoted to head of department

grand, -e adj big ▫ **grande distribution** mass distribution; **grand magasin** department store; Ordinat **grand réseau** wide area network; **grandes et moyennes surfaces** large and medium commercial outlets; **grande surface** superstore, hypermarket; **grande surface spécialisée** specialist superstore

grand-livre nm Compta ledger; **porter qch au grand-livre** to enter an item in the ledger ▫ **grand-livre d'achats** purchase ledger; **grand-livre auxiliaire** subledger; **grand-livre de la dette publique** Br National Debt register, Am public debt register; **grand-livre général** nominal ledger; **grand-livre de ventes** sales ledger

graphe nm graph, chart ▫ **graphe en ligne** line chart

grapheur nm Ordinat graphics package

graphique nm (schéma) graph, chart; **tracer un graphique** to plot a graph; **faire le graphique de qch** to chart sth; Ordinat **graphiques** graphics ▫ **graphique d'acheminement** flow (process) chart; **graphique des activités** activity chart; **graphique à** ou **en barres** ou **bâtons** bar chart; **graphique circulaire** pie chart; **graphique en colonnes** bar chart; **graphique d'évolution** flow chart; **graphique financier** financial chart; **graphique de gestion** management chart, business graphic; **graphiques de présentation** presentation graphics; **graphique à secteurs** pie chart; **graphique à tuyaux d'orgue** bar chart; **graphique de type camembert** pie chart; **graphique de type lignes** line chart

graphisme nm Ordinat graphics ▫ **graphisme en couleur** colour graphics

graphiste nmf graphic artist

grappe nf Ordinat (de terminaux) cluster

gras 1 adj bold
2 nm bold; **en gras** in bold

graticiel, gratuiciel nm Ordinat freeware

gratification nf (pourboire) gratuity, tip; (prime) bonus

gratis 1 adj free
2 adv gratis, free (of charge)

gratuit, -e adj (échantillon, livraison) free; (crédit) interest-free; **à titre gratuit** free of charge

gratuitement adv free of charge

graver vt Ordinat (CD) to burn

graveur de CD-ROM nm Ordinat CD-ROM burner or writer

gré nm **au gré de l'acheteur** at buyer's option; **au gré du vendeur** at seller's option; **le bail est renouvelable au gré du locataire** the tenant has the option of renewing the lease; **de gré à**

gré by (mutual) agreement; **vendre de gré à gré** to sell by private contract, to sell privately

greffe nm Fin (de société par actions) registry

greffier nm Fin registrar

grève nf strike, walkout; **faire grève** to (be on) strike; **lancer un ordre de grève** to call a strike; **se mettre en grève** to (go on) strike ▫ **grève d'avertissement** token strike; **grève bouchon** disruptive strike; **grève générale** general strike; **grève perlée** go-slow; **grève avec préavis** official strike; **grève sauvage** unofficial strike, wildcat strike; **grève de solidarité** sympathy strike; **grève surprise** lightning strike, walkout; **grève symbolique** token strike; **grève sur le tas** sit-down strike, sit-in; **grève tournante** staggered strike; **grève du zèle** work to rule; **faire la grève du zèle** to work to rule

> "
> Venus des hôpitaux de Metz-Thionvile, Forbach (Moselle) et Briey (Meurthe-et-Moselle), des infirmiers anesthésistes et de blocs opératoires, ont brûlé leurs diplômes devant la préfecture de Metz. En **grève perlée** depuis le 16 janvier, ils s'estiment lésés par les négociations salariales et remettent en cause les "quotas d'accès aux grades supérieurs".
> "

grever vt (**a**) (pouvoir d'achat) to restrict; **grevé d'impôts** weighed down or burdened with tax (**b**) Jur (propriété) to mortgage

gréviste nmf striker

GRH nf (abrév **gestion des ressources humaines**) HRM

griffe nf (marque) label

grille nf grid ▫ **grille d'analyse par fonction** functional analysis chart; **grille d'avancement** career structure; **grille de gestion** managerial grid; Compta **grille d'imputation** table of account codes; **grille indiciaire** salary structure or scale; **grille de rémunération** salary scale; Ordinat **grille de saisie** input grid; **grille des salaires** salary scale

gros, grosse 1 adj (bénéfices, somme) big; **la plus grosse partie de nos affaires** the bulk of our business; **le nouvel impôt touchera principalement les gros salaires** the new tax will have the biggest effect on top wage earners; **on a réussi à récupérer plusieurs de leurs gros clients depuis leur faillite** we have managed to pick up some of their biggest customers since they went bankrupt; **un gros consommateur** a heavy user ▫ Ordinat **gros système** mainframe
2 adv **gagner gros** to make a lot (of money); **cette opération m'a rapporté gros** the deal

made me a lot of money *or* a healthy profit
3 *nm* (**a**) *(majorité)* bulk; **le gros de la cargai-son** the bulk of the cargo (**b**) *(en commerce)* wholesale (trade); **acheter en gros** to buy wholesale; *(en grosse quantité)* to buy in bulk; **vendre en gros** to sell wholesale; **faire le gros et le détail** to sell wholesale and retail; **de gros** *(prix, commerce)* wholesale
4 *nf* **grosse** *(douze douzaines)* gross

grossiste *nmf* wholesaler, wholesale dealer
❑ **grossiste importateur** import wholesaler

grossoyer *vt Jur (document)* to engross

grouillot *nm Bourse* messenger

groupage *nm (de paquets)* bulking; *(de com-mandes, d'envois, de livraisons)* groupage, consolidation

groupe *nm* group; *Bourse* crowd ❑ **groupe d'assurance** insurance group; *Mktg* **groupe cible** target group; *Écon* **groupe de consom-mateurs** consumer group; **groupe de détail-lants** retailer co-operative; *Ordinat* **groupe de discussion** discussion group; **groupe d'étude** study group; **groupe financier** financial group; **groupe hôtelier** hotel group; **Groupe des Huit** Group of Eight; **groupe industriel** industrial group; **groupe d'intervention** task force; **groupe de médias** media group; **groupe multi-média** multimedia group; *Ordinat* **groupe de nouvelles** newsgroup; **groupe de presse** press group, newspaper group; **groupe de pression** pressure group; **groupe de prix** price bracket; *Mktg* **groupe de prospects** prospect pool; **groupe de référence** reference group; **Groupe des Sept** Group of Seven; **groupe socio-éco-nomique** socio-economic group; **groupe stra-tégique** strategic group; *Mktg* **groupe suivi** control group; *Mktg* **groupe témoin** control group; *Mktg* **groupe test de consommateurs** consumer test group; **groupe de travail** work-ing party, work group; **groupe volontaire** vol-untary group

groupé, -e *adj (commandes, envois, livraisons)* grouped, consolidated

groupe-cible *nm Mktg* target group

groupement *nm* (**a**) *(association)* group ❑ **groupement d'achat** purchasing group, bulk buying group; *Écon* **groupement de consom-mateurs** consumer group; **groupement de dé-fense des consommateurs** consumers' association; **groupement de détaillants** re-tailers' group; **groupement européen d'inté-rêt économique** European Economic Interest Group; **groupement à l'export** consolidation

for export; **groupement financier** financial pool; **groupement d'intérêt économique** eco-nomic interest group; **groupement profes-sionnel** trade association; **groupement syndical** *Br* trade *or Am* labor union bloc (**b**) *(action) (d'intérêts, de ressources)* pooling

grouper *vt (intérêts, ressources)* to pool; *(pa-quets)* to bulk; *(commandes, envois, livraisons)* to group, to consolidate

groupeur *nm* consolidator ❑ **groupeur de fret aérien** air freight consolidator; **groupeur ma-ritime** maritime freight consolidator; **groupeur routier** road haulage consolidator

GSM *nm Tél (abrév* **global system for mobile communications**) *(système)* GSM; *Belg (télé-phone portable)* mobile (phone)

GSS *nf (abrév* **grande surface spécialisée**) spe-cialist superstore

> **❝**
> La quasi totalité des secteurs représentés dans les galeries commerciales ont profité du courant d'achat de décembre. Les ventes des grandes surfaces à dominante alimen-taire ont progressé de 5,3% et celles de **GSS** de 6,2%.
> **❞**

guelte *nf* commission, percentage *(on sales)*

guérilla *nf Mktg* guerilla attack

guerre *nf* **guerre économique** economic war-fare; **guerre des prix, guerre des tarifs** price war

guichet *nm Banque* position, window, *Am* wick-et; **payer au guichet** to pay at the counter; **gui-chet fermé** *(sur panneau)* position closed ❑ *Banque* **guichet automatique (de banque)** *Br* cash dispenser, cashpoint, *Am* ATM; **gui-chet d'enregistrement** check-in desk; **guichet de réservation** booking office

guichetier, -ère *nm,f (dans une banque)* coun-ter clerk, teller

guide *nm* guide ❑ *Mktg* **guide d'entretien** in-terview guide; **guide des rues** (street) direct-ory; **guide de l'utilisateur** instruction manual, user manual

guillemet *nm* quotation mark, *Br* inverted comma; **entre guillemets** in quotation marks, *Br* in inverted commas ❑ **guillemets fermants** closing quotes; **guillemets ouvrants** opening quotes; **guillemets simples** single quotes

gulden *nm Anciennement* guilder

Hh

habiliter *vt Jur* to empower, to entitle; **être habilité (à faire qch)** to be empowered *or* entitled (to do sth); **habilité à signer** *(employé de banque)* authorized to sign

habillage *nm* **(a)** *(de marchandises)* packaging ❏ *habillage transparent* blister pack **(b)** *Compta (d'un bilan)* window-dressing **(c)** *Ordinat* text wrap

habiller *vt* **(a)** *(marchandises)* to package **(b)** *Compta (bilan)* to window-dress

habitant, -e *nm,f* inhabitant; **par habitant** per person, per capita

habitude *nf* habit ❏ *Mktg* **habitudes d'achat** purchasing habits

hacker *nm Ordinat* hacker

halle *nf* (covered) market

harcèlement sexuel *nm* sexual harassment

hardware *nm Ordinat* hardware

hausse *nf* **(a)** *(des prix, du chômage, du coût de la vie)* increase, rise **(de** in); **une hausse de quatre pour cent** a four percent rise; **accuser une hausse** to show a rise; **être à la hausse** to go up; **les prix ont subi une forte hausse** prices have increased sharply, prices have shot up ❏ *hausse de prix déguisée* hidden price increase

(b) *Bourse (des cours, des valeurs)* rise; **à la hausse** *(tendance, marché, position)* bullish; **en hausse** *(actions)* rising; **jouer** *ou* **spéculer à la hausse** to speculate on a rising market, to bull the market; **pousser les actions à la hausse** to bull the market; **les cours sont orientés à la hausse** there is an upward trend in share prices; **provoquer une hausse factice** to rig the market

hausser 1 *vt (prix, taux de l'escompte)* to raise, to put up; **le prix a été haussé de dix pour cent** the price has gone up by ten percent

2 *vi* to rise; **faire hausser les prix** to force up prices

haussier, -ère *Bourse* **1** *adj (marché)* bullish

2 *nm,f* bull

haut, -e 1 *adj* **(a)** *(prix, salaire)* high; **de haute vitesse** high-speed ❏ *Ordinat* **haute densité** high density; **haute résolution** high resolution;

2 *nm* **(a)** *Mktg (du marché)* high end, top end **(b)** *Compta* **haut de bilan** *(fonds propres)* shareholders' funds

hauteur *nf* **participer à hauteur de 30 pour cent** to contribute up to 30 percent; **un actionnaire à hauteur de cinq pour cent** a shareholder with five percent of the shares

haut-parleur *nm* speaker

HD *adj Ordinat* (*abrév* **haute densité**) HD

hebdomadaire 1 *adj* weekly

2 *nm (journal, revue)* weekly

hébergement *nm Ordinat (de site Web)* hosting; **hébergement de sites Web** Web hosting

héberger *nm Ordinat (site Web)* to host

hébergeur *nm Ordinat (de site Web)* host

HEC *nfpl* (*abrév* **Hautes Études Commerciales**) = prestigious business school in France

héritage *nm* inheritance

hériter 1 *vt* to inherit

2 hériter de *vt ind* to inherit

hétérogène *adj (marché, produits)* heterogeneous

héritier, -ère *nm,f* heir, *f* heiress

heure *nf* hour; **engager qn à l'heure** to employ sb by the hour; **être payé à l'heure** to be paid by the hour; **il est payé 55 euros (de) l'heure** he is paid 55 euros an hour ❏ *heures d'affluence* rush hour; *heure d'arrivée* arrival time, time of arrival; *heures de bureau* office *or* business hours; *Bourse* **heures de cotation** trading time; *heures creuses* off-peak hours; *heure de départ* departure time, time of departure; *heure d'embarquement* boarding time; *heure de fermeture (d'un magasin)* closing time; *(d'une usine, d'un bureau)* finishing time; *heure machine* machine hour; *heures d'ouverture, heures ouvrables (d'un magasin, d'une agence)* opening hours; *(d'un bureau)* business *or* office hours; *heures de pointe* rush hour; *heures de réception (dans une administration)* opening hours; *heures supplémentaires ou Fam* **sup'** overtime; **faire des heures supplémentaires** to do *or* work overtime; *heures de travail* working hours

> **"**
>
> Ironie du sort, ceux qui font encore des **heures sup'** n'en touchent plus aussitôt les dividendes: avec l'annualisation du temps de travail, les entreprises en effet préfèrent souvent attendre la fin de l'année pour calculer les heures et payer.
>
> **"**

hexadécimal, -e *adj* hexadecimal

hiérarchie *nf* hierarchy

hiérarchique *adj (organisation, structure)* hierarchical; **c'est mon supérieur hiérarchique** he's my immediate superior; **passer par la voie hiérarchique** to go through the official channels

hiérarchisation *nf* (**a**) *(structure)* hierarchical structure (**b**) *(de tâches)* prioritization

hiérarchiser *vt* (**a**) *(personnel)* to grade; **hiérarchiser les salaires** to create a salary structure (**b**) *(tâches)* to prioritize

histogramme *nm* histogram

historique *nm Ordinat (de document)* log; *(dans un logiciel de navigation)* history list

holding *nm Fin* holding company

homme *nm* **homme d'affaires** businessman; **homme de métier** expert, professional

homogène *adj (marché, produits)* homogeneous

homologation *nf (d'un prototype)* approval, certification; *(d'un prix)* authorization; *(d'un accord, d'une décision, d'un document)* ratification; *(d'un testament)* probate

homologue *nmf* counterpart

> "
> L'opérateur de télécommunications finlandais et son **homologue** suédois s'unissent en vue de former le premier groupe nordique du secteur, avec 9 millions d'euros de chiffre d'affaires.
> "

homologué, -e *adj (prix)* authorized

homologuer *vt (prototype)* to approve, to certify; *(prix)* to authorize; *(accord, décision)* to ratify; *(document)* to obtain legal ratification of; *(testament)* to probate

honneur *nm* **faire honneur à qch** *(facture, chèque, traite)* to honour, to meet; **nous avons l'honneur de vous informer que...** we are pleased to inform you that...

honorable *adj (entreprise)* of high standing

honoraire **1** *adj (membre)* honorary
   2 *nmpl* **honoraires** fee, fees

honorer *vt (facture, chèque, traite)* to honour, to meet; *(signature)* to honour

horaire **1** *adj* hourly
   2 *nm* timetable, schedule; *(d'un magasin)* opening hours □ **horaires à la carte, horaires flexibles** flexitime; **horaires de travail** working hours

horizontal, -e *adj (concentration, intégration)* horizontal

horloge *nf* **horloge horodatrice** time clock;

horloge pointeuse time clock; *Ordinat* **horloge du système** system clock; *Ordinat* **horloge en temps réel** real-time clock

horodaté, -e *adj* stamped with time and date

horodateur *nm* time and date stamp

hors *prép* **hors bilan** off-balance sheet; **hors Bourse** after hours; **hors budget** not included in the budget; **hors commerce** not for sale to the general public; **hors pointe** off-peak; **hors saison** off-season; **hors série** made-to-order, custom-built; **hors taxe** exclusive of tax; *(à la douane)* duty-free; **hors TVA** net of VAT

hors-cote *Bourse* **1** *adj* unlisted
   2 *nm* unlisted securities market

hors-média(s) **1** *adj* below-the-line
   2 *nm* below-the-line advertising

> "
> A l'inverse, le **hors-médias** comme les documents adressés (32% des citations) ou les imprimés sans adresse (56,9%) dont l'exposition est forte, restent très consultés avant l'achat des produits alimentaires, de vêtements ou de l'électroménager.
> "

hôtel *nm* (**a**) *(pour l'hébergement)* hotel □ **hôtel d'affaires** business hotel (**b**) *(bâtiment) Admin* **hôtel des impôts** tax office; **l'Hôtel de la Monnaie** ≃ the Royal Mint; **hôtel des ventes** sale room, auction room; **hôtel de ville** town hall

hôtelier, -ère **1** *adj* **l'industrie hôtelière** the hotel industry *or* trade
   2 *nm,f* hotel keeper, hotelier

hôtellerie *nf* **l'hôtellerie** the hotel trade

HT *adj (abrév* **hors taxe***)* exclusive of tax

HTML *nm Ordinat (abrév* **HyperText Markup Language***)* HTML

HTTP *nm Ordinat (abrév* **HyperText Transfer Protocol***)* HTTP

hub *nm Ordinat* hub

huissier *nm* bailiff

huit **1** *adj* **dans huit jours** in a week's time
   2 *nm* **lundi en huit** a week next Monday

hyperinflation *nf* hyperinflation

hyperlien *nm Ordinat* hyperlink

hypermarché *nm* hypermarket

hypermédia *nm Ordinat* hypermedia

hypersegmentation *nf Mktg* hypersegmentation

hypertexte *adj & nm Ordinat* hypertext

hypertoile *nf Ordinat* World Wide Web

hypothécable *adj* mortgageable

hypothécaire *adj* mortgage

hypothèque *nf* mortgage; **franc** *ou* **libre d'hy-**

pothèques unmortgaged; **prendre une hypothèque** to take out a mortgage; **emprunter sur hypothèque** to borrow on mortgage; **avoir une hypothèque sur une maison** to have one's house mortgaged; **purger une hypothèque** to pay off or clear or redeem a mortgage; **propriété grevée d'hypothèques** encumbered estate ◻ *hypothèque générale* blanket mortgage; *hypothèque de premier rang* first legal mortgage

hypothéquer vt (a) *(propriété, titres)* to mortgage (b) *(dette)* to secure by mortgage

Ii

IA *nf Ordinat (abrév* **intelligence artificielle)** AI

icône *nf Ordinat* icon

idée de vente *nf Mktg* selling idea

identificateur *nm* (**a**) *Ordinat* identifier (**b**) *Mktg* **identificateur de marque** brand identifier

identification *nf* (**a**) *Ordinat* **identification de l'utilisateur** user identification, user ID (**b**) *Mktg* **identification des besoins** need identification; *Mktg* **identification de marque** brand recognition

identité *nf* (**a**) *Admin* identity (**b**) *Mktg* **identité graphique** logo; **identité de marque** brand identity

IEP *nm (abrév* **Institut d'études politiques)** = higher education institute of political science

IGP *nf (abrév* **indication géographique protégée)** = designation of a product which guarantees its authentic origin and gives the name protected status

illégal, -e *adj* illegal, unlawful

illégalement *adv* illegally, unlawfully

illégalité *nf (caractère)* illegality, unlawfulness; *(acte)* unlawful act

illicite *adj (profits, transactions)* illicit

illimité, -e *adj (crédit, responsabilité)* unlimited

illisible *adj Ordinat* unreadable

îlot *nm Mktg* gondola □ **îlot de vente** (display) stand, island

ILV *nf Mktg (abrév* **information sur le lieu de vente)** point-of-sale information

image *nf* image □ *Ordinat* **image cliquable** clickable image; *Mktg* **images à compléter** picture completion; *Ordinat* **image digitalisée** digitized image; *Mktg* **image de l'entreprise** corporate image; *Compta* **image fidèle** true and fair view; **image institutionnelle** corporate image; **image de marque** *Mktg (d'un produit)* brand image; *(d'une société)* corporate image *or* identity; **image de produit** product image; **images de synthèse** computer-generated images, CGI

imbattable *adj (prix)* unbeatable

IME *(abrév* **Institut monétaire européen)** EMI

imitation *nf (d'un produit)* imitation; *(d'une signature, d'un billet)* forgery □ **imitation de marque** brand imitation

imiter *vt (produit)* to imitate; *(signature, billet)* to forge

immatériel, -elle *adj Fin (actif, valeurs)* intangible

immatriculation *nf (d'un document, d'une société, des marchandises)* registration

immatricule *nf* registration

immatriculer *vt (document, société, marchandises)* to register; **être immatriculé à la Sécurité Sociale** to have a Social Security number

immeuble 1 *adj Jur* real, fixed
  2 *nm* (**a**) *(bâtiment)* building □ **immeuble de bureaux** office block; **immeuble (à usage) commercial** business premises; **immeuble locatif, immeuble de rapport** rental property (**b**) *Jur* real estate, landed property, *Am* realty; **placer son argent en immeubles** to invest in property

immobilier, -ère 1 *adj Br* property, *Am* real-estate
  2 *nm* **l'immobilier** the *Br* property *or Am* real-estate business; **l'immobilier d'entreprise** the commercial *Br* property *or Am* real-estate business; **l'immobilier locatif** the *Br* rental property *or Am* real-estate rental business

immobilisation *nf* (**a**) *Compta* asset; **immobilisations** fixed *or* capital assets; **faire de grosses immobilisations** to carry heavy stocks □ **immobilisations de capitaux** capital assets, financial assets; **immobilisations corporelles** tangible (fixed) assets; **immobilisations financières** long-term investments; **immobilisations incorporelles** intangible (fixed) assets; **immobilisations non financières** physical fixed assets
  (**b**) *Jur* conversion into real estate
  (**c**) *Fin (de capital)* locking up, tying up, immobilization; *(d'actif, de valeurs)* freezing

immobilisé, -e *adj Fin (capital)* locked-up, tied up, immobilized; *(actif, valeurs)* frozen

immobiliser *vt* (**a**) *Jur* to convert into real estate (**b**) *Fin (capital)* to lock up, to tie up, to immobilize; *(actif, valeurs)* to freeze

immunité *nf* immunity □ **immunité fiscale** immunity from taxation

impact *nm (d'une publicité, d'une campagne)* impact

impartir *vt* (**a**) *Jur (droit, faveur)* to grant (**à** to) (**b**) *(délai)* to grant, to allow; **faire qch dans les délais impartis** to do sth to schedule

impasse *nf* (**a**) *(blocage)* impasse, deadlock; **être** *ou* **se trouver dans une impasse** to be at a dead end; **sortir de l'impasse** to break the deadlock; **les négociations sont dans l'impasse** the talks have reached a deadlock *or* are deadlocked (**b**) *Fin* **impasse budgétaire** budget deficit

impayé, -e 1 *adj* (**a**) *(dette, facture)* unpaid, outstanding; *(comptes)* unsettled (**b**) *(effet)* dishonoured
  2 *nm* outstanding payment

impératif, -ive 1 *adj Jur (loi, disposition)* mandatory
  2 *nm (exigence)* requirement; **nous avons des impératifs de livraison** we have delivery dates that we must respect

implantation *nf* (**a**) *(installation)* setting up, establishment; *(d'un produit sur le marché)* establishment (**b**) *(d'une usine, du matériel)* layout ❏ *implantation fonctionnelle* functional layout

implanter 1 *vt (magasin, rayon)* to locate; *(établir)* to set up; **implanter un produit sur le marché** to establish a product on the market; **cette entreprise japonaise a plusieurs usines implantées en France** this Japanese company has a number of factories located in France
  2 s'implanter *vpr (magasin, rayon)* to be located, to be sited; *(être établi)* to be set up; **l'usine s'est finalement implantée au Mexique** the factory was eventually sited in Mexico; **s'implanter sur un marché** to establish oneself in a market

implication *nf Mktg (du consommateur)* involvement

impliquer *vt (dépenses)* to entail

import *nm* import ❏ *Ordinat* **import de données** data import

importable *adj* importable

importance *nf* (**a**) *(d'une somme, d'un projet)* size; **une usine de moyenne importance** a medium-sized factory (**b**) *(des dégâts)* extent (**c**) *(d'une société)* position, standing

important, -e *adj* (**a**) *(grand)* large, considerable; **nous ne pouvons pas vous accorder un crédit plus important** we cannot allow you credit beyond this limit (**b**) *(sérieux) (rôle, négociations)* important

importateur, -trice 1 *adj* importing; **les pays importateurs de pétrole** the oil-importing countries
  2 *nm,f* importer; **c'est l'importateur exclusif de cette marque pour la France** they are the sole French importers of this brand

importation *nf* (**a**) *(activité)* importing ❏ *importation en franchise* duty-free importation; *importation temporaire* temporary importation (**b**) *(produit)* import ❏ *importation grise* grey import; *importations invisibles* invisible imports; *importations parallèles* parallel imports; *importations visibles* visible imports

importer *vt* (**a**) *(marchandises)* to import; **importer des marchandises des États-Unis en France** to import goods from the United States into France (**b**) *Ordinat* to import (**depuis** from)

import-export *nf* import-export; **travailler dans l'import-export** to work in the import-export business

imposable *adj (personne, marchandises)* taxable, liable to tax; *(revenu)* taxable; *(propriété)* rateable

imposé, -e 1 *adj (soumis à l'impôt)* taxed; **être lourdement imposé** to be heavily taxed
  2 *nm,f* taxpayer; *(d'une propriété)* ratepayer

imposer *vt (personne, marchandises)* to tax; *(propriété)* to levy a rate on; **imposer des droits sur qch** to tax sth

imposition *nf* taxation ❏ *imposition en cascade* cascade taxation; *imposition forfaitaire* basic-rate taxation; *imposition progressive* progressive taxation; *imposition à la source* taxation at source

impôt *nm* tax; **avant impôt** before tax; **après impôt** after tax; **frapper qch d'un impôt** to tax sth; **payer 5000 euros d'impôts** to pay 5,000 euros in tax(es) ▫ *impôt sur les bénéfices* profit tax; *Bourse impôt de Bourse* transaction tax; *impôt sur le capital* capital tax; *impôt sur le chiffre d'affaires* turnover tax; *impôt à la consommation* output tax; *impôt dégressif* sliding scale taxation, degressive taxation; *impôt déguisé* hidden tax; *impôt différé* deferred tax; *impôt direct* direct tax; *impôt sur les dividendes* dividend tax; *impôt sur les donations et les successions* gift and inheritance tax; *impôt extraordinaire* emergency tax; *impôt foncier* land tax, property tax; *impôt sur les gains exceptionnels* windfall tax; *impôt indiciaire* wealth tax; *impôt indirect* indirect tax; *impôts locaux* *Br* council tax, *Am* local taxes; *impôt de luxe* tax on luxury goods; *impôt sur la masse salariale* payroll tax; *impôt négatif sur le revenu* negative income tax; *impôt sur les plus-values* capital gains tax; *impôt à la production* input tax; *impôt progressif* progressive tax; *(sur le revenu)* graduated income tax; *impôt de quotité* coefficient tax; *impôt retenu à la base ou à la source* tax deducted at source, *Br* pay-as-you-earn tax, *Am* pay-as-you-go tax; *impôt sur le revenu* income tax; *impôt sur les sociétés* *Br* corporation tax, *Am* corporation income tax; *impôt de solidarité sur la fortune* wealth tax; *impôt du timbre* stamp duty; *impôt sur le travail* payroll tax

imprescriptibilité *nf Jur* imprescriptibility, indefeasibility

imprescriptible *adj Jur* imprescriptible, indefeasible

impression *nf Ordinat* printing ▫ *impression en arrière-plan* background (mode) printing; *impression couleur* colour printing; *impression écran* screen dump; *impression ombrée* shadow printing; *impression en qualité brouillon* draft quality printing

imprévu, -e 1 *adj (dépenses)* unforeseen, incidental
　2 *nm* hidden expense, contingency

imprimante *nf Ordinat* printer ▫ *imprimante à bulles* bubble-jet printer; *imprimante couleur* colour printer; *imprimante feuille à feuille* sheet-fed printer; *imprimante à impact* impact printer; *imprimante à jet d'encre* ink-jet printer; *imprimante (à) laser* laser printer; *imprimante à marguerite* daisy-wheel printer; *imprimante matricielle* dot-matrix printer; *imprimante parallèle* parallel printer; *imprimante PostScript®* PostScript® printer; *imprimante série* serial printer; *imprimante thermique, imprimante thermoélectrique* thermal printer

imprimé, -e 1 *adj* printed
　2 *nm* (a) *(formulaire)* form; **remplir un imprimé** to fill in *or* out a form ▫ *imprimé publicitaire* ad-

vertising leaflet, publicity handout (**b**) **imprimés** *(journaux, prospectus)* printed matter

imprimer *Ordinat* **1** *vt* to print (out)
　2 s'imprimer *vpr (document)* to print

imprimerie *nf (établissement)* printing works, printer's; *(industrie)* printing industry ▫ *l'Imprimerie nationale* = the French government stationery office, *Br* ≃ HMSO, *Am* ≃ the Government Printing Office

imprimeur *nm (industriel)* printer; *(ouvrier)* printer, print worker

improductif, -ive *adj (capitaux)* unproductive, idle

impulsion *nf Tél* pulse

imputable *adj Fin* chargeable (**sur** to)

imputation *nf Fin (des dépenses)* charge, charging; **l'imputation d'un paiement** the appropriation of money *(to the payment of a debt)*; **imputation à** charge to; **imputation d'une somme au crédit/débit d'un compte** crediting/debiting an amount to an account ▫ *imputations budgétaires* budget allocations; *imputation des charges* cost allocation

imputer *vt* (**a**) *(déduire)* to deduct; **imputer qch sur qch** to deduct sth from sth (**b**) *Fin (attribuer)* to charge sth to sth; **imputer des frais à un compte** to charge expenses to an account; **imputer une somme à un budget** to allocate a sum to a budget

inabordable *adj (prix, produit, service)* unaffordable

inacceptation *nf (d'un effet)* non-acceptance

inacquitté *adj (effet)* unreceipted

inactif, -ive 1 *adj* (**a**) *Écon (personne)* non-working; **la population inactive** the non-working population (**b**) *(marché)* sluggish, dull (**c**) *(fonds)* unemployed, idle
　2 *nm,f Écon* **un inactif** a person without paid employment; **les inactifs** the non-working population

inactivité *nf (du marché)* sluggishness, dullness

inamical, -e *adj (offre publique d'achat)* hostile

inamovible *adj (fonctionnaire, poste)* permanent

inanimé, -e *adj (marché)* sluggish, dull

INC *nm (abrév* **Institut national de la consommation***)* = French consumer research organization

incapacité *nf* (**a**) *(incompétence)* **incapacité (professionnelle)** inefficiency, incompetence (**b**) *(invalidité)* disablement, disability ▫ *incapacité de travail* (industrial) disablement (**c**) *(impossibilité)* incapacity, inability; **nous sommes dans l'incapacité de satisfaire à votre demande** we are unable to meet your request

incertain nm Bourse, Fin variable exchange; **coter** ou **donner l'incertain** to quote on the exchange rate

incessibilité nf Fin non-transferability

incessible adj Fin non-transferable

inchangé, -e adj unchanged

incidence nf impact, repercussions; **l'incidence d'un impôt sur le consommateur** the impact of a tax on the consumer; **l'incidence des salaires sur les prix de revient** the impact or repercussions of wage levels on production costs

incitation nf incentive ❑ **incitation à l'achat** buying incentive; **incitation fiscale** tax incentive; **incitation à la vente** sales incentive

inclure vt (**a**) (dans un courrier) to enclose (**dans** with or in) (**b**) (comprendre) to include (**c**) Jur (clause) to insert

inclus, -e adj (**a**) (dans un courrier) enclosed; **le chèque est inclus dans la lettre** the cheque is enclosed with the letter (**b**) (compris) inclusive, included; **jusqu'au 30 juin inclus** until 30 June inclusive, Am through 30 June; **les frais de main-d'œuvre pour l'installation sont inclus dans la somme totale à payer** the labour costs for installation are included in the total sum due

inclusivement adv inclusively; **du vendredi au mardi inclusivement** from Friday to Tuesday inclusive, Am Friday through Tuesday; **jusqu'au 30 avril inclusivement** until 30 April inclusive, Am through 30 April

incompatibilité nf incompatibility (**avec** with)

incompatible adj incompatible (**avec** with)

incompétent, -e adj (**a**) Jur (tribunal) not competent, incompetent (**b**) (incapable) incompetent

inconvertible adj Fin inconvertible

incorporation nf Fin **incorporation des réserves au capital** capitalization of reserves

incorporel, -elle adj (actif, valeurs, biens) intangible

incoté, -e adj Bourse unquoted

incoterms nmpl incoterms

indemnisable adj entitled to compensation

indemnisation nf (**a**) (action) compensating (**b**) (paiement) compensation, indemnity

❝
Les décisions de la chambre sociale de la Cour de cassation, qui porte sur vingt-neuf affaires, permettent l'**indemnisation** intégrale des victimes de l'amiante. On ne peut que s'en féliciter.
❞

indemniser vt to compensate, to indemnify (**de** for); **indemniser totalement qn** to compensate sb in full; **indemniser qn de ses frais** to reimburse sb his/her expenses, to pay sb's expenses

indemnitaire 1 adj compensatory
2 nmf beneficiary of compensation

indemnité (**a**) (pour perte encourue) compensation, indemnity; (pour délai, non-livraison) penalty; **à titre d'indemnité** by way of compensation; **recevoir une indemnité** to receive compensation; **demander une indemnité** to put in a claim ❑ **indemnité en argent** cash compensation; **indemnité d'assurance** insurance money; **indemnité de clientèle** compensation for loss of custom; **indemnité compensatrice** compensation; **indemnité compensatrice de congés payés** pay in lieu of holidays; **indemnité contractuelle de départ** ou **de licenciement** golden parachute; **indemnité de départ, indemnité de licenciement** severance pay, redundancy pay, Am lay-off pay; **indemnité de retard** late payment penalty; **indemnité de rupture** severance pay; **indemnité de rupture abusive** compensation for breach of contract
(**b**) (allocation) allowance, grant ❑ **indemnité de cherté de vie** cost-of-living allowance, Br weighting; **indemnité de chômage** unemployment benefit; **indemnité complémentaire** additional allowance; **indemnité conventionnelle** contractual allowance; **indemnité de déménagement** relocation grant or allowance; **indemnité de déplacement** travel or travelling or transport allowance; **indemnité de fonction** entertainment allowance; **indemnité journalière** daily allowance; **indemnité kilométrique** ≃ mileage allowance; **indemnité de logement** accommodation allowance; **indemnité de maladie** sickness benefit; **indemnité de représentation** entertainment allowance; **indemnité de résidence** housing allowance; **indemnité de séjour** living expenses or allowance; **indemnité de transport** travel or transport allowance; **indemnité de vie chère** cost-of-living allowance, Br weighting

indépendant, -e 1 adj (travailleur) self-employed; (traducteur, journaliste, photographe) freelance
2 nm,f (travailleur) self-employed worker; (traducteur, journaliste, photographe) freelancer

indépensé, -e adj unspent

index nm Ordinat (d'une base de données) index

indexation nf Écon index-linking, indexation; **l'indexation des salaires sur les prix** the index-linking of salaries to prices

indexé, -e adj Écon index-linked, indexed

indexer vt (**a**) Écon to index-link, to index (**sur**

to) (**b**) *Ordinat (base de données)* to index

indicateur *nm* indicator ❑ *indicateurs d'alerte* economic indicators, business indicators; *indicateur clé* key indicator; *Fin indicateur (d'activité) économique* economic indicator; *indicateur de marché* market indicator; *indicateur statistique* statistical indicator; *indicateur de tendance* market indication

indicatif, -ive 1 *adj (prix)* approximate; **à titre indicatif** for information only
2 *nm* (**a**) *Tél* **indicatif (téléphonique)** *Br* dialling code, *Am* dial code ❑ *indicatif du pays* international *Br* dialling code *or Am* dial code (**b**) *Ordinat* prompt ❑ *indicatif (du) DOS* DOS prompt

indication *nf* indication; **il n'y a aucune indication de prix dans ce catalogue** there is no indication of the price in the catalogue; **sauf indication contraire** unless otherwise stated ❑ *indication d'origine, indication de provenance* place of origin

indice *nm* index ❑ *Mktg* **indice ad hoc** specific indicator; *Bourse* **indice boursier** share index; *Bourse* **l'indice CAC 40** the CAC 40 index; *Bourse* **indice composé, indice composite** composite index; *Écon* **indice corrigé des variations saisonnières** seasonally adjusted index; *Bourse* **indice des cours d'actions** share price index; *Écon* **indice du coût de la vie** cost-of-living index; *Écon* **indice de croissance** growth index; **indice de détail** retail price index; *Bourse* **l'indice Dow Jones** the Dow Jones index; *Bourse* **l'indice FTSE des 100 valeurs** the FTSE 100 share index; **indice de gros** wholesale price index; *Mktg* **indice des groupes cibles** Target Group Index; *Bourse* **l'indice Hang Seng** the Hang Seng index; *Bourse* **l'indice MidCAC** = Paris Stock Exchange index of 100 medium-range shares, ≃ MidCap index; *Bourse* **l'indice Nikkei** the Nikkei index; *Écon* **indice non-corrigé des variations saisonnières** non-seasonally adjusted index; **indice des prix** price index; **indice des prix à la consommation** consumer price index; **indice des prix de détail** retail price index; **indice des prix de gros** wholesale price index; **indice des prix et des salaires** wage and price index; **indice de profit** profit indicator; **indice de rentabilité** profitability index; *Mktg* **indice de richesse vive** consumer purchasing power index; *Bourse* **l'indice SBF** the SBF index *(broad based French Stock Exchange Index)*; *Bourse* **indice des titres** stock average; *Bourse* **indice des valeurs boursières** share index

indirect, -e *adj (coûts, vente)* indirect

indisponibilité *nf (de fonds)* unavailability, non-availability

indisponible *adj (fonds)* unavailable

individuel, -elle *adj* individual; *(fortune)* private

individuellement *adv Jur* severally; **responsables individuellement** severally liable

indivis, -e *adj Jur* undivided, joint

indivisaire *nmf Jur* joint owner

indivisément *adv Jur* jointly

indivision *nf Jur* joint possession

indu *nm* **l'indu** money not owed

induit, -e *adj (demande, investissement)* induced

industrialisation *nf* industrialization

industrialiser 1 *vt* to industrialize
2 s'industrialiser *vpr* to become industrialized; **l'agriculture s'est fortement industrialisée et a augmenté sa production** agriculture has become highly mechanized and has increased output

industrialisme *nm* industrialism

industrie *nf Écon* industry, manufacturing; **travailler dans l'industrie** to work in industry *or* in manufacturing ❑ *industrie agro-alimentaire* food-processing industry; *industrie artisanale* cottage industry; *industrie automobile* car *or* motor industry; *industrie de base* basic industry; *industrie du bâtiment* building trade *or* industry; *industrie clé* key industry; *industrie de consommation* consumer (goods) industry; *industrie en croissance rapide* growth industry; *industrie électronique* electronics industry; *industrie de fabrication* manufacturing industry; *industrie légère* light industry; *industrie des loisirs* leisure industry; *industrie lourde* heavy industry; *industrie de luxe* luxury goods industry; *industrie manufacturière* manufacturing industry; *industrie mécanique* engineering; *industrie des métaux* metal industry; *industrie nationalisée* nationalized *or* state-owned industry; *industrie de niche* niche industry; *industrie pétrochimique* petrochemical industry; *industrie pétrolière* oil *or* petroleum industry; *industrie de pointe* high-tech industry; *industrie de précision* precision industry; *industrie primaire* primary industry; *industrie secondaire* secondary industry; *industrie subventionnée* subsidized industry; *industrie de transformation* processing industry

> ❝
> En outre, l'accent est mis sur le développement d'une **industrie de pointe** proprement irlandaise, reposant sur la vente de produits et services à forte valeur ajoutée.
> ❞

industriel, -elle 1 *adj* industrial
2 *nm,f* manufacturer, industrialist

industriellement *adv* industrially

inemployé, -e *adj* unemployed, unused

inescomptable *adj Fin* undiscountable

inexact, -e *adj* incorrect, wrong

inexécuté, -e *adj (contrat)* unfulfilled; *(travaux)* not carried out

inexécution *nf (d'un contrat)* non-fulfilment; **inexécution des travaux** failure to carry out work

inexigible *adj (remboursement, dette)* irrecoverable

infecter *vt (fichier, disque)* to infect

inférieur, -e 1 *adj* (**a**) *(dans une hiérarchie)* inferior; **d'un rang inférieur** of a lower rank; **être rétrogradé à l'échelon inférieur** to be demoted to the grade below; **de qualité inférieure** inferior quality
(**b**) *(dans une comparaison)* **inférieur à** *(qualité)* inferior to; *(quantité)* less than; **les bénéfices réalisés sont inférieurs aux prédictions** the profits are lower than predicted *or* forecast; **votre paiement est inférieur de 1000 euros à la somme prévue** your payment falls short of the agreed amount by 1,000 euros
2 *nm,f* subordinate

inflation *nf* inflation; **contenir l'inflation** to contain *or* curb inflation; **le gouvernement a eu recours à l'inflation** the government resorted to inflation □ **inflation par les coûts** cost-push inflation; **inflation par la demande** demand-pull inflation; **inflation fiduciaire** inflation of the currency; **inflation galopante** galloping *or* rampant inflation; **inflation monétaire** monetary inflation; **inflation des prix** price inflation; **inflation rampante** creeping inflation; **inflation des salaires** wage inflation

inflationnisme *nm* inflationism

inflationniste 1 *adj* inflationary
2 *nmf* inflationist

infléchir 1 *vt (faire diminuer)* to cut, to reduce
2 s'infléchir *vpr (diminuer) (cours)* to fall

inflexion *nf (diminution)* reduction, fall

influenceur *nm Mktg* influencer

infographe *nmf Ordinat* graphics artist

infographie *nf Ordinat* computer graphics

infographique *adj Ordinat* graphics

infographiste *nmf Ordinat* graphics artist

informaticien, -enne *nm,f* computer scientist

information *nf* (**a**) *(renseignement)* piece of information; **informations** information; **(devoirs d')information financière** disclosure; **nous vous adressons ce catalogue à titre d'information** we are sending you this catalogue for your information □ *Mktg* **information commerciale** market intelligence; *Mktg* **information sur le lieu de vente** point-of-sale information;

informations primaires primary data; **informations secondaires** secondary data
(**b**) *Ordinat* data, information
(**c**) *Jur (enquête)* inquiry; *(instruction préparatoire)* preliminary investigation; **ouvrir une information** to set up a preliminary investigation

informatique *nf Ordinat* data processing; *(science)* computer science, information technology, IT; **elle travaille dans l'informatique** she works in computing □ **informatique d'entreprise** business data processing; **informatique de gestion** administrative data processing; **informatique individuelle** personal computing

informatisation *nf Ordinat* computerization

informatiser *vt Ordinat* to computerize

infraction *nf Jur* offence □ **infraction pénale** criminal offence

infrarouge *nm* infrared

infrastructure *nf* infrastructure

infructueux, -euse *adj (investissements)* unprofitable

ingénierie *nf* engineering; *(service)* engineering department □ *Ordinat* **ingénierie assistée par ordinateur** computer-aided engineering; *Fin* **ingénierie financière** financial engineering; **ingénierie des systèmes assistée par ordinateur** computer-aided software engineering, CASE

ingénieur *nm* engineer □ **ingénieur civil** civil engineer; **ingénieur commercial** sales engineer; **ingénieur constructeur** civil engineer; **ingénieur d'études** design engineer; **ingénieur informaticien** computer engineer; **ingénieur de méthodes** methods engineer; **ingénieur en organisation** work study engineer; **ingénieur projecteur** design engineer; **ingénieur des travaux publics** civil engineer

ingénieur-conseil *nm* engineering consultant, consultant engineer

inhibiteur *nm* inhibitor

initial, -e *adj (coût, capitaux)* initial

initialisation *nf (d'ordinateur, modem)* initialization

initialiser *vt (d'ordinateur, modem)* to initialize; **non initialisé** uninitialized

initiateur *nm* initiator

initié, -e *nm,f Bourse* insider

injecter *vt (argent, capitaux)* to inject (**dans** into); **il faudrait injecter quelques idées nouvelles dans ce projet** we need to inject a few fresh ideas into the project; **injecter des millions dans une affaire** to inject *or* pump millions into a business

"

Pendant la première vague de privatisations, entre 1986 et 1988, il n'est pas question de toucher à Renault: Georges Besse, son président récemment désigné, a été assassiné par Action directe. Surtout, la Régie est exsangue et l'Etat doit, au contraire, **injecter** 12 milliards de francs (1,83 milliards d'euros) pour la sauver.

"

injection *nf (d'argent, de capitaux)* injection (**dans** into)

innovateur, -trice 1 *adj (entreprise, procédé)* ground-breaking, innovative
2 *nm,f Mktg* innovator ◻ *innovateur continu* continuous innovator; *innovateur tardif* laggard

innovation *nf* innovation ◻ *Mktg innovation continue* continuous innovation; *innovation de produit* product innovation

innover *vi* to innovate; **c'est l'incapacité de notre entreprise à innover qui nous empêche de gagner des parts de marché** it's our inability to innovate that is preventing this company from gaining a market share

inondation *nf (du marché)* flooding

inonder *vt (marché)* to flood; **le marché des produits de luxe est inondé de contrefaçons** the luxury goods market is flooded with imitation products; **nous sommes inondés de réclamations** we have been inundated with complaints

inopérant, -e *adj Jur* inoperative

inscription *nf* (**a**) *(action) (de renseignements, d'un nom, d'une date)* writing down, noting down; *(dans un journal, un registre)* entering, recording
(**b**) *Compta (dans un livre de comptes)* entry ◻ *inscription comptable* accounting entry; *inscription sur le grand-livre* journal entry
(**c**) *(à un organisme)* registration; *inscription en ligne* on-line registration
(**d**) *Fin* scrip
(**e**) *Bourse* **inscription à la cote** quotation on the (official) list; **faire une demande d'inscription à la cote** to apply for admission to the official list, to seek a share quotation

inscrire 1 *vt (renseignements, nom, date)* to write down, to note down; *(dans un journal, un registre)* to enter, to record; **inscrire une adresse sur qch** to address sth; **inscrire une question à l'ordre du jour** to put *or* place a question on the agenda; **inscrire une dépense au budget** to include an item in the budget
2 s'inscrire *vpr* (**a**) *(sur une liste)* to register, to put one's name down; **s'inscrire au chômage** to register as unemployed
(**b**) *(faire partie de)* **s'inscrire dans** to come

within the framework of; **ces licenciements s'inscrivent dans la stratégie globale de restructuration de l'entreprise** these redundancies are in keeping with *or* are part of the overall restructuring policy of the company
(**c**) *Bourse* **s'inscrire en baisse** to fall; **s'inscrire en hausse** to rise; **les valeurs industrielles s'inscrivent en baisse de 13 points à la clôture** industrial shares are closing 13 points down

inscrit, -e *adj Bourse* **inscrit à la cote officielle** listed; **non inscrite** unlisted

INSEE *nm (abrév* **Institut national de la statistique et des études économiques**) = French national institute of statistics and information about the economy

insérer *vt* (**a**) *(inclure)* to insert; **insérer une clause dans un contrat** to insert a clause in an agreement; **insérer une annonce dans un journal** to put an advertisement in a newspaper
(**b**) *Ordinat* to insert

insertion *nf* (**a**) *(dans la presse)* advertisement; **tarif des insertions** advertising rates ◻ *insertion publicitaire* advertisement (**b**) *(intégration)* integration; **l'insertion professionnelle des jeunes est de plus en plus tardive** it is taking longer and longer for young people to enter the job market ◻ *insertion sociale* social integration (**c**) *Ordinat* insertion ◻ *insertion de caractère* character insert

insolvabilité *nf* insolvency

insolvable *adj* insolvent

inspecter *vt* to inspect, to examine

inspecteur, -trice *nm,f* inspector; *(dans un magasin)* supervisor; *(dans une usine)* foreman ◻ *inspecteur des contributions directes* tax inspector; *inspecteur des contributions indirectes* customs and excise official; *inspecteur des douanes* customs inspector; *Inspecteur des Finances* ≃ general auditor *(of the Treasury)*; *inspecteur du fisc* tax inspector; *inspecteur général* inspector general; *inspecteur des impôts* tax inspector; *inspecteur du travail* factory inspector; *inspecteur de la TVA* VAT inspector, VAT man

inspection *nf* inspection, examination; **faire l'inspection de qch** to inspect sth, to examine sth ◻ *inspection du travail* factory inspection

instabilité *nf (du marché, du change, des prix)* instability

instable *adj (marché, change, prix)* instable

installation *nf* (**a**) *(d'une machine)* installation, setting up; *(d'un logiciel)* installation; *(d'une usine, d'un atelier)* fitting out, equipping (**b**) installation; **installations** *(d'un atelier)* fittings ◻ *installations électriques* electrical fittings *or* equipment; *installation frigorifique* refrigeration plant; *installations portuaires* port installations; **installations techniques** plant and machinery; **installations touristiques** tourist facilities

installer vt (machine) to install, to set up; (logiciel) to install; (usine, atelier) to fit out, to equip

instance nf (a) (organisme) authority □ **instances communautaires** EC authorities; **instances économiques** economic authorities (b) Jur (legal) (proceedings) (c) **en instance** (dossier, affaire) pending; (courrier) ready to go out

institut nm (organisme) institute □ **Institut d'études politiques** = higher education institute of political science; **institut monétaire** lender of last resort; **Institut monétaire européen** European Monetary Institute; **Institut national de la consommation** = French consumer research organization; **Institut national de la statistique et des études économiques** = French national institute of statistics and information about the economy; **institut de sondage** polling company; **Institut universitaire de technologie** = vocational higher education college

institution nf (a) (création) institution, establishment; (d'une loi) introduction (b) (organisme) institution □ **institution financière** financial institution

institutionnel, -elle 1 adj institutional **2** nmpl institutional investors

"
Le leader mondial de la restauration collective, qui réalise la moitié de son chiffre d'affaires outre-Atlantique, ne compte que 5% d'**institutionnels** américains à son capital. Un handicap qu'une cotation à New York et l'amélioration de la notoriété qu'elle implique peuvent tenter de limiter.
"

instruction nf (a) (ordre) instruction; **instructions** (mode d'emploi) instructions; **conformément aux instructions** as directed, according to instructions; **nous attendons vos instructions** we await your instructions □ **instructions permanentes** standard operating procedure (b) (circulaire) (official) memo, circular (c) Ordinat instruction

instruire vt (a) (informer) **instruire qn de qch** to inform sb of sth (b) Jur **instruire un dossier** to set up a preliminary enquiry

instrument nm (a) (document) instrument; Jur (legal) instrument □ **instrument de commerce** instrument of commerce; **instrument de couverture** hedging instrument; **instrument de crédit** instrument of credit; **instrument financier** financial instrument; **instrument financier à terme** financial future; **instrument négociable** negotiable instrument; **instrument de négociation** trading instru-

ment; **instrument de placement** investment instrument

(b) (moyen d'évaluation) tool; **c'est un instrument d'analyse de l'inflation** it's a tool for analysing inflation □ **instrument de vente** sales tool

insuffisance nf insufficiency □ **insuffisance de capitaux** insufficient capital; **insuffisance d'espèces** cash shortage; **insuffisance de personnel** staff shortage; **insuffisance de provision** insufficient funds (to meet cheque); **insuffisance de ressources** insufficient resources

insuffisant, -e adj insufficient; **nous avons des effectifs insuffisants** we're understaffed, our workforce is too small; **c'est insuffisant pour ouvrir un compte** it's not enough to open an account with

intégral, -e adj complete; **la somme intégrale de vos dépenses s'élève à 800 euros** your expenses amount to 800 euros

intégralement adv completely, in full; **rembourser intégralement une somme** to repay a sum in full; **intégralement libéré, intégralement versé** (capital) fully paid-up

intégration nf Écon integration □ **intégration en amont** backward integration; **intégration ascendante** backward integration; **intégration en aval** forward integration; **intégration descendante** forward integration; **intégration économique** economic integration; **intégration globale** full consolidation; **intégration horizontale** horizontal integration; **intégration verticale** vertical integration

intégré, -e adj Ordinat (fax, modem) integrated

intelligence marketing nf marketing intelligence

intenter vt Jur **intenter un procès à** ou **contre qn** to institute proceedings against sb; **intenter une action contre qn** to bring an action against sb

intention d'achat nf Mktg intention to buy

interactif, -ive adj Ordinat interactive

interactivité nf Ordinat interactivity

interbancaire adj interbank

interdiction nf ban □ **interdiction de commerce** trade ban; **interdiction d'exportation** ou **d'exporter** export ban; **interdiction d'importation** ou **d'importer** import ban

interdire vt to forbid, to prohibit; **l'exportation de l'or est formellement interdite** the export of gold is strictly prohibited; **interdire qch d'exportation/d'importation** to impose an export/import ban on sth

interdit, -e 1 adj (a) (défendu) forbidden, pro-

hibited (**b**) *Ordinat* **interdit d'écriture** *(disquette)* write-protected
 2 *nm* **interdit bancaire** ban on writing cheques; **être frappé d'interdit bancaire** to be banned from writing cheques

"
Le système de l'**interdit bancaire** a été conçu pour éviter et en tout cas décourager les délinquants économiques récidivistes. Il visait essentiellement l'émission des chèques sans provision, les fameux "chèques en bois".
"

interenterprises *adj* inter-company

intéressé, -e 1 *adj* (**a**) *(financièrement)* **être intéressé dans une entreprise** to have a financial interest in a business (**b**) *(concerné)* **les parties intéressées** the interested parties, the persons concerned
 2 *nm,f* **l'intéressé** the interested party, the person concerned

intéressement *nm* **intéressement (aux bénéfices)** profit-sharing scheme; **l'intéressement des salariés aux bénéfices de l'entreprise devrait avoir un effet bénéfique sur la productivité** profit-sharing should have a positive effect on productivity

intéresser *vt* **intéresser qn aux bénéfices** to give sb a share of the profits; **notre personnel est intéressé aux bénéfices** our staff gets a share of the profits, we operate a profit-sharing scheme

intérêt *nm* (**a**) *Fin* interest; **emprunter/prêter à intérêt** to borrow/lend at interest; **laisser courir des intérêts** to allow interest to accumulate; **payer des intérêts** to pay interest; **rapporter des intérêts** to yield *or* bear interest; **placer son argent à sept pour cent d'intérêt** to invest one's money at seven percent interest; **à sept pour cent d'intérêt** with seven percent interest; **sans intérêt** interest-free ▫ **intérêts arriérés** back interest; **intérêt bancaire** bank interest; **intérêt du capital** interest on capital; **intérêts compensatoires** damages; **intérêts composés** compound interest; **intérêts courus** accrued interest; **intérêts cumulatifs** cumulative interest; **intérêts débiteurs** debit interest; **intérêts pour défaut de paiement** default interest; **intérêts à échoir** accruing interest; **intérêts échus** accrued interest; **intérêts exigibles** interest due and payable; **intérêt fixe** fixed interest; **intérêts moratoires** default interest, penalty penal *or* interest; **intérêt négatif** negative interest; **intérêts à payer** interest charges; **intérêt pécuniaire** insurable interest; **intérêt sur prêt** interest on a loan; *Bourse* **intérêt de report** contango; **intérêt de retard** interest on arrears; **intérêt simple** simple interest; **intérêt à taux flottant** floating-

rate interest; **intérêt variable** variable-rate interest
 (**b**) *(dans une entreprise, une affaire)* share, stake; **avoir des intérêts dans une société** to have a financial interest in a company; **les intérêts économiques de notre pays dans cette région** our country's economic interests in that region; **mettre qn hors d'intérêt** to buy sb out
 (**c**) *(avantage)* interest, advantage; **agir dans l'intérêt de la société** to act in the interests of the company ▫ *Mktg* **intérêt du consommateur** consumer welfare

interface *nf Ordinat* interface ▫ **interface commune de passerelle** common gateway interface; **interface graphique** graphic interface; **interface parallèle** parallel interface; **interface série** serial interface; **interface utilisateur** user interface; **interface utilisateur graphique** graphical user interface; **interface vidéo numérique** digital video interface; **interface WIMP** WIMP

intérieur, -e *adj (national)* home, domestic

intérim *nm (travail intérimaire)* temporary work, temping; **par intérim** *(fonction, employé, personnel)* temporary; *(directeur)* acting; **faire de l'intérim** to do temporary work, to temp; **assurer** *ou* **faire l'intérim (de qn)** to deputize *or* stand in (for sb)

"
Les jeunes sont de plus en plus nombreux à décrocher leur premier emploi par le biais de l'intérim. Selon une récente enquête du Cereq … 21% des jeunes sortis du système éducatif en 1998 … indiquent avoir obtenu leur premier expérience professionnelle grâce à l'intérim.
"

intérimaire 1 *adj (fonction, employé, personnel)* temporary; *(directeur)* acting
 2 *nmf* (**a**) *(employé)* temporary worker, temp; **travailler comme intérimaire** to temp, to work as a temp (**b**) *(fonctionnaire)* official holding a temporary appointment

interlignage *nm Ordinat* line spacing ▫ **interlignage double** double spacing; **interlignage simple** single spacing

intermédiaire 1 *adj (biens, produits)* intermediate
 2 *nmf* (**a**) *(personne)* intermediary, go-between; *(dans une transaction)* middleman; **sans intermédiaire** directly; **je préfère vendre sans intermédiaire** I prefer to sell directly to the customer ▫ **intermédiaire agréé** authorized dealer; **intermédiaire financier** financial intermediary (**b**) *Bourse* market maker ▫ **intermédiaire négociateur** trading member; **intermédiaire remisier (en Bourse)** intermediate broker

3 *nm* par l'intermédiare de qn/qch through (the intermediary of) sb/sth

international, -e 1 *adj* international
2 *nm* l'international *(l'étranger)* world markets; **notre entreprise est très tournée vers l'international** our company is very export-oriented

internaute *nmf Ordinat* Internet user

interne *adj* internal; *(de l'entreprise)* in-house

Internet *nm Ordinat* Internet; **naviguer sur l'Internet** to surf the Internet; **acheter/vendre qch par l'Internet** to buy/sell sth over the Internet

interpolation *nf* interpolation

interprétariat *nm (dans une autre langue)* interpreting; **faire de l'interprétariat** to work as an interpreter

interprétation *nf (dans une autre langue)* interpreting

interprète *nmf (dans une autre langue)* interpreter; **servir d'interprète (à qn)** to interpret (for sb) ❑ *interprète de conférence* conference interpreter

interpréter *vt (dans une autre langue)* to interpret

interprofessionnel, -elle *adj* interprofessional

interrogation *nf Ordinat (d'une base de données)* inquiry, query; *(activité)* interrogation ❑ *interrogation à distance* remote access

interrogeable à distance *adj Tél (répondeur)* with a remote-access facility

interroger *vt* **(a)** *Mktg* to interview, to question; **60 pour cent des personnes interrogées ont déclaré n'avoir jamais entendu parler de ce produit** 60 percent of those questioned said that they had never heard of this product **(b)** *Ordinat (base de données)* to query, to interrogate

interrompre *vt Mktg (produit)* to discontinue

interrupteur *nm* switch ❑ *interrupteur DIP* DIP switch

intersyndical, -e *adj* inter-union

intervenant, -e *nm,f* **(a)** *(dans une conférence, un débat)* speaker **(b)** *Jur (dans une transaction)* intervening party **(c)** *Mktg* **intervenant sur le marché** market participant

intervenir *vi* **(a)** *(avoir lieu)* to happen, to occur; **un accord est intervenu entre la direction et les syndicats** an agreement has been reached between management and unions **(b)** *(prendre la parole)* to speak up, to intervene; **le délégué syndical est intervenu plusieurs fois pendant la réunion** the union representative intervened several times during the meeting

(c) *(agir)* to intervene; **l'État a dû intervenir pour renflouer la société** the state had to intervene to keep the company afloat
(d) *Jur* to intervene

intervention *nf* **(a)** *(action)* intervention; **l'intervention d'un médiateur n'a pas été suffisante pour régler le conflit** the intervention of a mediator was not enough to resolve the dispute **(b)** *(prise de parole)* intervention; **j'ai approuvé son intervention** I agreed with what he said **(c)** *Jur* intervention

interventionnisme *nm* interventionism

interventionniste *nmf* interventionist

intestat *Jur* **1** *adj* **décéder** *ou* **mourir intestat** to die intestate
2 *nm* intestacy

intitulé *nm* **(a)** *(d'un compte)* name **(b)** *Jur (d'un acte)* premises

Intranet *nm Ordinat* Intranet

intransférable *adj* not transferable; *Jur (droit)* unassignable

introduction *nf* **(a)** *(importation)* importing **(b)** *Bourse (de valeurs)* introduction ❑ *introduction en Bourse* flotation, listing on the Stock Market, *Am* initial public offering **(c)** *(de mesures, de nouveaux produits)* introduction **(d)** *Ordinat* **introduction de données** data input

> **"**
>
> D'autres investissements se sont révélés malheureux, comme l'acquisition du français Air Liberté, revendu après avoir accumulé des pertes. Ou une participation dans Iberia : l'**introduction en Bourse** de l'espagnol a été retardée, et sa valorisation divisée par quatre en raison de la flambée des prix du carburant !
>
> **"**

introduire 1 *vt* **(a)** *(importer)* to bring in, to import **(b)** *Bourse (valeurs)* to introduce, to bring out **(c)** *(mesures, nouveaux produits)* to introduce; **nous allons bientôt introduire un nouveau produit sur le marché** we are soon going to launch a new product on the market **(d)** *Ordinat* **introduire des données** to input *or* enter data
2 s'introduire *vpr Ordinat* **s'introduire en fraude dans un réseau** to hack into a network

intrus, -e *nm,f Ordinat (dans un réseau, dans un système)* hacker

invalidation *nf Jur* invalidation

invalide *adj* **(a)** *Jur* invalid **(b)** *Ordinat (mot de passe, nom du fichier)* invalid

invalidité *nf Jur* invalidity

invendable *adj* unmarketable, unsaleable

invendu, -e 1 *adj* unsold
2 *nm* unsold item

inventaire *nm* (**a**) *(de marchandises) (procédure)* stocktaking; *(liste)* Br stocklist, Am inventory; **faire** *ou* **dresser un inventaire** Br to stocktake, Am to take the inventory ▫ *inventaire effectif* physical inventory; *inventaire d'entrée* incoming inventory; *inventaire intermittent* periodical inventory; *inventaire des marchandises* inventory of goods; *inventaire périodique* periodic inventory; *inventaire permanent* perpetual inventory; *inventaire physique* physical inventory; *inventaire de sortie* outgoing inventory; *inventaire de stock* physical inventory; *inventaire théorique* theoretical inventory
(**b**) *(liste)* inventory; **faire** *ou* **dresser un inventaire** to draw up an inventory; **faire l'inventaire des ressources d'un pays** to assess a country's resources
(**c**) *Compta* **inventaire (comptable)** book inventory ▫ *inventaire de fin d'année* accounts for the end of the Br financial or Am fiscal year
(**d**) *Fin (d'un portefeuille de titres)* valuation

invention *nf* invention ▫ *invention brevetée* patented invention

inventorier *vt* to make an inventory of; *(marchandises)* to make a Br stocklist or Am inventory of

investi, -e *adj (argent, capitaux)* invested

investir 1 *vt* (**a**) *(argent, capitaux)* to invest (**dans** in); **investir des capitaux à l'étranger** to invest capital abroad
2 *vi* to invest (**dans** in); **investir à court terme** to make a short-term investment; **investir à long terme** to make a long-term investment

investissement *nm* investment; *(action)* investing, investment; **faire des investissements** to invest (money) ▫ *investissement de base* core holding; *investissement de capitaux* capital investment; *investissement à court terme* short-term investment; *investissement direct* direct investment; *investissement éthique* ethical investment; *investissements à l'étranger* outward or foreign investment; *investissement de l'étranger* inward investment; *investissement immobilier* investment in real estate, property investment; *investissement indirect* indirect investment; *investissement industriel* investment in industry; *investissements initiaux* initial investment; *investissement institutionnel* institutional investment; *investissement locatif* investment in rental property; *investissement à long terme* long-term investment;

investissement lourd heavy investment; *investissement privé* private investment; *investissement de productivité* productivity investment; *investissement à revenu fixe* fixed-rate investment; *investissement à revenu variable* floating-rate investment; *investissement en valeurs de redressement* ou *de retournement* failure investment

investisseur *nm* investor ▫ *investisseur étranger* foreign investor; *investisseur institutionnel* institutional investor; *investisseur minoritaire* minority investor; *investisseur privé* private investor

invisible *Écon* 1 *adj (exportations, importations)* invisible
2 *nm* **invisibles** invisibles

invite *nf Ordinat* prompt ▫ *invite (du) DOS* DOS prompt

IRC *nm Ordinat (abrév* **Internet Relay Chat**) IRC

IRSM *nm (abrév* **impact sur la rentabilité de la stratégie marketing**) PIMS

irréalisable *adj Fin (valeurs)* unrealizable

irrécouvrable *adj (argent, créance)* irrecoverable

irrégularité *nf (infraction)* irregularity; **il y a des irrégularités dans les comptes** there are some irregularities in the accounts ▫ *irrégularité comptable* accounting irregularity

ISBN *nm (abrév* **International Standard Book Number**) ISBN

ISF *nm (abrév* **impôt de solidarité sur la fortune**) wealth tax

> **“**
> L'**ISF** s'applique par ménage, que le couple vive marié, pacsé ou en union libre. Comme la preuve du concubinage est à la charge du fisc, nombre de riches concubins organisent leur célibat et "oublient" de faire une déclaration commune d'**ISF**. Contrairement à l'impôt sur le revenu, l'**ISF** s'applique aux pacsés dès la première année.
> **”**

ISO *nf (abrév* **International Standards Organization**) ISO

itératif, -ive *adj Ordinat* iterative

itinérance *nf Tél* to roam

itinérer *vi Tél* roaming

IUT *nm (abrév* **Institut universitaire de technologie**) = vocational higher education college

Jj

jargon *nm* jargon ❑ *jargon administratif* administrative jargon; *jargon journalistique* journalistic jargon, journalese; *jargon publicitaire* advertising jargon

JAT *adj (abrév* **juste à temps***)* JIT

jauge *nf (de navire)* tonnage ❑ *jauge brute* gross registered tonnage; *jauge nette* net registered tonnage

jaugeage *nm* measurement *(of tonnage)*

jauger 1 *vt (mesurer la capacité de)* to gauge, to measure the capacity of; *(navire)* to measure the tonnage of
  2 *vi* **un pétrolier qui jauge quarante mille tonneaux** a forty thousand-ton tanker

Java® *nm Ordinat* Java®

Javascript® *nm Ordinat* Java® script

jetable *adj (emballage, produit)* disposable

jeter *vt (mettre au rebut)* to throw away; **jeter des marchandises sur le marché** to throw goods onto the market

jeton de présence *nm (honoraires)* director's fees

jeu *nm* **(a)** *Bourse* speculating ❑ *jeu de Bourse* gambling on the Stock Exchange, Stock Exchange speculation; *jeu sur les reports* speculating in contangos
  (b) *(série) (de connaissements, de lettres de change)* set ❑ *Ordinat jeu de caractères* character set; *jeu de fiches* card index
  (c) *Compta jeu d'écritures* paper transaction
  (d) *(marge de manœuvre)* leeway
  (e) *(action)* force; **laisser faire le jeu de la concurrence** to allow the free play of competition; **le jeu de la concurrence ne peut pas s'exercer si seules certaines entreprises sont subventionnées par l'État** the forces of competition cannot come into play if only some companies receive State grants

jingle *nm* jingle

JO *nm Admin (abrév* **Journal officiel***)* = French government publication giving information to the public about new laws, government business, new companies etc, *Br* ≃ Hansard, *Am* ≃ Federal Register

joindre *vt* **(a)** *(ajouter)* to add (**à** to); *(dans une lettre, dans un colis)* to enclose, to attach; *Ordinat (document, fichier)* to attach (**à** to); **joindre l'intérêt au capital** to add the interest to the capital; **l'échantillon joint à votre lettre** the sample attached to your letter; **veuillez joindre CV et photo d'identité** please attach a copy of your *Br* CV *or Am* résumé and a photograph
  (b) *(contacter)* to get in touch with; **joindre qn par téléphone/par lettre** to contact sb by phone/in writing; **j'ai téléphoné, mais je n'ai pas réussi à le joindre** I phoned but I couldn't get hold of him; **où pourrai-je vous joindre?** how can I get in touch with you *or* contact you?

joint, -e *adj (documents, échantillons)* enclosed, attached

joint-venture *nf Fin* joint venture

joker *nm Ordinat* wildcard

jouer 1 *vt Bourse* **jouer la livre à la baisse/à la hausse** to speculate on a falling/rising pound
  2 *vi* **(a)** *Bourse* to speculate, to play the market; **jouer à la Bourse** to speculate *or* gamble on the Stock Exchange; **jouer à la hausse** to gamble on a rise in prices, to bull the market; **jouer à la baisse** to gamble on a fall in prices, to bear the market
  (b) *(s'appliquer)* to be operative, to operate; **l'augmentation des salaires joue depuis le 1ᵉʳ janvier** the rise in salaries has been operative since 1 January
  (c) *(fonctionner)* to work; **une livre forte joue contre les exportateurs britanniques** a strong pound puts British exporters at a disadvantage

tout simplement s'en servir comme d'un parachute. Reste à savoir utiliser les instruments "indiciels" correspondant à votre profil.

"

joueur, -euse *nm,f Bourse* speculator ❏ *joueur à la baisse* bear; *joueur à la hausse* bull

jouissance *nf* (a) *Jur (usage)* use; **avoir la jouissance de qch** to have the use of sth; **avoir la (pleine) jouissance de ses droits** to enjoy one's (full) rights; **à vendre avec jouissance immédiate** *(sur panneau)* for sale with vacant possession; **la période de jouissance est de sept ans** the period of tenure is seven years ❏ *jouissance en commun (d'un bien)* communal tenure; **jouissance locative** tenure (b) *Fin jouissance d'intérêts* entitlement to interest

jour *nm* (a) *(journée)* day; **quinze jours** *Br* a fortnight, *Am* two weeks ❏ *jour d'action* day of action; *Admin jour chômable, jour chômé* public holiday; *jour de congé* day off; *jour de l'échéance* due date; *jour férié* public *or* bank holiday; *jour franc* clear day; *Fin jours d'intérêt* interest days; *jour non-ouvrable* non-trading day; *jour ouvrable* working day; *jour de paie* pay day; *jour plein* clear day; *jour de repos* day off (b) *(date)* day; **à ce jour** up until now, to date; **à ce jour la facture que nous vous avons envoyée reste impayée** to date the invoice we sent you remains unpaid; **intérêts à ce jour** interest to date ❏ *jour de livraison* delivery date (c) **à jour** up to date; **notre catalogue n'est pas à jour** our catalogue is not up to date; **mettre qch à jour** to bring sth up to date, to update sth; **tenir les livres à jour** to keep the books *or* the accounts up to date (d) *Bourse* day ❏ *jour de Bourse* trading day; *jour de la déclaration des noms* ticket day; *jour de grâce* day of grace; *jour de la liquidation* account day, settlement day; *jour d'option* option date; *jour d'ouverture* opening day; *jour de paiement, jour de règlement* payment day, prompt day, settlement day; *jour de la réponse des primes* option day; *jour des reports* contango day; *jour du terme* term day; *jour de valeur* value day

journal *nm* (a) *(publication)* paper, newspaper ❏ *journal d'annonces* advertising newspaper; *Fin journal de banque* bank book; *journal sur CD-ROM* CD-ROM newspaper; *journal électronique* electronic newspaper; *journal d'entreprise* in-house *or* company magazine; *journal gratuit* giveaway paper; *journal interne (d'entreprise)* in-house *or* company magazine; *journal en ligne* on-line newspaper; *Admin Journal officiel* = French government publication giving information to the public about new laws, government business, new

companies etc, *Br* ≃ Hansard, *Am* ≃ Federal Register; *journal professionnel* trade journal (b) *Compta* ledger, account book ❏ *journal des achats* purchase ledger, bought ledger; *journal analytique* analysis ledger; *journal de banque* bank book; *journal de caisse* cash book; *journal des effets à payer* bills payable ledger; *journal des effets à recevoir* bills receivable ledger; *journal factures-clients* sales invoice ledger; *journal factures-fournisseurs* purchase invoice ledger; *journal de paie* wages *or* payroll ledger; *journal des rendus* returns ledger *or* book; *journal de trésorerie* cash book; *journal des ventes* sales ledger (c) *Ordinat* log

journalier, -ère *adj (production, recette, salaire)* daily

journaliser *vt Compta* to enter, to write up in the books

journalisme *nm* journalism ❏ *journalisme électronique* electronic news gathering

journaliste *nmf* journalist ❏ *journaliste économique* economics correspondent *or* journalist; *journaliste politique* political correspondent *or* journalist

journalistique *adj* journalistic

journée *nf* day; **faire la journée continue** *(magasin)* to remain open at lunchtime; *(personne)* to work through lunch; **être payé à la journée** to be paid by the day *or* on a daily basis; **travailler à la journée** to work on a daily basis ❏ *journée comptable* accounting day; *journée portes ouvertes Br* open day, *Am* open house; *journée de travail (quantité de travail)* day's work; *(durée)* working day; *journées de travail perdues* lost working days

JPEG *nm Ordinat (abrév* **Joint Photographic Experts Group**) JPEG

judiciaire *adj Jur (pouvoir, enquête, acte)* judicial; *(aide, autorité)* legal; *(vente)* court-ordered, by order of the court

judiciairement *adv Jur* judicially

juge *nm Jur* judge ❏ *juge consulaire* judge in commercial court; *juge d'instance* conciliation magistrate *(in commercial cases)*; *juge d'instruction Br* examining magistrate, *Am* committing magistrate; *juge des référés* judge in chambers

jugement *nm Jur* (a) *(décision)* judgement, decision, ruling; *(dans une cause criminelle)* sentence ❏ *jugement contentieux* judgement in disputed matter; *jugement déclaratif de faillite* adjudication in bankruptcy, declaration of bankruptcy; *jugement exécutoire* enforceable judgement; *jugement mis en délibéré* reserved judgement (b) *(d'une affaire)* trial; **passer en jugement** to stand trial

juger vt Jur (**a**) *(affaire, prévenu)* to try (**b**) *(demande, litige)* to adjudicate

juguler vt *(inflation, chômage)* to check, to curb

junk bond nm Bourse junk bond

juré, -e nm,f Jur juror

juridiction nf Jur (**a**) *(compétence)* jurisdiction; **tomber sous la juridiction de** to come under the jurisdiction of □ **juridiction commerciale** commercial jurisdiction (**b**) *(tribunaux)* courts

juridique adj *(système, environnement)* judicial, legal; *(texte, frais)* legal

juriste nmf lawyer □ **juriste d'entreprise** company lawyer

jury nm jury □ Mktg **jury des consommateurs** focus group

juste 1 adj (**a**) *(équitable)* *(prix, salaire)* fair (**b**) *(exact)* correct, accurate (**c**) Mktg **juste à temps** *(achat, distribution, production)* just-in-time
  2 adv exactly, precisely; **le prix calculé au plus juste** the minimum price

justice nf *(système judiciaire)* law, legal proceedings; **recourir à la justice, aller en justice** to go to law; **poursuivre qn en justice** to institute legal proceedings against sb, to take legal action against sb; **être traduit en justice** to be tried, to be taken to court

justificatif, -ive 1 adj supporting, jusitificatory
  2 nm (**a**) Admin written proof; Compta receipt; **à adresser à la Comptabilité avec justificatifs** to be sent to the accounts department with all necessary receipts □ **justificatif de domicile** proof of address (**b**) *(journal)* = free copy of newspaper sent to those who have an advertisement in it

justification nf (**a**) *(preuve)* proof □ **justification de paiement** proof of payment (**b**) Ordinat justification □ **justification à droite** right justification; **justification à gauche** left justification; **justification verticale** vertical justification

justifier 1 vt (**a**) *(légitimer)* to justify, to warrant (**b**) Ordinat to justify; **justifié à gauche/à droite** left/right justified
  2 vi **justifier de qch** to prove sth

juteux, -euse adj Fam *(transaction)* juicy, lucrative; **une affaire juteuse** a money spinner, a goldmine

Kk

Kb nm Ordinat (abrév **kilobit**) Kb

KF nm Anciennement (abrév **kilofranc**) thousand francs; **son salaire annuel est de 200 KF** she earns 200,000 francs a year

kilobaud nm Ordinat kilobaud

kilobit nm Ordinat kilobit

kilofranc nm Anciennement thousand francs

kilomètre-passager nm (en avion) passenger-kilometre

kilo-octet nm Ordinat kilobyte

kit nm Ordinat kit □ **kit d'accès, kit de connexion** connection kit; **kit d'évolution, kit d'extension** upgrade kit; **kit de téléchargeur** download kit

KO nm Ordinat (abrév **kilo-octet**) K, KB; **une disquette de 720 KO** a 720K disquette

ko/s Ordinat (abrév **kilo-octets par seconde**) kbps

krach nm (financial) crash □ **krach boursier** Stock Market crash; **le krach de Wall Street** the Wall Street Crash

> **"**
>
> ... les e-milliardaires (souvent virtuels, mais pas toujours) apparaissent dans le haut de classement des grandes fortunes, des entreprises sans revenus brûlent leur "cash" pour mieux flamber en Bourse, jusqu'à dépasser la valorisation d'entreprises établies et rentables ... On connaît la suite : le réveil brutal, les premières faillites, le **krach boursier**, le rejet ...
>
> **"**

Ll

label *nm* (**a**) *(étiquette)* label ❑ **label d'exporta-tion** export label; **label de garantie** guarantee label; **label NF, label norme française** *(délivré par l'AFNOR)* = French industry standards la-bel; **label d'origine** certificate of origin; **label de qualité** quality label (**b**) *Ordinat* **label de vo-lume** volume label

laboratoire d'idées *nm* think tank

lâcher *Ordinat* **1** *nm* **lâcher d'icônes** icon drop
2 *vt (icône)* to drop

laissé-pour-compte 1 *adj (article, marchan-dise)* rejected, returned
2 *nm (article, marchandise)* reject

laissez-faire *nm Écon* laissez-faire

laissez-passer *nm* pass, permit; *Douanes* transire

lancement *nm* (**a**) *(d'un projet, d'une société, d'un produit, d'un modèle)* launch ❑ *Mktg* **lance-ment sur le marché** market entry; *Mktg* **lance-ment tardif** late entry
(**b**) *Bourse (d'une société)* flotation; *(de titres boursiers, d'un emprunt)* issuing, issue; *(d'une souscription)* start
(**c**) *Ordinat (d'impression)* start; *(de pro-gramme)* running

lancer 1 *vt* (**a**) *(projet, société, produit, modèle)* to launch; **lancer un nouveau produit sur le marché** to launch a new product on the mar-ket; **lancer un appel d'offres** to invite tenders
(**b**) *Bourse (société)* to float; *(titres boursiers, emprunt)* to issue; *(souscription)* to start; **lancer des titres sur le marché** to issue shares
(**c**) *Ordinat (impression)* to start; *(programme)* to run, to start (up)
2 se lancer *vpr* **se lancer dans les affaires** to set oneself up in business; **se lancer sur le marché** to enter the market

langage *nm Ordinat* language ❑ **langage as-sembleur** *ou* **d'assemblage** assembly lan-guage; **langage auteur** authoring language; **langage de commande** command language; **langage Java®** Java® script; **langage machine** machine language; **langage naturel** natural language; **langage de programmation** pro-gramming language; **langage source** source language; **langage utilisateur** user language

languissant, -e *adj (marché)* dull, sluggish; *(affaires, activité)* slow

largeur de bande *nf Ordinat* bandwidth

laser *nm Ordinat* laser

l/c *nf Fin (abrév* **lettre de crédit***)* L/C

LCR *nf Fin (abrév* **lettre de change relevé***)* bills of exchange statement

leader *nm Mktg* leader; **cette entreprise est le leader mondial de la micro-informatique** this firm is the world leader in microcomputing ❑ **leader sur le marché** market leader; **leader d'opinion** opinion former, opinion leader

> "
> Giuseppe Panini ... a compris que ce bout de carton appelé "image" – qui avait fait rêver les jeunes depuis la fin du XIXᵉ siècle – pouvait véhiculer aussi les rêves modernes, qui ont l'avantage d'être collectifs. La Panini devien-dra grâce à lui **leader mondial** des fabricants d'images avec 80% de part de marché.
> "

leasing *nm* lease financing; **acheter qch en leasing** to lease sth, to buy sth on lease

lèche-vitrines *nm* window-shopping; **faire du lèche-vitrines** to window-shop

lecteur *nm Ordinat* reader; *(de disque, de dis-quettes)* drive ❑ **lecteur de bande audionu-mérique** DAT drive; **lecteur de cartes magnétiques** magnetic card reader; **lecteur de carte à mémoire** smart card reader, card reader; **lecteur de carte à puce** smart card rea-der; **lecteur de CD-ROM** CD-ROM drive; **lec-teur de courrier** mail reader; **lecteur DAT** DAT drive; **lecteur par défaut** default drive; **lecteur de destination** destination drive; **lec-teur de disque dur** hard disk drive; **lecteur de disque optique** CD-ROM drive; **lecteur de disquettes** disk drive, floppy (disk) drive; **lec-teur de documents** document reader; **lecteur non connecté** off-line reader; **lecteur OCR** OCR reader; **lecteur optique** optical drive; **lec-teur optique de caractères** optical character reader; **lecteur de pages** page scanner; **lecteur Zip®** Zip® drive

lectorat *nm (d'un journal)* readership, readers

lecture *nf Ordinat* read; **en lecture seule** in read-only mode; **mettre un fichier en lecture seule** to make a file read-only ❑ **lecture sur dis-que** reading to disk; **lecture optique** optical reading; **lecture au scanneur** scan

lecture-écriture *nf Ordinat* read-write (mode); **être en lecture-écriture** to be in read-write (mode)

légal, -e *adj* legal; *(action)* legal, lawful; **avoir recours aux moyens légaux** to take legal action, to institute legal proceedings; **suivre la procédure légale** to follow the legal procedure; **par les voies légales** legally, by legal means

légalement *adv* legally, lawfully

légalisation *nf* (a) *(d'un produit, d'une pratique)* legalization (b) *(d'une signature)* authentication, certification

légaliser *vt* (a) *(produit, pratique)* to legalize (b) *(signature)* to authenticate, to certify

légalité *nf* legality, lawfulness; **ils ont réussi à échapper à cet impôt tout en restant dans la légalité** they managed to avoid paying the tax by legal means

légataire *nmf* legatee, heir

légende *nf (commentaire)* caption

léger, -ère *adj (amélioration, reprise)* slight

législation *nf* legislation □ *législation anti-dumping* anti-dumping laws; *législation antitrust* Br anti-monopoly or Am antitrust legislation; *législation bancaire* banking legislation; *législation douanière* customs legislation; *législation fiscale* tax laws; *législation du travail* industrial or labour legislation

légitime *adj* legitimate

legs *nm Jur* legacy, bequest; **faire/recevoir un legs** to leave/receive a legacy □ *legs particulier* personal or private legacy; *legs universel* residuary legacy

léguer *vt Jur* to leave, to bequeath

LEP *nm Banque (abrév* **livret d'épargne populaire**) = special tax-exempt savings account

lettre *nf* (a) *(courrier)* letter; **adresser une lettre à qn** *(écrire l'adresse sur)* to address a letter to sb; *(écrire)* to write a letter to sb □ *lettre d'accompagnement* covering letter; *Fin lettre accréditive* letter of credit; *lettre d'affaires* business letter; *lettre d'affectation* letter of appointment; *lettre d'agrément* letter of consent; *Bourse lettre d'allocation* letter of allotment; *Fin lettre d'aval* letter of guaranty; *lettre d'avis* advice note; *Fin lettre de change* bill or letter of exchange; *Fin lettre de change à l'extérieur* foreign bill; *Fin lettre de change relevé* bills of exchange statement; *lettre circulaire* circular; *lettre commerciale* business letter; *lettre de confirmation* letter of confirmation; *lettre de couverture* cover note; *Fin lettre de créance* letter of credit; *Banque lettre de crédit* letter of credit; **émettre une lettre de crédit** to open a letter of credit; *Banque lettre de crédit circulaire* circular letter of credit;

Banque lettre de crédit directe direct letter of credit; *Banque lettre de crédit documentaire* documentary letter of credit; *Banque lettre de crédit irrévocable* irrevocable letter of credit; *lettre de demande d'emploi* letter of application *(for job)*; *lettre de démission* resignation letter; *lettre d'embauche* written offer of employment; *lettre d'envoi* covering letter, advice note; *lettre d'excuse* letter of apology; *Douanes lettre d'exemption* bill of sufferance; *lettre explicative* covering letter; *lettre exprès* express letter; *Fin lettre de gage* debenture bond; *(pour hypothèque)* mortgage bond; *Fin lettre de garantie* letter of guarantee; *Banque lettre de garantie bancaire* bank guarantee; *Banque lettre de garantie d'indemnité* letter of indemnity; *Jur lettre d'intention* letter of intent; *lettre de licenciement* letter of dismissal; *Douanes lettre de mer* clearance certificate; *lettre de motivation* covering letter *(accompanying curriculum vitae)*; *Fin lettre de nantissement* letter of hypothecation; *lettre de nomination* letter of appointment; *lettre notificative* letter of notification; *lettre de poursuite* letter threatening legal action, chasing letter; *lettre de rappel* reminder; *lettre de réclamation* letter of complaint; *lettre de recommandation* letter of recommendation, reference; *lettre recommandée* registered letter; *lettre recommandée avec accusé de réception* registered letter with confirmation of receipt; *lettre de relance* follow-up letter; *lettre de relance des impayés* debt-chasing letter; *Banque lettre de signatures autorisées* mandate form; *Bourse lettre de souscription* letter of application; *lettre de transport aérien* air waybill; *lettre type (pour mailing)* form letter; *lettre de vente* sales letter; *lettre de voiture* waybill, consignment note

(b) *(de l'alphabet)* letter; **écrire une somme en (toutes) lettres** to write an amount in words (not figures) □ *lettres majuscules* capital letters, capitals, upper case; *lettres minuscules* small letters, lower case

levée *nf* (a) *(du courrier, des impôts)* collection; **quand la levée du courrier a-t-elle lieu?** when is the mail or Br post collected? (b) *(d'embargo, de sanctions)* lifting; *(de séance)* closing, adjourning (c) *Bourse, Fin (des actions, d'une option)* taking up □ *Banque levées de compte* personal withdrawals

lever *vt* (a) *(courrier, impôts)* to collect (b) *(embargo, sanctions)* to lift; *(séance)* to close, to adjourn (c) *Bourse, Fin (actions, option)* to take up

levier *nm Écon* leverage

liaison *nf* (a) *(dans les transports, les télécommunications)* link □ *liaison aérienne* air link; *liaison ferroviaire* rail link; *liaison maritime* sea link; *liaison postale* postal link; *liaison rail-aéroport* rail-air link; *liaison routière* road link; *liai-*

son par satellite satellite link; **liaison spéciali-sée** dedicated line; **liaison de télécommunica-tions** telecommunications link; **liaison téléphonique** telephone link or communications
  (**b**) (contact) contact, liaison; **travailler en liai-son avec qn** to liaise with sb, to work closely with sb; **assurer la liaison entre deux personnes/ser-vices** to liaise between two people/departments; **les différents services sont en liaison** the va-rious departments are in contact or liaise closely (with each other); **être en liaison permanente (avec)** to be constantly in touch (with); **se mettre en liaison avec qn** to get in touch with sb; **rester en liaison avec qn** to stay in touch with sb
  (**c**) Ordinat connection

liasse nf (de billets de banque) wad; (de docu-ments) bundle

libellé nm wording; Compta (d'une écriture) particulars

libeller vt (**a**) Admin (document, acte, contrat) to word, to draw up; **libellé comme suit…** wor-ded as follows… (**b**) (chèque, facture) to make out; **un chèque libellé à l'ordre de Y. Mourier** a cheque made out or payable to Y. Mourier; **li-bellé en euros** (chèque) made out in euros; (cours) quoted or given in euros; **être libellé au porteur** to be made out to bearer, to be made payable to bearer

libéral, -e Écon **1** adj (économie, doctrine) free-market
  2 nm,f free-marketeer

libéralisation nf Écon deregulation, easing of restrictions; **la libéralisation du commerce** the easing of trade restrictions, the deregulation of trade; **la libéralisation complète de l'écono-mie** the application of free-market principles throughout the economy

> **"**
> Elle court le risque, en outre, de voir affluer sur son marché plusieurs dizaines de mil-lions de tonnes d'acier produites au Japon, en Corée du Sud, en Australie ou au Brésil. Plus grave, cette poussée de fièvre protec-tionniste américaine menace les fragiles ac-cords sur la **libéralisation** des échanges récemment conclus à Doha.
> **"**

libéraliser vt Écon to deregulate, to ease res-trictions on; **libéraliser l'économie** to reduce state intervention in the economy

libéralisme nm Écon free-market economics, free enterprise

libération nf (**a**) (déréglementation) (des prix) deregulation ☐ **libération des changes** relaxing of foreign exchange controls; **libération des échanges commerciaux** deregulation of trade, relaxing of exchange controls
  (**b**) (d'une dette) payment in full, discharge;

(d'un engagement) release; (d'une action, du ca-pital) paying up; (d'un débiteur) discharge, re-lease; (d'un garant) discharge ☐ Fin **libération intégrale** (d'une action) payment in full

libératoire adj **avoir force libératoire** to be le-gal tender

libéré, -e adj Fin (action) (fully) paid-up; **non (entièrement) libéré, partiellement libéré** partly paid-up; **un titre de 1000 euros libéré de 750 euros** ou **libéré à 75%** a 1,000-euro share of which 750 euros are paid up; **libéré d'impôt** tax paid

libérer 1 vt (**a**) (déréglementer) (prix, échanges commerciaux) to deregulate
  (**b**) (dette) to free; (engagement) to release; (action, capital) to pay up; (débiteur) to dis-charge, to release; (garant) to discharge; **libé-rer entièrement une action** to make a share fully paid-up, to pay up a share in full; **libérer qn de la responsabilité légale** to relieve sb of legal liability
  2 se libérer vpr (se dégager) **se libérer de qch** (dette) to redeem sth, to liquidate sth; (engage-ment) to free oneself from sth

liberté nf (déréglementation) (des prix, des échanges commerciaux) freedom ☐ **liberté du commerce** freedom of trade; **liberté de com-munication** freedom of communication; **li-berté d'entreprise** (right of) free enterprise; **liberté d'information** freedom of information; **liberté de la presse** freedom of the press; **li-berté syndicale** freedom to join a union, union rights

libertel nf Ordinat freenet

libre adj (**a**) (non réglementé) free ☐ **libre circula-tion** (des marchandises, des personnes, des capi-taux) free movement; **libre concurrence** free competition; **libre entreprise** free enterprise; **libre service** (technique de vente) self-service; (magasin) self-service shop (**b**) (disponible) free; **la ligne n'est pas libre** the line's Br enga-ged or Am busy ☐ **libre possession** vacant pos-session (**c**) **libre d'hypothèque** free from mortgage; **libre d'impôt** tax-free

libre-échange nm Écon free trade

libre-échangisme nm Écon free trade

libre-échangiste Écon **1** adj (politique, théo-rie) free-trade
  2 nmf free trader

libre-service nm self-service; (magasin) self-service shop

licence nf (**a**) (permis) licence; (pour l'utilisation d'un logiciel) registration card; **obtenir une li-cence** to obtain a licence; **fabriqué sous li-cence** manufactured under licence ☐ **licence de débit de boissons** licence to sell beer, wines and spirits, Am liquor licence; **licence exclusive** exclusive licence; **licence d'exploitation d'un**

brevet licence to use a patent; *licence d'expor-tation* export licence; *licence de fabrication* manufacturing licence; *licence d'importation* import licence; *Ordinat licence individuelle d'utilisation* single user licence; *licence de vente* selling licence **(b)** *(diplôme)* degree; **une licence en droit/en économie** a law/econo-mics degree

licenciement *nm (pour raisons économiques)* redundancy; *(pour faute professionnelle)* dismis-sal ❑ *licenciement abusif* unfair *or* wrongful dismissal; *licenciement collectif* mass redun-dancy; *licenciement économique* redundan-cy; *licenciement sans préavis* dismissal without notice; *licenciement sec* = redundan-cy without any form of statutory compensation

❝
Négociations difficiles entre l'Unice, repré-sentant les employeurs européens, et la Commission. Celle-ci veut réduire le coût social des restructurations. Et réclame la mise en place de solutions alternatives (ré-duction du temps de travail, par exemple) pour éviter les **licenciements secs**.
❞

licencier *vt* **licencier qn** *(pour raisons économi-ques)* to make sb redundant; *(pour faute profes-sionnelle)* to dismiss sb

licite *adj* licit, lawful

licitement *adv* licitly, lawfully

lié, -e *adj (marchés)* related; *(opérations)* combined; *(emprunts)* tied; **tous les emplois liés à l'industrie automobile sont affectés par cette grève** this strike has affected all jobs connected with the motor industry

lien *nm Ordinat* link ❑ *lien hypertexte* hyper-text link

lier *vt* **(a)** *(par contrat)* to bind; **ce contrat vous lie** you are bound by this agreement; **votre con-trat ne vous lie pas à la société** your contract does not bind you to the company **(b)** *Ordinat* to link **(à** to)

lieu *nm* **(a)** *(endroit)* place; **vider les lieux** to va-cate the premises ❑ *Fin lieu d'émission* place of issue; *lieu de livraison* place of delivery, point of delivery; *lieu de naissance* place of birth; *lieu de paiement* place of payment; *lieu de rendez-vous, lieu de réunion* meeting place; *lieu de travail* place of work; **sur le lieu de tra-vail** in the workplace; *lieu de vente* point of sale **(b)** **avoir lieu** *(se dérouler)* to take place; **la réunion aura lieu vendredi** the meeting will take place *or* will be held on Friday

ligne *nf* **(a)** *Tél* line; **être en ligne** to be on a call; **la ligne est occupée** the line is *Br* engaged *or* *Am* busy; **la ligne a été coupée** I've/we've/*etc* been cut off; **il y a quelqu'un sur la ligne**

there's someone on the line; **vous êtes en ligne** you're connected, you're through; **il est déjà en ligne** he's on another line; **la ligne est en dé-rangement** the line is out of order ❑ *ligne d'abonné numérique* digital subscriber line, DSL; *ligne commutée* dial-up line; *ligne di-recte* direct line; *ligne directe accessible 24 heures sur 24* 24-hour hotline; *ligne exté-rieure* outside line; *ligne ouverte* open line; *ligne privée* private line; *ligne RNIS* ISDN line; *ligne spécialisée* dedicated line; *ligne télépho-nique* telephone line; *ligne téléphonique di-recte* direct-dial line; *ligne terrestre* land line **(b)** *Mktg (de produits)* line, range; **ligne pour hommes** range for men **(c)** *Fin ligne de crédit* line of credit, credit line; *Bourse ligne de cotation* line of quotation; *Banque ligne de découvert* line of credit, credit line; *Banque ligne de substitution* backup line **(d)** *(principe)* **les grandes lignes, les lignes di-rectrices** *(d'un projet)* the broad outline **(e)** *Compta* **au-dessus de la ligne** *(dépenses)* above-the-line **(f)** *(dans les transports)* line ❑ *ligne aérienne* airline; *ligne intérieure* domestic route; *ligne maritime, ligne de navigation* shipping line **(g)** *Ordinat* line; **en ligne** on-line; **sur ligne** on-line; **hors ligne** off-line ❑ *ligne d'état* status line

limitatif, -ive *adj Jur (clause)* limiting, restric-tive

limitation *nf* limitation, restriction; **ils appli-quent une limitation volontaire de leurs ex-portations** they set voluntary limits on their exports ❑ *limitation des dégâts* damage limita-tion; *limitation des prix* price control; *limita-tion de responsabilité* limitation of liability; *limitation des salaires* wage restraint

limite *nf* **(a)** *(maximum ou minimum)* limit; **dans la limite des stocks disponibles** while stocks last ❑ *limite d'âge* age limit; *limite de crédit* credit limit; *limite d'endettement* borrowing limit; *limite de poids* weight limit; *limite de prix* price limit **(b)** *Bourse* limit ❑ *limite de la baisse* limit down; *limite de la hausse* limit up; *limite inférieure* limit down; *limite de po-sition* position limit; *limite supérieure* limit up

limité, -e *adj* limited; *Can* **Desrochers et Cie Limitée** Desrochers and Co. Ltd.

linéaire 1 *adj (programmation)* linear
2 *nm* shelf space; *(étalage)* shelf display; **ce pro-duit n'apparaît pas dans les linéaires de ma-gasins non spécialisés** non-specialist shops do not stock this product

❝
Numéro cinq mondial de l'agroalimentaire, Campbell Soup est spécialisé dans la fabri-cation de potages et bouillons industriels.

> Pour développer ce segment et améliorer sa position dans les **linéaires**, Campbell France s'est doté d'un logiciel de merchandising pour la gestion des rayons et de l'espace magasin. **"**

lingot *nm* ingot ◻ *lingot d'or* gold ingot *or* bar; *lingots en or* gold bullion

liquidateur, -trice *nm,f Jur* liquidator ◻ *liquidateur judiciaire* official liquidator; *Bourse* *liquidateur officiel* official assignee

liquidatif, -ive *adj Jur* pertaining to liquidation

liquidation *nf* (a) *Jur* liquidation; **être en liquidation** to have gone into liquidation; **entrer en liquidation** to go into liquidation; **mettre en liquidation** to put into liquidation, to liquidate ◻ *liquidation des biens* liquidation of assets; *liquidation forcée* compulsory liquidation; *liquidation (par décision) judiciaire* official receivership; *liquidation volontaire* voluntary liquidation
(b) *(d'un compte, d'une dette)* settlement, clearing
(c) *Bourse* settlement; *(d'une position)* liquidation ◻ *liquidation en espèces* cash settlement; *liquidation de fin de mois* end-of-month settlement; *liquidation de quinzaine Br* fortnightly settlement, fortnightly account, *Am* mid-month settlement, mid-month account
(d) *(de stocks)* selling off, clearance; *(d'un commerce)* closing-down, *Am* closing-out ◻ *liquidation totale (sur panneau)* closing down sale, everything must go

liquide 1 *adj Fin* liquid; **peu liquide** illiquid
2 *nm* (a) *(espèces)* (ready) cash; **je n'ai pas assez de liquide** I haven't enough cash; **vous payez par chèque ou en liquide?** are you paying by cheque or cash? (b) *liquide correcteur* correction fluid, liquid paper

liquider (a) *Jur (entreprise)* to liquidate (b) *(compte, dette)* to settle, to clear (c) *Bourse (position)* to liquidate (d) *(stocks)* to sell off, to clear; *(commerce)* to close down, *Am* to close out

liquidité *nf Fin* liquidity; **être à court de liquidité** to be short of funds; **liquidités** liquid assets, monetary assets ◻ *liquidités excédentaires* excess liquidities; *liquidités obligatoires* mandatory liquid assets; *liquidité du portefeuille* portfolio liquidity

lire¹ *nf (unité monétaire)* lira

lire² *vt Ordinat (disquette)* to read; **lire au scanneur** to scan

lisible *adj Ordinat* **lisible par ordinateur** machine-readable

lissage de caractères *nm Ordinat* character smoothing

liste *nf* list; **faire** *ou* **dresser** *ou* **établir une liste** to draw up or to make out a list; *Tél* **être sur la liste rouge** to be *Br* ex-directory *or Am* unlisted ◻ *liste des actionnaires* list of shareholders; *liste d'adresses* mailing list, address list; *liste des arrivées* arrivals list; *liste d'attente* waiting list; *liste de clients* customer *or* client list; *liste de colisage* packing list; *liste de contrôle* checklist; *liste des départs* departure list; *liste de diffusion* mailing list; *liste d'émargement* payroll; *liste d'envoi* mailing list; *Douanes* **liste d'exemptions** free list; *Ordinat* **liste de fichiers à imprimer** print list, print queue; *liste des importations* import list; *Douanes* **liste des marchandises importées en franchise** free list; *Can* **liste de paie** payroll; *liste de prix* price list; *liste de publipostage* mailing list; *liste à puces* bulleted list; *Ordinat* **liste rapide** draft; *liste des signatures autorisées* authorized signatory list; *Ordinat* **liste de signets** bookmark list, hot list; *Fin* **liste des souscripteurs** list of applications; *Fin* **liste de souscriptions** subscription list; *liste des tarifs* price list, tariff

listing *nm Ordinat* listing, printout

litige *nm (conflit)* dispute; *(procès)* lawsuit; **être en litige** to be in dispute; **régler un litige** to settle a dispute ◻ *litige commercial* commercial dispute

litigieux, -euse *adj (question)* contentious

livrable *adj* (a) *(marchandises)* ready for delivery; **les marchandises ne sont pas livrables à domicile** goods cannot be delivered (b) *Fin* deliverable

livraison *nf* (a) *(action, marchandises)* delivery; **faire** *ou* **effectuer une livraison** to make a delivery; **faire la livraison de qch** to deliver sth; **prendre livraison de qch** to take delivery of sth ◻ *livraison à domicile (sur panneau)* door-to-door delivery, we deliver; *livraison échelonnée* staggered delivery; *livraison franco* free delivery, delivered free; *livraison franco à domicile* free home delivery; *livraison franco par nos soins* carriage paid; *livraison gratuite* free delivery, delivered free; *livraison immédiate* immediate delivery; *livraison le jour même* same-day delivery; *livraison lendemain* next-day delivery; *livraison partielle* short delivery; *livraison contre remboursement Br* cash on delivery, *Am* collect on delivery; *livraison retardée* late delivery
(b) *Bourse, Fin (des titres)* delivery ◻ *livraison au comptant, livraison immédiate* spot delivery; *livraison à terme* future delivery, forward delivery

livre¹ *nf (unité monétaire)* pound; **un billet de cinq livres** a five-pound note ◻ *Anciennement* *livre irlandaise* Irish pound, punt; *livre sterling* pound (sterling); *UE* **livre verte** green pound

livre² nm (registre) book; Compta **tenir les livres** to keep the accounts or the books; **vérifier les livres** to check the books ❑ Compta **livre des achats** bought ledger, purchase ledger; Bourse **livre d'actionnaires** register of shareholders; **livre blanc** official report; (publié par le gouvernement) white paper; Compta **livre de caisse** cash book; **livre de commandes** order book; Compta **livre de commerce, livre de comptabilité, livre de comptes** ledger, account book; Compta **livre des créanciers** accounts payable ledger; Compta **livre des débiteurs** accounts receivable ledger; Compta **livre du dehors** out book; Compta **livre de dépenses** cash book; **livre d'échantillons** sample book, pattern book; Fin **livre d'échéance** bill book; Compta **livre des effets à payer** bills payable ledger; Compta **livre des effets à recevoir** bills receivable ledger; Ordinat **livre électronique** e-book; Compta **livre des entrées** purchase ledger; Compta **livre fractionnaire** day book, book of prime entry; **livre d'inventaire** stock book, inventory book; Compta **livre journal** journal, day book; **livre de magasin** warehouse book; Ordinat **livre numérique** e-book; **livre de paie** pay or wages ledger; **livre de petite caisse** petty cash book; **livre des réclamations** claims book; **livre des rendus** returns ledger; **livre des sorties** sales ledger; **livre de stock** stock book; **livre de trésorerie générale** general cash book; Compta **livre des ventes** sales ledger

livrer vt (a) (marchandises) to deliver; **nous avons bien été livrés** we have received the delivery; **livrer une commande** to deliver an order; **nous livrons à domicile** we deliver to your door; **vous serez livrés dès demain** you will receive delivery tomorrow; **livré franco domicile** delivered free at domicile; **livrer une usine clés en mains** to hand over a turnkey factory (b) Bourse, Fin to deliver; **livrer à terme fixe** to deliver at a fixed term; **prime pour livrer** seller's option; **vente à livrer** sale for delivery

livret nm book ❑ Banque **livret A** = tax-exempt savings account issued by the French National Savings Bank and the Post Office; **livret de banque** passbook; **livret de caisse d'épargne** bank book, passbook; **livret de compte** bank book; **livret de dépôt** deposit book, passbook; **livret d'épargne-logement** Br ≃ building society passbook, Am ≃ savings and loan association passbook; Banque **livret d'épargne populaire** (compte) = special tax-exempt savings account; (carnet) savings book, passbook

livreur, -euse nm,f (a) (qui effectue des livraisons) delivery man, f delivery woman (b) Bourse, Fin deliverer

LJM nf (abrév **livraison le jour même**) same-day delivery

LMDS nm (abrév **local multipoint distribution system**) LMDS

LOA nf (abrév **location avec option d'achat**) lease financing

lobby nm lobby, pressure group

lobbying nm lobbying

> ❝
>
> Pourquoi n'a-t-on jamais eu un ministre de l'Industrie issu du monde de l'entreprise ? Le problème, c'est que les chefs d'entreprise n'ont pas le temps de se consacrer au **lobbying** de réseau qui leur permettrait d'être décideurs à la fois politique et économique.
>
> ❞

lobbyist nmf lobbyist

lobbysme nm lobbying

local, -e 1 adj (autorités, industrie, personnel) local

2 nm premises ❑ **locaux commerciaux** business premises, commercial property; **locaux à louer** premises to let; **local professionnel** premises used for professional purposes; **locaux à usage commercial** business premises, commercial property

localisation nf localization

localiser vt to localize

locataire nmf (de logement) tenant; (pensionnaire) lodger ❑ Jur **locataire à bail** lessee, leaseholder

location nf (a) (de voiture, d'équipement) (par le locataire) renting, Br hiring; (par le propriétaire) renting out, Br hiring out; **prendre qch en location** to rent sth, Br to hire sth; **donner qch en location** to rent sth out, Br to hire sth out ❑ **location d'équipement** plant hire; **location de voitures** car rental, Br car hire

(b) (de logement) (par le locataire) renting; (par le propriétaire) renting out, Br letting (out); **prendre qch en location** to rent sth; **donner qch en location** to rent sth out, Br to let sth (out) ❑ **location avec option d'achat** lease financing; **location à vie** life tenancy

(c) (appartement, maison) rented Br accommodation or Am accommodations

location-gérance nf = agreement with a liquidator to manage a company in liquidation

location-vente nf hire purchase, Am installment plan; **acheter qch en location-vente** to buy sth on hire purchase or Am on the installment plan

lock-out nm lockout

lock-outer vt (personnel) to lock out

logement nm Br accommodation, Am accommodations ❑ **logement locatif** rented Br accommodation or Am accommodations

logiciel nm Ordinat software; **un logiciel** a software package; (programme) a piece of software ❏ **logiciel d'application** application software; **logiciel auteur** authoring software; **logiciel de bureautique** business software; **logiciel client** client software; **logiciel de communication** communications software, comms software; **logiciel de comptabilité** accounts software; **logiciel de conception assistée par ordinateur** computer-aided design software; **logiciel contributif** shareware; **logiciel de conversion** conversion software; **logiciel convivial** user-friendly software; **logiciel de courrier électronique** e-mail software; **logiciel de dessin** art package, drawing program; **logiciel d'exploitation** system software; **logiciel grapheur, logiciel graphique** graphics software; **logiciel intégré** built-in or integrated software; **logiciel de lecture de nouvelles** news reader; **logiciel de mise en page** desktop publishing software; **logiciel multi-utilisateur** multi-user software; **logiciel de navigation** (Web) browser; **logiciel d'OCR** OCR software; **logiciel de PAO** desktop publishing software; **logiciel de planification** scheduler; **logiciel de présentation** presentation software; **logiciel de reconnaissance vocale** voice recognition software; **logiciel de réseau** network software; **logiciel système** system software; **logiciel de système d'exploitation** operating system software; **logiciel de télémaintenance** remote-access software; (pour base de données) server software; **logiciel de traitement de texte** word-processing software; **logiciel utilisateur** user software; **logiciel utilitaire** utility program

logistique 1 adj logistic
  2 nf logistics ❏ **logistique commerciale** marketing mix

logo nm logo

loi nf law ❏ **loi antitrust** Br anti-monopoly or Am antitrust law; **lois contre la diffamation** libel laws; **loi de Finances** Finance Act; **la loi de la jungle** the law of the jungle; **loi de l'offre et de la demande** law of supply and demand; **loi parlementaire** act of parliament; **loi des rendements décroissants** law of diminishing returns; **lois tarifaires** tariff laws

loi-programme nf framework legislation

long, longue adj long; **longue distance** (appel) long-distance; Fin **à longue échéance** long dated; **à long terme** long-term; Fin **emprunter à long terme** to borrow long

longévité nf (d'un produit, des capitaux) life

longitudinal, -e adj (étude, recherche) longitudinal, continuous

lot nm (**a**) (de marchandises) batch ❏ **lot dépareillé** odd lot; **lot d'envoi** consignment (**b**) (aux enchères) lot (**c**) (de terrain) plot, lot (**d**) Bourse (d'actions) parcel

lotir vt (**a**) (marchandises) to divide into batches (**b**) (terrain à bâtir) to divide into building plots

lotissement nm (**a**) (fait de diviser) (de marchandises) dividing into batches; (de terrain à bâtir) division into plots (**b**) (terrain à bâtir) building plot (**c**) (ensemble d'habitations) housing estate or development

lotisseur, -euse nm,f property developer

louage nm **prendre qch à louage** to rent sth ❏ **louage de services** contract of employment

louer 1 vt (**a**) (donner en location) (logement) to rent out, Br to let (out) (**à** to); (voiture, équipement) to rent out, Br to hire out (**à** to); **maison à louer** house Br to let or Am for rent (**b**) (prendre en location) (logement) to rent (**à** from); (voiture, équipement) to rent, Br to hire
  2 se louer vpr (logement) to be rented or Br let; (voiture, équipement) to be rented or Br hired; **les locaux situés au centre de la capitale se louent à prix d'or** city centre premises are very expensive to rent

loueur, -euse nm,f renter, Br hirer

lourd, -e adj (industrie, investissement) heavy; **la crise en Asie est lourde de conséquences pour bien des entreprises en Europe** the crisis in Asia has serious consequences for many European companies

loyal, -e adj honest, fair; **un bon et loyal inventaire** a true and accurate inventory; **c'est quelqu'un de parfaitement loyal en affaires** he's a scrupulously fair businessman

loyalement adv honestly, fairly

loyauté nf honesty, fairness

loyer 1 nm (**a**) (de logement) rent; **être en retard sur son loyer, avoir des arriérés de loyer** to be behind with one's rent; **devoir trois mois de loyer** to owe three months' rent; **prendre une maison à loyer** to rent a house ❏ **loyer de bureau** office rent; **loyer trimestriel** quarterly rent (**b**) Fin **le loyer de l'argent** the interest rate, the price of money
  2 nmpl **loyers** lease revenue

lucratif, -ive adj (travail, activité, commerce) lucrative, profitable

luxe nm luxury; **de luxe** (produits) luxury

Mm

machine nf (**a**) (de bureau) machine; **écrire** ou **taper une lettre à la machine** to type a letter □ **machine à additionner** adding machine; **machine à affranchir** Br franking machine, Am postal meter; **machine à calculer** calculator; **machine à écrire** typewriter; **machine à facturer** invoicing machine; **machine de traitement de l'information** data processor; **machine de traitement de texte(s)** word processor
(**b**) (dans l'industrie, l'agriculture) machine; **les machines** (the) machinery; **fait à la machine** machine-made
(**c**) (organisation) machinery □ **machine administrative** administrative or bureaucratic machinery

machine-outil nf machine-tool

machinerie nf machinery

macrocommande nf Ordinat macro (command)

macroéconomie nf macroeconomics

macroéconomique adj macroeconomic

macroenvironnement nm macroenvironment

macro-instruction nf Ordinat macro instruction

macrolangage nm Ordinat macro language

macromarketing nm macromarketing

Madame nf (titre) Mrs; (au début d'une lettre) Dear Madam

Mademoiselle nf (titre) Miss; (au début d'une lettre) Dear Madam

magasin nm (**a**) (commerce) shop, Am store; **tenir un magasin** to keep a shop or Am store □ **magasin de détail** retail shop or Am store, retail outlet; **magasin détaxé** duty-free shop or Am store; **magasin de discount** discount shop or Am store; Ordinat **magasin électronique** on-line shop or Am store; **magasin d'exposition** showroom; **magasin franchisé** franchise; **magasin sous franchise exclusive** tied outlet; **magasin à grande surface** hypermarket; **magasin hors taxe** duty-free shop or Am store; **magasin libre-service** self-service shop or Am store; **magasin de luxe** luxury-goods shop or Am store; **magasin minimarge** discount shop or Am store; **magasin d'occasions** second-hand shop or Am store; **magasin à prix unique** one-price shop or Am store; **magasin de proximité** local shop; **magasin à succursales multiples** chain store; **magasin d'usine** factory shop or Am store, factory outlet; **magasin de vente au détail** retail shop or Am store
(**b**) (entrepôt) store, warehouse; **avoir qch en magasin** to have sth in stock □ Douanes **magasins généraux** bonded warehouse
(**c**) Mktg **magasin laboratoire** = model test-shop used to monitor consumer behaviour

magasinage nm (**a**) (de marchandises) warehousing, storing; (frais) warehouse or storage charges (**b**) Can shopping

magasiner vi Can **aller magasiner** to go shopping

magasinier nm warehouseman, warehouse keeper

magazine nm magazine □ **magazine d'actualités** current affairs magazine; **magazine électronique** e-zine, ezine; **magazine d'entreprise** in-house magazine, company magazine; **magazine d'information** news magazine

magnat nm magnate, tycoon □ **magnat des médias** media tycoon; **magnat du pétrole** oil magnate or tycoon; **magnat de la presse** press baron or tycoon

magouiller vi Fam to scheme, to wheel and deal

magouilles nfpl Fam scheming, wheeling and dealing

mailing nm (**a**) (procédé) mailing; **ce sont des clients que nous avons eus par mailing** we acquired these customers through a mailshot (**b**) (envoi de prospectus) mailshot; **faire un mailing** to do or send a mailshot

main nf (**a**) (membre) hand; **faire/fabriquer qch à la main** to do/to make sth by hand; **fait (à la) main** hand-made; **payer de la main à la main** to pay cash in hand; **passer la main (à)** to stand down (in favour of); **changer de mains** (entreprise, propriété) to change hands; **camion d'occasion de première main** second-hand truck (with only one previous owner); Ordinat, Tél **mains libres** hands-free
(**b**) Compta **main courante** cash book; **main courante de caisse** counter cash book; **main courante de dépenses** paid cash book; **main courante de recettes** received cash book

> On les comprend, les acheteurs piaffent à la porte, servis par des taux d'intérêt bas et une économie pas encore déprimée. Après un petit creux à la veille de l'été 2001, une paralysie attentiste après les événements du 11 septembre à New York, les ventes ont repris dès novembre et culminé en décembre. Quelque 616000 logements ont **changé de mains** l'an passé, contre 600400 en 2000, une année historique.

main-d'œuvre *nf* manpower, workforce; *Écon* labour; **embaucher de la main-d'œuvre** to take on workers; **cela vous coûtera 10 000 euros, main-d'œuvre comprise** that will cost 10,000 euros, including labour costs; **main-d'œuvre et fournitures** labour and material □ *main-d'œuvre contractuelle* contractual labour; *main-d'œuvre directe* direct labour; *main-d'œuvre étrangère* foreign labour; *main-d'œuvre féminine* female labour; *main-d'œuvre indirecte* indirect labour; *main-d'œuvre non spécialisée* unskilled labour; *main-d'œuvre occasionnelle* casual labour; *main-d'œuvre productive* productive labour; *main-d'œuvre qualifiée* skilled labour; *main-d'œuvre spécialisée* semi-skilled labour; *main-d'œuvre syndiquée* organized labour; *main-d'œuvre temporaire* temporary labour

mainlevée *nf Jur* withdrawal; *(d'une hypothèque)* withdrawal, release □ *mainlevée de saisie* restoration of goods *(taken in distraint)*, replevin

mainmise *nf (sur une propriété)* seizure (**sur** of); **la mainmise d'une seule société sur le marché du logiciel en inquiète plus d'un** many people are worried about a single company having a stranglehold on the software market □ *mainmise économique* economic stranglehold

maintenance *nf (de matériel)* maintenance (service) □ *maintenance à la demande, maintenance périodique* routine maintenance

maintenir 1 *vt* to maintain, to keep; **dividende maintenu à cinq pour cent** dividend maintained at five percent; **maintenir le change au-dessus du gold-point** to maintain the exchange above the gold-point; **maintenir les prix fermes** to keep prices firm *or* steady; **on accuse le gouvernment de maintenir cette entreprise en activité de façon artificielle** the government has been accused of using artificial means to keep the company operating
2 **se maintenir** *vpr* to hold up; **la hausse des prix se maintient à quatre pour cent** the rise in prices remains at four percent; **la livre se maintient par rapport au dollar** the pound is holding its own against the dollar; *Bourse* **ces**

actions se maintiennent à 57,5 euros these shares remain firm at 57.5 euros

maintien *nm (à un niveau donné)* maintenance; **maintien continu du plein emploi** continuous full employment; **le maintien de l'euro** maintaining the level of the euro; **le maintien du pouvoir d'achat des salariés doit être une priorité** maintaining wage-earners' purchasing power must be a priority

maison *nf (entreprise)* **maison (de commerce)** firm, company, business; **notre comptable a 25 ans de maison** our accountant has been with the firm for 25 years; **elle n'a pas l'esprit maison** she's got no company spirit □ *Banque maison d'acceptation Br* accepting house, *Am* acceptance house; *maison affiliée* affiliated company, *Am* affiliate; *maison de banque* banking house; *maison de commission* commission agency; *maison de courtage* brokerage house; *maison de détail* retail company; *maison d'édition* publishing company *or* house; *maison d'escompte* discount house; *maison d'expédition* forwarding house; *maison d'exportation* export firm; *maison de gros* wholesale firm; *maison d'importation* import firm; *maison mère* parent company; *maison de prêt* loan office *or* company; *maison de rabais* discount store; *maison à succursales multiples* chain store; *Fin maison de titres* securities firm; *maison de vente par correspondance* mail-order company

maître *nm (artisan)* skilled tradesman; **être maître du marché** to lead the market □ *maître bâtisseur* master builder; *maître d'œuvre* chief architect, project manager; *maître d'ouvrage* works owner; *Ordinat maître des postes* postmaster

maîtrise *nf* (a) *(dans une entreprise)* supervisory staff (b) *(diplôme)* ≃ master's degree

majeur, -e *adj (important)* major; **la majeure partie de nos exportations** the major part of our exports

majoration *nf* (a) *(de prix)* increase, mark-up (b) *(sur une facture)* additional charge, surcharge; **frapper un immeuble d'une majoration de cinq pour cent** to put five percent on the valuation of a building □ *majoration fiscale, majoration d'impôt* surcharge on taxes (c) *(d'actif)* overestimation, overvaluation

majorer *vt* (a) *(prix, tarif)* to increase, to raise (**de** by) (b) *(facture)* to make an additional charge on; **majorer une facture de dix pour cent** *(faire payer en plus)* to put ten percent on an invoice; *(faire payer en trop)* to overcharge by ten percent on an invoice; **tous les impôts impayés avant la fin du mois seront majorés de cinq pour cent** there will be a five percent additional charge on all taxes not paid by the end of the month (c) *(actif)* to overestimate, to overvalue

majoritaire *Bourse, Fin* **1** *adj* majority; **se rendre (largement) majoritaire** to acquire a majority interest *or* shareholding; **il a une participation majoritaire dans la société** he has a majority interest *or* shareholding in the company
2 *nmf* majority shareholder

majorité *nf* majority; **une majorité de(s) deux tiers** a two-thirds majority; **une décision prise à la majorité (des voix)** a majority decision; **la majorité des consommateurs se sont déclarés satisfaits de ce produit** most customers said that they were happy with the product □ *Mktg* **majorité absolue** absolute majority; *Mktg* **majorité conservatrice** late majority; *Mktg* **majorité innovatrice** early majority; *Mktg* **majorité précoce** early majority; Mktg **majorité qualifiée** supermajority; *Mktg* **majorité simple** simple majority; *Mktg* **majorité tardive** late majority

majuscule 1 *adj* upper-case
2 *nf* upper case

mal *adv* badly; **mal calculer un compte** to miscalculate an account; **mal gérer une affaire** to mismanage a business; **mal renseigner qn** to misinform sb; **il est très mal payé** he is very badly paid

maladie professionnelle *nf* occupational disease

malfaçon *nf* (a) *(travail de mauvaise qualité)* bad workmanship (b) *(défaut)* defect

malus *nm Assur* surcharge, extra premium

malversation *nf* embezzlement, corrupt administration (of funds)

"

Le procureur l'a impliqué dans le détournement, en 1999, de 4 millions d'euros destinés aux pauvres, délit passible de quatre à vingt ans de détention. La somme a été retournée depuis. Akbar Tandjung, qui était à l'époque secrétaire d'Etat, nie toute **malversation**.

"

---

management *nm* management □ **management des ressources humaines** human resource management

manager¹ *nm* manager

manager² *vt (projet, équipe commerciale)* to manage

mandant, -e *nm,f Jur* principal *(in transaction)* □ **mandant et mandataire** principal and agent

mandat *nm* (a) *(mission) (de député)* mandate; *(de président)* term of office; **exercer un mandat** to fill an elected position
(b) *Jur (ordre)* warrant □ **mandat d'action** receiving order (in bankruptcy); **mandat d'amener** ≃ summons; **mandat de dépôt** committal order

(c) *(mode de paiement)* order; **toucher un mandat** to draw on *or* to cash a money order; **un mandat sur la Banque de France** an order on the Bank of France □ **mandat international** international money order; **mandat de paiement** order to pay; **mandat postal, mandat poste** *Br* postal order, *Am* money order; *Fin* **mandat du Trésor** Treasury warrant; **mandat de virement** transfer order
(d) *(autorité)* mandate
(e) *Jur (procuration)* power of attorney, proxy; **donner mandat à qn** to give sb power of attorney

mandataire *nmf* (a) *(représentant)* proxy, representative (b) *Jur* authorized agent, assignee □ **mandataire général** general agent; **mandataire liquidateur** official receiver

mandat-carte *nm Br* postal order, *Am* money order *(in postcard form)*

mandat-contributions *nm Br* postal order, *Am* money order *(for paying income tax)*

mandatement *nm* = payment by means of a money order

mandater *vt* (a) *(représentant)* to appoint, to commission (b) *(somme)* to pay by *Br* postal order *or Am* money order

mandat-lettre *nm Br* postal order, *Am* money order *(which may be sent as a letter in an envelope)*

mandat-poste *nm Br* postal order, *Am* money order

maniement *nm (d'une affaire, de fonds)* handling, management

manier *vt (affaire, fonds)* to handle, to manage

manifeste *nm* manifest □ **manifeste de chargement** manifest; **manifeste de douane** customs manifest; **manifeste d'entrée** inward manifest; **manifeste de fret** freight manifest; **manifeste de sortie** outward manifest

manipulation *nf* (a) *Bourse, Fin* manipulation, rigging □ **manipulations comptables** creative accounting; **manipulation monétaire** currency manipulation (b) *Ordinat* **manipulation de documents** document handling; **manipulation de données** data manipulation

manœuvre¹ *nf* (a) *Bourse* **manœuvre boursière** stock market manipulation (b) *Jur* **manœuvres frauduleuses** swindling

manœuvre² *nm* unskilled labourer *or* worker; **travail de manœuvre** unskilled labour *or* work □ **manœuvre qualifié** skilled worker; **manœuvre spécialisé** semi-skilled worker

manquant *nm* shortfall, shortage □ **manquant en caisse** cash shortage; **manquant en stock** stock shortage

manque *nm* (a) *(pénurie)* lack, shortage □ **man-**

que à l'embarquement short-shipped goods; **manque à gagner** loss of profit *or* earnings; **manque à la livraison** short delivery (**b**) *Compta* shortfall ◻ **manque de caisse** cash unders; **manque de capitaux** capital shortfall

> **❝**
>
> Il s'agit de compenser un **manque à gagner**. Les salariés ont souscrit à l'époque des actions coûtant environ 48 euros et qui n'en valent plus que 16. Ceux qui avaient pris un crédit remboursent actuellement cet engagement.
>
> **❞**

manquement *nm* breach ◻ **manquement à la discipline** breach of discipline, misconduct; **manquement à l'obligation de prudence** negligence

manquer 1 *vt (occasion)* to miss, to lose; **manquer une affaire** to miss one's chance of doing business; **manquer un contrat** to lose a contract
2 *vi* (**a**) *(faire défaut)* to be lacking; **manquer en magasin** to be out of stock (**b**) *(être absent)* to be missing (**à** from); **manquer à un rendez-vous** to fail to keep an appointment
3 manquer de *vt ind (argent, main-d'œuvre)* to be short of, to lack
4 *v impersonnel* **il nous manque les capitaux nécessaires** we are short of the necessary capital

manuel¹, -elle 1 *adj (travail, travailleur)* manual
2 *nm,f (personne)* manual worker

manuel² *nm* manual, handbook ◻ **manuel d'entretien** service manual; **manuel d'utilisation** user manual

manufacturé, -e *adj* manufactured, factory-made

manufacturer *vt* to manufacture

manufacturier, -ère *adj (industrie)* manufacturing

manutention *nf (de marchandises)* handling ◻ **manutention industrielle** industrial handling

manutentionnaire *nmf* warehouseman, *f* warehousewoman

manutentionner *vt (marchandises)* to handle

mapping *nm Mktg* mapping

maquette *nf* (**a**) *(de livre)* dummy (**b**) *(d'une construction architecturale)* (scale) model; *(de mise en page)* paste-up, layout (**c**) *(dans l'industrie)* mock-up

maquettiste *nmf* layout artist

maquignonnage *nm* shady dealing, wheeling and dealing

> **❝**
>
> Les manœuvres tacticiennes auxquelles a donné lieu le sommet de Laeken, la désignation de Valéry Giscard d'Estaing, le véritable **maquignonnage** entre la présidence belge, la France et l'Italie, d'autant plus compliqué que l'attribution des sièges d'une douzaine d'agences européennes faisait parti du marché ... ne doivent pas cacher les véritables causes des blocages de l'Union.
>
> **❞**

maquignonner *vi* to wheel and deal

maquillage *nm (d'un chèque, d'un document, d'un bilan)* falsification

maquiller *vt (chèque, document, bilan)* to falsify

marasme *nm Écon* stagnation, slump; **le marasme économique actuel** the present economic slump; **le marasme des affaires** the slump in business; **l'économie des pays d'Asie traverse actuellement une période de marasme** Asian economies are currently going through a period of stagnation

> **❝**
>
> Le fabricant d'ordinateurs Gateway a mis fin à son activité, provoquant la suppression de 2000 postes. Un vrai électrochoc pour les Irlandais. Le **marasme** de cette industrie a fait chuter la croissance économique, tombée de 11% en 2000 à 6% en 2001, et à 3,5% selon les dernières prévisions pour cette année.
>
> **❞**

marchand, -e 1 *adj (quartier, ville)* commercial
2 *nm,f (dans un magasin) Br* shopkeeper, *Am* storekeeper; *(de tableaux, de meubles)* dealer ◻ **marchand de biens** *Br* ≃ estate agent, *Am* ≃ realtor, real estate agent; **marchand au détail** retailer; **marchand en gros** wholesaler, wholesale dealer

marchandage *nm* (**a**) *(sur le prix d'un article)* bargaining, haggling (**b**) *Jur* illegal subcontracting of labour *(whereby the worker receives less than a fair wage)*

marchander 1 *vt* (**a**) *(prix, article)* to bargain over, to haggle over (**b**) *Jur* to subcontract illegally
2 *vi* to bargain, to haggle

marchandeur, -euse *nm,f* (**a**) *(sur le prix d'un article)* haggler, bargainer (**b**) *Jur* illegal subcontractor of labour

marchandisage *nm* marketing, merchandising

marchandise *nf* merchandise, commodity; **marchandises** goods, merchandise ◻ *Bourse* **marchandises et biens physiques** actuals; **marchandises de contrebande** contraband goods; **marchandises au détail** retail goods; **marchandises en entrepôt** warehoused goods, goods in storage; *Douanes* bonded goods, goods in bond; **marchandises à l'export** export goods; **marchandises en gros** wholesale goods; **marchandises à l'import** import goods; *Bourse* **marchandises livrables au comptant** spot goods; **marchandises en magasin** stock in hand; **marchandises d'origine** = goods of guaranteed origin; **marchandises sur palette(s)** palletized goods; **marchandises périssables** perishable goods, perishables; **marchandises de qualité** quality goods; **marchandises sèches** dry goods; **marchandises en souffrance** unclaimed goods; **marchandises en stock** stock in hand; **marchandises en transit** goods in transit; **marchandises de vente courante** goods that have a ready sale; **marchandises en vrac** bulk goods

marchandiser *vt* to merchandise

marchandiseur *nm* merchandiser

marche *nf* (**a**) *(fonctionnement)* running, working; **en état de marche** in working order; **la bonne marche d'une entreprise** the smooth running of a firm (**b**) **marche à suivre** procedure (**c**) *Bourse* **marche aléatoire** random walk

marché *nm* (**a**) *Écon, Mktg* market; **mettre** *ou* **lancer un nouveau produit sur le marché** to put *or* to launch a new product on the market; **ce produit n'a pas de marché** there is no market for this product; **conquérir un marché** to break into a market; **arriver sur le marché** to come onto the market; **mettre qch sur le marché** to put sth on the market; **retirer qch du marché** to take sth off the market ▫ **marché d'acheteurs** buyers' market; *Bourse* **marché des actions** share market, stock market; **marché actuel** existing market; *Bourse* **marché à la baisse, marché baissier** buyers' *or* bear market; **marché des besoins** need market; **marché boursier** stock market; **marché cambiste** foreign exchange market; **marché de capitaux** capital market, investment market; **marché captif** captive market; **marché des céréales** grain market; *Bourse* **marché des changes** currency (exchange) market, foreign exchange market; *Bourse* **marché des changes à terme** forward exchange market; **marché cible** target market; *Anciennement* **le Marché commun** the Common Market; *Fin* **marché au comptant** spot market; **marché de concurrence** competitive marketplace; **marché des consommateurs, marché de consommation** consumer market; *Bourse* **marché continu** continuous *or* all-day trading; *Bourse* **marché des contrats à terme** futures market; *Bourse* **marché de cotation** securities market; **marché en coulisse** outside market; **marché demandeur** buyers' market; *Fin* **marché des denrées et matières premières** commodity market;

marché des devises (étrangères) foreign exchange market; *Bourse* **marché dirigé par les cotations** quotation-driven market; *Bourse* **marché dirigé par les ordres** order-driven market; *Fin* **marché du disponible** spot market; **marché effectif** available market; *Bourse* **marché électronique privé** ECN, electronic communications network; **marché de l'emploi** job market; **marché des entreprises** business market; **marché environnant** substitution market; **marché d'équipement** capital goods market; **marché de l'escompte** discount market; **marché étranger** overseas market; **marché de l'eurodevise** euromarket, eurocurrency market; **marché existant** existing market; **marché à l'exportation** export market; **marché extérieur** foreign market, overseas market; **marché financier** money *or* financial market; **marché générique** generic market; **marché global** global market; **marché grand public** consumer market, mass market; **marché de gré à gré entre banques** interbank wholesale market; *Bourse* **marché gris** grey market; **marché à la hausse, marché haussier** sellers' *or* bull market; *Bourse* **marché hors Bourse** street market; *Bourse* **marché hors cote** unlisted securities market, *Am* over-the-counter market; **marché hypothécaire** mortgage market; **marché de l'immobilier** property market, housing market; **marché industriel** industrial market; **marché de l'information** information market; **marché interbancaire** interbank market; **marché intérieur** home market, domestic market; **marché des intermédiaires** middleman's market; **marché libre** *Écon* free market; *Bourse* open market; **marché libre des capitaux** open money market; **marché locatif** rental market; *Bourse* **marché lourd** heavy market; **marché marginal** fringe market; **marché de masse** mass market; *Fin* **marché des matières premières** commodity market; **marché mondial** world *or* global market; *Bourse* **marché mondial des actions** global equities market; **marché monétaire** money market; **marché monétaire international** international money market; **marché monopolistique** monopoly market; *Bourse* **marché mort** dead market; **marché national** national market, home market; *Bourse* **marché du neuf** primary market; **marché noir** black market; **faire du marché noir** to buy and sell on the black market; *Bourse* **marché des nouvelles émissions** new issue market; *Bourse* **marché obligataire, marché des obligations** bond market; **marché officiel** official market; **marché à** *ou* **des options** options market; *Bourse* **marché des options négociables de Paris** Paris traded options exchange, *Br* ≃ London International Financial Futures Exchange, *Am* ≃ Chicago Board Options Exchange; **marché de l'or** gold market; **marché d'outre-**

mer overseas market; **marché parallèle** parallel or black market; **marché pétrolier** oil market; **marché porteur** growth market; **marché des prêts** loan market; Bourse **marché primaire** primary market; **marché à primes** options market; **marché principal** core market; Bourse **marché à prix affichés** quotation-driven market; Jur **marché public** market overt; **marché de référence** core market, benchmark market; Bourse **marché du règlement mensuel** forward market; **marché de renouvellement** repurchase market; **marché de revente** second-hand market; Bourse **marché RM** forward market; Bourse **marché secondaire** secondary market; **marché témoin** control market, test market; Fin **marché à terme** futures market, forward market; Bourse **marché à terme de devises** forward exchange market; **Marché à terme des instruments financiers** financial futures or derivatives market; **Marché à terme international de France** = body regulating activities on the French stock exchange, Br ≃ LIFFE, Am ≃ CBOE; **marché test** test market; Bourse **marché des titres** securities market; **marché des transactions hors séance** Br unlisted securities market, Am over-the-counter market; **marché du travail** labour market; **le Marché unique (européen)** the Single (European) Market; **marché utile** addressable market; Bourse **marché des valeurs mobilières** stock exchange, securities market; Bourse **marché des valeurs de premier ordre** gilt-edged market, gilts market; **marché vendeur** sellers' market; **marché visé** target market (**b**) (accord) deal, bargain; (plus officiel) contract; **faire** ou **conclure un marché** to strike a deal or bargain, to clinch a deal ◻ **marché compensatoire** compensation deal; **marché de gré à gré** mutual agreement, private contract

> ❝
> De fait, 78% des cadres qui ont quitté leur entreprise en 2000 l'ont fait de leur propre initiative. Bien sûr, la situation du **marché de l'emploi** influe fortement sur la volonté de changement. Les cadres y sont d'autant plus enclins que la conjoncture est favorable.
> ❞

marchéage nm Mktg marketing mix, marketing spectrum ◻ **marchéage de distribution** retailing mix

marcher vi (**a**) (travail, projet) to be going well; (entreprise, nouveau produit) to do well; **les affaires marchent/ne marchent pas fort** business is brisk/slack; **notre nouveau modèle marche bien/mal** our new model is doing well/badly; **ça fait marcher le commerce** it's good for business (**b**) (machine, appareil) to

work, to run; **faire marcher qch** to work or operate sth

marge nf margin; **avoir une faible/forte marge** to have a low/high (profit) margin; **nous faisons 30 pour cent de marge sur ce produit** we make a 30 percent margin on this product ◻ Mktg **marge arrière** refund (given to distributors at end of financial year); Compta **marge d'autofinancement** cash flow; Compta **marge d'autofinancement disponible** free cash flow; **marge bénéficiaire** profit margin; **marge brute** gross (profit) margin; Compta **marge brute d'autofinancement** cash flow; **marge commerciale** trading profit; **marge commerciale brute** gross profit margin; **marge commerciale nette** net profit margin; **marge de crédit** credit margin; **marge du détaillant** retailer margin; **marge du distributeur** distributor's margin; **marge d'erreur** margin of error; Fin **marge étroite** fine price; Fin **marge de flottement, marge de fluctuation** (d'une monnaie) margin of fluctuation, fluctuation band; **marge du grossiste** wholesaler margin; **marge de l'importateur** importer margin; **marge avant impôt** pre-tax margin; **marge initiale** initial margin; **marge d'intérêt** margin of interest; **marge nette** net (profit) margin; **marge nette d'exploitation** operating margin; **marge de profit** profit margin; **marge sectorielle** segment margin; **marge de sécurité** safety margin; **marge de tolérance** tolerance margin

marger Ordinat **1** vt (page) to set the margin(s) for
2 vi to set the margin(s); **marger à droite/à gauche** to set the right/left margin

marginal, -e adj Écon marginal

margoulin nm Fam (**a**) (à la Bourse) petty speculator (**b**) (escroc) shark, swindler

> ❝
> Ces deux conflits ont montré que les plans sociaux ne sont pas adaptés aux drames industriel et humain. Dans les deux situations, nous aurions préféré le maintien de l'activité, et rien n'indique que c'était impossible. La preuve ? Les ouvrières de chez Lacoste ont obtenu un repreneur, Vesta, qui est un industriel sérieux, pas un **margoulin**, alors que celles de Cellatex pointent à l'ANPE.
> ❞

mariage nm Bourse matched bargain

maritime adj (droit, législation, risque) maritime

mark nm (**a**) Anciennement (monnaie allemande) (German) mark, Deutschmark (**b**) (monnaie finlandaise) markka

marketer nm marketing expert, marketing consultant

marketing *nm* marketing ❑ *marketing après-vente* after-sales marketing; *marketing ciblé* niche *or* target marketing; *marketing commercial* trade marketing; *marketing concentré* concentrated marketing; *marketing de contact* direct marketing; *marketing de différenciation, marketing différencié* differentiated marketing; *marketing direct* direct marketing; *marketing écologique* green marketing; *Ordinat marketing électronique* on-line marketing; *marketing global* global marketing; *marketing de grande consommation* mass marketing; *marketing indifférencié* undifferentiated marketing; *marketing industriel* industrial marketing; *marketing interactif* interactive marketing; *marketing international* global marketing; *marketing interne* internal marketing; *marketing de masse* mass marketing; *marketing sur mesure* customized marketing; *marketing mix* marketing mix; *marketing multinational* multinational marketing; *marketing non commercial* non-business marketing; *marketing non lucratif* not-for-profit marketing; *marketing de nouveaux produits* new product marketing; *marketing one to one* one-to-one marketing; *marketing opérationnel* operational marketing; *marketing de relance* remarketing; *marketing relationnel* relationship *or* direct marketing; *marketing de réseau* multi-level marketing; *marketing sélectif* selective marketing; *marketing de stimulation* stimulation *or* incentive marketing; *marketing stratégique* strategic marketing; *marketing téléphonique* cold calling, telemarketing; *marketing vert* green marketing; *marketing viral* viral marketing

> ❝
> Le **marketing viral** peut être comparé au concept de "bouche à oreille". On parle de **marketing viral** sans friction quand l'utilisateur fait connaître un service en l'utilisant (ex Hotmail) et de **marketing viral** actif quand l'utilisateur est incité à faire connaître le service à ses connaissances (système de parrainage, de recommandations).
> ❞

marquage *nm* branding, marking

marque *nf* (**a**) *(de produit)* brand; *(de voiture)* make; *(sur l'article)* trademark; **grande marque** famous make, well-known brand; **de marque** *(produit)* branded ❑ *marque d'appel* loss leader brand; *marque clé* key brand; *marque collective* label; *marque de commerce* trademark, brand (name); *marque déposée* registered trademark; *marque de distributeur* distributor's brand name, own brand; *marque dominante* dominant brand; *marque économique* budget *or* economy brand; *marque de fabricant* manufacturer's brand name; *marque de fabrique* trademark, brand (name); *marque de garantie*

certification mark; *marque générale* family brand; *marque générique* generic brand; *marque globale* global brand; *marque grand public* consumer brand; *marque de magasin* store brand; *marque multiple* multibrand; *marque ombrelle* umbrella brand; *marque d'origine* maker's mark; *marque de service* mark of quality, quality guarantee *(on range of services offered by company or manufacturer)*; *marque de tête* brand leader; *marque de valeur* value brand
(**b**) *(cachet)* stamp
(**c**) *Ordinat* marker, flag, tag ❑ *marque d'insertion* insertion marker; *marque de paragraphe* paragraph mark

marquer *vt* (**a**) *(article, produit)* to brand, to label, to mark (**b**) *Ordinat* to mark, to flag, to tag

marqueur *nm* (**a**) *(feutre)* marker pen (**b**) *Ordinat* marker, flag, tag ❑ *marqueur de fin de texte* end-of-text marker

masse *nf* (**a**) *Fin* fund, stock; *(de personnes)* body ❑ *masse active* assets; *masse des créanciers* (general) body of creditors; *masse monétaire* money supply; *masse des obligataires* body of debenture holders *or* bondholders; *masse passive* liabilities; *masse salariale* wages bill, payroll (**b**) *Ordinat (d'informations)* bulk

> ❝
> Contrairement aux idées reçues, la **masse salariale** a augmenté sensiblement plus vite que les profits, ce qui ne s'était pas produit depuis vingt ans; la politique fiscale et sociale a allégé de quelque 5 milliards d'euros les prélèvements sur la moitié supérieure de la population, mais pour la moitié inférieure le gain a été de l'ordre de 6 milliards.
> ❞

mass(-)média(s) *nmpl* mass media

matérialiser *vt Fin* to realize

matériel, -elle 1 *adj* material
2 *nm* (**a**) *(équipements)* equipment ❑ *matériel de bureau* office equipment; *matériel d'entretien* maintenance equipment; *matériel à longévité élevée* long-life equipment; *matériel lourd* heavy equipment *or* plant; *matériel et main-d'œuvre* material and labour (**b**) *Mktg* material ❑ *matériel de PLV* point-of-sale material; *matériel de présentation* display material; *matériel de promotion* promotional material; *matériel publicitaire* advertising material (**c**) *Ordinat* hardware ❑ *matériel informatique* computer hardware

matière *nf* (**a**) *(substance)* material ❑ *matière brute* unprocessed material; *matière et façon* material and labour; *matière non travaillé* unrefined material; *matières premières* raw materials; *Bourse matières premières et denrées* commodities (**b**) *(domaine)* matter ❑ *matière juridique* legal matter (**c**) *Fin matière imposable* taxable income

MATIF *nm* (**a**) *(abrév* **Marché à terme d'instruments financiers**) financial futures *or* derivatives market (**b**) *(abrév* **Marché à terme international de France**) = body regulating activities on the French stock exchange, *Br* ≃ LIFFE, *Am* ≃ CBOE

matinée de Bourse *nf* morning session

matraquage *nm Fam Mktg* plugging, hype ❑ *matraquage marketing, matraquage publicitaire* plugging, hype

> **"**
> La bataille des consoles de jeux va bientôt commencer. A grands coups de pilonnage publicitaire et de **matraquage marketing**. Deux mois après son concurrent Microsoft et sa Xbox, Nintendo lance à son tour une nouvelle console baptisée Game Cube (sortie prévue le 3 mai).
> **"**

matraquer *nm Fam Mktg* to plug, to hype

matrice *nf* (**a**) *Admin* register (**b**) *Ordinat* matrix; *(de données)* array (**c**) *Mktg* **matrice BCG** Boston matrix; *matrice croissance-part de marché* growth-share matrix

matricule *nf* registration certificate

maturité *nf* maturity; **économie en pleine maturité** mature economy; **mon compte d'épargne n'est pas encore arrivé à maturité** my savings account hasn't matured yet

mauvais, -e *adj* bad; **en mauvais état** in bad condition; **de mauvaise qualité** poor-quality, inferior; **faire de mauvaises affaires** to be doing badly; **faire de mauvais placements** to make bad investments, to invest unwisely ❑ *mauvaise administration* mismanagement; *mauvaise créance* bad debt; *mauvaise gestion* mismanagement, bad management; *mauvais payeur* bad payer

maximal, -e *adj* maximum

maximalisation *nf* maximization, maximizing

maximaliser, maximiser *vt* to maximize

maximum 1 *adj (prix, tarif, cours)* maximum **2** *nm* maximum; **maximum de rendement** highest performance, maximum efficiency; **au maximum** *(au plus)* at the most; *(le plus possible)* to the highest degree; **porter la production au maximum** to maximize production

Mb *nm Ordinat (abrév* **mégabit**) Mb

MBA *nf Compta (abrév* **marge brute d'autofinancement**) cash flow

Mbps *Ordinat (abrév* **mégabits par seconde**) Mbps

m-commerce *nm* m-commerce

MDD *nf Mktg (abrév* **marque de distributeur**) distributor's brand name, own brand

mécanisation *nf* mechanization

mécanisé, -e *adj* mechanized

mécaniser *vt* to mechanize

mécanisme *nm* mechanism ❑ *mécanisme administratif* administrative machinery; *mécanisme bancaire* banking machinery *or* mechanism; *mécanisme budgétaire* budgetary mechanism; *Écon, UE mécanisme de change* Exchange Rate Mechanism; *Écon, UE mécanisme de change européen* European Exchange Rate Mechanism; *mécanismes économiques* economic machinery; *mécanisme de l'escompte* discount mechanism; *mécanisme du marché* market mechanism; *mécanisme de l'offre et de la demande* supply and demand mechanism; *mécanisme des prix* price mechanism

mécénat *nm* sponsorship ❑ *mécénat d'entreprise* corporate sponsorship

> **"**
> Le **mécénat** culturel des entreprises privées européennes atteint un montant annuel de 1,1 milliard d'euros. Ce chiffre représente environ 4 % du montant du financement de la culture, dans les 11 pays (l'Union hors Danemark, Finlande, Luxembourg et Portugal) sur lesquels porte une étude ... Bruxelles affirme vouloir développer un environnement juridique et fiscal favorable au **mécénat**, notamment dans les futurs Etats membres.
> **"**

mécompte *nm* miscalculation, error in reckoning

MÉDAF *nm Fin (abrév* **modèle d'évaluation des actifs**) CAPM

médecin *nm* doctor ❑ *médecin d'entreprise* company doctor; *médecin du travail* medical officer

MEDEF *nm (abrév* **Mouvement des entreprises de France**) French employers' association, *Br* ≃ CBI

média *nm* medium; **les médias** the media; **une campagne publicitaire dans tous les médias** a media-wide advertising campaign ❑ *médias électroniques* electronic media; *média de masse* mass media; *médias numériques* digital media; *médias numériques interactifs* interactive digital media; *média planner* media planner; *média planning* media planning; *média publicitaire* advertising media; *médias de télécommunication* telecommunications media

médialisation *nf* media planning

médialogie *nf* media research

médiaplaneur, médiaplanneur *nm* media planner

médiaplanning *nm* media planning

médiateur, -trice 1 *adj* mediatory, mediating 2 *nm,f* mediator; *Admin* ombudsman; *(dans l'industrie)* arbitrator, conciliator; **agir en médiateur** *ou* **servir de médiateur (entre)** to act as mediator (between) □ **médiateur d'entreprises** arbitrator

médiation *nf (de conflit, de crise)* mediation

médiatique *adj* media; *(personne, société)* media-friendly; **un événement médiatique** a media event; **il est très médiatique** *(il passe bien à la télévision)* he comes over very well on television, he's very mediagenic; *(il exploite les médias)* he uses the media very successfully, he's very media-conscious

> L'entrée en Bourse d'Afflelou, le plus **médiatique** des opticiens français, commençait à prendre des airs d'Arlésienne. Cette fois, plus question de reculer: ce 4 avril, Alain Afflelou introduit sa société au second marché de la Bourse de Paris.

médiatisation *nf* media coverage; **la médiatisation d'un événement** the media coverage given to an event

médiatiser *vt (populariser)* to popularize through the media; *(événement)* to give media coverage to; **il est très médiatisé** he's got a high media profile

médiologie *nf* mediology

médium *nm (support)* medium

méga *nm Ordinat* megabyte, meg

mégabit *nm Ordinat* megabit; **mégabits par seconde** megabits per second

mégafusion *nf* mega-merger

mégahertz *nm* megahertz

mégaoctet *nm Ordinat* megabyte

meilleur, -e *adj* (a) *(comparatif de bon)* better; **meilleur marché** cheaper, less expensive; **acheter qch (à) meilleur marché** to buy sth cheaper; **payer qch meilleur marché** to pay less for sth; **ce produit est de meilleure qualité** this product is of better quality (b) *(superlatif de bon)* best; **veuillez nous faire profiter de votre meilleur prix** please give us your best price

mél, mel *nm Ordinat (courrier électronique)* e-mail; *(adresse électronique)* e-mail address

membre 1 *adj (pays, État)* member 2 *nm (participant)* member □ **membre associé** associate member; *Bourse* **membre de compensation** clearing member; **membre fonda-**

teur founding member; **membre honoraire** honorary member; **membre permanent** permanent member; **membre suppléant** deputy member

mémoire 1 *nm* (a) *(note)* account, bill; **présenter un mémoire** to send a detailed account *or* bill (b) *Compta* report 2 *nf* (a) *Ordinat* memory; **cet ordinateur possède 32 mégaoctets de mémoire RAM** this computer has 32 megabytes of RAM; **mettre un dossier en mémoire** to write a file to memory □ **mémoire bloc-notes** scratchpad memory; **mémoire centrale** main memory; **mémoire disponible** available memory; **mémoire à disque** disk memory; **mémoire haute** high memory; **mémoire intermédiaire** buffer memory; **mémoire de masse** mass storage; **mémoire morte** read-only memory; **mémoire RAM dynamique** dynamic RAM; **mémoire tampon** buffer memory; **mémoire tampon de texte** text buffer; **mémoire vive** random access memory; **mémoire vive dynamique** dynamic random access memory; **mémoire vive statique** static random access memory (b) **pour mémoire** for the record

mémoire-cache *nf Ordinat* cache (memory); **mettre en mémoire-cache** to cache

mémomarque *nf Mktg* brand name recall

mémorandum *nm* (a) *(circulaire)* memorandum, memo (b) *(à un fournisseur)* written order

mémorisation *nf* (a) *Ordinat* writing to memory (b) *Mktg* recall □ **mémorisation un jour après** day-after recall; **mémorisation de la marque** brand-name recall

mémoriser *vt Ordinat* to write to memory

menace *nf (d'un concurrent, d'un produit)* threat

ménage *nm Écon* household; **les revenus des ménages** household incomes

> Car, outre le climat social alourdi par la remontée du chômage, c'est la hausse du pétrole, plus importante que prévu mais peut-être provisoire, qui motive une baisse de forme de la consommation des **ménages**.

ménager, -ère *adj Écon* household

mener *vt* (a) *(groupe, équipe)* to lead (b) *(négociation, étude)* to carry out

meneur, -euse *nm,f* leader □ **meneur de grève** strike leader

mensualisation *nf (d'un salaire, d'un paiement)* paying by the month, monthly payment; **pour vos règlements, pensez à la mensualisation** don't forget that you can pay in monthly instalments

mensualiser *vt* to pay monthly; **il est payé au trimestre mais il a demandé à être mensualisé** he is paid quarterly but has asked to be paid monthly

mensualité *nf* (**a**) *(paiement)* monthly payment; **payer par mensualités** to pay by monthly instalments; **il a payé son ordinateur en 36 mensualités** he paid for his computer in 36 monthly instalments □ **mensualité de remboursement** monthly repayment (**b**) *(salaire)* monthly salary

❝
S'ils décident d'augmenter leur **mensualité** de 100 euros à partir de la vingtième, ils économiseront 51 mois et 4 515 euros sur le coût de leur crédit. S'ils décident de l'augmenter de 150 euros, toujours à partir de la vingtième, ils gagneront 58 mois et 6 351 euros.
❞

mensuel, -elle **1** *adj (rapport, publication, relevé)* monthly
2 *nm,f (employé)* employee paid monthly
3 *nm (revue)* monthly (magazine)

mensuellement *adv (tous les mois)* monthly, every month; *(une fois par mois)* once a month

mention *nf* (**a**) *(fait de citer)* mention; **faire mention de qn/qch** to mention sb/sth, to refer to sb/sth (**b**) *(indication)* note, comment; *Admin* **rayer les mentions inutiles** *(sur formulaire)* delete where inapplicable; **le dossier porte la mention "confidentiel"** the file is marked "confidential" □ **mention de réserve** copyright notice

mentionner *vt* to mention; **mentionné ci-dessus** above-mentioned, aforementioned

menu *nm Ordinat* menu □ **menu d'aide** help menu; **menu en cascade** cascading menu; **menu déroulant** pull-down menu; **menu fichier** file menu; **menu d'impression** print menu; **menu local** pop-up menu; **menu principal** main menu

mercantile *adj* mercantile, commercial

mercantilisme *nm* mercantilism

mercaticien, -enne *nm,f Mktg* marketing expert, marketing consultant

mercatique *nf* marketing

merchandisage *nm* merchandising

merchandising *nm* merchandising

mercuriale *nf Bourse* commodity *or* market price list

message *nm* (**a**) *(communication)* message; **prendre un message** to take a message; **veuillez laisser un message après le signal sonore** please leave a message after the tone; **laisser un message à l'attention de qn** to leave a message for sb □ **message électronique** e-mail; envoyer un message électronique à qn to e-mail sb; **message enregistré** recorded message; *Mktg* **message principal** core message; *Mktg* **message publicitaire** advertisement; **message système** broadcast message; **message téléphonique** telephone message; **message télex** telex (message); *Tél* **message texte** text message (**b**) *Ordinat (à l'écran)* message □ **message d'accueil** welcome message; **message d'aide** help message; **message d'alerte** warning message, alert box; **message d'attente (du système)** (system) prompt; **message d'erreur** error message; **message d'invite** prompt

messagerie *nf* (**a**) *(service de transports)* courier company □ **messageries aériennes** air freight company; **messageries maritimes** shipping company (**b**) *Ordinat* **messagerie de dialogue en direct** chat; **messagerie électronique** e-mail; **messagerie vocale** voice mail (**c**) *(entreprise de routage)* **messagerie de presse** newspaper distribution service

mesure *nf* (**a**) *(initiative)* measure, step; **le gouvernement a pris des mesures pour réduire le chômage des jeunes** the government has taken measures to reduce youth unemployment □ **mesures déflationnistes** deflationary measures; **mesure disciplinaire** disciplinary measure; **mesure économique** economic measure; **mesures préventives** preventive measures; **mesures protectionnistes** protectionist measures; **mesures provisoires** temporary measures; **mesures de sécurité** safety measures *or* precautions; **par mesure de sécurité** as a safety precaution; **mesures d'urgence** emergency measures
(**b**) *(action)* measurement, measuring; *(résultat)* measurement; **la mesure de la productivité a été améliorée grâce à de nouvelles techniques** productivity measurement has been improved thanks to new techniques □ *Mktg* **mesure d'audience** audience measurement; *Mktg* **mesure d'impact** impact measurement; *Mktg* **mesure de satisfaction de la clientèle** customer satisfaction measurement (**c**) **être en mesure de faire qch** to be in a position to do sth, to be able to do sth; **l'entreprise n'est pas en mesure de fournir les quantités nécessaires** the company is unable to supply the necessary quantities

mesurer *vt* (**a**) *(déterminer la dimension de)* to measure (**b**) *(estimer)* to assess; **mesurer l'ampleur d'un problème** to assess the size of a problem (**c**) *(adapter)* **mesurer ses dépenses sur ses profits** to gear one's expenditure to one's profits (**d**) *(limiter)* to limit; **on nous mesure les crédits** our funds are limited

métal *nm Fin* metal □ **métal en barres** bullion; **métal en lingots** ingots

métallique *adj Fin (monnaie)* metallic

méthode *nf (façon de procéder)* method ❑ *Compta* **méthode d'achat** purchase method; **méthodes administratives** systems and procedures; *Compta* **méthode d'amortissement dégressif** declining balance method; *Compta* **méthode d'amortissement linéaire** straight line depreciation method; **méthode d'analyse statistique** method of statistical analysis; *Mktg* **méthode de la boule de neige** referral system; *Compta* **méthode de capitalisation du coût entier** full cost accounting (method); **méthode du chemin critique** critical path method; **méthode de classement** filing system; *Compta* **méthode de comptabilité** accounting method; *Compta* **méthode de comptabilité des coûts variables** direct cost accounting; **méthode des coûts marginaux** cost pricing; *Compta* **méthode du coût de revient complet** full costing, full cost accounting (method); **méthode des coûts proportionnels** ou **variables** direct costing; *Compta* **méthode des coûts standards** standard cost accounting, standard costing; *Mktg* **méthode d'échantillonnage** sampling method; *Compta* **méthode par** ou **à échelles** daily balance interest calculation; **méthode estimative** judgemental method; **méthode expérimentale** experimental method; **méthode d'exploitation** method of working *or* operation; **méthode de fabrication** manufacturing method; **méthode linéaire** straight line method; *Mktg* **méthode non probabiliste** non-probability method; **méthodes et organisation** organization and methods; *Mktg* **méthode probabiliste** probability method; **méthode prospective** projected benefit valuation method; *Mktg* **méthode des quotas** quota sampling method; *Mktg* **méthode de sélection** selection method; *Mktg* **méthode de sondage** polling method, sampling method; *Mktg* **méthode de vente** sales technique, selling technique; *Mktg* **méthode de vente agressive** hard sell techniques; *Mktg* **méthode de vente non agressive** soft sell techniques

méthodologie *nf* methodology

métier *nm* (**a**) *(profession)* profession, occupation; **exercer** ou **faire un métier** to carry on a trade *or* a profession; **il exerce le métier de comptable** he is an accountant; **il est du métier** he's in the trade *or* the business ❑ **métier manuel** manual trade (**b**) *(savoir-faire)* experience; **avoir du métier** to have experience, to be experienced; **manquer de métier** to lack experience, to be inexperienced

métrage *nm (métier)* quantity surveying

mètre linéaire *nm* linear metre

> ❝
> Le temps de parcours d'un client pour venir et revenir de son magasin est de vingt à vingt-cinq minutes. Il vient d'y passer cin-

quante minutes. Il a soif. Lorsqu'un hypermarché dispose d'une *vending machine*, il réalise 1 000 000 F de chiffre d'affaires au **mètre linéaire** et des marges de 30 à 40%.
> ❞

métrer *vt* (**a**) *(mesurer)* to measure *(in metres)* (**b**) *(dans le bâtiment)* to survey

métreur, -euse *nm,f* **métreur (vérificateur)** quantity surveyor

mettre *vt* (**a**) *(placer)* to put, to place; **mettre son argent à la banque** to put *or* deposit one's money in the bank; **mettre sa signature à un contrat** to put one's signature to a contract, to sign a contract
(**b**) *(investir)* to put, to invest; **mettre son argent en immeubles** to put *or* to invest one's money in property; **je ne peux pas y mettre tant que ça** I can't afford as much as that
(**c**) *(établir)* **mettre qch en œuvre** *(produit, campagne)* to implement sth
(**d**) *Ordinat* **mettre en forme** to format; **mettre à jour** *(logiciel)* to update; **mettre en ligne** to put on-line

meuble 1 *adj* movable
2 *nm* (**a**) *(élément du mobilier)* piece of furniture; **meubles** furniture ❑ **meubles de bureau** office furniture (**b**) *Jur* movable; **meubles** movables, personal property ❑ **meubles corporels** tangible assets *or* movables; **meubles à demeure** fixtures; **meubles gagés** furniture under distraint; **meubles incorporels** intangible assets *or* movables

mévente *nf* slump (in sales), slack period; **c'est une période de mévente dans l'immobilier** there is a slump in the property market

> ❝
> Dans la région caladoise, il reste un tissu économique de petites PME, avec un taux de chômage supérieur à la moyenne départementale, après la disparition des deux secteurs industriels forts de la métallurgie et du textile. Les cours des vins du Beaujolais se sont effondrés, l'année 2001 a été très difficile, ponctuée de **mévente** et de faillites.
> ❞

micro 1 *nm* (**a**) *Ordinat* (abrév **micro-ordinateur**) micro(computer) (**b**) *(abrév* **microphone**) mike
2 *nf Ordinat* (abrév **micro-informatique**) microcomputing

microéconomie *nf* microeconomics

microéconomique *adj* microeconomic

microédition *nf Ordinat* desktop publishing, DTP

microfiche *nf* microfiche

microfilm *nm* microfilm

micro-informatique *nf Ordinat* microcomputing, microprocessing

micromarketing *nm* micromarketing

micro-ordinateur *nm* Ordinat micro(computer) ❑ *micro-ordinateur de bureau* desktop computer; *micro-ordinateur portable* laptop (computer)

microprocesseur *nm* Ordinat microprocessor

microprogramme *nm* Ordinat firmware

microsite *nm* Ordinat microsite

MidCAC *nm* Bourse le MidCAC, l'indice Mid-CAC = Paris Stock Exchange index comprised of 100 medium-range shares, ≃ MidCap

mieux 1 *adv* Bourse **acheter/vendre au mieux** to buy/sell at best
2 *nm* (amélioration) improvement; **on constate un léger mieux par rapport aux ventes du mois dernier** a slight improvement on last month's figures can be observed

milieu *nm* (entourage) environment; **dans les milieux autorisés, on s'accorde à dire que la société n'est plus viable** informed sources are agreed that the company is no longer viable ❑ *milieux commerciaux* business circles; *milieux financiers* financial circles

millésime *nm* (a) (sur une monnaie) date (b) (d'un produit) year of manufacture

milliard *nm* billion; **10 milliards de dollars** 10 billion dollars

milliardaire *adj & nmf* billionaire

million *nm* million; **un million d'euros** a million euros; **un chiffre d'affaires de deux millions** a turnover of two million

millionnaire *adj & nmf* millionaire

mine *nf* mine ❑ *mine de charbon* coal mine; *mine d'or* gold mine

minerai *nm* ore ❑ *minerai de fer* iron ore

mineur *nm* miner

minier, -ère *adj* (industrie, secteur) mining

minimal, -e *adj* minimum

minimarge *nm* discount store

mini-message *nm* Tél text message; **envoyer un mini-message à qn** to send sb a text message

❝
L'opérateur mobile Orange, filiale de France Télécom, qui est en train de créer une grille de programmes thématiques consultables sur les futurs écrans des téléphones portables multimédias, a fait des contenus sportifs l'un de ses chevaux de bataille. L'idée est de proposer toute une gamme de services payants aux abonnés – du suivi des résultats par **mini-messages** à la vente de billets en passant par la diffusion d'images des meilleurs moments des matchs ...
❞

minimisation *nf* minimization, minimizing

minimiser *vt* (pertes, dépenses, coûts) to minimize

minimum 1 *adj* minimum
2 *nm* minimum; **au minimum** (au moins) at least; (le moins possible) to a minimum; **il y en aura cinq au minimum** there will be a minimum of five, there will be at least five; **réduire les frais au minimum** to reduce expenses to a minimum ❑ *minimum imposable* tax threshold; *minimum vieillesse* = basic old-age pension; *minimum vital* minimum living wage

mini-ordinateur *nm* minicomputer

ministère *nm* department, Br ministry ❑ *ministère des Affaires étrangères* Br ≃ Foreign Office, Am State Department; *le ministère du Commerce* Br ≃ the Department of Trade and Industry, Am ≃ the Department of Commerce; *le ministère du Commerce extérieur* Overseas Trade Department, Br ≃ the Department of Trade and Industry; *le ministère de l'Économie et des Finances* Br ≃ the Treasury, Am ≃ the Treasury Department; *le ministère de l'Industrie* Br ≃ the Department of Trade and Industry, Am ≃ the Department of Industry; *le ministère de l'Intérieur* Br ≃ the Home Office, Am ≃ the Department of the Interior; *le ministère de la Santé et de la Sécurité sociale* Br ≃ the Department for Work and Pensions, Am ≃ the Department of Health and Human Services; *le ministère des Transports* Br ≃ the Department for Transport, Am ≃ the Department of Transportation; *le ministère du Travail* Br ≃ the Department of Education and Employment, Am ≃ the Department of Labor

ministre *nmf* minister, Am secretary ❑ *ministre des Affaires étrangères* Br ≃ Foreign Secretary, Am ≃ Secretary of State; *ministre du Commerce* Br ≃ Secretary of State for Trade and Industry, Am ≃ Secretary of Commerce; *ministre du Commerce extérieur* Overseas Trade Minister, Br ≃ Secretary of State for Trade and Industry; *ministre de l'Économie et des Finances* Finance Minister, Br ≃ Chancellor of the Exchequer, Am ≃ Secretary of the Treasury; *ministre de l'Industrie* Br ≃ Secretary of State for Trade and Industry, Am ≃ Industry Secretary; *ministre de l'Intérieur* Br ≃ Home Secretary, Am ≃ Secretary of State; *ministre de la Santé et de la Sécurité sociale* Br ≃ Secretary of State for Work and Pensions, Am ≃ Secretary for Health and Human Services; *ministre des Transports* Br ≃ Secretary of State for Transport, Am ≃ Transportation Secretary; *ministre du Travail* Br ≃ Secretary of State for Education and Employment, Am ≃ Labor Secretary

Minitel® *nm* viewdata service, Br ≃ Prestel®, Am ≃ Minitel®

minitéliste *nmf* Minitel® user

mini-tour *nf Ordinat* mini tower

minoritaire *adj* minority

minorité *nf* minority; **être en minorité** to be in the *or* a minority ▫ **minorité de blocage** blocking minority

minuscule 1 *adj* lower-case
2 *nf* lower case
minutage *nm* (*d'un contrat*) drafting
minute *nf* (*d'un contrat*) minute; (*d'un acte notarié*) record; **faire la minute d'un contrat** to minute *or* draft a contract

minuter *vt* (**a**) (*contrat*) to minute, to draft; (*acte notarié*) to record (**b**) (*chronométrer*) to time; **sa journée est soigneusement minutée** his day is carefully planned, his day is run to a tight schedule

MIPS *nm Ordinat* (*abrév* **million d'instructions par seconde**) mips

mise *nf* (**a**) (*placement*) putting ▫ **mise en application** implementation; **mise en circulation** (*de l'argent*) circulation; **mise en commun de fonds** pooling of capital; **mise en demeure** formal demand; **mise en demeure de payer** final demand; **mise en dépôt** warehousing; **mise en disponibilité** leave of absence; *Can* layoff; **mise en distribution** distribution; **mise en examen** indictment; **mise de fonds** (capital) investment; **faire une mise de fonds** to put up capital; **ma première mise de fonds a été de 1000 livres** my initial outlay was £1,000; **mise en gage** pawning, pledging; **mise en garde** warning; **mise hors** (*action*) disbursement; (*somme*) sum advanced; **mise à jour** updating; **mise en œuvre** implementation; **mise en page** page design, page layout; *Fin* **mise en paiement** (*d'un dividende*) payment; *Fin* **mise en pension** borrowing against securities, pledging; **mise à pied** suspension; *Can* layoff; **mise sur pied** setting up; **mise en place** putting into place; **mise au point** (*d'une technique*) perfecting; (*d'un document, d'un rapport*) finalization; (*d'un produit*) development; **mise à la retraite anticipée** early retirement; **mise en route** start-up; **mise en service** (*d'une machine*) commissioning, putting into service; **mise sociale** = capital brought into a business by a partner; **mise en valeur** *Fin* (*d'un investissement*) turning to account; (*d'une propriété, d'un terrain*) development; **mise en vente** (*d'une propriété*) putting up for sale; (*d'un produit*) bringing onto the market, launching; **mise en vigueur** implementation
(**b**) (*à une vente aux enchères*) bid; **doubler la mise** to double the stakes ▫ **mise à prix** reserve price, upset (price)
(**c**) *Mktg* **mise en avant** special display; **mise en place marketing** marketing implementation
(**d**) *Tél* **mise en attente d'appels** call holding
(**e**) *Ordinat* **mise en attente des fichiers à im-**

primer printer spooling; **mise en forme** formatting; **mise en ligne** putting on-line; **mise en mémoire** saving; **mise à niveau** upgrade; **mise en relation** (*avec un service*) log-on; **mise en réseau** networking; **mise hors tension** power-down; **mise sous tension** power-up

miser 1 *vt* (*somme*) to bid
2 miser sur *vt ind* (**a**) (*parier sur*) to bet on; *Bourse* **miser sur une hausse/une baisse** to speculate on a rising/falling market (**b**) (*compter sur*) to count on; **nous misons sur une reprise des exportations** we are counting on a recovery in exports

mission *nf* (**a**) (*groupe*) mission, delegation; **une mission commerciale japonaise** a Japanese trade mission (**b**) (*tâche*) assignment; **partir en mission** to go away on business ▫ *Mktg* **mission d'activité** business mission; *Mktg* **mission d'entreprise** business mission

mi-temps *nm* part-time job; **travailler à mi-temps** to work part-time

mix *nm Mktg* (*marchéage*) mix ▫ **mix média** media mix; **mix de produits** product mix

mixte *adj* (*cargaison, économie*) mixed; (*commission*) joint

MJPEG *nm Ordinat* (*abrév* **Moving Joint Photographic Experts Group**) MJPEG

Mo *nm Ordinat* (*abrév* **mégaoctet**) MB

mobile 1 *adj* mobile; **la main-d'œuvre en Europe est moins mobile qu'aux États-Unis** the European workforce is less mobile than the workforce in the US
2 *nm* (**a**) (*téléphone*) mobile phone (**b**) *Mktg* **mobile d'achat** buying inducement, purchasing motivator; **mobile publicitaire** advertising mobile

mobilier, -ère 1 *adj Jur* movable
2 *nm* furniture ▫ **mobilier de bureau** office furniture

mobilisable *adj Fin* (*capital*) realizable; (*actif, biens immobiliers*) mobilizable

mobilisation *nf Fin* (*de capital*) realization, (*d'actif, de biens immobiliers*) mobilization; (*de fonds*) raising

mobiliser *vt Fin* (*capital*) to realize; (*actif, biens immobiliers*) to mobilize; (*fonds*) to raise

mobilité *nf* (*du capital, des travailleurs*) mobility ▫ **mobilité sociale** upward mobility

> **"**
>
> On a souvent l'impression que les gens à faible revenu sont très nombreux et que pour la majorité d'entre eux, c'est une condition de vie permanente. Cette perception est, en fait, contraire à la réalité. La permanence de la pauvreté est une des questions auxquelles les recherches sur la **mobilité**

sociale permettent de répondre. Une grande **mobilité sociale** rend possible une meilleure adaptation aux changements constants de la vie économique.
— **"**

modalité *nf* method; *Fin* **modalités** *(d'une émission)* terms and conditions ❏ *modalités d'application de la loi* = means of enforcing the law; *modalités de financement* financing terms *or* conditions; *modalités de paiement, modalités de règlement* methods *or* terms of payment; *modalités de souscription* conditions of application

mode *nm* (**a**) *(manière)* method ❏ *Compta mode d'amortissement linéaire* straight line depreciation method; *mode de classement* filing system; *mode d'emploi* directions for use; *mode de fabrication* manufacturing method; *mode de fonctionnement* method of operation; *mode de gestion* management method *or* style; *Compta mode linéaire* straight line method; *mode de paiement* method *or* means of payment; *mode de règlement* method *or* means of payment
(**b**) *Ordinat* mode; **en mode point** *(image)* bitmapped, bitmap ❏ *mode autonome* off-line mode; *mode brouillon* draft mode; *mode connecté* on-line mode; *mode continu* continuous mode; *mode démarrer* start-up mode; *mode de dialogue* dialogue mode; *mode édition* edit mode; *mode graphique* graphics mode; *mode d'impression rapide* draft mode; *mode d'insertion* insert mode; *mode paysage* landscape mode; *mode portrait* portrait mode; *mode réponse* *(d'un modem)* answer mode; *mode de superposition* overwrite mode; *mode survol* browse mode; *mode texte* text mode

modèle 1 *adj (usine, employé)* model
2 *nm* (**a**) *(exemplaire)* model; **le nouveau modèle de chez Renault** the new model from Renault; **ce modèle existe aussi en rouge** this model also comes in *or* is also available in red; **petit/grand modèle** small-scale/large-scale model ❏ *modèle de démonstration* demonstration model; *modèle déposé* registered design; *modèle familial* family model
(**b**) *(représentation schématique)* model ❏ *modèle de comportement d'achat* purchasing behaviour model; *modèle du chemin critique* critical path model; *modèle de décision, modèle décisionnel* decision model; *modèle de décision en arborescence* decision-tree model; *modèle déterministe* decision model; *modèle économique* economic model; *modèle d'entreprise* corporate model; *Fin modèle d'évaluation des actifs* capital asset pricing model; *modèle de lettre* standard letter; *modèle de prévision des ventes* sales forecast model; *modèle prévisionnel* econometric model; *modèle de prise de décision* de-

cision-making model; *modèle de relations réciproques* reciprocal relationships model; *modèle de signature* specimen signature
(**c**) *(référence)* model; **prendre modèle sur qch** to use sth as a model; **le modèle américain/japonais** the American/Japanese model
(**d**) *Ordinat (pour un programme)* template

modem *nm Ordinat* modem; **envoyer qch à qn par modem** to modem sth to sb, to send sth to sb by modem ❏ *modem externe* external modem; *modem interne* internal modem; *modem Numéris* ISDN modem; *modem réseau commuté* dial-up modem; *modem RNIS* ISDN modem

modem-câble *nm Ordinat* cable modem

modem-fax *nm Ordinat* fax modem

modération *nf* reduction ❏ *modération de droit* tax reduction *or* rebate

modéré, -e *adj* moderate; **une baisse, même modérée, des taux d'intérêt permettrait de relancer la consommation** even a moderate drop in interest rates would boost consumption

modernisation *nf* modernization

moderniser 1 *vt* to modernize
2 se moderniser *vpr (industrie, secteur)* to modernize

modeste *adj (salaires, revenus, prix)* modest, low

modicité *nf (des salaires, des revenus, des prix)* lowness

modification *nf* modification, alteration; *(d'un loi)* amendment; **apporter des modifications à qch** to modify sth, to alter sth

modifier *vt* to modify, to alter; *(loi)* to amend

modique *adj (salaires, revenus, prix)* modest, low

module d'extension *nm Ordinat* plug-in

moins *adv* (**a**) *(comparatif)* less; **je gagne moins que vous** I earn less than you (do); **moins de** *(argent)* less; *(travailleurs, magasins)* fewer; *(avec un nombre)* less than; **celui-ci coûte dix euros de moins que l'autre** this one costs ten euros less than the other one; **il y a eu 20 pour cent de clients de moins ou en moins par rapport à l'année dernière** there have been 20 percent fewer customers than last year
(**b**) *(superlatif)* **le moins** the least; **le moins disant** the lowest bidder; **c'est le produit le moins cher de tous** it's the cheapest product of all

moins-perçu *nm* amount due, outstanding amount

moins-value *nf Fin* depreciation, drop in value; *(après une vente)* capital loss

mois *nm* (**a**) *(période)* month; **au mois d'août** in the month of August, in August; **le 12 de ce**

mois the 12th of this month; **le mois dernier** last month; **un mois de crédit** a month's credit; **être payé au mois** to be paid by the month; **elle gagne 18 000 euros par mois** she earns 18,000 euros a month ❑ **mois civil** calendar month; *Bourse* **mois d'échéance** trading month; **mois légal** thirty days; *Bourse* **mois de livraison** delivery month
(**b**) *(salaire mensuel)* monthly salary; **toucher son mois** to receive one's (month's) salary ❑ **mois double** = extra month's salary paid as an annual bonus

moitié *nf* half; **à moitié prix** at half price; **réduit de moitié** reduced by half; **être de moitié dans une entreprise** to have a half share in a business; **partager les frais moitié-moitié** to share the cost fifty-fifty

monde *nm (univers, milieu)* world; **ce produit est disponible dans le monde entier** this product is available worldwide *or* all over the world ❑ **le monde des affaires** the business world *or* community; **le monde de la haute finance** the world of high finance, the financial world; **le monde de la publicité** the advertising world, the world of advertising

mondial, -e *adj (cours, prix, production)* world, worldwide; *(commerce, consommation)* worldwide, global; **à l'échelle mondiale** on a worldwide scale; **leur réseau de distribution mondial est leur atout principal** their worldwide distribution network is their main asset

mondialisation *nf* globalization

mondialiser 1 *vt* to globalize
2 se mondialiser *vpr* to become globalized

Monep *nm Bourse (abrév* **marché des options négociables de Paris)** Paris traded options exchange, *Br* ≃ LIFFE, *Am* ≃ CBOE

monétaire *adj (circulation, politique, système, zone)* monetary; *(marché, masse)* money

monétarisme *nm Écon* monetarism

monétariste *adj & nmf Écon* monetarist

Monétique®, monétique® *nf Fin* electronic money, e-money

> ❝
> Les Allemands, pour leur part, se préoccupent de la taille des portefeuilles, car certains billets en euros seront plus grands que les deutsche marks ... Pas vraiment adeptes des cartes de crédit et de la **monétique**, les Allemands utilisent beaucoup plus les espèces que les autres Européens. C'est en grande partie pour eux qu'une coupure de 500 euros a été créée.
> ❞

moniteur *nm Ordinat* monitor ❑ **moniteur couleur** colour monitor; **moniteur à écran plat** flat screen monitor; **moniteur SVGA** SVGA monitor

monnaie *nf* (**a**) *Fin (argent)* money; *(d'un pays)* currency ❑ **monnaie d'appoint** fractional money; **monnaie d'argent** silver money; **monnaie de banque** bank money, deposit money; **monnaie bloquée** blocked currency; **monnaie circulante** active money; *UE* **monnaie commune** common currency; **monnaie de compte** money of account; **monnaie de compte convertible** convertible money of account; **monnaie convertible** convertible currency; **monnaie courante** legal currency; **monnaie dirigée** managed *or* controlled currency; **monnaie divisionnaire** divisional money; **monnaie électronique** electronic money, e-money; **monnaie étrangère** foreign currency; **monnaie faible** soft currency; **monnaie fiduciaire** paper money, *Am* fiat money; **monnaie flottante** floating currency; **monnaie forte** hard currency; **monnaie légale** legal tender; **monnaie locale** local currency; **monnaie de marchandise** commodity money; **monnaie non convertible** blocked currency; **monnaie d'or** gold money; **monnaie de papier** paper money; **monnaie de réserve** reserve currency; **monnaie scripturale** bank money, deposit money; *Fam* **monnaie de singe** Monopoly money; *UE* **monnaie unique** single currency; **monnaie verte** green currency
(**b**) *(pièces)* change; **donner la monnaie de 50 euros** to give change for 50 euros *or* a 50-euro note; **faire de la monnaie** to give change; **petite monnaie, menue monnaie** small change

monnayable *adj Fin* convertible into cash

monnayer *vt Fin (terrains, biens, actif)* to convert into cash

monnayeur *nm Fin* change machine

monopole *nm* monopoly; **avoir le monopole de qch** to have a monopoly on sth; **exercer un monopole sur un secteur** to monopolize a sector ❑ **monopole commercial** commercial monopoly; **monopole d'émission** issuing monopoly; **monopole d'État** State monopoly; **monopole d'exploitation** operating monopoly; **monopole de fabrication** manufacturing monopoly; **monopole des prix** price ring; **monopole de vente** sales monopoly

monopoleur, -euse 1 *adj* monopolistic
2 *nm,f* monopolist

monopolisateur, -trice 1 *adj* monopolistic
2 *nm,f* monopolist

monopolisation *nf* monopolization

monopoliser *vt* to monopolize, to have a monopoly on

monopoliste 1 *adj* monopolistic
2 *nmf* monopolist

monopolistique *adj* monopolistic

monoposte *nm Ordinat* stand-alone

monotâche *adj & nm Ordinat* single-tasking

Monsieur *nm (titre)* Mr; *(au début d'une lettre)* Dear Sir

montage *nm* **(a)** *Fin* **montage financier** financial arrangement; **le montage financier a été difficile** it wasn't easy getting the money together; **le montage financier du projet sera le suivant** money for the project will be provided as follows **(b)** *(fabrication)* assembling, assembly

> **❝**
> Une étude de la Direction de la Législation fiscale (DLF) a en effet montré que ce type de **montage financier** innovant était légalement en vigueur dans une trentaine d'autres grandes entreprises du CAC 40.
> **❞**

montant *nm (somme)* amount, sum; **quel est le montant du chèque/de la facture?** how much is the cheque/invoice for?; **cinq versements d'un montant de 500 euros** five payments of 500 euros (each); **j'ignore le montant de mes dettes** I don't know what my debts amount to ❑ **montant brut** gross amount, gross total; *UE* **montants compensatoires (monétaires)** subsidies, compensatory amounts; **montant exonéré de TVA** VAT exempt amount; **montant forfaitaire** lump sum; **montant net** net amount, net total; **montant prévisionnel des ventes** forecast sales level; *Compta* **montant à reporter** amount brought forward; **montant du retour net** net return; **montant total** total (amount)

monté, -e *adj (équipé)* **être bien monté (en qch)** to be well stocked (with sth)

monte-charge *nm* hoist, *Br* goods lift, *Am* goods elevator

montée *nf (des prix, des salaires)* increase, rise **(de** in); **face à la montée en flèche des prix du pétrole** faced with rocketing *or* soaring oil prices

> **❝**
> Ces ratios boursiers comportent un autre vice. Pour réaliser leurs prévisions, les analystes ont pris l'habitude de travailler non sur le résultat net, mais sur le résultat opérationnel calculé sans prendre en compte les intérêts des dettes et les amortissements. A partir de 1997, avec la **montée en flèche** de l'endettement, le résultat net et l'opérationnel ont commencé à ne plus correspondre.
> **❞**

monter 1 *vt* **(a)** *(atelier)* to fit out, to equip; *(machine)* to assemble **(b)** *(entreprise, affaire)* to set up; *(opération financière, campagne publicitaire)* to arrange, to set up

2 *vi (cours, prix)* to rise, to go up, to increase **(de** by); **empêcher les prix de monter** to keep prices down; **faire monter les prix** to raise prices, to send prices up; **les prix montent en flèche** prices are soaring

3 se monter *vpr* **se monter à** to amount to; **les frais se montent à des milliers d'euros** the expenses amount to thousands of euros; **la facture se monte à mille euros** the bill amounts *or* comes to a thousand euros

mops *nmpl Ordinat (abrév* **mégaoctets par seconde)** MBps

morale *nf* ethics ❑ **morale professionnelle** business ethics

moratoire *Fin* **1** *adj (paiement)* delayed by agreement
2 *nm* moratorium; **décréter un moratoire** to declare a moratorium; **le moratoire des loyers** the moratorium on rents

> **❝**
> Les manifestations de ces épargnants avaient déjà fait chuter le président Fernando de la Rua et son éphémère successeur qui avait déclaré un **moratoire** unilatéral sur la dette publique du pays (141 milliards de dollars).
> **❞**

moratorium *nm* moratorium

mort, -e *adj (marché)* dead; *(argent)* lying idle

morte-saison *nf* slack season, off season

mosaïque *nf Ordinat* **afficher en mosaïque** *(fenêtres)* to tile

mot *nm* word ❑ *Ordinat* **mot clé** keyword; *Ordinat* **mot de passe** password

moteur de recherche *nm Ordinat* search engine

motif *nm* **(a)** *Mktg (intention)* motive ❑ **motif d'achat** buying motive **(b)** *(raison)* reason **(de** for); **c'est sa troisième absence sans motif valable** it's the third time that he has been absent without a good reason ❑ **motif de licenciement** grounds for dismissal

motion *nf* motion, proposal; **faire une motion** to propose a motion; **adopter une motion** to carry a motion; **appuyer une motion** to second a motion; **présenter une motion** to present *or Br* to table a motion; **ajourner une motion** to defer *or Am* to table a motion; **rejeter une motion** to reject a motion ❑ **motion de censure** vote of no confidence

motivation *nf* motivation, incentive ❑ *Mktg* **motivation d'achat** buying motive; *Mktg* **motivation de consommateur** consumer motivation; **motivation du personnel** staff motivation; **motivation par le profit** profit motive

mouchard électronique nm Ordinat cookie

mouvement nm (**a**) (déplacement) movement; (tendance) trend ❏ **mouvement ascensionnel** upward trend; **mouvement de baisse** downward trend; Compta **mouvement de caisse** cash transaction; Fin **mouvement des capitaux** movement or flow of capital; Compta **mouvement d'espèces** cash transaction; Fin **mouvement de fonds** movement or flow of capital; **mouvement de hausse** upward trend
  (**b**) (fluctuation) fluctuation ❏ **mouvement boursier** stock market fluctuation; Bourse **mouvement des cours** price fluctuation; **mouvement des devises** currency fluctuation; **mouvement du marché** market fluctuation; **mouvement des prix** change or fluctuation in prices; **mouvement des valeurs** share fluctuation
  (**c**) (renouvellement) turnover ❏ **mouvement du personnel** staff turnover; **mouvement des stocks** stock turnover
  (**d**) (dans un port, un aéroport) traffic ❏ **mouvement des marchandises** goods or freight traffic
  (**e**) (groupe) movement ❏ **mouvement de défense des consommateurs** consumer protection movement; **mouvement syndical** Br trade union or Am labor union movement

moyen¹, -enne adj (**a**) (prix, salaire, consommation) average; **de taille moyenne** medium-sized ❏ Mktg **moyenne des ventes** sales average (**b**) (ni bon ni mauvais) average

moyen² nm (**a**) (façon, possibilité) means ❏ **moyens de communication** means of communication; **moyens de paiement** means of payment; **moyens de production** means or method of production; **moyens de transport** means of transport
  (**b**) **moyens** (financiers) means; **vivre au-dessus de ses moyens** to live beyond one's means ❏ **moyens financiers** financial means; **moyens liquides** liquid resources; **moyens de trésorerie** financial means

moyennant prép (in return) for; **moyennant paiement de 500 euros** on payment of 500 euros; **moyennant finance** for a fee

moyenne nf average, mean; **en moyenne** on average; **il gagne en moyenne 100 euros (de) l'heure** on average he earns 100 euros an hour; **établir la moyenne de qch** to average sth ❏ **moyenne horaire** hourly average; Compta **moyenne mobile** moving average; Compta **moyenne pondérée** weighted average

MP3 nm Ordinat MP3

MPEG nm Ordinat (abrév **Moving Pictures Experts Group**) MPEG

MS-DOS nm Ordinat (abrév **Microsoft Disk-Operating System**) MS-DOS

multidevise adj multicurrency

multi-écran nm Ordinat split screen

multifonctions adj multipurpose

multilatéral, -e adj multilateral

multimarque nf multibrand

multimédia adj & nm multimedia

multimillionnaire adj & nmf multimillionaire

multinational, -e 1 adj multinational
  2 nf **multinationale** multinational

multiple adj multiple

multiplex Tél **1** adj multiplex
  2 nm multiplex ❏ **multiplex numérique** digital multiplex

multiplexage nm Tél multiplexing

multiplexeur nm Tél multiplexer

multiplier vt to multiply (**par** by); **notre chiffre d'affaires a été multiplié par deux en cinq ans** our turnover has doubled in five years

multipostage nm Mktg volume mailing

multiposte adj Ordinat multi-station

multiprocesseur nm Ordinat multiprocessor

multipropriété nf timeshare; **investir dans la multipropriété** to invest in a timeshare

❝
Les formules juridiques de la **multipropriété** varient d'un pays à l'autre. Les professionnels de la **multipropriété** ont beau assurer que les résidences qu'ils gèrent peuvent offrir une solution de vacances souple et économique, il n'en reste pas moins que nombre de propriétaires se sentent piégés dans cette formule et que le secteur est sans cesse secoué de scandales financiers.
❞

multirisque adj (assurance) all-in, all-risk; (pour un véhicule) comprehensive

multitâche adj & nm Ordinat multitasking

multitraitement nm Ordinat multiprocessing, multithreading

multi-utilisateur adj Ordinat multi-user

municipalité nf local authority

mur coupe-feu nm Ordinat firewall

mutation nf (**a**) (de personnel) transfer; **demander/obtenir sa mutation** to ask for/be given a transfer (**b**) Douanes **mutation d'entrepôt** transfer of bonded goods (to another bonded warehouse) (**c**) Jur change of ownership, transfer

muter vt (personnel) to transfer

mutualisme nm Assur mutual insurance

mutualiste Assur **1** adj (caisse, banque) mutual

2 *nmf* member of a mutual insurance company

mutualité *nf Assur* mutual insurance

mutuel, -elle *Assur* **1** *adj (service, assurance)* mutual

2 *nf* **mutuelle (d'assurance)** mutual insurance company, *Br* ≃ friendly society, *Am* ≃ benefit society

myopie marketing *nf* marketing myopia

Nn

nantir *vt Fin, Jur (créancier)* to give security to, to secure; *(valeurs)* to pledge; **entièrement/ partiellement nanti** *(créancier)* fully/partly secured

nantissement *nm Fin, Jur* (**a**) *(action)* pledging (**b**) *(gage)* pledge, collateral; **déposer des titres en nantissement** to lodge stock as security; **emprunter sur nantissement** to borrow on security □ *Bourse* **nantissement d'actions** lien on shares; *Banque* **nantissement flottant, nantissement général** floating charge

nation *nf* nation □ **nation commerçante** mercantile nation; **les Nations unies** the United Nations

national, -e *adj (produit, dette, fortune, grève)* national; *(marché)* domestic

nationalisation *nf* nationalization

nationalisé, -e *adj* nationalized

nationaliser *vt* to nationalize

nationalité *nf Admin* nationality; **prendre la nationalité française** to take French nationality

nature *nf* (**a**) *Admin* **nature du contenu** nature of contents (**b**) **payer en nature** to pay in kind

navette *nf* shuttle; **faire la navette** to commute; **il y a une navette entre la gare et l'aéroport** there is a shuttle between the station and the airport

> **"**
>
> Laurence Danon a enchaîné avec ce sens aigu de l'organisation de ces femmes managers et mères de famille. "Dans ma vie professionnelle passée, je me partageais entre New York et Paris où mes enfants vivaient" ... Aujourd'hui, c'est son mari, Pierre Danon, cadre dirigeant de British Telecom à Londres, qui **fait la navette** entre leurs deux bases de vie.
>
> **"**

navetteur, -euse *nm,f Belg* commuter

navigateur *nm Ordinat* browser

navigation *nf* (**a**) *(maritime)* navigation, shipping □ **navigation côtière** coastal trade (**b**) *Ordinat* □ **navigation sur l'Internet** Internet surfing; **navigation rapide** rapid browsing; **navigation sécurisée** secure browsing

naviguer *vi Ordinat* **naviguer sur l'Internet** to surf the Net, to browse the Web

navire *nm* ship □ **navire de charge** freighter, cargo ship; **navire de commerce** merchant ship; **navire frigorifique** refrigerated vessel; **navire marchand** merchant ship; **navire mixte** mixed passenger and cargo ship; **navire de passagers** passenger ship; **navire porte-conteneurs** container ship

navire-citerne *nm* tanker

néant *nm Admin* none, nil

négatif, -ive *adj (balance, impôt)* negative

négligence *nf Jur* negligence; **par négligence** through negligence □ **négligence coupable, négligence criminelle** criminal negligence; **négligence grave** gross negligence; **négligence professionnelle** professional negligence, malpractice

négoce *nm* (**a**) *(commerce)* trade; **faire le négoce de qch** to trade in sth (**b**) *Bourse (de titres, d'actions)* dealing

négociabilité *nf Fin* negotiability

négociable *adj* (**a**) *(salaire, prix, conditions d'emploi)* negotiable; **non négociable** not negotiable, non-negotiable (**b**) *Fin (bon, traite)* negotiable, transferable, trad(e)able; **négociable en banque** bankable; **négociable en Bourse** negotiable on the Stock Exchange

négociant, -e *nm,f* (**a**) *(dans le commerce)* wholesale merchant *or* dealer, wholesaler □ **négociant en vins** wine merchant (**b**) *Bourse* trader □ **négociant courtier** broker dealer

négociateur, -trice *nm,f* negotiator

négociation *nf* (**a**) *(de traité, de paix)* negotiation (**sur** on); **entamer des négociations** to enter into negotiations; **rompre des négociations** to break off negotiations; **en négociation** *(conditions)* under negotiation; **nous sommes en négociation avec la direction** we are negotiating *or* we are in negotiation with the management □ **négociation(s) collective(s)** collective bargaining; **négociations commerciales** trade negotiations; **négociation(s) de conventions collective(s)** collective bargaining; **négociations paritaires** joint negotiations; **négociations salariales** pay talks (**b**) *Bourse (transaction)* negotiation, transaction; *Fin (d'un effet)* negotiation □ **négociations**

de bloc block trading; **négociations de Bourse** Stock Exchange transactions; **négociations de change** exchange transactions; *Bourse* **négociations au comptant** spot trading; *Bourse* **négociation à la criée** open-outcry trading; *Bourse* **négociations à prime** options trading; *Bourse* **négociations à terme** futures trading

> ❝
> Les Britanniques négocient sur le plan local. Parallèlement à l'affaiblissement des syndicats, qui ont perdu la moitié de leurs adhérents en vingt ans et apparaissent de moins en moins comme la courroie de transmission du Parti travailliste, la **négociation collective** s'est décentralisée. Il y a de moins en moins de **négociations** de branche. Une majorité de salariés britanniques ne sont plus couverts par une convention collective, le phénomène étant particulièrement marqué dans le secteur privé.
> ❞

négocier 1 *vt* (**a**) *(traité, paix, salaire, prix)* to negotiate; **modalités/prix à négocier** terms/price negotiable (**b**) *Bourse* to trade
2 *vi (traiter, discuter)* to negotiate (**avec** with)
3 se négocier *vpr* (**a**) *(traité, paix, salaire, prix)* to be negotiated (**b**) *Bourse* **se négocier à** *(titres, valeurs)* to be trading at, to trade at

Net *nm Ordinat* **le Net** the Net

net, nette 1 *adj (bénéfice, valeur, poids)* net; **il reçoit un salaire net de 250 livres par semaine** he nets £250 a week; *Compta* **net après cessions** net of disposals; **net d'impôt** tax-free; **net de tout droit** exempt of *or* free from duty
2 *adv* **cent euros net** a hundred euros net; **cela m'a rapporté 100 euros net** I cleared *or* netted 100 euros, I made a net profit of 100 euros
3 *nm* net; **net à payer** *(sur bulletin de paie)* net pay, net payable ❑ *Compta* **net commercial** net profit; *Compta* **net financier** net interest income; *(à payer)* net interest charges

netéconomie *nf* Internet economy

netiquette *nf Ordinat (sur l'Internet)* netiquette

neuf, neuve 1 *adj (machine, matériel, locaux)* new; **à l'état neuf** as new
2 *nm* **remettre qch à neuf** *(machine, matériel)* to recondition sth; *(locaux)* to renovate sth

newsgroup *nm Ordinat* newsgroup

news magazine *nm* news magazine, current affairs magazine

NF *nf (abrév* **norme française)** = label indicating compliance with official French standards, *Br* ≃ BS, *Am* ≃ US standard

niche *nf* (market) niche

niveau *nm* (**a**) *(degré)* level; **l'indice des actions** est descendu à son plus bas niveau/est monté à son plus haut niveau the share index has reached an all-time low/an all-time high; **maintenir les prix à un niveau élevé** to maintain prices at a high level; **les bénéfices ont atteint un niveau record** profits have reached a record level; **ces deux candidats ont un niveau de qualification équivalent** the two candidates have the same level of ability ❑ *Ordinat* **niveau d'accès** *(dans un réseau)* access level; **niveau des besoins** need level; *Bourse* **niveau de cours des actions** stock price level; *Bourse* **niveau de dépôt requis** margin requirement; **niveau général des prix** general price level; **niveau général des salaires** general wage level; *Ordinat* **niveau de sécurité** security level; **niveau des stocks** stock level, inventory level; **niveau de vie** standard of living
(**b**) *(échelon)* level; **c'est au niveau de la distribution qu'il nous faut faire un effort** we need to make an effort at the distribution level

niveler *vt (prix, taux, salaires)* to level, to even up; **niveler par le bas** to level down

nivellement *nm (des prix, des taux, des salaires)* levelling; **nivellement par le bas** levelling down

N° *(abrév* **numéro)** No.

nœud *nm Ordinat* node

noir *nm* **acheter au noir** to buy on the black market; **vendre au noir** to sell on the black market; **travailler au noir** to moonlight

> ❝
> Difficile d'embaucher aussi quand les apprentis manquent pour assurer la relève. Jean Perrat n'imagine pas pouvoir recruter: "Si demain j'emploie un boulanger et que je lui demande de faire 35 heures pour ne pas lui payer d'heures supplémentaires, il ira faire six heures de plus chez un concurrent. **Au noir**, bien sûr."
> ❞

nolisement *nm (de navire, d'avion)* chartering

noliser *vt (navire, avion)* to charter

nom *nm* name; **nom... prénoms...** *(sur formulaire)* surname... first name...; **nom et prénoms** full name; **agir au nom de qn** to act on behalf of sb; **les actions sont à mon nom** the shares are in my name; **le chèque est libellé au nom de M. Dufour** the cheque is made out to Mr Dufour; **un nom bien connu dans le monde des affaires** a big name in the business world; **se faire un nom** to make a name for oneself ❑ **nom du bénéficiaire** name of payee; *Ordinat* **nom de champ** field name; **nom commercial** company name; **nom déposé** registered (trade) name; *Ordinat* **nom de domaine** domain name; *Bourse* **nom d'emprunt** nominee name; **nom de famille** surname; *Mktg* **nom de**

famille global blanket family name; *Ordinat* **nom de fichier** file name; *Ordinat* **nom de fichier erroné** *(message d'erreur)* bad file name; *Mktg* **nom générique** generic name; **nom de jeune fille** maiden name; *Mktg* **nom de marque** trade name; *Mktg* **nom de marque sous licence** licensed brand name; *Ordinat* **nom de l'utilisateur** user name

nomade *nmf Ordinat, Tél* road warrior

nombre *nm* number; **nombre à trois chiffres** three-digit number; **un grand nombre de** a large number of, many ❑ *nombre index* index number

nomenclature *nf* list ❑ *nomenclature douanière* customs classification

nominal, -e *Bourse, Fin* **1** *adj* nominal, par **2** *nm (d'une action)* nominal value; *(d'une obligation)* par value

nominatif, -ive 1 *adj* **(a)** *(carte d'adhérent, billet)* non-transferable **(b)** *Bourse (liste)* nominal; *(titres, actions)* registered **2** *nm Bourse* **un dividende au nominatif** a dividend on registered securities

nomination *nf (à un poste)* appointment **(à** to); **elle a obtenu** *ou* **reçu sa nomination au poste de directrice** she was appointed (to the post of) manager

nommer *vt (à un poste)* to appoint **(à** to); **nommer qn président** to appoint sb chairman *or* president; **il a été nommé à Lille** he was appointed to a post in Lille

non-acceptation *nf (de marchandises)* refusal; *Banque (d'une lettre de change)* non-acceptance

non-accomplissement *nm (d'un contrat)* non-fulfilment

non-autorisé, -e *adj Ordinat (nom de fichier)* illegal

non-compensé, -e *adj Banque (chèque)* uncleared

non-connecté, -e *adj Ordinat* off-line

non-consigné, -e *adj* non-returnable

non-coté, -e *adj Bourse* unquoted

non-disponibilité *nf* non-availability

non-encaissé, -e *adj (chèque)* uncashed

non-exécution *nf (d'un contrat)* non-fulfilment, non-performance

non-formaté, -e *adj Ordinat* unformatted

non-garanti, -e *adj* unsecured

non-initialisé, -e *adj Ordinat* uninitialized

non-lieu *nm Jur (d'une affaire)* withdrawal, dismissal; **bénéficier d'un non-lieu** to be discharged through lack of evidence

non-livraison *nf* non-delivery

nonobstant *prép Jur* notwithstanding, in spite of; **nonobstant toute clause contraire** notwithstanding any provision to the contrary

non-paiement *nm* non-payment

non-réception *nf* non-delivery

non-reconduction *nf Admin (de contrat)* failure to renew

non-récupérable *adj Ordinat* non-recoverable

non-résident, -e *adj* non-resident, non-domiciled

non-responsabilité *nf Jur* non-liability

non-salarié, -e 1 *adj* self-employed **2** *nm,f* self-employed person

non-souscrit, -e *adj (action, émission)* undersubscribed

non-syndiqué, -e 1 *adj* non-union **2** *nm,f* non-union worker

non-valeur *nf* **(a)** *Fin (créance)* bad debt; *Bourse* worthless security **(b)** *Jur (caractère improductif)* unproductiveness

non-vente *nf* no sale

non-vérifié, -e *adj Compta* unaudited

normal, -e 1 *adj* **(a)** *(dans la norme)* normal **(b)** *(moyen)* standard **2** *nf* **normale** standard; **au-dessus/au-dessous de la normale** above/below standard

normalisation *nf (de produits, de procédures)* standardization

normaliser *vt (produits, procédures)* to standardize

norme *nf* norm, standard ❑ *norme d'application* relevant standard; *normes d'application obligatoires* compulsory standards; *normes de conformité* trading standards; *normes européennes* European standards; *normes financières* financial standards; *norme française* French standard, *Br* ≃ British standard, *Am* ≃ US standard; *norme de prix de revient* cost standard; *norme de production* production norm; *norme de productivité* productivity norm; *normes publicitaires* advertising standards; *normes de sécurité* safety standards; *norme technique* technical standard; *norme de travail* work standard; *Ordinat* **norme USB** USB, universal serial bus

notaire *nm Jur* notary (public); **dressé par-devant notaire** drawn up before a notary

notarial, -e *adj Jur* notarial

notarié, -e *adj Jur* legally drawn up

notation *nf* **(a)** *(évaluation)* rating ❑ *notation du personnel* personnel rating, merit rating **(b)** *Bourse* rating ❑ *notation AA* double-A rating; *notation AAA* triple-A rating

note *nf* **(a)** *(facture)* bill; *(dans un hôtel) Br* bill,

Am check; **régler** *ou* **payer une note** to pay a bill ❑ **note de frais** expense account; *(présentée après coup)* expenses; *(facture)* expenses claim form; **mettre qch sur sa note de frais** to put sth on one's expense account; **note de rappel** reminder; **note de téléphone** phone bill

(**b**) *(communication écrite)* note, memo; **prendre qch en note** to note sth down ❑ **note d'avis** advice note; **note d'avoir** credit note; *Fin* **note de commission** commission note, fee note; *Bourse* **note de contrat** contract note; **note de couverture** cover note; **note de crédit** credit note; **note de débit** debit note; *Douanes* **note de détail** details, description *(of parcel)*; **note de fret** freight note; **note d'information** memo; **note de poids** weight note; **note de service** memo

(**c**) *(annotation)* note ❑ **note explicative** explanatory note; **note marginale** marginal note

(**d**) *Ordinat* **note de fin de document** endnote

noté, -e *adj Bourse* rated; **noté AA** double-A rated; **noté AAA** triple-A rated

notebook *nm Ordinat* notebook

noter *vt* (**a**) *(écrire)* to note down, to make a note of (**b**) *(évaluer)* to rate, to evaluate; **c'est l'employé le mieux noté du service** he's the highest-rated employee in the department

notice *nf (mode d'emploi)* instructions ❑ **notice explicative** directions for use; *Bourse* **notice d'information** information prospectus; **notice publicitaire** advertising brochure; *(dans un journal)* advertisement; **notice technique** technical instructions, technical handbook

notificatif, -ive *adj* notifying

notification *nf* notification, notice; **donner à qn notification de qch** to notify sb of sth, to give sb notification of sth; **recevoir notification de qch** to be notified of sth

notifier *vt* **notifier qch à qn** to notify sb of sth; **veuillez notifier par écrit** please inform us in writing

notoriété *nf Mktg* **notoriété assistée** aided recall; **notoriété de la marque** brand awareness; **notoriété du produit** product awareness; **notoriété publicitaire** advertising awareness; **notoriété spontanée** spontaneous recall

nouveau, -elle *adj* new; **créer de nouveaux débouchés au commerce** to open up new channels for trade; **jusqu'à nouvel ordre** until further notice; *Bourse* until cancelled; **pour une nouvelle période de trois mois** for a further three months ❑ *Bourse* **nouvelle émission** new issue; **nouveaux emprunts** new borrowings; *Écon* **nouveau pays industrialisé** newly industrialized country; *Mktg* **nouveau produit** new product; *Mktg* **nouvel utilisateur** first-time user

nouveauté *nf* new product, innovation; **il est**

allé voir les nouveautés au salon de l'informatique he went to see the latest innovations at the IT fair

nouvelle *nf* piece of news; **nouvelles** news

novateur, -trice **1** *adj (produit, entreprise)* innovative
2 *nm,f* innovator

novation *nf Jur* novation, substitution ❑ **novation de créance** substitution of debt

nover *vt Jur* to novate, to substitute

noyau *nm* (**a**) *Ordinat* node (**b**) *Bourse* **noyau dur** = group of stable shareholders chosen for a company by the government on its flotation

❝
La solution retenue par le gouvernement italien lors de la vente d'Autostrade a consisté à créer un **noyau dur** d'actionnaires autour de la famille Benetton et à verrouiller le capital pour empêcher un actionnaire unique d'en prendre la majorité. Apparemment, la France n'est pas parvenue à faire de même, car Vinci, candidat évident au **noyau dur**, aurait soulevé des problèmes de concurrence.
❞

NPI *nmpl Écon (abrév* **nouveaux pays industrialisés**) newly industrialized countries, NIC

nue-propriété *nf Jur* bare ownership

nuit *nf* night; **être de nuit** to be on night shift, to work nights

nul, nulle *adj Jur* **nul et de nul effet, nul et non avenu** null and void; **considérer une lettre comme nulle et non avenue** to consider a letter cancelled; **rendre qch nul** to invalidate sth, to render sth void

nullité *nf Jur* invalidity, nullity; **frapper qch de nullité** to invalidate sth, to render sth null and void

numéraire **1** *adj* **espèces numéraires** legal tender
2 *nm* cash; **payer en numéraire** to pay in cash ❑ **numéraire fictif** paper currency

numérique *adj* (**a**) *(analyse, valeur, liste)* numerical (**b**) *Ordinat* digital; *(données, pavé)* numerical

numériquement *adv* (**a**) *(en nombres)* numerically (**b**) *Ordinat* digitally

numérisation *nf Ordinat* digitization

numériser *vt Ordinat* to digitize

numériseur *nm Ordinat* digitizer ❑ **numériseur d'image** image digitizer

numéro *nm* (**a**) *(chiffre)* number; **le numéro un du verre** the number one company in the glass industry ❑ *Ordinat* **numéro d'accès** *(à un fournisseur d'accès)* access number; *Banque* **nu-**

méro de chèque cheque number; **numéro de commande** order number; *Banque* **numéro de compte** account number; **numéro d'enregistrement** booking number; **numéro de fabrication** serial number; **numéro d'immatriculation** registration number; *Ordinat* **numéro Internet** Internet number; *Ordinat* **numéro IP** IP number; *Ordinat* **numéro de licence** registration number; **numéro de lot** batch number; *Bourse, Fin* lot number; **numéro de nomenclature** catalogue number, inventory number; **numéro d'ordre** serial number; **numéro de référence** reference number; **numéro de série** serial number
 (b) *Tél* number; **composer** *ou* **faire un numéro** to dial a number ❑ **numéro azur** = special telephone number for which users are charged at the local rate irrespective of the actual distance of the call; **numéro de fax** fax number; **numéro de poste** extension number; **numéro de téléphone** telephone number; **numéro d'urgence** hot line, emergency number; **numéro vert** *Br* ≃ Freefone® number, 0800 number, *Am* ≃ 800 number, toll-free number (c) *(d'un journal, d'une magazine)* issue ❑ **numéro spécial** special issue

numérotation *nf* (a) *(attribution d'un numéro)* numbering ❑ *Ordinat* **numérotation alphanumérique** alphanumeric numbering (b) *Tél* dialling ❑ **numérotation abrégée** speed dial

numéroter *vt* to number

nu-propriétaire *nmf Jur* bare owner

Oo

obérer *vt* *(entreprise, pays)* to burden with debt; **la facture pétrolière obère le budget de l'État** the oil bill is a burden on the country's budget

objectif *nm* objective, goal, aim □ *objectif de croissance* growth target; *objectif global* overall objective; *objectif lointain* long-term objective; *objectif de production* production target; *objectif de profit* profit target; *objectif de vente* sales objective, sales target

objet *nm* (a) *(objectif)* object, aim; **la société a pour objet de...** the aim of the company is to... (b) *(dans une lettre)* **objet: confirmation de commande** re: confirmation of order (c) *(sujet)* *(d'une dispute, d'une discussion)* subject; *(d'un contrat)* purpose; **cette société fait l'objet d'une liquidation** this company is currently in liquidation (d) *(article)* article □ *objet de luxe* luxury item or article; *objet de valeur* valuable, article of value (e) *Ordinat* *(dans un document)* object; *(de courrier électronique)* subject

oblig *nf Fam Fin (titre)* bond, debenture

> "
> Il n'est que 9 heures, et un joyeux brouhaha règne désormais dans la salle. Des standards téléphoniques dont est équipé chaque opérateur fusent les commentaires de traders du monde entier. "Je suis short sur des **obligs** à court terme de la BEI, qui peut m'en vendre?" s'inquiète un Suisse.
> "

obligataire *Fin* 1 *adj (créancier, émission, intérêts, marché)* bond; *(dette, emprunt)* debenture 2 *nmf* bondholder, debenture holder

obligation *nf* (a) *Fin (titre)* bond, debenture □ *obligation amortissable* redeemable bond; *obligation à bon de souscription d'actions* bond with share warrant attached; *obligation cautionnée* guaranteed bond, secured bond; *obligation chirographaire* simple debenture; *obligation convertible* convertible bond, convertible; *obligation à coupon partagé* split coupon bond; *obligation à coupon zéro* zero coupon bond; *obligation de deuxième rang* second debenture; *obligation émise à coupon zéro* zero coupon bond; *obligation émise au pair* par bond; *obligation d'État* government

bond, Treasury bond; *obligation garantie* guaranteed bond; *obligation hypothécaire* mortgage bond; *obligation indemnitaire* indemnity bond; *obligation indexée* indexed *or* index-linked bond; *obligation à intérêt variable* floating-rate bond; *obligation à long terme* long-term bond; *obligations longues* long-dated securities, longs; *obligation à lots* prize bond, lottery bond, *Br* ≃ premium bond; *obligation multimarchés* global bond; *obligation nominative* registered bond; *obligation non amortissable* irredeemable bond; *obligation non garantie* unsecured debenture; *obligation or* gold bond; *obligation au porteur* bearer bond, coupon bond; *obligation de premier ordre* prime bond; *obligation à prime* premium bond; *obligation à prime d'émission* OID bond, original issue discount bond; *obligation remboursable* redeemable bond; *obligations remboursables en actions* redeemable bonds; *obligation à revenu fixe* fixed-rate bond; *obligation à revenu variable* variable-income bond, floating-rate bond; *obligation Samouraï* Samurai bond; *obligation sans garantie* naked debenture; *obligation de société* corporate bond; *obligation à taux fixe* fixed-rate bond; *obligation à taux variable* variable-income *or* floating-rate bond; *obligation transmissible, obligation transférable* transferable bond (b) *(engagement)* obligation, binding agreement; **contracter une obligation (envers qn)** to enter into a binding agreement (with sb); **honorer ses obligations** to honour *or* meet one's obligations; **avoir des obligations financières** to have financial obligations □ *obligation contractuelle* privity of contract; *obligation d'information* disclosure

obligatoire *adj* compulsory, obligatory; *Jur (ayant force)* binding

obligé, -e 1 *adj (reconnaissant)* grateful, obliged; **nous vous serions obligés de bien vouloir nous régler dans les meilleurs délais** we would be grateful *or* obliged if you would send us payment as soon as possible 2 *nm,f* (a) *Jur* obligee (b) *Fin* obliger *(guaranteeing a bill)*

oblique *nf* slash

OBSA *nf Fin (abrév* **obligation à bon de souscription d'actions)** bond with share warrant attached

observation *nf Mktg* ***observation en situation*** personal observation

obsolescence *nf* obsolescence; **le taux d'obsolescence des ordinateurs est très élevé** the obsolescence rate of computers is very high, computers very quickly become obsolescent ❑ ***obsolescence calculée, obsolescence planifiée, obsolescence prévue*** built-in *or* planned obsolescence

obsolescent, -e *adj* obsolescent

obtenir *vt* (*augmentation de salaire, avancement, contrat, délai, poste*) to get; (*prêt*) to get, to secure; (*accord*) to reach; **où peut-on obtenir ce produit?** where can you get this product?; **l'entreprise a obtenu d'excellents résultats l'année dernière** the company achieved excellent results last year; **les salariés ont réussi à obtenir de meilleures conditions de travail** the staff succeeded in obtaining better working conditions; **obtenir sa mutation** to be given a transfer

occasion *nf* (**a**) (*bonne affaire*) bargain; **pour ce prix-là, c'est une occasion** it's a real bargain at that price (**b**) (*article de seconde main*) second-hand item; **acheter qch d'occasion** to buy sth second-hand; **l'occasion** the second-hand trade; **l'occasion se vend bien** there's a brisk trade in second-hand goods (**c**) (*circonstance favorable*) opportunity ❑ *Mktg* ***occasion d'entendre*** opportunity to hear; *Mktg* ***occasion de voir*** opportunity to see

occasionnel, -elle *adj* (*travail, ouvrier*) casual; (*clientèle*) occasional

occulte *adj* secret

occupant, -e 1 *adj* occupying
2 *nm,f* occupier, occupant; *Jur* **premier occupant** occupant

occupation *nf* (*d'un lieu*) occupancy; **grève avec occupation des locaux** sit-in (strike)

occupé, -e *adj* (*ligne téléphonique*) *Br* engaged, *Am* busy; **la ligne est occupée** the line *or* number is *Br* engaged *or* *Am* busy; **ça sonnait occupé** I got the *Br* engaged *or* *Am* busy signal

occuper 1 *vt* (*détenir*) (*poste, fonction*) to have, to hold; **occuper un poste important** to hold an important post; **cette entreprise occupe une position enviable sur le marché** this company has an enviable market position (**b**) (*employer*) to employ; **occuper 20 ouvriers** to employ 20 workers (**c**) (*lieu*) to occupy; **occuper des locaux/une usine** (*lors d'une grève*) to occupy premises/a factory
2 s'occuper *vpr* **s'occuper de** to take care of; (*avoir pour responsabilité*) to be in charge of; **est-ce qu'on s'occupe de vous?** (*dans un magasin*) are you being attended to?; **c'est lui qui s'occupe de la comptabilité de l'entreprise** he is in charge of the company's accounts

occurrence *nf Ordinat* (*lors d'une recherche*) hit

OCDE *nf* (*abrév* **Organisation de coopération et de développement économiques**) OECD

OCR *nf Ordinat* (*abrév* **optical character recognition**) OCR

octal, -e *adj Ordinat* octal

octet *nm Ordinat* (eight-bit) byte

octroi *nm* (*de crédits, de subventions, d'un délai supplémentaire, d'un prêt*) granting

octroyer *vt* (*crédits, subventions, délai supplémentaire, prêt*) to grant (**à** to)

ODE *nf Mktg* (*abrév* **occasion d'entendre**) opportunity to hear

ODV *nf Mktg* (*abrév* **occasion de voir**) opportunity to see

offert, -e *adj* offered

office *nm* (**a**) (*poste*) office, post; **faire office de secrétaire** to act as secretary (**b**) (*organisation*) agency ❑ ***office de publicité*** advertising agency; ***office de régularisation de vente*** marketing board; ***office du tourisme*** tourist board (**c**) **d'office** ex officio; **être nommé d'office** to be automatically appointed; **être mis à la retraite d'office** to be automatically retired

officiel, -elle 1 *adj* official; **à titre officiel** officially, formally
2 *nm,f* official

officiellement *adv* officially

officieusement *adv* unofficially, off the record

officieux, -euse *adj* unofficial; **à titre officieux** unofficially

off-line *adj Ordinat* off-line

offrant, -e *nm,f* (*à une vente aux enchères*) **le plus offrant (et dernier enchérisseur)** the highest bidder; **vendre au plus offrant** to sell to the highest bidder

> **"**
>
> Pourtant, il est toujours possible de négocier. Obtenir au moins 10% est d'usage en insistant sur les défauts du logement: emplacement, électricité à refaire, chaudière à changer, fissures à combler, etc. Mais évitez de médire sur le goût des propriétaires: ce n'est pas toujours **le plus offrant** qui gagne dans ce domaine hautement émotionnel. Une maison de banlieue a ainsi été vendue au moins-disant, car celui qui proposait le plus s'était moqué des nains de jardin.
>
> **"**

offre *nf* (**a**) (*proposition*) offer, proposal; **recevoir/accepter une offre** to receive/accept an offer; **ils lui ont fait une offre avantageuse** they made him a worthwhile offer ❑ ***offre d'emploi*** job offer, offer of employment; ***offres***

d'emploi (dans un journal) situations vacant; *Bourse* **offre publique** public offering; *Fin* **offre publique d'achat** takeover bid; **faire** *ou* **lancer une offre publique d'achat (sur)** to make *or* launch a takeover bid (for); *Fin* **offre publique d'échange** exchange offer, takeover bid for shares; *Fin* **offre publique de vente** offer by prospectus, public share offer

(b) *Mktg* offer; **cette offre est valable jusqu'au 30 juin** this offer is valid until 30 June ❏ **offre de base** basic offer; **offre de bon de réduction** coupon offer; **offre d'échantillon gratuit** sampling offer; **offre d'essai** trial offer; **offre exceptionnelle** bargain offer; **offre de lancement** introductory offer; **offre à prix réduit** reduced-price offer; **offre promotionnelle** promotional offer; **offre de remboursement** money-back offer; **offre spéciale** special offer

(c) *Écon* supply; **l'offre et la demande** supply and demand; **lorsque l'offre excède la demande, les prix ont tendance à baisser** when supply exceeds demand, prices have a tendency to fall

(d) (à une vente aux enchères) bid

(e) (dans un appel d'offres) tender, bid

offrir vt (a) (proposer) to offer; **offrir ses services** to offer one's services; **offrir un emploi à qn** to offer sb a job; **offrir sa démission (à qn)** to tender *or* offer one's resignation (to sb)

(b) (présenter) to offer; **combien m'en offrez-vous?** how much will you offer *or* give me for it?; **offrir des marchandises à la vente** to offer goods for sale; **enchérir sur les prix offerts** to improve on the prices offered; **être offert à…** to be on offer at…; **ce genre d'investissement n'offre aucune garantie** this kind of investment offers no guarantee whatsoever; **ce placement offre un meilleur rendement** this investment gives *or* offers a better return

offshore adj (fonds, investissements, société) offshore

oisif, -ive adj (capital) uninvested, idle

OIT nf (abrév **Organisation internationale du travail**) ILO

oligopole nm *Écon* oligopoly

OMC nf (abrév **Organisation mondiale du commerce**) WTO

omission nf **sauf erreur ou omission** errors and omissions excepted; **sauf erreur ou omission de notre part, notre facture du 16 janvier reste impayée à ce jour** unless we are mistaken, our invoice of 16 January remains unpaid

omnium nm *Écon* combine

onduleur nm *Ordinat* UPS

onéreux, -euse adj costly, expensive; *Jur* **à titre onéreux** subject to payment, for a consideration

ONG nf (abrév **organisation non gouvernementale**) NGO

onshore adj (fonds, investissements, société) onshore

ONU nf (abrév **Organisation des Nations unies**) UNO

OP nm (abrév **ouvrier professionnel**) skilled worker

OPA nf *Fin* (abrév **offre publique d'achat**) takeover bid; **lancer une OPA (sur)** to make *or* launch a takeover bid (for) ❏ **OPA amicale** friendly takeover bid; **OPA hostile, OPA inamicale, OPA sauvage** hostile takeover bid

❝ Le second lui a volé la vedette la semaine dernière en lançant une **OPA amicale** sur le dernier britannique indépendant. L'opération, qui dépasse 6 milliards de dollars, constitue la fusion la plus importante depuis plus de deux ans. ❞

OPCVM nm *Bourse* (abrév **organisme de placement collectif en valeurs mobilières**) collective investment fund, *Br* unit trust, *Am* mutual fund ❏ **OPCVM actions** equity-based *Br* unit trust *or Am* mutual fund

OPE nf *Fin* (abrév **offre publique d'échange**) exchange offer, takeover bid for shares

opéable adj vulnerable to takeover bids

❝ En juin 2004, le pacte qui lie Elf et L'Oréal prendra fin, et le groupe pharmaceutique risque de devenir **opéable**, au moment où son père fondateur devrait prendre sa retraite. Le groupe devra-t-il, pour échapper à toute menace, changer de dimension? Compte tenu du prix élevé de l'action, c'est difficile: toute nouvelle fusion aurait un effet négatif pour les actionnaires actuels. ❞

open-market nm open market

OPEP nf (abrév **Organisation des pays exportateurs de pétrole**) OPEC

opérateur, -trice 1 nm,f (a) *Fin* trader; *Bourse* operator, dealer ❏ **opérateur à la baisse** operator for a fall, bear; **opérateur boursier** Stock Exchange dealer; **opérateur en couverture** hedger; **opérateur sur écran** screen trader; **opérateur à la hausse** operator for a rise, bull; **opérateur d'un jour** day trader

(b) *Tél* operator

(c) *Ordinat* **opérateur de PAO** DTP operator; **opérateur de saisie** keyboard operator, keyboarder; **opérateur système** systems operator, SYSOP

2 nm *Ordinat, Tél* operator

opération *nf* (**a**) *Banque, Fin (transaction)* transaction, deal, operation ❏ *opération blanche* break-even transaction; *Compta* **opération de caisse** counter transaction; *Compta* **opération en capital** capital transaction; **opération de clearing** clearing transaction; **opération en commun** joint venture; **opération comptable** accounting operation; **opération au comptant** cash transaction; *Compta* **opérations courantes** normal business transactions, ordinary activities; **opération d'escompte** discount operation; **opération de face à face** back-to-back operation; **opération de financement** funding operation; **opération financière** financial transaction; **opération imposable** taxable transaction; **opération de prêt** loan transaction
  (**b**) *Bourse* transaction, deal ❏ *opération à la baisse* bear transaction; **opération de Bourse** Stock Exchange transaction; **opération de change** exchange transaction, swap; **opération de change à terme** forward exchange transaction; **opérations de clôture** late trading, trading at the finish; **opération au comptant** spot deal, spot transaction; **opérations de couverture** hedging; **opération à découvert** short position; **opérations sur écran** screen trading; **opération à la hausse** bull transaction; **opération de journée** day trade; **opérations à option** option dealing *or* trading; **opération à prime** option deal; **opération à terme** futures transaction, forward transaction; **opérations à terme sur matières premières** commodity futures
  (**c**) *Ordinat* operation
  (**d**) *(activité)* operation; **le procédé comporte trois opérations** the process involves three operations ❏ *opération commerciale* business *or* commercial operation; **opération mercantile** mercantile operation
  (**e**) *(campagne)* operation, campaign ❏ *opération escargot* *Br* go-slow, *Am* slowdown *(by drivers)*; **une opération escargot a perturbé la circulation hier** a *Br* go-slow *or* *Am* slowdown by drivers disrupted traffic yesterday; **opération marketing** marketing campaign; **opération publicitaire** advertising campaign

opérationnel, -elle *adj* (**a**) *(coûts, efficacité)* operational (**b**) *(en service)* operational; **ce système sera opérationnel en 2008** this system will be operational *or* will be in operation in 2008

opérer **1** *vt (virement, paiement)* to make, to effect; *(changement)* to carry out, to implement; **opérer une restructuration au sein d'une entreprise** to restructure a company; **le pays tente d'opérer un redressement économique** the country is attempting to bring about an economic recovery
  2 *vi Bourse* **opérer à découvert** to take a short position, to go short
  3 **s'opérer** *vpr (changement, transformation)* to take place

opinion *nf* opinion (**de/sur** of/about) ❏ *opinion publique* public opinion

opposition *nf* **faire opposition à un chèque, faire opposition au paiement d'un chèque** to stop (payment of) a cheque

optimal, -e *adj* optimum, optimal

optimalisation *nf* optimization ❏ *optimalisation du profit ou des profits* profit optimization

optimaliser *vt* to optimize

optimisation *nf* optimization ❏ *optimisation du profit ou des profits* profit optimization

optimiser *vt* to optimize; *Ordinat (matériel, système)* to upgrade

optimiseur *nm Ordinat* optimizer

optimum **1** *adj* optimum, optimal
  2 *nm* optimum

option *nf* (**a**) *Bourse* option; **lever une option** to take up an option ❏ *option d'achat* call option, option to buy; **option d'achat vendue à découvert** naked option; **option sur actions** option on shares, share option; **option américaine** American-style option; **option à l'argent** at-the-money option; **option de change** foreign currency option; **option sur contrats à terme** futures option; **option cotée** traded option; **option au cours** at-the-money option; **option en dedans** in-the-money option; **option en dehors** out-of-the-money option; **option sur devises** foreign exchange option; **option du double** call of more; **option d'échange** swap option; **option européenne** European-style option; **option sur indice** index option; **option à la monnaie** at-the-money option; **option négociable** traded option; **option de titres** stock option; **option de vente** put option, option to sell

(**b**) *(choix)* option; **prendre une option sur qch** to have the option of purchase on sth □ **option d'achat** option to buy; **option de vente** option to sell

(**c**) *(accessoire)* optional extra; **le fax est en option sur ce portable** a fax is an optional extra with this laptop

(**d**) *Ordinat* option □ **option d'impression** print option; **option de menu** menu option; **option de sauvegarde** save option

optionnel, -elle *adj* optional

optique 1 *adj Ordinat* optical
2 *nf Mktg* outlook □ **optique marketing** marketing orientation; **optique produit** product orientation; **optique publicitaire** advertising approach; **optique vente** sales orientation, sales philosophy

OPV *nf Fin* (*abrév* **offre publique de vente**) offer by prospectus

or *nm* gold □ **or en barre** gold bars, gold bullion; *Fam* **ces actions, c'est de l'or en barre** these shares are a rock-solid investment; **or monnayé** gold coins

ORA *nfpl Fin* (*abrév* **obligations remboursables en actions**) redeemable bonds

ordinateur *nm* computer; **mettre qch sur ordinateur** to put sth on computer, to computerize sth □ **ordinateur autonome** stand-alone (computer); **ordinateur bloc-notes** notebook (computer); **ordinateur de bureau** business computer, desktop (computer); **ordinateur central** mainframe (computer); **ordinateur compatible** compatible computer; **ordinateur à écran tactile** touch-screen computer; **ordinateur frontal** front-end computer; **ordinateur de gestion** business computer; **ordinateur individuel** personal computer; **ordinateur multimédia** multimedia computer; **ordinateur de poche** palmtop (computer); **ordinateur portable** laptop (computer); **ordinateur en réseau** network computer

ordinateur-serveur *nm* host computer

ordinogramme *nm* flowchart

ordonnance *nf Jur* order, ruling □ **ordonnance de mise sous séquestre** receiving order, sequestration order; *Fin* **ordonnance de paiement** order *or* warrant for payment, order to pay; **ordonnance de saisie** writ of execution; **ordonnance de saisie-arrêt** garnishee order

ordonnancement *nm* (**a**) *(de production, de commandes)* scheduling, sequencing (**b**) *Fin* order to pay

ordonnancer *vt* (**a**) *(production, commandes)* to schedule, to sequence (**b**) *Fin (paiement)* to

authorize, to order; *(compte)* to initial, to pass for payment; *(dépense)* to sanction

ordonnateur, -trice *nm,f Admin* = official in charge of public expenditure and authorization of payment

ordre *nm* (**a**) *(classement)* order; **il faut traiter les affaires par ordre de priorité** the items must be dealt with in order of priority □ **ordre alphabétique** alphabetical order; **ordre croissant** ascending order; **ordre de date** order of date; **ordre décroissant** descending order; **ordre hiérarchique** hierarchical order; **ordre du jour** *(d'une réunion)* agenda; **inscrire qch à l'ordre du jour** to add sth to the agenda; *Jur* **ordre utile** ranking (of creditor)

(**b**) *(catégorie)* class, category; **de premier ordre** first-class, first-rate; **la hausse de l'inflation sera de l'ordre de cinq pour cent** the rise in inflation will be in the region of five percent

(**c**) *Banque, Bourse* order; **exécuter un ordre** to fill an order; **payez à l'ordre de J. Martin** pay to the order of J. Martin; **libeller** *ou* **faire un chèque à l'ordre de qn** to make a cheque payable to sb, to make out a cheque to sb; **c'est à quel ordre?** who should I make it out to?, who should I make it payable to?; **non à ordre** *(sur chèque)* not negotiable □ **ordre d'achat** purchase order; *Bourse* buy order; *Bourse* **ordre à appréciation** discretionary order; *Bourse* **ordre de Bourse** Stock Exchange order; *Fin* **ordre au comptant** cash order; *Bourse* **ordre conditionnel** contingent order; *Bourse* **ordre environ** discretionary order; *Bourse* **ordre lié** straddle; **ordre limite, ordre limité** limit order; **ordre au mieux** market order; *Bourse* **ordre de négociation** trading order; *Fin* **ordre de paiement** payment order; *Banque* **ordre permanent** standing order; *Banque* **ordre de prélèvement (permanent)** direct debit; *Bourse* **ordre à révocation** good-till-cancelled order; *Bourse* **ordre stop** stop order, stop-loss order; *Bourse* **ordre à terme** futures order; *Bourse* **ordre tout ou rien** all-or-none order; *Banque* **ordre de transfert permanent** banker's order, *Br* standing order; *Bourse* **ordre de vente** order to sell; *Bourse* **ordre de vente stop** stop-loss selling; *Fin* **ordre de virement** transfer order; *Banque* **ordre de virement automatique** *ou* **bancaire** banker's order, *Br* standing order

organe *nm Admin* **organe distributeur** distributing agency; **organe de publicité** advertising medium

organigramme *nm* organization chart, organigram; *Ordinat* (data) flow chart, flow diagram □ **organigramme de production** production flow chart

organisateur, -trice 1 *adj* organizing
2 *nm,f* organizer □ **organisateur de confé-**

rences conference organizer; *organisateur de voyages* tour operator

organisateur-conseil *nm* time and motion consultant

organisation *nf* (a) *(groupement)* organization ❑ *organisation à but lucratif* profit-making organization; *organisation à but non lucratif* *Br* non-profit-making organization, *Am* not-for-profit organization; *Organisation de coopération et de développement économiques* Organization for Economic Co-operation and Development; *Organisation internationale de normalisation* International Standards Organization; *Organisation internationale du travail* International Labour Organization; *Organisation mondiale du commerce* World Trade Organization; *Organisation des Nations unies* United Nations Organization; *organisation non gouvernementale* non-governmental organization; *organisation patronale* employers' association or organization; *Organisation des pays exportateurs de pétrole* Organization of Petroleum Exporting Countries; *organisation politique* political organization; *organisation professionnelle* professional body; *organisation squelettique* skeleton organization; *organisation syndicale* *Br* trade-union or *Am* labor-union organization

(b) *(façon de s'organiser)* organization ❑ *Ordinat* **organisation des données** data organization; *organisation fonctionnelle* functional organization, staff organization; *organisation hiérarchique* line organization; *organisation horizontale* functional organization, staff organization; *organisation mixte* line and staff organization; *organisation de la production* production engineering; *organisation scientifique du travail* organization and methods; *organisation verticale* line organization

organisé, -e *adj* organized

organiser 1 *vt* *(réunion, voyage d'affaires)* to organize

2 s'organiser *vpr* to organize (oneself), to get organized; *la main-d'œuvre s'est organisée en syndicat* the workforce has organized itself into a *Br* trade union or *Am* labor union

organiseur *nm* *Ordinat (logiciel)* organizer

organisme *nm* *(organisation)* organization, body ❑ *organisme de crédit* credit institution; *organisme de défense des consommateurs* consumer organization; *organisme international* international organization; *Bourse* **organisme de placement** investment fund; *Bourse* **organisme de placement collectif** collective investment scheme; *Bourse* **organisme de placement collectif en valeurs mobilières** *Br* unit trust, *Am* mutual fund; *organisme professionnel* professional body; *organisme de régle-*

mentation regulatory body; *organisme de tutelle* umbrella organization

> ❝
> En contrepartie de cette liberté de manœuvre retrouvée, la Commission abolit la directive de 1985 sur les normes prudentielles. Et publie un nouveau texte imposant des critères plus sélectifs. Les **organismes de placement collectif** disposeront d'un délai de cinq ans pour augmenter leurs fonds propres.
> ❞

orientation *nf* (a) *(tendance)* trend ❑ *orientation clientèle* customer orientation; *orientation du marché* market trend; *orientation du marché à la baisse* downward market trend; *orientation du marché à la hausse* upward market trend (b) *(conseil)* **orientation professionnelle** vocational or careers guidance

orienté, -e *adj* (a) *Bourse* **orienté à la baisse** bearish; **orienté à la hausse** bullish (b) *(économie, entreprise)* orientated; **une économie orientée vers les exportations** an export-orientated economy (c) *Ordinat* **orienté ligne** line-orientated; **orienté objet** object-orientated

original, -e 1 *adj* original

2 *nm* *(d'un document, d'une facture)* original; *(d'un fichier, d'une disquette)* master copy; **copier qch sur l'original** to copy sth from the original

origine *nf (d'un produit)* origin

OS *nm* *(abrév* **ouvrier spécialisé)** semi-skilled worker

oscillant, -e *adj* *Fin* fluctuating

oscillation *nf Fin* fluctuation, variation; **les oscillations du marché** the fluctuations of the market, the ups and downs of the market ❑ *oscillations saisonnières* seasonal fluctuations

osciller *vi* *Fin* to fluctuate

oseille *nf* *Fam (argent)* cash, *Br* dosh, *Am* bucks

OST *nf (abrév* **organisation scientifique du travail)** organization and methods, O & M

outil *nm* tool ❑ *outil d'aide à la décision* decision-making tool; *Ordinat* **outil auteur** authoring tool; *Ordinat* **outil de création de pages Web** Web authoring tool; *outil de gestion* management tool; *outil de marketing* marketing tool; *Ordinat* **outil de navigation sur le Web** Web browser; *outil de production* production tool; *outil de spéculation* trading instrument; *outil de travail* tool

outillage *nm* *(d'une usine)* plant, equipment, machinery

outplacement *nm* outplacement

outre-mer *adv* overseas

ouvert, -e *adj* open; *Mktg (question)* open-ended; **les bureaux sont ouverts de dix heures à cinq heures** the offices are open from ten to five

ouverture *nf* (**a**) *(d'un magasin, d'une entreprise, des frontières)* opening (up); *(d'un compte, d'un crédit, des négociations)* opening; **l'ouverture de nouveaux débouchés** the opening up of new markets ❑ *Ordinat* **ouverture de session** log-on (**b**) *Mktg* opening, window of opportunity; **l'ouverture de nouveaux débouchés** the opening up of new markets (**c**) *Bourse* start of trading; **à l'ouverture, le dollar était à 1,46 livres** at the start of trading, the dollar was at £1.46

ouvrage *nm* (**a**) *(travail)* work (**b**) *(œuvre)* piece of work, product

ouvrier, -ère **1** *adj* working

2 *nm,f* worker ❑ **ouvrier hautement qualifié** highly-skilled worker; **ouvrier à la journée** day labourer; **ouvrier non spécialisé** unskilled labourer; **ouvrier aux pièces** pieceworker; **ouvrier professionnel** skilled worker; **ouvrier qualifié** skilled worker; **ouvrier spécialisé** semi-skilled worker; **ouvrier syndiqué** worker belonging to a union; **ouvrier d'usine** factory worker

ouvrir **1** *vt* (**a**) *(magasin, entreprise, frontières)* to open (up); *(compte, crédit, négociations)* to open; **ouvrir un nouveau débouché à un produit** to open up a new market for a product

(**b**) *Ordinat (fichier, répertoire)* to open; **ouvrir une session** to log on

2 *vi* (**a**) *(magasin, entreprise)* to open; **nous ouvrons tous les jours à huit heures** we open every day at eight (o'clock); **les banques n'ouvrent pas les jours de fête** the banks do not open on public holidays

(**b**) *Bourse* to open; **ouvrir en baisse/en hausse** to open down/up; **les valeurs pétrolières ont ouvert ferme** oils opened firm

3 **s'ouvrir** *vpr* to open up; **leur pays s'ouvre peu à peu au commerce extérieur** their country is gradually opening up to foreign trade

P *nm Mktg* **les quatre P** the four Ps

P2P *nm* (*abrév* **peer to peer**) P2P

PAC *nf UE* (*abrév* **politique agricole commune**) CAP

package *nm Ordinat* package

PACS, pacs *nm* (*abrév* **Pacte civil de solidarité**) civil solidarity pact, = bill introduced in the French parliament in 1998 allowing unmarried heterosexual couples and homosexual couples to legally formalize their relationships

> **"**
> La signature d'un **pacs** est loin de résoudre tous les problèmes de succession entre partenaires. Comme le simple concubin, celui ou celle qui a signé un **pacs** n'a pas de droit dans la succession. Les partenaires doivent donc établir un testament s'ils souhaitent que le survivant puisse recueillir totalement ou partiellement les biens de la personne décédée.
> **"**

pacsé, -e *nm,f* = person who has signed a "PACS" contract

pacser 1 *vi* = to sign a "PACS" contract
2 se pacser *vpr* = to sign a "PACS" contract

pacson *nm Fam* **toucher le pacson** (*dans une affaire*) to make a bundle

pacte *nm* agreement □ **le pacte pour l'emploi** = job creation scheme for young people; *Jur* **pacte de paiement** pay agreement; **pacte de préférence** preference scheme

PAG *nf Douanes* (*abrév* **procédure accélérée générale de dédouanement**) accelerated customs clearance procedure

page *nf* (**a**) (*feuille*) page □ **page de garde** (*d'un fax*) cover sheet; *Tél* **les Pages jaunes**® the Yellow Pages® (**b**) *Ordinat* page □ **page d'accueil** home page; **page perso, page personnelle** personal home page; **page précédente** page up; **page suivante** page down; **page Web** Web page (**c**) **page de publicité** commercial break

page-écran *nf Ordinat* screen page

pagination *nf* pagination

paginer *vt* to paginate

paie *nf* pay, wages; **toucher sa paie** to draw one's wages, to get paid

paiement *nm* payment; (*d'un compte*) payment, settlement; **effectuer** *ou* **faire un paiement** to make a payment; **recevoir un paiement** to receive a payment; **contre paiement de 100 euros** on payment of 100 euros; **suspendre** *ou* **cesser les paiements** to stop payments □ **paiement par anticipation** payment in advance, advance payment; **paiement arriéré** payment in arrears; **paiement d'avance** payment in advance, advance payment; **paiement par carte** card payment, payment by card; **paiement par chèque** payment by cheque; **paiement à la commande** cash with order; **paiement (au) comptant** cash payment, payment in cash; **paiement différé** deferred payment; **paiement contre documents** payment against documents; **paiement échelonné** staggered payment; **paiement électronique** electronic payment, payment by electronic transfer; **paiement en espèces** payment in cash, cash payment; **paiement intégral** payment in full, full payment; **paiement par intervention** payment on behalf of a third party; **paiement libératoire** payment in full discharge from debt; **paiement en liquide** payment in cash, cash payment; **paiement à la livraison** *Br* cash *Am* collect on delivery, COD; **paiement en nature** payment in kind; **paiement partiel** partial *or* part payment; **paiements périodiques** periodic payments; **paiement préalable** prepayment; **paiement progressif** graduated *or* increasing payments; **paiement au prorata** payment pro rata; *Compta* **paiement reçu** inward payment; **paiement en souffrance** overdue *or* outstanding payment; **paiement à tempérament** payment by *or* in instalments; **paiement à terme** payment by *or* in instalments; **paiement transfrontalier** cross-border payment; **paiement par versements échelonnés** staggered payment

pair *nm Fin* par; **au-dessous/au-dessus du pair** below/above par; **au pair** at par □ **pair du change** par of exchange; **pair commercial** par; **pair intrinsèque** mint par

palette *nf* (**a**) *Ordinat* palette □ **palette graphique** graphics palette; **palette d'outils** tool palette (**b**) (*pour la manutention*) pallet

palette-avion *nf* air-freight pallet

palettisation *nf* palletization

palettiser *vt* to palletize

palier *nm* stage, level; **l'inflation a atteint un nouveau palier** inflation has reached a new level; **taxes imposées par paliers** graduated taxation

pancarte *nf (dans un magasin)* showcard

panel *nm Mktg* panel □ **panel ad hoc** ad hoc panel; **panel de consommateurs** consumer panel, shopping panel; **panel de détaillants** retail panel; **panel de distributeurs** distributor panel; **panel d'essayeurs de produits** product testing panel; **panel de téléspectateurs** television viewing panel

panéliste *nmf* panel member

panier *nm* (**a**) *Écon* **le panier de la ménagère** the shopping basket; **avec des conséquences sur le panier de la ménagère** with consequences for the food bill (**b**) *Mktg* dump bin □ **panier de présentation en vrac, panier présentoir** dump bin; **panier à la sortie** checkout display (stand); **panier vrac** dump bin (**c**) *Écon* **panier de devises, panier de monnaies** basket of currencies (**d**) *Bourse (d'actions)* basket

panne *nf* (**a**) *(de machine)* breakdown; **tomber en panne** to break down (**b**) *Ordinat* failure, crash □ **panne logicielle** software failure; **panne matérielle** hardware crash; **panne du système** system crash, system failure

panneau *nm* board □ **panneau d'affichage** *Br* notice board, *Am* bulletin board; *Ordinat* bulletin board; *Ordinat* **panneau de configuration** control panel; **panneau publicitaire** *Br* hoarding, *Am* billboard

PAO *nf Ordinat (abrév* **publication assistée par ordinateur)** DTP

paperasserie *nf* (**a**) *(documents)* papers, paperwork (**b**) *(d'un système bureaucratique)* red tape

papeterie *nf (produits)* stationery

papier *nm* (**a**) *(matière)* paper □ **papier à en-tête** headed notepaper; **papier d'impression** printer paper; **papier à lettres** writing paper, notepaper; **papier libre** plain paper; **papier machine, papier pour machine à écrire** typing paper; **papier quadrillé** graph paper
(**b**) *(document)* document, paper □ **papiers d'affaires** commercial documents; **papiers de bord** ship's papers; **papiers d'expédition** clearance papers; **papiers d'identité** identity papers; **papier libre** = official paper on which stamp duty has not been paid; **papier timbré** = official paper on which stamp duty has been paid
(**c**) *Fin* bill; **papiers à trois mois (d'échéance)** bills at three months □ **papier bancable** bankable paper; **papier de commerce, papier commercial** commercial *or* trade *or* mercantile paper; **papier commercial de premier ordre** prime bill; **papier sur l'étranger** foreign bill; **pa-**

pier fait guaranteed paper, backed bill; **papier de haut commerce** fine trade bill; **papier négociable** negotiable paper; **papier non bancable** unbankable paper; **papier à ordre** instrument to order; **papier au porteur** bearer paper; **papier de première catégorie** fine trade bill; **papiers valeurs** paper securities; **papier à vue** sight paper
(**d**) *Ordinat* paper □ **papier à bandes perforées** perforated paper; **papier continu** continuous paper *or* stationery; **papier couché** coated paper; **papier à étiquettes** sheets of labels; **papier d'impression** printer paper; **papier listing** listing paper; **papier multiple** multi-part stationery; **papier peint** wallpaper; **papier thermique, papier thermosensible** thermal paper

papier-monnaie *nm* paper money, paper currency

paquet *nm* (**a**) *(à expédier)* parcel, package; **expédier un paquet par la poste** to post a parcel, to send a parcel by post (**b**) *(marchandise emballée)* packet, pack □ *Mktg* **paquet échantillon** sample packet; **paquet économique** economy pack; **paquet familial** family-size pack; **paquet géant** giant-sized pack; **paquet individuel** individual pack; **paquet de présentation** display pack, presentation pack (**c**) *Bourse (d'actions, de valeurs)* parcel, block (**d**) *Ordinat* packet

paradis fiscal *nm* tax haven

> **❝**
>
> La mise en place demande un sens aigu de l'organisation. Primo, s'établir dans un pays d'où on démarche par téléphone les clients à l'autre bout du monde. Secundo: leur promettre un coup super, une OPA qui va faire bondir tel titre, par exemple. Le client vire alors ses économies sur le compte d'une banque connue, dans un **paradis fiscal** pas très regardant. Tertio: les escrocs disparaissent avec l'argent.
>
> **❞**

parafe = **paraphe**

parafer = **parapher**

parafiscal, -e *adj* parafiscal

parafiscalité *nf* = taxes paid to the state and used for administrative purposes

paragraphe *nm* (**a**) *(de lettre)* paragraph (**b**) *(de contrat)* sub-clause, paragraph

parallèle *adj* (**a**) *(marché)* unofficial (**b**) *Ordinat (imprimante, interface)* parallel

paralyser *vt (pays, industrie, économie)* to paralyse; **la grève des routiers a paralysé le pays pendant plusieurs jours** the *Br* lorry *or* *Am* truck drivers' strike paralysed the country for several days

paramétrable *adj Ordinat* configurable; **paramétrable par l'utilisateur** user-definable

paramétrage *nm Ordinat* configuration

paramètre *nm Ordinat* parameter, setting; *(du DOS)* switch

paramétrer *vt Ordinat* to configure

paraphe *nm Admin* initials; **mettre son paraphe au bas d'une page** to initial a page

parapher *vt Admin* to initial

parc *nm* (a) *(ensemble)* **parc automobile** *(d'un pays)* number of cars on the road; *(d'une entreprise)* fleet (of cars); **parc locatif** rental dwellings; **parc d'ordinateurs** computer population, total number of computers in service (b) *(zone)* park ❑ **parc d'activités** business park; **parc industriel** industrial park, *Br* industrial estate; **parc technologique** technology park

parcage *nm* (a) *Ordinat (de disque dur)* parking; **effectuer le parcage d'un disque** to park a disk (b) *Bourse (d'actions)* warehousing

parcourir *vt Ordinat (document)* to scroll through

parenthèse *nf* parenthesis, *Br* bracket; **entre parenthèses** in parentheses, *Br* in (round) brackets

parité *nf Bourse, Fin* parity; **à parité** at parity, at the money; **change à (la) parité** exchange at par *or* parity ❑ **parité du change** exchange rate parity, parity of exchange; **parité à crémaillère** crawling *or* sliding peg; **parité fixe** fixed parity; **parité des monnaies** monetary parity; **parité du pouvoir d'achat** purchasing power parity; **parité rampante** crawling peg

Parlement européen *nm* European Parliament

parquer *vt Ordinat (disque dur)* to park

parquet *nm Bourse* **le parquet** *(lieu)* the trading floor; *(personnes)* the Stock Exchange

parrain *nm Mktg* sponsor

parrainage *nm Mktg* sponsoring ❑ **parrainage d'entreprises** corporate sponsorship

parrainage-télévision *nm Mktg* television sponsoring

parrainer *vt Mktg* to sponsor

parraineur *nm Mktg* sponsor

part *nf* (a) *Fin* share, part ❑ **part d'association** partnership share; **part bénéficiaire** founder's share; **part de fondateur** founder's share; **part de marché** share of the market, market share; **part de marché relative** relative market share; **part patronale** employer's contribution; **part salariale** employee's contribution; **part sociale** share of capital, capital share; **part syndicataire** underwriting share; **part de voix** share of voice (b) **avoir part aux bénéfices** to have a share in the profits, to share in the profits; **mettre qn de part (dans une affaire)** to give sb a share in the profits

(c) **faire part de qch à qn** to inform sb of sth; **de la part de** on behalf of; **c'est de la part de qui?** *(au téléphone)* who's calling, please?

partage *nm (répartition)* division; *(de marchandises, de biens)* allotment, distribution; *(de tâches, de responsabilités)* sharing out; *Jur (d'une propriété)* partition ❑ **partage des bénéfices** profit sharing; *Ordinat* **partage des données** data sharing; **partage de l'emploi** job sharing; *Ordinat* **partage de fichiers** file sharing; *Ordinat* **partage d'imprimantes** printer sharing; **partage de temps** time sharing; **partage du travail** job sharing

partager *vt* (a) *(répartir)* to divide; *(marchandises, biens)* to allot, to distribute; *(tâches, responsabilités)* to share out; *Jur (propriété)* to parcel out; *Fin* **partager proportionnellement** to divide pro rata (b) *(utiliser en commun)* to share; **il partage les bénéfices avec son partenaire** he shares the profits with his partner

partagiciel *nm Ordinat* shareware

partenaire *nmf* partner ❑ **partenaire commercial** business partner, trading partner; **partenaire financier** financial partner; **partenaires sociaux** workers and management

partenariat *nm* (trading) partnership ❑ *Mktg* **partenariat télévision** television tie-in

participant, -e **1** *adj Fin (action, obligation)* participating
   2 *nm,f* participant (**à** in)

participation *nf* (a) *(fait de participer)* participation (**à** in); **nous comptons sur votre participation à la prochaine réunion** we are counting on your attendance at the next meeting (b) *(argent)* contribution ❑ **participation aux frais** contribution towards costs (c) *Fin* holding, share, interest (**à** in); **notre groupe a une participation de 25 pour cent dans cette société** our group has a 25 percent holding *or* share *or* interest in the company ❑ **participation aux bénéfices** profit sharing; **participation d'exploitation** working interest; **participation majoritaire** majority holding *or* interest; **participation minoritaire** minority holding *or* interest; **participation ouvrière** worker participation; **participation des salariés aux bénéfices** profit-sharing scheme

participer **participer à** *vt ind* (a) *(prendre part à)* to take part in, to participate in; **participer à la gestion d'une entreprise** to take part in the running of a firm; **participer à une réunion** to attend a meeting (b) *(financièrement)* to contribute to; **participer aux frais** to pay one's share of the costs, to contribute towards the costs (c) *(partager)* **participer aux bénéfices** to share in the profits

particulier, -ère **1** *adj (compte)* private, personal

2 *nm,f* (private) individual; **vente de particulier à particulier** private sale

partie *nf* (**a**) *(portion)* part; **faire partie du personnel** to be on the staff, to be a member of staff
(**b**) *Jur* party ❑ **partie concernée** interested party; **partie contractante** contracting party; **partie défaillante** defaulting party; **partie lésée** aggrieved party; **partie signataire** signatory
(**c**) **partie prenante** *Fin* payee; *(de biens)* recipient; **être partie prenante dans des discussions** to be a party to the discussions
(**d**) *Compta* **en partie double** double-entry; **en partie simple** single-entry

partiel, -elle *adj* part, partial

partiellement *adv* partially, in part; **payer partiellement** to pay in part

partir *vi* (**a**) *(s'en aller)* to go, to leave; **ceux qui partiront volontairement de l'entreprise recevront une prime** those who leave the company voluntarily will receive a bonus (**b**) **à partir de** starting from; **à partir d'aujourd'hui** starting from today, from today (onwards); **le directeur sera libre à partir de 10 heures** the manager will be free from 10 (o'clock) onwards; **imposé à partir de 30 000 euros** taxable from 30,000 euros upwards

parvenir parvenir à *vt ind (endroit, accord)* to reach; **faire parvenir qch à qn** to send *or* to forward sth to sb; **votre lettre m'est parvenue hier** I received your letter yesterday; **votre demande doit nous parvenir avant la fin du mois** your application must reach us by the end of the month

PASCAL *nm Ordinat* PASCAL

pas-de-porte *nm Jur (somme d'argent)* key money

passage *nm* (**a**) *(à l'euro, à l'économie de marché)* changeover, transition (**à** to) (**b**) *Ordinat* **passage automatique à la ligne (suivante)** autoflow, wordwrap

passager, -ère 1 *adj (crise, problèmes)* temporary
2 *nm,f* passenger ❑ **passager (en) stand-by** standby passenger

passation *nf* (**a**) *Compta (d'une écriture)* entering ❑ **une passation d'écriture** a journal entry; **passation par pertes et profits** write-off (**b**) *(d'un accord, d'un contrat)* signing; *(d'une commande)* placing (**c**) *Fin (d'un dividende)* payment (**d**) **passation de pouvoirs** handover *or* transfer of power

passe de caisse *nf* = allowance to cashier for errors

passeport *nm* passport

passer 1 *vt* (**a**) *(introduire)* **passer des marchandises à la douane** to clear goods through customs; **passer des marchandises en fraude** to smuggle in goods
(**b**) *Tél* **passer qn à qn** to put sb through to sb; **passez-moi M. Lecuyer** put me through to *or* get me Mr Lecuyer; **je vous passe le directeur** I'll put you through to the manager
(**c**) *(accord, contrat)* to enter into, to sign; *(commande)* to place (**de qch** for sth; **à qn** with sb); **passer un acte par-devant notaire** to draw up a document before a solicitor
(**d**) *Compta* to enter, to post; **passer un article au grand-livre** to post an entry in the ledger; **passer écriture d'un article** to post an entry; **passer une somme au débit/au crédit** to debit/credit an account with a sum; **passer une somme en perte** to charge an amount to an account; **passer une somme en profit** to credit an amount to an account; **passer par** *ou* **en pertes et profits** to transfer to profit and loss, to write off
(**e**) *(devenir)* **il est passé contremaître** he has been promoted to foreman
2 *vi* (**a**) *(aller)* **passer à la douane** to go through customs
(**b**) *(changer)* **passer de qch à qch** to go from sth to sth; **notre chiffre d'affaires est passé de deux à trois millions en cinq ans** our turnover has increased from two million to three million in five years
(**c**) *(représentant)* **passer chez un client** to call on a client

passerelle *nf Ordinat* gateway

passible *adj (d'une amende)* liable (**de** to); *(d'un impôt, d'une taxe)* liable, subject (**de** to)

passif *nm Compta, Fin* liabilities, debts; **l'actif et le passif** assets and liabilities; **inscrire** *ou* **passer une dette au passif** to enter a debt on the liabilities side ❑ **passif circulant** current liabilities; *passif éventuel* contingent liabilities; *passif exigible* current liabilities; *passif à long terme* long-term liabilities; *passif reporté* deferred liabilities

patentable *adj* subject to a licence, requiring a licence

patente *nf* (**a**) *(licence)* licence *(to exercise a trade or profession)*; **payer patente** to be duly licensed (**b**) *(impôt)* tax *(paid by self-employed people)*

patenté, -e *adj* licensed

patenter *vt* to license

patienter *vi* to wait; **faire patienter qn** *(au téléphone)* to ask sb to hold; **est-ce que vous désirez patienter?** would you like to hold?

patrimoine *nm Fin (d'un individu)* property, wealth, personal assets; *(actif net)* net assets ❑ *patrimoine immobilier* *Br* property assets, *Am* real-estate assets; *Banque* *patrimoine social* social assets

patron, -onne *nm,f* (**a**) *(d'une entreprise) (directeur)* employer; *(propriétaire)* owner; **les patrons** *(le patronat)* employers (**b**) *Fam (responsable)* boss (**c**) *(d'un hôtel)* proprietor

patronage *nm Mktg* sponsorship, sponsoring; **placé sous le patronage de...** sponsored by...; **sous le patronage de** under the sponsorship of

patronal, -e *adj* employers'

patronat *nm* employers; **le patronat et les syndicats** employers and unions

patronner *vt Mktg* to sponsor

pause *nf* pause

pavé *nm* (**a**) *Ordinat* keypad ❑ *pavé numérique* numeric keypad (**b**) *(publicité)* (large) display advertisement

pavillon *nm* flag; **battre pavillon libérien** to sail under a Liberian flag ❑ *pavillon de complaisance* flag of convenience

payable *adj* payable; **effet payable au 1ᵉʳ juillet** bill due on 1 July; **payable à 30 jours** payable at 30 days' date; **payable en 12 mensualités** payable in 12 monthly instalments; **payable à l'arrivée** payable on arrival; **payable à la banque** payable at the bank; **payable à la commande** cash with order, payable with order; **payable comptant** payable in cash; **payable sur demande** payable on demand; **payable à l'échéance** payable at maturity; **payable à la livraison** payable on delivery; **payable au porteur** payable to bearer; **payable sur présentation** payable on demand *or* on presentation; **payable à vue** payable on sight

payant, -e *adj* (**a**) *(non gratuit) (agence)* charging a fee; *(service)* with a charge (**b**) *(qui rapporte)* profitable

paye = **paie**

payement = **paiement**

payer *vt (facture, impôts, intérêts, loyer, personne)* to pay; *(marchandises, service)* to pay for; *(dette)* to pay (off), to settle; *(effet)* to honour; **payer qch à qn** to buy sth for sb; **payer qch cher** to pay a lot of money for sth; **payer qch bon marché** to buy sth cheaply; **payer d'avance** to pay in advance; **comment désirez-vous payer?** how are you paying?, how would you like to pay?; **payer par carte de crédit** to pay by credit card; **payer par chèque** to pay by cheque; **payer comptant** *ou* **en liquide** to pay cash; **payer à l'échéance** to pay at maturity *or* due date; **payer en espèces** to pay (in) cash; **payer intégralement** *ou* **en totalité** to pay in full; **payer à la livraison** to pay on delivery; **payer à l'ordre de...** *(sur chèque)* pay to the order of...; **payez au porteur** pay to bearer; **payer à présentation** to pay on presentation; **payer à vue** to pay at sight; **être payé à l'heure/à la semaine/au mois** to be paid by the hour/by the week/by the month; **être payé à la pièce** to be on piecework; **c'est une entreprise qui paie mal** that firm pays badly; **travail bien payé** well-paid job

payeur, -euse **1** *nm,f* payer; **c'est un bon/mauvais payeur** he is a good/bad payer **2** *nm Admin* pay clerk

pays *nm* country; **les pays d'Europe de l'Est** Eastern European countries ❑ *pays créditeur* creditor country, creditor nation; *pays débiteur* debtor country, debtor nation; *pays exportateur* exporting country; *pays importateur* importing country; *pays industrialisé* industrialized country; *pays membre* member state; *pays d'origine* country of origin; *pays pétrolier* oil-producing country; *pays de provenance* country of origin; *pays signataires* *(d'un accord)* signatory countries; *pays en voie de développement* developing country

paysage *nm* (**a**) *(situation)* scene, landscape; **le paysage politique/économique d'un pays** the political/economic landscape of a country (**b**) *Ordinat* **(mode) paysage** landscape (mode); **imprimer qch en paysage** to print sth in landscape

PC **1** *nm Ordinat (abrév* **personal computer***)* PC **2** *nf Fin (abrév* **pièce de caisse***)* cash voucher

PCG *nm Compta (abrév* **plan comptable général***)* chart of accounts

PCMCIA *nm Ordinat (abrév* **PC Memory Card International Association***)* PCMCIA

PCV *nm Tél (abrév* **payable chez vous***)* **(appel en) PCV** *Br* reverse-charge call, *Am* collect call; **appeler en PCV, faire un appel en PCV** *Br* to reverse the charges, *Am* to call collect

PDF *nm Ordinat (abrév* **portable document format***)* PDF

P-DG nm (abrév **président-directeur général**) Br Chairman and Managing Director, Am CEO

PDV nm Mktg (abrév **point de vente**) POS

PEA nm Fin (abrév **plan d'épargne en actions**) investment trust, Br ≃ PEP

pécuniaire adj financial; **améliorer sa situation pécuniaire** to improve one's financial situation

PEE nm Fin (abrév **plan d'épargne d'entreprise**) company savings scheme

> **"**
>
> L'argent versé sur un **PEE** est placé dans des fonds communs de placement d'entreprise (FCPE). La plupart des sociétés offrent le choix entre un fonds monétaire sans risque, un fonds obligataire et un fonds dynamique placé en actions. Ces fonds peuvent miser sur tous les marchés et sur tous les pays alors qu'un PEA ne peut être constitué que d'actions françaises.
>
> **"**

peine nf penalty □ **peine contractuelle** penalty for non-performance (of contract)

PEL nm Fin (abrév **plan épargne-logement**) Br ≃ building society account, Am ≃ savings and loan association account

pénal, -e adj (système, droit) penal

pénaliser vt (punir, désavantager) to penalize; **cette mesure pénalise les petits épargnants** this measure penalizes small savers

pénalité nf penalty □ Fin **pénalité libératoire** full and final penalty payment; **pénalité de retard** late payment penalty; (pour livraison tardive) late delivery penalty

pendant, -e adj Jur pending; **la question est toujours pendante** the matter is still pending or in abeyance

pénétration nf (d'un marché) penetration

pénétrer vt (marché) to penetrate, to enter into

pension nf (allocation) pension □ **pension de l'État** state pension; **pension d'invalidité** invalidity pension; **pension de retraite** (retirement or old-age) pension; **pension de réversion** survivor's pension; **pension viagère** life annuity; **pension à vie** life pension

pensionné, -e 1 adj (employé) pensioned; **elle est pensionnée à 75 pour cent** her pension represents 75 percent of her income **2** nm,f pensioner

pensionner vt to grant a pension to

pénurie nf (de matières premières, de capitaux, de devises) shortage, scarcity □ **pénurie de main-d'œuvre** labour shortage

PEP nm Fin (abrév **plan d'épargne populaire**) special savings account

pépinière d'entreprises nf enterprise zone, business incubator

PEPS nm (abrév **premier entré, premier sorti**) FIFO

PER nm Fin (abrév **plan d'épargne retraite**) retirement savings scheme

percée nf breakthrough; **leur société a fait une percée sur le marché de la micro-informatique** their company has broken into the micro-computer market □ **percée commerciale** market thrust; **percée technologique** technological breakthrough

> **"**
>
> Avec la société de l'information ou des réseaux, nous allons assister au phénomène inverse et à la **percée** empirique de nouvelles formes d'emploi comme le portage salarial.
>
> **"**

percepteur nm Admin collector of taxes, tax collector

perceptible adj Admin (impôt) collectable

perception nf (**a**) Admin (d'impôts, de droits, de loyer) collection, receipt □ Fin **perception de dividende** receipt of a dividend; **perception douanière** collection of customs duties; **perception à la source** tax deduction at source (**b**) Mktg (d'un consommateur, d'un client) perception □ **perception de marque** brand perception; **perception sélective** selective perception

percer vi **percer sur un marché** to break into a market

percevable adj Admin (impôt) collectable

percevoir vt Admin (impôts, droits, loyers) to collect; (revenus, indemnités, intérêts, commission) to receive, to be paid; **percevoir l'allocation chômage** to receive unemployment benefit; **cotisations à percevoir** contributions still due; **percevoir les impôts à la source** to collect tax at source

perdre vt (argent, procès, client, emploi) to lose; **perdre de sa valeur** to lose value; **l'euro a encore perdu par rapport à la livre** the euro has slipped further against the pound

perdu, -e adj (emballage) one-way

péremption nf lapsing

péréquation nf (des impôts, des salaires) equalization; **faire la péréquation des salaires** to equalize wages

perfectionnement nm (**a**) (d'une machine, d'une méthode, d'un procédé) perfecting; **notre but est le perfectionnement de nos techniques** our aim is to perfect our techniques (**b**) (formation) (further) training; **faire un stage de perfectionnement** to do an advanced training course

perfectionner 1 vt (machine, méthode, procédé) to perfect; (logiciel) to upgrade
   2 se perfectionner vpr (personne) to improve oneself; (technologie) to improve, to advance

perforation nf Ordinat (**a**) (action) punching (**b**) (trou) punch (hole)

perforatrice nf Ordinat card punch, (key) punch

perforer vt Ordinat (carte, bande) to punch

perforeuse nf Ordinat card punch, (key) punch

performance nf performance, achievement; **il faut améliorer les performances de notre entreprise/économie** we must improve the performance of our company/economy; **performance des cours de la Bourse** share price performance

performant, -e adj (employé) efficient; (investissement) profitable, high-yield; (entreprise) successful

péril de mer nm Assur risk and peril of the seas, sea risk

périmé, -e adj (coupon) out-of-date; (passeport) expired; (ticket) no longer valid; (mandat) lapsed

périmer se périmer vpr (document) to lapse, to expire

période nf period; **pendant une période de trois mois** for a period of three months, for a three month period □ **période d'activité** (d'une personne) period of active employment; Fin **période d'amortissement** depreciation period; **période comptable** financial period, accounting period, Am fiscal period; Bourse **période de cotation obligatoire** mandatory quote period; Anciennement UE **période de double circulation** (de la monnaie nationale et de l'euro) double circulation period; **période d'essai** probation or trial period; **période d'essai gratuit** free trial period; **période d'essor** boom; **période de grâce** tax holiday; **période d'inactivité** period of inactivity, dead period; **période de liquidation** phase-out period; **période de prospérité** boom, period of prosperity; **période de recouvrement** collection period; **période de réflexion** cooling-off period; **période de remboursement** payback period

périodique adj (inventaire, résultats) periodical

périphérique Ordinat **1** adj peripheral, device
   2 nm peripheral □ **périphérique d'entrée** input device; **périphérique d'entrée-sortie** input/output device; **périphérique externe** external device; **périphérique d'impression** printer peripheral; **périphérique de sortie** output device

périssable adj perishable

péritéléphonie nf peripheral telephone equipment

permanence nf (**a**) (lieu) (duty) office (**b**) (service) **il y a une permanence le dimanche** there is a 24-hour service on Sundays; **être de permanence** to be on duty; **en l'absence du directeur, M. Lenoir assure la permanence au conseil d'administration** in the director's absence, Mr Lenoir will head the board of directors

permanent, -e 1 adj (emploi) permanent; (comité) standing
   2 nm,f (d'une organisation) paid worker, worker on the payroll

permettre vt to allow, to permit

permis nm permit □ **permis de chargement** loading permit; **permis de conduire** Br driving licence, Am driver's license; **permis de construire** planning permission; **permis de débarquement** landing permit or order; **permis de douane** customs permit; **permis d'embarquement** shipping note; **permis d'entrée** (pour marchandises) import permit or licence; (pour bateau) clearance inwards; **permis d'exporter** ou **d'exportation** export permit or licence; **permis d'importer** ou **d'importation** import permit or licence; **permis poids lourd** HGV licence; **permis de séjour** residence permit; **permis de sortie** (pour marchandises) export permit or licence; (pour bateau) clearance outwards; **permis de transit** transit permit; **permis de travail** work permit

perquisition nf search

personnalisation nf (d'un service, d'une assurance, d'un produit) personalization, customization

personnaliser vt (service, assurance, produit) to personalize, to customize

personnalité juridique nf Jur legal status

personne nf person; **par personne** per person, per capita; **le prix est de 200 euros par personne** it costs 200 euros a head or per person; **les deux tiers des personnes interrogées ont déclaré ne pas connaître ce produit** two-thirds of those people interviewed said that they hadn't heard of the product □ Jur **personne à charge** dependant; Jur **personne fictive** fictitious person; Jur **personne morale** legal entity, corporate body; Jur **personne physique** individual entity

personnel, -elle 1 adj (entreprise, lettre) personal; **personnel** (sur document) private and confidential
   2 nm (d'une entreprise, d'un hôtel, d'une boutique) personnel, staff, employees; (d'une usine) workforce; **faire partie du personnel** to be on the staff, to be a member of staff, to be on the payroll; **manquer de personnel** to be understaffed or shorthanded □ **personnel administratif** administrative staff; Banque **personnel**

de back-office back office staff; *personnel de bureau* office staff, clerical staff; *personnel dirigeant* managerial staff; *personnel d'encadrement* management; *personnel d'entretien* maintenance staff; *personnel intérimaire* temporary staff; *personnel permanent* permanent staff; *personnel réduit* reduced or skeleton staff; *personnel de remplacement* replacement staff; *personnel saisonnier* seasonal staff; *personnel de service* staff on duty; *Mktg personnel de soutien commercial* sales support staff; *personnel à temps partiel* part-time staff; *personnel titulaire* permanent staff; *personnel de vente* sales personnel

personnellement *adv* personally, in person

perspective *nf* prospect, outlook ❑ *perspectives de carrière* job prospects; *perspectives commerciales* market prospects; *perspectives de croissance* prospects for growth; *perspectives économiques* economic prospects; *perspectives de profit* profit outlook

perte *nf (de marché, de clientèle, d'argent)* loss; *Assur* loss, damage; **travailler** *ou* **fonctionner à perte** to operate at a loss; **vendre qch à perte** to sell sth at a loss; **passer une perte par profits et pertes** to write off a loss; **subir de lourdes pertes** to suffer heavy losses; **il s'agit d'un secteur en perte de vitesse** it's a sector that's going downhill ❑ *perte de bénéfice* loss of profit; *Fin perte brute* gross loss; *Fin perte en capitaux* capital loss; *Fin perte de change* (foreign) exchange loss; *Ordinat perte de données* data loss; *Ordinat perte de données irréparable* irretrievable data loss; *Ordinat perte d'exploitation* operating loss; *Ordinat perte finale* terminal loss; *Ordinat perte de fin d'exercice* year-end loss; *Fin perte d'intérêts* loss of interest; *Fin perte latente* unrealized loss; *Fin perte nette* net loss; *Ordinat perte partielle* partial loss; *Ordinat perte présumée* presumptive loss; *Compta pertes et profits exceptionnels* extraordinary items; *Fin perte sèche* dead loss, clear loss; *Compta perte supportée* loss attributable; *Fin perte totale* total loss; *Assur perte totale effective* actual total loss; *Compta perte transférée* loss transferred

peser *vt (entreprise)* to be worth; **cette entreprise pèse 20 millions de dollars** this company is worth 20 million dollars

peseta *nf Anciennement* peseta

petit, -e *adj* small ❑ *petites annonces* classified advertisements, small ads; *petite caisse* petty cash; *Ordinat petites capitales* small caps, small capitals; *petit commerçant* small trader, shopkeeper; *le petit commerce* the small retail trade, *Br* the high street; *petit entrepreneur* small businessman; *petite entreprise* small business; *petits épargnants, la petite épargne* small savers; *la petite indus-*

trie small-scale industry; *petites et moyennes entreprises* small (and medium-sized) businesses; *petites et moyennes industries* small (and medium-sized) industries; *Fin petit porteur* small investor or shareholder

pétrodollar *nm* petrodollar

pétrole *nm* oil, petroleum; *Bourse* **les pétroles** oils, oil shares ❑ *pétrole brut* crude oil

pétrolier, -ère 1 *adj (prix, produits, marché)* oil; **les grandes sociétés pétrolières** the big oil companies
2 *nm* (oil) tanker

pétromonarchie *nf* oil kingdom

pétromonnaie *nf* petrocurrency

pèze *nm Fam* cash, *Br* dosh, *Am* bucks

phase *nf* phase, stage ❑ *Mktg phase de commercialisation* marketing stage; *phase de croissance* growth phase; **être en phase de croissance** to be growing; *Mktg phase de déclin* decline stage; **être en phase de déclin** to be on the decline; *Mktg phase de développement* development stage; *phase de fabrication* manufacturing stage; *Mktg phase de faisabilité* feasibility stage; *Mktg phase d'introduction* introduction stage

phoning *nm Mktg* telesales

❝

"Mais, au regard de l'investissement à déployer pour être vus, nous avons renoncé et préféré reporter notre budget sur le **phoning**. Le téléphone étant lui aussi un média très coûteux, notamment en B to B où il faut compter en moyenne quatre appels pour un contact", explique Sylvie Cartier.

❞

photocopie *nf* photocopy

photocopier *vt* to photocopy

photocopieur *nm* photocopier, photocopying machine

photocopieuse *nf* photocopier, photocopying machine

photocopillage *nm* = infringement of copyright through excessive use of photocopiers

photostyle *nm Ordinat* light pen

PIB *nm Écon (abrév* **produit intérieur brut)** GDP

pic *nm (d'une courbe)* peak

pièce *nf* **(a)** *(monnaie)* **pièce (de monnaie)** coin; **une pièce de deux euros** a two-euro coin ❑ *pièce d'or* gold coin
(b) *(exemplaire)* piece; **ils coûtent dix euros la pièce** they cost ten euros each; **ils se vendent à la pièce** they are sold separately or singly; **être payé à la pièce** to be paid piecework (rates); **travailler à la pièce** *ou* **aux pièces** to be on piecework, to do piecework

(**c**) *(document)* document, paper; **pièce à join-dre...** *(à une lettre)* please enclose... ❑ **pièce annexe** attachment; **pièce à l'appui** supporting document; *Compta* **pièce de caisse** cash voucher; **pièce d'identité** proof of identity; **pièce jointe** *(à une lettre)* enclosure; **pièce justificative** written proof, supporting document

(**d**) *(de machine)* **pièces détachées, pièces de rechange** spare parts, replacement parts

pige *nf Mktg (de la publicité concurrente)* monitoring

pignoratif, -ive *adj Fin* with a repurchase option

pilote **1** *adj (usine, échantillon, étude, prix)* pilot **2** *nm Ordinat* driver ❑ **pilote de mise en file d'attente** spooler

piloter *vt* (**a**) *(étude, campagne)* to pilot (**b**) *Ordinat* to drive; **piloté par menu** menu-driven

pilule empoisonnée *nf (contre-OPA)* poison pill

pionnier *nm (société, produit)* pioneer; **entrer en pionnier sur le marché** to be the first on the market

> 66
>
> Le **pionnier** du supermarché on-line continue à perdre de l'argent et ses performances boursières s'en ressentent. Sur les neufs premiers mois de 1997, le spécialiste américain de la livraison à domicile a perdu 8,8 millions de dollars.
>
> 99

piquet *nm* picket ❑ **piquets de grève** pickets; **piquets de grève volants** flying pickets

piratage *nm* piracy ❑ *Ordinat* **piratage informatique** (computer) hacking; *Ordinat* **piratage de logiciels** software piracy

pirate *nm* pirate ❑ *Ordinat* **pirate informatique** cracker, hacker

pirater *vt* to pirate; *Ordinat* to hack

piraterie *nf* piracy, pirating; *Ordinat* hacking ❑ *Ordinat* **piraterie informatique** hacking

piste *nf (de disque)* track ❑ *Ordinat* **piste d'amorçage** boot track; **piste magnétique** *(sur carte)* magnetic strip

piston *nm Fam* string-pulling; **avoir du piston** to have friends in high places; **il a eu le poste par piston** someone pulled some strings to get him the job

> 66
>
> C'est un système basé sur l'entraide, qui prend en compte les vrais besoins. Contrairement au marché formel, qui gâche tant de ressources intellectuelles ou manuelles, notre but, c'est que tout le monde soit productif. Dans ce réseau, on n'est pas rémunéré en

fonction des diplômes, de l'ancienneté ou parce qu'on **a du piston**, comme c'est le cas dans l'économie traditionnelle.

> 99

pistonner *vt Fam* to pull strings for

pivot *nm* key person

pixel *nm Ordinat* pixel

pixélisé, -e *adj Ordinat* bit-mapped, bitmap

placard *nm* poster, bill ❑ **placard publicitaire** advertisement *(in newspaper)*

place *nf* (**a**) *(emploi, poste)* job, post, position; **quitter/perdre sa place** to leave/to lose one's job; **il a trouvé une place de comptable** he found a job as an accountant; **le gouvernement en place** the government in office *or* power

(**b**) *(endroit)* place, location; **engager du personnel sur place** to hire staff locally; **s'approvisionner sur place** to use local suppliers; **avoir du crédit sur la place** to have credit (facilities) locally; **chèque encaissable sur la place** cheque cashable locally

(**c**) *Bourse* market ❑ **place boursière** stock market; **place financière** financial market; **le dollar est à la hausse sur la place financière de New York** the dollar has risen on the New York exchange

> 66
>
> Ainsi, l'avertissement sur résultats d'IBM, suivi de celui du canadien Nortel, et les craintes concernant les comptes de Cisco ont entraîné cette semaine les valeurs techno à la baisse sur toutes les **places financières**.
>
> 99

placement *nm* (**a**) *Fin (action)* investment, investing; *(argent)* investment; **faire des placements** to invest (money), to make investments; **faire un bon placement** to make a good investment ❑ **placement en actions** equity investment; **placement à court terme** short-term investment; **placement éthique** ethical investment; **placement financier** stock market investment; **placement à long terme** long-term investment; **placement obligataire** bond investment; **placement off shore** offshore investment; **placement de père de famille** gilt-edged investment, blue chip; **placement privé** private investment *or* placement; **placement à revenus fixes** fixed-income investment, fixed-yield investment; **placement à revenus variables** variable-income investment

(**b**) *Mktg* placement ❑ **placement de produit(s)** product placement

(**c**) *(fait de donner un emploi)* placement, placing

placer ▸ planche à billets

A présent, les **placements éthiques** se multiplient également en Europe. Ainsi, la Grande-Bretagne a adopté une loi qui engage les fonds de pension à indiquer clairement s'ils tiennent compte d'aspects sociaux et écologiques lors de la sélection des **placements**. Une loi similaire vient également d'être promulguée en Allemagne.

""

placer 1 vt (**a**) (procurer un emploi à) to find a job for; **placer qn comme apprenti chez qn** to apprentice sb to sb; **elle a été placée à la direction commerciale** she was appointed head of the sales department

(**b**) (vendre) to sell; **facile/difficile à placer** easy/difficult to sell

(**c**) Fin (argent) to invest; (actions) to place; **placer de l'argent dans les pétroles** to invest in oils; **placer à court terme/à long terme** to invest short-term/long-term; **placer à intérêts** to invest at interest; **placer de l'argent sur un compte** to put or deposit money in an account

2 se placer vpr (**a**) (trouver un emploi) to get or find a job; **se placer comme analyste-programmeur** to get a job as a systems analyst

(**b**) (se vendre) to sell; **ces marchandises se placent facilement** these goods sell easily

placier nm (**a**) (représentant de commerce) sales representative (**b**) (qui fait du porte-à-porte) door-to-door salesman

plafond nm (limite) ceiling; **l'euro a atteint son plafond** the euro has reached its ceiling or upper limit; **crever le plafond** to exceed the limit, to break the ceiling; **fixer un plafond à un budget** to put a ceiling on a budget, to cap a budget □ Banque **plafond d'autorisation de retrait** withdrawal limit; **plafond des charges budgétaires** spending limit, budgetary limit; **plafond du crédit** credit ceiling or limit; Banque **plafond de découvert** overdraft limit; **plafond de l'impôt** tax ceiling; **plafond de la production** production or output ceiling; Banque **plafond de retrait** withdrawal limit

plafonnement nm **le plafonnement des salaires** the ceiling imposed on salaries

plafonner 1 vt (salaires, prix, dépenses) to cap, to put a ceiling on; **être plafonné à** to have a ceiling of

2 vi to have reached a ceiling (**à** of); **la production plafonne** output has reached its ceiling; **cette année, l'inflation a plafonné à trois pour cent** inflation this year peaked at three percent

44

Jean-Charles Corbet ne le cache pas: les marges d'Air Lib Express **plafonneront** à 3 ou 4%, bien loin des juteux 15% de ses puissants concurrents.

""

plage nf (éventail) range, band □ **plage fixe** core time; **plage de prix** price range; **plage de taux** rate band

plaider vt & vi Jur to plead

plaignant, -e nm,f Jur plaintiff

plaindre se plaindre vpr to complain

plainte nf complaint

plan nm (**a**) (projet) plan, project □ **plan d'action** plan of action; Fin **plan d'actionnariat des salariés** Br employee share ownership plan, Am employee stock ownership plan; Mktg **plan d'activité** business plan; Compta **plan d'amortissement** depreciation schedule; **plan d'assainissement** stabilization plan; Écon, Fin **plan d'austérité** austerity programme; **plan de campagne** campaign plan; **plan de carrière** career plan; Compta **plan comptable** accounting plan; Compta **plan comptable général, plan de comptes** chart of accounts; **plan de développement** development plan; Mktg **plan de développement des produits** product planning; **plan directeur** master plan; **plan d'échantillonnage** sampling project; **plan d'échéances** instalment plan; **plan économique** economic plan; **plan d'embauche** recruitment plan; **plan d'ensemble** overall plan; Fin **plan d'épargne** savings scheme or plan; Fin **plan d'épargne en actions** investment trust, Br ≃ personal equity plan; Fin **plan d'épargne d'entreprise** company savings scheme; Fin **plan épargne-logement** Br ≃ building society account, Am ≃ savings and loan association account; Fin **plan d'épargne populaire** special savings account; Fin **plan d'épargne retraite** retirement savings plan or scheme; Compta **plan de financement** funding plan, financial plan; **plan de formation** training scheme; **plan d'investissement** investment plan; Mktg **plan de marketing** marketing plan; **plan média** media planning; **plan optionnel d'achat d'actions** stock option plan; Bourse **plan d'options sur titres** stock option plan; **plan prévisionnel** forecast plan; Mktg **plan prix** price plan; **plan de production principal** master production schedule; Écon **plan quinquennal** five-year plan; **plan de redressement de l'entreprise** company recovery plan; **plan de relance** revitalization plan; **plan de restructuration** restructuring plan; **plan de retraite** pension plan or scheme; **plan social** (du gouvernement) = corporate restructuring plan, usually involving job losses; Mktg **plan stratégique d'entreprise** strategic business plan; **plan de travail** planning; **plan de trésorerie** cash flow forecast; **plan d'urgence** contingency plan

(**b**) (point de vue) **sur le plan de** as regards; **sur le plan économique** economically, as far as the economy is concerned

planche à billets nf Fam **faire fonctionner la**

planche à billets to print money

plancher *nm* floor, lower limit ❑ *plancher des salaires* wage floor

planifiable *adj Écon* plannable

planificateur, -trice 1 *adj (autorité, mesures)* planning
2 *nm,f Écon* planner

planification *nf Écon* planning❑ *planification budgétaire* budget planning; *planification à court terme* short-term planning; *planification économique* economic planning; *planification de l'emploi* manpower planning; *planification de l'entreprise* company *or* corporate planning; *planification financière* financial planning; *planification à long terme* long-term planning; *planification des opérations* operational planning; *planification du produit* product planning; *planification stratégique* strategic planning; *Ordinat planification des systèmes* systems engineering; *planification des ventes* sales planning

planifié, -e *adj Écon (économie)* planned

planifier *vt* to plan

planigramme *nm Mktg* flowchart

planning *nm* plan, schedule; *(programme d'activités, de travail)* schedule; **nous avons un planning très chargé cette semaine** we have a very busy schedule this week ❑ *Compta planning des charges* expenditure planning; *planning de distribution* distribution planning; *planning de livraison* delivery schedule; *planning de la production* production planning

planté, -e *adj Fam* **être planté** *(réseau, ordinateur)* to be down

planter *vi Fam (réseau, logiciel)* to go down, to crash

plaquette *nf Ordinat* circuit board ❑ *Mktg plaquette publicitaire* advertising brochure

plate-forme *nf Ordinat* platform ❑ *plate-forme numérique* digital platform

plein, -e *adj* full; **agir de plein droit** to act by right; **avoir plein(s) pouvoir(s)** to have full power; *Jur* to have power of attorney; **être en plein travail** *(usine)* to be in full production; **payer plein tarif** to pay the full rate; **la pleine saison** the high season; **travailler à plein temps** to work full-time

plein-emploi *nm Écon* full employment

pli *nm (enveloppe)* envelope; **sous pli cacheté** in a sealed envelope; **sous pli séparé** under separate cover; **nous vous envoyons sous ce pli...** please find enclosed..., herewith...; **sous pli recommandé** by registered letter

plomber *vt Douanes (colis, wagon de marchandises)* to seal

plugiciel *nm Ordinat* plug-in

plus 1 *adv* **(a)** *(davantage)* more; **le plus** the most; **gagner plus de mille euros** to earn more than *or* over a thousand euros; **le taux le plus élevé** the top *or* highest rate of interest **(b)** **en plus** in addition, extra; **la TVA est en plus** there is VAT on top
2 *nm* plus, bonus; **le service après-vente est un plus que nous offrons à notre clientèle** the after-sales service is a plus that we offer all our customers
3 *conj* plus; **deux cents euros d'amende plus les frais** a two hundred euro fine plus costs; **le prix du produit plus la TVA** the price of the product plus VAT

plus-produit *nm Mktg* competitive advantage

plus-value *nf Écon, Fin (bénéfice)* capital gain, profit; *(augmentation de la valeur)* appreciation, increase in value; *(bénéfice)* profit; *(excédent)* *(d'impôts)* surplus; **réaliser une plus-value sur la vente d'un produit** to make a profit on the sale of a product; **les recettes présentent une plus-value de...** the receipts show an increase of...; **nos actions ont enregistré une plus-value** our shares have increased in value ❑ *plus-value sur titres* paper profit

PLV *nf (abrév* **publicité sur le lieu de vente)** point-of-sale promotion

PME 1 *nf (abrév* **petite et moyenne entreprise)** small business, SME
2 *nm (abrév* **porte-monnaie électronique)** electronic wallet, electronic purse

PMI *nf (abrév* **petite et moyenne industrie)** small industrial firm, SMI

PNB *nm Écon (abrév* **produit national brut)** GNP

PO *(abrév* **par ordre)** by order

pochette d'expédition de disquette *nf*
Ordinat disk mailer

poids *nm* (a) *(masse)* weight; **vendre au poids**
to sell by weight; **vendre à faux poids** to give
short weight; **poids et mesures** weights and
measures ▫ *poids brut* gross weight; *poids excédentaire* excess weight; *poids insuffisant*
short weight; *poids juste* full weight; *poids
minimum* minimum weight; *poids net* net
weight; *poids rendu* delivered weight; *poids
de taxation* chargeable weight
(b) *(dans un chargement)* load ▫ *poids en
charge* laden weight; *poids embarqué* loaded
weight, shipped weight; *poids mort* dead
weight; *Mktg (produit)* dog, dodo; *poids net à
l'emballage* net weight when packed; *poids
net embarqué* net shipped weight; *poids normal* standard weight; *poids utile* load-carrying
capacity
(c) *poids lourd* *Br* heavy goods vehicle, HGV,
Am heavy goods truck
(d) *(charge)* burden ▫ *poids de la fiscalité* tax
burden

poinçon *nm (sur l'or et l'argent)* hallmark

point *nm* (a) *(endroit)* point, place ▫ *point
d'achat* point of purchase; *point de chargement* loading point *or* place; *point de déchargement* unloading point *or* place; *point de
destination* destination; *Mktg point de distribution* distribution outlet; *point d'entrée de
l'or* import gold-point; *point d'expédition*
place of shipment; *Banque point retrait* cashpoint; *point de sortie de l'or* export gold-
point; *point de vente* *Mktg* point of sale,
POS; *(magasin)* sales outlet; **disponible dans
votre point de vente habituel** available at your
local stockist; *point de vente au détail* retail
outlet; *point de vente électronique* electronic
point of sale; *point de vente multimarque*
multibrand store
(b) *(dans un pourcentage, dans une échelle)*
point; **amélioration de trois points** improvement of three points, three-point improvement; **l'indice CAC 40 a perdu un point hier**
the CAC 40 index fell by a point yesterday
▫ *Mktg* **points cadeau** points *(awarded when
making a purchase and collected by the customer
to receive a discount off subsequent purchases)*;
point de part de marché share point; *point
prix* price point; *point de retraite* pension
point
(c) *(stade)* point ▫ *point critique* break-even
point; *Fin point mort* break-even point; **l'activité est au point mort dans ce secteur** activity
is at a standstill in this sector; *point de saturation* saturation point
(d) *(élément)* point, item; **il a présenté un plan
de redressement en trois points** he presented
a three-point recovery plan ▫ *point faible*
weak point; *point fort* strong point

(e) **mettre qch au point** *(produit)* to finalize
sth; *(procédé, technique)* to perfect sth; **mettre
les choses au point** *(clarifier la situation)* to get
things straight, to make things clear; **faire le
point (sur qch)** to take stock (of sth)
(f) *Ordinat* *point de césure* breakpoint, hyphenation point
(g) *(en fin de phrase)* *Br* full stop, *Am* period
▫ *Mktg* *point d'interrogation* *(produit)* question mark

pointage *nm* (a) *(d'articles, de noms)* checking,
ticking off (b) *(au travail)* *(à l'arrivée)* clocking
in; *(à la sortie)* clocking out

pointer 1 *vt* (a) *(articles, noms)* to check, to tick
off; **pointer un compte** to tick off items on an
account (b) *Ordinat (curseur)* to position (**sur**
on); **le mot pointé** the word where the cursor is
2 *vi (à l'arrivée)* to clock in; *(à la sortie)* to clock
out; **pointer à l'ANPE** *ou* **au chômage** to register unemployed

pointeur *nm Ordinat* pointer

pointeuse *nf (machine)* time clock

point-virgule *nm* semicolon

pôle *nm Écon* **les pôles de croissance** the main
centres of economic growth ▫ *pôle de reconversion* development *or* reconversion zone

police *nf* (a) *Assur* policy; **établir une police** to
draw up *or* make out a policy ▫ *police d'abonnement* floating policy; *police d'assurance* insurance policy; **souscrire à** *ou* **prendre une
police d'assurance** to take out an insurance policy; *police d'assurance accidents* accident policy; *police d'assurance maritime* marine
insurance policy; *police d'assurance mixte* mixed policy; *police d'assurance (sur la) vie* life
(assurance) policy; *police de chargement* bill
of lading; *police conjointe* joint policy; *police
flottante* floating policy; *police à forfait* policy for a specific amount; *police générale* master *or* general policy; *police globale (tous
risques)* blanket policy; *police individuelle
crédit acheteur* individual buyer credit policy;
police individuelle crédit fournisseur individual supplier credit policy; *police ouverte* open
policy; *police au porteur* policy to bearer; *police à terme* time policy; *police tous risques*
fully comprehensive policy; *police type* standard policy; *police universelle* worldwide policy
(b) *Ordinat* font ▫ *police bitmap* bitmap font;
police de caractères character font; *police par
défaut* default font; *police pixelisée* bitmap font;
police téléchargeable uploadable font

politique *nf (stratégie)* policy; **suivre** *ou* **adopter une nouvelle politique** to follow *or* adopt a
new policy; **pratiquer la politique de la chaise
vide** to make a political point by not attending
meetings ▫ *politique d'accommodement* give-
and-take policy; *politique d'achats centralisés*
centralized purchasing; *UE politique agricole*

commune Common Agricultural Policy; *poli-tique antiprotectionniste* free trade policy; *Mktg politique d'assortiment diversifié* mixed merchandising; *politique d'austérité* austerity policy; *politique budgétaire* budgetary policy; *politique commerciale* trade policy; *politique de commercialisation* marketing policy; *UE politique commune de la pêche* Common Fisheries Policy; *Mktg politique de communication* promotional policy; *politique conjoncturelle* economic policy *(responding to changes in the business cycle)*; *politique de crédit* credit policy; *politique de déflation, politique déflationniste* deflationary policy; *politique de distribution* distribution policy; *politique de dividendes* dividend policy; *politique économique* economic policy; *politique de l'emploi* employment policy; *politique de l'entreprise* company policy; *politique de l'environnement* environmental policy; *politique extérieure* foreign policy; *Fin politique fiscale* fiscal policy; *politique de gestion* business policy; *politique d'inflation, politique inflationniste* inflationary policy; *politique intérieure* domestic policy; *politique d'investissement* investment policy; *politique du laisser-faire* laissez-faire policy; *politique de libre-échange* free-trade policy; *politique de la main tendue* policy of the outstretched hand; **pratiquer la politique de la main tendue** to make friendly overtures, to be conciliatory; *Mktg politique de marque* brand policy; *politique en matière de change* exchange policy; *politique monétaire* monetary policy; *politique d'open-market* open-market policy; *politique de plein emploi* policy of full employment; *politique de la porte ouverte* open-door policy; *politique des prix* price policy, pricing policy; *politique des prix et des salaires* prices and incomes policy; *politique de produit/prix* product/price policy; *politique de promotion* promotional policy; *politique de responsabilité professionnelle* professional indemnity policy; *politique des revenus* incomes policy; *politique salariale, politique des salaires* wages policy; *politique de stabilité* stabilizing policy; *politique de la terre brûlée* scorched earth policy; *politique de vente* sales policy

polycopie *nf (procédé)* duplication; *(document)* duplicate

polycopié *nm* (duplicated) copy

polycopier *vt* to duplicate

polyvalence *nf (d'un employé)* adaptability, versatility

polyvalent, -e 1 *adj (produit)* multi-purpose; *(employé)* adaptable, versatile
2 *nm Admin* tax inspector

ponction *nf (retrait)* withdrawal; **faire une grosse ponction sur un compte** to withdraw a large sum from an account; **c'est une ponction importante sur mes revenus** it makes a big hole *or* dent in my income ▫ *Admin* **ponction fiscale** taxation; **ponction sociale** = contributions to the social security scheme, *Br* ≃ National Insurance contributions

ponctionner *vt (économies, pouvoir d'achat)* to make a hole *or* dent in; **on nous ponctionne un tiers de notre salaire en impôts** a third of our salary goes in tax

> Le ministre de la Santé appuie évidemment là où ça fait mal : le gouvernement Jospin, contre l'avis unanime des syndicats, avait choisi, l'an dernier, de **ponctionner** le budget de la Sécurité sociale quand les recettes du budget de l'Etat s'étaient révélées insuffisantes pour faire face aux importants allégements de charges sociales accordés aux entreprises dans le cadre de la mise en place des 35 heures.

ponctuel, -elle *adj* **(a)** *(paiement, impôt)* one-off; **l'État accorde une aide ponctuelle aux entreprises en difficulté** the state gives backing to companies to see them through periods of financial difficulty **(b)** *(employé)* punctual

pondérateur, -trice *adj Écon* balancing, stabilizing; **les éléments pondérateurs du marché** the stabilizing factors of the market

pondération *nf Écon (d'un indice, d'une moyenne)* weighting

pondéré, -e *adj Écon (indice, moyenne)* weighted

pondérer *vt Écon (indice, moyenne)* to weight

pont *nm* **(a)** *pont d'or* golden hello; **faire un pont d'or à qn** to offer a golden hello to sb **(b)** *(congés)* long weekend; *(jour)* = day off granted by an employer to fill the gap between a national holiday and a weekend; **faire le pont** to take a long weekend

pool *nm* **(a)** *Écon* pool, common stock ▫ *pool d'assurances* insurance pool; *pool bancaire* banking pool; *pool de l'or* gold pool **(b)** *(équipe)* pool ▫ *pool de dactylos, pool dactylographique* typing pool; *pool de secrétaires* secretarial pool

population *nf* population ▫ *la population active* the working population; *Mktg population cible* target population; *population mère* basic population; *population prévue* projected population

> En Finlande, plus on part tôt, plus la pension est maigre. Au début des années 90, en Finlande, le chômage approchait 20% de la **population active**, et les préretraites étaient massivement accordées.

port¹ *nm Ordinat* port; *(pour Internet)* socket ❏ *port de communication* comms port, communications port; *port d'extension* expansion port; *port d'imprimante* printer port; *port modem* modem port; *port parallèle* parallel port; *port série* serial port; *port série universelle* universal serial port; *port souris* mouse port

port² *nm (pour bateaux)* port, harbour; **le port du Havre** the port of Le Havre ❏ *port d'arrivée* port of arrival; *port d'attache* home port, port of registry; *port autonome* independent *or* autonomous port; *port de commerce* commercial port; *port pour conteneurs* container port; *port de déchargement* unloading port; *port de départ* port of departure; *port de destination* port of destination; *port d'embarquement* port of loading; *port d'entrée* port of entry; *port d'entrepôt* entrepôt port; *port d'escale* port of call; *port d'expédition* port of shipment; *port fluvial* river sea; *port franc* free port, entrepôt port; *port marchand* commercial port; *port maritime* sea port; *port ouvert* open port; *port pétrolier* oil port; *port de relâche* port of call; *port de transit* transit port

port³ *nm (de marchandises)* carriage; *(de paquet, de lettre, de télégramme)* delivery; **en port dû** carriage forward, freight collect ❏ *port avancé* carriage forward, freight collect; *port compris* postage included; *port dû* carriage forward; *port et emballage* postage and packing; *port franc (de revue, de journal)* postage paid; *(de marchandises)* carriage paid *or* free; *port en lourd* deadweight; *port payé (de revue, de journal)* postage paid; *(de marchandises)* carriage paid; *port payé, assurance comprise* carriage insurance paid

portable 1 *adj (machine à écrire)* portable; *(ordinateur)* laptop; *(téléphone)* mobile **2** *nm (ordinateur)* laptop; *(téléphone)* mobile (phone)

portage *nm* **(a)** *(transport) (de marchandises)* porterage, transport; *(de bateau)* portage **(b)** *Banque* piggy-backing

portail *nm Ordinat* portal

portatif, -ive 1 *adj (machine à écrire)* portable; *(ordinateur)* laptop **2** *nm (ordinateur)* laptop

porte-à-porte *nm* door-to-door selling; **faire du porte-à-porte** to be a door-to-door salesman, *f* saleswoman

porte-conteneurs *nm (avion)* container aircraft; *(navire)* container ship

porte-documents *nm* document case

portée *nf* **(a)** *(d'un navire)* burden, tonnage ❏ *portée en lourd* deadweight (capacity); *portée utile* load-carrying capacity **(b)** *(impact)* *(d'une décision, de mesures)* impact, effect; *(d'une publicité, d'une campagne)* reach; **il est encore trop tôt pour évaluer la portée de cette brusque hausse des taux d'intérêt** it is still too early to judge the impact of this sudden rise in interest rates

portefeuille *nm Fin* portfolio ❏ *portefeuille d'actions* share portfolio; *Mktg* **portefeuille d'activités** business portfolio, portfolio mix; *portefeuille d'assurances* insurance portfolio; *portefeuille effets* bills in hand, holdings; *portefeuille indexé* indexed portfolio; *portefeuille d'investissements* investment portfolio; *portefeuille avec mandat* discretionary portfolio; *Mktg* **portefeuille de marques** brand portfolio; *Mktg* **portefeuille de produits** product portfolio; *portefeuille de titres* securities portfolio

porte-monnaie électronique *nm* electronic wallet, electronic purse

> **“**
> Déjà disponible à Lyon, Bordeaux, Montpellier, Poitiers, ou encore en Indre-et-Loire et en Bretagne, le **porte-monnaie électronique** Moneo arrivera à Paris et en Ile-de-France le 6 novembre. Fin 2003, ce moyen de paiement pour les montants inférieurs à 30 euros devrait être accessible dans toute la France.
> **”**

porte-parole *nmf* spokesperson, spokesman, *f* spokeswoman; **se faire le porte-parole de qn** to speak on sb's behalf

porter 1 *vt* **(a)** *(signature, date)* to bear; **la lettre porte la date du 28 novembre** the letter is dated 28 November; **l'enveloppe portait la mention "confidentiel"** the envelope was marked "confidential"
(b) *(intérêts)* to bear
(c) *(transmettre)* **porter qch à la connaissance de qn** to bring sth to sb's attention; **je porterai votre proposition à la connaissance du conseil d'administration** I shall bring your suggestion to the notice of the board
(d) *(inscrire)* to enter, to inscribe; **porter un achat sur un compte** to enter a purchase on an account; **portez cela sur** *ou* **à mon compte** put that on my account, charge it to my account; **portez-le sur la note** put it on the bill; **porter une somme au crédit de qn** to credit sb's account with a sum
2 porter sur *vt ind (avoir pour sujet)* to concern, to be about; **les négociations portent sur la possibilité de fusion des deux sociétés** the negotiations concern a possible merger of the two companies; **le détournement de fonds porte sur plusieurs millions d'euros** the funds embezzled run into several millions of euros

3 se porter *vpr Jur* **se porter garant de qch pour qn** to stand surety for sb for sth; **se porter acquéreur de qch** to offer to buy sth

porteur, -euse 1 *adj* (*marché*) buoyant, flourishing; **l'informatique est un secteur porteur** computing is a flourishing *or* booming industry **2** *nm,f* (**a**) *Banque* (*d'un chèque*) bearer, payee; (*d'un effet*) bearer, holder, payee; **payer au porteur** (*sur chèque*) pay bearer; *Fin* **un gros/petit porteur** a big/small investor □ **porteur d'actions** shareholder, *Am* stockholder; **porteur d'actions nominatives** registered shareholder *or Am* stockholder; **porteur d'obligations** debenture holder, bondholder; **porteur de parts, porteur de titres** shareholder, *Am* stockholder (**b**) *Tél* carrier

portrait *nm Ordinat* (**mode**) **portrait** portrait (mode); **imprimer qch en portrait** to print sth in portrait

portuaire *adj* port; **Montréal est une ville portuaire** Montreal is a port

poser *vt* **poser sa candidature (à)** to apply (for)

position *nf* (**a**) *Fin* (*d'un compte*) balance; **demander sa position** to ask for one's balance □ **position de compte** balance; **position créditrice** credit balance; **position débitrice** debit balance; **position financière** financial position; **position de trésorerie** cash(flow) situation (**b**) *Bourse* position; **liquider une position** to close (out) a position; **prendre une position inverse sur le marché** to offset □ **position acheteur** long position, bull position; **position baissière** short *or* bear position; **position courte** short position; **position courte couverte** covered (short) position; **position couverte** covered position; **position élémentaire** simple position; **position longue** long position; **position non couverte** uncovered position; **position ouverte** open position; **position vendeur** short position, bear position (**c**) (*d'une entreprise, d'un produit*) position □ **position clé** key position; **position concurrentielle** competitive position; **position stratégique** strategic position

positionnement *nm* (**a**) *Fin* (*d'un compte*) calculation of the balance (**b**) *Mktg* (*sur un marché*) positioning □ **positionnement concurrentiel** competitive positioning; **positionnement sur le marché** market positioning; **positionnement de la marque** brand positioning; **positionnement de prix** price positioning; **positionnement du produit** product positioning; **positionnement par la qualité** quality positioning; **positionnement stratégique** strategic positioning

positionner 1 *vt* (**a**) *Ordinat* (*curseur, graphique*) to position (**b**) *Fin* (*compte*) to calculate the balance of (**c**) *Mktg* (*produit*) to position **2 se positionner** *vpr* **se positionner à la** hausse sur le marché to move upmarket; **se positionner par rapport à la concurrence** to position oneself in relation to the competition

possesseur *nm* owner; (*de valeurs, de titres*) holder □ **possesseur légitime** lawful owner

possession *nf* (**a**) (*de biens, de valeurs, de titres*) possession; **être en possession de qch** to be in possession of sth; **entrer en possession de qch** to come into possession of sth, to come by sth; **nous sommes en possession de votre lettre du 4 mars** we are in receipt of *or* have received your letter of 4 March □ *Jur* **possession de fait** actual possession (**b**) *Fin* **la possession** (*d'une société*) the assets

possibilité *nf* possibility; **achat avec possibilité de versements échelonnés** purchase with the option of payment by instalments; **son poste n'offre guère de possibilités de promotion** there is little possibility for promotion in his job □ *Ordinat* **possibilités d'extension** upgradeability

possible *adj* possible; **aussitôt que possible, le plus tôt (qu'il vous sera) possible** at your earliest convenience, as soon as possible

post-achat *adj Mktg* post-purchase

postal, -e *adj* (*tarif, services*) postal

postdater *vt* to postdate

poste¹ *nf* (**a**) (*service*) mail, *Br* post; **la Poste** *Br* ≃ the Post Office, *Am* ≃ United States Mail; **par poste aérienne** by airmail; **envoyer qch par la poste** to send sth by mail *or Br* by post; **mettre une lettre à la poste** to mail *or Br* post a letter (**b**) (*endroit*) **(bureau de) poste** post office □ **poste restante** poste restante

poste² *nm* (**a**) (*emploi*) post, position; **M. Dupont s'est vu confier le poste de directeur général** Mr Dupont was appointed general manager; **c'est un poste à responsabilités** it's a responsible job, it's a position of responsibility □ **poste clé** key post; **poste d'encadrement** managerial position; **poste évolutif** job with prospects (for promotion); **poste à pourvoir** (job) vacancy; **poste vacant** vacant post (**b**) (*lieu*) post, station □ *Ordinat* **poste autonome** stand-alone; **poste douanier** customs (post); *Ordinat* **poste terminal** terminal; *Ordinat* **poste de travail** workstation (**c**) (*de travail posté*) shift; **un poste de 12 heures** a 12-hour shift □ **poste de nuit** night shift (**d**) *Tél* extension; **poste 106** extension 106; **le poste est occupé** the extension is *Br* engaged *or Am* busy; **je vous passe le poste** I'm putting you through (**e**) *Compta* entry, item □ **poste de bilan** balance sheet item; **poste créditeur** credit item; **poste débiteur** debit item; **poste extraordinaire** extraordinary item; **poste de mémoire** reminder entry

poster vt (courrier) to mail, Br to post

PostScript® nm Ordinat PostScript®

post-test nm post-test

post-tester vt to post-test

postulant, -e nm,f applicant, candidate

postuler postuler à vt ind (poste) to apply for

pot-de-vin nm bribe; **verser des pots-de-vin à qn** to bribe sb

> 66
>
> Au Tibet, sont pourchassés ceux qui "accompagnent illégalement des fuyards vers la frontière", alors qu'au Guangdong, ce sont plutôt les crimes économiques que l'on vise : peuvent être exécutés des entrepreneurs qui ont fait de la contrebande et des fonctionnaires qui ont accepté des **pots-de-vin**.
>
> 99

potentiel, -elle 1 adj (acheteur, marché, ressources) potential

2 nm potential; **c'est une entreprise qui a du potentiel** it's a company with potential □ **potentiel de croissance, potentiel de développement** growth potential; **potentiel industriel** industrial potential; **potentiel sur le marché** (d'un produit) market potential; **potentiel de production** production potential or capacity; **potentiel publicitaire** advertising potential; **potentiel de revenu** (d'une personne) earning capacity, earning potential; **potentiel de vente** sales potential

poubelle nf Ordinat wastebasket, Am trash

pourcentage nm percentage; **travailler au pourcentage** to work on a commission basis

pourcompte, pour-compte nm = undertaking to sell goods on behalf of a third party

poursuites nfpl Jur (legal) proceedings; **engager** ou **intenter des poursuites (judiciaires) contre qn** to take or to institute proceedings against sb, to take (legal) action against sb □ **poursuites judiciaires** legal proceedings

poursuivre vt Jur poursuivre qn (en justice) to take (legal) action against sb, to sue sb; **poursuivre qn en dommages et intérêts** to sue sb for damages

pourvoi nm Jur appeal

pourvoir 1 vt (a) (équiper) pourvoir qn de qch to supply or provide sb with sth (b) (remplir) (emploi) to fill; **le poste est toujours à pourvoir** the post is still vacant or to be filled

2 **pourvoir à** vt ind (besoins) to provide or cater for; (frais) to cover, to pay

pourvoyeur, -euse nm,f supplier

poussée nf (des prix, d'une monnaie, de l'inflation) rise (**de** in) □ **poussée inflationniste** inflationary surge

> 66
>
> L'économie batave a non seulement suivi la chute de sa voisine allemande, mais elle l'a même précédée. Après quatre années à un rythme de 4%, le plus élevé des pays moyens européens, la croissance du PIB est tombée à 1,1% en 2001. Raisons principales: la réforme fiscale de janvier 2001 générant une hausse de la TVA, et une **poussée inflationniste** mal contrôlée sur un marché du travail artificiellement étroit.
>
> 99

pousser vt Écon pousser qch à la hausse/la baisse to have an inflationary/a deflationary effect on sth; **poussé par les profits** profit-driven; **pousser la vente de qch** to push the sale of sth; **pousser un article aux enchères** to up the bidding for sth; **pousser les enchères** to run up the bidding

pouvoir nm (a) (autorité) power □ **pouvoir de décision** decision-making power; **pouvoirs discrétionnaires** discretionary powers; **pouvoir exécutif** executive power; **pouvoir judiciaire** judicial power; **pouvoir législatif** legislative power; **les pouvoirs publics** the authorities (b) (possibilité) **pouvoir d'achat** purchasing or buying power; **pouvoir de négociation** bargaining power

> 66
>
> Ils perdent sur tous les tableaux: l'emploi (160 000 cadres inscrits au chômage en 1994), le salaire (leur **pouvoir d'achat** évolue moins vite que celui de l'ensemble des salariés depuis 1992) ou les avantages acquis (la prime d'ancienneté, par exemple) qui disparaissent à vue d'œil.
>
> 99

PPP nm (abrév **partenariat public-privé**) public-private partnership

ppp nm Ordinat (abrév **points par pouce**) dpi

pratique nf (a) (procédé) practice, procedure; **cette commission a été créée pour lutter contre les pratiques discriminatoires à l'embauche** the commission was set up to combat discriminatory recruitment practices; **c'est une pratique courante sur le marché boursier** it's common practice in the Stock Market; **la pratique de ce genre de vente est illégale en France** this kind of sales practice is illegal in France □ **pratique comptable** accounting procedure; **pratique courante** standard practice; **pratiques déloyales** unfair trading; **pratiques loyales** fair trading; **pratiques restrictives** restrictive practices

(b) (expérience) (practical) experience; **elle a décidé d'embaucher le candidat qui avait le plus de pratique** she decided to employ the candidate with the most experience

pratiquer 1 *vt* pratiquer des prix trop élevés to be too expensive; **les prix pratiqués sur le marché** the ruling *or* current market prices
2 se pratiquer *vpr (prix, salaires)* to be in force, to apply

préalable 1 *adj (accord, étude, budget)* preliminary; *(conditions)* prerequisite
2 *nm* prerequisite, precondition; **les prix doivent être négociés au préalable** prices must be negotiated beforehand *or* in advance

PréAO *nf Ordinat (abrév* **présentation assistée par ordinateur)** computer-assisted presentation

préavis *nm (notification)* (advance *or* prior) notice; *(au travail)* notice; **il a été licencié sans préavis** he was dismissed without notice; **donner un préavis d'un mois (à qn)** to give (sb) a month's notice; **exiger un préavis de trois mois** to require three months' notice; **préavis de dix jours francs** ten clear days' notice; *Banque* **dépôt à sept jours de préavis** deposit at seven days' notice ▫ *préavis de grève* strike notice; *préavis de licenciement* notice of dismissal

précis *nm (d'un article)* abstract

préciser *vt* to specify, to stipulate

précommercialisation *nf* pre-marketing

précompte *nm Fin* (a) *(d'un compte)* advance deduction (b) *(de cotisations, d'impôts)* deduction at source

précompter *vt Fin* (a) *(argent d'un compte)* to deduct in advance (b) *(cotisations, impôts)* to deduct at source; **précompter la sécurité sociale sur le salaire de qn** to deduct social security payments from sb's salary

préconditionné, -e *adj* pre-packed, pre-packaged

préconditionner *vt* to pre-pack, to pre-package

préconisateur *nm Mktg* influencer, opinion leader

prédécesseur *nm* predecessor

prédisposition à l'achat *nf Mktg* buyer-readiness

préemballé, -e *adj* pre-packed, pre-packaged

préemballer *vt* to pre-pack, to pre- package

préemption *nf Jur* pre-emption

pré-étude *nf* pilot study

préférence *nf* (a) *(d'un créancier)* priority (b) *Écon* **préférence pour la liquidité** liquidity preference (c) *Douanes* **préférences douanières** preferential duty (d) *Mktg* preference ▫ *préférence du consommateur* consumer preference

préférentiel, -elle *adj Douanes (tarif, taux)* preferential

préfinancement *nm Fin* advance funding, pre-financing

préfinancer *vt Fin* to fund in advance, to pre-finance

préformaté, -e *adj Ordinat* pre-formatted

préformater *vt Ordinat* to pre-format

pré-installé, -e *adj Ordinat* pre-installed

pré-installer *vt Ordinat* to pre-install

préjudice *nm* prejudice, detriment; **sans préjudice de nos droits** without prejudice (to our rights); **subir un préjudice matériel** to sustain damage; **subir un préjudice moral** to suffer mental distress; **porter préjudice à qn** to do sb harm; **au préjudice de qch** to the detriment of sth ▫ *préjudice financier* financial harm

préjudiciable *adj* detrimental

prélèvement *nm Fin (action)* deduction (**sur** from); *(somme prélevée)* amount deducted; **faire un prélèvement sur un compte** to debit an account; **le prélèvement sera effectué le dernier jour de chaque mois** the deduction will be made on the last day of each month ▫ *UE* **prélèvements agricoles** agricultural levies; *Banque* **prélèvement bancaire (automatique)** direct debit; *prélèvement sur le capital* capital levy; *prélèvement à l'exportation* export levy; *prélèvement fiscal* taxation; *prélèvement à l'importation* import levy; *prélèvement de l'impôt à la source* taxation at source; *prélèvement libératoire* deduction (of tax) at source; *prélèvements obligatoires* = tax and social security contributions; *prélèvement salarial, prélèvement sur salaire* deduction from wages; *prélèvement social* social security contribution

prélever *vt* to deduct in advance; *(compte)* to draw on; **prélever dix pour cent sur qch** to make an advance deduction of ten percent from sth, to deduct ten percent in advance from sth; **prélever une commission de deux pour cent sur une opération** to charge a two percent commission on a transaction; **dividende prélevé sur le capital** dividend paid out of capital; **prélever une somme sur un salaire** to deduct a sum from a salary; **prélever une somme sur un compte** to withdraw a sum from an account; **prélever qch à la source** to deduct sth at source

prémarketing *nm* pre-marketing

premier, -ère 1 *adj* first; **produit de premier choix** *ou* **première qualité** top-quality product; **la France est le premier exportateur de produits agricoles de l'Union européenne** France is the leading exporter of agricultural products in the EU ▫ *Premier ministre* Prime Minister
2 *nm* **premier entré, premier sorti** first in, first out

3 *nf Banque, Fin* **première de change** first of exchange

prendre *vt* (a) *(avion, bateau, train)* to take (b) *(faire payer)* to charge; **prendre 40 euros (de) l'heure** to charge 40 euros an hour (c) *(embaucher)* to take on, to hire; **prendre un associé** to take on a partner; **prendre qn comme secrétaire** to hire sb as one's secretary (d) *(noter) (lettre, coordonnées)* to take; **voulez-vous prendre une lettre?** will you take a letter? (e) *(charger) (marchandises)* to take in (f) **prendre qn/qch en charge** to take charge of sb/sth; **prendre des frais en charge** to cover costs (g) **prendre date** to fix a date; **prendre rendez-vous** to make an appointment

preneur, -euse *nm,f* buyer, purchaser; *(d'un chèque, d'une lettre de change)* payee; *Jur (d'un bail)* lessee, leaseholder; **nous sommes preneurs** we are interested in buying; **trouver preneur** to find a buyer □ *Jur* **preneur à bail** lessee, leaseholder

prépayer *vt* to prepay

préposé, -e *nm,f (employé)* employee □ **préposé à la caisse** cashier; **préposé des douanes** customs officer; **préposé à la location** booking clerk

préposer *vt* **préposer qn à une fonction** to appoint sb to a position; **préposer qn à la direction d'un service** to appoint sb as head of department

préprogrammé, -e *adj Ordinat* preprogrammed

préprogrammer *vt Ordinat* to preprogram

préretraite *nf* early retirement; **partir en préretraite** to take early retirement; **être mis en préretraite** to be given early retirement

❝

La ministre de l'Emploi et de la Solidarité a annoncé hier, au cours d'une conférence de presse, que les personnes atteintes de maladies professionnelles liées à l'amiante pourront désormais bénéficier d'une **préretraite** à partir de cinquante ans. "L'espérance de vie de ces personnes est fortement réduite et elles ne peuvent donc pas profiter normalement de leur retraite", a ainsi estimé la ministre.

❞

prérogative *nf* prerogative

prescripteur, -trice *nm,f Mktg* opinion leader

prescription *nf Fin* **prescription acquisitive** positive prescription; **prescription extinctive** negative prescription

prescrit, -e *adj* stipulated; **dans les délais prescrits par la loi** within the legally required time; **à la date prescrite** on the agreed date

présentateur, -trice *nm,f (d'une traite, d'un chèque)* presenter

présentation *nf* (a) *(d'une traite, d'un chèque)* presentation; **sur présentation de** on presentation of; **présentation à l'encaissement** *Banque* paying in, *Br* encashment; *Admin* presentation for collection; **présentation au paiement** presentation for payment (b) *Mktg* display □ **présentation sur le lieu de vente** point-of-sale display; **présentation en masse** mass display; **présentation du produit** product display; **présentation au sol** floor display; **présentation à la sortie** checkout display; **présentation en vrac** dump display (c) *(à un client potentiel)* presentation; **faire une présentation** to make a presentation (d) *(d'une lettre)* layout (e) *(apparence)* appearance; **excellente présentation exigée** *(dans une offre d'emploi)* excellent presentation required

présenter *vt* (a) *Fin* **présenter une traite à l'acceptation** to present a bill for acceptance; **présenter un chèque à l'encaissement** to present a cheque for payment (b) *(proposer)* **présenter une motion à l'assemblée** to put a motion to the meeting (c) *Mktg* to display (d) *(montrer)* to show; **votre compte présente un solde créditeur de 50 000 euros** your account shows a credit balance of 50,000 euros

présentoir *nm Mktg* display stand, display unit; *(panier)* dump bin □ **présentoir de caisse** checkout display; **présentoir au sol** floor display, floor stand

présérie *nf* pre-production, pilot run

présidence *nf* chairmanship, presidency; **être nommé à la présidence de qch** to be appointed chairman of sth; **les pays de l'UE se succèdent à la présidence tous les six mois** a different EU member state assumes the presidency every six months; **elle a été élue à la présidence de la société** she was elected chairwoman of the company

président, -e *nm,f* (a) *(d'une réunion, d'une commission)* chairperson, chairman, *f* chairwoman; **être élu président** to be voted into the chair, to be elected chairperson □ **président d'honneur** honorary chairperson *or* president (b) *(d'une entreprise) Br* chairman, *Am* president □ **président du conseil d'administration** *Br* chairman (of the board), *Am* president; **président-directeur général** *Br* Chairman and Managing Director, *Am* Chief Executive Officer; **président du directoire** *Br* chairman (of the board), *Am* president

présider 1 *vt (réunion, commission)* to preside over, to chair **2** *vi* **présider à une réunion** to preside over a meeting, to chair a meeting

presse *nf* **la presse** the press □ **presse finan-**

cière financial press; **presse nationale** national press; **presse d'opinion** quality press; **presse professionnelle** trade press; **presse de qualité** quality press; **presse spécialisée** specialist press

presse-papiers nm Ordinat clipboard

pression nf pressure; **la pression de la demande a entraîné des ruptures de stocks** the pressure on demand has led to stock shortages; **la pression de la concurrence les a contraints à baisser leurs prix** pressure from the competition forced them to lower their prices; **sous la pression des syndicats, la direction a finalement accepté de revoir les salaires à la hausse** under pressure from the unions, the management finally agreed to revise salaries upwards □ **pression fiscale** tax burden; **pression inflationniste** inflationary pressure

> ❝
> Au-delà de la bataille de chiffres, droite et gauche s'affrontent sur la philosophie de l'allégement de la **pression fiscale**.
> ❞

prestataire nmf (a) Admin person receiving benefits or allowances (b) (fournisseur) **prestataire de service** contractor, service provider

prestation nf (a) (allocation) benefit, allowance; **verser les prestations** to pay out benefits; **recevoir des prestations** to receive benefits □ **prestations familiales** family benefits; **prestation indemnitaire** allowance, benefit; **prestation d'invalidité** invalidity benefit; **prestations maladie** sickness benefit; **prestation de service** service fee; **prestations sociales** social security benefits (b) Admin, Jur **prestations locatives** service charge (c) (service) service □ **prestation de capitaux** provision of capital

prêt nm loan; **accorder/consentir un prêt** to allow/to grant a loan; **demander** ou **solliciter un prêt** to apply for a loan □ **prêt pour l'accession à la propriété** home loan; **prêts d'aide à l'investissement** ou **au développement des entreprises** loan guarantee scheme; **prêt bail** leasing; **prêt bancaire** bank loan; **prêt de banque à banque** interbank loan; **prêt bonifié** loan at reduced rate of interest, soft loan; **prêt conditionnel, prêt à condition** tied loan; **prêt à la consommation** consumer loan; **prêt à court terme** short(-term) loan; **prêt à découvert** overdraft loan; **prêt de démarrage** start-up loan; **prêt douteux** doubtful loan; **prêt entre banques** interbank loan; **prêt d'épargne-logement** home loan; **prêt à fonds perdus** loan without security; **prêt sur gage** loan against security; **prêt garanti** guaranteed or secured loan, collateral loan; **prêt d'honneur** loan on trust; **prêt hypothécaire, prêt sur hypothèque** mortgage loan; **prêt immobilier** Br home

or property or Am real-estate loan; **prêt initial** start-up loan; **prêt à intérêt** loan at interest, interest-bearing loan; **prêt sans intérêt** interest-free loan; **prêts au jour le jour** call loan, loan at call; **prêt du jour au lendemain** overnight loan; **prêt à long terme** long(-term) loan; **prêt sur nantissement** loan on collateral; **prêt non garanti** unsecured loan; **prêt participatif** equity loan; **prêt en participation** syndicated loan; **prêts aux particuliers** personal loans; **prêt personnalisé, prêt personnel** personal loan; **prêt à la petite semaine** = short-term loan at high rate of interest; **prêt remboursable sur demande** call loan, loan at call, loan repayable on demand; **prêt de remboursement** refunding loan; **prêt en souffrance** non-performing loan; **prêt à tempérament** instalment loan; **prêt à terme** loan at notice; **prêt à terme (fixe)** term loan; **prêt sur titres** loan against securities; **prêt à vue** call loan, loan at call

prétendant, -e nm,f Mktg challenger

prête-nom nm Fin (société) nominee company; (personne) figurehead

> ❝
> Noms de société-écran, comptes en Suisse et à New York, **prête-noms** multiples, valises de billets transitant entre Genève et Paris, mots de passe, etc. Une chose est sûre, les commissions versées par Elf à Christine Deviers-Joncour ont emprunté "une trajectoire tortueuse", des mots même de Sophie Portier, la présidente du tribunal correctionnel.
> ❞

prétention nf (a) (demande) claim (à to); **exposé détaillé des prétentions du demandeur** detailed statement of claim (b) (financière) expected salary; **envoyer curriculum vitae et prétentions (de salaire)** send CV and state salary requirements

prêter vt to lend, to loan; **prêter de l'argent à intérêt** to lend money at interest; **prêter à huit pour cent** to lend at eight percent; **prêter sur garantie** ou **gage(s)** to lend against security; **prêter à la petite semaine** to make a short-term loan at a high rate of interest

pré-test nm pre-test □ **pré-test publicitaire** copy test

pré-tester vt to pre-test

prêteur, -euse nm,f lender; Jur bailor □ **prêteur en dernier ressort** lender of last resort; **prêteur sur gages** pawnbroker; **prêteur sur titre** money broker

prêt-logement nm Br home or property or Am real-estate loan

prêt-relais nm Br bridging loan, Am bridge loan

préventif, -ive adj (mesure) preventive

prévision *nf* forecast; *(activité)* forecasting; **nous avons constitué des stocks en prévision d'une hausse subite de la demande** we have built up stocks in anticipation of a sudden increase in demand; **nos résultats sont inférieurs à nos prévisions** our results are lower than *or* below forecast ◻ *Mktg* **prévision de la base** grass-roots forecast; *(activité)* grass-roots forecasting; *Bourse* **prévision boursière** stock market forecast; *(activité)* stock market forecasting; **prévisions budgétaires** budget forecasts; *(activité)* budget forecasting; **prévisions conjoncturelles, prévisions économiques** economic forecasts; *(activité)* economic forecasting; *Mktg* **prévision par estimation** judgemental forecast; *(activité)* judgemental forecasting; *Mktg* **prévision événementielle** hazard forecasting; *Mktg* **prévisions hiérarchisées** top-down forecast; *(activité)* top-down forecasting; **prévision du marché** market forecast; *(activité)* market forecasting; *Mktg* **prévisions qualitatives** qualitative forecast; *(activité)* qualitative forecasting; *Mktg* **prévisions quantitatives** quantitative forecast; *(activité)* quantitative forecasting; **prévision de trésorerie** cash flow forecast; *(activité)* cash flow forecasting; **prévision des ventes** sales forecast; *(activité)* sales forecasting; **prévision des ventes et profits** sales and profit forecast; *(activité)* sales and profit forecasting

prévisionnel, -elle *adj (coût)* estimated; *(budget)* predicted

prévisionniste *nmf Écon* forecaster

prévisualisation *nf Ordinat* print preview

prévoir *vt (augmentation, baisse)* to foresee, to forecast; **les experts prévoient une baisse du chômage dans les mois à venir** the experts are forecasting a drop in unemployment over the coming months; **ventes prévues** projected sales; **il prévoit une baisse de quatre pour cent au mois de mai** he's projecting a four percent fall in May; **la mise en service de ces ordinateurs est prévue pour l'année prochaine** these computers are scheduled for installation next year; **la réunion est prévue pour demain** the meeting is arranged for *or* will be held tomorrow; **dépenses prévues au budget** expenses provided *or* allowed for in the budget; **selon les conditions prévues dans le contrat** according to the conditions set out in the contract; **le contrat prévoit une prime de licenciement** the contract provides for a severance payment

prévoyance *nf Fin* contingency, provision for the future ◻ **prévoyance sociale** social security provisions

prévu, -e *adj (augmentation, baisse, ventes)* forecast, projected

prier *vt* **nous vous prions de bien vouloir ac-** cepter l'assurance de nos sentiments les meilleurs *(dans une lettre)* *(à quelqu'un dont on connaît le nom)* Br yours sincerely, Am sincerely; *(à quelqu'un dont on ne connaît pas le nom)* Br yours faithfully, Am sincerely; **nous vous prions de bien vouloir vous présenter à l'accueil à 14 heures** please report to reception at 2 pm

prière *nf (utilisé dans la correspondance)* **prière de nous couvrir par chèque** kindly remit by cheque; **prière de faire suivre** please forward; **prière de bien vouloir confirmer votre commande** please confirm your order

primaire *Écon* **1** *adj (secteur)* primary
  2 *nm* primary sector

prime *nf* **(a)** *Assur* premium ◻ **prime annuelle** annual *or* yearly premium; **prime d'assurance** insurance premium; **prime majorée** loaded premium; **prime nette** pure premium; **prime de renouvellement** renewal premium; **prime unique** single premium
  (b) *Bourse, Fin* premium, option; **abandonner la prime** to forfeit *or* surrender the option; **acheter à prime** to give for the call; **donner la réponse à une prime, répondre à une prime** to declare an option; **faire prime** to stand at a premium; **lever la prime** to exercise *or* take up an option ◻ **prime à l'acheteur** buyer's option; **prime auto-payante** self-liquidating premium; **prime du change** agio, exchange premium; **prime de conversion** conversion premium; **prime sur le dollar** dollar premium; **prime d'émission** issue *or* share premium; **prime de fusion** merger premium; **prime d'illiquidité** illiquidity premium; **prime de l'or** premium on gold; **prime de remboursement** premium on redemption, redemption premium; **prime de risque** risk premium, yield gap; **prime au vendeur** seller's option
  (c) *(subvention)* subsidy, grant ◻ **prime de développement** (government) development subsidy *or* grant; **prime à l'exportation** export subsidy; **prime à l'investissement** investment subsidy; **prime de sauvetage** salvage money
  (d) *(sur salaire)* bonus ◻ **prime d'ancienneté** = bonus for long service; **prime de déménagement** relocation allowance; **prime de départ** severance pay, golden handshake; **prime d'efficacité** efficiency bonus; **prime d'encouragement** incentive bonus; **prime en espèces** cash bonus; **prime d'intéressement** reversionary bonus; **prime de licenciement** severance pay; **prime de mérite** merit bonus; **prime de productivité** productivity bonus; **prime de rendement** productivity bonus; *(suite à une mission réussie)* success fee; **prime de risque** danger money; **prime de transport** travel allowance; **prime de vie chère** cost-of-living allowance, *Br* weighting
  (e) *Mktg* free gift; **recette donnée en prime**

avec ce produit free recipe when you buy this product □ *prime contenant* container premium; *prime différée* on-pack offer; *prime directe* with-pack premium; *prime échantillon* free sample; *prime produit en plus* bonus pack

prime time *nm (à la télévision)* prime time

principal, -e 1 *adj* principal, main; **le vin est la production principale du pays** wine is the main product of the country; **un des principaux actionnaires** a major shareholder □ *principale compétence* core competence
2 *nm Fin* principal, capital sum; *(de l'impôt)* = original amount of tax payable before surcharges; **principal et intérêts** principal and interest

principe *nm* principle; **c'est un principe directeur de la politique de notre entreprise** it's a guiding principle of our company's policy □ *Compta* **principe de la continuité de l'exploitation** going-concern concept; **principes économiques** economic principles; *Compta* **principe d'indépendance des exercices** accruals concept; *Compta* **principe de la partie double** double-entry method; *Compta* **principe de la partie simple** single-entry method; *Compta* **principe de permanence, principe de la permanence des méthodes** consistency concept *or* principle; *Compta* **principe de prudence** conservatism concept *or* principle; *Compta* **principe de rattachement à l'exercice** accruals concept; *Compta* **principe du rattachement des produits et des charges** matching principle

prioritaire *adj* priority; **être prioritaire** to have priority; **notre projet est prioritaire sur tous les autres** our project has priority over all the others

priorité *nf* priority; *Jur* priority of claim; **avoir la priorité** to have priority; **il faut établir une liste des priorités pour l'entreprise** we must draw up a list of priorities for the company; **la recherche de nouveaux débouchés est une priorité absolue pour notre société** finding new outlets is an absolute priority for our company

pris, -e *adj (occupé)* busy; **elle est très prise en ce moment** she's very busy at the moment; **je suis pris mercredi toute la journée** I'm busy all day Wednesday

prise *nf* □ *Fin* **prise de bénéfices** profit-taking; *prise en charge (de frais)* payment, covering; *prise de contrôle (majoritaire)* takeover; *prise de décision* decision-making; *prise à domicile* receipt at domicile; *prise de participation (dans une entreprise)* acquisition of an interest in a company; *Bourse* **prise de position** position taking

> ❝
> Accueillie dans un scepticisme général, la **prise de contrôle** de Nissan par Renault va se révéler un succès phénoménal. Grâce à Nissan, Renault est sorti de son statut de constructeur régional pour jouer dans la cour des grands, ceux qui produisent et vendent dans le monde entier.
> ❞

privatif, -ive *adj (droit)* exclusive, private

privatisation *nf* privatization

privatiser *vt* to privatize

privé, -e *adj (banque, entreprise, propriété, secteur, investisseur)* private

privilège *nm* **(a)** *Banque* **privilège d'émission** = exclusive right to issue banknotes **(b)** *Fin, Jur* preferential right; **avoir un privilège sur qch** to have a lien *or* charge on sth □ *privilège du créancier* creditor's preferential claim; *privilège fiscal* tax privilege; *privilège général* general lien; *privilège spécial* particular lien

privilégier *vt* **(a)** *(personne, groupe)* to privilege; *(facteur, aspect)* to prioritize; **les augmentations en pourcentage privilégient les hauts salaires** percentage increases work in favour of high salaries **(b)** *(banque)* to grant a charter to; *(créancier)* to give preference to

prix *nm* **(a)** *(coût)* price; **à moitié prix** half price; **acheter qch à bas prix** to buy sth at a low price *or* cheaply; **je vous ferai un prix (d'ami)** I'll let you have it cheap; **mettre un prix à qch** to price sth, to put a price to sth; **prix à débattre** *(dans une annonce)* price negotiable □ *prix de l'abonnement* subscription rate; *Mktg* **prix d'acceptabilité** psychological price; *prix d'achat* purchase price; *prix adapté au marché* market-based price; *prix d'adjudication* auction price; *prix affiché* sticker price, displayed price; *prix d'appel* loss leader price; *(à une vente aux enchères)* starting price; *prix cassés* knock-down prices; *prix (de) catalogue* catalogue price; *prix (au) comptant* cash price; *prix conseillé* recommended retail price; *prix conseillé par le fabricant* manufacturer's recommended price; *prix contractuel* contract *or* contractual price; *prix courant* current price; *prix courant du marché* current market price; *prix coûtant* purchase price, cost price; **acheter/vendre qch au prix coûtant** to buy/sell sth at cost; *prix demandé* asking price; *prix démarqués* double pricing; *prix de demi-gros* trade price; *prix de départ (à une vente aux enchères)* upset price; *prix départ usine* price exworks, factory price; *prix de détail* retail price, *Am* end price; *prix directeur* price leader; *prix d'écrémage* skimming price; *prix d'équilibre* target price; *prix exceptionnel* bargain price; *prix à l'exportation, prix (à l')export* export price; *prix de fabrique* cost price, manufacturer's price; **prix de facture, prix facturé** invoice or invoiced price; **prix faible** discount price; **prix de faveur** preferential or special price; **prix fixe** fixed price, all-inclusive price; **prix forfaitaire, prix à forfait** fixed price, all-inclusive price; **prix fort (de vente)** full or top price; **prix franco** franco price; **prix de gros** wholesale price; **prix homologué** authorized price; **prix hors taxe** price net of tax, price before tax; **prix à l'importation, prix (à l')import** import price; **prix imposé** fixed price, Am administered price; **prix indicatif** approximate price; **prix initial** starting price; **prix de lancement** introductory price; **prix limite** upper price limit; **prix de liquidation** closing-down price, break-up price; **prix loco** loco price; Mktg **prix magique** odd numbers price; **prix de la main-d'œuvre directe** direct labour cost; **prix marchand** trade price; **prix du marché** market price; **prix marqué** marked price; **prix maximum** maximum price; **prix minimum** minimum price; (à une vente aux enchères) reserve price; **prix minimum rentable** break-even price; **prix moyen** average price; **prix net** net price; (sur un menu) price inclusive of service; **prix nominal** nominal price; **prix offert** offered or selling price; **prix officiel** standard price; **prix de l'offre** supply price; **prix optimum** optimal price; Mktg **prix de pénétration** penetration price; **prix pétroliers** oil prices; **prix sur place** loco price; Écon **prix plafond** ceiling price; Écon **prix plancher** bottom price; **prix pratiqué** current price; **prix préférentiel** preferential price; Mktg **prix de prestige** premium price, prestige price; **prix à la production** price ex warehouse; **prix promotionnels** promotional pricing; Mktg **prix psychologique** psychological price; Mktg **prix psychologique optimum** optimal psychological price; **prix public** posted price, list price; **prix à quai** landed cost; **prix de rabais** reduced or discount price; **prix recommandé** recommended retail price; **prix réduit** reduced or discount price; **prix réel** actual price; **prix de référence** reference price; **prix à la reprise** trade-in price; **prix de revient** cost price; **prix de revient unitaire** unit cost; UE **prix seuil** threshold price, floor price; **prix de solde, prix soldé** bargain price, sale price; UE **prix de soutien** support price; **prix spécial** special price; **prix standard** standard price; **prix taxé** standard price; **prix taxe comprise** price inclusive of tax; **prix tout compris, prix tous frais compris, prix toutes taxes comprises** all-inclusive price; **prix de transport** freight price; **prix unique** one price, single price; **prix unitaire, prix à l'unité** unit price; **prix d'usine** factory price; **prix à la vente** sticker price, displayed price; **prix de vente** sale or selling price; **prix de vente imposé** resale price maintenance

(b) Bourse, Fin price; **ces actions sont cotées au prix de...** these shares are quoted at the rate

of... □ **prix acheteur, prix d'achat** bid price; **prix de l'argent** price of money; **prix du change** (exchange) premium; **prix (au) comptant** spot price; **prix de conversion** conversion price; **prix du disponible** spot price; **prix d'émission** issue price; **prix d'exercice** exercise price; (d'option d'achat) exercise price, striking price; **prix du marché** market price; **acheter/vendre au prix du marché** to buy/sell at market price; **prix de négociation** trade price; **prix de l'option** option price; **prix de rachat** redemption price; **prix du report** contango rate; **prix à terme** forward price; **prix vendeur** offer price

> **❝**
>
> La France devrait également s'opposer à l'intention prêtée à la Commission de demander, dans le cadre de la révision prévue du montant des aides dans certains secteurs, une baisse de 5% du **prix de soutien** des céréales.
>
> **❞**

prix-courant nm price list, catalogue

prix-étalon nm standard cost or price

probatoire adj (période) probationary

problème nm problem □ **problème de logiciel** software problem

procédé nm process □ **procédé comptable** accounting procedure; **procédé de fabrication** manufacturing process; **procédé de travail** operating process

procédure nf (a) (méthode) procedure □ Ordinat **procédure de chargement** loading procedure; **procédure disciplinaire** disciplinary procedure; **procédure douanière** customs procedure; **procédure de licenciement** dismissal procedure (b) Jur proceedings; **engager une procédure contre qn** to institute proceedings against sb □ **procédure de faillite** bankruptcy proceedings

procès nm Jur proceedings; (civil) lawsuit; (criminel) trial; **intenter un procès à qn** to institute proceedings against sb

processeur nm Ordinat processor □ **processeur central** central processing unit, CPU; **processeur de données** data processor

processus nm process □ **processus d'achat** purchasing process; **processus décisionnel, processus de décision** decision-making process; **processus de diffusion, processus de distribution** distribution process; **processus de fabrication** manufacturing process; **processus de prise de décision(s)** decision-making process

procès-verbal nm (official) report; (d'une réunion) minutes; **dresser un procès-verbal** to draw up a report; **tenir le procès-verbal de la**

réunion to keep the minutes of the meeting; **le procès-verbal de la dernière séance a été approuvé** the minutes of the last meeting were approved □ **procès-verbal des avaries** protest

procuration *nf Jur* proxy, power of attorney; **signé par procuration** signed by proxy; **agir par procuration** to act by proxy; **donner procuration à qn** to give sb power of attorney; **avoir procuration sur un compte** to have power of attorney over an account □ **procuration générale** full power of attorney

procurer 1 *vt* to get, to obtain (**à** for); **procurer un emploi à qn** to get sb a job
2 se procurer *vpr* to get *or* obtain for oneself

procureur *nm Jur* prosecutor

producteur, -trice 1 *adj* productive; **producteur d'intérêt** interest-bearing; **les pays producteurs de pétrole** the oil-producing countries
2 *nm,f* producer; **ce pays est le premier producteur d'acier du monde** this country is the world's largest steel producer

productif, -ive *adj* productive; **productif d'intérêts** interest-bearing

production *nf* (**a**) *(fait de produire)* production; *(quantités produites)* production, output; **augmenter la production** to increase production; **ralentir la production** to slow down production; **la production ne suit plus la consommation** production is failing to keep up with demand □ **production à la chaîne** mass production; **production sur** *ou* **à la commande** production to order; **production continue** continuous flow production; **production dirigée** planned production; **production discontinue** production in batches; **production globale** aggregate production; *Fin* **production immobilisée** = fixed assets produced for use by the company; **production intérieure brute** gross domestic product; **production JAT** JIT production; **production juste à temps** just-in-time production; **production par lots** batch production; **production à la machine** machine production; **production manufacturée** secondary production; **production de masse** mass production; **production de matières premières** primary production; **production planifiée** planned production; **production en série** mass production
(**b**) *(produit)* product □ *Compta* **production stockée** *(poste de bilan)* stored production, production left in stock; *Compta* **production vendue** sales

productique *nf* production engineering

productivité *nf* productivity, productive capacity □ **productivité marginale** marginal productivity

produire 1 *vt* (**a**) *(documents)* to produce (**b**) *(intérêt)* to bear, to yield (**c**) *(marchandise, produit)* to produce, to manufacture; **produire qch en masse** to mass-produce sth; **produire qch en série** *ou* **à la chaîne** to produce sth on an assembly line
2 *vi Écon* to produce, to be productive

produit *nm* (**a**) *(article)* product □ **produits d'achat courant** convenience goods; **produits alimentaires, produits d'alimentation** food products; *Mktg* **produit d'appel** loss leader; **produit augmenté** augmented product; **produit de base** staple commodity *or* product; **produit ciblé** niche product; **produits de consommation** consumable goods; **produits de consommation courante** consumer goods; **produits en cours** work in progress; **produits de dépannage** emergency goods; **produits dérivés** by-products, derivatives; *Mktg* **produit drapeau** own-brand product; **produit écologique** green product; **produit d'élite** premium product; **produits étrangers** foreign produce *or* goods; **produit final** end product; **produit fini** finished product; *Mktg* **produit générique** generic product; **produits de grande consommation** consumer products; **produit de haut niveau** high standard product; *Mktg* **produit d'imitation** imitative product; **produit industriel** industrial product; **produit innovateur** innovative product; **produits intermédiaires** semi-finished products; **produit sous licence** licensed product; **produits de luxe** luxury goods; **produits manufacturés** manufactured goods *or* products; **produit de marque** branded *or* brand-name product; **produit à marque de distributeur** own-brand product; **produit sans marque** unbranded product; *Mktg* **produit sans nom** no-name product; *Mktg* **produit novateur** (in)novative product; **produits d'origine nationale** home(-grown) produce; **produit ouvré** finished *or* end product; **produits du pays** home produce; **produits périssables** non-durable goods; **produits pétroliers** oil products; **produit de première nécessité** essential *or* staple product; **produit de prestige** premium product; *Écon* **produit principal** main product; **produits de rejet** waste products; **produits de second choix** seconds, rejects; **produit semi-fini** semi-finished product; **produit semi-ouvré** semi-manufactured product; **produits spécialisés** speciality goods; *Mktg* **produit substituable** substitutable product; **produit de substitution, produit substitut** substitute product; *Mktg* **produit tactique** me-too product; *Mktg* **produit vert** green product
(**b**) *(profit)* yield; *(recette)* proceeds; **le produit de la journée** the day's takings *or* proceeds □ *Compta* **produits accessoires** sundry income; *Compta* **produits annexes** incidental income; *Compta* **produit brut** gross proceeds, gross income; *Compta* **produit constaté**

d'avance prepaid *or* deferred income; *Compta* **produits courants** current income; **produit national** home product; *Compta* **produits exceptionnels** extraordinary income; *Compta* **produits d'exploitation** operating income, income from operations; *Compta* **produits financiers** interest received, interest and dividend income; *Compta* **produits de gestion courante** income from operations; *Écon* **produit intérieur brut** gross domestic product; *Écon* **produit intérieur net** net domestic product; **produit moyen** average revenue; *Écon* **produit national** national product; *Écon* **produit national brut** gross national product; *Écon* **produit national net** net national product; *Compta* **produit net** net proceeds, net income; *Compta* **produits à recevoir** accrued income, accruals

(**c**) *Banque* **produit bancaire** banking product; **produit de taux** interest-bearing financial product

> **"**
>
> Le **produit intérieur brut** (PIB) irlandais, qui mesure la totalité de la richesse créée, est supérieur de 30% au **produit national brut** (PNB), mesure de la richesse créée par les entreprises nationales. Cela s'explique simplement par le poids des multinationales américaines, dont la valeur ajoutée en Irlande est comptabilisée dans le PNB des Etats-Unis.
>
> **"**

profession *nf* profession; **être sans profession** to be out of a job

professionnalisme *nm* professionalism

professionnel, -elle *adj & nm,f* professional

profil *nm* profile; **quel est le profil du candidat idéal?** what is the profile of the ideal candidate?; **elle a le profil requis pour ce genre de poste** she has the right profile for this kind of job ❏ *Mktg* **profil de la clientèle** customer profile; *Mktg* **profil du consommateur** consumer profile; **profil démographique** demographic profile; **profil d'entreprise** company profile; *Mktg* **profil du marché** market profile; *Banque* **profil patrimonial** personal assets profile; *Mktg* **profil de produit** product profile; **profil psychologique** psychological profile; **profil socio-démographique** sociodemographic profile

profit *nm* profit; **vendre à profit** to sell at a profit; **profit de 12 pour cent** 12 percent profit ❏ **profit aléatoire** contingent profit; **profit annuel** annual profit; **profit brut** gross profit; **profit espéré** anticipated profit; **profits exceptionnels** windfall profits; **profits de l'exercice** year's profits; **profit d'exploitation** operating profit; **profits fictifs** paper profits; **profits inattendus** windfall profits; **profits mis en réserve** capital reserves; **profit net** clear profit; **profits**

non matérialisés paper profits; **profits et pertes** profit and loss; **profits rapides** quick returns; **profit réel** real profit; **profit tout clair** clear profit

profitable *adj* profitable

profiter 1 profiter de *vt ind* to take advantage of; **ils ont profité de la baisse des taux d'intérêt** they took advantage of the drop in interest rates

2 profiter à *vt ind* to benefit; **la chute de la livre a profité aux exportateurs** the fall in the value of the pound benefited exporters

profiteur, -euse *nm,f* profiteer

pro forma *adj* pro forma

progiciel *nm Ordinat* software package ❏ **progiciel de communication** comms package; **progiciel de comptabilité** accounting package; **progiciel intégré** integrated package

programmateur, -trice *nm,f Ordinat* programmer

programmation *nf* (**a**) *(planning)* programming, planning ❏ **programmation de la production** production scheduling (**b**) *Ordinat* programming ❏ **programmation par objets, programmation orientée objet** object-oriented programming

programme *nm* (**a**) *(planning)* programme, schedule; **arrêter un programme** to draw up *or* arrange a programme ❏ *Mktg* **programme d'amélioration de la qualité** quality improvement programme; *Mktg* **programme des annonces** advertising schedule; **programme de développement** development programme; **programme de fabrication** production programme *or* schedule; *Mktg* **programme de fidélisation** frequent user programme; **programme de formation** training programme; *Fin* **programme d'investissement** investment programme; **programme de maintenance** maintenance programme; **programme de production** production programme *or* schedule; **programme de recherche(s)** research programme; *Mktg* **programme de stimulation** incentive scheme; *Mktg* **programme des ventes** sales programme *or* schedule

(**b**) *Ordinat* program ❏ **programme antivirus** antivirus program; **programme d'application** application program; **programme de commande d'impression** printer driver; **programme de commande de la souris** mouse driver; **programme de conversion** conversion program; **programme de courrier électronique** e-mail program; **programme en cours d'éxécution** active program; **programme de création de pages Web** Web authoring program; **programme de dessin** drawing program, paint program; **programme de diagnostic** diagnostic program; **programme**

de gestion driver; **programme informatique** computer program; **programme d'installation** setup program, installer; **programme senti-nelle** watchdog program; **programme utili-taire** utility program; **programme virus** virus program

programmé, -e *adj Ordinat* programmed

programmer 1 *vt* (**a**) *Ordinat* to program; **pro-grammer en assembleur** to program in assem-bly language (**b**) *(prévoir)* to plan, to schedule **2** *vi Ordinat* to program

programmeur, -euse *nm,f Ordinat* (compu-ter) programmer

progrès *nm* progress; **faire des progrès** to make progress

progressif, -ive *adj (développement, crois-sance)* progressive, gradual; *(impôt, taux)* gradu-ated, progressive; **l'amélioration progressive du rendement** the gradual improvement in pro-ductivity

progression *nf* (**a**) *(de la situation économique)* upturn; *(d'un secteur)* expansion; *(des bénéfices)* increase; *Bourse (des actions)* rise, improve-ment; **être en progression** *(secteur)* to be growing *or* expanding; **les ventes sont en pro-gression par rapport à l'année dernière** sales are on the increase compared with last year (**b**) *(dans une carrière)* progress, advancement

progressivement *adv* progressively, gradual-ly; **adopter qch progressivement** to phase sth in

progressivité *nf* progressivity □ *Fin* **progres-sivité de l'impôt** progressive increase in taxa-tion

prohibé, -e *adj (marchandises)* prohibited

prohibitif, -ive *adj (prix, tarif)* prohibitive

prohibition *nf* prohibition, ban □ **prohibition d'entrée, prohibition à l'importation** import prohibition *or* ban; **prohibition de sortie** ex-port prohibition *or* ban

projection *nf* projection □ **projection de dia-positives** *(sur écran d'ordinateur)* slide show; *Mktg* **projection des ventes** sales projection

projet *nm* plan, project; **être à l'état de projet** to be at the planning stage □ **projet de budget** budget estimates; **projet de contrat** draft contract; **projet d'entreprise** business plan; *Jur* **projet de loi** bill

projeter *vt* to plan; **ils projettent d'ouvrir une nouvelle usine au Mexique** they are planning to open a new factory in Mexico

projet-pilote *nm* pilot project, pilot scheme

prolongation *nf* extension; **obtenir une pro-longation de congé** to get an extension of leave

prolonger *vt (délai)* to extend

promener se promener *vpr Ordinat* to browse; **se promener dans** to browse through

promesse *nf* (**a**) *Mktg* claim □ **promesse men-songère** false claim; **promesse produit** claim *(made about a product)*; **promesse unique de vente** unique selling point, USP (**b**) *Fin* under-taking □ **promesse d'achat** undertaking *or* pro-mise to purchase; **promesse écrite** written undertaking; **promesse de vente** undertaking *or* promise to sell

> **"**
>
> Un deal est conclu en juillet 2001: Financière Pinault prend 30% du holding de tête du groupe Harwanne et obtient une **promesse de vente** sur le solde dans un délai de deux à cinq ans.
>
> **"**

promo *nf Fam* promo

promoteur, -trice *nm,f* promoter □ **promo-teur immobilier** property developer; **promo-teur des ventes** sales promoter

promotion *nf* (**a**) *(d'un employé)* promotion □ **promotion à l'ancienneté** promotion by se-niority; **promotion des cadres** executive pro-motion; **promotion interne** internal promotion (**b**) *(offre spéciale)* promotion; **articles en pro-motion** items on promotion *or Am* on special; **notre promotion de la semaine** this week's special offer *or Am* special; **faire une promo-tion sur un produit** to promote a product; **faire la promotion de qch** to promote sth □ *Mktg* **promotion collective** tie-in promotion; *Mktg* **promotion d'entreprises** corporate iden-tity; *Mktg* **promotion immobilière** property development promotion; *Mktg* **promotion sur le lieu de vente** point-of-sale promotion; *Mktg* **promotion "on-pack"** on-pack promotion; *Mktg* **promotion sur point d'achat** point-of-purchase promotion; *Mktg* **promotion de pres-tige** prestige promotion; *Mktg* **promotion spé-ciale** special promotion; *Mktg* **promotion des ventes** sales promotion

promotionnel, -elle *adj (brochure)* promo-tional; *(tarif)* special; *(budget)* promotional, pu-blicity

promouvoir *vt* (**a**) *(donner de l'avancement à)* to promote; **être promu** to be promoted (**b**) *(article)* to promote, to publicize

pronostic *nm* forecast □ **pronostic du marché** market forecast

propension *nf Écon* propensity □ **propension à consommer** propensity to consume; **propen-sion à épargner** propensity to save

proportion *nf* proportion

proportionnalité *nf (rapport)* balance; *(ré-partition)* equal distribution □ *Fin* **proportion-nalité de l'impôt** fixed rate system of taxation

proportionnel, -elle *adj* proportional (**à** to); *(impôt, droit)* ad valorem

proportionnellement *adv* proportionally (à to)

proposer *vt (service, prix)* to recommend; *(candidat)* to nominate; **être proposé pour un emploi** to be recommended for a job; **proposer une motion** to propose a motion

proposition *nf (suggestion)* suggestion, proposal; *(offre)* offer; **faire** *ou* **formuler une proposition** to make a proposal; **dernière proposition** final offer ❑ *proposition d'affaires* business proposition; *proposition d'assurance* insurance proposal; *proposition de loi* bill; *proposition de paiement* payment proposal; *proposition de prix* price proposal; *proposition de rachat* offer to buy; **faire une proposition de rachat à une entreprise** to make an offer to buy a company; *Mktg* **proposition unique de vente** unique selling point, USP

propriétaire *nmf (d'une entreprise, d'un hôtel)* owner, proprietor; *(des actions)* holder ❑ *propriétaire foncier* landowner; *propriétaire individuelle* individual owner; *propriétaire indivis* joint owner; *propriétaire légitime* rightful *or* legal owner; *propriétaire occupant* owner-occupier; *propriétaire terrien* landed proprietor; *propriétaire unique* sole owner

propriété *nf* **(a)** *(fait de posséder)* ownership, proprietorship ❑ *propriété artistique* copyright; *propriété collective* collective ownership, social ownership; *propriété commerciale* = commercial tenant's right to security of tenure or compensation; *propriété commune* joint ownership; *propriété foncière* land ownership; *propriété individuelle* individual ownership; *propriété indivise* joint ownership; *propriété privée* private ownership; *propriété publique* public ownership
(b) *(chose ou terre possédée)* property, estate ❑ *propriété de l'État* government property; *propriété foncière* landed estate *or* property; *propriété immobilière* real estate, *Am* realty; *propriété industrielle* patent rights, industrial property; *propriété intellectuelle* intellectual property; *propriété mobilière* personal estate; *propriété privée* private property; *propriété publique* public property; *propriété territoriale* landed estate *or* property; *propriété à vendre* property for sale

prorata *nm* proportion; **au prorata** proportionately, pro rata; **au prorata de qch** proportionately to sth

prorogation *nf* extension of time limit; *(d'un contrat, d'un bail)* extension, renewal

proroger *vt* to extend; *(contrat, bail)* to extend, to renew; **proroger l'échéance d'un billet** to extend the maturity of a bill

prospect *nm Mktg* prospective customer, prospect ❑ *prospects à forte potentialité* hot prospect pool

prospecté, -e *nm,f Mktg* prospective customer, prospect

prospecter 1 *vt (client)* to canvass; *(marché)* to explore; **prospecter la clientèle** to canvass for new business
2 *vi* to prospect

prospecteur, -trice *nm,f* canvasser

prospectif, -ive *adj* prospective

prospection *nf Mktg* canvassing, prospecting; **faire de la prospection** to explore the market ❑ *prospection des marchés* market exploration; *prospection téléphonique* telephone marketing; *prospection sur le terrain* field research

prospectus *nm* **(a)** *Bourse* **prospectus (d'émission)** prospectus **(b)** *(de publicité)* leaflet; *(de plusieurs pages)* brochure; *(donnant renseignements de base)* fact sheet

prospère *adj* prosperous, thriving

prospérer *vi* to prosper, to thrive

prospérité *nf* prosperity

protecteur, -trice *adj Écon (droits, tarif)* protective

protection *nf* **(a)** *(défense)* protection (**contre** from *or* against) ❑ *protection du consommateur* consumer protection; *protection de l'emploi* job protection, employment protection; *protection de l'environnement* environmental protection, protection of the environment; *protection fiscale* tax shield; *protection sociale* social welfare (system)
(b) *Écon* protection(ism)
(c) *Ordinat* protection ❑ *protection contre la copie* copy protection; *protection contre l'écriture* *ou* *en écriture* write-protection; *protection de fichiers* file protection; *protection de l'information* data protection; *protection par mot de passe* password protection

protectionnisme *nm Écon* protectionism

protectionniste *adj Écon* protectionist

> ❝
> Le processus reste fragile. A preuve: le bras de fer avec Washington sur l'acier. George Bush ayant décidé d'appliquer des mesures **protectionnistes** pour défendre une industrie de l'acier archaïque, la Commission a porté plainte auprès de l'OMC et annonce, le 28 mars dernier, des mesures de sauvegarde.
> ❞

protégé, -e *adj* **(a)** protected; **protégé contre l'inflation** inflation-proof **(b)** *Ordinat* **protégé contre la copie** copy-protected; **protégé contre l'écriture** *ou* **en écriture** write-protected; **protégé par mot de passe** password-protected

protéger vt (**a**) *Écon (industrie)* to protect; *Bourse (position)* to hedge; **protéger qch par un brevet** to patent sth (**b**) *Ordinat* **protéger contre l'écriture** ou **en écriture** to write-protect; **protéger contre la copie** to copy-protect

protestable *adj Fin (effet)* protestable

protester vt *Fin (effet)* to protest

protêt *nm Jur* protest; **dresser un protêt** to make a protest; **signifier un protêt** to give notice of a protest ▫ **protêt authentique** certified protest; **protêt faute d'acceptation** protest for non-acceptance; **protêt faute de paiement** protest for non-payment

protocole *nm* (**a**) *(procès-verbal)* protocol ▫ **protocole d'accord** draft agreement, heads of agreement; **protocole d'achat et de vente** buy-sell agreement; **protocole d'intention** statement of intent; **protocole de vente** sale agreement
(**b**) *Ordinat* protocol; *(de réseau)* frame format; *(de traitement)* procedure ▫ **protocole HTTP** HTTP protocol; **protocole Internet** Internet protocol; **protocole point à point** point-to-point protocol; **protocole POP** post office protocol, POP; **protocole PPP** PPP; **protocole de téléchargement** download protocol; **protocole de transfert anonyme** anonymous FTP; **protocole de transfert de fichier** file transfer protocol; **protocole de transmission** transmission protocol
(**c**) *(cérémonial)* protocol, etiquette

❝
Dans le **protocole d'accord** final signé en décembre par la direction, les salariés ont pourtant obtenu deux jours de repos supplémentaires ainsi qu'une prime annuelle de 180 euros équivalant à un jour et demi de congés. Une formule qui déçoit les syndicats.
❞

prototype *nm* prototype

provenance *nf* origin; **de provenance française** of French origin

provision *nf* (**a**) *Banque, Fin* funds; **verser une provision** ou **des provisions** to deposit funds; **manque de provision** *(sur chèque)* no funds; **provision insuffisante** *(sur chèque)* insufficient funds; **provision d'une lettre de change** consideration for a bill of exchange; **faire provision pour une lettre de change** to provide for or protect a bill of exchange
(**b**) *Compta* provision, reserve ▫ **provision pour amortissement** provision for depreciation, depreciation allowance; **provision pour créances douteuses** provision for bad debts; **provision pour dépréciation** provision for depreciation, depreciation allowance; **provision pour risques et charges** contingency and loss provision

(**c**) *Jur (payé à un avocat)* retainer
(**d**) *(stock)* store, stock, supply; **faire provision de qch** to build up a stock of sth

provisionnement *nm* funding

provisionner vt *Banque, Fin (compte)* to pay money into, to deposit funds into; *(lettre de change)* to provide for, to protect

provisoire *adj (situation, bilan, état des comptes)* temporary; *(gérant)* temporary, acting; **à titre provisoire** on a temporary basis

prud'homme *nm* member of an industrial tribunal; **cette affaire va être portée devant les prud'hommes** this case will be taken to an industrial tribunal

❝
Prenons un exemple: un jeune cadre à qui l'on a refusé un emploi parce qu'il a un nom à consonance maghrébine et à qui le même employeur dit oui parce qu'il a donné un nom bien français peut aujourd'hui aller devant les **prud'hommes**.
❞

psychologie *nf* psychology ▫ *Mktg* **psychologie commerciale** psychology of marketing; *Mktg* **psychologie des consommateurs** consumer psychology; **psychologie industrielle** industrial psychology; *Mktg* **psychologie de la publicité** advertising psychology

psychométrique *adj* psychometric

PU *nm (abrév* **prix unitaire**) unit price

pub *nf Fam (abrév* **publicité**) (**a**) *(secteur)* advertising; **elle travaille dans la pub** she works in advertising; **faire de la pub pour qch** to advertise sth (**b**) *(message)* ad

public, -ique 1 *adj* public; *(entreprise)* public, government-owned
2 *nm* (**a**) *(secteur)* **le public** the public sector; **placer des actions dans le public** *(société)* to go public (**b**) **le grand public** the general public (**c**) *(d'un produit, d'une publicité)* audience

publication *nf* (**a**) *(fait de publier)* publication, publishing ▫ *Ordinat* **publication assistée par ordinateur** desktop publishing; *Fin* **publication des comptes** disclosure (of accounts) (**b**) *(document)* publication, published work

publiciste, publicitaire 1 *adj (dépenses, campagne)* advertising
2 *nmf (personne)* advertising executive; **c'est une publiciste** she works in advertising

publicité *nf (secteur)* advertising; *(message)* advert, advertisement; *(couverture)* advertising, publicity; **être dans la publicité** to be in advertising; **faire de la publicité pour qch** to advertise or publicize sth ▫ **publicité par affichage** poster advertising; **publicité agressive** hard sell; **publicité d'amorçage** advance publicity; **publicité de bouche-à-oreille** word-of-mouth advertising; **publicité collective** group advertising; **publicité comparative** comparative advertising; **publicité concurrentielle** competitive advertising; **publicité directe** direct advertising; **publicité d'entreprise** corporate advertising; **publicité extérieure** outdoor advertising; **publicité générique** generic advertising; **publicité goutte-à-goutte** drip advertising; **publicité informative** informative advertising; **publicité institutionnelle** corporate or institutional advertising; **publicité intensive** saturation advertising; **publicité sur le lieu de vente** (activité) point-of-sale advertising; (promotion) point-of-sale promotion; **publicité de marque** brand advertising; **publicité média** media advertising, above-the-line advertising; **publicité mensongère** misleading advertising; (message) misleading advertisement; **publicité sur panneau** billboard advertising; **publicité périphérique** perimeter advertising; **publicité au point de vente** instore promotion; **publicité presse** newspaper advertisement, print advertisement; (action) newspaper advertising, print advertising; **publicité de prestige** prestige advertising; **publicité de produit** product advertising; **publicité par publipostage** direct mail advertising; **publicité rédactionnelle** advertorial; **publicité à réponse directe** direct response advertising; **publicité subliminale** subliminal advertising; **publicité télévisée** television advertising; (message) television advertisement; **publicité par voie d'affiches** poster advertising

publicité-médias nf media advertising, above-the-line advertising

publicité-produit nf product advertising

publier vt (document, page Web) to publish

publi-information nf special advertising section, advertorial

publiphone® nm public telephone ❑ **publiphone**® **à carte** cardphone

publipostage nm Mktg mail shot, mailing; **faire un publipostage** to send a mailshot or mailing ❑ **publipostage groupé** volume mailing

publireportage nm special advertising section, advertorial

puce nf Ordinat (a) (composant) (micro)chip ❑ **puce à mémoire** memory chip (b) (symbole) bullet

puissance nf power; **une grande puissance économique** a major economic power ❑ **puissance d'achat** buying power; **puissance de vente** selling power

punaise nf Br drawing pin, Am thumbtack

pupitre nm Ordinat **pupitre (de commande)** console (desk); **pupitre de visualisation** visual display unit

purger vt (hypothèque) to pay off

put nm Bourse put (option)

PVD nm (abrév **pays en voie de développement**) developing country

pyramide des salaires nf wage pyramid

Qq

QCM nm Mktg (abrév **questionnaire à choix multiple**) multiple-choice questionnaire

quadrimestriel, -elle adj four-monthly

quai nm (**a**) (dans un port) quay, wharf; **à prendre** ou **livrable à quai** (marchandises) ex quay, ex wharf; **rendu** ou **livré franco à quai** free on quay (**b**) (dans une gare) platform ❏ **quai de chargement** loading platform; **quai de déchargement** off-loading platform; **quai d'embarquement** loading platform

qualification nf (**a**) (compétence) qualification; **posséder les qualifications nécessaires pour un poste** to have the necessary qualifications for a job ❏ **qualifications professionnelles** professional qualifications (**b**) Bourse, Fin qualification (by acquisition of shares)

qualifié, -e adj qualified; (ouvrier) skilled; **être qualifié pour faire qch** to be qualified to do sth

qualitatif, -ive adj qualitative

qualitativiste nmf Mktg market researcher

qualité nf (**a**) (d'un produit) quality; **de bonne qualité, de qualité supérieure** good-quality, high-quality; **de mauvaise qualité, de qualité inférieure** poor-quality; **de première qualité** high-grade, of the best quality ❏ **qualité loyale et marchande** fair average quality; **qualité marchande** fair average quality; Mktg **qualité perçue** perceived quality; **qualité prescrite** stipulated quality; **qualité supérieure** top quality (**b**) (qualification) qualification, skill; **avoir qualité pour agir** to be qualified or authorized to act; **posséder les qualités requises pour un poste** to have the necessary qualifications for a job; ❏ **qualités de gestionnaire** management or managerial skills (**c**) (fonction) capacity; **en sa qualité de directeur général** in his capacity as managing director (**d**) Ordinat quality ❏ **qualité brouillon** draft quality; **qualité courrier** (near) letter quality; **qualité d'impression** print quality

quantitatif, -ive adj quantitative

quantité nf quantity; **acheter qch en grande quantité** to buy sth in bulk or in large quantities ❏ **quantité économique de commande** economic order quantity; **quantité économique de production** economic manufacturing quantity; **quantité économique de réapprovisionnement** economic lot size

quantum nm (montant) amount; (proportion) proportion, ratio; **fixer le quantum des dommages-intérêts** to fix the amount of damages

quartier nm area ❏ **quartier des affaires** business area; **quartier commerçant** shopping area

quasi-contrat nm Jur quasi contract, implied contract

quasi-espèces nfpl Compta cash equivalents

quasi-trésorerie nf Compta cash equivalents

question nf question ❏ Mktg **question à choix multiple** multiple-choice question; **question de confiance** vote of confidence; Mktg **question dichotomique** dichotomous question; **questions diverses** (à l'ordre du jour) general business; Mktg **question fermée** closed-ended question; Mktg **question filtre** check question; Mktg **question ouverte** open-ended question

questionnaire nm Mktg questionnaire ❏ **questionnaire à choix multiple** multiple-choice questionnaire

questionnaire-pilote nm Mktg pilot questionnaire

Quinze n **les Quinze** = the member states of the European Union

quittance nf receipt ❏ **quittance comptable** accountable receipt; **quittance de douane** customs receipt; **quittance finale, quittance libératoire** receipt in full; **quittance de loyer** rent receipt; **quittance pour solde** receipt in full; Banque **quittance pour solde de tout compte** closing account balance; **quittance valable** proper receipt

quittancer vt to receipt

quitter vt (**a**) Ordinat **quitter le système** to quit (**b**) (au téléphone) **ne quittez pas** hold on, hold the line

quitus nm Compta final or full discharge

quorum nm quorum; **constituer un quorum**

to have a quorum; **le quorum n'est pas atteint** we don't have a quorum

quota *nm* quota ❑ *quota d'échantillonnage* sampling quota; *quota d'exportation* export quota; *quota d'importation* import quota; *quota de ventes* sales quota; *quotas volontaires à l'export* voluntary export restraint

quote-part *nf* share, quota; **apporter** *ou* **payer sa quote-part** to contribute one's share; **quote-part des bénéfices** share in the profits

> ❝
>
> Théoriquement, les pays européens doivent financer 47,5 % de l'AMA, mais l'Union européenne a renoncé en décembre, pour respecter ses propres règles budgétaires, à payer sa part. Libre choix était alors laissé aux gouvernements européens de payer ou non leur propre **quote-part**.
>
> ❞

quotidien, -enne *adj* daily

quotient *nm* quotient, ratio ❑ *quotient familial* = income tax relief system based on number of dependents

quotité *nf* (a) *(part)* quota, share; **la quotité du dégrèvement fiscal** the portion of income not subject to taxation ❑ *Jur* **quotité disponible** disposable portion *(of estate);* **quotité imposable** taxable portion of income (b) *Bourse, Fin (d'actions)* minimum number

Rr

rabais *nm* reduction, discount; **un rabais de 500 euros** a 500-euro reduction *or* discount; **acheter/vendre qch au rabais** to buy/sell sth at a discount *or* at a reduced price; **faire** *ou* **accorder un rabais sur qch** to give a discount on sth; **il nous a fait un rabais de 20 pour cent** he gave us a 20 percent discount; **certains patrons profitent de la situation pour se procurer de la main-d'œuvre au rabais** some employers are taking advantage of the situation by taking on cheap labour ❑ *rabais différé* deferred rebate

rabattre *vt* to take off, to deduct; **il a rabattu cinq pour cent sur le prix affiché** he took five percent off the marked price

raccordement *nm Ordinat* link

raccorder *Ordinat* **1** *vt* to connect
2 se raccorder *vpr* **se raccorder à** to link up to

raccourci *nm Ordinat* shortcut ❑ *raccourci clavier* keyboard shortcut

raccrocher *vi (au téléphone)* to hang up

rachat *nm* (**a**) *(par le vendeur)* repurchase, buying back; *Jur* **avec faculté de rachat** with option of repurchase
(**b**) *(de police d'assurance)* surrender; *(de valeur, de dette, d'obligation)* redemption ❑ *Compta rachat des créances* purchase of debts *or* of accounts receivable; *rachat forfaitaire des créances* lump-sum purchase of debts *or* of accounts receivable
(**c**) *(d'une entreprise)* buy-out ❑ *rachat d'entreprise par la direction* management buy-out; *rachat d'entreprise financé par l'endettement* leveraged buy-out; *rachat d'entreprise par les salariés* staff *or* employee buy-out
(**d**) *Bourse (d'actions)* repurchase, buyback ❑ *rachat gagnant* repurchase at a profit

rachetable *adj* repurchasable

racheter *vt* (**a**) *(au propriétaire)* to repurchase, to buy back (**à** from) (**b**) *(police d'assurance)* to surrender; *(valeur, dette, obligation)* to redeem (**c**) *(entreprise)* to buy out; **racheter les parts de qn** to buy sb out (**d**) *Bourse (actions)* to repurchase, to buy back; **se couvrir en rachetant** to cover a short position by buying back

racine *nf Ordinat* root directory

radiation *nf* (**a**) *(d'une liste)* crossing out; *(d'une dette)* cancellation (**b**) *Bourse* **radiation**

de la cote delisting

radier *vt* (**a**) *(d'une liste)* to cross out; *(dette)* to cancel (**b**) *Bourse* **radier qch de la cote** *(société, actions)* to delist sth

radio *nf* radio

radiocommunication *n* radiocommunication

raffermir se raffermir *vpr (prix, marché)* to steady

raffermissement *nm (des prix, du marché)* steadying

rafraîchir *vt Ordinat* to refresh

rafraîchissement *nm Ordinat* refresh

raid *nm Bourse* raid; **lancer/financer un raid** to mount/to finance a raid

raider *nm Fin* (corporate) raider

raison *nf* (**a**) *(nom)* **raison commerciale** trade name; **raison sociale** (company *or* corporate) name (**b**) **à raison de** at the rate of; **le travail est payé à raison de 20 euros l'heure** the work is paid at the rate of 20 euros an hour

> «
>
> Soucieux de tourner la page après l'affaire des frégates de Taïwan, Denis Ranque, PDG de Thomson-CSF, annonce en décembre 2000 la transformation de sa **raison sociale** en Thales. Avantage supplémentaire: en changeant de nom, il coupe le lien historique qui unissait encore les activités d'électronique civile et militaire à celles, grand public, de Thomson Multimedia.
>
> »

raisonnable *adj (prix, revenu)* reasonable

rajustement *nm* adjustment; **les syndicats réclament un rajustement des salaires** the unions are demanding an adjustment of the wage structure

rajuster *vt (taux d'intérêt)* to adjust, to revise; **rajuster les salaires** to readjust the wage structure

ralentir *vt & vi (affaires, production, croissance économique)* to slow down

ralentissement *nm (des affaires, de la production, de la croissance économique)* slowing down

rallonge *nf Fam* extra money; **une rallonge de 1000 euros** an extra 1,000 euro(s)

RAM *nf Ordinat* RAM ❑ *RAM sur carte* on-board RAM

ramassage *nm* (**a**) *Bourse (d'actions)* buying up (**b**) *(transport)* picking up; **un service de ramassage et de livraison** a pick-up and delivery service

ramasser *vt Bourse (actions)* to buy up

rang *nm* (**a**) *(dans une hiérarchie)* rank; **cette entreprise occupe le premier rang mondial du marché des composants électroniques** this company is number one in the world in the electronic component market; **l'entreprise a été reléguée au cinquième rang pour la production d'appareils électroménagers** the company has slipped to fifth place in the white goods market (**b**) *Fin (d'une créance, d'une hypothèque)* rank

ranger *vt* (**a**) *(marchandises)* to stow (**b**) *Ordinat* **ranger en mémoire** to store

rapidité *nf Ordinat* speed ❑ *rapidité d'impression* print speed; *rapidité de traitement* processing speed

rappel *nm* (**a**) *Fin (de paiement)* reminder ❑ *rappel de compte* reminder; *rappel d'échéance* prompt note; *rappel de salaire* back pay (**b**) *Fin (d'une somme déjà avancée)* calling in (**c**) *Ordinat* calling up (**d**) *Tél* **rappel du dernier numéro** redial feature (**e**) *(de marchandises défectueuses)* recall (**f**) *(en publicité)* follow-up

rappeler *vt* (**a**) *(au téléphone)* to call *or* phone back; **il est en réunion, voulez-vous qu'il vous rappelle?** he's in a meeting, would you like him to call you back?; **je vous rappelle dans une minute** I'll call you back in a minute (**b**) *(faire figurer)* to quote; **dans votre réponse, veuillez rappeler la référence FK/FJ** when replying please quote reference FK/FJ; **prière de rappeler ce numéro** in reply please quote this number (**c**) *Ordinat (faire revenir)* to call up (**d**) *(marchandises défectueuses)* to recall

rapport *nm* (**a**) *(compte-rendu)* report; **faire** *ou* **rédiger un rapport (sur)** to make *or* to draw up a report (on); **soumettre un rapport à qn** to submit a report to sb ❑ *Fin rapport d'activité* progress report; *rapport des affaires sociales* social report; *rapport annuel* annual report; *rapport annuel de gestion* annual report; *rapport d'avancement des travaux* *(dans la construction)* progress report; *rapport collectif* joint report; *rapport commercial* market report; *rapport du commissaire aux comptes* auditor's report; *rapport d'étude de marché* market study report; *rapport d'expertise* valuation, expert's report; *Compta rapport d'exploitation* operating statement; *rapport de faisabilité* feasibility report; *rapport financier* financial report; *rapport de gestion* management report; *rapport intérimaire* interim re-

port; *rapport périodique* progress report; *rapport du président* chairman's report; *rapport récapitulatif* summary report; *Compta rapport réservé* qualified report; *Bourse rapport de situation journalière* daily trading report; *rapport de vente* sales report

(**b**) *Fin (profit)* yield, return; **en rapport** *(capital)* interest-bearing, productive; **d'un bon rapport** profitable; **d'un mauvais rapport** unprofitable

(**c**) *(proportion)* ratio, proportion ❑ *rapport cours-bénéfice* price-earnings ratio; *rapport coût-profit* cost-benefit ratio; *rapport de parité* parity ratio; *rapport profit sur ventes* profit-volume ratio; *rapport qualité-prix* quality-price ratio, value for money; **être d'un bon rapport qualité-prix** to be good value for money

(**d**) *(relation)* **mettre qn en rapport avec qn** to put sb in touch with sb; **rapports** relations; **avoir des rapports avec qn** to have dealings with sb; **nous avons de bons rapports avec la filiale française** we're on good terms with the French subsidiary ❑ *rapports patrons–syndicats* relations between the employers and the unions

rapporter 1 *vt* (**a**) *(faire le compte-rendu de)* to report, to give an account of; **vous me rapporterez ses commentaires** let me know what he says

(**b**) *Fin (bénéfices, intérêts)* to yield; **rapporter de l'argent** to be profitable; **le compte d'épargne vous rapporte 7,5 pour cent** the savings account carries 7.5 percent interest

(**c**) *Compta (écriture)* to post

2 *vi (être rentable)* to be profitable, to yield a profit; **c'est un métier qui rapporte** it's a profitable career; **l'affaire a beaucoup rapporté à l'entreprise** the deal brought in a lot of money for the company; **ça ne rapporte pas** it doesn't pay, there's no money in it; **ça peut rapporter gros** it can be very profitable

> **"**
>
> Le droit, à condition de viser juste et d'être bilingue en anglais – business is business – peut aussi **rapporter gros**. Les experts en fiscalité, mais aussi en droit des affaires, droit social, droit européen ou encore les diplômés des formations de juriste conseil raflent la mise.
>
> **"**

rapprochement bancaire *nm Compta* bank reconciliation

rapprocher *vt Compta* to reconcile

raquer *vi Fam* to pay up

rare *adj (ressources, argent)* scarce

raréfaction *nf (de ressources, d'argent)* growing scarcity

rareté *nf (de ressources, d'argent)* scarcity

rassemblement *nm (de documents)* collation; *Ordinat (de données)* gathering

rassembler *vt (documents)* to collate; *Ordinat (données)* to gather

ratification *nf* ratification

ratifier *vt* to ratify

ratio *nm* ratio □ *ratio d'activité* activity ratio; *ratio des bénéfices d'exploitation sur le capital employé* primary ratio; *ratio de capitalisation* capitalization ratio; *ratio capital-travail* capital-labour ratio; *ratio capitaux empruntés-fonds propres* debt-to-equity ratio; *ratio comptable* accounting ratio; *ratio Cooke* capital adequacy ratio; *ratio cours-bénéfice* price-earnings ratio; *ratio de couverture de l'intérêt* interest coverage; *ratio de distribution* distribution ratio; *ratio d'endettement* debt *or* gearing ratio; *ratio d'endettement global* overall gearing ratio; *ratio d'endettement à terme* long-term gearing ratio; *Compta ratio d'exploitation* performance ratio, operating ratio; *ratio de gestion* financial *or* activity ratio; *ratio d'intensité de capital* capital-output ratio; *ratio de levier* leverage; *ratio de liquidité (générale)* liquidity ratio; *ratio de liquidité immédiate, ratio de liquidité restreinte* quick ratio, acid test ratio; *ratio de rentabilité (nette)* (net) profit ratio; *ratio de solvabilité* solvency ratio; *Compta ratio de trésorerie* cash ratio; *ratio des ventes* sales ratio; *ratio de volume de bénéfices* profit/volume ratio, P/V

rationalisation *nf Écon (d'une industrie)* rationalization, streamlining; **rationalisation des choix budgétaires** planning-programming-budgeting system

rationaliser *vt Écon (industrie)* to rationalize, to streamline

rationnel, -elle *adj* rational; *Écon* **l'organisation rationnelle de l'industrie** the rationalization *or* streamlining of industry

rattachement *nm Compta* matching

rattrapage *nm Écon* adjustment

rattraper *vt* **(a)** *(combler)* to make up **(b)** *(arriver au même niveau que)* to catch up with; **il est impératif que nous rattrapions nos principaux concurrents** we have to catch up with our main competitors **(c)** *Écon* to adjust

rayon *nm* **(a)** *rayon d'action (d'une entreprise)* range of activities; *(d'une campagne publicitaire)* range **(b)** *(dans un magasin)* department; *(d'une étagère)* shelf; **nous n'en avons plus en rayon** we're out of stock □ *rayon des soldes* bargain counter

rayonnage *nm* shelving, shelves

RCB *nf (abrév* **rationalisation des choix budgétaires)** PPBS

RCS *nm (abrév* **Registre du commerce et des sociétés)** register of companies

R-D *nf (abrév* **recherche et développement)** R & D, R and D

réabonnement *nm* renewal of subscription

réabonner 1 *vt* **être réabonné à qch** to have renewed one's subscription to sth
2 se réabonner *vpr* **se réabonner à qch** to renew one's subscription to sth

réachat *nm Mktg* rebuy, repurchase □ *réachat modifié* modified rebuy

réacheminement *nm (de marchandises)* re-routing; *Ordinat (de message)* redirecting

réacheminer *vt (marchandises)* to reroute; *Ordinat (message)* to redirect

réacheter *vt* to rebuy, to repurchase

réaction *nf* reaction; *(des consommateurs)* feedback; *Bourse* **il y a eu une vive réaction de la livre sterling sur le marché des changes** sterling has reacted sharply on the exchange market □ *Mktg* **réaction émotionnelle** emotional response; *réaction des ventes* sales response

réactique *nf* business intelligence system

réaffectation *nf* **(a)** *(de ressources, de subventions)* reassignment, reallocation **(b)** *(d'un employé)* reassignment; **il a demandé sa réaffectation à son poste initial** he asked to be reassigned to his original job **(c)** *Ordinat* reallocation

réaffecter *vt* **(a)** *(ressources, subventions)* to reassign, to reallocate; **réaffecter une subvention à sa destination première** to reallocate funds to their original use **(b)** *(employé)* to reassign; **réaffecter qn à son poste initial** to reassign sb to his/her original job **(c)** *Ordinat* to reallocate

réafficher *vt Ordinat* to redisplay

réajustement, réajuster = rajustement, rajuster

réalignement *nm (des taux de change)* realignment □ *réalignement monétaire* realignment of currencies

réaligner *vt (taux de change)* to realign

réalisable *adj* **(a)** *Banque, Fin (avoirs)* realizable **(b)** *(projet)* realizable; *(but)* achievable

réalisation *nf* **(a)** *Banque, Fin* realization; *(d'actions)* selling out; *(d'un bénéfice)* making □ *réalisation du stock* clearance sale **(b)** *(d'un projet)* realization; *(d'un but)* achievement

réaliser *vt* **(a)** *Banque, Fin* to realize; *(actions)* to sell out; *(bénéfice)* to make; **réaliser un capital** to realize an asset, to convert an asset into cash; **réaliser un chiffre d'affaires de 10 millions d'euros** to have a turnover of 10 million euros; **réaliser des économies** to economize **(b)** *(projet)* to realize; *(but)* to achieve

réalité virtuelle *nf Ordinat* virtual reality

réaménagement *nm (d'un magasin)* refit

réaménager *vt (magasin)* to refit

réamorcer *Ordinat* **1** *vt* to reboot
2 se réamorcer *vpr* to reboot

réapprovisionnement *nm* restocking

réapprovisionner 1 *vt (magasin)* to restock (**en** with); *(personne)* to resupply (**en** with)
2 se réapprovisionner *vpr* to stock up again (**en** with)

réassortiment *nm* (**a**) *(fait de réassortir)* restocking (**b**) *(nouveau stock)* new stock

réassortir *vt* to restock
2 se réassortir *vpr* to replenish one's stock; **se réassortir en qch** to renew one's stock of sth

réassurance *nf* reinsurance

rebaisser *vi (prix)* to go back down

rebond *nm (d'actions, de marché, de monnaie)* recovery

> ❝
> ... tous les indicateurs semblaient au rouge pour les fabricants d'équipements destinés à l'industrie des puces électroniques. Pourtant, les chiffres publiés le 29 mars par la Semiconductor Industry Association font apparaître un **rebond** de la demande en puces au début de l'année.
> ❞

rebondir *vi (actions, marché, monnaie)* to pick up again, to recover

rebut *nm (article)* reject

recapitalisation *nf* recapitalization

recapitaliser *vt* to recapitalize

recensement *nm (de marchandises)* inventory ❑ *recensement des distributeurs* census of distribution; *recensement des entreprises* company census; *recensement de la production* census of production

recenser *vt (marchandises)* to inventory, to take stock of

recentrage *nm (modification)* reorientating, refocussing

recentrer *vt (modifier)* to reorientate, to refocus; **le nouveau directeur a décidé de recentrer la politique de l'entreprise sur l'exportation** the new manager decided to refocus the company's activities on exporting

récépissé *nm* receipt ❑ *récépissé de dépôt* deposit receipt; *récépissé de douane* customs receipt; *récépissé d'entreposage* warehouse receipt; *récépissé d'entrepôt* warehouse receipt; *récépissé postal* postal receipt

réceptif précoce *nm Mktg* early adopter

réception *nf* (**a**) *(d'une lettre, d'une commande,*

de biens) receipt; **accuser réception de qch** to acknowledge receipt of sth; **à payer à la réception** *Br* cash *or Am* collect on delivery ❑ *réception définitive* final acceptance; *réception des travaux* acceptance of work (**b**) *(accueil)* reception (desk); **demandez à la réception** ask at reception

réceptionnaire *nmf (de marchandises)* consignee, receiving agent

réceptionner *vt (marchandises)* to take delivery of

réceptionniste *nmf* receptionist

réceptivité des consommateurs *nf Mktg* consumer acceptance

récession *nf Écon* recession ❑ *récession économique* economic recession

recette *nf* (**a**) *Fin* takings, earnings, revenue; **faire recette** to be profitable *or* a success; **on a fait une bonne/mauvaise recette** the takings were good/poor; **recettes et dépenses** receipts and expenditure, incomings and outgoings ❑ *recette annuelle* annual income *or* revenue; *recette brute* gross income *or* earnings; *recettes de caisse* cash receipts; *recettes fiscales* tax revenue; *recettes non gagées* unassigned *or* unpledged revenue; *recette journalière* daily takings; *recette nette* net income *or* receipts; *recettes publiques* government revenue
(**b**) *(d'argent dû)* collection; *(bureau)* tax office; **faire la recette de l'argent/des contributions** to collect the money/contributions

> ❝
> Avec une croissance moins forte, l'Etat va encaisser moins de **recettes fiscales** que prévu. Pour compenser ce manque à gagner, le gouvernement va simplement laisser filer le déficit. Le déficit public devrait donc représenter cette année près de 2% de notre PIB et non 1,4% comme promis.
> ❞

recevable *adj (marchandises)* fit for acceptance

receveur, -euse *nm,f* (**a**) *(de marchandises)* receiver (**b**) *Admin receveur des contributions* tax collector; *receveur des douanes* customs officer; *receveur des Finances* district tax collector; *receveur des impôts* receiver general; *receveur des postes* postmaster, *f* postmistress

recevoir *vt (courrier, coup de téléphone)* to get, to receive; *(salaire, somme)* to get, to receive, to be paid; **nous avons bien reçu votre lettre du 20 juin** thank you for your letter of 20 June, we acknowledge receipt of your letter of 20 June; **vous avez reçu un appel de Londres** you've had *or* received a call from London; **recevoir**

des ordres de qn to take orders from sb; **recevez, Monsieur, l'assurance de mes sentiments distingués** (dans une lettre) (à quelqu'un dont on connaît le nom) Br yours sincerely, Am sincerely; (à quelqu'un dont on ne connaît pas le nom) Br yours faithfully, Am sincerely; **bien reçu** duly received; Fin **à recevoir** (effets, intérêts) receivable

rechange nm (a) (remplacement) replacement; **de rechange** spare (b) Banque, Fin (d'un effet) redraft

recharge nf Tél top-up card

recharger vt Ordinat to reload; Tél (téléphone portable) to charge up

recherche nf (a) Mktg research; **faire des recherches (sur qch)** to do research (into sth) ❏ **recherche ad hoc** ad hoc research; **recherches sur les besoins des consommateurs** consumer research; **recherche commerciale** marketing intelligence; **recherche et développement** research and development; **recherche documentaire** desk research; **recherche longitudinale** longitudinal research, continuous research; **recherche marketing, recherche mercatique** market research; **recherche de motivation** motivation research; **recherche opérationnelle** Br operational research, Am operations research; **recherches par panel** panel research; **recherche sur les prix** pricing research; **recherche de produits** product research; **recherche par sondage** survey research; **recherches sur le terrain** fieldwork (b) Ordinat find, search ❏ **recherche arrière** backward search; **recherche avant, recherche vers le bas** forward search; **recherche binaire** binary search; **recherche booléenne** Boolean search; **recherche dichotomique** binary search; **recherche documentaire** information retrieval; **recherche de données** data retrieval; **recherche globale** global search; **recherche vers le haut** backward search; **recherche et remplacement** search and replace; **recherche et remplacement global** global search and replace (c) **recherche de personne** paging (service)

recherché, -e adj (produit) in demand, sought-after

recherche-développement nf research and development

rechercher vt Ordinat to search, to do a search for; **rechercher et remplacer qch** to search and replace sth; **rechercher en arrière** ou **vers le haut** to search backwards; **rechercher en avant** ou **vers le bas** to search forwards

réciproque adj (bénéfices, accord, concessions) reciprocal

réclamation nf (a) (plainte) complaint; **faire** ou **déposer une réclamation** to make or lodge

a complaint; **toutes réclamations devront être adressées au service clientèle** all complaints should be addressed to the customer services department (b) (revendication) claim; **faire** ou **déposer une réclamation** to make a claim ❏ Jur **réclamation en dommages-intérêts** claim for damages; **réclamation d'indemnité** claim for compensation

réclame nf (a) (publicité) advertising; (annonce) advertisement; **faire de la réclame pour qch** to advertise sth (b) (promotion) **en réclame** on offer

réclamer 1 vt (a) (revendiquer) (dommages-intérêts, allocation, indemnité) to claim (b) (demander) to ask for; (exiger) to demand; **réclamer son argent** to ask for one's money back; **ils réclament la semaine de 35 heures** they are demanding a 35-hour week
2 vi to complain (**auprès de** to)

reclassement nm (a) (de poste) reassignment (b) (de personnel, de salaires) regrading

reclasser vt (a) (poste) to reassign (b) (personnel, salaires) to regrade

recommandation nf (a) (parrainage) recommendation; (lettre) (letter of) reference; **elle a été embauchée sur la recommandation du chef de service** she was recruited on the recommendation of the head of department (b) (d'une lettre, d'un colis) recording

recommandé, -e 1 adj (a) (produit, prix) approved, recommended (b) (lettre, colis) recorded
2 nm **en recommandé** (lettre, colis) by recorded delivery

recommander 1 vt (a) (personne, produit) to recommend (b) (lettre, colis) to record
2 **se recommander** vpr **se recommander de qn** (pour un emploi) to give sb's name as a reference

recommercialiser vt to remarket

recomposer vt (numéro de téléphone) to redial

reconditionner vt (marchandises) to repackage

reconduction nf (d'un bail, d'un contrat) renewal

reconduire vt (bail, contrat) to renew

reconfiguration nf (d'une société) reengineering

reconfigurer vt Ordinat to reconfigure

reconnaissance nf (a) Ordinat **reconnaissance de caractères** character recognition; **reconnaissance optique de caractères** optical character recognition; **reconnaissance de la parole** speech recognition; **reconnaissance vocale** speech recognition (b) Mktg (identification) recognition ❏ **reconnaissance des be-**

soins need recognition; **reconnaissance de dette** *(document)* IOU

reconstituer *vt* (**a**) *(stocks)* to rebuild, to build up again (**b**) *(entreprise)* to reconstruct

reconstitution *nf* (**a**) *(de stocks)* rebuilding (**b**) *(d'une entreprise)* reconstruction

reconversion *nf* (**a**) *(de l'économie)* turnaround; *(d'un site industriel, d'une région, d'une entreprise)* conversion, changeover (**b**) *(d'un salarié)* retraining

reconvertir **1** *vt* (**a**) *(économie)* to turn around; *(site industriel, région, entreprise)* to convert, to change over (**b**) *(salarié)* to retrain
  2 se reconvertir *vpr* (**a**) *(site industriel, région, entreprise)* to convert, to change over (**dans** to) (**b**) *(salarié)* to retrain; **il s'est reconverti dans la comptabilité** he retrained as an accountant

record *adj* *(chiffre)* record; **l'inflation a atteint le chiffre record de 45 pour cent** inflation has reached an all-time high of 45 percent

recoupement *nm* cross-checking; **faire le recoupement (de qch)** to cross-check (sth); **moyen de recoupement** cross-reference

recouponnement *nm* Bourse, Fin renewal of coupons

recouponner *vt* Bourse, Fin to renew the coupons of

recours *nm* (**a**) *(utilisation)* recourse, resort; **avoir recours à l'arbitrage** to go to arbitration (**b**) *Jur* appeal ❏ **recours en cassation** appeal; **recours contre des tiers** recourse against third parties; *Assur* **s'assurer contre le recours des tiers** to insure against a third-party claim

recouvrable *adj* *(argent, dette)* recoverable; *(impôt)* collectable

recouvrement *nm* (**a**) *(d'argent, d'une dette)* recovery; *(de l'impôt)* collection; **faire un recouvrement** to recover a debt; **l'impôt est mis en recouvrement après le 31 octobre** payment of tax is due from 31 October (**b**) **recouvrements** *(dettes)* outstanding debts

recouvrer *vt* *(argent, dette)* to recover; *(impôt)* to collect

recrutement *nm* recruitment; **le recrutement du personnel s'effectue par concours** staff are recruited by competitive examination

recruter **1** *vt* to recruit; **l'entreprise recrute des ingénieurs en informatique** the company is recruiting computer engineers
  2 se recruter *vpr* to be recruited; **les ingénieurs se recrutent sur diplôme** engineers are recruited on the basis of their qualifications

rectangle de sélection *nm* selection box

rectificatif, -ive **1** *adj* rectifying, correcting
  2 *nm* rectification, correction

rectification *nf* rectification, correction; *Compta, Fin (d'un compte)* adjustment ❏ **rectification saisonnière** seasonal adjustment

rectifier *vt* to rectify, to correct; *Compta, Fin (compte)* to adjust

recto *nm* front; **recto verso** recto verso, on both sides

reçu *nm* receipt ❏ *Can* **reçu de caisse** (till) receipt; **reçu certifié** accountable receipt; **reçu en duplicata** receipt in duplicate; **reçu d'espèces** cash receipt; **reçu libératoire** receipt in full discharge; **reçu du transitaire** forwarding agent receipt

recueil *nm* ❏ *Mktg* **recueil des données** data collection; *Jur* **recueil des lois** statute book

recul *nm* decline, drop; **le recul de l'industrie textile** the decline of the textile industry; **les ventes ont subi un recul** sales have dropped; **le recul du yen par rapport au dollar** the fall of the yen against the dollar

reculer *vi* *(baisser)* to decline, to drop; **le yen recule par rapport au dollar** the yen is falling against the dollar

récupérabilité *nf* *(de marchandises, de cargaison)* salvage value

récupérable *adj* (**a**) *(dette)* recoverable; *(TVA)* reclaimable (**b**) *(marchandises, cargaison)* salvageable (**c**) *(temps)* recoverable; **les heures supplémentaires sont récupérables** additional time off may be taken in lieu (**d**) *Ordinat* retrievable, recoverable

récupération *nf* (**a**) *(d'une dette)* recovery; *(de TVA)* reclaiming (**b**) *(des débours)* recoupment (**c**) *(de marchandises, de cargaison)* recovery, salvage (**d**) *(du temps)* making up; **la récupération des heures supplémentaires** time off in lieu (**e**) *Ordinat (d'un fichier, de données)* retrieval, recovery

récupérer *vt* (**a**) *(dette)* to recover; *(TVA)* to reclaim (**b**) *(débours)* to recoup (**c**) *(marchandises, cargaison)* to recover, to salvage (**d**) *(temps)* to make up; **récupérer des heures supplémentaires** to take time off in lieu; **on récupère ce jour férié samedi prochain** we are making up for this public holiday by working next Saturday (**e**) *Ordinat (fichier, données)* to retrieve, to recover

recyclage *nm* (**a**) *(du personnel)* retraining; **suivre un stage de recyclage** to retrain (**b**) *(de matières)* recycling

recycler **1** *vt* (**a**) *(personnel)* to retrain (**b**) *(matières)* to recycle
  2 se recycler *vpr (personnel)* to retrain

rédacteur, -trice *nm,f* editor ❏ **rédacteur en chef** chief editor; **rédacteur politique** political editor; **rédacteur publicitaire** copywriter

rédaction *nf* (**a**) *(poste)* editorship; *(personnel)* editorial staff; *(département)* editorial department; *(activité)* editing ❑ **rédaction électronique** on-line publishing; **rédaction publicitaire** copywriting **(b)** *(de lettre, de contrat, de facture)* drawing up

rédactionnel, -elle *adj* editorial

reddition *nf Fin (de comptes)* rendering

redéfinir *vt Ordinat (touche)* to redefine

redémarrage *nm* **(a)** *(de l'économie, du commerce)* recovery **(b)** *Ordinat* reboot, restart

> ❝
>
> Pour les fabricants d'équipements, très en amont de la chaîne, il faudra patienter jusqu'au quatrième trimestre pour voir les commandes repartir. Mais il n'y a pas d'incertitude quant à la réalité du **redémarrage** de l'activité.
>
> ❞

redémarrer *vi* **(a)** *(économie, commerce)* to recover, to take off again **(b)** *Ordinat* to reboot, to restart

redéploiement *nm Écon* redeployment

redéployer *vt Écon* to redeploy

redevable *adj* **être redevable de qch à qn** to be accountable to sb for sth; **être redevable de l'impôt** to be liable for tax; **vous êtes redevable d'un acompte provisionnel** you are liable for an interim payment

redevance *nf (pour un service)* fees ❑ **redevance pétrolière** oil royalty; **redevance téléphonique** rental charge

rédhibition *nf* = cancellation of a sale due to a material defect in the article or product

rédhibitoire *adj (prix)* prohibitive; *(conditions, salaire)* unacceptable

rédiger *vt (lettre, contrat, facture)* to draw up

redimensionnement *nm* **(a)** *(d'une entreprise)* downsizing, rightsizing **(b)** *Ordinat* resizing

redimensionner *vt* **(a)** *(entreprise)* to downsize **(b)** *Ordinat* to resize

redorer *vt (société, image)* to repackage

redressement *n* **(a)** *(d'une erreur)* rectification; *Compta (d'un compte)* adjustment ❑ **redressement financier** gearing adjustment; *Admin* **redressement fiscal, redressement d'impôt** tax adjustment **(b)** *(d'une monnaie, de l'économie)* recovery ❑ **redressement économique** economic recovery **(c)** **redressement judiciaire** receivership; **être mis en redressement judiciaire** to go into receivership

> ❝
>
> Les deux actionnaires phares d'AOM-Air Liberté, Swissair et Marine-Wendel, refusent de recapitaliser l'entreprise, qui dépose son bilan le 15 juin, avant d'**être mise en redressement judiciaire**.
>
> ❞

redresser **1** *vt (erreur)* to rectify; *Compta (compte)* to adjust

2 se redresser *vpr (monnaie, économie)* to recover, to rally

redresseur d'entreprise *nm* company doctor

redû *nm* balance due, amount owed

réduction *nf* **(a)** *(des prix, des taux d'intérêt, des impôts)* reduction (**de** in), lowering (**de** of); *(des dépenses, des frais, du personnel, des salaires)* reduction (**de** in), cutting (**de** of); *(des stocks)* running down; *Fin (du capital)* writing down; **on nous a demandé d'accepter une réduction de salaire** we were asked to take a cut in wages; **ils ont promis une réduction des impôts** they promised to reduce *or* lower taxes; **ils nous ont imposé une réduction des dépenses** they've reduced *or* cut our expenditure ❑ **reductions d'impôts** tax cuts
(b) *(rabais)* reduction; **faire une réduction de 15 pour cent (à qn)** to give (sb) a 15 percent reduction

réduire *vt* **(a)** *(prix, taux d'intérêt, impôts)* to reduce, to lower; *(dépenses, frais, personnel, salaires)* to reduce, to cut; *(stocks)* to run down; *Fin (capital)* to write down; **la société réduit progressivement ses opérations en Allemagne** the company is winding down its operations in Germany **(b)** *Ordinat (fenêtre)* to minimize

réduit, -e *adj (prix)* reduced; **depuis la vague de licenciements l'entreprise fonctionne avec un effectif réduit** since the wave of redundancies the company is operating with a reduced workforce

rééchelonnement *nm Fin (de dette)* rescheduling, restructuring

rééchelonner *vt Fin (dette)* to reschedule, to restructure

réel, -elle *adj (coût, revenu)* real

réembaucher *vt* to re-employ; **elle a été licenciée puis réembauchée en tant que freelance** she was made redundant and then re-employed *or* taken on again as a freelancer

réemploi *nm* re-employment

réemployer = **remployer**

rééquilibrer *vt (budget)* to rebalance

réescompte *nm Fin* rediscount

réescompter *vt Fin* to rediscount

réessayer *vi Ordinat* to retry

réévaluation *nf (d'une monnaie, de l'actif)* revaluation; *(d'une propriété, des prix, d'un budget)* reassessment; *(des salaires)* reappraisal

réévaluer *vt (monnaie, actif)* to revalue; *(propriété, prix, budget)* to reassess; *(salaires)* to reappraise

réexpédier vt (à une autre adresse) to forward, to send on; (à l'expéditeur) to send back, to return

réexpédition nf (à une autre adresse) forwarding, sending on; (à l'expéditeur) sending back, returning

réexportation nf (activité) re-exportation; (produit) re-export

réexporter vt to re-export; **produits réexportés** re-exports

réf nf (abrév **référence**) ref; **N/Réf** our ref; **V/Réf** your ref

réfaction nf (de biens endommagés ou de qualité inférieure) allowance, rebate

refaire vt (a) (opération, commande) to redo (b) Tél (numéro) to redial

référence nf (a) (sur une lettre, sur un document) reference; **en référence à** with reference to; **adresser sous référence RL3U, référence à rappeler RL3U** when replying please quote reference RL3U (b) **références** (recommandation) reference; **avoir de bonnes références** to have good references; **références exigées** (sur offre d'emploi) references required (c) Mktg (produit) benchmark, listed product (d) Compta **référence au meilleur** benchmarking

référencé, -e adj **être référencé** to have a reference number; **votre lettre référencée 450/198** your letter reference number 450/198

référencement nm (d'un produit) listing

référencer vt (a) Ordinat to reference (b) (échantillon) to classify in a sample book

refinancement nm refinancing

refinancer vt to refinance

refluer vi **faire refluer le dollar/yen** to keep down the value of the dollar/yen

reformatage nm Ordinat reformatting

reformater vt Ordinat to reformat

réforme nf reform □ **réforme monétaire** monetary reform

refrain publicitaire nm (advertising) jingle

refus nm (d'une invitation, d'une demande) refusal; (d'une proposition, d'une offre, des marchandises) rejection □ **refus d'acceptation** non-acceptance; **refus d'insertion** refusal to publish; **refus de paiement** non-payment; **refus de vente** refusal to sell

refuser vt (invitation, demande) to refuse; (proposition, offre, marchandises) to reject; (chèque) to bounce

regagner vt (après perte) to win back; **le dollar a regagné quelques cents sur le marché des changes** the dollar has regained a few cents on the foreign exchange market

régénération de l'écran nf Ordinat screen refresh

régie (a) Admin (gestion) management, control; (d'un domaine) administration, stewardship; **en régie** in the hands of trustees (b) (entreprise publique) public corporation, state-owned company; **la régie Renault** the Renault company □ **régie publicitaire** advertising sales agency (c) Admin **régie des impôts indirects** excise (administration), Br ≃ Customs and Excise department; Can **Régie des Loyers** rental board

régime nm (système) scheme, system □ **régime d'assurance vieillesse** old age pension fund or scheme; **régime douanier** customs system; **régime fiscal** tax system; Fin **régime du forfait** standard assessment system, fixed-rate tax assessment system; **régime d'imposition** tax system; Douanes **régime préférentiel** preferential rates of duty; Fin **régime du réel** full assessment system; **régime de retraite** pension scheme or plan; **régime de retraite par capitalisation** funded pension scheme or plan; **régime de retraites complémentaires** = graduated pension scheme or plan; **régime de retraite des artisans, commerçants et professions libérales** self-employed pension; **régime de Sécurité sociale** social security system; Fin **régime simplifié** simplified system; **régime de transit** transit system; **le régime du travail** the organization of labour

> ❝
> L'Arrco, le **régime de retraite** complémentaire des salariés cadres et non cadres, est dans une position plutôt enviable. Avec quatre actifs cotisants pour seulement trois retraités à l'horizon 2020, le rapport démographique reste confortable. Mais en fait, dès 2012, le **régime** commencera à perdre de l'argent. Le montant de sa perte annuelle pourrait dépasser les 14,5 milliards d'euros à l'horizon 2040.
> ❞

région nf region, area □ Mktg **région test** test area

régional, -e 1 adj (conseil) local **2** nm Tél area telephone system

régir vt to govern, to rule; **les prix sont régis par la demande** prices are governed by demand; **les conditions régissant votre compte** the terms for the conduct of your account

registre nm (a) (de comptes) account book; (des délibérations) minutes book; **inscrire/rapporter un article sur un registre** to enter/to post an item in a register; **signer le registre** (d'un hôtel) to sign the register □ Bourse **registre des actionnaires** register of shareholders, shareholders' register; Bourse **registre des actions** share register; **registre du commerce** trade register; **s'inscrire au registre du commerce** to enter oneself in the trade register; **Re-**

gistre du commerce et des sociétés register of companies; *registre de comptabilité* account book, ledger; *registre foncier* land register; *registre international des marques* international trademark register; *registre des obligataires* debenture register; *registre des procès-verbaux* minutes book; *registre des salaires* payroll; *Bourse registre des transferts* transfer register (**b**) *Ordinat* register ❏ *registre d'accès mémoire* memory access register

réglages *nmpl Ordinat* settings

règle *nf* (**a**) *(mesure)* rule ❏ *Compta* **règles comptables** accounting rules; *règles d'exploitation* operating rules; *règles de sécurité* safety regulations (**b**) **en règle** *(document)* in due form; *(papiers, passeport)* in order; **tenir sa comptabilité en règle** to keep one's accounts in order (**c**) *Ordinat (sur écran)* ruler line

règlement *nm* (**a**) *(d'un compte)* settlement; *(d'une facture, d'une dette)* payment; **en règlement de** in settlement of; **faire un règlement par chèque** to pay by cheque; **pour règlement de tout compte** in full settlement ❏ *règlement à la commande* cash with order; *règlement contre documents* cash against documents; *règlement en espèces* cash payment, cash settlement; *règlement en nature* settlement in kind; *règlement en perte totale* total loss settlement

(**b**) *(règles)* regulations ❏ *règlement intérieur* internal regulations

(**c**) *Bourse* settlement ❏ *règlement mensuel* forward market

(**d**) *Jur (résolution)* settlement ❏ *règlement à l'amiable* amicable settlement; *(sans procès)* out-of-court settlement; *règlement arbitral, règlement par arbitrage* settlement by arbitration; *règlement de gré à gré* amicable settlement, settlement by negotiation; *règlement judiciaire* liquidation; **être en règlement judiciaire** to be in the hands of the receiver(s); **se mettre en règlement judiciaire** to go into liquidation *or* receivership

réglementaire *adj* statutory, prescribed

réglementation *nf* (**a**) *(fait de réglementer)* control, regulation ❏ *réglementation des changes* exchange control; *réglementation des prix* price control *or* regulation (**b**) *(règlement)* regulations, rules ❏ *réglementation douanière* customs regulations; *réglementation sur l'hygiène et la sécurité* health and safety regulations; *réglementation du travail* labour regulations *or* legislation

réglementer *vt* to regulate, to control; *(prix)* to control

régler 1 *vt* (**a**) *(compte)* to settle; *(facture, dette, personne)* to pay, to settle; *(achat)* to pay for; **régler qch en espèces** to pay cash for sth; **régler qch par chèque** to pay for sth by cheque

(**b**) *Jur (résoudre)* to settle; **régler qch à l'amiable** to settle sth amicably; *(sans procès)* to settle sth out of court (**c**) *Assur (sinistre)* to settle

2 *vi* to pay

réglette *nf Ordinat (pour un clavier)* template

régresser *vi (ventes, production)* to decline

régression *nf (des ventes, de la production)* decline

regrèvement *nm* tax increase

regroupement *nm* (**a**) *(de sociétés)* amalgamation, merger (**b**) *Fin (de comptes)* consolidation

regrouper 1 *vt* (**a**) *Fin (sociétés)* to amalgamate, to merge (**b**) *Fin (comptes)* to consolidate

2 se regrouper *vpr (sociétés)* to amalgamate, to merge

régularisation *nf (d'une situation)* regularizing; *Fin (de dividende)* equalization; *(d'un compte, des stocks, des charges)* adjustment

régulariser *vt (situation)* to regularize; *(document)* to put into proper form; *Fin (dividende)* to equalize; *(compte, stocks, charges)* to adjust

régularité *nf (d'une décision, d'une situation)* legality; *Fin* **régularité et sincérité des charges** true and fair nature of expenses

régulateur, -trice *adj* regulating

régulation *nf (de la Bourse)* regulation; *(de l'économie)* control; **la régulation du marché des changes** foreign exchange control

réhabilitation *nf* (**a**) *Jur (de failli)* discharge (**b**) *(d'immeuble, de quartier ancien)* rehabilitation, renovation

réhabilité, -e *nm,f* discharged bankrupt

réhabiliter *vt* (**a**) *(failli)* to discharge (**b**) *(immeuble, quartier ancien)* to rehabilitate, to renovate

réimportation *nf* (**a**) *(activité)* re-importation, re-importing (**b**) *(produit)* re-import

réimporter *vt* to re-import

réimposer *vt Fin (produit)* to reintroduce tax on, to retax

réimposition *nf Fin* retaxation

réinitialisation *nf Ordinat* reset; *(de la mémoire)* reinitialization

réinitialiser *vt Ordinat* to reset; *(mémoire)* to reinitialize

réinjecter *vt (bénéfices)* to plough back (**dans** into)

réinscriptible *adj Ordinat (support)* rewritable

réinscription *nf Ordinat* re-entry, re-registering

réinscrire *vt Ordinat* to re-enter, to re-register

réinsérer *vt Ordinat (bloc)* to reinsert

réinsertion professionnelle *nf* = getting back into the job market

réinstaller *vt Ordinat* to reinstall

réintégration *nf (d'un employé)* reinstatement

réintégrer *vt (employé)* to reinstate; **réintégrer qn dans ses fonctions** to reinstate sb

réinvestir *vt* to reinvest; *(bénéfices)* to plough back

rejet *nm (d'une offre)* rejection; *(d'une dépense)* disallowance

rejeter *vt (offre)* to reject; *(dépense)* to disallow

relais *nm* relay, shift; **travail par relais** shift work

relance *nf* (**a**) *(de l'économie, de la production, des ventes, du commerce)* revival (**b**) *(d'un produit, d'une marque, d'une entreprise)* relaunch (**c**) *(d'un débiteur)* chasing up; *(d'un client)* follow-up □ **relance téléphonique** telephone follow-up

> **"**
> Devant ces révoltes de la population, le président Abdelaziz Bouteflika a annoncé en grande pompe cet été "un plan de soutien à la **relance économique**" . Enfreignant la règle d'orthodoxie financière, chère au FMI et à la Banque mondiale, plus de 352 milliards de dinars devraient être injectés dans l'économie algérienne.
> **"**

relancement *nm (d'un produit)* relaunch

relancer *vt* (**a**) *(économie)* to boost, to revive; *(production, ventes, commerce)* to boost (**b**) *(produit, marque, entreprise)* to relaunch (**c**) *(débiteur)* to chase up; *(client)* to follow up (**d**) *Ordinat (programme)* to rerun; *(logiciel)* to restart

relatif, -ive *adj (part de marché)* relative

relation *nf* (**a**) *(rapports entre personnes)* relations; **être en relation avec qn** to be in touch with sb; **mettre qn en relation avec qn** to put sb in touch with sb; **être en relations d'affaires avec qn** to have business relations with sb, to deal with sb □ **relations d'affaires** business relations; **relations clientèle** customer relations; **relations commerciales** business relations; **relations industrielles** industrial relations; **relations presse** press relations; **relations publiques** public relations; **relations sociales** labour relations

(**b**) *(personne)* acquaintance; **avoir des relations** to have contacts □ **relation d'affaires** business acquaintance

relationniste-conseil *nm* account executive

relevé *nm* statement □ **relevé d'achat** purchase report; *Mktg* **relevé d'achat journalier** diary; **relevé de caisse** cash statement; **relevé de compte** bank statement; **relevé des dépenses** statement of expenditure; **relevé des dettes actives et passives** statement of assets and liabilities; **relevé de factures** statement of invoices; **relevé de fin de mois** end-of-month statement, monthly statement; **relevé d'identité bancaire** = document giving details of one's bank account; **relevé d'identité postal** = document giving details of one's post office account; **relevé remis** account tendered; **relevé de vente** sales report

relèvement *nm* (**a**) *(des salaires, d'un tarif, d'un impôt, des taux d'intérêt)* raising, increasing (**b**) *(des affaires, de l'économie, d'une industrie)* recovery, revival

relever 1 *vt* (**a**) *(salaires, tarif, impôt, taux d'intérêt)* to raise, to increase; **relever le cours de l'euro** to raise the value of the euro (**b**) *(affaires, économie, industrie)* to revive (**c**) *(adresse, coordonnées)* to take down; **relever un compte** to make out a statement of account

2 se relever *vpr (affaires, économie, industrie)* to recover, to revive; *(cours)* to recover; **l'entreprise ne s'est jamais relevée de la perte de ce marché** the company has never recovered from the loss of this market

relief *nm Ordinat* highlight; **mettre en relief** to highlight

relier se relier *vpr Ordinat* to link up

reliquat *nm* remainder; *(d'un compte)* balance

relutif, -ive *adj Fin* **avoir un effet relutif** to strengthen the equity capital of a company

relution *nf Fin* strengthening of equity capital

remballage *nm* repacking

remballer *vt* to repack

rembours *nm Douanes* drawback

remboursable *adj Fin (prêt)* repayable; *(caution, versement)* refundable; *(obligation, coupon)* redeemable; **remboursable sur une période de 25 ans** repayable over (a period of) 25 years; **remboursable au pair** repayable at par

remboursement *nm Fin (des dépenses)* repayment, reimbursement; *(d'un prêt)* repayment; *(d'une caution, d'un versement, d'un achat, des frais)* refund; *(d'une obligation, d'un coupon)* redemption; *(d'un effet)* retirement □ **remboursement anticipé** redemption before due date; **remboursement in fine** bullet repayment

rembourser *vt Fin* (**a**) *(dépenses)* to repay, to reimburse; *(prêt)* to repay; *(caution, versement, achat, frais)* to refund; *(obligation, coupon)* to redeem; *(effet)* to retire (**b**) *(personne)* to repay, to reimburse

remembrement *nm Admin (de terres)* reallocation, regrouping

remembrer *vt Admin (terres)* to reallocate, to regroup

réméré *nm Banque, Bourse* repurchase, repo

remettant *nm Banque* = person who pays money or a cheque into a current account

remetteur, -euse *Banque* **1** *adj (banque)* remitting
2 *nm,f* remitter

remettre *vt* (**a**) *(donner)* to remit; **remettre un chèque à l'encaissement** to cash a cheque; **remettre sa démission** to hand in one's notice (**b**) *(ajourner)* to postpone, to put off; **la réunion a été remise à lundi** the meeting has been put off *or* postponed until Monday (**c**) *(lettre, colis)* to deliver (**d**) *(dette)* to cancel

remise *nf* (**a**) *Fin (fait de remettre)* remittance; **payable contre remise du coupon** payable on presentation of the coupon; **faire une remise à qn** to send sb a remittance □ *remise documentaire* documentary remittance; *remise de fonds* remittance of funds; *remise à vue* demand deposit
  (**b**) *(rabais)* discount, reduction; **une remise de dix pour cent** a discount of ten percent, ten percent off; **faire une remise sur qch** to allow a discount on sth; **faire une remise à qn** to give sb a discount □ *remise de caisse* cash discount; *remise de fidélité (au client)* (customer) loyalty discount; *remise de marchandisage* merchandising allowance; *remise sur marchandises* trade discount; *remise professionnelle* trade discount; *remise promotionnelle* promotional discount; *remise quantitative, remise pour quantité, remise sur la quantité* bulk discount, quantity discount; *remise sur quantité non cumulable* non-cumulative quantity discount; *Fin remise pour règlement rapide* settlement discount; *remise saisonnière* seasonal discount; *remise d'usage* trade discount
  (**c**) *(d'une lettre, d'un colis)* delivery
  (**d**) *(d'une dette)* cancellation; **faire remise d'une dette** to cancel a debt
  (**e**) *(ajournement)* postponement

remisier *nm Bourse* half-commission man, intermediate broker

remontée *nf (d'une monnaie, des valeurs, des prix)* recovery; **faire une belle remontée** to make a good recovery

remonter *vi (monnaie, valeurs, prix)* to go back up

remplacement *nm* replacement; **de remplacement** *(coût)* replacement; *(produit)* substitute; *(marché)* alternative

remplacer *vt* to replace; **doit-on accepter que l'euro remplace notre monnaie nationale?** should we accept that our national currency be replaced by the euro?; **il a remplacé Luc Le-**

blanc à la direction de l'entreprise he has replaced Luc Leblanc *or* taken over from Luc Leblanc as manager of the company; *Ordinat* **tout remplacer** replace all

remplir *vt* (**a**) *(formulaire, questionnaire)* to fill in, to fill out, to complete; *(chèque)* to write, to make out (**b**) *(condition, obligation)* to comply with, to fulfil

remployer *vt* (**a**) *(personne)* to re-employ (**b**) *(argent, fonds)* to reinvest

remue-méninges *nm Mktg* brainstorming

rémunérateur -trice *adj* remunerative, profitable; *(placement)* interest-bearing

rémunération *nf* (**a**) *(somme versée)* remuneration, payment (**de** for); **en rémunération de vos services** as payment for your services □ *rémunération du capital* return on capital; *rémunération au temps passé* time rate (**b**) *(salaire)* salary □ *rémunération de départ* starting salary

rémunérer *vt* (**a**) *(travail, services)* to pay for (**b**) *(salaires)* to pay

renchérir 1 *vt (marchandises, main-d'œuvre)* to raise the price of; *(prix)* to raise
2 *vi* (**a**) *(marchandises, main-d'œuvre)* to go up in price; *(prix)* to go up, to increase (**b**) **renchérir sur qn** *(aux enchères)* to outbid sb

renchérissement *nm (de marchandises, de main-d'œuvre)* price increase; *(d'un prix)* increase; *(d'une devise)* rise in value

> **"**
> Pour profiter de la reprise, l'Allemagne devra, par ailleurs, attendre que les commandes internationales de biens d'équipement redécollent et que les capacités de production de ses grands concurrents soient saturées. Toujours du côté des exportations, un **renchérissement** de l'euro pourrait provoquer un retard à l'allumage.
> **"**

rendement *nm* (**a**) *Fin (d'un investissement, d'une obligation)* yield, return, profit; *(des actions)* earnings; **à gros rendement** *(investissement, obligation)* high-yield; *(actions)* high-earning □ *rendement actuariel brut* gross actuarial return, gross redemption yield; *rendement annuel* annual return; *rendement brut* gross yield *or* return; *rendement constant* fixed yield; *rendement coupon* coupon yield; *rendements décroissants* diminishing returns; *rendement à l'échéance* yield to maturity, redemption yield; *rendement sur fonds propres* return on equity; *rendement marginal du capital* marginal return on capital; *rendement moyen* average yield; *rendement net* net return; *rendement réel* inflation-adjusted yield
  (**b**) *(d'un ouvrier)* output; *(d'une usine)* output,

production; *(d'un processus, d'un ordinateur)* throughput; **travailler à plein rendement** to work to full capacity; **l'usine tourne à plein rendement** the factory is operating at full capacity ❑ *rendement d'ensemble, rendement global* aggregate output; *rendement à l'heure, rendement horaire* output per hour; *rendement individuel* output per person; *rendement maximum* maximum output; *rendement minimum* minimum output; *rendement moyen* average output; *rendement optimal* peak output; *rendement total* aggregate or total output

(**c**) *(d'une machine)* efficiency ❑ *rendement économique* commercial efficiency; *rendement effectif* performance rating; *rendement global* overall efficiency

rendez-vous *nm* appointment; **fixer un rendez-vous** *ou* **donner rendez-vous (à qn)** to make or fix an appointment (with sb) ❑ *rendez-vous d'affaires* business appointment

rendre *vt* (**a**) *(redonner)* to give back, to return; *(argent)* to repay, to pay back; *(article)* to return; *Fam* **rendre son tablier** to resign (**b**) *(sujet: investissement)* to yield (**c**) *(livrer)* to deliver; **rendu à domicile** delivered to your door; **rendu franco à bord** (delivered) free on board

> **❝**
>
> ... ses ventes ont reculé de 2% en 2001, et son résultat d'exploitation de 40%. Au point que son président, Gilles Oudot, un ancien d'Habitat, a dû **rendre son tablier** après dix-huit mois. En cinq ans, le BHV aura connu cinq patrons.
>
> **❞**

rendu *nm* returned article, return; **faire un rendu** to return or exchange an article

renflouer *vt (entreprise, personne)* to bail out, to keep afloat

renommer *vt Ordinat (fichier)* to rename

renouvelable *adj (contrat)* renewable

renouveler *vt* (**a**) *(changer) (personnel)* to renew; *(stock, matériel)* to renew, to replace (**b**) *(répéter) (commande)* to repeat; *(passeport, abonnement, demande)* to renew; **renouveler sa candidature** *ou* **sa demande d'emploi** to reapply (for a job) (**c**) *(prolonger) (traite, bail, contrat)* to renew, to extend; *(crédit)* to extend

renouvellement *nm* (**a**) *(de personnel)* turnover; *(du stock, du matériel)* renewal, replacement (**b**) *(d'une commande)* repetition; *(d'un passeport, d'un abonnement, d'une demande)* renewal (**c**) *(d'une traite, d'un bail, d'un contrat)* renewal, extension; *(d'un crédit)* extension

renseignement *nm* (**a**) *(information)* piece of information; **renseignements** information; **pour tout renseignement complémentaire,** **veuillez appeler ce numéro** for information or if you have any queries, please call this number; **je vous envoie à titre de renseignement...** I am sending you for your information...; **demander/donner des renseignements sur qn/qch** to ask for/to give (some) information about sb/sth; **prendre des renseignements sur qn/qch** to make enquiries or to enquire about sb/sth; **aller aux renseignements** to go to find out or to make enquiries ❑ *renseignements classés secrets* classified information; *Fin renseignements de crédit* status or credit enquiry; *renseignements statistiques* statistical data; *renseignements techniques* data (**b**) *Tél* **renseignements** *Br* directory enquiries, *Am* information

renseigner 1 *vt* **renseigner qn (sur qch)** to give sb (some) information (about sth), to inform sb (about sth)

2 se renseigner *vpr* to make enquiries; *(sur un point précis)* to find out (**sur** about)

rentabilisation *nf* making profitable; **la rentabilisation de l'affaire prendra peu de temps** it won't be long before the business becomes profitable or starts to make a profit

> **❝**
>
> Même si d'immenses profits sont dégagés par la **rentabilisation** du travail, ils ne répondent pas aux exigences des actionnaires. Ces derniers poussent à des délocalisations là où un retour sur investissements de 15 % à 20 % est possible. Ce qui se traduit par la destruction de pans entiers d'industries rentables économiquement, sans compter celle du secteur vital des petites et moyennes entreprises.
>
> **❞**

rentabiliser *vt* to make profitable; **l'industrie exige de gros investissements longs à rentabiliser** industry requires heavy investment which takes a long time to show a profit

rentabilité *nf* profitability, cost-effectiveness (**de** of); *(d'un investissement, des ventes)* return (**de** on) ❑ *rentabilité directe du produit* direct product profitability; *rentabilité nette d'exploitation* net operating profit

rentable *adj* profitable, cost-effective; **l'opération n'a pas été très rentable** the operation has not been very profitable

rente *nf* (**a**) **rentes** *(revenu)* private income; **avoir cinquante mille euros de rentes** to have a private income of fifty thousand euros (**b**) *(pension)* annuity, pension ❑ *rente annuelle* annuity; *rente à paiement différé* deferred annuity; *rente de situation* guaranteed income; *rente à terme* terminable annuity; *rente viagère* life annuity, life interest

(**c**) *Fin (emprunt d'État)* government loan or

bond ❑ **rentes amortissables** redeemable stock or loans; **rentes sur l'État** government stock or funds; **rentes perpétuelles** irredeemable securities
  (d) *Écon* rent ❑ **rente foncière** ground rent

rentier, -ère *nm,f (qui vit de ses rentes)* person of independent means ❑ **rentier viager** annuitant

rentrée *nf (d'argent)* receipt; **rentrées** income, money coming in; **avoir des rentrées d'argent** to have a regular income or money coming in regularly ❑ *Compta* **rentrées de caisse** cash receipts; **rentrées de devises** foreign exchange inflows; **rentrées fiscales** tax revenue; **rentrées journalières** daily takings; *Compta* **rentrées et sorties de caisse** cash receipts and payments

rentrer *vi* **rentrer dans ses frais** to recover one's expenses, to get one's money back, to break even

renvoi *nm* (a) *(de lettre, de marchandises, de colis)* return, sending back (b) *(d'un employé)* dismissal (c) *(ajournement)* postponement; *Jur* adjournment (d) *Jur (devant une autre juridiction)* transfer, referral (**devant** to) (e) *Ordinat* cross-reference

renvoyer *vt* (a) *(lettre, marchandises, colis)* to return, to send back (b) *(employé)* to dismiss (c) *(ajourner)* to postpone; *Jur* to adjourn (d) *Jur (devant une autre juridiction)* to transfer, to refer (**devant** to) (e) *Ordinat* to cross-refer

réorganisation *nf (du personnel, des ressources)* reorganization

réorganiser *vt (personnel, ressources)* to reorganize

réouverture *nf (d'un magasin, d'un marché)* reopening; *(de négociations)* resumption

réparation *nf* (a) *(action)* repairing; *(résultat)* repair; **être en réparation** to be under repair ❑ **réparation d'entretien** maintenance; **réparations locatives** repairs incumbent on the tenant (b) *Jur* compensation ❑ **réparation civile** compensation; **réparation de dommages** damages; **réparation légale** legal redress

réparer *vt* (a) *(appareil, défaut)* to repair (b) *(erreur)* to rectify; *(pertes, dommage)* to make good

répartir *vt* (a) *(distribuer) (tâches, argent)* to divide, to distribute; *Fin (dividende)* to distribute; *(coûts)* to break down; *Bourse (actions)* to allot, to allocate (b) *(étaler) (versements, dépenses)* to spread (out) (c) *(impôts)* to assess; *Assur (avarie)* to adjust

répartiteur, -trice *nm,f Admin* (**commissaire**) **répartiteur** tax assessor ❑ *Assur* **répartiteur d'avaries** average adjuster, loss adjuster

répartition *nf* (a) *(de tâches, d'argent)* division,

distribution; *(d'une dividende)* distribution; *(de coûts)* breakdown; *Bourse (d'actions)* allotment, allocation; **première et unique répartition** first and final dividend; **nouvelle répartition** second dividend; **dernière répartition** final dividend ❑ **répartition optimale des ressources** optimal resource allocation
  (b) *(des versements, des dépenses)* spreading (out) ❑ **répartition des risques** risk spreading
  (c) *(des impôts)* assessment ❑ *Assur* **répartition d'avarie** average adjustment

répercuter **1** *vt* to pass on; **la taxe sera répercutée sur les consommateurs** the tax will be passed on to the consumers
  2 se répercuter *vpr (effets, crise)* to have repercussions (**sur** on)

répertoire *nm* (a) *Ordinat* directory ❑ **répertoire central, répertoire principal** main directory, root directory (b) *(carnet)* address book *(with alphabetical index)*; *(liste)* list ❑ **répertoire d'adresses** directory; **répertoire des métiers** trade directory

répertorier *vt* to list

répétition *nf Jur* claiming back ❑ **répétition d'indu** recovery of payment made in error

repli *nm Bourse* fall, drop ❑ **repli stratégique** *(du marché)* strategic withdrawal

replier se replier *vpr Bourse* to fall back, to drop

répondant, -e *nm,f Jur* surety, guarantor

répondeur *nm* answering machine, answerphone ❑ **répondeur automatique** answering machine, answerphone; **répondeur enregistreur** answering machine; **répondeur interrogeable à distance** answering machine with remote-access facility; **répondeur téléphonique** telephone answering machine

répondre répondre à *vt ind* (a) *(question, lettre)* to reply to, to answer (b) *Bourse, Fin (prime)* to declare

réponse *nf* (a) *(à une question, à une lettre)* answer, reply; **en réponse à votre lettre** in reply or response to your letter; **réponse payée** reply paid ❑ *Bourse* **réponse des primes** declaration of options; *Mktg* **réponse stimulée** stimulus response (b) *Ordinat* answering ❑ **réponse automatique** unattended answering

report *nm* (a) *(renvoi à plus tard) (d'un rendez-vous, d'une réunion)* postponement ❑ *Fin* **report d'échéance** extension of due date; **report de livraison** extension of delivery date
  (b) *Compta (en bas de page)* (balance) carried forward; *(en haut du page)* (balance) brought forward ❑ **report déficitaire sur les exercices précédents** loss carry back; **report déficitaire sur les exercices ultérieurs** loss carry forward; **report de l'exercice précédent** carried forward from the previous financial year; **report à l'exercice suivant** carried forward to the next

financial year; **report à nouveau** carried forward
(**c**) *Compta (d'une écriture)* entering up, posting (**d**) *Bourse* contango, continuation; **en report** *(actions, titres)* taken in, carried over; **prendre des actions en report** to take in *or* carry over shares

reporté, -e *nm,f Bourse (d'actions)* giver

reporter *vt* (**a**) *(remettre à plus tard) (rendez-vous, réunion)* to postpone (**b**) *Compta (balance, total) (en bas de page)* to carry forward; *(en haut de page)* to bring forward; **solde à reporter** balance carried forward (**c**) *Compta (écriture)* to enter up, to post (**d**) *Bourse* to continue, to contango; **(faire) reporter des titres** to carry stock; **(faire) reporter un emprunteur** to take in stock for a borrower; **se faire reporter** to be carried over

reporteur *nm Bourse (d'actions)* taker

repositionnement *nm Mktg (d'un produit)* repositioning □ *repositionnement réel* real repositioning

repositionner *Mktg* **1** *vt (produit)* to reposition
2 se repositionner *vpr* to reposition oneself; **se repositionner à la baisse** to move downmarket; **se repositionner à la hausse** to move upmarket

> **"**
> A l'hétérogénéité de la clientèle s'ajoute un autre problème: l'arrivée de nouveaux concurrents. La Samaritaine, située aussi rue de Rivoli, et rachetée par LVMH, va **se repositionner** sur les jeunes, les touristes, le textile et la décoration légère.
> **"**

reprendre **1** *vt* (**a**) *(employé, marchandises)* to take back (**b**) *(recommencer)* **reprendre le travail** to return to work (**c**) *(acheter) (entreprise)* to take over, to buy out (**d**) *Ordinat (programme)* to restart, to resume
2 *vi (affaires)* to rally, to recover, to pick up; **les cours ont repris** the market rallied

repreneur *nm* purchaser, buyer

représentant, -e *nm,f* representative, agent; **je suis représentant en électroménager** I'm a representative for an electrical appliances company □ *représentant de commerce, représentant commercial* sales representative; *représentant dûment accrédité* duly authorized representative; *représentant exclusif* sole agent; *représentant fiscal* fiscal agent; *représentant multi-carte* representative for several companies; *représentant du personnel* staff representative

représentatif, -ive *adj (échantillon)* representative

représentation *nf* representation; *(agence)* agency; **faire de la représentation, être dans la représentation** to be a (sales) representative □ *représentation exclusive* sole agency; **avoir la représentation exclusive de...** to be sole agents for...

représenter *vt* (**a**) *(agir au nom de)* to represent, to act for (**b**) *(correspondre à)* to account for, to represent; **ceci représente dix pour cent du budget** this represents ten percent of the budget

repris, -e *adj* **non repris** *(emballage)* non-returnable

reprise *nf* (**a**) *(des affaires, des cours)* recovery; *(des travaux)* resumption □ *reprise économique* economic recovery, upswing *or* upturn in the economy; *reprise de travail* return to work; **les grévistes ont voté la reprise de travail** the strikers have voted to return to work
(**b**) *(de marchandises invendues, d'articles en solde)* taking back □ *Compta reprises sur provisions* recovery of provisions, write-back of provisions
(**c**) *(rachat)* takeover □ *reprise de l'entreprise par ses salariés* employee buy-out
(**d**) *Ordinat (d'un programme)* restart

> **"**
> De nombreuses enquêtes de conjoncture indique un futur rebond de l'activité dans la zone euro. Cette **reprise** devrait normalement intervenir en juin ou en juillet, ce qui représente un décalage de sept à neuf mois avec la **reprise** américaine, qui a débuté en octobre ou novembre 2001.
> **"**

reproduction *nf (d'un document)* reproduction, duplicating

reproduire *vt* (**a**) *(document)* to reproduce, to duplicate (**b**) *(répéter)* to repeat; **la nouvelle direction a reproduit les mêmes erreurs** the new management repeated the same mistakes

reprogrammable *adj Ordinat (touche)* reprogrammable

reprogrammer *vt* (**a**) *(livraison)* to reschedule (**b**) *Ordinat* to reprogram

reprographie *nf* reprography, repro

reprographier *vt (polycopier)* to duplicate; *(photocopier)* to photocopy

réputation *nf* reputation, standing; **avoir (une) bonne/mauvaise réputation** to have a good/bad reputation

requérant, -e *Jur* **1** *adj* **partie requérante** claimant
2 *nm,f* claimant

requête *nf Ordinat* query

requin *nm* **requin (de la finance)** shark, raider

RES *nf Fin* (*abrév* **rachat de l'entreprise par ses salariés**) staff *or* employee buy-out

réseau *nm* (**a**) *(dans le commerce, dans les télécommunications)* network; **mettre en réseau** to network ❑ *réseau d'affichage* outdoor network; *réseau analogique* analogue network; *réseau câblé* cable network; *réseau commercial* sales network; *réseau de communication* communication network; *réseau de distribution* distribution network; *réseau multimédia* multimedia network; *réseau de télécommunications* telecommunications network; *réseau téléphonique* telephone system *or* network; *réseau de transport intégré* integrated transport network; *réseau de vente* sales network

(**b**) *Ordinat* network ❑ *réseau en anneau à jeton* token ring network; *réseau de communication* communications network; *réseau de communication de données* datacomms network; *réseau connecté en étoile* star network; *réseau de données* data network; *réseau en étoile* star network; *réseau informatique* computer network; *réseau local* local area network, LAN; *réseau longue distance* wide area network, WAN; *réseau national d'interconnexion* backbone; *réseau neuronal* neural network; *réseau numérique* digital network; *réseau numérique à intégration de services* integrated services digital network; *réseau de télématique* datacomms network; *réseau d'utilisateurs* user network

réservation *nf* reservation, booking ❑ *réservation à l'avance* advance reservation *or* booking; *réservation électronique* electronic reservation; *réservation télématique* automated reservation

réserve *nf* (**a**) *(stock)* reserve; **en réserve** in reserve, set aside; **avoir qch en réserve** to have sth in stock *or* in reserve; **mettre qch en réserve** to put *or* set sth aside; **puiser dans les réserves** to draw on the reserves; **sans réserve de retour** non-returnable, no-return; **avec réserve de retour** on a sale or return basis ❑ *réserve d'achat* credit limit; *réserves bancaires* bank reserves; *réserves de change* monetary reserves; *réserve pour créances douteuses* bad debts reserve; *réserves en devises (étrangères)* (foreign) exchange reserves; *réserves en espèces* cash reserves; *réserves excédentaires* excess reserves; *réserve latente* hidden reserve; *réserve légale* legal reserve; *réserve liquide* liquid assets, cash reserve; *réserve métallique* bullion reserve; *réserves mondiales (de matières premières)* world reserves; *réserves monétaires* monetary reserves; *réserves monétaires internationales* international monetary reserves; *réserves non distribuées* capital reserves; *réserves obligataires* federal fund; *réserve occulte* secret reserve; *réserve d'or* gold reserve; *réserve de pré-voyance* contingency reserve; *réserve statutaire* statutory reserve; *réserve visible* visible reserve

(**b**) *(restriction)* reservation; *Jur* **sous toutes réserves** without prejudice; **sous réserve de la signature du contrat** subject to contract

(**c**) *(magasin)* storeroom, warehouse

réserver *vt* (**a**) *(chambre, place)* to reserve, to book (**b**) *(mettre de côté)* to set aside; **réserver des fonds pour qch** to put money aside for sth

réservoir de main-d'œuvre *nm* labour pool

résident, -e 1 *adj (personne)* resident
2 *nm,f (personne)* resident

résiliable *adj (bail, contrat)* that may be terminated

résiliation *nf (d'un bail, d'un contrat)* termination

résilier *vt (bail, contrat)* to terminate

résistance des consommateurs *nf Mktg* consumer resistance

résoluble *adj (bail, contrat)* that may be terminated

résolution *nf* (**a**) *(d'un bail, d'un contrat)* termination; *(d'une vente)* cancellation (**b**) *(décision)* resolution; **prendre** *ou* **adopter une résolution** to pass *or* adopt a resolution (**c**) *Ordinat* resolution

résorber *vt (surplus, déficit)* to absorb; *(inflation, chômage)* to reduce, to bring down; *(stocks)* to reduce; *(dettes)* to clear

résoudre *vt (bail, contrat)* to terminate

respecter *vt* to respect; *(clause)* to comply with

responsabilité *nf (morale)* responsibility (**de** for); *Jur (légale)* liability (**de** for); **avoir la responsabilité de qch** *(en avoir la charge)* to be in charge of sth; **elle a la responsabilité du service après-vente** she's in charge of the after-sales department; **"la direction décline toute responsabilité en cas de vol"** *(sur panneau)* the management accepts no responsibility in case of theft; **on lui a confié de nouvelles responsabilités au sein du groupe** he was given new responsibilities within the group; **il a un poste à responsabilités** he has a position of responsibility ❑ *Jur responsabilité civile* public liability, third-party liability, civil liability; **être assuré responsabilité civile** to have public liability insurance; *Jur responsabilité collective* collective liability; *Jur responsabilité conjointe* joint liability; *Jur responsabilité conjointe et solidaire* joint and several liability; *Jur responsabilité contractuelle* contractual liability; *responsabilité de l'employeur* employer's liability; *responsabilité du fabricant* manufacturer's liability; *Fin responsabilité illi-*

mitée unlimited liability; *Jur* **responsabilité individuelle** several liability; *Fin* **responsabilité limitée** limited liability; **responsabilité patronale** employer's liability; *UE* **responsabilité du produit** product liability; *Jur* **responsabilité solidaire et indivise** joint and several liability; **responsabilité au tiers** third-party liability; **être assuré responsabilité au tiers** to carry third-party insurance

responsable 1 *adj (moralement)* responsible (**de** for); *(légalement)* liable (**de** for); **être responsable de qch** *(en avoir la charge)* to be in charge of sth; **elle est responsable du service après-vente** she's in charge of the after-sales department
2 *nmf (coupable)* person responsible (**de** for); *(personne qui a la charge)* person in charge (**de** of) ❏ **responsable de budget** account manager; **responsable commercial** business manager; **responsable des comptes-clients** account handler, account executive; **responsable des conférences** conference organizer; **responsable des congrès** conference organizer; **responsable d'entrepôt** warehouse manager; **responsable de groupe** group leader; **responsable du marketing** marketing manager; **responsable de projet** project manager; **responsable des relations avec la presse** press officer; **responsable des relations publiques** public relations officer; **responsable syndical** union official

resserrement du crédit *nm Écon* credit squeeze

ressort *nm (d'un tribunal)* competence; **cette affaire est du ressort du chef du personnel** this is a matter for the personnel manager; **ce conflit est du ressort du tribunal des prud'hommes** this conflict falls within the jurisdiction of the industrial tribunal

ressources *nfpl* resources ❏ **ressources d'appoint** additional (sources of) income; **ressources du budget** budgetary resources; **ressources de l'État** government resources; **ressources financières** financial resources; **ressources fiscales** tax resources; **ressources humaines** human resources; **ressources naturelles** natural resources; **ressources personnelles** private means

restant *nm* rest, remainder; *(d'un compte)* balance ❏ **restant en caisse** cash surplus

restauration *nf Ordinat (de fichier, texte, données)* restore

restaurer *vt Ordinat (fichier, texte, données)* to restore

reste *nm* rest, remainder; **vous pouvez payer le reste par mensualités** you can pay the balance in monthly instalments

restituable *adj* repayable

restitution *nf* repayment, refund ❏ *Douanes* **restitution des droits d'entrée** drawback; *UE* **restitution à l'exportation** export refund; **restitution d'impôts** tax refund; *Jur* **restitution d'indu** return of payment made in error

restreindre *vt (crédit, dépenses, production)* to restrict, to limit

restreint, -e *adj (crédit, dépenses, production)* restricted, limited

restrictif, -ive *adj (pratique, endossement)* restrictive; *(clause)* limitative

restriction *nf* restriction ❏ *Ordinat* **restriction d'accès** access restriction; **restrictions budgétaires** budget restrictions; **restriction de concurrence** trade restraint; **restriction du crédit** credit squeeze *or* restrictions; **restrictions à l'exportation** export restrictions; **restrictions à l'importation** import restrictions; **restrictions salariales, restrictions des salaires** wage restraint; *Fin* **restrictions de transfert** transfer restrictions; **restriction volontaire des exportations** voluntary export restraint

restructuration *nf* (**a**) *(d'une industrie, d'une entreprise)* restructuring (**b**) *(de dette)* rescheduling

❝
Lorsque l'entreprise envisage une **restructuration** entraînant une compression d'effectif, le comité d'entreprise doit être réuni deux fois au lieu d'une (un débat sur la **restructuration** doit avoir lieu en préalable à celui sur les licenciements), avec toujours la possibilité pour lui de se faire assister par un expert-comptable.
❞

restructurer *vt* (**a**) *(industrie, entreprise)* to restructure (**b**) *(dette)* to reschedule

résultat *nm* (**a**) *Compta* profit ❏ **résultat brut** gross return; **résultat courant** profit before tax and extraordinary items; **résultat économique** economic profit; **résultat exceptionnel** extraordinary profit or loss; **résultat de l'exercice** profit or loss for the financial year, statement of income; **résultat d'exploitation** operating profit or loss; **résultat final** final statement; **résultat financier** financial profit or loss; **résultats à longue échéance** deferred results; **résultat net** net return; **résultat net consolidé** consolidated statement of net income; **résultat de la période** profit or loss for the financial period; **résultats prévisionnels** earnings forecast (**b**) *Mktg* performance ❏ **résultats antérieurs** past performance; **résultats perçus** perceived performance

rétablir 1 *vt (économie, échanges commerciaux)* to re-establish, to restore; **rétablir un budget déficitaire** to balance an adverse budget; **rétablir qn (dans ses fonctions)** to reinstate sb

2 se rétablir *vpr (économie)* to recover, to pick up again; *(entreprise, monnaie)* to recover

retard *nm* delay; **en retard** *(compte, paiement)* outstanding, overdue; **ils sont en retard dans leurs paiements** they're behind *or* in arrears with their payments ❑ *retard de livraison* delay in delivery, late delivery; *retard de paiement* delay in payment, late payment

retarder *vt* to delay; *(paiement)* to defer, to delay; **la grève des routiers a retardé les livraisons** deliveries were delayed because of the *Br* lorry *or Am* truck drivers' strike

retenir *vt* (**a**) *(somme)* to keep back, to deduct (**sur** from) (**b**) *(offre)* to accept (**c**) *(chambre, table, place)* to reserve, to book

rétention *nf (d'un message publicitaire)* retention ❑ *rétention sélective* selective retention

retenue *nf (d'une somme)* deduction; **faire une retenue de cinq pour cent sur les salaires** to deduct *or* withhold five percent from salaries ❑ *retenue fiscale* withholding tax; *retenue à la source* payment (of income tax) at source, *Br* ≃ PAYE, *Am* ≃ pay as you go

> ❝
>
> C'est aussi la question que les contribuables se sont posée en rédigeant leur déclaration 2001: la **retenue à la source** de l'impôt sur le revenu serait-elle un plus ou un moins pour les particuliers?
>
> ❞

retirer 1 *vt* (**a**) *(argent)* to withdraw, to take out; **retirer des marchandises de la douane** to take goods out of bond (**b**) *(commande, candidature)* to withdraw; *(ordre de grève)* to call off (**c**) *Fin (effet)* to retire, to withdraw; *(monnaies)* to withdraw from circulation, to call in

2 se retirer *vpr* **se retirer des affaires** to retire from business

retombées *nfpl* repercussions; **la grève aura des retombées sur les prix** the strike will have repercussions on prices

retour *nm* (**a**) *(de marchandises, d'une lettre)* return; **marchandises de retour, retours** returns; **vendu avec possibilité de retour** sold on a sale or return basis; **répondre par retour du courrier** to reply by return of post; **retour à l'envoyeur** *ou* **à l'expéditeur** return to sender; **en retour d'une somme de 50 euros** in consideration of a sum of 50 euros ❑ *retour en charge* loaded return; *retour sans frais* return free of charge; *retour d'information* feedback; *retour à vide* empty return

(**b**) *(amortissement)* return ❑ *retour sur achat* purchase return; *retour sur investissement* return on investment, ROI; *retour sur ventes* return on sales

(**c**) *Fin* dishonoured bill, bill returned dishonoured

(**d**) *Ordinat (sur clavier)* return ❑ *retour arrière* backspace

retourner *vt (effet, lettre, colis, marchandises)* to return; **retourner à l'envoyeur** *ou* **à l'expéditeur** to return to sender; **prière de nous retourner l'accusé de réception ci-joint, revêtu de votre signature** please sign and return the enclosed acknowledgement

retrait *nm* (**a**) *(d'argent)* withdrawal; **faire un retrait** to make a withdrawal; **faire un retrait de 1000 euros** to withdraw 1,000 euros ❑ *retrait automatique* automated withdrawal; *retrait d'espèces* cash withdrawal (**b**) *(d'une commande, d'une candidature)* withdrawal; *(d'un ordre de grève)* calling off (**c**) *Fin (d'un effet)* withdrawal; *(de monnaies)* withdrawal from circulation, calling in (**d**) *Ordinat* **mettre en retrait** to indent

retraite *nf* (**a**) *(de la vie active)* retirement (from work); **âge de la retraite** retirement age; **être à la retraite** to be retired; **mettre qn à la retraite** to pension sb off, to retire sb; **prendre sa retraite** to retire; **partir en retraite** to retire, to go into retirement ❑ *retraite anticipée* early retirement; *retraite forcée* compulsory retirement

(**b**) *(pension)* pension ❑ *retraite par capitalisation* loanback pension; *retraite complémentaire* private pension; *retraite indexée sur le revenu* earnings-related pension; *retraite minimum* guaranteed minimum pension; *retraite vieillesse* retirement pension

retraité, -e 1 *adj* retired
2 *nm,f* pensioner

retrancher *vt* to deduct, to take off

rétribuer *vt (employé, service, travail)* to pay; **bien rétribué** highly-paid; **mal rétribué** badly-paid

rétribution *nf* payment

rétroactif, -ive *adj* retrospective, retroactive; **augmentation avec effet rétroactif au 1er septembre** increase backdated to 1 September

rétrocéder *vt* to resell

rétrocession *nf* resale

rétroéclairage *nm Ordinat (d'écran)* backlight

rétroéclairé, -e *adj Ordinat (écran)* backlit

rétroprojecteur *nm* overhead projector

rétrospective *nf Fin* review

réunion *nf* (**a**) *(assemblée)* meeting; *(d'un comité)* session, sitting; **le directeur est en réunion** the manager is in a meeting ❑ *réunion d'actionnaires* shareholders' meeting; *réunion de comité* committee meeting; *réunion du conseil d'administration* board meeting; *réunion des créanciers* creditors' meeting; *réunion électorale* election meeting; *Mktg*

réunion de groupe group meeting; **réunion paritaire** round-table conference; **réunion préparatoire** briefing; **réunion publique** public meeting; *Mktg* **réunion de remue-méninges** brainstorming session; **réunion de représentants** sales meeting; **réunion syndicale** union meeting (**b**) *(de deux services)* merger, amalgamation

réunir 1 *vt* (**a**) *(somme)* to collect, to get together (**b**) *(personnes)* to bring together; **réunir un comité** to convene a committee, to call a committee meeting; **la conférence a réuni les dirigeants de plusieurs multinationales** the conference brought together executives from several multinationals
2 se réunir *vpr* (**a**) *(personnes)* to meet, to convene (**b**) *(sociétés)* to amalgamate, to merge

revalorisation *nf* (**a**) *Fin (d'une monnaie)* revalorization, revaluation (**b**) *(des salaires, des retraites)* upgrading

revaloriser *vt* (**a**) *Fin (monnaie)* to revalorize, to revalue (**b**) *(salaires, retraites)* to upgrade

revendable *adj* resaleable

revendeur, -euse *nm,f* retailer; *(d'articles d'occasion)* second-hand dealer

revendicatif, -ive *adj (mouvement)* protest

revendication *nf (de travailleurs)* claim, demand (**sur** on) □ **revendications salariales, revendications salaires** wage claims; **revendications syndicales** union demands *or* claims

> **"**
> Car la hausse des prix reste l'un des maux de l'économie irlandaise. Elle a atteint jusqu'à 7% en 2000, avant de ralentir actuellement à 5%. Dans un contexte de tensions sur le marché de l'emploi (le chômage est tombé à 4% l'année dernière), l'inflation a alimenté les **revendications salariales**.
> **"**

revendiquer *vt* to claim, to demand; **les salariés revendiquent de meilleures conditions de travail** the employees are demanding better working conditions

revendre 1 *vt* to resell; *Bourse (titres)* to sell out
2 se revendre *vpr* **ce genre de produit ne se revend pas facilement** this sort of product isn't easy to resell `

revenir *vi* to cost; **revenir cher** to be expensive; **sa maison lui est revenue à 750 000 euros** his house cost him 750,000 euros; **cet article vous reviendra à 100 euros** this item will cost you 100 euros

revente *nf* resale; *Bourse (de titres)* selling out

revenu *nm* (**a**) *(d'une personne, d'une entreprise)* income; *(de l'État)* revenue; **avoir de gros/petits revenus** to have a large/small income □ **revenus accessoires** incidental income; **revenus**

actuels current earnings *or* income; **revenu annuel** annual income; **revenu brut** gross income; **revenu brut global** total gross income; **revenu cumulé** cumulative revenue; **revenu disponible** disposable income; **revenus de l'exportation** export revenue; *Admin* **revenu familial** family income; **revenu fictif** notional income; **revenu fixe** fixed income; **revenu imposable** taxable income; **revenu imposable après déduction des abattements fiscaux** taxable income after deduction of tax allowances; **revenus indépendants** independent income; **revenu des intérêts** earned interest, interest income; **revenu locatif** rental income; **revenu marginal** marginal revenue *or* income; **revenu minimum d'insertion** *Br* ≃ income support, *Am* ≃ welfare; *Écon* **revenu national** national income; *Écon* **revenu national brut** gross national income; *Écon* **revenu national net** net national income; **revenu net** net income; **revenu net global** total net income; **revenu personnel disponible** disposable personal income; **revenu pétrolier** oil revenue; **revenu réel** real income; **revenu résiduel** residual income; **revenus salariaux** earned income; *Écon* **revenus du secteur public** public sector earnings; **revenu de société** corporate income; **revenu du travail** earned income (**b**) *(d'un investissement)* yield, return □ **revenu(s) obligataire(s), revenu(s) des obligations** income from bonds; **revenu variable** income from variable-yield investments

> **"**
> L'objectif est de réduire l'écart … entre le **revenu net** perçu par les salariés et son coût global pour l'entreprise.
> **"**

reversement *nm Fin* transfer *(of funds from one account to another)*

reverser *vt Fin (somme)* to transfer (**à** *ou* **sur** to); *(impôt)* to pay

revêtir *vt (document)* to sign, to validate

révisable *adj (prix) (qui peut changer)* subject to alteration *or* to modification; *(négociable)* open to offer, negotiable

réviser *vt (clause, contrat)* to revise; *(compte)* to check; **réviser une estimation à la hausse/baisse** to revise an estimate upwards/downwards; **il a fallu réviser à la baisse les prévisions pour l'an prochain** the projected figures for next year have had to be scaled down

réviseur *nm Fin* **réviseur (comptable)** auditor; **réviseur externe** external auditor; **réviseur interne** internal auditor

révision *nf (d'un contrat, des salaires, des prix)* review

révoquer *vt* (**a**) *(commande, contrat)* to revoke, to countermand; *(ordre de grève)* to call off (**b**) *(fonctionnaire)* to dismiss, to remove from office

revue *nf (publication)* magazine; *(spécialisée)* journal ❏ *revue économique* economic journal; *revue financière* financial journal; *revue professionnelle* trade journal

RH *nfpl (abrév* **ressources humaines***)* HR

RIB *nm (abrév* **relevé d'identité bancaire***)* = document giving details of one's bank account

riche 1 *adj* rich, wealthy
  2 *nmf* wealthy person; **les impôts indirects touchent davantage les pauvres que les riches** indirect taxes penalize the poor more than the rich

richesse *nf* (**a**) *(d'une personne, d'un pays)* wealth ❏ *Mktg* **la richesse vive** consumer purchasing power (**b**) **richesses** *(ressources)* resources

RIP *nm (abrév* **relevé d'identité postale***)* = document giving details of one's post office account

RISC *nm Ordinat (abrév* **reduced instruction set chip** *ou* **computer***)* RISC

risque *nm Assur, Fin* risk; **couvrir un risque** to cover a risk; **souscrire un risque** to underwrite a risk; **aux risques et périls du propriétaire** *(sur panneau)* at owner's risk ❏ *risque accru* overexposure; *risque assuré* risk subscribed or taken up; *Bourse* **risque de baisse** downside risk; *risque de change* exchange *or* currency risk; *risque collectif* collective risk; *risque de contrepartie* credit risk; *Bourse* **risque de hausse** upside risk; *risque d'incendie* fire risk; *risque locatif* tenant's third-party risk; *Bourse* **risque de marché** market risk; *risque maritime, risque de mer* sea risk; *risque du métier* occupational hazard; *risques mixtes* mixed risks; *risque perçu* perceived risk; *risque de perte et d'avaries* loss risk; *risque du recours du tiers* third-party risk; *risque de vol* theft risk

risque-pays *nm* country risk

> **❝**
>
> Dans cette situation économique, la pire depuis trois ans, le **risque-pays** du Brésil, paramètre utilisé par les investisseurs étrangers pour apprécier la défiance vis-à-vis des emprunts d'Etat, s'approche tous les jours de son record historique, 1 770 points, établi le 14 janvier 1999, au lendemain de la dévaluation.
>
> **❞**

ristourne *nf* (**a**) *(rabais)* discount; **une ristourne de 15 pour cent** a 15 percent discount; **faire une ristourne à qn** to give sb a discount ❏ *ristourne de fidélité* customer loyalty discount; *ristourne de prime* premium discount (**b**) *Assur* repayment, refund

ristourner *vt (réduire)* to give a discount of; **il nous a ristourné 15 pour cent du prix** he gave us a 15 percent discount

rival, -e *nm,f & adj* rival

rivaliser *vi* **rivaliser avec qn** to compete with sb; **ils rivalisent avec nous pour la conquête du marché** they're competing with us to dominate the market

RMI *nm (abrév* **revenu minimum d'insertion***)* *Br* ≃ income support, *Am* ≃ welfare

RNIS *nm Ordinat (abrév* **réseau numérique à intégration de services***)* ISDN; **envoyer qch par RNIS** to ISDN sth, to send sth by ISDN

roaming *nm Ordinat, Tél* roaming

robotique *nf* robotics

ROC *nf Ordinat (abrév* **reconnaissance optique des caractères***)* OCR

rôle *nm (liste)* roll, register ❏ *Admin* **rôle des contributions** tax roll; *rôle d'impôt* tax roll

ROM *nf Ordinat (abrév* **read only memory***)* ROM

rompre *vt (négociations)* to break off; *(contrat)* to break

rompu *nm Bourse (d'actions, de titres)* odd lot

rotation *nf (des stocks)* turnover ❏ *rotation des capitaux* capital turnover; *Fin* **rotation des clients** debtors' turnover; *rotation des fournisseurs* creditors' turnover; *rotation du personnel* staff turnover; *Fin* **rotation de portefeuille** churning; *Fin* **rotation de portefeuille-action** equity switching; *Fin* **rotation de portefeuille-obligation** gilt switching; *rotation des postes* job rotation; *rotation des stocks* *Br* stock turnround, *Am* inventory turn; **le délai de rotation des stocks est de quatre mois** stocks are turned round every four months

rouge *nm* **être dans le rouge** to be in the red; **sortir du rouge** to get out of the red

> **❝**
>
> S'il prétend ne pas le faire, sauf pour les revenus du patrimoine, il faut en conclure qu'il a antidaté le moment où les finances publiques de la France **sortiront du rouge**.
>
> **❞**

roulage *nm (de marchandises)* carriage, haulage

roulant, -e *adj Fin (fonds, capital)* working

roulement *nm* (**a**) *Fin (de fonds)* circulation; *(de capitaux)* turnover (**b**) *(de personnel)* turnover

rouler *vi Fin (argent)* to circulate freely

roulier *nm* RORO (ship)

routage nm (**a**) *(de documents, de lettres)* sorting and mailing (**b**) *Ordinat* routing

route nf *(itinéraire)* route; **en cours de route** in transit ❑ *route commerciale* commercial route, trade route; *route à péage* toll road

routeur nm *Ordinat* router

routier, -ère 1 *adj* road
2 nm,f Br long-distance lorry driver, Am truck driver

rouvrir vt *(compte)* to reopen

RSVP *(abrév* **répondez s'il vous plaît)** RSVP

RTGS nm *Banque, UE (abrév* **Real-Time Gross Settlement)** RTGS; **système RTGS** RTGS system

RTT nf *(abrév* **réduction du temps de travail)** = reduction of the working week in France from 39 to 35 hours, introduced by the government of Lionel Jospin in 1998 and phased in from 2000 onwards

44

Une enquête de la Dares (ministère de l'emploi) indique que, pour 59% des salariés bénéficiant d'une réduction du temps de travail (**RTT**), celle-ci a été "dans le sens d'une amélioration" de leur vie quotidienne. Ils passent davantage de temps avec leurs enfants, se reposent plus ou profitent de vacances courtes.

77

ruiner vt to ruin, to bankrupt

rupture nf (**a**) *(de négociations)* breaking off ❑ *rupture de contrat* breach of contract; *rupture de garantie* breach of guarantee; *rupture de stock* stock outage; **être en rupture de stock** to be out of stock (**b**) *(transbordement)* *rupture de charge* transhipment of cargo

rythme nm rate; **à quel rythme dois-je vous les envoyer?** what rate should I send them to you at? ❑ *rythme annualisé* annually compounded rate; *rythme des livraisons* delivery rate; *rythme de production* rate of production

Ss

SA *nf* (*abrév* **société anonyme**) *Br* ≃ public limited company, plc *Am* ≃ listed compnay

sacquer *vt Fam* to sack, to fire

sacrifié, -e *adj* (*prix*) rock-bottom; (*article*) at a rock-bottom price

sacrifier *vt* (*marchandises*) to sell at rock-bottom prices

saisie *nf* (**a**) (*de marchandises, de capitaux*) seizure; (*d'un bien pour non-paiement des traites*) repossession □ **saisie conservatoire** seizure of goods (*to prevent sale*) (**b**) (*d'une hypothèque*) foreclosure (**c**) *Ordinat* keying □ **saisie automatique** automatic input; **saisie de données** data capture; **saisie manuelle** manual input

saisir *vt* (**a**) (*marchandises, capitaux*) to seize (**b**) (*hypothèque*) to foreclose on (**c**) *Ordinat* (*données*) to capture (**d**) *Jur* (*tribunal*) to refer a case to; **la juridiction compétente a été saisie** the case was referred to the appropriate jurisdiction

saison *nf* season; **la haute saison** the busy *or* high season; **la basse saison** the off season, the slack season; **hors saison** off season; **pendant la saison** in season □ **saison creuse** off season, slack season; **saison touristique** tourist season

saisonnier, -ère 1 *adj* seasonal
2 *nm,f* seasonal worker

salaire *nm* (*mensuel*) salary; (*hebdomadaire, journalier*) wage □ **salaire annuel** annual salary; **salaire annuel garanti** annual guaranteed salary; **salaire après impôts** after-tax salary; **salaire de base** basic salary *or* pay; **salaire brut** gross salary *or* pay; **salaire de congé** leave pay; **salaire de départ** starting salary; **salaire fixe** fixed salary *or* pay; **salaire hebdomadaire** weekly pay *or* wage; **salaire horaire** hourly wage *or* pay; **salaire indexé** index-linked salary; **salaire indirect** fringe benefits; **salaire mensuel** monthly salary; **salaire minimum** minimum wage; **salaire minimum interprofessionnel de croissance** index-linked guaranteed minimum wage; **salaire minimum interprofessionnel garanti** guaranteed minimum wage; **salaire net** net salary *or* pay; **salaire nominal** nominal wages; **salaire à la pièce** piece rate; **salaire plafonné** wage ceiling; **salaire réel** real salary; **salaire au rendement** performance-related pay

salarial, -e *adj* (*mensuel*) salary; (*hebdomadaire, journalier*) wage

salariat *nm* wage-earning population; **le salariat et le patronat** employees and employers

salarié, -e 1 *adj* (**a**) (*travailleur*) (*payé au mois*) salaried; (*payé à la semaine*) wage-earning (**b**) (*travail*) paid
2 *nm,f* (*payé au mois*) salaried employee; (*payé à la semaine*) wage earner; **les salariés de l'entreprise se sont mis en grève** the employees went on strike

salarier *vt* (*tous les mois*) to pay a salary to; (*toutes les semaines*) to pay a wage to

salle *nf* room □ **salle d'accueil (de la clientèle)** reception room; **salle d'attente** waiting room; *Bourse* **salle des changes** trading room; *Banque* **salle des coffres** vaults; **salle de conférence** conference room; **salle du conseil** boardroom; **salle de démonstration** showroom; **salle d'embarquement** departure lounge; **salle d'exposition** showroom; (*pour une foire*) exhibition hall; *Banque* **salle des guichets** front office; *Bourse* **salle des marchés** trading *or* dealing room; **salle de réception (de la clientèle)** reception room; **salle de réunion** boardroom, meeting room; **salle des ventes** auction room, salesroom

salon *nm* exhibition, trade fair □ **le Salon de l'informatique** = information technology trade fair

sanction *nf* (**a**) (*punition*) sanction; **prendre des sanctions contre un pays** to impose sanctions on a country □ **sanctions économiques** economic sanctions (**b**) (*approbation*) sanction

sans-emploi *nmf* unemployed person; **les sans-emploi** the unemployed

sans-travail *nmf* unemployed person; **les sans-travail** the unemployed

sapiteur *nm Assur* (*de cargaison*) valuer

saquer = **sacquer**

SARL *nf* (*abrév* **société à responsabilité limitée**) limited (liability) company, *Br* ≃ private limited company

satellite *nm* satellite □ **satellite de télécommunication** telecommunications satellite; **satellite de télédiffusion** broadcast satellite; **satellite de télévision** television satellite

satisfaction *nf* satisfaction □ **satisfaction de**

la clientèle customer satisfaction; *satisfaction du consommateur* consumer satisfaction; *satisfaction dans le travail* job satisfaction

satisfaire 1 *vt* to satisfy
  2 satisfaire à *vt ind (demande, condition, besoins)* to satisfy; *(règlement, normes de sécurité)* to comply with; *(obligation)* to fulfil

satisfait, -e *adj* satisfied; **j'espère que vous en serez entièrement satisfait** I trust it will give you complete satisfaction

saturation *nf Mktg (du marché)* saturation; **arriver à saturation** to reach saturation point

saturé, -e *adj Mktg (marché)* saturated

sauf *prép* except; **sauf avis contraire** unless I/we hear to the contrary; **sauf stipulation contraire** unless otherwise stated; *Compta* **sauf erreur ou omission** errors and omissions excepted

saut *nm Ordinat* **saut de ligne** line break; **saut de ligne manuel** hard return; **saut de page** page break

sauter *Ordinat* **1** *vt (commande)* to skip
  2 *vi (réseau)* to crash

sauvegarde *nf Ordinat* saving, backup; **faire la sauvegarde d'un fichier** to save a file ❑ *sauvegarde automatique* automatic backup; *sauvegarde sur bande* tape backup

sauvegarder *vt* (**a**) *(protéger)* to safeguard, to protect; **sauvegarder les intérêts des actionnaires** to protect the interests of shareholders (**b**) *Ordinat (fichier)* to save, to back up; **sauvegarder un fichier sur disquette** to save a file to disk; **sauvegarder automatiquement** to autosave

SAV *nm (abrév* **service après-vente)** after-sales service

SBF *nf (abrév* **Société des bourses françaises)** = company which runs the Paris Stock Exchange, ≃ *Br* LSE, ≃ *Am* NYSE; **le SBF 120** = French stock exchange index based on the share value of 120 companies; **le SBF 250** = French stock exchange index based on the share value of 250 companies

> **"**
> Sur les 250 plus grosses sociétés cotées, qui forment l'indice **SBF 250** de la Bourse de Paris, plus de la moitié appartient à la sphère du capitalisme familial.
> **"**

scanner¹ *nm Ordinat* scanner; **passer qch au scanner** to scan sth; **insérer qch par scanner** to scan sth in; **insérer qch par scanner, capturer qch au scanner** to scan sth in ❑ *scanner à main* handheld scanner; *scanner optique* optical scanner; *scanner à plat* flatbed scanner; *scanner à tambour* drum scanner

scanner² *vt Ordinat* to scan

scannérisation *nf Ordinat* scanning

scanneur = **scanner¹**

sceau *nm* seal; **apposer son sceau à qch** to set one's seal to sth

sceller *vt (apposer son sceau à)* to seal

scénario d'achat *nm Mktg* buying situation

schéma *nm* (**a**) *(dessin)* diagram, plan ❑ *Ordinat* *schéma de clavier* keyboard map; *schéma d'entreprise* organization chart (**b**) *(résumé)* summary, outline

schématique *adj* (**a**) *(sous forme de dessin)* diagrammatic (**b**) *(sous forme de résumé)* schematic, simplified

schématiser *vt* (**a**) *(dessiner)* to make a diagram of (**b**) *(résumer)* to schematize, to simplify

schilling *nm Anciennement* schilling

science *nf* **sciences économiques** economics; **science de la gestion** management science

scinder *vt (société)* to break up, to split

scission *nf (d'une société)* demerger; *Fin (d'actif)* divestment

> **"**
> On la croyait affaiblie par son procès pour "abus de position dominante" et par les menaces de **scission** prononcées l'année dernière ? Elle est aujourd'hui assurée d'échapper au démantèlement, et ses ventes n'ont jamais été aussi florissantes.
> **"**

score *nm Mktg* score ❑ *score d'agrément* approval rating, approval score; *score d'attribution* attribution score; *score de mémorisation* recall score; *score de reconnaissance* recognition score

SCP *nf (abrév* **société civile professionnelle)** professional *or* non-trading partnership

SCPI *nf (abrév* **société civile de placement immobilier)** = company which owns and manages rented accommodation

> **"**
> La **SCPI** collecte des fonds pour acheter des immeubles destinés à la location et distribue les loyers qu'elle perçoit à ses associés. Dans la pratique, c'est une société de gestion, liée ou non à une banque, qui décide de la création de la **SCPI**, émet des parts, les distribue dans le public et gère les immeubles et la société.
> **"**

script *nm Fin* scrip

scriptural, -e *adj* cashless

scrutin *nm* vote, ballot; **dépouiller le scrutin** to count the votes

SCSI *nf Ordinat* (*abrév* **small computer systems interface**) SCSI

SDRAM *nf Ordinat* (*abrév* **synchronous dynamic random access memory**) SDRAM

séance *nf* (*réunion*) session, meeting; *Bourse* (trading) session; **être en séance, tenir séance** to be sitting *or* in session; **la séance s'ouvrira/sera levée à huit heures** the meeting will open/adjourn at eight o'clock; **je déclare la séance ouverte** I declare the meeting open; **en séance publique** at an open meeting □ *Bourse* **séance boursière** trading session; **séance de clôture** closing session; **séance de créativité** brainstorming session; **séance de concertation** policy meeting; **séance du conseil de discipline** disciplinary hearing; **séance d'information** briefing (session); **séance d'ouverture** opening session; **séance supplémentaire** additional session

second, -e *adj* second □ **second associé** junior partner; *Bourse* **second marché** secondary market, unlisted securities market

secondaire *Écon* **1** *adj* (*secteur*) secondary **2** *nm* secondary sector

secours *nm* (**a**) (*aide*) help, assistance □ **secours d'argent** financial assistance (**b**) *Ordinat* **de secours** (*copie, fichier, disquette*) backup

secret *nm* **secret de fabrication** trade secret; **secret professionnel** = obligation to respect the confidentiality of sources; **enfreindre le secret professionnel** to betray a confidential source

secrétaire *nmf* secretary □ **secrétaire de direction** personal assistant; **secrétaire général** company secretary; **secrétaire particulier** private secretary

secrétariat *nm* (**a**) (*fonction*) secretaryship (**b**) (*bureau*) secretary's office; (*d'un organisme international*) secretariat (**c**) (*métier*) secretarial work

secteur *nm* (**a**) *Écon* (*d'une activité*) sector □ **secteur d'activité** field *or* sphere of activity; **secteur du bâtiment** building industry *or* sector; **secteur de croissance** growth sector; **secteur économique** economic sector; **secteur en expansion** growth area *or* sector; *Mktg* **secteur de la grande distribution** mass distribution sector; **secteur des grandes entreprises** corporate sector; **secteur industriel** branch *or* sector of industry; **secteur primaire** primary sector; **secteur privé** private sector; **secteur privé à but non lucratif** private non-profit sector; **secteur public** public sector; **secteur sanitaire** health sector; **secteur secondaire** secondary sector; **secteur des services** service *or* tertiary sector; **secteur tertiaire** tertiary secteur (**b**) (*d'un représentant*) area, patch □ **secteur de vente** sales area *or* territory

(**c**) *Ordinat* sector □ **secteur endommagé** bad sector; **secteur d'initialisation** boot sector

section *nf* (**a**) (*d'un service, d'un syndicat*) branch (**b**) (*d'un document*) section

sectoriel, -elle *adj* (*revendications, crise*) sector-based

Sécu *nf Fam* (*abrév* **Sécurité sociale**) = French social security system providing public health benefits, pensions, maternity leave etc

> **"**
>
> Le contrat d'orientation : pour les jeunes de moins de 22 ans non titulaires d'un diplôme professionnel rencontrant des difficultés d'accès à l'emploi. Le salaire varie de 30 à 65 % du SMIC selon l'âge. L'employeur est tenu de faire participer le jeune à des actions d'orientation et de formation représentant 20 % du temps de travail. Il bénéficie d'une exonération des cotisations patronales de **Sécu**, et parfois d'une prise en charge des frais de formation.
>
> **"**

sécuriser *vt* (*paiement*) to securitize; *Fin* **sécuriser un financement** to guarantee a loan

sécurité *nf* security □ *Ordinat* **sécurité des données** data security; **sécurité de l'emploi** job security; *Admin* **Sécurité sociale** = French social security system providing public health benefits, pensions, maternity leave etc

séduction *nf Mktg* appeal □ **séduction du client** customer appeal

segment *nm Mktg* segment □ **segment démographique** demographic segment; **segment géodémographique** geodemographic segment; **segment géographique** geographic segment; **segment de marché** market segment; **segment socio-démographique** sociodemographic segment

segmentation *nf Mktg* segmentation □ **segmentation par avantages recherchés** benefit segmentation; **segmentation comportementale** behaviour segmentation; **segmentation démographique** demographic segmentation; **segmentation fondée sur les besoins** needs-based segmentation; **segmentation géodémographique** geodemographic segmentation; **segmentation géographique** geographic segmentation; **segmentation du marché** market segmentation; **segmentation psychographique** psychographic segmentation; **segmentation socio-démographique** sociodemographic segmentation; **segmentation stratégique** strategic segmentation; **segmentation par styles de vie** lifestyle segmentation

segmenter *vt Mktg* (*marché*) to segment

seing *nm Jur* **un acte sous seing privé** a private contract

sélecteur nm Ordinat chooser

sélectif, -ive adj Ordinat **en mode sélectif** in veto mode

sélection nf (a) (fait de choisir) selection; (de candidats) screening, shortlisting □ **sélection de portefeuille** portfolio selection; **sélection de titres** stockpicking (b) Mktg (échantillon) selection □ **sélection au hasard** random selection

sélectionner vt (a) (choisir) to select (b) Ordinat (texte) to block, to select; **sélectionner qch par défaut** to default to sth

self-service nm self-service

selon prép (a) (d'après) according to (b) (conformément à) in accordance with

semaine nf (a) (période) week □ **semaine de travail** working week (b) (rémunération) week's pay, weekly wages

semainier nm (a) (feuille) weekly time sheet (b) (agenda) desk diary (with sections for each day of the week)

semestre nm (a) (période) half-year, six-month period; **les bénéfices du premier semestre** the first-half profits (b) (rémunération) six months' pay (c) (loyer) six months' rent

semestriel, -elle adj half-yearly, six-monthly

semestriellement adv half-yearly, every six months; **réviser les salaires semestriellement** to review salaries every six months

semi-fini, -e adj Écon (produit) semi-finished

semi-ouvré, -e adj Écon (produit) semi-finished

semi-produit nm semi-manufactured product

sens nm **sens des affaires** business sense or acumen; **sens du commerce** sales acumen

sensibilité nf Mktg sensitivity □ **sensibilité compétitive** competitive awareness; **sensibilité aux marques** brand sensitivity; **sensibilité aux prix** price sensitivity

sensible adj (hausse, baisse) marked, noticeable; Mktg **sensible aux marques** brand-sensitive; **sensible aux prix** price-sensitive

SEO Compta (abrév **sauf erreur ou omission**) E & OE

séparateur nm Ordinat separator

séparation automatique des pages nf Ordinat automatic pagination

séquence nf Ordinat sequence □ **séquence de caractères** character string, sequence of characters; **séquence de commandes** command sequence

séquentiel, -elle adj sequential

séquestre nm Jur sequestration; **mettre qch sous séquestre** to sequester or seize sth

séquestrer vt Jur to sequester, to sequestrate

série 1 adj Ordinat serial
2 nf (de marchandises) range, line; **fabriquer qch en série** to mass-produce sth; **hors série** custom-made, custom-built □ Écon **série économique** economic batch; **série économique de production** economic manufacturing quantity

sérieux, -euse adj (a) (offre, acheteur) genuine, serious (b) (entreprise) reliable

serpent nm Fin, UE (currency) snake □ **serpent monétaire (européen)** (European) currency snake

> ❝ ——————
>
> La situation rappelle donc fortement les événements de 1973-1978, lorsque se créa le **serpent monétaire européen**, ancêtre de l'euro, qui reposait sur l'idée que chaque monnaie se voyait imposer une marge de fluctuation par rapport aux autres, une fourchette dont elle ne devait pas s'écarter. Le Deutsche Mark, par exemple, valait autour de 3,46 francs français. Aucune des deux monnaies ne pouvait s'éloigner trop de cet équilibre.
>
> ————— ❞

serrure nf lock □ **serrure de combinaison** combination lock

serveur nm Ordinat server □ **serveur de courrier** mail server; **serveur distant** remote server; **serveur de fichiers** file server; **serveur FTP** FTP server; **serveur mandataire** proxy server; **serveur Minitel®** Minitel service provider; **serveur de nouvelles** news server; **serveur de procuration, serveur proxy** proxy server; **serveur de réseau** network server; **serveur sécurisé** secure server; **serveur télématique** bulletin board (system); **serveur de terminaux** terminal server; **serveur Web** Web server

service nm (a) (département) department □ **service des achats** purchasing department; **service d'action commerciale** marketing department; **service administratif** administrative department; **service après-vente** after-sales department; **service clientèle, service clients** customer service department; **service des commandes** order department; **service commercial** sales department; **service commercial export** export department; **service de (la) comptabilité** accounts department; **service consommateurs** customer service department; **service du contentieux** legal department; **service contrôle qualité, service de contrôle de qualité** quality control (department); **service du courrier** mail room; **service des crédits** credit or loan department; Compta **service des émissions** issue department; **service de l'entretien** maintenance department; **service d'études** research department; **service d'étude marketing** market research department; **service des expéditions** forwarding *or* dispatch department; **service des exportations, service export** export department; **service export intégré** integrated export service; **service de facturation** invoice department; **service de groupage** joint-cargo service; **service informatique** computer department; **service juridique** legal department; **service du marketing, service mercatique** marketing department; **service marketing-vente** sales and marketing department; **service des méthodes** methods office; **service du personnel** personnel department; **service de planification, service de planning** planning department; **service premier** premium service; **service de presse** press department *or* office; **service (de) production** production department; **service de la prospection** new business department; **service de publicité** advertising *or* publicity department; **service de recherche** research department; **service des réclamations** complaints department; **service de recouvrement** collecting department; **service de relation clientèle** customer service (department); **service des renseignements** information office; **service des renseignements commerciaux** status enquiry department; **service technique** technical department; **service des titres** securities department; **service des ventes** sales department; **service vente-marketing** sales and marketing department (**b**) *(prestation)* service; **offrir ses services (à qn)** to offer one's services (to sb) ❏ **service après-vente** after-sales service; **service d'assistance** *(téléphonique)* help desk, help line; **service d'assistance technique** consultancy service; **service de bavardage Internet** Internet Relay Chat; *Banque* **services de caisse** counter services; **service clientèle, service clients** customer service; **service consommateurs** customer service; *Ordinat* **service de dépannage** breakdown service; **service de la dette** debt servicing; **services aux entreprises** business services; **services financiers** financial services; **service d'informations** information services; **services d'investissement** investment services; **service de livraison** delivery service; **service de médiation** conciliation service; **service de messageries** courier service; **service d'orientation professionnelle** careers service; **service perçu** perceived service; **services postaux** postal services; **service premier** premium service; **service public** public utility; **service de renseignements** advisory service; **service de répondeur téléphonique** answering service; **services du secteur tertiaire** business services; **services de soutien** support services; *Ordinat* **service de télétraitement** dial-up service

(**c**) *Écon* **services** *(secteur)* services; **les biens et les services** goods and services

(**d**) *(travail)* duty; **être de service** to be on duty; **prendre/quitter son service** to go on/off duty; **il a été licencié après 25 ans de service** he was dismissed after 25 years' service ❏ **service de jour** day shift; **service de nuit** night shift

(**e**) *(dans un restaurant)* service; **service compris** service included; **service non compris** service not included

(**f**) *Fin (d'un emprunt, d'une dette)* servicing; **assurer le service d'un emprunt/d'une dette** to service a loan/debt

(**g**) *Admin* **service des douanes** customs service; **service postal, service des postes** postal service(s); **service public** *Br* public utility, *Am* utility

(**h**) *(dans les transports)* service ❏ **service de marchandises** goods *or* freight service; **service de voyageurs** passenger service

(**i**) *(d'une machine)* service; **en service** in service; **hors service** out of order, not in use; **mettre qch en service** to bring sth into service

serviette *nf (cartable)* briefcase

servir *vt* (**a**) *(client)* to serve, to attend to (**b**) *(dette)* to pay, to service; **servir une rente à qn** to pay an annuity to sb

servitude *nf Jur (droit d'usage)* easement

SET *nf Ordinat (abrév* **secure electronic transaction**) SET®

seuil *nm* threshold; **la dette a atteint le seuil critique des deux milliards** debt has reached the critical level *or* threshold of two billion ❏ *Bourse* **seuil d'annonce obligatoire** disclosure threshold; **seuil d'imposition** tax threshold; **seuil de pauvreté** poverty line; **seuil de prix** price threshold; **seuil de réapprovisionnement** reorder level *or* point; **seuil de rentabilité** break-even point; **atteindre le seuil de rentabilité** to break even, to reach break-even point

> **"**
>
> Mais, surtout, exporter une livraison ou installer ses propres entrepôts dans plusieurs villes, cela constitue autant d'opérations coûteuses pour les opérateurs, qui ont besoin de vendre de gros volumes pour atteindre le **seuil de rentabilité**.
>
> **"**

SGAO *nm Ordinat (abrév* **système de gestion assisté par ordinateur**) computer-assisted management system

SGBD *nm Ordinat (abrév* **système de gestion de base de données**) DBMS

SGDBR *nm Ordinat (abrév* **système de gestion de bases de données relationnelles**) RDBMS

SGDG (abrév **sans garantie du gouvernement**) without government guarantee

SGML nm Ordinat (abrév **Standard Generated Markup Language**) SGML

shareware nm Ordinat shareware

SICAF, sicaf nf Fin (abrév **société d'investissement à capital fixe**) closed-end investment company

SICAV, sicav nf Fin (abrév **société d'investissement à capital variable**) (a) (organisme) Br ≃ unit trust, Am ≃ mutual fund ❑ **sicav actions** equity-based unit trust; **sicav éthique** ethical investment fund; **sicav mixte** split capital investment trust; **sicav monétaire** money-based unit trust; **sicav obligataire** bond-based unit trust (b) (action) ≃ share in a Br unit trust or Am mutual fund

> 66
>
> Les **sicav** indicielles sont destinées aux débutants. Elles sont censées répliquer le mieux possible l'indice parisien. On classe aussi dans cette catégorie les fonds dits tiltés, investis dans les actions du Cac, avec de légères "améliorations", et qui ont pour objectif de battre l'indice.
>
> 99

SICOB nm (abrév **salon des industries du commerce et de l'organisation du bureau**) = annual information technology trade fair in Paris

SICOVAM, Sicovam nf Bourse (abrév **société interprofessionnelle pour la compensation des valeurs mobilières**) = French central securities depository

siège nm (d'une organisation, d'une société) headquarters ❑ **siège administratif** administrative headquarters; **siège social** head office, registered office

signal nm (a) Tél **signal d'appel** call waiting service (b) Ordinat **signal numérique** digital signal

signaler vt Ordinat to post

signataire 1 adj (pays) signatory
2 nmf (d'un contrat, d'un accord) signatory ❑ **signataire autorisé, signataire accrédité** authorized signatory

signature nf signature; **avoir la signature** to be authorized to sign; **la lettre portait la signature du président** the letter was signed by the chairman; **pour signature** (sur lettre) for signature ❑ **signature collective** joint signature; Ordinat **signature électronique, signature numérique** digital signature; **signature musicale publicitaire** (advertising) jingle; **la signature sociale** the signature of the company

signer vt to sign; **signer à la réception de marchandises** to sign for goods on reception; **signez au bas de la page** sign at the bottom of the page

signet nm Ordinat bookmark; **créer un signet sur une page** to bookmark a page

silver-point nm silver point ❑ **silver-point d'entrée** silver import point; **silver-point de sortie** silver export point

SIM nm (abrév **système d'information marketing**) MIS

SIMM nm (abrév **single in-line memory module**) SIMM

simple adj (a) (intérêts) simple (b) Ordinat **simple densité** single density

simplex Ordinat, Tél 1 adj simplex
2 nm simplex

simulateur nm simulator ❑ **simulateur de réalité virtuelle** virtual reality simulator

simulation nf simulation ❑ **simulation sur ordinateur** computer simulation

simuler vt to simulate

sinistre nm disaster; Assur loss; **déclarer un sinistre** to put in a claim ❑ **sinistre maximum prévisible** maximum foreseeable loss; **sinistre partiel** partial loss

SIT nm (abrév **Système Interbancaire de Télécompensation**) = interbank automated clearing system, Br ≃ CHAPS

site nm Ordinat site; Mktg (emplacement) site; ❑ Ordinat **site FTP** FTP site; Ordinat **site marchand** e-commerce site; Ordinat **site miroir** mirror site; Ordinat **site Web** web site

situation nf (a) (état) state, condition; (d'un compte) balance; (circonstances) situation; **la situation de l'économie/de l'emploi** the economic/employment situation ❑ Mktg **situation d'achat** buying situation; **situation en banque** financial position or situation; **situation de caisse** cash balance; **situation de compte** account balance; **situation financière** financial situation or position; Fin **situation nette** (d'une société) net assets, net worth; Mktg **situation de nouvel achat** new buy situation; Fin **situation de trésorerie** cash flow situation (b) (document) report, return; Fin statement of finances ❑ **situation de caisse** cash statement; **situation hebdomadaire** (de la Banque de France) weekly report (c) (emploi) position, job; **avoir une belle situation** to have a good job; **chercher une situation** to look for a job; **perdre sa situation** to lose one's job

SIVP nm (abrév **stage d'initiation à la vie professionnelle**) = training scheme for young unemployed people

slogan nm slogan ❑ **slogan publicitaire** advertising slogan

SME nm (a) (abrév **système monétaire européen**) EMS (b) (abrév **serpent monétaire européen**) European currency snake

SMIC, Smic nm (abrév **salaire minimum inter-professionnel de croissance**) index-linked guaranteed minimum wage

> ❝
>
> Décidés en 1993 par la droite, amplifiés en 1997 par la gauche, ces allègements auraient permis la création de près de 400 000 emplois peu qualifiés, en réduisant le coût du travail au niveau du **Smic**.
>
> ❞

smicard, -e nm,f minimum wage earner

smiley nm Ordinat smiley, emoticon

SMS nm Tél (abrév **short message service**) SMS

SNC nf (abrév **société en nom collectif**) partnership

social, -e adj (**a**) (qui a trait à la société) social (**b**) (qui a trait à une entreprise) company

socialisation nf Écon (du capital, des industries) socialization, collectivization

socialiser vt Écon (capital, industries) to socialize, to collectivize

sociétaire nmf (**a**) (membre) member (**b**) (d'une société anonyme) Br shareholder, Am stockholder

société nf (**a**) (entreprise) company, firm; **se monter en société** to set up in business □ **société par actions** Br joint-stock company, Am incorporated company; **société d'affacturage** factoring company; **société affiliée** Br affiliated company, Am affiliate; **société anonyme** Br public limited company, Am listed company; **société d'assurances** insurance company; **société de Bourse** stockbroking or brokerage firm; **société de capital-risque** venture capital company; Mktg **société cible** target company; **société civile** non-trading company; **société en commandite** limited partnership; **société en commandite par actions** partnership limited by shares; **société en commandite simple** limited partnership; **société de commerce international** international trading corporation; **société commerciale** business firm; **société commune** joint venture; **société de conseil en investissement** investment consultancy; **société coopérative** cooperative; **société cotée (en Bourse)** listed company; **société cotée à la Cote officielle** quoted company; **société non cotée** unquoted company; **société de crédit immobilier** Br ≃ building society, Am ≃ savings and loan association; **société de crédit mutuel** mutual insurance company, Br ≃ friendly society; **société d'économie mixte** semi-public company; **société écran** shell company; **société émettrice** issuing company; **société enregistrée** incorporated company; **société d'État** state-owned or public company;

société d'études research company or firm; **société d'études de marché** market research company; **société d'exploitation, société exploitante** development company; **société d'exploitation en commun** joint venture (company); **société d'exportation** export company or house; **société de factoring** factoring company; **société fictive** dummy company; **société fiduciaire** trust company; **société financière** finance company; **société de gestion** management company; **société de gestion de portefeuille** Br ≃ unit trust, Am ≃ mutual fund; **société (en) holding** holding company; **société immobilière** real-estate company; **société d'import-export** import-export company; **société industrielle** manufacturing firm; **société d'investissement** investment company; **société d'investissement à capital fixe** closed-end investment fund; **société d'investissement à capital variable** Br ≃ unit trust, Am ≃ mutual fund; **société de leasing** leasing company; **société de location** rental firm; **société de location de voitures** Br car hire company, Am car rental company; **société de marketing, société de mercatique** marketing company or firm; Bourse **société membre** member corporation; **société mère** parent company; **société multinationale** multinational (company); **société de mutualité** mutual insurance company, Br ≃ friendly society; **société nationale** state-owned or public company; **société de négoce** trading company; **société en nom collectif** partnership; **société off-shore** offshore company; **société opéable** target company; **société en participation** joint venture; **société de personnes** partnership; **société pétrolière** oil company; **société de placement** investment trust; **société à portefeuille** holding company; **société de prévoyance** provident society; **société privée** private company; **société à responsabilité illimitée** unlimited company; **société à responsabilité infinie** unlimited company; **société à responsabilité limitée** limited (liability) company, Br ≃ private limited company; **société de secours mutuel(s)** mutual insurance company, Br ≃ friendly society; **société de sécurité** guarantee company; **société de services** service company; **société sœur** sister company; **société de traitement à façon** service bureau; **société de transport** transport company; **société d'utilité publique** Br public utility company, Am utility; **société de vente par correspondance** mail order company (**b**) (communauté) society □ **société d'abondance** affluent society; **société de consommation** consumer society

sociodémographique adj sociodemographic

sociologique adj (enquête) sociological

socio-style nm lifestyle group

socket nf Ordinat socket

software nm Ordinat software

solde nm (**a**) (de compte) balance; **pour solde** in settlement; **pour solde de tout compte** in full settlement; **régler le solde** to pay the balance □ **solde actif** credit balance; **solde bancaire, solde en banque** bank balance; **solde bénéficiaire** credit balance; **solde de** ou **en caisse** cash balance; **solde créditeur** credit balance; **solde cumulé** cumulative balance; **solde débiteur** debit balance; Banque overdraft; **solde à découvert** outstanding balance; **solde déficitaire** debit balance; **solde disponible** available balance; **solde de dividende** final dividend; **solde dû** balance due; **solde final** bottom line; **solde de fin de mois** end-of-month balance; Compta **solde à nouveau** balance brought forward; Compta **solde nul** nil balance; **solde d'ouverture** opening balance; **solde passif** debit balance; Compta **solde reporté** balance brought forward; Compta **solde à reporter** balance carried forward; Compta **solde de trésorerie** cash balance

(**b**) (promotion) sale; (marchandise) sale item; **en solde** (marchandise) Br in the sale, Am on sale; **acheter** ou **avoir qch en solde** to buy or get sth Br in the sale or Am on sale; **mettre** ou **vendre qch en solde** to sell sth off □ **solde de fermeture** closing-down sale; **solde de fin de saison** end-of-season sale; **solde après inventaire** stocktaking sale

solder 1 vt (**a**) Fin (compte) to balance, to close; (dette) to settle, to pay (off); **solder l'arriéré** to make up back payments (**b**) (stock) to sell off, to clear

2 se solder vpr (**a**) Fin **se solder par qch** to show sth; **les comptes se soldent un bénéfice/un déficit de 10000 euros** the accounts show a profit/a deficit of 10,000 euros (**b**) **se solder par qch** (avoir pour résultat) to end in sth; **les négociations se sont soldées par un échec** the negotiations ended in failure

> ❝
>
> "Gouverner, c'est prévoir, et vous n'avez rien vu, rien prévu", fustige à son tour cet actionnaire marseillais, habitué à donner des leçons – il enseigne l'économie. L'allusion vise les comptes 2001, qui **se soldent par 13,6 milliards d'euros de pertes**, après notamment 15 milliards de dépréciations d'actifs, achetés ou fusionnés au plus haut de la bulle des valeurs médias et technologie.
>
> ❞

soldeur, -euse nm,f discount trader

solidaire adj Jur jointly liable or responsible

solidairement adv Jur **conjointement et solidairement** jointly and severally

solidarité nf (**a**) Jur joint and several liability, joint responsibility (**b**) (soutien) solidarity; **faire grève** ou **débrayer par solidarité** to come out in sympathy

solide adj (entreprise) sound, well-established

solidité nf (d'une entreprise) soundness

solvabilité nf solvency, creditworthiness

solvable adj solvent, creditworthy

sommaire nm (d'un article) abstract

somme nf (**a**) (d'une addition) sum, total amount; **la somme s'élève à 100 euros** the total comes to 100 euros □ **somme due** amount due, total due; **somme en excédent** sum in excess; **somme nette** net amount; Compta **sommes payables** sums payable; **somme totale** total amount, sum total (**b**) (argent) **somme (d'argent)** sum (of money); **payer une grosse** ou **forte somme** to pay a large sum or amount of money; **dépenser une somme de 500 euros** to spend (a sum of) 500 euros □ **somme forfaitaire** lump sum

sommet nm (réunion) summit (meeting) □ **sommet du G8** G8 summit

sommier nm Compta cash book, ledger

sonal nm (advertising) jingle

sondage nm Mktg (enquête) poll, survey; (activité) sampling; **faire un sondage** to carry out a poll or survey □ **sondage aléatoire** random sampling; **sondage d'opinion** opinion poll; **sondage par quotas** quota sampling

sondé, -e nm,f Mktg respondent

sonder vt (dans une enquête) to poll; **sonder l'opinion** to carry out or to conduct an opinion poll; **dix pour cent de la population sondée** ten percent of those polled

sortant, -e adj (élu) retiring, outgoing

sortie nf (**a**) (d'un nouveau produit) launch (**b**) Ordinat exit; (information) output □ **sortie (sur) imprimante** printout; **sortie (sur) papier** (computer) printout; **sortie parallèle** parallel output; **sortie série** serial output (**c**) (de marchandises, de devises) export; (de capital) outflow (**d**) Fin **sorties** outgoings; **ce mois-ci il y a eu plus de sorties que de rentrées** outgoings have exceeded incomings this month □ **sorties de fonds** expenses, outgoings; **sorties de trésorerie** cash outgoings

sortir 1 vt (**a**) (nouveau produit) to bring out, to launch (**b**) Ordinat to output

2 vi (**a**) **sortir sur le marché** (produit) to come onto the market (**b**) Ordinat to exit, to quit; **sortir d'un programme** to exit a program;

souche nf (de chèque, de ticket) counterfoil, stub

souffrance nf **en souffrance** (coupon, dette)

outstanding, unpaid; *(effet)* overdue, outstanding; *(marchandises)* held up, awaiting delivery; *(travail)* pending

soulte *nf Fin* equalization payment

> **"**
> Nous avons un véritable problème avec les retraites … Parmi les solutions possibles, se trouve celle de la **soulte** de 5,7 milliards d'euros, versée en 1997 par l'opérateur téléphonique à l'Etat, qui a pris à sa charge, en contrepartie, le paiement des retraites des agents de la société.
> **"**

soumettre *vt (document, loi)* to submit, to refer; **soumettre un document à la signature** to submit *or* present a document for signature

soumis, -e *adj (à une loi)* subject (**à** to); *(à un impôt)* liable, subject (**à** to); **soumis à l'impôt sur le revenu** liable to income tax; **soumis au (droit de) timbre** subject to stamp duty; **soumis aux fluctuations du marché** subject to fluctuations in the market

soumission *nf* (a) *(offre)* tender, bid; **par (voie de) soumission** by tender; **faire une soumission pour un travail** to tender for a piece of work ❑ *soumission cachetée* sealed tender (b) *Douanes* **soumission (en douane)** bond; *soumission cautionnée* secured bond

soumissionnaire *nmf* tenderer

soumissionner *vt (travail)* to tender *or* bid for; **soumissionner à une adjudication** to tender *or* bid for a contract

source *nf* source; *Fin* **imposé à la source** taxed at source ❑ *Ordinat source de données* data source; *source de revenus* source of revenue

> **"**
> De plus, l'employeur est tenu de s'assurer que le travailleur étranger conclut une assurance maladie. Le revenu des ressortissants étrangers qui ne sont pas au bénéfice d'un permis d'établissement C et qui exercent une activité lucrative en Suisse, est **imposé à la source**. La responsabilité incombe à l'employeur qui est tenu de déduire l'impôt sur le revenu directement sur le salaire et de le verser à l'administration fiscale.
> **"**

souriant *nm Ordinat* smiley

souris *nf Ordinat* mouse ❑ *souris à infrarouge* infrared mouse; *souris optique* optical mouse; *souris sans fil* cordless mouse; *souris tactile* touchpad mouse; *souris à trois boutons* three-button mouse

sous-agence *nf* sub-agency

sous-agent *nm* sub-agent

sous-bail *nm* sublease

sous-capitalisation *nf Écon* under-capitalization, underfunding

sous-capitalisé, -e *adj Écon* under-capitalized, underfunded

sous-chef *nm* assistant manager

sous-comité *nm* sub-committee

sous-commission *nf* sub-committee

sous-compte *nm* subsidiary account

sous-consommation *nf Écon* under-consumption

sous-contractant, -e *nm,f* subcontractor

souscoté, -e *adj (action, marché, monnaie)* undervalued

souscripteur, -trice *nm,f* (a) *Fin (d'un emprunt)* subscriber (**de** to) (b) *Bourse (des actions)* applicant (c) *Assur* policy holder

souscription *nf* (a) *Fin (à un emprunt)* subscription (**à** to) (b) *Bourse (à des actions)* application (**à** for) (c) *Assur (d'une police d'assurance)* taking out (d) *(somme)* subscription, contribution; **lancer une souscription** to start a fund; **verser une souscription** to pay a subscription

souscrire 1 *vt* (a) *(abonnement)* to take out (b) *Assur (police d'assurance)* to take out (c) *Bourse (actions)* to apply for
 2 souscrire à *vt ind* (a) *Fin (emprunt)* to subscribe to (b) *Bourse (actions)* to apply for

sous-développé, -e *adj Écon (pays, économie)* underdeveloped

sous-développement *nm Écon* underdevelopment

sous-directeur, -trice *nm,f* assistant manager, deputy manager

sous-emploi *nm Écon* underemployment

sous-employé, -e *adj Écon* underemployed

sous-équipé, -e *adj Écon* underequipped

sous-équipement *nm Écon* under-equipment

sous-estimation *nf* undervaluation

sous-estimer *vt* to undervalue

sous-évaluation *nf* undervaluation

sous-évaluer *vt* to undervalue

sous-jacent, -e *adj (fonds, titre)* underlying

sous-locataire *nmf* subtenant, sublessee

sous-location *nf* (a) *(par le locataire)* subletting (b) *(par le sous-locataire)* subrenting

sous-louer *vt* (a) *(sujet: locataire)* to sublet (b) *(sujet: sous-locataire)* to subrent

sous-menu *nm Ordinat* submenu

Sous-ministre *nm Can Admin* Deputy Minister ❑ *Sous-ministre adjoint* Assistant Deputy Minister

sous-payer *vt* to underpay

sous-préfet, -ète *nm,f Admin* subprefect

sous-production *nf Écon* underproduction

sous-produit *nm* by-product

sous-programme *nm Ordinat* subroutine, subprogram

sous-répertoire *nm Ordinat* subdirectory

sous-seing *nm* private agreement

soussigné, -e *adj & nm,f* undersigned; **je soussigné, Gérard Manvussat, déclare que ...** I, the undersigned, declare that…

sous-total *nm* subtotal

sous-traitance *nf* subcontracting; **donner qch en sous-traitance** to subcontract sth, to contract sth out

sous-traitant, -e 1 *adj* subcontracting **2** *nm,f* subcontractor

sous-traité *nm* subcontract

sous-traiter *vt* to subcontract

sous-utiliser *vt* to underutilize

soutenir *vt* (**a**) *Écon* (*monnaie, économie*) to support, to bolster up; **soutenir des cours par des achats** to support prices by buying (**b**) *(dépense)* to meet

soutenu, -e *adj (marché)* steady

soutien *nm* support, backup ❑ **soutien commercial** sales support; **soutien de famille** breadwinner; **soutien financier** financial support; *Écon* **soutien des prix** price pegging

spammer *vt Ordinat* to spam

spamming *nm Ordinat* spamming

spécialisation *nf* specialization

spécialisé, -e *adj (travail)* specialized; *(ouvrier, main-d'œuvre)* semi-skilled; *Ordinat (terminal, ligne)* dedicated; **non spécialisée** unskilled

spécialiser se spécialiser *vpr* **se spécialiser dans qch** to specialize in sth; **il s'est spécialisé dans l'import-export** he has specialized in import-export

spécialiste *nmf* specialist; **c'est un spécialiste du marketing** he's an expert in marketing ❑ *Mktg* **spécialiste produit** product specialist

spécialité *nf Br* speciality, *Am* specialty ❑ *Fin* **spécialité budgétaire** budgetary speciality; **spécialité pharmaceutique** patent medicine

spécification *nf* specification ❑ **spécification de la fonction** job specification

spécifier *vt* to specify; *Bourse* **spécifier un cours** to make a price

spécimen *nm* specimen; *Mktg (d'un livre)* specimen copy ❑ **spécimen de signature** specimen signature

spéculateur, -trice *nm,f Bourse, Fin* speculator ❑ **spéculateur à la baisse** bear; **spéculateur sur devises** currency speculator; **spéculateur à la hausse** bull; **spéculateur à la journée** day trader, scalper; **spéculateur sur plusieurs positions** position trader

spéculatif, -ive *adj Bourse, Fin* speculative

spéculation *nf Bourse, Fin* speculation ❑ **spéculation à la baisse** bear trading; **spéculation à la hausse** bull trading; **spéculations immobilières** property speculation; **spéculation à la journée** day trading

spéculer *vi Bourse, Fin* to speculate; **spéculer en Bourse** to speculate on the Stock Market; **spéculer à la baisse** to speculate for a fall *or* on a falling market, to go a bear; **spéculer à la hausse** to speculate for a rise *or* on a rising market, to go a bull; **spéculer sur les valeurs pétrolières** to speculate in oils

spirale *nf (hausse rapide)* spiral; **monter en spirale** *(prix)* to spiral ❑ **spirale inflationniste** inflationary spiral; **spirale prix-salaires** wage-price spiral

> **❝**
> Le foot est entré dans une **spirale inflationniste**. En France, les droits de télévision sont passés de 5 millions de francs (760 000 euros) en 1984 – avant la création de Canal+ et la privatisation de TF1 – à 2,6 milliards de francs (396 millions d'euros) en 2001.
> **❞**

sponsor *nm* sponsor, backer

sponsorat *nm* sponsorship

sponsoring *nm* sponsorship

sponsorisation *nf* sponsorship

sponsoriser *vt* to sponsor

spot *nm Mktg* **spot (publicitaire)** advert, commercial; **spot télé** TV commercial

spouleur *nm Ordinat* spooler

spread *nm Bourse* spread ❑ **spread horizontal** horizontal spread; **spread vertical** vertical spread

SS *nf Admin* (*abrév* **Sécurité sociale**) = French social security system providing public health benefits, pensions, maternity leave etc

stabilisateur, -trice *adj* stabilizing; **exercer une action stabilisatrice sur les prix** to have a stabilizing effect on prices

stabilisation *nf (d'une monnaie, des prix, du marché)* stabilization

stabiliser 1 *vt (monnaie, prix, marché)* to stabilize

  2 se stabiliser *vpr (monnaie, prix, marché)* to stabilize, to level off, to level out; **la Bourse a**

fini par se stabiliser après une chute vertigi-neuse the stock exchange eventually stabilized after plunging dramatically

stabilité *nf (d'une monnaie, des prix, du marché)* stability, steadiness

stable *adj (monnaie, prix, marché)* stable

stage *nm (cours)* training course; *(expérience professionnelle) Br* (work) placement, *Am* internship; **faire un stage** *(cours)* to go on a training course; *(expérience professionnelle)* to do a work placement □ *stage de formation* training course; *stage de perfectionnement* advanced training course; *stage de reconversion* retraining course

stagflation *nf Écon* stagflation

stagiaire *adj & nmf Br* trainee, *Am* intern

stagnant, -e *adj (économie, prix, marché)* stagnant

stagnation *nf (de l'économie, des prix, du marché)* stagnation; **en stagnation** at a standstill, stagnant

stagner *vi (économie, prix, marché)* to stagnate

stand *nm (d'exposition)* stand □ *stand d'exposition* exhibition stand

standard 1 *adj (modèle, prix)* standard
  2 *nm* **(a)** *(critère)* standard □ *standards budgétaires* budgetary standards **(b)** *Tél* switchboard

standardisation *nf* standardization

standardiser *vt* to standardize

standardiste *nmf Tél* (switchboard) operator

stand by *nm Fin* standby agreement

star *nf Mktg (produit)* star

start-up *nf* start-up

> **"**
>
> En fait, le PDG de LVMH est fasciné par l'envolée du Nasdaq. Dès 1995, il s'aventure à investir ses deniers personnels dans une petite **start-up** qui fabrique des équipements pour les réseaux: Cisco.
>
> **"**

station *nf Ordinat (d'un réseau)* station, node □ *station d'accueil* docking station; *station de travail* workstation

statisticien, -enne *nm,f* statistician

statistique 1 *adj* statistical
  2 *nf* statistics □ *statistiques démographiques* demographics

statuer **statuer sur** *vt ind* to rule on

statut *nm* **(a)** *Jur (état)* status □ *statut juridique, statut legal* legal status **(b)** **statuts** *(d'une société)* articles of association, statutes; **statuts et règlements** rules and regulations

statutaire *adj* statutory; *(actions)* qualifying; *(gérant)* appointed according to the articles

statutairement *adv* in accordance with the regulations

stellage *nm Bourse* put and call (option), double option

sténo 1 *nf (abrév* **sténographie**) shorthand; **prendre qch en sténo** to take sth down in shorthand
  2 *nmf (abrév* **sténographe**) stenographer

sténodactylo 1 *nf* shorthand typing
  2 *nmf* shorthand typist

sténodactylographie *nf* shorthand typing

sténographe *nmf* shorthand typist

sténographie *nf* shorthand

sténographier *vt* to take down in shorthand

sterling *adj* sterling

stimulant *nm (pour relancer)* stimulus; *(pour encourager)* incentive □ *stimulants de la production* production incentives; *stimulants de vente* sales incentives

stimulation *nf Mktg* incentive □ *stimulation financière* cash incentive

stimuler *vt* to stimulate; **l'exportation stimule la production** exports stimulate production; **pour stimuler les employés, la direction a décidé de les intéresser aux bénéfices de la société** as an incentive to employees, management has decided to give them a share in the company's profits

stipulation *nf (d'un contrat)* stipulation □ *stipulation particulière* special provision

stipuler *vt* to stipulate; **le contrat stipule que toutes les réparations seront à la charge du locataire** the contract stipulates that the tenant shall be responsible for all repairs

stock *nm (des marchandises)* stock; *Compta* **stocks** *Br* stock, *Am* inventory; **en stock** in stock; **nous n'avons plus ce modèle en stock** we no longer have this model in stock, this model is out of stock; **dans la limite des stocks disponibles** while stocks last, subject to availability; **constituer des stocks** to build up stocks; **épuiser les stocks** to deplete *or* exhaust stocks □ *stock d'alerte* minimum stock level; *stock de dépannage* buffer stock; *stock de départ* initial stock; *stock existant* stock in hand; *stock final* closing stock; *stock initial* opening stock; *stock à l'inventaire* closing stock; *stock en magasin* stock in hand; *stock d'or (d'une Banque d'État)* gold reserve; *stock d'ouverture* opening stock; *stocks régulateurs* buffer stocks; *stocks de réserve* stockpile; *stock de sécurité* safety stock; *stock stratégique* perpetual inventory; *stock tampon* safety stock

stockage *nm* **(a)** *(des marchandises)* stocking; *(en grande quantité)* stockpiling □ *stockage mécanisé* mechanized stocking **(b)** *Ordinat* storage ❏ *stockage de données* data storage; *stockage en mémoire tampon* buffering

stocker *vt* (**a**) *(marchandises)* to stock; *(en grande quantité)* to stockpile (**b**) *Ordinat (informations)* to store

stockiste *nmf Br* stockist, *Am* dealer

stock-option *nf Bourse* stock option

stop-vente *nf Bourse* stop-loss selling

stratégie *nf* strategy ❏ *stratégie commerciale* business strategy; *stratégie de communication* communication strategy; *stratégie conjoncturelle* economic strategy; *stratégie de croissance* growth strategy; *stratégie de différenciation* differentiation strategy; *stratégie de distribution* distribution strategy; *stratégie de distribution intensive* intensive distribution strategy; *stratégie de diversification* diversification strategy; *stratégie d'entreprise* corporate strategy, business strategy; *stratégie financière* financial strategy; *stratégie fonctionnelle* functional strategy; *stratégie de globalisation* globalization strategy; *Mktg stratégie d'imitation* imitation strategy, me-too strategy; *stratégie marketing, stratégie mercatique* marketing strategy; *Mktg stratégie de la marque* brand strategy; *stratégie opérationnelle* operations strategy; *Mktg stratégie de pénétration* (market) penetration strategy; *Mktg stratégie de positionnement* positioning strategy; *stratégie promotionnelle* promotional strategy; *Mktg stratégie publicitaire* advertising strategy; *Mktg stratégie pull* pull strategy; *Mktg stratégie push* push strategy

streamer *vt Ordinat* to stream

streaming *n Ordinat* streaming

structure *nf* (**a**) *(enquête, organisation)* structure ❏ *structure des coûts* cost structure; *structure de l'entreprise* corporate *or* company structure; *structure hiérarchique* line organization; *structure du marché* market structure; *structure de(s) prix* price structure; *structure des salaires* salary *or* wage structure (**b**) *Ordinat* structure ❏ *structure en anneau* ring structure; *structure arborescente* directory *or* tree structure; *structure en arbre* tree structure; *structure de bloc* block structure; *structure en bus* bus structure; *structure en étoile* star structure; *structure de fichier* file structure

structuré, -e *adj Mktg (enquête)* structured

structurer *vt* to structure

style de vie *nm (du consommateur, du client)* lifestyle

stylo *nm* pen ❏ *stylo bille* ballpoint pen; *Ordinat stylo optique* light pen

subalterne *adj (position)* subordinate; *(employé)* junior

subordonné, -e *nm,f (employé)* subordinate

subrogation *nf Jur* subrogation

subside *nm* subsidy, grant

substitut *nm* substitute ❏ *Mktg substitut rapproché* close substitute

substitution *nf* substitution

subvention *nf* subsidy, grant ❏ *subventions en capital* capital grants; *subvention d'équipement* equipment subsidy; *subvention de l'État* government grant; *subvention d'exploitation* operating subsidy; *subvention des exportations* export subsidy; *subvention d'investissement* investment grant

> "
> Dans ce domaine, l'Europe ne peut s'arc-bouter sur certains privilèges hérités du passé. Elle se doit de remettre en cause certains de ses passe-droits, et en tout premier lieu sa politique de **subventions des exportations**, notamment agricoles.
> "

subventionné, -e *adj* subsidized; **subventionné par l'État** State-aided

subventionner *vt* to subsidize, to grant financial aid to

succéder **succéder à** *vt ind* to take over from, to succeed

successeur *nm* successor (**de** to)

succession *nf* (**a**) *Jur (héritage)* inheritance; *(biens)* estate (**b**) *(remplacement)* succession; **prendre la succession de qn** to take over from sb; **la succession du poste sera assurée par M. Dupont** Mr Dupont will take over the post

succursale *nf* branch

suite *nf* (**a**) *(dans une lettre)* **(comme) suite à votre lettre du 15 août** with reference to *or* further to your letter of 15 August; **(comme) suite à notre conversation téléphonique** further to our telephone conversation (**b**) **donner suite à qch** *(demande, lettre)* to follow sth up; *(commande)* to deal with sth; **pour suite à donner** *(sur document)* (passed to you) for action (**c**) **sans suite** *(article)* discontinued (**d**) *Ordinat* *suite logicielle* suite

suivant¹ *prép (conformément à)* in accordance with; **suivant inventaire** as per stock list

suivant², -e **1** *adj* following; **aux conditions suivantes** on the following terms
  2 *nm,f Mktg* follower; *(sur le marché)* market follower ❏ *suivant immédiat* early follower

suiveur *nm Mktg* follower; *(sur le marché)* market follower

suivi, -e **1** *adj (demande)* steady, persistent; *(achats)* consistent
  2 *nm* follow-up; **assurer le suivi de qch** *(de-*

mande, lettre) to follow sth up; *(commande)* to deal with sth

suivre 1 *vt* (**a**) *(dossier)* to follow up; *(commande)* to deal with (**b**) *(article)* to continue to stock; **nous n'avons pas suivi cet article** we have discontinued this item
 2 *vi* **faire suivre une lettre** to forward a letter, to redirect a letter; **(prière de) faire suivre** *(sur enveloppe)* please forward

sujet, -ette *adj* **sujet à** *(soumis à)* subject or liable to; **ce contrat est sujet au droit de timbre** this agreement is subject to stamp duty

superdividende *nm Fin* surplus dividend

superficie *nf (des locaux)* surface area; **l'entrepôt fait 3000 m² de superficie** *ou* **a une superficie de 3000 m²** the warehouse has a surface area of 3,000 m²

supérieur, -e 1 *adj* (**a**) *(produit, marchandises)* of superior quality; *(qualité)* superior (**b**) *(rang, grade)* higher; *(cadre)* senior (**c**) *(offre)* higher
 2 *nm,f* superior

supermarché *nm* supermarket

super-ordinateur *nm Ordinat* supercomputer

superposer *vt Ordinat* **superposer une écriture** to overwrite

superprofits *nmpl* very large profits

superviser *vt* to supervise

superviseur *nm* supervisor

supplément *nm* (**a**) *(surcroît)* supplement; **un supplément d'information/de travail** additional *or* extra information/work; **en supplément** extra, additional (**b**) *(somme)* additional charge, supplement

supplémentaire *adj* supplementary, additional

support *nm* (**a**) *Ordinat* medium, support ❏ **support de données** data carrier; **support de sortie** output medium; **support de souris** mouse support; **support de stockage** storage medium; **support technique** technical support (**b**) *(médium)* medium ❏ **support de publicité, support publicitaire** publicity *or* advertising medium

supporter *vt (frais, coût)* to bear; **l'acheteur supporte les frais** the fees are borne by the purchaser

suppression *nf* (**a**) *(de crédits, d'aide)* withdrawal; *(d'un impôt)* abolition (**b**) *(d'emplois)* axing; **il y a eu beaucoup de suppressions d'emplois dans la région** there were many job losses in the area

supprimer *vt* (**a**) *(crédits, aide)* to withdraw; *(impôt)* to abolish (**b**) *(emplois)* to shed, to axe (**c**) *Ordinat* to delete

sûr, -e *adj (placement)* safe, secure; *(entreprise)* of good standing

surabondance *nf* surfeit, glut

surassurance *nf* overinsurance

surcapacité *nf Écon* overcapacity, excess capacity

surcapitalisation *nf Fin* overcapitalization

surcapitalisé, -e *adj Fin* overcapitalized

surcharge *nf* (**a**) *(d'un véhicule)* overloading ❏ *surcharge permise* permissible overload (**b**) *(de bagages)* excess weight (**c**) *(surcroît)* **une surcharge de travail** excess *or* extra work (**d**) *(sur un mot)* alteration; **sans rature ni surcharge** *(sur document administratif)* without deletions or alterations

surcharger *vt* (**a**) *(véhicule)* to overload (**b**) *(marché)* to glut, to overload (**c**) *(accabler)* **surcharger qn d'impôts** to overburden sb with taxes (**d**) *(chèque, écriture)* to alter

surchauffe *nf Écon* overheating

surconsommation *nf Écon* overconsumption

surcoté, -e *adj (action, marché, monnaie)* overvalued

surcoût *nm* extra charge

surcroît *nm* addition, increase; **un surcroît de dépenses/travail** additional *or* extra expenditure/work

surdéveloppé, -e *adj Écon* highly developed; *(excessivement)* overdeveloped

surdéveloppement *nm Écon* high state of development; *(excessif)* overdevelopment

surdon *nm* (**a**) *(indemnité)* = compensation allowable to purchaser for damage to goods (**b**) *(droit)* = right to non-acceptance of damaged goods

sureffectif *nm* overmanning

surémission *nf Fin* overissue

suremploi *nm Écon* overemployment

surenchère *nf* higher bid, overbid; **faire une surenchère sur qn** to outbid sb

surenchérir *vi* to bid higher; **surenchérir sur qn** to outbid sb, to bid higher than sb

❝

Le groupe Euronext pourrait **surenchérir sur** l'OPA hostile lancée sur le marché londonien par le groupe suédois OM Gruppen. Ce dernier gère la Bourse de Stockholm et a lancé son offre hostile le 29 août. Euronext, qui doit naître de la fusion le 22 septembre des places boursières de Paris, d'Amsterdam et de Bruxelles, pourrait, selon le Figaro, lancer une offre à son tour.

❞

surenchérissement *nm* further rise in prices

surenchérisseur, -euse *nm,f* outbidder

surendetté, -e *adj Écon* overindebted

surendettement *nm Écon* excessive debt; **courir un risque de surendettement** to run a risk of getting into excessive debt

suréquipement *nm* overequipment

suréquiper *vt* to overequip

surestarie *nf* demurrage

surestimation *nf* overestimate, overvaluation

surestimer *vt* to overestimate, to overvalue; **l'entreprise a surestimé ses capacités de production** the company overestimated its production capabilities

sûreté *nf (garantie)* surety, guarantee □ **sûreté personnelle** surety; **sûreté réelle** (real) security

surévaluation *nf* overestimate, overvaluation

surévaluer *vt* to overestimate, to overvalue

surexploitation *nf* over-exploitation, excessive exploitation

surexploiter *vt* to overexploit

surface *nf* **(a)** *(aire)* surface □ *Mktg* **surface d'affichage, surface d'exposition, surface de présentation** display area *or* space; **surface au sol** floor space; **surface de vente** sales area **(b)** *Fin* **surface financière** financial standing **(c)** *Ordinat* **surface d'affichage** display area; **surface d'enregistrement** read-write surface

surfacturation *nf* overbilling

surfaire *vt (marchandises)* to overprice

surfait, -e *adj (prix)* excessive

surfer *vi Ordinat* **surfer sur (l')Internet** to surf the Internet

surfin, -e *adj* of the highest quality

surimposer *vt* **(a)** *(augmenter l'impôt sur)* to increase the tax on **(b)** *(frapper d'un impôt trop lourd)* to overtax

surimposition *nf* **(a)** *(augmentation de l'impôt)* increase of taxation **(b)** *(excessif)* overtaxation

surindustrialisation *nf* overindustrialization

surinvestissement *nm Fin* overinvestment

surligneur *nm* highlighter (pen)

surmarquage *nm* overpricing

surmarquer *vt* to overprice

surmédiatisation *nf* media overkill, overexposure

> **"**
>
> La SNCF avait pourtant réussi l'examen de l'inauguration, elle annonçait un avenir plus que prometteur, mais la **surmédiatisation**

l'attendait au tournant : la moindre défaillance, le moindre couac aurait transformé la performance en un fiasco.
>   **"**

surnombre *nm* **en surnombre** excess; **personnel en surnombre** surplus staff

suroffre *nf* **(a)** *(surenchère)* counterbid, higher bid **(b)** *Écon (surabondance)* excess supply

surpaie, surpaye *nf* overpayment

surpayer *vt (personne)* to overpay; *(produit)* to pay too much for

surplus *nm* **(a)** *(excédent)* surplus, excess; *(revenu)* disposable income □ **surplus acquis** acquired surplus; **surplus des bénéfices** excess profits; **surplus exceptionnels, surplus extraordinaires** excess profits; **surplus d'importation** import surplus; *Fin* **surplus monétaire** monetary surplus; **surplus de productivité** productivity surplus **(b)** *(supplément)* (à un prix) surcharge; **payer le surplus** to pay the difference

surpositionnement *nm* over-positioning

surpositionner *vt* to over-position

surprime *nf Assur* extra *or* additional premium

surprix *nm* excess price

surproduction *nf Écon* overproduction

surproduire *vt & vi Écon* to overproduce

surprofit *nm Écon* excessive profit

surremise *nf* additional discount

surréservation *nf* overbooking; **faire une surréservation de qch** to overbook sth

sursalaire *nm* bonus, extra pay

sursis *nm Jur* respite, delay □ **sursis de paiement** extension of deadline for payment

sursouscription *nf Fin* oversubscription

sursouscrire *vt Fin* to oversubscribe

sursouscrit, -e *adj Fin* oversubscribed

surtaux *nm* excessive rate

surtaxe *nf* **(a)** *(en sus)* surtax, surcharge □ **surtaxe à l'importation** import surcharge; **surtaxe progressive** progressive surtax **(b)** *(taxe excessive)* excessive tax

surtaxer *vt* **(a)** *(frapper d'une taxe supplémentaire)* to surtax, to surcharge; *(lettre)* to surcharge **(b)** *(frapper d'une taxe excessive)* to overtax

survaleur *nf* goodwill

> **"**
>
> Cette différence entre valeur boursière et valeur comptable, conséquence de la prise en compte d'actifs non financiers (part de marché, valeur de la marque …), c'est le fameux goodwill, cette **survaleur**, qui est en

ce moment dépréciée à grands coups de pertes exceptionnelles. Traduction, par exemple, pour le groupe d'électronique de défense Thales, qui vient d'inscrire 460 millions d'euros en amortissement exceptionnel de **survaleur** après l'acquisition du britannique Racal. **"**

surveillance *nf (de travail)* supervision; *(des prix)* monitoring; *(de la production)* control

surveillant, -e *nm,f (dans une usine, sur un chantier)* supervisor

surveiller *vt (travail)* to supervise; *(prix)* to monitor; *(production)* to control

survendre *vt* to overcharge for

survente *nf* overcharging

survoler *vt Ordinat* to browse through

sus *adv* **en sus** in addition, extra; **les frais d'expédition sont en sus** postage is extra

suscription *nf Admin (sur une lettre)* address

susdit, -e *adj & nm,f* above-mentioned, aforesaid

susmentionné, -e *adj & nm,f* above-mentioned, aforesaid

susnommé, -e *adj & nm,f* above-named

suspendre *vt* (**a**) *(paiement, travail)* to suspend, to stop; **suspendre le paiement d'un chèque** to stop a cheque (**b**) *(employé)* to suspend (**c**) *Ordinat* **suspendre l'exécution d'un programme** to abort a program

suspens en suspens *adv* pending, outstanding

suspension *nf* (**a**) *(d'un paiement, de travail)* suspension (**b**) *(d'un employé)* suspension (**c**) *Ordinat* **suspension d'exécution** *(d'un programme)* abort, aborting

SVGA *nm (abrév* **Super Video Graphics Array**) SVGA

SVP *(abrév* **s'il vous plaît**) please

swap *nm Bourse* swap ❑ **swap d'actifs** asset swap; **swap de change** exchange rate swap

symbole *nm* ❑ **symbole du dollar** dollar sign; **symbole de l'euro** euro sign; **symbole de la livre** pound sign

symbolique *adj (loyer)* nominal; *(paiement, somme)* token; *Jur* **obtenir le franc symbolique de dommages-intérêts** to be awarded token damages

syndic *nm* (**a**) *Jur* receiver ❑ **syndic de faillite** trustee in bankruptcy (**b**) *Admin* **syndic d'immeuble** property manager

syndical, -e *adj (Br* trade *or Am* labor) union

syndicalisme *nm* (**a**) *(mouvement)* (*Br* trade *or Am* labor) unionism (**b**) *(activité)* **faire du syndicalisme** to be involved in union activities

syndicaliste 1 *adj (Br* trade *or Am* labor) union

2 *nmf (Br* trade *or Am* labor) unionist

syndicat *nm* (**a**) *(de salariés, d'ouvriers)* (*Br* trade *or Am* labor) union (**b**) *(d'employeurs)* federation; *(de producteurs, de propriétaires)* association; *(de financiers)* syndicate ❑ **syndicat d'enchères** tender pool; **syndicat financier** (financial) syndicate; **syndicat de garantie** underwriting syndicate; **syndicat industriel** industrial pool; **syndicat d'initiative** tourist information office; **syndicat patronal** employers' federation; *Fin* **syndicat de prise ferme** underwriting syndicate; **syndicat de producteurs** producers' association; **syndicat professionnel** trade association *or* body

syndicataire 1 *adj* syndicate

2 *nmf* member of a syndicate

syndiqué, -e 1 *adj* (**a**) *(membre d'un syndicat financier)* belonging to a syndicate (**b**) *(membre d'un syndicat de travailleurs)* belonging to a (*Br* trade *or Am* labor) union; **être syndiqué** to be a member of a (*Br* trade *or Am* labor) union

2 *nm,f (Br* trade *or Am* labor) union member

syndiquer 1 *vt* to unionize

2 se syndiquer *vpr* (**a**) *(se constituer en syndicat)* to form a (*Br* trade *or Am* labor) union (**b**) *(adhérer à un syndicat)* to join a (*Br* trade *or Am* labor) union

syntaxe *nf Ordinat* syntax

synthétiseur de paroles *nm Ordinat* voice synthesizer

sysop *nm Ordinat (abrév* **Systems Operator**) SYSOP

systématique *adj* systematic

système *nm* (**a**) *(structure)* system ❑ **système bancaire** banking system; **système du budget à base zéro** zero base budgeting; *Banque* **système de compensation** clearing system; **système comptable** accounting system; **système de contrôle de stocks** stock control system; **système de direction** management system; **système de distribution** distribution system; **système d'entrepôt** warehousing system; **système de fabrication** manufacturing system; **système de fabrication flexible** flexible manufacturing system; **système fiscal** tax system; **système d'information mercatique** *ou* **marketing** marketing information system; *Bourse* **système informatique de cotation** computerized trading system; **système informatisé de transaction** screen-trading system; **système intégré de gestion** integrated management system; **système d'inventaire** inventory method; *Écon* **système monétaire** monetary system; *Écon* **système monétaire européen** European Monetary System; **système de participation aux bénéfices** profit-sharing scheme; **système de primes** bonus scheme, incentive scheme; **système de retraite** pension scheme; ***système de retraite par répartition*** contributory pension plan

(**b**) *Ordinat* system ❑ ***système à boîtier vertical*** tower system; ***système expert*** expert system; ***système d'exploitation*** operating system; ***système d'exploitation de*** *ou* ***à disques*** disk operating system; ***système d'exploitation réseau*** network operating system; ***système de gestion de bases de données*** database management system; ***système de gestion de fichiers*** file management system; ***système informatique*** computer system; ***système informatisé*** computerized information system; ***système intégré de gestion*** integrated management system; ***système d'intelligence marketing*** marketing intelligence system; ***système multi-utilisateur*** multi-user system; ***système de nom de domaine*** domain name system, DNS; ***système en réseau*** networked system; ***système de sauvegarde*** backup system; ***système de sauvegarde sur bande*** tape backup system; ***système de secours*** backup system; ***système serveur*** host system; ***système à tour*** tower system; ***système de traitement de l'information*** data processing system

Tt

table nf (**a**) *(liste, recueil)* table ❑ *Assur* **tables d'actualisation** present value tables; **tables d'espérance de vie** life expectancy tables, actuarial tables; **table des intérêts** interest table; **table des matières** table of contents; **tables de mortalité** life expectancy tables, actuarial tables; **table des parités** parity table, table of par values; *Ordinat* **table de recherche, table de référence** look-up table
(**b**) *(meuble)* table ❑ **table de conférence** conference table; **table des négociations** negotiating table; **s'asseoir à la table des négociations** to get round the negotiating table; **table ronde** round table

tableau nm (**a**) *(liste)* list, table; **disposer qch en tableau** to tabulate sth ❑ **tableaux d'activité économique** economic activity tables; **tableau d'affichage** notice board; *Compta* **tableau d'amortissement** depreciation schedule; **tableau d'avancement** promotions list; **tableau d'avancement de commandes** order flowchart; **tableau de bord** management chart; **tableau comptable** (financial) statement; *Compta* **tableau des emplois et ressources** funds flow statement, cash flow statement; *Compta* **tableau de financement** funds flow statement, cash flow statement; **tableau des flux de trésorerie** cash flow statement; **tableau de marche** progress schedule; **tableau de prix** price list; **tableau de service** rota; **tableau statistique** statistical table
(**b**) *Ordinat* control panel

tablette nf *Ordinat* **tablette graphique** graphics tablet; **tablette tactile** trackpad

tableur nm *Ordinat* spreadsheet ❑ **tableur de graphiques** graphics spreadsheet

tabulation nf tab, tabulator; **délimité par des tabulations** tab-delimited

tâche nf (**a**) *(travail)* task, job; **travailler à la tâche** to do piecework (**b**) *Ordinat* task ❑ **tâche d'arrière-plan** background task or job; **tâche de fond** background task or job

tacite adj *(convention)* tacit ❑ *Jur* **tacite reconduction** renewal (of lease) by tacit agreement

tactique **1** adj tactical
2 nf tactics ❑ **tactique commerciale** marketing tactics; **tactiques de défense contre-OPA** defensive tactics

taille nf (**a**) *Ordinat (de fichier)* size (**b**) *Bourse*

taille boursière market size (**c**) *Mktg (du marché, de part de marché, d'un segment)* size

talon nm (**a**) *(de chèque)* counterfoil, stub (**b**) *Fin (de coupon)* talon (**c**) **talon à retourner** reply slip

tampon nm *(cachet, instrument)* rubber stamp ❑ **tampon dateur** date stamp; **tampon encreur** ink pad

tantième nm *(de bénéfices)* percentage, quota; **le tantième des administrateurs** the directors' percentage of the profits

taper **1** vt (**a**) *Ordinat* to key; **tapez entrée ou retour** select enter or return (**b**) *(dactylographier)* **taper qch (à la machine)** to type sth
2 vi *(dactylographier)* **taper (à la machine)** to type; **taper au toucher** to touch-type

tapis de souris nm *Ordinat* mouse mat or pad

tare nf (**a**) *(dépréciation)* depreciation, loss in value *(owing to damage or waste)* (**b**) *(pour calculer le poids net)* tare; **faire la tare** to allow for the tare ❑ **tare commune, tare par épreuve, tare moyenne** average tare; **tare réelle** actual tare

tarer vt *(emballage, caisse)* to tare

TARGET nm *(abrév* **Transferts Express Automatisés Transeuropéens à Réglement Brut en Temps Réel)** TARGET

tarif nm (**a**) *(prix)* rate; *(d'un billet d'avion, de train)* fare ❑ **tarif apex** APEX fare; **tarif de base** basic rate; **tarif colis postal** parcel rates; **tarif dégressif** sliding-scale tariff, tapering charge; **tarif d'encaissement** collection rate; **tarif fixe** flat rate; **tarif forfaitaire** fixed rate; **tarif groupage** groupage rate; **tarif hors saison** off-season tariff; **tarif (des) imprimés** printed paper rate; **tarif des insertions** advertising rates; **tarif lettres** letter rate; **tarif marchandises** goods or freight rate; **tarif minimum** minimum charge; **tarif normal** ordinary rate, first-class (rate); **tarif de nuit** night rate; **tarifs postaux** postal rates; *Fin* **tarif préférentiel** preferential rate; **tarif de la publicité** advertising rates; **tarif réduit** cheap or reduced rate; **tarif des salaires** salary scale; **tarif syndical** trade union tariff; **tarif uniforme** flat rate
(**b**) *(tableau des prix)* price list, *Br* tariff
(**c**) *Douanes (droit)* tariff, rate; *(liste)* list ❑ **tarif ad valorem** ad valorem tariff; **tarif différentiel** differential tariff; **tarif douanier** customs tar-

iff; **tarif douanier commun** common customs or external tariff; **tarif d'entrée** import list; **tarif préférentiel** preferential rate or tariff; **tarif de sortie** export list

tarifaire adj (accord, lois) tariff

tarifer vt to fix the price of

tarification nf pricing □ **tarification en fonction de la valeur perçue** perceived value pricing; **tarification géographique** geographic pricing; **tarification de pénétration du marché** market penetration pricing

> **"**
> Malgré tout, "ces services ne marquent pas un différentiel majeur entre les FAI. C'est bien sur la **tarification** que se fait la différence", note Olivier Beauvillain, analyste chez Jupiter MMXI. Sur ce point, Tiscali est confronté à une difficulté: rentabiliser un fonds de commerce attiré en premier lieu par les promesses du gratuit.
> **"**

tassement nm (du marché, des valeurs) weakening, downturn, drop; **l'augmentation de la TVA a provoqué un léger tassement de nos ventes** the rise in VAT has caused a slight drop in our sales

tasser se tasser vpr (marché, valeurs) to weaken

taux nm (a) (montant, pourcentage) rate; **à taux fixe** fixed-rate; **taux de huit pour cent** rate of eight percent; **emprunter à un taux de sept pour cent** to borrow at seven percent □ **taux d'accroissement** rate of increase or of growth; Écon **taux d'activité** participation rate; Compta **taux d'actualisation** net present value rate, rate of discount; **taux actuariel** yield to maturity; Mktg **taux d'adoption** rate of adoption; Compta **taux d'amortissement** rate of depreciation, depreciation rate; **taux annualisé** annual percentage rate, APR; **taux annuel effectif** effective annual rate; Fin **taux de l'argent** money rate; Fin **taux de l'argent au jour le jour** overnight rate; **taux d'assurance** insurance rate; **taux d'attribution** attribution rate; **taux d'autofinancement** cash flow rate; **taux bancaire** bank rate; **taux de base (bancaire)** (bank) base rate; Compta **taux de capitalisation** price-earnings ratio; **taux de change** exchange rate, rate of exchange; **taux de change à l'achat** bank buying rate; **taux de change concertés** dirty float; **taux de change en cours** current rate of exchange; **taux de change fixe** fixed exchange rate; **taux de change flottants** floating exchange rate; **taux de change libres** floating exchange rate; **taux de change multiple** multiple exchange rate; **taux de change à la vente** bank selling rate; **taux de chômage** unemployment level, unemployment rate;

taux de conversion conversion rate; **taux de corrélation** relative strength; **taux à court terme** short rate; **taux de couverture** cover ratio; **taux de couverture du dividende** dividend cover; **taux de crédit export** export credit rate; **taux de crédit immobilier** mortgage rate; **taux de croissance** growth rate; Compta **taux dégressif** decreasing rate; **taux de déport** backwardation rate; **taux de désintéressement** drop-dead rate; **taux directeur** intervention rate; **taux d'échange** rate of exchange, exchange rate; **taux effectif global** annual percentage rate; Banque **taux d'emprunt** borrowing rate; **taux d'épargne** savings rate; **taux d'escompte** discount or discounted rate; **taux d'escompte bancaire préférentiel** prime rate; **taux d'escompte hors banque** market rate of discount; **taux d'exclusivité à la marque** brand exclusivity rate; **taux d'expansion** growth rate; **taux d'expansion économique** economic growth rate; **taux de faveur** special rate; **taux flottant** floating rate; **taux du fret** freight rates; **taux horaire** hourly rate; **taux d'imposition** rate of taxation; **taux d'imposition effectif** Br effective or Am average tax rate; **taux d'inflation** rate of inflation, inflation rate; **taux interbancaire offert** interbank offered rate; **taux d'intérêt** interest rate, rate of interest; **taux d'intérêt à court terme** short-term interest rate; **taux d'intérêt croisé** cross-currency interest rate; **taux d'intérêt légal** official rate of interest; **taux d'intérêt à long terme** long-term interest rate; **taux d'intérêt nominal** nominal rate; **taux d'intervention** intervention rate; **le taux du jour** today's rate; **taux légal** legal rate; Fin **taux linéaire** straight-line rate; Banque **taux de liquidité** liquidity ratio; Banque **taux Lombard** Lombard rate; Bourse **taux long obligataire** long-term bond rate; **taux du marché** market rate; **taux de marge** mark-up ratio; **taux de marque** mark-up ratio; **taux marginal d'imposition** marginal tax rate; **taux maximum** top rate, maximum rate; **taux de mémorisation** recall rate; **taux minimum** bottom rate, minimum rate; Fin **taux moyen du marché monétaire** money-market rate; **taux nominal** nominal yield; **taux normal** standard rate; Mktg **taux de notoriété** (d'un produit) awareness rating; **taux officiel** official rate; Banque **taux officiel d'escompte** minimum lending rate; **taux de panne** failure rate; Mktg **taux de pénétration** (d'un marché) penetration rate; **taux plafonné** cap; Can Banque **taux préférentiel** prime rate; Banque **taux de prêt** lending rate; **taux privé** market rate; **taux de production** rate of production; **taux de profit net** net profit ratio; **taux proportionnel** (d'un crédit) annual percentage rate; **taux de réabonnement** subscription renewal rate; Fin **taux de rachat** repo rate; Mktg **taux de réachat** rebuy or repurchase rate; *Fin* **taux réduit** reduced rate; *Banque* **taux de référence** reference rate; **taux de référence interbancaire** interbank reference rate; *Mktg* **taux de refus** refusal rate; **taux de rendement** rate of return; *Fin* **taux de rendement actuariel brut** gross annual interest return; **taux de rendement courant** current yield; **taux de rendement à l'échéance** yield to maturity; *Mktg* **taux de renouvellement** rate of renewal; **taux de rentabilité** rate of return; **taux de rentabilité interne** internal rate of return; **taux de répétition** frequency rate; **taux de réponse** response rate; **taux de report** contango rate; **taux de rotation des stocks** turnover rate; **taux des salaires** wage rate; **taux standard** standard rate; **taux de TVA** VAT rate; **taux uniforme** uniform *or* flat rate; *Fin* **taux d'usure** penal rate; *Compta* **taux d'utilisation des actifs** asset utilization ratio; *Banque, Fin* **taux variable** floating *or* variable rate; **taux vert** green rate; **taux zéro** zero rating; **taxer à taux zéro** to zero-rate

(**b**) *Ordinat* rate ▫ **taux d'actualisation** refresh rate; **taux de compression** compression rate; **taux de rafraîchissement d'images** image refresh rate; **taux de transfert** transfer rate

> **"**
>
> En outre, si le prix du baril continue d'augmenter, l'inflation totale que la Banque centrale européenne (BCE) surveille pourrait approcher 3%. Ce qui devrait embarrasser l'organisme et l'obliger, selon sa propre boussole, à envisager une hausse prochaine de son **taux directeur**.
>
> **"**

taxable *adj* taxable

taxation *nf (par l'impôt)* taxation; *(contrôle)* assessment ▫ **taxation d'office** special rate of taxation; **taxation au poids** tax on weight; **taxation à la valeur** tax on value, valuation tax

taxe *nf* (**a**) *(prélèvement)* tax; **hors taxes** exclusive of tax; **toutes taxes comprises** inclusive of tax ▫ **taxe à l'achat** purchase tax; **taxe d'aéroport** airport tax; **taxe d'apprentissage** = tax paid by businesses to fund training programmes; **taxe sur le chiffre d'affaires** turnover tax; **taxe exceptionnelle** exceptional tax, special levy; **taxe à l'exportation** export duty *or* tax; **taxe foncière** property tax; **taxe à l'importation** import duty *or* tax; **taxe d'habitation** local tax; **taxe locale** local tax; **taxe de luxe** tax on luxury goods, luxury tax; *Admin* **taxe parafiscale** exceptional tax, special levy; **taxe professionnelle** = tax paid by businesses and self-employed people; **taxe sur la valeur ajoutée**, *Can* **taxe sur les ventes** *Br* value-added tax, *Am* sales tax

(**b**) *(prix)* charge, rate; *Tél* call charge ▫ **taxe forfaitaire** flat rate; **taxe postale** postal

charge; **taxe supplémentaire** surcharge

(**c**) *(prix fixé)* controlled price; **vendre des marchandises à la taxe** to sell goods at the controlled price

> **"**
>
> Cela signifie que des professeurs doivent nouer et gérer ces relations, trouver des stages, promouvoir le placement de leurs élèves : autant d'initiatives qui réclament des moyens, obtenus en prospectant des soutiens d'entreprise, notamment sous forme de **taxe d'apprentissage**, compte tenu des budgets souvent misérables des universités.
>
> **"**

taxer *vt* (**a**) *(personne, alcool, cigarettes)* to tax; **taxer qch à dix pour cent** to put a ten percent tax on sth (**b**) *(prix)* to regulate, to fix; *(salaire)* to regulate the rate of; *Tél (appel)* to charge for

taylorisme *nm Écon* Taylorism, time and motion studies

TCI *nmpl* (*abrév* **termes commerciaux internationaux**) incoterms

TCP/IP *nf Ordinat* (*abrév* **transmission control protocol/Internet protocol**) TCP-IP

technicien, -enne *nm,f* technician ▫ **technicien en informatique** computer technician

technico-commercial, -e 1 *adj (service)* technical sales; **agent technico-commercial** sales technician *or* engineer

2 *nm,f* sales technician *or* engineer

technique 1 *adj* technical; *(service)* engineering

2 *nf* technique ▫ **techniques commerciales** marketing techniques; **techniques de défense contre-OPA** defensive tactics; **techniques de gestion** management techniques; *Mktg* **techniques marchandes** merchandising techniques; *Mktg* **techniques promotionnelles** promotional techniques; *Mktg* **techniques de sondage d'opinion** opinion measurement techniques; *Mktg* **techniques de vente** sales techniques

technologie *nf* technology ▫ **technologie de l'information** information technology, IT

TEG *nm Fin* (*abrév* **taux effectif global**) APR

téléachat *nm (d'articles présentés à la télévision)* teleshopping *(where articles are offered on television and ordered by telephone or Minitel®)*; *(par l'Internet)* on-line shopping

téléassistance *nf Ordinat* remote help

Télécarte® *nf* phonecard

téléchargeable *adj Ordinat* downloadable

téléchargement *nm Ordinat* download, downloading; *(vers un serveur)* upload, uploading

télécharger *vt Ordinat* to download; *(vers un serveur)* to upload; **peut être téléchargé à partir de notre site Web** available to download from our web site

télécommunications *nfpl* telecommunications

téléconférence *nf (conférence)* conference call, teleconference; *(procédé)* teleconferencing

télécopie *nf* fax (message)

télécopier *vt* to fax

télécopieur *nm* fax (machine)

télécourtage *nm* telebroking

tel écran-tel écrit *adj Ordinat* WYSIWYG

télédémarchage *nm Mktg* telephone canvassing

téléfax® *nm* fax machine

télégestion *nf Ordinat* teleprocessing, remote processing

télégramme *nm* telegram; **envoyer un télégramme à qn** to send a telegram to sb □ *télégramme téléphoné* = telegram delivered over the phone, *Br* ≃ telemessage

télégraphe *nm* telegraph

télégraphier *vt & vi* to telegraph

téléimprimeur *nm Br* teleprinter, *Am* teletypewriter; **liaison par téléimprimeur** teleprinting

téléinformatique *nf Ordinat* teleprocessing

télémarketing *nm* telemarketing

télématique *Ordinat* **1** *adj (serveur, service, réseau)* data retrieval
2 *nf* telematics

téléphone *nm* telephone, phone; **appeler qn au téléphone, donner un coup de téléphone à qn** to telephone sb, to phone sb; **être abonné au téléphone** to be on the phone; **coup de téléphone** telephone *or* phone call □ *téléphone cellulaire* cellular phone; *téléphone Internet* Internet phone; *téléphone mobile Br* mobile phone, *Am* cellphone; *téléphone portable Br* mobile phone, *Am* cellphone; *téléphone sans fil* cordless telephone; *téléphone à touches* touch-tone telephone; *téléphone WAP* WAP phone

téléphoner *vi* to telephone, to phone; **téléphoner à qn** to telephone sb, to phone sb

téléphonie *nf* telephony □ *téléphonie sans fil* wireless telephony; *téléphonie sur l'Internet* Internet telephony; *téléphonie mobile* mobile telephony; *téléphonie portable* mobile telephony;

téléphonique *adj* telephone

téléphoniste *nmf* telephone operator, *Br* telephonist

téléréunion *nf* teleconference

téléscripteur *nm Br* teleprinter, *Am* teletypewriter

téléspectateur, -trice *nm,f* television viewer

Télétex® *nm Ordinat* teletex

télétexte *nm* teletext

télétraitement *nm Ordinat* teleprocessing, remote data processing

télétypiste *nmf* teletypist

télévendeur, -euse *nm,f* telesales person

télévente *nf* telephone selling; **téléventes** telesales

télévision *nf* television □ *télévision numérique* digital television; *télévision numérique par satellite* digital satellite television; *télévision numérique terrestre* digital terrestrial television

télex *nm* telex; **envoyer un télex à qn** to send sb a telex; **envoyer qch par télex** to send sth by telex, to telex sth

télexer *vt* to send by telex, to telex

télexiste *nmf* telex operator

Telnet *nm Ordinat* Telnet

tel-tel *nm Ordinat* WYSIWYG

témoignage *nm* **(a)** *Jur* testimony **(b)** *Mktg (publicité)* testimonial advertising

TEMPÉ *nm Fin (abrév* **Taux Moyen Pondéré en Euros)** EONIA

tempérament *nm* **à tempérament** on hire purchase, *Am* on the installment plan; **acheter qch à tempérament** to buy sth on hire purchase *or Am* on the installment plan

temporaire *adj (mesures, personnel, travail)* temporary

temps *nm* time; **à plein temps, à temps complet** *(emploi, travail)* full-time; **travailler à plein temps** *ou* **à temps complet** to work full time; **à temps partiel, à mi-temps** *(emploi, travail)* part-time; **travailler à temps partiel** *ou* **à mi-temps** to work part time □ *Ordinat* **temps d'accès** access time; *Ordinat* **temps d'accès disque** disk access time; **temps d'arrêt** down time, idle time; **temps improductif** down time, idle time; **temps mort** down time, idle time; *Ordinat* **temps réel** real time; *Ordinat* **temps de réponse** response time; *Ordinat* **temps de traitement** processing time

tendance *nf* tendency, trend □ *tendance ascensionnelle* upward trend; *tendance à la baisse* downward trend *or* tendency, downtrend; *Bourse* bearish tendency; *tendances conjoncturelles* economic trends; *tendances de la consommation* consumer trends; *tendance de croissance* growth trend; *tendance économique* economic trend; *tendance géné-*

rale general trend *or* tendency; **tendance à la hausse** upward trend *or* tendency; *Bourse* bullish tendency; **tendance du marché** market trend

tendu, -e *adj Bourse (cours)* steady, firm

teneur¹ *nf* (**a**) *(d'un document, d'un discours)* content; *(d'un contrat)* terms (**b**) *(quantité)* content; **teneur en or** gold content

teneur², -euse *nm,f* **teneur de livres** bookkeeper; **teneur de marché** market maker

tenir *vt* (**a**) *(s'occuper de)* to keep; **tenir la caisse** to be in charge of the cash; **tenir la comptabilité** *ou* **les livres** to keep the accounts *or* the books (**b**) *Fin* **tenir qch à bail** to hold a lease on sth

tenu, -e *adj Bourse (cours)* steady, firm

tenue *nf* (**a**) *(d'une assemblée)* sitting, session; **pendant la tenue du conseil** during the council meeting (**b**) *Bourse (des cours)* steadiness, firmness; *(du marché)* state (**c**) *(fait d'administrer)* *Compta* **tenue de caisse** petty cash management; **tenue des comptes, tenue des livres** bookkeeping; **tenue des stocks** stock keeping

terme *nm* (**a**) *Fin* **à court terme** *(effet)* short-dated; *(emprunt, placement, crédit)* short-term; *(argent)* at short notice, at call; **à long terme** *(effet)* long-dated; *(emprunt, placement, crédit)* long-term; **à terme fixe** fixed-term; **arriver à terme** *(plan d'épargne)* to reach fruition ▫ **terme d'échéance** tenor
(**b**) *Bourse* settlement; **à terme** *(compte, cours, livraison, marché)* forward; **livrable à terme** for forward delivery; **acheter à terme** to buy forward; **vendre à terme** to sell forward; **placer de l'argent à terme** to invest in futures
(**c**) *(versement)* instalment; **acheter à terme** to buy on credit; **payable en deux termes** payable in two instalments
(**d**) *(loyer)* quarter's rent; *(date de paiement d'un loyer)* rent day
(**e**) **termes** *(d'un accord, d'un contrat)* terms; **aux termes de l'article 12** in accordance with the terms of article 12, under article 12 ▫ **termes commerciaux internationaux** incoterms; **termes d'échange** terms of exchange; **termes de paiement** terms of payment

terminal *nm* (**a**) *Ordinat* terminal, VDU ▫ **terminal distant** remote terminal; **terminal électronique de paiement** electronic payment terminal; **terminal éloigné** remote terminal; **terminal intelligent** smart terminal; **terminal de paiement connecté** on-line cash desk terminal; **terminal de paiement en ligne** on-line cash desk terminal; **terminal point de vente** point-of-sale terminal (**b**) *(dans un aéroport)* terminal

terminateur *nm Ordinat* terminator

terminer 1 *vt (discours, réunion)* to end, to close (**par** with)

2 *vi (actions)* to close
3 se terminer *vpr* to end, to come to an end

terrain *nm* (**a**) *(terre)* piece *or* plot of ground ▫ **terrain à bâtir** building plot; **terrain à lotir** development site (**b**) **perdre du terrain** *(monnaie, entreprise)* to lose ground; **gagner du terrain** *(monnaie, entreprise)* to gain ground; **l'entreprise regagne du terrain sur le marché français** the company is making up lost ground on the French market (**c**) *Mktg (lieux d'étude)* field; **sur le terrain** in the field

> **"**
> Assis sur 30 milliards de dollars de cash, le leader mondial du logiciel aligne d'excellents résultats et déclenche, cet automne, un tir groupé de nouveautés : une version améliorée de son logiciel pour agendas électroniques (Pocket PC, qui **gagne du terrain** sur le Palm), un téléphone mobile intelligent (Stinger, en phase d'expérimentation), et sa console de jeu Xbox, annoncée pour novembre aux Etats-Unis et mars en Europe.
> **"**

terre *nf (propriété)* **une terre** a piece of land; **des terres** land ▫ **terres en non-valeur** unproductive land

territoire *nm (d'un représentant)* territory ▫ **territoire exclusif** exclusive territory; **territoire de vente** sales territory

tertiaire *Écon* **1** *adj (secteur)* tertiary
2 *nm* tertiary *or* service sector

tertiairisation, tertiarisation *nf Écon* tertiarization, growth of the tertiary *or* service sector

> **"**
> En dix ans, ce sont les effectifs des professions intermédiaires qui ont le plus progressé. Une population cadre en forte croissance à l'ouest, poursuite de la **tertiarisation** du Sud-Est et régression du nombre d'ouvriers dans presque toutes les régions : telles sont quelques-unes des grandes évolutions observées par l'Insee entre les deux recensements de 1990 et 1999.
> **"**

test 1 *adj (zone, département)* test; *(période)* trial
2 *nm Mktg* test ▫ **test d'acceptabilité** acceptance test; **test d'aperception thématique** thematic apperception test; **test en aveugle** blind product test; **tests auprès des consommateurs** consumer testing; **test comparatif** comparison test; **test de concept** concept test; **test du lendemain** day-after recall test; **test de marché** market test; **test de mémorisation** memory *or* recall test; **test monadique** monadic test; **test de performance** performance

test; **test de performance du produit** product performance test; **test sur place** field test; **test de préférence** preference test; **test de produit** product test; **test de rappel** recall test; **test de reconnaissance** recognition test; **test de vente** market test

testament nm will; **faire un testament** to make a will

tester vt Mktg to test; **tester qch sur le marché** to test-market sth

tête nf head; **par tête** per capita, per head; **être à la tête de qch** (à la direction de) to be in charge or at the head of sth ▫ **tête de gondole** aisle end display, gondola end; Ordinat **tête d'impression** print head; Ordinat **tête de lecture-écriture** read-write head

texte nm text ▫ Ordinat **texte ASCII** ASCII text; **texte de départ** source text; **texte publicitaire** advertising copy

texteur nm Ordinat word or text processor

texto nm Fam Tél text message

TG nf (abrév **tête de gondole**) aisle end display, gondola end

théorie nf theory ▫ Compta **théorie de la contingence** contingency theory; Mktg **théorie de la décision** decision theory; **théorie de la gestion de l'entreprise** management theory; **théorie de l'information** information theory; Mktg **théorie des jeux** game theory; Écon **théorie quantitative** quantity theory

théorique adj (profits) paper

thésaurisation nf Écon building up of capital; (par des particuliers) hoarding

thésauriser vi Écon to build up capital; (particuliers) to hoard money

> En France, vu le très bas niveau des remboursements de la Sécurité sociale, le non-accès à une complémentaire maladie est un facteur structurel de l'exclusion. D'où notre proposition de créer un fonds de mutualisation nationale géré par l'ensemble du mouvement mutualiste français. Aujourd'hui, on pousse les mutuelles à **thésauriser** une à une. Elles détiennent 50 milliards de francs de réserve.

TIBEUR nm Fin (abrév **Taux Interbancaire Européen**) EURIBOR

ticket nm ticket ▫ **ticket de caisse** Br till receipt, Am sales slip; **ticket d'entrée** = cost of entering the market

ticket-repas, ticket-restaurant nm Br luncheon voucher, Am meal ticket

tiers, tierce 1 adj third ▫ **tiers bénéficiaire** (d'un chèque, d'un effet) beneficiary; **tierce cau-**

tion contingent liability; **tierce détenteur** third-party holder; Ordinat **tierce partie de confiance** trusted third party; **tierce personne** third person or party; **tierce porteur** second endorser; **tiers possesseur** third-party owner; **tiers souscripteur** third-party subscriber

   2 nm (**a**) (individu) third party (**b**) Fin (impôt) interim tax payment (equal to one third of tax paid in the previous year)

tiers-monde nm le tiers-monde the Third World

tiers-saisi nm Jur garnishee

timbre nm (**a**) (pour le courrier) (postage) stamp (**b**) (marque) stamp ▫ **timbre fiscal** revenue stamp; **timbre de quittance** receipt stamp (**c**) (instrument encreur) stamp ▫ **timbre dateur** date stamp

timbre-poste nm postage stamp

timbrer vt to put a stamp/stamps on

TIOP nm Banque (abrév **taux interbancaire offert à Paris**) PIBOR

TIP nm Banque (abrév **titre interbancaire de paiement**) bank giro transfer

TIR nm (abrév **transport international routier**) TIR

tirage nm (**a**) Banque, Fin (d'un chèque, d'une lettre de change) drawing, emission; (d'un prêt) drawdown ▫ **tirage en l'air, tirage en blanc** kite flying, kiting (**b**) (de loterie) draw (**de** for); **les obligations sont rachetées par voie de tirage** debentures are redeemed by lot ▫ **tirage au sort** drawing lots (**c**) (d'un journal) circulation; **un tirage de 50 000** circulation figures or a circulation of 50 000; **à fort tirage** with large circulation figures (**d**) Ordinat hard copy

tiré, -e nm,f Banque, Fin (d'un chèque, d'une lettre de change) drawee

tirer Banque, Fin **1** vt (chèque, lettre de change) to draw (**sur** on); **avez-vous tiré des chèques depuis cette date?** have you written any cheques since then?; **ce chèque a-t-il déjà été tiré?** has this cheque cleared yet?

   2 vi **tirer à découvert** to overdraw; **tirer à vue** to draw at sight

tiret nm (de dialogue) dash; (en fin de ligne) rule; (trait d'union) hyphen

tireur, -euse nm,f Banque, Fin (d'un chèque, d'une lettre de change) drawer ▫ **tireur en l'air** kite flyer; **tireur à découvert** kite flyer

tiroir-caisse nm till, cash register

titre nm (**a**) Bourse, Fin (valeur) security; (certificat) certificate; **titres** stocks and shares, securities, Am stock; **prendre livraison de titres** to take delivery of stock; **vendre des titres** to sell stock ▫ **titre d'action** share certificate; **titre commercial** commercial bill; **titre de créance** loan note, debt instrument; **titre de**

crédit proof of credit; **titres déposés en nantissement** securities lodged as collateral; **titres détenus en garantie** stocks held as security; **titres dilués** watered stock; **titres émis** issued securities; **titres fiduciaires** paper securities; **titres flottants** shares available on the market; **titres libérés** fully paid-up securities; **titres longs** long-dated securities, longs; **titre à lots** lottery loan bond; **titres négociables** negotiable stock; **titre nominatif** registered security; **titre d'obligation** loan or bond note; **titre de paiement** document of payment; **le titre de paiement doit être envoyé à…** remittance by cheque or money order to be sent to…; **titre participatif, titre de participation** equity investment or loan; **titres de placement** marketable securities; **titres en portefeuille** securities (in portfolio); **titre au porteur** bearer bond, negotiable instrument; **titre de prêt** loan certificate; **titre provisoire** scrip certificate; **titres ramassés** takeover stock; **titre de rente** government bond; **titres à revenu fixe** fixed-rate securities; **titres à revenu variable** floating-rate securities; **titre sous-jacent** underlying security; **titres subordonnés à durée indéterminée** subordinated perpetuals; **titres en suspens** fungible securities; **titres à terme** futures; **titre universel de paiement** (joint à la facture) payment form, universal payment order (**b**) **à titre de** by way of; **à titre d'essai** on approval; **à titre gratuit** free (of charge); Jur **à titre onéreux** subject to payment, for a consideration; **à titre provisoire** provisionally (**c**) Jur title □ **titre (constitutif) de propriété** title deed (**d**) (d'une personne) title □ **titre de civilité** (dans une lettre) salutation

titrisation nf Bourse, Fin securitization

titulaire 1 adj Admin (fonctionnaire) with a permanent contract **2** nmf (**a**) (d'un droit, d'un titre, d'un certificat, d'un compte, d'une carte) holder; (d'un passeport) holder, bearer □ **titulaire d'action** shareholder (**b**) (d'un poste) incumbent

titularisation nf Admin (d'un fonctionnaire) granting of a permanent contract; **en stage de titularisation** on probation

titulariser vt Admin **titulariser qn** to grant sb a permanent contract

TJJ nm Fin (abrév **taux d'argent au jour le jour**) overnight rate

TMM nm (abrév **taux moyen du marché monétaire**) money-market rate

Toile nf Ordinat **la Toile** the Web

tolérance nf Douanes **tolérance (permise)** tolerance, allowance

tomber vi (**a**) (prix, valeurs) to fall, to drop (**b**) **tomber en panne** (ordinateur) to crash

tonalité nf Tél Br dialling or Am dial tone □ **tonalité d'appel** ringing tone, ringtone

toner nm toner

tonnage nm tonnage □ **tonnage de jauge** registered tonnage; **tonnage net** registered tonnage

tonne nf metric ton, tonne □ **tonne d'affrètement** freight ton; **tonne courte** short ton; **tonne métrique** metric ton

tort nm (dommage) wrong; **la livre forte fait du tort aux exportateurs britanniques** the strong pound is harming British exporters

total, -e 1 adj total **2** nm total; **le total des recettes et des dépenses** total revenue and expenditure; **faire le total des bénéfices** to add up the profits, to calculate the total profit; **le total s'élève à 10 000 euros** the total comes to 10,000 euros □ **total de l'actif** total assets; **total global** grand total; **total du passif** total liabilities; **total à payer** total payable

totaliser vt (**a**) (additionner) to total up, to add up (**b**) (avoir au total) to have a total of

totalité nf **la totalité de** all of; **l'entreprise exporte la totalité de sa production** the company exports its entire production; **payer qch en totalité** to pay sth in full

touchable adj (chèque) that can be cashed; (effet) collectable

touche nf Ordinat (de clavier) key □ **touche d'aide** help key; **touche d'alimentation** power-on key; **touche alt** alt key; **touche d'arrêt de défilement, touche Arrêt défil** scroll lock key; **touche à bascule** toggle key; **touche contrôle** control key; **touche de curseur** cursor key; **touche début** home key; **touche de défilement** scroll key; **touche de déplacement du curseur** cursor movement key; **touche de déplacement vers le bas** down arrow key; **touche de déplacement vers la droite** right arrow key; **touche de déplacement vers le haut** up arrow key; **touche de direction** arrow key;

touche Echap esc key; *touche d'échappement* escape key; *touche d'effacement* delete key; *touche d'effacement arrière* backspace key; *touche (d')entrée* enter key; *touche d'espacement arrière* backspace key; *touche fin* end key; *touche fléchée, touche (à) flèche* arrow key; *touche flèche vers le bas* down arrow key; *touche flèche vers la droite* right arrow key; *touche flèche vers la gauche* left arrow key; *touche flèche vers le haut* up arrow key; *touche (de) fonction* function key; *touche Impr écran* print screen key; *touche d'insertion* insert key; *touche d'interruption* break key; *touche majuscule* shift key; *touche des majuscules* shift key; *touche multifonction* multifunctional key; *touche numérique* number key; *touche page précédente* page up key; *touche page suivante* page down key; *touche Pause* pause key; *touche personnalisée* hot key; *touche de raccourci* shortcut key; *touche de répétition* repeat-action key; *touche retour* return or enter key; *touche de retour arrière* backspace key; *touche de tabulation* tab key; *touche de verrouillage du clavier numérique* num lock key; *touche du verrouillage des majuscules* caps lock key

toucher *vt* (salaire) to get, to draw; (chèque) to cash; (intérêts, pot-de-vin) to receive, to get; (traite) to collect

tour¹ *nm* (a) *Banque, Fin* **tour de table** pool, backers (b) **à tour de rôle** in turn, by rotation

tour² *nf Ordinat* tower

tourisme *nm* tourism ❑ *tourisme vert* green tourism

tournée de présentation *nf Mktg* road show

tourner *vi Ordinat* **ce logiciel tourne sous DOS** this software runs on DOS; **faire tourner un programme** to run a program

tourniquet *nm Mktg* (présentoir) stand, spinner

tour-opérateur *nm* tour operator

TPC *nf Ordinat* (abrév **tierce partie de confiance**) TTP

TPV *nm* (abrév **terminal point de vente**) point-of-sale terminal

traceur *nm Ordinat* plotter

trackball *nm ou nf Ordinat* trackball

tract *nm* leaflet

trade marketing *nm* trade marketing

trader *nm* trader

traducteur, -trice 1 *nm,f* translator 2 *nm Ordinat* translator

traduction *nf* translation (**de/en** from/into) ❑ *traduction assistée par ordinateur* computer-assisted translation, machine translation;

traduction automatique machine translation; *traduction simultanée* simultaneous translation

traduire 1 *vt* (a) (texte, terme) to translate (**de/en** from/into) (b) *Ordinat* to translate 2 **se traduire** *vpr* **se traduire par qch** (avoir pour résultat) to result in sth; **le ralentissement de l'activité économique s'est traduit par de nombreux licenciements** the slowdown in economic activity brought about numerous redundancies

trafic *nm* (a) (activité illégale) trafficking ❑ *Jur trafic d'influence* influence peddling (b) (circulation) traffic ❑ *trafic aérien* air traffic; *Ordinat trafic de réseau* network traffic; *trafic routier* road traffic

traficoter *vi Fam* to be on the fiddle, to be involved in shady dealing

> Hier, on a eu droit à la confirmation que sa filiale Ecopia avait obtenu $21 millions en placement privés, et que son entrée en bourse pourrait se faire bientôt, de même que la redistribution des quotes-parts aux actionnaires de TH. Je me demande si les zinzins **traficotent** pas un peu actuellement avec le titre de façon à ce que le déblocage coïncide avec l'exercice des attributions supplémentaires sur les 366,900 actions auxquels les preneurs fermes ont droit suite au dernier financement.

trafiquant, -e *nm,f* trafficker

trafiquer *vt* to traffic in

train *nm* (a) (pour le transport) train ❑ *train de marchandises* goods or freight train; *train mixte* passenger and goods train (b) (ensemble) set, package; **un train de mesures économiques/fiscales** a set or package of economic/tax measures ❑ *train de propositions* package deal (c) (niveau) *train de vie* standard of living

trait d'union *nm* hyphen

traite *nf Fin* (lettre de change) (banker's) draft, bill (of exchange); **encaisser une traite** to collect a bill; **escompter une traite** to discount a bill; **présenter une traite à l'acceptation** to present a bill for acceptance; **tirer une traite** to draw a bill ❑ *traite contre acceptation* acceptance bill; *traite en l'air* fictitious bill, kite; *traite avalisée* guaranteed bill; *traite bancaire* bank draft; *traite de complaisance* accommodation bill; *traite à courte échéance* short-dated bill; *traite à date fixe* time bill; *traite documentaire* documentary bill; *traite domiciliée* domiciled bill; *traite sur l'étranger, traite sur l'extérieur* foreign bill; *traite sur l'intérieur* inland bill; *traite libre* clean bill; *traite à longue échéance* long-dated bill; *traite de plaisance* accommodation bill; **traite pro forma** pro forma bill; **traite 'sans frais'** bill 'without protest'; **traite à terme** term draft, time draft; **traite à vue** sight draft

traité *nm (accord)* treaty ❏ *Assur* **traité facultatif obligatoire** open cover

traitement *nm* (**a**) *Ordinat* processing ❏ **traitement automatique des données** automatic data processing; **traitement des données** data processing; **traitement électronique de l'information** electronic data processing; **traitement d'images** image processing; **traitement de l'information** data processing; **traitement par lots** batch processing; **traitement séquentiel** sequentiel processing; **traitement de textes** word processing; *(logiciel)* word processor, word processing software; **réaliser qch par traitement de texte** to word process sth (**b**) *(rémunération des fonctionnaires)* pay, salary; **sans traitement** *(secrétaire)* honorary; *(magistrat)* unsalaried ❏ **traitement de base** basic pay *or* salary; **traitement fixe** fixed salary; **traitement initial** starting salary (**c**) *(d'une commande, d'une plainte, d'une demande)* processing (**d**) *(de matières premières)* processing

traiter **1** *vt* (**a**) *Ordinat* to process (**b**) *(commande, plainte, demande)* to process, to handle (**c**) *(matières premières)* to process **2** *vi* **traiter avec qn** to deal with sb; *(créancier)* to negotiate with sb

tranche *nf (de chiffres)* group, block; *(d'actions)* block, tranche; *(d'un crédit, d'un emprunt)* instalment; *(d'assistance financière internationale)* tranche; *(d'un programme immobilier)* stage, portion; *Admin* **par tranche de 1000 euros ou fraction de 1000 euros** for every complete sum of 1,000 euros or part thereof ❏ **tranche d'âge** *(dans une étude de marché)* age group; **tranche d'imposition** tax bracket; **tranche de revenus** income bracket; **tranche de salaire** income bracket

> ❝
> Et, malgré cela, il perdra près de 70% de son pouvoir d'achat avec une pension de 2195 euros par mois. Pour maintenir son train de vie, il n'a que deux possibilités. La première, c'est de demander à sa caisse de retraite de cotiser dans la **tranche de revenus** immédiatement supérieure. Si, comme le lui permet sa caisse, la Cipav, il verse ainsi 1200 euros de plus chaque mois, il pourra espérer obtenir, en 2030, un complément de 310 euros par mois sur sa retraite.
> ❞

tranquille *adj (marché)* quiet

transaction *nf (opération)* transaction, deal; **transactions** transactions, dealings ❏ **transac-**

tion **bancaire** bank transaction; **transaction boursière** Stock Exchange transaction; *Banque* **transaction par carte** card transaction; *Bourse* **transaction de clôture** closing transaction; **transaction commerciale** business transaction; *Bourse* **transaction au comptant** spot *or* cash transaction; **transaction à crédit** credit transaction; **transactions intersociétés** intercompany transactions; *Bourse* **transactions à terme** futures

transbordement *nm* transshipment

transborder *vt* to transship

transcription *nf (texte)* transcript

transcrire *vt (recopier)* to transcribe; *Compta* **transcrire le journal au grand-livre** to transfer journal entries into the ledger

transférable *adj* transferable, negotiable

transférer *vt* (**a**) *(argent, actions, effets)* to transfer; **transférer un billet par voie d'endossement** to transfer a bill by endorsement; **il a transféré son argent sur un compte suisse** he's transferred his money into a Swiss account (**b**) *Ordinat (données)* to transfer

transfert *nm* (**a**) *(d'argent, d'actions, d'effets)* transfer ❏ *Tél* **transfert d'appel automatique** automatic call transfer; *Banque* **transfert par CCP** giro transfer; *Compta* **transfert de charges** transfer of charges; *Compta* **transfert de compte à compte** book entry transfer; *Compta* **transfert de créances** assignment of accounts receivable *or* of debts; **transfert de devises** currency transfer, foreign exchange transfer; *Banque* **transfert télégraphique** telegraphic transfer (**b**) *Ordinat (de données)* transfer ❏ **transfert électronique de fonds** electronic funds transfer; **transfert de fichiers** file transfer; **transfert de fonds électronique** electronic funds transfer, EFT; **transfert de fonds électronique au point de vente** electronic funds transfer at point of sale, EFTPOS

transfert-paiement *nm Fin* transfer of account *(from one savings bank to another)*

transformation *nf (de matières premières)* processing

transformer *vt (matières premières)* to process

transiger *vi* to compromise, to come to an arrangement (**avec** with); **transiger avec ses créanciers** to come to terms with one's creditors

transit *nm* transit; **en transit** *(marchandises, passagers)* in transit ❏ **transit communautaire** community transit; **transit douanier** customs transit

transitaire **1** *adj* transit **2** *nmf* forwarding agent, transport agent

transiter **1** *vt (marchandises)* to forward **2** *vi (marchandises, voyageurs)* to pass in transit (**par** through)

translation *nf Jur (de propriété)* conveyancing

transmettre *vt Jur (propriété)* to transfer, to convey; *(actions, brevet)* to assign

transmissible *adj* (**a**) *Jur (propriété)* transferable; *(actions, brevet)* assignable (**b**) *Fin* **transmissible par endossement** transferable by endorsement

transmission *nf* (**a**) *Ordinat (de données)* transfer, transmission □ **transmission par modem** modem transmission (**b**) *Jur (de propriété)* transfer, conveyance; *(d'actions, d'un brevet)* assignment (**c**) *Fin* **transmission par endossement** transfer by endorsement

transpalette *nf* pallet truck

transport *nm* (**a**) *(de marchandises, de passagers)* transport; **cela permet d'effectuer les transports urgents par avion** this enables urgent freight to be sent by air □ **transport aérien** air transport, airfreight; **les transports aériens** (the) airlines; **transports en commun** public transport; **transport ferroviaire** rail transport; **transport maritime** transport by sea, shipping; **transports routiers** road transport *or* haulage; **transport terrestre** surface transport; **transport urbain** urban transport
(**b**) *Jur (de droits)* transfer
(**c**) *Banque (de fonds)* transfer *(from one account to another)*
(**d**) *Compta* transfer

transport-cession *nm Jur* transfer, conveyance

transporter *vt* (**a**) *(marchandises)* to transport; **transporter qch par avion/par mer** to transport sth by air/by sea; **transporter par route/par chemin de fer** to transport by road/by rail (**b**) *Jur (droits)* to transfer, to assign (**c**) *Banque (fonds)* to transfer *(from one account to another)* (**d**) *Compta* to transfer

transporteur *nm* carrier, forwarding agent

travail *nm* (**a**) *(activité)* work □ **travail de bureau** office work, clerical work; **travail à la chaîne** assembly line work, production line work; **travail complémentaire** follow-up work; **travail en cours** work in progress; **travail à domicile** work done at home; **travail à l'entreprise** contract work, work by *or* on contract; **travail par équipes** shift work; **travail d'équipe** teamwork; **travail en équipe** shift work; **travail à façon** job work; **travail à forfait** fixed-price work; **travail à l'heure** time work; **travail à la machine** machine work; **travail manuel** manual labour, manual work; **travail (au) noir** moonlighting; **travail de nuit** night work; **travail à la pièce, travail aux pièces** piece work; **travail à plein temps** full-time work; **travail posté** shift work; **travail de secrétaire** secretarial work; **travail à la tâche** piecework; *(intermittent)* jobbing (work); **tra-**

vail au ralenti go-slow; **travaux de recherche** research work; **travail par roulement** shift work; **travail en sous-traitance** contract work; *Ordinat* **travail en temps partagé** time sharing; **travail à temps partiel** part-time work; **travaux sur le terrain** fieldwork
(**b**) *(emploi)* employment, job; **être sans travail** to be out of work, to be unemployed
(**c**) *(lieu)* work; **il est à son travail** he's at work
(**d**) *(tâche)* piece of work, job; **entreprendre un travail** to undertake a piece of work, to take on a job
(**e**) **travaux** *(réparations)* work; *(sur panneau)* work in progress □ **travaux publics** *(secteur)* public works

travailler *vi* (**a**) *(effectuer une tâche)* to work; **travailler à son compte** to work for oneself, to be self-employed; **travailler à la pièce** to do piecework; **travailler au ralenti** to go slow; **travailler à la tâche** to do piecework; **travailler à temps partiel** to work part time, to have a part-time job (**b**) *(fructifier)* **faire travailler son argent** to make one's money work for one

travailleur, -euse *nm,f* worker □ **travailleur à domicile** home worker; **travailleur indépendant** self-employed person; **travailleur manuel** manual worker; **travailleur à mi-temps** part-time worker; **travailleur occasionnel** casual worker; **travailleur à la pièce** pieceworker; **travailleur à plein temps** full-time worker; **travailleur posté** shiftworker; **travailleur à la tâche** pieceworker; **travailleur à temps partiel** part-time worker

treizième mois *nm* = extra month's salary paid as an annual bonus

trente-cinq heures *nfpl* **les trente-cinq heures** 35-hour working week in France, introduced by the government of Lionel Jospin in 1998 and phased in from 2000 onwards

> **❝**
> Les **35 heures**, officiellement étendues à l'ensemble des entreprises au 1er janvier 2002, ont déjà révélé l'essentiel de leur effet emploi, surtout dans les grandes entreprises.
> **❞**

trésor *nm* treasury; **le Trésor (public)** *(institution)* = department dealing with the State budget, *Br* ≃ the Treasury, *Am* ≃ the Treasury Department; *(finances publiques)* public funds *or* finances

trésorerie *nf* (**a**) *(fonction de trésorier)* treasurership (**b**) *(bureau) (gouvernemental)* public revenue office; *(d'une entreprise)* accounts department (**c**) *(ressources)* funds, finances; **avoir des problèmes de trésorerie** to have cash flow problems (**d**) *(gestion)* accounts

trésorier, -ère *nm,f* treasurer □ **trésorier de banque** bank treasurer

tri nm (**a**) *(de candidats)* selection, screening; *(de courrier)* sorting (**b**) *Ordinat* sort; **effectuer un tri** to do a sort ◻ *tri alphabétique* alphasort; *tri en ordre croissant* ascending sort; *tri en ordre décroissant* descending sort

tri-bande *adj Tél* tri-band

tribunal nm court ◻ *tribunal arbitral* arbitration court; *tribunal de commerce* commercial tribunal *or* court; *tribunal d'instance* ≃ magistrates' court

trier 1 vt (**a**) *(candidats)* to select, to screen; *(courrier)* to sort; **trier qn/qch sur le volet** to hand-pick sb/sth (**b**) *Ordinat* to sort; **trier par ordre alphabétique** to sort in alphabetical order, to alphasort
   2 se trier vpr *(fichier, données)* to sort

trieuse nf *Ordinat* sorter; *(logiciel)* sort program

trimestre nm (**a**) *(période)* quarter, three months; **par trimestre** quarterly (**b**) *(salaire)* quarter's salary; *(loyer)* quarter's rent

trimestriel, -elle adj quarterly

trimestriellement adv quarterly, every three months

triple adj triple; **en triple exemplaire** in triplicate

tripotage nm *Fam* scam, *Br* fiddle

troc nm barter; **faire du troc** to barter

3G nf *Tél (abrév* **troisième génération**) 3G

trois-huit nmpl **les trois-huit** = shift system based on three eight-hour shifts; **ils font les trois-huit** they work eight-hour shifts

❝

De nombreuses entreprises ont recours aux CAT afin de réduire leurs coûts, pour un délai semblable à n'importe quel sous-traitant. De fait, il arrive que les cadences des chaînes de production soient telles qu'elles ne puissent être suivies par certains ouvriers, ce qu'ils vivent comme un échec. Il arrive de plus en plus souvent qu'on aboutisse au départ en stage de l'ouvrier, pour cause de manque de productivité, vers une structure aux rythmes plus souples. Certains CAT, qui fonctionnent à flux tendu, pratiquent même les **trois-huit**.
❞

trombone nm *(agrafe)* paper clip

trop-perçu nm *Fin (d'impôts)* excess payment; **rembourser le trop-perçu** to refund the excess payment

troquer vt to exchange, to barter

trouver vt *Ordinat* **trouver et remplacer** to find and replace

trust nm *Fin* trust; **un trust de l'acier/du pétrole** a steel/an oil cartel ◻ *trust commercial* commercial monopoly; *trust industriel* industrial monopoly; *trust de placement* investment trust; *trust de valeurs* holding company; *trust vertical* vertical trust

truster *Fin* **1** vt to monopolize, to form into a monopoly
   2 vi to form a monopoly

trusteur nm *Fin* organizer *or* administrator of a trust

TTC *(abrév* **toutes taxes comprises**) inclusive of tax, tax inclusive

tuyau nm *Fam (information)* tip ◻ *tuyau de Bourse* Stock Exchange tip

TVA nf *(abrév* **taxe sur la valeur ajoutée**) *Br* VAT, *Am* sales tax; **soumis à la TVA** subject to *Br* VAT *or Am* sales tax ◻ *Compta* **TVA encaissée** output tax; *Compta* **TVA récupérée** input tax

type 1 adj **échantillon type** representative sample; **lettre type** standard letter
   2 nm *(sorte)* type

Uu

UAS *nf* (*abrév* **unité d'activité stratégique**) SBU

UE *nf* (*abrév* **Union européenne**) EU

UEM *nf* (*abrév* **union économique et monétaire**) EMU

ultérieur, -e *adj* (*date*) later; (*commandes*) further

ultracompétitif, -ive *adj* very highly competitive

ultraportatif *nm Ordinat* palmtop

UME *nf* (*abrév* **union monétaire européenne**) EMU

UMTS *nm Tél* (*abrév* **Universal Mobile Telecommunications Services**) UMTS

unanime *adj* (*vote, consentement*) unanimous

unidirectionnel, -elle *adj Tél* simplex

unification *nf* (**a**) *Fin* (*des crédits*) consolidation (**b**) (*fusion des entreprises*) merger

unifié, -e *adj Fin* (*crédits*) consolidated

unifier *vt Fin* (*crédits*) to consolidate

uniforme *adj* uniform, across-the-board

unilatéral, -e *adj* (*contrat*) unilateral

union *nf* (**a**) (*association*) union, association ◻ **Union des annonceurs** = organization which defends the interests of advertisers; **union douanière** customs union; **union économique** economic union; **union économique et monétaire** Economic and Monetary Union; **l'Union européenne** the European Union; **union monétaire européenne** European monetary union (**b**) *Jur* **union des créanciers** = agreement on the part of creditors to take concerted action in bankruptcy proceedings

unique *adj* sole, single

unitaire *adj* (*prix, coût*) unit

unité *nf* (**a**) (*article*) unit; **actions émises en unités** shares issued in ones; **la production a dépassé les 3000 unités** production has passed the 3,000-unit mark; **acheter/vendre qch à l'unité** to buy/sell sth individually *or* singly (**b**) (*département*) unit ◻ **unité d'activité stratégique** strategic business unit; **unité administrative** administrative unit; **unité de fabrication** factory unit; **unité de prise de décision(s)** decision-making unit; **unité de** *Mktg* **production** production unit (**c**) *Ordinat* unit, module ◻ **unité d'affichage** display unit; **unité arithmétique et logique** ALU, arithmetic logic unit; **unité de bande** tape unit; **unité centrale** central processing unit; (*de disque*) drive; **unité de destination** destination drive; **unité de disque** disk drive; **unité de disque dur** hard drive; **unité de disquettes** floppy (disk) drive; **unité externe** external drive *or* unit; **unité interne** internal drive *or* unit; **unité périphérique** peripheral device *or* unit; **unité de sauvegarde** backup device; **unité de sauvegarde sur bande** tape backup unit; **unité de sortie** output device; **unité de stockage** storage device; **unité de traitement de texte** text processor; **unité de visualisation** display unit (**d**) (*étalon*) unit ◻ *Écon* **unité de compte** unit of account; *UE* **unité de compte européenne** European currency unit; **unité de consommation** unit of consumption; **unité de coût** cost unit; **unité monétaire** monetary unit, unit of currency; *UE* **unité monétaire européenne** European currency unit; **unité de poids** unit of weight; **unité de production** unit of production; *Bourse* **unité de transaction** lot size; **unité de travail** unit of labour, man-work unit

univers *nm* (*nombre de personnes dans un groupe, ou un segment*) universe

> **"**
>
> Certes, le consommateur achète rarement des draps et des serviettes le même jour, mais les fournisseurs – communs aux deux **univers** – conçoivent leurs collections de lit et de salle de bains autour des mêmes thèmes.
>
> **"**

UNIX *nm Ordinat* Unix; **basé sur UNIX** Unix-based

urbanisme *nm* town planning

urbaniste *nmf* town planner

urgence *nf* **d'urgence** immediately; **veuillez répondre d'urgence** please reply without delay *or* immediately

urgent, -e *adj* urgent

URL *nf Ordinat* (*abrév* **uniform resource locator**) URL

URSSAF *nf* (*abrév* **Union de recouvrement des**

cotisations de Sécurité sociale et d'Alloca-tions familiales) = organization which collects social security and family allowance payments

usage *nm* (**a**) *(utilisation)* use; **à usages multiples** multi-purpose; **locaux à usage commercial** business *or* commercial premises (**b**) *Jur* **avoir l'usage de qch** to have the right to sth (**c**) *(coutume)* custom, practice; **je peux vous fournir les références d'usage** I can supply you with the usual references; **suivant les usages bancaires** according to normal banking practice

usagé, -e *adj* used

usager *nm* user

usance *nf* usance; **à deux usances** at double usance; **à usance de trente jours** at thirty days' usance

Usenet *nm Ordinat* Usenet

usinage *nm* (**a**) *(fabrication industrielle)* manufacturing (**b**) *(à la machine-outil)* machining, tooling

usine *nf* factory, plant; **travailler en usine** to work in a factory ❑ *usine d'assemblage* assembly plant; *usine d'automobiles* car factory; *usine modèle* model factory

usine-pilote *nf* pilot factory

usiner *vt* (**a**) *(fabriquer)* to manufacture (**b**) *(à la machine-outil)* to machine, to tool

usufruit *nm Jur* usufruct

usufruitier, -ère *nm,f Jur* life tenant

usure¹ *nf (intérêt, délit)* usury

usure² *nf (action de s'user)* wear and tear ❑ *usure en magasin* shelf depreciation; *usure normale* fair wear and tear

usurier, -ère *nm,f* usurer

utile *adj (nécessaire)* necessary; **en temps utile** in (good) time, within the prescribed time; **prendre toutes dispositions utiles** to make all necessary arrangements

utilisable *adj* usable; *Fin* **utilisable à vue** *(crédit)* available at sight

utilisateur, -trice *nm,f* user; *Ordinat* **pour utilisateurs multiples** multi-user ❑ *Mktg* **utilisateur final** end user; *Mktg* **utilisateur pilote** lead user; *Mktg* **utilisateur tardif** late adopter

utiliser *vt (produit)* to use

utilitaire 1 *adj* utilitarian
2 *nm Ordinat* utility, utility program

utilité *nf Écon* utility ❑ *utilité marginale* marginal utility

Vv

vacance *nf* (**a**) *(poste)* vacancy; **suppléer à une vacance** to fill a vacancy; **il y a une vacance à la comptabilité** the accounts department has a vacancy (**b**) **vacances** *Br* holiday(s), *Am* vacation; **un mois de vacances** a month's holiday, a month off

vacant, -e *adj* vacant

vache à lait *nf Fin, Mktg (produit, société)* cash cow

> **"**
>
> Si le modèle économique de cette dernière rend le pari très incertain, les perspectives d'Orange, la **vache à lait** du groupe, et d'Equant sont attrayantes sur le long terme.
>
> **"**

vague *nf (mouvement)* wave; *(de publicités)* run, series; **l'annonce a provoqué une vague de protestations** the announcement provoked a wave of protest ❑ *vague de prospérité* boom, wave of prosperity; *vague de spéculation* wave of speculation; *vague de vente* sales wave

valable *adj* valid; **ce billet est valable pour un mois** this ticket is valid for one month; *Bourse* **valable jusqu'à nouvel ordre** good until cancelled

valeur (**a**) *(prix)* value, worth; **prendre/perdre de la valeur** to go up/down in value; **avoir de la valeur** to be of value; **être sans valeur** to be of no value ❑ *valeur d'achat* purchase value; *Compta valeur d'actif* asset value; *Compta valeur d'actif net* net asset value; *Compta valeur actionnariale* shareholder value; *Compta valeur actualisée* discounted (present) value; *Compta valeur actualisée nette* discounted cash flow; *Compta valeur actuelle* current value, present value; *Compta valeur actuelle nette* current net value, net present value; *Écon valeur ajoutée* added value, value added; *Compta valeur amortie* written-down cost or value; *valeur assurable* insurable value; *valeur d'assurance* insurance value; *valeur assurée* insured value; *valeur attendue* expected value; *Compta valeur de bilan* book value, total asset value; *Compta valeur bilantielle* book value, total asset value; *valeur en Bourse* market value; *valeur boursière* market value; *valeur brute* gross value; *valeur capitalisée* capitalized value, future value; *valeur à la casse* break-up value, scrap value; *valeur compensée* cleared value; *Compta valeur comptable* book value; *Compta valeur comptable nette* net book value; *Banque valeur en compte* value in account; *Compta valeur cyclique* cyclical stock; *valeur déclarée* declared value; *Ordinat valeur par défaut* default value; *valeur de départ* initial value; *Mktg valeur distinctive* distinctive value; *valeur en douane* customs value, value for customs purposes; *valeur d'échange* exchange value, value in exchange; *Fin valeur à l'échéance* maturity value, value at maturity; *valeur effective* real value; *Fin valeur à l'encaissement* value for collection; *valeur d'émission* issue price; *valeur enregistrée* registered value; *valeur extrinsèque* extrinsic value; *(d'une monnaie)* legal *or* fictitious value; *valeur faciale (d'une action)* face value, nominal value; *(d'un timbre) Br* face value, *Am* face amount; *valeur de facture* invoice value; *Fin valeur fictive (de la monnaie fiduciaire)* face value; *valeur future* prospective value; *valeur initiale* original value; *valeur intrinsèque* intrinsic value; *Compta valeur d'inventaire* balance sheet value, break-up value; *Banque valeur jour* same-day value; *valeur de liquidation, valeur liquidative* value at liquidation; *Fin* cash-in value; *valeur locative* rental value; *valeur locative imposable* rateable value; *valeur marchande* commercial value, market value; *valeur marginale* marginal value; *valeur minimale* minimal value; *valeur monétaire* monetary value; *valeur monétaire escomptée* expected monetary value; *valeur négociable* market value, commercial value; *valeur nette* net value *or* worth; *valeur à neuf* replacement value; *valeur nominale Fin (d'une obligation)* par value; *Bourse (d'une action)* nominal value, face value; *valeur numéraire* legal-tender value; *valeur à l'origine, valeur d'origine* original value; *valeur au pair* par value, parity value; *valeur perçue* perceived value; *Bourse valeur de rachat* redemption value, surrender value; *valeur de rareté* scarcity value; *valeur réalisable* realizable value; *valeur réalisable nette* net realizable value; *valeur de récupération* salvage value; *valeur réelle* real value, actual value; *valeur de remboursement* redemption value; *Assur valeur de remplacement* replacement value; *valeur de rendement (d'une entreprise)* profitability value; **valeur de reprise** trade-in value; **valeur résiduelle** residual value; **valeur résiduelle nette** net residual value; **valeur à la revente** resale value; *Bourse* **valeur temporelle** time value; **valeur totale assurée** total insured value; **valeur transactionnelle** settlement value; **valeur d'usage** value as a going concern, value in use; **valeur vénale** fair market value **(b)** *Bourse (titre)* **valeur (boursière)** security, share ❑ *Bourse* **valeur aurifère** gold share; **valeurs bancaires** bank shares; **valeurs de bourse** quoted securities; *Fin* **valeurs classées** investment stock; **valeurs au comptant** securities dealt in for cash; **valeurs de croissance** growth shares *or* stocks; **valeur dirigeante** leading share; **valeurs immobilières** property shares; **valeurs industrielles** industrial shares, industrials; **valeurs à intérêt fixe** fixed-interest securities; **valeurs à lot** lottery bonds, prize bonds; **valeurs mobilières** stocks and shares, transferable securities; **valeurs mobilières de placement** marketable securities; **valeurs nanties** pledged securities; **valeurs négociables** marketable securities; **valeurs nominatives** registered securities; **valeur non cotée** unlisted *or* unquoted security; **valeurs de père de famille** blue chip stock; **valeurs pétrolières** oil shares; **valeurs de placement** investment securities; **valeurs de** *ou* **en portefeuille** portfolio securities; **valeurs au porteur** bearer securities, bearer bonds; **valeurs de premier choix** blue chip stock; **valeurs de premier ordre** blue chip stock; **valeurs réalisables** realizable *or* marketable securities; *Bourse* **valeurs de rendement** income bonds; **valeurs de retournement** recovery shares; **valeurs à revenu fixe** fixed-income securities; **valeurs à revenu variable** floating-rate *or* variable-rate securities; **valeurs du second marché** unlisted securities; **valeurs des sociétés industrielles** industrials; **valeurs spéculatives, valeurs de spéculation** speculative securities; **valeurs à terme** futures; **valeurs de tout repos** gilt-edged securities; **valeur vedette** leading share **(c)** **valeurs** *(capital)* assets ❑ **valeurs actives** assets; **valeur en capital** capital assets; **valeurs disponibles** available *or* liquid *or* current assets; **valeur en espèces** cash, bullion; **valeurs immatérielles** fixed assets; **valeurs immobilisées** fixed assets; **valeurs incorporelles** intangible assets, intangibles; **valeurs liquides** liquid assets *or* securities; **valeurs matérielles** tangible assets, tangibles; **valeurs passives** liabilities

> Cette crise a fait prendre conscience au gouvernement irlandais de la fragilité d'une économie fondée, souvent, sur des "usines tournevis", à faible **valeur ajoutée**, où la recherche et le développement font cruellement défaut.

valeur-or *nf Fin* value in gold currency

valeur-temps *nf* extrinsic value

validation *nf* **(a)** *(d'un contrat)* ratification **(b)** *(d'un document)* authentication, validation

valide *adj (contrat, document)* valid

valider *vt* **(a)** *(contrat)* to ratify; *(document)* to authenticate, to validate **(b)** *Ordinat (option)* to confirm; *(cellule, case)* to select

validité *nf (d'un contrat, d'un document)* validity

valoir *vi* **(a)** *(avoir comme valeur)* to be worth; **valoir cher** *(objet en vente)* to be expensive; *(objet précieux)* to be worth a lot **(b)** *(fructifier)* **faire valoir son argent** to invest one's money profitably **(c)** **à valoir** *(paiement, somme)* to be deducted, on account; **payer 200 euros à valoir** to pay 200 euros on account; **verser un acompte à valoir sur une somme** to pay a deposit to be set off against *or* deducted from a sum

valorisateur de fonds *nm Compta* fund accountant

valorisation *nf* **(a)** *(augmentation de la valeur)* *Fin* increase in value, valorization; *Compta (d'un inventaire)* valuation ❑ *Compta* **valorisation de fonds** fund accounting **(b)** *Écon* development

valoriser 1 *vt* **(a)** *(bien, monnaie)* to increase the value of **(b)** *Écon (région)* to develop **2 se valoriser** *vpr* to increase in value

valse *nf* **valse des étiquettes** constant price rises; **valse des prix** spiralling prices

> La **valse des prix** a-t-elle déjà eu lieu ? Les Français se plaignent de plus en plus d'une hausse des prix depuis le passage à l'euro. Le ministre de l'Economie et des Finances, Laurent Fabius, a admis certains dérapages, notamment dans les cafés restaurants. L'enquête de la DGCCRF sur les prix sera publiée mardi.

VAN *nm Compta (abrév* **valeur actuelle nette**) current net value

variabilité *nf* variability

variable 1 *adj* variable **2** *nf Ordinat* variable ❑ **variable de mémoire** memory variable

variation *nf* variation; *(des cours, du marché)* fluctuation ❑ **variations annuelles** annual variations; **variation de cours minimale** minimum fluctuation; **variations cycliques** cyclical variations; **variation maximale autorisée** maximum fluctuation; **variations saisonnières** seasonal variations

varier *vi* to vary, to change; *(cours, marché)* to fluctuate; **les prix varient d'un magasin/d'un**

jour à l'autre prices vary from one shop/day to another; **les salaires proposés varient suivant l'expérience des candidats** the salaries offered vary according to the experience of the candidates

vedette *nf Mktg (produit)* star

véhicule *nm* (a) *(moyen de transport)* vehicle ❑ **véhicule commercial** commercial vehicle; **véhicule industriel** industrial vehicle, goods vehicle; **véhicule de transport de marchandises** freight vehicle, goods vehicle; **véhicule utilitaire** commercial vehicle (b) *(moyen de transmission)* vehicle ❑ **véhicule médiatique** media vehicle

véhiculer *vt* (a) *(transporter)* to transport (b) *(transmettre)* to convey; *Mktg* **véhiculer une image** to convey an image

veille *nf* (a) *Ordinat* standby mode, sleep mode; **en veille** in standby mode, in sleep mode (b) *Mktg* **veille marketing** marketing intelligence

vendable *adj* saleable, sellable

vendeur, -euse *nm,f* (a) *(particulier)* seller; *Jur* vendor (b) *(dans un magasin)* Br sales assistant, Am (sales) clerk; *(dans une entreprise)* sales representative ❑ **vendeur à domicile** door-to-door salesman; **vendeur export** exporter; **vendeur par téléphone** telesales person (c) *Bourse* seller; *(d'une prime)* giver ❑ **vendeur à découvert** short seller, bear seller

vendre 1 *vt* to sell; *(commercialiser)* to market; **vendre qch à qn** to sell sb sth, to sell sth to sb; **vendre moins cher que qn** to undersell sb; **vendre comptant** to sell for cash; **vendre à crédit** to sell on credit; *Bourse* **vendre à découvert** to sell short, to go a bear; **vendre au détail** to sell retail, to retail; **vendre en entrepôt** to sell in bonded warehouses; **vendre de gré à gré** to sell privately; **vendre en gros** to sell wholesale; **vendre à perte** to sell at a loss; *Bourse* **vendre à terme** to sell forward

2 **se vendre** *vpr (produit, article)* to be sold; **le nouveau modèle ne se vend pas bien** the new model isn't selling well

vente *nf (transaction)* sale; *(activité)* selling; **réaliser une vente** to make a sale; **la vente** *(secteur)* sales; **elle est dans la vente** she's in sales; *Compta* **ventes** sales, turnover; **en vente** for sale, on sale; **en vente libre** freely available; **mettre qch en vente** to put sth up for sale, to offer sth for sale; **en vente dans tous les grands magasins** on sale at all leading stores; **vente et marketing** sales and marketing ❑ *Suisse* **vente action** bargain offer; **vente agressive** hard sell (techniques); **vente à l'amiable** sale by private agreement, private sale; **vente à l'arrivée** sale at arrival; **ventes de base** baseline sales; **vente par catalogue** mail-order (selling); **vente à (la) commission** commission sale; **vente (au) comptant** cash

sale; **vente aux comptes-clés** key-account sale; **vente par correspondance** mail-order (selling); **vente à crédit** credit sale; *(à tempérament)* hire purchase, *Am* installment plan; **vente à découvert** *(activité)* retailing, retail selling; *Bourse (transaction)* short or bear sale; *Mktg* **vente sur description** sale by description; **vente au détail** *(activité)* retailing, retail selling; *(transaction)* retail sale; **vente directe** *(activité)* direct selling; *(transaction)* direct sale; **vente à distance** in-home shopping; **vente à domicile** door-to-door selling; **vente domiciliaire** home (party) selling, party-plan selling; **vente sur échantillon** sale by sample; **vente en l'état** sale as seen; *Ordinat* **vente électronique** on-line selling; **vente aux enchères** (sale by) auction; **vente à l'essai** sale on approval; **ventes export** export sales; **ventes à l'exportation** export sales; **vente avec faculté de retour** sale or return; **vente ferme** firm sale; **vente forcée** forced sale; **vente à froid** cold selling; **vente de gré à gré** sale by private agreement, private sale; **vente en gros** wholesaling; **vente sans intermédiaire** direct selling; **vente judiciaire** sale by order of the court; **vente jumelée** twin-pack selling; *Ordinat* **vente en ligne** on-line selling; **vente de liquidation** closing-down sale; **vente par lot** banded pack selling; **vente et marketing assistés par ordinateur** computer-aided sales and marketing, CASM; **ventes sur le marché intérieur** home sales; *Bourse* **vente nue** naked sale; **vente parallèle** parallel selling; **vente personnelle** personal selling; **vente à perte** sale at a loss; **vente de porte-à-porte** door-to-door selling; **ventes de précaution** panic selling; **vente à prime** premium selling; **vente à prix réduit** sale at a reduced price; **vente promotionnelle** promotional sale; **ventes de prospection** missionary selling; **vente publique** public sale; **vente pyramidale** pyramid selling; **vente rapide** quick or ready sale; **vente réclame** bargain sale; **vente de référence** reference sale; **vente répétée** repeat sale; **vente à réméré** sale with option of repurchase; **vente par réseau coopté** multi-level marketing; **vente sans intermédiaire** direct selling; **vente en semi-gros** small wholesale selling; *Bourse* **vente spéculative** speculative selling; **vente par téléphone** *(méthode)* telephone selling; **ventes par téléphone** *(transactions)* telephone sales, telesales; **vente à tempérament** hire purchase, *Am* installment plan; *Bourse* **vente à terme** forward sale

> **"**
>
> Elle constate qu'elle "a pu sauver les meubles grâce à la **vente à découvert**", une pratique qui consiste à vendre des actions que l'on ne possède pas en pariant sur la baisse des cours avant la transaction effective.
>
> **"**

vente-marketing *nf* sales and marketing

ventilation *nf* (**a**) *(décomposition) (des prix, des dépenses)* breakdown (**b**) *(répartition) (de crédits, d'équipments)* allocation

ventiler *vt* (**a**) *(décomposer) (prix, dépenses)* to break down (**b**) *(répartir) (crédits, équipements)* to allocate; **ventiler un lot** to break down bulk

vépéciste *nm* mail-order company

> **"**
>
> "Et ce qui compte, comme dans tout commerce, c'est de proposer de bons produits, de bons prix et de bons services pour fidéliser une clientèle," assure Régis Saleur. "Comment un site qui a deux ans d'existence pourrait-il rivaliser avec un monstre comme La Redoute, par exemple, qui fait de la VPC depuis cinquante ans?" Le site Redoute.fr ne pèse certes que 4% du chiffre d'affaires total du **vépéciste**. Mais il est rentable depuis l'été dernier…
>
> **"**

verbal, -e *adj (convention, offre)* verbal

véreux, -euse *adj (affaires, financier)* shady, dubious

vérificateur, -trice 1 *nm,f* inspector, examiner □ **vérificateur de comptes** auditor; **vérificateur externe** external auditor; **vérificateur interne** internal auditor
2 *nm Ordinat* **vérificateur orthographique** spellchecker

vérification *nf* (**a**) *(de déclarations) (activité)* checking, verification; *(résultat)* check, verification; *(du travail)* inspection, examination □ *Compta* **vérification de comptes** auditing of accounts; **vérification en douane** customs examination (of goods); **vérification d'écritures** auditing of accounts; **vérification externe** *(activité)* external auditing; *(résultat)* external audit; **vérification fiscale** *(activité)* tax auditing; *(résultat)* tax audit; **vérification interne** *(activité)* internal auditing; *(résultat)* internal audit; *Compta* **vérification à rebours** audit trail; **vérification des stocks** stock control (**b**) *Ordinat* check □ **vérification antivirale** antivirus check; **vérification orthographique** spellcheck

vérifier *vt* to check; *(comptes)* to audit; *(références)* to take up; **vérifié et revérifié** checked and double-checked

verr num *Ordinat (abrév* **verrouillage numérique***)* num lock

verrouillage *nm Ordinat* lock □ **verrouillage du clavier numérique** num lock; **verrouillage des fichiers** file lock; **verrouillage en lecture seule** read-only lock; **verrouillage en majuscule(s)** caps lock; **verrouillage du pavé numérique** num lock, numbers lock

verrouiller *vt Ordinat (fichier, disquette)* to lock on; **verrouiller en écriture** *(fichier)* to lock; **verrouillé en majuscule(s)** *(clavier)* with caps lock on

versement *nm (paiement)* payment; *(paiement partiel)* instalment; **en plusieurs versements** by *or* in instalments; **premier versement** down payment □ **versement annuel** yearly payment; **versement à la commande** down payment; **versement comptant** cash payment; **versements échelonnés** staggered payments, instalments; **versement d'espèces** cash deposit; **versement libératoire** final instalment; **versement en numéraire** payment in cash; **versement partiel** instalment

verser *vt* (**a**) *(argent, intérêt, salaire)* to pay; *(sur un compte)* to deposit; **verser qch au crédit de qn** to credit sb with sth; **verser un acompte** to make a down payment; **verser de l'argent sur son compte** to pay money into one's account; *Bourse* **verser un premium** to pay *or* deposit a premium (**b**) *(joindre)* to add; **verser un document au dossier** to add a document to the file

version *nf (d'un projet, d'un document)* draft

verso *nm (d'un effet, d'un chèque)* back

vertical, -e *adj Écon (concentration, intégration)* vertical

veto *nm* veto; **mettre** *ou* **opposer son veto à qch** to veto sth

vétusté *nf* obsolescence

VGA *nm Ordinat (abrév* **Video Graphics Array***)* VGA

VI *nf Compta (abrév* **valeur d'inventaire***)* balance sheet value, break-up value

viabilisé, -e *adj Admin (terrain)* serviced, with services

viabiliser *vt Admin (terrain)* to service

viabilité *nf (d'un projet, d'un système)* viability, workability

viable *adj (projet, système)* viable, workable

viager, -ère 1 *adj (rente)* life
2 *nm* life annuity; **placer son argent en viager** to invest one's money in a life annuity; **acheter une propriété en viager** = to acquire a property by paying pre-determined instalments until the death of the owner(s)

vice *nm* fault, defect, flaw □ **vice apparent** obvious defect; **vice caché** hidden defect; **vice de construction** construction fault; **vice de fabrication** manufacturing defect; **vice de forme** legal flaw; **vice inhérent** inherent defect; **vice propre** inherent defect; **vice rédhibitoire** material defect

vice-gérance *nf* deputy managership

vice-gérant, -e *nm,f* deputy manager

vice-présidence *nf (d'état, d'organisation)*

vice-presidency; *(d'entreprise)* vice-chairman-ship

vice-président, -e *nm,f (d'état, d'organisation)* vice-president; *(d'entreprise)* vice-chairman

vidage (de) mémoire *nm Ordinat* memory dump

vide *adj* (**a**) *(emballage, conteneur)* empty; **vide en retour** empty on return (**b**) *Ordinat (disquette, écran)* blank

vidéo *nf* video ❏ *vidéo d'entreprise* corporate video; *vidéo institutionnelle* corporate video; *vidéo numérique* digital video; *vidéo promotionnelle* promotional video

vidéoconference *nf (conférence)* videoconference; *(procédé)* videoconferencing

vidéotex *nm Ordinat* Videotex®, Viewdata®

vider *vt* (**a**) *Ordinat* **vider l'écran** to clear the screen; **vider la corbeille** to empty the wastebasket *or Am* the trash (**b**) *Fam (congédier)* to kick out

vie *nf Écon* living, livelihood; **gagner sa vie** to earn one's living ❏ *vie économique (d'un produit)* economic life; *vie physique (d'une machine)* productive life

vierge *adj Ordinat (ligne, espace)* blank; *(disquette)* blank, unformatted

vignette *nf* manufacturer's label *(of quality, guarantee)*; *Ordinat* thumbnail

vigueur *nf* **en vigueur** *(règlement, loi)* in force; **entrer en vigueur** to come into force; **cesser d'être en vigueur** to lapse

village planétaire *nm* global village

> **"**
>
> La mondialisation est souvent idéalisée par la désormais classique image du "**village planétaire**", observait Madjid Cherikh, au nom de la FNME-CGT, "mais la pauvreté s'accumule de telle façon qu'elle compromet l'avenir du village dans son ensemble". De ce point de vue, la formation initiale et professionnelle représente "une des conditions majeures pour que la mondialisation cesse d'être cette machine à exclure". Comme l'énergie, elle est un passage obligé.
>
> **"**

ville *nf* town ❏ *ville champignon* boom town; *ville industrielle* industrial town; *Mktg* **ville test** test city

violation *nf* infringement, violation; **en violation de la loi** in breach *or* violation of the law ❏ *violation du droit de reproduction* copyright infringement; *violation de garantie* breach of warranty

violer *vt (accord, loi)* to break, to violate

virement *nm* (**a**) *Banque* (credit) transfer ❏ *virement automatique* automatic transfer; *virement bancaire* bank transfer; *virement par courrier* mail transfer; *virement de crédit* credit transfer; *virement interbancaire* interbank transfer; *virement postal* post office transfer; *virement télégraphique* cable transfer; *virement par télex* telex transfer (**b**) *Admin* *virement de fonds* = transfer (often illegal) of funds from one article of the budget to another

virer *vt* (**a**) *Banque (somme)* to transfer; *(chèque)* to clear; **il vire 1000 euros tous les mois sur mon compte** he transfers 1,000 euros into my account every month (**b**) *Fam (congédier)* to sack

virgule *nf* comma ❏ *Ordinat* **virgule flottante** floating point

virtuel, -elle *adj* virtual

virus *nm Ordinat* virus; **désactiver un virus** to disable a virus ❏ *virus informatique* computer virus; *virus de macro* macro virus

visa *nm* (**a**) *(pour passeport)* visa ❏ *visa de la douane* customs visa; *visa de transit* transit visa (**b**) *(signature)* signature; *(initiales)* initials; *(tampon)* stamp (**c**) *(de chèque)* certification (**d**) *Bourse* **visa de la COB** permission to deal

viser *vt* (**a**) *(passeport)* to visa (**b**) *(document) (signer)* to countersign; *(apposer ses initiales à)* to initial; *(tamponner)* to stamp (**c**) *(chèque)* to certify; *Compta* **viser des livres de commerce** to certify the books (**d**) *Mktg (clientèle, public)* to target

visible *adj (biens, importations, exportations)* visible

visioconférence *nf (conférence)* videoconference; *(procédé)* videoconferencing

visiophone *nm* videophone

visiophonie *nf* video teleconferencing

visite *nf* (**a**) *(d'un représentant)* call, visit ❏ *visite d'affaires* business call; *visite à froid* cold call; *visite de relance* follow-up visit (**b**) *(inspection)* inspection, examination ❏ *visite de douane, visite douanière* customs inspection

visiter *vt* (**a**) *(client)* to call on (**b**) *(inspecter)* to inspect, to examine

visualisation *nf Ordinat* display ❏ *visualisation sur écran* soft copy; *visualisation de la page à l'écran* page preview

visualiser *vt Ordinat* to display; *(codes, document)* to view

visuel *nm Ordinat* visual display unit, VDU

vitesse *nf* (**a**) *(rapidité)* speed, rate; **être en perte de vitesse** *(entreprise, économie, monnaie)* to be losing ground ❏ *Fin* **vitesse de rotation** *(des stocks)* turnover rate, turnround rate; *Écon* **vitesse de transformation des capitaux**

income velocity of capital (**b**) *Ordinat* speed □ *vitesse d'accès* access speed; *vitesse d'affichage* display speed; *vitesse de calcul* processing *or* computing speed; *vitesse de clignotement* blink rate; *vitesse de clignotement du curseur* cursor blink rate; *vitesse d'écriture* write speed; *vitesse d'exécution* execution speed; *vitesse de frappe (à la machine à écrire, à l'ordinateur)* typing speed; *vitesse de frappe à la minute/à l'heure* keystrokes per minute/hour; *vitesse d'impression* print speed, printer speed; *vitesse du processeur* processor speed; *vitesse de traitement* processing speed; *vitesse de transfert* transfer speed

> ❝
> Le gérant se propose de faire la meilleure répartition des actions du Cac dans le fonds, en "sous-pondérant" des titres ou des secteurs **en perte de vitesse** et, au contraire, en augmentant la part d'une valeur ou d'un secteur en croissance. Le but de la manœuvre est de faire mieux que l'indice.
> ❞

vitrine *nf Br* shop window, *Am* store window; **mettre des marchandises en vitrine** to display goods in the window

VMP *nfpl Fin* (*abrév* **valeurs mobilières de placement**) marketable securities

voie *nf* (**a**) *(route)* way, road; **par voie aérienne** by air; **par voie ferrée** by rail; **par voie maritime** by sea; **par voie terrestre** by land, overland (**b**) *Admin* **la voie hiérarchique** the official channels; **suivre la voie hiérarchique** to go through the official channels (**c**) *(cours)* **en voie d'achèvement** nearing completion (**d**) *Jur* **voie de droit** recourse to legal proceedings; *voie de recours* grounds for appeal (to a higher court) (**e**) *Ordinat* **voie d'accès** path; *voie de transmission de données* data link

voiture *nf* (**a**) *(automobile)* car □ *voiture de fonction* company car; *voiture de livraison* delivery van; *voiture de location* rented car, *Br* hire car; *voiture de louage* rented car, *Br* hire car; *voiture de luxe* de luxe car; *voiture d'occasion* secondhand car, used car; *voiture de société* company car (**b**) *(wagon) Br* coach, *Am* car

voix *nf* (individual) vote; **donner sa voix à qn** to vote for sb; **mettre une question aux voix** to put a question to the vote, to take a vote on a question □ *voix prépondérante* casting vote

vol *nm* flight □ *vol charter* charter flight; *vol direct* direct flight; *vol avec escale* flight with stopover

volant, -e **1** *adj (personnel)* mobile
2 *nm* (**a**) *Écon, Fin* reserve □ *volant de sécurité* reserve fund; *volant de trésorerie* cash reserve

(**b**) *(de carnet)* tear-off portion; **talon et volant** *(de chèque)* counterfoil and leaf

volatil, -e *adj Bourse (option)* volatile

volatilité *nf Bourse (d'une option)* volatility

volet *nm (d'un chèque)* tear-off portion; *(d'un document)* section

volontaire *adj (liquidation)* voluntary

volonté *nf* **payable à volonté** payable on demand

volume *nm* volume □ *volume d'achat* purchase volume, volume of purchases; *volume d'activité* volume *or* level of activity; *volume d'affaires* volume of business; *volume annuel de production* annual (volume of) production; *volume des échanges commerciaux* volume of trade; *volume des exportations* volume of exports; *volume des importations* volume of imports; *volume de production* volume of production; *volume de la production courante* volume of current output; *volume des ventes* sales volume, volume of sales

votant, -e *nm,f* voter

vote *nm* vote; **déclarer le résultat d'un vote** to declare the result of the voting; **prendre part au vote** to vote, to take part in the voting □ *vote de confiance* vote of confidence; *vote par correspondance* postal vote; *vote de défiance* vote of no confidence; *vote majoritaire* majority vote; *vote préférentiel* preferential voting; *vote à l'unanimité* unanimous vote

voter **1** *vt (crédit)* to vote; *(loi)* to pass; *(projet de loi)* to vote for
2 *vi* to vote; **voter à main levée** to vote by a show of hands; **voter par procuration** to vote by proxy

voyage *nm* journey, trip □ *voyage d'affaires* business trip; *voyage d'aller* outward voyage; *voyage de retour* homeward journey

voyager *vi* (**a**) *(personne)* to travel; **voyager pour affaires** to travel on business; **voyager pour une maison de commerce** to represent a firm (**b**) *(marchandises)* to be transported; **le vin voyage mal** wine doesn't travel well

voyageur, -euse *nm,f* traveller; *(passager)* passenger □ *voyageur de commerce* sales representative; *voyageur représentant placier* sales representative; *voyageur en transit* transfer passenger

voyagiste *nm* tour operator

VPC *nf (abrév* **vente par correspondance**) mail order selling

vrac *nm* **en vrac** *(marchandises)* loose; *(cargaison)* bulk; **faire le vrac, transporter le vrac** to transport goods in bulk

VRAM *nf Ordinat (abrév* **video random access memory**) VRAM

vraquier *nm* bulk carrier

VRC *nf Mktg* (*abrév* **vente par réseau coopté**) MLM, multilevel marketing

V/Réf (*abrév* **votre référence**) your ref

VRML *nm Ordinat* (*abrév* **virtual reality modelling language**) VRML

VRP *nm* (*abrév* **voyageur représentant placier**) sales rep □ *VRP multicarte* freelance rep

vue *nf* (**a**) *Fin* **à sept jours de vue** seven days after sight (**b**) **en vue** on view; **mettre des marchandises bien en vue** to display goods prominently

Ww Xx Yy

W3 *nm Ordinat (abrév* **World Wide Web**) WWW, W3

wagon *nm* (**a**) *(de passagers) Br* carriage, *Am* car; *(de marchandises) Br* wagon, *Am* car ▫ *wagon frigorifique* refrigerated van; *wagon de marchandises Br* goods wagon, *Am* freight car (**b**) *(contenu) Br* wagonload, *Am* carload (**de** of)

WAIS *nm Ordinat (abrév* **wide area information service** *or* **system**) WAIS

WAP *nm Tél (abrév* **wireless applications protocol**) WAP

warrant *nm* warrant ▫ *warrant à l'achat* call warrant; *warrant hôtelier* hotel warrant; *warrant industriel* industrial warrant; *warrant en marchandises* produce warrant; *warrant à la vente* put warrant

warrantage *nm* issuing of a warehouse warrant

warranté, -e *adj* covered by a warehouse warrant

warranter *vt* to issue a warehouse warrant for

Web *nm Ordinat* **le Web** the Web

webcam *nf Ordinat* Web cam

webcast *nm Ordinat* webcast

webcasting *nm Ordinat* webcasting

Webmaître, Webmaster, Webmestre *nm Ordinat* Web master

webphone *nm Ordinat* webphone

webzine *nm Ordinat* webzine

World Wide Web *nm Ordinat* **le World Wide Web** the World Wide Web

WORM *Ordinat (abrév* **write once read many times**) WORM

WWW *nm Ordinat (abrév* **World Wide Web**) WWW

Wysiwyg *nm Ordinat* WYSIWYG

X-Dax *nm Bourse* **le X-Dax** the X-Dax (index)

Xetra-Dax *nm Bourse* **le Xetra-Dax** the Xetra-Dax (index)

XMCL *nm Ordinat (abrév* **Extensible Media Commerce Language**) XMCL

XML *nm Ordinat (abrév* **Extensible Markup Language**) XML

yen *nm* yen

Z z

ZAC *nf* (*abrév* **zone d'aménagement concerté**) = area developed through cooperation between public and private sectors

ZAD *nf* (*abrév* **zone d'aménagement différé**) = area earmarked for future development

ZEP *nf* (*abrév* **zone d'environnement protégé**) = environmentally protected zone

zéro *nm* zero; **tomber à zéro** *(action)* to fall to zero; **zéro défaut** zero defect

ZI *nf* (*abrév* **zone industrielle**) industrial estate

zinzin *nm Fam Fin* institutional investor

zipper *vt Ordinat* to zip

zone *nf* **(a)** *(espace)* area, zone ◻ **zone d'aménagement concerté** = area developed through cooperation between public and private sectors; **zone d'aménagement différé** = area earmarked for future development; **zone de chalandise** catchment area *(of shop)*; **zone commerciale** retail park; **zone de développement** development area; **zone de développement d'entreprises** enterprise zone; **zone dollar** dollar area; **zone sous douane** customs zone; **zone d'environnement protégé** environmentally-protected zone; *UE* **zone euro** euro zone, euro area; *Anciennement* **zone franc** franc area; *Écon* **zone franche** free zone; **zone franchise** duty-free zone; **zone frontière** frontier zone; **zone grise** grey zone; **zone industrielle** industrial estate *or* park; **zone de libre-échange** free-trade area; **zone monétaire** monetary area; **zone postale** postal area; **zone sterling** sterling area; *Mktg* **zone test** test area; *Admin* **zone à urbaniser en priorité** = priority development area

(b) *Ordinat* **zone d'affichage** display area; **zone d'amorçage** boot sector; **zone de dialogue** dialogue box; **zone d'écriture** write area; **zone d'état** status box; **zone tampon** *(en mémoire)* (memory) buffer; **zone de travail** work area

(c) *Admin* **zone de salaire** wage zone *or* bracket

> **"**
>
> Cette année, les vacanciers français en voyage dans la **zone euro** vont goûter aux joies de la monnaie unique: ils pourront utiliser à discrétion leur carte bancaire. Jusqu'ici, le prix des opérations dans les pays de la **zone euro** pouvait représenter jusqu'à 7% de la transaction! Mais, depuis le 1er juillet, en conformité avec un règlement de la Commission européenne, les banques sont obligées d'étendre à toute la **zone** les tarifs qu'elles pratiquent à l'intérieur de leurs frontières.
>
> **"**

ZUP *nf* (*abrév* **zone à urbaniser en priorité**) = priority development area

SUPPLEMENT

Contents

FRENCH COMMUNICATION GUIDE

Contents

Basic Principles

When sending a letter or other written communication, particular attention should be paid to the grammar and spelling as these are sensitive topics. Spelling mistakes and grammatical errors in a letter are considered very bad form, even in private correspondence.

The style should be simple and clear. It is a good idea to keep sentences short and to use active rather than passive verbs. Each paragraph should deal with one idea only. The idea is presented in the first sentence of the paragraph and is then developed. A new idea is expressed in a new paragraph.

Beginnings

The opening greetings and endings used in letters written in French follow certain well-established rules:

- If you do not know the person you are writing to, whether you know their name or not, or if you know them only slightly:

Monsieur
Madame

The greetings *Monsieur* and *Madame* are equivalent of *Dear Sir* and *Dear Madam* in English.

Mademoiselle

Mademoiselle is used for an unmarried young woman. If in doubt, use *Madame*.

- When you are unsure whether the recipient of the letter is male or female:

Madame, Monsieur

- When the letter is addressed to a company rather than to an individual:

Messieurs

- When writing to the head of a company or institution:

Monsieur le Directeur	*Madame la Directrice*
Monsieur le Président	*Madame la Présidente*

- When writing to a minister, to the Prime Minister or the President:

Monsieur le Ministre
Madame le Ministre

The form *Madame la Ministre* is equally acceptable now.

Monsieur le Premier Ministre
Madame le Premier Ministre

Monsieur le Président de la République
Madame la Présidente de la République

- When writing to a lawyer or solicitor:

Cher Maître

This form is used irrespective of whether one is addressing a man or woman in this context.

- When you know the person you are writing to and want to sound less formal:

Cher Monsieur
Chère Madame
Chère Mademoiselle
(for an unmarried young woman)

These greetings are never followed by the name of the person. The equivalent of *Dear Mr Allen* is *Monsieur* if you don't know him very well, or *Cher Monsieur* if you know him better and want to sound less formal. Always write the title in full and avoid abbreviations like *M.*, *Mme* and *Mlle*.

If you are writing to more than one person, you need to repeat *Cher* before each title: *Cher Monsieur, Chère Madame,*

- When you are writing to a colleague you do not know or know only slightly:

  Cher collègue
  Chère collègue

  The titles ***Cher confrère*** and ***Chère consœur*** are used between professionals such as doctors and lawyers.

  Cher confrère
  Chère consœur

  Cher ami
  Chère amie

  The titles ***Cher ami*** and ***Chère amie*** are still slightly formal and are not used between friends but between colleagues or acquaintances.

- When you are writing to a colleague with whom you are on first name terms:

  Cher Olivier
  Chère Sandrine

Endings

Although the formal endings of French business or administrative letters may appear slightly florid or pompous, it must be remembered that this is all part of a code of politeness integral to French correspondence etiquette. The complimentary close should correspond in form and tone to the opening greeting. The title used at the beginning (Monsieur, Cher Monsieur, etc) is always repeated in the ending of the letter:

This form is used when addressing a lawyer or solicitor specifically.

- The most neutral endings are:

  Veuillez agréer, Monsieur (Madame), mes salutations distinguées.
  Veuillez recevoir, Monsieur (Madame), mes salutations distinguées.
  Veuillez agréer, Monsieur (Madame), l'expression de mes sentiments distingués.
  Je vous prie d'agréer, Monsieur le Directeur (Madame la Directrice), mes salutations distinguées.
  Je vous prie d'agréer, cher Maître, mes salutations distinguées.
  Je vous remercie d'avance et vous prie d'agréer, Monsieur (Madame), mes salutations distinguées.
  Dans l'attente d'une réponse de votre part, veuillez agréer, Messieurs, nos salutations distinguées.

- If you want to end on a more respectful note, such as when writing to a superior:

  Veuillez agréer, Monsieur (Madame), l'expression de ma considération distinguée.
  Je vous prie d'agréer, Monsieur (Madame), l'expression de mon profond respect.
  Veuillez agréer, je vous prie, Monsieur le Président (Madame la Présidente), l'expression de ma respectueuse considération.

- If you want to show your gratitude:

  Veuillez agréer, Monsieur (Madame), l'expression de ma profonde gratitude.
  Veuillez agréer, Monsieur (Madame), l'expression de ma respectueuse reconnaissance.
  Croyez, Monsieur (Madame), à toute ma reconnaissance.
  Croyez, Monsieur (Madame), à ma sincère gratitude.

- Although still formal, the following endings are more friendly:

  Veuillez agréer, cher Monsieur (chère Madame), l'expression de mes sentiments les plus cordiaux.
  Veuillez croire, cher Monsieur (chère Madame),
  à mon meilleur souvenir.
  Veuillez recevoir, cher ami (chère amie), mes plus cordiales salutations.
  Croyez, cher Olivier (chère Sandrine), à mon amical souvenir.

  > As noted above, the expression *cher ami*, although more friendly, is still formal and should not be used for a friend.

- Simplified and more informal endings are becoming more common. The following endings can be found more and more in everyday business letters, e-mails and faxes:

  Salutations distinguées.
  Cordialement. (more friendly)
  Bien à vous. (even more friendly)

Addresses and Postcodes

- You might often see "bis" and "ter" after the street number in a French address. For example:

  3 bis, rue des Lilas
  11 ter, avenue de Bernay

They indicate that there is more than one residence, whether in the form of a self-contained apartment or an annexe to the main house or premises, at the address in question. "Bis" is used to indicate that there is a second residential (or business) unit, "ter" a third, the equivalent of 3b or 11c in English.

- The first two numbers of a French postcode correspond to the administrative code number of the relevant "département". All postcodes for Paris begin with 75. This system also applies to vehicle licence plates. For example:

  20, boulevard Arago
  75013 Paris

In the example above, the first two numbers indicate the city of Paris while the last two figures indicate that the address is located in the thirteenth "arrondissement" (district) of the city.

- The abbreviation "Cedex" is often found in French business addresses. For example:

  Société Delacour
  77170 Fontainebleau Cedex

This is a special postcode ensuring rapid delivery of mail to businesses and certain institutions. In these cases, the first two figures, as in other postcodes, denote geographical location but the following three figures denote an individual code assigned to the company in question.

- In Belgium addresses are often written with the street number coming after the street name, and the postcode before the town. For an apartment or a house where there are more than three letterboxes it is usual to add the letterbox number (not the apartment number) after the street number. For example:

**Monsieur Luc Dujardin
Amiel Électronique
rue du Clocher 143, bte 12** ———— The abbreviation for **boîte**.
1040 Bruxelles

• Swiss addresses are also usually written with the street number appearing after the street name, and the postcode before the town. If writing from outside Switzerland one may include the abbreviation CH (for "Confederatio Helvetica" or the Swiss Confederation). For example:

**Monsieur André Roux
Express Distribution
Avenue du Peyrou 4
CH - 2000 Neuchâtel**

• In Canada, it is usual to write the name of the town or municipality, followed by the abbreviation corresponding to the province in which it is located, followed by the postcode, all on the same line. For example:

**Madame Chantal Lemoine
DLD Industrie
3567 rue Drummond
Montréal (Québec) H3G 1M8** ————

The name of the province is usually given in brackets after the name of the town or municipality. Alternatively, an abbreviation can be used to designate the province: for example **QC** for **Québec**. If the abbreviated form is used then there is no need for brackets.

The websites of the various postal services in French-speaking countries are a useful source of information regarding addresses and postcodes in particular.

France: www.laposte.fr   Switzerland: www.poste.ch
Belgium: www.post.be   Luxembourg: www.pt.lu
Canada: www.canadapost.ca

Envelopes

The French postal services recommend that no punctuation be used on the envelope (no commas at the end of lines, no comma after the street number etc) and that the name of the town should be written in capital letters, without any accents or hyphens.

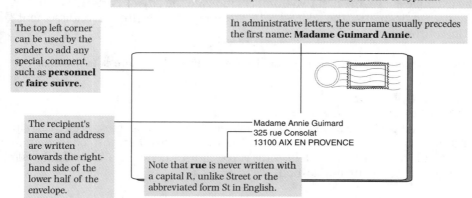

The top left corner can be used by the sender to add any special comment, such as **personnel** or **faire suivre**.

In administrative letters, the surname usually precedes the first name: **Madame Guimard Annie**.

The recipient's name and address are written towards the right-hand side of the lower half of the envelope.

Madame Annie Guimard
325 rue Consolat
13100 AIX EN PROVENCE

Note that **rue** is never written with a capital R, unlike Street or the abbreviated form St in English.

It is standard practice to write a return address on the back of the envelope at the top, in case the letter gets lost.

Model Letters

- **Business to Business (general)**

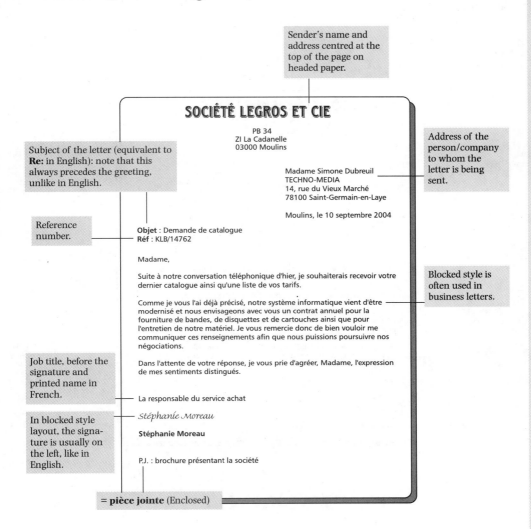

Sender's name and address centred at the top of the page on headed paper.

Address of the person/company to whom the letter is being sent.

Subject of the letter (equivalent to **Re:** in English): note that this always precedes the greeting, unlike in English.

Reference number.

Job title, before the signature and printed name in French.

In blocked style layout, the signature is usually on the left, like in English.

Blocked style is often used in business letters.

= **pièce jointe** (Enclosed)

SOCIÉTÉ LEGROS ET CIE

PB 34
ZI La Cadanelle
03000 Moulins

Madame Simone Dubreuil
TECHNO-MEDIA
14, rue du Vieux Marché
78100 Saint-Germain-en-Laye

Moulins, le 10 septembre 2004

Objet : Demande de catalogue
Réf : KLB/14762

Madame,

Suite à notre conversation téléphonique d'hier, je souhaiterais recevoir votre dernier catalogue ainsi qu'une liste de vos tarifs.

Comme je vous l'ai déjà précisé, notre système informatique vient d'être modernisé et nous envisageons avec vous un contrat annuel pour la fourniture de bandes, de disquettes et de cartouches ainsi que pour l'entretien de notre matériel. Je vous remercie donc de bien vouloir me communiquer ces renseignements afin que nous puissions poursuivre nos négociations.

Dans l'attente de votre réponse, je vous prie d'agréer, Madame, l'expression de mes sentiments distingués.

La responsable du service achat

Stéphanie Moreau

Stéphanie Moreau

P.J. : brochure présentant la société

Useful Phrases:

En réponse à votre lettre du...,
Nous avons bien reçu votre lettre du... et nous vous en remercions.
Nous sommes tout particulièrement intéressés par...
Nous vous remercions de l'intérêt que vous portez à notre société et nous restons à votre disposition pour toutes informations complémentaires.

- ## Placing an Order

A letter placing an order needs to specify the items required, as well as the conditions of delivery and payment.

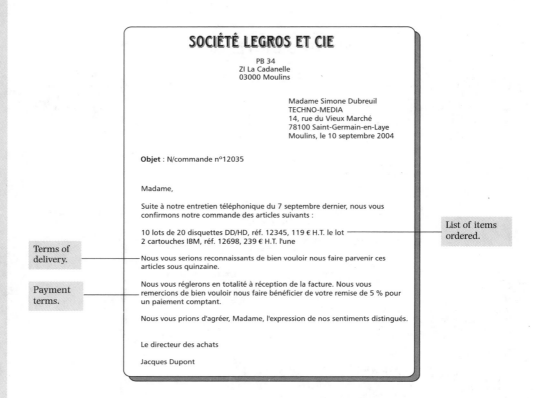

SOCIÉTÉ LEGROS ET CIE

PB 34
ZI La Cadanelle
03000 Moulins

Madame Simone Dubreuil
TECHNO-MEDIA
14, rue du Vieux Marché
78100 Saint-Germain-en-Laye
Moulins, le 10 septembre 2004

Objet : N/commande n°12035

Madame,

Suite à notre entretien téléphonique du 7 septembre dernier, nous vous confirmons notre commande des articles suivants :

10 lots de 20 disquettes DD/HD, réf. 12345, 119 € H.T. le lot — *List of items ordered.*
2 cartouches IBM, réf. 12698, 239 € H.T. l'une

Terms of delivery. — Nous vous serions reconnaissants de bien vouloir nous faire parvenir ces articles sous quinzaine.

Payment terms. — Nous vous réglerons en totalité à réception de la facture. Nous vous remercions de bien vouloir nous faire bénéficier de votre remise de 5 % pour un paiement comptant.

Nous vous prions d'agréer, Madame, l'expression de nos sentiments distingués.

Le directeur des achats

Jacques Dupont

Useful Phrases:

Veuillez nous faire parvenir les articles suivants...
Nous vous prions de bien vouloir nous expédier...
Nous vous passons commande de...
Veuillez trouver ci-joint notre bon de commande n°...

- ## Replying to an Order

Monsieur,

Nous avons bien reçu votre commande de 9 octobre.

Nous avons le plaisir de vous informer que les 300 mallettes de jeux vous ont été expédiées ce jour selon vos instructions.

Nous vous rappelons que nos délais de livraison sont de 10 jours minimum et que si vous désirez un nouvel envoi avant Noël, il serait prudent de nous prévenir par fax.

Nous vous prions d'agréer, Monsieur, l'expression de nos sentiments dévoués.

Marie-Françoise Durand

Marie-Françoise Durand
Directrice des ventes

- ## Informing a Customer

TECHNO-MEDIA
14, rue du Vieux Marché
78100 Saint-Germain-en-Laye
http:\\www.technomedia.fr

Saint-Germain-en-Laye, le 10 septembre 2004

Monsieur,

Nous avons le plaisir de vous informer que vous pouvez désormais consulter notre catalogue et passer vos commandes sur notre site Web.

Notre site est entièrement sécurisé. Si vous souhaitez bénéficier de nos services en ligne, il suffit de vous enregistrer en vous connectant à :
http:\\www.technomedia.fr

Dans l'espoir que ce nouveau service vous donnera entière satisfaction, nous vous prions d'agréer, Monsieur, nos meilleures salutations.

La responsable du site Web

Sylvie Legrand

Useful Phrases:

Nous vous informons que...
Nous vous annonçons que...
Nous tenons à vous signaler que...
Nous restons à votre entière disposition pour tous renseignements complémentaires.
Veuillez noter notre nouvelle adresse à partir du...
Notre magasin ouvrira ses portes le... à notre nouvelle adresse.

- **Letter of Complaint**

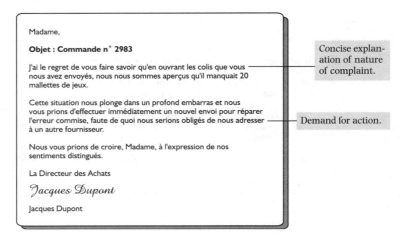

Madame,

Objet : Commande n° 2983

J'ai le regret de vous faire savoir qu'en ouvrant les colis que vous nous avez envoyés, nous nous sommes aperçus qu'il manquait 20 mallettes de jeux.

Cette situation nous plonge dans un profond embarras et nous vous prions d'effectuer immédiatement un nouvel envoi pour réparer l'erreur commise, faute de quoi nous serions obligés de nous adresser à un autre fournisseur.

Nous vous prions de croire, Madame, à l'expression de nos sentiments distingués.

La Directeur des Achats

Jacques Dupont

Jacques Dupont

Concise explanation of nature of complaint.

Demand for action.

- **Dealing with a Customer Complaint**

When replying to a customer complaint, it is necessary to give an explanation for what happened. If the complaint is justified, the company must apologize and offer a solution.

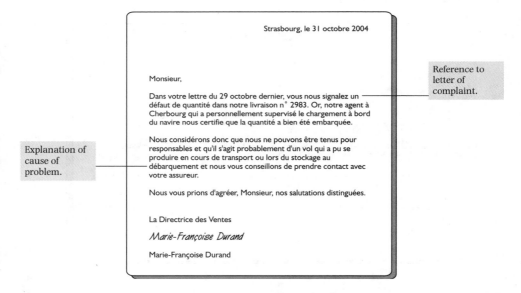

Strasbourg, le 31 octobre 2004

Monsieur,

Dans votre lettre du 29 octobre dernier, vous nous signalez un défaut de quantité dans notre livraison n° 2983. Or, notre agent à Cherbourg qui a personnellement supervisé le chargement à bord du navire nous certifie que la quantité a bien été embarquée.

Nous considérons donc que nous ne pouvons être tenus pour responsables et qu'il s'agit probablement d'un vol qui a pu se produire en cours de transport ou lors du stockage au débarquement et nous vous conseillons de prendre contact avec votre assureur.

Nous vous prions d'agréer, Monsieur, nos salutations distinguées.

La Directrice des Ventes

Marie-Françoise Durand

Marie-Françoise Durand

Reference to letter of complaint.

Explanation of cause of problem.

Useful Phrases:

Nous vous prions de bien vouloir nous excuser pour cette regrettable erreur.
Veuillez accepter nos excuses pour le dérangement que nous avons pu vous causer.
Nous avons pris des mesures pour que cela ne se reproduise plus.
Nous espérons que ce contretemps n'aura pour vous aucune conséquence préjudiciable.

• Invoice

A company is free to choose the layout of its invoices provided all the essential information is included.

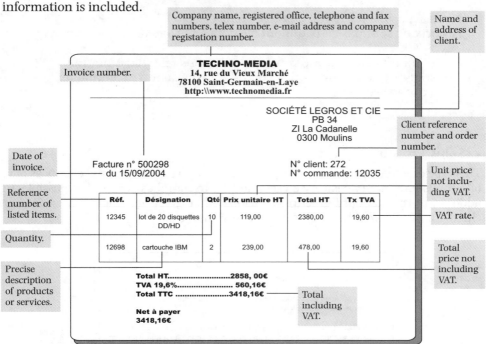

Company name, registered office, telephone and fax numbers, telex number, e-mail address and company registation number.

Name and address of client.

Invoice number.

TECHNO-MEDIA
14, rue du Vieux Marché
78100 Saint-Germain-en-Laye
http:\\www.technomedia.fr

SOCIÉTÉ LEGROS ET CIE
PB 34
ZI La Cadanelle
0300 Moulins

Client reference number and order number.

Date of invoice.

Facture n° 500298
du 15/09/2004

N° client: 272
N° commande: 12035

Unit price not including VAT.

Reference number of listed items.

Quantity.

Réf.	Désignation	Qté	Prix unitaire HT	Total HT	Tx TVA
12345	lot de 20 disquettes DD/HD	10	119,00	2380,00	19,60
12698	cartouche IBM	2	239,00	478,00	19,60

VAT rate.

Total price not including VAT.

Precise description of products or services.

Total HT.............................2858, 00€
TVA 19,6%..........................560,16€
Total TTC ....3418,16€

Total including VAT.

Net à payer
3418,16€

Total including VAT.

• Reply to Invoice

You only need to reply to an invoice if you are contesting it.

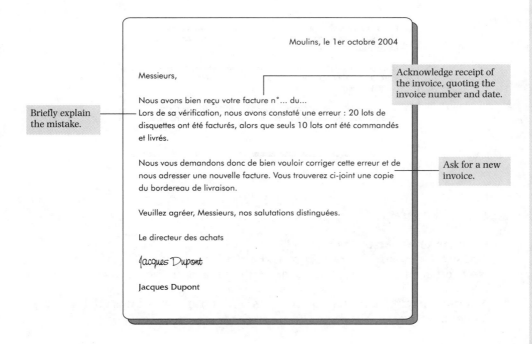

Moulins, le 1er octobre 2004

Messieurs,

Acknowledge receipt of the invoice, quoting the invoice number and date.

Nous avons bien reçu votre facture n°... du...

Briefly explain the mistake.

Lors de sa vérification, nous avons constaté une erreur : 20 lots de disquettes ont été facturés, alors que seuls 10 lots ont été commandés et livrés.

Nous vous demandons donc de bien vouloir corriger cette erreur et de nous adresser une nouvelle facture. Vous trouverez ci-joint une copie du bordereau de livraison.

Ask for a new invoice.

Veuillez agréer, Messieurs, nos salutations distinguées.

Le directeur des achats

Jacques Dupont

Jacques Dupont

- ## Sales Promotion Letter

This type of letter, known as a "circulaire", is sent to many potential clients as part of a mailshot. The style is very direct and tries to sound as personal as possible. In addition to the standard greetings, various other greetings might be used: Cher client/Chère cliente, Cher Monsieur/Chère Madame etc.

Note the typical greeting.

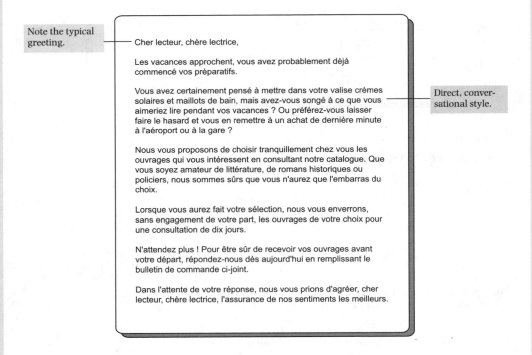

Cher lecteur, chère lectrice,

Les vacances approchent, vous avez probablement déjà commencé vos préparatifs.

Vous avez certainement pensé à mettre dans votre valise crèmes solaires et maillots de bain, mais avez-vous songé à ce que vous aimeriez lire pendant vos vacances ? Ou préférez-vous laisser faire le hasard et vous en remettre à un achat de dernière minute à l'aéroport ou à la gare ?

Nous vous proposons de choisir tranquillement chez vous les ouvrages qui vous intéressent en consultant notre catalogue. Que vous soyez amateur de littérature, de romans historiques ou policiers, nous sommes sûrs que vous n'aurez que l'embarras du choix.

Lorsque vous aurez fait votre sélection, nous vous enverrons, sans engagement de votre part, les ouvrages de votre choix pour une consultation de dix jours.

N'attendez plus ! Pour être sûr de recevoir vos ouvrages avant votre départ, répondez-nous dès aujourd'hui en remplissant le bulletin de commande ci-joint.

Dans l'attente de votre réponse, nous vous prions d'agréer, cher lecteur, chère lectrice, l'assurance de nos sentiments les meilleurs.

Direct, conversational style.

Employment

Cover Letter

When applying for a job in France, it is customary to write the cover letter ("lettre de motivation") by hand. Apart from adding a more personal touch, it is not unusual for French companies to use the services of a graphologist who analyses the applicants' handwriting.

A letter of application is quite formal in its presentation. It should be concise, properly structured in paragraphs and have the standard opening and closing formulas. You should cover the following points:

- Emphasize what you consider important in your CV
- Add information about your objectives
- Explain why you are interested in the company
- Convince the reader that you are the right person for the job

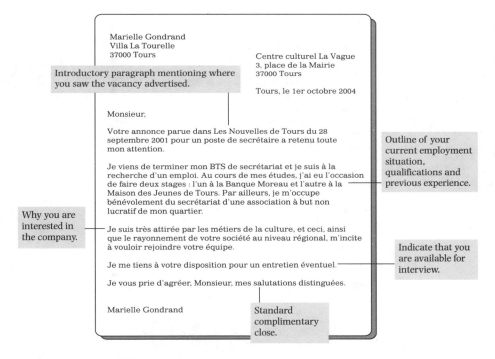

Marielle Gondrand
Villa La Tourelle
37000 Tours

Centre culturel La Vague
3, place de la Mairie
37000 Tours

Tours, le 1er octobre 2004

Introductory paragraph mentioning where you saw the vacancy advertised.

Monsieur,

Votre annonce parue dans Les Nouvelles de Tours du 28 septembre 2001 pour un poste de secrétaire a retenu toute mon attention.

Je viens de terminer mon BTS de secrétariat et je suis à la recherche d'un emploi. Au cours de mes études, j'ai eu l'occasion de faire deux stages : l'un à la Banque Moreau et l'autre à la Maison des Jeunes de Tours. Par ailleurs, je m'occupe bénévolement du secrétariat d'une association à but non lucratif de mon quartier.

Outline of your current employment situation, qualifications and previous experience.

Why you are interested in the company.

Je suis très attirée par les métiers de la culture, et ceci, ainsi que le rayonnement de votre société au niveau régional, m'incite à vouloir rejoindre votre équipe.

Je me tiens à votre disposition pour un entretien éventuel.

Indicate that you are available for interview.

Je vous prie d'agréer, Monsieur, mes salutations distinguées.

Marielle Gondrand

Standard complimentary close.

Useful Phrases:

En réponse à votre annonce parue dans Les Nouvelles de Tours du..., je me permets de vous adresser mon curriculum vitae pour le poste de secrétaire.
Je dispose de plusieurs années d'expérience dans différentes entreprises.
Au cours de mes cinq années d'expérience auprès de la société X, j'ai acquis une bonne maîtrise de...
Je souhaite élargir mon expérience professionnelle tout en acquérant de nouvelles responsabilités et serais donc ravi d'intégrer une entreprise aussi dynamique et réputée que la vôtre.
En espérant que ma candidature retiendra votre attention, je vous prie d'agréer, Madame, Monsieur, l'expression de mes sentiments distingués.

- Asking for a Work Placement

Work placements are very popular in France and are a compulsory part of many courses. It is therefore advisable to send your request well in advance.
This type of letter is always handwritten in French (see Cover Letter p.15).

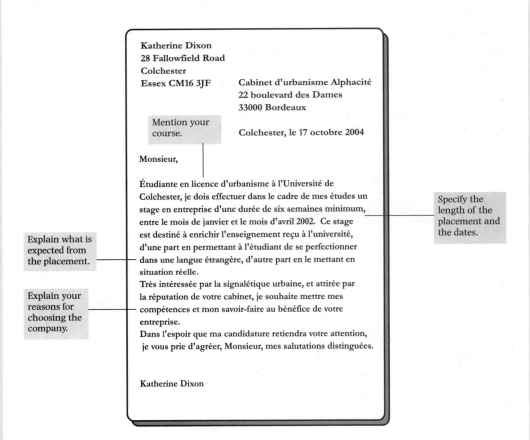

Katherine Dixon
28 Fallowfield Road
Colchester
Essex CM16 3JF   Cabinet d'urbanisme Alphacité
22 boulevard des Dames
33000 Bordeaux

Mention your course.   Colchester, le 17 octobre 2004

Monsieur,

Étudiante en licence d'urbanisme à l'Université de
Colchester, je dois effectuer dans le cadre de mes études un
stage en entreprise d'une durée de six semaines minimum,
entre le mois de janvier et le mois d'avril 2002. Ce stage
est destiné à enrichir l'enseignement reçu à l'université,
d'une part en permettant à l'étudiant de se perfectionner
dans une langue étrangère, d'autre part en le mettant en
situation réelle.
Très intéressée par la signalétique urbaine, et attirée par
la réputation de votre cabinet, je souhaite mettre mes
compétences et mon savoir-faire au bénéfice de votre
entreprise.
Dans l'espoir que ma candidature retiendra votre attention,
je vous prie d'agréer, Monsieur, mes salutations distinguées.

Katherine Dixon

Specify the length of the placement and the dates.

Explain what is expected from the placement.

Explain your reasons for choosing the company.

Useful Phrases:

Vous trouverez ci-joint mon curriculum vitae.
Je vous remercie de l'attention que vous porterez à ma demande et reste
à votre disposition pour un entretien.
Je reste à votre disposition pour vous rencontrer et vous fournir tout
autre renseignement.
En vous remerciant à l'avance de bien vouloir examiner ma demande, je
vous prie d'agréer...

Curriculum Vitae

The presentation of a CV in French is in many ways similar to an English or American CV. The following points should be noted.

- The title "Curriculum Vitae" should never be included in a French CV.
- Only mention hobbies if they add something personal to your profile or if they are particularly relevant to the job. It is assumed that everybody likes reading, going to the cinema, listening to music and travelling.
- Do not include referees on your CV: references are not commonly used in France apart from certain occupations where personal recommendation would be expected such as catering, cleaning, child care, building etc.
- Even if you do not complete your degree, you can mention the fact that you studied for it by using the word "niveau", for example "niveau licence".

- **Experienced (French)**

Laure Battisto
25, rue des Arquebusiers
76000 Rouen
Tél : 02 24 24 45 73   41 ans
Télécopie : 02 24 21 13 39   divorcée
E-mail : lbattisto@battisto.com.fr   un enfant (10 ans)

Consultante en Ressources humaines
13 ans d'expérience

Expérience professionnelle
1991 - 1996   Consultante en Ressources humaines, Cabinet Battisto-Langlade, Rouen : conseil auprès d'entreprises, audit, recrutement

1987 - 1990   Directrice des Ressources humaines, Conseil général, Le Havre : recrutement, planification des formations, suivi du personnel

1985 - 1986   Assistante du Directeur des Ressources humaines, Société Pierre et Fils, Le Havre

Formation
1983   Master of Business Administration, Boston University

1981 - 1982   DEA 'Langage et Médias' - Paris X

1980   Maîtrise d'Histoire - Paris IV

1976   Baccalauréat Mathématiques - Académie de Paris

Autres expériences
1984 - 1985   Voyage en Afrique dans le cadre d'une mission Médecins sans frontières

Langues
Bilingue anglais
Espagnol : lu, écrit, parlé

Divers
Bonne maîtrise du traitement de texte sur PC et sur Mac
Responsable d'une association bénévole luttant contre l'analphabétisme

- ## Experienced (American)

John Farmer
18 rue de Turenne
75004 Paris
Tél: 01 42 22 37 89
E-mail: jfarmer@nxl.fr

Né le 17 juin 1962
Marié, 2 enfants (11 et 14 ans)
Nationalité américaine

Directeur des ventes : 8 ans d'expérience
17 ans d'expérience dans la fonction commerciale
Connaissance approfondie du marché informatique

Depuis 1996	Softlux France, Paris Directeur des ventes Europe · Encadrement d'une équipe de 20 commerciaux · Diversification et développement des marchés existants · Ouverture de 3 nouveaux marchés (Grèce, Portugal, Espagne) · Augmentation du chiffre d'affaires (+ 53 %)

1988-1996	ICN Europe, Amsterdam
	Directeur commercial
	· Responsable de la politique commerciale et du marketing
	  opérationnel
	· Recrutement et encadrement d'une équipe de 7 commerciaux
	· Définition des objectifs commerciaux
	· Dépassement des objectifs fixés:
	  1994: 118 %, 1993: 110%, 1992: 108 %

1983-1987	Société ADB, Paris Ingénieur commercial grands comptes · Responsable du développement des ventes pour le secteur de la grande distribution sur la région parisienne · Ouverture de nouveaux comptes · Atteinte des objectifs fixés

Formation

1988	MBA, Harvard Business School
1984	MS (équivalent de la maîtrise) en Économie et Gestion, Yale University
1980	High school diploma (équivalent du baccalauréat)

Langues
Anglais : langue maternelle ; Français : bilingue ; Espagnol : notions

- ## Experienced (British)

Mary Grant
198 Francis Avenue
Leicester LE4 9PQ
Grande-Bretagne
Tél : 00 44 1493 767 33 36
E-mail: mgrant@USA.net

38 ans, célibataire
Nationalité britannique

EXPÉRIENCE PROFESSIONNELLE

Depuis septembre 1994	Directrice des exportations, Gannett UK Ltd, Leicester (Fabrication et distribution de produits cosmétiques) » mise en place d'un réseau commercial (40 représentants et 10 agents) » négociations avec les points de vente » études de marchés Augmentation du C.A. de 62 %
1990 - 1994	Responsable des exportations Europe, Simon & Co plc, Leicester (prêt-à-porter enfants) » prospection » contrôle des ventes » ouverture de deux nouveaux marchés (Espagne et Italie) Augmentation du C.A. de 53 % en 4 ans

FORMATION

1989 - 1993	MA (équivalent de la Maîtrise) en Gestion, Université d'Édimbourg
1989	A Levels (équivalent du baccalauréat) : économie, mathématiques, histoire et français (Lycée Harfield Comprehensive, Leicester)
1988	GCSE (premier examen de fin de scolarité) : anglais, mathématiques, français, économie, informatique et histoire (Lycée Harfield Comprehensive, Leicester)

AUTRES ACTIVITÉS

1993 - 1994	Séjour d'une année à Paris : enseignement de l'anglais commercial à la Chambre de commerce et d'industrie franco-britannique

LANGUES
Anglais : langue maternelle ; Bilingue français (mère française) ; Espagnol : lu, écrit, parlé

DIVERS
Bonne maîtrise de l'outil informatique sur PC et sur Mac
Chant choral

- ## Recent Graduate (French)

Isabelle Murat
30, impasse de la Colline
75004 Paris   25 ans
Tél : 01 40 22 57 93   Célibataire

Formation

septembre 01 - juin 2003	École Technique Supérieure, Bordeaux : Section Statistiques et Prévisions
septembre 00 - juin 01	Mathématiques spéciales (Lycée Louis Leduc, Paris)
septembre 99 - juin 00	Mathématiques supérieures (Lycée Louis Leduc, Paris)
juin 1999	Baccalauréat C (mention bien)

Expérience professionnelle

avril - mai 2002	Stage de 3 mois au Cabinet Desmoulin-Marketing et Communication, 44, rue des Francs-Bourgeois, 75004 Paris : relance et suivi de la clientèle
juillet - septembre 1999	Animatrice dans un camp d'adolescents à Port-de-Bouc (13)

Langues
Bilingue allemand
Anglais courant

Divers

juillet 2001	Séjour de deux mois en Allemagne, à Dortmund
juin 1999	Obtention du diplôme du BAFA (Brevet d'aptitude aux fonctions d'animateur)
juillet 93 - juin 95	Séjour d'un an à Munich

Loisirs
Course à pied, vélo, aérobic
Théâtre dans une troupe d'amateurs
Cours de cuisine

- ## Recent Graduate (American)

Martha Jacobs
493 Huntington Avenue
Boston
MA 02575
États-Unis
Tél : (617) 267-1680   23 ans, célibataire
E-mail: mjacobs@totem.com   Nationalité américaine

Traductrice anglais/français/espagnol
Début de spécialisation en informatique

FORMATION

2001 - 2003	Diplôme de traducteur technique Université McGill, Montréal
1997 - 2001	BA (équivalent de la licence) en français et espagnol, mention très bien Université de Boston
1996	High school diploma (équivalent du baccalauréat)

EXPÉRIENCE PROFESSIONNELLE

1999 - 2002	**Éditions Dulis**, Montréal Travaux de traduction en free-lance
juin 1997 - septembre 1998	**Société AX Networks**, Boston Stage de 3 mois dans le service de traduction : adaptation de logiciels pour le marché européen
1996 - 1997	**Lycée Dupuis**, Grenoble Assistante de français

LANGUES
Anglais : langue maternelle
Français : bilingue (2 ans à Montréal, 1 an à Grenoble)
Espagnol : courant

CONNAISSANCES INFORMATIQUES
Word, Excel et Access (sur PC et Mac)

LOISIRS
Escrime, violoncelle

- ## Recent Graduate (British)

Stephen Forbes
81 Lincoln Walk
Stevenage
Herts SE19 2DN
Tél: 00 44 1283 456789
E-mail: sforbes@teaser.org.uk

23 ans, célibataire
Nationalité britannique

Formation

1998 - 2002	BSc (équivalent de la licence) en Biologie, Université de Swansea, Grande-Bretagne.
1998	A Levels (équivalent du baccalauréat) : Mathématiques, Chimie, Biologie et Français, Lycée Whitton Comprehensive, Bristol, Grande-Bretagne.
1997	GCSE (premier examen de fin de scolarité) : Anglais, Mathématiques, Chimie, Biologie, Français, Histoire et Informatique, Lycée Whitton Comprehensive, Bristol, Grande-Bretagne.

Expérience professionnelle

juillet - septembre 2002	Stage de 3 mois auprès du service d'hématologie de l'hôpital Frenchay de Bristol : analyse de prélèvements sanguins.
octobre 1998 - novembre 1999	Enseignement de l'anglais langue étrangère, École de langues Babel, Osaka, Japon.

Langues
anglais : langue maternelle
français : courant
japonais : notions

Divers
Bonnes connaissances informatiques : animateur du club d'informatique d'une maison des jeunes et de la culture (Bristol)

Titulaire du brevet de secourisme

Faxes

Faxes, which are by definition a form of rapid communication, can generally be drafted in a more casual and concise way than letters. The endings are usually short and simplified.

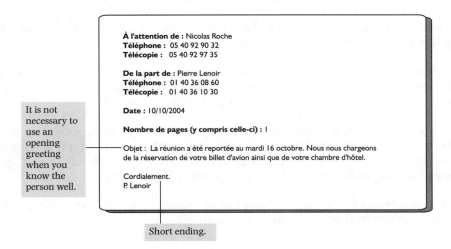

À l'attention de : Nicolas Roche
Téléphone : 05 40 92 90 32
Télécopie : 05 40 92 97 35

De la part de : Pierre Lenoir
Téléphone : 01 40 36 08 60
Télécopie : 01 40 36 10 30

Date : 10/10/2004

Nombre de pages (y compris celle-ci) : 1

Objet : La réunion a été reportée au mardi 16 octobre. Nous nous chargeons de la réservation de votre billet d'avion ainsi que de votre chambre d'hôtel.

Cordialement.
P. Lenoir

It is not necessary to use an opening greeting when you know the person well.

Short ending.

- **Booking a Hotel Room**

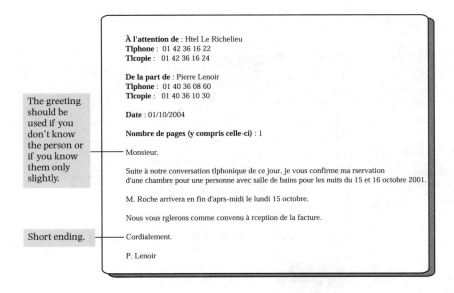

À l'attention de : Htel Le Richelieu
Tlphone : 01 42 36 16 22
Tlcopie : 01 42 36 16 24

De la part de : Pierre Lenoir
Tlphone : 01 40 36 08 60
Tlcopie : 01 40 36 10 30

Date : 01/10/2004

Nombre de pages (y compris celle-ci) : 1

Monsieur,

Suite à notre conversation tlphonique de ce jour, je vous confirme ma rservation d'une chambre pour une personne avec salle de bains pour les nuits du 15 et 16 octobre 2001.

M. Roche arrivera en fin d'aprs-midi le lundi 15 octobre.

Nous vous rglerons comme convenu à rception de la facture.

Cordialement.

P. Lenoir

The greeting should be used if you don't know the person or if you know them only slightly.

Short ending.

- Alternative endings:
  Salutations.
  Salutations distinguées.
  Bien à vous. (more friendly)

E-mail

• E-mail addresses are made up of two parts, the first being the user's name and the second being the domain name. The two parts are separated by the symbol @ (pronounced "arrobas" or "arobase" in French). It is important to type the exact address – get a single character wrong and the e-mail will not get through.

• Because of the nature of the medium, e-mails are not subject to the formal code of letter-writing that is prevalent in French.

• E-mail is becoming more and more widely used in the French working environment, although it is probably not yet as well established a method of business correspondence as it is in the English-speaking world.

• E-mails in French are often written in slightly less telegraphic style than tends to be the case in English, this being mainly due to the fact that French contains fewer of the abbreviated forms that characterize so much of this type of communication in English. Endings are usually rather informal.

• The same rules of "netiquette" apply as in English, so avoid typing entire words in capital letters as this is equivalent to shouting.

• **Within a Company**

The headings are often in English as many French firms use American-manufactured software.

Informal greeting. It can also be omitted.

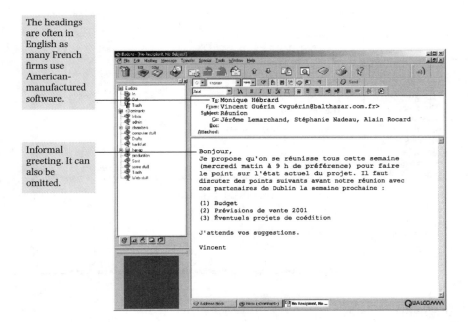

- **Business to Business**

The ending is never as formal as in a letter.

Greetings are often omitted.

- **To an ISP**

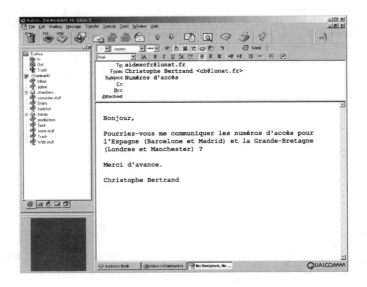

Abbreviations and Acronyms: e-mail and Internet

Below is a list of French abbreviations which are used in e-mail correspondence and in newsgroups. These abbreviations should only be used when you are sure that the person to whom you are sending the message understands what they mean. Some are familiar in register (labelled *Fam*) and therefore should only be used in casual correspondence with friends or very close colleagues.

Note that because English is the main language of the Internet, English abbreviations (see section in French supplement) are much more well established than French ones.

A+ *Fam*	à plus tard (see you/talk to you etc later)	**ex.**	exemple (example)
actu *Fam*	actualités (news, current affairs)	**fr**	français (French)
alld	allemand (German)	**impr.**	impression; imprimer; imprimante (printout; print; printer)
alp *Fam*	à la prochaine (see you!; until we're next in touch!)	**info** *Fam*	information
ama *Fam*	à mon avis (in my opinion)	**K7** *Fam*	cassette
amha *Fam*	à mon humble avis (in my humble opinion)	**Ltr**	lettre (letter)
		m	même (even; same)
angl	anglais (English)	**Mdr** *Fam*	mort de rire (hilarious)
bcp *Fam*	beaucoup (a lot; many)	**MMS** *Fam*	mes meilleurs souvenirs (Best regards)
BAL	boîte à lettres (mailbox)	**nvx**	nouveaux (new)
B.D.	base de données (database)	**p**	pour (for)
dc	donc (then, therefore)	**pb, pbm**	problème (problem)
doc.	documents (documents, documentation)	**pr**	pour (for)
		quoi 2/9 *Fam*	quoi de neuf? (what's new?)
Doss	dossier (file)	**RAS** *Fam*	rien à signaler (nothing to report)
ds	dans (in)	**suiv.**	suivant (following)
envoy.	envoyer (please send)	**svt**	souvent (often)
err	erreur (error)	**urgt**	urgent
esp	espagnol (Spanish)	**we**	weekend

Abbreviations and Acronyms: General Correspondence

ac	argent comptant; année courante; acompte (ready money; current year; on account)		exchange statement)
		LJM	livraison le jour même (same-day delivery)
AG	assemblée générale (General Meeting, GM)	**M**	Monsieur (sir)
		Me	Maître (title applied to lawyers)
arr.	arrondissement (district)	**Melle(s)**	Mademoiselle/Mesdemoiselles (Miss(es))
art	article (article)		
AV	avis de virement (transfer advice)	**MM.**	Messieurs (Messrs.)
bd	boulevard	**Mme**	Madame (Madam)
BP	boîte postale (PO Box)	**Mon, Mson**	maison (firm)
CA	chiffre d'affaires (turnover)	**n.**	notre, nos (our)
C&A	coût et assurance (cost and insurance, C and I)	**NB**	Nota Bene
		N°	numéro (number, No.)
c-à-d.	c'est-à-dire (that is to say)	**N/Réf**	notre référence (our ref)
CAF	coût, assurance, fret (cost, insurance and freight, cif)	**p/c**	pour compte
		P.-D.G.	Président-Directeur Général (Chairman and Managing Director)
c-c.	compte courant (current account)		
CCP	compte chèque postal (post office account)		
		p.j.	pièce jointe (enclosure, enc)
Cedex	courrier d'entreprise à distribution exceptionnelle (postal code for business mail)	**PO**	par ordre (by order)
		p.p.	par procuration (by proxy)
		P.T.T.	Postes, Télégraphes et Téléphones (General Post Office)
Cie	compagnie (company)		
cpt	comptant (cash)	**réf**	référence (reference, ref)
CR	compte-rendu (minutes)	**R.F.**	République Française (French Republic)
CV	curriculum vitae		
Dépt	département (administrative subdivision of France)	**r.p.**	réponse payée (reply paid)
		R.S.V.P.	répondez, s'il vous plaît (Please reply)
Dest.	destinataire (recipient)		
DRH	Directeur(trice) des Resources Humaines (Human Resources Manager)	**S.A.**	Société Anonyme (Limited Company)
		SARL	société à responsabilité limitée (limited (liability) company)
E.O.O.E	erreur ou omission exceptée (errors and omissions excepted)		
		s.e. ou o.	sauf erreur(s) ou omission(s) (errors and omissions excepted)
esc.	escompte (discount)		
Ets	établissements (factory; premises)	**SS**	Sécurité Sociale (social security)
Exp.	expéditeur (sender)	**SVP**	s'il vous plaît (please)
Fres	Frères (brothers)	**TEG**	taux effectif global (annual percentage rate, APR)
F.S.	faire suivre (please forward)		
hon.	honorée ("favour"; letter)	**Tél.**	téléphone (telephone)
HT	hors taxe (exclusive of tax)	**T.S.V.P.**	tournez s'il vous plaît (please turn over, PTO)
id.	idem (ditto)		
incl.	inclus (included)	**v.**	votre, vos (your)
j./jr(s)	jour(s) (day(s))	**Ve; Vve**	veuve (widow)
l/c	lettre de crédit (letter of credit)	**V/Réf**	votre référence (your ref)
LCR	lettre de change relevé (bills of		

Telephone Calls

Pronunciation of telephone numbers

When giving their phone numbers, French people say them two by two: 01 45 67 44 32: zéro un, quarante-cinq, soixante-sept, quarante-quatre, trente-deux.

This can be a little disconcerting for the English speaker and you may have to ask them to repeat giving one number at a time.

Typical Phrases

- ### Asking for information from the operator or switchboard

Est-ce que vous pouvez me passer les renseignements, s'il vous plaît ?
J'essaie d'obtenir un numéro à Marseille.
Quel est l'indicatif pour le Maroc, s'il vous plaît ?
Comment fait-on pour appeler à l'extérieur ?

- ### Answering the telephone

Informally:
Allô?
To which the caller replies:
Allô, (c'est) Georges? or *Salut, Georges, c'est Christophe etc*
More formally:
Allô, Hélène Chapsal à l'appareil (, je vous écoute).
In a company or institution:
Déménagements Leclerc, bonjour.
Éditions Paoli, bonjour.

- ### Asking to speak to someone:

Je voudrais parler à Monsieur Dupont.
Pouvez-vous me passer le service du/des ..., s'il vous plaît ?
Pouvez-vous me passer le poste 321, s'il vous plaît ? (pronounced **trois cent vingt-et-un**)

- ### Phrases used by a receptionist or secretary taking a call

Qui dois-je annoncer ?
C'est de la part de qui ?
When putting a caller through:
Je vous le passe.
Ne quittez pas, je vous le passe.
When the caller cannot be connected immediately:
C'est occupé.
Il est en communication, voulez-vous patienter ?
Asking the caller if he or she wishes to leave a message:
Voulez-vous lui laisser un message ?
To which the caller may reply:
Pouvez-vous lui demander de me rappeler ?

- Recorded messages

If you are put through to an answering machine, the usual recorded message while waiting is :

Nous vous demandons de bien vouloir patienter quelques instants. Nous allons donner suite à votre appel.

If you have to leave a message, you will hear the following standard set of sentences:

Vous êtes bien en communication avec... Nous ne pouvons répondre à votre appel. Veuillez nous laisser votre nom et numéro de téléphone après le signal sonore et nous vous rappellerons dès que possible. Merci.

FRENCH BUSINESS MEETINGS

by Maddy Glas

Maddy Glas, Docteur de la Sorbonne, has worked in many EU countries and now teaches business French in the language department of the French business school INSEAD.

Contents

Introduction

The word "réunion" in French is used to refer to meetings which lie outside the scope of the typical business meeting discussed below: we find, in particular, "la réunion d'information" which is more of a conference or a seminar where, without any agenda, a speaker makes a presentation of an issue which may or may not be followed by a question-and-answer session.

The run-of-the-mill business meeting (with a chairperson, a secretary, an agenda, minutes, a fixed slot in the week's or month's business diary, and largely the concern of the same limited group of colleagues) resembles only superficially the business meeting conducted in the UK and US.

Glossary

a business meeting	**une réunion d'affaires**
a seminar/conference	**une réunion d'information**
a board meeting	**une réunion du conseil d'administration**
a sales meeting	**une réunion de vente**
a brainstorming session	**un brainstorming**
a planning committee	**un comité d'orientation**
an informal meeting	**une conférence**
a management meeting	**une réunion de la direction**
the meeting room	**la salle de réunion**
the boardroom	**la salle de direction**

---

1. Preparing the Meeting

Preparation implies fixed objectives, thus an agenda ("l'ordre du jour") has to be established and distributed beforehand to those taking part ("les participants"). Usual expressions are:

Je dois assister à une réunion/participer à une réunion	I have to attend/take part in a meeting

The agenda is the responsibility of the chairperson ("président(e) de la réunion/animateur(trice)"), so placing an item on the agenda requires his or her assent.

Practice varies, and in many small businesses ("PME-PMI") the agenda is drawn up at the beginning of the meeting on the basis of the current preoccupations of its participants.

The agenda, on which the date ("la date"), the time ("l'heure"), and the place ("le lieu") are mentioned, acts as a summons ("une convocation"). Should one or another of these parameters be different from normal practice, the chairperson's secretary ("la secrétaire de direction") will normally inform the participants personally beforehand to confirm their availability.

In French business, hierarchies tend to be strictly formal, so any excuse for absence has to be negotiated with the chairperson in person. Greater latitude is given to the demands of one's private life than in the UK (for example, sick children, or picking up the car from the garage), but repeated absence is not recommended.

The existence of a more formal hierarchy in French business largely explains the different function of the business meeting in the two countries. Since in France, decision-making is the prerogative of the hierarchical superior (the chair – "l'animateur(trice)"), the business meeting is more of a forum for the formulation and exchange of ideas. A bad idea, brilliantly proposed, may have more impact than a good idea poorly presented. This has obvious consequences both for the agenda and for the conduct of the meeting.

As far as the agenda is concerned, a reading of the previous minutes is not a formal item, and the idea of AOB tends to be relegated to the realm of non-sense. Responsibility for presenting items on the agenda is often delegated to the participants (thankfully forewarned), leaving the newcomer with the impression of attending a seminar. There is no pressure from the chairperson to get through the agenda, or even to finish the agenda: the wider discussion can range, the better. The agenda, in other words, is no more than an approximation of what the participants are expected to and will in fact discuss. Effective participation thus demands a thorough grasp of company politics, and a high level of preparation for those items relevant to one's interests.

2. Running the Meeting

Before the meeting starts, do not forget to shake hands with all those you have not previously shaken hands with that day. The chairperson starts the proceedings by referring to the agenda and suggesting any changes in the order of the items down for discussion. The tone is often stiffly formal, a strange contrast to the generally relaxed atmosphere of such meetings in English-speaking countries. He or she uses such expressions as:

Nous sommes ici pour...	We are here today in order to...
Aujourd'hui, nous allons examiner...	Today, we are going to discuss...
Le but de notre réunion est de...	The purpose of today's meeting is to...

A lot of UK businesspeople are surprised by the apparent aimlessness of such meetings compared to the conventions they are used to, where a chairperson guides the participants through the agenda with a firm hand, cuts short speakers who tend not to stick to the point, or who stray from the cut and thrust of opinion and argument demanded by the various items. Here, the role of the chairperson is to encourage the widest discussion possible with a view to later synthesizing the different positions adopted by the participants. As decisions are the prerogative of the chairperson, his or her aim is to have the possibilities examined from all conceivable angles. Should you remain reticent, he or she will often explicitly demand your opinion:

Nous n'avons pas encore bénéficié du point de vue de Monsieur...	We haven't heard from Mr... yet
Et vous, Monsieur, quelle est votre opinion à ce sujet?	And what do you think about this, Mr...

First names are rarely used, and in the absence of a lead from the chairperson, "Nous pouvons nous tutoyer, je crois"(I think it is appropriate to use the "tu" form of address), you would be advised to stick to the "vous" form. Even using the "vous" form does not exempt the participant from a formal display of respect which can border on caricature:

Je suis d'accord avec vous, Monsieur	I totally agree with you, sir
Monsieur, avec tout le respect que je vous dois...	With all due respect, sir,...

Even a certain intimacy between participants is subtly suppressed: a close collaborator of the chairperson, on first-name terms, would address him or her as "Monsieur"/"Madame"or "Monsieur le Président"/"Madame la Présidente". The use of the blunt "Monsieur"/"Madame" however, to someone with whom you are on close terms, would be taken as a rebuke. French also includes a highly developed form of gestural expression: it is often necessary to catch the chairperson's eye by lifting a finger; opening both palms may express either agreement or disagreement, but above all a desire to speak; putting the thumb and the index finger together underlines the importance of a point, or a desire for precision. By contrast, an open palm pointing upwards means you have made your point, but without conviction.

Most contributors use a common stock of phrases:

À mon avis...	In my opinion/if you ask me
Je trouve que.../Je pense que...	I think that...
Je voudrais préciser mon point de vue...	I'll try to be more clear...
Je désire mettre en évidence...	I'd like to draw your attention to...
J'aimerais suggérer...	May I suggest...
Je tiens à préciser que...	I'd like to point out that...
Je voudrais ajouter un point qui me paraît important...	I'd like to add a point I think is important...

Agreement may be expressed as follows:

Je suis d'accord avec...	I agree with...
Je partage l'opinion de...	I share ...'s opinion
J'approuve ce point de vue	I'm of the same opinion
Vous avez absolument raison	You are quite right
Excellente idée	What a good idea

Disagreements, on the other hand, can be expressed in the following way:

Je ne suis pas d'accord	I don't agree
Je crains que...	What worries me is/I'm afraid...
Je désapprouve l'idée	I'm not happy with the idea
Je ne suis pas de votre avis	I don't share your viewpoint
Je déplore...	I'm sorry to say...
Je doute que...	I doubt if...

And, of course, there is always the infamous:

Oui, mais...	Yes, but...

Disagreement is often preceded by an apparently innocent request for further information:

Que voulez-vous dire par...?	What do you mean when you say...?
Qu'entendez-vous exactement par...?	What does... mean exactly?
Pourriez-vous m'expliquer...?	Can you explain...?

Interrupting requires diplomacy:

Je suis désolé(e) de vous interrompre...	Excuse me for interrupting...
Si vous me permettez une seconde...	If I may interrupt for just a second...

To which one may retort:

Vous permettez que je termine ?	Let me finish what I'm saying
Laissez-moi continuer	Please don't interrupt

3. Follow-up

The writing and circulating of the minutes ("le compte-rendu") is the responsibility of the secretary. As the reading of the previous minutes does not figure on the agenda, serious complaints should be raised at the start of the following meeting, but in a highly diplomatic form:

Juste un détail sur le compte-rendu de notre dernière réunion... Si ma mémoire est bonne...	Just a small point concerning the minutes... If I remember correctly...

4. General Observations

A. *Punctuality*

The French notion of time is quite different from that in northern Europe. Not only do meetings tend to be open-ended (discussion can continue for hours), but they rarely begin on time. At first, British people may interpret this as sloppiness, downright rudeness, or some other form of "inefficiency". However, it is neither better nor worse than a Briton's "respect"of time: it is just different, and reflects deeper aspects of Latin culture. If you start to calculate by how much you can be late for a meeting or an appointment, you have not begun to understand the difference. Nobody arrives late on purpose, but nobody will break off a conversation because it is "time" to be somewhere else.

B. *The presentation of an argument*

Since high school, a particular method for writing and presenting an argument has been drummed into French children: "thèse", "antithèse" and "synthèse". Thus it is not surprising that business arguments and presentations revolve around this logic: first, the points in favour; second, the points against; and finally, a judicious summing up of the strengths and weaknesses.

Two different strategies can be identified. First, a description of the present situation followed by an analysis of its strengths and weaknesses, leading to suggestions as to how the situation can be improved or reformed. Second, the analysis of a problem in terms of known causes and standard remedies, followed by the recommendation of a particular solution.

C. *Losing face*

Being mistaken, or being responsible for an error, means losing face. Consequently, errors and mistakes are not openly recognized and admitted. This aspect of French culture raises two problems: how to cover up for one's own mistakes, and how to indicate the mistakes of others.

The first requires a certain aplomb. Whereas Britons tend to assume responsibility for the mistakes of others, the French make no reservations in detecting the "culprit"and detailing the disciplinary measures taken to avoid similar mistakes in the future. This is considered "good management".

The second requires elegance:

Ne pensez-vous pas que la meilleure solution aurait été de...?	Don't you think with hindsight that it might have been better to...?
Avec les données d'aujourd'hui en main, il aurait peut-être fallu...	Knowing what we know today, don't you think it might have been better to...?

WORKING WITH AN INTERPRETER

In today's international business environment, interpretation is becoming increasingly common as a means of helping people from different countries to communicate. In order to get your message across to an international audience, it is essential to understand how best to work with interpreters.

There are three types of interpreting:

- Simultaneous
- Consecutive
- Whispering

Simultaneous is the most common form for conferences and business meetings. A microphone relays the speaker's voice to the interpreters who are sitting in soundproof booths. They then interpret instantaneously into the relevant language and the delegates listen to the interpretation via headsets.

Consecutive is used when simultaneous interpretation would not be practical, eg for factory visits or over dinner. The interpreter stands or sits next to you and interprets what you have said after you have said it, sometimes taking notes.

Whispering is the least common form of interpretation. The interpreter sits next to the delegates and whispers the translation of the presentation while it is being made.

Making a Presentation to an International Audience

If you know that your presentation is being interpreted into other languages, bear in mind the following points:

- Adapt the content of your speech to reflect the fact that it will be listened to by people from different cultures. Jokes rarely translate well and may even seem inappropriate to people from certain cultures. Culture-specific references are also usually meaningless to delegates from other countries. Colloquial or very technical language can be hard to translate, so stick to everyday vocabulary wherever possible.

- If you have written your speech out in advance, always provide a copy for the interpreters. Ideally, they should receive it a couple of weeks before the presentation, but if this is impossible, at least distribute it to them just before you speak, along with copies of any transparencies or other documents you may be discussing. Background information on the subject of the presentation is also useful if provided in advance of the conference.

- When using simultaneous interpretation, you will be speaking into a microphone. The sound from the microphone is what the interpreters hear, and if they cannot hear what you are saying, they cannot interpret it. First, make sure your microphone is switched on and the interpreters can hear you. Direct your voice towards the microphone, but slightly over the top of it rather than straight at it. Remain at a constant distance from the microphone – if you keep moving towards it and then away, the volume will keep going up and down. When turning to point to a screen behind you, remember that if you speak with your back to the microphone, it will not pick up what you say. To avoid this problem, people using transparencies often wear a small microphone attached to their tie or lapel. If you are using one of these, remember that if you brush against it with your hand or jacket while speaking, the interpreters will only be able to hear a loud crackling noise.

- When using an overhead projector, make sure the screen is positioned so that the interpreters can see it. It is important to take the audience through the content of each transparency, otherwise only those people who speak the language in which they are written will understand them.

- The most common mistake made by people speaking to an international audience is to speak too quickly. Interpreters don't simply repeat what you say, they have to translate it first, so they inevitably need more time than you do. Consider also that many European languages (including French) are up to one third longer than English. Furthermore, there may be delegates listening to your speech in the language you are making it in, even though it is their second language.

- One way to ensure you keep to a reasonable pace is to pause at the end of every sentence. This allows the listeners time to digest what you have said and gives the interpreters time to finish translating. A good speaker will wait until he or she hears that the interpreters have stopped speaking before continuing with his or her presentation.

- It is essential to speak clearly. Interpreters can only translate what they hear; if you mumble they will not be able to communicate your message.

If you bear all these points in mind next time you attend a multilingual conference or business meeting, you will be doing your bit to improve international communication and understanding.

Do's and don'ts when working with an interpreter

✓ Do:
- Provide a copy of your speech, transparencies and reference material in advance.
- Switch your microphone on and use it correctly.
- Speak slowly and clearly.

✗ Don't:
- Use too many jokes or culture-specific references.
- Turn away from the microphone when speaking about transparencies.
- Change language in the middle of a sentence.

Please note that the French name for the countries has been given in the second column. In order to find the French terms for the currencies and languages, please refer to the corresponding table in the French supplement.

Note also that the abbreviations given for currencies are the internationally recognised standard abbreviations established by the ISO and used in international financial transactions, rather than locally used abbreviations.

English name	French name	Local name	Official language(s)	Currency
Afghanistan	Afghanistan	Afghānestān	Dari, Pushtøu	1 Afghani (AFA) = 100 puls
Albania	Albanie	Shqïpëri	Albanian	1 Lek (ALL) = 100 qindarka
Algeria	Algérie	Al-Jazā'ir (Arabic), Algérie (French)	Arabic	1 Algerian Dinar (DZD) = 100 centimes
Andorra	Andorre	Andorra	Catalan, French, Spanish	1 Euro (EUR) = 100 cents
Angola	Angola	Angola	Portuguese	New Kwanza (AOK) = 100 weil
Argentina	Argentine	Argentina	Spanish	1 Peso (ARS) = 100 centavos
Armenia	Arménie	Hayastani Hanrapetut'yun	Armenian	1 Dram (AMD) =100 louma
Australia	Australie	Australia	English	1 Australian Dollar (AUD) = 100 cents
Austria	Autriche	Österreich	German	1 Euro (EUR) = 100 cents
Azerbaijan	Azerbaïdjan	Azarbaijan	Azeri (Azerbaijan)	1 Manat (AZM) =100 gopik
The Bahamas	Bahamas	Bahamas	English	1 Bahamian Dollar (BSD) = 100 cents
Bahrain	Bahreïn	Dawlat al-Bahrayn	Arabic	1 Bahrain Dinar (BHD) = 1,000 fils
Bangladesh	Bangladesh	Gana Prajatantri Bangladesh	Bengali	1 Taka (BDT) = 100 poisha
Barbados	Barbade	Barbados	English	1 Barbados Dollar (BBD) = 100 cents
Belarus	Biélorussie	Belarus	Belarussian	1 Rouble (BYB) =100 kopeks
Belgium	Belgique	Belgique (French), België (Flemish)	Flemish, French, German	1 Euro (EUR) = 100 cents
Belize	Belize	Belize	English	1 Belize Dollar (BZD) = 100 cents
Benin	Bénin	Bénin	French	1 CFA Franc (XOF) = 100 centimes
Bhutan	Bhoutan	Druk-Yul	Dzongkha	1 Ngultrum (BTN) = 100 chetrum
Bolivia	Bolivie	Bolivia	Spanish	1 Boliviano (BOB) = 100 centavos

English name	French name	Local name	Official language(s)	Currency
Bosnia-Herzegovina	Bosnie-Herzégovine	Bosnia-Herzegovina	Serbo-Croat	1 Dinar (BAD) = 100 paras
Botswana	Botswana	Botswana	English	1 Pula (BWP) = 100 thebe
Brazil	Brésil	Brasil	Portuguese	1 Real (BRL) = 100 centavos
Brunei	Brunei	Brunei	Malay	1 Brunei Dollar (BND) = 100 sen
Bulgaria	Bulgarie	Bălgarija	Bulgarian	1 Lev (BGL) (*pl* Leva) = 100 stotinki (*sing* stotinka)
Burkina Faso	Burkina	Burkina Faso	French	1 CFA Franc (XOF) = 100 centimes
Burma ▶ Myanmar	Birmanie			
Burundi	Burundi	Burundi	French, Kirundi	1 Burundi Franc (BIF) = 100 centimes
Cambodia	Cambodge	Preah Reach Ana Pak Kampuchea	Khmer	1 Riel (KHR) = 100 sen
Cameroon	Cameroun	Cameroon	English, French	1 CFA Franc (XAF) = 100 centimes
Canada	Canada	Canada	English, French	1 Canadian Dollar (CAD) = 100 cents
Cape Verde	Cap-Vert	Cabo Verde	Portuguese	1 Escudo Caboverdiano (CVE) = 100 centavos
Central African Republic	République centrafricaine	République Centrafricaine	French, Sango	1 CFA Franc (XAF) = 100 centimes
Chad	Tchad	Tchad	French, Arabic	1 CFA Franc (XAF) = 100 centimes
Chile	Chili	Chile	Spanish	1 Chilean Peso (CLP) = 100 centavos
China	Chine	Zhongguo	Chinese	1 Renminbi Yuan (CNY) = 10 jiao = 100 fen
Colombia	Colombie	Colombia	Spanish	1 Colombian Peso (COP) = 100 centavos
Comoros	Comores	Comores	French, Comorian	1 Comorian Franc (KMF) = 100 centimes
Congo	Congo	Congo	French	1 CFA Franc (XAF) = 100 centimes
Congo, Democratic Republic of	Congo	Congo	French, Lingala	1 New Zaïre (ZRN) = 100 makuta (*sing* likuta)
Costa Rica	Costa Rica	Costa Rica	Spanish	1 Costa Rican Colón (CRC) (*pl* Colones) = 100 céntimos
Côte d'Ivoire	Côte d'Ivoire	Côte d'Ivoire	French	1 CFA Franc (XOF) = 100 centimes
Croatia	Croatie	Hrvatska	Serbo-Croat	1 Kuna (HRK) = 100 lipas
Cyprus	Chypre	Kipros (Greek), Kibris (Turkish)	Greek, Turkish	1 Cyprus Pound (CYP) = 100 cents
Czech Republic	République tchèque	Česká Republika	Czech	1 Koruna (CZK) = 100 haléřu

English name	French name	Local name	Official language(s)	Currency
Denmark	Danemark	Danmark	Danish	1 Danish Krone (DKK) (*pl* Kroner) = 100 øre
Djibouti	Djibouti	Djibouti	Arabic, French	1 Djibouti Franc (DJF) = 100 centimes
Dominica	Dominique	Dominica	English, French, Creole	1 East Caribbean Dollar (XCD) = 100 cents
Dominican Republic	République Dominicaine	República Dominicana	Spanish	1 Dominican Republic Peso (DOP) = 100 centavos
Ecuador	Équateur	Ecuador	Spanish	1 Sucre (ECS) = 100 centavos
Egypt	Égypte	Jumhuriyat Misr al-Arabiya	Arabic	1 Egyptian Pound (EGP) = 100 piastres
El Salvador	Salvador	El Salvador	Spanish	1 Colón (SVC) (*pl* Colones) = 100 centavos
Equatorial Guinea	Guinée Équatoriale	Guinea Ecuatorial	Spanish	1 CFA Franc (XAF) = 100 centimes
Eritrea	Érythrée	Eritrea	Tigrinya, Arabic	1 Ethopian Birr (ETB) = 100 cents
Estonia	Estonie	Eesti Vabariik	Estonian	1 Kroon (EEK) = 100 sents
Ethiopia	Éthiopie	Ityopiya	Amharic	1 Ethiopian Birr (ETB) = 100 cents
Faroe Islands	Îles Féroé	Faroyar/ Faeroerne	Faroese, Danish	1 Danish Krone (DKK) (*pl* Kroner) = 100 øre
Fiji	Îles Fidji	Matanitu Ko Viti	English	1 Fiji Dollar (FJD) = 100 cents
Finland	Finlande	Suomen Tasavalta	Finnish, Swedish	1 Euro (EUR) = 100 cents
France	France	République française	French	1 Euro (EUR) = 100 cents
French Guiana	Guyane	Guyane française	French Creole	1 Euro (EUR) = 100 cents
French Polynesia	Polynésie française	Territoire de la Polynésie française	Polynesian, French	1 CPA Franc (XPF) = 100 centimes
Gabon	Gabon	République gabonaise	French	1 CFA Franc (XAF) = 100 centimes
The Gambia	Gambie	Gambia	English	1 Dalasi (GMD) = 100 butut
Georgia	Géorgie	Sakartvelos Respublica	Georgian, Russian	1 Lari (GEL) = 100 tetri
Germany	Allemagne	Bundesrepublik Deutschland	German	1 Euro (EUR) = 100 cents
Ghana	Ghana	Ghana	English	1 Cedi (GHC) = 100 pesewas
Greece	Grèce	Elliniki Dimokratia	Greek	1 Euro (EUR) = 100 cents
Greenland	Groenland	Grønland (Danish), Kalaallit Nunaat	Danish, Greenlandic	1 Danish Krone (DKK) (*pl* Kroner) = 100 øre

English name	French name	Local name	Official language(s)	Currency
Guatemala	Guatemala	Guatemala	Spanish	1 Quetzal (GTQ) (*pl* Quetzales) = 100 centavos
Guinea	Guinée	République de Guinée	French	1 Guinea Franc (GNF) = 100 centimes
Guinea-Bissau	Guinée-Bissau	Republica da Guiné-Bissau	Portuguese	1 CFA Franc (GWP) = 100 centimes
Guyana	Guyana	Guyana	English	1 Guyana Dollar (GYD) = 100 cents
Haiti	Haïti	République d'Haïti	French	1 Gourde (HTG) = 100 centimes
Holland ▸ Netherlands, The	Hollande			
Honduras	Honduras	Honduras	Spanish	1 Lempira (HNL) = 100 centavos
Hungary	Hongrie	Magyar Koztarsasag	Hungarian	1 Forint (HUF) = 100 fillér
Iceland	Islande	Ísland	Icelandic	1 Króna (ISK) = 100 aurar (*sing* eyrir)
India	Inde	Bhārat (Hindi)	Hindi, English	1 Indian Rupee (INR) = 100 paisa
Indonesia	Indonésie	Republik Indonesia	Bahasa Indonesia	1 Rupiah (IDR) = 100 sen
Iran	Iran	Jomhoori-e-Islami-e-Iran	Farsi	1 Iranian Rial (IRR) = 100 dinars
Iraq	Irak	Jumhouriya al Iraquia	Arabic	1 Iraqi Dinar (IQD) = 1,000 fils
Ireland	Irlande	Poblacht na hEireann	Irish, English	1 Euro (EUR) = 100 cents
Israel	Israël	Medinat Israel	Hebrew, Arabic	1 Shekel (ILS) = 100 agora
Italy	Italie	Repubblica Italiana	Italian	1 Euro (EUR) = 100 cents
Ivory Coast ▸ Côte d'Ivoire	Côte d'Ivoire			
Jamaica	Jamaïque	Jamaica	English	1 Jamaican Dollar (JMD) = 100 cents
Japan	Japon	Nihon	Japanese	1 Yen (JPY) = 100 sen
Jordan	Jordanie	Al'Urdun	Arabic	1 Jordanian Dinar (JOD) = 1,000 fils
Jugoslavia ▸ Yugoslavia	Yougoslavie			
Kampuchea ▸ Cambodia	Cambodge			
Kazakhstan	Kazakhstan	Kazak Respublikasy	Kazakh, Russian	1 Tenge (KZT) = 100 tiyn
Kenya	Kenya Kenya	Jamhuri ya	(Ki) Swahili, English	1 Kenyan shilling (KES) 100 cents
Korea, North	Corée du Nord	Chosōn Minjujuüi In'min Konghwaguk	Korean	1 Won (KPW) = 100 chon

English name	French name	Local name	Official language(s)	Currency
Korea, South	Corée du Sud	Taehan-Min'guk	Korean	1 Won (KRW) = 100 chon
Kuwait	Koweït	Dowlat al-Kuwayt	Arabic	1 Kuwaiti Dinar (KWD) = 1,000 fils
Kyrgyzstan	Kirghizistan	Kyrgyz Respublikasy	Kyrgyz	1 Som (KGS) = 100 tyiyn
Laos	Laos	Lao	Lao	1 Kip (LAK) = 100 at
Latvia	Lettonie	Latvijas Republika	Latvian	1 Lats (LVL) (*pl* Lati) = 100 santimi (*sing* santims)
Lebanon	Liban	Al-Lubnān	Arabic	1 Lebanese Pound/Livre (LBP) = 100 piastres
Lesotho	Lesotho	Lesotho	English, Sesotho	1 Loti (*pl* Maloti) (LSL) = 100 lisente
Liberia	Liberia	Liberia	English	1 Liberian Dollar (LRD) = 100 cents
Libya	Libye	Lībyā	Arabic	1 Libyan Dinar (LYD) = 1,000 dirhams
Liechtenstein	Liechtenstein	Furstentum Liechtenstein	German	1 Swiss Franc (CHF) = 100 centimes/rappen
Lithuania	Lituanie	Lietuva	Lithuanian	1 Litas (LTL) (*pl* litai) = 100 centai (*sing* centas)
Luxembourg	Luxembourg	Lëtzebuerg (Letz), Luxembourg (French), Luxemburg (German)	French, German, Letzebuergesch	1 Euro (EUR) = 100 cents
Macedonia	Macédoine	Republika Makedonija	Macedonian	1 Denar (MKD) = 100 paras
Madagascar	Madagascar	Republikan'i Madagasikara	Malagasy, French	1 Malagasy Franc (MGF) = 100 centimes
Malawi	Malawi	Dziko la Malaŵi	Chichewa, English	1 Kwacha (MWK) = 100 tambala
Malaysia	Malaisie	Federation of Malaysia	Bahasa Malaysia	1 Malaysian Dollar/Ringgit (MYR) = 100 cents
Maldives	Maldives	Maldives Divehi Jumhuriya	Divehi	1 Rufiyaa (MVR) = 100 laari
Mali	Mali	Mali	French	1 CFA Franc (XOF) = 100 centimes
Malta	Malte	Malta	English, Maltese	1 Maltese Lira (MTL) = 100 cents = 1,000 mils
Martinique	Martinique	Martinique	French, Creole	1 Euro (EUR) = 100 cents
Mauritania	Mauritanie	Mauritanie (French), Mūrītāniyā (Arabic)	Arabic	1 Ouguiya (MRO) = 5 khoums
Mauritius	Île Maurice	Mauritius	English	1 Mauritian Rupee (MUR) = 100 cents
Mexico	Mexique	México	Spanish	1 Mexican Peso (MXN) = 100 centavos
Micronesia	Micronésie	Micronesia	English	1 US Dollar (USD) = 100 cents

English name	French name	Local name	Official language(s)	Currency
Moldova	Moldavie	Republica Moldove-neascā	Moldavian	1 Leu (MDL) (*pl* lei) = 100 bani (*sing* ban)
Monaco	Principauté de Monaco	Monaco	French	1 Euro (EUR) = 100 cents
Mongolia	Mongolie	Mongol Ard Uls	Halh Mongol	1 Tugrik (MNT) = 100 möngö
Morocco	Maroc	Mamlaka al-Maghrebia	Arabic	1 Dirham (MAD) = 100 centimes
Mozambique	Mozambique	República de Moçambique	Portuguese	1 Metical (MZM) = 100 centavos
Myanmar	Myanmar	Myanmar	Burmese	1 Kyat (MMK) = 100 pyas
Namibia	Namibie	Namibia	English	1 Namibian Dollar (NAD) = 100 cents
Nauru	Nauru	Naeoro (Nauruan), Nauru (English)	Nauruan, English	1 Australian Dollar (AUD) = 100 cents
Nepal	Népal	Nepal Adhirajya	Napali	1 Nepalese Rupee (NPR) = 100 paise/pice
The Netherlands	Pays-Bas	Koninkrijk der Nederlanden	Dutch	1 Euro (EUR) = 100 cents
New Zealand	Nouvelle-Zélande	New Zealand	English	1 New Zealand Dollar (NZD) = 100 cents
Nicaragua	Nicaragua	Nicaragua	Spanish	1 Córdoba Oro (NIO) = 100 centavos
Niger	Niger	Niger	French	1 CFA Franc (XOF) = 100 centimes
Nigeria	Nigéria	Nigeria	English, French	1 Naira (NGN) = 100 kobo
Norway	Norvège	Kongeriket Norge	Norwegian	1 Norwegian Krone (NOK) = 100 øre
Oman	Oman	Saltanat 'Uman	Arabic	1 Omani Rial (OMR) = 1,000 baiza
Pakistan	Pakistan	Pākistān	Urdu, English	1 Pakistan Rupee (PKR) = 100 paisa
Panama	Panamá	Panamá	Spanish	1 Balboa (PAB) = 100 centésimos
Papua New Guinea	Papouasie-Nouvelle-Guinée	Papua New Guinea	English, Tok Pïsin, Hiri Motu	1 Kina (PGK) = 100 toea
Paraguay	Paraguay	Paraguay	Spanish	1 Guaraní (PYG) = 100 céntimos
Peru	Pérou	Perú	Spanish	1 New Sol (PEN) = 100 centavos
Philippines	Philippines	Pilipinas	Filipino, English	1 Philippine Peso (PHP) = 100 centavos
Poland	Pologne	Rzeczpospolita Polska	Polish	1 Złoty (PLN) = 100 groszy (*sing* grosz)
Portugal	Portugal	Portugal	Portuguese	1 Euro (EUR) = 100 cents

English name	French name	Local name	Official language(s)	Currency
Puerto Rico	Porto Rico	Puerto Rico	Spanish, English	US Dollar (USD) 100 cents
Qatar	Qatar	Dowlat Qatar	Arabic	1 Qatar Riyal (QAR) = 100 dirhams
Romania	Roumanie	Romănia	Romanian	1 Leu (ROL) (Lei) = 100 bani (*sing* ban)
Russia	Russie	Rossiya	Russian	1 Rouble (RUR) = 100 kopeks
Rwanda	Rwanda	Rwanda	(Kinya) Rwanda, French, English	1 Rwanda Franc (RWF) = 100 centimes
Samoa	Samoa	Samoa	Samoan, English	1 Tala (WST) = 100 sene
San Marino	Saint-Marin	San Marino	Italian	1 Euro (EUR) = 100 cents
Saudi Arabia	Arabie Saoudite	Al-'Arabīyah as Sa'ūdīyah	Arabic	1 Saudi Arabian Riyal (SAR)= 20 qursh = 100 halala
Senegal	Sénégal	Sénégal	French, Wolof	1 CFA Franc (XOF) =100 centimes
Seychelles	Seychelles	Seychelles	Creole French, English, French	1 Seychelles Rupee (SCR) = 100 cents
Sierra Leone	Sierra Leone	Sierra Leone	English	1 Leone (SLL) = 100 cents
Singapore	Singapour	Singapore	Chinese, English, Malay, Tamil	1 Singapore Dollar (SGD)/ Ringgit = 100 cents
Slovakia	Slovaquie	Slovenska Republika	Slovak	1 Koruna (CSK) = 100 haléru
Slovenia	Slovénie	Republika Slovenija	Slovene	1 Tolar (SIT) =100 stotin
Solomon Islands	Îles Salomon	Solomon Islands	English	1 Solomon Islands Dollar (SBD) = 100 cents
Somalia	Somalie	Somaliya	Arabic, Somali	1 Somali Shilling (SOS) = 100 cents
South Africa	Afrique du Sud	South Africa	English, Afrikaans	1 Rand (ZAR) = 100 cents
Spain	Espagne	España	Spanish	1 Euro (EUR) = 100 cents
Sri Lanka	Sri Lanka	Sri Lanka	Sinhala, Tamil	1 Sri Lankan Rupee (LKR) = 100 cents
The Sudan	Soudan	As-Sūdān	Arabic	1 Sudanese Dinar (SDD) = 10 pounds
Surinam	Surinam	Suriname	Dutch	1 Surinam Guilder (SRG)/ Florin = 100 cents
Swaziland	Swaziland	Umbouso we Swatini	Swazi, English	1 Lilangeni (SZL) (*pl* Emalangeni) = 100 cents
Sweden	Suède	Konungariket Sverige	Swedish	1 Swedish Krona (SEK) = 100 øre
Switzerland	Suisse	Schweiz (German), Suisse (French), Svizzera (Italian)	French, German, Italian, Romansch	1 Swiss Franc (CHF) = 100 centimes/rappen
Syria	Syrie	As-Sūrīyah	Arabic	1 Syrian pound (SYP) = 100 piastres
Taiwan	Taiwan	T'aiwan	Chinese	1 New Taiwan Dollar (TWD) = 100 cents

English name	French name	Local name	Official language(s)	Currency
Tajikistan	Tadjikistan	Jumkhurii Tojikistan	Tajik	1 Tajik Rouble (TJR) = 100 tanga
Tanzania	Tanzanie	Tanzania	(ki)Swahili, English	1 Tanzanian Shilling (TZS) = 100 cents
Thailand	Thaïlande	Prathet Thai	Thai	1 Baht (THB) = 100 satang
Togo	Togo	Togo	French	1 CFA Franc (XOF) = 100 centimes
Tonga	Tonga	Tonga	English, Tongan	1 Pa'anga/Tongan Dollar (TOP) = 100 seniti
Trinidad and Tobago	Trinité-et-Tobago	Trinidad and Tobago	English	1 Trinidad and Tobago Dollar (TTD) = 100 cents
Tunisia	Tunisie	Tunisiya	Arabic, French	1 Tunisian Dinar (TND) = 1,000 millimes
Turkey	Turquie	Tūrkiye	Turkish	1 Turkish Lira (TRL) = 100 kurus
Turkmenistan	Turkménistan	Turkmenostan	Turkmenian	1 Manat (TMM) = 100 tenesi
Uganda	Ouganda	Uganda	English, Kiswahili	1 Uganda Shilling (UGX) = 100 cents
Ukraine	Ukraine	Ukraina	Ukrainian, Russian	1 Hryvna (UAK) = 100 kopiykas
United Arab Emirates	Émirats Arabes Unis	Ittihād al-Imārāt al-'Arabīyah	Arabic, English	1 Dirham (AED) = 100 fils
United Kingdom	Royaume-Uni	United Kingdom	English	1 Pound Sterling (GBP) = 100 pence
United States of America	États-Unis	United States of America	English	1 US Dollar (USD) = 100 cents
Uruguay	Uruguay	Uruguay	Spanish	1 New Uruguayan Peso (UYU) = 100 centésimos
Uzbekistan	Ouzbékistan	Uzbekistan	Uzbek	1 Sum (UZS) = 100 tiyin
Vanuatu	Vanuatu	Vanuatu	Bislama, English, French	1 Vatu (VUV) = 100 centimes
Vatican City	cité du Vatican	Citta' del Vaticano	Italian	1 Euro (EUR) = 100 cents
Venezuela	Venezuela	Venezuela	Spanish	1 Bolívar (VEB) (pl bolívares) = 100 céntimos
Vietnam	Vietnam	Viêt-nam	Vietnamese	1 Dông (VND) = 10 hào = 100 xu
Yemen	Yémen	Al-Yamaniya	Arabic	1 Yemeni Riyal (YER) = 100 fils
Yugoslavia	Yougoslavie	Jugoslavija	Serbo-Croat (Serbian)	1 New Dinar (YUN) = 100 paras
Zaire	Zaïre			

▶ Congo, Democratic Republic of

English name	French name	Local name	Official language(s)	Currency
Zambia	Zambie	Zambia	English	1 Kwacha (ZMK) = 100 ngwee
Zimbabwe	Zimbabwe	Zimbabwe	English	1 Zimbabwe Dollar (ZWD) = 100 cents

ADMINISTRATIVE DIVISIONS

FRANCE

Region	Administrative centre	Region	Administrative centre
Alsace	Strasbourg	Lorraine	Nancy
Aquitaine	Bordeaux	Midi-Pyrénées	Toulouse
Auvergne	Clermont-Ferrand	Nord-Pas-de-Calais	Lille
Brittany (Bretagne)	Rennes	Normandy, Lower (Basse-Normandie)	Caen
Burgundy (Bourgogne)	Dijon		
Centre	Orléans	Normandy, Upper (Haute-Normandie)	Rouen
Champagne-Ardennes	Reims		
Corsica (Corse)	Ajaccio	Pays de la Loire	Nantes
Franche-Comté	Besançon	Picardy (Picardie)	Amiens
Île-de-France	Paris	Poitou-Charentes	Poitiers
Languedoc-Roussillon	Montpellier	Provence-Alpes-Côte d'Azur	Marseille
Limousin	Limoges	Rhône-Alpes	Lyon

FRENCH DÉPARTEMENTS

Département	Code	Administrative centre	Region	Telephone code
Ain	01	Bourg-en-Bresse	Rhône-Alpes	4
Aisne	02	Laon	Picardie	3
Allier	03	Moulins	Auvergne	4
Alpes-de-Haute-Provence	04	Digne-les-Bains	Provence-Alpes-Côte d'Azur	4
Alpes (Hautes-)	05	Gap	Provence-Alpes-Côte d'Azur	4
Alpes-Maritimes	06	Nice	Provence-Alpes-Côte d'Azur	4
Ardèche	07	Privas	Rhône-Alpes	4
Ardennes	08	Charleville-Mézières	Champagne-Ardennes	3
Ariège	09	Foix	Midi-Pyrénées	5
Aube	10	Troyes	Champagne-Ardennes	3
Aude	11	Carcassonne	Languedoc-Roussillon	4
Aveyron	12	Rodez	Midi-Pyrénées	5
Belfort (Territoire de)	90	Belfort	Franche-Comté	3
Bouches-du-Rhône	13	Marseille	Provence-Alpes-Côte d'Azur	4
Calvados	14	Caen	Basse-Normandie	2
Cantal	15	Aurillac	Auvergne	4
Charente	16	Angoulême	Poitou-Charentes	5
Charente-Maritime	17	La Rochelle	Poitou-Charentes	5
Cher	18	Bourges	Centre	2
Corrèze	19	Tulle	Limousin	5
Corse-du-Sud	2A	Ajaccio	Corse	4
Corse (Haute-)	2B	Bastia	Corse	4
Côte-d'Or	21	Dijon	Bourgogne	3
Côtes-d'Armor	22	Saint-Brieux	Bretagne	2
Creuse	23	Guéret	Limousin	5
Dordogne	24	Périgueux	Aquitaine	5
Doubs	25	Besançon	Franche-Comté	3
Drôme	26	Valence	Rhône-Alpes	4
Essonne	91	Évry	Île-de-France	1
Eure	27	Évreux	Haute-Normandie	2
Eure-et-Loire	28	Chartres	Centre	2

Département	Code	Administrative centre	Region	Telephone code
Finistère	29	Quimper	Bretagne	2
Gard	30	Nîmes	Languedoc-Roussillon	4
Garonne (Haute)	31	Toulouse	Midi-Pyrénées	5
Gers	32	Auch	Midi-Pyrénées	5
Gironde	33	Bordeaux	Aquitaine	5
Hauts-de-Seine	92	Nanterre	Île-de-France	1
Hérault	34	Montpellier	Languedoc-Roussillon	4
Ille-et-Villaine	35	Rennes	Bretagne	2
Indre	36	Châteauroux	Centre	2
Indre-et-Loire	37	Tours	Centre	2
Isère	38	Grenoble	Rhône-Alpes	4
Jura	39	Lons-le-Saunier	Franche-Comté	3
Landes	40	Mont-de-Marsan	Aquitaine	5
Loir-et-Cher	41	Blois	Centre	2
Loire	42	Saint-Étienne	Rhône-Alpes	4
Loire (Haute-)	43	Le-Puy-en-Velay	Auvergne	4
Loire-Atlantique	44	Nantes	Pays de la Loire	2
Loiret	45	Orléans	Centre	2
Lot	46	Cahors	Midi-Pyrénées	5
Lot-et-Garonne	47	Agen	Aquitaine	5
Lozère	48	Mende	Languedoc-Roussillon	4
Maine-et-Loire	49	Angers	Pays de la Loire	2
Manche	50	Saint-Lô	Basse-Normandie	2
Marne	51	Châlons-en-Champagne	Champagne-Ardennes	3
Marne (Haute-)	52	Chaumont	Champagne-Ardennes	3
Mayenne	53	Laval	Pays de la Loire	2
Meurthe-et-Moselle	54	Nancy	Lorraine	3
Meuse	55	Bar-le-Duc	Lorraine	3
Morbihan	56	Vannes	Bretagne	2
Moselle	57	Metz	Lorraine	3
Nièvre	58	Nevers	Bourgogne	3
Nord	59	Lille	Nord-Pas-de-Calais	3
Oise	60	Beauvais	Picardie	3
Orne	61	Alençon	Basse-Normandie	2
Paris (Ville de)	75		Île-de-France	1
Pas-de-Calais	62	Arras	Nord-Pas-de-Calais	3
Puy-de-Dôme	63	Clermont-Ferrand	Auvergne	4
Pyrénées-Atlantiques	64	Pau	Aquitaine	5
Pyrénées (Hautes-)	65	Tarbes	Midi-Pyrénées	5
Pyrénées-Orientales	66	Perpignan	Languedoc-Roussillon	4
Rhin (Bas-)	67	Strasbourg	Alsace	3
Rhin (Haut-)	68	Colmar	Alsace	3
Rhône	69	Lyon	Rhône-Alpes	4
Saône (Haute-)	70	Vesoul	Franche-Comté	3
Saône-et-Loire	71	Mâcon	Bourgogne	3
Sarthe	72	Le Mans	Pays de la Loire	2
Savoie	73	Chambéry	Rhône-Alpes	4
Savoie (Haute-)	74	Annecy	Rhône-Alpes	4
Seine-Maritime	76	Rouen	Haute-Normandie	2
Seine-et-Marne	77	Melun	Île-de-France	1
Seine-Saint-Denis	93	Bobigny	Île-de-France	1
Sèvres (Deux)	79	Niort	Poitou-Charentes	5
Somme	80	Amiens	Picardie	3
Tarn	81	Albi	Midi-Pyrénées	5
Tarn-et-Garonne	82	Montauban	Midi-Pyrénées	5
Val-de-Marne	94	Créteil	Île-de-France	1

Département	Code	Administrative centre	Region	Telephone code
Val-d'Oise	95	Pontoise	Île-de-France	1
Var	83	Toulon	Provence-Alpes-Côte d'Azur	4
Vaucluse	84	Avignon	Provence-Alpes-Côte d'Azur	4
Vendée	85	La-Roche-sur-Yon	Pays de la Loire	2
Vienne	86	Poitiers	Poitou-Charentes	5
Vienne (Haute-)	87	Limoges	Limousin	5
Vosges	88	Épinal	Lorraine	3
Yonne	89	Auxerre	Bourgogne	3
Yvelines	78	Versailles	Île-de-France	1

DÉPARTEMENTS ET TERRITOIRES D'OUTRE-MER/ COLLECTIVITÉS LOCALES

Département	Code	Administrative centre	Region
Guadeloupe	971	Basse-Terre	DOM
Martinique	972	Fort-de-France	DOM
Guyane	973	Cayenne	DOM
Réunion	974	Saint-Denis	DOM
Nouvelle-Calédonie	98	Nouméa	TOM
Wallis-et-Futuna	98	Mata-Utu	TOM
Polynésie-Française		Papeete	TOM
Terres australes et antarctiques françaises			TOM
Mayotte	976	Mamoudzou	CT
Saint-Pierre-et-Miquelon	97500	Saint-Pierre	CT

BELGIUM

Province	Capital	Province	Capital
Antwerp	Antwerp	Limburg	Hasselt
Brabant	Brussels	Luxembourg	Arlon
E Flanders	Ghent	Namur	Namur
Hainaut	Mons	W Flanders	Bruges
Liège	Liège		

SWITZERLAND

Canton	Capital	Canton	Capital
Aargau	Aarau	Nidwalden[1]	Stans
Appenzell Außer-Rhoden[1]	Herisau	Obwalden[1]	Sarnen
Appenzell Inner-Rhoden[1]	Appenzell	St Gall (Sankt Gallen)	St Gall
Basle (Basel-Landschaft)[1]	Liestal	Schaffhausen	Schaffhausen
Basle (Basel-Stadt)[1]	Basel	Schwyz	Schwyz
Berne	Berne	Solothurn	Solothurn
Fribourg	Fribourg	Thurgau	Frauenfeld
Geneva (Genève)	Geneva	Ticino	Bellinzona
Glarus	Glarus	Uri	Altdorf
Graubünden (Fr: Grisons)	Chur (Coire)	Valais	Sion
Jura	Delémont	Vaud	Lausanne
Lucerne (Luzern)	Lucerne	Zug	Zug
Neuenberg (Neuchâtel)	Neuchâtel	Zürich	Zürich

[1]Demi-canton – functions as a full canton.

FRENCH FINANCIAL STATEMENTS

As time goes by, national differences in the presentation and calculation of financial information are becoming less marked, but this must be seen against a historical context where accounting traditions are quite different:

- French accounting has been regulated by government since the seventeenth century and has its roots in taxation and management of the economy.
- British and American accounting are regulated in detail by the accounting profession, within a government framework, and have their roots in the industrial revolution, when it became necessary to monitor the financing of industrial projects.
- Historically, the balance sheet is the oldest financial statement. It originated when businesses established the practice of making an annual inventory of their property less their debts to estimate their wealth, with the difference between two annual inventories representing the gain or loss in the intervening year.

Modern financial reporting, however, does not typically carry out annual valuations, but maintains a database of financial transactions (the general or nominal ledger) from which the annual reports are derived. These reports are (a) the balance sheet, (b) the profit and loss account (or income statement), (c) the cash flow statement and (d) the notes to the accounts.

- The **balance sheet** ("bilan") shows, on the one hand, the sources of the company's finance (divided between that provided on a permanent basis by the owners – equity – and that which is borrowed and must be repaid – debt), and on the other hand, the production facilities and trading items – assets – which the finance is supporting. The assets are normally split between long-term productive capacity (fixed assets) and short-term trading items such as stocks of goods and invoiced amounts due from clients (current assets).
- The **profit and loss account** ("compte de résultat") gives a detailed picture of revenues and expenses for the year.
- The **cash flow statement** ("tableau des flux de trésorerie") analyses the changes in the financial structure of the company over the same year: how much cash has been generated from operations, how much has been invested in new capacity, and the consequences for these two flows on the company's debt position.
- The **notes to the accounts** ("annexe") have the same regulatory status as the prime statements and are generally used for the provision of supplementary analysis.

Financial reporting is done on what is called the "accruals" basis: it aims to record transactions when any contractual event takes place (e.g. when a product is delivered to the customer), not just cash flows (when clients pay their outstanding invoices). The profit and loss account is therefore an economic assessment, which is why there is a need for the cash flow statement which looks at the narrower cash aspect in isolation. All the economic transactions revert to cash in time, but accounting tries to track all economic events as they occur.

While the financial statements from different countries all give broadly the same information, presentation differs to some degree. The main building blocks of the balance sheet – equity, debt, fixed assets, current assets – are, however, preserved and easily recognised. The balance sheet works on the basis that the total of financing sources (debt and equity) will always equal the total of the uses of that finance (assets, fixed and current).

- The European Union has been a major force in harmonizing the presentation of financial information, but recognizes several formats. France and the UK generally use different formats within this constraint.

- France allows large companies to use international formats, and so not all French balance sheets necessarily look alike.

- There is a tradition in Europe that while recognized formats must be respected, companies are free to give additional information.

- In the US, there are no prescribed formats, although there are minimum categories of information. Formats for US companies will therefore vary, but majority practice is that shown in this book.

- Regulators generally accept a degree of fluidity between the financial statements and the notes. US and British companies have a tendency to keep their balance sheet presentation very simple, using highly aggregated figures, and put the detailed information in the notes.

Sample French Financial Statements

Previous year's comparative figures are obligatory

Compte de résultat
(en milliers d'euros)

	Exercice 20X2	Exercice 20X1
Produits d'exploitation		
Ventes de production	232 488	211 788
Autres produits	1 723	1 634
Total	234 211	213 422
Charges d'exploitation		
Matières premières et charges externes	86 739	80 645
Frais de personnel	92 865	86 320
Dotations aux amortissements	18 543	18 023
Dotations aux provisions	2 678	—
Total	200 825	184 988
Résultat d'exploitation	33 386	28 434
Produits financiers		
Participations	2 178	2 106
Reprise sur provisions	200	—
Total	2 378	2 106
Charges financières		
Intérêts	5 653	5 832

Vertical presentation now common, but may be presented as two columns with revenue to the right and expenses to the left

EU requires split between trading operations and purely financial transactions

Dotations aux provisions	486	—
Total	6 139	5 832

Résultat financier	(3 761)	(3 726)

Résultat courant avant impôts	29 625	24 708

Unusual or non-trading items shown separately ← Produits exceptionnels

Produits exceptionnels		
Cession d'immobilisations	5 887	678
Reprise d'amortissements dérogatoires	312	310
Total	6 199	988

Charges exceptionnelles		
Dotations aux amortissements dérogatoires	659	583
Cession d'immobilisations	6 677	—
Total	7 336	583

Résultat exceptionnel	(1 137)	405

Résultat avant impôts	28 488	25 113

Larger French companies must share profits with staff ← Participation des salariés

Participation des salariés	1 267	1 188
Impôts sur les bénéfices	10 766	8 344

Résultat net de l'exercice	16 455	15 581

Bilan
au 31 décembre
(en milliers d'euros)

Must show original cost as well as accounting value at balance sheet date

The EU requires that fixed assets be split between intangible, tangible and financial

ACTIF	Montants bruts	Amortis-sements et provisions	20X2 Montants nets	20X1 Montant nets
Immobilisations incorporelles				
Marques	2 560	1 670	890	1 100
Immobilisations corporelles				
Terrains	4 890	—	4 890	4 890
Constructions	2 763	578	2 185	2 240
Installations techniques	1 326	652	674	805
Autres	1 547	662	885	968
Total	10 526	1 892	8 634	8 903
Immobilisations financières				
Participations	7 867	680	7 187	7 409
Créances rattachées	1 500	—	1 500	1 500
Total	9 367	680	8 687	8 909

Actif immobilisé	22 453	4 242	18 211	18 912
Actif circulant				
Stocks et en cours	13 266	1 215	12 051	12 897
Créances clients	51 683	2 528	49 155	47 488
Placements de trésorerie	3 400	—	3 400	—
Banques et caisses	10 243	—	10 243	2 758
Total	78 592	3 743	74 849	63 143

Classified within fixed or current assets in UK/US accounting

Charges constatées d'avance	1 324	—	1 324	1 415
Charges à répartir sur plusieurs exercices	2 240	896	1 344	1 792
Total de l'actif	104 609	8 881	95 728	85 262

Figures shown before and after allocation of the year's profit to dividend and reserves

PASSIF		20X2	20X1
	Avant répartition	Après répartition	Après répartition
Capitaux propres			
Capital social	5 657	5 657	5 657
Primes d'émission, de fusion et d'apport	17 244	17 244	17 244
Ecarts de réévaluation	218	218	218
Réserve légale	566	566	566
Réserves réglementées	357	387	357
Autres réserves	12 780	25 035	12 780
Report à nouveau	1 543	2 343	1 543
Résultat de l'exercice	16 455	—	—
Provisions réglementées	2 868	2 868	2 521
Total	57 688	54 318	40 886
Provisions			
Provisions pour risques	3 000	3 000	3 000
Provisions pour charges	5 362	5 362	2 398
Total	8 362	8 362	5 398
Emprunts obligataires	5 000	5 000	5 000
Emprunts et dettes auprès des établissements de crédit	4 331	4 331	9 876
Dettes d'exploitation			
Dettes fournisseurs	12 486	12 486	11 734
Dettes fiscales et sociales	7 438	7 438	6 854
Autres dettes	423	3 793	5 514
Total	29 678	33 048	38 978
Total du passif	95 728	95 728	85 262

Provisions are potential liabilities and part of the "debt" block in the balance sheet

Long-term debts shown separately from current operating items

Tableau des Flux de Trésorerie

(en milliers d'euros)	Exercice 20X2	Exercice 20X1
Format recommended by Ordre des Experts Comptables		
Opérations d'exploitation		
Résultat net	16 455	15 581
Élimination des charges et produits sans incidence sur la trésorerie ou non liés à l'exploitation		
amortissements et provisions	3 720	1 367
variations de stocks	846	(1 289)
transferts de charges du compte de charges à repartir	539	539
(plus) et moins values de cession	790	—
Incidence de la décalage de trésorerie sur opérations d'exploitation	(4 515)	(2 834)
Flux de trésorerie provenant de l'exploitation	17 835	13 364
Opérations d'investissement		
Décaissements provenant de l'acquisition d'immobilisations	(2 292)	(7 595)
Encaissements provenant de la cession d'immobilisations	5 887	—
Flux de trésorerie provenant des (affecté aux) opérations d'investissment	3 595	(7 595)
Opérations de financement		
Dividendes versés aux actionnaires	(4 900)	(3 943)
Remboursements d'emprunts	(5 545)	
Flux de trésorerie provenant des (affecté aux) opérations de financement	(10 545)	(3 943)
Variation de la trésorerie	10 885	1 826
Trésorerie à l'ouverture	2 758	932
Trésorerie à la clôture	13 643	2 758

Difference in balances over year explained by analysis

Sources of English Quotes
Sources de citations anglaises

A

ABC1 *Marketing* 1999
ABOVE-THE-LINE *The Guardian* 2001
ACCRUED *Business Wire* 2001
ACTUALS *Healthcare Financial Management* 2001
ADSPEND *Marketing* 1998
ADVERTORIAL *Marketing* 1999
AFFINITY *The Guardian* 2000
AFLOAT *DSN Retailing Today* 2001
AFTER-SALES *The Guardian* 2001
AIM *The Guardian* 1999
ANCHOR STORE *PR Newswire* 2001
ARTICLE *Business Wire* 2000
A-SHARE *The Economist* 1999
ASPIRATIONAL *Marketing* 1999
AVC *Moneywise* 1999

B

B2B *http://news.bbc.co.uk* 2000
BABY *The Economist* 1998
BACS *The Guardian* 2000
BAD *South China Morning Post* 1999
BANCASSURANCE *The Observer* 1999
BANNER *Marketing* 1998
BARGAINING *Aftermarket Business* 2000
BELOW-THE-LINE *Marketing* 1998
BEST-PERCEIVED *Marketing* 1998
BIG *The Guardian* 2002
BI-MEDIA *MediaGuardian* 2001
BLITZ *The Drum* 1998
BORROWING *The Financial Times* 2000
BRAIN-DRAIN *Computer Weekly* 1999
BRAND-LED *Marketing Week* 1999
BREAK-EVEN *The Guardian* 2001
BUILD *Marketing* 1998
BULL *Bloomberg Money* 1999
BULLISH *Chemical Market Reporter* 2001
BUNDLE *Video Store* 2000
BUSINESS *Your Business* 1994
BUYBACK *The Observer* 1999
BUYING *The Observer* 2001

C

CAPITAL *Bloomberg Money* 1999

CEILING *Business Times* 2002
CHAEBOL *Korea Times* 1999
CHAPTER 11 *PR Newswire* 2002
CHARITY *PR Newswire* 2000
CHURN *The Guardian* 2002
CLICKS-AND-MORTAR *http://news.bbc.co.uk* 2000
COLLATERAL *The Financial Times* 2002
COLLECTIVE *The Wall Street Journal* 2002
COMMODITY *Bloombery Money* 1999
COMPETITIVE *Brandweek* 2000
CONSUMER *Computer Weekly* 2001
CONTRARIAN *The Guardian* 2001
COOLING-OFF PERIOD *Newsbytes* 2000
CORPORATE *CNN Money* 2002
COST-OF-LIVING *Journal of Accountancy* 2000
COUNTERBID *Investors Chronicle* 1999
CREDIT *The Scotsman* 1999
CROSS-HOLDING *The Guardian* 1999
CUSTOMER-DRIVEN *The Guardian* 2002
CYBERSQUATTING *The Guardian* 2001

D

DAILY *PR Newswire* 2000
DAUGHTER COMPANY *PR Newswire* 2002
DEAD *The Guardian* 2001
DEBTOR *Challenge* 2000
DECISION-MAKING WIN *News* 2001
DECONTROL *The Guardian* 2000
DEED *The Guardian* 2001
DEFAULT *Newsbytes* 2000
DEMERGER *The Guardian* 2002
DEMOGRAPHICS *http://news.bbc.co.uk* 2000
DEMUTUALIZATION *The Guardian* 1999
DEPRESSED *The Guardian* 2001
DEPTH *www.decisionanalyst.com* 2001
DESKILL *New Statesman* 2000
DIGITAL *The Irish Times* 1999
DIMINISHING *The Guardian* 2000
DIRTY *CFO* 2001
DIVERSIFY *The Financial Times* 1999
DOG *Marketing Week* 1999
DOLLARIZATION *Foreign Policy* 2001
DOTCOM *The Guardian* 2002
DOWNSIZING *http://news.bbc.co.uk* 2001
DRAWDOWN *The Financial Times* 1999
DRESS-DOWN FRIDAY *The Observer* 2002

E

EARNOUT *America's Network* 2000
E-BUSINESS *The Guardian* 2001

E-COMMERCE *Sloan Management Review* 2000
EDGAR *PS Newswire 2000*
EEOC *Business Horizons* 2000
E-GOVERNMENT *Accountancy Age* 2002
ELECTRONIC *Business Wire* 2000
E-MARKETER *Business Wire* 2001
EMOTIONAL *Marketing* 1999
EMPLOYMENT *The Financial Times* 2002
EMPOWERMENT *The Guardian* 2002
ENDOWMENT *The Financial Times* 2002
ENTERPRISE *DSN Retailing Today* 2000
E-TAILER *PR Newswire* 2001
EURO-CURRENCY *Profile Data* 2002
EXCLUSIVITY *Business Wire* 2001
EX-GROWTH *The Financial Times* 2002
EXPANDING *The Guardian* 2002
EXTRAORDINARY *The Financial Times* 2002

F
FACE *Broadcasting & Cable* 1999
FACTORING *The Financial Times* 2002
FANNIE MAE *The Guardian* 2001
FAT CAT *The Guardian* 2002
FEATHER BED *The Guardian* 2001
FED *Emerging Markets Week* 2001
FEDERAL *Business Wire* 2001
FIAT (MONEY) *Federal Reserve Board* 2002
FIREWALL *The Guardian* 2002
FIRST-TIME *The Financial Times* 2002
FLAGSHIP *Accountancy Age* 2002
FLEET STREET *The Guardian* 2002
FLEXIBLE *The Guardian* 2001
FLOOR *Moneywise* 1999
FOCUS *The Guardian* 2002
FOOTFALL *Marketing* 1999
FOOTSIE *The Financial* 2002
FOREIGN *AFX Europe* 2002
FOREX *The Observer* 1999
FORTUNE *500 PR Newswire* 2002
FREE *The Guardian* 2002
FRONT-END *The Scotsman* 2000
FULL *Accountancy Age* 2002
FUTURES *Business Wire* 2000

G
GAGGING ORDER *The Guardian* 2000
GAP *The Guardian* 2002
GATEKEEPER *Elements of Marketing* 1987
GAZUMPING *New Statesman* 1999
GILT-EDGED *The Guardian* 2001

GLASS CEILING *The Scotsman* 2002
GLOBAL *Marketing* 1998
GLOBALIZE *Financial Post* 2002
GNOME *New Statesman* 2000
GOODWILL *CFO Magazine for Senior Financial Executives* 2000
GREENFIELD SITE *The Guardian* 2002
GROW *Unigram X APT Data Services Ltd*, 1993

H

HAIRCUT *Los Angeles Business Journal* 2000
HANDS-ON *The Guardian* 2002
HATCHET MAN *The Industry Standard* 2001
HEADHUNT *Scotland on Sunday* 2002
HEDGE *The Financial Times* 2002
HIGHLY-GEARED *The Financial Times* 2002
HOLDING *The Financial Times* 2002
HORSE-TRADING *Communications Today* 2001
HOSTILE TAKEOVER BID *The Guardian* 2002
HURDLE RATE *Graphic Arts Monthly* 2000

I

IFA *The Guardian* 2002
INCENTIVIZE *The Observer* 2002
INDEMNIFY *PR Newswire* 2002
INDEX *The Irish Times* 1999
INELASTIC *Industry Standard* 2000
INFLATIONARY *The Financial Times* 2002
INFLUENCE PEDDLING *Insight* 2001
INFORMAL ECONOMY *Private Banker International* 2001
INFORMATION *The Guardian* 2002
INSIDER *The Financial Times* 2002
INSTANT-ACCESS *The Financial Times* 2002
INTEGRATION *The International Economy* 2001
INTERIM *The Financial Times* 1999
INTERNATIONAL *PR Newswire* 2002
INTRAPRENEUR *PR Newswire* 2000
INVISIBLE *The Guardian* 2002
IPO *The Times* 1999
ISA *Moneywise* 1999
ISDN *Computer Weekly* 2001

J

JOB *Career Development Quarterly* 2001
JUMBO *Investment Dealers' Digest* 2001
JUNK *Financial Post* 2002

K

KEIRETSU *The Guardian* 2000
KERB *Dow Jones Newswires* 2002

KEY-ESCROW *The Irish Times* 1999
KITING *Business Wire* 2001

L
LADDERED PORTFOLIO *Medical Economics* 2002
LAME DUCK *The Guardian* 2002
LAUNDER *BBC Monitoring Service* 2002
LAYOUT *Marketing* 1999
LEARNING CURVE *Business Wire* 2002
LEISURE INDUSTRY *The Guardian* 2002
LEVERAGED *The Guardian* 2002
LIFFE *The Financial Times* 2002
LINEAR *Marketing* 1999
LLOYD'S NAME *The Guardian* 2002
LOCAL *The Guardian* 2001
LOYALTY *Debrief* 1998

M
MAILSHOT *The Guardian* 2002
M&A *Venture Capital Journal* 1999
MANIPULATE *American Metal Market* 2000
MARGIN *Purchasing* 2001
MARKET *American Enterprise* 2000
MARKET-DRIVEN *The Guardian* 2002
MARZIPAN LAYER *www.thisismoney.com* 2000
MASTERBRAND *Marketing* 1998
MATTRESS MONEY *The Observer* 2001
M-COMMERCE *TelecomWorldWire* 2002
MEANS-TEST *The Guardian* 2000
MEDIA MIX *Marketing Week* 1992
MENTORING *The Guardian* 2002
MERIT *HR Magazine* 2000
MEZZANINE *Investment Dealers' Digest* 2000
MICROMANAGE *Travel Weekly* 2001
MIND SHARE *Multichannel News* 2000
MISBRAND *PR Newsire* 2001
MISERY INDEX *www.worldbank.org* 2000
MISSION *The Guardian* 2001
MISSION-CRITICAL *The Guardian* 2000
MMC *Buyouts* 2000
MONEY *The Guardian* 1999
MORAL HAZARD *British Medical Journal* 2000
MOST-FAVOURED NATION *European Report* 2000
MOUSETRAP *Business Horizons* 2001
MOVER *Real Estate Weekly* 2000
MPC *The Guardian* 1999
MUST-HAVE *Professional Builder* 2001
MUTUAL *New Statesman* 2000
MYSTERY *Nation's Restaurant News* 2001

N

NARROW *The Guardian* 1999
NATURAL *Newsbytes News Network* 2001
NEGATIVE *Asian Economic News* 2001
NEST EGG *Medical Economics* 2002
NET *Investors Chronicle* 1999
NETWORKING *Training and Development* 2001
NICHE *Travel Weekly* 2002
NINE-TO-FIVER *Infoworld* 2000
NOTICE *Internet World* 2000
NUISANCE TAX *Contra Costa Times* 2002

O

OFF-BRAND *National Home Center News* 2000
OFFICIALESE *The Scotsman* 2001
OFT *Business Wire* 2001
ONE-DAY FALL *business a.m.* 2002
ON-LINE *Marketing* 1999
OPEN *Labor History* 2001
OPPORTUNITY *Marketing* 1999
ORGANIC GROWTH *The Guardian* 2002
OUTLOOK *Emerging Markets Week* 2001
OUTPLACEMENT *Business Wire* 2001
OUTREACH *The Independent* 2002
OUTSOURCING *Journal of Management* 2000
OUTTURN *OECD Economic Outlook* 2000
OVERBOUGHT *The Guardian* 1999
OVERTIME *Newsbytes* 2000

P

P *Elements of Marketing* 1987
PAC MAN DEFENSE *www.jonesday.com* 2002
PAPER *The Guardian* 1999
PARLAY *Brandweek* 2001
PATERNITY LEAVE *The Industry Standard* 2001
PAYE *The Independent* 2001
PAYROLL *Workforce* 2002
PEOPLE-FOCUSED *PR Newswire* 2000
PERCEPTION *Marketing* 1999
PERK *The Industry Standard* 2002
PERMATEMP *Workforce* 2000
PETER PRINCIPLE *Medical Economics* 2002
PINK *The Independent* 2002
PITCH *Marketing* 1998
PLAYER *Marketing Week* 1999
POACH *Electronic Times* 2000
POISON PILL *CFO* 2001
POLICY WONK *New York Observer* 2001
PONZI SCHEME *Los Angeles Business Journal* 2001
PORTFOLIO *The Guardian* 2002

POSTER *PR Newswire* 2000
POWER *PR Newswire* 2000
POWERBROKER *The Guardian* 2002
PREDATORY *Airline Industry Information* 2000
PRESELL *Brandweek* 2001
PRICE *The Observer* 1999
PROACTIVE *The Independent* 2002
PROFIT *The Guardian* 1999
PROFIT-TAKING *First Call/Thomson Financial Insiders' Chronicle* 2000
PROJECT *Electronic Designs* 2000
PROSPECT *PR Newswire* 2000
PUNTER *The Guardian* 2001
PYRAMID *The Guardian* 2001

Q
QUANGO *New Statesman* 2001

R
RAKE OFF *Dollar & Sense* 2001
RATE *Communications News* 2000
RAT RACE *The Independent* 2002
REBRANDING *Marketing* 1999
RECAPITALIZE *Investors Chronicle* 1999
RECEIVER *Eurofood* 2001
RED *The Guardian* 2002
REENGINEERING *The Independent* 2002
REFLATION *New Statesman* 2002
REFUSAL *The Independent* 2002
RELOCATION *The Industry Standard* 2000
REMUNERATION *The Guardian* 2002
REPOSITIONING *Hotel & Motel Management* 2001
RESTRUCTURING *PR Newswire* 2002
RETAIL Nation's *Restaurant News* 2001
RIG *Insight on the News* 2000
RIGHTSIZE *PR Newswire* 2002
RIP-OFF *Internet Magazine* 2001
ROADSHOW *Marketing* 1999
ROBBER BARON *The Chief Executive* 2002
ROGUE TRADER *The Independent* 2002
RSI *American Fitness* 2001
RUST BELT *The Independent* 2002

S
SALESMANSHIP *The Guardian* 2001
SATCASTER *Variety* 2000
SAYE *The Independent* 2002
SCORCHED EARTH POLICY *www.news.bbc.co.uk* 2000
SEASONALLY *The Independent* 2002
SELF-ASSESSMENT *The Independent* 2002
SELF-INSURANCE *Entrepreneur* 2000

SERPS *Challenge* 2000
SET-ASIDE *European Report* 2000
SEXY *Brandweek* 2000
SHAKE-UP *Computer Weekly* 2001
SHELF *The Independent* 2002
SHORT *Financial Management* 2002
SHORTFALL *The Independent* 2002
SHOWCASE *Business Wire* 2000
SHRINKAGE *PR Newswire* 2001
SICK *HR Magazine* 2000
SIGHT *Brandweek* 2000
SLUSH FUND *Japan Policy and Politics* 2001
SMEAR CAMPAIGN *The Independent* 2002
SNAIL MAIL *Newsbytes* 2000
SOFT *Econtent* 2001
SOUNDBITE *The Independent* 2002
SPAM *Newsbytes* 2001
SPEND *Food & Drink Weekly* 2002
SPIN *The Independent* 2002
SPIN-OFF *The Guardian* 1999
SQUARE *The Independent* 2002
STAG *Newsbytes* 1999
STAKEHOLDER *The Independent* 2002
STANDSTILL *American Metal Market* 2001
STATE-OF-THE-ART *Business Wire* 2000
STEERING COMMITTEE *The Guardian* 2001
STOCKBROKER *The Guardian* 2000
STRAPLINE *Marketing* 1999
STREAMLINE *The Guardian* 2002
STRIP MALL *Kiplinger's Personal Finance Magazine* 2000
SUNRISE INDUSTRY *The Guardian* 2001
SWAPTION *The Guardian* 1999
SWEAT EQUITY *Black Enterprise* 2000
SWOT *Business Horizons* 1999

T
TAKER *Los Angeles Business Journal* 2000
TAPER RELIEF *The Guardian* 2001
TAX *The Guardian* 1999
TAXMAN *The Independent* 2002
TEETHING TROUBLES *Internet Magazine* 2000
TELECOMMUTING *InfoWorld* 2001
TELEWORKING *Computer Weekly* 2000
THINK TANK *Asian Economic News* 2001
TIE-IN *Nation's Restaurant News* 2000
TIME *Business Wire* 2000
TIN PARACHUTE *Journal of Accountancy* 2001
TMT *The Independent* 2002
TOP-DOWN *Business Wire* 2002
TRADING *American Metal Market* 2000

TREASURY *American Metal Market* 2000
TRICKLE-DOWN THEORY *The Guardian* 2002
TRIPLE WITCHING HOUR *The Risks Digest* 1987
TROUBLESHOOTER *The Independent* 2002

U
UMBRELLA *The Independent* 2002
UNDERCUT *The Guardian* 2002
UNDERWATER *www.fed.org* 2001
UPSCALE *Travel Agent* 2000
UPTICK *The Independent* 2002
URBAN *Japan Policy and Politics* 2001
USER-FRIENDLY *Travel Agent* 2000

V
VAT *The Independent* 2002
VENTURE *The Financial Times* 1999
VIRAL MARKETING *The Guardian* 2002
VISITING FIREMAN *The Indian Ocean Newsletter* 2000

W
WATCHDOG *The Independent* 2002
WEIGHTING *The Independent* 2002
WHEELING AND DEALING *American Metal Market* 2001
WHIZ-KID *Private Banker International* 2000
WIN-WIN *Purchasing* 2000
WINDOW *The Guardian* 2002
WORK *The Guardian* 2002
WRONGFUL *Computer Weekly* 2000

Sources de citations françaises

Sources of French Quotes

A
ABUS *L'Humanité* 2002
ACCESSION *L'Humanité* 2002
ACCORD *CB News* 1998
ACHAT *LSA* 1998
ACQUIS *L'Express* 2002
ACTEUR *Stratégies* 1999
ACTIONNARIAT *Le Monde* 1999
ADÉQUATION *L'Humanité* 2002
AFFAIRISME *L'Humanité* 2001
AFFLUX *Le Monde* 1999
AGROALIMENTAIRE *L'Humanité* 2002
ALLÈGEMENT *Enjeux* 2002
AMÉLIORER *Challenges* 2002
AMORTISSEMENT *Enjeux* 2002
ANCIENNETÉ *Le Nouvel Economiste* 2002
APPORT *L'Expansion* 1994
APPROVISIONNEMENT *Enjeux* 2002
ARGENT *L'Humanité* 2002
ARGENTIER *Le Monde* 2001
ASSAINISSEMENT *Valeurs Actuelles* 2002
AUTOFINANCEMENT *L'Humanité* 2002
AVERTISSEMENT *La Vie Financière* 2002
AVOIR *Mieux Vivre Votre Argent* 1999

B
BAILLEUR *Le Monde* 2002
BAISSE *La Vie Financière* 2002
BANCASSURANCE *Le Monde* 1999
BANQUE *L'Expansion* 1999
BARÈME *Challenges* 2002
BARRE *L'Usine Nouvelle* 2002
BAS *Valeurs Actuelles* 2002
BIEN *L'Humanité* 2002
BON *Le Monde* 1999
BONUS-MALUS *Challenges* 2002
BOURSICOTER *Valeurs Actuelles* 2002
BULLE *Enjeux* 2002
BUSINESS *Le Revenu* 1999

C
CAC *La Vie Française* 1999
CAISSE *Le Nouvel Economiste* 2002
CANAL *Enjeux* 2002
CANDIDATURE *Challenges* 2002

CAPÉ *Le Nouvel Economiste* 2002
CAPITALISATION *Capital* 2002
CAPITALISME *Enjeux* 2002
CAPITAL-RISQUEUR *Le Revenu* 1999
CASH-FLOW *La Vie Française* 1999
CDI *Enjeux* 2002
CESSATION *Enjeux* 2002
CESSION *Le Monde* 1999
CHAEBOL *L'Humanité* 2000
CHÈQUE *L'Expansion* 2002
CHEVALIER *Le Monde* 1999
CHUTE *Challenges* 2002
CODEVI *Le Monde* 1999
CŒUR DE CIBLE *Stratégies* 1999
COMMISSAIRE *Enjeux* 2002
COMPTE-TITRES *Mieux Vivre Votre Argent* 1999
CONGÉ *Enjeux* 2002
CONJONCTURE *Challenges* 2002
CONSOMMATION *La Vie Française* 2002
CONTRACTUEL *L'Humanité* 2001
CONTRE-OFFRE *Le Monde* 1999
CONTRIBUABLE *Enjeux* 2002
COQUILLE VIDE *Le Monde Hebdomadaire* 2001
COTISATION *La Vie Financière* 2002
COUPE *L'Humanité* 2002
COUPURE *Challenges* 2002
CRÉANCE *Enjeux* 2002
CRÉATEUR *L'Humanité* 2002
CRÉDIT-BAIL *La Vie Française* 1999
CRÉNEAU *Enjeux* 2002
CROISSANCE *Libération* 2001
CYBER-RECRUTEMENT *Challenges* 2002
CYCLE *La Vie Financière* 2002

D
DÉBIT *L'Usine Nouvelle* 2002
DÉBLOQUER *Libération* 1998
DÉBOUCHÉ *Le Nouvel Observateur* 2002
DÉCONFITURE *Enjeux* 2002
DÉCOTE *Challenges* 2002
DÉFAILLANCE *Challenges* 2002
DÉFICITAIRE *Challenges* 2002
DÉGROUPAGE *L'Usine Nouvelle* 2002
DÉLIT *Le Nouvel Observateur* 2002
DÉLOCALISER *Enjeux* 2002
DÉMANTELER *L'Usine Nouvelle* 2002
DÉMEMBREMENT *Challenges* 2002
DENIER *Le Nouvel Observateur* 2002
DÉPART *Challenges* 2002
DÉPOSER *Le Nouvel Economiste* 2002

DÉRAPAGE *Challenges* 2002
DÉSENDETTEMENT *Le Nouvel Observateur* 2002
DÉSINTÉRESSER *Le Nouvel Observateur* 2002
DÉTAXER *Challenges* 2002
DEVANCER *L'Usine Nouvelle* 2002
DIRIGISME *Challenges* 2002
DIVERSIFICATION *Challenges* 2002
DOMAINE *Le Nouvel Observateur* 2002
DOPER *Le Nouvel Economiste* 2002
DOSSIER *Le Nouvel Economiste* 2002
DUMPING *Le Nouvel Observateur* 2002

E

ÉCART *Challenges* 2002
ÉCHELON *Challenges* 2002
ÉCONOMIE *La Vie Financière* 2002
ÉCOTAXE *Enjeux* 2002
EFFONDREMENT *L'Usine Nouvelle* 2002
EMBALLEMENT *Challenges* 2002
EMPLACEMENT *Challenges* 2002
ENCOURS *Le Nouvel Observateur* 2002
ENDETTEMENT *Enjeux* 2002
ENSEIGNE *L'Expansion.com* 2001
ENVELOPPE *Mieux Vivre Votre Argent* 1999
ENVOLÉE *L'Usine Nouvelle* 2002
ÉPONGER *Challenges* 2002
ÉQUILIBRE *Valeurs Actuelles* 2002
E-RECRUTEMENT *Challenges* 2002
ESPRIT *Challenges* 2002
ÉTAT-MAJOR *Challenges* 2002
EUROPE *Challenges* 2002
ÉVASION *L'Entreprise.com* 2001
EXERCICE *Challenges* 2002
EXTERNALISER *Enjeux* 2002

F

FACTURE *Les Echos* 2002
FAILLITE *Enjeux* 2002
FIDÉLISER *Challenges* 2002
FISC *Challenges* 2001
FISCALITÉ *Les Echos* 1999
FLAMBÉE *Valeurs Actuelles* 2002
FONCTION *Le Nouvel Observateur* 2002
FONDS *L'Usine Nouvelle* 2002
FORME *Enjeux* 2002
FOYER *Challenges* 2002
FRAUDE *L'Humanité* 2002
FRUCTIFIER *Challenges* 2002
FUITES *Le Monde* 2002
FUSION *Le Nouvel Economiste* 2002

G
GAIN *L'Usine Nouvelle* 2002
GARANT *Le Nouvel Economiste* 2002
GÉANT *L'Usine Nouvelle* 2002
GOULOT D'ÉTRANGLEMENT *Capital* 2002
GRÈVE *L'Humanité* 2001
GSS *LSA* 1998

H
HEURES *Le Nouvel Observateur* 2002
HOMOLOGUE *Challenges* 2002
HORS-MÉDIAS *L'Usine Nouvelle* 2002

I
IMPACT *Stratégies* 1999
IMPLANTER *Le Nouvel Economiste* 2002
IMPOSABLE *Challenges* 2002
INDEMNISATION *L'Usine Nouvelle* 2002
INDUSTRIE *Challenges* 2002
INJECTER *Le Nouvel Observateur* 2002
INSTITUTIONNEL *L'Usine Nouvelle* 2002
INTERDIT *L'Humanité* 2001
INTÉRIM *La Vie Financière* 2002
INTRODUCTION *Challenges* 2000
ISF *Challenges* 2000

J
JEU *Challenges* 2002
JOUER *Challenges* 2002

K
KRACH *Enjeux* 2002

L
LEADER *Challenges* 2002
LICENCIEMENT *Enjeux* 2002
LINÉAIRE *Marketing* 2002
LOBBYING *L'Usine Nouvelle* 2002

M
MAIN *Challenges* 2002
MALVERSATION *Le Monde* 2002
MANQUE *Valeurs Actuelles* 2002
MAQUIGNONNAGE *L'Humanité* 2001
MARASME *Challenges* 2002
MARCHÉ *L'Express* 2002
MARGOULIN *L'Humanité* 2000
MARKETING *Journal du Mail* 2002
MASSE *Le Nouvel Observateur* 2002

MATRAQUAGE *Challenges* 2002
MÉCÉNAT *Le Monde* 2002
MÉDIATIQUE *Challenges* 2002
MÉNAGE *Le Nouvel* Observateur 2002
MENSUALITÉ *Le Nouvel Economiste* 2002
MÈTRE LINÉAIRE *LSA* 1998
MÉVENTE *L'Humanité* 2002
MINI-MESSAGE *Le Monde* 2001
MOBILITÉ *www.iedm.org* 2001
MONÉTIQUE® *L'Humanité* 2001
MONTAGE *Le Nouvel Observateur* 2002
MONTÉE *Challenges* 2002
MORATOIRE *Challenges* 2002
MULTIPROPRIÉTÉ *Le Monde* 2002

N

NAVETTE *Challenges* 2002
NÉGOCIATIONS *Challenges* 2002
NOIR *Challenges* 2002
NOYAU *www.newsbourse.com* 2002

O

OBLIG *Challenges* 2002
OFFRANT *Challenges* 2002
OPA *Valeurs Actuelles* 2002
OPÉABLE *Challenges* 2002
OPÉRATEUR *Libération* 2002
OPÉRATION *www.fr.news.yahoo.com* 2002
ORGANISME *Enjeux* 2002

P

PACS *Le Monde* 2002
PARADIS FISCAL *Le Nouvel Observateur* 2002
PASSATION *Le Nouvel Observateur* 2002
PASSER *Enjeux* 2002
PEE *Le Revenu* 1999
PERCÉE *Enjeux* 2002
PHONING *Marketing* 2000
PIONNIER *Stratégies* 1998
PISTON *Le Nouvel Observateur* 2002
PLACE *La Vie Financière* 2002
PLACEMENT *www.ubs.com* 2001
PLAFONNER *Enjeux* 2002
PLEIN-EMPLOI *Challenges* 2001
PME *L'Usine Nouvelle* 2002
PONCTIONNER *L'Humanité* 2002
POPULATION *Challenges* 2002
PORTE-MONNAIE *Le Monde* 2002
POT-DE-VIN *L'Humanité* 2002
POUSSÉE *Challenges* 2002

POUVOIR *L'Humanité* 2002
PRÉRETRAITE *L'Humanité* 1998
PRESSION *Enjeux* 2002
PRÊTE-NOM *L'Humanité* 2001
PRISE *Le Nouvel Observateur* 2002
PRIX *Le Monde* 2002
PRODUIT *Challenges* 2002
PROMESSE *Challenges* 2002
PROTECTIONNISTE *Le Nouvel Economiste* 2002
PROTOCOLE *Le Nouvel Observateur* 2002
PRUD'HOMME *Le Nouvel Observateur* 2002

Q
QUINZE *Le Nouvel Economiste* 2002
QUOTE-PART *L'Humanité* 2002

R
RAISON *Challenges* 2002
RAPPORTER *Le Nouvel Observateur* 2002
REBOND *L'Usine Nouvelle* 2002
RECETTE *Le Nouvel Observateur* 2002
REDÉMARRAGE *L'Usine Nouvelle* 2002
REDRESSEMENT *Enjeux* 2002
RÉGIME *Le Nouvel Observateur* 2002
RELANCE *Le Nouvel Observateur* 2001
RENCHÉRISSEMENT *Challenges* 2002
RENDRE *Challenges* 2002
RENTABILISER *L'Humanité* 2001
REPOSITIONNER *Challenges* 2001
REPRISE *Challenges* 2002
RESTRUCTURATION *L'Entreprise* 2002
RETENUE *Challenges* 2002
REVENDICATION *Challenges* 2002
REVENU *Les Cahiers Français* 1994
RISQUE-PAYS *Le Nouvel Economiste* 2002
ROUGE *Valeurs Actuelles* 2002
RTT *Le Monde* 2002

S
SBF *Le Monde* 2002
SCISSION *Challenges* 2001
SCPI *Le Monde* 2002
SÉCU *L'Humanité* 2002
SERPENT *www.courrierinternational.com* 2002
SEUIL *Challenges* 2002
SICAV *Challenges* 2002
SMIC *Enjeux* 2002
SOLDER *Challenges* 2002
SOULTE *Le Monde* 2002
SOURCE *www.swiss-intermediary.com* 2001

SPIRALE *Challenges* 2002
START-UP *Challenges* 2002
SUBVENTION *Le* Monde 2002
SURENCHÉRIR *L'Humanité* 2000
SURMÉDIATISATION *L'Humanité* 2001
SURVALEUR *Challenges* 2002

T

TARIFICATION *Le Nouvel Observateur* 2002
TAUX *Challenges* 2002
TAXE *Le Nouvel Observateur* 2001
TERRAIN *Le Nouvel Observateur* 2001
TERTIAIRISATION *Le Monde* 2002
THÉSAURISER *L'Humanité* 1998
TOILE *Le Nouvel Observateur* 2002
TRAFICOTER *www.webfin.com* 2000
TRANCHE *Le Nouvel Observateur* 2002
TRENTE-CINQ HEURES *Enjeux* 2002
TROIS-HUIT *L'Humanité* 2001

U

UNIVERS *LSA* 1998

V

VACHE À LAIT *Le Nouvel Economiste* 2002
VALEUR *Challenges* 2002
VALSE *www.tf1.fr* 2002
VENTE *Valeurs actuelles* 2002
VÉPÉCISTE *Challenges* 2002
VILLAGE PLANÉTAIRE *L'Humanité* 2001
VITESSE *Challenges* 2002

Z

ZONE *Challenges* 2002

Organization Chart of a Large French Company
Organigramme d'une grande entreprise française

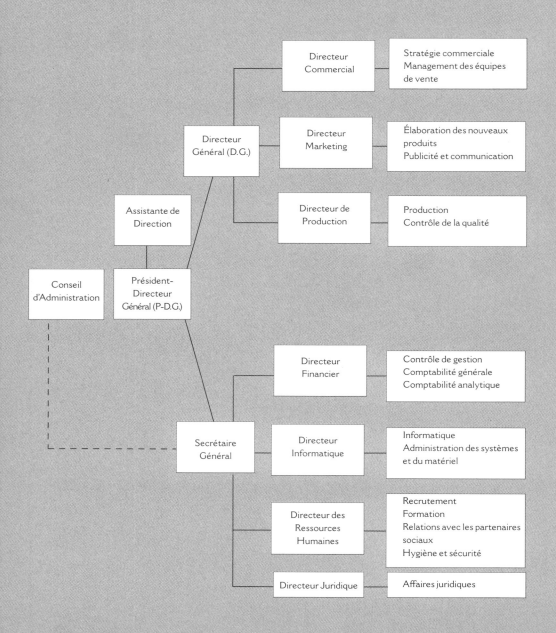